Garlick's Methodist Registry 1983

Garlick's Methodist Registry 1983

Edsall of London

This is the best known portrait of John Wesley, painted in 1765 when he was 62. The portrait, by the Irish painter Robert Hunter, hangs in the John Wesley Museum, City Road, London, England.

The front endpaper shows Wesley's Tree at Winchelsea, Sussex, where John Wesley preached his last open air sermon in 1790. The endpaper at the back of the book depicts John Wesley at the first Methodist Conference at the City Road Chapel, London, in 1779

ISBN 0 902623 32 X

Typeset by Wayside Graphics, Clevedon, England.
Printed by Hazell Watson & Viney Ltd, Aylesbury, England.
Design and typography by Sadlergraphics, West Byfleet, England.
Picture of John Wesley and endpapers by kind permission of Reverend Dr Ronald C Gibbins, Superintendent Minister of Wesley's Chapel, London, England.

Contents

TO THE PEOPLE CALLED METHODISTS

It has been necessary to use a number of books and records in compiling the Registry. I have also received help from the Conference Office, and from a number of people who were able to supply information that has not hitherto been published, and I am most grateful to them all.
Every care has been taken to make the information correct. In such a work involving so many figures and so much detail there may still be some omissions or errors. In such cases I would be grateful to be informed of any mistakes discovered.
The biographical details were all provided by Ministers themselves.
London April 1983

Exordium

I, IN THE SPIRIT of John Wesley, write to my heirs and children in 1983. I must remind you immediately of your first and over-riding task. It is to facilitate direct communion between God and human beings. This is what I meant when I said, 'You have nothing to do but to save souls'. Over centuries you have taken my own Aldersgate Street experience of May 24, 1738, out of its proper context. I wanted you to attend to the whole of my *Journal* and my total literary deposit. You have consistently presented me and my journey with God in too narrow and too straightforward context. This blinds you today to the enormously varied ways in which the incomprehensible mystery of God is encountered in the human heart. Some of you have even lost confidence in the possibility of God meeting the human personality. There can be no knowledge of God without knowledge of the self. Christian fellowship and pastoral counselling ought to be used to help people to face more reality about themselves, not less; to explore more deeply life's hurts, ambiguities, loneliness and despair. The church should be a community in which we find the courage to question God. Time, patience and sensitivity are crucial to this. But almost every contemporary Methodist, and especially the Minister, is too busy. You run away from experience of God in your frenetic activity.

I ALSO COMMEND to you silence and meditation. Every human being has a rich store of outstanding experience to recollect, to enjoy freshly, and for which to be thankful. Reflection on life's goodness can point to God. Quiet meditation is valuable corporately as well as privately. But whenever Methodists come together, all I hear is noise. You are intolerably talkative. You are unpractised in silence. So your spiritual lives are impoverished.

NEVER BE AFRAID of mystical religious experience. Alongside it, however, continue to attend to the instituted means of grace—especially prayer, the study of the Bible, the sacraments and the work of the church. I am thrilled that you Methodists have produced a succession of outstanding biblical scholars (though I wish you had as much expertise in the Old Testament as you have in the New). In the last generation liturgical scholarship has flourished in a way that would have been unthinkable 50 years ago. *The Methodist Service Book* marks the handsome progress since 1936, when *The Book of Offices* was produced.

WHAT IS COMMENDABLE in the scholarly leadership has, however, passed by so many Methodists. Why are my people no longer deeply immersed in the scriptures? Why have the Ministers failed for too long to nourish in our congregations students of the Bible? Your biblical illiteracy is embarassing. I also have a question about Holy Communion: Why has it not yet become normative and central in your worship? You have the *Sunday Services*; many Methodists crave for its frequent use. But once a month is as much as the church can provide in many places. You justify this in terms of numbers of Ministers. I know how I struggled on this subject during my lifetime for over 30 years. In the end I realised that discipline must be adjusted to make it the servant of faith. Learn from my struggle. Think again on my sermon 'The Duty of Constant Communion'. Listen to what Neville Ward and Jack Burton are saying to you on the spirituality of the sacrament.

LET ME MAKE it plain that I am not being dogmatic at this point. I simply desire your spiritual well-being. You live in a century which is as conscious as any of the horrendous evil that human beings can perpetrate on one another. Guernica, Hiroshima and Belsen are etched in your minds, and must never be forgotten. So I ask myself what sort of resources you need to sustain the possibility of faith in the face of such monstrosity? The eucharist can keep you alert to sin and evil, and mediates God's saving grace. I hold to Charles Kingsley's conviction after visiting the victims of cholera: 'If I had not had communion at church today to tell me that Jesus does reign, I should have blasphemed in my heart, I think, and said the Devil is king'.

IN THE 18TH CENTURY, 'Justification by Faith' was one of my central doctrines. Today this gospel truth is communicated as a promise of 'freedom'. Jesus means freedom.

Moreover, the word 'freedom' is linked to the word 'friend'. So Christian freedom is discovered and enjoyed in the fellowship of Christian friends. Through the introduction of bands, classes and societies I did so much to help you understand the necessity of intimate, charismatic fellowship in the Christian life. Throughout the 19th century, cut adrift from the Church of England, you struggled so painfully and divisively to sort out whether you should be a charismatic society or an institutional church. You needed to be both! The union of 1932 weighted the balance towards Methodism as an institutional church. Thank goodness you learned something from your history; you devised an institution with many checks and balances built into it, to inhibit a rigid hierarchy fascinated by power. I applaud your representative democracy, your commitment to women as equal in status to men (though I wish you had the courage to take this to its logical conclusion: when will you have a woman Chairman of District, and how long will it be before a woman sits in my chair?).

NO INSTITUTION is perfect. Since the Wesleyans made so much of what they called the 'Pastoral Office' (Jabez Bunting: 'I believe that we are teachers to instruct and pastors to govern the people'), there has been deep in your system a hint of authoritarianism. Ministers are still not alert enough to the dangers of power in Christian leadership. Ministers should be more trusting: they do not need ministerial sessions of Synod and Conference; they do not need equal numerical representation with lay people in representative sessions of Synod and Conference any more than they do at Circuit and Local Church meeting. The other complaint I have against your institution is its fascination with bureaucracy. You overwhelm yourselves with administration, consultative procedures, and structural changes. Most of these are directed 'downwards' from the Conference. The church cannot cope with so much ecclesiastical business. The Conference must reform itself: it is too large and expensive; it is not clear enough about its priorities; it is too grandiose and ambitious. Limited time and resources mean that work is done hastily and badly.

MORE IMPORTANT than the reform of the institution is the recovery among Methodists of the necessity and value of the intimate, free, fellowship of friends. The House Group movement has touched but a tiny proportion. The Methsocs which promised so much have become feeble: the intellectual and spiritual immaturity of Methodism's ablest young people is terrible to behold. Ironically you have lost the essence of what I gave you in the classes precisely in the century when the dynamics of groups, their potential and their limitations, are better understood than ever before. Why have not Methodists been pioneers in applying social psychology to the renewal of the church?

TURN NOW to what I consider to be your hardest test. Methodism is deeply divided. I bring these divisions to your attention not to threaten you, but to enable you to see the hard work that must be done. 'All true unity commences in consciousness of differences' (Auden). So do not attempt to reach a superficial unity which blurs differences. You will need to live with sharp differences of conviction for many years yet, perhaps for evermore. The range of opinions in Methodism will become wider than it has ever been before. You are becoming a more catholic community of faith.

SOME OF YOU will be fearful that divisions within the family of Methodism will rob you of the energy you need for evangelism and mission. However, part of your mission is to share with men and women the honest pilgrimage of exploration into truth in which you are engaged in the church. Successful evangelism is not guaranteed by simplistic agreements or by your so-called 'convergences' of theological belief. Evangelism requires integrity at its root. It is not division itself which undercuts the credibility of the gospel, but rather the inability of Christians to live together with their differences without mutual suspicion and hatred. Do all in your power not to repeat the schisms of the 19th century. Have you imbibed in this generation my advocacy of 'catholic love'?

I CANNOT STRESS too greatly the cost of Christian loving in the face of division and conflict. Arguments within the family are always more demanding and violent than those with relative strangers. But this is your passion—your commitment and your suffering. Never give up the fearless pursuit of truth. Be fearful only of indifference, woolly thinking and carelessness in your discipleship. They will push people away from faith, as Sartre testified: 'I was led to unbelief not through conflicting dogma but through my grandparents' indifference'.

YOUR MOST SERIOUS divide is apparent in theological controversy: conservative evangelical *versus* those in the liberal-critical tradition *versus* sacramentalists *versus* radicals. You each have your support group. But you have not learned to live together creatively with a theological pluralism which at times borders on theological contradiction. The disputes over the report on human sexuality, especially the section on homosexuality, illustrate this. We need to be more honest about the different theological approaches to this subject, and their implications. Of course the Bible is against homosexuality. But such an observation cannot possibly close the argument today. It is not at all inconceivable for a Christian to state his position thus: 'The Bible is against homosexuality, but there are situations today where it is good and right for a homosexual partnership to be nurtured, and to be blessed by the church'. If the truth were known, some similar form of argument needs to be deployed in relation to our understanding of marriage. In the scriptures a picture of marriage is presented in which the husband and wife are not equal partners in the relationship. The husband always has priority of the wife, even though in some passages considerable effort is expended to limit the cruel and authoritarian use of his status. Yet today many of you rightly admire a companionate form of marriage, in which husband and wife operate jointly and equally, and in which relationship each respects the other's right to independence and privacy. Some of you are beginning to do creative thinking about the possibilities for friendship between married persons and members of the other sex to whom they are not married. (I only wish for myself that marriage had been a topic of theological thinking in the 18th century!).

WHAT IS BEING uncovered in these disputes is a whole range of issues: some deep, unresolved questions about authority; the relationship of tradition in the church to contemporary moral and theological thinking; and the unconscious feelings aroused by a topic such as sexuality. You are reaping the consequences of allowing a whole generation of Methodists to emerge without good leadership and education in theology. Many of you who ought to know better do not even know how a true theologian goes about his task, how he relates his work to that of the biblical critic, the philosopher, the historian, the artist and the scientist. Inspire in the next generation some theologians of stature. In the meanwhile I must unveil my alarm that the vacuum in theological thinking is being filled by a neofundamentalism. This is quite foreign to the tradition of experiential and critical theology I bequeathed to you. I must return to this subject again.

ANOTHER AREA of division in contemporary Methodism is worship. The furore over the proposal for a new hymn-book indicates your traditionalism and your fears. My brother and I inaugurated a glorious era of creative hymn-writing and singing in English Christianity. Our hymns resonated with the experience of our generation, and they stretched the imagination and knowledge of the early Methodists with their sophisticated biblical imagery. Poetry thus became the handmaid of spiritual growth. We are glad some of our work has stood the test of time; but do not idolise us. We hoped our successors would continue to pioneer creative work in words and music. This has not happened. So I find the new hymn-book will contain about 70% of what you have already in your hymn-books! From another point of view, I notice a growth of spiritual nursery rhymes: scriptural texts in unversified, and largely unsingable form, disposed of as quickly as the duplicator produces them. This is no food for the mature Christian pilgrim.

THERE IS A comparable divide between tradionalism and triviality in your forms of worship. Some of you take seriously only traditional and formal preaching services; others will attend only informal or family services. The rigid divide is what is unhelpful. A congregation grows through all its members sharing gladly in a variety of forms of worship—sacramental and non-sacramental, formal and informal, traditional and experimental. In my lifetime I encouraged something of this kind by recommending Methodists to attend both the Parish Church and the Society Meetings.

IN SOME FORMS of worship the worshippers will be relatively passive, will have their imaginative life quickened by quiet attention to the suggestive symbols of our faith, and will ponder the great gaps between God's Kingdom and the world and the church as we know them. They will find resources of courage to change the world and to reform the church. By contrast there are other styles of worship which highlight the notion of celebration; they stress the new life of the Kingdom already given to believers; they facilitate free and joyful participation by the worshippers in every aspect of the service.

I COMMEND TO YOU the need to think clearly about the balance between various forms of worship. Here is a suggestion. Normally share in forms of worship which maximise the contributions individual worshippers make to the well-being of the whole community; this is best done in relatively small congregations or groups. Occasionally (once a month?) join together in a large assembly for a more formal, tightly structured act of worship. Such a policy will need to be agreed by groups of congregations in a locality. It will demand a radical revision of your attitudes to church buildings, their size and use, and the emotional attachment you give to them.

IF A POLICY anything like this were to be adopted, there will need to be considerable re-education not only for congregations but also for preachers, lay and ministerial. Most preachers are still individualists. They are too detached from the congregations where they lead worship. The relationship of Local Preachers to local churches needs radical revision, so that the Local Preachers share in pastoral care of the congregation alongside the Minister. Furthermore all preachers need help to see the full implications of a shared ministry with a congregation in the preparation and conduct of worship. Preachers must interpret their role as identifying, encouraging and developing gifts within the congregation which will build up the whole community at worship. There is little future in a preacher appearing as a relative stranger to lead a pre-arranged service without any consultation with a congregation, and without providing in advance material with which the congregation can prepare themselves for worship.

I MENTIONED EARLIER church buildings. This leads me to reflect on a matter of great concern: you have signally failed to bring to your churches, and to your worship generally, a bold use of the contemporary arts. Where in the church's life are the riches of music and design, of art, literature and sculpture from the late twentieth century? You worship in a cultural backwater; or is it a desert? I recognise your dilemma here. Not only do you need to draw upon the work of contemporary creativity to facilitate worship of the Creator, but you must also be faithful to your puritan heritage. 'In all religions the hermit, the ascetic, the puritan visionary reject the beautiful because the intoxication of the mystery they seek comes to them from another, immediate union with the unknown' (Bronowski). This links with my very first paragraph, about the importance of personal religious experience. The clue to this apparent conflict may lie in a new and deeper appreciation among you of the importance of both individual and corporate religious experience. (In my generation I emphasised too much the individualistic view of personality. I must return to this later, when I touch on my teaching of holiness). So you must be open to the possibility of intense, mystical, private experience of God (into which art is an intrusion); and simultaneously you must enrich your corporate worship through the sensual and imaginative experience provoked by human creativity. The whole range of the personality can be explored and offered in worship only by using a variety of buildings and settings for worship.

THE FINAL divisive topic on which I wish to write briefly is ecumenism. By and large you have a good record here. You have supported the ecumenical agencies, you have imbibed some of the scholarship and liturgy of other denominations, and you have worked hard to create visible unity among the church in England, locally and nationally. I am aware, however, that every ecumenical adventure produces division and criticism. The introduction of episcopacy will be no exception. May I make one appeal that may help to minimise the friction among you on this issue? Do everything possible to construct a style of bishop who has as little *power* as possible within the institution of the church. It would be wise not to graft your new bishops into the tradition of Superintendents; and do not make your Chairmen into bishops. Here is an unparalleled opportunity to do a new thing in Christian ministry; let novelty and imagination flourish to produce bishops who cannot be authoritarian, who are less influential institutionally than Circuit Ministers, who can lead as Francis and Ignatius Loyola led the church—as beggars.

I RETURN NOW to a topic I have touched on earlier: the need for the whole church to learn to do theology. In the first instance a recovery of theology in the church depends on leadership. So I appeal to the Ministers and those who train them. Set great store by a cultured and learned ministry. By a cultured ministry I do not mean a middle-class ministry! I refer, rather, to a ministry that is open to, at ease with, and contributing to the whole range of human affairs and human achievement. Ministers are so often appallingly bound by the ecclesiastical ghettos where they work. They even feel guilty if they spend time enjoying the rich, secular life God has given all his children. Lay Methodists too need to broaden their interests and expertise. Here are some examples of sectors of secular life where Methodism is weak: economics; Marxism; non-Christian religions and issues produced by ethnic and religious pluralism; international affairs, especially in Europe, the Middle East and at the United Nations; public policy; contemporary art, science and philosophy.

A LACK OF SERIOUS critical reflection in these areas of human life is so important that the President's Council should immediately take action to encourage its Ministers and appropriate laity to make a life-time's commitment to the study of and participation in these sectors. The experience and expertise gained must be made available to the whole church. This will require a drastic overhaul of communication in the church. The tragic failure of the Publishing House and of the *Methodist Recorder* in these areas must be reversed.

DO NOT misunderstand me. I acknowledge the well-meant compassion and social concern which has always characterised Methodism. You have always supported fashionable crusades, like development in the Third World and nuclear disarmament. But has your thinking kept ahead of your compassionate action? Some of your social teaching—the statement on gambling is a good example—is hopelessly out of date. Other social issues are not probed deeply enough to prise open the underlying questions.

YOU DO NOT have enough information and commitment to research to be able to form judgments independent of the prevailing political ideologies and established attitudes. So many of you allow your views to be formed by the *Guardian* newspaper, and wrongly suppose that this is the same as a genuinely theological appraisal.

IT IS IMPORTANT to me to put stress on critical and creative theological work in the church. In my lifetime it is fair to say that I argued that church order is variable but the faith is fixed. I was a child of my times. If you are to make a contribution in your own day and age, you must be children of your times. The twentieth century is rich in theological exploration and discovery. Thank God for continental protestantism, for the Roman Catholic church, and for North and South America. To illustrate the need for a new theological seriousness I bring to your attention some of my own emphases which are in need of radical investigation: holiness and assurance. I had much to say of importance here. I put holiness on the agenda of every Christian's life. It is not a subject reserved for ascetics, monks and nuns. I also underlined the truth that holiness is to be pursued in the midst of secular duties; it is not won in a sacred ghetto separated from the real world. But my teaching now needs to be taken further in the light of contemporary anthropology. You in the twentieth century have learned the hard way that human life is dogged as much by a corporate malady as by individual sinfulness. World wars have brought home to you in a harsh way the insights by psychologists and sociologists: evil is released into human society by group actions which no individual in the group approves; by unconscious aggression and irrational energies, by suffering and pain, by cultural and historical blindness. What are the legitimate aims of holiness for Christians aware of the social as well as the individual dimensions of personality? Is 'perfection' still a credible ideal?

DOING THEOLOGY is more than creative thinking about human culture, the scriptures and your distinctive theological tradition. Theology is a way of reflecting on experience and faith which probes deep into our individual self-awareness. (Remember what I said earlier about the connexion between self-knowledge and the knowledge of God). This means two things. First, every Christian can be a theologian. The church needs the insights and work of all its members in the task of discovering God's presence and purposes in today's world. Second, theology involves action. Action guided and inspired by theological reflection in the whole church is mission. You are truly my heirs in this: you have always underlined the centrality of mission and evangelism, in this country and throughout the world.

IN PRACTICE you have settled for only certain parts of the world (notably the West Indies, parts of Africa, India and the Far East), just as you have found yourselves operating in this country in some sectors and social classes but not in others. Limited resources prevent you doing everything. More will be done when you work thoroughly ecumenically. However, you must always be flexible, willing to transfer your resources to new objectives and areas, as circumstances change. I have always hinted that you need to be more alert to parts of the world outside the traditional mission fields. Europe, so important to me in my struggle for faith, has formed a new economic and political identity; but your Methodist churches are so terribly English and un-European. However, I commend you most heartily for the drastic transformation you have made in your understanding of world mission. You have surrendered paternalisitic attitudes; you have gladly encouraged indigenous structures and leaders; you have broadened the skills which contribute to the true development of nations. Now press ahead with the implications of partnership between home and overseas churches: receive from abroad many more Ministers and other resources for mission and evangelism in England.

WITHIN THIS country you need to be alert to the diverse needs of human beings in different social settings: inner-city, suburbs, small town, new town, countryside. Do not romanticise the inner-city at the expense of the other sectors of your society; though I am only too aware of the extraordinary costly mission that is required precisely there. It is apparent to me that you can no longer retain the fairly uniform style of connexionalism which has stood you in good stead up to now. Varied social settings require equally varied responses by the church. You can no longer spread your resources of Ministers and money thinly or equally everywhere. This policy will require a revolution in administration, in assessments, in stationing. It is one more example of what I have touched on several times already. You are moving into an era where you must revise your understanding of what it is to be a church in a more catholic direction: a community which lives harmoniously with differences, with variety verging on contradiction; yet united by mutual respect and trust, a recognition of a community of interests, and above all by love and service.

I COMMEND YOU for grasping the political implications of mission. In 1739 I urged you 'nakedly to follow the naked Jesus'. I hinted in my concerns for education, slaves, prison reform, health, and in my teaching on the use of money, at the political and social dimensions of following the poor and humble Jesus. My 'Twelve Rules of a Helper', like the Rules of Francis and Ignatius Loyola before them, could not guarantee a body of Christians who would remain happy to be alongside the poor, serving them in suffering love, enabling them to discover in themselves resources for change, for growth in dignity, responsibility, compassion and common action. So you need to discover afresh for yourselves in your generation a style of life which owes more to Gethsemane and Calvary than to suburbia. Never lose sight of your priorities. 'It is the unimportant, the unattractive, the downtrodden, the indifferent, the wearisome for whom the church was urged to show special concern' (Schweizer). And who are such today? The unemployed, ethnic minorities, those who live in the deprived inner cities and the depopulated rural communities, single parent families, the elderly.

SIMPLE LIVING, identifying with the poor and oppressed, political action for justice and harmony will win few friends. The message of the cross is as likely to empty churches as to fill them. Which brings me to your recurring obsession: numbers. I confess my contribution to this. I regularly exaggerated the size of my congregations; I did suppose numerical growth was a providential sign. But history should have taught you new and better lessons. You have been in numerical decline (measured as a percentage of the population) since 1850. At your much vaunted union in 1932 your membership was over 840,000; today it stands at less than 488,000. You still feel falsely guilty if you do not report membership increases; you continue to admire large congregations as ends in themselves. Benson of Cowley was wiser than I: 'The experience of Christianising countries leads one to believe that the country is Christianised at the expense of souls, and when all are Christians none are'. The trouble was that I, like you, had not fully absorbed the theological meaning of my devotion to the Holy Communion. (I have mentioned this already). The grace of God mediated to us in the sacrament is not in proportion to the size of the fragment of bread we consume or the sip of wine we drink. So neither is the transforming love of God set free in the world in proportion to the size of the sacramental body of the church. It is a thoroughly un-Christian idea to suppose that influence is related to size. We have always worshipped a God whose unparalleled act of influence on human history was achieved in humiliation, powerlessness and death—at Golgotha. His secret was pure love. If my determined advocacy of holiness and perfection was worth anything at all, it was to keep the theme of love at the centre of the Christian life and to demonstrate the fundamental hopefulness of love, and therefore its creative possibiliities for personal growth. In spite of what some of my commentators have suggested, I did not believe in the optimism of God's grace but its hopefulness. Putting it this way enables me to look squarely at the prospect of Methodism dying. If that happened, I should grieve for a while, but I should not despair. Better movements than ours have arisen and will arise to witness humbly to the infinite love of God and to the lives of holy love which experience of God nourishes; and to sing His praise.

A brief survey of Methodist history

WHO ARE THE METHODISTS, and how did they originate? The history of the various branches of the Methodist family span nearly two hundred and fifty years. Two of the Connexions besides the Methodist Church in Great Britain still maintain their witness, the Independent Methodists and the Wesleyan Reform Union. There are some historians who date the beginning from the date of the first Conference or Assembly of the Connexion, but this can hardly be so because often the work was well established before a complete administrative body was defined. In one or two cases it is difficult to determine the exact date a Connexion ceased to be effective. It is very probable that there were some members in small groups that lasted for a number of years. The Chronological Table of the Methodist Connexions is given in the Appendices.

The Wesleyan Methodists 1739–1932

THE FOUNDERS of Wesleyan Methodism were two brothers, John and Charles Wesley. They were the sons of Samuel and Susanna Wesley, their father being the Rector of Epworth, Lincolnshire. Both received instruction from their mother in the early years. In 1714 John went to Charterhouse, and in 1720 went up to Christ Church, Oxford. Charles went to Westminster in 1716, and to Christ Church in 1726. John was ordained Deacon by Dr John Potter, Bishop of Oxford, on September 19th 1725, at Christ Church. He was made a Fellow of Lincoln College, Oxford, in March 1726, and gained his MA degree in 1727. For a short time John was Greek Lecturer and Moderator of the Classes, and then obtained leave to assist his aged father at Epworth, being recalled to Oxford in 1729. On his return he found that his brother Charles and one or two fellow students had been meeting for prayer and the study of the Greek Testament, and they regularly attended Holy Communion. Outside the University they visited the poor and needy of the city and the prisoners in Oxford gaol. John immediately joined the group, and in a very short time became its leader. It soon became known by the name given it by critical students as the 'Holy Club'. When Samuel Wesley heard of it he wrote, 'I hear my son has the honour of being styled the Father of the Holy Club, and if that be so, I must be the grandfather of it', and: 'I have the highest reason to bless God that he has given me two sons together at Oxford to whom he has given grace and courage to turn the war against the world and the devil'. It was the members of the Holy Club who were nicknamed by their fellow students the 'Methodists' and within ten years the Methodist Societies were meeting.

General James Oglethorpe, a Member of Parliament, in 1733 established a colony in Georgia in America for the settlement of debtors released from prison and other displaced persons. After two years he returned home to seek help to develop what he called a 'rag-tag' community. He had known Samuel Wesley, having been a subscriber to his work on *Job*. He was known and admired by Samuel Wesley, Jun, and had also heard of the Holy Club. He invited John Wesley to go to Georgia as a missionary to the Indians for the Society for the Propagation of the Gospel. John's only hesitation was on account of his widowed mother who, when he consulted her replied, 'Had I twenty sons, I should rejoice that they were so employed, though I should never see them more'. His mother's wisdom was his guide in this as it had been before and was to be again. Two members of the Holy Club, Benjamin Ingham, just ordained, and Charles Delamottee, decided to join John, and James Oglethorpe invited Charles Wesley to go as his private secretary.

Though at the time Charles was not at all keen, John persuaded him to obtain ordination before setting out. He was ordained Deacon by Dr John Potter, Bishop of Oxford, on Sunday, September 21st, 1735, and Priest by Dr Edmund Gibson, Bishop of London, on Monday, September 29th.
The party set sail for America in October 1735, and after considerable delay arrived in February 1736. It was on this journey that John Wesley first met the Moravians, who greatly influenced him by their calmness in the storm and their hymn singing.
John Wesley faithfully carried out his duties as a priest of the Church of England, ministering to the English settlers, and working among the Indians. But he found the results of his labours unrewarding, and reurned home, arriving in February 1738. He records: 'I went to America to convert the Indians, but oh! who shall convert me?'. After his homecoming he was very unsettled, but fortunately met up with the Moravians, and discussed his problems with Peter Bohler. It was he who urged Wesley to 'Preach faith till you have it; and then, because you have it, you will preach faith'.
Almost from the beginning, Charles Wesley was unhappy in Georgia. His health was affected, his work as secretary to Oglethorpe was not satisfying and after only about six months he returned home in April 1736, resigning his secretaryship.
Chronologically it was Charles who first experienced evangelical conversion. About the middle of May 1738 he had been lent a copy of Martin Luther's *Commentary of Galatians*, and was surprised to find that Luther said nothing at variance with the doctrines of the Church of England, in fact helping his understanding. The words of Paul that struck at the heart of Charles Wesley were: 'Who loved me and gave himself for me'. On Whit-Sunday, May 21st 1738, John Wesley arrived at the house belonging to John Bray in Little Britain where Charles was staying. At nine in the morning, with some friends, they sang a Pentecostal Hymn, and when his brother and friends had left, Charles began to seek for and pray for the gift of the Holy Spirit. It came, and he found himself at peace with God, 'and rejoiced in the hope of loving Christ'. Two days later he started to write a hymn on his conversion which was significantly finished the next day. (Methodist Hymn Book 361)
As for John Wesley's evangelical conversion, his own words describe it best. It happened on May 24th, 1738, 'I think it was about five this morning, that I opened my Testament on those words, 'There are given to us exceeding great and precious promises, even that ye should be partakers of the divine nature'. (2 Peter 1:4) Just as I went out, I opened it again on those words, 'Thou art not far from the kingdom of God'.' In the afternoon I was asked to go to St Paul's. The anthem was 'Out of the deep have I called to thee, O Lord: Lord, Hear my voice.' In the evening I went very unwillingly to a Society in Aldersgate Street where one was reading Luther's *Preface to the Epistle to the Romans.* About a quarter before nine, while he was describing the change which God works in the heart through faith in Christ, I felt my heart strangely warmed. I felt I did trust in Christ, Christ alone for salvation; and an assurance was given me that he had taken away my sins, even mine, and saved me from the law of sin and death'.
The proclamation of 'Salvation by Faith' was not welcomed in the parish churches where the Wesleys had freely preached before, and soon they were closed to them, except by their clergy friends. In late March 1739, John Wesley was invited to Bristol by George Whitefield, a former member of the Holy Club. He records in the *Journal* for March 31st 1739. 'In the evening I reached Bristol, and met Mr Whitefield there. I could scarce reconcile myself at first to the strange way of preaching in the fields, of which he set me an example on Sunday; having been all my life (till very lately) so tenacious of every point relating to decency and order, that I should have thought the saving of souls almost a sin if it had not been done in a church.' For Monday, April 4th, he records, 'At four in the afternoon I submitted to be more vile, and proclaimed in the highways the glad tidings of salvation, speaking from a little eminence in a ground adjoining the city, to about three thousand people.'
This was for John Wesley, and shortly afterwards for Charles, the beginning of

a ministry which was to advance the cause of Methodism more than anything else. Within a month of his first service in the open-air, John Wesley laid the foundation stone of what he called the 'New Room' in the Horsefair, Bristol, the first Methodist Chapel in England, which is still standing. On returning to London, Wesley preached at Blackheath, Moorfields and Kennington Common, field preaching making a deep impression. Wesley writes, 'In the latter part of 1739, eight or ten persons came to me in London, who appeared to be deeply convinced of sin, and earnestly groaning for redemption. They desired (as did one or two more the next day) that I would spend some time with them in prayer, and advise them how to flee from the wrath to come, which they saw continually hanging over their heads. That we might have more time for this great work, I appointed a day when they might all come together, which from thenceforth they did every week, namely on Thursday, in the evening.'

In a very short time more than a hundred were gathering every week. 'This was the rise of the United Societies, first in London, and then in other places. At Moorfields there was a disused foundery which had suffered an explosion in 1716. Wesley took it over at a cost of £115, plus repairs costing a further £800. The first services were held on Sunday, November 11th 1739, and this building became the London headquarters of Methodism for almost forty years, until the erection in City Road, London, a site so near to the Old Foundery, of the 'New Chapel' in 1778, which we now call Wesley's Chapel.

About the beginning of 1740 a young man named Thomas Maxfield, who had been converted under John Wesley's preaching in Bristol, came to London to assist him at the Foundery. He conducted classes of instruction and led the prayer meetings and in Wesley's absence began to preach. As soon as Wesley was told, he dashed back to London and his mother, who was at this time living in an apartment at the Foundery, noticing he was most upset, asked why. He replied: 'Thomas Maxfield has turned preacher, I find', to which his mother replied 'John, you know what my sentiments have been. You cannot suspect me of favouring readily anything of this kind. But take care what you do with respect to that young man; for he is as surely called of God to preach as you are. Examine what have been the fruits of his preaching and hear him yourself'.

Again Wesley accepted his mother's advice, and submitted to what he believed to be the will of God, and soon afterwards began to employ Lay Preachers, the forerunners of the Methodist ministry, although they were always referred to by Wesley as Preachers, never ministers.

From the beginning, the Wesley brothers were one in heart and mind, but in 1749 Charles married Sarah Gwynne which meant he began to live a more settled life and ceased to intinerate as much as formerly. He lived first in Bristol, later moving to London where he continued to preach in the Methodist Societies as before. He continued to support John in all that he did to extend Methodism, attending most Methodist Conferences, but taking little part in organization and administration. He died in London in March 1788. His outstanding contributions were the six thousand hymns he wrote for Methodism and which remain his enduring monument.

The first Wesleyan Methodist Conference was held in June, 1744, at the Foundery. It is almost certain that there was a Conference every year thereafter, but unfortunately the full records are not extant until 1765 when we have the *Annual Minutes of the Conference*. For forty years the Conference was composed of those whom John Wesley invited or allowed to be present, and outside Methodism it had no legal status. In 1783, some of the more senior preachers began to wonder what would happen to the Methodist Societies after John Wesley's death, and when he was approached he saw the wisdom of their anxiety. With the help of Dr Thomas Coke, a clergyman of the Church of England, with a degree in Civil Law, who had joined Wesley in 1776, he drew up what he called a 'Deed of Declaration' which he enrolled in Chancery in February 1784. This Deed set up the Legal Conference of the people called Methodists, which was composed of One Hundred Methodist Preachers, all chosen by Wesley. The Deed laid down regulations for the replacement of preachers who died, were superannuated, resigned or expelled. Another important feature of the Deed was that a *Journal* had to be kept of the proceedings of the Conference and to give all resolutions the force of law, the President and the Secretary of the Conference (two officers required by the Deed) must sign it. Until his death John Wesley was always President, while Thomas Coke was Secretary and the *Journal* does not record any elections having taken place. A further important feature of the Deed was to preserve the itinerant system of Preachers. No preacher could be stationed in a Circuit for more than three successive years. This strict itinerancy was peculiar to Wesleyan Methodism.

In 1769 Wesley, when asked for help from the Methodists of New York who had just built a preaching-house, asked the Conference if any were willing to go, and two preachers, Richard Boardman and Joseph Pilmoor, offered. A collection was taken immediately and realised £70, of which £50 was allotted towards the cost of the new preaching-house, and £20 for passage fees. In the stations for 1770 we find that America is Circuit No. 50 and required two more preachers and another appeal was made. Five preachers were willing, and Wesley chose two, Francis Asbury and Richard Wright. In 1784 John Wesley sent Thomas Coke to America to ordain Francis Asbury General Superintendent, a man for the time and the task.

When John Wesley died in March 1791, membership of the Methodist Church in Great Britain and Ireland was 72 477 and the first real controversy in Wesleyan Methodism came a year after his death. Wesley had ordained Preachers for work in America and Scotland between 1784–1788 and in 1789 ordained Henry Moore and Thomas Rankin for England. Some of the ordained preachers claimed that they had the right to administer the Sacraments, and if their ordination meant anything that must have been so. But Wesley had never permitted other than Anglican ordained Preachers to administer the Sacraments in Methodist chapels or preaching-houses in England, and urged members to take Communion at their parish church. By 1792, the feeling that Methodist Preachers appointed to Circuits should be permitted to administer the Sacraments, at least among their own people, had grown among Preachers and people and the matter was debated at the 1792 Conference, and rejected.

The next year the matter was debated again at Conference which now decided to allow Preachers to administer the Sacraments wherever the Society was unanimous in wishing it, provided the service was held in the evening and the Anglican form of service was used.

In 1795, Conference passed, though not unanimously, the 'Plan of Pacification' allowing Preachers to administer the Sacraments in their own Circuits providing the majority of Trustees and Leaders approved. The planning of the Communion Service had to be under the direction of the Superintendent, only those in full connexion being allowed to preside, and there were no dispensations of any kind.

It took time for regular administration of the Sacraments to become the norm in all Methodist chapels, and Church Methodists, as they were called, did not give in easily. In the very early days a Preacher was received into Full Connexion with the Conference after one year, but in 1784 the probation period was increased to four years. It was not until 1836 that ordination was by the imposition of hands.

The Wesleyan Conference was composed of ministers only until 1877 when a new constitution was adopted, dividing the Conference into two sessions. The first was the Pastoral Session, consisting of 240 ministerial representatives elected by the ministers of the District Synod, and of such other ministers as the Conference should determine. The Representative Session followed and was composed of the 240 ministerial representatives who were present at the Pastoral Session, plus 240 lay representatives. Of these, 210 were elected by the District Synod, and 30 by the Representative Session itself. The Legal Conference had to ratify all resolutions passed by either session, and the President and Secretary designate had to have been elected to the Legal Hundred. Between 1877 and 1932 there were various changes in the number of ministerial and lay representatives, and although by 1877 Wesleyan Methodism had come a long way to satisfying those who in former years had deserted it, nevertheless it still lacked the freedom of other branches of Methodism.

The Methodist New Connexion 1797–1907

ABOUT THE SAME time as the controversy of the Sacraments was going on, there was also a feeling that lay people ought to have a more prominent part in the government of the Connexion. Both the Conference and District Meetings, which were formed in 1792, were composed of Preachers only.

One of the chief leaders of the agitation for greater lay participation was Alexander Kilham who had entered the itinerancy in 1785. Like the founders of Methodism, he was a native of Epworth, and at first was content to go round the Connexion speaking of the necessity for reform. He then began to publish pamphlets setting out his ideas, and gained supporters in some areas and Circuits. In 1795 he published a pamphlet entitled, *The Progress of Liberty amongst the People called Methodists*, to which is added the Outlines of a Constitution.' Kilham's argument can be summarised thus:

1 That instead of the Preachers admitting and expelling members, this should be done by lay people or their representatives.
2 That lay members should have a choice in the appointment of their leaders.
3 That Local Preachers, instead of being appointed by Circuit Preachers should be examined by the Leaders' and Quarterly Meetings.
4 That Quarterly Meetings have a vote in recommending Preachers to travel.
5 That lay delegates should be appointed by Quarterly Meetings to attend the District Meetings.
6 That with submission to the Preachers and the Connexion at large, one or two lay delegates should be appointed from every District Meeting to attend the Conference.

The Conference of 1796 met in London, under the Presidency of Thomas Taylor, a one time supporter of Kilham. No charge was made on Kilham's moral or religious character, or his efficiency as a Preacher. It was for the publication advocating reform, which was against the rules at the time, that he was put on trial.

A good many Methodists supported the suggested reform and at the 1797 Conference held at Leeds, seventy delegates were sent by supporters of reform to urge the Conference to reconsider lay representation at Conference and District level. The Conference refused to listen and some representatives met, with others, in Ebenezer Chapel, in Leeds and formed the Methodist New Connexion. William Thorn, a member of the Legal Hundred and a Preacher of twenty-three years standing, having been expelled by the Methodist Conference for supporting the dissidents, joined Kilham and, at their first Conference on August 9th 1797 in Leeds, was elected President of the Methodist New Connexion, Kilham being elected Secretary.

The Constitution of the New Connexion was based on Kilham's proposals and among other things required Conferences and District Meetings to consist of an equal number of Preachers and Laymen.

The new organization grew apace and a year later it was reported to the 1798 Conference that membership had grown to 5037. By 1907 the New Connexion had the largest membership of the three uniting Connexions at 41 875.

Independent Methodists 1805

THE INDEPENDENT Methodist Connexion has never been very large and it is, and has been, confined mainly to the North of England. Perhaps this is the reason why the historians of Wesleyan Methodism, William Myles, Dr George Smith, Benjamin Gregory and others, do not refer to them at all. Fortunately there are at least three historians of the Connexion, Arthur Mountford, George Hunter, and James Vickers, who have at various times given an account of the rise and progress of this denomination.

Those responsible for the formation of the Connexion were not, in the strict sense, seceders. No ministers were involved and, as far as we know, there were no expulsions from the parent body. The events that brought it to birth took place in Warrington, Lancashire in 1796. When it was in the Wesleyan Northwich Circuit from 1791 to 1792, it had been at the head of a Circuit, and had the transfer of Warrington not taken place that year, there might have been no Independent Methodists. The Northwich Circuit had never had, since its formation in 1792, more than two ministers stationed by the Conference, though it must be said that some of the foremost ministers of the time were appointed, it would appear that Warrington either did not get its fair share of appointments from the ministers, or the pastoral care that was needed.

The members of the Society began to organize extra meetings in addition to the ordinary Class Meetings, which were held in their own homes. These 'Cottage Meetings', as they were called, were regarded by the Superintendent of the Circuit, John Booth, as unconstitutional, and he said they must cease. One of the small groups involved took no notice of the ban and continued to meet, though they did not leave the Methodist Society at the time. Within a year or two the separate Society, as it had become, began to grow, and it is at this point that they probably left Wesleyan Methodism. They were joined by some Quakers who, for some reason, left their own meeting, and began meeting together in a room in Bridge Street, Warrington. Shortly afterwards, one of the Quakers, Peter Wright, opened his home for another meeting, which later became the second meeting room. We know that the Quakers had a marked effect on the former Methodists because they began to dress and speak in the same way as was the practice of the Quakers, and became known as the Quaker Methodists, not of their own desire, but by others.

One of the members of the Warrington Society named Peter Phillips, though a very young man at the time, but obviously already showing the qualities of leadership, began a careful study of the New Testament and became convinced that 'the Church in the New Testament is a model for all Ages, and that its simplicity, ministry and freedom from wordly entanglements should be copied by every generation'. Arthur Mountford writes: 'Sometimes Quaker Methodists have been described as Christians who who do not believe in ministers. It would be more correct to say they became separated from the Wesleyan Methodist Church because they did not believe in a ministry'. This is much the same as the view of George Fox, the Founder of the Quakers: 'We must all minister according to our light, but not for hire'.

In 1802 the Quaker Methodists built their first Chapel at Friars' Green, Warrington. It was largely built by the members themselves, and during its use was enlarged twice, and a gallery was added. This building was used till 1859, when it was demolished and a larger one was built on the same site.

In 1805, an American evangelist, Lorenzo Dow, visited England. Soon after landing at Liverpool he began to hold revival meetings in a house in Edmund Street. At the time Peter Phillips was visiting Liverpool, and went to one of the meetings and invited Lorenzo Dow to Warrington. The invitation was accepted and Dow began to hold revival meetings in the chapel and in the open air, which attracted people from miles around. Hugh Bourne, one of the future founders of Primitive Methodism heard Lorenzo Dow, who was to be instrumental in the 'Camp Meetings' some two or three years later in Staffordshire.

In 1805, a meeting was held in Manchester with representatives of the Quaker Methodist congregations at which it was decided to form the 'Independent Quaker Methodist Society'. In 1806, another meeting was held, but unfortunately the records of both these meetings are not extant. James Vickers says: 'We date our origin from 1805, the year when the association of our earliest Churches commenced.' We do not know exactly when the title 'Independent Methodist Connexion' was first used, but James Vickers again says: 'How the title was agreed upon can only be conjectured'. There is evidence that one or two different titles were used over the years, but in 1898 the Annual Meeting decided that their name would be the Independent Methodists Connexion.

At the fourth Conference in 1808, held in Macclesfield, it was reported that there were five Societies, Macclesfield, Manchester, Warrington, Stockport and Old-

ham, with a total membership of 1219.
As has already been said, the Connexion has mainly been confined to the North of England. The Year Book for 1981–82 reports 15 Circuits all, with the exception of Bristol and Loughborough, in the North. The total membership was 4399.
The following is taken from the Independent Methodist Connexion's publication, *Our Faith*.
'Our worship is similar to that of the Methodist and other Free Churches but we should make it clear how we differ from the Methodists. Each of our churches has the power to manage its own internal affairs without any overuling central authority.
We do not pay our Ministers. They are self supporting and our Ministry is open to any member who gives evidence of God's calling and passes the set examinations based on study courses.
In keeping with our belief, our Ministers have no clerical titles or special dress but are recognised by the State as accredited Ministers of Religion.
Although our Ministry is unpaid, full time workers can be appointed to establish new churches, conduct missions, and help the weaker churches, and we have missionaries in overseas work. These, while doing this work, receive financial aid from the Connexion.
We believe in the equality of all members, men and women, in sharing the running of a church and holding its offices.
Churches are grouped together in Circuits, but except on rare occasions Circuit decisions are in no way binding on a particular church. Circuits exist for the mutual help of member churches and for purposes of shared Christian action in the locality.
Circuits are represented on a Connexional Committee and once a year Circuit and Church representatives meet together for the Connexional Annual Meeting. This examines the year's work, debates topics of interest to Connexion and the Christian Church generally, and looks to the future.'
The Registered Office and the Bookroom is 95 Orrell Road, Wigan.

Band Room Methodists 1806

THIS SMALL SECESSION from Wesleyan Methodists was led by John Broadhurst, a member of the Wesleyan Methodist North Street Society, Manchester. In 1803 he began to hold meetings in what he called 'The Band Room', a not unfamiliar term in Methodism. In the earlier days there were a good many Methodist chapels that had such a room, presumably because the 'Band Meeting' was held there. Such meetings were another form of Class Meeting, and there were Band Leaders and Band Tickets. The Band Ticket was distinguished from the normal Class Ticket by the printing of the letter 'B' in the centre under the text. Broadhurst's meetings were not official Methodist meetings. He had not obtained the permission of the Leader's Meeting to hold them, and when they began to attract large numbers, the Superintendent, William Jenkins, took action by writing to Broadhurst to tell him that the meetings must cease. Broadhurst ignored the order and continued his meetings, yet remaining a member of the Society.
In December, 1805, the Manchester Circuit decided to hold the annual Covenant Service on the first Sunday of the New Year, it being thought the most convenient date for most of the members. It was to be a united service and held in one of the town chapels. The Leaders of North Street agreed to close their chapel, yet for some unknown reason, a service was still held there. When investigations were made, it was found that not only had the service been held, but people who were not members of the Society had been admitted, even though only members who could show their Methodist Class tickets could be admitted to the Covenant service. It was decided that in future when such a service was planned in any of the three town chapels, North Street should close. When such a service was held in North Street no person without a Class Ticket or a note from one of the Preachers of the Circuit should be admitted.
The North Street members, no doubt being influenced by John Broadhurst, regarded the action taken as a censure motion. After a number of unsuccessful meetings to try to resolve the matter, some members withdrew. Broadhurst be-

came their acknowledged leader, and they called themselves the 'Band Room Methodists'. Within two years there were sixteen congregations, all of them in Lancashire and Cheshire. There was no real growth, though there were still a very small number in existence in the 1850's.

Primitive Methodists 1810–1932

THE PRIMITIVE METHODISTS did not originate out of a secession or division. The founders were Hugh Bourne and William Clowes, both converts to Wesleyan Methodism, who became Local Preachers. Both were attracted to open-air preaching, and they lighted on the idea of holding what they termed a 'Camp Meeting', the first of which was held on May 31st, 1807 on a prominent hill called 'Mow Cop', and between 1807 and 1810 several such meetings were held.

At the Wesleyan Conference following the first Camp Meeting, in July–August, 1807, a debate was held on the judgment of the Conference concerning what are called Camp Meetings. The Conference's answer was: 'It is our judgment, that, even supposing such meetings are allowable in America, they are highly improper in England and, likely to be productive of considerable mischief'.

The reference to America was no doubt a reference to the help of the American evangelist Lorenzo Dow, who two years previously, preaching in Liverpool, had impressed one of the founders of the Independent Methodists, Peter Phillips. The action of the Conference did nothing to prevent Bourne and Clowes from carrying on their evangelistic labours and, as a consequence, Bourne was expelled from the Methodist Society in 1808, and Clowes in 1810. They each set up Society Classes, because pastoral care was refused by the Wesleyans, and late in 1810 these two groups of Classes were brought together. In 1811 the first Class Tickets were issued, whose text is not without significance. 'But we desire to hear what thou thinkest; for as concerning this sect, we know that everywhere it is spoken against'.

The first printed plan was authorised in 1812, and the denomination took its name from a speech of John Wesley in the Chester Circuit in 1790, when he declared that he was a 'Primitive Methodist'. There is little doubt that he would have approved of open-air evangelism, for never before or since has there been a more enthusiastic supporter. He records. 'It were better for me to die, than not to preach the Gospel; yea, and in the fields, either where I may not preach in the church, or where the church will not contain the congregation.'

The growth of the Primitive Methodists was nothing short of phenomenal. The thrust started from Staffordshire, going on through Yorkshire to the North East, and through Lancashire to the North West, then to the Midlands and the South. The first reported official membership figure in 1820 was 7842, and within two years the number was 25 294. The industrial towns, mining and farming communities were attracted to Primitive Methodism. Many local councillors, trade union officials and later Members of Parliament came from the denomination in far greater proportion than any other. At Methodist Union, in 1932, the membership of the Primitive Methodist Connexion was 222 021.

The first Primitive Methodist Conference met in 1820. Unfortunately, although we have extant records of the Minutes of the Conference, there are gaps for some years between 1821–24, 1827–28, 1830–41 with regard to who was the President, and for the years 1820–24, 1827–28, 1830–36, 1838–40, who was Secretary. The Conference was composed of ministerial and lay representatives in the proportion of two laymen for every minister. The President or Secretary could be either ministerial or lay. In 1872 the Conference decided to elect annually a Vice-President, and again this office was open to both ministers and laymen, though in fact it was usually a layman.

The late Dr W E Sangster, speaking of those who attended the first Camp Meeting wrote. 'Tired but happy, those devout souls went home quite unaware that they had made history and that, in after years, one vital stream of Methodism would look back to that praying day as a time of spiritual re-birth, and Mow Cop became a name of reverence all round the world'.

The Bible Christian Methodists 1815–1907

THE BIBLE CHRISTIANS, like the Primitive Methodists, did not secede from Wesleyan Methodism. The founder of the denomination was William O'Bryan. He joined the Methodist Society when he was seventeen years old, and some five years later became a local preacher. Almost from the beginning he was prone to wander from place to place. One of the Preachers in the Bodmin Circuit, Joseph Wormersley, suggested that his labours might be more useful in the regular ministry, but the superintendent, Edward Millward, did not share his colleagues' view, and did nothing to encourage O'Bryan to offer as a candidate for the ministry. However, in 1810 O'Bryan appeared before the District Meeting as a candidate, but was told by the Chairman of the District, John Woodrow, that he could not be recommended on account of his family responsibilities. O'Bryan had married in 1803. After being rejected, he took to his wanderings again, and went to Newquay where at the time there was no Methodist Society which, in a very short time, he formed. As a result of his lack of obedience to Methodist discipline he was expelled from the Society in the latter part of 1810, in the very chapel he had himself built and had given to the Connexion at Gunwen.

O'Bryan was invited to preach at Lake Farm, Shebbear, the home of the Thorne family. After the service he was asked to form a Society and twenty-three joined, three of the Thorne sons being among them. John, who was a farmer and remained so, Samuel, who for a time was a Bible Christian minister who became a printer, and James, the second to enter the ministry of the Connexion.

By the end of 1815 there were eleven Societies and 237 members. This time James Thorne was invited to become a local preacher, and within ten weeks he was an intinerant. The first Quarterly Meeting was held in January 1816 at Holsworthy. In the same year, O'Bryan heard some of his followers referred to as 'Bible Christians'. He adopted the name but prefixed it with 'Arminian' to express his theological point of view, but this was eventually dropped. In 1816 the membership was 600. The first 'Rules of Society' were drawn up by O'Bryan in 1817, and were very similar to those which John Wesley had drawn up in 1743.

The first Bible Christian Conference was held in 1819 in the house in which O'Bryan was living at Launceston. O'Bryan was elected President, and James Thorne Secretary. The membership at the time was 2,000 and influence of the denomination grew, especially in the West country, there were Circuits in London, Kent, the Isle of Wight, Yorkshire and Northumberland.

Unfortunately, in 1829 there was a disagreement between O'Bryan and the Conference, and James Thorne was accused of misdemeanours by O'Bryan. The Conference looked into the matter and found they were groundless. Although O'Bryan adjourned the Conference, it carried on without him and he withdrew from the ministry, going shortly afterwards to America. He died in New York in 1868.

Richard Pyke says: 'Though we must accord to William O'Bryan the honour of founder, it was to the lad who was less than nineteen when the first Society was formed that the denomination was to be indebted more than to any other one person. He was its main pillar; and without his courage, wisdom and endurance it is doubtful if the denomination would have attained a stable organization'.

James Thorne was President of the Conference five times, Secretary ten, Connexional Editor 1828–1869 and Governor of Edgehill College for Girls, 1841–70. At the union with the Methodist New Connexion and the United Methodist Free Churches in 1907, the Bible Christian membership was 32,202.

The Tent Methodists 1820

THE TENT METHODISTS comprise an association of Churches who use tents in which to preach the Gospel. The founder was George Pocock, a Methodist Local Preacher in Bristol. It was a revival movement, and as with the Primitive Methodists and the Bible Christians, though on a very much smaller scale, the Wesleyan Connexion frowned on it. It was a point of discipline that brought Pocock and his movement into prominence. He was told, probably by his superintendent (though there is no record), that he must not employ any at his meetings other than accredited Methodist Local Preachers. This he refused, and connexion with Wesleyan Methodism ceased.

He set up his own Board of Management which became known as 'The Friends of Tent Preaching'. Pocock said that his committee were as capable of choosing who were proper to be employed as Tent Preachers as the Conference itself. At the first Annual Meeting in May 1822, at Bristol,, 'The Rules of the Tent Methodist Society' were adopted. One of Pocock's early supporters, John Pyer, is said to have brought Congregational terminology into tent Methodism, and eventually he left the movement and entered the Congregational ministry.
George Pocock was a man of considerable means. He bore the financial responsibility almost from the beginning. He built seven chapels in seven years himself. The first volume of 'The Tent Methodist Magazine' was published in 1823, and as far as I know that was the only one. How long the Tent Methodist Societies existed is hard to determine. That they did 'no damage to the Wesleyan cause, nor did it call forth any statement of policy or principle' is certain.

The Wesleyan Protestant Methodists 1829–1836

IT MAY SEEM strange to modern Methodists that a secession should occur as a result of the installation of an organ in a Methodist Chapel, but it was so. The event is known as the 'Leeds Organ Case'.
In 1825 Leeds Brunswick Chapel was opened. It was large and from the start it attracted large congregations. Early in 1827 the Trustees decided that it would be desirable to install an organ, but in 1820 the Conference passed a rule respecting organs in chapels: 'We think that in some of the larger Chapels, where some Instrumental Music may be deemed expedient in order to guide the Congregational Singing, Organs may be allowed, by Special Consent of the Conference: but every Application for such Consent shall first be made at the District Meeting; and if it obtain their sanction, shall then be referred to a Committee at the Conference, who shall report their opinion as to the proprietory of acceding to the Request, and also as to the Restrictions with which the permission to erect an Organ ought, in that particular case, to be accompanied'.
The Trustees made application according to rule, but as soon as it was known they had done so, the Leaders and Local Preachers objected, informing the District Meeting that an organ was not necessary. The District Meeting met, and after a long discussion the decision by 13 votes to 7 decided that 'it is not desirable to grant permission to place an organ in Brunswick Chapel'. The matter should have ended there, but the Trustees, some of them influential men, decided quite unconstitutionally to apply direct to the Conference, which broke its own rule, reversed the decision of the District Meeting and granted permission for an organ to be installed.
This Conference decision angered most of the Leaders and Local Preachers and they resorted to holding illegal meetings, the ringleader being Matthew Johnson, a Local Preacher, who was suspended for his part in the affair by Edmund Grindrod, Superintendent of the Leeds East Circuit and Chairman of the District. In December 1827 Grindrod called a Special District Meeting, which was quite constitutional, to consider the matter further, and probably to try and prevent a secession. The meeting was presided over by the President of the Conference, John Stephens, who brought with him as his 'Official Adviser' Jabez Bunting, at the time Secretary of the Conference. Grindrod also invited George Marsden, John Burdsall, Robert Newton and his predecessor Thomas Stanley. Richard Watson and John Hannah were also invited, but could not attend. There were two unconsitutional errors. There was no provision for an 'Official Adviser', and the other Preachers attending were not the three nearest Superintendents, as they should have been. The meeting, which went on by successive adjournments from the 5th to the 11th of December, regarded the protestors as 'rebels' and upheld Grindrod's suspension of Matthew Johnson.
When the Conference of 1828 upheld this decision of the Special District Meeting, the dissidents, led by Matthew Johnson, seceded and styled themselves 'The Wesleyan Protestant Methodists'.
The first Yearly Meeting of the Wesleyan Protestant Methodists was held in September 1829, in the New Chapel, Caroline, Leeds. James Sigston was elected President and Joah Mallinson and Matthew Johnson the Secretaries. It was reported that there were six Circuits (Barnsley, Leeds, Newark, Preston, York and

Wallsend), with a total membership of 2490. The membership returns for the following six years were; 1830, 3977; 1831, 3590; 1832, 3627; 1833, 3735; 1834, 3517; 1835, 3964.
During 1835 a Committee of the Protestant Methodists met with representatives from the seceders over the formation of the Wesleyan Theological Institution which in 1836 became the Wesleyan Methodist Association. Unfortunately, we have no record of the membership of the Protestant Methodists for 1836, but we do know that thirteen Preachers, one in full connexion, and twelve on probation, were recognised.
It has been said that the 'Leeds Organ Case' cost Leeds Methodism a thousand pounds and a thousand members.

Arminian Methodists 1833–1837

THIS SMALL SECESSION began in Derby, and because of this they are sometimes referred to as 'The Derby Faith Methodists'. The secession only amounted to about 600 in the Derby Circuit and was the only secession which took place on doctrinal grounds. It was said that they regarded saving faith as of purely human origin, a bare intellectual acceptance of facts.
The movement began in 1831, though it took no organized form till 1833. The leader and founder was Henry Breedon, a schoolmaster, who was a Wesleyan Methodist Local Preacher showing some sympathy towards the seceders, who invited him to take charge of their affairs. He accepted. He travelled the areas of Derbyshire, Leicestershire, and Worcestershire holding revival meetings, taking over the Temple Chapel in London Road, Derby. In his autobiography Breedon says: 'The first Assembly of the Arminians was held at the Temple, Derby, in June, 1833. The vote by ballot for the Presidency during the year placed me in that office. The meeting was a very pleasant one, and truly agreeable; and the Connexion again showed a considerable amount of prosperity. The rules and regulations were all passed about as prepared unanimously. At this meeting I was formally examined and placed by a unanimous vote of the Assembly in full connexion as the First Arminian Methodist Minister'.
The Arminian Methodist Connexion was almost wholly confined to the Midlands, but there was a small Society in Manchester. The second Annual Assembly was at the Temple, Derby, and Henry Breedon was again elected President in 1834. No figures are reported, but simply that the circuits were still enjoying prosperity.
The third Assembly was held in 1835 at the New Chapel, Derby, when it was reported that several Itinerants were taken into full connexion, the names of only John Wright and James Slack having been preserved. Henry Breedon was again elected President.
There are no details of the Fourth Annual Assembly if one was held. Breedon says that as President of the Arminian Methodists he received a communication from the Wesleyan Methodist Association which had just been formed (1836), respecting a union between the two Connexions. He was favourable from the beginning, and sought the support of the Arminian Circuits. This he did, and writes: 'I attended in the month of May, 1837, a Connexional Committee Meeting of the Association, held in Stevenson's Square Tabernacle, Manchester. And it was there arranged that Henry Breedon, John Wright, and James Slack, should be received as Ministers in full connexion with the Association. And that the Ministers on trial should be received in the same standing as they had amongst the Arminians, (Samuel Sellars and William Mackenney). That the following Circuits should be received as such, namely: Derby, Nottingham, Leicester, Nuneaton, and Redditch. And that our societies in Birmingham, Manchester and all other places should be included in the Association Circuits of such places'.
On July 26th, 1837, Henry Breedon and other representatives of the Arminian Methodist Connexion went to the Wesleyan Association Annual Assembly, held in Bold Street Music Hall, Liverpool, the Association ratified the arrangements made with the Arminians, and the union was completed.
It is obvious that the Arminians must have had a change of mind with regard to doctrine, or the Wesleyan Methodist Association would never have offered an invitation for union. It may well have been that in the very early days that there

was some doubts about saving faith and these were exaggerated. It is quite clear that Henry Breedon was a revivalist preacher, and it is very probable that he was instrumental in bringing the membership back to the fold as far as Methodist doctrine is concerned.

There are no records of membership figures for the Arminians, 1837 being the first year when the Association recorded membership figures, which included the Wesleyan Protestant Methodists, who joined in 1836, and the Arminians. The figure was 21 277, with 24 Preachers in full connexion and 33 Probationers, 53 Circuits, 167 Chapels, and 362 Meeting rooms and Preaching places.

Wesleyan Methodist Association 1836–1857

AT THE FIRST Conference of 1744, the following question was asked: 'Can we have a seminary for labourers?' The answer was: 'If God spare us till another Conference'. At the second Conference, in 1745, the question was asked again: 'Can we have a seminary for labourers yet?' The reply was: 'Not till God give us a proper tutor'. The subject came before Conferences a number of times, but it was not until the Conference of 1833, that a Committee was appointed to provide a scheme for the education of preachers on the list of reserve.

The Committee met in October 1833 when an elaborate report was prepared and published under the title of: 'Proposals for the formation of a Literary and Theological Institution, with a design to promote the improvement of the Junior Preachers of the Methodist Connexion'.

The Conference of 1834 accepted the proposals with little alteration. The Committee nominated Preachers to fill the principal offices of President, House-Governor, Theological Tutor and Classical Tutor and there is little doubt that the Committee went further than its brief by so doing. At a meeting at which Dr Jabez Bunting, the Senior Secretary at the Mission House, was not present, it was resolved that 'he should be requested to allow himself to be nominated as the President of the proposed Institution'. It was thought by those who wanted this, that arrangements could be made so that he could manage both jobs with help at the Mission House. It was further proposed that Dr Bunting should be the Theological Tutor, and still retain his appointment at the Mission House.

At this point the trouble began. Dr Samuel Warren did not object in the Committee to what had been done, nor in the Conference, until the proposal of Dr Bunting as Theological Tutor. Dr Warren characterized this as 'The astounding proposal that Dr Bunting should not only be the President of the Institution, but also Theological Tutor, and at the same time retain the responsible and influential office of Senior Secretary of our Foreign Missions'. He turned to Dr Bunting and said: 'To such an extraordinary assumption of power I would never give my consent'.

With this we must agree, and from this time onwards Dr Warren vigorously opposed the Institution. Some have thought that he himself expected to be appointed one of the tutors, but we have no evidence for this.

Warren launched a vigorous attack on the Conference, and founded 'The Grand Central Association' in November 1834, at Manchester, where he was the Superintendent of the Manchester First Circuit (Oldham Street). In 1835 he was expelled from the ministry and appealed to the civil courts against the Conference decision, first to the Vice-Chancellor's court, where his appeal was dismissed. He then appealed to the Lord Chancellor, Lord Lyndhurst, and again lost. It ought to be said that it is probably near to the truth to say that Warren's quarrel was not with the scheme itself, but rather with the way in which it had been planned. 'Despite the fierceness of this tempest, the Theological Institution scheme weathered the storm.'

Dr Warren's expulsion resulted in the secession of about a thousand members who designated themselves the Wesleyan Methodist Association, whose first Assembly was held in Manchester, 1836, when Dr Warren was elected the first President. During 1835 negotiations took place with the Wesleyan Protestant Methodist Association about an amalgamation and the 1836 Assembly confirmed the decision to amalgamate reached by the Joint Committee, and Matthew Johnson, formerly a Wesleyan Protestant Methodist, was appointed Secretary. In 1837 the Arminian Methodists (sometimes known as the Derby Faith

Methodists) also amalgamated with the Wesleyan Methodist Association, which Dr Warren left in 1838 to enter the ministry of the Church of England. He died in 1862.

In 1837, the first time any records are reported, there were 21 275 members, 57 Preachers and 53 Circuits. There was missionary work in Ireland, Germany, Australia, and the West Indies. In 1857, with the amalgamation with the Wesleyan Reformers, the membership was 20 873, 93 Preachers, 381 Chapels and 161 Preaching Places.

Wesleyan Methodist Reformers 1849–1857

THE SECESSION WHICH gave birth to this branch of Methodism has been called 'The great upheaval of Methodism'. It is said that over 100 000 members left the Wesleyan Methodist Connexion, and the financial loss was about £100 000.

In 1844 there appeared an anonymous publication which was sent to all Wesleyan Methodist ministers. It was the first of five such publications between 1844 and 1849, and which were called 'Fly Sheets'.

All were an attack on the constitution and administration of Wesleyan Methodism. It was alleged that far too many officials had been stationed in London for a number of consecutive years, that they moved from one London Circuit to another, that among them there was an intrigue and that they met together in secret to form proposals for policy.

A number of ministers were alluded to by their office, rather than by name, but one who was certainly named was Dr Jabez Bunting, Senior Secretary at the Mission House, to which he had been first appointed in 1833, remaining there for the rest of his active ministry. He had been the President of the Wesleyan Theological Institution from its inception in 1834, had two periods as Secretary of the Conference, 1814–1819 and 1824–1827, and by 1844 had been elected President of the Conference four times, the only minister to have been so elected up to then, and only later equalled by his friend and supporter, Robert Newton.

A further allegation was that all the Connexional Committees met in London, and that most of the Connexional Secretaries, if their office was not a stationed appointment, were found a London Circuit. It was said that Secretaries stationed in administrative posts were too secular and deficient in their calling as Methodist ministers, they had high allowances and lived in commodious houses. Complaints were made about the way the President of the Conference was nominated for election, favouritism playing a large part in the choice of Connexional Secretaries and members of Committees.

There is little doubt that there is some truth in some of these allegations, and if complaints had been made about them in the Conference and debated there, at least an answer could have been made. But, as Dr John Bowmer rightly said, 'It was done with an invective which amounted to slander'.

As was to be expected, Jabez Bunting said, 'the Fly Sheets must be put down', and Conference permitted the Revd George Osborn to issue a 'Declaration' sent to every minister asking that they should sign to the effect that they had not written or had any part in writing the 'Fly Sheets'.

At the Conference of 1849 it was found that thirty-six ministers had refused, for different reasons, to sign the Declaration, a number far too high for the Conference to deal with, so it was decided to interrogate only a few.

There is no doubt that there were some suspicions, with the Revd James Everett, who had entered the ministry in 1807, at the top of the list. He was a prolific writer and had spoken his mind on constitutional matters on more than one occasion. He was not present at the Conference, so was sent for, to appear before it to be questioned about authorship of the 'Fly Sheets'. His request for the name of his accuser, and the nature of the charge against him, was refused, and after a very long debate, and many points of order, he too flatly refused to answer, and on that account was expelled from the ministry.

It has never been proved who was the author of the 'Fly Sheets', but Dr John Kent may not be far from the truth when he says that if James Everett 'did not write them, then he must have been green with envy of the person who did'.

Two other ministers among those who refused to sign the Declaration were also brought to the bar of the Conference, and when both of them were asked if they had played any part in the writing of the 'Fly Sheets', refused to answer. Samuel Dunn, who entered the ministry in 1819, was more specifically charged with starting the publication of a monthly periodical called 'The Wesley Banner', which gave its support to reform. He was told that if he would promise to cease publication the charge against him would be dropped, but he refused and was forthwith expelled from the ministry.

William Griffith, Jun, a son of the manse, who father was still in the ministry, and who himself entered it in 1836, was charged with making contributions to a newspaper called 'The Wesleyan Times', which also supported the Reform Movement. If he would promise to refrain from further contributions he would be allowed to remain in the ministry. He refused, and was expelled.

When the expulsions had taken place there was widespread criticism of the Conference, the London Times declaring that it had 'taken a step which smacks more of the inquisition than a British tribunal . . . and we pronounce them at once a gross outrage on all our English principles of fair play'. Such remarks must have caused Bunting and his followers much pain, all of them loyal to Tory sentiments.

Very soon after the Conference had concluded, a large meeting was held in Exeter Hall, London, which was the first of a series of meetings throuhgout the country, with widespread support for the Reformers. Many superintendents, when they discovered there were members in their Circuits who supported reform, had to take measures for their explusion.

In 1850 four hundred delegates representing reform congregations met in Albion Street Chapel, London, and sought a meeting with the President of the Conference, but he refused to meet any of them. Between 1850 and 1856, Reform Delegates met at the same time and place as the Wesleyan Conference. They wrote letters asking for the reinstatement of the expelled ministers, and that the principles should at least be debated, and in most cases agreed to, but it was of no avail.

The United Methodist Free Churches 1857–1907

FOR A CONSIDERABLE time the Wesleyan Methodist Association was looking for the possibility of amalgamation with another branch of the Methodist family, one or two attempts being made without result. There is little doubt that the Wesleyan Reformers were more akin than any other branch and in 1854, Hildreth Kay of London, a leading layman, of the Reformers, moved in the Delegate Meeting, 'that communications be opened with the other branches of the Wesleyan family'. He was appointed Secretary of the Committee of Investigation.

The Methodist New Connexion were only prepared to consider any plan for union based on its own constitution. In November, 1854 the Wesleyan Methodist Association appointed twelve representatives (six ministers and six laymen) to meet a similar number of Reformers. The Committee met in Nottingham in 1855. The Reformers prepared a paper giving details of their principles, and these were fully discussed. A further meeting took place in June the same year, where 'A draft basis of union was agreed upon with almost perfect unanimity'. The constitution was agreed at the Wesleyan Methodist Association Assembly in 1855, who suggested a Joint Assembly in 1856. The Reformers held their Delegate Meeting at the same time as the Assembly and proposed one or two slight amendments, but stipulated that two-thirds of the membership of their churches must give approval, a proviso which put the whole matter back for a year. In 1856 agreement was reached on all points and the required number of Reformers were agreeable. In 1857 the Wesleyan Methodist Association Assembly together with the Reformers who were joining, met in Baillie Street Chapel, Rochdale, one of the most important items to discuss being the name of the new denomination. Several were suggested, and after a long debate The United Methodist Free Churches was chosen. James Everett was elected first President of the Assembly, and Robert Eckett first Secretary. At the time of union, the Wesleyan Association membership was 20 873, the Reformers who joined 19 113, totalling 19 986. Some Reformers joined later, but those who did not, formed themselves into the Wesleyan Reform Union in 1859, and still, though small, exist today.

The Wesleyan Reform Union 1859

THERE ARE SOME Wesleyan Reformers who did not wish to join with the Wesleyan Methodist Association in 1857, and at a Delegate meeting held in 1859, it was decided that a 'Declaration of Principles' should be drawn up, with the declared objects: 'To extend brotherly love and increase fraternal intercourse among the Churches comprising the Union. To promote unity of exertion in whatever way may best serve the cause of Christ'.
The first Annual Meeting (later called Conference) met at Bethesda Chapel, Bradford in 1860, when it was reported that the membership was 17 000. The Conference appoints annually a President and Secretary, and both offices are open to both ministers and laymen. It is perhaps not insignificant that the Union uses the Methodist Hymn Book in its worship.

The Methodist Church 1932

WHILE THE NEGOTIATIONS were taking place to form what was to be the United Methodist Church between 1902–1907, feelers were being put out by some Wesleyan Methodists for fuller Methodist Union. As was suggested above, the formation of the United Methodist Church in 1907 gave impetus to those who were seeking wider union. A leading Wesleyan layman, Robert W Perks (later Sir), proposed a Committee of Inquiry should meet representatives of the other Methodist denominations in 1903. Approaches were made to the Methodist New Connexion, but they rejected the proposals.
In 1912 John Lewis introduced a motion on Methodist Union into the Wesleyan Conference, and the following year Robert Perks secured another Committee of Inquiry. In 1916 Samuel Horton persuaded the Primitive Methodist Conference to set up a Committee to investigate Primitive Methodist and United Methodist Union. In 1920 a 'Tentative Scheme' for Methodist Union was published, and the three Conferences sent it down to their Districts for consideration. All Synods criticized it. In 1922 opposition to union was expressed by some leading United Methodists, and in 1924 by some Primitive Methodists. In 1925 the Wesleyan Conference decided that a 75 per cent vote in favour must be secured both in the Conference and Districts for any proposal on union. In 1926 major revisions to doctrinal and sacramental clauses were made. The Wesleyan Synods failed to get a 75 per cent vote for an Enabling Bill, although the Representative Session of the Conference voted in favour of the 'Scheme'. In 1927 the Wesleyan Synods again failed to get the requisite vote, and the Representative Session of the Conference now withdrew its support for union. In 1927 the Wesleyan Conference appointed a Committee of four, Henry Carter, John Hornabrook, J Ernest Rattenbury, and John H Rider, to investigate, 'the basis of a Draft of Agreement'. They presented 'A Policy of Three Stages: acceptance of the Enabling Bill in 1928; a final vote for Union in 1931, and a Uniting Conference in 1932; the first Conference of the United Church in 1933. 'The interim period was to be devoted to active preparation, and the 75 per cent formula was to be observed throughout'.
The Primitive Methodist and the United Methodist leaders accepted these Three Stages, as did subsequently their Conferences. The Representative Session of the Wesleyan Conference, and the Primitive Methodist and United Methodist Conferences all accepted the proposal for Methodist Union, the Pastoral Session of the Wesley Conference accepting it by one vote, the other two Conferences not having a Pastoral Session.
In 1929 The Methodist Church Union Act was passed by Parliament, and the Methodist Church in Great Britain was formed in 1932, the Uniting Conference meeting in the Royal Albert Hall, London, on September 20th 1932, in the presence of their Royal Highnesses, the Duke and Duchess of Gloucester, represent ing King George V and Queen Mary.
The Deed of Union was read and signed. The Revd John Scott Lidgett, MA DD, was elected the first President, Sir Robert W Perks, Bart, Vice-President, and the Revd Robert Bond, Secretary of the Conference.
The 1932 Deed of Union was superseded in 1976 by The Methodist Church Act.

Methodist ministers

ADAMS, Deryck Underwood, 2 Linthurst Newtown, Blackwell, Bromsgrove, Worcs. B60 1BP. (021-445 1022) *b. 8 Feb 1917, Harrogate. m. 11 April 1944: 4s.*
Education: 1925–9 St. Olaves (Prep); 1929–35 Wycliffe; 1937–40 Didsbury Coll. *Appointments:* 1940–41 St. Vincent; 1941–52 Georgetown, Br. Guiana; 1952–53 Morecambe; 1953–62 Guernsey; 1962–68 Southend; 1968–75 London Mission, Broomwood and Clapham; 1975–82 Northampton; 1982– Bromsgrove.
Connexional Committees: 1965–71 Healing; 1972–78 D.S.R. Community Relations.

ADAMS, John Clifford, 18 Bushmead Rd., Luton, Beds. LU2 7EU. (0582-29916) – MA Leeds, BD Lond. *b. 20 April 1927, Halesowen. m. 7 March 1981; 1d., 2s.*
Education: 1940–42 Halesowen Tech. and Comm. Sch., Halesowen; 1951–55 Hartley Victoria Coll.; 1954–57 Poly of Central London, London. *Appointments:* 1955–56 Belper; 1956–8 Morley; 1958–66 Manchester NE; 1966–70 Bramhall; 1970–75 Industrial Chaplain, London SE District; 1975–76 Nigeria; 1976–80 Pontefract and Normanton; 1980– Luton Industrial College.
Connexional Committees: 1971–73 'July' Committee. *Publications:* Chester House 1974, *The Work of God and Man.*
Special Interests: Industrial Mission, Ministerial Training, Biblical Theology, Social and Political Ethics, Liturgy. *Hobbies and Recreations:* Sport, Music, Walking, Gardening.

ADAMS, Maurice Malcolm, 41 Abbotsham Rd., Bideford, Devon EX39 3AF. (023-72 2352) – BA (Open). *b. 13 Feb 1933, Leicester. m. 9 June 1956: 2d., 1s.*
Education: 1938–40 Coleman Rd. Prim.; 1940–44 Humberstone Jnr.; 1944–49 Gateway, Leicester; 1958–61 Handsworth. *Appointments:* 1961–64 St. Just; 1964–67 Redruth; 1967–72 St. Ives; 1972–77 Isles of Scilly; 1977– Bideford.
Local Council Committees: 1972–77 Isles of Scilly Education Committee.
Hobbies and Recreations: Music, Photography, History of the Cinema, Walking.

AGER, Edward James, 98 Chiltern Gardens, Dawley, Telford TF4 2QJ. (0592-502007) *b. 9 Jan 1942, Irthlingborough. m. 4 April 1970: 1d., 1s.*
Education: Irthlingborough C.P. Sch.; 1953–58 Wellingborough Gram. Sch.; 1963–67 Richmond Coll. *Appointments:* 1967–72 Winsford; 1972–79 Kendal; 1979– Telford South.
Local Council Committees: 1975–79 Age Concern, South Lakeland; 1981– Age Concern, Wrekin; 1982– Telford Community Council.
Special Interests: Ecumenical Work – World Development, Community Development. *Hobbies and Recreations:* Gardening, Walking.

AINSWORTH, Alan Patterson, 18 Clarence Road, Leighton Buzzard, Beds. LU7 8EJ. (0525-372289) – BD Lond. *b. 1920, Blackburn. m. 1949: 3s.*
Education: Wilsons Gram. Sch., Camberwell, 1947–49 Wesley Coll., Bristol. *Appointments:* 1945–46 Presidents List; 1946–47 Matlock; 1947–50 Bristol Coll.; 1950–54 Bury; 1954–61 Salisbury; 1961–66 West Wight; 1966–72 Portsmouth and Southsea.

ALDERSON, James, Beckstones Yard, Gayle, Hawes, N. Yorks. DL8 3SA. (096-97 513) *b. 23 May 1909, Gayle, N. Yorks. m. 19 Aug 1939: 3s.*
Education: 1914–23 Hawes; 1932–36 Didsbury Coll. *Appointments:* 1931–33 Horncastle; 1936–39 Dursley and Stonehouse; 1939–41 Farringdon; 1941–6 Witney; 1946–50 Leeds, Richmond Hill; 1950–56 Boston; 1956–63 Farringdon; 1963–74 Dursley and Stonehouse.
Publications: Under Wetherfell.
Special Interests: Local History.
Hobbies and Recreations: Woodwork, Walking.

ALDRIDGE, Derek Albert, 9 Newcastle Rd., Chester le Street, Co. Durham DH3 3TS. (0385-883374) *b. 27 Oct 1947, Chelsea. m. 2 Oct 1968: 1d., 1s.*
Education: 1976–79 Wesley Coll., Bristol. *Appointments:* 1979– Chester le Street.

ALLAN, Donald George, 'The Manse', 29 Dundalk Lane, Cheslyn Hay, Walsall, W. Midlands WS6 7BA. (0922-414156) *b. 7 Sept 1931, Barrow-in-Furness. m. 1 Aug 1959: 2d., 1s.*
Education: 1936–40 Holker St. Inf., Barrow-in-Furness; 1940–41 Rawlinson St. Jnr., Barrow-in-Furness; 1941–43 Coniston C.E. Prim.; 1943–51 Ulverston Gram. Sch.; 1953–54 Norwood Tech. Coll., W. Norwood; 1955–58 Handsworth. *Appointments:* 1958–59 Attleborough; 1959–63 Shrewsbury; 1963–68 Stoke-on-Trent, Hanley; 1968–74 Stoke-on-Trent, Burslem; 1974– Cannock Chase; (1976– Part-time Chaplain Featherstone Prison).
Special Interests: Ministry of Healing,

Religious Drama. *Hobbies and Recreations:* Philately, Matchstick Modelling.

ALLCOTT, Barrie Armell, Asbury House, 3(B) Cambridge Rd., Colchester CO3 3NS. (0206-73061) – BA (Open). *b. 16 April 1939, Birmingham. m. 6 April 1963: 2s. Education:* 1950–56 King Edwards, Birmingham; 1962–63 Westhill Coll.; 1970–72 Open Univ.; 1959–62 Didsbury. *Appointments:* 1963–68 Bristol Mission; 1968–73 London, Streatham and Dulwich; 1973–81 Kingston upon Thames; 1981– Colchester. *Connexional Committees:* 1981– National Children's Home; 1976–79 Connexional Candidate; 1980– Division of Social Responsibility. *Publications:* London Union of Youth Clubs 1978, *Decisions Decisions*, An Investigation into Community Education.
Special Interests: Broadcasting: Regular Contributor 'Prayer for the Day' Radio 4; Television with Anglia TV. *Hobbies and Recreations:* Cricket, Swimming, Boating.

ALLEN, Lemuel Thompson Marsden, Cedar Lawn, Welcombe Rd., Stratford-upon-Avon, Warwicks. CV37 6YR. *b. 30 March 1898, Wimbledon. m. 26 Jan 1921: 1d., 1s. Education:* Dondonald El. Sch., Rutlish Sec. Sch., Merton, Surrey; 1924–27 Richmond. *Appointments:* 1927–31 Hastings; 1931–34 Selby; 1934–38 Higham Ferrers; 1938–42 Leicester, King Richards Rd.; 1942–46 Leamington; 1946–52 Lancaster, Sulyard St.; 1952–59 London, Wandsworth; 1959–63 London, Brentford.
Special Interests: Theology, Prison Chaplaincy.

ALLEN, Michael John, 62 King George's Ave., Leiston, Suffolk IP14 4JG. (0728-830733) – BSc (B'ham), MA (Cantab). *b. 25 Jan 1942, King's Lynn. m. 1 April 1982: 1d., 1s. Education:* 1947–49 St. Michael's CE, King's Lynn; 1949–52 St. Margarets CE, King's Lynn; 1952–60 King Edward VII Gram. Sch., King's Lynn; 1960–63 Birmingham Univ.; 1963–66 Fitzwilliam House, Cambridge Univ.; 1963–66 Wesley House. *Appointments:* 1966–68 Kent Mission; 1968–69 Wadhurst; 1969–73 Ipswich; 1973–78 Wellingborough; 1978– Lowestoft and E. Suffolk. *Special Interests:* Charismatic Renewal in Methodism. *Hobbies and Recreations:* Music, Ornithology.

ALLEN, Percy O., 57 Mill Lane, Saxilby, Lincoln LN1 2HN. (0522-702327) *b. 7 June 1918, Somerset. m. 14 Sept 1944: 1d., 3s. Appointments:* 1969–74 Barnsley East; 1974–79 Forest of Dean; 1979– Lincoln North.

ALLEN, Richard, 117 Hastings Rd., Swadlincote, Burton-on-Trent, Staffs DE11 9AL. (0273 217110) *b. Wynberg, Cape. m. 9 Feb 1951: 1d., 1s.*
Education: 1959–62 Richmond. *Appointments:* 1962–68 Kenya; 1966–71 Jersey; 1971–76 Stour Valley; 1976–81 Portland; 1981– South Derbyshire.
Connexional Committees: 1966–71 Christian Citizenship.

ALLEN, Thomas Leslie, 'Trevone', South Rd., Hythe, Kent CT21 6AT. (0303-66281) – BD Lond. *b. 5 Dec 1944, Wandsworth. m. 18 Sept 1965: 1d., 2s.*
Education: 1956–63 Sir Roger Manwoods Gram. Sch., Sandwich; 1966–69 Richmond. *Appointments:* 1969–71 Boston; 1971–77 Doncaster; (1971–74 Doncaster West); 1977– Folkestone.
Special Interests: Training. *Hobbies and Recreations:* Board Games, Music.

ALLEN, Trevor David, 93 Mountnessing Rd., Billericay, Essex CM12 9EZ. (02774-3085) – BA Bristol. *b. 19 Aug 1939, Kingham. m. 14 April 1962: 2d., 1s.*
Education: 1951–57 Chipping Norton Gram. Sch.; 1958–62 Bristol Univ.; Didsbury. *Appointments:* 1962–64 Canterbury and Faversham; 1964–67 Mansfield West; 1967–75 Nottingham Central; 1975– Romford. *Connexional Committees:* 1973–75 Candidates Committee.
Hobbies and Recreations: All Sport, Gardening.

ALLINSON, John Bernard, 15 Oakley Close, Addlestone, Weybridge, Surrey KT15 2LT. (0932-46330) *b. 10 July 1929, Middleton-in-Teesdale. m. 28 Dec 1957.*
Education: 1934–42 Middleton-in-Teesdale Elem.; 1957–61 Hartley Victoria. *Appointments:* 1961–63 Uttoxeter; 1963–67 Nantwich; 1967–74 Aldershot; 1974– Woking/Walton-on-Thames.
Special Interests: Hospital Chaplaincy. *Hobbies and Recreations:* Photography, General D.I.Y., Walking, Caravans, Boats.

ALLISON, Roy Christopher, 35 Alcove Rd., Bristol BS16 3DS. (0272-651089) – MA Cantab. *b. 10 May 1932, Grimsby. m. 3 June 1961: 2s.*
Education: 1942–50 Pears Lane Prim. Sch.; 1950–51 Clee Gram. Sch.; 1951–57 Hymers Coll., Hull; 1957–61 Cambridge Univ.; 1961–63 Hartley Victoria. *Appointments:* 1963–68 Manchester SE; 1968–71 Manchester and Salford Mission; 1971–76 Plymouth and Devonport Mission; 1976– Bristol Mission.
Local Council Committees: 1970–71 Committee to implement Seebohm Report in Salford; 1974–76 Devon Education Authority, Plymouth Area, Youth Service Committee and Grants Sub-Committee.
Special Interests: The needs of the poor, Welfare Benefits, Employment of Young People, United Nations Association. *Hobbies and Recreations:* Providing 'fellowship' holiday tours, Loooking for a small property we can afford to purchase.

ALLPORT, Ralph Edward, Downlands, Farrington Rd., Paulton, Bristol, Avon BS18 5LP. (0761-414778) *b. 19 Aug 1901, Quarry Bank. m. 30 June 1927: 1d.*
Education: 1905–13 Quarry Bank Council Sch.; 1913–17 King Edward VI Gram. Sch., Stourbridge; 1923–25 Hartley Victoria. *Appointments:* 1921–23 Lowestoft and Beccles; 1923–25 Hartley; 1925–32 Radstock;

1932–44 Weymouth; 1944–53 Worcester; 1953–59 Chippenham; 1959–64 Paulton.
Hobbies and Recreations: Football, Gardening.

ALTON, William Herbert, 7 Castle View, Sherriff Hutton, York. YO6 1PR. *b. 5 Feb 1907, Ripon. m. 26 July 1934: 1d., 1s.*
Education: 1917–21 Ashville Coll., Harrogate; Didsbury Coll., Manchester. *Appointments:* 1931–50 South China District.
Connexional Committees: 1955–63 General Committee MMS.
Special Interests: Overseas Church (China). *Hobbies and Recreations:* Cantonese, Pig Farming, Bowling.

AMBLER, George Robson, The Manse, Allendale Town, Hexham, Northumberland NE47 9BZ. (Allendale 344) – BD. *b. 1 Dec 1923, Ryton on Tyne. m. 15 Oct 1955: 2d., 1s.*
Education: 1928–29 Crookhill Inf. Sch., Ryton; 1929–31 Featherstone Park CE Sch.; 1931–34 Herdley Bank Sch., Coanwood; 1934–40 Queen Elizabeth Gram. Sch.; Hexham; 1950–53 Manchester Univ.; 1950–53 Hartley Victoria. *Appointments:* 1953–60 Leeward Islands, W. Indies; 1960–65 Br. Guiana; 1965–70 Macclesfield; 1970–75 South Shields; 1975–80 Stanley; 1980–82 Allendale.
Connexional Committees: 1982 Memorials Committee. *Council Member:* 1967–69 Chaplain to Village Chairman, Bollington; 1978–79 Chaplain to District Chairman, Derwentside.
Special Interests: Music, Drama, Theology, History, Geography, Poetry, Philosophy, Psychology, Sport, People. *Hobbies and Recreations:* Sport, Reading, Poetry, Drama, Music, Chess, Scrabble, Crosswords, Mathematical Puzzles.

AMERY, Frank Maples, 83 Mellish Rd., Walsall WS4 2DF. (0922-28723) – MA. *b. 8 July 1922, Crowle. m. 1952: 2s.*
Education: 1927–33 Crowle Council Sch.; 1933–37 Clee Gram. Sch., Cleethorpes; 1937–40 Alford Gram. Sch., Lincs; 1940–42 Wadham Coll., Oxford Univ.; 1946–48 Didsbury, Bristol. *Appointments:* 1948–49 Halifax, St. Johns; 1949–53 Gainsborough; 1953–57 Market Rasen and Caistor; 1957–62 Hull, Trinity; 1962–68 Holbach; 1968–69 Lincoln, N.; 1969–78 Chairman, Sheffield District; 1979–81 Walsall; 1981– Walsall and Darlaston.
Connexional Committees: Chairman, Day Schools Committee, Division of Education and Youth Convenor, Methodist Representative on Free Church Federal Council.

AMERY, Martin John, Wesley Manse, 46 Doncaster Rd., Bawtry, Doncaster DN10 6NU. (0302-710354) – BA Dunelm, MA Cantab. *b. 9 June 1953, Gainsborough. m. 10 Aug 1974: 1d., 1s.*
Education: 1963–68 Spalding Gram. Sch.; 1968–69 Lincoln Sch.; 1969–71 King Edward VII Sch., Sheffield; 1971–75 St. Cuthberts Society, Durham Univ.; 1975–77 Fitzwilliam Coll., Cambridge Univ.; 1975–78 Wesley House, Cambridge. *Appointments:* 1978–82 Redcar, Saltburn and Guisborough; 1982– Doncaster.
Special Interests: Foreign Languages, Spanish Evangelical Church, Hebrew and Greek, Hymnology. *Hobbies and Recreations:* Bridge, Chess.

AMES, Frank, 994 Anlaby Rd., Hull, N. Humberside HU4 6AT. (0482-561571) – BA Lond., MA Surrey.
Education: 1946–47 Handsworth.
Appointments: 1947–50 Walkden; 1950–55 Long Eaton; 1955–60 Darlington, N.; 1960–69 Stockton on Tees; 1969–74 Leigh on Sea; 1974–79 Purley; 1979– Hull, W.
Connexional Committees: 1969–74 Restructuring; 1970–75 Conference Memorials Secretary; 1976– Conference Record Secretary; General Purposes.

ANDERSON, Brian John, 26 Linkside, New Malden, Surrey KT3 4LB. (01-942 0333) – BSc(Hons) Liverpool; Post Grad. Cert. in Education, Birmingham; Post Grad. Cert. in Theology, Cambridge. *b. 3 Feb 1939, Wallasey. m. 29 Aug 1964: 2s.*
Education: 1950–57 Wallasey Gram. Sch.; 1957–61 Liverpool Univ.; 1961–62 Birmingham Univ.; 1974–76 Wesley House, Cambridge. *Appointments:* 1976–81 Cambridge; 1981– Kingston-upon-Thames.
Hobbies and Recreations: Railways, Walking, Gardening, Maps.

ANDERSON, Brian Vaughan, 30 Marlborough Rd., Castle Bromwich, Birmingham B36 0EH. (021-747 2517) – BD. *b. 3 Mar 1922, Algburth. m. 23 Mar 1954: 1d., 1s.*
Education: 1932–39 Liverpool Institute; 1948–51 Handsworth.
Appointments: 1946–48 Marlborough; 1951–52 Poole; 1952–55 Sunderland W.; 1955–58 Poole; 1958–60 Macclesfield; 1960–63 Keighley; 1963–69 Southampton; 1969–71 West Wight; 1971–76 Southport; 1976–82 Richmond, Yorks.
Parliamentary Service: 1982– Birmingham Elmdon.
Special Interests: Opera. *Hobbies and Recreations:* Walking, Cycling, Old Churches.

ANDERSON, George Wishart, 51 Fountainhall Rd., Edinburgh EH9 2LH. (031-667 2945) – MA St. Andrews & Cantab., Hon. DD St Andrews, Hon. Teol. D. Lund, FBA, FRSE. *b. 25 Jan 1913, Arbroath. m. (1) 14 June 1941; (2) 27 July 1959: 1d., 1s.*
Education: 1920–24 Inverbrothock Elem. Sch.; 1925–31 Arbroath High Sch.; 1931–35 Univ. of St. Andrews; 1935–38 Fitzwilliam House, Cambridge; 1938–39 Univ. of Lund, Sweden; 1935–38 Wesley House, Cambridge. *Appointments:* 1939–41 Asst. Tutor, Richmond Colll; 1941–46 Chaplain H.M.F.; 1946–56 Tutor in O.T. Language and Literature, Handsworth Coll.; 1956–58 Lecturer in O.T. Literature and Theology, St. Andrews Univ.; 1958–62 Professor of O.T. Studies, Durham Univ.; 1962–68 Professor of O.T. Literature and Theology, Edinburgh Univ.; 1968–82 Professor of Hebrew and O.T. Studies, Edinburgh Univ.
Council Member: 1966 Memorial; 1969 Fernley-Hartley; 1976–80 Speaker's Lectures, Oxford; 1978 Henton Davies. *Offices Held:* In Society for O.T. Study – 1957–66 Editor of *Book List*; 1963 President; 1964–73 Hon. Foreign Secretary. In

International Organization for the Study of the O.T. – 1950–75 Member of Editorial Board of *Vetus Testamentum*; 1953–71 Hon. Secretary; 1971–74 President. Edinburgh Council of Christians and Jews – 1969–73 Joint Chairman. Friends of St. Andrews, Jerusalem – 1970– Joint President. *Award:* British Academy's Burkitt Medal for Biblical Studies 1982. *Publications Editor:* 1967 *A Decade of Bible Bibliography; 1970 Aage Bentzen, King and Messiah*, 2nd edn.; 1979 *Tradition and Interpretation*; *Lectureships:* Ryder Smith. *Publications: Books:* 1959 *Critical Introduction to the Old Testament;* 1966 *History and Religion of Israel. Translations:* 1956 *He That Cometh*, from the Norwegian of S. Mowinckel; 1965 *The Ras Shamra Discoveries and the Old Testament*, from the Norwegian of A. S. Kapelrud. Articles in learned journals and collected works.
Hobbies and recreations: Reading, Music.

ANDERSON, James William,
41 Hummersknott Ave., Darlington, Co. Durham DL3 8LQ. (0325-64320) *b. 7 Oct 1904, Cohoes, Albany, U.S.A. m.: 1d.*
Education: 1920–24 Openshaw Tech.; 1928–31 Hartley Victoria. *Appointments:* 1931–32 S.E. London Mission; 1933–35 Carlisle, Cecil St.; 1935–37 Whitehaven Low St.; 1937–40 Brighouse; 1940–46 Chaplain H.M.F.; 1946–56 Gateshead; 1956–60 Consett; 1960–65 Stanley; 1965–69 Shildon.

ANDERSON, Kenneth, 6 Epworth Lodge, 51 Barker Rd., Hong Kong. (Hong Kong 5-96632) *b. 18 April 1928, Middlesborough. m. 19 Mar 1955: 1d., 2s.*
Education: 1942–44 Bootle Jnr. Tech. Coll.; 1951–54 Hartley Victoria. *Appointments:* 1960–64 Barbados and Trinidad; 1964–68 Liverpool Mission; 1968–72 Blackpool N.; 1972–78 Liverpool S.E.; 1978–82 Wallasey; 1982 Appointed to Hong Kong (English District) as Chairman and General Supt.
Special Interests: Politics and Current Affairs. *Hobbies and Recreations:* Water Colour Painting and Cartooning, Reading, History.

ANDERSON, Thomas Alan,
7 Parkside, Park End, Middlesborough, Cleveland TS3 0BP. (0642-314401) – BA, ALA.
Education: 1957–1966 The High Sch. of Glasgow; 1967–69 Robert Gordon's Inst. of Technology, Aberdeen; 1971–72 Jordanhill Coll. of Education, Glasgow; 1973–77 Univ. of Birmingham; 1973–77 Queen's Coll., Birmingham. *Appointments:* 1977–81 Wombwell and Hoyland; 1981– Middlesborough and Eston.

ANDREWS, Frederick Arthur,
32 Winchester Ave., Lancaster LA1 4HX. (60854) *b. 28 Nov 1909, Portsmouth. m. 6 Sept 1940: 1d., 1s.*
Education: Keighley Gram.; 1934–37 Handsworth. *Appointments:* 1937–45 Jamaica Dt., W. Indies; 1945–49 Nottingham, Central; 1949–53 Wellingborough; 1953–61 Aireborough; 1961–67 Chorley; 1967–72 Bolton Wesley; 1972–75 Goole.

ANDREWS, William John,
19 Velindre Rd., Whitchurch, Cardiff, S. Glamorgan CF4 7JE. (0222-66316) – BA Keele, BA Cambridge. *b. 5 Dec 1936, Abingdon. m. 19 Aug 1961: 2s.*
Education: 1948–51 Penzance Gram.; 1951–55 Devonport High; 1955–59 Keele Univ.; 1959–61 Wesley House. *Appointments:* 1961–64 Bourne; 1964–71 Louth; 1971–79 Bath; 1979– Cardiff.
Special Interests: Ecumenical Movement. *Hobbies and Recreations:* Sports and Games, Reading.

ANFIELD, Harold Arthur, The Manse, Summer Lane, Dudley, W. Midlands DY3 2HA. (0384-52114) *b. 27 June 1924, Hull. m. 4 Aug 1951: 2s.*
Education: 1929–32 Wheeler St. Sch.; 1932–37 Paisley St. Sch., Hull; 1937–39 Hull Coll. of Commerce; 1946–48 Headingley. *Appointments:* 1948–50 South Devon Mission; 1950–52 Loftus and Staithes; 1952–54 Scarborough, St. Sepulchre St.; 1954–60 Sowerby Bridge; 1960–64 Wellington, Shropshire; 1964–71 Droxford; 1971–74 Leigh-on-Sea; 1974–79 Sherburn; 1979– Gornal and Sedgley.
Special Interests: Convention Ministry, Gardening. *Hobbies and Recreations:* Gardening.

ANKERS, Arthur Reginald,
19 Dawes Close, Worthing, W. Sussex BN11 2LB. (0903-37618) – MA Bristol, Hon. DD, High Point U.S.A. *b. 19 April 1909, York. m. 24 July 1940: 1d.*
Education: 1915–20 Priory St. Wesleyan Higher Grade Sch., York; 1920–25 Nunthorpe Gram. Sch., York; 1937–40 Bristol Univ.; 1941–42 St. Deiniol's Coll., Hawarden; 1933–37 Didsbury Coll., Manchester. *Appointments:* 1936–37 Didsbury; 1937–38 President's List; 1938–41 Minehead and Dunster; 1941–45 Chaplain H.M.F.; 1945–50 Darlington South; 1950–56 Middlesborough; 1956–63 Wolverhampton, Trinity; 1963–70 Bournemouth; 1970–74 Worthing.
Publications: Articles in the Wolverhampton Magazine, The Dalesman (Yorkshire), The Journal of the Kipling Society.
Special Interests: Literary History and Biography; Guide at the National Trust Property called 'Bateman's', Burwash, East Sussex; Lecturer on various literary celebrities; Sport of all kinds; Travel.

ANNAND, Alexander Robertson,
13 Long Bank, Wrekenton, Gateshead, Tyne and Wear NE9 7HE. (875131) *b. 27 Jan 1936, Aberdeen. m. 3 Mar 1962: 1d., 1s.*
Education: Hanover St. Jnr., Aberdeen; Frederick St. Sec. Mod., Aberdeen; 1962–63 Selly Oak Colls; 1969–70 Newcastle Univ.; 1978–81 Queens.
Appointments: 1981 Gateshead and Jarrow.
Local Council Committees: Methodist Dist. Rep. North of England Boy's Brigade Dist. Council.
Special Interests: Community Care, Boy's Brigade, Elderly and Physically Handicapped. *Hobbies and Recreations*: Music, Gardening.

ANSLEY, John William,
153 Rockingham Rd., Corby, Northants NN17 1JW. (05366-3065) *2s.*

Education: 1955–58 Richmond. *Appointments*: 1958–61 Pocklington; 1961–67 East Nigeria Dt; 1967–72 Ossett and Horbury; 1972–76 Staines and Feltham; 1976–81 London Mission Broomwood and Clapham; 1981 Kettering and Corby. *Connexional Committees*: 1973–76 Home Committee of Overseas Missions.

APPLEBY, John Richard, 17 Thornewill Drive, Stretton, Burton-on-Trent, Staffs DE13 0HY. (0283-63096) – BD(Lond). *b. 3 Jan 1931, Nottingham. m. 16 Aug 1958: 1d., 1s.*
Education: Lenton Prim., Nottingham; Mundella Gram., Nottingham; 1946–48 Leicester Coll. of Arts and Crafts; 1955–58 Headingley. *Appointments*: 1958–61 Sheffield (South); 1961–66 Barnsley (East); 1966–69 Hyde and Denton; 1969–74 Loughborough; 1974–79 Cheltenham; 1979– Burton-on-Trent.
Hobbies and Recreations: Collecting Stamps, Watching Cricket, Gardening, Continental Travel.

APPLEYARD, Michael Russell, 54 Whitecote Hill, Bramley, Leeds LS13 2HU. (0532-570563) – MA(Cantab), BD(Lond). *b. 3 April 1932, Yorkshire. m. 10 Aug 1957: 3s.*
Education: 1937–39 Pontefract Rd. Inf., Castleford; 1939–42 Glass Houghton Jnr., Castleford; 1942–51 The Kings Sch., Pontefract; 1954–57 Wesley; 1957 St. Andrew's, Selly Oak. *Appointments*: 1958–70 Southern Rhodesia Dt; 1970–76 Epworth Tech. Coll (Principal 1971–76); 1971–72 Chairman Salisbury Area Council; 1976– Leeds, Horsforth and Bramley. *Connexional Committees*: 1976– Overseas Division Central Committee. *Council Member*: 1965–68 Christian Council of Rhodesia. *Local Council Committees*: 1965–68 Secretary Salisbury Council of Churches. *Publications*: Contributed to *Ideas for Worship*, ed. R. G. Jones.
Special Interests: Industrial Mission, Ecumenical Movement. *Hobbies and Recreations*: Philately, Walking.

ARCHER, David Brian, The Manse, Portessie, Buckie, Banffshire AB5 1SX. (0542-32240) – MA. *b. 30 Nov 1949, Norwich. m. 18 Aug 1973: 1d., 1s.*
Education: 1962–68 Royal High Sch., Edinburgh; 1968–71 Manchester Univ.; 1973–75 Wesley House; 1975–76 Kingsmead. *Appointments*: 1976–79 Livingstone, Zambia; 1979– North of Scotland Mission.
Special Interests: One World Issues, Christian Communication (Local Radio, Drama, Music). *Hobbies and Recreations*: Photography, Philately.

ARLAND, William John, 40 Reeth Rd., Middlesborough, Cleveland TS5 5JX. (0642-822661) *b. 2 Jan 1921, Leicester. m. 15 Aug 1950: 1d., 1s.*
Education: 1926–32 Hinckley Rd., Leicester; 1932–37 Alderman Newton's Boys Sch., Leicester; 1947–49 Handsworth. *Appointments*: 1946–47 Dursley and Stonehouse; 1949–51 Leith and Tranent; 1951–56 Hexham; 1956–61 North of Scotland Mission; 1961–65 Barnard Castle; 1965–71 Hinckley; 1971–78 Hillingdon; 1978– Middlesborough and Eston.
Connexional Committees: 1967–71 Church Membership.

ARMITSTEAD, Kenneth Stephen, Flat 4, 96 London Rd., St. Leonards-on-Sea, East Sussex TN37 6LR. BD, MTh. *b. 21 Aug 1916, Gillingham, Kent.*
Education: 1928 Hastings Gram. Sch.; 1937–41 Richmond. *Appointments*: 1941–44 Luton (Hightown); 1944–47 Stoke on Trent (Stoke); 1947–49 Smethwick; 1949–52 Huddersfield (Gledholt); 1952–57 Bradford (Manningham); 1957–61 Salford (Swinton); 1961–64 Stoke on Trent (Burslem); 1964–69 Frodsham; 1969–71 Sheffield North; 1971–75 Bolton, Farnworth; 1975–80 Sheffield North-East.

ARMSON, Barry Robert, 2 West Bank Avenue, Mansfield, Notts NG19 7BN (0632 23659) *b. 21 June 1946, Sedgley, Staffs. m. 26 Mar 1966: 2s.*
Education: 1957–62 Dudley Gram. Sch.; 1977–79 Queens. *Appointments*: 1979– Mansfield (West).

ARNOLD, Bernard Donald Arnold, 89a Pitt's Lane, Earley, Reading, Berks RG6 1DD. (0734-663914) *b. 5 Sept 1942, Bournemouth. m. 16 Aug 1969: 1d., 1s.*
Education: 1947–57 Sheringham County Prim.; 1957–59 King's Lynn County Tech. Coll.; 1967–70 Bristol; 1971 Kings Mead. *Appointments*: 1971–77 M.C.C.A.; 1977– Reading. *Connexional Committees*: 1977 National Children's Home General Committee, 1978– Caribbean Advisory Committee, 1979 Overseas Division Central Committee. *Council Member*: 1978–81 Reading Council for Community Relations.
Special Interests: Boy's Brigade, Peace Movement, Third World Issues, The Fabian Society, National Children's Home, Prison Chaplaincy. *Hobbies and Recreations*: Books: Wesleyana, Rare, Theology, Third World Thought; Music.

ARNOLD, Clifford, 49 Hightown Rd., Ringwood, Hants BH24 1NQ. (04254-6727) *b. 22 Dec 1902, Portsmouth.*
Education: 1914–18 Portsmouth Boys Sec. Sch.; 1918–21 Portsmouth Dockyard Sch. (part-time); 1924–25 Cliff. *Appointments*: 1964–66 Forest of Dean; 1966–70 Goole; 1970–74 London, Bow Mission.
Special Interests: Youth Work (Club and Scouting), Biography Reading. *Hobbies and Recreations*: Motoring, Camping, Travel.

ARNOLD, Henry George, Sandacre, 4 Morley Close, Burton, Christchurch, Dorset BH23 7LA. (484048) *b. 18 Aug 1896, Peckham. m. 24 Aug 1926: 3s.*
Education: Private School (Kindergarten); Peckham Wesleyan Sch.; 1921–24 Richmond. *Appointments*: 1919–20 Devon and Dorset Mission; 1920–21 Supply; 1921–24 Richmond Coll.; 1924–26 South Molton; 1926–29 Chatham Garrison; 1929–23 Kent Mission; 1933–37 Gravesend; 1937–41 S. Norwood; 1941–47 Colchester; 1947–51 Guildford; 1951–57 Kent Mission; 1957–62 Wiltshire Mission.
Hobbies and Recreations: Cricket, Music, Poetry, Gardening.

ARNOLD, Thomas Peter, 33 Church St., Wath upon Dearne, Rotherham, S. Yorks S63 7RF. (0709-873281) – BA(Sheffield). *b. 13 Feb 1933, Sheffield. m. 13 Aug 1958: 1d., 1s.* *Education*: 1939–42 Eccleshall CE Inf./Jnr.; 1942–51 King Edward VII Sch., Sheffield; 1951–55 Sheffield Univ.; 1955–58 Headingley. *Appointments*: 1958–63 Worcester; 1963–68 Shrewsbury; 1968–76 Sheffield (Victoria); 1976– Wath and Mexborough.
Connexional Committees: 1975–81 Property Division. *Council Member*: 1975–76 President, Sheffield Free Church Federal Council.
Hobbies and Recreations: Gardening, Music, Sport.

ASHBERRY, Bryan, 2 King's Ave., Whitefield, Manchester M25 7SH. (061-766-3291) *b. 22 Dec 1937, Boston, Lincs. m. 15 Aug 1964: 2d., 4s.* *Education*: 1948–53 Boston Gram.; 1963–67 Handsworth. *Appointments*: 1967–69 Newark; 1969–72 Helston; 1972–74 Hayle; 1974–80 St. Ives and Hayle; 1980 Cheetham Hill and Prestwich.
Special Interests: Education. *Hobbies and Recreations*: Philately, All Sports.

ASHBY, Howard William Frederick, 33 Quantock Rd., Weston-super-Mare, Avon BS23 4DD. (0934-24091) – BSc. *b. 23 May 1924, Croydon. m. 29 Mar 1947: 2d., 1s.* *Education*: 1934–42 Caterham Sch., Surrey; 1942–44 Imperial Coll., London; 1947–48 Westminster Coll., London; 1961–62 Richmond.
Appointments: 1962–66 Upwell and Manea; 1966–72 Folkestone; 1972–79 London (Enfield); 1979– Weston-super-Mare.
Connexional Committees: 1974–77 Candidates Committee, 1976– Overseas Pastoral Committee.
Hobbies and Recreations: Music (Piano and Organ), D.I.Y.

ASHLEY, Alan Lord, The Manse, Caxton Close, Park South, Swindon, Wilts SN3 2HS. (0793-23074) – BD(Lond). *b. 18 Jan 1924, Salford. m. 16 April 1955: 2d., 2s.*
Education: 1930–38 Old Trafford Prim. and Sec.; 1950–53 Headingley. *Appointments*: 1953–56 Nigeria; 1956–59 Macclesfield; 1959–74 Nigeria; 1974–79 London Mission, Hammersmith; 1979– Swindon.
Connexional Committees: 1974–79 Overseas Division Central Committee; 1978– Overseas Division Pastoral Committee. *Local Council Committees*: 1974–79 Hammersmith Community Relations.
Special Interests: Multi-Racial Community Relations. *Hobbies and Recreations*: Swimming, Calligraphy.

ASHMAN, Laurence Arthur, Wesley House, 15 Bassett Wood Drive, Southampton SO2 3PT. (0703-769508) – BD. *b. 6 Sept 1924, Brighton. m. 26 July 1952: 1d., 3s.* *Education*: 1936–41 Eastleigh County High Sch.; 1948–51 Richmond. *Appointments*: 1946–48 Andover; 1951–53 Swindon; 1953–56 West Wight; 1956–61 London (Willesden); 1961–68 Portsmouth and Southsea; 1968–75 Gosport and Fareham; 1975–77 Hunmanby Hall Sch. (Chaplain); 1977– Chairman, Southampton District.
Connexional Committees: 1977– General Purposes Committee, 1977– Home Mission Board; 1981– Social Responsibility Board; 1981– President's Council.

ASHMAN, Ronald George, Avoncroft, 3 Morley Close, Burton, Christchurch, Dorset BH23 7LA. (0202-485606) – MA(Cantab), MA(Glasgow), PhD(Wales). *b. 16 Jan 1914, Tredegar. m. 24 July 1942.* *Education*: 1925–30 West Monmouth Sch.; 1933–36 Glasgow Univ.; 1937–40 Cambridge Univ., Fitzwilliam Coll.; 1946–49 University Coll., Cardiff; 1937–40 Wesley House. *Appointments*: 1940–42 Brynmawr; 1942–46 Cardiff (Canton); 1946–52 Cardiff (Penarth and Barry); 1952–57 Bristol (Clifton and Redland); 1957–60 Southport (South); 1960–70 Cardiff (Wesley); 1970–78 Reading.
Connexional Committees: 1945–73 Connexional Youth Council; 1973–79 Divisional Board, Education and Youth; 1975–81 Board of Home Mission; 1980– Board of Trustees Homes for Aged; 1970–79 Methodist Stewardship Organisation. *Local Council Committees*: 1970–73 Reading Education Authority; 1973–78 Berks Education Authority. *Special Interests*: Methodist and Reformation History, The Boys' Brigade.

ASHPLANT, John Douglas, 71 Stanwell Rd., Penarth, S. Glamorgan CF6 2LR. (0222-707013) *b. 10 Oct 1920, Bideford. m. 26 Dec 1941: 1d., 1s.*
Education: 1928–37 Bideford Gram. Sch.; 1946–48 Didsbury. *Appointments*: 1948–54 Northampton (Gold St.); 1954–61 Corby New Town; 1961–65 Edinburgh Mission; 1965–72 Plymouth and Devonport Mission; 1972–81 Cheddar Valley; 1981– Penarth.
Connexional Committees: 1963–70 General Purposes; 1965–70 H.M.; 1968–82 Radio and T.V. (off and on). *Publications*: Book: *Faith For Life*, collection of T.V. talks published 1981. *Special Interests*: Broadcasting (Radio and T.V.) – Advisor to Westward T.V. and TSW from 1965 to present.
Hobbies and Recreations: Sport, Reading, Coin Collecting, Gardening.

ASHTON, Neville, 9 Allandale, St. Albans, Herts AL3 4NG. (0727-57826) – BD(Lond). *b. 15 Oct 1929, Hadfield, Derbyshire. m. 27 July 1957: 2d.*
Education: 1933–41 Hadfield CE Prim. Sch.; 1941–46 Glossop Gram. Sch.; 1967–68 Manchester Univ.; 1953–57 London Univ.; 1953–57 Handsworth. *Appointments*: 1957–62 Middlesborough ; 1962–65 Doncaster Coalfields Mission; 1965–67 Fairfield High Sch., Droylsden; 1968–70 Ilkley Gram. Sch.; 1978 St. Albans.
Special Interests: History, Social and Political and International Affairs, Liturgy, Church Journalism. *Hobbies and Recreations*: Gardening, Cookery and Confectionery, Snooker, Football, Cricket, Golf, Poetry, Music, Travel, Writing.

ASHWORTH, Gordon, 56 Spencer Park, London SW18 2SX. (01-874-8509) *b. 22 June 1943, Accrington. m. 17 July 1971: 1d., 1s.*

Education: St. Peters Jun. Sch., Accrington; Rhyddings County Sec., Oswaldtwistle; 1966–67 Wesley, Headingley; 1968–69 Wesley, Bristol. *Appointments*: 1969–75 London Mission (Lambeth); 1975–78 London Mission (Broomwood and Clapham); 1978– London Mission (Battersea Central).
Connexional Committees: Home Mission Inner City Committee. *Local Council Committees*: 1978– ILEA Divisional Youth Committee, Wandsworth; 1974–78 ILEA Divisional Youth Committee, Lambeth; Joint ILEA/Wandsworth Borough Council Holiday Playschemes Committee.
Special Interests: Inner City. *Hobbies and Recreations*: Video, Photography, Walking.

ASPEY, Albert, Rua Do Molhe 555, Foz Do Douro, 4100 Porto, Portugal. (Porto 681849) *b. 1 June 1911, Leeds. m. 25 Oct 1941: 1d., 1s.*
Education: 1915–22 Elem. Woodside St. James' National; 1922–27 Yeadon and Guiseley Sec. Sch.; 1927–31 Leeds Univ.; 1931–34 Victoria Park and Hartley. *Appointments*: 1934–37 Bristol Mission; 1937–39 London Mission Poplar; 1939–44 Chaplain H.M.F.; 1944–48 West Hartlepool; 1948–51 Nottingham Mission; 1951–55 Derby Mission; 1955– Chairman Portugal District and Minister of Mirante Methodist Church, Oporto.
Publications: *Por Este Caminho*, 1970, a history of Portuguese Methodism till 1900.
Hobbies and Recreations: Gardening and Reading.

ASTON, Gwyron Wesley James, 4 Penyghent View, Settle, North Yorkshire BD24 9JJ. (07292-2554) – BA(Hons)(Theol.)(B'ham). *b. 7 Nov 1931, Gruting, Shetland. m. 8 Aug 1953: 1d., 1s.* JEAN MEAKIN
Education: 1942–47 King Edward VI Gram. Sch., Retford, Notts; 1969–72 Birmingham Univ.; 1969–70 Handsworth; 1970–72 Queens. *Appointments*: 1972–78 Canterbury; 1978– Settle.
Special Interests: Methodist History. *Hobbies and Recreations*: Philately, Photography.

ATHERTON, Malcolm J. W., 122a Main Street, Halton, Runcorn, Cheshire WA7 2PW. (09285-66299) *b. 13 Aug 1944, Prescot, Lancs. m. 2 April 1966: 1d., 2s.*
Education: 1949–55 St. Michaels CE Prim. Sch.; 1955–59 Huyton Hey Sec. Mod. Sch.; 1959–61 St. Helens Tech. Coll.; 1969–72 Manchester Univ.; 1968–72 Hartley Victoria. *Appointments*: 1972–74 Lytham St. Annes; 1972–79 Plymouth, Devonport; 1979– Runcorn.
Special Interests: Music, Work with Schools. *Hobbies and Recreations*: Sea, Coarse and Game Angling, Aquarian.

ATKINS, Martyn David, 176 Town St., Middleton, Leeds LS10 3TH. (0532-716818) – BA. *b. 16 June 1955, Bradford. m. 1980.*
Education: 1968–72 Prince Henry Gram. (Comp.) Sch., Otley, Yorks; 1972–74 Bradford Coll. of Art and Tech.; 1977–81 Manchester Univ.; 1977–81 Hartley Victoria. *Appointments*: 1981– South Leeds.
Special Interests: Modern Gospel Music, both listening to it and playing it (Guitars). Initiation Theology in Methodism. *Hobbies and Recreations*: Badminton, Growing Vegetables, House Decoration!! and Reading and 'Writing' Novels.

ATKINSON, Benjamin Kaines, 2 Epworth Mount, Ocker Hill, Randwick, Stroud, Glos GL6 6HU. (04536-78583) *b. 23 May 1906, Sheffield. m. 15 Aug 1934: 2s.*
Education: Doncaster Rd. Board Sch., Rotherham; South Grove Sch., Rotherham; 1918–23 Rotherham Gram. Sch.; 1928–31 Didsbury. *Appointments*: 1931–33 Mid-Norfolk Mission; 1933–34 Saddleworth; 1934–37 Wantage and Wallingford; 1937–39 Chesterfield, Saltergate; 1939–42 Pontefract, Horsefair; 1942–45 Ripon; 1945–49 Norwich, Calvert St., 1949–54 Loughborough; 1954–60 Wem; 1960–64 Hitchin; 1964–67 Hyde and Denton; 1967–71 Hindley.
Connexional Committees: 1945–49 Overseas Missions East Anglia Rep.
Special Interests: Art, Music. *Hobbies and Recreations*: Art, Organist.

ATKINSON, John Hilary, The Close, Mayfield Grove, Baildon, Shipley, West Yorkshire BD17 6DZ. (0274-582729) – BA(Leeds), MA(Leeds). *b. 24 Nov 1927, Knaresborough, Yorkshire. m. 29 July 1955: 1s.*
Education: 1937–45 Harrogate Gram. Sch.; 1945–48 Leeds Univ.; 1947–48 and 1949–50 Headingley. *Appointments*: 1950–53 Bradford, Woodhouse Grove; 1953–57 Wakefield; 1957–61 Bradford, Shipley; 1961–66 Union Theological Seminary, Jamaica; 1966–71 Colwyn Bay and Llandudno; 1971–79 Christian Citizenship Department/Division of Social Responsibility; 1979– Chairman, West Yorkshire District.
Connexional Committees: Currently member of Property and Home Mission Boards, Connexional General Purposes Committee, Stationing Committee, Faith and Order Committee. Several other committees in past, including 1975–80 President's Council. *Publications*: *Ways Towards Oneness* (SPCK 1965); *Doctors' Dilemmas* (Epworth 1976); *Abortion Reconsidered* (ed.) (Epworth 1977); *What Does Methodism Think?* (ed.) (DSR 1978); *The Media: A Christian View* (Epworth 1979); 1980 Beckly Lecture, 'People & Medicine' (pub. 1981 by Churches' Council for Health & Healing); regular contributor to IBRA books.
Special Interests: Music, the Countryside, Cricket, Current Affairs. *Hobbies and Recreations*: Being Outdoors (walking, camping, caravanning, even gardening), Photography, Reading (almost anything), some Television, as much Music as possible.

ATKINSON, Philip, 72 Henbury Rd., Westbury-on-Trym, Bristol BS10 7AA. BSc. *b. 24 Sept 1955, Stourbridge, Worcs. m. 30 Sept 1978: 1d., 1s.*
Education: 1959–64 Summberbank; 1964–65 Park View CP Sch.; 1965–68 Rydal Prep. Sch.; 1968–73 Rydal Sch.; 1974–78 U.M.I.S.T.; 1981– Bristol.
Special Interests: Evangelism, Children's Work, C.E.I.M. *Hobbies and Recreations:* Genealogy, D.I.Y., Collecting.

ATKINSON, Ronald, 13 Lawn Way, Stockton Lane, York YO3 0JD. (0904-24953) *b. 8 May 1921, Oldham, Lancs. m. 17 Aug 1949: 2d.*
Education: Hollinwood Council Sch.; Oldham High Sch.; 1945–48 Headingley. *Appointments*: 1948–49 Withernsea; 1949–53 Peel, I.O.Man; 1953–58 St. Helens and Prescott; 1958–66 Harrogate; 1966–74 York Clifton and Monkgate; 1974–75 Filey; 1975– Chairman York and Hull District.
Connexional Committees: 1973– Stewardship Sub-Committee; 1975– General Purposes, Home Mission; 1980– Home Mission Executive; 1978– Division Finance.
Special Interests: Ministries. *Hobbies and Recreations*: Cricket, Tennis, Philately, Music.

AUDSLEY, Alwyne, Ashcroft, 17 Spilsby Rd., Wainfleet, Skegness, Lincs PE24 4LN. (0754-880201) *b. 14 Jan 1924, Bradford, Yorkshire. m. 7 June 1947: 1d., 1s.*
Education: 1935–39 Carlton High Sch., Bradford; 1960–62 Hartley Victoria. *Appointments*: 1962–69 Chorley; 1969–77 Bury and Heywood; 1977– Skegness and Wainfleet.
Connexional Committees: 1969–72 Education Committee; 1969–72 Day Schools' Committee. *Local Council Committees*: 1971–74 Bury Education Committee Free Church Rep.
Hobbies and Recreations: Sport.

AUSTIN, Alfred John, Brig-y-Don, 26 Old Rd., Llanelli, Dyfed SA15 3HP. (05542-2474) *b. 26 Feb 1943, Woodsetton, Staffs. m. 15 July 1967.*
Education: 1947–55 Tipton Green County Prim.; 1955–59 Dudley Gram. Sch.; 1964–67 Didsbury; 1967–68 Bristol. *Appointments*: 1968–70 Port Talbot; 1970– Llanelli and Carmarthen.
Hobbies and Recreations: Motor Vehicle Maintenance and Repair.

AUSTIN, Joseph, Walton Place, Holcombe, Bath BS3 5ED. (0761-232638) *b. 21 July 1909, Burslem, Stoke-on-Trent. m. 27 Aug 1936.*
Education: 1914–23 Burslem Elem.; 1930–33 Didsbury. *Appointments*: 1929–30 Wimborne; 1933–36 Shaftesbury; 1936–38 Marlborough; 1938–39 St. Helens and Prescott; 1939–42 Manchester, Harpurhey; 1942–46 Chaplain H.M.F.; 1946–49 Manchester, Chorlton; 1949–52 Sheffield North; 1952–56 Jersey; 1956–61 Devonport; 1961–64 St. Ives; 1964–66 Thirsk; 1966–69 Pontypool; 1969–73 Tipton.
Hobbies and Recreations: Motoring, Photography.

AUSTIN, Robert Alan, The Manse, Reedham Rd., Acle, Norwich NR13 3DE. (0493-750275) *b. 27 March 1938, Clacton-on-Sea, Essex. m. 19 March 1960: 2d.*
Education: 1943–49 St. Osyth Rd. Prim. Sch., Clacton-on-Sea; 1949–54 Pathfields Sec. Mod.; 1954–57 N.E. Essex Tech. Coll., Colchester (day release); 1961–64 Richmond.
Appointments: 1964–70 Peterborough and Oundle; 1970–76 Norwich, Calvert St.; 1976– Acle.
Connexional Committees: Overseas Division Home Committee 1973–76.
Special Interests: Current Affairs.
Hobbies and Recreations: Music, Brass Band, Reading, Singing, Rug-Making.

AYLOTT, William Roy, 19 Panmuir Rd., London SW20 0PZ. (01-946-6239) *b. 6 May 1906, S. Woodford, Essex. Widower. 2s.*
Education: Lindisfarne Coll., Westcliffe-on-Sea, Essex; 1927–30 Hartley Victoria. *Appointments*: 1926 Louth; 1927–30 College; 1930–50 Wenchow Dist. China; 1951–54 East Ham; 1955–57 Rhondda; 1958–1962 Fulham; 1962–68, 1972–74 Sarawak.
Publications: Journalism in various dailies, etc.
Special Interests: Human Rights, International Affairs. *Hobbies and Recreations*: Music, Art, Geology, Travel.

AYRE, Arthur, Glen Millans, Ambleside, Cumbria LA22 9AG. (09663-3232) *b. 18 Nov 1919, Darlington. m. 6 Aug 1949: 1d., 1s.*
Education: 1930–36 Darlington Gram. Sch.; 1946–48 Headingley.
Appointments: 1948–50 Edinburgh, Nicholson Square; 1950–53 Leeds Mission; 1953–59 Bradford, Woodhouse Grove; 1959–65 Stockton; 1965–72 Scunthorpe; 1972–80 Watford; 1980– Ambleside and Windermere.
Special Interests: Music, Ornithology.
Hobbies and Recreations: Photography, Walking, Gardening.

BACON, Christopher Donald, St. Edmund's, Westbury, Sherborne, Dorset DT9 3RA. (Sherborne 2189) – BA(Wales), BD(Manchester). *b. 11 Nov 1915, Shrewsbury. m. 2s.*
Education: 1922–25 Church St. Council Sch., Wallasey; 1925–27 Arnold House Sch., Blackpool; 1927–33 Kingswood Sch.; 1933–36 Univ. of Wales (Bangor); 1937–40 Manchester Univ.; 1937–40 Didsbury. *Appointments*: 1940–42 Assistant Tutor, Headingley College; 1942–47 Leeds, Horsforth; 1947–54 Stockport, Mount Tabor/Hazel Grove and Poynton; 1954–61 London, Harrow; 1961–69 Sec. Youth Dept.; 1969–73 Chairman, Nottingham and Derby District; 1973–79 General Sec. Division of Ministries.
Connexional Committees: 1943–54 Ministerial Training Committee; 1956–69 Youth Department; 1973–79 Ministries. *Publications*: *The World of Young Children* (M.Y.D. 1963); (with Margaret Bacon) *Praying with Beginners* (N.C.E.C. 1968).
Hobbies and Recreations: Photography, Gardening.

BADCOCK, Albert John, 1 Orchard Bank, Heath Green Road, Studland, Swanage, Dorset BH19 3BX. (0929-44335) – MA. *b. 7 Oct 1905, Stourbridge, Worcs. m. 18 Aug 1934: 2s.*
Education: Openshaw Jun. Tech. Sch., Manchester; 1945–49 Liverpool Univ.; 1927–30 Hartley Victoria.
Appointments: 1930–32 Bletchley; 1932–34 Northwich; 1934–36 Market Weighton; 1936–41 Hull North; 1941–44 Hull Coltman St.; 1944–49 Wallasey; 1949–52 Birkenhead; 1952–58 Southport; 1958–65 Wallasey; 1965–70 Reading; 1965–70 Chaplain to Reading University.
Connexional Committees: 1964–68 Local Preachers Connexional Committee. *Local Council Committees*: 1938–42 Hull Education Committee;

1958–65 Governor of Oldershaw Grammar School, Wallasey.
Special Interests: Books.

BADDLEY, George Donald, 269 Ingrow Lane, Keighley, West Yorkshire BD22 7DS. (602669) *b. 20 Mar 1919, Manchester. m. 5 Apr 1947: 1d., 2s.*
Education: 1924–27 Wheeler St. Beginners, Openshaw; 1927–30 Wheeler St. Elem., Openshaw; 1930–34 Varna St., Central Manchester; 1935 Ardwick Central; 1935–38 Manchester Coll. of Tech.; 1945–47 Hartley Victoria. *Appointments*: 1947–50 Bacup; 1950–52 Islington, Higher Ardwick; 1952–55 Manchester and Salford Mission; 1955–59 Otley; 1959–64 Darlington; 1964–70 Lincoln South; 1970–79 Huddersfield East; 1979 Keighley and Worth Valley.
Special Interests: Local Council of Churches. *Hobbies and Recreations*: Photography.

BAGGS, Frederick Peter, Palawan, 27 Coffee Lake Meadow, Lostwithiel, Cornwall PL22 0AW. (0208-873093) *b. 19 May 1917, Croydon. m. 1 June 1946: 1d.*
Education: St. Hilda's Sch., Moseley, Birmingham; King's Norton Sec. Sch., Birmingham; 1974–76 Queens.
Appointments: 1976–82 Liskeard and Looe.
Hobbies and Recreations: Walking, Birdwatching, Gardening.

BAGULEY, Edward C., 1 Aldford Way, Winsford, Cheshire CW7 2HL. (06065-53726) – MA, PhD (Leeds). *b. 13 July 1912, Melton Mowbray. Widower, m. 20 Apr 1940: 3d., 3s.*
Education: 1917–20 CE Prim., Melton Mowbray; 1920–26 Melton Mowbray Boys Sch.; 1932–33 Cliff Coll.; 1935–38 Leeds Univ.; 1935–39 Headingley. *Appointments*: 1939–44 Glasgow Paisley Rd.; 1944–49 Paisley Mission; 1949–52 Lincoln Aldersgate; 1952–57 Leeds Mission; 1957–63 Bramley and Farsley; 1963–69 Normanton; 1969–77 Middlewich.
Hobbies and Recreations: Reading, Photography.

BAGWELL, Frederick Henry, 51 Vicarage Rd., Tywardreath, Par, Cornwall PL24 2PH. (072-681-2773) *b. 22 Nov 1925, Exeter. m. 7 Aug 1954: 1d., 1s.*
Education: 1937–42 Hele's School, Exeter; 1949–52 Didsbury. *Appointments*: 1948–49 Guildford; 1952–54 Devonport; 1954–57 Penzance Central; 1957–62 Tiverton; 1962–71 Plymouth East; 1971–76 Saltash; 1976– St. Austell.

BAILEY, Allan Roy, The Manse, 46 School Lane, Fulford, York YO1 4LS. (0904-33190) *b. 14 Sept 1931, Nottingham. m. 29 Mar 1969: 1d.*
Education: 1943–48 Loughborough Gram. Sch.; 1948–53 Nottingham and District Tech. Coll.; 1953–56 Richmond. *Appointments*: 1956–59 Weardale; 1959–61 Bishop Auckland; 1961–62 Missionary Training; 1962–64 N. Rhodesia Dist; 1964–78 Resigned; 1978 Reinstated; 1979– York Centenary (South).
Special Interests: The work of the Overseas Church. *Hobbies and Recreations*: Photography, Wildlife and Ornithology.

BAILEY, Arthur, 102a Gawsworth Rd., Macclesfield SK11 8UE. (0625-28276) *b. 22 June 1900, Newchapel, Staffs. m. 28 July 1932: 1d., 3s.*
Education: Harrishead; Didsbury.
Appointments: 1925–26 Supply; 1929–32 London Mission, Poplar; 1932–34 Grosvenor St., Manchester; 1934 Longton Zion; 1934–39 London Mission, Central; 1939–45 Hebden Bridge; 1945–49 Bradford Gt. Horton; 1949–55 Birstall; 1955–61 Malton; 1961–65 Farnham; 1965–69 Highgate.
Council Member: Malton Urban District. *Local Council Committees*: All committees.
Special Interests: Social Problems, Local Preacher Training, Church Architecture and Buildings. *Hobbies and Recreations*: Philately, Gardening.

BAILEY, John Martin, 31 Southern Avenue, South Norwood, London SE25 4BT (01 653-2424) – BD(Lond). *b. 10 Jan 1937, Doncaster, Yorks. m. 7 Aug 1963: 1d., 1s.*
Education: 1942–48 Beechfield Inf. & Jun. Mixed, Doncaster; 1948–53 Doncaster Gram. Sch.; 1953–54 Doncaster Tech. Coll.; 1960–63 London Univ.; 1960–63 Richmond.
Appointments: 1963 Sutton; 1964–66 East Dereham; 1966–68 Newhall and Woodville; 1968–71 Grantham; 1971–77 Southend-on-Sea; 1977– Croydon.
Special Interests: The Holy Land – Israel; Ministry of Healing. *Hobbies and Recreations*: Music, Amateur Dramatics, Travel, Aircraft, Swimming, Dog.

BAILEY, John Reginald, 39 Eighth Avenue, Bristol BS7 0QS. (0272-691123) *b. 9 Sept 1907, Worksop, Notts. m. 23 June 1936: 1d., 1s.*
Education: 1930–33 Didsbury.
Appointments: 1928–29 West Monmouth Mission; 1933–34 Ely; 1934–39 Bletchley; 1939–42 Rantenstall; 1943–45 Chaplain H.M.F.; 1945–50 London, Finsbury Park and Southgate; 1950–59 Portsmouth; 1959–66 Jersey; 1966–72 Bristol, Clifton and Redland. 1956–58 Secretary Portsmouth District Synod; 1959–62 Secretary Channel Islands District Synod; 1962–66 Chairman Channel Islands District Synod; 1955 President Portsmouth and District Free Church Council; 1969 President Bristol Free Church Federal Council; 1969 Joint Chairman Bristol Council of Christian Churches.
Hobbies and Recreations: Golf, Gardening, *The Times* Crosswords.

BAINES, Geoffrey, Flat 2, Didsbury House, Wesley College, Henbury Rd., Westbury-on-Trym, Bristol BS10 7QD. (0272-500494) *b. 27 July 1959, Stokesley, N. Yorks. m. 23 Aug 1980: 1s.*
Education: 1970–74 Stokesley Comp.; 1974–75 Scalby Comp., Scarborough; 1975–77 Scarborough Sixth Form Coll.; 1977–78 Cliff Coll.; 1980– Bristol.
Special Interests: Church Growth and Renewal (in services, meetings, etc. membership). *Hobbies and Recreations*: Art and Photography, Sports.

BAIRD, Thomas Charles, 25 St John St., Whithorn, Wigtownshire DG8 8PD. (0988-5446) – MA(Cantab.),

BA, BD, MTh, PhD (Lond.). *b. 18 Oct 1914, Edinburgh. m. 19 July 1941: 3s.* *Education*: 1921–26 George Watsons Boys Coll., Edinburgh; 1926–33 Highgate Sch., London; 1933–36 London Univ.; 1936–39 Cambridge Univ.; 1936–39 Wesley House. *Appointments*: 1939–40 Headingley Coll. (Asst. Tutor); 1940–43 London Westminster; 1943–45 Chaplain H.M.F.; 1945–50 Liverpool N.; 1950–55 Kingston-on-Thames; 1955–68 Rhodesia; 1969–72 Manchester and Salford Mission; 1972–75 Downham Market.
Connexional Committees: 1969–78 Overseas Division General Committee (and General Purposes Committee); 1973–75 Ministries General Committee. *Local Council Committees*: 1941–43 Hon. Sec. Westminster City Youth Council. *Publications*: Asst. Ed. of *Violence in Southern Africa* (S.C.M. 1970); *Now Let It Work* (St James) (Epworth Press 1953); Chapter on *The Last Things* in *Approach to Christian Doctrine* (ed. G. P. Lewis) (Epworth Press 1954).
Special Interests: New Testament Ethics for Today. *Hobbies and Recreations*: Words, Language, Reading, Walking.

BAKER, Blanche Mary, 46a Lyford Rd., London SW18 3LS. (01-870-1742) *b. 25 Aug 1913, Sale, Cheshire.* *Education*: Sale County High Sch. for Girls; Loreburn College, Manchester; 1965 William Temple Coll., Rugby; 1937–39 Wesley Deaconess Coll. *Appointments*: 1974–75 Matlock; 1975–80 Grays, Essex.
Connexional Committees: 1980– N.C.H. Committee; 1958–61 Wesley Deaconess Committee.
Special Interests: Methodist Peace Fellowship. *Hobbies and Recreations*: Gardening, Dressmaking, Reading, Walking, Theatres, Concerts.

BAKER, Bryan Henry, 574 Chorley Old Rd., Bolton, Lancs BL1 6AA. (0204-43609) *b. 21 Dec 1933, Barnstaple. m. 29 July 1961: 3s.*
Education: 1947–53 Ecclesfield Gram. Sch., Sheffield; 1957–61 Handsworth. *Appointments*: 1961–66 Bolton; 1966–71 Newark-on-Trent; 1971–75 Kenya Dt.; 1975–82 Brampton; 1982– Bolton.
Connexional Committees: 1976–82 Overseas Division Central Committee. *Council Member*: 1975–82 Diocese of Carlisle, Council for Agriculture and Rural Life. *Publications*: *African Short Stories* (E.A.F.S. Stockholm, 1976). *Special Interests*: Overseas Development, Small Communities Development. *Hobbies and Recreations*: Music, Watching Soccer and Rugby League, Reading.

BAKER, Eric William, 19 Moorhouse Gdns, Hetton-le-Hole, Houghton-le-Spring, Tyne and Wear DH5 0AD. (0783-266281) – BA (Open Univ.). *b. 6 Mar 1926, Liverpool.*
Education: 1931–36 Bedford Rd. Elem. Sch., Bootle; 1936–40 Merchant Taylors Sch., Gt. Crosby; 1954–58 Hartley Victoria. *Appointments*: 1958–60 Presteigne and Kington; 1960–64 Oldham West; 1964–69 Bodmin; 1969–78 Ramsey, I.O.M.; 1978– Hetton-le-Hole.

BAKER, Norman John, Hothfield, Coombe Rd., Salisbury, Wilts SP2 8BT. (0722-20858) *b. 3 May 1937, Wolverhampton. m. 23 June 1962: 2d., 1s.*
Education: 1947–52 Elmfield Sch., Cheltenham; 1975–76 Westminster Coll., Oxford; 1960–64 Handsworth. *Appointments*: 1964–66 Lowestoft; 1966–71 Witney; 1971–76 Wantage and Abingdon; 1976– Salisbury.
Special Interests: Travel. *Hobbies and Recreations*: Photography.

BAKER, William Harold, 209 Bassaleg Road, Newport, Gwent NPT 3PZ. (66048)
Education: 1914–15 and 1919–21 Handsworth. *Appointments*: 1921–24 East Coast Mission; 1924–27 Wigan; 1927–31 Mansfield; 1931–35 Nottingham, Tennyson St.; 1935–39 Leeds, Headingley; 1939–42 Cleckheaton; 1942–47 Wakefield; 1947–51 Leeds, Richmond Hill; 1951–57 Newport, Gwent.

BALES, Stephen David, The Manse, 142 Princess Drive, Grantham, Lincs NG31 9PY. (0476-4191) *b. 28 Aug 1947, Bradford. m. 12 Aug 1978: 1s.*
Education: 1958–63 Harrogate Gram. Sch.; 1976–9 Queens. *Appointments:* 1979– Grantham.
Special Interests: Family. *Hobbies and Recreations:* Gardening, Music, Poetry.

BALL, Albert, Wesley Manse, The Crescent, Ramsey, Isle of Man. (0624-812385) *b. 3 Dec 1923, Ashton-under-Lyne. m. (1) 28 July 1951: 2d. (2) 11 Apr 1977: Stepchildren 3d., 1s.*
Education: 1935–40 Ashby-de-la-Zouch Boys' Gram. Sch.; 1947–49 Handsworth. *Appointments:* 1946–49 Liverpool Mission; 1949–52 Whitehaven; 1952–56 Burnley; 1956–61 Preston (Lune St. & Orchard St.); 1961–64 Grimsby (George St.); 1964–71 Stoke-on-Trent (Hanley Trinity); 1971–75 Lancaster; 1975–79 Tadcaster; 1979– Ramsey (Isle of Man).
Connexional Committees: 1958–61 Youth Committee. *Local Council Committees:* 1966–69 Stoke-on-Trent Education Committee.
Publications: Opportunity for Mission (BBC Local Radio, Stoke-on-Trent Publication); 1968–71 Religious Programmes Producer, Radio Stoke-on-Trent; at present Religious Programmes Presenter on Manx Radio.
Special Interests: Radio Production.
Hobbies and Recreations: Reading, Music, Gardening.

BALL, David, 10 Park Way Close, Southwick, Brighton, Sussex BN4 4LE. (0273-592608) – BA(Manch.) *b. 7 May 1909, Manchester. m. 7 Aug 1935: 1d., 1s.*
Education: 1914–19 Crumpsall Lane Elem. Sch., Manchester; 1919–25 Queen Elizabeth's Gram. Sch., Middleton, Lancs; 1934–36 Manchester Univ.; 1930–34 Victoria Park.
Appointments: 1929–30 Leeds West; 1934–36 Bury, Brunswick; 1936–37 Bury and Ramsbottom; 1937–40 Guernsey English; 1940–42 Petersfield and Haslemere; 1942–45 Leeds South; 1945–48 Bradford Mission; 1948–53 Bristol East; 1953–58 Plymouth East; 1958–64 Bristol Ebenezer; 1964–67 Brighton and Hove; 1967–70 Finchley and Hendon; 1970–73 Grimsby West.
Connexional Committees: 1955–56

Stationing Committee; 1955–56 Home Missions; 1955–56 General Purposes; 1955–56 Educational.

BALL, Ernest Albert, 9 Springfield, Old Totnes Rd., Buckfastleigh, S. Devon TQ11 0LQ. (03644-3212) *b. 21 June 1915, Saltash, Cornwall. m. 8 Jan 1946 (w.): 1d., 1s.*
Education: Saltash Prim. Sch.; Saltash Boys' Sch.; Saltash County Sec. Sch.; 1939–41 Richmond; 1941–42 Headingley. *Appointments:* 1942–46 Barnstaple (Thorne Memorial); 1946–50 Ludlow; 1950–53 Launceston; 1953–58 Longton and Fenton; 1958–61 Derby South; 1961–66 Bodmin; 1966–75 Totnes; 1975–80 Chepstow and Caldicot.
Hobbies and Recreations: Poster Writing (Graphics).

BALL, Raymond Oliver, Pencraig Cottage, Llechryd, Cardigan, Dyfed SA43 2NR. (023 987-219) *b. 13 Mar 1908, Liverpool. m. 28 July 1939: 2d., 1s.*
Education: 1913–16 Penny Lane Inf. Sch.; 1916–19 Sefton Park Board Sch.; 1919–25 Hendon Gram. Sch.; 1927–28, 1929–30 St. Andrews Coll., Univ. of Saskatchewan, Canada; 1936–37 Westhill Coll. (Selly Oak, Birmingham); 1933–34 Victoria Park; 1934–36 Hartley Victoria. *Appointments:* 1932–33 Knighton (West St.); 1937–38 Youth Lecturer Portsmouth and Southampton District; 1938–41 Cannock Chase; 1941–45 Coventry; 1945–48 Buxton Rd., Huddersfield; 1948–53 Middleton (Manchester); 1953–56 St. Helens, Lancs.; 1956–59 Stratford on Avon; 1959–65 Tadcaster; 1965–73 Boroughbridge.
Connexional Committees: 1946–48, 1949–53 Youth Committee; 1950–61(?) Hartley Victoria College Committee. *Council Member:* 1968–73 Boroughbridge Parish Council. *Local Council Committees:* 1941–45 Coventry Youth Committee; 1945–48 Huddersfield Youth Committee.
Special Interests: Probation Work (Accredited Volunteer), Senior Citizens (Chairman of local organisation), Marriage Guidance (President of local Support Group), Preaching, Adult Literacy (Treasurer of local Day Centre). *Hobbies and Recreations:* Dog Walking, Painting and Making Love Spoons (when time).

BAMFORD, Roland, 43 Scott Park Rd., Burnley, Lancs BB11 4JR. (0282-24946) – BA(Manch.) *b. 17 Dec 1931, Oldham, Lancs. m. 7 Aug 1965: 2d.*
Education: 1942–49 Chadderton Gram. Sch., Oldham, Lancs; 1954–58 Manchester Univ.; 1954–58 Hartley Victoria. *Appointments:* 1958–60 Aberdare; 1960–68 Pontypool (Eastern Valley); 1968–74 London Mission (North and Central); 1974– Burnley.
Local Council Committees: 1980– Burnley, Pendle and Rossendale Community Health Council.
Special Interests: Hospital Chaplaincy, Care of the Elderly, Terminal Care (Community Health Council), Boys' Brigade, Prison Chaplaincy, Non-Directive Leadership. *Hobbies and Recreations:* Crosswords, Walking, Television, Sport (watching).

BANKS, Arthur Wyatt, 80 Holmfield Rd., Leicester LE2 1SB. (0533-737675) – MA(Cantab.), BSc(Lond.) *b. 15 Aug 1910, Audley. m. 5 May 1938: 3s.*
Education: County Sec. Sch., Crewe; 1928–30 North Staffs Tech. Coll., Stoke-on-Trent; 1930–31 Kingsmead Coll, Selly Oak, Birmingham; 1931–34 Wesley House. *Appointments:* 1934–36 Missionary Society; 1936–55 Gold Coast District, West Africa; 1955–56 Missionary Committee; 1956–64 St. Andrew's College; 1964–69 Guildford; 1969–71 Farnham; 1971–72 Supernumerary; 1972–76 Cardiff.
Connexional Committees: 1956–68 MMS Western and General Committees; 1958–67 Connexional Candidates Examination Committee.
Publications: *Teaching Religion:* Teacher's Handbook for use with Agreed Syllabus, 1953 *God and His People*; 1959 *Christ and His Church;* 1960 *Plans for Bible Study.*
Special Interests: African Affairs, Religion and Culture, Church's World Mission. *Hobbies and Recreations:* Sport.

BANKS, Charles, 155 Surrenden Rd., Brighton BN1 6ZA. (0273-503348) – MA(Cantab.), BA(Lond.). *b. Oldham. m.*
Education: 1932–41 Gt. Yarmouth Gram. Sch.; 1941–45 University Coll., London; 1947–49 Fitzwilliam Coll., Cambridge; 1947–49 Wesley House.
Appointments: 1949–50 Worcester; 1950–54 Edinburgh Mission; 1954–60 Birmingham South-West; 1960–66 Glasgow (St. John's); 1966–71 Bristol (Clifton and Redland); 1971–73 Bournemouth; 1973–74 Streatham and Dulwich; 1974–81 Stockport; 1981– Brighton (Dome Mission).
Connexional Committees: 1960–79 Radio & Television Committee; 1960–64 World Methodist Council; 1971–75 Exchange of Pastorate Committee.
Special Interests: Music. *Hobbies and Recreations:* Painting.

BANKS, John, 224 Wilbraham Rd., Manchester M16 8GN. (061 881-7701) – BA(Lond.), MA(Cantab.). *b. 11 Dec 1919, Ackworth, Yorks. m. 16 July 1942: 2d.* d 2007
Education: 1931–38 Gt. Yarmouth Gram. Sch.; 1938–40 University Coll., London; 1948–50 Univ. of Cambridge; 1948–50 Wesley House. *Appointments:* 1943–45 Cwm and Kingstone; 1946–48 Harrow and Sussex Mission (while on President's List); 1946–48 Brighton and Hove; 1950–55 Manchester and Salford Mission; 1955–60 Great Barr and Kingstanding; 1960–68 Leeds (Brunswick); 1968– Manchester and Salford Mission.
Connexional Committees: 1961–67 OM; 1968–72 HM; 1960s Deaconess Committee; 1974–82 Inner City Committee; 1970s City Centre Committees.
Publications: 1961 *A People Prepared;* 1964 *The Church in Your House;* 1964 *What Goes Up Must Come Down;* 1968 *Is There a Word from the Lord?* 1970s *Fun in the Lake; In the Dales; In London; On the Waterways.*
Special Interests: Antiques, Wesleyana, Methodist History, Writing.
Hobbies and Recreations: Birdwatching, Reprographics, Travel, Cottage Renovation.

BANNISTER, David, 99 Nettleham Rd., Lincoln LN2 1RU. (0522-25617)

BARBER, Alan Otter, 39 Victoria Park Rd., Malvern Link, Worcs WR14 2JX. (06845-61224) *b. 23 Aug 1919, Carlton-in-Lindrick, Notts. m. 17 Aug 1950: 2d.*
Education: 1931–35 King Edward VI Gram. Sch., East Retford; 1942 Royal Naval Coll., Greenwich; 1945–48 Handsworth. *Appointments:* 1948–49 London (Blackheath and Lee); 1949–52 Burnley; 1952–56 London (Blackheath and Lee); 1956–62 Doncaster N.E.; 1962–68 Derby (South); 1968–74 Bath; 1974–80 Chairman Cumbria District; 1980– Malvern and Ledbury.
Conference Appointments: 1960–64 Asst. Record Secretary; 1965–67 Record Secretary; 1968–74 Asst. Secretary. *Connexional Committees:* 1967–80 General Purposes; 1974–80 Home Mission; 1969– Law and Polity; 1967–80 Stationing Committee; 1978–80 President's Council; 1972–74 Commission on Restructuring of the Conference (Convenor).
Local Council Committees: 1975–80 Cumbria Education Committee (and sub-cttees).
Special Interests: Methodist History. *Hobbies and Recreations:* All Sports, Walking.

BARBER, Donald Charles Langley, 62 Southampton Rd., Fareham, Hants PO16 7EA. (0329-232105) – BA.
Education: 1964–66 Didsbury.
Appointments: 1966–70 Bristol (Clifton and Redland); 1970–75 Shrewsbury; 1975–81 Bristol (Kingswood); 1981– Gosport and Fareham.

BARBER, Peter E., The Manse, Victoria Rd., Camelford, Cornwall PL32 9XA. (0840-213321) – BSc., BA. *b. 16 June 1954, Nottingham. m. 26 July 1975: 2d.*
Education: 1965–72 Fairham Comp. Sch., Clifton Estate, Nottingham; 1972–75 Univ. Coll. of Wales, Aberystwyth; 1976–78 Cambridge Univ.; 1976–79 Wesley House.
Appointments: 1979– Camelford and Wadebridge.
Special Interests: Ornithology and Ecology. *Hobbies and Recreations:* Photography and Woodwork.

BARDSLEY, Warren Robert, 76 Brockhurst Rd., Hodge Hill, Birmingham B36 8JD. (021-783-3259) – BA(Open Univ.) *b. 18 May 1939, Hillingdon, Middx. m. 18 Aug 1962: 2s.*
Education: 1950–55 Chadderton Gram. Sch.; 1976–79 Open Univ.; 1958–62 Hartley Victoria. *Appointments:* 1962–64 Watton and Rocklands; 1964–73 Sierra Leone (MMS); 1973–77 Bedford (North); 1977– Birmingham (Elmdon).
Connexional Committees: 1973–77 Overseas Service Committee.
Special Interests: World Development, Peace and Justice Issues.
Hobbies and Recreations: Reading, Sport (esp. Cricket).

BAREHAM, Eric William, 49 Brudenell Rd., Leeds LS6 1HA. (0532-789841) *b. 17 Mar 1913, Sible Hedingham, Essex. m. 19 Aug 1939: 2s.*
Education: 1924–29 Sudbury Gram. Sch.; 1948–50 Headingley. *Appointments:* 1946–48 Easingwold; 1950–55 Leeds (Brunswick); 1955–61 Leeds (Headingley); 1961–65 Otley; 1965–74 Dewsbury; 1974–78 Birstall and Birkenshaw.
Connexional Committees: 1956–62 Education and Youth; 1961–62 National Vice-President MAYC.
Council Member: 1962–64 Chaplain Otley UDC.
Special Interests: Member of Brontë Society.

BARKER, Alan Marshall, 1 Shetland Close, St. John's Park Estate, Ladywood, Birmingham. (021-455-8054) – B.Tech(Brad.), B.A.(Bristol). *b. 18 May 1956, Leeds. m. 15 Aug 1981.*
Education: 1967–74 The Perse Sch. for Boys, Cambridge; 1975–79 Bradford Univ.; 1979–82 Bristol Univ.; 1979–82 Wesley, Bristol. *Appointments:* 1982– Birmingham West.
Hobbies and Recreations: Natural History.

BARKER, David Anthony, 6 Mandeville Gdns, Walsall, W. Midlands WS1 3AT. (0922-25681) *b. 1 Nov 1939, Leeds. m. 15 Aug 1964: 2s.*
Education: 1944–51 Hunslet Moor C.P. Sch.; 1951–55 Pitmans Coll.; 1959–63 Hartley Victoria. *Appointments:* 1963–65 Welshpool; 1965–71 Willenhall; 1971–77 Cannock Chase; 1977– Walsall Mission.
Connexional Committees: 1973–79 DSR Board. *Local Council Committees:* 1977– Walsall Metropolitan Borough Education Committee.

BARKER, Horace Felstead, 24 Chamber Rd., Shaw, Oldham OL2 7AR. (0706-847393) *b. 1924, Kingston upon Hull. m. 1953: 1d., 2s.*
Education: 1935–40 Hull Gram. Sch.; 1950–53 Wesley, Headingley.
Appointments: 1949–50 Motherwell and Wishaw; 1953–58 Shipley; 1958–62 Wakefield; 1962–68 Paisley Mission; 1968–75 Motherwell and Wishaw; 1975–82 Shaw and Royton; 1982– Sandbach and Alsager.
Connexional Committees: 1964–70 Christian Citizenship. *Local Council Committees:* 1958–62 West Riding of Yorkshire County Youth Committee; 1962–68 Min. of Labour, Local Youth Employment Committee.
Hobbies and Recreations: D.I.Y.

BARKER, John Hubert, 71 Wallbridge Drive, Leek, Staffs ST13 8HY. (0538-372569) *b. 10 Nov 1914, Kalmunai, Sri Lanka. m. 22 Mar 1944: 2d., 1s.*
Education: 1923–24 Kingswood; 1924–28 Airdrie Academy; 1928–31 Kings Lynn Gram.; 1936–39 Handsworth. *Appointments:* 1939–47 Bengal Dt. India; 1947–51 Burton-on-Trent, George St.; 1951–54 Bengal Dt., India; 1954–58 Uttoxeter; 1958–63 Ashbourne; 1963–70 Newport (Gwent); 1970–75 Chesterfield; 1975–79 Midsomer Norton (Avon).
Connexional Committees: 1951–54 Overseas Missions.
Special Interests: Methodist History (member W.H.S.). *Hobbies and Recreations:* Gardening.

BARKER, Peter T., 1 Savile Rd., Elland, W. Yorks HX5 0LA. (0422-72388) – BA(Leeds), BD(Manch.). *b.*

5 May 1937, Bradford. m. 20 Feb 1965: 1d., 1s.
Education: 1941–44 Haworth Rd. Inf., Bradford; 1944–47 Daisy Hill Prim., Bradford; 1947–55 Bradford Gram. Sch.; 1955–58 Leeds Univ.; 1958–61 Manchester Univ.; 1958–61 Hartley Victoria. *Appointments:* 1961–66 Sale; 1966–71 Cadishead; 1971–77 South Craven; 1977–82 Ilkley; 1982– Elland; 1976–82 Synod Secretary.
Connexional Committees: 1972–75(?) Candidates Committee.
Special Interests: The Worship of the Church, Church Buildings, Administration, Ministries. *Hobbies and Recreations:* Music, Photography, Walking, Arts and Crafts, Drama.

BARKER, Philip John, 64 Aberdour Rd., Goodmayes, Ilford IG3 9PG. (01-590-2841) – MA(Cantab.) *b. 17 Dec 1944, Chelmsford, Essex. m. 5 Aug 1967: 2d.*
Education: 1949–56 Broomfield County Prim. Sch.; 1956–63 King Edward VI Gram. Sch., Chelmsford; 1964–67 Wesley House. *Appointments:* 1967–70 Epworth and Crowle; 1970–76 Margate; 1976– London, Ilford.
Publications: 1981– Partners in Learning Theme-Writers Panel.
Hobbies and Recreations: Organist, Gardening.

BARKER, Robert, 120 Church Rd., New Mills, Stockport SK12 4PF. (New Mills 42331) *b. 2 Dec 1927, Leek, Staffs. m. 24 Jan 1959: 1s.*
Education: 1933–39 West St. Methodist, Leek, Staffs; 1939–42 St. Edward's CE Sen. Elem., Britannia St., Leek, Staffs.; 1951–54 Hartley Victoria.
Appointments: 1954–55 South Devon Mission; 1955–57 Market Weighton; 1957–61 Walkden; 1961–64 Northallerton; 1964–67 Gateshead East; 1967–72 Wigan, Standishgate; 1972–76 Saddleworth and Lees; 1976–79 Oldham and Saddleworth; 1979 New Mills.
Local Council Committees: 1977–79 Free Church representative, Oldham Metropolitan Borough Education Committee.
Hobbies and Recreations: Bridges, Music (Jazz and Opera), Biographies.

BARKER, Stanley James, The Manse, 27 Theydon Ave., Woburn Sands, Milton Keynes, Bucks MK17 8PN. (0908-582055) – BA(Bristol). *b. 2 Jan 1945, Whiston, Lancs. m. 21 July 1979.*
Education: 1956–63 Baines Gram. Sch., Poulton-le-Fylde, Lancs; 1963–66 Poulton-le-Fylde Teacher's Training Coll.; 1976–77 Cliff Coll.; 1978–81 Bristol Univ.; 1978–81 Wesley, Bristol. *Appointments:* 1981– Milton Keynes; 1981– Free Church Chaplain, Edgbury Hospital, Woburn Sands.
Hobbies and Recreations: Playing Clarinet, Singing, Gardening, ASA Teacher's Certificate (Swimming).

BARKER, William George, c/o Whitechapel Mission, 212 Whitechapel Rd., London E1 1BJ. (01-247-8280) *b. 3 Aug 1913, Harwich, Essex. m. (divorced) 20 Aug 1955: 1d., 2s.*
Education: 1925–31 Harwich County High Sch.; 1932 Gregg Sch., Ipswich.
Appointments: 1949–50 Isles of Scilly; 1950–52 Sudbury; 1952–55 Ludlow; 1963–66 Rhymney Valley; 1966–70 Halifax (North); 1970–73 Leigh; 1973–75 Pontypool.
Special Interests: Writing Verses in Acrostic Form on People's Names for Birthdays, Weddings and other occasions. Making and Distributing Cards ("Ministry of Cards"). Interest in Trees, Wild Flowers, etc.

BARLEY, John Alexander Hurd, 4 Splash Lane, Castor, Peterborough PE5 7BD. (073-121-247) *b. 14 Nov 1917, Lincoln. m. 29 Mar 1947: 3s.*
Education: 1927–34 Woking County Gram. Sch.; 1945–47 Handsworth; 1966–67 Westminster, Oxford;
Appointments: 1947–50 Romford; 1950–53 Manningtree and Harwich; 1953–57 Longton and Fenton; 1957–62 Waltham Abbey and Hertford; 1962–63 Wakefield; 1963–66 Chipping Norton; 1967–80 Head of Religious Education, John Mansfield School, Peterborough.
Publications: Book Reviews in *Journal of Moral Education.*
Special Interests: Education; W.E.A. Lecturer on World Religion and Church History. *Hobbies and Recreations:* Sketching.

BARNARD, Geoffrey Henry Edgar, 10 Mere Rd., Formby, Liverpool L37 2JX. (07048-75869) – BA(Leeds). *b. 17 Mar 1937, Caister-on-Sea, Norfolk. m. 6 April 1966: 2d.*
Education: 1942–48 Caister-on-Sea Prim. Sch.; 1948–55 Gt. Yarmouth Gram. Sch.; 1957–61 Leeds Univ.; 1957–61 Wesley, Headingley.
Appointments: 1961–71 N. Rhodesia District; 1971–76 Liverpool South; 1976–81 United World College of Southern Africa, Mbabane, Swaziland; 1981– Liverpool, Crosby.
Connexional Committees: 1974–75 Overseas Division.
Special Interests: Media. *Hobbies and Recreations:* Photography, Outdoor Activities.

BARNES, Anthony, 14 Glebelands Ave., South Woodford, London E18 2AB. (01-989-3264) – MA(Cantab). *b. 25 Dec 1946, Penzance, Cornwall. m. 9 Aug 1975.*
Education: 1958–65 Humphrey Davy Gram. Sch., Penzance; 1966–70 Wesley House. *Appointments:* 1970–72 Romiley; 1972–77 Torquay and Paignton; 1977–82 Dover and Deal; 1982– Wanstead and Woodford.
Hobbies and Recreations: Music, Piano Playing, Reading, Walking.

BARNETT, John Patrick, 35 Salisbury Ave., Goole, North Humberside DN14 5JW (0405-3762) *b. 13 Aug 1947, Oxford. m. 2 Sept 1967: 2d.*
Education: Wallingford County Gram; Bicester County Gram.; 1975–79 Wesley, Bristol. Appointments: 1979– Goole.
Special Interests: Children's Work, Hospital Chaplaincy. *Hobbies and Recreations:* Walking, Gardening, Bird Watching, Fish Keeping.

BARNETT, Leonard Palin, 26 Cromwell Ave., Bromley, Kent BR2 9AQ. (01-460-0669) – BD, LitD. *b. 11 April 1919, Crewe, Cheshire. m. 26 Dec 1945: 2s.*
Education: 1930–36 Crewe Gram. Sch.; 1939–42 Hartley Victoria.
Appointments: 1942–43 Holyhead; 1943–46 Nantwich; 1946–49 Guernsey; 1949–58 Nat. Sec. MAYC; 1958–62 Priory Place, Doncaster;

1962–68 Sutton (Epsom); 1968–74 Finchley, London and Hendon; 1974– Bromley.
Connexional Committees: 1948–60 Youth Committees. *Council Member:* 1949–58 British Council of Churches Youth Department. *Publications:* About 20 or more titles over the years; most significant, *Adventure with Youth* (1953) MAYC leaders text-book; *Way to the Stars* and *High Cost of Living* (sermons); *Sex and Young Lovers* (NCCE); *Homosexuality: Time to tell the Truth* (Gollancz); *What is Methodism?* (1981).
Special Interests: Radio, TV, Communications, Journalism (weekly or monthly feature writer for *Methodist Recorder, Nat. Sun. Sch. Chronicle, British Weekly* and currently *YOURS*); play writing. *Hobbies and Recreations:* Swimming.

BARNETT, Philip, 12 Kenelm Rd., Rhos-on-Sea, Colwyn Bay, Clwyd LL28 4EE. (0492-44737) *b. 29 Mar 1943, Bebington, Cheshire. m. 13 Sept 1969: 2s.*
Education: 1954–60 Birkenhead Sch.; 1964–68 Hartley Victoria. *Appointments:* 1968–70 Bristol South; 1970–75 Shrewsbury; 1975–82 Stockton-on-Tees; 1982– Colwyn Bay and Llandudno.
Connexional Committees: 1980– Chairman Connexional Youth & Community Committee.
Special Interests: Music, Methodism, Youth. *Hobbies and Recreations:* Gardening, Sheepdogs.

BARNSBY, John Raymond, The Gables, 105 High St., Henley in Arden, Solihull B95 5AU. (Henley in Arden 2627) *b. 14 Nov 1915, Chapel End, Nuneaton. m. (1) 1946, d. 1977. (2) 1982: 3d.*
Education: Galley Common Council Sch., Nuneaton; 1938–39 Cliff; 1939–42 Hartley Victoria. *Appointments:* 1942–44 Stour Valley Mission; 1944–46 South Molton; 1946–50 Walthamstow; 1950–53 Clacton; 1953–57 Wellingborough; 1957–63 Luton; 1963–68 Leicester South; 1968–73 Leighton Buzzard; 1973–76 Old Hill; 1976–82 Darlaston.
Special Interests: Building and modernisation of Churches (New Darlaston Church built to my design 1980). *Hobbies and Recreations:* Gardening and Designing & decorating wedding cakes.

BARRACLOUGH, Gerald, 26 Slaithwaite Rd., Meltham, Huddersfield HD7 3PG. (0484-850385) – BD(Lond) 1958, MTh(Lond) 1964. *b. 20 Aug 1930, Leeds. m. 31 July 1958: 2d., 1s.*
Education: 1935–44 Upper Wortley Council, Leeds; 1944–46 Leeds Central High Sch.; 1953–57 Handsworth. *Appointments:* 1957–59 Cheadle; (1959–60 Selly Oak Training; 1960–61 Sierra Leone; 1961–68 Nigeria); 1968–71 Hanley Trinity; 1971–78 St. Mary's College, Newcastle upon Tyne; 1978– Holmfirth.
Special Interests: New Testament Studies, Islamic Studies. *Hobbies and Recreations:* Spectator Sports, Walking, Cricket, Crosswords, Music.

BARRETT, Charles Kingsley, 8 Prince's St., Durham DH1 4RP. DD(Cantab), Hon.DD(Hull), Hon.DD(Aberdeen), Hon.DTheol (Hamburg) FBA. *b. 4 May 1917, Salford. m. 16 Aug 1944: 1d., 1s.*
Education: 1923–28 Linden Hall; 1928–35 Shebbear College; 1935–38 Pembroke Coll., Cambridge; 1938–42 Wesley House. *Appointments:* 1942–43 Wesley College, Headingley Asst. Tutor; 1943–45 Darlington South; 1945–82 Per Durham University.
Publications: The Holy Spirit and the Gospel Tradition (1947); *The Epistle to the Romans* (1957); *Luke the Historian in Recent Study* (1961); *From First Adam to Last* (1962); *The Pastoral Epistles* (1963); *Jesus and the Gospel Tradition* (1967); *The 1st Epistle to the Corinthians* (1968); *The Signs of an Apostle* (1970); *New Testament Essays* (1972); *The 2nd Epistle to the Corinthians* (1973); *The Gospel According to St. John* (2nd edn., 1978); *Essays on Paul* (1982); *Essays on John* (1982); other books and many articles.

BARRETT, Donald Dunstan, 13 Glendale, Chapel Rd., Swanmore, Southampton, Hants SO3 2QY. (04893-4884) *b. 19 Nov 1919, Ripponden, West Yorkshire. m. 17 Mar 1951: 1d.*
Education: 1925–31 Stones Council Sch., Ripponden; 1931–37 Sowerby Bridge Gram. Sch. *Appointments:* 1948–55 Methodist Church of South Africa; 1955–59 Ashton-under-Lyne; 1959–62 Altrincham; 1962–66 Manchester (South East); 1966–71 Devonport; 1971–74 Birkenhead; 1974–75 Port Talbot; 1975–76 Poole; 1976–78 North Hill; 1978–82 Droxford.

BARRETT, John Charles Allanson, Hartley, Fonthill Rd., Bath BA1 5RG. (0225-314744) – BA(Newcastle), MA(Cantab). *b. 8 June 1943, King's Lynn, Norfolk. m. 1967: 1d., 1s.*
Education: 1951–61 Culford Sch., Bury St. Edmunds; 1965 Newcastle upon Tyne; 1967 Fitzwilliam, Cambridge; 1965–68 Wesley House. *Appointments:* 1968–69 Chaplain and Lecturer in Divinity, Westminster College, Oxford; 1969–71 Asst. Tutor, Wesley College, Bristol; 1971–73 Stoke-on-Trent (Hanley); 1973– Chaplain and Head of Religious and General Studies, Kingswood School, Bath.
Connexional Committees: 1972–80 Local Preachers Committee; 1980– Candidates Examination Committee; 1981– British Committee (World Methodist Council) Assistant Secretary; 1981– European Relations Committee. *Council Member:* 1981– World Methodist Council; 1981– Executive Committee, World Methodist Council. *Publications: Family Worship* (Epworth, 1982); *What is a Christian School?* – Discussion paper (Methodist Residential Schools); articles in *Epworth Review, Worship and Preaching, Bloxham Review.*
Special Interests: Drama; World Development Movement; World Disarmament Campaign. *Hobbies and Recreations:* Rugby Football, Art.

BARRETT, William Hubert, Wesley Manse, 61 Newland, Sherborne, Dorset DT9 3JG. (093-581-3220) *b. 26 Feb 1923, Leyton, London. m. 24 May 1947: 2d., 3s.*
Education: 1928–34 Newport Rd. Sch., Leyton; 1934–39 Leyton County High Sch.; 1950–53 Richmond.

Appointments: 1949–50 London, Poplar and Bow Mission; 1953–56 East Suffolk; 1956–61 Thetford; 1961–67 Newport (Mon.); 1967–71 Nottingham South; 1971–77 Clay Cross; 1977– Sherborne.

BARRITT, Gordon Emerson, 85 Highbury Park, London N5 1UD and 10 Cadogan Gdns, Grange Park, London N21 1ER. (01-226 2033) – OBE, MA(Cantab), BA(Manchester). *b. 30 Sept 1920, Stockport, Cheshire. m. 7 Aug 1947: 1d., 2s.* *Education:* 1930–39 William Hulme's Gram. Sch., Manchester; 1939–41 Manchester Univ.; 1945–47 Cambridge Univ.; 1945–47 Wesley House. *Appointments:* 1947–52 Kempston; 1952–57 Newcastle-under-Lyme; (1953–57 Chaplain to University of Keele); 1957– National Children's Home – Principal of NCH since 1969. *Committees:* 1970–72 Treasurer, National Council of Voluntary Child Care Organisations (chm, 1970–72); 1968–71 Member Home Office Advisory Council on Child Care; National Children's Bureau; Founder Member British Association of Social Workers; International Union for Child Welfare; UK and International Committees, Council of Selly Oak Colls, Birmingham; Board of Management of Methodist Residential Schools. *Publications: The Edgworth Story* (1972); (ed.) *Many Pieces – One Aim* (1975); (ed.) *Family Life* (1979); *Residential Care* (1979); Contrib. *Caring for Children* (1969); Contrib. *Giving Our Best* (1982). *Special Interests:* Social work – national and international. *Hobbies and Recreations:* Music, Do-It-Yourself.

BARRON, Colin George, 19 Hollyhurst Rd., Sutton Coldfield, Birmingham B73 6SY. (021-354-1454) *b. 12 May 1937, Birmingham. m. 24 July 1965: 1d., 1s.* *Education:* 1940–48 Arnside House Private Sch.; 1948–54 King Edward VIth Gram. Sch., Camp Hill, Birmingham; Bristol Univ.; 1963–65 Didsbury, Bristol. *Appointments:* 1966–71 Looe; 1971–76 Birmingham Smethwick; 1976–81 Cannock Chase; 1981– Birmingham Asbury. *Special Interests:* Working with Young People, Community Involvements. *Hobbies and Recreations:* Choral Singing, Gardening, DIY.

BARTON, Eric Tomlin, 15 Greenacres Drive, Poringland, Norwich, Norfolk NR14 7JG. (050-86 2126) – BD(London). *b. 7 Sept 1906, Edmonton, Middx. m. 2 July 1935: 1d., 1s.* *Education:* 1911–20 Crouch End Council Sch., N. London; 1920–23 Owens Sch., Islington; 1929–33 Richmond. *Appointments:* 1928–29 Oundle; 1933–45 N. China; 1945–46 Hornsea Mkt. Pl.; 1946–51 N. China; 1951–59 Newmarket M.; 1959–66 Sussex M.; 1966–71 Romford. *Connexional Committee:* 1951–59 Overseas Missions. *Special Interests:* Theology, Christianity in China. *Hobbies and Recreations:* Woodcarving.

BASSETT, Arthur Vivian, 7 Cavie Cres., Braunton, N. Devon EX33 1DU. (0271-814-031) *b. 8 Dec 1911, Helston, Cornwall. m. 13 July 1937.* *Education:* 1920s Helston Council, formerly Wesleyan, Sch.; 1957–58 Didsbury, Bristol. *Appointments:* 1958–61 New Forest Mission; 1961–66 Grimsby, Flottergate, Grimsby West; 1966–71 Newbury; 1971–77 Fleetwood. *Connexional Committees:* 1964–65 Connexional Youth Committee; 1973–76 Home Committee of Overseas Missions. *Hobbies and Recreations:* Walking, Gardening.

BASTIN, Ernest Albert, 11 Beech grove, Moffat, Dumfriesshire, Scotland DH10 9RS. (0683-20426) – MBE. *b. 24 Mar 1893, Plumstead, London. m. (1) 26 Apr 1924; (2) 25 June 1955: 1d., 2s.* *Education:* London County Council Schools; Roan Sch., Greenwich, London; Army Coll. of the Rhine Army of Occupation; 1914–15 and 1920–21 Handsworth. *Appointments.* 1916–19 HMF; 1921–33 South China Dt.; 1933–36 London Woolwich; 1936–39 Birmingham Belmont Row; 1939–41 Altrincham; 1941–47 Chaplain HMF; 1947–50 Birmingham Belmont Row; 1950–56 Kenya Dt. East Africa; 1956–58 Wigan (Welsey and Standishgate). *Special Interests:* Cricket. *Hobbies and Recreations:* Homecrafts.

BATE, Phillip, 13 Langland Rd., Mumbles, Swansea, W. Glam. SA3 4ND. (0792-66712) *b. 6 June 1925, Aberavon, Glam. m. 15 Aug 1953: 1d., 1s.* *Education:* 1939–43 Port Talbot Sec.; 1949–51 Handsworth. *Appointments:* 1953–58 Manchester Droylsden and Openshaw; 1958–63 Birmingham Wesley; 1963–68 Oxford; 1968–75 Cardiff; 1975– Swansea. *Hobbies and Recreations:* Hill Walking, Cycling.

BATES, Edmund Ralph, 3 Hansford Close, Combe Down, Bath BA2 5LW. (0225-833857) *b. 2 Dec 1896, Weedon, Aylesbury, Bucks. m. 11 Aug 1937: 1d., 1s.* *Education:* 1902–09 Hardwicke (Bucks) CE; 1909–13 Aylesbury Gram.; War Service, Royal Naval Div., Wounded at Passchaendale Oct 1917; 1919–23 Didsbury. *Appointments:* 1923–24 President's Assistant; 1924–28 Bristol Mission; 1928–31 Bath; 1931–37 London, Blackheath; 1937–40 Leigh-on-Sea; 1940–45 London, Brixton Hill; 1945–50 Liverpool North; 1950–56 Liverpool, Grove St.; 1956–62 Birmingham S.W.; 1962–65 Wokingham; 1969–72 Warden, New Room, Bristol. *Connexional Committees:* 1948–50 Overseas Missions; 1941–69 Local Preachers; 1939–69 L.P. Studies Board; 1957–63 Care of Overseas Students. *Local Council Committees:* 1941–45 Lambeth Borough Youth Committee. *Publications: Langton St. Chapel, Bristol (Centenary History, 1928); Methodism in Wokingham (1817–1967)* (1967); *Rise of Methodism in the Vale of Aylesbury 1772–1791* (1972); *Captain Thomas Webb: Anglo-American Methodist Pioneer* (1975); Articles in *Proceedings W.H.S.; Methodist History* (U.S.A.), etc. *Special Interests:* English Social

History, Methodist History. *Hobbies and Recreations:* Historical Research, Gardening, Philately.

BATES, James Bamford, 3 Queensmere Rd., London SW19 5PD. (01-946-1761) – BA(Theology) Bristol. *b. 5 Sept 1925, Belper, Derbyshire. m. 6 Aug 1952: 1d., 1s.*
Education: 1931 Westhill Kindergarten, Selly Oak; 1931–36 Lescudjack Elem. Sch., Penzance; 1936–41 Truro Sch.; 1941–43 Manchester Gram. Sch.; 1948–51 Bristol Univ.; 1948–51 Didsbury, Bristol. *Appointments:* 1947–48 Hunts Mission; 1951–52 Wells (Somerset); 1952–55 Brandon and Deerness Valley; 1955–62 Kent College, Canterbury (Chaplain); 1962– Southlands College (Roehampton Institute).
Publications: Worship & Preaching (with Morrow & Billington, 1965); *In Church* (Contribution, 1971); *The Methodist Church* (R.E.P., 1977); Poetry (in *Words for Worship,* 1969, and *Worship for Today,* 1968); Contributed to *Learning for Life* (I.L.E.A., 1968), *Seeds of Life & Living Traditions* (Merton Education Authority, 1980 & 1982).
Special Interests: Religious Education; Religion and Art and Architecture; London and its Churches; Methodist History; World Religion. *Hobbies and Recreations:* Art, Architecture, Walking, Swimming.

BATES, Peter Kenneth,
25 Sycamore Drive, Patchway, Bristol BS12 5ET. (0272-696088) *b. 6 Aug 1949, Wolverhampton. m. 26 July 1973: 1d., 1s.*
Education: 1957–68 Tettenhall Coll.; 1968–71 Madeley Coll. of Ed.; 1981– Wesley, Bristol.
Connexional Committees: 1976–78 Connexional Day Schools Committee; 1979–81 Christian Education Development Committee.
Hobbies and Recreations: Football, Squash, Cricket, Music, Reading.

BATES, Trevor Sydney, 71 South Parade, Pudsey, West Yorks LS28 8NX. (0532-571880) *b. 7 Oct 1928, Bootle, Lancs. m. 12 June 1957: 1s.*
Education: 1951–54 Richmond; 1960–61 Westhill Coll., Birmingham; 1980– Sch. of Peace Studies, Bradford Univ. *Appointments:* 1954–69 Leeward Islands District; 1969–72 Belize and Honduras District; 1972–81 Leeds North East; 1981– Pudsey and Farsley.
Connexional Committees: 1974– Overseas Division Central Committee; 1978–81 Inner City Committee.
Council Member: 1973– Leeds Council for Community Relations.

BATSON, Samuel John, 20 Percy Rd., Boscombe, Bournemouth BH5 1JF. (0202-301971) – BA(Manch.) *b. 29 Oct 1912, Barrow-in-Furness, Cumbria. m. 27 Feb 1940: 1d.*
Education: Barrow-in-Furness Gram. Sch.; 1932–36 Manchester Univ.; 1932–36 Hartley Victoria. *Appointments:* 1936–38 Shebbear Coll.; 1938–42 Stockport, Mt. Tabor; 1942–45 Manchester, Withington; 1945–50 Stockport, Trinity; 1950–53 Bradford, Woodhouse Grove; 1953–59 Scarborough, Queen St.; 1959–65 Hoylake and West Kirby; 1965–71 Wallasey; 1971–77 Southampton.
Connexional Committees: 1940–50 Division of Education and Youth; 1970–82 Finance Division.
Hobbies and Recreations: Gardening, Travel, Reading Biographies, Football, Cricket.

BATTY, Harry, The Manse, Reeth, Richmond, North Yorks DL11 6SN. (0748-84336) *b. 1 Mar 1924, Sunderland. m. 6 Aug 1951: 1d., 2s.*
Education: 1929–35 Fulwell; 1935–40 Monkwearmouth Central; 1946–49 Headingley. *Appointments:* 1949–50 Northallerton; 1950–51 Kirkoswald; 1951–53 British Guiana Dt.; 1953–56 Essequibo, British Guiana; 1956–61 Thirsk; 1961– Reeth.
Hobbies and Recreations: Golf, Electrical Repairs.

BAUGH, George, 18 Malzeard Rd., Luton, Beds LU3 1BD. (0582-30129) *b. 25 July 1918, Pontefract, Yorkshire. m. 18 Apr 1949: 2d.*
Education: 1923–32 Council Sch., Love Lane, Pontefract; 1945–48 Handsworth. *Appointments:* 1948–49 Loftus and Staithes; 1949–54 Gateshead (West); 1954–57 Sheffield (Mission); 1957–60 Sheffield (Brunswick); 1960–68 London (Wimbledon); 1968–76 Romford; 1976– Luton (North); USA Exchange 1967, 1975, 1979, 1982.
Connexional Committees: 1971–76 London Mission. *Council Member:* 1964–68 London Borough of Merton – Member of Education Committee.
Special Interests: Travel, Photography, Methodist History.

BAXENDALE, Janet Anne, The Manse, 4 Titness St., Buckie, Moray District, Grampian Region, Banffs. (Buckie 31176) – BA(Birmingham). *b. 28 Apr 1956, Bolton.*
Education: 1968–74 Canon Slade G.S., Bolton; 1976–80 Birmingham Univ.; 1976–80 Queen's Coll., Birmingham; 1980–81 St. Paul's Coll., Limuru, Kenya. *Appointments:* 1981– North of Scotland Mission.
Hobbies and Recreations: Music.

BAXENDALE, Norman,
101 Netherton Lane, Netherton, Wakefield, West Yorks WF4 4HG. (0924-275730) *b. 24 Dec 1917, Old Trafford, Manchester. m. 26 Aug 1944: 2d.*
Education: 1923–28 Seymour Park Council Sch., Old Trafford, Manchester; 1928–31 Old Trafford Snr. Boys, Old Trafford. *Appointments:* 1953–58 Tunstall; 1958–65 Dewsbury; 1965–75 Ossett and Whorbury; 1975–82 Sheffield North East.
Special Interests: Music – Listening and Playing (Violin); D.I.Y.; Gardening; Reading; The Theology of Peter Taylor Forsyth.

BAXTER, Alfred Stanley, 6 Trinity Ave., Northampton NN2 6JJ. (0604-718747) *b. 15 Apr 1930, Harrow. m. 6 Aug 1960: 1d., 2s.*
Education: 1944– Belmont Elem.; 1950–53 Cliff Coll.; 1954–58 Didsbury, Bristol. *Appointments:* 1958–60 Home Mission Caravans; 1960–65 Rugby; 1965–71 Leamington Spa; 1972–75 M.C.C.A. (Trinidad); 1975–80 Barnsley; 1980– Northampton.
Hobbies and Recreations: Gardening, Walking.

BAYLEY, Peter, c/o Rev. C.R. Wolsey Gilbert, R.N. Army & R.A.F. Board, 1 Central Buildings, Westminster,

London SW1H 9NH. (01-222-8702) *b. 25 Sept 1938, Stoke-on-Trent, Staffs. m. 4 Oct 1958: 2d., 1s.* *Education:* 1950–55 Wolstanton Gram. Sch., Newcastle-under-Lyme; 1955–56 Cliff Coll.; 1962–65 Hartley Victoria. *Appointments:* 1965–70 Stoke-on-Trent (South); 1970– Chaplain H.M.F.
Special Interests: H.M. Forces.
Hobbies and Recreations: Singing, Jogging, Family.

BAYLISS, Roger Owen, 119 Norfolk Rd., R.A.F. Marham, Kings Lynn, Norfolk. (0760-337261 ext. 225 office, 529 home) *b. 21 July 1944, Nottingham. m. 21 Aug 1976: 2s.* *Education:* 1949–55 Junior Schs.; Sir Philip Magnus Tech. Coll., Kings Cross; Clarks Coll., Walthamstow; Highfield Comp., Oxon; 1976–78 Moorlands Bible Coll., Sopley; 1978–81 Wesley, Bristol. *Appointments:* 1981– Chaplain H.M.F.
Special Interests: To work mainly amongst unchurched in field of Evangelism and Church Growth.
Hobbies and Recreations: Squash, Gliding, Stamp Collecting, Chess, Running.

BEAR, Kenneth Alfred, Ballabruin, Top Flat, 253 Upper Grosvenor Rd., Tunbridge Wells, Kent TN1 2EJ. (0892-37662) – BA. *b. 26 Jan 1912, Dovercourt, Essex. m. 20 Aug 1941.* *Education:* 1918–21 Bury St. Edmunds Gram. Sch.; 1921–24 Belmont Jun. Sch. for Mill Hill; 1924–27 King's Sch., Chester; 1927–29 High Sch., Glasgow; 1929–32 Brighton Tech. Coll.; 1932–35 Cambridge Univ.; 1932–35 Wesley House. *Appointments:* 1935–37 Barnet; 1937–41 Croydon; 1941–47 South Norwood; 1947–52 Colchester; 1952–57 Ilford; 1957–64 Torquay and Paignton; 1964–69 Harrow; 1969–75 Douglas (I.O.M.); 1972–75 Chairman Isle of Man District; 1976–82 National Guild Secretary (Supernumary).
Connexional Committees: 1964–67 Central Committee (Overseas Missions); 1972–75 General Purposes Committee and Home Missions Committee; 1976–82 Division of Ministries.
Special Interests: Wesley Guild, Member of Chesterton Society, English Literature generally. *Hobbies and Recreations:* Reading, Walking, and all kinds of travel, especially Railways.

BEARD, George Murray, Kirklands, 17 Athens Drive, Barrow-in-Furness, Cumbria LA13 9ND. (0229-31137) *b. 25 Aug 1912, Gloucester. m. 18 Feb 1942: 3d., 1s.*
Education: 1918–20 Denmark Road High Sch.; 1920–28 Crypt Gram. Sch., Gloucester; 1928–29 Bedford Modern Sch.; 1935–39 Handsworth.
Appointments: 1939–42 South Petherton; 1942–45 Rhondda; 1945–49 Keswick and Cockermouth; 1949–51 Cheltenham; 1951–55 Peterborough; 1955–59 Loughborough; 1959–62 Saddleworth; 1962–68 Holsworthy; 1968–74 Connah's Quay and Hawarden, Buckley and Deeside, 1974–77 Wrexham.
Hobbies and Recreations: Photography, Painting.

BEARD, John Gordon, 38 Horsebrook Pk., Calne, Wilts SN11 8EY. (0249-813340) *b. 21 Mar 1927, Cinderford, Glos. m. 2 Apr 1956: 2d., 2s.*
Education: 1939–45 East Dean Gram. Sch.; 1950–53 Bristol Univ.; 1950–53 Didsbury. *Appointments:* 1953–55 Barnstaple; 1955–62 Chelmsford; 1962–69 Clacton-on-Sea; 1969– Mid-Wiltshire.
Special Interests: Religious Films.
Hobbies and Recreations: Sport, Photography.

BEARD, Stanley, 14 Lums Hill Rise, Matlock, Derbyshire DE4 3FX (0629-4443) – BD. *b. 14 June 1920, Scunthorpe, Lincs. m. 24 July 1948: 2d.*
Education: 1931–37 King Edward VI Sch., Retford. *Appointments:* 1940–45 National Service; 1945–46 Birstall; 1946–48 Handsworth Coll.; 1948–53 Banbury; 1953–59 Sheffield (Ecclesall); 1959–64 London (Highgate); 1964–72 Romford; 1972–79 Birmingham (Sutton Park); 1979– Matlock.

BEARDSALL, Reginald Trevor Hill, 39 Barnes Way, Worcester WR5 3AP. (0905-353916) – BA(Manch.), BD(Manch.). *b. 31 Jan 1926, Wombwell, Yorkshire. m. (1) 1952–58. (2) 1962. 1d., 1s.*
Education: 1931–33 Private Tutor; 1933–34 Barnsley Rd. Primary, Wombwell; 1934–36 St. John's Jun., Wombwell; 1936–43 Wath-upon-Dearne Gram. Sch.; 1943– Liverpool Univ.; 1949–52 Manchester Univ.; 1949–52 Hartley Victoria. *Appointments:* 1947–48 St. Albans; 1948–49 Bletchley; 1952–54 Manchester, Pendleton; 1954–58 Chesterfield; 1958–64 Morecambe; 1964–69 Manchester and Salford Mission; 1969–76 Exeter; 1976– Worcester.
Special Interests: Christian Aid; Ecumenical; Amnesty International; Social Concerns. *Hobbies and Recreations:* Photography; Ornithology; Stamp Collection; Gardening; Scouting; Fell-walking.

BEARDSLEY, John Alan, 72 South St., Cottingham, North Humberside HU16 4AT. (0482-847164) – BA (Durham), MA(Cambridge). *b. 26 Jan 1943, North Yorkshire. m. 5 Aug 1967: 2d.*
Education: 1954–56 Kings Sch., Pontefract; 1956–60 Holme Valley Gram. Sch.; 1960–63 St. Cuthbert's Society, Univ. of Durham; 1964–67 Wesley House. *Appointments:* 1967–71 Gateshead (East); 1971–80 Sunderland (North); 1980– Hull (West), with chaplaincy at Hull University.
Connexional Committees: 1972–76 Church Membership; 1977–79 Candidates; 1982– Board of Division of Ministries. *Local Council Committees:* 1977–80 Sunderland Education Committee (Free Church representative).
Special Interests: Church History; Ministries; Student chaplaincy.
Hobbies and Recreations: Railways, Philately, Walking.

BEARDSLEY, Kenneth Denys, 90 Bolton Rd., Silsden, Keighley, West Yorkshire BD20 0JT. (0535-52353) – BA(Manch.), BD(London). *b. 23 Oct 1928, Sutton-in-Ashfield, Notts.*
Education: Elem; 1940–44 Middlesborough High Sch.; 1944–46 Stockton Sec. Sch.; 1946–49 Manchester Univ.; 1949–51 Headingley. *Appointments:* 1951–54 Pickering; 1954–59

Durham; 1956–65 Keighley; 1965–71 Otley; 1971–76 Bradford (Woodhouse Grove); 1976–81 Hexham; 1981– South Craven.
Special Interests: Music. *Hobbies and Recreations:* Hill-walking.

BECK, Brian Edgar, Wesley House, Jesus Lane, Cambridge CB5 8BJ. (0223-350609) – MA(Cantab.) *b. 27 Sept 1933, London. m. 9 Aug 1958: 3d.*
Education: –1944 Sellincourt Rd., LCC Jun., Tooting; 1944–52 City of London Sch.; 1952–55 Corpus Christi Coll., Cambridge; 1955–57 Wesley House. *Appointments:* 1957–59 Handsworth College, Asst. Tutor; 1959–62 East Suffolk; 1962–68 Methodist Church in Kenya, St. Paul's United Theological College, Limuru; 1968–80 Wesley House, Cambridge, Tutor; 1980– Principal.
Connexional Committees: 1968–74, 1975–78 Overseas General/Central Committee (and Sub-Committees); 1968– Division of Ministries. *Local Council Committees:* 1978– University of Cambridge Faculty Board of Divinity. *Publications: Reading the N.T. Today* (Lutterworth, 1977); *The Language of Luke and Acts, New Testament Studies* (April 1977); *"Imitatio Christi" and the Lucan Passion Narrative in Suffering and Martyrdom in the N.T.* (ed. Horbury & McNeile, C.U.P. 1981); Fernley Hartley Lecturer 1978, "Christian Character in the Gospel of Luke" (in *Epworth Review* 1979); Contributor to *Christian Belief: A Catholic-Methodist Statement* (1970); Contributor to *Unity the Next Step* (ed. P. Morgan, 1972).
Special Interests: Secretary Worship and Liturgy Committee, East African Church Union Consultation 1963–68; Member British Methodist/R.C. Commission; World Methodist Council, Council Member 1966–71, 1981–; Worship and Liturgy Committee Secretary 1971–81; Oxford Institute of Methodist Theological Studies, Secretary from 1969, Joint Chairman since 1976.
Hobbies and Recreations: Walking, Woodworking, Reading, T.V., Music.

BECK, George S., 12 Osborne Ave., Great Yarmouth, Norfolk NR30 4EE. (0493-2070) *b. 1 Jan 1924, Yorkshire.*
Education: 1948–50 Hartley Victoria. *Appointments:* 1947–48 Manchester, City Rd.; 1948–50 Hartley Victoria; 1950–52 Hyde and Denton; 1952–57 Bolton (Wesley); 1957–62 Sheffield Mission; 1962–67 Hull Mission; 1967–72 Burslem Mission; 1972–79 Bradford Mission; 1979– Great Yarmouth.

BECK, Keith Maylott, MA(Bristol). *b. 4 April 1930, Torquay. m. 8 Aug 1956: 1d., 3s.*
Education: 1935–41 Ellacombe Prim. and Jun.; 1941–46 Torquay Boys Gram. Sch.; 1951–54 Didsbury, Bristol. *Appointments:* 1950–51 Nantwich; 1954–55 Colchester; 1956–59 Bath; 1960–62 Birmingham (Moseley Road and Sparkhill); 1963–65 Aldershot and Farnborough; 1966–81 Toc H; 1982– Birmingham (Sutton Park).
Publications: West Midland Lines of the GWR (1982).
Special Interests: Church History, Church Architecture, Worship, Politics. *Hobbies and Recreations:* Birdwatching, Gardening, Classical Music, Railway History (especially GWR).

BECKERLEGGE, Oliver Aveyard, 74 Grange Garth, York YO1 4BS. (0904-34599) – MA 1936; Dip Ed 1936; PhD 1940. *b. 1 Oct 1913, Sheffield. m. 3 May 1951: 2d., 1s.*
Education: 1919–24 Sharrow Lane Council Sch., Sheffield; 1924–32 Central Sec. Sch. for Boys; 1932–38 Univ. of Sheffield; 1934 Univ. of Göttingen; 1946–47 Richmond.
Appointments: 1945–46 Higham Ferrers; 1947–48 Glasgow (Paisley Road); 1948–51 Greenock; 1951–54 Alston; 1954–59 Settle; 1959–64 Camborne; 1964–68 Roseland; 1968–71 Sheffield South; 1971–73 Hanley Bethesda; 1973–76 Superannuated (serious ill health); 1974–76 Active Sup. in Waltham Abbey and Hertford Ct.; 1976–81 Brigg; 1975–76 Librarian of United Kingdom Alliance (established library).
Connexional Committees: 1951–54 Educational Committee; 1976– Archives Committee; 1976– Necessitous Local Preachers' Committee; 1978– Texts Sub-Committee and Wesley Corpus Sub-Committee of New Hymnbook. *Publications:* Critical edn. of Pierre d'Abernun's *Secré de Secrez* (1944); *Fifty Years* (History of Meersbrook Park, Sheffield, S.S.U., 1938); *A New Book of German Songs with Music* (1942); *A School Certificate Revision Course in German* (1944); *The Youth Club Shakespeare* (Vol. 1) (1948); *How to Read the Bible* (1952; 2nd edn. 1955); *The ABC of Salvation* (1953; 2nd edn. 1966); *The United Methodist Free Churches* (1957); *Free Methodism in Cornwall* (1961); *The Story of the Bible* (1965); *Methodism in Roseland* (1966); Edn. of Wesley's *Roman Catechism* (1968); *United Methodist Ministers and their Circuits* (1968); *History of Mosborough Queen St. Meth. Ch.* (1969); *Our Methodist Doctrines and why we must preserve them* (1972); *Methodism in Barnetby* (1972); (now in press: with Franz Hildebrandt and James Dale: *Edn. of Hymns for the Use of the People called Methodists;* Vol. VII of Oxford Edn. of *Wesley's Works*).
Special Interests: Hymnology; Philately; Collecting early Bibles; Collecting Wesleyana; Editor of *VMA* since its inception, 1965; Contributor to *WHS Proc.* etc.; Editor of the abortive independent *Methodist Magazine* (10 issues, 1971); Governor of Ashville College 1971–.

BEDFORD, Derek, Rhosynfa, Erw Wen, Welshpool, Powys SY22 7HN. BA(Open). *b. 23 June 1932, Oldham. m. 15 Dec 1962: 1d., 2s.*
Education: 1936–43 All Saints CE; 1943–46 Grange St. Council Sch., Oldham; 1956–60 Didsbury, Bristol.
Appointments: 1960–62 Home Missions Caravan; 1962–66 Oldham East; 1966–71 Hattersley Mission; 1971–78 Farnworth; 1978–80 President's List; 1980– Welshpool and Bro Hafren.
Connexional Committees: 1967–71 Cooperation with other Communions Building Committee. *Council Member:* 1975–79 Bolton Metropolitan District Council. *Local Council Committees:* 1975 Parks, Arts. 1977

Industrial Development. 1977–79 Education and Social Services. *Special Interests:* Liberal Party, Self-sufficiency, Farming, Canals, History, Building Churches, Restoring Houses. *Hobbies and Recreations:* Reading, Gardening, Writing Novels, Music Appreciation.

BEDFORD, Peter, 17 Stanhope Ave., Hartlepool, Cleveland TS26 9QY. (0429-73700) – BA(Manch.) *b. 11 June 1944, Darlington. m. 1 Apr 1967: 2s.*
Education: 1968–69 Salford Univ.; 1975–78 Manchester Univ.; 1975–78 Hartley Victoria.

BEDFORD, Reginald Callear, 46 Ashley Way, Westone, Northampton NN3 3EB. (0604-412598) – Chevalier d'Ordres National de Cote d'Ivoire, BA(Sheffield), Dip Ed(Sheffield). *b. 17 Aug 1916, Abersychan, Mon. m. 2 Jan 1943: 2s.*
Education: 1927–32 Purbrook Park County High Sch., Hants; 1932–35 Colne Gram. Sch., Lancs; 1935–39 Sheffield Univ.; 1948–49 Richmond. *Appointments:* 1945–48 Deal; 1949–54 Guernsey; 1954–58 Hull (East); 1958–67 Secretary Methodist Youth Dept. and Secretary Methodist Association of Youth Clubs; 1967–71 Elland and Greetland; 1971–77 Northampton; 1977–81 Colchester. *Connexional Committees:* 1949–70 Youth (now Division of Education and Youth); 1958–82 Division of Social Responsibility (formerly Department of Christian Citizenship); World Methodist Council; Oxford 1951, Oslo 1961, London 1966, Denver 1971: also member British Committee World Methodist Council; 1958–67 British Council of Churches Youth Dept.; 18 times representative to Methodist Conference (never ex officio). *Local Council Committees:* 1973–77 Northants Youth Service Committee. *Publications: Let's Get Involved* (1965); *They Volunteered* (1968); *Why Total Abstinence?* (1963); *I Believe But...* (with Rosalind Thomas, 1965); *The World of Young People* (1963). Lectures: "Total Abstinence and the Teenager" (1960); "The New Look in Temperance Work" (1963); "Reply to the Trade" (1966). Regular contributor to *BLC Lessons* and *Partners in Learning*. *Special Interests:* Social Questions especially Alcohol Problems (formerly President, United Kingdom Alliance); since 1959 Director Methodist Holiday Hotels Ltd; 1981–82 Vice-Chairman; 1982– Chairman.
Hobbies and Recreations: Journalism, Radio and Television, Watching Football – supporter of Hull City.

BEE, Herbert Charles, 16 Beechway, Exmouth, Devon EX8 3HP. (03952-3897) – MA(Birmingham). *b. 14 June 1900, Lincoln. m. 6 Aug 1930: 1s.*
Education: Rosemary Lane Wesleyan Day Sch. (till 1916) then evening classes at Lincoln Municipal Tech. Sch.; 1924–27 Handsworth; 1939–42 Leeds Univ. *Appointments:* 1923–27 Stratford on Avon; 1927–30 Loftus and Staithes; 1930–33 Llandrindod Wells; 1933–34 Redruth; 1934–37 Newquay; 1937–42 York Centenary; 1942–47 Newark; 1947–50 Bristol, King Street; 1950–56 Bristol, East; 1956–62 St. Albans; 1962–66 Exmouth.
Special Interests: Social Anthropology. *Hobbies and Recreations:* Gardening, Photography.

BEECH, John (A), 3 Twyford Avenue, London N2 9NU. (01-883-5096) – Dip Theol(London). *b. 29 July 1926, Biddulph Moor, Staffs. m. 7 Apr 1956: 2s.*
Education: Local Prim. and County Sec.; 1950–54 Handsworth; 1953–54 Visiting Student, Selly Oak. *Appointments:* 1949–50 Wishaw; 1954–58 Gold Coast/Ghana, 1958–61 West Bromwich; 1961–68 Methodist Missionary Society; 1968– London Mission (North and Central).
Local Council Committees: 1969–78 Member Islington Area Youth Committee; 1970–78 Chairman Islington ILEA Detached Youth Work Project. *Publications:* Associate Editor of the *MMS* (1966–68); Contributor to Magazines and Handbooks.
Special Interests: Local Community affairs, Evangelism. *Hobbies and Recreations:* Gardening.

BEECH, Malcolm John, Epworth, 215 Long Lane, Holbury, Southampton SO4 1PD. (Fawley 891679) *b. 21 Dec 1934, Pontefract, Yorkshire. m. 28 Mar 1964.*
Education: 1940–44 Bridgetown Inf. and Boys Sec. Sch., Staffs; 1944–49 St. Augustines CE Sec. Sch., Broxbourne, Herts; 1958–60 Cliff Coll.; 1960–64 Didsbury, Bristol. *Appointments:* 1964–66 Forest of Dean; 1966–72 Bristol, Bedminster; 1972–74 Cardiff, Wesley; 1979– Southampton.
Special Interests: Singing. *Hobbies and Recreations:* Gardening, Photography, Wine Making.

BEEDEN, Albert Edward, The Brushes, Retford Rd., Walesby, Newark, Notts NG22 9PE. (0623-860044) *b. 2 Feb 1902, London. m. 4 Aug 1932: 2s.*
Education: 1906–09 Snowsfields Inf., Bermondsey; 1909–16 Owler Lane, Sheffield, Council Sch.; 1925–28 Victoria Park. *Appointments:* 1928–30 Faversham; 1930–32 Barrow-in-Furness; 1932–34 Manchester (Oxford Rd.); 1934–40 Huddersfield (High St.); 1940–46 Nottingham (North); 1946–50 Long Eaton; 1950–56 Cleethorpes (Trinity); 1956–61 Lancaster; 1961–66 Wigton; 1966–69 Whitehaven.

BEER, Stephen, 9 Ramsay Rd., Headington, Oxford OX3 8AY. (0865-63676) – MA; STM.
Education: 1971–75 Hartley Victoria. *Appointments:* 1975–80 Northampton; 1980– Oxford.

BEETHAM, Thomas Allan, 17 Grosvenor Cres., Dorchester, Dorset DT1 2BA. (0305-65691) – MA. *b. 13 Mar 1906, Ilford, Essex. m. (2) 11 Dec 1971: 3s.*
Education: 1918–23 City of London Sch.; 1923–26 Kings Coll., London; 1926–28 Wesley House. *Appointments:* 1928–36 Gold Coast, W. Africa; 1936–39 Haworth and Oakworth; 1939–50 Gold Coast, W. Africa; 1950–60 Missionary Secretary; 1960–67 Conference of Missionary Societies; 1967–70 Kingsmead College (Warden).

BEGG, Michael Birnie, 88 Rock Ave., Gillingham, Kent ME7 5PS. (0634-52429) *b. 24 Sept 1940, Dublin. m. 2 Apr 1966: 1d., 1s.*
Education: Dromore Rd. Prim. Sch., Warren Point, Co. Down, N. Ireland; Newry Gram. Sch., Downshire Rd., Newry, Co. Down; 1960–61 Cliff Coll.; 1962–66 Headingley. *Appointments:* 1966–68 Wymondham and Attleborough; 1968–71 Diss; 1971–76 Ipswich; 1978–81 West Indies (Jamaica); 1981– Medway Towns.
Special Interests: Christian Aid, Third World, Church Union, Pastoral Counselling. *Hobbies and Recreations:* Photography.

BELBEN, Howard Albert George, 7 Derriman Grove, Sheffield S11 9LE. (0742-367620) – MA(Cantab.), BD(London). *b. 8 June 1914, Sherborne, Dorset. m. 27 July 1948: 2d., 1s.*
Education: 1925–32 Weymouth Coll.; 1932–35 Emmanuel Coll., Cambridge; 1935–38 Richmond.
Appointments: 1938–40 Guildford; 1940–44 Shepton Mallet; 1943–47 Chaplain and Lecturer in Divinity, Southlands Training College; 1944–47 Weston-super-Mare; 1947–53 Cliff College Tutor; 1953–57 Wolverhampton (Darlington St.); 1957–60 Sheffield Mission; 1960–65 Cliff College Tutor; 1965–77 Principal.
Connexional Committees: 1944–47, 1948–53 Connexional Youth Council; 1950–52, 1962–64, 1969–71 Connexional Candidates Examination Committee; 1965–77 Connexional Home Mission Committee. *Publications: Evangelistic Counselling* (1965); *The Misson of Jesus* (1970); *The Evangelical Methodist* (CEIM Lecture, 1978); *Old Testament Notes* (1979).
Special Interests: Old Testament.
Hobbies and Recreations: Genealogy.

BELFIELD, Christopher Evan, 55 Charnock Dale Rd., Sheffield 12. (0742-392462) *b. 13 Dec 1943, Manchester. m. 28 July 1979.*
Education: 1949–55 Brookdale Park Prim.; 1955–60 Ducie Tech. High; 1970–71 Cliff Coll.; 1971–75 Hartley Victoria. *Appointments:* 1975–78 Ashton under Lyne; 1978– Sheffield South.
Special Interests: Methodist History.
Hobbies and Recreations: Transport History.

BELFIELD, Michael, The Methodist Manse, 58 Victoria Rd., Maldon, Essex CM9 7HF. (Maldon 53423) – BA(Bristol). *b. 3 Aug 1952, Stockport, Cheshire. m. 16 June 1978: 2s.*
Education: 1963–70 Hulme Gram. Sch., Oldham; 1974–77 Bristol Univ.; 1973–77 Wesley, Bristol. *Appointments:* 1978–79 Andros, Bahamas; 1979–81 Abaco, Bahamas; 1981– Chelmsford.
Hobbies and Recreations: Making and Drinking Wine, Tropical Fish, Gardening.

BELL, Clifford, Wesley House, 10 Victoria Rd., Sidmouth, Devon EX10 8TZ. (03955-3384) *b. 28 Apr 1922, Bradford, Yorkshire. m. 16 Dec 1950: 1s.*
Education: 1927–34 Brownhill Sch., Harehills, Leeds; 1934–39 Salt Boys' High Sch., Shipley; 1948–50 Headingley. *Appointments:* 1946–48 St. Albans; 1950–52 South Devon Mission; 1952–56 Goole; 1956–62 Nottingham South; 1962–68 Leicester West; 1968–75 Nottingham West; 1975–81 Plymouth; 1981– Sidmouth and Bridport.

BELL, Frederick John, 58 Middleton Ave., Newcastle-upon-Tyne NE4 9NB. *b. 1 June 1893, Newcastle.*
Education: 1919–21 Handsworth.

BELL, Geoffrey William, 89 Eastover Rd., High Littleton, Bristol BS18 5JB. (0761-70722) *b. 8 Mar 1928, Stoke-on-Trent, Staffs. m. 14 Mar 1959: 2d., 1s.*
Education: 1934–37 Hartshill Inf. Sch.; 1937–39 Hartshill Jun.; 1939–42 Hartshill Sen., Stoke-on-Trent; 1951–54 Hartley Victoria. *Appointments:* 1954–57 Camelford and Wadebridge; 1957–62 Hayle; 1962–67 Midsomer Norton.
Special Interests: Roman History, The Social and Political History of England, English Churches, Hadrian's Wall, Cinema History. *Hobbies and Recreations:* Metal Detecting, Woodworking and Joinery, Coin Collecting, Reading Novels (Thrillers), Tennis, Rowing, Swimming, Old Films (esp. Westerns), Playing and Listening to Music.

BELL, Reuben, 22 Borrowdale Ave., Seaburn Dene, Fulwell, Sunderland SR6 8LJ. (0783-486740) *b. 30 Oct 1912, Choppington, Northumberland. m. 1 June 1938 (Widower): 1d., 1s.*
Education: Bothal Sch., Ashington; 1945–47 Hartley Victoria. *Appointments:* 1947–51 Consett; 1951–56 Sunderland North; 1956–61 Heaton and Wallsend; 1961–67 Leeds North; 1967–72 Guernsey; 1972–78 Stoke-on-Trent.
Connexional Committees: 1953–72 Temperance and Social Welfare.
Hobbies and Recreations: Bowls, Golf, Football and Cricket.

BELLHOUSE, A. Gordon, 50 High St., Ecclesfield, Sheffield S30 3XD. (0742-467556) *b. 2 Apr 1915, Manchester. m. 6 June 1942: 2d.*
Education: 1920–26 Romiley Council Sch.; 1926–31 Hyde County Sch.; 1946–48 Hartley Victoria.
Appointments: 1944–45 National Service; 1945–46 Stour Valley Mission; 1948–52 Oldham (Wesley); 1952–61 West Indies Dt. (Jamaica); 1961–66 Aireborough; 1966–75 Sheffield (Brunswick); 1975–81 Stockport.
Connexional Committees: 1968–76 Overseas Division.
Special Interests: Ethnic Minorities; Peace (member of F.O.R. over 40 years). *Hobbies and Recreations:* Gardening, Walking.

BENNETT, James Ashworth, 58 Captain's Clough Rd., Bolton, Lancs BL1 5RS. (Bolton 46937) *b. 2 Dec 1890, Castleton, Lancs. m. 26 Jul 1920 (Widower): 1s.*
Education: 1911–12 Cliff Coll.; 1913–16 Handsworth. *Appointments:* 1916–17 H.M. Forces; 1917–19 Chaplain, H.M.F.; 1919–22 Manchester Mission; 1922–26 Sunderland Mission; 1926–29 Lancaster; 1929–32 Stockton, Brunswick; 1932–36 Gateshead, High

7.5.95 – CH. ANN. THE HILL.
m. d. 1978
f. ae 90 – HOME AT COVENTRY

West St., and East; 1936–40 Hull, Waltham St.; 1940–44 Barnoldswick; 1944–48 Bolton, Farnworth; 1948–52 Bolton, Wesley; 1952–56 Bolton, Park St.; 1956–58 Chorley.

BENNETT, John D., 31 Raikeswood Rd., Skipton, N. Yorks BD23 1NB. (0756-3551) – BA(Open). *b. 7 Apr 1944, Farnborough, Kent. m. 31 Aug 1971: 2d.*
Education: 1957–59 Tottenham Tech. Coll.; 1968–70 Handsworth; 1971 Queens. *Appointments:* 1971–76 West Bromwich; 1976–81 Nottingham East; 1981– Skipton.
Special Interests: Christian Aid, World Disarmament Movement. *Hobbies and Recreations:* Travel, Modern Art, Open University Courses.

BENSON, George Victor, The Manse, Baugy Vale, Guernsey, C.I. (0481-44264) – BD(London). *b. 11 Feb 1932, Bedlington, Northumberland. m. 13 Dec 1958: 2d.*
Education: 1937–43 Bedlington County Prim.; 1943–48 Bedlington Gram.; 1956–59 Headingley.
Appointments: 1959–61 Preston (Lune St.); 1961–65 Kenya Dt.; 1965–69 Pontefract; 1969–76 Ealing and Acton; 1976– Guernsey.
Connexional Committees: 1977– Central Committee O.D.
Hobbies and Recreations: Soccer, Badminton, Theatre.

BENT, Herbert, 12 Burrowmoor Rd., March, Cambs PE15 9RD. (03542-3322) – Academic Diploma of Theology (London). *b. 11 Nov 1922, Oldham. m. 16 Aug 1947: 2d.*
Education: Waterhead Elem.; Clarksfield Jun.; Waterloo Central; 1946–47 Richmond. *Appointments:* 1947–50 North Isles (Shetland); 1950–53 Bacup; 1953–57 King's Lynn; 1957–62 Waltham Abbey and Hertford; 1962–67 Newmarket; 1967–73 Newport (Mon.); 1973–81 Bridgend; 1981– Fenland.
Connexional Committees: 1968–74 Local Preachers.
Special Interests: Industrial Mission (Chaplain 1967–81), Mission to Rural Communities (Chaplain 1981–).
Hobbies and Recreations: Car Maintenance, Gardening, Photography.

BENTON, Malcolm John, 5 Tregothnan Rd., Falmouth, Cornwall TR11 2DR. (0326-312464) *b. 6 Jul 1943, Selston, Notts. m. 22 Jul 1967: 3s.* m. CHARMAINE AP. 1995
Education: 1948–54 Selston Prim. Sch.; 1954–59 Magnus Gram. Sch., Newark-on-Trent, Notts; 1961–63 Cliff Coll.; 1963–67 Handsworth.
Appointments: 1967–69 Dorchester; 1969–70 Leeds N.E.; 1970–78 Callington and Gunnislake; 1978– Falmouth. NEWTON ABBOTT
Hobbies and Recreations: Gardening, Camping.

BERNARD, Henry Walter, Le Gron, St. Saviour's, Guernsey, C.I. (For all correspondence: c/o Mrs. E. Mahy, 250 Brooklyn Rd., Cheltenham, Glos GL51 8ED.) L.es.L. *b. 27 Aug 1908, Nîmes, Gard, France. m. 20 Aug 1935 (Widower). 2d.*
Education: Lycée education in France; 1926–28 Sorbonne (Paris); 1928 Eglise Réformée Theol. Coll., Paris; Université de Poitiers.
Appointments: 1941–45 French Church; 1946–58 Jamaica Dt.; 1958–64 Jersey Dt.; 1964–67 North Somercotes.
Special Interests: Until retirement through infirmity: Photography, Ornithology, Sport, Writing and Translation.

BERRY, John Reay, Tillydrine, Todholes Rd., Cleator Moor, Cumbria. (0946-810428) *b. 12 Mar 1915, Barrow-in-Furness. m. 27 Aug 1946: 1d., 2s.*
Education: 1926–32 Barrow Gram. Sch.; 1935–38 Didsbury. *Appointments:* 1938–40 Army Chaplain (India); 1940–46 Combatant Officer (Indian Army); 1946–50 Bexhill; 1950–53 Grays; 1953–59 Army Chaplain; 1965–80 Director of Religious Studies, the Manchester Grammar School.
Publications: The Carpenter's Son (1980). *Special Interests:* N.T. Studies, History. *Hobbies and Recreations:* Water colour painting, Fell walking, Travel, Lecturing.

BERRY, Ronald, Greystones, 36 Carleton Rd., Pontefract, W. Yorks WF8 3NF. (0977-702591) – BD(London). *b. 11 Nov 1925, Bury, Lancs. m. 18 Jul 1953: 2d., 2s.*
Education: 1936–40 Altrincham Gram. Sch.; Handsworth. *Appointments:* 1947 Birmingham Mission; 1948–49 Manchester (City Rd.); 1949–52 Handsworth Coll.; 1952–53 Gainsborough; 1953–57 Gateshead (West); 1957–61 Gateshead (East); 1961–65 Dudley; 1965–71 Wantage and Abingdon; 1972–76 Hull (East); 1976– Pontefract and Normanton.
Connexional Committees: 1968–79 Faith and Order Committee; 1979– Joint Building Schemes Committee.
Publications: Article *Scottish Journal of Theology* (March 1961).
Special Interests: N.T. Theology, Liturgy. *Hobbies and Recreations:* Music.

BERRYMAN, Norman, The Manse, 37 Main St., Seahouses, Northumberland NE68 7RF. (0665-720349) *b. 25 Dec 1923, Scarborough. m. 10 Aug 1957.*
Education: 1927–29 Scarborough (Central); 1929–36 Hull (Newlands); 1936–38 Scarborough (Friarage); 1951–54 Hartley Victoria. *Appointments:* 1954–57 Coatbridge/Airdrie/Arnadale; 1957–62 Hetton-le-Hole; 1962–69 Ryton and Prudhoe; 1969–75 Seamens Mission, Queen Victoria, London (Chaplain); 1975–81 Gibraltar (Wesley House); 1981– Seahouses.
Connexional Committees: 1963–73 Christian Citizenship Committee.
Council Member: 1969–75 Chaplain & Welfare Officer Queen Victoria Seamens Rest; 1975–81 Officiating Chaplain to H.M. Forces Gibraltar.
Local Council Committees: 1962–69 Ryton Urban District Council Accident Prevention & Road Safety Committee.
Special Interests: History (local and national) and Social Affairs. *Hobbies and Recreations:* Photography, Philately and Walking.

BESLEY, William Jess, 75 Dunstan Cres., Worksop, Notts S80 1AG. (0909-472609) *b. 28 Apr 1915, Rotherham. m. 3 Feb 1940: 2d.*
Education: 1920–25 Doncaster Rd. Prim. Sch.; 1925–31 Rotherham Gram. Sch.; 1945–47 Handsworth.
Appointments: 1947–49 Wallasey;

1949–52 Stanley; 1952–56 Bury; 1956–61 Fleetwood; 1961–68 Skegness; 1968–75 Bridlington; 1975– Worksop and Kiveton.
Special Interests: Methodist History and Doctrine, General Secretary of The Voice of Methodism Association 1977–82. *Hobbies and Recreations:* Electronics and Printing.

BETHEL, William Edward, 89 Ledbury Rd., Hereford HR1 1RQ. (0432-272877) – BA. *b. 30 Oct 1934, Madeley, Shropshire. m. 20 Jun 1959: 2s.*
Education: 1946–51 Coalbrookdale High Sch.; 1974–79 Open University; 1957–60 Headingley. *Appointments:* 1960–63 Melton Mowbray; 1963–67 Hinckley; 1967–72 Zambia Dt.; 1972–78 Holsworthy; 1978– Hereford.
Hobbies and Recreations: Gardening, Tennis, Swimming, Badminton, Walking.

BEUZEVAL, Philip McRoberts, 32 Mast Lane, Cullercoats, North Shields, Tyne and Wear NE30 3DE. (0632-526541) – BA(Cantab.), LlB(London). *b. 23 Jun 1937, St. Helier, Jersey. m. 18 Mar 1967: 2s.*
Education: 1942–45 Durham Rd. Inf. Sch., Newport, Mon.; 1945–48 Victoria Coll., Jersey, Prep. Sch.; 1948–56 Victoria Coll., Jersey; 1956–59 University Coll., London; 1960–63 Wesley House. *Appointments:* 1963–66 Assistant Tutor Richmond College; 1966–72 Leicester Central Mission; 1972–79 Leicester South East; 1979– North Shields and Whitley Bay.
Connexional Committees: 1959–60 Church Membership Committee; 1970–73, 1977–80 Candidates Examination Committee.
Hobbies and Recreations: Gardening, Sport, Walking.

BEWICK, Wilfrid Moseley, 12 Manor Court, Barrow-on-Trent, Derby DE7 1HB. (0332-700540) – BA. *b. 14 Aug 1908, Liverpool. m. 30 Nov 1940: 2s.*
Education: Epworth Coll., Rhyl, N. Wales; 1929–33 Handsworth.
Appointments: 1933–47 Trichinopoly District, S. India; 1947–50 Oldham; 1950–53 Liverpool (Central); 1953–58 Sheerness; 1958–63 Faversham; 1962–67 Bury St. Edmunds; 1967–73 Haverfordwest.

BHOGAL, Inderjit Singh, The Manse, Leacroft Ave., Low Hill, Wolverhampton WV10 9BE. (0902-732689/782847) – BA. *b. 17 Jan 1953, Nairobi, Kenya.*
Education: 1958–64 Khalsa Boys and Girls Sch., Nairobi; 1964–70 Blue Coat C of E; 1970–73 Dudley Tech. Coll.; 1973–74 Cliff Coll.; 1975–79 Hartley Victoria. *Appointments:* 1979– Wolverhampton, Darlington St.
Connexional Committees: 1981– Overseas Missions Central Committee.
Special Interests: Inter-faith dialogue, Race Relations, The Peace Movement, The Sikh Religion. *Hobbies and Recreations:* Photography, most sports activities, Mountain climbing.
PRESIDENT OF CONF. 2000-2001

BIBB, Andrew Derek McKinley, 21 Trowbridge Gdns, Luton, Beds LU2 7JY. (0582-391409) *b. 9 Sept 1942, St. Pancras, London.*
Education: 1947–53 Kender Prim. Sch.; 1953–59 Samuel Pepys County Sec. Sch.; 1959–61 Addey and Stanhope Sch.; 1971–75 Queens.
Appointments: 1975–78 London, Lambeth Mission; 1978– Luton North.
Special Interests: Politics, Peace Movement, Railways. *Hobbies and Recreations:* Photography.

BICKLE, Jack Rodney, The Manse, Bossinex Rd., Tintagel, Cornwall PL34 0AJ. (0840-770237) *b. 22 Apr 1921, Plymouth. m. 18 Aug 1951: 1s.*
Education: 1926–32 Mount St., Plymouth; 1932–37 Plymouth Public; 1947–49 Wesley, Bristol. *Appointments:* 1946–47 Portsmouth Mission; 1949–51 Trowbridge and Bradford-on-Avon; 1951–56 Malton; 1956–63 Helston; 1963–68 Brighton and Hove; 1968–73 Redruth; 1973–79 Ripley; 1979– Camelford and Wadebridge.
Special Interests: Politics and Current Affairs. *Hobbies and Recreations:* Gardening, Stamp Collecting, Football, Cricket.

BIDNELL, Alan Roy, 90 Nottingham Rd., Long Eaton, Nottingham NG10 2BZ. (060-76-2045) – BA(Sheffield), BA(Bristol). *b. 25 Sept 1936, Luton. m. 5 Aug 1961: 2d., 1s.*
Education: 1941–44 Denbigh Rd. Inf., Luton; 1944–48 Denbigh Rd. Jun., Luton; 1948–55 Luton Gram. Sch.; 1955–58 Sheffield Univ.; 1958–61 Bristol Univ.; 1958–61 Didsbury, Bristol. *Appointments:* 1961–63 Wolverton and Bletchley; 1963–68 Stanley; 1968–73 King's Lynn; 1973–80 Eastbourne; 1980– Long Eaton.
Connexional Committees: 1969–73 Connexional Youth Committee.
Special Interests: Music – play piano and organ.

BIDNELL, Roger Stuart, 100 Harrow Rd., Wollaton Park, Nottingham NG8 1FN. (0602-293630) – MA, LLB. *b. 13 Mar 1940, Luton. m. 16 Apr 1968: 1d., 2s.*
Education: 1945–51 Denbigh Rd. County Prim., Luton; 1951–58 Luton Gram. Sch.; 1958–61 Sheffield Univ.; 1963–66 Cambridge Univ.; 1963–66 Wesley House. *Appointments:* 1966–68 London, Rivercourt and Shepherds Bush Road; 1968–75 Birmingham (Elmdon); 1975– Nottingham West.
Local Council Committees: 1973–75 Family Practitioners Committee, Solihull.
Special Interests: Clinical Theology, Team Ministry (Ecumenical), Communities, International Twinning Arrangements. *Hobbies and Recreations:* Photography, Gardening.

BIELBY, Richard, 38 Macaulay Drive, Balderton, Newark, Notts NG24 3QQ. (0636-704412) – BA(Open).
Appointments: 1981– Newark.

BIGGIN, Harry, 4a Collaton Rd., Torquay TQ2 7HL. (0803-64372) *b. Sheffield. m. 1933: 2s.*
Education: Elem.; 1928–31 Hartley Victoria. *Appointments:* 1927–28 Kingsbridge; 1932–35 Leeds; 1935–38 Margate; 1938–44 Southampton; 1944–50 Barnstaple; 1950–55 Salisbury; 1955–60 Bridgwater; 1960–64 Romford; 1964–66 Jersey; 1966–69 Portsmouth Mission.
Hobbies and Recreations: Gardening, Bowls.

BINGHAM, John Hiram, 349 Orrell Rd., Orrell, Wigan WN5 8QZ. (0695-623334) *b. 4 May 1936, Blackwell,*

Derbyshire. m. 22 Aug 1964: 2s.
Education: Blackwell, Tibshelf Sec. Mod.; 1971–73 Hartley Victoria. *Appointments:* 1973–78 Droylsden and Openshaw; 1978– Orrell and Lamberhead Green.
Special Interests: Football; Cricket; Chaplain of Stockport County F.C. since 1973. *Hobbies and Recreations:* Gardening, Breeding Tropical Fish.

BINKS, John Arthur James, 88 Cranleigh Drive, Whitfield, Dover, Kent. BD. *b. 21 Jan 1912, Dover. m.*
Education: 1933–36 Headingley.
Appointments: 1937–48 Madras District; 1948–70 Church of S. India; 1970–76 Huntingdon Mission.

BINNEY, Alfred, Ringinglow, 73 Felpham Way, Felpham, Bognor Regis, West Sussex PO22 8PU. (0243-863518) *b. 23 Nov 1910, Rotherham, Yorks. m. 22 Jul 1937: 2s.*
Education: Wellgate Inf. and Jun. Sch., Rotherham; Rotherham Gram. Sch.; 1930–33 Handsworth. *Appointments:* 1933–36 Guildford; 1936–37 Shaftesbury; 1937–39 Grays; 1939–42 Higham Ferrers; 1942–47 Rugby; 1947–52 London, Kilburn and Hampstead; 1952–56 Harrow; 1956–65 Cambridge; 1965–70 Redhill; 1970–76 Chichester and Bognor.
Connexional Committees: 1948–1954 Christian Citizenship; 1947– Seamen's Mission. *Publications: City Road Diary* (Joint Editor, 1978).
Special Interests: Early Church History, Early Methodist History, Education. *Hobbies and Recreations:* Keen cricketer from teens to forties.

BIRCH, Kenneth, "Andermatt", St. Andrews Ave., Morley, Leeds LS27 0JT. (0532-532079/534051) – BA(Leeds). *b. 27 Jul 1927, Leek, Staffs.*
Education: 1932–38 St. Luke's CE, Leek; 1938–44 Leek High Sch.; 1951–54 Leeds Univ.; 1956–57 London Univ.; 1951–54 Headingley.
Appointments: 1954–56 Swinton and Pendlebury; 1956–76 Resigned; 1976 Morley.
Special Interests: Biblical Studies. *Hobbies and Recreations:* Astronomy, Detective Fiction.

BIRD, Arthur Henry, 17 Capper Close, Newton Poppleford, Nr Sidmouth, Devon EX10 0HD. *b. 3 Apr 1909, Brough, Cumbria. m. 25 Mar 1940: 2d., 2s.*
Education: Brough Council Sch.; Appleby Gram. Sch. *Appointments:* 1953–58 Nottingham South; 1958–63 Barnstaple; 1963–66 Tony Pandy; 1966–71 London, Bow Mission (Old Ford); 1971–73 Oldham; 1973–74 Brinkworth.
Connexional Committees: Church Membership Committee; Christian Citizenship Committee. *Council Member:* Malmesbury Town Council; 1979–80 Mayor of Malmesbury. *Local Council Committees:* On various Council Committees as Councillor and Mayor. *Publications: Victory* (Religious Play); *Adventure in Evangelism* (1968); Editor *International Youth Review* (1944–50).
Special Interests: Work amongst elderly, Public House evangelism with aid of piano accordion, Journalism, International youth work. *Hobbies and Recreations:* Philately – Chairman Methodist Philatelic Association for 5 years, Walking, Photography.

BIRD, Harold, 33 Chapel St., Penzance, Cornwall TR18 4AQ. (0736-4760) *b. 10 May 1901, Hellifield, Yorks. m. 4 Nov 1974: 2s., 1d.*
Education: 1921–24 Didsbury.
Appointments: 1924–67 Hyderabad District and Church of South India Diocese of Dornakal, 1948–52 Hayle.

BIRNIE, Merson Burnett, 46 Dale Ave., Stratford-upon-Avon, Warwicks CV37 7EW. (0789-68578) – MA(Bristol). *b. 1 Jul 1904, Edinburgh. m. 28 Jul 1932: 2d.*
Education: 1914–19 Boroughmuir Sch., Edinburgh; 1939–42 Bristol Univ.; 1925–28 Didsbury. *Appointments:* 1928–32 London Finsbury Park; 1932–35 Sunderland S.E.; 1935–38 Buxton; 1938–41 Bristol, King St.; 1941–46 Bristol, Clifton; 1946–51 Reading; 1951–58 Leamington; 1964–65 Liverpool North; 1965–70 Evesham.

BIRTWELL, Norman, 34 Malvina Place, Perth PH1 5DY. (0738-31927) *b. 1 Aug 1916, Rochdale, Lancs. m. 3 Aug 1949: 1d., 1s.*
Education: 1923–30 Lowerplace Prim. & Castlemere Central; 1933–36 Loreburn Coll., Manchester; 1945–47 Hartley Victoria. *Appointments:* 1947–49 Reeth; 1949–53 Wensleydale; 1953–58 Redcar, Saltburn and Guisborough; 1958–65 Glasgow (West); 1965–81 Dundee, Perth and Blairgowrie; 1969–77 Secretary of Methodist Synod in Scotland. Secretary of Negotiating Committee for Union with Church of Scotland, 9 years; Multilateral Church Conversations in Scotland, 9 years.
Connexional Committees: 1960–69 Overseas.
Special Interests: Ecumenical. *Hobbies and Recreations:* Philately and Gardening.

BISHOP, Christopher John, 3 Elm Gardens, East Finchley, London N2 0TF. (01-883-3994) *b. 30 Nov 1942, Bally Castle, N. Ireland. m. 12 Aug 1970: 2d., 1s.*
Education: 1954–60 Harborne Collegiate; 1960–63 Birmingham Coll. of Art and Craft; 1966–70 Hartley Victoria. *Appointments:* 1970–73 Coventry Mission; 1973–76 Hawley Trinity; 1976– Finchley and Hendon.
Local Council Committees: 1979– Borough of Barnet Art Committee.
Special Interests: Industrial Mission. *Hobbies and Recreations:* Badminton, Reading, Camping.

BISHOP, Edna Phyllis, 29 Growstone Avenue, Westcliff on Sea, Essex SS0 8HT. (0702-42091) *b. 8 Aug 1924, Hastings, Sussex.*
Education: 1936–40 Gosport County Sch.; 1946–48 Wesley Deaconess Coll. *Appointments:* 1974–75 Devonport; 1975–80 Bury and Heywood; 1980– Southend on Sea.

BISHOP, Frank Edward, 18 Kingswood Rd., Shrewsbury, Shropshire SY3 8OX. (0743-62638) – BD(London). *b. 1 Mar 1937, Wickhambrook, Suffolk. m. 19 Aug 1961: 3d.*
Education: 1948–53 King Edward VI Gram. Sch., Bury St. Edmunds; 1958–61 Richmond. *Appointments:* 1961–64 Wadhurst; 1964–67

Epworth and Crowle; 1967–72 Sandbach and Alsager; 1972–79 Oxford; 1979– Shrewsbury. *Connexional Committees:* 1974–77 Social Responsibility Committee. *Special Interests:* Community Relations – Member of Executive Committee Oxford Committee for Community Relations 1973–79. *Hobbies and Recreations:* Soccer Referee, Camping, Gardening.

BISHOP, Harold Alfred, 32 Copley Lodge, Murton, Bishopston, Swansea SA3 3JJ. (0792-828-2568) *b. 11 Aug 1900, Walsall, Staffs. m. 10 Jul 1979.* *Education:* Sec. Sch., Maidenhead, Berks; 1926–29 Richmond. *Appointments:* 1925–26 Llanelli; 1926–29 Richmond College; 1929–32 Cowbridge; 1932–33 Ferndale; 1933–35 Rhondda Ely Valley; 1935–39 Newport, Stow Hill; 1939–42 Warrington; 1942–48 Kidderminster; 1948–55 Gower.
Special Interests: Sunday Services.

BISHOP, John Walter, Epworth, Woodham Rd., Woking, Surrey GU21 4DP. (04862-61289) – BA, MTh (London). *b. 7 June 1919, Harrogate, Yorkshire. m. 23 Oct 1948.* *Education:* –1930 Markland Hill Sch., Bolton; 1930–36 Bolton Sch.; 1944–47, 1949–52 Univ. of London; 1947–49 Richmond. *Appointments:* 1945–47 Bury St. Edmunds; 1947–49 Richmond College; 1949–54 Leytonstone and Forest Gate; 1954–63 Romford; 1963–68 Wolverhampton (Trinity); 1968–76 Kilburn and Hampstead; 1976– Woking and Walton on Thames.
Connexional Committees: 1963–69 Candidates Examination Committee; 1966–80 Methodist Youth Camps Conference Committee.
Special Interests: Hospital Chaplaincy Work, Philosophy, Theology. *Hobbies and Recreations:* Photography, Music, Varied Sports – Football, Cricket, Tennis.

BISHOP, Peter Douglas, 8 Scarletts Close, Uckfield, Sussex TN22 2BA. (0825-2171) – MA(Manchester), BD, PhD(London). *b. 30 June 1934, Seaford, Sussex. m. 12 Aug 1961: 1d., 1s.* *Education:* County Gram. Sch., Sutton, Surrey; 1962–64 Univ. of Manchester; 1968–73 Univ. of London; 1958–61 Richmond. *Appointments:* 1961–64 Middleton; 1964–71 Church of South India (Diocese of Madras); 1971–76 Tunbridge Wells; 1976– Brighton Polytechnic (Senior Lecturer in History of Religions).
Connexional Committees: 1972–75 Central Committee, MMS (Overseas Division). *Publications: Books:* *Sermons from St. John's*, CLS/ISPCK, Madras & Delhi, 1971; *World Religions – A Glossary and A Guide*, Brighton Polytechnic, 1977; *Words in World Religions*, SCM, 1979; *A Technique for Loving: Non-Violence in Indian and Christian Traditions*, SCM, 1981. *Articles:* Towards a Christian Yoga, *The Expository Times*, LXXXVII, No. 12, 1976; Ahimsa and Satyagraha, *Indian Journal of Theology*, Vol. 27, No. 2, 1978; God and the Absolute in Vivekananda and Aurobindo, *Indian Journal of Theology*, Vol. 31, No. 1, 1982. *Lectures* include: Christian Theology in Multi-Cultural Britain – The Question of Race, LPMA Aggregate, June 1982; Proclaiming the Gospel in Europe Today – Peace and Reconciliation, Consultative Conference of European Methodist Churches, Herrnhut, GDR, September 1982. *Special Interests:* Modern Indian History and Religion, Inter-Religious Dialogue, CND, Tutor for the Open University, Chairman, Friends of Vellore, UK. *Hobbies and Recreations:* Indifferent Tennis and leisurely Walking.

BLACKBURN, Philip, 3 The Grove, Harrogate, North Yorkshire HG1 5NN. (0432-504362) – MA(Cantab.) *b. 17 Apr 1923, Loughborough, Leicestershire. m. 30 Jul 1957: 1d., 1s.* *Education:* 1929–33 Mapperley Plains Sch., Nottingham; 1933–41 Nottingham High Sch.; 1941–42 University Coll., Nottingham; 1946–48 and 1954–55 Fitzwilliam House; 1946–48 and 1954–55, Wesley House. *Appointments:* 1948–54 Jamaica Dt. West Indies; 1954–55 Wesley House, Cambridge; 1955–61 Jamaica Dt. West Indies; 1962–67 Bahamas Dt. West Indies; 1967–74 Leeds (North East); 1974–82 Leeds (Horsforth and Bramley); 1982– Harrogate.
Connexional Committees: 1969–74 Overseas Missions. *Council Member:* 1964–66 Chairman: Bahamas Christian Council. *Local Council Committees:* 1962–66 Member Nassau Prison Visiting Committee, Member Nassua Mental Hospital Committee, Member Bahamas Advisory Council on Education, Member Nassua Children's Emergency Hostel Committee.
Special Interests: Philately, Numismatics, Air Training Corps (Squadron Chaplain 1971–77, West Riding Wing Chaplain 1977–82), Tramways.

BLACKBURN, Raymond Hugh, 23 Park Ave., Sleaford, Lincs NG34 7JJ. (0526-303169) *b. 23 Nov 1909, Coningsby, Lincs. m. 11 Aug 1937: 1d., 3s.*
Education: 1919–26 Queen Elizabeth's Gram. Sch., Horncastle; 1931–34 Headingley. *Appointments:* 1930–31 Bardney; 1934–37 Leeds Richmond Hill; 1937–39 Knaresborough; 1939–46 Chaplain HMF; 1946–50 Boston; 1950–54 Brigg; 1954–60 Market Rasen; 1960–65 Barton on Humber; 1965–70 Sleaford; 1970–74 The Peak.
Local Council Committees: 1965–70 Kesteven (Lincs) Education Committee.
Hobbies and Recreations: Art and Natural History.

BLACKBURN, Wilfred, 47 Buttermere Drive, Kendal, Cumbria LA9 7PA. (0539-25902) – BA(Open). *b. 8 Sept 1909, Skipton, Yorkshire. m. 31 Mar 1951.*
Education: Ermplids Gram. Sch., Skipton; 1977–80 Open Univ.; 1946–49 Hartley Victoria. *Appointments:* 1946 London Mission, West Ham; 1949–52 Manchester and Salford Mission; 1952–56 Sheffield North East; 1956–61 Carlisle; 1961–66 Birkenhead; 1966–71 Bloxwich; 1971–76 Kendal.
Connexional Committees: 1956–61 Youth; 1971–75 Social Responsibility.

Special Interests: Religion and Politics. *Hobbies and Recreations:* Golf, Walking, Reading.

BLAINEY, Edward, 23 Pyghtle Close, Trunch, North Walsham, Norwich NR28 0QF. (0263-721341) *b. 15 Aug 1914, Oldham. m. 1d., 1s.*
Education: 1919–28 Hathershaw Council, Oldham; 1948–50 Hartley Victoria. *Appointments:* 1947–48 Aylesham; 1948–50 Hartley Victoria; 1950–53 Stockport Mount Tabor and South; 1953–57 Northwich London Rd.; 1957–63 Buckley and Mold; 1963–68 St. Helens and Prescot; 1968–73 North Walsham and Aylsham; 1973–79 Camelford and Wadebridge.

BLAKEY, John William Wesley, 39 Delamere Ave., Salford, Lancashire M6 7NS. (061-736-3158) *b. 9 Aug 1947, Newcastle-upon-Tyne. m. 3 Jan 1970: 1d., 1s.*
Education: 1952–58 Shiney Row Inf. and Jun. Sch.; 1958–64 Washington Gram. Sch.; 1967–71 Hartley Victoria.
Appointments: 1971–76 Wigan; 1976– Swinton.
Hobbies and Recreations: Gardening, Squash, Jogging.

BLANCHARD, Bernard William, Wesley Villa, New St., Sedbergh, Cumbria LA10 5AF. (0587-20329) – AIBA. *b. Hull. m.*
Education: Hull Gram. Sch.; Hymers Coll., Hull; Hull Sch. of Architecture.
Appointments: 1976–82 Blaydon; 1982– Sedbergh.
Connexional Committees: 1958–63 Connexional General Purposes; 1964–71 Archives Committee, 1970–74 Property Division. *Publications:* Thesis: Nonconformist Architecture in East Yorkshire.
Special Interests: Methodist Buildings, Methodist Hymnody. *Hobbies and Recreations:* Fell Walking, Music.

BLANCHFLOWER, David, The Manse, 59 Top Rd., Kingsley, Cheshire WA6 8BY. (0928-88277) *b. 17 Aug 1944, Salford, Lancashire. m. 20 June 1970: 1d., 2s.*
Education: 1948–55 New Windsor Prim. Sch.; 1955–59 Clarendon Sec. Mod. Sch., Salford; 1968–72 Wesley, Bristol. *Appointments:* 1972–75 Sheffield North East; 1975–79 Leeds (Richmond Hill); 1979– Frodsham. 1980– Assistant Secretary Synod, Chester and Stoke-on-Trent District.
Publications: Up and Away (Poems) 1978; *Half Time* (Poems) 1979; *Mainly People* 1982.
Special Interests: Poetry, Music, Politics, Friends.

BLAND, Arthur, 23 South Drive, Timperley, Altrincham, Cheshire WA15 6QJ. (061-973-8768) – BA, BD(London). *b. 13 July 1912, Manchester. m. 2 Mar 1946: 1d., 1s.*
Education: 1924–28 Manchester Central High Sch.; 1938–41 Headingley. *Appointments:* 1941–44 Bromsgrove New Road; 1944–46 Liverpool North; 1946–50 Wigan (Standishgate); 1950–53 St. Helens; 1953–58 Cheetham Hill; 1958–63 Hinckley (Albert Road); 1963–68 Leicester North; 1968–72 Wolverhampton (Trinity); 1972–77 Walsall Mission.

BLAND, John David, 3 Leslie Close, Littleover, Derby DE3 7AW. (0332-517132) *b. 11 Dec 1937, Warrington, Cheshire. m. 20 May 1961: 2d.*
Education: 1943–49 Stockton Heath County Inf. Sch.; 1949–55 Lymm Gram. Sch.; 1961–65 Hartley Victoria.
Appointments: 1965–70 Edinburgh (Nicolson Square); 1970–74 Tadcaster; 1974–75 Home Missions (Chaplain, Gibraltar); 1975–79 Derby Mission.
Connexional Committees: 1971–74 DSR Board; 1976–79 Home Missions Central Mission Sub-Committee.
Publications: Prayers in Fellowship 1982.
Special Interests: Inner City Work – Healing and Counselling. *Hobbies and Recreations:* Music, Photography.

BLANDFORD, Gwendolyn Elizabeth, 34 Holly Lane, Smethwick Warley, West Midlands B67 7JD. (021-558-1792) – LRAM. *b. 26 Jan 1930, Bilston, Staffs.*
Education: 1940–47 High Sch. for Girls, Wolverhampton; 1947–51 Coll. of Technology, Wolverhampton (Music Dept.); 1958–59 Royal Coll. of Music; 1967–68 Reading Univ.; 1980–81 Queens. *Appointments:* 1981– Birmingham West.
Special Interests: Unemployed, Multi-Ethnic, Ecumenical, Prayer & House Groups, Counselling, Neighbourhood Groups. *Hobbies and Recreations:* Music, Walking, Gardening, Reading, Theatre.

BLANTERN, John Bruce, 21 The Drive, Kilner Park, Ulverston, Cumbria LA12 0DT. (0229-53198) *b. 22 Jan 1936, Coventry. m. 30 June 1962: 2d.*
Education: 1947–52 John Gulson, Coventry; 1958–62 Handsworth.
Appointments: 1962–63 Penistone; 1963–68 Barnsley West; 1968–76 Birmingham, Moseley Road and Sparkhill; 1976–81 Bradford Great Horton; 1981– Ulverston.
Special Interests: Children's Work, Audio-Visual Aids, Recent Folk Hymnody.

BLATHERWICK, David, 4 Sydney Rd., Cradley Heath, Warley, W. Midlands B64 5BA. (0384-69892) – LlB(Nottingham), BA(Cantab). *b. 30 Dec 1937, Newark-on-Trent, Notts. m. 27 Jul 1963: 2s.*
Education: 1948–55 Rydal Sch.; 1955–58 Nottingham Univ.; 1958–61 Cambridge Univ.; 1961–62 Göttingen Univ.; 1958–61 Wesley House.
Appointments: 1962–64 Assistant Tutor, Headingley; 1964–66 Shooters Hill; 1966–69 London Mission (Plumstead); 1969–71 Grimsby (West); 1971–75 British Council of Churches (Ecumenical Officer for England); 1975–80 Warrington; 1980– Cradley Heath.
Connexional Committees: 1967– Local Preachers Studies Board; 1971–78 Ecumenical Affairs Committee.
Publications: This Stab of Fire (Epworth 1971); *Adventures in Unity* (BCC 1975); *Mark as Storyteller* (Fearnley-Hartley Lecture 1977).
Special Interests: New Testament Studies. *Hobbies and Recreations:* Music, Poetry.

BLIZZARD, Russell H. B. H., 33 Highclere Rd., Manchester M8 6NU. (061-795-7812)
Education: 1935–38 Handsworth.
Appointments: 1938–49 Jamaica Dt.;

1949–52 St. Just; 1952–53 Pontypool, E. Valley; 1953–56 Sherburn; 1956–59 Driffield; 1959–62 South Normanton; 1962–64 Garstang; 1964–67 Hindley; 1967– Padiham.

BLOOMFIELD, Jeffrey Frank, 220 Shepherds Lane, Dartford, Kent DA1 2PW. (0322-20058) – BA. *b. 22 Oct 1933, Oxford. m. 20 April 1960: 3d. Education:* Oxford Sec. Tech. Sch.; 1954–57 Handsworth. *Appointments:* 1957 Thetford; 1958–61 Cromer and Sherringham; 1960–63 Boston; 1963–69 London (Blackheath and Lee); 1969–75 Bromley (Kent); 1975–78 Wantage and Abingdon; 1978– Gravesend and Dartford.
Connexional Committees: 1981– Connexional Candidates' Committee. *Local Council Committees:* 1964–69 Lewisham Borough Youth Committee; 1981– Dartford Council/ Churches Liaison Committee.
Special Interests: History of Science; Order of St. John; St. John Ambulance Brigade; Secretary, Local Council of Churches; Save the Children President; Rotary Vice-President. *Hobbies and Recreations:* The family and gardening.

BLOUNT, Cyril Derek, 142 Balne Lane, Wakefield, West Yorkshire WF2 0DN. (0924-373287) – BA(Open), Cert FE (Teachers Certificate for Adult and Further Education). *b. 8 June 1930, Crewe, Cheshire. m. 10 Aug 1957: 1d., 1s.*
Education: 1935–38 Edleston Rd. Inf. Sch., Crewe; 1938–41 Edlestone Rd. Boys Sch., Crewe; 1941–48 Crewe County Gram. Sch.; 1972–78 Open Univ.; 1953–56 Headingley. *Appointments:* 1952–53 Gravesend and Dartford; 1956–57 Home Missions; 1957–59 Hull Mission; 1959–62 Harlow Mission; 1962–66 St. Neots; 1966–71 Norwich (St. Peters); 1971–76 Wymondham, Attleborough and Watton; 1976–79 York North; 1979– Wakefield.
Connexional Committees: 1976–82 Standing Committee on World Development.
Special Interests: Astronomy (Fellow of Royal Astronomical Society, Member of the British Astrononical Association, Secretary of Norwich Astronomical Society for 7 years); Adult Education, especially Psychology of Learning. *Hobbies and Recreations:* Computing (have Texas Instruments 99/4a Computer), Butterflies (maybe insect life generally), Reading Science Fiction; Genealogy (have traced family to 1736), have a caravan in Wensleydale, Photography.

BLOW, William Ralph, 24 Higham Station Ave., Chingford, London E4 9AZ. (01-527-6932) – MA. *b. 10 Jul 1923, Kodai Kanal, S. India. m. 12 Nov 1952: 2d., 1s.*
Education: 1934–42 Kingswood Sch., Bath and Uppingham; 1942–44 Brasenose Coll., Oxford; 1949–51 Wesley House. *Appointments:* 1951–67 Bengal District; 1967–68 Bingley; 1968–69 Kent College (Chaplain); 1969–74 London, Streatham and Dulwich; 1974–82 London Mission South; 1982– London, Walthamstow and Chingford.
Special Interests: "The Church in the Community"; Inter-personal relations (counselling training with Westminster Pastoral Foundation).
Hobbies and Recreations: Pragmatic practicalities (buildings, automotive, electronics), Horology, Camping and Open Air.

BLOXHAM, Kenneth George, 6 Beaufort Drive, Wimborne, Dorset BH21 1BB. (0202-886634) – BD(London). *b. 4 Feb 1906, Clapham, London. m. (1) died 1 Jan 1937. (2) 30 Oct 1940: 1d., 1s.*
Education: 1910–18 Charlotteville Sch., Guildford; 1918–23 Royal Gram. Sch., Guildford; 1928–31 London Univ.; 1932–33 Marburg Univ., Germany (Research Student); 1928–31 Richmond. *Appointments:* 1927–28 Pateley Bridge; 1931–32 Richmond College Asst. Tutor and President's Asst.; 1932–33 President's List; 1933–34 North Cornwall Mission, Chairman's Asst.; 1934–53 Chaplain (staff) to Toc H; 1934–39 SW England; 1939–40 Southampton; 1940–44 Birmingham; 1944–48 Manchester and NW England; 1948–53 South Australia; 1953–57 Nicolson Square, Edinburgh; 1957–64 London, Ealing and Acton; 1964–69 Wimbledon; 1969–73 Birmingham, Sutton Park.
Connexional Committees: 1955– General Committee NCH; 1960–65 District Chairman's Finance; 1959–67 Richmond College Committee.
Publications: Toc H Treasury of Prayers and Praises, 1938; *To Conquer Hate* (ed.) writings of Revd. P. B. Clayton CH, DD. MC. Published 1963, Epworth Press.
Special Interests: Toc H work across the world – am now a President of this world-wide family of Christian social workers. *Hobbies and Recreations:* Organs and Organ-building, Travel, Painting.

BLUCK, David Edwin, Hawthornden Lodge, 20 Bramshall Rd., Uttoxeter, Staffs ST14 7PG. (088-93-2764) *b. 30 Nov 1905, Royston, Yorks. m. (2) July 1933: 3d., 1s.*
Education: 1908–18 Royston; 1927–29 Hartley Victoria. *Appointments:* 1929–33 Birmingham; 1933–35 Hornsea; 1935–36 Middleton in Teesdale; 1936–39 Blackwood W. Mon. Mission; 1939–42 Liverpool North; 1942–45 Newcastle-upon-Tyne, NE; 1945–48 Stockton-on-Tees; 1948–53 Sunderland South; 1953–57 Pudsey; 1957–63 Newcastle-upon-Tyne (Heaton and Wallsend); 1963–68 Long Eaton.
Hobbies and Recreations: Electronics, Sports, General Reading.

BLUNDRED, Frederick, 28 Northgate Vale, Market Weighton, York YO4 3EA. (0696-72879) *b. 15 Nov 1912, Stoke-on-Trent, Staffs. m. 16 Dec 1944: 3s.*
Education: 1917–26 Uttoxeter Rd. Sch., Stoke-on-Trent; 1937–40 Hartley Victoria. *Appointments:* 1941–45 Hunan Dt. China; 1945–51 Great Harwood; 1951–57 Cross Hills and Silsden; 1957–64 Ottley; 1964–71 Hull East; 1971–77 Market Weighton.
Special Interests: Reading. *Hobbies and Recreations:* Figure Drawing and Writing.

BOGGIS, Arthur Richard Walter, 25 St. Philip's Ave., Eastbourne, E. Sussex BN22 8LU. (0323-23338) *b.*

15 Aug 1909, West Raynham, Norfolk. m. (1) died 1 Oct 1967; (2) 8 Aug 1968: 1s. 1 step-d., 1step-s.
Education: 1916–23 Helhoughton Boys Elem., Norfolk; 1928–29 Cliff; 1932–35 Richmond. *Appointments:* 1935–38 London, East End Mission; 1938–41 Ilford plus officiating Chaplaincy (other denominations) RAF (Hornchurch); 1941–45 Mansfield (Bridge St.); 1945–50 Leigh-on-Sea; 1950–56 London, Tooting Mission; 1956–64 Brighton and Hove; 1964–71 London, Ealing and Acton; 1971–75 Eastbourne.
Connexional Committees: 1974–77 Connexional Panel for the Nomination of Chairmen of Districts; 1966–77 General Committee of the National Children's Home.
Special Interests: Pastoral and Ecumenical. *Hobbies and Recreations:* Reading, Gardening.
d. 05.09.04 ae 95

BOLD, Wyndham Eric, 12 Llywn-y-Grant Rd., Cardiff CF3 7ET. (0222-486751) *b. 1 Sept 1917, Caldicot, Gwent. m. 20 Jul 1946: 1d., 2s.*
Education: 1929–34 Chepstow Gram.; 1939–41 Richmond; 1941–42 Headingley. *Appointments:* 1942–46 Cromer, Sheringham and Holt; 1946–51 Sirhowy Valley; 1951–61 Newport (Gwent); 1961–66 Cardiff (Canton); 1966–71 Pontypool (Eastern Valley); 1971– Chairman of the Cardiff and Swansea District.
Special Interests: Local Methodist History. *Hobbies and Recreations:* Photography, Hill Walking, Camping.

BOLT, Alastair Vivian Charles, 23 Dane Ave., Barrow-in-Furness, Cumbria. (0229-30844) – MA, BSc. *b. 11 Nov 1950, Bristol. m. 15 Jul 1981: 1d.*
Education: Bristol Cathedral Sch.; 1969–75 Univ. Coll. of Wales, Aberystwyth; 1975–78 Wesley House. *Appointments.* 1978– South West Cumbria.
Connexional Committees: 1982– Education and Youth Board.
Special Interests: Philosophy, Church Growth and Renewal, Religious language. *Hobbies and Recreations:* Geology, Railways.

BOLT, Peter Harold, 7 St. Lawrence Rd., Plymouth PL4 6HN. (0752-663869) – BD(London). *b. 5 Feb 1925, Princetown. m. 26 Nov 1946: 1d., 1s.*
Education: 1935–37 Tavistock Gram.; 1937–40 Plympton Gram.; 1943–44 Loughborough Coll.; 1947–48 Nottingham Univ.; 1950–53 Didsbury, Bristol. *Appointments:* 1949–50 Preston (Clubland); 1953–54 Wolverton and Bletchley; 1954–60 Northampton; 1960–64 Nottingham Mission; 1964–69 Exeter (Mint); 1969–73 Leys School, Cambridge; 1973–81 Truro; 1981– Plymouth.
Connexional Committees: 1954–65 Youth; 1965–82 WMC; 1976–82 Central Committee OD; 1972–82 Transfer of Authority; 1972–82 Exchange of Pastorates. *Council Member.* 1965, 1971, 1976, 1981 World Methodist Council (Programme Sec. 1971, 1976); 1966–82 World Methodist Council Executive. *Publications: A Way of Loving*, Epworth 1978; *Encyclop. Britannica Book of Year: Religion: Methodists*, 1973–82; *Childrens Encyclopaedia Britannica: Religion: Methodists*, 1979.
Special Interests: Praisemaker Youth Choirs, Truro and Plymouth, Local Church Missions (mainly in America 1975–82). *Hobbies and Recreations:* Music, Walking.

BOLTON, John Robert, RN Army and RAF Board, 1 Central Bldgs, Westminster, London SW1. *b. 29 Apr 1936, Goldthorpe, Yorks, m. 30 Jul 1960: 2d.*
Education: 1941–47 Goldthorpe Jnr.; 1947–52 Bolton-on-Dearne Sec. Mod.; 1952–54 Barnsley Tech. Coll.; 1956–57 Cliff; 1957–60 Hartley Victoria. *Appointments:* 1960–63 Ipswich, Museum Street; 1963–66 Burnley; 1966– Chaplain HMF.
Special Interests: Modern Theology; Modern Teaching Methods. *Hobbies and Recreations:* Reading, Soccer (Referee Class 1), Squash.

BOND, Frederick Charles, 31 Broad Reaches, Ludham, Gt. Yarmouth, Norfolk NR29 5PD. (069-252-631) *b. 29 June 1908, Blaina, Gwent. m. 12 June 1940: 1s.*
Education: Elem. – Blaina Central Boys'; Sec. – Abertillery County Sch. *Appointments:* 1950–54 Liverpool Mission; 1954–60 Liverpool North East; 1960–64 Bardney; 1964–70 Horncastle and Bardney; 1970–76 Epworth and Crowle.
Connexional Committees: Church Membership Committee; Church in Rural Life Committee.

BONE, Hugh Temple, 49 Pages Lane, Muswell Hill, London N10 1QB. (01-833-2350) – MA(Cantab) (Theology Tripos). *b. 4 May 1918, Gt. Driffield, Yorks. m. (1) 19 Apr 1954; (2) 3 Nov 1979: 1d.*
Education: 1923–26 Hill House Kindergarten; 1926–27 Upminster Council Sch.; 1927–34 City of London Sch.; 1946–49 Fitzwilliam Coll., Cambridge, 1946–49 Wesley House. *Appointments:* 1949–50 Castletown, Isle of Man; 1950–53 Stafford; 1953–59 Stockton-on-Tees; 1959–67 Watford; 1967–76 Orpington; 1976–82 Birmingham, Sutton Park; 1982– London, Highgate.
Connexional Committees: 1954–68 Youth Council; 1966–81 Epworth Board; 1967– Stewardship Committee; 1974– Church Membership Committee; 1980– Ministries Board. *Local Council Committees:* 1951–53 Stafford Youth Leaders Committee; 1955–59 Stockton-on-Tees Youth Leaders Committee; 1960–65 Watford Youth Leaders Committee; 1956–59 Herts Education Committee. *Publications: Stewardship the Christian Way of Life*, 1974; Anonymously with others: Booklets and Leaflets for Church Membership Committee.
Special Interests: Youth Work, Hospital Chaplaincies, NCH Chaplaincy, Suburban Church Work, especially Christian Stewardship, Church Membership and House Fellowships. *Hobbies and Recreations:* Badminton, Tennis, Golf, Rock-Climbing, Mountains, Walking, Travel, Reading, Classical Music, Football.

BONNAR, Edward Donald, Maranatha, Brent, Polperro, Looe, Cornwall PL13 2JJ. (0503-72384) *b. 3 June 1908, Shoeburyness, Essex. m.*

15 Feb 1978: 3d.
Education: 1915–20 Angel Rd., Norwich; 1920–24 City of Norwich, Norwich; 1930–33 Hartley Victoria.
Appointments: 1929–30 Penzance (Alexander Road); 1933–35 Preston; 1935–38 Cheddar Valley; 1938–42 Halifax (St. Johns); 1942–47 Plymouth (East); 1947–51 Bingham; 1951–55 Clevedon; 1955–61 Looe; 1961–69 Ringsash; 1969–73 North Hill; 1943–47 District Probationers' Secretary; 1938–42 District Guild Secretary.
Connexional Committees: 1938–42 Methodist Guild.
Special Interests: Methodist Peace Fellowship, FOR, Toc H.

BOOTH, Howard, 13 Staimburn Rd., Workington, Cumbria CA14 1SW. (0900-2468) *b. 22 May 1923, Belper, Derbys. m. July 1951: 1d., 1s.*
Education: 1928–34 Private Sch.; 1934–39 County Gram. Sch., Long Eaton; 1948–50 Handsworth.
Appointments: 1945–46 West Auckland; 1946–48 Liverpool North; 1950–52 Preston Clubland; 1952–57 Liverpool Grove and Woolton; 1957–64 Uxbridge, Hayes and Yiewsley; 1964–72 London, East Ham Mission; 1972–80 London, Harrow; 1980– Workington.
Connexional Committees: 1966–70 Home Missions; 1976–80 Ministers' Retirement Fund; 1973– Division of Social Responsibility; 1979– Chairman Healing and Pastoral Committee; 1983– to be Chairman of new DSR Standing Committee on Family, Healing and Personal Concerns. *Local Council Committees:* 1977 Founder Chairman London Borough of Barking Community Relations Council; now Member West Cumbria Community Health Council. *Publications: On Parade!* (Epworth Press 1964); *Growing in Christian Confidence* (Div. Ministries 1978); *Towards Health and Healing* (DSR 1979); *Prayer Tools for Health and Healing* (Grail Publication 1980); *Stepping Stones to Christian Maturity* (Bible Reading Fellowship & Grail 1980).
Special Interests: Health and Healing.
Hobbies and Recreations: Fell Walking, Writing, Creative Use of Duplicator.

BOOTH, Mark Robert, 98 Wycombe Rd., Marlow, Bucks SL7 3JE. (06284-3985) *b. 2 Jan 1949, Birmingham. m. 20 June 1970: 1d.*
Education: 1960–66 King Edward VI Gram. Sch. (Boys), Aston, Birmingham; 1972–74 Birmingham Poly; 1967–69 Cliff; 1980–82 Wesley, Bristol. *Appointments:* 1982– High Wycombe.
Special Interests: Social Work (Childcare); Dr. Samuel Johnson.
Hobbies and Recreations: Daughter, Dog, Books, Theatre.

BOOTH, Rufus, 8 Bylands Gdns, Sunderland, Tyne and Wear SR3 1NF. (0783-281456) *b. 11 Aug 1909, Grange Moor, Yorks. m. 27 Mar 1943: 1d., 1s.*
Education: 1935–42 Cliff.
Appointments: 1950–54 Newcastle Mission; 1954–59 Newcastle North East; 1959–66 Morpeth and Bedlington; 1966–71 Sunderland South; 1971–76 Gateshead SW.
Hobbies and Recreations: Music, Gardening.

BOOTH, Sidney, 29 Kingsley Park Grove, Sheffield S11 9HL. (0742-369813)
Education: 1949–52 Handsworth.
Appointments: 1947–49 Glasgow, Cathcart Rd.; 1949–52 Handsworth College; 1952–54 Bloxwich, Pinfield; 1954–60 Stourbridge and Brierley Hill; 1960–65 Sheffield North; 1965–72 Sheffield, Ecclesall; 1972–78 Colwyn Bay and Llandudno; 1978– Chairman Sheffield District.

BOOTH, Thomas James, 175 Watling St. Rd., Fulwood, Preston PR2 4AE. (0772-700206) *b. 28 Feb 1925, Liverpool. m. 25 Jul 1953: 1d., 3s.*
Education: 1930–32 Prince Edwin St. Prim. Sch., Liverpool; 1932–39 Roscommon St. Council Sch.; 1949–51 Hartley Victoria. *Appointments:* 1947–49 Liverpool (South); 1951–53 Uttoxeter and Ramsor; 1953–58 Sheffield (Surrey Street); 1958–63 South Bank and Eston; 1963–66 St. Helens (Lancs); 1966–74 Liverpool (South); 1974–79 Great Harwood (Lancs); 1979– Preston (Trinity).
Connexional Committees: 1966–73 Christian Citizenship; 1975–80 Social Responsibility.
Hobbies and Recreations: Photography, Freelance Writing.

BOSHIER, Brian William, 29 Whitehouse Drive, Sedgefield, Cleveland TS21 3BX. (0740-20692) *b. 25 June 1922, Godalming, Surrey. m. 19 Aug 1953: 2d., 1s.*
Education: 1927–33 Berne Leigh Jnr. Sch., Godalming; 1933–38 County Sch., Godalming; 1948–50 Richmond.
Appointments: 1946–48 Guildford; 1948–50 Richmond Coll.; 1950–52 Cheddar Valley; 1952–56 London Seamen's Mission; 1956–58 South East London Mission; 1958–63 Leeds (South); 1963–68 South Bank and Eston; 1968–75 Hartlepool; 1975–82 Spennymoor and Ferryhill.
Connexional Committees: 1964–67 Youth Committee. *Local Council Committees:* 1969–75 Chairman of Disablement Income Group.
Special Interests: Trade Unions, Rural employment, Mental Health. *Hobbies and Recreations:* Gardening, Golf, Walking and Cycling.

BOSTOCK, David Gerald, 35 Willowbrae Ave., Edinburgh EH8 7HE. (031-661-4289) – MA(Cantab), PhD(Manchester). *b. 8 Apr 1938, Nottingham. m. 29 Sept 1967: 2d., 1s.*
Education: 1949–57 Nottingham High Sch.; 1957–60 Kings Coll., Cambridge; 1962–65 Hartley Victoria. *Appointments:* 1965–67 Leeds North East; 1967–71 Wakefield; 1971–74 Swindon; 1974–80 Darlington; 1980– Edinburgh and Forth.
Publications: "Egyptian Influence on Origen" in *Origeniana*, 1975; "Quality and Corporeity in Origen" in *Origeniana Secunda*, 1980; "Jesus as the New Elisha" in *The Expository Times*, Nov 1980; "Origen and Reincarnation" in *The Christian Parapsychologist*, Dec 1981.
Special Interests: Steam Trains.
Hobbies and Recreations: Music, Golf, Walking.

BOUNDS, Kenneth, 41 Roker Park Ave., Audenshaw, Manchester M34 5NJ. (061-370-2635) *b. 10 Apr 1914, Chester. m. 11 Aug 1942: 3d., 1s.*
Education: 1924–28 Love St., Chester; 1919–24 St. Mary C of E; Glasgow Bible Training Inst.; 1950–52 Headingley. *Appointments:* 1950–56 Birstall; 1956–62 Blackburn, Trinity; 1962–69 Preston Trinity; 1969–77 Ashton under Lyne; 1977–81 Kinsley Stephen and Appleby and Tebay.
Connexional Committees: 1955–69 Church Membership Committee.
Publications: Various Booklets. "Prayers of the Bible", 1970–1980.

BOURNE, Wilfrid Harry, 48 Grovehill Rd., Redhill, Surrey RH1 6BD. (Redhill 69184 & 68998) – FPS. *b. 30 Jan 1897, Horsham, Sussex. m. 3 Aug 1926: 1d., 1s.*
Education: 1905–10 Chichester Central; 1919 Mildmay (London).
Appointments: 1922–26 Whitehaven; 1926–30 Newcastle-upon-Tyne Central; 1930–35 Eastleigh; 1935 London, Ilford; 1939–48 London, Thornton Heath; 1948–51 London, Bayswater; 1951–54 Bradford, West Brook; 1954–57 Bradford, Low Moor; 1957–62 Chichester.
Publications: Methodist New Connexion in Newcastle-on-Tyne, 1929; *Companioned by Angels*, 1934; *God Gave Me A Telephone*, 1957; *Preparation for Christian Healing*, 1960; *The Christian Telephone Ministry*, 1962.

BOWDEN, Jill Brainsby, 72 Lower Wortley Rd., Leeds LS12 4SN. (0532-637145) *b. 27 Nov 1935, Leeds.*
Education: 1946–50 Roundhay High Sch., Leeds; 1958–60 Wesley Deaconess Coll., Ilkley; 1976–77 Wesley House. *Appointments:* 1977– Leeds West.
Connexional Committees: 1976–82 Div. of Ministries, Candidates Committee; 1979–82 GP Executive; 1979–84 GP Committee; 1980–83 Minister Retirement Fund; 1978–81 Overseas Division.

BOWE, Kathleen Mary, 137 Windsor Drive, Wigginton, York YO3 8RZ. (0904-763886) – BEd(Leeds), BA(Bristol). *b. 8 Mar 1951, Bedale, N. Yorks.*
Education: 1956–62 Bedale C of E Prim. Sch.; 1962–69 Northallerton Gram. Sch.; 1969–73 City of Leeds and Carnegie Coll.; 1977–80 Bristol Univ.; 1977–80 Wesley, Bristol. *Appointments:* 1980– York (North).
Connexional Committees: 1981– Main Sub-Committee for the New Hymn Book.
Hobbies and Recreations: Walking, Music – Choral.

BOWEN, David John, 4 Kelso Close, Worthing, West Sussex BN13 1PL. (0903-42526) *b. 3 Sept 1898, Plymouth. m. 3 Aug 1927: 2d.*
Education: 1908–13 Higher Elem., Devonport; 1913–16 Royal Dockyard Sch.; 1919–20 Handsworth; 1920–22 Richmond. *Appointments:* 1922–25 Amble; 1925–26 Rock Ferry; 1927–30 Stourbridge; 1930–33 Birmingham, Bristol Road; 1933–36 Oldham, Manchester Street; 1936–39 South Shields; 1939–44 Sunderland, Durham Road; 1944–47 Brampton; 1947–50 Glasgow, Cathcart Road; 1950–54 Liverpool, Aigburth; 1954–58 Ashton-under-Lyne; 1958–63 Newcastle-under-Lyme.
Hobbies and Recreations: Archaeology, Bird Watching, Walking.

BOWERS, Allan John, 11 Poplar Tree Drive, Seaton, Devon EX12 2TW. *b. 2 Apr 1923, London. m. 7 Nov 1951: 1d.*
Education: 1948–50 Hartley Victoria.
Appointments: 1945 HM Forces; 1946–48 Matlock Trinity; 1948–50 Hartley Victoria College; 1950–51 Walton-on-Thames; 1951–57 Chaplain HMF (Army) Hong Kong, Korea, Home Counties; 1957–61 Grantham; 1961–67 Sheffield; 1967–74 Bebington; 1974–80 Wolverhampton Trinity; 1980– Sidmouth and Bridport.
Connexional Committees: 1967– Property Division; 1973– Board of Trustees for Methodist Church Purposes; 1973– Connexional Advance Fund.
Special Interests: Healing and Spirituality. *Hobbies and Recreations:* Painting, Wood carving, Writing, Music.

BOWERS, Robert, 82 Presthope Rd., Selly Oak, Birmingham B29 4NL. (021-475-8289) *b. 26 Mar 1905, Stoke-on-Trent. m. 15 Oct 1938: 1s.*
Education: 1910–18 Summerbank Rd., Tunstall; 1928–30 Cliff Coll.; 1931–34 Didsbury. *Appointments:* 1930–31 Chipping Norton; 1934–36 Altrincham; 1936–38 Ashford, Kent; 1938–40 Hulme and Whalley Range; 1940–43 Willington; 1943–48 Rochdale South; 1948–52 Wigan; 1952–58 Blackpool North; 1958–61 Bristol Kingswood; 1961–66 Clevedon; 1966–70 Shebbear.
Hobbies and Recreations: Music and Gardening.

BOWES, Harold Russell, 12 Devonshire Rd., Sheffield S17 3NT. (0742-363157) – BD. *b. Kingston upon Hull. m. 1956: 2d.*
Education: 1939–45 Malet Lambert High Sch., Hull; 1945–48 Hull Univ. Coll.; 1953–56 Headingley. *Appointments:* 1952–53 Saddleworth; 1956–60 Lerwick and North Isles; 1960–65 Gateshead South; 1965–71 Lincoln North; 1971–78 Sheffield North; 1978– Sheffield Ecclesall.
Connexional Committees: 1965–72 Connexional Youth Council. *Publications: Samuel Dunn's Shetland and Orkney Journal 1822–1825* (1976), and several related articles.
Special Interests: Methodist History, especially Shetland Isles.

BOWKER, Derek Westerdale, 16 Dunkirk Rd., Birkdale, Southport, Merseyside PR8 4QZ. (0704-67192) *b. 18 Oct 1938, Stockport, Cheshire. m. 1968: 1d., 1s.*
Education: 1949–55 Stockport Gram. Sch.; 1955–56 Liverpool Nautical Coll.; 1965–68 Handsworth. *Appointments:* 1968–70 Preston (Lune Street and Orchard); 1970–75 Burnley; 1975–81 York, Wesley; 1981– Southport.
Special Interests: Youth Work.
Hobbies and Recreations: Sailing, Reading, Photography.

BOWMAN, Michael John, 12 Cassiobury Park Ave., Watford WD1 7LB. (0923-21003) *b. 12 Apr 1940, Stoke-on-Trent. m. 2 Jul 1966: 1d., 1s.*
Education: 1945–55 Meir CP Jnr. and

Sec.; 1963–65 Cliff Coll.; 1965–69 Handsworth. *Appointments:* 1969–71 Wisbech; 1971–76 Worksop; 1976–81 Ilford; 1981– Watford. *Special Interests:* Disability and Handicap; Hospital Chaplaincy; Previous connections with Special School, Barnardos Handicapped Children and now Local MS Group, and Industrial Chaplaincy. *Hobbies and Recreations:* Canoeing.

BOWMER, John Coates, 1 Matfen Place, Gosforth, Newcastle upon Tyne NE3 3PR. (0632-852955) – BD (London), MA, PhD(Leeds). *b. 26 Aug 1911, Esh Village, Co. Durham. m. 16 Aug 1939: 1s.*
Education: Cornsay Colliery, Durham (Prim. and Jnr.) Johnston Sch., Durham; 1947–49, 1964–67 Leeds Univ.; 1933–34 Victoria Park, Manchester; 1935–37 Hartley Victoria. *Appointments:* 1932–33 Blackpool; 1937–39 Hull, St. George's Road; 1939–42 Jarrow; 1942–47 Ryton and Prudhoe; 1947–50 Castleford; 1950–52 Girvan; 1952–58 Seaham; 1958–62 Whitley Bay; 1962–76 Connexional Archives.
Connexional Committees: 1953–63 Local Preachers; Law and Polity; 1960–80 Archives. *Publications: The Sacrament of the Lord's Supper in Early Methodism*, 1951; *The Lord's Supper in Methodism, 1792–1960*, 1961; *Pastor and People*, 1975; many articles in *Proceedings WHS* and other journals. *Lectures: Wesley Historical Society, 1961; Fernley Hartley, 1975. President Emeritus of the Wesley Historical Society.*
Hobbies and Recreations: Music; Philately, Woodwork, Gardening, Photography, Hill-walking.

BOWN, John Emlyn Clark, 31 Cross Flatts Ave., Leeds, W. Yorks LS11 7BE. (0532-716641) *b. 15 Jul 1941, Caergwrle, Clwyd. m. 5 Sept 1964: 1d., 3s.*
Education: 1946–52 Lyminster County Prim. Sch.; 1952–57 Littlehampton Sec. Mod. Sch.; 1957–59 Clark's Coll., Brighton; 1963–64 Cliff Coll.; 1969 Kingsmead; 1965–68 Richmond. *Appointments:* 1969–72 Belize, Honduras Dt.; 1972–78 Market Rasen and Caistor; 1978– Leeds.
Publications: 1973– Frequent contributor of bible reading notes and sermon outlines to the International Bible Reading Association.
Special Interests: Ecumenical Work, Chaplaincies – Hospital, Industrial. *Hobbies and Recreations:* Interest in all sport, Rambling, Jogging, Tennis, Local History.

BOWYER, Frank Ewart, 88a Park Ave., Oswestry, Shropshire SY11 1AZ. (0691-50191) *b. 15 Jul 1903, Oswestry. m. 2 Jul 1930: 1d.*
Education: 1908–18 Oswestry Council Sch. and Oswestry Boys' High Sch.; 1926–28 Hartley Victoria. *Appointments:* 1924–26 Docking; 1926–28 Hartley College; 1928–30 S. Wales Mission; 1930–34 Minsterley; 1934–37 Liverpool, Everton Road; 1937–41 Downham Market; 1941–45 Chatteris; 1945–49 Dudley; 1949–55 Ellesmere; 1955–59 Northwich; 1959–62 Warrington; 1962–66 Batley. *Special Interests:* Music. *Hobbies and Recreations:* Gardening, Cricket.

BOWYER, William Basil, White Cottage, St. Martins Close, Sidmouth, Devon EX10 9JQ. *b. 14 Aug 1898, Dartford, Kent. m. (1) 31 Jul 1929, died 9 July 1976; (2) 6 Sept 1977.*
Education: –1909 Hextable (Kent) Jnr.; 1909–13 Birchwood, nr Swanley, Snr.; 1920–21 Cliff Coll.; 1922–25 Handsworth. *Appointments:* 1925–26 Isles of Scilly; 1926–28 Okehampton; 1928–29 South Molton; 1929–32 Wensleydale Mission; 1932–36 Devon and Dorset Mission; 1936–37 Swindon, Bath Road; 1937–42 Taunton; 1942–44 St. Austell, St. John's; 1944–48 Midsomer Norton and Radstock; 1948–50 Bristol, Bedminster; 1950–54 North Hill; 1954–56 South Petherton and Crewkerne; 1956–60 Oldham Wesley; 1960–63 Brynawr; 1963–64 Ebbw Vale.
Local Council Committees: 1940–41 President, Taunton Free Church Council.
Special Interests: Leader, Bethany Prayer Fellowship for Handicapped People (by correspondence).

BOYER, Horace, Wesley Manse, 12 Wrawby Rd., Brigg, South Humberside DH20 8DL. (0652-53253) *b. 9 Jul 1923, Buckfastleigh, Devon. m. 4 Nov 1963: 1d.*
Education: 1949–51 Didsbury, Bristol. *Appointments:* 1948–51 Llandrindod Wells; 1951–54 Northern Rhodesia Dt.; 1954–56 Hebden Bridge; 1956–59 Birstall and Birkenshaw; 1959–64 Rugby; 1964–70 Malmesbury; 1970–74 Salisbury; 1974–81 Louth; 1981– Brigg.
Hobbies and Recreations: Oil Painting, Photography, DIY, Gardening, Swimming.

BOYLE, David, 8 Carlton Close, Sutton Coldfield, West Midlands B75 6BX. (021-378-1615) – BA, MA. *b. 14 Mar 1934, Evesham, Worcs. m. 20 Jul 1957: 2d.*
Education: 1945–52 Prince Henry's Gram. Sch., Evesham; 1955–58 Birmingham Univ.; 1954–58 Handsworth. *Appointments:* 1958–72 Jamaica Dt.; 1972–82 Birmingham West; 1982– Birmingham Sutton Park.
Special Interests: Pastoral Care of the Mentally Ill. *Hobbies and Recreations:* Walking, Gardening, Model Railways.

BOYS, Donald John, 8 Corton Rd., Lowestoft, Suffolk NR32 4PL. (0502-3048) – BD(London), PhD(Leeds). *b. 6 Oct 1919, Northampton. m. 27 Dec 1946: 1d., 1s.*
Education: 1924–31 Daventry Abbey; 1931–36 Daventry Gram.; 1946–47 Handsworth. *Appointments:* 1943–46 Attleborough; 1947–50 Cannock Chase; 1950–57 Ripon; 1957–63 Harrogate; 1963–70 Eastbourne; 1970–75 Harrow; 1975–78 Glasgow (St. John's); 1978– Lowestoft.
Connexional Committees: 1950– Local Preachers' Department, Local Preachers' Studies Board.
Hobbies and Recreations: Collecting GCE Scripts.

BRADFIELD, Anne Elizabeth, 29 Carr Hill Drive, Calverley, Pudsey, W. Yorks LS28 5QA. (0532-565298) – MA(Cantab.), BD(London). *b. 8 Apr 1918, Liverpool.*
Education: 1924–31 Belvedere Sch., Liverpool; 1931–36 Farringtons, Chislehurst, Kent; 1937–42

Newnham Coll., Cambridge; 1957–68 The Deaconess Coll., Ilkley. *Appointments:* 1973–75 Stafford; 1975–81 Huddersfield East; 1957–69 Lecturer Wesley Deaconess College. *Connexional Committees:* Church Membership. Local Preachers' Studies Board; Local Preachers Committee; General Purposes; General Purposes Executive; Connexional Probationers Oversight Committee. *Council Member:* 1980– Presidents Council. *Publications: The Kingdom of God*, 1961; *The Challenge of Christ*, 1956; Manuals of Fellowship, Epworth. *Special Interests:* Old Testament studies. *Hobbies and Recreations:* Gardening, Dressmaking, Music.

BRADSHAW, Albert Arthur, 5 Taliesin St., Llandudno, Gwynedd, N. Wales LL30 2YE. (0492-79065) *b. 2 May 1917, Southfields, London. m. 10 Aug 1946: 2d.* *Education:* 1922–24 Inf. Sch., Ealing, London; 1924–28 Jnr. Sch., Ealing, London; 1928–33 Chiswick Central Sch., London; 1940–42 Hartley Victoria; 1942–43 Headingley. *Appointments:* 1939–40 Loftus and Staithes; 1943–44 Marazion; 1944–46 Knighton; 1946–49 Bilston; 1949–54 Manchester, Droylsden and Openshaw; 1954–59 Altrincham; 1959–65 Liverpool South; 1965–72 Grimsby West; 1972–77 Crewe; 1977–82 Ashton-under-Lyne. *Connexional Committees:* 1947–49 District Temperance and Social Welfare Secretary of the Wolverhampton and Shrewsbury District; 1955–59 District Christian Citizenship Secretary of the Manchester and Stockport District. Throughout both periods I was a member of the Connexional Committee. *Special Interests:* Most kinds of sport. *Hobbies and Recreations:* Walking, Water-colour Painting, Listening to music.

BRADSHAW, Raymond John, 2 Bounds Oak Way, Southborough, Tunbridge Wells, Kent TN4 0UB. (0892-28128) – FCA. *b. 4 Jan 1936, Merton, Surrey. m. 4 Mar 1961: 3d.* *Education:* 1948–53 Kingswood Sch., Bath; 1976–78 Wesley, Bristol. *Appointments:* 1978–82 Canterbury, Faversham; 1982– Tunbridge Wells. *Connexional Committees:* 1981– Central Finance Board.

BRADSHAW, Timothy J., Hollymount, 6 Crow Trees Brow, Chatburn, Clitheroe, Lancs BB7 4AA. (0200-41258) *m.* *Appointments:* 1981– Clitheroe.

BRADWELL, Ronald Joseph, 4 Sussex Ave., Melton Mowbray, Leics LE13 0AP. *b. 7 Aug 1913, Halifax. m. 13 Mar 1944: 2d.* *Education:* 1918–24 Salter Hebble Council Sch., Halifax; 1924–28 Halifax Sec. Sch.; 1928–30 Halifax Tech. Coll.; 1938–41 Hartley Victoria. *Appointments:* 1941–43 Stamford; 1941–46 Chaplain HMF; 1946–50 Chichester and Bognor; 1950–54 Loughborough; 1954–62 Northampton; 1962–65 Southport; 1965–72 Melton Mowbray; 1972–78 Ilkley. *Connexional Committees:* 1946–50 Temperance and Social Welfare; 1972–78 Methodist Homes for Aged. *Special Interests:* Healing, Prayer Circles; Youth Work. *Hobbies and Recreations:* Gardening, Rugby Union (Yorks trialist).

BRADY, Edwin, 1 Anne's Way, Chester CH4 7BA – BD(London). *b. 4 Nov 1897, Bedlington, Northumberland. m. 23 Sept 1930: 3s.* *Education:* 1907 Ocean Rd., South Shields; 1910 Hilton Rd., Sunderland; 1925–28 Hartley. *Appointments:* 1923–25 E. Dereham; 1925–28 Hartley Coll.; 1928–30 Bradford VII; 1930–34 Westgate; 1934–38 Walkden, 1938–42 Cheadle, 1942–46 Spennymoor; 1946–51 Douglas (Bucks Road), 1951–55 Guildford, 1955–61 Chester (George Street); 1961–64 Congleton (Kinsey Street).

BRAITHWAITE, Gilbert Denis, The Manse, Middleton-in-Teesdale, Barnard Castle, Co. Durham DL12 0SH. (0833-40329) – BA(Bristol). *b. 26 Jul 1939, Wallasey, Cheshire. m. 21 Jul 1971: 1d., 2s.* *Education:* 1944–50 Vaughan Rd. County Prim. Sch., Wallasey; 1950–58 Wallasey Gram. Sch.; 1958–61 Univ. of Bristol; 1961–62 Univ. of Nottingham; 1976–78 Wesley, Bristol. *Appointments:* 1978– Barnard Castle and Teesdale. *Special Interests:* The Educational Role of the Church. *Hobbies and Recreations:* Wesleyana, Transport, History.

BRAKE, George Thompson, 19 Bethell Ave., Ilford, Essex IG1 4UX. (01-554-3633) – ARHS. *b. 27 Apr 1917, Oldham. m. 29 Dec 1945: 1d., 1s.* *Education:* Prim. Schs. Docking and Walton, 1932–35 Downham Market Gram., Peterborough; 1935–36 Cliff Coll.; 1940–41 Richmond; 1941–42 Hartley Victoria; 1942–43 Headingley. *Appointments:* 1939–40 Kingsbrompton; 1943–45 Holyhead; 1945–46 Rhosymedare and Chisk; 1946–49 Beccles, Loddon and Bungay; 1949–52 Norwich Colvert Street; 1952–55 Wantage and Wallingford; 1955–63 Baptist Ministry; 1970– London, Ilford; 1974–80 Secretary London NE Synod. *Connexional Committees*: 1949–52 Education; 1953–54, 1969–79 Division of Social Responsibility. *Local Committees:* 1970– Director of Christian Economic and Social Research Foundation. *Publications: Inside the Free Churches*, Epworth 1967; *Drink Ups and Downs of Methodist Attitudes to Temperance*, Uplands 1974; *Methodist Attitudes to Temperance*, Beeby Lecture 1974; *Drink in Great Britain 1900–1979* (with G. Prys Williams) Edsall 1980; *The Limitation of Licensing Legislation (Joseph Malim Lecture 1981); Alcohol its Consumption and Control*, 1981 Edsall; *The English Public House in Transition* (with G. Prys Williams) 1982 Edsall. *Special Interests:* Social History of Alcohol, Contemporary Methodism. *Hobbies and Recreations:* Painting.

BRAMHALL, Frank, Wesley Manse, Brompton Rd., Northallerton, N. Yorks DL6 1DU. (0609-3620) *b. 1 May 1918, Barrow-in-Furness. m. 12 Aug 1961: 1d., 1s.* *Education:* 1929–36 Glossop Gram. Sch., Derbyshire; 1947–50 Handsworth. *Appointments:* 1946 Pickering; 1950 Middleton-in-Teesdale;

1950–53 Spennymoor; 1953–56 Morley; 1956–61 York (Centenary); 1961–66 York (Wesley); 1966–73 Smethwick; 1977– Northallerton. *Connexional Committees:* 1964–66 Local Preachers Committee; 1969–73 Church Membership.

BRAMLEY, Jeffrey, 39 Sunny Grove, Chaddesden, Derby DE2 6QP. (0332-673350) *b. 31 Jul 1937, Gotham, Nottingham.*
Education: 1942–52 Gotham Village Sch.; 1953–58 People's College, Nottingham; 1964–67 Headingley; 1967–68 Wesley, Bristol.
Appointments: 1968–69 Pontypool; 1969–74 Halifax; 1974–80 Barnsley; 1977–78 Year Exchange, California, USA; 1980– Derby (East).
Hobbies and Recreations: Stamp Collecting; Digitabulist, Swimming; Cricket; Golf.

BRAMWELL, Frederick Thomas, Flat 2, Orchard Bank, Heath Green Rd., Studland, Swanage, Dorset BH19 3BX. (0929-44-346) *b. 7 Aug 1900, Portsmouth. m. 10 Aug 1929: 1s.*
Education: 1922–25 Handsworth.
Appointments: 1925–28 Newbury; 1928–29 Poole; 1929–32 Maryport; 1932–35 Durham; 1935–40 Gateshead East; 1940–46 Newcastle-upon-Tyne West; 1946–53 Bolton Wesley; 1953–61 Leigh King St. and Leigh; 1961–66 West Bromwich Wesley; 1966–71 Chester-le-Street.
Publications: Paul – a play, Epworth 1934.

BRANDOM, Harold John, 25 Fairfield Rd., Uttoxeter, Staffs ST14 7JY. (088-93-2994) *b. 1 Apr 1920, Bletchley, Bucks. m. 22 Jul 1950: 3d., 1s.*
Education: 1947–49 Hartley Victoria.
Appointments: 1946–47 Buckingham and Brackley; 1949–50 Tiverton; 1950–53 Swindon, Regent St.; 1953–58 Stourbridge; 1958–63 Bournemouth; 1963–67 West Wight; 1967–72 Bistol, South Gloucestershire; 1972–75 Chepstow; 1975–80 Long Eaton; 1980– Dove Valley.

BRANFIELD, Edgar W., 1 Queen Mary Rd., Portchester PO16. *b. 9 Feb 1913, Clatworthy, Somerset. m. 30 Sept 1939.*
Education: 1919–27 Clatworthy CE Sch.; 1932–34 Cliff Coll. *Appointments:* 1962–63 Rhymney Valley; 1963–68 Yeovil; 1968–76 Portchester.
Special Interests: Music, Fishing; Painting.

BRANT, Peter Marlow, Wesley Villa, 1 St. James Terrace, Buxton, Derbys SK17 6HS. (0298-3556) – MA (Cantab). *b. 30 May 1944, Bletchley, Bucks. m. 11 Sept 1971: 2d.*
Education: 1955–56 Wolverton Gram. Sch.; 1956–63 Bletchley Gram. Sch.; 1963–66 Gonville and Caius Coll., Cambridge; 1978–81 Queens.
Appointments: 1981– Buxton.
Special Interests: Ethics, Economics; Wholeness and Health.

BRAZIER, Anthony, Hawthorn House, 38 Turnpike, Newchurch, Rossendale, Lancs BB4 9DU. (0706-215952) *b. 10 Aug 1942, Luton, Beds. m. 25 Sept 1965: 3s.*
Education: 1953–58 Denbigh Sec. Mod., Luton; 1958–61 Luton Coll. of F.E.; 1978–80 Wesley, Bristol.
Appointments: 1980– Rossendale.
Local Council Committees: 1980– Rossendale/M.S.C. District Liaison.
Special Interests: Industry and Commerce, Education (Governor of Bacup and Rawtenstall Gram. Sch. 1980–). *Hobbies and Recreations:* Philately, Driving, Gardening.

BREEZE, Arthur Edward, The Manse, Stibb Cross, Langtree, Torrington, Devon EX38 8LH. (08055-279) *b. 22 Mar 1921, Cannock, Staffs. m. 9 Aug 1952: 2s.*
Education: 1933–37 Queen Mary's Gram. Sch., Walsall, Staffs; 1948–50 Handsworth. *Appointments:* 1946–48 Knighton; 1950–51 Kimberley; 1951–52 Bloxwich Pinfold; 1952–55 Sunderland West; 1955–58 Atherstone; 1958–63 Hinckley Stockwell Head; 1963–66 Hazel Grove and Poynton; 1966–74 St Helens/Makerfield; 1974–79 Tipton; 1979– Shebbear.

BREEZE, George Edward, 6 Bank Villas, Mold, Clwyd CH7 1BN. *b. 14 Mar 1903, West Kirby. m. 16 Aug 1933.*
Education: 1908–13 Ffynnongroyw Sch.; 1927–29 Didsbury. *Appointments:* 1926–27 Barmouth/Dolgelley; 1929–31 Dinas Mawddwy; 1931–34 Llanfaircaereinion; 1934–37 Ystumtuen; 1937–39 Portmadog; 1939–45 Caernarfon; 1945–48 Ruthin; 1948–50 Llarnwst; 1950–52 Holyhead; 1955–65 Abercynon; 1965–68 Mold.
Publications: 1942–47, 5 Welsh Detective Novels.
Special Interests: Music.

BRENTON, Donald Henry, 3 Haslar Crescent, Waterlooville, Portsmouth. (0705-14-52767) *b. 21 Oct 1910, Portsmouth. m. 4 May 1940: 1d., 1s.*
Appointments: 1960–64 Castleford; 1964–67 Ebbw Vale; 1967–72 Swindon; 1972–77 Aberdare.

BRENTON, Leonard D., Fir Tree Cottage, Oaklands Rd., Hawkhurst, Kent TN18 4LL. (0585-2105) *b. 24 Jul 1913, Nanpean, Cornwall. m. 8 Mar 1945: 2s.*
Education: Elem.; 1939–40 Handsworth; 1940–41 Richmond; 1941–42 Headingley. *Appointments:* 1942–43 Brixton and Dartmouth; 1943–44 Bridgwater (King St.); 1944–47 Chaplain HMF; 1947–50 Ipswich (Museum St.); 1950–52 Boston; 1952–55 Oldham East; 1955–59 Liverpool (Grove St.); 1959–62 Wrexham; 1962–65 Southport (Banks and Hesketh Bank); 1965–70 Gt Harwood; 1970–73 Keighley; 1973–79 Stanley; 1979–81 Millom.

BREWER, Douglas Alfred, 22 Rothley Rd., Mountsorrel, Loughborough, Leics LE12 7JU. (0533-302538) – ABIC, Dip Theol (Lond). *b. 6 Feb 1938, Hove, Sussex. m. (2) 20 Apr 1981: 1d., 3s.*
Education: 1943–49 St. Lukes Prim. Sch., Brighton; 1949–53 Brighton and Hove Building and Engineering Sec. Sch.; 1953–57 Brighton Tech. Coll.; 1963–66 Richmond. *Appointments:* 1966–69 London Seamen's Mission; 1969–76 London, Leytonstone and Forest Gate; 1976– Loughborough; 1976–84 District Secretary for Industrial Affairs (Oxford and Leicester).
Special Interests: Industrial and community ministry, The development of

lay and team (collaborative) ministry. *Hobbies and Recreations:* Painting and Drawing; Walking, Carpentry and Joinery, Music, Crafts.

BREWIS, Noel R., 18 Orchard Drive, Watford, Herts WD1 3DY. (0923-20402) –BCom(Dunelm). *b. 25 Dec 1910, Gateshead. m. 18 Mar 1942: 4d.* *Education:* 1920–27 Royal Gram. Sch., Newcastle-upon-Tyne; 1928–32 Durham Univ. – Armstrong Coll., Newcastle; 1935–39 Manchester Univ.; 1935–39 Didsbury. *Appointments:* 1939–48 Hyderabad Dt., South India; 1948–58 Church of South India, Medak Diocese; 1959–69 British and Foreign Bible Society, Midlands District Secretary; 1969–76 North Thames Regional Secretary. *Special Interests:* Church Organisation – India and England, Ecumenical Activity with several denominations including Anglican, Educational work – including Headmaster of Belampalli High School, India, for 17 years. *Hobbies and Recreations:* Photography, Gardening.

BRICE, Derek Charles, 16 Newton Rd., Faversham, Kent ME13 8DY. (0795-532461) – MA, PhD. *b. 23 May 1940, Sittingbourne, Kent. m.* *Education:* 1951–58 Borden Gram. Sch., Sittingbourne; 1959–64 Nottingham Univ.; 1968–70 Cambridge Univ.; 1968–70 Wesley House. *Appointments:* 1970–75 Brigg; 1975– Mansfield, Bridge St. *Special Interests:* French history and literature, Church history with special reference to the Reformation Period, Arthurian studies. *Hobbies and Recreations:* Marathon running.

BRICE, Frank, 15 Axminster Rd., Roath, Cardiff CF2 5AR. (0222-495202) *b. 6 Dec 1918, Bloxwich, Staffs. m. 28 June 1947: 1d., 2s.* *Education:* 1923–32 Bloxwich CE Sch.; 1937–38 Cliff Coll.; 1940–41 Richmond; 1941–42 Hartley Victoria; 1942–43 Wesley, Headingley. *Appointments:* 1939–40 Kirby Moorside; 1943–45 Blackburn Mission; 1945–46 Wimborne; 1946–47 Todmorden; 1947–50 Morley Wesley; 1950–54 Birmingham, Belmont Row; 1954–59 Sheffield, Carver St.; 1959–61 Knaresborough; 1961–62 Supernumerary; 1962–69 Looe; 1969–72 Thame and Watlington; 1972–78 Barry; 1978– Cardiff. *Connexional Committees:* 1973–79 Building Schemes and Cooperation with other Communions. *Hobbies and Recreations:* Hymnology.

BRIDGE, John David, 138 Lambton Rd., London SW20 0TJ. (01-946-9551) – BA(Leeds), BD(Manchester). *b. 17 June 1937, Leigh, Lancashire. m. 15 Aug 1964: 2d.* *Education:* 1947–55 Kingswood Sch.; 1955–58 Leeds Univ.; 1958–60 Manchester Univ.; 1960–61 Geneva Univ.; 1958–61 Hartley Victoria. *Appointments:* 1961–64 Bramhall; 1964–68 Chester; 1968–75 Newcastle (Staffs); 1975–79 North Shields and Whitley Bay; 1979– Secretary, Home Missions Division. *Publications: Looking at Leisure* (Epworth, 1979); Contributor to *Experience of Ordination* (Epworth, 1980). *Special Interests:* Leisure, Cinema. *Hobbies and Recreations:* Camping, Theatre, Music, Playing with my children.

BRIDGE, Wilfred Herbert, 5 St. John's Close, Stratford-on-Avon CV37 9AB. (0789-5970) *b. 2 June 1906, Stoke Newington, London. m. 13 Aug 1932: 2d.* *Education:* Hackney Downs (Grocers) Sch.; 1926–29 Didsbury, Manchester. *Appointments:* 1925–26 Ledbury; 1926–29 Didsbury Coll.; 1929–32 Manchester Mission; 1932–33 H.M. Comm.; 1933–40 Southampton; 1940–44 Bournemouth, Punshon Memorial; 1944–49 London, Ilford and Romford; 1949–52 London Finsbury Park; 1952–57 Scarborough, Queen St.; 1957–63 Eastbourne; 1963–74 Birmingham District Chairman; 1974–77 Religious Adviser BBC Radio, Birmingham. *Publications: The Anvil of Faith*, 1964. *Hobbies and Recreations:* Art, Gardening, Countryside, Watching Sport.

BRIDGEMAN, Leonard George, 620 Leeds Rd., Outwood, Wakefield, West Yorkshire WF1 2LT. (0924-823113) – BD. *b. 22 Feb 1921, Swindon, Wilts. m. 8 Jan 1949: 1d., 1s.* *Education:* 1924–39 Westcott Elem. Sch.; 1932–37 Commonweal Sec. Sch., Swindon; 1945–48 Richmond. *Appointments:* 1948–49 Stour Valley Mission; 1949–52 Cardiff (Canton); 1952–58 Chaplain HMF; 1958–61 Liskeard; 1961–66 Bude; 1966–71 Devon and Dorset Mission; 1971–80 Slough; 1980– Wakefield. *Hobbies and Recreations:* Trailer tenting.

BRIDGES, Ethel Myfannwy (Beth), Wesley House, Warren St., Tenby, Dyfed SA70 7JT. *b. 21 Jan 1921, Farmborough, Bath, Som.* *Education:* 1926–32 Farmborough CE Sch,; 1932–37 Midsomer Norton County Sec. Sch.; 1937–38 Merchant Venturers' Tech. Coll.; 1945–47 Wesley Deaconess Coll., Ilkley. *Appointments:* 1973–78 Pocklington; 1978– Tenby and Pembroke. *Connexional Committees:* 1979– Board of Education and Youth; 1978– Joint Building Schemes Committee. *Special Interests:* Ecumenical and Multi Racial Affairs. *Hobbies and Recreations:* Local History and Tennis.

BRIDGES, John Arnot, 145 Richmond Rd., Accrington, Lancs BB5 0JB. (0254-33284) *b. 5 Aug 1953, South Wales. m. 1s.* *Education:* Abertaf Gram. Selective; Aberdare Boys Gram.; Cliff Coll.; 1976–80 Wesley, Bristol. *Appointments:* 1980– Accrington and Haslingden. *Special Interests:* Relating the Gospel and Implications to Modern Culture and Popculture, Youth Work. *Hobbies and Recreations:* Reading, Music, Football, Films, Art.

BRIGG, Gordon Teasdale, 4 Cronks Hill Close, Meadvale, Redhill, Surrey RH1 6LX. (07372-47154) – MA. *b. 6 Nov 1911, Bulawayo, S. Rhodesia. m. 27 Jul 1940: 2d., 1s.* *Education:* 1923–28 Kingswood Sch.; 1933–37 Didsbury. *Appointments.* 1937–40 Altrincham; 1940–43 Trowbridge; 1943–48 Chaplain HMF; 1948–52 Woodford and Wanstead; 1952–68 Chaplain HMF; (1962–68 Asst. Principal Chaplain); 1968–75

Bournemouth; 1975–77 Secretary Royal Army, Navy and Air Force Board. *Connexional Committees:* 1968– R.N., Army and R.A.F. Board; 1975–77 H.M. Board.
Special Interests: History. *Hobbies and Recreations:* Gardening, Golf, Ornithology.

BRIGHAM, George, 2 Pilton Rd., Westerhope, Newcastle-upon-Tyne NE5 4PP. (0632-869655) – BA. *b. 26 Aug 1940, Tynemouth, Northumberland. m. 26 Oct 1963: 1d., 1s.*
Education: 1951–55 Ralph Gardener Sec. Mod. Sch.; 1961–62 Cliff Coll.; 1972–75 Manchester Univ.; 1971–75 Hartley Victoria. *Appointments:* 1975–79 Denby Dale; 1979– Newcastle-upon-Tyne (West).
Special Interests: Ethics. *Hobbies and Recreations:* Aviation, Photography.

BRINDLEY, Ivan G., 10 Vernon Ave., Handsworth Wood, Birmingham B20 1DE. (021-554-2338) *b. 24 Sept 1932, Cannock, Staffs. m. 5 Apr 1958: 2d., 1s.*
Education: 1937–41 Hazel Slade Prim.; 1941–48 Rugeley Gram. Sch.; 1956–59 Hartley Victoria. *Appointments:* 1959–61 Uttoxeter and Ramsor; 1961–66 Bilston; 1966–68 Cradley Heath; 1968–75 Monmouth and Ross; 1975–81 Hereford; 1981– Birmingham (Asbury).
Connexional Committees: 1971–73 Church in Rural Life; 1972–75 Committee for Methodism in Wales. *Local Council Committees:* School Governors; 1970–75 Ross; 1981– Handsworth.
Hobbies and Recreations: Golf, Gardening.

BRINSLEY, Henry Sheridan, 22 Elsdon Rd., Durham DH1 5YL. (0385-49339) *b. 16 Dec 1915, Stellenbosch, S. Africa. m. 13 Jan 1943.*
Education: 1926–33 Richmond (Surrey) County Sch.; 1939–40 Didsbury. *Appointments:* 1940–43 Macclesfield; 1943–46 Bridlington (Central); 1946–49 Manchester (City Road); 1949–52 Leigh; 1952–56 Lower Bebington; 1956–61 Gateshead (West); 1961–64 St. Helens and Prescot; 1964–69 Grimsby (West); 1969–74 Danby; 1974–79 Berwick-on-Tweed.
Hobbies and Recreations: Gardening.

BRITTON, Kenneth, The Manse, Clutton, Bristol BS18 4TA. (0761-52331) – BD(London). *b. 13 June 1936, Bradford, Yorkshire. m. 18 Aug 1962: 2d., 1s.*
Education: 1940–46 Bradford Moor Inf. and Jnr.; 1946–47 Hambleton CE; 1947–52 King's Sch., Pontefract; 1969–74 London Univ. External Student; 1959–63 Headingley.
Appointments: 1963–64 President's List (Sept–Dec Huddersfield South; Jan–Aug Tunstall); 1964–67 Hindley; 1967–74 Peel, I.O.M.; 1974– Midsomer Norton.
Connexional Committees: 1968–74 Methodist Missionary Society.
Special Interests: Hermeneutics.
Hobbies and Recreations: Car, Garden, Children, Walking, Aircraft Recognition.

BROAD, Roger Anthony, 4 Tavistock Rd., Launceston, Cornwall PL15 9EZ. (0566-3169) *b. 2 Sept 1946, Truro.*
Education: 1951–57 Treliske Prep. Sch.; 1957–63 Truro Sch.; 1975–78 Wesley, Bristol. *Appointments:* 1978– Launceston.

BROADBENT, Alan, The Central Hall, Corporation St., Birmingham B4 6QW. (021-233-1915) *b. 2 Nov 1932, Bradford, Yorks. m. 21 June 1958: 1d., 1s.*
Education: 1943–48 Belle Vue Gram. Sch., Bradford. 1956–59 Handsworth. *Appointments:* 1959–63 Stoke-on-Trent (Hanley); 1963–66 East Grinstead and Oxted; 1966–77 Manchester and Salford Mission; 1977– Birmingham Mission.
Connexional Committees: 1975– Deaconess Committee; 1975–81 General Purposes; 1976–82 Home Mission Board; Many sub-committees.
Special Interests: Evangelism.
Hobbies and Recreations: Golf.

BROADBENT, Richard Martin, 5 Belgrave Rd., Bath BA1 6LU. (0225-312930) – BD(London). *b. 28 May 1939, Brighouse, Yorks. m. 27 Jul 1963: 1d., 1s.*
Education: 1950–57 Devizes Gram. Sch.; 1957–58 Jacksonville State Univ., Alabama; 1958–61 Exeter Univ.; 1962–65 Hartley Victoria.
Appointments: 1965–68 Bristol South; 1968–74 Paulton; 1974– Bath.
Connexional Committees: 1977– Division of Ministries and Executive (1979–82); 1975–80 Division of Education and Youth (and Executive); 1974–80 Connexional Local Preachers Committee; 1979– Connexional Regional Development Committee. *Local Council Committees:* District Youth Committees.
Publications: Epworth Review.
Special Interests: Ministry of Healing and Counselling, Student work.
Hobbies and Recreations: Fishing, Squash.

BROADHURST, Harold, 7 Southmead, Poynton, Stockport, Cheshire SK12 1EB. *b. 24 Aug 1917, Liverpool. m. 20 Dec 1941: 1s.*
Education: 1921–28 St. George's CE, Macclesfield; 1928–33 The Central Sch., Macclesfield; 1946–48 Headingley. *Appointments:* 1945–46 Wymondham; 1948–52 Wetton and Longnor; 1952–57 Biddulph; 1957–65 Downham Market; 1965–70 Thetford; 1970–76 Wigton; 1976–82 Old Hill.

BROADHURST, Kenneth, 10 Branksome Rd., Norwich, Norfolk NR4 6SN. (0603-54761) *b. 26 Dec 1917, Congleton, Cheshire. m. 4 Apr 1945: 4d.*
Education: 1922–26 Wagg St. Wesleyan Day Sch.; 1926–32 Congleton Council Sch.; 1938–41 Headingley. *Appointments:* 1941–45 Douglas (Victoria); 1945–49 Swansea; 1949–52 Blackpool South; 1952–55 Manchester and Salford Mission; 1955–62 Darlington South; 1962–69 Salisbury; 1969–71 Bedford South; 1971–76 Bedford South and Ampthill; 1976–78 Norwich Calvert St.; 1978– Norwich.

BROADHURST, Mark, 70 Chapel St., Hyde, Cheshire SK14 1DN. (061-368-2484) – BD(London). *b. 8 Feb 1946, Bollington, Cheshire. m. 20 Jul 1968: 1d., 1s.*
Education: 1951–52 Wetton Inf. Sch.;

1952–57 Biddulph County Prim.; 1957–64 Downham Market Gram. Sch.; 1965–69 Richmond. *Appointments:* 1969–74 Diss; 1974–79 Romiley; 1979–82 Oldham and Saddleworth; 1982– Hyde and Denton. *Special Interests:* Methodist History; Music. *Hobbies and Recreations:* Most sports (esp. Soccer and Cricket), Railways.

BROCK, Phyllis, 5 Plowman Close, Greenleys, Milton Keynes MK12 6AG. (0908-312043) *b. 13 Apr 1931, London.*
Education: 1952–54 Wesley Deaconess Coll. *Appointments:* 1976–77 Dudley; 1977– Milton Keynes.

BROCKLEHURST, John Charles, 48 The Oatlands, West Kirby, Wirral, Merseyside L48 7HN. (051-625-7965) *b. 13 Dec 1904, Liverpool. m. 7 Aug 1937: 1d., 1s.*
Education: 1910–17 Granton Rd., Liverpool; 1917–20 Liverpool Collegiate Sch.; 1931–34 Handsworth. *Appointments:* 1930–31 Knighton; 1934–37 Chatham Garrison and Naval Port Mission; 1937–40 Severn Valley Mission; 1940–46 Rochdale (South); 1946–50 Bolton (Park St.); 1950–56 Walkden and Worsley; 1956–61 Cadishead; 1961–65 Manchester (Charlton and Moss Side); 1965–72 Workington; 1946–50 Synod Secretary, Bolton and Rochdale; 1952–61 Synod Secretary, Manchester. *Connexional Committees:* 1953–70 General Chapel Committee. *Council Member:* 1947–66 Free Church Federal Council.

BROMLEY, John, 158 Cot Lane, Kingswinford, Brierley Hill, West Midlands DY6 9SB. (038-44-3509) *b. 20 Jul 1929, Stoke-on-Trent. m. 18 Aug 1956: 1d.*
Education: 1931–39 Woodlane CP Sch.; 1939–46 Wolstanton Gram. Sch.; 1950– Westhill; 1953–56 Handsworth. *Appointments:* 1956–59 Sirhowy Valley; 1959–63 Rotherham; 1963–69 Burslem Mission; 1969–76 Withington and Didsbury; 1976– Stourbridge and Brierley Hill. *Special Interests:* Rotary (Manchester and Brierley Hill). *Hobbies and Recreations:* Finance.

BROOK, Donald George, 40 Avenue Rd., Wimborne, Dorset BH21 1BT. (0202-880820) – MC. *b. 18 Sept 1895, Nottingham. m. 12 Aug 1925: 1d., 2s.*
Education: 1919–22 Didsbury. *Appointments:* 1922–25 Manningtree and Harwich; 1925–28 Stainland; 1928–31 Inverness; 1931–35 Altrincham; 1935–40 Bradford, Shipley; 1940–45 Chaplain HMF; 1946–51 London, Ilford; 1951–55 Wellingborough; 1955–59 Rye.

BROOKER, Lawrance Oscar, 8 Chenies Ave., Little Chalfont, Bucks HP6 6PR. (02404-3163) *b. 8 Mar 1892, Lynton, Kent. m. (1) 2 Feb 1932. (2) 7 Jan 1965. 1d.*
Education: 1897–1906 Elem. Sch.; Handsworth. *Appointments:* 1921–24 Litchfield; 1924–29 Derby, Greenhill; 1929–34 Birmingham, Wesley; 1934–44 Bradford Mission; 1944–52 London, Archway Central; 1952–57 Finchley and Hendon; 1951–57 Chairman of London NW District; 1957–62 Separated Chairman. *Connexional Committees:* Home Mission; Free Church Council; Chairman Hospital Chaplaincy Board 6 years.
Special Interests: Cricket.

BROOKES, George Lloyd, 120 Snowdon Drive, Ty Gwyn, Wrexham, Clywd. (0978-51377) *b. 22 Jun 1892, Llysfaen, Colwyn Bay. m. (2) 1921: 2d., 1s.*
Education: Llysfaen Elem. Sch.; Colwyn Bay High Grade Sch.; Cliff Coll.; 1915 Headingley; 1919–21 Didsbury. *Appointments:* 1914–15 Ystumtuen; 1915–19 Headingley and HM Forces; 1919–21 Didsbury; 1921–22 Coedpoeth Welsh; 1922–25 Dinas Mawd Welsh; 1925–28 Mold Welsh, 1928–31 Treorchy Welsh; 1931–36 Holywell Welsh; 1936–37 Llanrhaeadr Welsh; 1937–39 Machynlleth Welsh; 1939–42 Llanfyllin; 1942–44 Chaplain HMF; 1944–50 Mold Welsh; 1950–55 Badillt Welsh; 1955–60 Coedpoeth Welsh. *Special Interests:* Reading. *Hobbies and Recreations:* None, except interest in young people and old.

BROOKES, Malcolm, The Manse, Coast Rd., La Rocque, Jersey, Channel Islands. (0534-52327) *b. 17 Feb 1941, Thurnscoe, S. Yorkshire. m. 13 Aug 1966: 3d.*
Education: 1952–56 The Hill, County Sec., Thurnscoe; 1956–58 Barnsley Coll. of Technology; 1958–59 Wath-upon-Dearne Gram. Sch.; 1960–62 Cliff Coll.; 1962–66 Handsworth.
Appointments: 1966–70 Leominster; 1970–75 Welwyn; 1975–77 Exeter; 1977–82 Hornsea; 1982– Jersey.
Special Interests: History of Methodism, Pastoral Psychology, Christian Unity. *Hobbies and Recreations:* Walking, Jogging, Reading.

BROOKS, Michael Anthony, 25 Beechwood Ave., Stanwix, Carlisle, Cumbria CA3 9BW. (0228-24834) – Dip Theol. *b. 13 June 1935, Bolton. m. 12 Aug 1970: 1d., 1s.*
Education: 1940–46 Overton (Village Sch., nr Morecambe); 1946–50 Balmoral Rd. Sec. Mod., Morecambe; 1962–65 Rhodes Univ., Grahamstown, S. Africa. *Appointments:* 1960–62 and 1965–70 South West Africa; 1970–77 Newcastle-upon-Tyne West; 1977– Carlisle.
Publications: Wrestling for God, Christian Journals Ltd, 1976.
Special Interests: Evangelism, Revival, Evangelical Theology. *Hobbies and Recreations:* Wrestling, Formerly Champion in 12 stone Class, Cumberland and Westmorland Style, also Middleweight Free Style Champion of South West Africa, Gardening, Nature study, Bird watching.

BROOKS, Peter, 188 Heathwood Rd., Cardiff CF4 4BR. (0222-63678) – MA(Oxon), BA(Cantab). *b. 24 Sept 1938, Hallatrow, Somerset. m. 20 Aug 1964: 2d., 1s.*
Education: 1949–56 Sexey's Sch., Bruton, Som.; 1959–62 Oxford Univ.; 1962–64 Wesley House. *Appointments:* 1964–66 Romford; 1966–70 Tavistock; 1970–76 South Petherton and Crewkerne; 1976–82 Nelson (Lancs); 1982– Cardiff.

BROUGHTON, Robert Cannell, 3 Clevelands Ave., Silverdale, Carnforth, Lancs LA5 0RP. (0524-701382) – BD(London). *b. 2 Sept 1910, Ramsey, I.O.M. m. 12 Aug 1940: 1s.*
Education: 1922–26 Lancaster Royal Gram. Sch.; 1933–37 Didsbury.
Appointments: 1937–40 Towcester; 1940–42 Leicester, Hinckley Rd.; 1942–44 Melton Mowbray; 1944–46 Chaplain RAF; 1946–50 Penrith; 1950–54 St. Helens; 1954–58 Nelson; 1958–63 Clitheroe; 1963–68 Hinckley; 1968–69 Derby South; 1969–75 Spennymoor and Ferryhill.

BROWN LAWSON, Albert, 9 Trent Ave., Huntington, York YO3 9SE. (0904-761711) – BD(Lond); MLitt (Dunelm); PhD(Sheffield). *b. 17 Jan 1924, Wakefield, W. Yorks.*
Education: 1927–30 St. John's CE Prim.; 1930–33 Cathedral CE Jnr.; 1932–34 St. John's Jnr.; 1935–40 Thornes House Gram. Sch.; 1947–50 London; 1953–60 Durham; 1961–74 Sheffield; 1947–50 Richmond.
Appointments: 1945–46 Minehead and Dunster; 1946–47 Towcester; 1950–51 Leigh and Hindley Green; 1951–53 Barnstaple (Thorne Memorial); 1953–55 Kirkby Stephen, Appleby and Tebay; 1955–60 Macclesfield; 1960–63 Huddersfield (West); 1963–70 Lancaster; 1970–71 Blackburn; 1971–75 Sector Ministry Teaching; 1975– York.
Academic Posts: 1971– Course Tutor and Tutor Counsellor, Open University; Former WEA Lecturer; Examiner (Assistant) Cambridge Schools Examination Syndicate; 1966 Qualified Schoolteacher. *Publications: John Wesley and the Christian Ministry*, SPCK 1963; Publications in Historical Journals etc.; Article on John Wesley's Ordinations in *Encyclopaedia of Methodism*, 1970.
Special Interests: Ecclesiastical History and History of Christian Doctrine, Psychical Studies, Spiritual Healing; Education, Officiating Chaplain HMF, Strensall, King's Depot.
Hobbies and Recreations: Music, Nature Studies, Animal Welfare.

BROWN, Arthur McGregor, The Beeches, 8 Grove Rd., Horbury, Wakefield WF4 6AQ. (0924-272616)
Education: 1954–58 Hartley Victoria.
Appointments: 1958–60 Wirksworth; 1960–64 Bingham; 1964–68 Ripley; 1968–74 Sheffield (Brunswick); 1974–80 Liverpool North; 1980– Ossett and Horbury.

BROWN, Brian Dennis, 3 St. Peter's Crescent, Bicester, Oxon. (08692-41765) – BA(Bristol); BD(London): MA(Birmingham); MA(Leicester). *b. 18 June 1936, Bristol. m. 12 Apr 1958: 2d., 1s.*
Education: 1941–47 Kingsdown Council Sch., Bristol; 1947–54 Cotham Gram. Sch., Bristol; 1954–57 Bristol Univ.; 1968–70 Birmingham Univ.; 1975–77 Birmingham Univ.; 1977–78 Leicester Univ.; 1957–60 Handsworth. *Appointments:* 1960–62 Hunts Mission; 1962–66 Secretary Younger School Leavers Student Christian Movement in Schools; 1966–71 Lecturer Dudley College of Education; 1971–75 Head Religious Studies Lady Spencer-Churchill College of Education, Oxford; 1975–82 Senior Lecturer Subject Leader Sociology of Education, Oxford Polytechnic; 1982– Leader Television and Child Research Unit, Oxford Polytechnic.
Connexional Committees: 1964–68 Education Committee; 1976– MDEY Training Advisory Committee.
Publications: Alternative Syllabus, (Lancs Education Cttee) 1968; *Living Together*, (CEM) 1965; *Making Sense of Living; Making Sense of Loving*, (Arnold) 1969; *The Choice; The Search*, (Arnold) 1970; *Theology and Culture*, (unpublished thesis Birmingham) 1970; *A Time for Candour*, (Epworth) 1975; *The Final Frontier*, (Coulson Lecture, Luton Indust. College); *Clubchat*, (Chester House) 1976; *Work and Witness* (editor), Home Missions 1977; *Methodism, the Labour Movement and the 1926 General Strike*, (thesis) 1977; *Curriculum Change in Religious Education*, (thesis Leicester) 1978.
Special Interests: Moral and Religious Education, Television, Children.
Hobbies and Recreations: Qualified professional swimming coach, Coach to club county and national level swimmers.

BROWN, Brian Joseph, 13 Deerings Rd., Reigate, Surrey RH2 0PW. (07372-43075) – BA. *b. 5 Oct 1938, Cape Town, S. Africa. m. 2 Nov 1963: 1d., 2s.*
Education: Sea Point Boys Jnr. & Snr., Cape Town; 1955–58 Cape Town Univ.; 1959–61 Rhodes Univ.
Appointments: 1962–78 South Africa Conf.; 1978–80 Denby Dale; 1980– British Council of Churches.
Council Member: British Council of Churches – an Executive Secretary of Division of International Affairs.
Publications: Divine or Civil Obedience, Christian Institute 1975; *Facing the Facts – Analysis of SA Society*, Anglican Panel 1982.
Special Interests: Church-State Relations, Prophetic Ministry.

BROWN, Clifford, Thorn Lea, 52 Sefton St., Southport, Merseyside PR8 6SD. (0704-42798) *b. 28 Sept 1904, Lincoln. m. 30 Jun 1932: 2d.*
Education: Stoneyholme Council Sch., Burnley, Lancs; 1925–28 Hartley Victoria. *Appointments:* 1928–32 Nantwich; 1932–35 Market Drayton; 1935–39 Stafford; 1939–44 Great Harwood; 1944–48 Accrington; 1948–52 York (Monkgate); 1952–56 Blackburn; 1956–61 Bradford (Great Horton); 1961–66 Whaley Bridge; 1966–73 Rawtenstall.
Special Interests: Bible-Study Groups, Youth Fellowships, Men's Fellowships.
Hobbies and Recreations: Gardening, House Decoration, Woodwork, Snooker.

BROWN, Gerald W., The Manse, 41 Burbage Rd., London SE24 9HB. (01-274-6633)
Education: 1953–56 Didsbury, Bristol. *Appointments:* 1956–59 South Molton; 1959–64 Launceston; 1964–69 Kingsbridge and Salcombe; 1969–75 Sutton (Surrey); 1975– London, Streatham and Dulwich.

BROWN, James Richard, 39 Ashley Rd., Thornton Heath, Surrey. (01-689-9531) *b. 24 May 1926, Eton, Bucks. m. 4 Aug 1956: 1d., 1s.*
Education: 1936–40 St. Martin's CE Sch., West Drayton; 1951–54 Cliff Coll.; 1951–54 Richmond. *Appointments:* 1950–52 Snaith; 1956–60

Sheffield Mission; 1960–64 Andover; 1964–69 Slough; 1969–72 London, Blackheath; 1972–77 Croydon. *Local Council Committees:* 1970–72 Lewisham Borough Youth Committee. *Special Interests:* Church Drama and Music. *Hobbies and Recreations:* Astronomy, Ornithology, Amateur Dramatics, Badminton, Singing.

BROWN, Kenneth Roy, Ingledene, 5 Overton Rd., Sheffield S6 1WG. (0742-345008) – BA(Open). *b. 12 Sept 1924, Firsby, Lincs. m. 14 Aug 1953.*
Education: 1935–40 King Edward VI Gram. Sch., Spilsby, Lincs; 1970–76 Open Univ.; 1949–52 Headingley. *Appointments:* 1947–49 Glasgow (East Mission); 1952–53 Motherwell; 1953–58 Spennymoor and Ferryhill; 1958–61 Burnley (Wesley); 1961–70 Wakefield; 1970–75 Ashington and Newbiggin; 1975– Sheffield (North). *Publications: Count Me Out*, a Passion Play, 1975.
Special Interests: Methodist Ministry. *Hobbies and Recreations:* Camping, Hill Walking, Tourism.

BROWN, Leonard, 18 Spring Crescent, Portswood, Southampton SO2 1GA. (0703-552371) – MA, BD. *b. 6 Dec 1906, Manchester. m. (Widower) 12 Aug 1936: 1d., 3s.*
Education: 1911–18 Wheler St. Elem. Sch., Hr. Openshaw, Manchester; 1918–22 Manchester Central High Sch.; 1923–27, 1930–34 Manchester Univ.; Hartley Victoria. *Appointments:* 1934–35 Gateshead; 1935–36 London, East End Mission; 1936–39 Farsley, Pudsey and Yeadon; 1939–42 Sheffield North-East; 1942–47 Middlesborough; 1947–50 Chester-le-Street; 1950–56 London, Upper Tooting; 1956–60 Peterlee; 1960–65 Stoke-on-Trent, Hanley; 1965–68 Hull, Princes Avenue; 1968–71 Dudley.
Connexional Committees: 1951–72 Division of Social Responsibility; 1960–70 Division of Ministries.
Council Member: 1965–81 World Methodist Council (Family Life Committee). *Local Council Committees:* 1972–81 Dudley Community Relations Council; 1970–80 Dudley Temperance Society. *Publications: Proceedings of Wesley Historical Society:* Articles: *Origins of Primitive Methodism; William Clowes in the North of England; Hugh Bourne: A Bicentenary Reflection* (1972).
Special Interests: Primitive Methodist History, Community Relations; Alcohol Problems. *Hobbies and Recreations:* Wesleyana, Staffordshire Pottery Figures, Local History.

BROWN, Michael George, 339 Millhouses Lane, Ecclesall, Sheffield S11 9HY. (0742-361490) – BD(London), BD(Manchester). *b. 14 Aug 1938, Coventry. m. 21 Aug 1965: 1d., 2s.*
Education: 1943—49 Prim. Sch.; 1949–56 King Henry VIII Gram. Sch., Coventry; 1956–59 London Bible Coll.; 1963–65 Hartley Victoria.
Appointments: 1965–66 Missionary Training; 1966–74 Ceylon Conf. and Sri Lanka; 1974–81 Durham and Deerness Valley; 1981– Sheffield (Ecclesall).
Connexional Committees: 1977–81 Overseas Division Central Committee. *Special Interests:* Baptism. *Hobbies and Recreations:* Music.

BROWN, Robert Raymond, Royal Navy, Army and Royal Air Force Board, 1 Central Bldgs, Westminster, London SW1H 9NU. BA(Leeds), BD(Manchester). *b. 24 Mar 1936, Stockport. m. 18 Jul 1959: 1d., 3s.*
Education: 1947–53 Stockport Sch.; 1953–56 Leeds Univ.; 1956–59 Manchester Univ.; 1956–59 Hartley Victoria. *Appointments:* 1959–64 Luton Industrial Mission; 1964–67 Bramhall; 1967– Chaplain HMF.
Special Interests: Adult Christian Education. *Hobbies and Recreations:* Music (Singing), Drama.

BROWN, Ronald Henry, Wesley Manse, 10 Wordsworth St., Penrith, Cumbria CA11 7QY. (0768-62787) *b. 24 Nov 1919, Dover, Kent. m. 16 Jul 1949: 1s.*
Education: Barton Rd. Prim./Elem. Sch., Dover; Dover County Gram. Sch., Dover; 1946–48 Hartley Victoria.
Appointments: 1948–49 Matlock; 1949–54 Chesterfield; 1954–61 Manchester and Salford Mission; 1961–67 Carlisle (Central Hall); 1967–75 Barrow-in-Furness; 1975–80 Workington; 1980– Penrith.
Special Interests: Poetry, Music. *Hobbies and Recreations:* Drama Groups, Theatre, Music.

BROWN, Stanley, 1 Rockery Terrace, Fernleigh Rd., Grange over Sands, Cumbria LA11 7HS. (044-84-3946) – BA(Leeds). *b. 18 Jun 1913, Barrowford, Lancs. m. 18 Jun 1946: 1d., 1s.*
Education: 1918–27 Barrowford Council Sch.; 1930–33 Nelson Tech.; 1936–40 Leeds Univ.; 1936–40 Headingley. *Appointments:* 1940–58 Sierra Leone Dt.; 1958–63 Orrell and Lamberhead Green; 1963–68 Warrington; 1968–75 Sierra Leone Dt.; 1975–79 Holmfirth.
Special Interests: World Peace.

BROWN, Stephen James, 46 Gawsworth Rd., Broken Cross, Macclesfield, Cheshire SK11 8UE. (0624-24361) – BSc. *b. 10 Apr 1949, Grimsby. m. 7 Sept 1974: 1d.*
Education: 1960–67 Grimsby Wintringham Boys' Gram. Sch.; 1967–71 Nottingham Univ.; 1975–77 Birmingham Bible Institute; 1977–80 Queen's Coll., Birmingham. *Appointments:* 1980– Macclesfield.
Hobbies and Recreations: Gardening, Bird-watching.

BROWN, Thomas Clifford, Abbeyfield, 181 Heysham Rd., Morecambe LA3 1DF. (0524-414236) *b. 19 Apr 1895, Lightcliffe, W. Yorks. m. 28 Jul 1932.*
Education: 1898–1911 Lightcliffe National Sch.; 1919–20 Cliff Coll.; 1922–25 Didsbury. *Appointments:* 1922–23 Supply; 1923–26 Didsbury College; 1926–27 Ledbury; 1927–30 Blandford; 1930–31 Kirby Moorside; 1931–34 Mansfield; 1934–37 Selby; 1937–40 Kirkby Stephen; 1940–45 Settle; 1945–48 Leeds Rothwell; 1948–52 East Cornwall Mission; 1952–57 Forest of Dean; 1957–60 Barrow in Furness.
Special Interests: Peace Movement (FOR). *Hobbies and Recreations:* Handicraft, Chess.

BROXHOLME, John Derek, 1 Fir Tree Close, Skelmersdale, Lancs WN8 9AW. (0695-22402) *b. 25 Sept 1925, Melton Mowbray, Leics. m. 15 Feb*

1958: 2s.
Education: 1929–40 County (Prim., Jnr. & Snr.), Melton Mowbray; 1949–51 Handsworth. *Appointments:* 1948–49 Raunds; 1952–62 Burma District; 1962–66 Malton; 1966–69 Hull, Trinity; 1969–73 Northampton; 1973–79 Harlow Mission; 1979– Skelmersdale.
Special Interests: Ecumenical Work, Church Overseas. *Hobbies and Recreations:* Music, Photography.

BRUCE, Geoffrey Temple, 625 Yarm Rd., Eaglescliffe, Stockton-on-Tees, Cleveland TS16 9BS. (0642-782147) – BA(Dunelm), BD(Lond). *b. 9 Sept 1934, Gateshead, Co. Durham. m. 18 Jul 1959: 1d., 2s.*
Education: 1939–46 Springwell Prim. Sch.; 1946–53 Washington Gram. Sch.; 1953–56 Durham Univ.; 1956–59 Headingley. *Appointments:* 1959–64 Bolton (Wesley); 1964–70 Walsall; 1970–78 Redcar, Saltburn and Guisborough; 1978–82 Stockton.
Special Interests: The Countryside, Music. *Hobbies and Recreations:* Five-a-Side Football, Walking.

BRUCE, George Edward, 144 Henrietta St., Ashton-under-Lyne, Lancs OL6 8PH. (061-330-1644) *b. Limerick, Eire. m.: 1d., 1s.*
Education: Didsbury, Bristol.
Appointments: 1956–57 Hunts Mission; 1957–62 Rhymney Valley; 1962–65 Pately Bridge; 1965–68 Kineton; 1968–71 Preston; 1971–75 Danby Dale and Clayton West; 1975–77 Port Talbot; 1977–82 Mid Glam Mission; 1982– Ashton-under-Lyne.
–1992 Newark.

BRUNSKILL, Robinson, 50 Bridle Rd., Woodford, Cheshire SK7 1QJ. (061-439-6902) *b 28 Dec 1902, Gateshead. m. 2 Jul 1932: 1s.*
Education: 1927–31 Northern Baptist Coll., Manchester. *Appointments:* 1931–46 Baptist Church; 1946–49 Gt Harwood; 1949–53 Blackpool; 1953–57 Lytham St. Annes; 1957–62 Stretford; 1962–66 Newcastle-upon-Tyne (Heaton and Wallsend); 1966–69 Jarrow.

BRYANT, Thomas Henry, 4 Exning Rd., Newmarket, Suffolk CB8 0AB. (0638-662837) *b. 4 Aug 1922: Docking, Norfolk. m. 10 Jun 1961: 2d., 1s.*
Education: 1927–36 Docking CE Sch.; 1951–54 Didsbury, Bristol. *Appointments:* 1954–56 Attleborough; 1956–61 Aylsham, Briston and Reepham; 1961–66 Thetford; 1966–71 Birmingham (Moseley Road and Sparkhill); 1971–75 Swaffham; 1975– Newmarket.

BRYON, David John, 210 Main St., Calverton, Nottingham NG14 6LU. (0602-652446) – BA(Birmingham). *b. 3 Jul 1940, Watford, Herts. m. 15 Jul 1972: 2s.*
Education: 1945–51 Chater J&I Sch.; 1951–56 Watford Gram. Sch. for Boys; 1956–59 Watford Tech. Coll.; 1959–63 Regent St. Poly.; 1968–71 Birmingham Univ.; 1968–70 Handsworth; 1970–72 Queens. *Appointments:* 1972–76 Nottingham (West); 1976–81 Belper; 1981– Nottingham (Central).

BUCKMASTER, Reginald John, 3 Rose Cott., Broads Green, Gt Waltham, Chelmsford CM3 1DS. (0245-360235) *b. 17 Nov 1901, Battersea, London. m. 11 Aug 1934: 1d.*
Education: 1914–18 Sheerness Higher Elem.; 1919–20 Chichester Lancastrian; 1928–30 Hartley Victoria. *Appointments:* 1930–34 London Mission (S.E.); 1934–37 London Mission (Plumstead); 1937–45 London Mission (South); 1945–48 Darlaston; 1948–59 London Mission (Hackney and Clapton); 1959–63 London Mission (North and Central); 1963–69 Upwell and Manga; 1969–70 Fenland.

BUCKROYD, Clifford, 12a Silurian Close, Leominster, Hereford HR6 8SR. (0568-4582) – BA. *b. 19 May 1909, Leeds. m. 6 Jun 1945: 1s.*
Education: Leeds Boys Mod.; 1928–32 Leeds; 1932–35 Cambridge; 1932–35 Wesley House. *Appointments:* 1936–38 Truro Sch.; 1938–47 Liskeard; 1947–50 Sheffield (Carver St.); 1950–54 Hanley Trinity; 1954–61 Congleton; 1961–66 Nantwich; 1966–70 Leigh (Lancs); 1970–75 Rossendale; 1975–79 Church Stretton.
Special Interests: Music, Photography, Gardens.

BUCKROYD, Elizabeth Ann, 7 Lyme Ave., Macclesfield, Cheshire SK11 7RS. (0625-25604) *b. 14 Jul 1936, Leeds.*
Education: 1947–55 Roundhay High Sch., Leeds; 1955–57 Sunderland Teacher Training Coll.; 1957–58 Supp. Cert. in History Course; 1968–69 Durham Univ. Inst. Ed.; 1973–76 Wesley, Bristol. *Appointments:* 1976–81 Sale; 1981– Macclesfield.
Connexional Committees: 1978–81 Connexional Candidates; 1980– Text Committee of the New Hymn Book (app. by Faith and Order Comm.).
Publications: Wesley Historical Society Proceedings Vol. XLI, Part 4, Feb 1978, "Hymns for Children"; Robert Raikes Historical Society Annual Lecture Oct 1978, printed by NCEC, "Education or Indoctrination? The Role of Authorized Hymnody in the Early Sunday Schools of the Wesleyan Methodist Connexion".
Special Interests: Children's Hymnody, The role of education within the context of the Church.
Hobbies and Recreations: Music, Reading, Gardening.

BUGLASS, Anthony Edward, 3 King's Rd., Wallsend, Tyne and Wear NE28 7QT. (0632-620121) – BA (Bristol). *b. 4 Sept 1953, North Shields. m. 12 Aug 1978.*
Education: 1958–65 Western Jnr. Sch.; 1965–72 Tynemouth Gram. Tech. Sch.; 1974–75 Cliff Coll.; 1976–79 Bristol Univ.; 1976–80 Wesley, Bristol. *Appointments:* 1980– Newcastle, Heaton and Wallsend.
Connexional Committees: 1981– Methodist Study Centre.
Special Interests: Biblical Studies, Political Theology. *Hobbies and Recreations:* Modern Military History, Aircraft and Warship Modelling, Wine-Making, Music (incl. Guitar playing).

BULCOCK, Keith, 134 Pioneer Ave., Desborough, Kettering, Northants NN14 2PB. (0536-760651) *b. 23 Mar 1935, Liverpool. m. 29 Jul 1961: 3d.*
Education: 1940–42 South Bank, Liverpool; 1942–46 Duncombe Rd., Liverpool; 1946–51 Quarry Bank Gram. Sch., Liverpool; 1957–61 Hartley Victoria. *Appointments:*

1961–63 Holyhead; 1963–65 Horden and Easington Colliery; 1965–68 Billingham New Town; 1968–71 Bude; 1971–73 St Budeaux; 1973–80 Dove Valley; 1973–80 Chaplain HM Prison Sudbury; 1976–80 Chaplain Pastures Psychiatric Hospital Derby; 1980– St Giles Anglican-Methodist Church Desborough.
Special Interests: Preaching, Evangelism, Church History, Church Unity, Episcopacy, Ecology and Conservation. *Hobbies and Recreations:* Meteorology, Tides, Transport.

BULLICK, Brian, 14 Woodlands, Todmorden, W. Yorks OL14 5LT. (070-681-3640) *b. 19 Aug 1936, Stockton-on-Tees, Co. Durham. m. 17 Jun 1961: 1d., 2s.*
Education: 1941–48 Dormanstown Inf. & Jnr.; 1948–53 Archbishop Holgate's GS, York.; 1959–63 Headingley. *Appointments:* 1963–65 Albert Hall, Nottingham; 1965–70 Ashfield; 1970–77 Halifax; 1977– Todmorden.
Council Member: 1978– Todmorden Town Council; 1982–83 Mayor of Todmorden.
Special Interests: Choral Society (Halifax and Todmorden); Assocn. Football Referee, Yorks C.C. Member. *Hobbies and Recreations:* Member of Rotary, Schools Manager.

BULLOCK, Tony, 20 Heatherley Rd., Camberley, Surrey GU15 3LX. (0276-63084) *b. 26 Jul 1935, Northampton. m. 20 Jun 1959: 2d.*
Education: 1946–51 Northampton Town and County Gram. Sch.; 1957–61 Hartley Victoria. *Appointments:* 1961–66 Barnstaple; 1966–71 Bromsgrove; 1971–78 Amersham; 1978– Aldershot.
Special Interests: American Methodism, Theology, Youth Work; Evangelism. *Hobbies and Recreations:* Watching all sport, The Countryside, Reading.

BULLOCK, Vernon Thomas, 12 Meriden Close, Cannock, Staffs WS11 1QG. (054-35-3195) – BA (Liverpool), BA(Bristol), MLitt (Dunelm). *b. 15 Dec 1933, Great Wyrley, Staffs. m. 10 Nov 1962: 2d.*
Education: 1945–52 Rugeley Gram. Sch.; 1952–56 Liverpool Univ.; 1956–59 Bristol Univ.; 1956–59 Didsbury, Bristol. *Appointments:* 1959–61 Whitehaven; 1961–68 Stockton-on-Tees; 1968–74 Lecturer in Religious Studies, Neville's Cross College, Durham; 1974–78 Lecturer in Religious Studies, West Midlands College, Walsall; 1978– Senior Lecturer in Religious Studies, West Midlands College of Higher Education, Walsall.
Publications: Various articles in *Handbook of Suggestions for Religious Education*, Durham Education Committee 1972–74.
Special Interests: Modern Theological Thought, World Religions, Classical Music, Architecture and Design.

BUMPHREY, David Leslie, The Manse, North Rd., Holsworthy, Devon EX22 6HF. (0409-253286) – Dip Theol. *b. 8 Dec 1926, Costessey, Norfolk. m. 14 Aug 1954: 1d., 1s.*
Education: 1932–38 St. Augustines Prim. Sch., Costessey; 1938–39 Hellesdon Central Sch.; 1939–41 Jnr. Tech. Sch., Norwich; 1941–47 Norwich Tech. Coll. and Sch. of Art (part-time); 1949–51 Richmond.
Appointments: 1948–51 Upwell and Manea; 1951–54 South Molton; 1954–58 Oldbury Wesley; 1958–63 Birmingham Elmdon; 1963–67 Douglas (I.o.M.); 1967–74 Ipswich; 1974–81 Sidmouth and Bridport; 1981– Holsworthy.
Connexional Committees: 1963–66 Division of Social Responsibility. 1966–67 Secretary I.o.M. Synod.
Hobbies and Recreations: Gardening.

BURCH, Arthur Roy, The Beeches, 9 Lower East Coker Rd., Yeovil, Somerset BA20 2LH. (0935-4112) *b. 7 May 1907, Belmont, Surrey. m. 13 Aug 1935: 2s.*
Education: Sutton High Sch., Surrey; Bethany House Sch., Goudhurst, Whitgift Sch.; 1929–32 Richmond.
Appointments: 1928–29 Epworth; 1932–35 North of Scotland Mission; 1935–38 Lerwick and North Roe; 1938–41 North of Scotland Mission; 1941–45 Carlisle, Fisher St.; 1945–49 Arbroath and Montrose; 1949–53 Birmingham, Sutton Park; 1953–57 St. Leonards and Bexhill; 1957–63 Reading; 1963–66 Southport North; 1966–71 Somerset Mission.
Special Interests: Biography, Travel, Philately, Chess, Fishing, Gardening.
Hobbies and Recreations: Photography, Fishing, Travel.

BURCH, Michael David, 1 Roseacre St., Portsoy, Banff AB4 2QX. (02614-2745) *b. 30 May 1930, Tattingstone, E. Suffolk. m. 16 Aug 1956: 2d.*
Education: 1941–49 Doncaster Gram. Sch.; 1951–54 Headingley.
Appointments: 1954–56 Beverley; 1956–57 Barton-on-Humber; 1957–62 Market Rasen and Caistor; 1962–67 York (Clifton and Monkgate); 1967–70 North of Scotland Mission; 1970–73 Social Worker, Dundee; 1973–77 Probation Officer, Notts; 1977– Social Worker, Grampian Region.
Hobbies and Recreations: Railways.

BURCHELL, Keith, 14 Frankland Rd., Coventry CV6 7HE. (0203-86115) – BSc(Eng). *b. 13 Oct 1941, Gloucester. m. 9 Apr 1969: 1d., 1s.*
Education: 1952–60 King's Coll. Sch., Wimbledon; 1960–63 Southampton Univ.; 1977–80 Manchester Univ.; 1977–80 Hartley Victoria. *Appointments:* 1980– Coventry.
Special Interests: Administration.
Hobbies and Recreations: Railways.

BURDEN, John Paul, Derlwyn, 3 Heol Arenig, Bala, Gwynedd IL23 7AH. (0678-520621) *b. 27 Nov 1914, Erith. m. 18 Aug 1951: 2d.*
Education: Glasgow, Leeds and Blackwood (Prim. & Jnr.); Lewis's Sch., Pengam (Gram.); Shaftesbury Gram., West Mon. Gram. Sch.; 1934–37 Handsworth. *Appointments:* 1937–46 Bombay Dt., India; 1946–50 Stoke-on-Trent, Burslem, Hill Top; 1950–55 Bebington; 1955–58 Northwick, London Rd and Nortwich; 1958–63 Haverford West and Milford Haven; 1963–69 Port Talbot; 1969–71 Pontypridd; 1971–78 Cross Keys and Risca.
Special Interests: Moral Re-armament.
Hobbies and Recreations: Tennis.

BURGE, Cyrus, Helsayle, 14 Lennard Rd., Crediton, Devon EX17 2AP. (03632-2185) *b. 15 Oct 1901, Ebbw*

Vale, Mon. m. 3s.
Education: Waun-Llwyd S.; 1920–22 Richmond. *Appointments:* 1923–24 Helston; 1924–27 Richmond; 1927–30 Wye Valley Mission; 1930–32 Brixham and Dartmouth; 1932–35 Camborne; 1935–38 Swansea and Gower; 1938–44 Shepton Mallett; 1944–47 Newbury; 1947–52 Redruth; 1952–56 Penzance, Chapel St.; 1956–64 Pontypridd; 1964–66 Hyde.

BURGESS, Arthur George Edward, 3 Andrew Way, Lowestoft, Suffolk NR33 8PY. (0502-66072) – BA (Bristol), STM(Union Theological Seminary, New York). *b. 19 Feb 1934, Edgware, Middx. m. 31 Dec 1960: 1d., 1s.*
Education: 1945–52 Haberdashers' Aske's Hampstead Sch.; 1954–57 Bristol Univ.; 1957–58 Union Theological Seminary, New York; 1954–57 Didsbury, Bristol. *Appointments:* 1958–60 SCM in Schools; 1960–62 Towyn; 1962–64 Burton-on-Trent; 1964–70 Chaplain, Ashville College, Harrogate; 1970–72 Nicholas Sch., Basildon; 1972– Harris Middle School, Lowestoft.
Special Interests: Education; Liturgy, French and German. *Hobbies and Recreations:* Walking, Ornithology, Amateur Radio.

BURGESS, Donald Henry, 70 Serpentine Rd., Wallasey, Merseyside L44 0AZ. (051-639-1713) *b. Widnes, Lancs. m.: 2d.*
Education: 1965–69 Hartley Victoria. *Appointments:* 1969–74 Manchester, Cheetham Hill and Prestwich; 1974–79 Worsley; 1979– Wallasey.

BURGESS, Ernest William Guthrie, Peerie Voe Cott., 5 Harrison Place, Glusburn, Keighley, W. Yorks BD20 8QS. (0535-35684) *b. 7 May 1914, Preston, Lancs. m.*
Education: 1959–62 Richmond. *Appointments:* 1962–64 Bolton (Park St.); 1964–71 South Craven; 1971–79 Halifax.

BURGESS, Stephen John, 20 Rochester Ave., Bromley, Kent BR1 3DD. (01-460-1437) – BA, BSc. *b. 10 Jul 1949, London. m. 21 Jul 1979.*
Education: 1954–57 Talbot Rd. County Prim. Sch., Leeds; 1957–60 Westbury-on-Trym CE, Bristol; 1960–67 Cotham Gram. Sch., Bristol; 1968–72 Thames Poly. (Woolwich); 1977–80 Birmingham Univ.; 1974–75 Westminster Coll., Oxford; 1977–80 Queen's. *Appointments:* 1980– Bromley, Kent (P.T. Farrington School Chaplain).
Special Interests: Education; Science. *Hobbies and Recreations:* Sailing (esp. with London Sailing Project), Music, Theatre.

BURGESS, Stuart John, 954 Bristol Rd., Selly Oak, Birmingham B29 6NB. (021-472-0314) – BD(London), MEd, MTh(Nottingham). *b. 18 Mar 1940, Birmingham. m. 17 Jul 1965: 2d.*
Education: 1951–58 Moseley Gram. Sch., Birmingham; 1959–61 St. Peters Coll., Saltley, Birmingham; 1962–65 Headingley. *Appointments:* 1965–68 Leeds, Headingley; 1968–81 Nottingham West; 1981– Birmingham South-West.
Connexional Committees: 1980– Doctrinal Committee.
Special Interests: Communities esp. Taize, Local radio, Worship, Eastern Europe. *Hobbies and Recreations:* Travelling, Tennis, Squash.

BURGON, George, Chapel Cott., Langcliffe, Settle, N. Yorks BD24 9NH. *b. 7 Jan 1899, Newcastle-upon-Tyne. m. 9 Aug 1927 (Widower): 1s.*
Education: 1917–29 Rutherford Coll., Newcastle-upon-Tyne; 1920–23 Hartley Victoria. *Appointments:* 1923–25 Skipton; 1925–27 N. Cornwall; 1927–33 Doncaster; 1933–38 London, Hither Green; 1938–44 Swindon; 1944–50 Crosshills; 1950–55 Batley; 1955–63 Madeley.
Special Interests: Reading; Music; Travel. *Hobbies and Recreations:* Tennis, Photography, Walking fells.

BURNETT, Edwin Richard, Waverley, Beckfoot, Silloth, Carlisle, Cumbria. (0965-31597) – BA, BD (Lond). *b. 4 Jan 1904, Halesowen. m. (Widower) 7 Jul 1931: 1d., 2s.*
Education: 1909–10 Private Sch., Miss Fairgraves, Liverpool; 1910–12 Wesleyan Sch.; 1912–15 Council Sch., Sturminster Newton; 1915–18 Cirencester Gram. Sch.; 1918–20 Churcher's Coll., Petersfield; 1925–27 Hartley. *Appointments:* 1927–29 Southampton; 1929–31 Wymondham; 1931–33 Pateley Bridge; 1933–37 Wigton; 1937–39 Brandon and Deerness Valley; 1939–44 Shildon; 1944–47 Redcar; 1947–48 Castleford; 1948–51 Blaenavon; 1951–55 Midsomer Norton; 1955–57 Radstock; 1957–63 Kirkby Steven, Appleby and Tebay; 1963–67 Hetton le Hole.
Publications: Many Magazine Articles from about 1923 to present.
Special Interests: Photography; Scottish History. *Hobbies and Recreations:* Photography.

BURNS, Francis Victor, Richmond, 27 Victoria Rd., Exmouth, Devon EX8 1DW. (03952-70420) – BD(Lond). *b. 2 Apr 1912, Exeter, Devon. m. 30 Jul 1938: 3s.*
Education: 1922–28 Hele's Sch., Exeter; London Univ.; 1931–35 Richmond. *Appointments:* 1935–46 Bahamas District; 1946–50 Teddington; 1950–57 Windsor and Maidenhead; 1957–64 Slough; 1964–74 Richmond and Hounslow.
Connexional Committees: 1952–56 MMS General Committee; 1964–72 Ministerial Training Committee.
Publications: Commentary on St. Luke's Gospel for W. Indies Local Preachers, 1955.
Hobbies and Recreations: Swimming, Tennis.

BURRIDGE, William Ernest, Green Pastures, 17 Burton Rd., Branksome Pk, Bournemouth BH13 6DT. (0202-764776) *b. 30 Sept 1919, Fenny Stratford. m. 28 Jul 1949: 3d.*
Education: 1924–33 Bletchley Council Sch.; 1947–49 Hartley Victoria. *Appointments:* 1945–47 Abergavenny; 1949–52 Neath and Port Talbot; 1952–56 Barry; 1956–63 Guernsey; 1963–72 Bournemouth; 1972– Green Pastures Director and Chaplain.
Connexional Committees: 1949–56 Youth Committee; 1972– Pastoral and Healing Committee. *Publications: Healing Transformation; Renewal in Green Pastures.*
Special Interests: Ministry of Healing.

Hobbies and Recreations: Caravanning, Music, Photography.

BURROWS, Norman, Trinity Manse, Lingfield Rd., East Grinstead, West Sussex RH19 2HA. (0342-25877) *b. 6 Dec 1931, Sheffield. m. 4 Apr 1953: 1d., 1s.*
Education: 1934–38 Lound Inf., Sheffield; 1938–42 Burncross Jnr., Sheffield; 1942–46 Ecclesfield Gram., Sheffield; 1961–64 Hartley Victoria.
Appointments: 1964–70 Mansfield, Bridge St.; 1970–75 High Wycombe; 1975–80 Leighton Buzzard and Stewkley; 1980– Redhill and East Grinstead.
Special Interests: Revival. *Hobbies and Recreations:* Stamp Collecting, Walking.

BURT, Gerald Matthison, Division of Social Responsibility, 1 Central Bldgs, Westminster, London SW1H 9NH. (01-222-8589) – MA(Oxon), BA(Cantab). *b. 11 Aug 1929, Newhaven, Sussex. m. 28 Jul 1956: 2d.*
Education: 1934–41 Newhaven Prim. and Boys Jnr. Schs.; 1941–44 Rye Gram. Sch.; 1944–48 Lewes County Gram. Sch. for Boys; 1950–53 St. Edmund Hall, Oxford; 1953–56 Wesley House. *Education:* 1956–57 Methodist Missionary Society; 1957–61 Birmingham, Elmdon; 1961–67 Hull North; 1967–72 Southampton; 1972–74 Canterbury and Faversham; 1974–79 Division of Ministries; 1979– Division of Social Responsibility.
Connexional Committees: 1970–73 Ecumenical Committee; 1974–79 Board of Division of Ministries; 1979– Board of Division of Social Responsibility; 1979– President's Council; 1979– GP Committee.
Special Interests: Ethics; Worship; Ministry. *Hobbies and Recreations:* Walking, Bird-watching.

BURTON, Albert Dennis, 39 Thorncliffe Rd., Astley Bridge, Bolton BL1 7ER. (0204-51074) – BA. *b. 30 Mar 1942, Leeds. m. 4 Apr 1970: 1d., 2s.*
Education: 1948–52 Martin Frobisher Sch.; 1953–60 Normanton Boys Gram. Sch.; 1960–63 York Diocesan Teacher Training Coll. of St. John; 1975–78 Manchester Univ.; 1975–78 Hartley Victoria. *Appointments:* 1978– Bolton.
Connexional Committees: 1979– Methodist Drama Committee. *Publications:* Plays: *Carol for Christmas*, 1967; *Treasure for Christmas*, 1968; *Boy and a Drum*, 1971; *Life in Time* (on lives of Methodist Preachers), 1980; *Song of Christmas*, 1981.
Special Interests: Christian Drama and Music, training others to use creative media in evangelism, especially with youth. *Hobbies and Recreations:* Clock Restoration and Antique Renovation.

BURTON, David, 177 Redcar Lane, Redcar, Co. Cleveland TS10 2EJ. (0642-483927) – BA(Newcastle). *b. 26 Oct 1946, Radcliffe, Manchester. m. 17 Jun 1972: 2s.*
Education: –1958 St. Paul's Methodist Jnr. Sch., Radcliffe, Manchester; 1958–59 Radcliffe Sec. Mod. Sch.; 1959–65 Stand Gram. Sch. for Boys, Whitefield, Manchester; 1965–68 Newcastle Univ.; 1970–72 Liverpool Univ.; 1976–78 Wesley, Bristol. *Appointments:* 1978–82 Colne; 1982– Redcar.

BURTON, Frederick Wilfred, 31 Springfield Rd., Halesowen, W. Midlands B62 8JY. (021-422-2698) – Inter BD. *b. 18 Dec 1916, Bala. m. 8 Jul 1947: 2d.*
Education: 1921–26 Market Drayton National; 1926 Chester Rd. Jnr., Port Sunlight; 1926–28 Acton Park Jnr., Wrexham; 1928–34 Grove Park Gram., Wrexham; 1948 St. Andrews, Selly Oak; 1946–48 Richmond.
Appointments: 1948–54 Bengal Dt; 1954–59 Sheffield N.E.; 1959–61 Fleetwood; 1961–67 Blackburn Trinity; 1967–72 Holmfirth; 1972–77 Radcliffe; 1977–82 Birmingham, Blackheath.
Connexional Committees: MMS General Committee (Sheffield Dt. OM Sec.)–1959; MMS General Committee (N. Lancs Dt. OM Sec.)–1965; Church in Rural Life Committee (W. Yorks Dt. rep.).
Hobbies and Recreations: National Trust, RSPB, Steam Railways.

BURTON, Jack Robert, 11 Colegate, Norwich NR3 1BN. *b. 17 Oct 1939, Norwich. m. 13 Jun 1961: 2d., 1s.*
Education: 1951–56 City of Norwich; 1959–63 Handsworth. *Appointments:* 1963–65 Glasgow (Paisley Road, Govan); 1965–68 Ely (Littleport); 1968– Norwich (Sector Ministry, Bus Driver).
Publications: Message Delivered, (pseudonymously 1967); *Transport of Delight*, 1976 (Won the Winifred Mary Stanford Book Prize 1978); *Our Common Humanity*, 1980 (The Third Michael Harding Memorial Address); *The Richest Legacy*, 1981.
Special Interests: Worship and Liturgy; Church Unity. *Hobbies and Recreations:* Natural History, Local Studies.

BURTON, Keith John, St Cyprien, Church Lane, Lower Broadheath, Worcester WR6 2QY. (0905-641757) – BD. *b. 11 Aug 1935, Leicester. m. 28 Jun 1964: 2s.*
Education: 1946–51 Gateway Sch., Leicester; 1961–65 Headingley.
Appointments: 1965–67 Oswestry; 1967–70 Ludlow; 1970–74 Brighouse; 1974– Worcester Technical College.

BURTON, Lewis, 429 Wakefield Rd., Huddersfield HD5 8DB. (0484-24822) – BA(Bristol), BA(Lond), PhD(Lond), MPhil(Leeds). *b. 22 May 1929, Leeds. m. 14 Jul 1956: 1d., 2s.*
Education: 1934–42 Broad Lane Elem. Sch., Bramley; 1942–44 Jnr. Tech. Sch., Leeds; 1952–55 Bristol Univ.; 1956–62, 1964–72 London Univ., 1974–79 Leeds Univ., 1951–55 Didsbury, Bristol. *Appointments:* 1950–51 Barnstaple; 1955–60 Hebden Bridge; 1960–65 Wolverhampton (Darlington St.); 1965–74 Leeds (South); 1974–81 Pudsey and Farsley; 1981– Huddersfield East.
Connexional Committees: Methodist Sociological Group. *Publications:* PhD Thesis, *Class Structure of the Local Church*, Univ. London Library 1972; MPhil Thesis, *Community and Recruitment in the Local Church*, Univ. Leeds Library 1979.
Special Interests: D.I.Y., Railways.

BUSSEY, Dennis, Pine Trees, 52 Lake Rd., Verwood, Wimborne, Dorset BH21 6BT. (0202-822718) *b. 20 May 1932, Bradford, Yorks. m. 7 Aug 1958: 1d.*
Education: 1943–48 Rastrick Gram. Sch.; 1970–71 Birmingham Univ.; 1955–58 London Univ.; 1955–68 Richmond. *Appointments:* 1958–61 Bacup; 1961–67 Wimborne; 1967–70 Grays; 1971–72 Farnham and Alton. Appointed to Dorset Probation Service 1973, and now at Christchurch Office.
Council Member: Dorset County Council 1973–77.
Special Interests: Local government – especially Education; Juvenile Crime. *Hobbies and Recreations:* Theatre.

BUTLER, Margaret Mary, 12 Didsbury Pk, Manchester M20 0LJ. (061-445-3539) *b. 1 Jun 1930, Darlington, Co. Durham.* d. 8.8.04
Education: 1935–41 Dodmire Inf. and Jnr. Schs.; 1941–47 Darlington High Sch.; 1951–53 Wesley Deaconess Coll., Ilkley; 1973–74 Wesley, Bristol. *Appointments:* 1974–79 Cadishead and Eccles; 1979– Manchester, Withington.
Connexional Committees: 1980– Connexional Probationers Sub Committee.
Special Interests: Languages. *Hobbies and Recreations:* Swimming; Walking; Golf, Cinema, Theatre, Knitting.

BUTLER, William Graeme, 21 Dunsford Rd., Exeter EX4 1LG. (0392-55791) *b. 12 Jul 1931, Ashton-under-Lyne, Lancs. m. 10 Aug 1956: 1d., 1s.* ~~d. 8.8.04~~
Education: 1942–47 Ashton-under-Lyne GS; 1951–54 Handsworth.
Appointments: 1954–57 Tipton (Park Lane); 1957–62 Walsall; 1962–69 Wymondham and Attleborough; 1969–80 South Petherton and Crewkerne; 1980– Exeter.
Connexional Committees: 1982– President's Council.

BUXTON, John Douglas, 258 Felmongers, Harlow, Essex CM20 3DR. (0279-22998) – MA (Cantab). *b. 16 Apr 1938, Fulham, London. m. 11 Aug 1962: 1d., 1s.*
Education: 1942–48 Peterborough Rd. Inf. and Jnr., Fulham; 1948–56 Christ's Hospital; 1956–59 Manchester Univ.; 1959–62 Cambridge Univ.; 1959–62 Wesley House. *Appointments:* 1962–72 South East Asia Conference; 1972–79 Wrexham; 1979– Harlow Mission.
Connexional Committees: 1976–79 Consultative Council for Methodism in Wales. *Local Council Committees:* 1982– Essex County Religious Education Conference.

BYWATER, Stephen Michael, 63 St. Kingsmark Ave., Chepstow, Gwent. (02912-2100) *b. 28 Feb 1945, Preston, Lancs. m. 4 Apr 1970: 2s.*
Education: 1955–61 Picklenash County Prim., Newent, Glos; Newent Sec. Mod.; 1964–65 Gloucester Coll. of Agriculture; 1968–69 Brooksby Agricultural Coll., Leicester; 1972–75 Queens, Birmingham. *Appointments:* 1975–80 Buckfastleigh; 1980– Chepstow and Caldicot.
Special Interests: Evangelism; The work of the Holy Spirit; Rural outreach. *Hobbies and Recreations:* Gardening, Motor mechanics, Property.

CAINK, David Miller, The Beeches, 104 Ware Road, Hertford SG13 7HN. (0992-53644)–Dip/Design. *b. 7 Aug 1924, Walton, Wakefield, Yorkshire. m. 15 March 1961: 1d., 2s.*
Education: 1933–1936 Wakefield Academy; 1936–1938 Manorside Secondary Modern, Finchley; 1938–1942, 1946–1948 Willesden Poly., 1951–1954 Handsworth.
Appointments: 1950–1951 Chelmsford; 1954–1955 Penzance; 1955–1961 Bolsover; 1961–1966 King's Lynn; 1966–1972 Lowestoft; 1972-1977 Shooters Hill; 1977– Waltham Abbey and Hertford.
Connexional Committees: 1968–1972 Methodist Education Committee.
Special Interests: Art and Architectural History, Writing, Broadcasting. *Hobbies and Recreations:* Painting, Music, Walking, Tennis.

CAINK, Graham, 35 Vicarage Road, St Agnes, Cornwall TR5 0TF. (087 255–2363) *b. 9 May 1921, Whitchurch, Cardiff, Glamorgam. m. 12 Aug 1953: 2d.*
Education: 1926–27 Private; 1927–32 Sandal Endowed Sch., (CE); 1932–35 Silcoates Sch., Wakefield; 1946–47 Cliff Coll.; 1949–51 Hartley Victoria. *Appointments:* 1948–49 Yeovil; 1951–52 Glasgow (Admiral St); 1952–53 Amble and Alnwick; 1953–57 Peak and Bradwell; 1957–62 Consett; 1962–67 Chelmsford; 1967–74 Callington and Gunnislake; 1974–79 Kidderminster and Stourport; 1979– Newquay Perranporth and St. Agnes.
Local Council Committees: 1963–67, 1969–74 School Manager in Essex and Cornwall.
Special Interests: Church and Methodist History, Member of C.E.I.M. and M.R.F. *Hobbies and Recreations:* Walking, Cycling and Railway Studies.

CALDWELL, Martin Victor, The Manse, 32 East Street, Newquay, Cornwall TR7 1BH. (063 73–3087) *b. 6 March 1937, York. m. 1 April 1967: 2d.*
Education: 1942–48 Poppleton Road Prim. Sch., York; 1948–51 Barnard Castle Sch.; 1951–1953 Archbishop Holgate's Grammar Sch.; 1960–64 Wesley Coll., Headingley.
Appointments: 1964–66 Marazion; 1966–71 St. Austell; 1971–73 Newquay; 1973-79 Division of Education & Youth and MAYC Secretary; 1979– Newquay, Perranporth and St. Agnes; 1979–82 Cornwall District Synod Secretary.
Connexional Committees: 1967–79 MYD Youth & Community Committee (1970–72 Chairman, 1973–79 Secretary); 1973–79 Most DEY Committees; 1980– DEY Central Committee for Regional Development.
Special Interests: Youth Work, Worship, Church Management, Music. *Hobbies and Recreations:* Youth Work, Music.

CALLISTER, Frank, Mountford, Eleanora Drive, Douglas, Isle of Man. (0624–21056)–MA (Glasgow), BD, PhD (Lond), Dip Ed (Lond). *b. 9 July 1916, Douglas.*

Education: 1927–35 Douglas High Sch. for Boys; 1935–39 London (External Department); 1942–46 Glasgow; 1935–39 Didsbury Coll., Manchester. *Appointments:* 1939–42 Glasgow (Cathcart Road); 1942–46 Wishaw; 1946–51 Dewsbury (Centenary); 1951–56 Sheffield (Carver Street); 1956–76 Sectors R.I.; 1976–78 President's List; 1978–81 St. Just. *Publications: Bible Plays for the Morning Assembly* 1958 (Epworth); *The Vacant Throne* 1960 (Epworth); *Living in the Kingdom* 1963 (Epworth) with H. F. Mathews; *One World Not Two* 1968 (R.E.P.).

CALVER, Martin William, 88 Wolsey Croft, Sherburn-in-Elmet, Leeds LS25 6DP. (0977-682230) (LRAM) 1974. *b. 20 Sept 1944, Strensall, York. m. 5 April 1975: 2d., 1s.*
Education: 1949–55 Strensall Prim.; 1955–59 Joseph Rowntree Secondary Modern (York); 1959–61 York Coll. of Further Education; 1959–61 (Full time) York Coll. of Further Education; 1961–67 (Part time) York Coll. of Further Education; 1978–80 Wesley, Bristol.
Appointments: 1980– Snaith and Selby.
Special Interests: Sport of all kinds, Work among young people, Voluntary probation worker. *Hobbies and Recreations:* DIY, Travel, Football, Cricket.

CALVERT, David G. A., 7 Burton Crescent, Headingley, Leeds LS6 4DN. (0523-751141)–MA(Cantab.), BD(Lond.), PhD(Leeds). *b. 1 July 1940, Huddersfield. m. 15 Aug 1964. 2d.*
Education: King James's Grammar Sch., Almondsbury; 1959–62 King's Coll. Univ. of London; 1962–64 Wesley House, Cambridge.
Appointments: 1964–67 Headingley, Asst. Tut.; 1967–70 Methodist Church in Kenya; 1970–74 Chaplain, Univ. of Leeds; 1977 Ecumenical Lecturer, Lincoln Theological Coll.; 1977– Headingley.
Connexional Committees: 1979– Division of Ministries, Member of Board and Executive Committee.
Publications: Companion to The Lectionary, Prefaces to the Lessons, 1982.
Special Interests: Christology.
Hobbies and Recreations: Walking.

CALVERT, Walter Ivor, 14 Kirklands, Strensall, York YO3 5WX. (0904-490026) *b. 23 Sept 1915, Stickney, Lincs. m. 10 April 1944: 1s.*
Education: 1920–27 Stickney C.E., 1927–31 Magdalen Coll. Sch., Wainfleet, Lincs.; 1934–35, Cliff Coll.; 1937–40 Didsbury.
Appointments: 1940–44 Bradford Mission; 1944–47 London Mission (East); 1947–52 Leeds, Headingley; 1952–56 Keighley; 1956–62 Leeds, Chapel Allerton; 1962–69 Harrow, (including 1 year exchange US Pastorate, East Bloomfield, Western NY, Conf., 1968–69); 1969–76 Ilford; 1976–1980 Ryedale.
Connexional Committees: 1949–72 Christian Citizenship.
Hobbies and Recreations: In earlier years, Football, Cricket (as spectator), more recent years, Crossword Compiling.

CANDELAND, Arthur, Wesley Manse, Durham Road, Annfield Plain, Stanley, Co. Durham DH9 7UG. (0207-34397)–MA(Oxford), MA(Cantab.). *b. 31 Dec 1917, Chester. m. 30 July 1949: 2d, 3s.*
Education: 1923–29 Wirral House Sch., Chester; 1929–37 King's Sch., Chester; 1937–40 and 1945–46 Worcester Coll., Oxford; 1946–48 Wesley House, Cambridge.
Appointments: 1948–49 Assistant Tutor, Didsbury Coll., Bristol; 1949–53; Paisley Mission; 1953–56 Keswick and Cockermouth; 1956–60 Gateshead (South); 1960–66 Newcastle (Heaton and Wallsend); 1966–70 Newcastle (West); 1970–74 Whitehaven; 1974–79 Shildon; 1979– Stanley.
Connexional Committees: 1961–70 Local Preachers Cttee.
Publications: The Preacher's Quarterly, Vol 10, nos 3,4, Vol 11, No.1 (1964–65); *Psalms and The Preacher, The Preacher's Handbook,* No.9 (1965); *The Book of Daniel.*
Special Interests: Old Testament Studies (Member of S.O.T.s) 1956–76. *Hobbies and Recreations:* Music, Fell-Walking, Sports.

CANNING, Vincent Graham, The Manse, Carno Road, Caersws, Powys SY17 5JA. (068684-8139)–BA(Birm.), *b. 30 June 1945, Rhiwabon, Clwyd. m. 12 Sept 1966: 2d, 1s.*
Education: 1949–56 New Broughton County Prim. Sch.; 1956–63 Grove Park Grammar Sch. for Boys, Wrexham; 1973–76 Birmingham Univ.; 1973–76 Queen's Coll., Birmingham.
Appointments: 1976–81 Pontypool; 1981– Welshpool and Bro Hafren.
Publications: Nothing book form, occasional poems in *Free Press of Monthmouthshire,* between 1976 and 1981, and in other magazines.
Special Interests: Folk Art, Poetry, Railways, Rugby, Cricket. *Hobbies and Recreations:* Railway Modelling, Poetry.

CANNON, Arthur Michael, 119 Carshalton Park Road, Carshalton, Surrey SM5 3SJ. (01-647-2147)–MA(Oxon), MSc, BD(Lond.), ARCO. *b. 8 May 1929, Kingston-Upon-Hull. m. 11 Aug 1962: 1d, 2s.*
Education: 1941–48 Kingswood Sch., Bath; 1950–53 Keble Coll., Oxford; 1963–65 Richmond Coll.
Appointments: 1965–69 Blackburn; 1969–74 Bournemouth, 1974– Sutton (Surrey).
Hobbies and Recreations: Organ Playing, Woodwork.

CAPSTICKS, Thomas Edward, 17 Farside Road, West Ayton, Scarborough, North Yorkshire YO13 9LE. *b. 24 April 1913, Darlington, Co Durham. m. 9 July 1938: 1d.*
Education: 1918–24 Reid Street, Darlington; 1924–27 Central Commercial, Darlington; 1946–48 Headingley.
Appointments: 1945–6 Pickering, Hungate; 1948–51 Haltwhistle; 1951–55 Durham Coast; 1955–60 Whitehaven; 1960–62 Burnley, Wesley; 1962–65 Burnley; 1965–70 Sherburn; 1970–71 Halifax North; 1971-75 Halifax; 1975–78 Sunderland; 1978–81 Sherburn.

Special Interests: Preaching, Methodism. *Hobbies and Recreation:* Gardening, D.I.Y.

CARDEW, John David, 430 Ashfield Road, Whiteholme, Blackpool, Lancashire FY5 3JA. (0253-867197/866976)–BA(Bristol), BSc(Lond.). *b. 30 Sept 1930, Columbo, Sri Lanka. m. 15 Dec 1956: 1d, 1s.*
Education: 1939–44 Brighton Coll. Jun. Sch.; 1944–49 Brighton Coll.; 1951–54 King's Coll., London; 1956–59 Bristol Univ.; 1956–59 Didsbury, Bristol.
Appointments: 1959–64 Harrow; 1964–69 Sutton; 1969–76 Wembley and Golders Green; 1976 Blackpool North.
Special Interests: Counselling and Social Welfare (Specialist in Grief Counselling). *Hobbies and Recreations:* Music, Reading, Squash, General interest in Sport.

CARR, Henry James, 5 Red Hill, Lodge Park, Redditch, Worcs B98 7JE. (0527–27318). *b. 27 Aug 1910, Nevilles Cross, Durham City. m. 30 July 1942: 2d.*
Education: 1915 Bearpark Colliery Prim.; 1916–21 Newtown (Stockton-on-Tees) Jun.; 1921–25 Richard Hind Central Sch.; 1935–38 Hartley Victoria.
Appointments: 1938–42 London Mission (South East); 1942–47 North Walsham; 1947–52 Huddersfield (Fartown); 1952–58 Bristol (Bedminster); 1958–64 Guernsey (Victoria) and Sark; 1964–71 Saltash; 1971–78 Rotherham.
Special Interests: Industrial and Hospital Chaplaincies. *Hobbies and Recreations:* In younger days—Football, Cricket etc., Cycling, Walking.

CARR, John, The Birches, Crosthwaite Road, Keswick, Cumbria CA12 5PG. (0596-72379). *b. 24 Feb 1932, Blyth, Northumberland. m. 22 Aug 1953: 2d, 2s.*
Education: 1937–45 New Delaval, Blyth; 1958–59 Cliff Coll.; 1960–63 Headingley.
Appointments: 1963–70 Weardale; 1970–78 Redcar, Salturn and Guisborough; 1978– Keswick and Cockermouth.
Connexional Committees: 1967–71 M.Y.D. (MAYC District President 1968); 1973–78 D.S.R. Asst. Sec.; 1979–85 Property Division Dist. Sec.
Special Interests: Family Man. *Hobbies and Recreations:* Gardening and generally D.I.Y.

CARTER, R. Graham, 25 Eaton Rd., West Derby, Liverpool L12 7JJ. (051-226-3217)–MA.
Education: 1964–67 Hartley Victoria.
Appointments: 1967–71 Newcastle-upon-Tyne, Brunswick and Central; 1971–74 Blyth and Seaston Delaval; 1974–81 Birkenhead; 1981– Liverpool North and Central.

CARTER, William Gregory, Yew Tree Cottage, 37 High Street, Roade, Northampton NN7 2NW. (0604-862570) *b. 1918, Northampton. m. 1949: 1d, 1s.*
Education: 1947–49 Handsworth.
Appointments: 1945–47 Aberdare; 1949–53 Peterborough; 1953–58 Bedford (North); 1958–63 Bournemouth; 1963–66 Somerset Mission; 1966–73 Petersfield and Haslemere; 1973–1982 Nottingham (Central).
Special Interests: People. *Hobbies and Recreations:* Painting, Woodcarving, Walking.

CARTLEDGE, Maurice, 409 Ford Green Rd., Norton, Stoke on Trent, Staffs ST6 8LX. (0782-534013)–MA, BD. *b. 6 Aug 1925, Pendleton, Salford, Lancs. m.6 Oct 1956: 1d, 1s.*
Education: 1930–31 London St. Elem., Salford, Lancs.; 1931–36 S. Hornchurch Jun. Mixed, Essex; 1936–41 S.E. Essex Technical Coll. Day Sch.; 1941–43 S.E. Essex Technical Coll. Architectural Dept.; 1952–53 Marburg Univ., Germany; 1949–52 Richmond.
Appointments: 1947–49 Tamworth; 1953–56 Chislehurst; 1956–58 Llanelli and Camarthen; 1958–62 Spalding; 1962–67 Hemel Hempstead and Berkhamsted; 1967–71 Colchester; 1971–74 Lytham St. Annes; 1974–79 Middlesbrough and Eston; 1979– Stoke on Trent (Burslem).
Publications: Worlds Apart—Radicalism and the Gospel (lecture 12pp 1977) *Special Interests:* Old Testament and Semitics. *Hobbies and Recreations:* Music, Piano Playing.

CARTWRIGHT, Alfred, 11 Hudson St., Burnham-on-Sea, Somerset TA8 1PR. (0278-789487). *b. 24 April 1907, Carlisle. m. 11 Aug 1936: 1d, 2s.*
Education: 1916–20 Calabar, Jamaica; 1920–24 Kingswood; 1929–32 Richmond.
Appointments: 1932–34 Waltham Abbey and Hertford Mission; 1934–36 Diss; 1936–39 Home Missions (Maesteg); 1939–44 Wolverhampton (Darlington Street); 1944–45 Aylesbury; 1945–48 Jamaica (Port Antonio); 1948–51 British Honduras; 1951–55 Aylesbury; 1955–60 Teignmouth; 1960–63 Bude; 1963–70 Chichester and Bognor; 1970–74 Alderley Edge and Knutsford.

CASH, Barrie James, 24 Woodside Ave., Rosyth, Dunfermline KY11 2SJ. (0383-413292)–BA(Leics.) DipTh (Bristol). *b. 15 Nov 1943, Hull. m. 23 July 1966: 2d.*
Education: 1954–62 Ashville Coll., Harrogate; 1963–66 Leicester Univ.; 1970–71 Bristol Univ; 1970–72 Wesley, Bristol.
Appointments: 1972–74 Sierra Leone Dt; 1974–76 Woking and Walton; 1976– Edinburgh & Forth.
Connexional Committees: 1979–82 Division of Social Responsibility Board; 1982 Methodist Homes for Aged Board; 1978–81 Rosyth Community Council Chairman.
Special Interests: Counselling (1980– Chairman Fife Marriage Guidance Council), Community care projects. *Hobbies and Recreations:* Music, Rugby, Cricket, Walking, Fishing.

CASLEY, Arthur Frank, The Manse, Torbay Close, Castle Cary, Somerset BA7 7DN. *b. 11 June 1923, St. Thomas, Exeter, Devon. m. 25 July 1953: 2s.*
Education: 1927–33 Lyndhurst Grove Jun. Sch., Cimberwell; 1933–

35 Bexleyheath Central Sch.; 1935–38 Dartford County Technical Coll.; 1950–53 Hartley Victoria.
Appointments: 1949–50 Chatham Garrison and Naval Port Mission; 1953–56 Dewsbury; 1956–60 Ashton-under-Lyne; 1960–64 Swinton-Pendlebury and Salford; 1964–69 Liskeard; 1969–74 Bodmin; 1974–80 Penzance; 1980– Somerset Mission.
Special Interests: Scouting, Commonwealth Period, Christian Education. *Hobbies and Recreations:* Model Making, Walking, Swimming, Crosswords.

CASTLE, Howard Francis Wade, Centre For Christ, Burstone Manor, Bow, Crediton, Devon EX17 6LB. (036-33-261). *b. 31 Jan 1931, Folkestone, Kent. m. 9 Aug 1961: 1d, 1s.*
Education: 1945–47 Kent Coll., Canterbury; 1958–61 Richmond.
Appointments: 1961–66 Tiverton; 1966–75 Ringsash; 1975–78 Northlew; 1978– Minister with outside Appointment, viz., Administrator, Centre for Christ, Conference and Training Centre.
Special Interests: Farming, Building, Railways, Local History, Etymology, Philately, Architecture, World Affairs in relation to Biblical Teaching and Prophesy, Professional and Human Interest in People.

CATHERALL, Noel, 19 Langdale Rd., Ribbleton, Preston, Lancs PR2 6AN. (0772-792473). *b. 9 Dec 1918, Buckley, Clwyd, N. Wales. m. 29 July 1950: 1d.*
Education: 1922–32 St. Matthew's CE; 1948–50 Hartley Victoria.
Appointments: 1946–48 Loftus and Staithes; 1950–56 Thornley; 1956–63 St. Helens and Prescot; 1963–70 Sale; 1970–78 Ormskirk; 1978– Preston (Lune St., and Orchard); 1960 President of Free Church Fed. Council, St. Helens; 1979 Preston; 1979–81 President of Preston & District Christian Endeavours Union.
Special Interests: The continuing contribution Methodism can make in the service of the Kingdom of God. *Hobbies and Recreations:* Clocks, Walking.

CAWTHERA, Thomas F., 24 Ashurst Drive, Goring-by-Sea, Worthing, West Sussex BN12 4SW. (0903-45799). *b. 19 Nov 1924, Bradford, Yorks. m. 19 July 1952: 1d, 1s.*
Education: 1934–39 Priestman Central Sch., Bradford; 1948–50 Hartley Victoria.
Appointments: 1947–50 Stoke-on-Trent (Hanley); 1950–52 Newmarket; 1952–55 Ilkeston Central and Kimberley; 1955–60 Nottingham Central; 1960–64 Leicester East; 1964–69 Leamington; 1969–77 Harrow; 1977 Worthing.
Special Interests: Ecumenical Co-operation. *Hobbies and Recreations:* Music, Photography, Wildlife, Walking.

CHALLENER, Stanley, Crawley, 12 Kelston Gdns., Westbury-on-Trym, Bristol, Avon BS10 5FY. (0272-504601). *b. 1 March 1903, London. m. 1935 (w.): 2d, 2s.*
Education: Ilford County High Sch., Essex; 1927–30 Victoria Park.
Appointments: 1926–27 Leeds West; 1930–39 Kenya Dt.; 1939–52 Leeward Island, Dt., West Indies; 1952–57 Hereford; 1957-62 Nuneaton; 1962–67 Cannock Chase; 1967–70 Wolstanton and Audley.

CHALLONER, Eric, 25 Leek Rd., Cheadle, Stoke-on-Trent ST10 1JE. (0538-75-3467). *b. 27 Feb 1918, Long Lane Farm, Over Peover, Nr. Knutsford, Cheshire. m. 16 Aug 1950: 2s.*
Education: 1930–34 City and County Sch., Chester; 1937 Cheshire Sch. of Agriculture, Reasheath; 1948–50 Handsworth.
Appointments: 1946–48 Ashby and Coalville, 1950–53 Rawtenstall; 1953–59 Whitchurch (Shropshire); 1959–66 Alsager; 1966–73 Alderley Edge and Knutsford; 1973– Cheadle, Staffs.
Hobbies and Recreations: Gardening, Walking.

CHAMBERLAIN, Frank, New Chapter, 16 Lennard Rd., Crediton, Exeter, Devon EX17 2AP. (03632-2005)—Dip Rel (Lond.) 1921. *b. 16 June 1896, West Ealing, London. m. 9 Aug 1922: 1d.*
Education: 1903–06 Beaudesert Boys Sch., Leighton Buzzard; 1906–1912 Dunstable Grammar Sch.; 1913–14 Cliff Coll.; 1919 Didsbury; 1919–21 Handsworth.
Appointments: 1921–24 Attleborough; 1924–26 Southwold & Lowestoft; 1926–29 Dunstable; 1929–33 Holsham; 1933–36 Brentford; 1936-39 Bristol; 1939–46 Bognor Regis; 1946–48 Bournemouth; 1948–53 Tunbridge Wells; 1953–57 Folkestone; 1957–59 Berkhamsted; 1959–65 Sherborne.
Connexional Committees: 1955–56 President, London Wesley Guilds; TocH Chaplain at Horsham, Southborough, Tunbridge Wells.
Local Council Committees: 1929–33 British Legion Chaplain, Horsham; 1940–46 Bognor Regis; 1949–53 Southborough, Tunbridge Wells; 1954–57 Folkestone; 1960–66 Milborne Port, Sherborne; 1962–66 Member of Somerset BL County Committee.
Special Interests: Music, Piano, Conducting Choirs, Hockey and Tennis. *Hobbies and Recreations:* Gardening and Photography.

CHAMBERLAYNE, John Henry, 7 Wickham Ave., Shirley, Croydon CRO 8TZ. (01-656-0742)—BA, BD, MA(Sociology), MTL(Comparative Religion), PhD(Comparative Religion) (Lond.). *b. 6 Feb 1917, South Norwood, London SE25. m. (Wesley Deaconess), 4 Nov 1944: 1d, 2s.*
Education: 1926–36 City of London Sch.; 1937–38 King's Coll., Lond. Univ.; 1944–45 Sch. of Oriental and African Studies, Lond. Univ.; 1939–42 Headingley.
Appointments: 1942–43 South Molton; 1943–44 South East London Mission; 1944–48 Croydon; 1947–48 Chungsiang (Hupeh District); 1948–51 S. Devon Mission; 1951–56 Plymouth (Peverell Park); 1956–60 London (Barry Rd.); 1960–64 Orpington; 1964–65 Emory Univ., (Candler Sch. of Theology); 1965–70 London (Muswell Hill); 1970–75 Tonbridge; 1975–82 London, Whitechapel Mission.
Connexional Committees: 1952–56 Connexional Youth Council; 1966–

82 N.C.H. General Committee. *Council Member:* 1959 Dulwich Free Church Federal Council President; 1956–60 Registrar (Fellowship of the Kingdom); Hospital Chaplaincies: 1952–56 South Brent Hospital; 1956–60 Maudsley Hospital; 1975–82 The London Hospital; 1982 Warlingham Park Hospital. *Publications: People's Religion in China* (PhD Thesis–unpublished); *Man in Society* (Fernley Hartley Lecture, 1966); *The Quest of Faith* (REP, 1969); Monographs in *Numen* (1962–68); Articles in *British Journal of Sociology, London Quarterly, Preacher's Quarterly,* etc. *Special Interests:* History of Religions, The Place of the Family in World Cultures. *Hobbies and Recreations:* Swimming (S. Counties Representative & Surrey), Cycling, Reading, Scouting (N. London County Chaplain 1966–70).

CHAMBERS, Arthur Liddell, 12 Old Castle Rd., Weymouth, Dorset. (0305-785358). *b. 7 Aug 1906, Whitley Bay, Northumberland. m. 25 July 1936.*
Education: 1920–23 The Leys, Cambridge; 1930–34 Didsbury.
Appointments: 1929 Lond. Central Mission; 1934–36 Lond. Mission Poplar; 1937–42 West Wickham; 1942–47 Bristol, Redland; 1947–52 Weston-super-Mare; 1952–58 Poole; 1958–64 Hove; 1964–71 Higham Ferrers.
Special Interests: British and Foreign Bible Society. *Hobbies and Interests:* Bowls.

CHAMBERS, Gordon, 37 Knebworth Rd., Bexhill, East Sussex TN39 4JJ. (0424-216444)–BD. *b. 21 Nov 1936, Worthing, Sussex. m. 19 Aug 1961: 2s.*
Education: 1943–46 Private Tutor, Glenster House, Prep.; 1946–55 Goring Hall, Worthing; 1958–62 Richmond.
Appointments: 1962–64 Yeovil; 1964–71 Eastleigh; 1971–1981 Worthing; 1981– Hastings, Bexhill and Rye.
Connexional Committees: 1967–70 Youth Council.
Hobbies and Recreations: Gardening, Caravanning, Photography, Boating.

CHAMBERS, John Bryan, 33 Dyne Rd., Kilburn, London NW6 7XG. (01-624-3075). *b. 21 April 1945, Wales. m. 19 July 1969: 1d, 1s.*
Education: 1956–60 Belfairs High Sch., Leigh-on-Sea; 1967–68 Cliff Coll.; 1970–73 Queens Coll.
Appointments: 1973–76 Romford; 1976– Lond. Mission (North West).

CHANDLER, Winifred Emily, Whingarth, High Ghyllhead, Moresby Parks, Whitehaven, Cumbria CA28 8UT. *b. 11 April 1920.*
Education: Ampthill Rd. Sch., Bedford; Wesley Deaconess Coll., Ilkley.
Appointments: 1974–77 Worksop and Kiveton; 1977–82 Wrexham.
Hobbies and Recreations: Gardening.

CHANT, Albert William, 202 Furlong Rd., Goldthorpe, Rotherham S63 9PR. (0709–893209). *b. 25 Feb 1920, Milborne Port, Somerset. m. 11 Aug 1951: 1s.*
Education: 1925–31 Milborne Port Council Sch.; 1931–37 Yeovil Sch.; 1947–50 Richmond.
Appointments: 1945–46 Newbury; 1946–47 Llandrindod Wells; 1950–51 Leominster; 1951–57 Bodmin; 1957–60 Winsford; 1960–65 Leigh; 1965–71 Sheffield North East; 1971–76 Derby East; 1976–81 Manchester (Droylsden and Openshaw); 1981– Wath and Mexborough.

CHANTLER, John Brian, 101 Higher Ainsworth Rd., Radcliffe, Manchester M26 0JJ. (061-764-1331)–MA(Cantab.). *b. 10 Oct 1934, Dunham Massey, Cheshire. m. 19 April 1965: 1d.*
Education: 1946–53 Altrincham County Grammar Sch. for Boys; 1953–56 Fitzwilliam Coll., Cambridge; 1956–60 Didsbury, Bristol.
Appointments: 1960–61 Birkenhead; 1961–69 Bury; 1969–77 Chester; 1977– Radcliffe.
Local Council Committees: 1977– Chairman of Governors, Radcliffe Wesley controlled Prim. Sch.
Special Interests: History, Music.
Hobbies and Recreations: Football (1953–69 Referee), Cricket (Member Lancs. Cricket Club since 1946), Crown Green Bowls.

CHAPMAN, Derek Robert, 14 Crane Drive, Verwood, Wimborne, Dorset BH21 6QB. (0202-822212). *b. 20 May 1934, Newcastle-upon-Tyne. m. 29 Aug 1959: 1d, 1s.*
Education: 1939–45 Walkergate; 1945–48 Heaton Grammar Sch.; 1948–50 Gosforth Grammar Sch.; 1956–60 Headingley.
Appointments: 1960–65 Dewsbury; 1965–68 Blackpool (North); 1968–72 Stoke-on-Trent (Hanley Trinity); 1972–77 Guernsey (Victoria) and Sark; 1977– Wimborne.
Connexional Committees: 1975–77 Education and Youth; 1979– Ministries.
Hobbies and Recreations: Gardening, Photography.

CHAPMAN, Eric George Monk, Pantiles, 89 Church Rd., Ferndown, Dorset BH22 9ET. (0202-873441)–BD(Lond.). *b. 12 Nov 1908, Stelling Minnis, nr Canterbury, Kent. m. 3 Aug 1937: 2s.*
Education: 1913–18 Bossingham Sch., Stelling Minnis (CE); 1918-22 Craven Park, Clapton, Lond. E4; 1922–25 Sch. of Engineering and Navigation, Poplar; 1931–34 Lond. Univ.; 1931–34 Richmond.
Appointments: 1930–31 S. Hants Mission; 1931–34 Richmond Coll.; 1934–35 London, Tottenham; 1935–37 London, Enfield; 1937–41 Newmarket Mission; 1941–46 Chaplain HMF; 1946–50 High Wycombe; 1950–55 London, Brixton Hill; 1954–60 London, Highgate; 1960–66 Romford.
Publications: Lectures too numerous to recall details, from 1966-73.
Special Interests: Reading, Sport, Collecting, in a modest way, Inexpensive Antiques. *Hobbies and Recreations:* Gardening and Home Decorating, plus Maintenance of Car.

CHAPMAN, John Bailey, 7 The Paddocks, London Rd., Newark, Notts NG24 1SS. (0636-71505). *b. 13 Dec 1909, Basingstoke, Hants. m. 11 Aug 1938: 2s.*
Education: 1920–26 Magnus Grammar Sch., Newark, Notts.; 1932–35 Headingley.
Appointments: 1931–32 Doncaster; 1935–36 President's List; 1936–38 Becoles and Loddon; 1938–40 Marlborough; 1940–44 Wolverton; 1944–47 Uttoxeter; 1947–50 Hartlepools; 1950–54 Dudley; 1954–57 Redditch; 1957–62 Holbeach; 1962–68 Ripley; 1968–74 Ashbourne.
Special Interests: English Literature. *Hobbies and Recreations:* Gardening, Bowls, as spectator—Cricket, Football, Reading.

CHAPMAN, Philip Ingram, 12 Pollards Hill East, Norbury, London SW16 4UT. (01-764-1775)– BA(Birmingham) BSc(Bristol). *b. 3 Oct 1938, Hornchurch, Essex. m. 28 July 1962: 3s.*
Education: 1947–54 Westcliff HS; 1954–57 Bristol Univ.; 1960–63 Birmingham Univ.; 1960–63 Handsworth.
Appointments: 1963–64 Miss. Training; 1964–65 Abidjan; 1965–70 Adzope; 1970–71 Grand Bassam; 1971–78 San Pedro Mission; 1978– Streatham and Dulwich.
Special Interests: Community Work, Overseas Missions. *Hobbies and Recreations:* Computers, Gardening.

CHAPMAN, William Robert, Albert Cottage, Pin Mill, Ipswich, Suffolk IP9 1JT. MC. *b. 3 Nov 1893, Easington Lane, County Durham. m. 29 June 1921 (w.): 1d., 1s(d).*
Education: 1898–1907 Easington Lane, Elem.; 1915, 1919–1921 Hartley Victoria.
Appointments: 1921–24 Leeds III; 1924–27 Barnsley II; 1923–30 Woodfalls; 1930–35 Jersey (Aquila Rd.); 1935–37 Gravesend and Dartford; 1937–39 Sheringham; 1939–45 Chaplain HMF; 1945–50 Ramsgate; 1950–54 Southern Rhodesia Dt.
Local Council Committees: 1932–35 Jersey Poor Law Commission.
Publications: 1930–45 Church and Army Magazine Articles; 1930–35 Journalism.
Special Interests: Philosophy and Poetry. *Hobbies and Recreations:* Landscape and Portrait Painting.

CHARITY, Harold William, 19 Ascot Close, Borough Green, Sevenoaks, Kent TN15 8HL. (0732-882201). *b. 15 June 1899, Grantham, Lincolnshire. m. 20 July 1929: 1d., 2s.*
Education: 1905–19 CE Day Sch.; 1923–24 Victoria and Hartley.
Appointments: 1922–25 Camelford and Wadebridge; 1925–26 Chirk; 1926–27 South Yorkshire Mission; 1927–28 Blackburn; 1928–29 Oldham (King St.); 1929–32 Bolton (Hanover); 1932–34 Downham Market; 1934–38 Kent Mission; 1938–40 London (Broomwood); 1940–43 Doncaster (Priory Place); 1943–46 Hull North; 1946–50 Hebden Bridge; 1950–53 Oldham, Manchester St.; 1953–56 Launceston; 1956–59 Malmesbury; 1959–64 Swaffham.
Publications: For Those Who Are Ill, a book of prayers in orders of worship for special occasions, some of which have been published by the Epworth Press and others published locally, some in local newspapers or magazines (1920).
Special Interests: English Literature and Writing, some articles published in the Fellowship of the Kingdom Bulletin, others in Methodist magazines and newspapers. *Hobbies and Recreations:* Motoring, Walking, Scouting.

CHARLTON, Jack, 5 Avonlea Close, Ilkeston, Derbyshire DE7 5BL. (0602-326042). *b. 25 May 1912, Seacombe, Wallasey, Cheshire. m. 8 Sept 1936: 1d., 1s.*
Education: 1945–47 Hartley Victoria.
Appointments: 1947–50 Ripley; 1950–57 Burton-on-Trent; 1957–64 Ashby-de-la-Zouch; 1964–1974 South Derbyshire; 1974–1977 Ilkeston.
Hobbies and Recreations: Organs, Railways.

CHARLTON, Ronald Stanley, 56 Greenways, Standish, Wigan WN6 0AF. (0257-421154). *b. 30 Oct 1922, Worsley, Manchester. m. 11 Aug 1951: 2d.*
Education: Little Hulton East Council Sch.; Walkden Moor Methodist Sch.; Farnworth Grammar Sch.; 1946–47, 1949–51 Hartley Victoria; 1947–49 Wesley, Headingley.
Appointments: 1945–46 Spilsby; 1946–47, 1949-51 Manchester and Salford Mission; 1951–55 Worksop; 1955–58 Bolton Mission; 1958–68 Rochdale (South); 1968– Wigan Mission.
Connexional Committees: 1962–68 Social Responsibility; 1968– Property Board.
Special Interests: Ecumenical Cooperation and Church Unit, Health and Healing, Pastoral Counselling, Samaritan Work. *Hobbies and Recreations:* Golf, Bowls, Billiards, Walking (with dog).

CHATTERS, Leonard Edwin, 1 Greaves Lane, Stannington, Sheffield, S. Yorks S6 6BB. (0742-344610) *b. 15 Oct 1918, West Mersea, Colchester, Essex. m. 26 May 1945: 2d.*
Education: 1929–34 Colchester Royal Grammar Sch.; 1945–47 Hartley Victoria.
Appointments: 1947–50 Spalding; 1950–53 Halifax North; 1953–58 Manningtree and Harwich; 1958–63 Beccles, Loddon and Bungay; 1963–70 March; 1970–76 Raunds; 1976–80 Scunthorpe; 1980– Sheffield, Carver St.
Hobbies and Recreations: Gardening, Word Puzzles.

CHATTERTON, Geoffrey Brant, St John's Manse, 4 Seaton Rd., Arbroath, Angus DD11 5DX. (0241 72021) *b. 8 Aug 1913, Brighouse, Yorks.*
Education: 1925–30 Ashville Coll., Harrogate.
Appointments: 1973–78 Newcastle upon Tyne West; 1978–81 Dumfries.
Special Interests. TOC.H. *Hobbies and Recreations:* Gardening.

CHEATER, Kenneth, 21 Woodstock Rd., Witney, Oxon OX8 6EB. (0993-3178) *b. 9 July 1917, Bournemouth.*

m. 2d., 3s.
Education: 1946–48 Headingley.
Appointments: 1948–50 Stanley; 1950–54 Holsworthy; 1954–58 Tavistock; 1958–65 Poole; 1965–72 Kineton; 1972–79 Belper; 1979– Witney and Farringdon.
Hobbies and Recreations: Watercolour Painting, Gardening.

CHEESEMAN, Christopher John, The Manse, Northlew, Okehampton, Devon EX20 3BP. (040-922-252) *b. 22 July 1947, Carshalton, Surrey. m. 6 Sept. 1969: 1d., 1s.*
Education: 1952–58 Collingwood Prep. Sch.; 1958–64 Wallington Independent Grammar Sch.; 1965–67 Kingsway Coll.; 1971–74 YMCA National Coll./N.E. Lond. Poly.; 1980–82 Queens.
Appointments: 1982– Northlew.
Special Interests: MAYC Division of Education and Youth, Ministerial Training. *Hobbies and Recreations:* Cricket, Football, Music.

CHEFFINGS, Ronald, 25 Barrow Lane, Hessle, North Humberside HU13 0PJ. (0482-649142)–BD(Lond.) *b. 27 Dec 1922, Louth, Lincolnshire. m. 1951: 1d., 1s.*
Education: 1934–41 King Edward VI Grammar Sch., Louth; 1947–50 Richmond.
Appointments: 1946–47 Spilsby; 1951–55 Ivory Coast Dt; 1955–62 Dahomey-Benin Dt; 1962–69 Bridlington; 1969–76 Easingwold and York North; 1976– Hull West; Central Cttee. (Overseas Div.).
Connexional Committees: 1966–73 Central Cttee. (Overseas Div.).
Special Interests: Industrial Society, Stewardship. *Hobbies and Recreations:* French Language, Photography.

CHESTER, Michael Arthur, 11 Broad St., Syston, Leicester LE7 8GH. (0533-607626)–BA(Bristol), STM(Saskatchewan) *b. 30 Dec 1945, Southall, Middlesex. m. 18 July 1970: 1d., 1s.*
Education: 1957–63 St Clement Dane's Grammar Sch.; 1968–71 Univ. of Bristol; 1971–72 St Andrew's Coll., Univ. of Saskatchewan (Canada); 1972–73 Univ. of Oxford; 1968–71 Wesley, Bristol.
Appointments: 1973–78 Middlesbrough and Eston; 1978– Leicester (North).
Hobbies and Recreations: Gardening and Animal Husbandry, Badminton, Canal-Boating, Reading.

CHESWORTH, Clifford Wharmby, 17 Belgrave Ave., Penwortham, Preston PR1 0BH. (0772-745627) *b. 3 June 1917, Hawarden, North Wales. m. 28 April 1945: 3s.*
Education: 1927–29 Brampton Secondary Sch.; 1929–32 Colne Grammar Sch.; 1939–41 Hartley Victoria.
Appointments: 1937–38 Nantwich and Burland; 1938–39 Hyde (Cheshire); 1941–42 Hadleigh; 1942–43 Pateley Bridge; 1943–46 Chaplain HMF; 1946-51 Dewsbury; 1951–56 Preston (Lune St); 1956–63 St Annes; 1962–74 Preston Trinity; 1974–78 Wigan; 1978–81 Chorley.
Connexional Committees: 1965–81 Church Membership.
Special Interests: Theology. *Hobbies and Recreations:* Tennis, Table Tennis, Travel, Reading, Writing, Lecturing.

CHESWORTH, Stanley King, 37 Long Buftlers, Harpenden, Hertfordshire AL5 1JF. (05827-60567) *b. 21 Feb 1926, Brampton, Cumbria. m. 15 Jan 1955: 1d., 1s.*
Education: 1948–50 Hartley Victoria.
Appointments: 1945 National Service; 1946–48 London, Poplar and Bow Mission; 1950–52 Barton on Humber; 1952–57 Blackpool (South); 1957–62 Morecambe and Heysham; 1962–69 Lytham St Annes; 1969–74 Birmingham (Elmdon); 1974–80 Harpenden; 1980 Chairman, London N.W. District.

CHILDE, Donald Braithwaite, 74 Filsham Rd., St. Leonards-on-Sea, E. Sussex TN38 0PG. (0424-422429) *b. 2 Nov 1901, Drighlington, Nr. Bradford, West Yorkshire. m. 25 Oct 1932: 3d.*
Education: Morley Grammar Sch.; 1927–30 Handsworth.
Appointments: 1926 Reserve List; 1927–30 Handsworth; 1930–49 S. China District; 1949–65 Miss. Soc.; 1965–66 Miss. Soc.
Connexional Committees: 1952–59 Stationing Committee; 1966–69 (Overseas) Missionary Committee.
Publications: Various Reports through the MMS on Secretarial Visits Overseas: Report on Secretarial Visit to Burma, North India and Hong Kong (with Mrs. R. A. Ladlay), Nov. 1952 April 1953; *China Now* (1955); *Asia Survey,* Report on Secretarial Tour of S.E. Asia, Burma and Hong Kong, Aug. 1957 to April 1958; Report on Secretarial Visit to The Church of South India, Dec. 1959 to April 1960; Report on Secretarial Visit to Ceylon, *Ceylon Crucible,* 1960.

CHILDS, John, Rehoboth, King Street, Mortimer, Reading, Berks RG7 3RS. (0734-332952) *b. 31 Mar 1916, Hackney, London. m. 14 Sept 1940: 2d.*
Education: London Schs.
Appointments: 1976–79 Camelford and Wadebridge.
Hobbies and Recreations: Gardening, Woodwork, Reading.

CHILDS, Leonard Arthur, 25 Sapcote Drive, Melton Mowbay, Leicester LE13 1HG. (0664-69888) *b. 3 Feb 1915, Reading, Berkshire. m. 27 Aug 1938: 1s.*
Education: 1920–34 Elem.
Appointments: 1950–51 Shetland; 1951–55 North Scotland; 1955–61 Worksop; 1961–63 Mansfield; 1963–64 Denby Dale; 1964–70 Camberley; 1970–73 Ipswich; 1973–76 Liskeard/Looe; 1976–80 Hunts Mission.
Hobbies and Recreations: Tapestry, Reading, Marquetry, Follow most sports–do not participate, DIY.

CHILVERS, Philip Adrian, 2 The Close, Grimsby, South Humberside DN34 4PE. (0472-54553) *b. 9 Jan 1948, Barnsley, South Yorks. m. 11 Sept 1971.*
Education: 1953–59 Agnes Rd. Inf./Jun. Sch., Barnsley; 1959–63 Racecommon Rd., Secondary Sch.; Queens Coll. *Appointments:* 1977–82 Louth; 1982– Grimsby West.
Connexional Committees: 1981– Divisional Board of Youth and

Education.
Special Interests: Music–I am a keen pianist and choir singer. *Hobbies and Recreations:* Walking, Cycling, Model Railways.

CHISNALL, Gordon, 37 Glen Ave., Blackley, Manchester M9 1EU. (061-205-3285)—Dip Theol.(Lond.) *b. 30 June 1941, Nelson, Lancs. m. 26 Aug 1967: 2s.*
Education: 1952–55 Keighley Grammar; 1955–57 Nelson Grammar; 1964–68 Hartley Victoria.
Appointments: 1968–71 Newcastle-u-Lyme; 1971–76 Swinton; 1976–79 Burnley; 1979– Manchester (North) and Middleton.
Connexional Committees: 1973–76 Education and Youth.
Hobbies and Recreations: Walking, Squash.

CHORLEY, Kenneth Edmund, 8 Julian Rd., Ludlow, Shropshire SY8 1HA. (0584-2831) *b. 14 Feb 1934, Southampton. m. 1958: 2d., 1s.*
Education: Southamptom Technical Coll.; 1955–58 Richmond.
Appointments: 1958–64 South India Church; 1964–69 West Indies Dt; 1969–73 Minsterley; 1973–78 Dudley.

CHURCHILL, Ronald, George, Hebden Lodge, Dacre Banks, Harrogate, N. Yorks HG3 4EW. (0423-780357) *b. 22 June 1916, Evesham. m. 24 Jan 1942: 1d.*
Education: Badse County Sch.
Appointments: 1974– Pateley Bridge.
Local Council Committees: 1969–74 Chairman Badsey Parish Council; 1968 74 Chairman Badsey County Jun. Sch.
Hobbies and Recreations: Photography.

CLAPP, Gerald John, 19 Sunset Heights, Barnstaple, Devon EX32 8DH. (0271-39776)—BD (Lond.) *b. 12 June 1925, Exmouth. m. 25 July 1953: 1d., 1s.*
Education: 1930–36 Lympstone Sch., (Prim.); 1936–41 Exmouth Grammar Sch.; 1949–52 Didsbury, Bristol. *Appointments:* 1947–49 Buckingham and Brackley; 1952–53 Tiverton; 1953–58 Barnstaple; 1958-65 Newton Abbot; 1965–72 Bristol Frome Valley; 1972–80 Stafford; 1980– Barnstaple.
Connexional Committees: 1957–61 Local Preachers.
Hobbies and Recreations: Sailing, Walking.

CLARK, Charles Arthur, 100 Glenfield Frith Drive, Glenfield, Leicester LE3 8PS. (0533-872200)—BD (Lond.). *b. 13 Sept 1913, Swadlincote, S. Derbys. m. 23 Dec 1944: 1d., 1s.*
Education: Burton on Trent Grammar Sch.; 1938–40 Didsbury; 1940–42 Hartley Victoria.
Appointments: 1942–48 Derby South; 1943–46 Chaplain HMF; 1948–54 Bath; 1954–58 Bebington; 1958–64 Southport North; 1964–70 Birmingham SW; 1970–73 Cardiff Wesley; 1973–80 Leicester Central; 1980 President, Leicester Free Church Federal Council; 1964–70, 1973–82 Free Church Hospital Chaplain. *Connexional Committees:* 1951–79 Local Preachers; 1946–58 Youth; 1966–70 Church Membership. *Publications: Introducing the Old Testament* (Co-Author) (1974).
Special Interests: Training Local Preachers. *Hobbies and Recreations:* Gardening.

CLARK, David Nelson, 26 St. Floras Rd., Littlehampton, W. Sussex BN17 6BB. (090-64-3506) *b. 24 April 1936, Norwich. m. 29 Aug 1959: 3d., 1s.*
Education: 1948–53 City of Norwich; 1957–60 Richmond. *Appointments:* 1960–63 Minehead and Dunster; 1963–67 Bolton (Bridge St.); 1967–76 Ipswich; 1976– Chichester and Bognor.
Special Interests: Buildings. *Hobbies and Recreations:* DIY, Gardening.

CLARK, Geoffrey Laurence, 31 Victoria Ave., Cheadle Hulme, Cheshire SK8 5DJ. (061-485-1160) *b. 11 Dec 1936, Hull.* d. 22.05.2007
Education: 1955–56 Cliff Coll.; 1957–61 Wesley Coll., Leeds.
Appointments: 1961–66 Bolton (Farnworth); 1966–72 Manchester and Salford Mission; 1972–81 Newcastle upon Tyne (Brunswick and Central); 1981– Bramhall.

CLARK, John Reginald, 243 Wigan Rd., Deane, Bolton. (0204-62519)—BA (Hull), BD (Manchester). *b. 15 March 1940, Macclesfield, Cheshire. m. 14 Aug 1971.*
Education: 1944–49 Beech Lane Prim. (CE) Sch., Macclesfield, Cheshire; 1949–53 Beech Hall Preparatory Sch.; 1953–58 Rydal School, Colwyn Bay, North Wales; 1958–61 Univ. of Hull; 1961–63 Univ. of Manchester; 1976–79 Hartley Victoria.
Appointments: 1979–81 Preston (Orchard and Lune St.); 1981– Bolton.

CLARK, Joseph Alan, 30 Guisborough Rd, Great Ayron, Middlesbrough, Cleveland TS9 6ND. (0642-722437)—BA. *m. 2d.*
Education: 1972–75 Manchester Univ.; 1971–75 Hartley Victoria.
Appointments: 1975– Stokesley.

CLARK, Malcolm, 4 High Rd., Rayleigh, Essex SS6 7AA. (0268-774189) *b. 28 Jan 1935, Letchworth Garden City, Hertfordshire. m. 1 July 1961: 2d.*
Education: 1946–51 Letchworth Grammar Sch.; 1958–61 Handsworth.
Appointments: 1961–64 Driffield; 1964–70 King's Lynn; 1970-78 Leighton Buzzard; 1978– Leigh-on-Sea.

CLARKE, Charles Joseph, 35 Kimberley Rd., Little Wakering, Southend-on-Sea, Essex SS3 0JP. *b. 22 March 1903, Hawkwell, Essex. m. 11 June 1964: 2s.*
Education: Barling Sch.; 1927–30 Hartley Victoria. *Appointments:* 1925–27 Dover; 1930–32 Chelmsford; 1932–36 Kings Lynn; 1936–43 Bradford; 1943–48 Hull; 1948–52 Newmarket Miss., 1952–56 Southampton; 1956–61 Cowes; 1961–64 Horsbury; 1964–67 Ely.
Publications: Pattern of Revival (1964); *Pioneers of Revival* (1970); *Worldwide Revival* (1980).

Special Interests: History of Revivals. *Hobbies and Recreations:* Gardening and Painting.

CLARKE, David Frederick, 21 Ladbrook Rd., Coventry CV5 7JW. (0203-464603)–BA MPhil. *b. 20 April 1933, Drybeck, Appleby, Westmorland. m. 8 Aug 1959: 1d., 2s.*
Education: 1939–44 Oakbeck; 1944–52 Appleby; 1955–58 Leeds; 1955–59 Headingley. *Appointments:* 1959–61 Pateley Bridge; 1961–65 Bacup; 1965–70 Lancaster; 1970–75 Coalville; 1975–81 Coventry; 1981–82 Coventry Mission; 1982– Permission to Study.
Council Member: Coventry Free Church FC. *Publications:* PWHS Article on Benjamin Ingham (1972 Dec.); Catherine Holme Methodist Church Centenary Booklet.
Special Interests: Methodism in the Upper Eden Valley. *Hobbies and Recreations:* Music, Photography.

CLARKE, Ernest Alexander, 61 Dunkeld Ave., Filton, Bristol BS12 7RQ. (0272-692036) *b. 12 Mar 1924, Brixton, London. m. 6 Aug 1953: 3s.*
Education: 1930–35 The Ecclesbourne Sch., Thornton Heath; 1935–39 John Ruskin Sch., Croydon; 1940–41 Pitmans College, Croydon; 1950–53 Didsbury, Bristol.
Appointments: 1949–50 Belper; 1950–53 Didsbury; 1953–55 Missionary Society; 1955–59 New Mills; 1959–64 Wolverton and Bletchley; 1964–75 Bristol (South); 1975– Bristol (North).
Connexional Committees: 1967–71 Youth Department; 1975– John Wesley's Chapel, The New Room, Bristol; 1981– Methodist Publishing House.
Special Interests: Ecumenical Affairs. *Hobbies and Recreations:* Philately and Conjuring.

CLARKE, Frederick Stuart, 18 Woodland View, Southwell, Nottinghamshire NG25 0AG. (0636-812166)–MA (Oxon.), BA (Cantab.). *b. 2 Sept 1930, Doncaster. m. 16 Aug 1958: 2d., 1s.*
Education: 1936–41 Newbold CE Inf./Jun., Chesterfield; 1941–48 Chesterfield Grammar Sch.; 1950–53 Worcester Coll., Oxford; 1977–81 Nottingham Univ. (Part Time); 1953–56 Wesley House, Cambridge. *Appointments:* 1956–58 Carlisle; 1958–62 Nottingham North; 1962–66 Glasgow (Cathcarr Rd., and Pollokshaws); 1966–72 Stoke-on-Trent (Tunstall); 1972–77 Bradford (Great Horton); 1977– Newark. *Publications:* The Theology of Arminius article, *London Quarterly and Holborn Review,* 1960; Gave paper on John Wesley's Doctrine of Justification, another on Arminius's View of Calvin, Durham 1980, printed in *Evangelical Quarterly,* Jan-Mar, 1982.
Special Interests: Historical Theology, especially the Doctrine of Predestination. *Hobbies and Recreations:* Walking.

CLARKE, George Doubleday, 25 Wells Rd., Folkestone, Kent CT19 4PW. (0303-75697) *b. 2 May 1911, Swallowrest, Sheffield. m. 1 Aug 1938: 1s.*
Education: Elementary Sch.; 1932–33 Cliff Coll.; 1945–46 Handsworth. *Appointments:* 1945–46 Ashby-de-la-Zouch; 1946–47 Handsworth Coll.; 1947–48 Wetton and Longnor; 1948–52 Ashby-de-la-Zouch, St. John's; 1952–58 Burton-on-Trent, Trinity; 1958–63 Leicester West; 1963-68 Leicester South; 1968–71 Manchester, South East; 1971–77 Mansfield, Bridge St.
Connexional Committees: Youth and Property.

CLARKE, Harold Stockley, 29 Victoria Park St., Whiteinch, Glasgow G14 9QA. (041-959-1548) *b. 29 Oct 1940, Hexham, Northumberland. m. 1 Sept 1962: 1d., 1s.*
Education: 1945–54 Westerhope County Prim.; 1954–1955 Wallbottle County Secondary; 1955–1961 Rutherford Coll. of Technology; 1962 Gateshead Technical; 1963–67 Headingley (1966–67 William Temple, Rugby). *Appointments:* 1967–73 Airdrie Coatbridge and Armadale; 1973–78 Glasgow West; 1978– Glasgow West Industrial Chaplain.
Connexional Committees: 1976–82 Board of Education and Youth; 1982– Connexional Church in Industry Cttee. *Publications: Ministering to the Unemployed* (Home Missions 1981).
Special Interests: Effects of Redundancy, Role of Work in Society, Vehicle Building. *Hobbies and Recreations:* Assn. Football, Wine Making.

CLARKE, John Edward, 21 Mount Pleasant, Stockton, Rugby, Warks. CV23 8JW. (092-681-7092)–BD (Lond.) *b. 20 March 1934, Wigston, Leicester. m. 14 Oct 1960: 2s.*
Education: 1945–50 Wyggeston Boys Grammar Sch., Leicester; 1958–59 St. Andrews Coll., Selly Oak; 1955–58 Didsbury, Bristol.
Appointments: 1959–69 Kenya District; 1969–76 Leominster, Presteigne and Kingston; 1976–81 Ormskirk; 1981– Leamington Spa.
Connexional Committees: 1963– Church in Rural Life. *Publications: Mission in Rural Communities* (I&M Publications 1980).
Special Interests: Ministry, Mission of the Church in Rural Areas. *Hobbies and Recreations:* Walking, Gardening, Music, Sport, Reading.

CLARKE, Leslie Roy, 66 High View Ave., Grays, Essex RM17 6RX. (0375-72924) *m.*
Education: 1946–48 Headingley.
Appointments: 1945–46 Nat. Service; 1948 Leone Dt, West Africa; 1953–56 Shooters Hill; 1956–61 Burnley, Fulledge; 1961–66 Colchester; 1966–69 Southend-on-Sea; 1969–76 Walthamstow and Chingford; 1976 Grays.
Connexional Committees: 1974–80 Overseas Missions.

CLARKE, Philip Allan, 69 Lowther St., Penrith, Cumbria CA11 7UF. (0768-62476)–MA (Dunelm), BA (Wales), BA (Cantab.). *b. 12 Feb 1954, Manchester. m. 11 Aug 1979.*
Education: 1965–67 Ducie High Sch., Manchester; 1967–70 Fulwood High Sch., Preston; 1970–72 Hutton Grammar Sch., Preston; 1972–75 St Davids Univ. Coll., Lampeter; 1975–

76 St Chad's Coll., Univ. of Durham; 1977–79 Fitzwilliam Coll., Cambridge; 1977–80 Wesley House. *Appointments:* 1980–83 Penrith. *Publications: New Wine, New Wineskins* (Study Pamphlet 1982); *Historical Geography of Settlement in Ancient Palestine* (Thesis 1976). *Special Interests:* Evangelism, Youth Work. *Hobbies and Recreations:* Sport, Fell Walking, Travel, Art, Photography.

CLARKE, Richard James, 34 Sycamore Drive, Banbury, Oxon OX16 9HF. (0295-62784)–BA. *12 Oct 1950, Bournemouth, Dorset. m. 17 July 1971: 1d., 1s.* *Education:* 1962–69 Blandford Grammar Sch., Blandford Forum, Dorset; 1969–72 Nottingham Univ.; 1972–75 Wesley, Bristol. *Appointments:* 1975–78 Skipton; 1978–79 Woodhouse Grove; 1979– Banbury.

CLARKSON, David A, 39 Brentwood Ave., Crosby, Liverpool L23 2UY. (051-924-4472)–MA. *m. 2d., 1s.* *Education:* Beverley Grammar Sch.; Leeds Univ.; Cambridge Univ.; 1952–53 Wesley House. *Appointments:* 1953–57 Banbury; 1957–64 Birmingham Mission; 1964–67 Birmingham Elmdon; 1967–74 Shipley; 1974–81 Liverpool South; 1981– Crosby, Liverpool. *Connexional Committees:* Connexional Property Board.

CLAY, Graham Charles, Park House, Queen St., Barrowford, Nelson, Lancs BB9 6HU. (0282-64500) *b. 5 June 1953, Cardiff. m. 6 Sept 1975: 3s.* *Education:* 1958–64 Marlborough Rd. Prim. and Jun. Sch.; 1964–70 Ty Celyn Sec. Mod.; 1974–75 Cliff Coll.; 1976–80 Wesley Coll., Bristol. *Appointments:* 1980– Nelson. *Special Interests:* Printing and Bookbinding. *Hobbies and Recreations:* Sport and Philately.

CLAY, John Arnold, 41 Tudor Rd., Hampton, Middlesex TW12 2NG. (01-979-4174) *b. 5 Jan 1947, Wisbech, Cambridgeshire. m. 11 Aug 1973: 1 d., 1s.* *Education:* 1952–55 St. Mary's Inf. Sch., Peterborough; 1955–56 Eastholme Jun. Sch., Peterborough; 1956–58 Walnut Tree Ave. Jun. Sch., Cambridge; 1958–63 Coleridge Sch., Cambridge; 1969–71 Cliff Coll.; 1971–75 Wesley, Bristol. *Appointments:* 1975–77 Camborne; 1977–82 Telford North; 1982– Teddington. *Publications: What is the Lord's Supper* (1979). *Special Interests:* Evangelism and Preaching. *Hobbies and Recreations:* Railways, Swimming.

CLAYTON, John Arthur, 29 Drury Lane, Dore, Sheffield S17 3GG. (0742-367392) *b. 19 Sept 1912, Bentley, Doncaster. m. 29 July 1939.* *Education:* 1933–36 Didsbury. *Appointments:* 1932–33 Daventry; 1936–39 Birkenhead; 1939–42 Liverpool (Grove St. and Woolton); 1942–44 Ellesmere Port; 1944–47 Sunderland West; 1947–52 Sheffield NE; 1952–57 Stockport (Tiviot Dale); 1957–62 Leicester (West); 1962–69 Sheffield (Ecclesall); 1969–74 Torquay; 1974–79 Sheffield (Brunswick). *Special Interests:* Art History, Music. *Hobbies and Recreations:* Painting, Fell Walking.

CLAYTON, Thomas Stanley, The Manse, Ferrand Lane, Gomersal, West Yorks BD19 4DA. (0274-873859) *b. 20 Jan 1922, Keighley, West Yorkshire. m. 9 Aug 1950: 1d., 2s.* *Education:* Keighley Boys' Grammar Sch.; Keighley Technical Coll.; 1946–48 Headingley. *Appointments:* 1948–50 Coatbridge and Airdrie; 1950–51 Edinburgh (Nicholson Square); 1951–54 Ilkley; 1954-57 London, Leytonstone and Forest Gate; 1957–62 Sheffield (Norfolk); 1962–67 Bradford (Manningham); 1967–74 Doncaster; 1974–81 Bradford (Gt. Horton); 1981– Birstall and Birkenshaw. *Connexional Committees:* 1975–77 Property Board.

CLEAVER, Horace, 8 Abbey Gate, Kirkhill, Morpeth, Northumberland NE61 2XJ. (0670-514585)–BD (Lond.). *b. 1903.* *Education:* 1914–20 Wyggeston Grammar Sch., Leicester; 1923–25 Victoria Park. *Appointments:* 1921–26 Barnstaple; 1926–27 North Shields; 1928–33 Sunderland South; 1933–38 Newcastle upon Tyne; 1938–42 Blackpool North; 1942–44 Bradford, Shipley; 1944–48 Manchester, Leicester Rd.; 1948–54 Gloucester; 1954–56 Bristol Redland; 1956–62 Middlesbrough; 1962– Penrith. *Connexional Committees:* 1943–58 Local Preacher Committee. *Publications: God Spake these Words* (1933); *An Approach to the Old Testament* (1955); *God makes History* (1946).

CLEMENTS, Robert Reginald, 33 Forest Rd., Heswall, Wirral, Merseyside L60 5SN. (051-342-6675)–MBE. *b. 27 March 1909, Leicester. m. Lyall, 15 April 1946: 1d.* *Education:* 1920–25 Alderman Newton's Boy's Sch., Leicester; 1932–35 Hartley Victoria. *Appointments:* 1935–6 President's List; 1936–38 Sunday School Dept.; 1938–40 Southend; 1940–47 Chaplain RAF; 1947–53 Portsmouth and Southsea; 1953–60 Birmingham (Moseley Rd. and Sparkhill); 1960–67 Salisbury; 1967–75 Coventry; 1975–79 Hoylake and West Kirby. *Connexional Committees:* 1950–68 Youth Council; 1969–75 Home Missions. *Special Interests:* Work of the Bible Lands Soc.–Member of Exec. Middle East Affairs; *Hobbies and Recreations:* Music, Photography, Gardens.

CLEMENTS, Ronald William, Maison Binet, Gorey Village, Jersey, Channel Islands. (0534-54290). *Appointments:* 1957–60 Derby South; 1960–65 Buckfastleigh; 1965–70 Camborne; 1970–77 Jersey.

CLIFF, Frank Alan, 13 Spring Rd., Wrexham, Clwyd LL11 2LU. (0978-261006)–MA (Oxon), MA (Cantab.), Dip Theol (Oxon). *b. 30 Jan 1936,*

Morecambe. m. 16 July 1960: 2d., 2s.
Education: 1944–54 Lancaster Royal Grammar Sch.; 1954–58 Oxford; 1958–60 Cambridge; 1958–60 Wesley House. *Appointments:* 1960–65 Great Yarmouth and Gorleston; 1965–74 Edinburgh Mission; 1974– Wrexham.
Connexional Committees: 1977–80 Home Mission Division.
Hobbies and Recreations: Railway Enthusiast.

CLIFFORD, Fredrick William Homantin, 5 Hop Row, Haddenham, Cambs. (0353-740663) *b. 5 Jan 1917, West Hartlepool, Co. Durham. m. 7 April 1945: 1s.*
Education: Elem. up to Age of 14; Adult Education Coll. and Battersea Poly.; 1939–40 Handsworth; 1940–41 Richmond. *Appointments:* 1941–46 London SE Mission; 1946–51 Darlington; 1951–56 Sevenoaks; 1956–61 Middlesbrough; 1961–67 Wimbledon; 1967–74 Bromley; 1974–82 London, Finsbury Park and Southgate.
Connexional Committees: 1969–71 Connexional Candidates; 1970–82 Healing and Latterly Healing Pastoral; 1975–Present time NCH; 1957–75 Correspondence Secretary (Conference); Further Training Courses under the Dir. of Ministries.
Local Council Committees: 1962–66 Boards of Management and Governors—Wimbledon Education Committee.
Special Interests: Counselling—Marriage, Family and Psycho-Therapeutic. *Hobbies and Recreations:* Golf, Painting, Gardening, Theatre.

CLIFTON, Paul Edward, 34 Eastonville Rd., London SW17 7SL. (01-672-8387).
Education: Didsbury. *Appointments:* 1962–63 Barry; 1963–65 Barnsley West; 1965–68 Worksop; 1968–73 Bristol, Kingswood; 1973–78 Bristol, Parkway; 1978– Wimbledon.

CLOUGH, James Leonard, 33 Delavale Rd., Winchcombe, Cheltenham, Gloucestershire GL54 5YL. (0242-603464) *b. 24 Sept 1909, Consett, Co. Durham. m. 16 Aug 1938: 1d., 2s.*
Education: Consett Grammar Sch.; 1930–33 Hartley Victoria.
Appointments: 1933–34 Scarborough; 1934–38 Tunbridge Wells; 1938–41 St Leonards and Bexhill; 1941–47 Torquay; 1947–52 Portsmouth; 1952–61 Gosport and Fareham; 1961–66 Southampton; 1966–75 Basingstoke.
Connexional Committees: Property; *Publications: A Guide to Daily Prayer* (Epworth Press 1938); *Power to Live* (Lutterworth Press 1943).
Special Interests: Youth Work and Youth Camps in Scotland, Wales and Ireland. *Hobbies and Recreations:* Caravanning in France, Travelling—Hong Kong and Philippines, Hill Walking in Wales, Letter-Writing.

CLOWES, David, Epworth House, Carr Lane, Pilling, Preston PR3 6HH. (039-130-277)—BA (Manchester). *b. 8 Feb 1945, Ellesmere Port, Wirral, Cheshire, England. m. 20 Aug 1966: 2s, and 1 Foster Son.*
Education: 1950–56 William Stockton (Prim. and Jun.) Sch., Ellesmere Port; 1956–59 The Grange, Secondary Modern, Ellesmere Port; 1959–60 Peel Moat Secondary Modern, Stockport; 1972–75 Manchester Univ.; 1971–75 Hartley Victoria. *Appointments:* 1975–77 Preston (Lune St. and Orchard); 1977– Garstang; 1979–81 Assistant Secretary of the Synod; 1981– Secretary of the North Lancashire District.
Special Interests: Cricket, C.E.I.M., Tropical Fish. *Hobbies and Recreations:* Rambling, Book-binding, Gardening, Classical Music.

CLULOW, Arnold Harrison, 11 Hasborough Rd., Folkestone, Kent CT19 6BD. (0303-58080)—BA, BD (Manchester). *b. 23 June 1908, Atherton, Lancashire. m.8 Aug 1934: 1d., 2s.*
Education: Golborne, Lancs., Prim.; Heywood, Lancs., Grammar; Hull Technical Coll.; Manchester Univ.; 1926–31 Hartley Victoria.
Appointments: 1931–32 Dukinfield; 1932–34 Rochdale; 1934–37 Waltham St., Hull; 1937–41 Cleethorpes; 1941–45 Grimsby (Wheelsby Rd.); 1945–49 Scarborough (Jubilee); 1949–55 Sutton, Surrey; 1955–61 Wimbledon; 1961–67 Woking; 1967–73 Folkestone.
Connexional Committees: 1951–55 South London District Youth Secretary and Committee.

CLUTTERBUCK, Francis Frederick, 15 Park Crescent, St. George, Bristol BS5 7AT. (0272-517283) *b. 23 April 1894, Bristol. m. 19 Sept 1918: 1d., 1s.*
Education: Redfield Sch., Bristol; St. George Grammar Sch., Bristol; Private Tuition; Western Coll., Bristol.
Appointments: 1923–25 Chirk; 1925–29 Framlingham; 1929–1931 Portland; 1931–39 Bristol East; 1939-48 Bristol South; 1948–57 Bristol, Kingswood; 1957–1960 Dursley and Stonehouse.
Special Interests: Reading, Philately.
Hobbies and Recreations: Gardening, Walking.

CLUTTERBUCK, John Owen, 6 Coppice Beck Court, Coppice Drive, Harrogate, N. Yorks., HG1 2JE. (0423-509803) *b. 7 March 1907, Newark, Notts. m. 1 Nov 1937: 3d.*
Education: 1917–19 Nottingham High Sch.; 1919–22 Hucknall Pupil Teachers Centre; 1930–33 Didsbury.
Appointments: 1929–30 Wensleydale Mission; 1933–36 Wimborne; 1936–39 Poole; 1939–44 Derby King St.; 1944– 49 York Centenary; 1949–55 Luton; 1955–60 Torquay; 1960–65 Bideford; 1965–72 Weston-super-Mare.

CLUTTERBUCK, Richard Nigel, 6 The Meadow Way, Harrow Weald, Harrow, Middx HA3 7BW. (01-427-3447)—BA(Birmingham), MA(Hull). *b. 28 Aug 1952, Newark, Notts. m. 7 Aug 1979: 1d.*
Education: 1963–70 Newark Magnus Grammar; 1970–72 Bradford Univ.; 1974–77 Birmingham Univ.; 1977–78 Irish Sch. of Ecumenics (Dublin); 1974–77 Queen's. *Appointments:* 1979–81 Tutor Sia 'A Toutai Theological Coll., Tonga; 1981–82 Leeds NE; 1982– London, Harrow.

Publications: Kung and Chirico on Infallibility, One in Christ (pp 131–142 1981 No2).
Special Interests: Ecumenism, Systematic Theology. *Hobbies and Recreations:* Photography, Music.

COATES, Bryan Frederick, 8 Thornhill Rd., Streetly, Sutton Coldfield, West Midlands B74 3EH. (021-353-2728)–BD. *b. 22 Oct 1942, Wolverhampton. m.4 July 1970: 3s.*
Education: 1954–59 Wolverhampton Grammar Sch.; 1967–68 Westhill Coll.; Birmingham Univ.; 1964–67 Richmond.
Appointments: 1968–71 Ashford, Kent; 1971–79 United Church of Zambia; 1979– Birmingham, Sutton Park.
Connexional Committees: 1980– M.C.O.D. Central Committee.
Special Interests: World Development, Overseas Missions. *Hobbies and Recreations:* Ornithology, Philately.

COCHRAN, Peter Gregory, 10 Iddesleigh Rd., Bournemouth BH3 7JR. (0202-296305) *b. 17 Oct 1913, Northampton. m. 11 July 1946: 3d., 1s.*
Education: 1921–31 Northampton Town and County Grammar; Handsworth. *Appointments:* 1939–61 Madras Dt, India; 1962–67 Canterbury and Faversham; 1967–1972 Leicester South; 1972–81 Madras and Coimbatore Diocese (CSI).
Council Member: 1963–72 Asian Committee (MMS). *Publications: Indian Short Stories* (MMS). *Hobbies and Recreations:* Golf, Chess, Cooking, Knitting.

COCKING, Graham George, Methodist Manse, Mowcroft Rd., Hartcliffe, Bristol BS13 0LT. (0272-643100)–BA(Open Univ.). *b. 13 Jan 1948, Lincoln. m. 16 Dec 1972.*
Education: 1959–66 Wigan Grammar Sch.; 1966–69 St Katherines Coll. of Education (Liverpool); 1978–81 Wesley, Bristol.
Appointments: 1981– Bristol South.
Special Interests: Developing Nations, Travel. *Hobbies and Recreations:* Walking, Music, Reading, Travel.

COLBECK, Harold, 29 Roman Rd., Steyning, West Sussex BN4 3FN. (0903-812863) *b. Aug 1910, Leeds. m. (w.): 2s.*
Education: 1929–32 Victoria Park.
Appointments: 1932–36 Stockton-on-Tees; 1936–37 Rochdale; 1937–41 Blackpool (South); 1941–46 Lytham St Annes; 1946–49 Richmond and Barnes; 1949–56 Croydon; 1956–62 Kilburn and Hampstead; 1962–69 Kingston-upon-Thames; 1969–75 Enfield.
Connexional Committees: Overseas Missions Committee, Candidates for the Ministry Committee.

COLCLOUGH, Colin Campbell, 122 Osborne Rd., Jesmond, Newcastle-upon-Tyne NE2 2TE. (0632-812309)–BA. *b. 14 Dec 1925, Alsager, Cheshire. m. 12 Aug 1961: 2d.*
Education: 1930–33 Inf. Sch., Alsager; 1933–34 Senior Sch., Alsager; 1934–44 Newcastle High Sch., Staffs.; 1948–50 Durham Univ.; 1951–54 Richmond. *Appointments:* 1954–57 Liverpool (Crosby); 1957–60 Newcastle upon Tyne, Heaton and Wallsend; 1960–65 Ashfield; 1965–70 Newcastle Staffs; 1970–75 Manchester (Withington); 1975– Newcastle (Brunswick/Central).
Connexional Committees: 1971–83 Church Membership; 1978– Board of Division of Ministries.
Special Interests: Worship, World Development Movement, Ecumenical Movement, Peace Movement (F.O.R. Member). *Hobbies and Recreations:* Philately, Gardening, Walking.

COLE, Cuthbert, Pendenys, Green Lane, Marazion, Cornwall TR17 0EY. (0736-710529) *b. 11 Aug 1919, Bolsover, Derbyshire. m. 9 Aug 1947: 4s.*
Education: Clay Cross County Secondary Sch.; King Edward VI Grammar Sch., Retford; Lincoln School; 1947–49 Hartley Victoria.
Appointments: 1944–45 Aberdare; 1947–53 Lookwaar Banarar District, India; 1953-60 Port Talbot; 1960–67 Chelmsford; 1967–74 Mid Wilts; 1974– Bristol Clifton and Redland; 1981– St Marazion.
Connexional Committees: 1969–80 Church in Rural Life Committee (Sub Committee of Connexional H.M); 1955–57 OM Ctte.

COLE, Owen Taylor, 33 Abbeygate, Thetford, Norfolk IP24 1AX. (0842-3819)–BD(Lond.). *b. 24 April 1926, Newport, Mon. m. 22 Oct 1956: 3s.*
Education: 1936–39 Sutton Village Sch. in Suffolk; 1939–44 Woodbridge Grammar Sch.; 1950–53 London Univ.; 1950–53 Richmond.
Appointments: 1949–50 Camelford and Wadebridge; 1953–72 Church of South India; 1972–79 Ramsey, Isle of Man; 1979 Thetford.
Connexional Committees: 1974–79 Central Committee of Overseas Division.
Special Interests: Local, National and Church History. *Hobbies and Recreations:* Stamp Collecting, Visiting Places of Historical Interest, Reading, Sport, Cricket, Soccer, Rugby, Tennis.

COLEMAN, Graham Owen, 9 The Banks, Bingham, Nottingham NG13 8BL. (0949-37330) *b. 6 July 1931, Leamore, Walsall, Staffs. m. 20 April 1957: 2d., 1s.*
Education: 1936–42 Woden Ave. Prim. Sch., Wednesfield, Wolverhampton; 1942–45 Lichfield Rd. Senior Sch., Wednesfield, Wolverhampton; 1945–48 County Commercial Coll., Wood Green, Wednesbury, Staff.; 1954–57 Hartley Victoria. *Appointments:* 1957–60 Glasgow, Paisley Rd.; 1960–63 Shaw and Royton; 1963–68 Kimberley; 1968–73 Ashby-de-la-Zouch; 1973–81 Long Eaton; 1981– Bingham.
Connexional Committees: 1980–81 OM Central Committee; 1979–80 OM (Home) Committee.
Hobbies and Recreations: Football, Cricket (Spectator!).

COLEMAN, Thomas Brian, Northgate, Woodhouse Grove School, Apperley Bridge, Bradford BD10 0NR. (0532-502389)–BA(Leeds). *b. 25 April 1920,*

Wallsend-on-Tyne. m. 9 Aug 1950: 1d., 1s.
Education: 1930–31 Heaton Ave. Prim., Cleckheaton; 1931–32 South Parade Modern, Cleckheaton; 1933–39 Whitcliffe Mount Grammar, Cleckheaton; 1947–50 Leeds Univ.; 1947–50 Headingley. *Appointments:* 1950–54 Hebden Bridge; 1954–58 Bath; 1958–64 Reading; 1964–73 Truro Sch. (Chaplain); 1973–79 Bournemouth (Punson Memorial); 1979– Woodhouse Grove Sch. (Chaplain).
Connexional Committees: 1960– Division of Education and Youth; Rep. of Chester House Publications Committee. *Council Member:* 1970–73 Chairman, Dorset Council of Christian Education; 1970–73 Member of Dorset County Education Committee (Free Church Rep).
Publications: Co-Music Editor *Partners in Praise.*
Special Interests: Education, Music, Hynmology. *Hobbies and Recreations:* Playing Piano and Organ, Walking.

COLES, Francis H, Colway, Bond's Hill, Chardleigh Green, Wadeford, Chard, Somerset TA20 3AP. (046-06-2409) *b. Wolverton, Bucks.*
Education: Wolverton County Secondary; 1929–30 Richmond; 1930–32 Headingley. *Appointments:* 1928–29 Newbury; 1929–32 Richmond and Headingley; 1932–33 Chelmsford; 1933–36 Ludlow; 1936–38 Withernsea; 1938–41 Winchester and Eastleigh; 1941–44 Gower; 1944–47 Louth; 1947– Shaftesbury and Gillingham.

COLLINGS, Maurice Lee, 11 Bradfield Ave., Buckingham, Bucks MK18 1PR. (02802-3862) *b. 8 Oct 1917, Lydcott Farm, Morval, Cornwall. m. 12 July 1947: 3d., 1s.*
Education: Trenode Primary and Liskeard County Secondary (now Grammar); 1945–47 Hartley Victoria. *Appointments:* 1940–43 Nat Service; 1943–44 Plymouth; 1944–46 Camelford and Wadebridge; 1946–47 Hartley Victoria Coll.; 1947–50 South China Dt; 1950–54 Bude; 1954–58 Radstock; 1958–62 Cannock Chase; 1962–67 Wellingborough; 1967–71 Wantage and Abingdon.
Special Interests: Cricket, Old Architecture, including Parish Churches. *Hobbies and Recreations:* Gardening, some Snooker.

COLLINGWOOD, Deryck Cuthbert, The Mansel, Church Rd., Little Baddow, Chelmsford, Essex CM3 4BE. (024541-3355)– BA(Leeds). *b. 8 Jan 1916, Rangoon, Burma. m. 21 Aug 1943: 2d., 2s.*
Education: 1927–35 Whycliffe Coll., Stonehouse, Glos.; 1937–40 Leeds Univ., Headingley.
Appointments: 1940–43 Retford; 1943–46 Barnsley (East); 1946–52 Leicester (King Richard's Rd.); 1952–61 Birmingham (Wesley); 1961–69 Penarth; 1969–72 Sutton (Surrey); 1972–82 Chairman London NE Dt.
Connexional Committees: 1972–82 GP; '60s MTC; '60s Things Spiritual; 1968–72 Restructuring; 1972–82 Wesley's Chapel; 1972–82 NCH; 1974–77 Overseas Division (c); 1972–76 Archives.
Special Interests: Comparative Religions, Archaeology, Old Testament (Psalms), Church Growth, Lay Ministry. *Hobbies and Recreations:* Music, English Literature and History, Travel, Sport, Drama.

COLLINGWOOD, Peter Joseph, Sunnyside, New St., Torrington, Devon EX38 8BY. (080-52-3172)– BA(Cantab.), MA. *b. 14 June 1929, March, Cambridgeshire. m. 29 July 1967: 3s.*
Education: 1939–48 March Grammar Sch.; 1948–52 Downing Coll., Cambridge; 1952–54 Wesley House.
Appointments: 1954–63 East Nigeria Dt; 1963–65 Nigerian Conf.; 1965–67 St Andrew's Coll.; 1967–76 Zimbabwe Conf.; 1976 Bideford.
Connexional Committees: 1965–67, 1982– Overseas Division Central Committee. *Publications:* 1954 Wesley Historical Society Essay Prize.

COLLINS, Glyn Gordon, 182 Church Rd., Hanwell, London W7. (01-567-9360) *b. 7 Sept 1933, Hedge End, Southampton. m. 14 Aug 1965: 2d., 1s.*
Education: 1945–50 Taunton Grammar Sch., Southampton; 1962–66 Handsworth. *Appointments:* 1966–70 Nelson (Lancs); 1970–77 Hitchin and Letchworth; 1977–82 Harrow; 1982– London, Ealing and Acton.

COLLINS, Kenneth Howard, 229 Verity Way, Stevenage, Herts SG1 5PS. (0438-54740) *b. 14 March 1937, Dudley, West Midlands. m. 30 June 1962: 2d.*
Education: 1948–53 Dudley Grammar Sch.; 1973–75 Lanchester Poly., Coventry; 1959–62 Richmond.
Appointments: 1962–65 Swansea; 1965–70 London East Ham Mission; 1970–73 Banbury; 1973–75 Coventry; 1975– Stevenage.
Special Interests: Social Work.
Hobbies and Recreations: Reading, Listening to Music, Watching Football, DIY.

COLLINSON, David James, 14 Knowl Rd., Mirfield, West Yorkshire WF14 8DQ. (0924-492308)– BA(Durham), MA(Cantab.). *b. 4 Jan 1944, Newcastle-upon-Tyne. m. 30 Dec 1972: 2d., 1s.*
Education: 1949–52 North Heaton Prim. Sch.; 1952–55 Newcastle Royal Grammar Sch. Jun. Sch.; 1955–62 Newcastle Royal Grammar Sch.; 1962–65 Durham Univ.; 1965–68 Wesley House. *Appointments:* 1968–73 Leigh-on-Sea; 1973–78 Durham and Deerness Valley; 1978 Dewsbury.
Publications: Article *Mining Village Methodism: A Study in Church Decline,* in *Epworth Review* (Jan 1981).
Special Interests: Pastoral Counselling and the Ministry of Healing; Charismatic Movement; Work of Southport Holiness Convention; Church Life Behind the Iron Curtain. *Hobbies and Recreation:* Anything to do with Ships, Music, Mountain Walking.

COLLINSON, Geoffrey William, 1 Willow Rd., Farncombe, Godalming, Surrey GU7 3SP. (0424-21923) *b. 10 Feb 1910, York. m. 28 July 1939 (w.): 1d., 3s.*

Education: 1915–18 Acomb Prep. Sch. (Private), York; 1918–22 Priory St., Elem. Sch. (Wesleyan), York; 1922–26 Nunthorpe Secondary (Grammar) Sch.; 1932–36 Didsbury. *Appointments:* 1936–38 London Wesley's Chapel; 1938–42 Bromley (Kent); 1942-46 Teddington; 1946–50 Maidenhead, Windsor and Slough; 1950–53 Leeds (Morley); 1953–57 Waltham Abbey and Hertford; 1957–64 Cambridge; 1964–69 Chingford; 1969–75 Guildford.
Hobbies and Recreations: Walking, Gardening, Tennis, Painting.

COLLINSON, Joseph Frederick, 7 New Rd., Crook, Co. Durham DL15 8QE. (0388-762587) *b. 26 April 1928, Doncaster. m. 21 Aug 1954: 2d., 1s.*
Education: 1939–46 Maltby Grammar Sch., WRCC; 1949–52 Headingley. *Appointments:* 1948–49 Kirkoswald; 1952–57 Northallerton; 1957–62 Withernsea; 1962–68 Whitby; 1968–73 Hull (West); 1973–78 Barnard Castle; 1978– Crook.

COLLINSON, Nigel Thomas, 26 Upland Park Rd., Oxford OX2 7RU. (0865 59026)–MA(Cantab), (Hull). *b. 14 Mar 1941, Stoke-on-Trent. m. 30 July 1964: 2d.*
Education: 1946–52 Forster Street Inf./Jun., Tunstall, Stoke-on-Trent; 1952–59 Hanley High Sch., Stoke-on-Trent; 1959–62 Hull University; 1962–64 Cambridge; 1962–64 Wesley House. *Appointments:* 1964–67 Clifton and Redland, Assistant Student Chaplain, Victoria Meth. Church; 1967–72 Stroud and Cirencester; 1972–80 Wolverhampton Trinity; 1980– Oxford, Chaplain to Methodist Students in Oxford.
Connexional Committees: 1975– Connexional Candidates Examination Committee, 1982– Wesley Deaconess Order Committee.
Special Interests: Philosophy of Religion (particularly the Contemporary Experience of God and The Language We Use), Christianity and Politics. *Hobbies and Recreations:* Sports, Walking.

CONNELL, Richard John, Beaudesert, East Drive, Ham Manor, Angmering, Sussex BN16 4HJ. (090-62-3940)–MBE, BA, BD. *b. 18 March 1906, Luton, Bedfordshire. m. 2 Aug 1934: 1d., 1s.*
Education: 1914–19 Luton, Dallow Rd.; 1920–25 Luton Grammar; 1926–31 Manchester Univ.; 1931–32 Halle Wittenberg, Germany; 1934–37 Cambridge Univ.; 1926–31 Hartley. *Appointments:* 1932–34 Bournemouth Winton; 1934–37 Cambridge; 1937–40 Northampton, Kettering Rd.; 1940–45 Loughborough; 1945–50 Leicester, Claremont St.; 1950–54 London, Highgate; 1954–75 General Secretary Methodist Homes for the Aged (Supernumerary).
Connexional Committees: 1956–75 Homes for Aged; Ministers Housing Society.
Hobbies and Recreations: Reading, Golf, Bowls.

CONNOLLY, Samuel, 63 The Hundred, Romsey, Hampshire SO5 8BZ. (0794-512387) *b. 18 July 1918, Luton, Bedfordshire. m. 13 Aug 1949.*
Education: 1923–32 Aspinal, Manchester; 1937–39 Northampton Poly. (London); 1947–49 Hartley Victoria. *Appointments:* 1949–52 Belper; 1952–59 Newmarket; 1959–66 Leigh-on-Sea; 1966–77 Mid-Sussex; 1977– Romsey.
Connexional Committees: 1968–73 Home Mission Prison Committee.
Local Council Committees: 1953–71 Sch. Managers & Governors; 1972–77 Careers Council; 1959–77 Youth Advisory Councils.
Special Interests: Prison Chaplaincy, Education & Youth, Holy Land Pilgrimages, Council Member of 'Highway Holidays Ltd'. *Hobbies and Recreations:* Photography (Member of 'Methodist Pen & Camera Club'), Overseas Travel, Various Sporting Activities.

CONSTANTINE, Leonard, 25 Moorview Way, Skipton, N. Yorks BD23 2JW. (0756-5101)–BA(Manchester), MA(Cantab.). *b. 14 Aug 1907, Accrington, Lancs. m. 20 Aug 1935 (w.).*
Education: 1918–24 Accrington Grammar Sch.; 1924–28 Manchester Univ.; 1928–31 Wesley House. *Appointments:* 1931–51 Central China Univ., Wuchang, China; 1951–57 London, Brixton Hill; 1957–60 Kingston-upon-Thames; 1960–66 Bradford, Woodhouse Grove; 1966–72 Ilkley.
Connexional Committees: 1951–66 Overseas Missions Committee; 1957–66 Faith and Order Committees.
Publications: 1944–51 Contributed Articles on China to the *Manchester Guardian. The Gospel to Communists* (International Review of Missions 1952).
Special Interests: Politics and World Affairs. *Hobbies and Recreations:* Gardening.

COOK, Alfred Ernest, 93 Tilworth Rd., Hull HU8 9BW. (0482-74555)–MBE. *b. 24 April 1911, Hull. m. 23 July 1938: 1d., 1s.*
Education: 1921–25 Constable St. Elem. Sch., Hull; 1931–34 Headingley. *Appointments:* 1934–43 Eastern Nigeria Dt; 1944–66 Chaplain HMF; 1966–71 Scarborough; 1971–76 Hull East.
Connexional Committees: 1966–70 Royal Navy, Army and Royal Air Force Board.
Hobbies and Recreations: Music, Cricket, Golf.

COOK, Frederick Gilbert Arthur, Ravdox, Colwall, Malvern WR13 6ER. (0684-40278) *b. 10 Oct 1903, Bournemouth. w. 1930: 1d.*
Education: 1922–26 Hartley Victoria. *Appointments:* 1926–28 Dartmouth; 1928–34 Stoke and Longton, 1934–40 Stoke-on-Trent; 1940–58 Chaplain HMF.

COOK, Herbert John, 36 Templemore Drive, Great Barr, Birmingham B43 5HE. (021-358-5424)–BA, MA(Birmingham). *b. 7 Dec 1910, Northampton. m. 9 Aug 1939: 1d.*
Education: 1923–27 Northampton Town and County Grammar Sch.; 1933–36, 1946–47 Birmingham Univ.; 1933-36 Handsworth. *Appointments:* 1932–33 Wellington (Shropshire); 1936–47 British

Honduras Dt; 1947–61 Jamaica Dt; 1961–67 Headingley Coll. Tu.O.T.; 1967–70 Handsworth Coll. Tu.O.T.; 1970–78 West Bromwich.
Connexional Committees: 1961–79 Connexional Probationers' Oversight Committee. *Publications: The People of God in the Old Testament* (1957); Manual for Membership in the Methodist Church (1957); *Pekah* (Vetus Testamentum 1965); *Baptism and Confirmation* (1966); *The A Text of the Greek Versions of the Book of Esther* (ZATW 1969); *Why Should it Happen to Me?* (1980).

COOK, John Fillingham, 1 Horsley Hill Rd., South Shields, Tyne and Wear NE33 3ET. (0632-562211)–BA(Wales), MA(Cantab.). *b. 16 Jan 1935, Prescot, Lancs. m. 19 Aug 1961: 1d., 1s.*
Education: 1940–42 County Inf. Sch., Prescot; 1942–46 County Jun. Sch., Prescot; 1946–53 Prescot Grammar Sch.; 1953–56 Univ. Coll. of N. Wales, Bangor; 1956–59 Wesley House. *Appointments:* 1959–61 University Road, Belfast; 1961–64 London, Ilford; 1964–69 Middlesbrough; 1969–76 Hull (West); 1976– South Shields.
Connexional Committees: 1966–69 Local Preachers' Committee; 1974–76 Ministries Committee.

COOKE, Barrie Godfrey, 5A Gladstone Rd., Chesterfield S40 4TE. (0246-32189) *b. 7 Sept 1933, Selston. m. 20 Aug 1960: 3d.*
Education: 1938–45 Selston CE; 1945–47 Selston Matthew Holland County Secondary Sch.; 1947–49 Mansfield Technical Sch.; 1951–54 Cliff Coll.; 1954–58 Hartley Victoria.
Appointments: 1958–60 Liverpool Linacre Mission; 1960–64 Middleton; 1964–69 Manchester Withington; 1969–75 Redditch; 1975– Chesterfield.
Connexional Committees: 1964–77 Ministries; 1964–77 Probationers' Oversight; 1980– Board of Ministries.
Hobbies and Recreations: Golf.

COOKE, C. Brian, 10 Berwyn, Nant Parc, Johnstown, Wrexham, Clwyd LL14 1YE. (0978-87463)–Dip Theol(Rhodes). *b. 5 Aug 1934, Urmston, Lancs.*
Education: 1943–44 Bridlington Sch.; 1944–52 King Edward VI Sch., Stafford; 1952–55 Royal Air Force; 1960–62 Rhodes Univ., South Africa.
Appointments: 1955–56 Cwm and Kingstone; 1957–71 Methodist Church of South Africa; 1971–74 Louth; 1974–76 Ilkeston; 1976–79 Edinburgh; 1979–82 Netherton; 1982– Wrexham.
Council Member: 1972–74 Grimsby Branch RSPCA Auxiliary Secretary.
Special Interests: Animal Welfare, Life Member—The Cats Protection League. *Hobbies and Recreations:* Reading, Collecting Old Postcards, Walking.

COOKE, Frank William, 1 Ickworth Rd., Sleaford, Lincs NG34 7LJ. (0529-302289) *b. 5 Jan 1928, Cooling, Rochester, Kent. m. 14 Feb 1953: 2d., 1s.*
Education: 1932–42 Cooling and Cliffe Council Schs.; 1942–51 Medway Tech. Coll.; Richmond
Appointments: 1964–67 Frome and Shepton Mallet; 1967–73 West Bromwich; 1973–80 Coventry; 1980– Sleaford.
Connexional Committees: 1972–78 Central Committee of MMS.
Special Interests: Hospital Chaplaincy Work, Ecumenical Activities. *Hobbies and Recreations:* Gardening and Bowls, Interested in Cricket, Football, Tennis, Boxing, Show Jumping.

COOKE, John Alfred, 1 Collington St., Beeston, Nottingham NG9 1FJ. (0602-255601)–BD(Lond.), MA(Birmingham). *b. 26 June 1944, Shrewsbury, Shropshire.*
Education: 1955–63 Adam's Sch., Wem.; 1964–68 Hartley Victoria; 1968–69 Handsworth.
Appointments: 1969–72 Castleford; 1972–74 Assistant Chaplain—Westminster Coll., Oxford; 1974–81 Chaplain Univ. of Lancaster; 1981– Chaplain Univ. of Nottingham.
Special Interests: Religion and the Arts, Liturgy, Politics. *Hobbies and Recreations:* Theatre, Music, Novels, Poetry, Art, Walking, Cooking, Wine Tasting.

COOKE, Kathleen Hilary, 121 Chapeltown Rd., Ecclesfield, Sheffield S30 3WD. (0742-467215) *b. 12 March 1947, Shrewsbury, Shropshire.*
Education: 1952–58 Loppington CE Prim. Sch.; 1958–65 Priory Grammar Sch. for Girls; 1965–66 Ealing Technical Coll.; 1968–70 Handsworth; 1970–71 Queens; 1974–75 Hartley Victoria.
Appointments: 1975–80 Bristol (Kingswood); 1980– Sheffield (North-East).
Hobbies and Recreations: Poetry, Crosswords, Walking, Drama.

COOMBS, David Frank Lewis, 76 Elm Rd., Leigh-on-Sea. (0702-75384) *b. 20 July 1931, Gillingham, Kent. m. 26 July 1958: 2d., 2s, also 1 Foster Daughter.*
Education: 1936–37 Napier Rd. Sch.; 1937–42 Byron Rd. Sch.; 1942–48 Gillingham County Grammar Sch. for Boys; 1953–54 Cliff Coll.; 1954–58 Hartley Victoria; 1958–59 St Andrews (Birmingham); 1959 Union Theological Seminary, Kingston, Jamaica. *Appointments:* 1959–60 Bahamas District, North Eleuthera; 1960–62 Bimina and Grand Bahama; 1962-64 Abaco; 1964–69 Launceston; 1969–74 Milton Keynes; 1974–82 Waltham Abbey and Hertford; 1982– Leigh-on-Sea.
Council Member: Milton Keynes Council of Social Service and Marriage Guidance Council, Bletchley Youth Council, Hoddesdon and Broxbourne Carnival Committee.
Publications: Professional Views magazine for immigrant communities, March/April 1975; *Uganda Asian Resettlement NIE* (Nationwide Initiate in Evangelism 1980); Passion/Drama Report, Cliff Withers, 1981; Report on NIE.
Special Interests: Secretary/Treasurer NIE, Herts County Group, Wesley Day and NE District Precentor, Cliff Coll. Committee (Interviewing potential students). *Hobbies and Recreations:* Photography, Singing, Reading, Drama.

COOPER, Arnold Herbert, 69 Griffins Brook Lane, Bournville, Birmingham B30 1QB. (021-459-8664)—BA. *b. 11 Oct 1911, Newcastle-on-Tyne. m. 16 June 1943: 2d.*
Education: 1921–25 Manchester Grammar Sch. (Prep. Sch.); 1925–30 Epworth Coll., Rhyl, N. Wales; 1930–33 Manchester Univ.; 1933–36 Headingley. *Appointments:* 1936–37 Rochdale Mission; 1937–38 Brampton (Cumb.); 1938–45 Liverpool North; 1945–48 Ilncley (Yorks.); 1948–52 Scarborough (Queen St.); 1952–57 Filey (Trinity); 1948–57 Chaplain to Hunmanby Hall; 1957–62 London Hinde St.; Chaplain to London Univ., to Pentonville Prison, to the Middlesex Hospital and to Southlands Coll., 1962–66 Leicester (Bishop St.); 1966–76 Columbo South Circuit, Sri Lanka. *Connexional Committees:* Connexional Youth Committee; Committee for Spiritual Direction; Convener, Committee on Worship; Candidates Committee; Overseas Missions Candidates Committee; Church Membership Committee; Connexional Panel for Nomination of Chairman of Districts; In 1977 I was appointed Chaplain to HM Remand Centre, Brockhill, and to Hewell Grange Borstal, Nr. Redditch, I hope to continue to Aug 1983. *Publications:* Wrote Report of the Committee on Worship in the Methodist Church, presented to Conference in 1960.
Hobbies and Interests: Listening to Music, Reading, Gardening and all DIY Jobs.

COOPER, Colin Stanley, Hartwood, 80 Westwood Rd., Leek, Staffs. ST13 8DH. (0538-383090)—BD. *b. 7 March 1934, Dudley, Worcs. m. 15 Aug 1959: 3d., 1s.*
Education: 1944–49 Halesowen Grammar Sch.; 1955–59 Handsworth. *Appointments:* 1959–61 Stafford, 1961–66 Manchester Mission; 1966–70 Southport (North); 1970–79 Runcorn; 1979– Leek.
Connexional Committees: 1978– Ecumenical Sub-committee.
Hobbies and Recreations: Gardening.

COOPER, David, Burnside, Scalloway, Shetland ZE1 0UA. (059-588-204)—BA. *b. 6 Nov 1949, Seaham, Co. Durham. m. 11 Sept 1971: 1d.*
Education: 1961–68 Bede Grammar Sch. for Boys, Sunderland; 1968–72 Univ. of London; 1972–76 Univ. of Manchester; 1976–77 Univ. of Ghana; 1972–76 Hartley Victoria.
Appointments: 1977–80 Morpeth; 1980– Lerwick.
Connexional Committees: 1980– Division of Social Responsibility; 1980– Division of Ministries Board.
Local Council Committees: 1982– Shetland Island Council Education Committee.
Special Interests: Contemporary Theology and Society. *Hobbies and Recreations:* Classical Music, Walking, The Liberal Party, Gardening.

COOPER, David William, 31 Winchester Drive, Burbage, Hinckley, Leicestershire LE10 2BA. (0455-634168)—BA(Manchester). *b. 25 Sept 1949, Ilford, Essex. m. 2d., 1s.*
Education: 1961–68 Buckhurst Hill County High (Essex); 1970–73 Manchester Univ.; 1970–73 Hartley Victoria; 1973–74 Wesley House.
Appointments: 1974–79 Halifax; 1979– Hinckley.
Special Interests: Music Generally, Playing the Organ, Running a Youth Choir, Pipe Organs especially, I have built/rebuilt 5 organs for Methodist Churches, and do some organ advisory work for MCMS.
Hobbies and Recreations: Canals.

COOPER, Frank Mitchel, 2 Imaden Cresc., Lindford, Nr Bordon, Hants GU35 0PH. (04203-2680)—MM. *b. 27 April 1896, Batley, Lancs. m. 27 Dec 1927: 2d.*
Education: 1906–1912 Bolton Municipal Secondary, Orme Boys' Grammar, Newcastle, Staffs.; 1919–1921 Nottingham Univ. Coll.
Appointments: 1923–24 Nelson; 1924–25 Newcastle Sandyford; 1927–27 Faversham; 1927–30 Nelson; 1930–34 Farsley; 1934–41 Bristol South; 1941–45 Weston-super-Mare; 1945–50 Newcastle Central and Sandyford; 1950–54 Sunderland West; 1954–58 Bristol, Brookland; 1958–61 Clay Cross.
Special Interests: Reading, Writing Stories for Children, Youth Club Work. *Hobbies and Recreations:* Walking Long Distances, Travel Abroad, often with Organised Parties as Leader.

COOPER, James L, 14 Henrietta Rd., Thame, Oxon OX9 3TJ. (084421-2019) *m.*
Education: 1950-53 Richmond.
Appointments: 1949–50 New Forest Mission; 1950–53 Richmond Coll.; 1853–56 Darwen; 1956–61 Kings Lynn; 1961–64 Biggleswade; 1964–68 Ashby-de-la-Zouch; 1968–75 Mid Sussex; 1975–80 Basingstoke; 1980– Thame and Watlington.

COOPER, Norman Barratt, 256 Cranbrook Rd., Ilford, Essex IG1 4UR. (01-554-2757) *b. 3 July 1909, Andover. m. 3 July 1946.*
Education: 1915–19 Westfield House Sch., Andover; 1919–25 Andover Grammar Sch.; 1932–35 Handsworth. *Appointments:* 1931–32 Thetford; 1943–35 Handsworth; 1935–38 Ledbury; 1938–42 London, Finchley and Hendon; 1942–45 Wakefield; 1945–48 Nottingham Mission; 1948–53 Barnet; 1953–60 The Seaman's Mission, London; 1960–70 British Sailors Society (Port Chaplain, Southampton); 1970–74 Streatham and Dulwich.
Connexional Committees: 1953–60 Home Mission. *Local Council Committees:* 1953–60 Port Welfare Committee, London; 1960–70 Port Welfare Committee, Southampton.
Special Interests: Music and the Theatre.

COOPER, Percival Edward, The Corner, Limpenhoe, Norwich NR13 3HA. (0493-700432) *b. 18 Aug 1902, Aldershot. m. 1 July 1931: 1d., 1s.*
Education: 1924–27 Hartley Victoria.
Appointments: 1927–28 Marple; 1928–31 Dover and Folkestone; 1931–32 Weobley; 1932–36 Scholes; 1936–39 Kirkby Stephen, Appleby and Tebay; 1939–42 Bedale; 1942–46 West Aukland; 1946–51 Wigton;

1951–57 Market Weighton; 1957–62 Sheffield (South); 1962–67 Acle. *Special Interests:* Music and Art.

COOPER, Robert, 56 Grosvenor Drive, Whitley Bay, Tyne and Wear NE26 2JS. (0632-521655) *b. 2 Feb 1950, m. 17 May 1980: 2d.* *Education:* 1972–76 Wesley, Bristol. *Appointments:* 1976–79 Wigan; 1979–82 Huddersfield East; 1982– North Shields and Whitley Bay. *Publications: Bruised Echoes* (Outposts Publications 1978).

COOTE, David Frank, 29 Fairfield Rd., Viewsley, Middx. UB7 8EY. (08954-43392). *Education:* 1971–74 Queens. *Appointments:* 1974–78 Birmingham (Elmdon); 1978– Hillingdon.

COPE, Harold Karl Jordan, 38 Greenhow St., Sheffield S6 3TP. (0742-343438) *b. 18 Feb 1910, Peckham, London. m. 26 Aug 1939: 1d., 1s.* *Education:* –1923 Woods Rd. Elem. Sch., Peckham, London; 1923–26 Wilson's Grammar Sch., Camberwell, London; 1933-36 Handsworth. *Appointments:* 1932–33 Home Mission Commmittee; 1933–36 Handsworth Coll.; 1936–46 Bombay District, India; 1946–51 Huddersfield and Gledholt; 1951 Hartlepool; 1955–61 Great Harwood; 1961–66 Blackheath and Langley Green; 1966–72 Sheffield North East. *Connexional Committees:* 1947–51 and 1955–63 Overseas Missions; 1967–75 Property Division. *Special Interests:* History of Methodism. *Hobbies and Recreations:* Reading (Especially British History), Cricket, Football (Soccer and Rugby), Gardening.

COPE, Norman Newton Gerhardt, Red Roofs, 18 Penpethy Rd., Brixham, Torbay TQ5 8NW. (08045-3925) *b. 26 April 1912, Peckham, S. London. m. 11 Feb 1942.* *Education:* 1917–26 Woods Rd., Peckham, S. London; Richmond. *Appointments:* 1940–43 London M., Downham; 1943–7 Dorking and Horsham; 1947–52 Haverfordwest; 1952–58 Wolverhampton; 1958–62 Coventry; 1962–67 Cleethorpes; 1967–77 Brixham. *Connexional Committees:* 1945–68 Methodist Book Room; 1963–76 Property Committee. *Publications: Poems of Sunlight and Shadow* (1936); *The Night is Ending* (1945); *Five Minutes to Wake the Dead* (1952). *Special Interests:* Classical Music, History Social Studies. *Hobbies and Recreations:* Formerly Cricket, Walking, DIY, Gardening.

COPESTAKE, Reginald Henry, 29 Stanwell Drive, Middleton Cheney, Banbury OX17 2RE. (0295-710660) *b. 28 July 1909, Liverpool. m. 24 July 1937: 2d., 1s.* *Education:* 1913–22 Rathbone Sch., Liverpool; 1922–24 Old Swan Technical Institute, Liverpool; 1931–35 Didsbury. *Appointments:* 1937–40 Wye Valley Mission; 1940–44 St. Helens and Prescot; 1944–47 Louth; 1947–50 Alford; 1950–56 London, Walthamstow; 1956–60 Great Bentley; 1960–64 London, Enfield; 1964–71 Rhondda; 1971–74 Risca. *Publications: Ten Words to Christian Disciples* (1947); *The Methodist Way* (1951, Reprinted 1955,55,60); *All That Jesus Began* (1956); *How the Church Began* (1981); *How the Church Grew* (1981); *The Apostle Paul* (1982); *Francis of Assissi* (1982). *Hobbies and Recreations:* Carpentry, Wood Carving, Music, Gardening, Home-Decoration and Repair.

COPPACK, Norman Roy, The Manse, 2 Repps Rd., Martham, Great Yarmouth, Norfolk NR29 4QT. (0493-740237)–Dip Theol(Lond.). *b. 7 July 1941, Fleetwood. m. 26 June 1965: 1d., 1s.* *Education:* 1945–48 Flakefleet Inf. Sch., Fleetwood, Lancs.; 1948–52 Milton St. Jun. Sch., Fleetwood, Lancs.; 1952–57 Baines Grammar Sch., Poulton-Le-Fylde; 1962–66 Hartley Victoria. *Appointments:* 1966–71 East Dereham; 1971–76 Barrow-in-Furness; 1976– Martham. *Connexional Committees:* 1974–76 Overseas; 1981– Overseas. *Special Interests:* Mental Health (Chairman in Barrow & Here), Youth Management Affairs, Finance. *Hobbies and Recreations:* Philately, Music.

CORDY, Andrew, 288 Ash Bank Rd., Werrington, Stoke-on-Trent ST9 0JS. (078130-2323)–BA(Bristol). *b. 1 Nov 1949, Selston, Nottingham. m. 4 April 1970: 2d.* *Education:* 1962–69 Frederick Gent County Secondary Sch., South Normanton, Derbyshire; 1978–81 Univ. of Bristol; 1977–81 Wesley, Bristol. *Appointments:* 1981 Stoke-on-Trent (Hanley).

CORKER, Margaret, 37 Victoria St., Stocksbridge, Sheffield S30 5FY. (0742-882210). *Appointments:* 1974–78 Doncaster; 1978– Sheffield North.

CORNAH, Albert William, Wesley Manse, 17 Clifford St., Appleby in Westmoreland, Cumbria CA16 6TS. (0930-51244)–MA(Bristol), BD(Lond.). *b. 27 Feb 1919, Liverpool. m. 24 June 1948: 2s.* *Education:* 1924 Christchurch CE Prim. Sch., Preston; 1925–29 Ashton Wesleyan Sch., Preston; 1929–34 Preston Grammar Sch.; 1934–36 King George Vth Sch., Southport; 1946–48 Headingley. *Appointments:* 1948–51 Stockton; 1951–55 Bristol (Clifton and Redland); 1955–59 Dundee and Perth; 1959–64 Sunderland (South); 1964–69 Colchester; 1969–74 London (Wanstead and Woodford); 1974–77 Gateshead and Jarrow; 1977–81 Portsmouth Mission; 1981– Kirkby Stephen, Appleby and Tebay. *Connexional Committees:* 1968– Press and Information Committee (then Press Service); 1970–72 Education Committee; 1963–69 Connex. Youth Committee; 1965 till dissolution, MYD Trade Committee; 1964–65 Chairman MYD Executive; 1964–65 National President MAYC; 1963–71 Production Team MAYC Display. *Publications:* Sundry Articles Humorous in *F.K. Bulletin, Methodist Magazine, The Choir, Methodist Recorder*; Series of Articles on Preaching in Youth (NB. all these periodicals except *Methodist*

Recorder and *FK Bulletin* are now defunct).
Special Interests: Reading, Humour, Organs, Hymnody, Script-Writing. *Hobbies and Recreations:* Organ Playing, Pottering.

CORNAH, Cyril, 48A Hawkshead St., Southport, Merseyside PR9 9BP. (0704-815254) *b. 13 Feb 1912, Blackpool. m. 14 Sept 1938: 3s.*
Education: 1918–26 Various Liverpool Council Schs.; 1949–50 Richmond Coll. *Appointments:* 1948–49 Thornley; 1950–52 Crooke; 1952–56 Wigan (Wesley); 1956–61 Liverpool (South); 1961–64 Chester; 1964–67 Bristol (Kingswood); 1967–74 Wigan; 1974–79 Birmingham (Elmdon).
Connexional Committees: 1962–75 Christian Citizenship Department, General Committee; 1981–82 DSR Board Member.

CORNELL, Christine, 16 St. Lesmo Rd., Edgeley, Stockport SK3 0TX. (061-480-3501).
Appointments: 1976– Mid-Glamorgan Mission.

CORNELL, Geoff, 16 St. Lesmo Rd., Edgeley, Stockport SK3 0TX. (061-480-3501).
Appointments: 1976– Mid-Glamorgan Mission.

CORNER, Clarence Vincent, 1 Manor Grove, Kennington, Oxford OX1 5QY. (0865-735730) *b. 1 June 1909, Thornaby on Tees, Cleveland. m. 11 April 1938: 3s.*
Education: Arthur Head Sch., Thornaby; The High Sch., Middlesbrough; 1930–33 Hartley Coll. *Appointments:* 1933 Chinnor; 1933-37 Hull; 1937–39 Middlesbrough Mission; 1939–41 Market Weighton; 1941–45 Goole; 1945–50 Birmingham, Moseley Rd.; 1950–55 London, Walthamstow; 1955–64 Portsmouth; 1964–68 Edinburgh, Nicolson Square, 1968–73 Chairman of the Lincoln District.
Connexional Committees: 1955–64 Division of Social Responsibility; 1968–73 General Purposes, Stationing, Property etc.; At present Methodist World Council Board of Trustees, Epworth Rectory. *Local Council Committees:* 1968–73 Lincolnshire Education Committee.
Special Interests: Philosophy of Religion. *Hobbies and Recreations:* Walking and Watching Sport.

CORNER, Ronald Arthur, 76 Howard Rd., Leicester LE2 1XH. (0533-708074)–BA. *b. 2 Oct 1914, Cardiff. m. Yendle, 15 Nov 1942: 2s.*
Education: 1926–32 Howard Gardens Secondary Sch.; 1936–40 Birmingham; 1936–1940 Handsworth. *Appointments:* 1940–42 Tamworth and Lichfield; 1942–45 Chaplain HMF; 1945–49 Salisbury; 1949–53 Stroud and Cirencester; 1953–59 Truro; 1959–64 Helston; 1964–71 Leicester (South); 1971–76 Leamington; 1976–79 Coventry.
Connexional Committees: 1947–67 Youth Committee (Council); 1975–79 Home Missions Secretary, Birmingham Dt. *Local Council Committees:* c1950 District Youth Secretary in Oxford and Leicester, 1954–59 in Cornwall.
Special Interests: Music, at times Synod Precentor in Oxford and Leicester and Cornwall, 1945–59 Youth Club Leadership. *Hobbies and Recreations:* Music, Tape-Recording, Local Radio 1964–71.

CORNEY, Michael Ritson, 382 Landseer Rd., Ipswich, Suffolk IP3 9LX. (0473-76280) *b. 14 April 1943, Halesworth, Suffolk. m. 29 July 1967: 2s.*
Education: 1948–54 Dell Rd. Prim. Sch., Lowestoft; 1954–59 Alderman Woodrow Secondary Modern Sch., Lowestoft; 1968–71 Wesley, Bristol. *Appointments:* 1971–73 Shildon; 1973–78 Middlesbrough and Eston; 1978– Ipswich.
Connexional Committees: 1981– Division of Education and Youth. *Local Council Committees:* 1976–77 Cleveland County Council
Hobbies and Recreations: Painting, Music, Theatre, Gardening.

CORNFIELD, Redvers G., Kewstoke, 1 Cecil Rd., Swanage BH18 1JJ. (092-92-2523) *b. 23 March 1923, Blaenavon, Gwent, S. Wales. m. 23 March 1947: 1d.*
Education: 1928–33 Blaenavon Roman Catholic Prim.; 1933–34 Blaenavon Comprehensive Sch.; 1934–36 Abersychan Technical Sch.; 1950–52 Handsworth.
Appointments: 1948–49 Hawkhurst (Kent); 1953–58 Paulton; 1958–64 Bristol (South); 1964–70 Portsmouth and Southsea; 1970–75 Midsomer Norton; 1975–81 Fareham (Hants); 1981– Swanage.
Special Interests: Pastoral Counselling. *Hobbies and Recreations:* Origami, Woodwork, Walking.

COSTAIN, Thomas Frederick, Yn Aaie, 1 Cronk Reayrt, Glenfaba Park, Peel, Isle of Man. *b. 14 Jan 1913, Colby, Isle of Man. m. 19 Aug 1943: 1s.*
Education: Douglas High Sch.; 1936–39 Didsbury. *Appointments:* 1939–40 Warrington/Wantage; 1940–43 Rhosymedre and Chirk; 1943–44 Market Rasen and Caistor; 1944–47 Widnes; 1947–51 Ellesmere Port; 1951–55 Derby (Derwent); 1955–57 Buckley and Mold; 1957–64 Wolstanton and Audley; 1964–69 Cannock Chase; 1969–75 Winsford; 1975–82 Northwich.
Special Interests: Local Methodist History, Conservation, Wild Life. *Hobbies and Recreations:* Gardening, Rambling.

COTTRELL, Frederick Walter James, Hill View, Doynton, Bristol BS15 5SU. (027582-2612) *b. 26 June 1900, Bristol. m. (1) 12 Dec 1925, (2) 22 March 1969: 2d, 1s (deceased).*
Education: 1912–1914 St. George Secondary, Bristol; 1919–1920 Cliff Coll.; 1920–23 Victoria Park.
Appointments: 1923–42 SW China Dt; 1942–45 Chaplain RAF; 1945–51 Home Organisation Sec. MMS; 1951–58 London, Highgate St.; 1955–57 Torquay (Union St.); 1957-63 Chairman, Bristol District.
Connexional Committees: 1945–55 MMS; 1957–63 Stationing Comm.
Special Interests: Philology. *Hobbies and Recreations:* Cricket, Reading, Music.

COULAM, Charles Eric, Rookland, 9 Warfield Villas, Highfield Rd., Ilfracombe, N. Devon EX34 9NZ. (0271-62175)–Dip Theol(Leeds). *b. 28 Nov 1930, Farlesthorpe, Nr. Alford, Lincolnshire. m. 11 Aug 1956: 1d., 2s.*
Education: Elem., left school at 14 years; 1953–56 Headingley.
Appointments: 1956–59 Upwell and Manea; 1959–64 Chipping Norton and Stow; 1964–67 Radstock; 1967–72 Hayle; 1972–79 Penzance; 1979– Ilfracombe; 1973–79 Secretary, Cornwall District Synod.
Hobbies and Recreations: Gardening, Walking, Sport (Spectator).

COULDWELL, Norma Beryl, 30 Green Lane, Bolton, Lancs BL3 2EF. (0204-22816) *b. 14 March 1934, Bolton, Lancs.*
Education: Local Prim., Jun. and Secondary Sch.; 1955–57 Ilkley Deaconess Coll.; 1977–78 Wesley, Bristol. *Appointments:* 1978 Bolton. *Connexional Committees:* 1973–74 Women's Fellowship 21 Committee. *Special Interests:* Industrial Chaplaincy and Hospital Chaplaincy. *Hobbies and Recreations:* A Little Gardening.

COUPLAND, Edwin Paul, 34 St. Mary's Hall Rd., Crumpsall, Manchester M86 6DZ. (061-740-1824)–BA(Leeds). *b. 5 July 1926, Berry Brow, Huddersfield. m.23 July 1955: 2d.*
Education: 1931–38 Berry Brow Council Inf. and Jun.; 1938–42 Huddersfield Coll.; 1950–53 Leeds Univ.; 1950–53 Headingley.
Appointments: 1949–50 Ashby-de-la-Zouch; 1953–55 Snaith; 1955–58 Bury; 1958–62 Manchester South East; 1962–66 Stoke-on-Trent (Burslem); 1966–73 Manchester North and Middleton; 1973–81 Swinton; 1981– Cheetham Hill and Prestwich.
Publications: Hymn Tunes: *In Places Where They Swing* (1964); *More For Swinging Places* (1966), Methodist Youth Department.
Special Interests: Listening to Classical and Swing Music, using Tape Recorder to good effect, Historical and Political Scene.
Hobbies and Recreations: Piano Playing and Composing Tunes, Seeing Plays/Films, either on TV or in Cinema, Watching Sports of various kinds, being present at Big Events like Test Matches.

COURTENAY, George Albert, 16 Forth An Nance, Portreath, Redruth, Cornwall TR16 4NQ. (0209-842098) *b. 6 Nov 1940, Totnes, Devon. m. 17 June 1967: 1d., 1s.*
Education: 1945–51 Totnes Prim. Sch., Totnes Jun. Sch.; 1951–55 Redruth Secondary Modern; 1961–62 Cliff Coll.; 1963–67 Didsbury, Bristol.
Appointments: 1967–69 Swindon; 1969–74 Pocklington; 1974–80 Swansea; 1980– Redruth.
Connexional Committees: 1970–72 Rural Life Committee.
Special Interests: School Governor at Portreath Inf./Jun. Sch. *Hobbies and Recreations:* Walking, Reading.

COUSIN, Peter Hedley, 20 The Copice, Sutton-in-Craven, Keighley, West Yorkshire BD20 8BT. (0535-35140)–MA(Cantab.), BD(Manchester). *b. 29 June 1943, Bradford, Yorkshire. m. 29 July 1967: 1d., 1s.*
Education: 1954–62 Whitcliffe Mount Grammar Sch., Cleckheaton, Yorkshire; 1962–65 Christ's Coll., Cambridge; 1965–66 Nottingham Univ.; 1972–74 Manchester Univ.; 1972–74 Hartley Victoria.
Appointments: 1974–77 Bradford Mission; 1977– South Craven.
Special Interests: Psychotherapy.
Hobbies and Recreations: Walking, Listening to Music.

COUSTICK, Alan Robert, 12 Golf Links Cresc., Tadcaster, North Yorkshire LS24 9HG. (0937-833358)–MA(Cantab.). *31 Dec 1948, Solihull. m. 25 April 1981.*
Education: 1953–56 Hall Green Inf. Sch., Birmingham; 1956–59 Hall Green Jun. Sch., Birmingham; 1959–66 King Edward's Sch., Birmingham; 1967–70 Selwyn Coll., Cambridge; 1970–72 Univ. of Manchester; 1973–75 Univ. of Birmingham; 1973–76 Queen's. *Appointments:* 1976–81 Shildon; 1981– Tadcaster.

COWBURN, Charles Edward Brian, South View, Hickling Rd., Sutton, Norwich NR12 9SH. (0692-80481) *b. 5 May 1894, Hull. m. (2) 31 July 1950: 1d., 2s.*
Educations: 1900–07 Hull Elementary; 1907–1909 Hull Municipal Technical Coll.; 1915–16 Headingley; 1919–20 Didsbury.
Appointments: 1921–22 Nottingham (Arkwright St.); 1922–24 Ripley; 1924–28 Birmingham (Smethwick); 1928–31 Hull (Queen's Road); 1931–34 Cromer; 1934–37 King's Lynn; 1937–45 Stockton (Brunswick); 1945–48 Hebden Bridge (Salem); 1948–52 Lincoln (Aldersgate); 1952–56 Rotherham; 1956 The Peak.
Special Interests: History and Travel.

COWDELL, John Mervyn, The Manse, Temple St., Fenton, Stoke-on-Trent ST4 4NW. (0782-411281) *b. 6 March 1946, Nottingham. m. 10 July 1971: 1d., 1s.*
Education: 1951–57 Ruddington St. Peter's Sch.; 1957–62 Braincote Hills Secondary/Technical; 1971/2 Matlock Coll. of Education; 1968–72 Richmond. *Appointments:* 1972–79 Mansfield West; 1979– Stoke-on-Trent (South).
Special Interests: Youth Work, Church in Industry. *Hobbies and Recreations:* Golf, Football, Cricket, Badminton, Politics.

COWELL, Leslie George, The Grove Manse, Town St., Horsforth, Leeds LS18 4RJ. (0532-582678)–MA(Cantab.). *b. 11 Aug 1924, Chadwell Heath, Essex. m. 22 June 1957: 3d.*
Education: 1929–1935 Melford House, Chingford; 1935–43 Leyton County High Sch.; 1946–49 St Catharine's Coll., Cambridge; 1949-51 Wesley House. *Appointments:* 1951–66 Burma District; 1966–69 Upwell and Manea; 1969–74 Ipswich; 1974–82 Leeds (South); 1982– Leeds (Hosforth and Bramley).
Connexional Committees: 1969–74 Methodist Missionary Society, Asia Committee; 1971–74 MMS General Committee. *Local Council*

Committees: 1975–78 Leeds Community Education Development Council.

COX, Alan, 32 Finch Rd., Berkhamsted, Herts. HP4 3LQ. (04427-6324) *b. 21 July 1926, Lingfield, Sussex. m. 13 Aug 1955: 1d., 2s.*
Education: 1930–40 Beacon Hill, Hindhead; 1940–41 Guildford Jun. Technical School; 1948–49 Cliff Coll., Sheffield; 1950–53 Hartley Victoria. *Appointments:* 1949–50 Sutton and Cheam; 1953–55 Liverpool NE; 1955–60 Liverpool Mission; 1960–65 High Wycombe; 1965–79 Staines and Feltham; 1979– Hemel Hempstead and Berkhamsted.

COX, Alan Geoffrey, 12 Hartop Close, Puntoe, Bedford MK41 8HF. (0234-52514) *b. 27 Sept 1931, Bromsgrove, Worcestershire. m. 10 Aug 1957: 1d, 1s.*
Education: 1942–48 Bromsgrove County High Sch.; 1948–51 Birmingham Coll. of Technology; 1955–57 Handsworth.
Appointments: 1957–60 Hindley; 1960–63 Bolton (Bridge St.); 1963–70 Tunstall; 1970–78 Runcorn; 1978– Bedford (North).
Connexional Committees: 1974–79 Ecumenical Committee; 1979– Joint Bldg–Co-operation with other Communions.
Special Interests: Ecumenical Movement. *Hobbies and Recreations:* Golf, Reading, Sport.

COX, Anthony Charles, 53 Westwood Rd., East Peckham, Tonbridge, Kent TN12 5DB. (0622-871332) *b. 3 Oct 1944, Luton, Bedfordshire. m. 22 Aug 1970: 3s.*
Education: 1976–78 Queen's.
Appointments: 1978–82 London, Streatham and Dulwich; 1982– Tonbridge.

COX, John Gray, Norbria, Riding Mill, Northumberland NE44 6HE. (043-482-332) *b. 9 April 1912, Sunderland, Co. Durham. m. 19 April 1941: 2d., 1s.*
Education: 1960–61 Headingley.
Appointments: 1961–64 Thornley; 1964–69 Hexham; 1969–74 Whitehaven; 1974–78 Stanley.

COX, Leslie David, 17 Hensingham Rd., Whitehaven, Cumbria CA28 8PS. (0946-2280) *b. 28 August 1919, Bolsover, Derbyshire. m. 4 Aug 1949: 1d., 1s.*
Education: 1931–36 Staveley (Derbyshire) Grammar Sch.; 1947–49 Hartley Victoria. *Appointments:* 1946–47 High Wycombe; 1949–54 Manchester (Chorlton and Moss Side); 1954-59 Pudsey; 1959–63 Sunderland; 1963–68 West Hartlepool; 1968–71 Jarrow; 1971-78 Orrell and Lambermead Green; 1978– Whitehaven.
Special Interests: Boys Brigade Work. *Hobbies and Recreations:* Oil Painting.

COX, Roland Lee, 146 Stag Lane, Kingsbury, London NW9 0QR. (01-204-7756)—BD(Lond.). *b. 30 Aug 1903, Long Lawford, Rugby, Warwicks. m. 6 Aug 1930: 3s.*
Education: 1912–20 Lawrence Sheriff Sch., Rugby; 1922–23 Cliff Coll.; 1923–27 Richmond.
Appointments: 1927–30 Swansea; 1930–37 Birmingham (Sutton Park); 1937–40 Lytham St. Annes; 1940–49 Bournemouth; 1949–55 Sutton (Surrey); 1955–60 Newcastle-upon-Tyne (Brunswick); 1960–66 Bristol (Clifton and Redlands).
Special Interests: I taught Hebrew at Handsworth Coll., 1930–31, while Dr. North was in USA.

CRACKNELL, Kenneth Robert, 43 Granby St., Loughborough, Leics LE11 3DU. (0509-26384)—MA, BD. *b. 19 June 1935, Leigh-on-Sea. m. 1 Aug 1959: 3d.*
Education: 1946–54 Royal Liberty Sch., Romford; 1954–57 Oxford; 1957–59 London; 1961–62 Leeds; 1957–59 Richmond. *Appointments:* 1959–61 Bourne; 1961–62 Missionary Training; 1962–63 East Nigeria Dt.; 1963–68 Nigeria Conf., Loughborough; 1978– British Council of Churches.
Connexional Committees: 1973–77, 1979– MCOD Central Committee.; Ecumenical Committee.
Publications: *Why Dialogue* (1980); *Considering Dialogue* (1981); Numerous Articles and Papers.
Special Interests: Biblical Study, Other Faiths, Ecumenical Questions. *Hobbies and Recreations:* Walking, Railways, Theatre and Films.

CRACKNELL, Vernon Francis, 7 Grange Rd., Egham, Surrey TW20 9QW. (0784-37973) *b. 21 Feb 1944, Edmonton, North Lonodon. m. 8 Aug 1970: 2d.*
Education: 1949–55 St Michaels Inf. and Jun. Sch., Palmers Green; 1955–60 Michenden Grammar Sch., Southgate; 1968–72 Wesley, Bristol.
Appointments: 1972–76 Andover; 1976– Staines and Feltham.
Special Interests: Work among Children and Young People (currently District Children's Sec.).
Hobbies and Recreations: Philately, Photography, Music, Gardening, Reading.

CRAMB, Ian Guthrie, 91 Lower Oldfield Park, Bath BA2 3HR. (0225-25830) *b. 22 Dec 1935, Ashton-under-Lyne, Lancs. m. 5 Aug 1961: 1d., 1s.*
Education: 1948–52 King's Coll. Sch., Cardiff; 1952–54 Cardiff Coll. of Technology and Commerce; 1957–61 Didsbury, Bristol.
Appointments: 1961–66 Coatbridge, Airdrie and Armadale; 1966–71 Blaydon; 1971–79 Bristol (Frome Valley); 1979– Bath.
Connexional Committees: Division of Education and Youth Board; 1972–78 Synod Representative.
Hobbies and Recreations: Gardening, Sketching.

CRAWFORD, Andrew, Cartref, Balmoral Place, Green Lane, Redruth TR15 1LA. (0209-217032) *b. 30 Jan 1909, Bootle, Liverpool. m. 12 Aug 1938: 1d.*
Education: Bedford Rd., Elem., Bootle; 1932–35 Handsworth.
Appointments: 1931–32 Porthleven, Cornwall; 1935–6 Home Mission Comm.; 1936–38 Cannock Chase; 1938–40 Liverpool Mission; 1940–48 Loughborough; 1948–53 Plymouth East; 1953–56 Brighton & Hove;

1956–61 Bath; 1961–65 Cadishead; 1965–70 Bodmin; 1970–74 Redruth.

CRAZE, Leslie George, 1 Orchard Lea, Guildhall Lane, Wedmore, Somerset BS28 4AJ. (0934-712673) *b. 13 March 1914, Paignton, S. Devon. m. 7 Sept 1943: 2d.*
Education: 1924-30 Torquay Grammar Sch.; 1935–38 Handsworth Coll. *Appointments:* 1938–45 Bombay and Punjab Dist., India; 1946–53 Trichinopoly Dist. and Diocese (CSI), S. India; 1953–60 Redhill; 1960–67 East Grinstead; 1967–70 St Leonards and Bexhill; 1970–75 Hastings, Bexhill and Rye; 1975–81 Penarth.
Connexional Committees: 1955–70 Overseas Mission; 1977–80 Homes for the Aged; 1977–81 Commission of Covenanting Churches in Wales.
Special Interests: Ecumenism, Local History. *Hobbies and Recreations:* Music, Gardening.

CREAMER, Denis John, 32 Russells Cres., Horley, Surrey RH6 7DN. (02934-4896)–BSc(Lond.). *m. 29 July 1950: 2s.*
Education: Hazelwood Lane Prim. and Jun Sch.; Southgate County Grammar Sch.; 1942–45 London Sch. of Economics; 1948–50 Handsworth. *Appointments:* 1945–47 HM Forces; 1950–53 Poulton; 1953–57 Colchester; 1957–62 West Wight; 1962–66 Salisbury; 1966–71 Sevenoaks; 1971–72 London, Ealing and Acton; 1972–77 Sutton (Surrey); 1977–82 Redhill and East Grinstead.

CREAMER, John Malcolm, 150 Marlborough Ave., Hull HU5 3JX. (0482-493937) *b. 8 July 1942, Padgate, Nr. Warrington, Cheshire. m. 14 Aug 1965. 1d., 2s.*
Education: 1947–52 Padgate CE Prim.; 1952–58 Urmston Grammar; 1973–75 Wesley, Bristol.
Appointments: 1975–80 Chorley; 1980– Hull West.
Connexional Committees: 1981–82 Education and Youth.
Special Interests: Music, Sport, Community Work. *Hobbies and Recreations:* Golf.

CREAMER, Patricia Margaret (Née McBride), 56 Hanover St., Ashton-under-Lyne, Lancs. OL5 0HL. (045-75-5267)–BA, M.Th. *b. 13 Dec 1952, Hitchin, Herts. m. 12 July 1980.*
Education: 1964–71 Letchworth Grammar Sch.; 1971–74, 1975–77 Univ. of Nottingham; 1974–77 Wesley, Bristol. *Appointments:* 1977–80 Exeter; 1980– Ashton-under-Lyne.

CREBER, Alan, 103 High St. South, Stewkley, Leighton Buzzard, Beds LU7 0HU. (052-524-251) *b. 20 Dec 1923, Plymouth. m. 12 Aug 1953: 3d.*
Education: 1928–31 Montpelier Jun. Sch; 1931–34 St. Budeaux Jun. Sch.; 1934–38 Tamar Central Sch.; 1949–51 Richmond. *Appointments:* 1948–49 London Mission (East Ham); 1951–53 Chislehurst; 1953–56 Stoke-on-Trent (Burslem Hill Top); 1956–62 Cambridge; 1962–68 Watford; 1968–75 Windsor and Maidenhead; 1975–80 Paulton (Amalgamated with Midsomer Norton and Radstock 1979); 1980– Leighton Buzzard and Stewkley.
Connexional Committees: 1958–66 Local Preachers; 1981– Ministries Division.
Special Interests: Family, Reading, Music. *Hobbies and Recreations:* Gardening, DIY.

CREBER, John Charles, 4 Dale Close, Littleton, Winchester, Hants SO2 6RA. (0962-881602)–CBE. *b. 27 Feb 1924, Redruth, Cornwall. m. 23 May 1953.*
Education: 1935–39 Public Central Sch., Plymouth; 1948–51 Hartley Victoria. *Appointments:* 1947–48 Camelford and Wadebridge; 1951–54 Plymouth East; 1954–57 Royal Army Chaplins' Deptartment; 1957–81 Royal Navy Chaplain.

CREE. John Richard, Trinity Manse, 78 Gillibrand Walks, Chorley, Lancs PR7 2HE. (025-72-62515)–BA(Open). *b. 12 May 1944, Bolton on Dearne, Rotherham, S. Yorkshire. m. 8 June 1968: 1d., 1s.*
Education: Dearnside Secondary Modern; Mexborough Schofield Technical Sch.; 1971–74 Open University; 1966 Headingley; 1967–70 Wesley, Bristol; 1974 Kingsmead, Selly Oak. *Appointments:* 1970–72 Corby; 1972–74 Wigan; 1974–78 Freetown Central, Sierra Leone; 1978– Chorley, Lancs.
Local Council Committees: District Home Missions Secretary.
Publications: Theology of Mission in an Urban Industrial and Rural Context (1976); West African Urban Industrial Rural Committee of the All African Conference of Churches (Published Lecture).
Special Interests: Philosophy.
Hobbies and Recreations: Model Railways.

CRESSWELL, Amos Samuel, 18 Velwell Rd., Exeter, Devon EX4 4LE. (0392-72541)–MA(Cantab.), BA(Durham). *b. 21 April 1926, Walsall Wood, Walsall, Staffordshire. m. 11 Feb 1956: 1d., 2s.*
Education: 1937–44 Queen Mary's Grammar Sch., Walsall; 1944–47 Univ. Coll., Durham; 1950–52 Cambridge Univ., (Fitzwilliam Coll.); 1952–53 Theological Seminary, Bethei bei Belefeld, Westphalia, West Germany; 1950–52 Wesley House. *Appointments:* 1949–50 Clitheroe; 1953–56 Asistant Tutor Richmond Coll.; 1956–61 Darlaston; 1961–66 Cliff Coll. (N.T. Tutor); 1966–73 Bramhall; 1973–76 Welwyn; 1976– Chairman Plymouth and Exeter District.
Connexional Commitees: 1963–78 Christian Citizenship Social Responsibility; 1967–68 LP; 1975–78 OM; 1976– HM; 1976– GP; 1971–73 Education (before DEY); 1980– Property. *Publications: The Story of Cliff* (1965); *The Story They Told*—A Study of the Gospels (1966); *Life Powers and Hope*—A Study of The Holy Spirit (1972).
Special Interests: Rotary Clubs; 1956–72 Assistant Examiner 'O' Level Religious Studies; 1972– Chief Examiner; Roman Imperial Coins, The American Civil War, Reading Poetry. *Hobbies and Recreations:* Being with the Family, Reduced to Watching Sport wherever I live, Supporter of West Bromwich Albion

(Soccer), Worcestershire (Cricket), and anybody else who plays in the spirit of the game, Music (especially National Folk Songs), Travelling and Visiting Historic Sites.

CRESSWELL, Roger, 9 The Avenue, Gravesend, Kent DA11 0NA. (0474-52266) *b. 19 Dec 1940, Hatfield Peverel, Chelmsford, Essex. m. 31 July 1965: 1d., 2s.*
Education: 1945–51 Hatfield Peverel CE Prim.; 1951–59 Maldon Grammar Sch.; 1961–62 Cliff Coll.; 1966 Kingsmead Coll.; 1962–66 Handsworth. *Appointments:* 1967–77 Methodist Church in Kenya; 1977– Gravesend and Dartford.
Connexional Committees: 1978–82 Methodist Relief Fund; 1980– Divisional Board, Division of Ministries; 1978– Overseas Division, Pastoral Committee.
Hobbies and Recreations: Gardening, Walking, Photography, Rotary, Music.

CREW, Clifford, Maycliffe, 66 Hillview Rd., Minehead, Somerset TA24 8EF. (0643 2764) *b. 25 Feb 1902, Waunllwyd, Monmouthshire. m. 28 Aug 1930: 1d., 3s.*
Education: 1907–1910 Council Schs., Waunllwyd; 1910–15 Victoria, Mon.; 1923–26 Handsworth.
Appointments: 1923–24 South Molton; 1927–30 Chipping Norton; 1930–31 Huntington Mission; 1931–34 Ormskirk; 1934–37 Neath; 1937–40 Tamworth; 1941–43 Bishops Castle; 1943–47 Ludlow; 1947–50 Bridgend; 1950–53 Stroud; 1953–56 Sheffield South; 1956–60 Sheffield, Carver Street; 1962–65 Hayle; 1965–66 South Petherton.

CREW, Roy Peter, 17 Hadlow Rd., Sidcup, Kent DA14 4AA. (01-300-3253) *b. 29 July 1935, Winterbourne, Glos. m. 10 Sept 1960: 1d., 1s.*
Education: Didsbury, Bristol 1963–66. *Appointments:* 1966–68 Canterbury and Faversham; 1968–73 Ashford (Kent); 1973– Chislehurst.

CREWE, Elgin Percy, 3 Pen Yr Allt, Watford Parc, Caerphilly, Mid Glamorgan, CF8 1NP. (0222-866684) *b. 31 Oct 1933, Hawkesbury, Glos (now Avon). m. 15 Dec 1974: 1d., 1s.*
Education: 1939–44 Hawkesbury Upton CE Prim. Sch.; 1944-49 Kathleen Lady Berkeley Grammar Sch.; 1957–61 Handsworth.
Appointments: 1961–63 Loftus and Staines; 1963–68 Easingwold; 1968–73 Poole; 1973–76 Shaftesbury and Gillingham; 1976–82 Caerphilly; 1982 Monmouth.
Hobbies and Recreations: Walking, Photography, Gardening.

CREWES, Frederick Ronald, Central Hall, Warwick Lane, Coventry CV1 1HA. (0203-23564)–JP, MA, BD(Lond.). *b. 14 Feb 1934, Truro, Cornwall. m. 23 July 1960: 1d., 1s.*
Education: 1945–50 Truro Sch.; 1954–57, 1965–73 Univ. of London; 1954–57 Richmond. *Appointments:* 1957–58 Isles of Scilly; 1958–60 London East Ham Mission; 1960–65 London, Broomwood and Clapham; 1965–70 South London Mission; 1970–75 Chaplain Woodhouse Grove Sch.; 1975– Coventry Mission.
Connexional Committees: 1962–65 Youth Committee; 1978– Central Mission Committee. *Local Council Committees:* 1965–70 Lambeth London Youth Committee; 1979– City of Coventry Education Committee and Further Education Committee; 1979– JP; 1980– Court of Warwick Univ.
Special Interests: Music and Drama.
Hobbies and Recreations: Music, Drama, Rugby, Cricket.

CRIBBIN, Keith Murray, Hamilton House, Bulford Rd., Tidworth, Hants SP9 7RZ. BA(Hull), BD(Manchester). *b. 12 Sept 1940, Secunderabad, Hyderabad State, South India. m. 25 Aug 1968: 1d., 1s.*
Education: 1952–53 Wolsingham Grammar Sch., Co. Durham; 1953–59 Ashville Coll., Harrogate; 1959–62 Hull Univ.; 1962–65 Manchester Univ.; 1962–65 Hartley Victoria.
Appointments: 1965–70 Edinburgh Mission; 1970–73 Ashville Coll., Harrogate (Chaplain); 1973– Chaplain HMF.
Special Interests: Christian Education, Industrial Mission, Mission to the Forces. *Hobbies and Recreations:* Indian Cookery, Gardening, Beer and Wine Making, Cricket and Golf.

CROCKER, Herbert John, Porthilly Greys, Rock, Nr. Wadebridge, Cornwall PL27 6JX. (020886–2589) *b. 22 Feb 1907, Gwinear, Nr. Camborne, Cornwall. m.11 Aug 1934 (w): 1s.*
Education: 1914–18 Basset Rd Sch., Camborne; 1918–20 Redruth County Sch.; 1920–24 Bodmin County Sch.; 1925–26 Cliff Coll.; 1928–31 Richmond. *Appointments:* 1927–31 South Molton; 1931–33 South Devon Mission; 1933–37 London, East Ham Mission; 1937–40 South Devon Mission; 1940–43 Swindon (Bath Rd); 1943–45 St. Just; 1945–51 St. Columb and Padstow; 1951–57 Perranporth and St Agnes; 1957–60 North Hill; 1960–63 Great Bentley; 1963–69 Coningsby; 1966–69 Camborne; 1969–72 Wellington (Salop); Officiating Chaplain (1946–51 RN, 1940–42, 1969–72 Army, 1943–45, 1972–79 RAF).

CROCKER, William John, 31 Quedeley, Yate, Bristol BS17 4JJ. (0454-312439) *b. 26 Sept 1933, Okehampton, Devon. m. 23 May 1981: 1d., 3s.*
Education: 1938–44 Bridestowe CE Sch.; 1944–50 Okehampton Grammar Sch.; 1959–63 Didsbury, Bristol. *Appointments:* 1963–64 Shepton Mallet; 1964–68 Cheddar Valley; 1968–76 Watford; 1976– Bristol (From Valley).
Hobbies and Recreations: Philately.

CROFTON, John William, Henge Close, Furlong Way, Shrewton, Salisbury, Wilts SP3 4DB. (0980-620327) *b. 3 Dec 1908, Bill Quay, County Durham. m. 14 Aug 1937–1d., 1s.*
Education: 1916–24 South Bank Central Sch.; 1929–32 Hartley Victoria. *Appointments:* 1932–33 Edinburgh, Leigh; 1933–36 Pateley Bridge; 1936–37 Lydney; 1937–40 Crowle; 1940–46 Chaplain HMF; 1946–50 Woodhouse Grove Sch. Chaplain; 1950–52 Staines and Feltham; 1952–60 Chaplain HMF;

1960–65 Scunthorpe; 1954–70 Clevedon; 1970–74 Tewkesbury. *Special Interests:* Music, Drama. *Hobbies and Recreations:* Gardening, Sport.

CROSBY, Bernard, 2 Belmont Court, 2 Ramshill Rd., Scarborough, N. Yorks YO11 2QE. (0723-72489) *b. 1 Apr 1911, Scarborough. m. 4 Sept 1939: 2d., 2s.*
Education: 1916–22 Scarborough Central; 1922–26 Scarborough Boys' High Sch.; 1932–35 Hartley Victoria. *Appointments:* 1935–59 West Indies Dt; 1959–64 British Honduras Dt; 1964–69 Easingwold; 1969–76 Hornsea.
Connexional Committees: 1965 Transfer of Authority to Overseas Districts. *Publications:* 2 Essays in *London Quarterly and Holborn Review,* October 1944 (Eayrs Prize), July 1950.
Special Interests: Overseas Missions. *Hobbies and Recreations:* Sports, especially Cricket, Chess.

CROSBY, Geoffrey Herbert, 7 Watkin Rd., Boscombe, Bournemouth, Dorset BH5 1HP. (0202-301035)–MA(Cantab.), BA(Manchester). *b. 3 June 1913, Burton on Trent. m. 20 July 1940: 1d., 2s.*
Education: 1922–25 King Edward 6th Grammar Sch., Nuneaton; 1925–32 Kingswood Sch., Bath; 1932–35 Manchester Univ.; 1935–38 Wesley House. *Appointments:* 1938–39 Biggleswade; 1939–42 Sheringham; 1940–42 Cromer, Sheringham and Holt; 1942–44 Diss; 1944–49 Oxford; 1949–54 Dorking and Horsham; 1954–58 Leicester (West); 1958–66 Dorchester; 1966–73 Petersfield and Haslemere; 1973–77 Dover.
Publications: A Bird's-Eye View of Christianity (Epworth Press 1950).

CROSBY, Kenneth Hubert, 2 Burnside, Ewhurst Rd., Cranleigh, Surrey GU6 7EF. (048-66-274621)–BA, BD, PHd(Lond.). *b. 11 May 1904, Briton Ferry. m. 5 Aug 1931: 1d., 1s.*
Education: 1909–12 Miss Aslin's Sch., Ripon; 1912–15 Guild St. Sch., Burton-on-Trent; 1915–21 Kingswood Sch., Bath; 1924–27 Richmond. *Appointments:* 1927–29 High Wycombe; 1929–38 Sierra Leone District; 1938–42 London, Harrow; 1942–46 Liverpool Central; 1946–51 Birkenhead; 1951–58 Wellasey; 1958–59 Sutton, Surrey; 1959–71 Manchester and Stockport District Chairman.
Connexional Committees: 1959–71 Church Membership; 1959–71 Home Mission; 1939–62 Overseas Mission, with two or three yearly 99/1s. *Publications: The Lord Jesus Christ* (Epworth Press 1944); Part Author of *An Introduction to the Study of Mende* (Heffer 1944).

CROSS, Joseph Donald, 51 George St., Ettingshall, Wolverhampton, West Midlands WV2 2LY. (0902-41613)–BSc. b. 31 Aug 1937, Wolverhampton. m. 21 Jan 1961: 1d., 1s.
Education: 1942–47 Essington CE Prim.; 1947–56 Bilston Boys Grammar Sch.; 1956–59 Univ. Coll., Leicester; 1959–60 Univ. of Leicester; 1978–80 Wesley House.
Appointments: 1980– Bilston.
Connexional Committees: 1981– Church and Industry (Home Missions).
Special Interests: Industrial Chaplaincy. *Hobbies and Recreations:* Walking, Sport, Reading, Family.

CROSS, Thomas Dunning, Pentlands, Borrowby, Thirsk, North Yorkshire YO7 4QQ. (0845-537461)–MA. *b. 9 Sept 1911, Melton Mowbray, Leicestershire. m. 10 Aug 1938: 1s.*
Education: Bruntsfield Prim. and Boroughmuir Secondary Schs., Edinburty; 1930–33 Edinburgh Univ.; 1933–36 Wesley House.
Appointments: 1936–38 Fleetwood; 1938–41 Bath; 1941–44 Glossop; 1944–48 Manchester, Withington; 1948–51 Brighouse; 1951–56 Thirks; 1956–59 Lancaster; 1959–66 Burton upon Trent; 1966–72 Goole; 1972–76 Glasgow, South.

CROSSLAND, Kenneth, The Manse, Fernleigh Rd., Grange-over-Sands, Cumbria LA11 7HN. (044-84-3164) *b. 6 Sept 1920, Salford. m. 29 July 1950: 2d., 1s.*
Education: 1931–34 Grecian St. Central; 1948–50 Hartley Victoria.
Appointments: 1946–47 North Scotland Mission; 1947–48 Manchester Mission; 1948–50 Hartley Victoria; 1950–54 Barnsley West; 1954–59 Stretford and Urmston; 1959–65 Barrow-in-Furness; 1965–68 Blackpool South; 1968–75 Manchester North and Middleton; 1975–80 Swindon; 1980– Ulverston.
Hobbies and Recreations: Rotary, Caravan Club, Photography.

CROSSLEY, John Hubert Stephen, 22 West Ridge, Frampton Cotterell, Bristol BS17 2JA. (0454-772104)–MA(Oxon), MA(Cantab.). *b. 26 June 1926, London. m. 18 Aug 1954: 1d., 2s.*
Education: 1931–36 Montpelier Sch., Plymouth; 1936–44 Devonport High Sch.; 1944 and 1953 Sch. of Oriental and African Studies, London; 1947–50 Merton Coll., Oxford; 1950–52 Fitzwilliam House, Cambridge; 1954 Selly Oak Colls., Birmingham; 1950–53 Wesley House.
Appointments: 1954–72 Nigeria Dt; 1959–72 Islam in Africa Project; 1972–77 Birmingham South West; 1977– Bristol Frome Valley.
Publications: Explaining the Gospel to Muslims (1960); *Questions Muslims Ask* (1967); *Christian Witness among Muslims* (1971).
Special Interests: Church Growth and Charismatic Renewal, Counselling and Healing Ministry; Folk Arts in Worship. *Hobbies and Recreations:* Walking, Talking.

CROWDER, Frank, Holmlea, 11 Willow Close, Horncastle, Lincs. (065-82-2306) *b. 16 Jan 1910, Lincoln. m. 7 Aug 1939 (w.): 1d., 1s.*
Education: 1915–24 Elem. Sch., Grimsby; 1933–37 Hartley Victoria.
Appointments: 1932–33 Guildford; 1933–37 Hartley Victoria Coll.; 1937–42 Spalding; 1942–47 Alford; 1947–52 Hull East; 1952–59 Shipley; 1959–66 Bilston (Staffs.); 1966–71 Middlesbrough; 1971–76 Fleetwood.

Connexional Committees: 1955–59 Christian Citizenship (now Social Responsibility).
Hobbies and Recreations: Gardening and Photography.

CROWTHER, Stanley, 23 Priory Lane, Kents Bank, Grange-over-Sands, Cumbria LA11 7BH. (04484-3694)–BA, BD. *b. 26 July 1913. m.*
Education: Halifax; 1936–39 Didsbury. *Appointments:* 1939–41 Saddleworth; 1941–43 Spilsby; 1943–46 Newcastle Mission; 1946–52 Bradford Manningham; 1952–57 Bradford Shipley; 1957–64 Pudsey; 1964–75 Halifax Wesley.

CROXFORD, William Thomas, Ludham, Great Yarmouth, Norfolk NR29 5QN. (0493-556) *b. 16 Oct 1893, Heath and Reach, Leighton Buzzard, Beds. m. 1959. Education:* 1896–1909 Heath and Reach; 1913–15 Richmond. *Appointments:* 1915–19 Army; 1919–21 Blackheath and Lewisham; 1921–23 The Peak; 1923–6 Barnsley; 1926–29 Peterborough; 1929–32 Bournemouth; 1932–34 Jersey; 1934–44 Andover; 1944–49 Guildford; 1949–56 Camelford and Wadebridge; 1956–60 Forest of Dean; 1960–62 Taunton.
Hobbies and Recreations: Gardening.

CROZIER, Arthur Edward, 29 Newland Park, Hull HU5 2DN. (0482-42799) *b. 1 Nov 1929, Warrington, Lancs. m. 7 Aug 1958: 2d.*
Education: 1948–51 Cliff Coll.; 1953–56 Headingley. *Appointments:* 1956–58 Home Mission Caravans; 1958–63 Burslem Mission; 1963–71 Manchester Mission; 1971–74 Bloomington (USA) Wesley; 1974– Hull Mission.

CRUISE, David Stanbury, 41 South Cottage Gardens, Chorleywood, Herts WD3 5EH. (092-78-2370)–BD(Lond.), ThM(Princeton USA). *b. 18 Aug 1935, Bideford, Devon. m. Clarke, Susan Mary, 23 March 1968: 1d., 1s.*
Education: 1947–52 Whitgift Sch., Croydon; 1953–57 Law Society's Sch. of Law; 1963–64 Princeton Theological Seminary, USA; 1960–63 Richmond. *Appointments:* 1964–65 Orpington; 1965–69 London, Lambeth Mission; 1969–76 Zambia Dt; 1976–82 London Mission (Plumstead); 1982– Overseas Division Secretary.
Special Interests: Africa. *Hobbies and Recreations:* Squash, Rough Shooting.

CRUMP, Frank Charles, Poplar Farm, Barrons Rd., Cheddar, Somerset. *b. 11 Sept 1906, West Bromwich, Staffs. m. 8 Aug 1934: 2d., 1s.*
Education: King Edwards Grammar (Birmingham); 1927–30 Hartley.
Appointments: 1930–32 Cardiff; 1932–34 London Mission, Plumstead; 1934–36 Deal; 1936–37 Canterbury; 1937–41 London Clapton; 1941–46 Chaplain HMF; 1946–50 Plymouth, King St.; 1950–55 Bristol South; 1955–62 Bristol, South Gloucestershire; 1962–66 Minehead.
Connexional Committees: 1957–63 HM Prison Committee.
Hobbies and Recreations: Chamber Music, Bowls.

CUBBON, Robert Edward, St. Clairs, Mountain View, Peel, Isle of Man. (062-484-2973) *b. 18 June 1907, Peel, Isle of Man. m. 7 Aug 1934: 1d.*
Education: 1910–21 Peel Clothworkers Sch.; 1922–23 Peel Clothworkers Night Sch.; 1925–26 Cliff Coll.; 1927–30 Hartley.
Appointments: 1930–32 Northwich; 1932–34 Eyemouth (Berwick); 1934–37 Trowbridge; 1937–40 Talk of the Hill; 1940–46 Chaplain HMF; 1946–50 Croydon; 1950–55 Liverpool North; 1955–68 Liverpool, Linacre Mission; 1968–71 Southport.
Special Interests: Evangelism—Open Air Work. *Hobbies and Recreations:* Sea Fishing, Sailing, Woodwork, Gardening.

CULLINGTON, Richard, Lexden, 121 Bodmin Rd., Truro, Cornwall TR1 1BQ. (0872-74383) *b. 21 June 1915, Peterborough. m. 8 Jan 1944: 1d., 1s.*
Education: 1923–26 Hoe Grammar Sch., Plymouth; 1926–32 Truro Sch.; 1937–40 Richmond.
Appointments: 1940–42 Bude; 1942–47 Chaplain HM Forces; 1947–54 Launceston; 1954–60 Liskeard; 1960–67 Penzance; 1967–74 Salisbury; 1974–80 King's Lynn; 1948–65 Territorial Army Chaplain, Duke of Cornwall's Infantry, 1960 Awarded TD; 1961–67 Chaplain West Cornwall Methodist Sch. (Girls); 1964–67 Cornwall District Synod Secretary.
Hobbies and Recreations: Cine Photography.

CULLUM, John Arthur, Harwood Court, Methodist Home For The Aged, Highburn, Cramlington, Northumberland NE23 6AZ. (9945-712492) *b. 15 Aug 1902, Ferryhill, Co. Durham. m. 2 July 1932, (w.): 1s.*
Education: 1913–18 Alderman Wraith Secondary Sch., Spennymoor; 1925–28 Hartley. *Appointments:* 1928–30 Tranent, Scotland; 1930–32 Rochdale, Smith St.; 1932–36 West Auckland; 1936–42 Jarrow; 1942–47 Gateshead West; 1947–52 York Wesley; 1952–57 Darlington North; 1957–63 Bolton Park St.; 1963–70 Hexham.
Special Interests: Philosophy, Poetry, Theology. *Hobbies and Recreations:* Sport, Music.

CULSHAW, Joseph Clifford, 9 John St., Stratford on Avon, Warwickshire CV37 6UB. (0789-292557)–MA(Oxon), BA(Cantab.). *b. 13 Feb 1910, Darjeeling, India. m. 3 Aug 1940: 2d.*
Education: 1921–29 Bridlington Sch.; The Queen's Coll., Oxford; Wesley House. *Appointments:* 1934–38 Baukura Coll., Bengal; 1940–48 Bengal District; 1948–51 Aylesbury; 1951–53 Luton; 1953–61 Kingswood Sch., (Chaplain); 1961–66 Bramley; 1966–71 Haywards Heath; 1971–75 Newcastle (Brunswick).
Connexional Committees. 1950–53, 1963–66, 1972–75 MMS Central Committees; 1963–66, 1972–75 Candidates Committee; 1982 Methodist Representative to Waldensian Methodist Synod.

Publications: Sundry Papers on Botany, Ornithnology, Education, Biblical Historical Studies. *Special Interests:* Languages, Literature, Art, including Teaching of Latin, Greek and Italian. *Hobbies and Recreations:* Gardening, Botany, Photography, Opera.

CUMBERLAND, George Herbert, 9 Priory Cresc., Penwortham, Preston PR1 0AL. (0772-744075) *b. 27 April 1905, Rawmarsh. m. 1 Aug 1933: 1s.*
Education: Rawmarsh Central, Mexborough Secondary; 1927–30 Didsbury. *Appointments:* 1926–27 Dorchester; 1927–30 Didsbury Coll.; 1930–32 Ludlow; 1932–35 Oldbury; 1935–36 Lancaster, Moor Lane; 1936–39 Manchester Harpurley; 1939–44 Nuneaton and Atherstone; 1944–48 Nelson; 1948–52 Accrington; 1952–57 Padiham; 1957–60 Darwen; 1960–65 Jarrow; 1965–69 Preston Lune St. and Orchard.

CUMBERS, Frank Henry, 23 Littlebury Gardens, Colchester, Essex CO2 8TB. (0206-71207)–BA, BD, DD. *m.*
Education: 1927–31 Richmond. *Appointments:* 1926–27 Colchester; 1927–31 Richmond Coll.; 1931–34 London Kilburn and Hampstead; 1934–36 Shepton Mallett; 1936–40 Peterborough; 1940–45 London Kilburn and Hampstead; 1945–47 London Ealing and Acton; 1947–48 Asst. Book Steward; 1948–69 Book Steward.
Publications: Richmond College 1843–1943 (1943); *The Book Room* (1956).

CUMMINGS, Arthur D., 37 Louis Drive, East Rayleigh SS6 9DU. (0268-771224)–BA(Open). *b. 26 Nov 1911, Sunderland. m. 20 July 1940: 1d., 1s.*
Education: Open University; 1933–36 Didsbury. *Appointments:* 1936–38 Birkenhead; 1938–41 Liverpool Mission; 1941–43 Gainsborough; 1943–47 Stoke-on-Trent, Burslem; 1947–49 Slough Mission; 1949–52 Wednesbury Mission; 1952–55 Bradford Cent. Hall; 1955–61 Blackburn Mission; 1961–63 Rhondda; 1963–68 Swindon; 1968–71 London Kilburn and Hampstead; 1971–75 Tiverton; 1975–77 London Tottenham and Stoke Newington.
Publications: WHS Lecture 1962 Portrait in Pottery.
Special Interests: Methodist History.

CUPIT, Kenneth, 13 Westbury Gardens, Belper, Derby DE5 1LD. (077382-2162) *b. 19 April 1931, Ripley, Derbyshire. m. 21 July 1956.*
Education: 1935–39 Codnor, Mill Lane Inf.; 1939–42 Cross Hill CE Jun. Boys Sch.; 1942–49 Heanor Grammar Sch.; 1949–51 RAF; 1951–54 Hartley Victoria. *Appointments:* 1954–57 Dorchester; 1957–62 Birmingham (Quinton); 1962–67 Nottingham (Central); 1967–72 Castle Donington; 1972–79 Burton on Trent; 1979– Belper.
Connexional Committees: 1977– Board of Property.
Special Interests: Industrial Mission and Religious Broadcasting (Local Radio). *Hobbies and Recreations:* Gardening, Railways, Philately.

CURNOW, Howard, 3 Kingswood Terrace, Holsworthy, Devon EX22 6HH. (0409-253640)–BSc, AKC. *b. 28 Oct 1941, Cornwall, St. Anthony-in-Meneage. m. 6 Aug 1966: 2s.*
Education: 1946–52 Manaccan CP; 1952–60 Helston County Grammar; 1960–63 King's Coll.; 1963–64 Westminster Coll.; 1974–76 Wesley, Bristol. *Appointments:* 1974–82 Carlisle; 1982– Holsworthy.

CURNOW, John Stuart, 9 Wayville Rd., Dartford, Kent DA1 1RL. (0322 20514)–MA(St Andrews), BA(Bristol). *b. 20 December 1936, Beckenham, Kent. m. 11 Aug 1962: 3d., 1s.*
Education: 1942–47 Otford County Prim. Sch., Kent; 1947–55 Sevenoaks Sch., Kent; 1957–61 St. Andrews Univ., Scotland; 1961–65 Bristol Univ.; 1961–65 Didsbury, Bristol. *Appointments:* 1965–66 Assistant Tutor, Didsbury Coll.; 1966–70 Dursley and Stonehouse; 1970–76 Bristol East and Bristol, Frome Valley; 1976– Gravesend and Dartford.
Connexional Committees: 1972–74 Connexional Candidates Committee; 1974–76 Board of Division of Ministries; 1982– Religious Advisory Panel, Radio Medway.
Special Interests: Work of the Holy Spirit, Ministry of Healing, Circuit Work. *Hobbies and Recreations:* Ornithology, Philately, Family Life.

CURREY, Allan Hartley, 6 Grovelands, Lower Bourne, Farnham, Surrey GU10 3RQ. (0252-73681) *b. 19 March 1911, Maryport, Cumberland, Cumbria. m. 7 April 1942: 1d., 3s.*
Education: 1916–18 Kindergarten (Carlisle Girls High Sch.); 1918–21 CE Board Sch. (Stanwix); 1921–24 Carlisle Grammar Sch.; 1924–28 Rydal Sch., Colwyn Bay; 1931–35 Regent St., Poly. (Building Centre); 1935–38 Richmond. *Appointments:* 1938–40 President's Assistant in Southport (South) Circuit; 1940–44 Petersfield and Haslemere (OCF to HMS Mercury); 1944–48 Eastleigh (OCF Fleet Air Arm); 1948–52 Dorking and Horsham; 1952–57 Chichester and Bognor (OCF Tangmere RAF); 1957–62 London Harrow; 1962–67 Wanstead and Woodford; 1967–74 Camberley.
Special Interests: In past Scouting, TocH, Rotary. *Hobbies and Recreations:* Painting, Reading, Gardening, Walking, Nature Study.

CURRY, Peter Finch, 79 London Rd., Enfield, Middlesex EN2 6ES. (01-363-1035)–BA(Dunelm). *b. 14 Feb 1940, Stockton-on-Tees. m. 17 June 1963: 3d., 4s.*
Education: 1944–46 Queen Victoria High Sch., (Stockton); 1946–53 Red House Preparatory Sch. (Norton-on-Tees); 1953–58 Culford (Bury St Edmunds); 1958–61 Durham (Bede Coll.); 1961–63 Wesley House.
Appointments: 1964–68 Ashford; 1968–75 Purley; 1975– London, Enfield.
Connexional Committees: 1976– NCH General Committee.
Special Interests: Ecumenical.

CURTIS, Kenneth William, 34 Bowfell Close, Little Marton, Blackpool, Lancs FY4 45Q. (0253-691030) *b. 20 Feb 1912, Great Yarmouth, Gorleston. m. 2 Nov 1940: 2s.*
Education: East Anglian Sch., Bury St. Edmunds; 1932–35 Hartley Victoria. *Appointments:* 1935–37 Southsea; 1937–40 Petersfield and Haslemere; 1940–42 Banbury; 1942–44 East Suffolk; 1944–46 Swindon (Regent St.); 1946–50 East Suffolk; 1950–54 Norwich St. Peters; 1954–60 High Wycombe; 1960–65 Letchworth; 1965–69 Gt. Yarmouth and Gorleston; 1969–74 London Leytonstone and Forest Gate; 1974–78 Makerfield.
Publications: I Have Decided (Pamphlet Epworth Press); Hymn Tunes *A Creed, Guidance* (MYD); *Trusting, Little Lord Jesus* (Peace Bros.)
Special Interests: Music, Conducting Local Church Choirs. *Hobbies and Recreations:* Composing Hymn Tunes.

DABILL, Samuel Stafford, 20 Kenilworth Rd., Fleet, Hants GU13 9AT. (025 14 6374) *b. 6 Sept 1886, Hucknall, Notts. m. May 1915 (w.): 2d., 1s.*
Education: Spring Street, Hucknall, Notts; 1907–1910 Ranmoor, Sheffield. *Appointments:* 1910–12 St. Ives, Cornwall; 1912–16 Barnsley; 1916–21 (Sheffield) Surrey St.; 1921–24 Sheffield South; 1924–28 Dewsbury; 1928–35 (Barnsley) Ebenezer and West; 1935–45 (Salisbury) Milford St.; 1945–52 Christ Church, Cradley Heath.
Publications: 1974 Man at the Keyhole, (Autobiography).
Hobbies and Recreations: Golf.

DAGG, William, 11 The Garlands, Scarborough, N.Yorks YO11 2SU. (0723 61124)–BD *b. 25 Nov 1919, Hylton, Nr. Sunderland. m. 19 Aug 1947, (w.): 1s.*
Education: Wolsingham Grammar; 1942–45 London. 1939–42 Hartley Victoria. *Appointments:* 1942–46 (Manchester) City Rd.; 1946–50 Spennymoor and Ferryhill; 1950–59 North Shields and Whitley Bay; 1959–65 Scarborough; 1965–70 Sunderland South; 1970–79 Liverpool South East; 1979– Scarborough.
Connexional Committees: 1946–50 Overseas Missions; 1968–73 Methodist Stewardship.

DAIN, Sidney John, 10 Vivian Park, Swanage, Dorset BH19 1PJ. (0929 423236)–BD. *b. 15 May 1919, Wolverhampton. m. 5 Aug 1944: 1d., 1s.*
Education: 1930–35 Wolverhampton Grammar Sch.; 1938–40 Handsworth; 1940–42 Headingley. *Appointments:* 1942–44 Worcester; 1944–47 Chaplain H.M.F.; 1947–50 Newbury; 1950–52 Ashton-under-Lyne; 1952–57 Colwyn Bay and Llandudno; 1957–62 Bramhall; 1962–67 Reading; 1967–76 Swanage; 1976–81 Portsmouth and Southsea.
Connexional Committees: 1956–59 Candidates.
Hobbies and Recreations: Gardening, Crafts.

DAINTY, Peter Robin, 21 Tut Hill, Fornham All Saints, Bury St. Edmunds, Suffolk IP28 6LD. (0284 66976). BA(Leeds), BD(Manchester) *b. 27 Nov 1936, Leeds. m. Aug 1961: 2d., 1s.*
Education: 1948–50 Doncaster Grammar Sch. for Boys; 1950/52 Sir Joseph Williamson's Mathematical Sch. for Boys, Rochester, Kent; 1952–55 Aireborough Grammar Sch., Leeds; 1955–58 Leeds Univ.; Manchester Univ.; 1968 Bingley Coll. of Education; 1958–61 Hartley Victoria. *Appointments:* 1961–65 Brigg; 1965–68 Pontefract; 1972–82 Bury St. Edmunds; 1969–71 Schoolmaster, Lovelane J.M. Sch., Pontefract and 1971– Culford Sch.
Publications: Poems in *Worship and Preaching,* and *The Bridge* Magazines.
Hobbies and Recreations: Reading, Writing, Armchair sport, Gardening, Music.

DALBY, John, 38 Deepdale Lane, Nettleham, Lincoln LN2 2LT. (0522 751162)–MA. *b. 2 April 1898, Leeds. m. 1926, (w.): 2d.*
Education: 1909–1916 West Leeds High; 1919–22 Leeds Univ.; 1922–24 Oxford (Oriel Coll.); 1935–38 Headingley. *Appointments:* 1938–44 South Ceylon Dt; 1944–49 Lincoln; 1949–53 Pudsey; 1953–57 Sleaford; 1957–60 Lincoln (Central); 1960–63 Coninsby.
Special Interests: Overseas Missions. *Hobbies and Recreations:* Gardening.

DALE, Ralph William, Bourne Villa, Park Bank, Congleton Cheshire CW12 3DH. (026 02 2216) *b. 5 Oct 1925, Upperhulme, Leek, Staffs. m. 24 Sept 1960: 2s.*
Education: 1930–37 Ramshaw Sch.; 1937–43 Leek High Sch.; 1943 Manchester Art Sch.; 1944–45 Burslem Sch. of Art; 1953–56 Handsworth. *Appointments:* 1956–59 Leominster; 1959–63 Claycross; 1963–68 Retford; 1968–73 Macclesfield; 1973–80 Cheadle, Staffs; 1980 Congleton.
Special Interests: M.R.F., R.A.F.A., Art and Design. *Hobbies and Recreations:* Farm work and building.

DALE, Ronald William, 17 Aldrin Rd., Pennsylvania, Exeter EX4 5DN. (0392 38648) *b. 1 June 1934, Kingston upon Hull. m. 18 Aug 1962: 1d., 1s.*
Education: 1946–48 Sir Henry Cooper; 1948–49 Eastfield High Sch.; 1958–59 Cliff Coll.; 1960–64 Handsworth. *Appointments:* 1964–66 Bude; 1966–69 Oldham (East); 1969–74 Birmingham (Wesley); 1974–81 Newton Abbot; 1981– Exeter.
Special Interests: Broadcasting BBC and Commercial Radio, Industrial Mission.
Hobbies and Recreations: Childrens magic, Sport, Ornithology, History.

DALE, Trevor, 25 Bellway, Woburn Sands, Milton Keynes MK17 8UG. (0908 583857) *b. 17 July 1933, Cudworth, South Yorkshire. m. 23 Aug 1958: 2d.*
Education: 1938–44 Cudworth Primary Sch., 1944–49 Barnsley Holgate Grammar Sch.; 1952–55 Richmond Coll. *Appointments:* 1955–58 Ilkeston; 1958–62 Denby

Dale; 1962–67 Ilkley; 1967–71 Bradford Woodhouse Grove; 1971–81 Milton Keynes.
Connexional Committees: Church Membership, Industrial Committee, Appeals Committee. *Council Member:* Woburn Sands Town Council. *Local Council Committees:* 1977–78 Woburn Sands Town Mayor.
Special Interests: Industrial Mission. *Hobbies and Recreations:* Reading.

DAMS, Brian W, 85 Lord Haddon Rd., Ilkeston, Derbys DE7 8AX. (0602 325850)–MA(Cantab), BA(Dunelm). *Education:* 1954–56 Wesley House, Cambridge. *Appointments:* 1958–60 Great Yarmouth Temple; 1960–65 Ipswich; 1965–70 Hunstanton and Docking; 1970–77 Leicester West; 1977– Ilkeston.

DANIEL, Richard, 8 Moorsfield Avenue, Audlem, Crewe CW3 0LA. (0270 811659) *b. 5 Mar 1901, Ripley, Derbyshire. m. 15 July 1930: 2d.*
Education: 1906–1912 Ripley Council Sch.; 1912–15 Heanor Technical Sch.; 1924–27 Handsworth. *Appointments:* 1923–24 Oldbury; 1927–36 British Guyana Dist. W.I.; 1936–38 Barbados and Trinidad Dist. W.I.;1938–42 West Mon Mission; 1942–48 Barbados and Trinidad Dist. W.I.;1948–51 Northwich; 1951–54 Nantwich; 1954–56 Guyana Dist.; 1956–61 Buckley and Mold; 1961–67 Ossett and Horbury; 1957–61 Missionary Committee.

DANN, Brian, 302 Bowthorpe Rd., Norwich NR5 8AB. (0603 24576) *b. 23 Aug 1936, Middlesbrough. m.: 2d.*
Education: 1947–52 Acklam Hall, Middlesbrough; 1960–63 Didsbury Coll., Bristol; 1964–1977 Zimbabwe Conf.; 1978– Norwich.
Hobbies and Recreations: Squash, Chess.

DARE, Jeremy Charles, 84 Florida Rd., Thornton Heath, Surrey CR4 8EW. (01-764 2965)–BSc, BA(Bristol) *b. 8 Sept 1951, Brighton, Sussex. m. 23 June 1973.*
Education: 1963–70 Bexhill Grammar Sch. for Boys; 1971–75 North Staffordshire Polytechnic; 1978–81 Bristol Univ.; 1978–82 Wesley Coll., Bristol. *Appointments:* 1982– London, Streatham and Dulwich.
Special Interests: Methodist Class System. *Hobbies and Recreations:* Painting, Fell Walking, Gardening, Carpentry.

DARLINGTON, Thomas William Maurice, The Manse, Hay, St. Stephen, St. Austell, Cornwall PL26 7LF. (0726 822282) *b. 2 April 1921, Coombe-Bissoe, Truro, Cornwall TR4 8RF. m. 30 July 1950: 1s.*
Education: 1926–32 Cusgarn Council; 1932–37 Truro Sch.; 1948–50 Didsbury Coll., Bristol.
Appointments: 1946–48 Oundle; 1950–51 Yeovil; 1951–54 Tavistock; 1954–59 Porthleven; 1959–65 E. Cornwall Mission; 1965–70 Northlew; 1970–77 Chagford; 1977–82 Camelford and Wadebridge; 1982– St. Austell.
Connexional Committees: 1953–54 Christian Citizenship. *Publications:* Various letters in Press including *Methodist Recorder; 1957–58 Why These Examinations?* (Methodist L.P. Depts Preliminary Booklets No. 3); *1957–58 Histories of Carleen, Godolphim, Roseudgeon, Ashton-Breage, Porthleven Circuit.*
Special Interests: Theological Notes in very wide blank margin Bible and Relation of Theology to Social Responsibility as means of local evangelism, Evangelism through press correspondents. *Hobbies and Recreations:* Goat Keeping (1959–77 in 3 circuits), Gardening, Cornish Dialect as distinct from Celtic language.

DAVEY, Cyril James, 17 Yeomead, Nailsea, Bristol BS19 1JA. (0272 852354) *b. 31 May 1911, Liverpool. m. 19 Aug 1937: 2d., 1s.*
Education: Redruth County Sch.; 1930–33 Handsworth.
Appointments: 1937–39 Tonbridge; 1939–47 Bombay and Punjab District; 1947–51 Watford; 1951–56 Liverpool South; 1956–62 Epsom; 1962–65 Reigate; 1965–76 Home Secretary, Methodist Missionary Society.
Publications: Has published a steady stream of books since 1942.

DAVEY, Thomas Frank, 12 Garland Avenue, Emsworth, Hants PO10 7QA. (02434 3672)–OBE, CBE, MSc(London), MD(Manchester), MBChB(Manchester) *b. 26 March 1908, London. m. 1 Aug 1939.*
Education: 1919–26 Christs Coll., Finchley; 1926–28 London Univ.; 1930–35 Manchester Univ. Medical Sch.; 1929–35 Hartley Victoria Coll.
Appointments: 1936–59 Uzuakoli Leprosy Hospital, E. Nigeria; 1960–68 Medical Secretary, Methodist Missionary Society; 1968–73 Director, Victoria Hospital, Dichpalli, A.P. India; 1951–54 Leprosy Adviser Nigerian Govt.; 1954–59 Senior Specialist (Leprosy), Nigerian Government.
Connexional Committees: 1960–68 Methodist Missionary Society Officer; 1964, 1966, 1967, Late Member, World Council of Churches Founding Committees of the Christian Medical Commission; Vice President The Leprosy Mission; Vice President LEPRA.
Publications: Numerous scientific articles and lectures on Leprosy; Joint Editor *'Leprosy in Theory and Practice' 1964;* Editor *'Leprosy Review' 1974–79; 'Compassionate Years' 1964. Special Interests:* Leprosy, Religion and Medicine. *Hobbies and Recreations:* Music, Watercolorist (Member, Portsmouth Hampshire Art Society, Medical Art Society).

DAVIDSON, Derek, Epworth, 10 Church Rd., Leatherhead, Surrey KT22 8AY. (53 72743) *b. 8 May 1930, London. m. 11 June 1966: 2s.*
Education: 1935–41 Heston Prim. and Jun. Sch.; 1941–47 Isleworth County Grammar Sch.; 1952–56 Northampton Poly. (Univ. of London); 1958–63 City of London Literary Institute; 1963–66 Handsworth Coll. *Appointments:* 1966–69 Oldbury; 1969–74 Barnet; 1974–82 Alderley Edge and

Knutsford; 1982– Dorking and Horsham. *Connexional Committees:* 1966– Methodist Drama Committee (Chairman 1982); 1973– Division of Ministries (Board Member 1973–76); *Council Member:* Greater Manchester Ecumenical Council (1975–82 Local Radio sub-committee vice-chairman and Secretary).
Publications: Plays and programmes for radio and T.V. production; Lectures at various conferences and workshops.
Special Interests: Drama (Religious Drama in particular), Radio, Poetry, varied 'forms' of Worship. *Hobbies and Recreations:* Drama, Hi-Fi, Photography, Cricket, Walking, Family Life, Music.

DAVIES, Alan John, 7 Durham Avenue, Bromley, Kent BR2 0OA. (01-464 4745)–BA(Livp), MA(Cantab).
Education: Liverpool Univ.; 1953–56 Wesley House. *Appointments:* 1952–53 H.M. Comm.; 1953–56 Wesley House; 1956–61 Great Horwood; 1961–66 Leicester North; 1966–69 Wantage and Abingdon; 1969– Secretary H.M. Division.
Connexional Committees: 1969– Home Mission Division (Conference Journal Secretary).

DAVIES, Daniel, 54 Bryn Castell, Bow Street, Aberystwyth SY24 5DF. 0970/828880 *b. 3 Nov 1914, Capel Dewi, Llandysul. m. 9 Oct 1945: 1d.*
Education: 1936–39 Headingley.
Appointments: 1935–36 Llanrhaeder; 1939–42 Machynlleth; 1942–45 Llandeilo, Tirydeul; 1945–50 Swansea; 1950–55 Dolgelley; 1955–60 Swansea; 1960–65 Coedpoeth; 1965–80 Aberystwyth.

DAVIES, Edward Gordon, 9 Central Avenue, Church Stretton, Shropshire SY6 6EE. (0694 723650) *b. 27 Nov 1911, Eccles, Lancs. m. 20 April 1949.*
Education: 1920–25 Croxton Preparatory, Southport; 1925–28 Leys, Cambridge; 1932–36 Didsbury.
Appointments: 1937–38 President's List; 1938–40 Ambleside; 1940–43 H.M.Com. (Clubland); 1943–46 H.M.F. Chaplain; 1946–49 York (Wesley); 1949–52 London (Broomwood); 1952–58 H.M.F. Chaplain; 1958–63 Birmingham (Elmdon); 1963–70 London (Finsbury Park); 1970–75 Birmingham (South West); 1975–79 St. Austell.
Connexional Committees: 1976–79 Property Committee.

DAVIES, Enoc Thomas, Bryn Awew, Talsarnaw, Gwynedd LL47 6WH. (770/316) *b. 23 June 1910, Bont-y-Foel, Capel Dewi, Llandyssul, Dyfed. m. 8 April 1947.*
Education: 1915–24 Capel Dewi Prim. Sch.; 1924–28 Grammar Sch. Pencader; 1932–35 Headingley.
Appointments: 1931–32 Caernarfon; 1935–39 Llandeilo; 1939–45 Aberystwyth; 1945–50 Machynlleth; 1950–55 Llanrwst; 1955–60 Bangor; 1960–65 Conway; 1965–70 Abergele; 1970–75 De. Gwynedd.

DAVIES, Frederick Warren, Yonder, St. White's Rd., Cinderford, Glos. GL14 3ER. (0594 22210). *b. 10 Oct 1911, Acton, Middlesex. m. 31 Aug 1940: 1d., 1s.*
Education: 1916–1925 Lawn Lane L.C.C. Sch.; 1925–28 City of London Coll.; 1948–1950 Richmond Coll.
Appointments: 1947–48 Liverpool Central; 1950–53 Watton and Rockland; 1953–56 Thetford; 1956–61 Wallasey; 1961–67 Wimbledon; 1967–72 Shooters Hill; 1972–77 Newbury and Hungerford; 1977– Forest of Dean.
Special Interests: Hospital Chaplaincy, work among disabled people.
Hobbies and Recreations: Music Astronomy, Reading, Gardening.

DAVIES, George Herber, 99 Cranleigh Rd., Worthing, W.Sussex BN14 7QR. (0903 32658)–BD(London) *b. 2 July 1916, Colwyn Bay, N. Wales. m. 27 July 1950: 2d.*
Education: Coll. Sch., Colwyn Bay; Richmond. *Appointments:* 1941–43 Southall and Uxbridge Mission; 1943–47 Chaplain HMF; 1947–50 London, Chingford; 1950–55 London, Ilford; 1955–61 London, Harrow; 1961–64 Ipswich, Museum St.; 1964–69 London, Wesley's Chapel; 1969–75 Purley; 1975–81 Brighton and Hove.
Connexional Committees: 1964–69 Connexional Church Membership Committee.

DAVIES, Gwynfor, 14 Carmen Court, Eastbourne Rd., Lower Willingdon, Monmouth. (032 12 4907) *b. 30 Jan 1917, Treorchy, Mid. Glam. m. 10 Aug 1946: 1s.*
Education: 1930–35 Goole Grammar Sch.; 1938–39 Cliff Coll.; 1939–41 Didsbury, Bristol; 1941–42 Hartley Victoria. *Appointments:* 1942–43 Isles of Scilly; 1944–45 Southampton; 1946–48 Crosskeys; 1949–52 Helston; 1953–56 Faversham; 1957–61 Exeter; 1962–67 Oswestry; 1968–72 Neath; 1973–77 Cardiff; 1978–82 Monmouth and Ross; 1982 Supernumerary retiring to Eastbourne.
Hobbies and Recreations: Gardening, Music, Reading.

DAVIES, John Darrel, 93 St. Michael Rd., Lichfield, Staffordshire WS13 6SN. (05432 22368)–BA(Bristol), MA(Cantab) *b. 10 Feb 1940, Coseley, Bilston, Staffs. m. 17 Aug 1963: 1d., 1s.*
Education: 1945–51 Hurst Hill Prim.; Coseley Board Sch., Nr. Bilston; 1951–58 Wolverhampton Grammar Sch.; 1958–61 Univ. of Bristol; 1961–63 Wesley House. *Appointments:* 1963–64 Missionary Training; 1964–66 Birmingham Mission; 1966–70 Shebbear Coll., Chaplain; 1970–75 Stoke-on-Trent, South; 1975–80 Birmingham, Islington and Quinton; 1980– Lichfield.
Connexional Committees: 1977–79 Ministries Divisional Board.

DAVIES, Joseph Haines, Goleugell, 24 Cadwgan Rd., Colwyn LL29 9PY. (0492/55463) *b. 15 January 1917, Caernarfon. m. 2 April 1947: 1d., 1s.*
Education: C'fon Prim.; C'fon County; 1946–47 Handsworth.
Appointments: 1943–46 Glamorgan Mission, Welsh; 1947–48 Dogelley Do; 1948–49 Abercon Do;1949–53

Llandil Do; 1953–65 Aberystwyth Do; 1965–70 Holywell Do; 1970– Old Colwyn Do.
Council Member: Secretary Sunday Sch. Council for Wales; Secretary North Wales Free Church Council.
Local Council Committees: Colwyn Bay Council of Churches (President).
Special Interests: Sunday Sch.–Evangelism.

DAVIES, O. Prys, 4a The Oatlands, West Kirby, Wirral, Merseyside L48 7HN. (051-625 9530) *b. 5 Jan 1904, Llandecwyn, Ardudwy, Gwynedd. m. 31 July 1934: 2d.*
Education: 1916–20 Festiniog County Sch.; 1928–30 Handsworth.
Appointments: 1927–28 Bagillt, Flint; 1930–31 Dolgelley and Barmouth; 1931–35 Llanrhaedr, Llansilin; 1935–39 Llangollen; 1939–45 Llanasa, Ffynnongroew; 1945–50 Denbigh; 1950–55 and 1960–70 Liverpool; 1955–60 Bagillt; 1965 President of Welsh Assembly.

DAVIES, Percival, 59 Mount Crescent, Tupsley, Hereford HR1 1NJ. (0432/268476) *b. 13 Dec 1904, Woodseaves, Eardisley, Hereford. m. (1) 1 Jan 1936; (2) 7 Nov 1947: 1d (adopted 1 Jan 1936).*
Education: 1909–17 Great Oak, Eardisley; 1917–21 Lady Hawkins Grammar Sch., Kington; 1927–30 Hartley Victoria. *Appointments:* 1930–34 Colchester; 1934–37 South Molton; 1937–39 Camborne; 1939–45 Somerset Mission; 1945–48 Leominster; 1948–51 Wolverton; 1951–56 Knighton; 1956-62 Prees Green.
Special Interests: Ornithology, Poetry, Motors, Sailing. *Hobbies and Recreations:* Ornithology, Poetry, Motors, Sailing.

DAVIES, Richard Ward, 12 St. Giles Croft, Beverley, North Humberside HU17 8LA. (0482-882325)–BD(London) *b. 28 Dec 1928, Maesbrook, Oswestry, Shropshire. m. 19 July 1963: 1d., 1s.*
Education: Oswestry Boys High Sch.; 1951–54 Headingley.
Appointments: 1954–56 Isles of Scilly; 1956–57 Tiverton; 1957–61 Bishop Auckland; 1961–63 Stafford; 1963–68 Ashton-u-Lyne; 1968–73 Leicester (North); 1973–79 Market Drayton; 1979– Beverley.
Special Interests: Pastoral and Preaching. *Hobbies and Recreations:* Home Printing.

DAVIES, Robert, 32 Temple Drive, Swinton, Manchester M27 1EB. (061 794 1763) *b. 22 March 1940, Wrexham. m. 2s.*
Education: 1960–64 Hartley Victoria.
Appointments: 1964–65 Huddersfield Mission; 1965–69 Bolton; 1969–81 Leigh; 1981– Swinton.
Connexional Committees: 1973–76 Home Mission; 1977– Prison Committee.
Special Interests: Prison Chaplaincy.

DAVIES, Rupert Eric, 6 Elmtree Drive, Bishopsworth, Bristol BS13 8LY. (0272 641087)–MA(Oxon.), BA, BD(Cantab) *b. 29 Nov 1909, Shepherd's Bush, London. m. 7 Aug 1937: 2d., 2s., plus a foster daughter, a refugee from Nazi Germany.*
Education: 1918–1922 Colet Court Preparatory Sch., West Kensington; 1922–28 St. Paul's School, West Kensington; 1928–29 Foundation Scholar, Captain of the Sch.; Balliol College; 1934–35 Univ. of Tübingen, South Germany (Denyer and Johnson Scholar of the Univ. of Oxford); 1932–34 Wesley House.
Appointments: 1935–47 Chaplain of Kingswood Sch., Bath; 1947–50 Bedminster; 1950–52 Bristol King St.; 1952–67 Tutor Didsbury Coll., Bristol; 1967–73 Principal of Wesley Coll., Bristol; 1973–76 Bristol Bedminster; 1976–82 New Room, Bristol; 1970–71 President of the Conference.
Connexional Committees: 1949–75, 1976–79 Faith and Order Committee (Convenor 1958–70); 1952–73 Ministerial Training Committee; 1951–76 World Methodist Committee; 1967–73 Stationing Committee; 1953– History of Methodist Committee (Convenor); 1975– Sch. Board of Management; 1950– Governor of Kingswood School (1950–69 Secretary, 1975– Chairman); 1965–69 Anglican-Methodist Unity Commission; 1951–73 World Methodist Council Executive; 1968 World Council of Churches; 1964–74 World Council of Churches Faith and Order Commission; 1966–73 Bristol Council of Churches; Numerous Working Parties of Methodist Churches and BCC; 1956–66 Bristol Education Committee; 1960– Council of Redland High School (Chairman 1976–); 1969–74 West Regional Advisory Council of BBC.
Publications: Co-editor of *History of Methodist Church in Great Britain* (1953); *Wesley's Works* (1971); Catholicity of Protestantism (1951); Co-author of *Circles of Community* (1982); Editor of *An Approach to Christian Education* (1956); *We Believe in God* (1968); Author of *The Problem of Authority in the Continental Reformation* (1946); *Reading your Bible* (1948); *Praying Together* (1950); *The Sunday School Today* (1952); *A Colony of Heaven* (1958); *Studies in I Corinthians* (1962); *Methodism* (1963); *Religious Authority in an Age of Doubt* (1968); *A Christian Theology of Education* (1974); *What Methodists Believe* (1976); *The Church in our Times* (1979); *Fernley Hartley Lecture* (1968); Wesley Historical Society Lecture (1982).
Special Interests: Ecumenism, Education, The Community of Women and Men. *Hobbies and Recreations:* Golf, Theatre and Gardening.

DAVIES, Thomas John, 30 Smith Crescent, Wrockwardine Wood, Telford, Salop TF2 7AX. (0952 612740)–BA *b. 3 Oct 1956, Crickhowell, S. Wales. m. 26 July 1980.*
Education: 1968–73 Monmouth Sch.; 1979–82 Bristol Univ.; 1979–82 Wesley Coll., Bristol. *Appointments:* 1982– Telford North.
Special Interests: Wesley's Theology, Methodist History. *Hobbies and Recreations:* Detective Fiction, The Civil War, Motoring, D.I.Y., Live Steam, Old Machinery.

DAVIES, Tom, Wesley Manse, The Avenue, Pontypridd, M.Glam. CF37 4DE. (0443 407890)–BD(Lond.) *b. 21 April 1932, Blackwood, Gwent. m. 27 July 1957: 2s.*
Education: 1937–43 Oakdale Prim. and Jun.; 1943–48 Pontllanfraith Grammar; 1954–57 Richmond.
Appointments: 1957–59 Pateley Bridge; 1959–64 Neath; 1964–67 Pontypool, Eastern Valley; 1967–71 London Westminster; 1971–79 Penarth; 1979– Mid Glamorgan Mission; 1976–82 Cardiff and Swansea District Hon.Sec.; 1982– Synod Sec.
Connexional Committee: 1970–72 Youth; 1976–82 Home Mission.
Publications: 1964 *Christian Leadership in the Youth Group* M.A.Y.C. King George VI Memorial Lecture.
Special Interests: Sport, Wales, Family. *Hobbies and Recreations:* Sport, D.I.Y.

DAVIES, Tudor, Araul, 13 Lôn-y-Meillion, Eithinog, Bangor, Gwynedd. (0248-2635) *b. 2 April 1923, Gwyddelwern, Nr. Corwen, Clwyd. m. 27 Aug 1952: 1d., 1s.*
Education: Gwyddelwern Village Sch.; 1948–50 Handsworth.
Appointments: 1945–46 Llanrhaeadr Welsh; 1946–47 Llandilo, 1947–48 Y Tu-Mtuen; 1948–50 Handsworth Coll.; 1950–55 Lampeter Welsh; 1955–60 Dogelley and Dogellau; 1960–65 Pwllheli; 1965–70 Blaenau Ffestiniog; 1970–72 Caernarfon; 1972 Arfon.
Connexional Committees: Overseas Mission, Division of Ministries, Local Preacher.
Publications: Occassional articles and Hymns in *Yr Eurgawn* the Welsh Wesleyan-Methodist Quarterly Magazine and other periodicals.
Special Interests: Hymnology and Welsh Literature. *Hobbies and Recreations:* Photography.

DAVIES, William James, 62 Polhill Avenue, Bedford MK41 9DU. (0234 61543) *b. 21 Jan 1935, Bradley, Staffs. m. 29 Aug 1959: 1d., 1s.*
Education: 1955–56 Cliff Coll.; 1957–60 Didsbury Coll., Bristol.
Appointments: 1960–63 Nottingham Central; 1963–68 Birmingham, Elmdon; 1968–73 Harpenden; 1973– Bedford North.
Connexional Committees: 1965–68 Local Preachers Committee; 1982 Superintendent Methodist Chaplain of Prisons and Secretary of the Home Mission Prison Committee.
Hobbies and Recreations: Photography, Golf, Philately.

DAVIES, William Rhys, Severn Lodge, Lister Lane, Bradford BD2 4LL; Also Eastbrook Hall, Leeds Road, Bradford BD1 5DT. (0274 637425 Home, 0274 22951 Office)–BD(Lond), MA (Manchester), PhD(Manchester) *b. 31 May 1932, Blackpool, Lancs. m. 9 Nov 1955: 1d., 1s.*
Education: 1937–43 Hawes Side Jun. Sch., Blackpool; 1943–45 Palatine Central Selective Sch., Blackpool; 1945–50 The Blackpool Grammar Sch.; 1956–59 and 1961–65 Univ. of Manchester; 1951–55 Hartley Victoria Coll. *Appointments:* 1955–60 Middleton; 1960–65 Fleetwood; 1965–66 Stockton-on-Tees; 1966–79 Padgate Coll. of Higher Education, Warrington; 1979– Bradford Mission.
Connexional Committees: 1974–77 and 1981– Cliff Coll. General Committee (Home Mission); 1975– Faith and Order Committee; 1979– Doctrinal Committee; 1982– Division of Social Responsibility Board.
Publications: The Charismatic Movement and Methodism (with Ross Peart) published Methodist Home Mission, 1973; *Spirit Baptism and Spiritual Gifts in Early Methodism,* published Cross-Fire Ministries USA, 1974; *Gathered Into One* (Archbishop of Canterbury's Lent Book) published Faith Press, 1975; *What About the Charismatic Movement?* (with Ross Peart) published Epworth Press, 1980.
Special Interests: Church History, Charismatic renewal and co-edit Dunamis a renewal magazine with 6,000 circulation (since 1972).
Hobbies and Recreations: Reading and Sport (especially soccer).

DAVIS, John Herbert, 3 Pwllycrochan Avenue, Colwyn Bay, Clwyd LL29 7DA. (0492 2589)–BA(Manchester) *b. 22 April 1926, Wellingborough, Northants. m. 19 May 1956: 1d., 1s.*
Education: 1937–42 Wellingborough Grammar Sch.; 1950–53 Manchester Univ.; 1950–53 Hartley Victoria. *Appointments:* 1953–55 Bolton Wesley; 1955–61 Bolton Park Street; 1961–66 Bolton Bridge St.; 1966–71 Manchester N.E.; 1971–78 Bangor; 1978– Colwyn Bay and Llandudno.
Connexional Committees: 1980– Connexional Church Membership Presidents Council; 1981– Precentor and Correspondence Secretary of the Conference.
Publications: A Short history of St. Johns Bangor (1975); *A Short History of St. Johns Conwy* (1981).
Special Interests: Music, Hymnology. *Hobbies and Recreations:* Gardening, D.I.Y.

DAVIS, Neville, White Hall, Queens Road, Darwen, Lancashire BB3 2LE. (0254 71413)–BA(Leeds) *b. 29 July 1935, Willenhall, Staffs. m. 5 July 1958: 3d., 1s.*
Education: 1946–53 Wolverhampton Grammar Sch.; 1956–59 Univ. of Leeds; 1956–59 Headingley. *Appointments:* 1959–63 Rotherham; 1963–65 Jersey; 1965– Bolton Tech. Coll.
Council Member: 1971–74 Darwen Borough Council. *Local Council Committees:* Darwen Borough Council; Management Board; Housing Committee, Parks, Baths and Library Committee; Highways; 1971–74 Development; 1971–74 Lancs. County Council Divisional Education Exec.
Publications: Give a Thought with F. H. Tucker (1968); Essay in *Investigations Essays on Church and Society* (1970); *Seven Days for Wholeness* (1970); Broadcasts–BBC Radio and TV, Channel TV, ABC TV, Granada.
Special Interests: Magistrate, School Governor. *Hobbies and Recreations:* Music, Song-writing, Animals, Gardening, Telephoning.

DAVIS, Peter William, The Manse, Lower Peasedown, Bath BA2 8AH. (0761 34672) *b. 4 Sept 1950, Leicester, m. 11 Aug 1979.*
Education: 1957–61 Braunstone Hall Jun. Sch.; 1961–66 Alderman Newton's Grammar Sch., Leicester; 1966–71 Leicester Coll. of Art and Technology; 1978–81 Wesley Coll., Bristol. *Appointments:* 1980– Midsomer Norton.
Hobbies and Recreations: Gardening, Modelmaking, Woodwork, D.I.Y.

DAVIS, Ruth Hilary, 25 Cartmel Road, Redcar, Cleveland TS10 4JT. (0642 484315)–MA *b. 13 May 1930, Cheadle Hulme, Cheshire. s.*
Education: 1935–40 Queens Road County Primary School, Cheadle Hulme; 1940–49 Cheadle Hulme Sch. (Manchester Warehousemen and Clerks Orphan Schools); 1949–52 Manchester Univ.; 1966–69 Liverpool Univ.; 1973–75 Cambridge Univ.; 1973–75 Wesley House.
Appointments: 1975–78 Lowestoft and East Suffolk; 1978– Redcar, Saltburn and Guisborough.
Connexional Committees: 1976–79 Candidates Exam Committee; 1981– Candidates Exam Committee (Psychology); 1980– Probationers Oversight Committee; DSR Main Committee Family Healing and Personal Concerns; 1981– Ministers Medical Sub-Committee (G.P.).
Special Interests: Pastoral Work; *Healing relating to Wholeness.*
Hobbies and Recreations: Choral Singing, Swimming, Walking, Skiing, Dressmaking, Attending Orchestral Concerts, Reading, Badminton, Watching sporting events on T.V., Gardening.

DAVIS, Stanley Bernard, 18 Little Gaynes Lane, Upminster, Essex RM14 2JJ. (040 22 23568) *b. 7 Sept 1926, Longton, Stoke-on-Trent. m. 12 Sept 1953: 1s.*
Education: Longton High Sch.; 1947–50 Handsworth.
Appointments: 1950–56 Church of South India; 1956–61 Mission House (Missionary Education Dept. Secretary); 1961–64 West Bromwich; 1964–76 Birmingham (Sutton Coldfield); 1976– Romford.
Connexional Committees: 1956–61 M.M.S. Home Organisation Committee.
Special Interests: India. *Hobbies and Recreations:* Tape Recording, Photography.

DAVISON, Richard Matthew, 39 Batcliffe Drive, Headingley, Leeds LS6 3QB. (0532-752793) *b. 4 Aug 1924, Consett, Co. Durham. m. 16 Aug 1952: 2d., 1s.*
Education: Various Council Schs.; 1936–39 Ashville Coll.; 1948–51 Richmond. *Appointments:* 1946–47 Edinburgh; 1947–48 Coatbridge and Airdrie; 1951–52 Snaith; 1952–56 Gateshead West; 1956–60 Newcastle West; 1960–65 Bradford, Woodhouse Grove; 1965–74 Middlesbrough; 1974– Leeds Mission.
Connexional Committees: 1961–65 Christian Citizenship: 1971–80 Connexional Team Ministry; 1975–81 Wesley Deaconess Committee; 1979– Commission on Evangelism.
Special Interests: City Centre Mission Work, Care of Prisoners and Prison Reform, Industrial Mission, Christian Pacifism, Literature. *Hobbies and Recreations:* Gardening, Reading and Walking.

DAVY, Kenneth, 21 Granville St., Grimsby, S.Humberside DN35 9NS. (0472 51105)–BD *b. 28 Jan 1933, Gainsborough, Lincs. m. 30 Aug 1958: 2d., 1s.*
Education: 1944–49 Queen Elizabeth Grammar, Gainsborough; 1955–59 Hartley Victoria.
Appointments: 1959–65 Ceylon Dt.; 1965–69 Brigg, 1969–73 Cleethorpes; 1973 Probation Officer, Humberside.
Special Interests: Divorce Court Welfare, Youth Work. *Hobbies and Recreations:* Photography (esp. Portraiture).

DAWES, Cecil, Garrigill, 4 Old Vicarage Close, Chilton Polden, Bridgwater TA7 9DY. (0278 722487) *b. 23 Jan 1914, Kensworth, Beds. m. 7 Aug 1946.*
Education: Dunstable Elem.; 1939–42 Hartley Victoria. *Appointments:* 1938–39 Alston; 1942–46 Tiverton; 1946–51 Taunton; 1951–58 Bridgwater; 1958–63 Bristol (South); 1963–70 Barnet; 1970–76 Luton North; 1976–79 Marlborough.
Connexional Committees: 1958–61 Youth.
Special Interests: Ecumenical Activity. *Hobbies and Recreations:* D.I.Y., Watching Sport.

DAWES, Charles Edward, 3 Admirals Way, Daventry, Northants NN11 4NT. (032 72 77071) *b. 30 Sept 1911, Brighton, Sussex. m. 31 May 1941: 1d.*
Education: 1916–25 St. John's CE, 1928–32 Brighton Technical Coll.; 1946–47 Richmond. *Appointments:* 1947–48 Ramsey (IOM) Waterloo Rd.; 1948–53 Brandon and Deerness Valley; 1953–58 King's Lynn; 1958–66 London, Walthamstow; 1966–71 Southport; 1971–1978 Wellingborough.
Connexional Committees: 1960–66 Governor Southlands; 1960–66 Education; 1966–70 Governor Trinity Hall; 1973–82 Property.
Local Council Committees: 1962–66 Free Church representative on Walthamstow Education Committee.
Hobbies and Recreations: Music, D.I.Y.

DAWSON, Alan Buley, The Manse, Newchurch Road, Tadley, Basingstoke, Hants RG26 6HN. (073 56 3892) *b. 8 June 1916, Gravesend. m. 31 March 1945: 1d., 1s.*
Education: 1922–26 Private Tuition owing to illness; 1926–34 County School for Boys, Gravesend; 1938–40 Richmond. *Appointments:* 1940–41 Medway Towns; 1941–44 Hastings; 1944–47 London, Blackheath and Eltham; 1947–53 Southsea; 1953–57 West Wight; 1957–65 Bristol East; 1965–72 Bridlington; 1972–77 Grays; 1977–82 Rinsash; 1982– Reading and Silchester.
Hobbies and Recreations: Music, Birdwatching.

DAWSON, John Gordon, 8 Orchard Hey, Eccleston Mere, St. Helens, Merseyside WA10 5AQ. (0744 29780) *b. 13 April 1923, Altrincham. m. 30 July 1953: 2s.*
Education: 1933–41 Boteler Grammar Sch.; 1947–49 Cliff Coll.;

1953–54 St. Andrew's, Selly Oak; 1949–51 Didsbury, Bristol. *Appointments:* 1951–54 Nantwich, Hospital St.; 1954–56 Leeward Islands Dt; 1956–76 Resigned; 1976– Prescot, St. Helens. *Council Member:* 1962–73 Runcorn R.District, Chairman 1970/1. *Local Council Committees:* Finance, Housing, Health, Divisional Roads, Div. Education. *Hobbies and Recreation:* Boats–sailing until 78.

DAWSON, Leslie, 37 Rainhall Rd., Barnoldswick, Colne, Lancs. (0282 813360) *b. 8 Aug 1928, Hardhorn-with Newton, Fleetwood, Lancs. m. 21 July 1957: 1d., 2s.* *Education:* 1939–44 Blackpool Grammar Sch.; 1950–52 Cliff College; 1953–56 Hartley Victoria; 1956–57 St. Andrew's, Selly Oak. *Appointments:* 1952–53 London Mission, Plumstead; 1957–58 N. Nigeria, Dt; 1958–60 Castleford; 1960–63 South Craven; 1963–67 Stockport, Tiviot Dale; 1967–72 Worsley; 1972–81 Bury; 1981– Barnoldswick.

DAWSON, Levi, 20 Heatherstone Rd., Worthing, West Sussex BN11 2HD. (0903 209138)–BD(Lond.), PhD(Edinburgh) *b. 18 Oct 1908. Ashford-in-the-Water, Derbyshire. m. 3 Aug 1938: 3d.* *Education:* 1919–25 Belle Vue High Sch., Bradford, Yorks.; 1932–35 London Univ.; 1951–54 Post Graduate Work at Edinburgh Univ.; 1932–35 Richmond. *Appointments:* 1931–32 Southend-on-Sea; 1935–37 London, Finsbury Park; 1937–40 London, Enfield; 1940–44 Luton; 1944–51 Liverpool North; 1951–54 Edinburgh Mission; 1954–57 Hastings; 1957–62 Bournemouth; 1962–64 Wallasey; 1964–67 Teaching, Coombe Girls Sch., New Malden; 1968–73 Tiffin Girls Sch., Kingston-upon-Thames; 1973–77 Guildford. *Connexional Committees:* 1946–51 Education Committee; 1948–51 Candidates Committee. *Local Council Committees:* 1951–54 Hastings Education and Library Committees; 1958–62 Bournemouth Education Committee. *Publications: The History and Religion of Israel* (Evans 1968). *Special Interests:* Education, Theatre–now serving as Actors' Church Union Chaplain, Connaught Theatre, Worthing. *Hobbies and Recreations:* Gardening, Wine-making.

DAY, Arthur Cecil, 16 Sandcroft Rd., Eastbourne, Sussex BN20 8HB. (0323 34717) *b. 8 Oct 1904, Leeds, Yorks. m. 2 Aug 1934: 1s.* *Education:* State Education; Didsbury and Headingley. *Appointments:* 1927–28 Wimborne; 1931–34 Nicolson Square, Edinburgh; 1934–35 Shotley Bridge and Consett; 1935–37 Severn Valley Mission; 1937–40 Rotherham; 1940–44 Manchester Street, Oldham; 1944–47 Bury; 1947–51 Manchester East; 1951–55 Oldham; 1955–59 Derby; 1959–64 Hill Top, West Bromwich; 1964–68 Bourne; 1968–71 Birstall and Birkenshaw. *Special Interests:* General, Biblical Studies. *Hobbies and Recreations:* Chess, Gardening on Retirement.

DAY, Brian Leslie, 50 Newport Road, Cowes, I.O.W. PO13 7PW. (0983 292748)–BD(Lond.) *b. 10 June 1924, London N22. m. 30 July 1953: 1d., 2s.* *Education:* 1935–39 Trinity Coun.; 1939–42 Eastbourne Grammar Sch.; 1944–47 Handsworth. *Appointments:* 1953–57 Watton; 1957–61 Burton-on-Trent; 1961–67 Bury; 1967–70 Swansea; 1970–74 Pontypool; 1974–77 Abertillery; 1977– Cowes. *Hobbies and Recreations:* Stamps, Music.

DAY, David George, 218 Liverpool Rd., Longton, Preston PR4 5YB (0772-612191) *b. 14 Dec 1916, York. m., 1d., 2s.* *Education:* 1921–30 Wawne St., Hull. *Appointments:* 1967–73 Birstall and Birkenshaw; 1973–81 Warrington; 1981– Preston Trinity. *Hobbies and Recreations:* Gardening.

DAY, Leslie Edward, 17 Farquharson Rd., Croydon, Surrey CR0 2UH. (01 688 3502) *b. 7 July 1923, Bethnal Green, East London. m. 4 Aug 1952: 2d.* *Education:* 1948–51 London Univ.; 1948–51 Richmond. *Appointments:* 1946–48 Camelford and Wadebridge; 1951–53 Chelmsford; 1953–56 London East End Mission; 1956–61 Southampton; 1961–63 Bristol North; 1963–68 London Mission Archway; 1968–73 Welling; 1973–78 London Streatham and Dulwich; 1978–80 London International House. *Connexional Committees:* 1954–55 President of London North East Methodist Association of Youth Clubs; 1967–68 Secretary of Methodist Peace Fellowship. *Council Member:* Fellowship of Reconciliation. *Special Interests.* Relation of Science to Religion, in particular the Evolution of Religion on basis of Darwin's Evolutionary Concept. *Hobbies and Recreations:* Golf, Bowls, Interest in most sports, Politics, Educational reading.

DEACON, David E. R., 16 St. Margaret's Grove, Plumstead, London SE18 7RL. (01 854 2385)–BSc, BA *m. 2s.* *Education:* 1947–54 Brighton Grammar Sch.; 1954–58 Brighton Technical Coll.; 1958–61 Didsbury, Bristol. *Appointments:* 1961–63 Whitehaven; 1963–66 Liverpool South; 1966–71 Bedford South; 1971–77 Manchester and Salford Mission; 1977– London Mission, Plumstead. *Special Interests:* Counselling.

DEAKIN, Edward Bruce, 1 Burton Close, Culcheth, Warrington WA3 4BW. (092 576 3218)–BD(Lond) *b. 17 July 1943, Holmfirth. m. 31 July 1971: 1d., 1s.* *Education.* 1948–54 Scholes County Prim. Sch.; 1954–62 Holme Valley Grammar Sch.; 1966–70 Hartley Victoria. *Appointments:* 1970–72 Seaham; 1972–76 Houghton-le-Spring; 1976– Leigh; 1979– Secretary of Synod, Bolton and Rochdale District.

DEAKIN, Thomas Ernest, 7 Ambleside Close, Mytchett, Camberley, Surrey GU16 6DG. (0252 543788) *b. 18 June 1901, Brownhills, West Midlands. m. 11 Aug 1927: 1d., 1s.*
Education: Council School, Watling St., Brownhills. 1919–20 Cliff College; 1923–26 Richmond Coll.
Appointments: 1922–23 West Mon. Mission; 1926–28 South Hants. Mission; 1928–29 Ticehurst; 1929–32 Shotley Bridge and Consett; 1932–37 Leek; 1937–40 Wakefield; 1940–42 Leeds South; 1942–47 East Wight; 1947–55 Portsmouth; 1955–60 Guildford; 1960–66 Medway Towns.
Special Interests: Music. *Hobbies and Recreations:* Gardening.

DEAN, John William, The Manse, Murcott Rd. East, Whitnash, Leamington Spa, Warwicks CV31 2JJ. (0926 26787) *b. 10 June 1939, Nottingham. m. 19 Dec 1970: 2s.*
Education: 1950–55 Queen Elizabeth's Grammar, Ashbourne; 1970 Cliff College; 1971–73 Queen's.
Appointments: 1973–77 Milton Keynes; 1977–80 Kidderminster; 1980– Leamington.
Hobbies and Recreations: Gardening, Music, Theatre.

DEEKS, Cecil G., 5 Windmill Row, Glemsford, Sudbury, Suffolk CO10 7QG. (0787 280588).
Education: 1929–32 Hartley.
Appointments: 1932–34 Bristol IV and Kingswood; 1934–36 Ipswich Ropewalk; 1936–40 Berwick-on-Tweed; 1940–44 Blyth and Seaton Delaval; 1944–56 Jamaica Dt; 1956–62 Acle; 1962–68 Wolsingham; 1968–72 Fakenham and Wells.

DEEKS, David Gerald, 31 Jesus Lane, Cambridge CB5 8BQ. (0223 51532)–MA(Cantab) *b. 5 July 1942, Chedburgh, Suffolk. m. 19 Aug 1967: 2d., 1s.*
Education: 1952–60 City of Norwich Sch.; 1960–63 Downing Coll., Cambridge; 1964–66 Wesley House.
Appointments: 1966–70 Assistant tutor, Richmond Coll.; 1970–74 Ecumenical Lecturer, Lincoln Theological Coll.; 1974–80 Maidstone; 1980– Tutor, Wesley House, Cambridge.
Connexional Committees: 1975– Faith and Order Committee; 1974– Connexional Probationers' Oversight Committee; 1981– Doctrinal Committee. *Publications: Calling God?* (1976); 3 chapters in *Doing Theology,* ed. J. Stacey (1972); Articles in various journals; *Fernley-Hartley Lecture* (1980).
Special Interests: New Testament, especially the Lukan literature; issues in Science and Religion and in Art and Religion. *Hobbies and Recreations:* Painting, Literature, Walking.

DELAP, Robert, Bramhope, Albert Rd., St. Saviour, Jersey C.I. (0534 22575)–BD(Lond.) *b. 1934, Newcastle-upon-Tyne. m. 3s.*
Education: 1958–62 Hartley Victoria.
Appointments: 1962–64 Hungerford; 1964–71 Blyth and Seaton Delaval; 1971–76 Great Barr and Kingstanding, Birmingham; 1976–82 Brunswick Central, Newcastle-upon-Tyne; 1982– Jersey.

DELVE, Trevor Arnold, 18 Weaver Avenue, Rainhill, Prescot, Merseyside L35 0NR. (051 426 0690) *b. 25 Oct 1921, Crosby, Merseyside. m. 10 June 1944: 1d., 2s.*
Education: 1926–30 Ballure House, Gt. Crosby; 1930–37 Waterloo Grammar Sch., Nr. Liverpool; 1930–37 Liverpool Technical Coll.; 1946–48 Southport Technical Coll.; Hartley Victoria. *Appointments:* 1977– St. Helens and Prescot.
Publications: Various papers and reports.
Special Interests: Ministry to the Underprivileged, Overseas Missions, Prisons, World Travel. *Hobbies and Recreations:* Sport, Reading, Philately, Music, Boys Brigade, Beavers and Cubs.

DEMORE, Timothy Patrick, The Manse, Peverell Terrace, Porthleven, Helston, Cornwall TR13 9DZ. (032 65 62301)–MA(Cambridge), BA(Lond.) *b. 2 Jan 1953, Guernsey, Channel Islands.*
Education: 1964–70 Elizabeth Coll., Guernsey; 1971–75 University Coll., London; 1976–79 Wesley House.
Appointments: 1979– Porthleven.
Special Interests: Languages.

DENNETT, Peter Robert, 9 Conway Drive, Aspull, Wigan, Lancs WN2 1XQ. (0942–831439) *b. 27 July 1926, Widnes, Lancs. m. 24 July 1956: 2d., 3s.*
Education: 1948 Cliff Coll.; 1950–53 Handsworth. *Appointments:* 1953–55 Coventry Mission; 1955–57 Crook; 1957–62 Wigan; 1962–65 Sheffield North; 1965–72 Leigh; 1972–79 Worsley; 1979– Wigan.
Connexional Committees: 1967–70 Church Membership.

DENNEY, Christopher, Ivor, The Manse, Willbrahams Walk, Audley, Stoke on Trent ST7 8HL. (0782 720267) *b. 18 Nov 1949, Consett, Co. Durham. m. 2 Aug 1975: 1d., 1s.*
Education: 1961–66 Moorside Secondary Modern, Consett; 1966–69 Durham Technical Coll.; 1971–75 Hartley Victoria. *Appointments:* 1975–76 Bedford South and Ampthill; 1976–81 Castletown, Isle of Man; 1981– Wolstanton and Audley.
Hobbies and Recreations: Walking, Camping, Reading.

DENNIGAN, Brian Joseph, Wesley House, 250 High Street, Cottenham, Cambridge CB4 4RZ. (0954 50242) *b. 5 June 1940, London.*
Education: 1962–66 Didsbury, Bristol. *Appointments:* 1966–70 Shrewsbury; 1970–75 Bloxwich; 1975–81 Liverpool Crosby; 1981– Cambridge.

DENNIS, Henry William, 93 Stanton Rd., Bebington, Wirral, Merseyside L63 3AT. (051 334 3177) *b. 21 January 1903, Thornaby-on-Tees, Cleveland. m. (1) Aug 1931; (2) June 1971 (w.): 1s.*
Education: Arthur Head Council Sch. (Elementary), Thornaby-on-Tees, Cleveland. *Appointments:* 1939–41 London East Ham Mission; 1941–46 Cannock Chase; 1946–52 Leeds Mission; 1952–58 Weston-super-Mare; 1958–67 Ghana, W.Africa; 1967–69 Mansfield, Bridge St.

Special Interests: Hymns and Writers (Hymnody); *Hobbies and Recreations:* Reading, Cricket and Football.

DENNY, Norwyn Ephraim, 49 Queen's Drive, Mossley Hill, Liverpool L18 2DT. (051 722 1219)–BD(Lond.) *b. 23 Oct 1924, Lowestoft, Suffolk. m. 29 July 1950: 3d.* *Education:* 1935–42 City of Norwich; 1946–50 Didsbury, Bristol. *Appointments:* 1950–54 Jamaica Dt; 1955–61 Peterborough; 1961–75 Notting Hill Group Ministry and Ecumenical Community; 1975– Liverpool District Chairman; 1982 President of the Conference. *Publications: Beware the Church* (co-author 1964); *News from Notting Hill* (co-author 1967); *Caring* (1976). *Special Interests:* Collaborative Ministry, Mission Alongside the Poor, Theological Formation of whole People of God. *Hobbies and Recreations:* Gardening, Astronomy, Association Football.

DENT, Brian Anthony, 33 Millfield Rd., Chorley, Lancashire PR7 1RF. (025 72 63251)–BA(Cambridge) *b. 7 Jan 1941, Bolton, Westmorland. m. 4 July 1964: 1d., 1s.* *Education:* 1946–52 Bolton Prim. Sch.; 1952–59 Appleby Grammar Sch.; 1959–61 Rheged Academy; 1961-64 Wesley House, Cambridge. *Appointments:* 1964–67 Bourne; 1967–73 Stafford; 1973–80 Minsterley; 1980– Chorley. *Special Interests:* Rural Methodism. *Hobbies and Recreations:* Rural Studies, Local History, Family History, Stamp Collecting, Walking, Reading.

DENT, John William, 20 Ridgewood Villas, South Gosforth, Newcastle upon Tyne NE3 1SH. (0632-855719) *b. 29 Sept 1900, Spital, Bowes. m. 28 July 1932 (w.): 3d.* *Education:* 1905–14 Scargill; 1923–24 Cliff College; 1926–29 Didsbury Coll. *Appointments:* 1925–26 Bedale; 1929–1933 Reeth; 1933–37 Redcar, Saltburn and Guisborough; 1937–40 Stockton Brunswick; 1940–48 Darlington; 1948–53 Stokes; 1953–59 South Bank and Eston; 1959–66 Barnard Castle. *Local Council Committees:* 1944–48 Voluntary Free Church Chaplain, Aycliffe Approved Sch.; 1945–46 Mayor's Chaplain, Darlington. *Special Interests:* Young People, Junior and Wesley Guild, Y. Clubs, Economics and Social Psychology. *Hobbies and Recreations:* Gardening.

DERHAM, Kenneth Walter, 19 King George Rd., Minehead, Som. TA24 5JD. (0643 3791) *b. 2 April 1921, Bristol. m. 28 Aug 1952: 2s.* *Education:* 1948–51 Richmond. *Appointments:* 1947–48 Trowbridge and Bradford on Avon; 1951–54 Leeward Islands Dt; 1954–56 Bury; 1956–61 Boston; 1961–66 Ramsgate; 1966–72 Taunton (B.F.B.S.); 1971–79 Port Talbot; 1979– West Somerset. *Connexional Committees:* 1957–66 Methodist Missionary Society General Committee. *Special Interests:* Ornithology, Geology, Railways, Lepidoptery. *Hobbies and Recreations:* Mountain Scrambling, Hill Walking, Motor Mechanics, Musical Appreciation.

DeVISME, Peter Henry Wilmot, 18 Third Close, East Molesey, Surrey KT8 9PW. (01 979 7073) *m. 21 Feb 1948: 1d., 1s.* *Education:* Hertford Grammar Sch.; 1938–40 Handsworth; 1940–41 Headingley. *Appointments:* 1941–51 Nigeria Ivory Coast Dt; 1951–55 Bolton Park St.; 1955–61 Bury; 1961–68 Wellington; 1968–73 Biggleswade; 1973–80 Tipton. *Connexional Committees:* 1950's Overseas Missions. *Hobbies and Recreations:* Gardening.

DEVLIN, T. David, 70 Gartree Rd., Leicester LE2 2FW. (0533 704270) *b. 15 Nov 1924, Egremont, Cumbria. m. 1d.,2s.* *Education:* 1935–40 Whitehaven Grammar; 1949–52 Hartley Victoria. *Appointments:* 1952–56 Middlesbrough; 1956–61 Hull West; 1961–64 York Centenary; 1964–70 Banbury; 1970–79 Leicester West; 1979– Leicester Central. *Publications: My Dear Friends* (1976); *Leave It To Berk* (1978). *Hobbies and Recreations:* Cricket, Writing.

DEW, Roy William, 2 Zealand St., Oldham, Lancs. OL4 2SA. (061-624 6538) *b. 3 May 1920, Wolverton, Bucks. m. 29 July 1950: 2d., 1s.* *Education:* 1925–34 Wolverton Boys Sch.; 1948–50 Handsworth. *Appointments:* 1947–48 London Southall Mission; 1948–50 Handsworth; 1950–51 Reeth; 1951–54 Oldham West; 1954–59 Rhosymedre and Chirk; 1959–65 London Mission, East Ham; 1965–69 London Mission Tooting; 1976–78 Welwyn; 1978–80 London Mission, East Ham; 1980– Oldham and Saddleworth.

DIBBEN, John Valentine, 5 Mantua, Warwick Court, Stratford upon Avon, Warwicks CV37 6YG. (0789 68608) *b. 30 April 1904,* 1992
Portsmouth. m. 29 July 1931: 1d., 1s. *Education:* 1924–27 Handsworth. *Appointments:* 1927–48 Lucknow Dt., India; 1948–53 Leamington; 1953–59 Birmingham, Belmont Row and Elmdon; 1959–64 Ashfield; 1964–71 Leamington.

DIBNAH, Herbert Clifford, 88 Park Avenue, Oswestry, Shropshire SY11 1AZ. *b. 24 May 1922, Hull. m. 28 July 1951: 2s.* *Education:* Chapman St. Council Sch., Hull; 1948–50 Didsbury, Bristol. *Appointments:* 1946–48 Brynmawr; 1948–50 Didsbury Coll.; 1950–52 Frome Wesley; 1952–57 Shrewsbury; 1957–61 Evesham; 1961–69 Middlewich; 1969–77 Sherborne; 1977– Oswestry, Ellesmere and Chirk.

DICKINSON, Joseph William, Wesley House, North Street, South Molton, Devon EX36 3AW. (076 95 2637) *m* *Education:* 1950–52 Headingley. *Appointments:* 1949–50 Cecil St., Carlisle; 1950–52 Headingley Coll.; 1952–57 Thornley; 1957–62 Ilkley; 1962–67 Doncaster N.E.; 1967–74 North Shields and Whitley Bay; 1974– South Molton, Devon.

DICKINSON, Paul, Parkside, 35 The High Street, Wolstanton, Newcastle, Staffs ST5 0SA. (0782 627963)–MA, PhD. *b. 5 July 1933, Penistone, Yorks. m. 25 Mar 1978. Education:* 1943–51 Penistone Grammar Sch.; 1951–56 University of Durham; 1956–58 Wesley House. *Appointments:* 1958–62 Hyde and Denton; 1962–65 Barnsley East; 1965–72 Resigned; 1972– Wolstanton and Audley (North Staffs. Poly.).
Publications: Medieval Land Surveys of County Durham (1960); *Bishop Hatfield's Survey* and *The Langley Survey;* Transcription and Translation (1961). *Special Interests:* Medieval agrarian land use.

DIFFEY, Frank Clifford, 5 Stepstone Lane, Knowle, Braunton, N.Devon EX33 2NB. (0271-813206) *b. 29 Sept 1909, Redhill, Surrey. m. 12 Aug 1942: 1d.*
Education: 1920–26 Reigate Grammar Sch.; 1931–34 Handsworth. *Appointments:* 1930–31 Wimborne; 1934–35 Sunderland S.E.; 1935–36 President's List; 1936–40 Ilfracombe; 1940–52 N.Walsham; 1942–45 Todmorden; 1945–49 Gloucester; 1949–53 Shaftesbury and Gillingham; 1953–57 King St., Plymouth; 1958–60 Supernumerary; 1960–64 Bude; 1964–69 Chichester and Bognor; 1969–72 Barnstaple.
Special Interests: Music (Tenor soloist).

DIGGLE, George Edward, 3 Carol Close, Patcham, Brighton BN1 8QG. (0273 557017) *b. 25 April 1911, Widnes, Lancs. m. (1) 17 March 1942; (2) 6 July 1968 (w.): 1d. 1s. Education:* 1916–22 Warrington Rd., Elem. Sch.; 1922–27 Wade Deacon Grammar Sch., Widnes; 1935–38 Didsbury. *Appointments:* 1938–39 Lytham; 1939 Preston, Lune St.; 1939–40 Bedford, St. Paul's; 1940–42 Hitchin; 1942–46 Beccles, Loddon and Bungay; 1946–50 Kings Lynn; 1950–56 Trinity Scunthorpe; 1956–62 Reading; 1962–67 Leeds, Richmond Hill; 1967–71 Ely; 1971–76 Tamworth. *Connexional Committees:* 1948–50 Christian Citizenship; 1960–62 Christian Citizenship.
Publications: History of Widnes (1961); *So You Want to be a Freelance Writer* (1971); *So You Want to be a Public Speaker* (1973); *Blighty* (1975); Numerous Articles in Religious and Secular Press. *Special Interests:* Methodist History, Social Problems, Preaching. *Hobbies and Recreations:* Gardening, Freelance Writing, Reading, Scrabble.

DIXON, Leslie Thomas, 3 Oakwood Drive, Ainsdale, Southport, Merseyside PR8 3HZ. (0704 75173) *b. 18 Jan 1908, Sheffield. m. 3 Aug 1936: 2d., 1s.*
Education: 1919–1923 King Edward VII Grammar Sch., Sheffield; 1929–30 Handsworth Coll.; 1930–32 Headingley. *Appointments:* 1932–38 Gold Coast Dt; 1938–41 Sheffield, Norfolk; 1941–45 Surrey St., Sheffield; 1945–50 Fisher St., Carlisle; 1950–53 Aireborough; 1953–60 Hexham; 1960–66 Sheffield N.E.; 1966–73 Nelson.
Connexional Committees: 1963–66 Overseas Missions General Committee.

DIXON, Malcolm Edwin, 45 Hitchin Street, Baldock, Herts SG7 6AQ. (0462-892004) *b. 11 June 1907, Wallasey, Cheshire. m. 25 July 1942: 1d., 2s.*
Education: 1918–22 Rotherham Grammar Sch.; 1922–24 Aberdeen Grammar Sch.; 1929–32 Richmond. *Appointments:* 1932–36 London, Ealing and Acton; 1936–38 London, Sydenham and Forest Hill; 1938–42 Chaplain, London, Regent St. Poly.; 1942–47 London, Kilburn and Hampstead; 1947–51 Carver St., Sheffield; 1951–55 Northwich; 1955–60 Altrincham; 1960–65 Bethesda, Hanley; 1965–68 Letchworth; 1968–72 London, Enfield.
Local Council Committees: 1960–64 Stoke-on-Trent Education Committee.
Special Interests: Most forms of sport. *Hobbies and Recreations:* Reading, Walking.

DIXON, Neil, 48 Station Road, Burley in Wharfedale, Ilkley, West Yorkshire LS29 7NG. (0943 863160)–BA(Leeds), MPhil(Lond.). *m. 1d., 1s.*
Education: 1958–65 Nelson Grammar Sch.; 1965–68 Leeds Univ.; 1968–70 London Univ.; 1968–70 Richmond Coll. *Appointments:* 1970-71 Wesley Coll., Bristol; 1971–75 Batley; 1975– Otley and Aireborough.
Connexional Committees: 1978– Local Preachers' Studies Board; 1979– Hymn Book Committee.
Publications: Approach With Joy (1975); *At Your Service* (1976); *Troubled Waters* (1979); (all published by Epworth). *Special Interests:* Liturgy and Church Music.

DIXON, Sidney Owen, 28 Gargrave Rd., Skipton, N.Yorks BD23 1QJ. (0756 3522) *b. 27 Mar 1924, Balderton, Nr. Newark, Notts. m. 9 Aug 1952: 1s.*
Education: 1929–38 Elementary; 1946–48 Richmond. *Appointments:* 1948–50 Frome, Radstock and Coleford; 1950–52 Fishponds, Bristol; 1952–55 Louth; 1955–59 East Cornwall Mission; 1959–65 Stokesley; 1965–72 Helston; 1972–78 Settle; 1978– Skipton.
Connexional Committees: 1968–71 Youth.
Publications: Cornish Methodist Historical Association Lecture *The Road to Unity in Cornish Methodism* (1971). *Special Interests:* Methodist History. *Hobbies and Recreations:* Railways, Bird Watching, Books.

DOBELL, Denis Marshall, 91 Elers Road, Ealing W13 9QE. (01 567 0172) *b. 19 Jan 1926, Tunbridge Wells, Kent. m. 16 Aug 1952. Education:* Pre 1937 St. John's CE; 1937–42 Skinners Sch., Tunbridge Wells; 1947–49 Handsworth.
Appointments: 1949–51 Dorchester; 1951–52 Boutport St., Barnstaple; 1952–54 Ilkeston Central; 1954–57 Haslingden; 1957–62 Higham Ferrers; 1962–67 Oxford; 1967–72 East Wight; 1972–78 Barnstaple; 1978– London, Ealing and Acton.
Publications: Occasional articles in *Dorset Year Book. Special Interests:*

Music and English Literature. *Hobbies and Recreations:* Model Railway, Philately.

DOBLE, Peter, Religious Education Centre, The Coll. of Ripon and York St. John, Lord Mayor's Walk, York YO3 7EX. (0904 56771 Ex.209)–MA. *b. 14 Dec 1929, Newport, Monmouthshire. m. 30 July 1955: 1d., 2s.*
Education: St. Julians High Sch., Newport; 1948–51 Univ. Cardiff; 1952–55 Fitzwilliam House, Cambridge; 1976–80 St. Edmund Hall, Oxford; 1952–55 Wesley House.
Appointments: 1955–59 Church of South India; 1960–64 Blackpool South; 1964–74 Resigned (Teaching); 1974–80 Culham College (Principal Lecturer); 1980– College of Ripon and York St. John (Director R.E. Centre).
Connexional Committees: 1978–81 Candidates Committee.
Publications: The Temptations **Expository Times,** Vol. 72; Articles on Wesley and Methodism in *Nelson's Dictionary of World History* (1973). *Special Interests:* Christian and Religious Education, Politics, Christology, and Steam Locomotives.
Hobbies and Recreation: Chess, Walking, Sailing, Music.

DOBSON, George Eric, 4 Palmyra Square, North, Warrington WA1 1JQ. (0925 35594) *b. 1 July 1922, Farndale, Kirbymoorside. m. 9 Aug 1951: 2d.*
Education: 1927–36 Low Farndale CE; 1946–47 Cliff Coll.; 1950–52 Wesley Coll., Bristol. *Appointments:* 1947–48 Bude; 1948–50 Wesley Coll.; 1950–52 Plymouth (King St. and Devonport); 1952–55 Leeds South; 1955–61 Bradford Mission; 1961–69 Blackburn Mission; 1969–77 South London Mission; 1977– Warrington Mission
Special Interests: Music, Classical and Traditional Jazz, Politicians and Politics. *Hobbies and Recreations:* Record Collecting, Photography.

DODD, Harry Alan, 31 Stoneleigh Avenue, Patcham, Brighton, Sussex BN1 8NP. (0273 501452) *b. 6 Dec 1926, Manchester. m. (2) 25 Oct 1975: 1d., 2s.*
Education: 1931–1937 Wilbraham Jun. Sch., Manchester; 1937–40 Heald Place, Senior Boys Sch. (Elementary), Manchester; 1954–57 Hartley Victoria. *Appointments:* 1957–61 Manchester, Gravel Lane; 1961–66 Cadishead; 1966–73 Bedford South; 1973–82 Teddington; 1982– Brighton and Hove.
Connexional Committees: 1977–82 Board of Division of Education and Youth.
Hobbies and Recreations: Gardening, Running, Cycling, Walking.

DODDRELL, John Henry, 1 Baldwin Avenue, Eastbourne BN21 1UJ. (0323 31471) *b. 17 Nov 1907, Bolton, Lancs. m. (2) 14 Aug 1953: 2d., 1s.*
Education: 1915–19 Sir George Moneaux Grammar Sch., Walthamstow; 1919–23 Kingswood School, Bath; 1928–31 Didsbury.
Appointments: 1931–34 Hunmanby Hall, Filey; 1934–37 London, Highgate; 1937–40 Camborne; 1940–45 Nottingham Central; 1945–47 Gold Coast, N.Ashanti Mission; 1947–53 Woking; 1953–58 Eastbourne; 1958–62 London, Willesden; 1962–67 Amersham; 1967–71 Cheddar Valley.
Connexional Committees: Overseas Missions Ministers' Retirement Fund.
Special Interests: Overseas Missions and World Development. *Hobbies and Recreations:* Chess and Gardening.

DODDS, Trevor Newton, 41 Brisbane Rd., Mickleover, Derby DE3 5LS. (0332-512663) *b. 23 Nov 1947, Darlington. m. 17 Aug 1973: 1d., 1s.*
Education: 1957–61 Hurworth House, Co. Durham; 1961–64 Scorton Grammar Sch., N.Yorkshire; 1967–69 Cliff College; 1969–70 Handsworth; 1970–73 Queens.
Appointments: 1973–76 Wigton; 1976–81 Hebden Bridge; 1981– Derby South.
Publications: Non-religious publication on *Film Music. Special Interests:* Tape Recording, Religion in the Cinema, Model Engineering, Film Music and Cinema.

DOIDGE, Peter William Edward, Epworth, Park Avenue, Scarborough, N.Yorks YO12 4AG. (0723 61488) *b. 26 April 1923, Plumstead, London SE18. m. 19 July 1952: 3d.*
Education: 1928–34 Bostall Lane, Abbey Wood SE2; 1934–35 Plumstead Central SE8; 1935–38 Owler Lane Intermediate, Sheffield; 1945–48 Handsworth.
Appointments: 1948–50 Allendale; 1950–52 Park Lane, Tipton; 1952–55 Hayle; 1955–58 Cannock Chase; 1958–63 Stanley; 1963–66 Glasgow West; 1966–73 South Shields; 1973–76 North Shields and Whitley Bay; 1976–81 St. Ives and Hayle; 1981– Scarborough.
Publications: Learning to Pray (1980). *Special Interests:* Spirituality.
Hobbies and Recreations: Music (Classical), Football and Cricket, The Countryside.

DOIDGE, Reginald James, 1 Tudor Wynd, North Heaton, Newcastle upon Tyne NE6 5UU. (0632 653360)–BScEcon(Lond.). *b. 28 April 1902, Plymouth. m. 14 May 1932 (w.).*
Education: 1922–25 Victoria Park.
Appointments: 1925–26 Bristol; 1926–28 Sheffield, Surrey St.; 1928–31 Preston Orchard; 1931–35 Oldbury; 1935–39 Central Hall, Coventry; 1939–47 Halifax West; 1947–54 Heaton and Wallsend, Newcastle-upon-Tyne; 1954–59 Newcastle-upon-Tyne West; 1959–61 Gateshead West; 1961–67 Blaydon.
Connexional Committees: 1933–45 Youth Committee.
Publications: Boys and Girls at Worship, Teenagers at Worship, Women at Worship (1967), *Epilogues for Youth Clubs etc.* (1948), *Time for Prayers* (1959); *Graded Teacher (Senior) Notes* (1939–48), R. J. & E. V. Eveline Doidge.

DOIDGE, Wilfrid John, 15 Marine Parade, Penarth, South Glamorgan CF6 2BG. (0222 707037)–BA,

BD(Lond.). *b. 15 Feb 1905, Plymouth. m. 1931: 1d.*
Education: 1915 Plymouth Grammar Sch.; 1916–22 Plymouth Coll.; 1924–27 Victoria Park. *Appointments:* 1927–29 Manchester IV; 1929–35 London, Walthamstow; 1935–38 London, Broomwood and Stockwell; 1938–43 London, South Norwood; 1943–51 Secretary of Methodist Youth Department; 1951–57 Sutton, Surrey; 1957–62 Bramhall; 1962–67 London, Finsbury Park and Southgate; 1967–72 Ipswich.
Connexional Committees: 1936–68 July Committee; 1943–56 Methodist Youth Department; 1944–50 Temperance and Social Welfare.
Council Member: 1940–74 British Lessons Council; 1955–67 Chairman of B.L.C.; 1960–61 National Christian Education Council, National President of NCEC; 1945–50 Westhill College Council, Secretary.
Publications: The Apostle to the Gentiles (1933); *Let's Read the Gospels* (1944); *Discovering the Bible* (1946–50); *(I.B.R.A. Vols) The Church and Its Children* (1948); *The Five Pound House* (1957).
Special Interests: Christian Education, History, Literature. *Hobbies and Recreations:* Gardening, Reading.

DOLBEY, George William, 17 Rutland Rd., Hazel Grove, Stockport, Cheshire. (0625-872856)–MA(Manchester), BD(Lond.). *b. 21 Feb 1914, Stoke Newington, London. m. 16 Sept 1939.*
Education: 1930–33 Northern Poly. Sch. of Architecture; 1947–49 Richmond Coll. *Appointments:* 1946–47 Southall, Hayes and Uxbridge; 1949–50 Crosby, Liverpool; 1950–54 Stockport; 1954–58 Hazel Grove and Poynton; 1958–63 Manchester, Cheetham Hill and Prestwich; 1963–66 Manchester and Salford Mission; 1966–79 Property Division Secretary.
Connexional Committees: 1966–79 Property Board; 1966– Trustees for Meth. Church Purposes; 1966–79 General Purposes and Home Missions; 1975– Law and Polity.
Publications: The Architectural Expression of Methodism (1962).
Special Interests: History and Architecture of Methodism.

DOLLING, John Scott, 46 Victoria Rd., Abingdon OX14 1DQ. (0235 20169)–MA(Cantab.). *b. 21 Feb 1932, Bitterly, Salop. m. 16 Aug 1958: 1d., 2s.*
Education: 1940–43 Inverness Royal Academy; 1943–51 Priors Court and Kingswood Sch.; 1955–58 Wesley House. *Appointments:* 1958–63 Ivory Coast District; 1963–64 Bristol South; 1964–69 Nottingham Central; 1969–76 Aberystwyth (English); 1976– Wantage and Abingdon.

DOLLING, Peter Munro, 32 Pennard Rd., Kittle, Swansea SA3 3JY. (044128 2867) *b. 20 Jan 1936, Craven Arms, Shropshire. m. 4 Sept 1965: 2s.*
Education: 1947–54 Ashville Coll., Harrogate; 1962–63 St. Andrews Coll., Selly Oak, Birmingham; 1958–59 Cliff Coll.; 1959–62 Handsworth Coll. *Appointments:* 1963–65 Skelmersdale; 1965–69 Tiruchirapalli Diocese C.S.I.; 1969 Bolton; 1969–73 Consett; 1973–80 Saltash; 1980– Swansea.
Special Interests: World Affairs.

DOLMAN, Robert Edward, 72 Millfield Lane, Hull Road, York YO1 3AL. (0904 410785)–MA(Cantab. and Birmingham). *b.28 Jan 1944, Whitley, Coventry, Warwickshire. m. 20 March 1971: 2d., 1s.*
Education: 1955–62 Bablake Sch., Coventry; 1962–66 Emmanuel College, Cambridge Univ.; 1973–75 The Queen's Coll. *Appointments:* 1975–78 Malvern and Ledbury; 1978–81 York (Centenary); 1981– York (South); 1978– Methodist Chaplain to York Univ.
Connexional Committees: 1980– Candidates' Examination Committee.
Special Interests: G. K. Chesterton, Ecumenical Movement. *Hobbies and Recreations:* History, Walking.

DONOGHUE, Stephen Richard, 57 Thames Avenue, Guisborough, Cleveland TS14 8AR. (0287 32770) *b. 18 Feb 1947, Windsor, Berkshire. m. 17 July 1976: 1d., 1s.*
Education: 1958–64 Maidenhead Grammar Sch.; 1976–79 The Queen's Coll. *Appointments:* 1979– Redcar, Saltburn and Guisborough.
Special Interests: Peace Movement, Ecumenical Activity. *Hobbies and Recreations:* Gardening, Sport, Reading.

DOREY, John Wilfred, 6 Herston Close, Aylesbury, Bucks HP21 7UR. (0296 88963) *b. 29 May 1919, Guernsey. m. 26 July 1950: 1d., 1s.*
Education: States Intermediate School, Guernsey; 1948–51 Richmond. *Appointments:* 1946–48 New Forest Mission; 1946–48 Chaplain HMF; 1951–53 Cradley Heath; 1953–56 Peterborough; 1956–62 Jersey; 1962–68 Sussex Mission; 1968–73 Richmond and Hounslow; 1973–78 London, Ealing and Acton; 1978– Aylesbury, Hospital Chaplain.
Special Interests: Sport, Handicrafts, Reading, Gardening, Horticulture (especially Pelargoniums). *Hobbies and Recreations:* Carpentry, Printing, D.I.Y.

DORMAN-SMITH, David John, 3 Eastfield Rd., Benton, Newcastle-upon-Tyne NE12 8BD. (0632–667260) *b. 8 Dec 1953, Rugby. m. 31 July 1976: 1d.*
Education: 1965–70 Herbert Kay, High Sch.; 1970–72 Dunsmore; 1976–80 Queens Coll.
Appointments: 1980– Newcastle upon Tyne, Brunswick.
Special Interests: Unemployment and Counselling of Related Problems. *Hobbies and Recreations:* Gardening, Photography.

DOUGILL, Geoffrey, 98 Kingston Rd., Willerby, Hull, North Humberside HU10 6LH. (0482 653214) *b. 2 Mar 1942, Stanhope, Weardale, Co. Durham. m. 29 July 1967: 1d., 1s.*
Education: 1946–47 Crawleyside Inf., Stanhope; 1947–53 Stanhope School; 1953–58 Wolsingham Grammar Sch.; 1964–68 Handsworth Coll. *Appointments:* 1968–72 Morpeth and Bedlington; 1972–79

Newcastle upon Tyne West; 1979– Hull West.
Connexional Committees: 1972–78 Division of Education and Youth.
Local Council Committee: 1972–78 Youth Advisory Committee, Newcastle-upon-Tyne.
Special Interests: Christian Aid.
Hobbies and Recreations: Gardening, Sport, Walking.

DOVER, John, 39 Town Moor Avenue, Doncaster DN2 6BP. (0302 23077)–MA(Cantab.). *b. 9 April 1933, Bedlington, Northumberland. m. 12 Aug 1959: 1d., 1s.*
Education: 1944–50 Queen Elizabeth Grammar Sch., Darlington; 1950–52 Bishop Wordsworth's, Salisbury; 1952–55 St. Catharine's Coll.; 1955–58 Wesley House.
Appointments: 1958–60 Assistant Tutor Headingley Coll., Leeds; 1960–66 Doncaster, Priory Place; 1966–71 Scarborough; 1971–80 Cambridge Univ., Chaplain; 1980– Doncaster.
Publications: To be a Christian (Epworth 1966); *The Words of the Crucified* (Epworth 1967); *Methodist Lent Book. Hobbies and Recreations:* Tennis, Reading, Television, Music.

DOWDING, Bernard Arthur George, 23 Ashleigh Rd., Solihull, West Midlands B91 1AF. (021–705 1392) *b. 1 Feb 1931, Romford, Essex. m. 19 July 1958: 3d.*
Education: 1944–48 Sevenoaks School; 1955–58 Richmond Coll.
Appointments: 1958–1961 Cheadle; 1961–66 Hemel Hempstead and Berkamsted; 1966–71 London, Finsbury Park and Southgate; 1971–77 Bromley; 1977– Birmingham, Elmdon.
Connexional Committees: 1973–75 Education and Youth.
Special Interests: Worship and Ecumenism; *Hobbies and Recreations:* Walking, Bird Watching and Photography.

DOWELL, Anton H., 2 Park Square, Wigton, Cumbria CA7 9PP. (0965-2468) *b. 15 Mar 1937, Redditch, Worcs. m. 19 Feb 1966: 1d., 2s.*
Education: 1948–55 Ashville Coll., Harrogate; 1956–57 Dundee Coll. of Technology; 1960–61 Cliff Coll.; 1961–65 Hartley Victoria.
Appointments: 1965–67 Alfreton and South Normanton; 1967–71 Spalding; 1971–76 Shaw and Royton; 1976–81 Leeds, Horsforth and Bramley; 1981– Wigton.
Special Interests: Pastoral Counselling (Group Dynamics, Transactional Analysis, Clinical Theology), working with deprived and handicapped. *Hobbies and Recreations:* Music, Fell-walking, Woodwork, Computers.

DOWELL, Joseph, 24 Cedar St., 24 Cedar Street, Merseyside PR8 6NG. *b. 15 Dec 1907, Coventry. m. (2) 1974: 1d., 1s.*
Education: 1912–1919 John Gulson Sch., Coventry; 1919–24 Bablake, Coventry; 1928–31 Hartley Victoria.
Appointments: 1931–35 Bottesford, 1935–38 Redditch; 1938–40 Newark; 1940–46 Chaplain, HMF; 1946–56 Champness Hall, Rochdale; 1956–60 Northampton; 1960–69 Cradley Heath; 1969–73 Wolverhampton.
Connexional Committees: 1963–72 Synod Secretary, Wolverhampton and Shrewsbury Dist.
Local Council Committees: 1947–54 Rochdale Education Committee.
Special Interests: Music, Hymnology, Violin (Orchestral Playing). *Hobbies and Recreations:* Gardening, Golf.

DOWNES, James Cyril Thomas, 33 Sandyland, Haxby, York YO3 8FG. (0904-761845)–MA(Liverpool), BD(Manchester), PhD(Edinburgh). *b. 14 May 1911, Liverpool. m. 23 Aug 1938: 1d., 1s.*
Education: 1922–29 Liverpool Institute; 1930–33 Liverpool Univ.; 1933–36 Manchester Univ.; 1959–61 Edinburgh Univ.; 1933–36 Hartley Victoria. *Appointments:* 1936–38 South East London Mission; 1938–39 Reading, London Road; 1939–45 Chaplain HMF; 1945–49 Leeds, Chapel Allerton, 1949–53 Scarborough, Queen Street; 1953–57 Chaplain, Woodhouse Grove Sch., Bradford; 1957–64 Nicolson Square, Edinburgh; 1964–70 Chairman York and Hull District.
Connexional Committees: 1949–64 Local Preachers Committee; 1949–52 July Committee; 1957–70 Connex Coll. Visitor; 1957–70 Home Missions; 1964–70 Overseas Missions.
Publications: Facts of the Faith (Epworth 1949); *The King in His Beauty* (Epworth 1955); *The Mormons* (Epworth 1963). *Special Interests:* Wesleyana and History of Methodism. *Hobbies and Recreations:* Music, Art, Cricket, Travel, Stamp Collecting.

DOWSON, Frederick Rodham, 6 Murray Rd., Selsey, Chichester, W. Sussex PO20 9AR. (0243 602370) *b. 5 Aug 1912, Haxby, York.* 1933–37 Hartley Victoria.
Appointments: 1937–40 Tiverton and Bampton; 1940–44 Hereford; 1944–48 Clifton, York; 1948–53 Brunswick, Sheffield; 1953–60 Purley; 1960–64 Bournemouth; 1964–69 Worcester; 1969–74 Park Lane, Norwich.

DREWERY, Benjamin, 35 Bramhall Lane South, Bramhall, Stockport, Cheshire SK7 2DN. (061 439 2165)–BA, MA(Oxford), BA(Cambridge). *b. 19 May 1918, Louth, Lincs. m. 30 July 1949: 4d.*
Education: 1923–1925 Lea Rd. Inf., Gainsborough; 1925–29 Pontefract Rd. Elem., Castleford; 1929–1934 Leeds Gramar Sch.; 1934–37 Manchester Grammar School; 1937–40 Corpus Christi College, Oxford; 1946–49 Wesley House, Cambridge.
Appointments: 1949–54 Middlesbrough; 1954–57 South Norwood, Croydon; 1957–64 Oxford, 1964–65 Worthing; 1965– Bishop Fraser (Senior) Lecturer in Ecclesiastical History, Univ. of Manchester.
Connexional Committees: 1964–72 Faith and Order; 1966–72 G.P.
Publications: Origin and the Doctrine of Grace (1960); Joint Editor of *Luther and Erasmus, Free Choice and Salvation* (1969); *Martin Luther (Documents of Modern History)* (1970); *History of Christian Doctrine* (1978). *Hobbies and Recreations:* Music (Organ, Choral).

DRIVER, David George, 36 Moor Crescent, Gosforth, Newcastle-upon-Tyne NE3 4AQ. (0632 853041)– BA(Nottingham), BD(Lond.). *b. 31 Aug 1934, Goole, Yorkshire. m. 25 July 1959: 1d., 2s.*
Education: 1938 and 1942 Pasture Rd. Inf. Sch., Goole, Yorkshire; 1939–42 Airmyn County School, Goole, Yorkshire; 1942–45 Lee Brig Jun. Sch., Altofts, Normanton, Yorks; 1945–47 Normanton Grammar Sch., Yorkshire; 1947–¡52 Royds Hall Grammar Sch., Huddersfield; 1952–55 Nottingham Univ.; 1957–60 Richmond Coll. *Appointments:* 1960–65 Manchester and Salford Mission; 1965–71 Coventry Mission; 1971–81 Croydon; 1981– Newcastle, Brunswick Central.
Connexional Committees: Home Mission Board; Faith and Order.
Publications: Occasional article in *Methodist Recorder* etc. *Special Interests:* History, Biography, Church Growth. *Hobbies and Recreations:* Reading, Exploring the countryside, Listening to music.

DRIVER, Roger Cumming, 23 Abbey Drive, Orrell, Wigan, Lancs. WN5 8RW. (0942 223172)– MA(Cantab), BD(Manchester). *b. 31 December 1933, Streatham, London SW16.*
Education: 1938–41 Private Sch.; 1941–46 The Friends Sch., Lancaster; 1946–52 Ashville Coll., Harrogate; 1952–55 Univ. of Cambridge; 1955–58 Univ. of Manchester; 1955–58 Hartley Victoria. *Appointments:* 1958–60 Orrell and Lamberhead Green; 1960–66 Liverpool North East; 1966–71 Sale; 1971–76 Romford; 1976– Orrell and Lamberhead Green.
Connexional Committees: 1962–66 Christian Citizenship Committee.
Special Interests: Methodist History, English Literature (Victorian and Modern). *Hobbies and Recreations:* Music, Walking.

DUCHARS, Leonard, 1 Groudle Rd., Onchan, Isle of Man. (0624-3018) *b. 1 Aug 1899, Middlesbrough. m. 29 June 1927 (w): 2s.*
Education: 1923–26 Hartley Coll.
Appointments: 1921–22 Enfield; 1922–23 Hartley Coll.; 1923–26 Banbury Coll.; 1926–27 Darlington; 1927–30 Burnley; 1930–34 Darlington; 1934–38 Middlesbrough; 1938–45 Birkenhead; 1945–51 Wallasey; 1951–57 Douglas, Isle of Man; 1957–63 Truro; 1963–67 St. Austell.
Connexional Committees: Youth Council.
Special Interests: Youth Work.
Hobbies and Recreations: Elocution, Music.

DUCKER, John Michael Frederick, 23 Belgrave Rd., Clifton, Bristol BS8 2AA. (0272 730134)– BD(Lond.). *b. 17 April 1932, Hartley, Witney, Hants. m. 20 Aug 1960: 1d., 2s.*
Education: 1935–39 County Inf. and Jun. Sch., Whitehall Rd., Uxbridge, Middx.; 1939–46 Woodhouse Grove Sch., Apperley Bridge, Yorks; 1950–53 Handsworth Coll. *Appointments:* 1953–55 Morpeth and Bedlington; 1955–56 Home Missions (Caravan Mission); 1956–59 Chaplain HMF; 1959–66 London East End Mission; 1966–71 Leigh-on-Sea; 1971–78 Guildford; 1978 Clifton and Redland, Bristol.
Connexional Committees: 1963–78 National Childrens Home; 1960–63 Candidates Examination; 1971–77 and 1981– R.N., Army and R.A.F. Board, 1976– Conference Memorials.
Local Council Committees: 1962–66 Bethnal Green Borough Youth Committee; 1962–66 B.G. Stepney and Poplar Youth Employment Committee.
Special Interests: Chaplaincy within all forms of Community. *Hobbies and Recreations:* Sailing and Walking.

DUCKER, Roger Francis, 35 Arundel Road, Cheam, Sutton, Surrey SM2 6EU. (01 642 1701)– MA(Cantab). *b. 1 Jan 1934, Luton, Beds. m. 6 Aug 1960: 3s.*
Education: 1939–42 Prim. Schools in Uxbridge and Halifax; 1942–50 Woodhouse Grove School, Apperley Bridge, Bradford, Yorks.; 1954–58 Cambridge Univ.; 1954–58 Wesley House. *Appointments:* 1958–60 Student Christian Movement; 1960–63 Watford; 1963–70 Richmond and Barnes; 1970–77 Rome (English Language and Liaison Officer with Methodist Church of Italy); 1977– Sutton, Surrey.
Publications: Ministers and Priests (Epworth Conversations Booklets 1964); *The Church At Ponte Sant Angelo* (English Transation of Italian Booklet by Giovanni Conti 1974).
Special Interests: Ecumenism, Travel, Astronomy, Italy–particularly Casa Materna Children's Home, Naples.
Hobbies and Recreations: Piano, Swimming.

DUERDEN, Tom, 61 Woodlands Rd., Cleadon, Sunderland, Tyne and Wear SR6 7UD. (0783 367007)– BA(Open Univ.). *b. 24 Jan 1934, Burnley, Lancs. m. 25 Sept 1954: 2s.*
Education: 1945– Healey Wood, Prim. Sch., Burnley; 1945–49 Towneley Technical High Sch.; 1958–61 Hartley Victoria.
Appointments: 1961–66 Haslingden; 1966–71 Blyth and Seaton Delaval; 1971–73 Newcastle Mission; 1973–78 Newcastle, Heaton and Wallsend; 1978– Sunderland North.
Hobbies and Recreations: Photography, Fishing, Model Railways.

DU FEU, Alfred George, 2 Balmoral Avenue, Spalding, Lincs. PE11 2RN. (0775 67636) *b. 26 Sept 1911, Trinity, Jersey. m. 13 Oct 1945: 4s.*
Education: 1918–21 Miss E. M. Du Feu's Sch., Jersey; 1921–27 St. Martin's Collegiate Sch., Jersey; 1935–38 Handsworth.
Appointments: 1938–41 E. Nigeria District; 1941–44 Matlock, Trinity; 1944–48 Southampton; 1948–54 Norton Radstock; 1954–63 St. Austell, 1963–67 Launceston; 1967–72 Spalding; 1972–75 St. Ives (Central); 1975–76 St. Ives and Hayle.
Connexional Committees: 1970– The Board of Trustees for Methodist Purposes; 1970– Chapel Affairs; 1973– Division of Property.
Hobbies and Recreations: Gardening and D.I.Y., Football, Hockey, Cricket, Tennis, Swimming, Table Tennis, Billiards and Snooker.

DU FEU, Philip Laurens, 3 Ashton Ave., Arnold, Nottingham NG5 8LL. (0602 206620) *b. 3 Sept 1912, St. Helier, Jersey, C.I. m. 27 Feb 1960: 2d.*
Education: 1924–28 Victoria Coll., Jersey; 1932–35 Handsworth Coll.
Appointments: 1935–52 Ivory Coast Dt, French West Africa; 1952–57 Lincoln Aldersgate; 1957–63 Ripley; 1963–68 Ashbourne; 1968–75 Chorley; 1975–80 Nottingham East.
Connexional Committees: 1955–57 and 1959–62 Overseas General Committee.
Hobbies and Recreations: Reading, Gardening, Philately.

DUGARD, Donald Robert, 8 Woodlands Drive., Harrogate, N.Yorks HG2 7AT. (0423 885680) *b. 28 Aug 1907, Birmingham. m. 29 Aug 1934: 1s.*
Education: 1927–30 Didsbury Coll.
Appointments: 1930–33 Per SCM; 1933–34 Airdrie and Coatbridge; 1934–36 Grove St. and Woolton, Liverpool; 1936–39 Newchurch in Rossendale; 1939–44 Harrogate; 1944–48 Hull, Cultman St.; 1948–56 London, South Norwood; 1956–61 London, Beckenham and Bromley; 1961–67 Whitby; 1967–69 York; 1969–73 Hull, Trinity.
Hobbies and Recreations: Music, Drama, Gardening.

DUGDALE, Richard Procter, 25 Little Dale, Pickering YO18 8PS. (0751 73847) *b. 25 May 1913, Lancaster. m. 1 Jan 1940: 1s.*
Education: 1919–25 Bowerham Council Sch.; 1925–29 Lancaster Royal Grammar Sch., 1932–35 Hartley Victoria. *Appointments:* 1935–39 Fernando Poo; 1939–42 Eastern Nigeria Dt; 1942–45 Macclesfield, 1945–50 Eastern Nigeria Dt; 1950–54 Macclesfield; 1954–67 Batley, 1967–70 Methodist Church Caribbean and Americas; 1970–75 Stokesley; 1975–77 Filey
Hobbies and Recreations: Art, Languages, Music.

DUNCAN, Ian Stewart, 16 Arbour Close, Kenilworth, Warwickshire CV8 2BA. (0926 52946)–LL.B., B.D. *b. 5 May 1933, Newcastle-upon-Tyne. m. 15 July 1961: 2d.*
Education: 1944–46 King Henry VIII Sch., Coventry; 1946–51 King Edwards Sch., Birmingham; 1951–54 Univ. of Birmingham; 1958–61 Headingley. *Appointments:* 1961–65 Huddersfield West; 1965–71 Liverpool North; 1971–77 Colwyn Bay and Llandudno; 1977– Leamington.
Connexional Committees: 1968– Law and Polity Committee; 1978– Board of Property.

DUNFORD, G. Henry, Southlands, 28 Churchill Drive, Spalding, Lincs. PE11 2RL. (0775 5129) *b. 21 Sept 1902, York. m. 3 Aug 1932: 1.*
Education: Elementary, CE; 1922–23 Cliff Coll.; 1926–29 Richmond.
Appointments: 1925–26 Stroud; 1926–29 Richmond Coll.; 1929–32 Hull, Waltham St.; 1932–35 Spalding; 1935–39 Scunthorpe; 1939–44 Gainsborough; 1944–47 Newcastle, Heaton and Wallsend; 1947–53 Dunstable; 1953–58 Small Heath, Birmingham; 1958–62 Wisbech; 1962–67 Spalding.
Special Interests: Reading, Gardening.

DUNN, Lawrence, 41 Keats Close, Wootton Bassett, Wilts SN4 8HH. (0793-853690) *b. 20 Sept 1901, Blackheath, Birmingham. m. 25 July 1936.*
Education: 1906–15 Lichfield Elem.; 1929–32 Headingley Coll.
Appointments: 1929–30 Dover; 1930–33 Headingley; 1933–35 North of Scotland Mission; 1935–39 London, Broomwood and Stockwell; 1939–49 London, Forest Hill and Sydenham; 1949–53 East Sussex M.; 1953–58 London Deptford and Greenwich; 1958–63 London, East Ham Mission; 1963–68 Brentford and Hounslow; 1968–73 Bedford South.
Special Interests: Rotary, English Literature, Club International
Hobbies and Recreations: Photography, Gardening, Microscopy.

DUNSTAN, Raymond Walters, 6 Friars Walk, Dunstable, Beds LU6 3JA. (0582 63639) *b. 13 Dec 1924, Bradworthy, N. Devon. m. 6 June 1952: 1d.*
Education: 1929–35 Horrabridge Council Sch.; 1935–43 Plympton Grammar Sch.; 1948–51 Headingley Coll. *Appointments:* 1946–47 Mid Somerset Mission; 1947–48 Snaith; 1951–58 Leeds South; 1958–67 North Shields and Whitley Bay; 1967–74 Wimbledon; 1974– Dunstable.
Local Council Committees: 1968–74 Education Committee of the London Borough of Merton.
Special Interests: Music, Methodist History. *Hobbies and Recreations:* Collecting Porcelain, Deltiology, Philately.

DUNSTONE, Robert Oliver, Methodist Church House, Church St., St. Mary's, Isles of Scilly. (0720 22406) *b. 16 Aug 1928, London. m. 9 July 1955: 1d., 1s.*
Education: Truro Sch.; 1953–55 Headingley. *Appointments:* 1952–53 Sheffield North East; 1953–55 Headingley Coll.; 1955–61 Barbados Dt.; 1961–65 Dunstable; 1965–67 Jamaica Dt.; 1967–71 Caribbean and Americas Conf.; 1971–82 Truro; 1982– Isles of Scilly.

DURRANT, Gordon A., 6A Waverley Rd., Bognor Regis, Sussex PO21 5NB. (0243-821736) *b. 5 Aug 1905, North Cove, Beccles, Suffolk. m. 15 Aug 1934: 2s.*
Education: Beccles Coll. Suffolk; 1928–31 Handsworth.
Appointments: 1927–28 Reserve List; 1931–32 Llandrindod Wells; 1932–35 Colchester; 1935–37 Grays; 1937–44 Grantham; 1944–49 Boston Central; 1949–54 Warrington; 1954–58 Reading; 1958–63 London Wandsworth; 1963–66 Wisbech; 1966–70 North Walsham.
Special Interests: Circuit Life and Ministry. *Hobbies and Recreations:* Woodwork, Gardening, Tennis.

DUTTON, Thomas B., Teasedale House, Easingwold, York YO6 3PN. (0347 21460) *b. 6 May 1923, Kelsall, Cheshire. m. 12 Aug 1953: 2d., 2s.*
Education: 1928–34 Kelsall; 1934–39 Chester City and County Sch.; 1946–48 Headingley. *Appointments:*

1948–51 Wellingborough; 1951–53 Leicester South; 1953–58 Richmond Hill, Leeds, 1958–64 North East Huddersfield; 1964–69 Edinburgh Mission; 1969–79 Lincoln North; 1979– York North.
Connexional Committees: 1965–68 Church Membership Committee.
Local Council Committee: 1971–74 Member of Lincoln Education Committee.
Hobbies and Recreations: Walking.

DYBDAHL, Christine Anne, 45 Jepson Lane, Elland, West Yorks HX5 0PY. (0422 72104) *b. 17 March 1948. Leicester.*
Education: Wyggeston Girls Grammar Sch., Leicester; 1976–79 Wesley, Bristol. *Appointments:* 1979– Elland and Greetland.

DYE, Alan, Westwood House, Wagg St., Congleton, Cheshire CW12 4BA. (026 02 2976)–BD(Lond.). *b. 2 March 1932, Norwich. m. 13 May 1960: 2d.*
Education: 1943–48 City of Norwich Sch.; 1956–60 Hartley Victoria.
Appointments: 1960–64 Douglas, Isle of Man; 1964–69 Eccles; 1969–75 Lincoln South; 1975–82 Colwyn Bay and Llandudno; 1982– Congleton.
Special Interests: Church Growth, Industrial Mission, Children's and Youth Work, Ministers' Fraternals.
Hobbies and Recreations: Photography, Music, Gardening, Conservation.

DYE, Michael Peter, 24 Southway, Eldwick, Bingley BD16 3EW. (0274 563227)–BA(B'Ham). *b. 30 Sept 1944, England. m. 3 April 1971: 1d., 2s.*
Education: 1949–57 Waterloo Secondary; 1957–60 Southport Tech.; 1969–73 Handsworth and Queens. *Appointments:* 1973–76 Huddersfield West; 1976– Shipley and Bingley.
Hobbies and Recreations: Ornithology.

DYER, Arthur Ronald, 47 Sketty Park Rd., Swansea, W.Glam. SA2 9AS. (0792 203938)–MA. *b. 9 June 1920, Cardiff. m. 10 Aug 1946: 3d., 1s.*
Education: 1925–32 Jun. Sch.; 1932–37 Cardiff High Sch.; 1937–41 Univ. Wales; 1941–44 Wesley House.
Appointments: 1944–46 Waltham Abbey and Hertford; 1946–51 St. Helens, Lancs.; 1951–56 Elland; 1956–63 London, Sydenham and Forest Hill; 1963–68 Sevenoaks; 1968–76 London, Walthamstow and Chingford; 1976– Swansea.
Special Interests: Drama, History.
Hobbies and Recreations: Walking, Gardening.

DYER, Ronald John, 26 Berkley St., Eynesbury, St. Neots, Cambs. PE19 2NE. (0480-73444) *b. 20 Dec 1931, Arkesden, Nr. Saffron Walden, Essex. m. 9 Dec 1972: 1d., 1s.*
Education: Newport, Essex County Prim. Sch.; 1957–58 Cliff Coll.; 1964–67 Handsworth.
Appointments: 1967–72 Melton Mowbray; 1972–80 Newmarket; 1980– St. Neots.
Connexional Committees: 1982 Overseas Missions.
Hobbies and Recreations: Sports, Varied aspects of collecting (e.g. Coins, Stamps, Postcards, Old Bottles), Gardening.

DYKES, Eric William, 4 The Serpentine, Lytham, Lytham St. Annes, Lancs. FY8 5NW. (0253 735466) *b. 30 Oct 1926, Castleford. m. 11 Aug 1954: 1d., 1s.*
Education: 1931–37 Pontefract Rd. Jun. Sch., Castleford; 1937–42 Castleford Grammar Sch.; 1949–52 Handsworth Coll. *Appointments:* 1948–49 Cheddar Valley; 1952–54 Glasgow Mission; 1954–59 Keighley; 1959–63 Cleethorpes (Trinity) and Grimsby (Central); 1963–66 Bradford (Manningham); 1966–73 Morecambe; 1973–80 Sunderland (South); 1980 Lytham St. Annes.
Connexional Committees: 1960–66, 1967–69; 1974–78 Social Responsibility; 1967–70 Church Membership; 1971–73 Home Mission.
Special Interests: Ecumenical Affairs, New Testament Studies, Current Affairs and Social Problems, Methodist History (Member of the W.H.S., Chairman of the N.E. Branch of the W.H.S. 1978–80). *Hobbies and Recreations:* Philately, Collecting Wesleyana, Great interest in the Lake District.

DYSON, Harry, 6 Cypress Avenue, Thornton, Cleveleys, Blackpool FY5 2JA. (03914 868840) *b. 23 Jan 1910, Keighley, Yorks. m. 27 July 1934: 2d., 1s.*
Education: Parkwood Elementary School; Keighley Boys Grammar Sch.; 1945–47 Handsworth.
Appointments: 1944–45 Chaplain H.M.F.; 1947–48 Sowerby Bridge; 1948–52 Buxton Rd., Huddersfield; 1952–55 Aireborough; 1955–59 Ripon; 1959–64 Rhosymedre and Chirk; 1964–67 Wrexham; 1967–73 Grassington; 1973–75 Skelmersdale.

EARL, John Ivor Harold, Wesley House, Baytree Hill, Liskeard, Cornwall PL14 4BG. (0579 42127) *b. 22 Aug 1922, London. m. Dec 1959: 4s.*
Education: Various Schools in London; 1948-1950 Handsworth.
Appointments: 1946–48 Wymondham; 1950–52 East Dereham; 1952–58 Boston; 1958–63 Spalding; 1963–69 Salisbury; 1969–80 Tavistock; 1980– Liskeard and Looe.
Special Interests: Music, Divine Healing, Writing Articles. *Hobbies and Recreations:* Walking.

EARL, Mark Wesley, 5 Stonydale, Ulverston, Cumbria LA12 9PQ. (0229 54517)–MA(B'Ham), BD(Lond). *b. 15 Sept 1915, Bentley, Yorks. m. 25 July 1940: 1d.*
Education: 1925–33 Brampton Secondary Sch.; Handsworth.
Appointments: 1937–46 N.China District; 1946–49 Stoke-on-Trent, Longton; 1949–54 Manchester, Cheetham Hill; 1954–60 Birmingham, Moseley Rd., 1960–65 Birkenhead; 1965–74 Carlisle Dist., Chairman; 1974–80 Newcastle-upon-Tyne Dt, Chairman.
Connexional Committees: Various.

EARLEY, Brian David, Carter Manse, 180 Loughborough Rd., Ruddington, Nottingham NG11 6LF. (0602 212146) *b. 13 June 1939,*

Trent, Nr. Sherbourne, Dorset. m. 12 Aug 1967: 1d., 1s.
Education: 1944–50 Trent Prim.; 1950–51 Foster's Grammar Sch., Sherbourne; 1951–55 Yeovil Grammar Sch.; 1955–56 Cliff Coll.; 1961–65 Didsbury, Bristol.
Appointments: 1965–67 North Walsham and Aylsham; 1967–70 Frome and Shepton Mallet; 1970–73 Roath, Cardiff; 1973–79 Shebbear; 1979– Nottingham, South.
Special Interests: Pastoral Work.
Hobbies and Recreations: Gardening, Walking, Tennis, Music.

EASTHOPE, J. H. Gordon, Epworth, 23 Golf Course, Givan, Ayrshire, Scotland KA26 9HW. (0465 2114).
Education: 1948–51 Brighton Grove Coll., Manchester Univ.
Appointments: 1952–58 Baptist Church, 1958–61 Burslem, Hill Top, Stoke-on-Trent; 1961–64 Swinton, Pendlebury and Pendleton, Manchester; 1964–67 Sheffield North East; 1967–68 Willington; 1968–71 Sunderland North; 1971–73 Todmorden; 1973–78 Newmarket/ Thetford; 1978– Paisley Mission.

EASTWOOD, Charles Cyril, Heathview, Monks Lane, Audlem, Nr. Crewe, Cheshire CW3 0HP. (0270 811383)–BD(Serampore), PhD(Lond), FRHistS. *b. 28 May 1916, Sheffield. m. 30 Nov 1944: 1d., 1s.*
Education: West Riding Council Sch.; 1937–40 Headingley.
Appointments: 1940–51 S. India; 1951–57 Waltham Abbey and Hertford; 1957–62 Harrogate, Trinity; 1962–65 London, Highgate; 1965–81 Keele Univ., Senior Lect. in Philosophy and Religion.
Connexional Committee: Doctrinal Comm. of Appeal, L.P. Committee, OM Comm., N.C.H. Comm.
Publications: Wanted on Voyage (Cargate Pr 1960); *The Priesthood of Believers* (Epworth 1960), *The Royal PRD of The Faithful* (Epworth 1963); *Life and Thought in the Ancient World* (Hodder 1963); *What You Make It* (Epworth 1967); *The Hidden Way* (Brechset 1982).
Hobbies and Recreations: Tennis, Cricket.

EASTWOOD, Harry Quarmby, Glyn Coed, St. Margarets Drive, Craig Y Don, Llandudno, Gwynedd LL30 1YD. (0492 78641) *b. 29 Dec 1906, Halifax, Yorkshire. m. 22 Aug 1935. 1d., 1s.*
Education: 1909–19 Battinson Rd. Sch., 1929 Didsbury; 1930–33 Headingley. *Appointments:* 1928–29 Holsworthy; 1933–35 Kirkoswold; 1935–37 Whitehaven; 1937–41 Ashton-u-Lyne; 1941–45 Blackpool South; 1945–49 Birkenhead; 1949–56 Wigan Mission; 1956–59 Huddersfield Mission; 1959–66 **Colwyn Bay and Llandudno (St. John's)**; 1966–72 Sunderland South.
Connexional Committees: 1940–41 Wesley Guild and Young Methodism; 1975– M.H.A.
Special Interests: Methodist Homes for the Aged, Marriage Guidance, Abbeyfield Housing for the Elderly
Hobbies and Recreations: Bee-keeping, Orchid Growing, Water-colour Painting.

EASTWOOD, Norman Arthur, 22 Fernside Rd., Talbot Park, Bournemouth BH9 2LB. (0202 515108) *b. 20 Nov 1913, Leeds. m. 21 Aug 1941.*
Education: 1922–25 Leeds Grammar Sch.; 1925–28 George Dixon's Secondary Sch., Birmingham; 1928–31 Cockburn High Sch., Leeds; 1932–36 Handsworth.
Appointments: 1936–37 President's List; 1937–39 Thorne Memorial, Barnstaple; 1939–41 Somerset Mission, 1941–42 Higham Ferrers; 1942–46 Kettering; 1946–50 Nottingham West; 1950–55 Nottingham South; 1955–62 Rhyl and Prestatyn; 1962–67 Bournemouth; 1967–72 Weymouth; 1972–75 Crosby, Liverpool; 1949–51 Nottingham District, Overseas Missions Secretary; 1951–55 Synod Secretary; 1946–50 Methodist Chaplain, Nottingham Univ.; 1967–72 Weymouth Coll. of Education.
Connexional Committees: 1949–51 Overseas Missions.
Hobbies and Recreations: Gardening and Photography.

EDDY, Geoffrey Thackray, 24 Townsend Rd., Norwich NR4 6RG. (0603 52257)–MA(B'ham), BD(Lond). *b. 15 Feb 1915, Prestwich, Lancs. m. 6 June 1942: 4d.*
Education: 1920–26 Inf. Sch., Hoyland, Hoyland Common Boys; 1926–33 Holgate Grammar Sch., Barnsley; 1933–38 Birmingham Univ.; 1936–38 Muirhead Post-Graduate Philosophy Scholarship; 1933–38 Handsworth.
Appointments: 1938–40 Tunbridge Wells; 1940–43 Birmingham (Islington); 1943–47 Birmingham (Wesley); 1947–51 Birmingham (Moseley Rd.); 1951–60 Gold Coast/ Ghana (Chairman 1954–60); 1960–63 Colwyn Bay; 1963–68 Lincoln District (Chairman); 1968–72 Methodist Missionary Society; 1972 East Anglia District (Chairman).
Connexional Committees: Doctrinal Committee of Appeal, Law and Polity, Faith and Order, Transfer of Authority, and others Ex. Officio as Chairman at various dates.
Publications: Manual of Fellowship on I Peter, Articles in *London Quarterly* and *Epworth Reviews,* etc.
Special Interests: Art. *Hobbies and Recreations:* Painting, Walking, Cycling.

EDDY, Graham Victor Carl, 15 North Road, Stokesley, Middlesbrough, Celeveland TS9 5DY. (0642 710358) *b. 1 Sept 1937, Lewes, Sussex. m. 30 April 1964: 2d.*
Education: 1942/43 Private House Sch., Chatham; 1943/45 Luton Rd. Jun., Chatham; 1945/46 Bisley Shaftesbury Home, Bisley; 1946/48 Luton Rd. Jun., Chatham; 1948–52 Highfield Secondary Modern, Chatham; 1962–66 London Univ.; 1962–66 Richmond. *Appointments:* 1966–68 Pickering; 1975–80 Norwich; 1968–72 Easingwold; 1980 Stokesley; 1972–75 Sleaford.
Connexional Committees: Sept 1982 Overseas Missions.
Hobbies and Recreations: Art, Photography.

EDDY, Sidney Austen, Trewirgie, Westward Rd., St. Ives, Cornwall

TR26 1JX. (0736 794297) *b. 26 Feb 1910, Cape Town, South Africa. m. 31 July 1940.*
Education: 1918–24 Rondebosch Boys High Sch., Cape Town; 1925–30 Truro Coll., Cornwall; 1930–32 Univ. of London (Kings Coll.); 1930–32 Westminster Coll.; 1933–37 Richmond Coll. *Appointments:* 1937–42 Holsworthy; 1942–55 Chaplain H.M.F.; 1955–61 St. Columb and Padstow; 1961–69 St. Ives, Cornwall; 1969–75 Long Eaton.
Special Interests: Cornish Methodism from Wesley and His Travels in the Duchy, Rotary. *Hobbies and Recreations:* Canvas Work, Upholstery, Bowls.

EDDYSHAW, Paul Francis, 17 Hazeloak Rd., Shirley, Solihull, W.Midlands B90 2AZ. (021 744 2830)–BD(Lond). *b. 31 Jan 1935, Newstead, Notts. m. 30 July 1960: 2d., 1s.* d. Jan 1990
Education: 1945–53 Henry Mellish Grammar Sch., Nottingham; 1957–60 Richmond. *Appointments:* 1960–64 Halifax N.; 1964–70 Leicester West; 1970–76 Chichester and Bognor; 1976 Birmingham (Moseley Rd. and Sparkhill).
Connexional Committees: 1967–70 Social Responsibility; 1973– Stewardship; 1974– Invalid Ministers Rest Fund; 1982 General Committee Division of Finance.
Publications: Progress in Stewardship (1973).
Special Interests: Stewardship and Ecumenism. *Hobbies and Recreations:* Sport, Gardening, Family.

EDEN, Frank Christopher, Oakdene, 140 Valley Road, Clacton on Sea, Essex CO15 6LX. (0255 421914) *b. 25 Dec 1900, Grendon, Northants. m. 11 Aug 1934: 2s.*
Education: Victoria Elementary Sch., Wellingborough; 1913–16 Wellingborough Public Sch.; 1927–30 Handsworth. *Appointments:* 1930–34 Birmingham (Islington); 1934–37 Tonbridge, 1939–42 Gravesend and Dartford; 1942–46 Sevenoaks; 1946–52 Luton; 1952–59 London (Kilburn and Hampstead); 1959–66 Romford; 1966–72 Chairman London NE.
Connexional Committees: 1936–46 Youth Comm.; 1966–72 Home Missions; 1966–72 General Purposes; 1966–72 Overseas Miss.
Council Member: Presidents Council one year, when formed; 1966–82 NCH; 1974–77 MHA Board; 1954–82 Seamens Mission.
Publications: Contributor, quarterly *Local Preachers and Class Leaders Magazine;* three volumes for *Class Leaders—Our Fellowship Below* (1954); *Together Travel On* (1955); *Experience will decide* (1956).
Hobbies and Recreations: Reading and Gardening, Golf until 1959.

EDMONDS, Reginald Charles, 528 Norwich Rd., Ipswich IP1 6JR. (0473 41274)–BD. *b. 20 Dec 1928, London. m. 18 Aug 1956: 3d.*
Education: 1939–43 Bexleyheath Secondary Sch.; 1955–56 Selley Oak Coll.: 1951–55 Hartley Victoria.
Appointments: 1956–64 Nigeria Dt; 1965–70 Callington and Gunnislake; 1970–77 Exeter; 1977 Ipswich.
Connexional Committees: Central Committee; Overseas Division from 82.
Special Interests: Ministry of Healing; New Testament. *Hobbies and Recreations:* Sport, Walking, Reading, Gardening.

EDMUNDSON, Brian, 44 Pollard Lane, Bradford BD2 4RW. (0274 637470) *b. 15 Dec 1938, Bolton, Lancs. m. 20 June 1964: 1d., 1s.*
Education: 1949–51 Bolton Grammar; 1951–52 Bolton Sch. of Commerce; 1961–65 Headingley.
Appointments: 1965–67 Boroughbridge; 1967–69 Selby; 1969–79 Morley; 1979– Bradford (Woodhouse Grove).

EDWARDS, Christopher G., 137 Priestsic Rd., Sutton in Ashfield, Notts NG17 4EA. (0623 554259) *b. 8 May 1932, Westcliff-on-Sea, Essex. m. 25 Sept 1965.* d. 08.07.14
Education: 1943–48 Westcliff High Sch.; 1955–58 Richmond Coll.
Appointments: 1958–59 Newport Hill St.; 1959–62 Sirhowy Valley; 1962–66 Sheffield North; 1966–69 Chesterfield; 1969–75 Old Hill; 1975–82 Coalville; 1982– Ashfield.
Special Interests: Member Churches Fellowship for Psychical and Spiritual Studies. *Hobbies and Recreations:* Astronomy, Lapidary.

EDWARDS, Eric, 12 Cavendish Square, Wrexham, Clwyd LL12 8AD. (0978 356818) *b. 27 March 1908, Coed-poeth, Nr. Wrexham, Denbighshire. m. 14 May 1940: 1d.*
Education: 5–12 years Coed-poeth, Nr. Wrexham Schs.; 12–16 years Grove Park, Wrexham County Sch.; 1933–36 Handsworth.
Appointments: 1932–33 Holyhead and Amlwch; 1936–39 Bagillt; 1939–40 Manchester (W); 1940–45 Llanrhaeadr-ym-Mochnant (Oswestry); 1945–47 Llanidloes; 1947–50 Bangor (W); 1950–55 Porthmadog; 1955–60 Holyhead and Amlwch; 1960–65 Tregarth; 1965–1970 Coedpoeth; 1970–75 Coedpoeth.
Connexional Committees: 1957–67 Epworth Book Committee.
Publications: Cylchdaith Coedpoeth (Circuit History 1975); *Yr Eglwys Fethodistaidd* (Statistical History of Welsh Methodism 1980); Welsh Methodist Historical Society Lectures 1967 and 1979.
Special Interests: Welsh Methodist History, Archives, Local History Journalism.

EDWARDS, James Edwin Prescott, 103 Railway Rd., Adlington, Chorley, Lancashire PR6 9QZ. (0257 480147) *b. 4 June 1911, Leigh, Lancashire. m. 27 Sept 1937: 1d., 1s.*
Education: Devonshire Rd. Sch., Blackpool; Palatine Sch., Blackpool; 1931–34 Didsbury. *Appointments:* 1934–44 Jamaica District; 1944–49 Clitheroe; 1949–52 Doncaster South; 1952–54 Lancaster; 1954–59 Paris; 1959–63 Morecambe; 1963–67 Preston; 1967–71 Kirkoswald; 1971–76 Bolton.
Connexional Committees: 1946–49, 1951–52, 1967–71 M.M.S. General Comm.

EDWARDS, Joseph Chapman, 54 Bishopton Lane, Ripon, N.Yorks. HG4 2QN. (0765 2071) *b. 10 Mar 1905, Cleethorpes. m. 14 Aug 1935:*

1s.
Education: 1910–12 St. Peter's Sch., Cleethorpes; 1912–19 Bursar St. Sch., Cleethorpes; 1928–31 Hartley Victoria. *Appointments:* 1931–35 Southend-on-Sea; 1935–40 Abergavenny; 1940–45 Pickering West; 1945–50 Skegness; 1950–56 Louth; 1956–62 Masham; 1962–71 Market Weighton.
Special Interests: Preaching. *Hobbies and Recreations:* Photography, Walking, German Language.

EDWARDS, Leonard Ralph, 27 Durleigh Rd., Bridgwater, Som. TA6 7HX. (0278 423529) *b. 5 Mar 1922, Watford, Herts. m. 17 July 1946: 1d.*
Education: 1933–38 Watford Boys Grammar Sch.; 1955–56 Didsbury, Bristol. *Appointments:* 1956–58 Wesley, West Bromwich; 1958–64 Radstock; 1964–69 Cheddar Valley; 1969–74 Gateshead and Jarrow; 1974–78 Dursley and Stonehouse; 1974– Bridgwater.
Connexional Committees: 1971–74, 1975–78, 1981–82 Property.

EDWARDS, Michael Stone, 118 Carlton Rd., Reigate, Surrey RH2 0JF. (Redhill 61241)–BA, MA(B'ham), MLitt(Bristol) *b. 18 June 1931, Catford, London SE6. m. 2 April 1959: 1d., 1s.*
Education: 1936–39 Sangley House Sch., Catford; 1940–42 Bromley Rd. Sch., Beckenham, Kent; 1942–48 Beckenham and Penge County Grammar Sch.; 1957–60 Univ. of Birmingham, part-time 1960–62; 1966–69 part-time Univ. of Bristol; 1956–60 Handsworth.
Appointments: 1960–65 Banbury; 1965–68 Penzance, 1968–73 Oxford, 1973–80 St. Pauls United Theological Coll., Limuru, Kenya; 1980– Redhill and East Grinstead.
Connexional Committees: 1964–77 Methodist Archives Committee.
Publications: Methodism in Boddington 1797–1965 (1965); *Joseph Rayner Stephens 1805–79* (1968); W.H.S. Lancashire and Cheshire Branch Lecture, 1967; *The Lime Walk Story, 1885–1972; S.E. Keeble, The Rejected Prophet* (1977); W.H.S. Lecture, (1972).
Special Interests: Church History including Methodist History. *Hobbies and Recreations:* Butterflies, Stamps, Wagnerian Opera.

EDWARDS, Richard Dilwyn, 71 Kings Drive, Bishopston, Bristol BS7 8JQ. (0272 45823)–BA(Bristol), BSc(Wales). *b. 1 Jan 1940, Wrexham, Clwyd. m. 21 July 1972: 2s.*
Education: 1945–51 Brymbo Inf./Prim. Sch.; 1951–59 Grove Park Boys Grammar Sch., Wrexham; 1959–62 Univ. Coll. of North Wales, Bangor; 1962–65 Didsbury, Bristol.
Appointments: 1965–67 Launceston; 1967–71 Truro; 1971–81 Basingstoke; 1981– Bristol North.
Special Interests: Science and Religion, Mathematical Statistics.
Hobbies and Recreations: Soccer, Photography, Computers.

EDWARDS, Wilfrid LeCato, Headmaster's House, Rookery Hill, Ashstead Park, Ashtead, Surrey KT21 1HY. (0327 72233)–BA(B'ham). *b. 29 April 1894, Sandwich, Kent. m. 3 Aug 1921: 2d.*
Education: 1903–10 Dunheved Coll., Launceston, Cornwall; 1914–15 Leeds Univ.; 1919–20 Birmingham Univ.; 1914–15 Headingly; 1919–20 Handsworth. *Appointments:* 1921–44 Hyderabad District, South India; 1945–47 Witney; 1947–55 Hyderabad District, South India; 1955–58 Epworth and Crowle; 1958–64 Warden Old Rectory, Epworth
Publications: In The Lands of The Lotus and Bamboo (Missionary Film Committee 1936); *Epworth The Home of The Wesley's* (Epworth Old Rectory 1959).
Special Interests: Photography, Eight Tours of the U.S.A. and Canada lecturing on The Message of the Mystic East and Epworth Old Rectory—the home of the Wesleys and its message for the world.

EGGLETON, Edward Martin, 22 Belmont Rd., Uxbridge, Middlesex. (0895 33997)–BA(Leeds), DMin. *b. 18 May 1938, Kensington, London. m. 25 July 1970. 2s.*
Education: 1943–49 Grove Rd., Harrogate; 1949–54 Harrogate Grammar Sch.; 1963–66 Univ. of Leeds; 1966–67 Kirchliche Hochschule, Wuppertal, W.Germany; 1962–66 Headingley. *Appointments:* 1967–75 Durham Univ. Chaplain; 1975–76 Schewectady, N.York State, U.S.A.; 1976– Chaplain, Brunel Univ.
Connexional Committees: 1970–73 Student Work Committee; 1981– Team Ministries.
Special Interests: Psychotherapy and Theology, The New Apologetic.
Hobbies and Recreations: Singing, Sport, Photography, Poetry.

EGLEN, Edmund, 3 Eastland Ave., Acomb, York YO2 4NZ. (0904-794947) *b. 8 Oct 1905, Newcastle-on-Tyne. m. 10 Aug 1935: 2d.*
Education: Newcastle-on-Tyne Technical Coll.; 1928–31 Hartley Victoria. *Appointments:* 1931–33 Ebbw Vale; 1933–37 Knaresborough; 1937–40 Pickering; 1940–45 Bury; 1945–50 Newcastle North West; 1950–53 Ryton-on-Tyne; 1953–60 Bishop Auckland; 1960–66 York Clifton; 1966–69 Filey, Yorks.

ELFORD, Gordon Neville, 156 Abbots Rd., Abbots Langley, Watford, Hert WD5 0BL. (092 77 63248) *b. 31 Oct 1938, Blandford Forum, Dorset. m. 22 Aug 1970: 1d.*
Education: 1949–54 Blandford Grammar Sch.; 1968–71 Richmond.
Appointments: 1971–76 Porthleven; 1976– Watford.
Hobbies and Recreations: Gardening and Flower Arranging.

ELGAR, Alan Francis, 119 Mere Rd., Leicester LE5 5GQ. (0533 58605)–BD(Lond). *b. 17 Aug 1929, London. m. 18 Aug 1956: 2d., 1s.*
Education: 1940–42 Coalville, Leics., Grammar Sch.; 1942–45 East Ham Grammar Sch. for Boys; 1952–56 Handsworth. *Appointments:* 1956–60 Bambury; 1960–61 Zimbabwe, Kwenda; 1961–66 Gatooma; 1967 Furlough; 1968 Epworth; 1968–74 Chibero; 1974–80 Cannock Chase; 1980– Leicester S.E.
Connexional Committees: 1974, 1978–80 Central Committee, Overseas Division.

Special Interests: Internationalism, Peace/War/Conflict Issues, Politics, Theology/Spirituality. *Hobbies and Recreations:* Music, Walking, Cricket.

ELLINGWORTH, Paul, 56 Craigton Rd., Aberdeen AB1 7UN. (0224 33674)–BA, MA(Oxon), BA(Cantab), PhD(Aberdeen). *b. 15 Nov 1931, Barnsley, Yorkshire. m. 23 May 1959: 3s.*
Education: 1936–39 The Weir High Sch., Hessle, Yorks.; 1939–40 Westgate Prim. Sch., Otley, Yorks; 1940–43 Privately; 1943–49 Midsomer Norton County Secondary Sch., Somerset; 1950–53 Worcester Coll., Oxford; 1956–57 University of Heidelberg, W.Germany; 1953–56 Wesley House. *Appointments:* 1959–68 Dahomey-Togo Dt, West Africa; 1968–71 Secretary Missionary Committee; 1971– United Bible Society.
Connexional Committees: European Relations Committee.
Publications: *Listening to the Conversations* (Epworth Press 1964); *The University: Theology, Legend and History* (Abbia 1967); *Biblical Revelation and African Beliefs* (Lutterworth Press 1969); *Towards an African Theology* (Department of Religious Studies, Aberdeen 1970); *A Translator's Handbook on Paul's Letters to the Thessalonians* (The United Bible Societies, Stuttgart, 1975); *Translation and Exegesis: a case study* (Biblica 1978).
Special Interests: Bible Translation, Hermeneutics, Chest, Heart and Stroke Association's Stroke Scheme.
Hobbies and Recreations: Music.

ELLIOTT, Andrew, 65 Haslemere Rd., Liphook, Hants. GU30 7BN. (0428 723234) *b. 1 Feb 1915, Lemington-on-Tyne. m. 21 March 1942: 1d., 1s.*
Education: 1920–26 Newburn Hall Council; 1926–31 Newbury-Lemington Secondary; 1935–39 Didsbury. *Appointments:* 1939–42 Liverpool South; 1942–46 Kirkby Stephen, Appleby and Tebay; 1946–48 Stretford, Manchester; 1948–52 Liverpool South; 1952–57 Heaton and Wallsend; 1957–65 Middlesbrough; 1965–74 Wimbledon; 1974–80 Farnham and Alton.
Publications: *The Geordie Bible* (1971); *A Geordie Life of Jesus* (1974); *The New Geordie Bible* (1977).
Special Interests: Dialect.

ELLIS, David Robert, The Manse, St. Buryan, Penzance TR19 6DB. (073 672 329) *b. 25 July 1950, Worthing, Sussex. m. 17 Aug 1974: 1d., 1s.*
Education: 1955–61 St. Brandons, Worthing; 1961–68 St. Andrews, Worthing; 1972–76 Wesley, Bristol.
Appointments: 1976–78 Launceston; 1978 St. Just.
Special Interests: Circuit Ministry.
Hobbies and Recreations: Sailing, Swimming, Model Railways.

ELLIS, Ifor Elfyn, Coronorion, 36 Rhodfa Glenys, St. Asaph, Clwyd LL17 0DW. (0745 582060)–MA(Cantab), BA(Wales). *b. 10 Aug 1908, Penanturch, Garthbeibio, Welshpool Powys. m. 15 Aug 1935: 4d.*
Education: 1914–20 Garthbeibio CE Prim.; 1920–22 Llanfair Caereinion County Sch.; 1922–27 Llanfyllin County Sch.; 1927–30 Univ. Coll. of North Wales, Bangor; 1930–33 Wesley House.
Appointments: 1933–35 Bangor; 1935–36 Manchester; 1936–37 Cefnmawr; 1937–42 Coedpoeth; 1942–45 Ruthin; 1945–50 Blaenan Ffestiniog; 1950–55 Rhyl; 1955–65 Coedpoeth; 1965–73 Denbigh.
Connexional Committees: 1951–55 Synod Secretary, First N.Wales District; 1955–71 District Chairman; 1961 President Welsh Assembly.

ELLIS, Irene Margaret (Mrs), 7 The Coppice, Clayton-le-Moors, Accrington, Lancashire BB5 5RU. (0254 35890)–BD. *b. 7 Oct 1933, East Ham, London. M. 8 April 1972.*
***Education:* 1939–45 Napier Rd., East Ham; 1945–47 Vicarage** Secondary Modern; 1947–53 East Ham Grammar for Girls; 1954–56 Dudley Training Coll.; 1963–65 Wesley Deaconess Coll.; 1979–80 Hartley Victoria. *Appointments:* 1979– Great Harwood.
Hobbies and Recreations: Reading, Photography, Music, Dress Making.

ELLIS, Richard Hiram, 9 Limetrees Gardens, Low Fell, Gateshead, Tyne and Wear NE9 5BE. (0632 771649)–BD. *b. Dewsbury.*
Appointments: 1945–47 Newmarket; 1949–53 Bishop Auckland; 1953–59 Stockton on Tees; 1959–69 South Shields; 1969–77 Sunderland North; 1977– Gateshead and Jarrow.

ELLIS, Thomas Griffith, Lluest, 24 Palmeira Gardens, Prestatyn, Clwyd. (07456 2896) *b. 18 Feb 1888, Aberdaron, Gwynedd. m. Feb 1923 (2): 2d., 2s.*
Education: 1893–1901 Aberdavon Council Sch.; 1909–12 Clynnog Grammar Sch.; 1913–16 Didsbury.
Appointments: 1912–13 Dinas Maud Welsh; 1913–16 Didsbury Coll.; 1916–17 Corwen Welsh; 1917–18 Dolgelly; 1918–22 Bagillt; 1922–25 Tregarth; 1925–28 Llanasa; 1928–31 Conway; 1931–36 Abegele; 1936–45 Denbigh; 1945–50 Holywell; 1950–54 Conway.
Connexional Committees: Local Preachers' Committee.
Special Interests: Popular Lecturer on Welsh Literature and Folk Music.
Hobbies and Recreations: Boating and Fishing.

ELVES, William Foster, 16 Meadowcroft Grove, Heysham, Morcambe LA3 1ND. (0524 51527) *b. 31 March 1909, Tudhoe, Spennymoor. m. 4 Aug 1937: 1d.*
Education: 1914–20 Tudhoe Sch.; 1920–28 Alderman Wraith Secondary Sch.; 1930–33 Hartley.
Appointments: 1933–34 Bournemouth; 1934–35 Llandudno; 1935–36 Chichester; 1936–39 Andover and Hurstbourne; 1939–44 Sunderland West; 1944–49 Bradford Great Horton; 1949–54 Eccles Wesley; 1954–59 Swinton; 1957–64 Cheetham Hill and Prestwich; 1964–70 Liverpool S.E.; 1970–74 Great Harwood.

ELVIDGE, George, 2 Worsfold Close, Allesley, Coventry CV5 9FT. (0203 403290)–BA, BD. *b. 3 June 1916, South Elmsall. m. 31 March 1944: 1s.*
Education: 1936–41 Manchester Univ.; 1936–39 Hartley Victoria. *Appointments:* 1941–48 Jamaica Dt; 1948–53 Cheetham Hill, Manchester; 1953–56 Grimsby West; 1956–63 Leicester South; 1963–71 Stourbridge and Brierley Hill; 1971–76 Scunthorpe; 1976–81 Blaydon.

ELWORTHY, Donald William, 8 Broadway, Ripley, Derby DE5 3LJ. (0773 43177) *b. Porth Rhondda, Glamorgan, S.Wales. m. 23 March 1940: 1d., 1s.*
Education: 1918–27 Islywyn Elem. Sch., Porth; 1927–28 Charles Church Senior Sch., Plymouth.
Appointments: 1964–67 Lune St., Preston; 1967–72 East Suffolk; 1972–75 Cambridge; 1975–79 South Derbyshire; 1979–80 Supernumerary; 1980– Ripley.
Hobbies and Recreations: Walking and Painting.

ELWORTHY, Kenneth Francis, 7 Hastings Ave., Barkingside, Ilford, Essex IG6 1DZ. (01 550 2460)–BD(Lond). *b. 16 Aug 1943, Torquay, Devon. m. 25 June 1966: 2d., 1s.*
Education: 1954–57 Callington Grammar Sch.; 1957–61 Lowestoft Grammar Sch.; 1963–67 Hartley Victoria. *Appointments:* 1967–69 Holyhead; 1969–72 Rotherham; 1972–78 Norwich (St. Peters) and Univ. Chaplain at Univ. of East Anglia; 1978– London (Ilford).

EMERSON, Albert Edward, 63 Cliff Rd., Paignton, Devon. (0803 558864)–MA, BD. *b. 27 Nov 1908, Aughnacloy, Northern Ireland. m: 1d., 1s.*
Education: Trinity Coll., Dublin; 1930 Edgehill, Belfast. *Appointments:* 1933–35 Kingstown; 1935–37 Dublin, Abbey St.; 1937–40 Edgehill Coll. (Tutor); 1940–48 West Nigeria Dt; 1948–49 Durham; 1949–55 Newcastle Brunswick; 1955–58 Liverpool, Crosby; 1958–65 Reading; 1965–70 York Centenary.

EMISON, David Robert, 29 Eldon Place, Patricroft, Eccles, **Manchester** M30 8QE. (061 789 1354)–Dip.Pas.Theol and Sociology (Manch.). *b. 28 April 1948, Haslingden, Lancashire. m. 18 Aug 1973: 2s.*
Education: 1953–59 St. James' CE Prim. Sch.; 1959–64 Haslingden County Secondary Sch.; 1969–73 Hartley Victoria. *Appointments:* 1973–76 London Mission (North West); 1976– Cadishead and Eccles.
Connexional Committees: 1981– Divisional Board of Education and Youth.
Special Interests: Youth Work, Pastoral Care. *Hobbies and Recreations:* Gardening.

ENGLISH, Donald, 44 Anne Boleyn's Walk, Cheam, Surrey SM3 8DF. (01 643 3679)–MA, DD. *b. 20 July 1930, High Westwood, Consett, County Durham. m. 28 July 1962: 2s.* d. 28.8.98
Education: 1935–37 Leadgate Inf. Sch., Co. Durham; 1937–41 Delves Lane Inf. and Jun. Sch.; 1941–48 Consett Grammar Sch.; 1948–53 Univ. Coll., Leicester; 1958–60 Cambridge Univ.; 1958–60 Wesley House. *Appointments:* 1960–62 Assistant Tutor, Wesley Coll., Headingley; 1962–65 Tutor in New Testament and Methodism, Trinity College, Umuahia, Eastern Nigeria; 1966–72 North Shields and Whitley Bay; 1972–73 Tutor in Historical Theology, Hartley Victoria Coll.; 1973–82 Tutor in Practical Theology and Methodism, Wesley Coll., Bristol; 1982– General Secretary of the Division of Home Mission; 1978 President of the Conference.
Connexional Committees: 1967–70 Overseas General Committee; 1968–80 Faith and Order Committee; 1979– Division of Education and Youth Board; 1982– Home Mission, Finance, Property.
Publications: Evangelism and Worship (1971); *God in the Gallery* (1975); *Christian Discipleship* (1977); *Windows on the Passion* (1978); *Anything to Declare?* (1980); Contributor to *About Faith* (1972); *Studying God's Word* (1972); *The Experience of Ordination* (1979).
Special Interests: Theology and Evangelism. *Hobbies and Recreations:* Reading, Gardening and Sport.

ENSOR, Peter William, Wesley Manse, Rodney Terrace, Masham, Ripon, N.Yorks MG4 4JA. (0765-89203)–MA(Oxon), MA(Cantab). *b. 28 July 1951, Croydon. s.*
Education: 1956–61 Winterbourne Prim. Sch., Thornton Heath, Surrey; 1961–64 Prior's Court Preparatory Sch., Newbury, Berks.; 1964–70 Kingswood Sch., Bath, Avon; 1970–74 Oriel Coll., Oxford; 1974–76 Fitzwilliam Coll., Cambridge; 1974–77 Wesley House. *Appointments:* 1977–79 Glossop; 1979– Ripon and Masham.
Special Interests: Editor of *Conservative Evangelicals in Methodism,* Newsletter. *Hobbies and Recreations:* Music, Fell-walking, Cross-country Running.

ENTICOTT, Raymond Frederick, 4 Portway Ave., Wells, Som. BA5 2QF. (0749 73296) *b. 3 Mar 1945, Edgeware, Middx. m. 25 July 1970: 1d., 1s.*
Education: 1950–60 Belmont Inf., Jun., Secondary Modern Sch.; 1966–70 Handsworth. *Appointments:* 1970–75 Sunderland North; 1975–82 Cheddar Valley; 1982– West Mendip.
Connexional Committees: 1981– Property Board.
Special Interests: Church's Ministry of Healing. *Hobbies and Recreations:* Philately, Needlework and Handcraft.

ERRINGTON, James William, 121 Burnham Av., West Denton Park, Newcastle upon Tyne NE15 8QQ. (0632 643547) *b. 14 May 1915, Annfield Plain, Co. Durham. m. 18 June 1949: 1d., 1s.*
Education: Annfield Plain Council Sch.; 1938–39 Cliff Coll.; 1946–47 Hartley Victoria. *Appointments:* 1947–49 Manchester Mission; 1949–53 Melton Mowbray; 1953–55 Leicester West; 1955–58 Manchester Mission; 1958–63 South Shields; 1963–69 Darlington; 1969–76

Newcastle upon Tyne (West); 1976–80 Ryton and Prudhoe.
Connexional Committees: 1964–73 Cliff Coll. Committee (Conference Appointed).
Special Interests: History, Preaching.
Hobbies and Recreations: Gardening, Walking, Soccer.

ETHERIDGE, W. Gordon, 24 Pearl Ave., Kirkby in Ashfield, Nottinghamshire NG17 7FE. (0623 752349)–BSc. *m.*
Education: 1971–74 Univ. of Bristol; 1977–79 Univ. of Birmingham; 1977–80 Queen's. *Appointments:* 1980–Ashfield.

EVAN, Peter John Russell, 33 The Green Rd., Ashbourne, Derbyshire DE6 1ED. (0335 42408) *b. 5 April 1928, Voorburg, Holland. m. 11 Aug 1956: 3s.*
Education: 1933–39 Harpenden CE Prim. Sch.; 1939–46 St. Alband's Sch.; 1946–48 Westminster Training Coll.; 1951–54 Richmond Coll.
Appointments: 1950–51 Ipswich; 1954–56 Thetford; 1956–59 Diss; 1959–62 Newmarket; 1962–69 Bristol East; 1969–75 Portsmouth; 1975–82 Peterborough; 1982–Ashbourne.

EVANS, Andrew John, 42 Yardley Drive, Northampton NN2 8PE. (0604 842442)–BD.
Education: 1964–67 Bemrose, Derbys; 1967–70 Richard Hale, Hertford; 1976–80 Wesley, Bristol.
Appointments: 1980– Northampton.

EVANS, David Graham, 6 Richmond Ave., St. Anns, Nottingham NE3 3AT. (0602 53302)–MA. *b. 4 Aug 1952, Manchester. m. 6 June 1981.*
Education: 1959–63 St. Johns CE, Nelson; 1963–70 Queen Elizabeth's Grammar Sch., Blackburn; 1970–73, 1975–76 Birmingham Univ.; 1972–76 Queens, Birmingham.
Appointments: 1977–81 Nottingham Central; 1981– Nottingham Mission.
Hobbies and Recreations: Sport, Fell Walking, Photography, The Lake District.

EVANS, David James, Trawscoed, 8 Wern Ave., Bagillt, Clwyd. (03526-3523) *b. 10 March 1910, Cnwch Coch, Crosswood, Nr Aberstwyth, Dyfed. m. 9 Aug 1939: 1d.*
Education: 1915–24 Llanfihangel-y-Creuddyn; 1930–31 Ystrad Maurig, Dyfed; 1931–32 Myrddin Carmarthen, Dyfed; 1933–36 Didsbury. *Appointments:* 1932–33 Mold; 1936–39 Lampeter; 1939–45 Tregarth; 1945–50 Llanrhaeadr-Yn-Mochnant; 1950–55 Llanasa; 1955–60 Corwen; 1960–65 Bagillt; 1965–70 Conway; 1970–75 Bagillt.
Connexional Committees: Home Mission (approx. 9 years to 1965); 1965–70 Property.
Hobbies and Recreations: Gardening.

EVANS, Douglas Reginald, 353 Devizes Rd., Salisbury, Wilts SP2 9NJ. (0722 20015)–MA(Edinburgh), MA(Cantab.). *b. 12 May 1911, Edinburgh. m. 18 Aug 1964.*
Education: 1923–29 Boroughmuir, Edinburgh; 1929–32 Edinburgh Univ.; 1932–35 Cambridge Univ.; 1932–35 Wesley House.
Appointments: 1935–36 York Wesley; 1936–37 Liskeard; 1937–40 Folkstone; 1940–45 Newport, Mon.; 1945–51 Brixton Hill, London; 1951–54 Walthamstow; 1954–58 Croydon and S. Norwood; 1958–64 Barry Road, London; 1964–69 Northwich; 1969–76 Shipley.
Connexional Committees: 1950–53 July Committee.
Special Interests: Antique English Porcelain. *Hobbies and Recreations:* Gardening, Reading, Music.

EVANS, Emrys Wyn, 12 Glasfryn Rd., Pontarddulais, Swansea, W.Glam. SA4 1LL. (0792 882381) *b. 21 Dec 1920, Caernarvon, Gwynedd. m. 8 Aug 1950: 1d.*
Education: 1926–32 Caernarvon Council Sch. for Boys; 1932–38 Caernarvon County Sch. (Grammar); 1945–48 Handsworth.
Appointments: 1944–45 Chaplain HMF; 1945–48 Handsworth Coll.; 1948–50 Bagillt Welsh; 1950–52 Brymawr; 1952–55 Llantwst; 1955–60 Tregarth; 1960–65 Bagillt; 1965–70 Dogellau and Barmouth; 1970–Morgannave.
Connexional Committees: 1955–65 Connexional Youth; 1974– Consultative Council for Methodism in Wales (Conference appointed committee).
Local Council Committees: 1973 South Wales Free Church Council President; 1976– Swansea Area Covenanted Churches Committee.
Publications: Many articles in Welsh on Biblical Archaeology and on Methodist Missionary history in the *Methodist Quarterly Magazine* (Welsh) *Yr Eurgrawn.*
Special Interests: Music, especially hymnology—conducting Sacred Song Festivals; Biblical Archaelogy and Folklore in general. *Hobbies and Recreations:* Soccer referee (1954–70), Sport, Bowls, Historical Reading.

EVANS, Harold, 7 Ashfield Drive, Baildon, Shipley, Bradford, West Yorks. BD17 6JA. (0274 591264) *b. 25 Oct 1916, Hartlepool, Co. Durham. m. 16 July 1946: 1d., 1s.*
Education: Elementary; 1938–41 Headingley. *Appointments:* 1941–43 Edinburgh; 1943–46 Glasgow Mission; 1946–48 Haworth and Oakworth; 1948–49 Accrington; 1949–54 Leek; 1954–57 Ilkley; 1957–60 Llanelli; 1960–67 Beverley; 1967–70 Bridgend; 1970–77 Bradford, Woodhouse Grove; 1977–81 Goole.
Hobbies and Recreations: Music, Golf, Photography.

EVANS, Huw Derryck, 42 St. Margarets Rd., Swindon. (0793 35696) *b. 21 June 1929, Barry, S.Glam. m. 1955: 4d., 1s.*
Education: 1940–45 St. Julians Grammar; Newport Technical College; Didsbury Bristol.
Appointments: 1964–69 Yate, Bristol; 1969–70 Kingswood, Bristol; 1970– Swindon.
Connexional Committees: 1978–82 Team Ministry; 1978–82 D.S.R. Housing.
Special Interests: Ecumenical Team Ministries, Housing Associations.
Hobbies and Recreations: Sailing, Reading.

EVANS, John Bonner, 6 Graif Terrace, Ferndale, Mid Glam. CF43 4EU. (0443 731574) *b. 25 March 1915, Aberystwyth, Dyfed. m. 21 Dec 1944: 1d.*
Education: Llanelli Grammar Sch.; 1938–39 Handsworth; 1940–41Headingley. *Appointments:* 1944–50 Glamorgan; 1941–42 President's List; 1942–44 Bangor and Ferndale; 1950–55 Aberdare; 1955–67 Caersws; 1967–78 Ferndale.
Connexional Committees: 1960–67 Overseas Division.
Special Interests: Welsh Affairs.
Hobbies and Recreations: Travel and Reading.

EVANS, Owen Ellis, Hafod Y Bryn, Lôn Tŷ Croes, Llanfairpwllgwyngll, Isle of Anglesey, Gwynedd LL61 5JL. (0248 714411)–MA(Leeds), BD(Lond.). *b. 23 Dec 1920, Barmouth, Merioneth, North Wales. m. 12 Aug 1953: 2d., 2s.*
Education: 1926–32 Barmouth Council Sch.; 1932–37 Barmouth County Intermediate Sch.; 1949–51 Univ. of Leeds (Post Graduate Research Student); 1946–49 Headingley. *Appointments:* 1945–46 Llanfair Caereinion, Welsh; 1948–52 Wesley Coll., Headingley, Leeds (Assistant Tutor); 1952–53 Pwllheli (Welsh); 1953–69 Hartley Victoria Coll., Manchester (Tutor in New Testament); 1969– Permitted to serve as Lecturer in Biblical Studies (Senior Lecturer since 1975) at Univ. Coll. of North Wales, Bangor.
Connexional Committees: 1969–78 Faith and Order; 1970–80 Connexional Probationers' Oversight Committee, Connexional Candidates' Examination Committee and Board of Studies.
Publications: The Gospel According to St. John (Epworth Preachers' Commentaries 1964); *Saints in Christ Jesus: A Study of the Christian Life in the New Testament* (J. Penry Press 1975); *On Translating the Bible* (Peake Lecture 1975); (Ed.) *The Passion Narrative of St. Luke, by Vincent Taylor* (Cambridge 1972); Other publications in Welsh.
Special Interests: New translation of the Bible into Welsh (Y Beibl Cymraeg Newydd); 1963–75 Chairman of New Testament Panel of Translators; 1975– Chairman of Apocrypha Panel; 1970–74 Deputy Director of Translation Project; 1974– Director; 1975– Honorary Member of Welsh Gorsedd of Bards.
Hobbies and Recreations: Motoring, Walking, Gardening, Choral Singing.

EVANS, Thomas Aneurin, 13 West Street, Prescot, Merseyside L34 1LE. (051 426 6157)–BA(Wales), BD(Lond.). *b. 21 Oct 1932, Manchester. m. 5 April 1962: 2s.*
Education: 1937–44 Manley Park, Manchester, C.P.; 1944–51 Chorlton High Sch., Manchester; 1951–54 Univ. Coll. of North Wales, Bangor; 1954–58 Wesley. *Appointments:* 1958–59 Douglas, Isle of Man; 1959–64 Wrexham; 1964–70 Liverpool North; 1970–75 Hoylake and West Kirby; 1975– St. Helens and Prescot.
Local Council Committees: 1976–82 Knowsley B.C. Education Committee.
Special Interests: Choral and Classical Music. *Hobbies and Recreations:* Photography, Woodwork, Gardening.

EVANS, Thomas Noel, Tegfryn, 27 Bryn Ave., Old Colwyn, Colwyn Bay, Clwyd LL29 8AH. (0492 55157)–BA, BD. *b. 23 Dec 1914, Penycae, Nr. Wrexham. m. 6 Aug 1948: 3d.*
Education: 1919–27 Church in Wales Sch., Rhos, Wrexham; 1927–33 Ruabon Grammar Sch.; 1935–39 Univ. of North Wales, Bangor; 1939–40 Hartley Victoria. *Appointments:* 1940–45 H.M.F.; 1945–46 Chaplain H.M.F.; 1946–47 Llanrhaeadr; 1947–49 Llandilo; 1949–50 Liverpool Mount Zion; 1950–53 Machyalleth; 1953–55 Holyhead and Almwch; 1955–60 Beaumaris; 1960–61 Ruthin; 1961–72 Resigned (Mental Welfare and Teaching); 1972–80 Social Work Dept., Cardiff Coll.

EVERITT, Roy Sydney, 19 Poltair Rd., Penryn, Cornwall TR10 8NZ. (0326 72543) *b. 26 Jan 1929, Feltham, Middlesex. m. 17 Aug 1957.*
Education: 1940–45 Hampton Grammar Sch.; 1952–55 Handsworth Coll., Birmingham. *Appointments:* 1951–52 Long Eaton; 1955–57 South Petherton and Crewkerne; 1957–62 Portland; 1962–69 Sherborne; 1969–73 Devon and Dorset mission; 1973–80 Christchurch and Lymington; 1980– Falmouth.
Special Interests: Listening to Chamber Music. *Hobbies and Recreations:* Astronomy, Gardening.

EVISON, Jack, 53 Forest Lane, Starbeck, Harrogate, North Yorkshire HG2 7HB. (0423 887586) *b. 29 March 1904, South Cockerington, Louth, Lincolnshire. m. 2 Oct 1940: 2s.*
Education: 1910–12 Ludford, CE; 1913–14 Kelstern County; 1914–17 Donington on Bain Wesleyan Methodist; 1933 Cliff Coll.
Appointments: 1964–66 Tunstall, Stoke on Trent; 1966–70 Market Rasen; 1970–72 Denby Dale.
Special Interests: Cricket, Football, Politics and Trade Unions. *Hobbies and Recreations:* Sports as spectator, Indoor Games, Draughts, Scrabble, Master Mind, Reading.

EWIN, John Bryan, 12 Warden Grove, Gillas Lane, Houghton-le-Spring, Tyne and Wear DH5 8HL. (0783 843206) *b. 24 Jan 1930, Appleby, Westmorland. m. 14 June 1969.*
Education: 1934–37 Ormside Council Sch.; 1937–44 Appleby Central County Sch.; 1944–45 Briggs Commercial Sch., Penrith; 1953–56 Headingley. *Appointments:* 1956–59 Howden Caves; 1959–63 Easingwold; 1963–68 Durham; 1968–73 Stanley; 1973–78 Seahouses; 1978– Houghton-le-Spring.
Special Interests: Methodism.
Hobbies and Recreations: Enjoying and Developing Country Cottage.

FACER, Harry, 16 Evening Hill Drive, Cockermouth, Cumbria CA13 0BP. (0900 823860) *b. 3 Nov 1915, Manchester. m. 2 April 1947: 1s.*
Education: 1920–26 Elementary Sch., Varna St., Openshaw, Manchester; 1926–30 Central High

Sch., Devonshire Rd., Ardwick, Manchester; 1945–47 Handsworth. *Appointments:* 1943–44 Settle; 1944–55 Retford; 1945–47 Handsworth Coll.; 1947–51 Islington, Birmingham; 1951–54 Ulverston; 1954–59 Barrow-in-Furness; 1959–64 Swansea; 1964–71 Kendal; 1971–77 Bexhill and Rye, Hastings; 1977–81 Ulverston.
Special Interests: Music and Hymnology; *Hobbies and Recreations:* Music, Organ, Piano.

FACEY, Barbara M, 1 Chapel Down Rd., Crediton, Devon EX17 2EB. (03632 2441) *b. 10 June 1924, Plymouth, Devon.*
Education: Devonport High Sch. for Girls, Plymouth; 1949–51 Wesley Deaconess Coll. *Appointments:* 1975–82 Northwich; 1982– Exeter.
Connexional Committees: Connexional Home Missions.

FAIL, John James, 121 Avon Rd., Devizes, Wilts. (0380 3535)–MBE, BA(Bristol). *b. 16 May 1930, Dudley, Northumberland. m. 24 Aug 1957 (w.): 1d., 1s.*
Education: 1943–48 Hammersmith Sch. of Art; 1951–54 Westminster Tech. Coll.; Bristol Univ.; 1954–57 Wesley, Bristol. *Appointments:* 1957–59 Wolverton; 1959– Chaplain H.M.F.
Hobbies and Recreations: Most Sports.

FAIRBEARD, Edward Rex, 41 Essa Rd., Saltash, Cornwall PL12 4EE. (075 55 2788)–BA. *b. 19 July 1937, Plymouth. m. 2 Aug 1961: 1d., 1s.*
Education: 1942–48 Montpelier Prim. Sch., Plymouth; 1948–55 Devonport High Sch.; 1957–61 Richmond. *Appointments:* 1961–63 New Forest Mission; 1963–67 Okehampton; 1967–73 Exeter; 1973–82 Plymouth; 1982– Saltash and St. German's.
Connexional Committees: Div. of Social Responsibility 1975–80.
Special Interests: Scouting (District Commissioner 1964–67), Drama.
Hobbies and Recreations: Camping, Photography, Insurance (agent for Ansvar Insurance Co. since 1963), Printing, Walking, Swimming, Travel.

FAIRHURST, Albert, 31 Trinity Close, Dereham, Norfolk NR19 2EP. (0362 5582) *b. 9 May 1917, Quarlton, Turton, Bolton, Lancs. m. 24 Oct 1942: 2d., 1s.*
Education: 1922–31 Edgworth Methodist; 1945–47 Hartley Victoria.
Appointments: 1947–49 Market Rasen and Caistor; 1949–52 Irlam and Cadishead; 1952–54 Haverfordwest; 1954–60 Louth; 1960–66 Bedford South; 1966–72 Hunstanton and Docking; 1972–1980 Skegness and Wainfleet; 1980– Dereham and Swaffham.
Council Member: 1952–54 Chairman North Somercotes Parish Council.
Local Council Committees: 1962–65 Chairman Bedford Area Youth Committee.
Publications: Sunday School Anniversary Programmes.
Special Interests: Church Building, Local Radio, R.A.F., and Hospital Chaplaincies.

FAIRHURST, Herbert Austin, 8 Meadow Close, Alresford, Hants SO24 9LA. (096 273 2931) *b. 29 May 1906, Bolton, Lancs. m. 28 July 1934 (w.): 2s.*
Education: 1911–18 Methodist Day Sch., Astley Bridge, Bolton; 1918–21 Municipal Secondary Sch., Bolton; 1927–30 Didsbury, Manchester.
Appointments: 1930–40 French West Africa District; 1941–44 Brunswick, Leeds; 1944–51 Gravesend and Dartford; 1951–61 Maidstone; 1961–67 Chislehurst; 1967–73 Dover and Deal.
Connexional Committees: 1944–67 Western Committee of the Overseas Division.
Hobbies and Recreations: Painting, Bird Watching, Cricket, Football.

FANNING, Phillip Neville, The Manse, Ballamillaghyn, Mount Rule, Parish of Braddan, Isle of Man. (0624 851975)–BA(Lond.), BD(Lond.). *b. 3 July 1950, Wallasey, Cheshire. m. 26 July 1975: 2d.*
Education: 1955–61 Riverside Inf. and Jun. Sch.; 1961–67, 1968–69 Wallasey Grammar Sch., 1967–68 Shadowschule, West Berlin; 1969–73 Southlands Coll.; 1969–73 London Univ.; 1978–81 London Univ.; 1978–81 Wesley, Bristol. *Appointments:* 1981– Douglas and Peel.
Special Interests: Scouts and other Youth Work; Citizen's Band Radio, Auxiliary Coastguard. *Hobbies and Recreations:* Sailing, Caving, Photography, Model Boats.

FARLEY, John Robert, The Methodist Manse, Sion, St. John, Jersey C.I. (0534 62497)–MA. *3 Feb 1920, Seven Kings, Ilford, Essex. m. 31 July 1952: 2d., 2s.*
Education: 1930–33 Ermysted's Grammar Sch., Skipton, Yorks; 1933–38 Blackpool Grammar Sch.; 1938–40 Univ. Coll., London; 1947–50 Cambridge Univ.; 1947–50 Wesley House. *Appointments:* 1946–47 South Molton; 1950–52 Assistant Tutor, Hartley Victoria Coll.; 1952–59 Rochdale North; 1959–63 W. Nigeria Dt; 1963–71 Sheffield Carver St.; 1971–74 Leicester South East; 1974–82 Peak; 1982– Jersey.
Connexional Committees: 1974–76 Education and Youth; 1974–82 Candidates' Examination Committee.
Publications: Manual of Fellowship, Four Friends of St. Paul (1957); Booklets on *Amos, Hosen, Isaiah* (all published in Nigeria between 1960 and 1963); *Key Book, The Good News of Jesus Christ* (U.S.C.I. 1962); *Manual of Fellowship, The Gospel of Human Rights* (1968).
Hobbies and Recreations: Sport (especially Rugby and Cricket), Reading, Walking, Swimming.

FARMER, Leslie George, 12 Elmwood Rd., London SE24 9NU. (01 274 2251)–BA(Open). *b. 31 Dec 1908, Brighton. m. 24 July 1937: 2d., 1s.*
Education: –1922 Downhills Central Sch., Tottenham; 1971–74 Open Univ.; 1931–34 Richmond.
Appointments: 1934–36 West London Mission; 1936–37 N.W. London Mission; 1937–39 South London Mission; 1939–45 Chaplain HMF; 1945–46 Seamen's Mission; 1947–50 South London Mission;

1951–54 Exeter; 1955–65 Bow Mission; 1966–68 Wandsworth and Fulham; 1969–72 Richmond.
Publications: We Saw the Holy City (Epworth 1944); *The Bow Story* (Epworth 1962); *Land of the Gospel* (Epworth 1963); *I Lack Nothing* (B.L.S. 1967); *Christ on Olivet* (B.L.S. 1974).
Special Interests: Biblical Geography, M.E. Affairs, London Methodist History. *Hobbies and Recreations:* Decorative Glasswork.

FARMEREY, William Hewson, Garbutt Place, Casterton Close, Mill Rd., Market Rasen, Lincs. LN8 3BP. (0673 842690) *b. 23 Sept 1909, Selby, Yorks. m. 12 Aug 1936.*
Education: 1921–28 The Grammar Sch., Drax, Yorks.; 1929–32 Handsworth Coll. *Appointments:* 1932–34 Llandrindod Wells; 1934–36 Pickering; 1936–39 Market Weighton; 1939–48 West Wight; 1948–51 Birmingham, Smethwick Broomfield; 1951–56 Newark; 1956–62 Mills Rd., Cleethorpes; 1962–68 Matlock; 1968–74 Bingham.
Special Interests: Local History.
Hobbies and Recreations: Gardening.

FARNELL, George H., 9 Kirkby Rd., Hillmorton, Rugby CV21 4HP. (0788 71104) *b. 8 Aug 1912, Nuneaton, Warwickshire. m. 2 Dec 1944: 2d.*
Education: 1938–41 Hartley Victoria.
Appointments: 1941–47 Sierra Leone, W.Africa; 1947–50 Oldham; 1950–56 Prestwich; 1956–61 Canton, Cardiff; 1961–66 Birmingham Wesley; 1966–73 Castle Donington; 1973–79 Matlock.
Connexional Committees: 1950–56, 1957–61 Overseas Missions.

FARRAR, John Anthony, 21 Belle Walk, Birmingham B13 9DE. (021 449 2414)–BA(Hons) Nottingham, MA(Cambridge). *b. 10 June 1943, Halifax. m. 28 Feb 1970: 1d., 1s.*
Education: 1948–54 Warley Rd., J/I, Halifax; 1954–61 Heath Grammar Sch., Halifax; 1961–64 Nottingham Univ.; 1964–66 Wesley House.
Appointments: 1966–70 Halifax (Wesley); 1970–71 Missionary Training; 1971–76 Runcorn; 1976– Birmingham (Moseley Rd. and Sparkhill).
Special Interests: Tutor—Methodist Study Centre, Local Community Groups, District Candidates Sec. 1978–. *Hobbies and Recreations:* Eating out with friends, Football, Cricket.

FARRELL, William, 2 Wesley Villas, Sowerby Rd., Thirsk, North Yorkshire YO7 1HX. *b. 29 June 1918, Bolton, Lancashire. m. 28 June 1941: 2d., 2s.*
Education: Oxford Grove Elementary Sch., Bolton; 1945–48 Hartley Victoria, Manchester. *Appointments:* 1948–51 Littleborough; 1951–56 Great Harwood; 1956–60 Bingley; 1960–66 Huddersfield West; 1966–71 Whaley Bridge; 1971–76 Alston; 1976– Thirsk and Boroughbridge.
Connexional Committees: 1973–76 Property.
Hobbies and Recreations: Photography, Caravanning.

FARRIMOND, John, Trinity Manse, 35 Bryntirion Drive, Prestatyn, Clwyd LL19 9NT. (07456 3483)–BA(Liverpool). *b. 7 Jan 1932, Birkenhead. m. 21 July 1956: 2d., 1s.*
Education: 1942–50 Rock Ferry High Sch.; 1950–53 Liverpool Univ.; 1953–56 Manchester Univ.; 1953–56 Hartley Victoria. *Appointments:* 1956–62 Glasgow (Cathcart Rd. and Pollokshaws); 1962–69 Keswick and Cockermouth; 1969–78 Nantwich; 1978– Rhyl and Prestatyn.
Hobbies and Recreations: Country Life, Woodwork, Music, Motorcycling (Editor of *Newsletter of Fellowship of Christian Motorcyclists).*

FARROW, Derek Robert, 1 Central Buildings, Westminster SW1H 9NP. (01 222 8868)–BA(Leeds) *b. 6 Aug 1925, Goodmayes, Essex. m. 26 Dec 1951: 2d., 1s.*
Education. 1936–41 Coopers Company's School; 1948–51 Leeds Univ.; 1948–51 Headingley.
Appointments: 1947–48 Colchester; 1951–53 Wolverton and Bletchley; 1953–60 London, East Ham Mission; 1960–67 Walthamstow; 1967–68 Harrow; 1968 Department of Connexional Funds, Division of Finance.
Publications: Meditations on Ministry (1977); *Through the Eye of a Needle* (1980).
Special Interests: Music and Poetry. *Hobbies and Recreations:* Oil Painting, Furniture Making, Photography.

FARTHING, Geoffrey Peter, Wesley Manse, 86 Mountford Close, Wellesbourne, Warwickshire CV35 9QQ. (0789-840433)–BA(B'ham), MA(B'ham). *b. 18 Oct 1945, London. m. 14 July 1973.*
Education: 1957–60 Wolverhampton Grammar Sch.; 1963–64 Cliff Coll.; 1975–79 Birmingham Univ.; 1979–81 Wesley, Bristol. *Appointments:* 1981– Stratford on Avon.
Special Interests: Research into Mathematical Methods for Defining the Relationships of Greek N.T. MSS.
Hobbies and recreations: Gardening, Micro Computing.

FAULKNER, Michael, 53 Kilnside Drive, Harpurley, Manchester M9 1QQ. (061 205 2031)–MA(Cantab). *b. 8 Nov 1948, Bradford, West Yorkshire. m. 28 March 1978.*
Education: 1953–60 Lidget Green Inf. and Jun. Sch.; 1960–67 Bradford Grammar Sch.; 1967–70 Christ's Coll., Cambridge; 1972–74 Wesley House. *Appointments:* 1974–77 South Wirral; 1977– Manchester North and Middleton.
Special Interests: The Church in the Inner City, World Development/ Third World, Chairperson Local Community Project. *Hobbies and Recreations:* Railways (Real and Model), Climbing and Walking.

FAULKS, Veronica Mary Suzanne, 2 Albany Way, Mill Lane, Warmley, Bristol BS15 5UA. (0272 679540)–BA. *4 Jan 1947, New Delhi, India. m. 6 July 1968: 1d., 1s.*
Education: 1958–58 Bletchley Grammar; 1959–66 Fowey Grammar; 1966–69 Bristol Univ.; 1975–78 Southwark N.R.T. *Appointments:* 1978–80 West Wight; 1980–

Kingswood, Bristol.
Connexional Committees: 1983– Candidates Committee.
Hobbies and Recreations: Theatre, Reading, Family Life.

FAWCETT, Graham Haden, Church House, 90A Revelstoke Way, Rise Park, Nottingham NG5 5EB. (0602 272611) *b. 20 June 1938, Chesterfield, Derbys. m. 17 Feb 1968: 1d., 1s.*
Education: 1942–49 Highfield Hall, Inf./Jun. Sch.; 1949–56 Chesterfield Sch.; 1958–60 Westminster Coll., London and Oxford; 1968–70 Handsworth. *Appointments:* 1970–73 Ashbourne; 1973–81 Highgate, London; 1981– Nottingham North. *Special Interests:* Pastoralia, Healing, Creativity. *Hobbies and Recreations:* Painting, Music, Gardening.

FEAST, Michael Philip, 8 Tower Rd., Kingswood, Bristol, Avon BS15 1PG. (0272 670141) *b. 30 Oct 1942, London. m. 7 March 1964; 3s.*
Education: 1954–59 Wandsworth Sch., Southfields, London; 1981 Wesley, Bristol.

FEATHERSTONE, Peter F., 37 Belle Vue Rd., Walthamstow, London E17 4DQ. (01 527 1849)–BSc. m.
Education: 1967–70 Sussex Univ.; 1978–80 Wesley, Bristol.
Appointments: 1980– Walthamstow and Chingford.

FEATHERSTONE, Thomas Denis, 15 St. Mark's Rd., Maidenhead, Berkshire SL6 6DG. (0628 26533) *b. 25 March 1918, Witton Park, Bishop Auckland, Co. Durham. m. 14 Aug 1945: 1d.*
Education: 1923–30 Witton Park Council Schs.; 1930–34 Cockton Hill Boy's Sch., Bishop Auckland; 1938–41 Hartley Victoria.
Appointments: 1941–45 Northallerton; 1945–49 Rotherham; 1949–50 Supply; 1950–53 Surrey St., Sheffield; 1953–50 Hereford; 1958–60 Rotherham Eastwood Mission; 1960–64 Cromer and Sheringham; 1964–68 Darlington; 1968–73 Manchester, Cheetham Hill and Prestwich; 1973–78 Cleethorpes; 1978– Windsor and Maidenhead.
Connexional Committees: 1981– Ministers Retirement Fund.
Publications: Dr. George Eayrs Prize Essay: *The Rise of Primitive Methodism* (1st prize shared, 1952); Dr. J. B. Paton Prize Essay: *An Approach to the Apostolic Experience* (3rd prize shared).
Special Interests: Methodist History, Psychology. *Hobbies and Recreations:* Painting, Music.

FELLOWS, William Alan,, 9 Croxton Close, Fairfield, Stockton on Tees, Cleveland TS19 7SW. (0642 587043)–BA(Leeds). *b. 26 Feb 1918, Stockton on Tees, Co. Durham. m. 8 Aug 1945. 3s.*
Education: 1923–26 Emerald St. Prep. Sch., Saltburn; 1927–34 Sir William Turners Sch., Coatham, Redcar, Yorks. 1937–40 Leeds Univ.; 1937–40 Headingley. *Appointments:* 1940–44 Loftus and Staithes; 1944–47 Middlesbrough; 1947–51 Nottingham (Central); 1951–57 Hinckley (Albert Rd.); 1957–62 Nottingham (East); 1962–65 Bradford (Manningham); 1965–70 Hull (West); 1970–75 Newmarket; 1975–79 Driffield.
Special Interests: Christian Unity.
Hobbies and Recreations: Music (especially Opera), History (including Methodist History).

FENNELL, Ralph Edward, 52 Styal Rd., Wilmslow, Cheshire SK9 4AQ. (0625 524911)–MA. *b. 22 Aug 1929, Sutton, Surrey. m. 13 Aug 1955: 1d., 3s.*
Education: 1940–47 Surbiton County Grammar Sch.; 1951–55 Fitzwilliam House, Cambridge; 1951–55 Wesley House. *Appointments:* 1950–51 Chislehurst; 1951–59 Bromley; 1959–63 Bournemouth; 1963–67 Deal; 1967–69 Ealing and Acton; 1969–74 Secretary Sector Ministry Committee; 1974–79 Chairman of West Yorks. District; 1979– Secretary Property Division.
Connexional Committees: 1969–74 Sector Ministry Committee; Various Ministerial Training Department and Division of Ministries Committees. 1970–79 Stationing Committee and other Ex Officio; Regional Development Committee, further training of the Ministry Committee, Property Division and Various Committees Ex Officio.

FERRIDGE, Dorothy M., 1A St. Edwards Close, Chilton Polden, Bridgwater, Somerset TA7 9DX. (0278 722639)–BD(Lond.). *b. 17 Sept 1921, Wimbledon.*
Education: 1932–37 Wimbledon County Sch.; 1946–47 Oakley Training College, Cheltenham.
Appointments: 1974–81 Bridgwater.
Special Interests: Education. *Hobbies and Recreations:* Music, Walking, Reading, Bird Watching, Crosswords, Gardening, Dress Making and Knitting.

FIELD, Douglas Osgood, 14 Westland Ave., Wolverhampton WV3 9NX. (0902 22560)–BA. *b. 11 Oct 1926, Reading, Berks. m. 16 Feb 1956: 1d., 1s.*
Education: King Edwards Aston, Birmingham; London Univ.; 1951–54 Didsbury. *Appointments:* 1954–65 Leeward Islands, West Indies; 1965–68 Luton (North); 1968–71 London, Kilburn and Hampstead; 1971–78 Newport (Gwent); 1978– Wolverhampton (Trinity).
Connexional Committees: 1972–78 Overseas Central Committee.

FIELD, Ian Haydn, 1 Ancaster Ave., Lincoln LN2 4AY. (0522 25064) *b. 22 Aug 1921, Port Talbot, Glamorgan. m. 27 July 1951: 2d.*
Education: 1927–30 Calstock, Cornwall Council Sch.; 1931–37 Orlestone Council Sch., Ashford, Kent; 1937–39 Ashford Technical Coll.; 1948–50 Handsworth.
Appointments: 1947–48 Worcester; 1948–50 Handsworth Coll.; 1950–55 Andover Trinity; 1955–60 Banbury; 1960–65 Witney; 1965–71 Southampton; 1971–79 East Wight; 1979– Lincoln North; 1971–79 Methodist Prison Chaplain, Parkhurst; 1979– Lincoln.
Hobbies and Recreations: Gardening.

FIELD, Ian Victor, 84 Peabody Rd., Farnborough, Hants. GU14 6DY. (0252 548146) *b. 30 July 1939, Barnet, Herts. m. 13 Aug 1966: 1d., 1s.*
Education: 1950–56 Cheshunt Grammar Sch.; 1961–62 Robert Montefiore Coll.; 1963–66 Headingley; 1966–67 Wesley, Bristol.
Appointments: 1967–73 Romford; 1973–80 Leigh on Sea; 1980– Aldershot, Farnborough and Camberley.
Connexional Committees: 1972– Childrens Work Committee.
Special Interests: Reading, Music.
Hobbies and Recreations: Squash, Walking.

FIELD, Stanley James John, 349 Westbourne Grove, Westcliff on Sea, Essex SS0 0PU. (0702 42327) *b. 24 Feb 1923, Mitcham, Surrey. m. 27 June 1973: 2s.*
Education: 1935–37 Haselrigge Rd. Elementary Sch., Clapham, London SW4; 1948–51 Headingley.
Appointments: 1951–53 Douglas (Victoria); 1953–56 Ramsey; 1956–61 Bebington; 1961–66 Stockport (South); 1966–70 Romiley; 1970–76 Woking; 1976– Southend on Sea.
Connexional Committees: 1960–79 Methodist Homes of the Aged.
Hobbies and Recreations: Photography.

FIELDER, Alfred Emanuel Hugh, Deer Path Cottage, Inval, Haslemere, Surrey GU27 1AH. (0428 51987)–BSc. *10 Sept 1904, Purbrook, Nr. Portsmouth, Hants. m. 12 Aug 1936: 1d., 3s.*
Education: 1910–15 Elementary Sch., 1915–19 Olivers High Sch., 1925–28 Kings' Coll., London; 1929–31 Manchester Univ.; 1931–32 Westhill, Selly Oak; 1929–31 Hartley Victoria. *Appointments:* 1932–36 East London and London Mission South East; 1936–40 Wimborne; 1940–43 Bolton, Highbridge St.; 1943–49 Nelson; 1949–65 North Rhodesia Dt; 1965–68 United Church of Zambia; 1968–72 Methodist International House, London (Warden).
Connexional Committees: At various times, Educational, Social Responsibility and Students Committee.
Special Interests: 1972– Marital and Individual Counselling, W.P.F., 1976– With my wife, responsibility for development of the Marriage Growth and Enrichment Movement in the U.K. *Hobbies and Recreations:* Garden and Outdoor Activities, Reading.

FIELDER, William George, 227 Wootton Rd., Gaywood, Kings Lynn, Norfolk PE30 3AN. (0553 672582)–BEM. *b. 15 Sept 1899, Eastleigh, Hants. m. 4 July 1938 (w.): 1d., 1s.*
Education: –1913 Chamberlayne Boys Sch.; 1923–25 Hartley Victoria.
Appointments: 1921–23 East Dereham; 1925–28 Loughborough; 1928–33 Bolsover; 1933–38 Skegness; 1938–45 Grimsby; 1945–49 Cleethorpes; 1949–55 Spalding; 1955–59 Lincoln Wesley.
Connexional Committees: 1949–58 Connexional Chapel Committee; 1952–57 Synod Secretary Lincoln District.

FINCH, Kenneth Thomas, 3 Chelveston Rd., Coventry CU6 1PF. (0203 594340)–BA. *b. Darlaston, South Staffordshire. m.*
Education: 1956–57 Cliff Coll.; 1958–61 Handsworth. *Appointments:* 1961–66 Blyth and Seaton Delaval; 1966–74 Burton-on-Trent; 1974– Coventry.

FINCH, Stanley, 5 Heathcliffe, Redhills Road, Arnside, Carnforth, Lancs. (0524 761131) *b. 23 April 1905, Barrow-in-Furness, Cumbria. m. 27 July 1935.*
Education: 1910–19 Holker St. Elem. Sch., Barrow-in-Furness; 1929–32 Didsbury. *Appointments:* 1928–29 Whitehaven; 1932–35 Spennymoor; 1935–38 Manchester (Hulme and Whalley Range); 1938–42 Withington, Manchester; 1942–46 City Road, Manchester; 1946–51 Cardiff (Wesley); 1951–57 Kendal; 1957–60 Preston (Trinity); 1960–65 Blackpool (North); 1965–70 Skipton.
Publications: Wordsworth's Flowers (1982).

Hobbies and Recreations: Water Colour Painting, Writing, Music, Walking, Sport.

FIRTH, George Eric, 22 Keep Hill Drive, High Wycombe, Bucks. HP11 1DU. (0494 23474) *b. 4 May 1903, Forest Gate, London E7. m. 30 Aug 1930: 1s.*
Education: 1908–13 Godwin Rd. Prim., Forest Gate; 1913–18 Coopers Company Sch., Tredegar Square, Bow; 1923–26 Richmond.
Appointments: 1926–29 Kettering (Chairman's Assistant); 1929–30 Stamford; 1930–50 Burma; 1945–49 Chairman of District (Burma); 1950–55 Harlesden, London; 1955–62 High Wycombe; 1962–68 Dunstable; 1968– Associate Secretary Church of South India Council; 1956–80 Hon. Secretary/Treasurer Ministers' Missionary Union.
Connexional Committees: 1956–68 Overseas.

FIRTH, Richard, 40 Reigate Rd., Reigate, Surrey RH2 0QN. (073 72 42167)–BA(Leeds). *b. 25 July 1938, Doncaster. m. 14 Aug 1965: 1d., 1s.*
Education: 1943–45 Balby Inf. Sch.; 1945–49 Balby Jun. Mixed Sch.; 1949–56 Doncaster Technical High Sch. for Boys; 1956–57 Nottingham Univ.; 1961–64 Leeds Univ.; 1959–61 Cliff Coll.; 1961–65 Headingley; 1967–67 Kingsmead, Birmingham.
Appointments: 1965–67 Leeds Central; 1968–71 Kwale, Kenya; 1971–78 Leeds South Circuit; 1978– Redhill and East Grinstead.
Connexional Committees: 1972–73 M.M.S. Home Committee; 1981– Division of Social Responsibility Board.
Special Interests: Relationship of Worship, Life and Faith of the Church to the Contemporary Situation.
Hobbies and Recreations: Gardening, Stamp and Coin Collecting.

FISHER, Allen Edward, 22 Chapel Lane, Banks, Southport, Lancs. PR9 8EY. (0704 28394) *b. 30 Oct 1929, Overton. m. 10 Aug 1957: 2d.*
Education: 1939–46 Ossett Grammar Sch.; 1949–51 Cliff Coll.; 1952–55 Hartley Victoria. *Appointments:* 1951–52 Tiverton; 1957–60

Doncaster Coalfields Mission; 1960–64 Cannock; 1964–74 Gornal and Sedgley; 1974– Banks and Hesketh Bank.
Local Council Committees: 1968–74 Dudley Education Committee.
Special Interests: Evangelism.
Hobbies and Recreations: Golf and Bee Keeping.

FISHER, Geoffrey Maxwell, 2 Ash Grove, South Elmsall, Pontefract WF9 2TA. (0977 42824) *b. 2 Nov 1941, Hitchin, Hertfordshire. m. 4 April 1964: 3d.*
Education: 1976–78 Queens.
Appointments: 1978– Pontefract and Normanton.

FISHER, Harold, 2 South Rd., Bishop's Stortford, Herts. CM23 3JH. (0279 54475) *b. 21 Nov 1925, Grendon, Nr. Atherstone, Warwickshire. m. 7 Aug 1954: 1d.*
Education: 1930–32 Baddesley Ensor Inf. Sch.; 1932–39 Baddesley Ensor Elem. Sch., Atherstone, North Warwickshire; 1949–52 Richmond.
Appointments: 1948–49 Matlock Trinity; 1952–58 Derby South; 1958–64 Leicester West; 1964–69 Leicester North; 1969–74 resigned; 1974–77 Leicester north; 1977– Bishop's Stortford.
Special Interests: Music, History, Poetry. *Hobbies and Recreations:* Gardening, Listening to Music, Writing Verse.

FISHER, John Arthur, 128 Centenary Rd., Goole, North Humberside DN14 6PE. (0405 2566) *b. 25 May 1946, Beverley, Yorkshire.*
Education: 1953–57 Hilderthorpe Jun. Sch., Bridlington; 1957–63 St. Georges Secondary Sch., Bridlington; 1964–66 Cliff Coll.; 1967–70 Handsworth. *Appointments:* 1966–67 Wombwell and Hoyland; 1970–73 Nelson, Lancs.; 1973–75 Great Harwood; 1975–81 South Shields; 1981– Goole.
Local Council Committees: 1976–81 South Tyneside Education Committee; 1979–81 Vice Chairman South Tyneside Community Health Council.
Special Interests: Politics, Music, and Opera.

FISHER, John Henry, 50 Nunney Rd., Frome, Som. (0373 65050) *b. 25 April 1910, Holybourne, Hants. m. 8 May 1945: 2d.*
Education: 1933–37 Richmond.
Appointments: 1932–33 Kent Mission; 1933–37 Richmond Coll.; 1937–42 Shaftesbury and Gillingham; 1942–45 Dorchester; 1945–49 West Wight; 1949–53 Coventry; 1953–60 Gosport and Fareham; 1960–72 Stroud and Cirencester; 1972–77 Frome and Shepton Mallet.
Special Interests: Methodist History.
Hobbies and Recreations: Sport.

FISHER, Kenneth Vernon, 47 King St., Pinxton, Nottingham, NG16 6NL. (0773 813604) *b. 8 Jan 1914, Pinxton, m. 5 Nov 1938: 2s.*
Education: 1919–21 Pinxton Wharf Inf.; 1922–23 Pinxton Jun.; 1924–28 Pinxton Kirkstead Sen. Boys; 1958–59 Headingley. *Appointments:* 1958–60 Castleford; 1961–65 Wakefield; 1966–68 Dove Valley; 1969–74 Sheffield South; 1975–78 Wombwell and Hoyland.
Hobbies and Recreations: Photography.

FISHER, Norman Bramley, 6 The Croft, Threlkeld, Keswick, Cumbria CA12 4SA. (059 683 311)–BA. *b. 5 May 1913, York. m. 29 April 1942: 3d.*
Education: –1924 Fishergate, York; 1924–29 Nunthorpe Grammar, York; 1936–39 Leeds Univ.; 1935–39 Headingley. *Appointments:* 1939–42 North of Scotland Mission; 1942–45 Falkirk, Wallacestone and Stirling; 1945–51 Crosshills, Silsden and Cowling; 1951–55 Halifax West; 1955–60 Huddersfield West; 1960–67 Keswick and Cockermouth; 1967–74 Preston Trinity; 1974–78 Whitehaven.

FISHER, Robert, 21 Dunbar Rd., Coalville, Leicester LE6 3RT. (0530 31757)–BA(Manchester). *b. 6 July 1947, Newcastle-upon-Tyne. m. 18 July 1970: 1d., 1s.*
Education: 1958–65 Johnston Grammar Technical Sch., Durham; 1965–66 V.S.O. Methodist Secondary Sch., Sibu, Sarawak–Assistant Teacher; 1966–67 Cliff Coll.; 1968–71 Manchester Univ.; 1967–71 Hartley Victoria. *Appointments:* 1971–73 Bury St. Edmunds; 1973–74 Ashton-under-Lyne; 1975–78 The Blue Coat CE Secondary Sch., Oldham–Assistant Teacher; 1978–King Edward VII Coll., Coalville–Head of Dept. of Religious Education.
Special Interests: Ecumenism (currently Chairman of Coalville and District Council of Churches), Worship and Preaching (Circuit L.P. Tutor), Education (Chairman Circuit Ministries Committee). *Hobbies and Recreations:* D.I.Y., Gardening, Philately, Model Railways.

FITZPATRICK, Brian, Penlan, Park Ave., Scarborough, North Yorks. YO12 4AH. (0723 61214) *b. 3 March 1935, Oldham, Lancs. m. 8 Aug 1964: 2d., 1s.*
Education: 1946–51 Chadderton Grammar Sch.; 1957–60 Headingley.
Appointments: 1960–65 Coventry Mission; 1965–70 Longton Mission; 1970–77 Carlisle; 1977– Scarborough.
Connexional Committees: Division of Ministries.
Special Interests: Care of the Dying.
Hobbies and Recreations: Golf.

FLEET, Wilfred Fletcher, Lane Side, Furzehill Rd., Torquay TQ1 3JG. (0803 27546)–BA(L'pool), BD, MA(Manch). *b. 20 Feb 1905, Bilston, Staffs. m. 10 July 1930: 2s.*
Education: 1916–22 Widnes Secondary Sch.; 1922–25 Liverpool Univ.; 1925–27 Manchester Univ. (1927–38 part time); 1932–34 Glasgow Univ.; 1938–39 London Univ.; 1925–27 Hartley Victoria.
Appointments: 1930–35 Glasgow (Pollokshaws); 1935–38 Runcorn; 1938–39 Harrow and Northwood; 1939–45 Chaplain H.M. Forces; 1945–48 Hoylake and West Kirby; 1948–55 Southport N; 1955–62 London Highgate.
Connexional Committees; 1957–60 July Candidates Committee; 1955–62 R.A.N.A.F. Board; 1960–72 Epworth Trust.

Local Council Committees: 1957–62 Southport L.E.A.
Publications: Translations for Lutterworth Press.
Special Interests: Linguistics, Archaeology, Liturgies. *Hobbies and Recreations:* Reading, Classical Music, Bridge.

FLEMINGTON, William Frederick, 204 Chesterton Rd., Cambridge CB4 1NE. (0223 314363)–MA(Oxon.&Cantab), BD(Cantab). *b. 24 May 1901, Barrowford, Lancashire. m. 27 June 1930: 1d., 1s.*
Education: 1909–12 Anfield Rd. Council Sch., Liverpool; 1912–15 Liverpool Collegiate Sch.; 1915–1920 Liverpool Coll.; 1920–24 Jesus Coll., Oxford; 1924–26 Fitzwilliam House Cambridge; 1938– Member of Jesus Coll., Cambridge, 1924–26 Wesley House. *Appointments:* 1925 Supply; 1926–30 Handsworth Coll. (Assistant Tutor); 1930–33 Stourbridge; 1933–37 West Bromwich (Wesley); 1937–43 Wesley House, Cambridge (N.T. Tutor); 1943–46 Cambridge; 1946–67 Wesley House, Cambridge (N.T. Tutor) (Principal 1955–67).
Connexional Committees: 1946–66 Healing Committee; 1963–68 Faith and Order Committee; 1950–56 Secretary of Doctrinal Committee of Appeal.
Publications: The New Testament Doctrine of Baptism (1948).
Hobbies and Recreations: Walking and Reading.

FLINTHAM, John Michael, 7 Shotford Rd., Harleston, Norfolk IP20 9JH. (0379-852474) *b. 22 July 1933, Leeds. m. 8 Aug 1959: 1d., 2s.*
Education: –1947 Warsop (Notts) County Sch.;1947–49 Mansfield Technical Sch.; 1956–59 Richmond. *Appointments:* 1959–64 Bodmin; 1964–69 Middleton; 1969–78 Bingham; 1978– Diss.
Special Interests: Christian Aid, Community Welfare, English Pubs, Politics. *Hobbies and Recreations:* Music, Gardening, Cricket, Wine Making; Cooking, W.E.A., Painting.

FLOWERS, Paul John, The Manse, New Street, Hill Top, West Bromwich, West Midlands B70 0HW. (021 556 1729)–BA(Bristol). *b. 5 June 1950, Portsmouth.*
Education: 1961–68 Barton Peveril Grammar Sch.; 1972–75 Bristol Univ.; 1975–76 World Council of Churches Ecumenical Institute, Geneva (Faculty of Protestant Theology, Geneva Univ.); 1972–76 Wesley Coll., Bristol. *Appointments:* 1976–78 West London Mission; 1978–81 Southampton; 1981 West Bromwich (Wesley).
Connexional Committees: 1976–82 European Relations Committee; 1982– Division of Ministries Local Preachers Committee; 1982– Committee for European Affairs.
Special Interests: Former Member of Council, Advertising Standards Authority; Chairman, Sandwell Citizens' Advice Bureau; Chairman, Sandwell Council for Voluntary Services Policy Committee. *Hobbies and Recreations:* Opera, Theatre, Travel, Politics.

FORBES, Alan Griffith, 33 Tredrea Lane, St. Erth, Hayle, Cornwall TR27 6JS. (0736 753989) *b. 27 Dec 1915, Radlett, Herts. m. 27 July 1946: 2d., 2s.*
Education: 1920–27 Churchtown CE Sch., Darley Dale; 1927–32 Lady Manners Grammar School, Bakewell, Derbys.; 1946–48 Hartley Victoria.
Appointments: 1948–58 Lucknow and Banaras Dist., N.India; 1958–62 Tarporley; 1962–67 Northwich; 1967–74 South Normanton; 1974–78 Peak; 1978–81 Marazion; 1962–74 District Overseas Sec.; 1979–81 Dist. G.P. Sec.
Connexional Committees: 1962–74 Central Committee Mission House.
Special Interests: Rotary Club, Faizabad (N.India), Northwich, Alferton, Bakewell, Penzance; Promoting Local Ecumenism, Choral Singing. *Hobbies and Recreations:* Gardening, Walking (formerly Rugby, Hockey, Tennis, Badminton).

FORD, Alfred Howard, 4 Welland View Rd., Cottingham, Market Harborough, Leics. LE16 8XU. (0536 771422)–BSc. *b. 14 Oct 1909, Erdington, Birmingham. m. 24 Aug 1940: 1d., 1s.*
Education; 1933–36 Hartley Victoria.
Appointments: 1932–33 London Central Mission; 1936–43 London, Tottenham and Enfield; 1943–46 Glasgow East Mission; 1946–51 Halifax West; 1951–55 Loughborough; 1955–64 East Wight; 1964–71 Slough; 1971–75 London Tottenham and Stoke Newington.

FORD, Douglas James, 22 Leighton Rd., Toddington, Dunstable, Beds. LU5 6AL. (052 55 2026)–BD. *b. 19 July 1927, Maldon, Essex. m. 16 Aug 1958: 1d., 1s.*
Education: 1932–38 Silver End County Prim., Essex; 1938–43 Braintree, Essex County High; 1953–57 Handsworth. *Appointments:* 1957–58 Nottingham (West); 1958–59 Ilkeston; 1959–64 Ashbourne; 1964–69 Stretford and Urmston; 1969–76 Witney and Faringdon; 1976– Dunstable.
Local Council Committees: 1966–69 Stretford Borough Education Committee.
Special Interests: Politics, Current Affairs, Church History (General), Methodist History. *Hobbies and Recreations:* Gardening, Walking, Golf.

FORD, Edgar John William, 3 Castle St., Deddington, Oxford. (0869 38024)–MA, PhD, DLitt. *b. 26 Nov 1918, Poughill, Bude, N.Cornwall. m. 9 Sept 1944: 1d.*
Education: Private, Bude; 1965–68 Geneva Theological Coll.
Appointments: 1968–73 Abertillery; 1973 78 Salisbury.
Council Member: General Secretary Philosophical Society of England; Governor Geneva Theological Coll.
Publications: 500 Years of Parliament (1960); *Bible Puzzle Book* (Methodist Publishing House 1978); *Words of Comfort* (1982).
Special Interests: Youth Work. *Hobbies and Recreations:* Gardening, Painting.

FORD, Kenneth Ivan, The Manse, 44 Wakeham, Easton, Portland, Dorset DT5 1HN. (0305 820489)–BA(B'ham), BD(Lond.), MTh(Lond.).

b. 30 June 1919, Derby. m. 6 Jan 1945; 2d., 1s.
Education: 1928–37 Bemrose Sch., Derby; 1937–38 Univ. Coll., Nottingham; 1938–42 Handsworth.
Appointments: 1942–45 Belper; 1945–48 Newcastle-on-Tyne (Heaton and Wallsend); 1948–52 Coventry Mission; 1952–58 Harrogate; 1958–71 Poole; 1971–81 Bournemouth; 1981 Portland.
Connexional Committees: 1954–72 Local Preachers.
Special Interests: Local Preachers Studies etc., Industrial Mission, Theology, Literature, History.
Hobbies and Recreations: Topography, Reading, The Countryside.

FORRESTER, Kenneth Charles, Sherwood, 38 Summer Shard, South Petherton, Somerset TA13 5DP. (4060 41038) *b. 17 July 1909, Hastings, Sussex. m. 12 Aug 1937: 2d.*
Education: Elementary and Private; 1931–35 Didsbury. *Appointments:* 1930–31 Coventry; 1935–36 President's List; 1936–39 Pontypridd; 1939–41 Cardiff (Roath Rd.); 1941–45 Bristol (Bedminster); 1945–46 Maryport and Wigton; 1946–50 Stourbridge and Brierley Hill; 1950–54 Bradford (Manningham); 1954–58 Walthamstow; 1958–62 Weston-super-Mare; 1962–65 Huddersfield N.E.; 1965–69 Hayle, Cornwall; 1969–70 Chesterfield; 1970–73 Bolsover; 1973–76 Thame and Watlington.
Connexional Committees: 1952–54 Connexional Youth Committee.
Special Interests: Music, Cookery, Art. *Hobbies and Recreations:* Music (chiefly piano), Cookery, Painting and Sketching.

FORSTER, Gerald, 16 Dene Close, Castle View Estate, Ovingham, Northumberland NE42 6BE. (0632 32089)–BA. *b. 22 Nov 1946, Newcastle-on-Tyne. m. 2 Nov 1974.*
Education: 1958–64 Hexham Grammar Sch.; Newcastle Coll. of Education; 1972–76 OU; 1968–72 Wesley, Bristol. *Appointments:* 1974–76 Blackpool North; 1976– Hexham (Minister in other appointment).
Special Interests: Education. *Hobbies and Recreations:* Sport.

FORSTER, John, Cumbrae, 3 Ledsham Park, St. Leonards-on-Sea, Sussex TN37 7LQ. (0424 754016)–BD(Lond.). *b. 28 Oct 1934, Carlisle. m. 14 July 1962: 2d.*
Education: 1939–45 Newtown Prim.; 1945–51 Creighton Sch.; 1971–73 Morray House Coll. of Education, Edinburgh; 1958–62 Hartley Victoria. *Appointments:* 1962–65 Wensleydale; 1965–70 Carlisle; 1970–75 Edinburgh, Nicholson Square; 1975– Chaplain and Head of Religious Studies Department (William Parker Sch., Hastings.
Special Interests: Photography.
Hobbies and recreations: Tennis, Table Tennis.

FORSTER, John Leslie, 47 Buckingham Rd., Bletchley, Milton Keynes, Bucks. MK3 5HN. (0908 73660)–BA(Open Univ.). *b. 18 July 1944, Wakefield, Yorkshire. m. 2 Nov 1968: 2d.*
Education: 1955–62 Thornes House Grammar Sch., Wakefield; 1962–65 Kitson Coll. of Engineering & Science, Leeds; 1965–68 Leeds Poly.; 1968–69 Doncaster Coll. of Technology; 1974–76 Open Univ.; 1971–75 Queen's. *Appointments:* 1975–80 Bilston (Industrial Chaplain—Rockwell Thompson and Northern Engineering Industries, Wolverhampton (P.T.)); 1980–Milton Keynes (Industrial Sector Minister with the Milton Keynes Christian Council (P.T.)).
Connexional Committees: 1979– Connexional Church-in-Industry Committee.
Publications: Responsibility for the Environment (Editor and Contributor, Luton Industrial Coll. 1972); *Changing Face of Work and the Contribution of Education* (NEAFE Journal 1981); *Industrial Festivals! ... What at My Church?* (with Rev. C. R. Smith) Home Missions.
Special Interests: Industrial Mission, New Technology, Energy Debate.
Hobbies and Recreations: Model Railways, Gardening, Oil Painting, Photography.

FORWARD, Martin Howard Frank, 16 Hinde St., London W1M 5AR. (01 935 9611)–BA(Manchester), MA(Cantab). *b. 23 Feb 1952, Manchester. m. 27 Dec 1980.*
Education: 1965–70 Burford Sch.; 1970–73 Manchester Univ.; 1973–75 Fitzwilliam Coll., Cambridge; 1973–75 Wesley House. *Appointments:* 1975–77 Church of South India; 1977–82 Chaplain to London Univ. (W. London Miss.).
Special Interests: World Religions especially Islam, Inter-faith Relationships, Indian History.
Hobbies and Recreations: Music and Reading.

FORWARD, Walter John Rossiter, 37 Chiltern Close, Warmley, Bristol BS15 5UL. (0272 672763) *b. 10 Dec 1915, Winscombe, Avon. m. 6 Feb 1945: 1s.*
Education: 1919–24 Winscombe Council Sch.; 1924–27 Corams Lane Jun. Sch., Wellington, Somerset; 1927–33 Wellington Sch., Som.; 1938–40 Handsworth; 1940–41 Headingley. *Appointments:* 1941–45 Poole; 1945–48 Portland; 1948–53 Plymouth (King Street and Devonport); 1953–56 South Petherton; 1956–61 Cheltenham; 1961–66 Bristol (Kingswood); 1966–70 Kingsbrompton and West Somerset; 1970–75 West Wight; 1975–80 Somerset Mission.
Connexional Committees: 1950–53 Christian Citizenship.
Special Interests: Prevention of Crime, Treatment and Rehabilitation of Offenders. *Hobbies and Recreations:* Sport, Bird Watching.

FORWAY, Donald John, Rose Morran, Mevagissey, Cornwall PL26 6RY. (0726 843381) *b. 13 Sept 1931, Chadwell St. Mary, Essex. m. 11 Dec 1954: 3d., 1s.*
Education: 1936–42 Arthur St., Grays, Essex; 1942–45 John Henry Burroughs, Grays, Essex; 1972–74 Wesley, Bristol. *Appointments:* 1974–80 Falmouth; 1980– St. Austell.
Connexional Committees: 1979–82

Property Board. *Council Member:* 1975–80 (1978–80 Mayor of Penryn).
Special Interests: Work for and among Mentally Handicapped Children and Adults, Local Government. *Hobbies and Recreations:* Driving, Rotary International, Angling.

FOSS, Henry Edward, 13 Rufford Rd., Ansdell, Lytham St. Annes, Lancs FY8 4AY. (0253 734312) *b. 8 May 1912, Guernsey, C.I. m. 22 March 1939: 1s.*
Education: 1924–27 Millom County Secondary; 1927–30 Workington County Technical and Secondary; 1931–34 Handsworth.
Appointments: 1934–36 President's List; 1936–38 Bedale; 1938–41 East Cornwall Mission; 1941–45 Bacup and Rawtenstall; 1945–49 Leigh; 1949–54 Coventry; 1954–57 Birmingham (Belmont Row); 1957–63 Redditch; 1963–67 Bishop Auckland; 1967–72 Lerwick; 1972–77 Trowbridge.
Connexional Committees: 1951–57 Local Preachers' Committee; 1967–72 Home Missions Committee.
Local Council Committees: 1972–77 Wiltshire County Education Committee.
Special Interests: History. *Hobbies and Recreations:* Philately, Reading, Walking.

FOSTER, Clifford, 60 Victoria Rd. East, Thornton Cleveleys, Blackpool, Lancs. FY5 5BT. (0253 855917) *b. 1 Jan 1920, Earby, West Riding, Yorks. m. 23 May 1942: 4d., 1s.*
Education: 1925–29 Council Sch., Earby; 1930–31 Lord St. Council Sch., Colne, Lancs.; 1931–34 Park Central Sch.; 1978–79 Hartley Victoria. *Appointments:* 1978 Fleetwood.
Special Interests: Peace and Reconciliation. *Hobbies and Recreations:* Caravanning, Script Writing.

FOSTER, Eric, 2 Coggles Causeway, Bourne, Lincs. PE10 9LN. (077 82 2258) *b. 26 June 1928, Hinckley, Leics. m. 27 March 1965: 1s.*
Education: 1939–45 Hinckley Grammar Sch.; 1956–59 Richmond.
Appointments: 1959–62 Ilkeston; 1962–67 Oldham; 1967–72 Shooters Hill; 1972–78 Leicester (West); 1978– Bourne.
Connexional Committees: 1974–78 Div. of Education and Youth.
Hobbies and Recreations: Horology, Gardening, Cycling.

FOSTER, Herbert, 4 Hawkstone Court, Bare, Morecombe, Lancs. LA4 6QH. (0524 424314) *b. 13 May 1916, Blencarn, Nr. Penrith, Cumberland. m. 29 Dec 1945.*
Education: 1921–24 Milburn; 1924–27 Culgaith; 1927–34 Penrith Grammar Sch.; 1939–40 Didsbury; 1940–42 Hartley Victoria.
Appointments: 1942–43 Amble; 1943–45 Allendale: 1945–46 Eyemouth (Berwick-upon-Tweed); 1946–49 Appleby, Tebay and Kirkby Stephen; 1949–53 Stoke/Trent; 1953–56 Stockport South; 1956–61 Bramhall; 1961–70 Fleetwood; 1970–73 Sunderland South; 1973–81 Morecambe and Heysham.
Connexional Committees: 1949–53 Youth Committee.
Hobbies and Recreations: Horticulture.

FOSTER, Philip Hedges, 7 Tillett Rd., Norwich NR3 4BJ. (0603 413413) *b. 8 Feb 1909, Banbury, Oxfordshire. m. 28 July 1938: 1d., 1s.*
Education: Council Sch., Norton-on-Tees; Secondary Sch., Stockton-on-Tees; 1932–34 Hartley Victoria.
Appointments: 1934–37 Barrow-in-Furness; 1937–39 Whitehaven; 1939–42 Bottesford; 1942–45 Chatterton; 1945–48 Banbury; 1948–54 Buckingham and Brackley; 1954–60 High Wycombe; 1960–65 London, Finsbury Park; 1965–70 Norwich, Calvert St.; 1970–74 Sleaford.
Special Interests: Chaplaincies–H.M. Prison (Grendon Underwood), H M R.E.M.E. and R.A.F. Bicester, Hospital Service, Norwich.

FOSTER, Raymond John, 36 St. Nicholas St., Bodmin, Cornwall PL31 1AD. (0208 2562) *b. 25 Sept 1931, Sandleheath, Fordingbridge, Hants. m. 2 Aug 1956: 1d., 1s.*
Education: 1936–41 Fordingbridge CE; 1941–46 Bishop Wordsworth Sch., Salisbury; 1953–56 Didsbury, Bristol. *Appointments:* 1956–62 Redruth; 1962–69 Perranporth and St. Agnes; 1969–76 Launceston; 1976– Bodmin.
Connexional Committees: 1964–68 Church Membership; 1969–72 Local Preachers; 1973–79 Division of Ministers Board.
Special Interests: Hospital Chaplaincy Work. *Hobbies and Recreations:* Walking and Motoring.

FOSTER, Robert, 8 Hazeldene Court, Valley Rd., Surrey CR2 5DJ. (01 660 6740) *b. 24 Dec 1915, Port-Glasgow. m. 6 Sept 1941: 2d., 1s (deceased).*
Education: –1931 Army Technical Coll.; 1958–59 Hartford Theol. Coll., Connecticut, U.S.A.
Appointments: 1954–76 Singapore; 1974–77 Gateshead and Jarrow; 1977–79 Enfield.
Connexional Committees: 1954–74 All Committees and Councils in Malasia and Singapore (Chairman at various times of seven, also Secretary); 1958–74 Secretary for Christian Literature.
Publications: Constitution, Doctrine and Discipline, Methodist Church, S.E. Asia General Conference (1968–76); *Editor of Minutes of Conference* (1954–74); *Malaya and Singapore Annual Conference;* Wrote *Membership Handbook; M. & S. Annual Conference; Home and Family Life.*
Special Interests: Commenced Marriage Guidance Council Bookroom (1946–51), 3 years East Brook Bookroom, Bradford (1951–54), Peace and Reconciliation, Managed Methodist Bookroom Singapore (1974–76); Treasurer Croydon Pastoral Foundation 1980–82. *Hobbies and Recreations:* Swimming, Walking.

FOSTER, Roderick Henry, Extra Cover, 27 Newstead Rd., Southbourne, Bournemouth, Dorset BH6 3HJ. (0202 420814) *b. 24 Nov 1908, Ealing, Middlesex. m. 27 July 1939: 1d.*

Education: 1916–21 Godwin Coll., Cliftonville (Prep.); 1922–28 Queen's Coll., Taunton; 1929–32 Didsbury. *Appointments:* 1932–36 Dover; 1936–37 Caterham and Aldershot (Army work); 1937–39 Barnstaple; 1939–42 Tavistock; 1942–45 London, Ilford; 1945–55 Queen's Coll.,Taunton; 1955–63 Bideford and 1963–71 Bournemouth; 1955–63 F.C.C. Hospital Chaplain, Bideford; 1963–76 Bournemouth. *Special Interests:* Hospital Chaplaincy, Visitation of Sick, Youth Work. *Hobbies and Recreations:* Philately, All Sport, Walking.

FOULGER, Thomas Robert, Greenways, Hawthorn Rd., Bognor Regis PO21 2UW. (0243 863479)–MA(Lond.). *b. 26 Dec 1891, Hastings. m. 8 Sept 1925 (w.).*
Education: c. 1910–14 Hastings Grammar Sch.; 1922–23 King's Coll., London; 1929–30 London Day Training Coll.; 1919–20 Handsworth; 1920–23 Richmond. *Appointments:* 1923–47 Madras District, India; 1947–60 Church of South India; Sometime Secretary and Chairman, Madras District; Sometime Vice-President Madras Diocesan Council and Convener, Legal Questions Committee, C.S.I. Synod.
Council Member: Univ. of Madras, Sometime Member of Senate and Academic Council; Sometime President, Faculty of Teaching; Sometime Chairman, Board of Studies in Teaching.

FOWKES, Ross, 12 Hull Rd., Withernsea, N. Humberside HU19 2DZ. (096 42 2521) *b. 23 Nov 1925, Cleethorpes.*
Education: 1948–51 Hartley Victoria. *Appointments:* 1945–48 H.M. Forces; 1948–51 Hartley Victoria Coll.; 1951–63 Barbados Dt; 1963–68 South London Mission; 1968–73 Ilford; 1973– Withernsea.

FOX, Frank Trevor, 6 Blagg Av., Nantwich, Cheshire. (0270 624821)–BA. *b. 4 Aug 1922, Hartshill, Stoke-on-Trent. m. 10 March, 1945: 2d., 2s.*
Education: Newcastle High Sch., Staffs.; 1946–48 Handsworth.
Appointments: 1945–48 Handsworth Coll.; 1948–52 Shrewsbury; 1952–57 Oakengates and Shifnal; 1957–60 Leeds, Richmond Hill; 1960–65 Gainsborough; 1965–69 Tarporley; 1969–77 Nantwich; 1977–81 Middlewich.
Hobbies and Recreations: Gardening, Music.

FOXON, Frank, 6 Burngreen, Kilsyth, Glasgow G65 0HT. (0236 822034) *b. 21 April 1917, Burton-on-Trent. m. 23 June 1949: 2s.*
Education: 1937–40 Didsbury.
Appointments: 1940–42 South Shields; 1942–44 Bradford; 1944–49 Edinburgh Mission; 1949–52 Carlisle, Fisher St.; 1952–57 Coventry Mission; 1957–63 Glasgow West; 1963–82 Kilsyth.

FOY, Whitfield, 120 Perse Way, Cambridge CB4 3SA. (0223 63636)–MC, BA(Leeds), BD(Lond.). *b. 1 Nov 1916, Blyth, Northumberland. m. 7 Aug 1943: 1s.*
Education: 1927–34 Blyth Grammar Sch.; 1937–40 Leeds Univ.; 1937–41 Headingley. *Appointments:* 1941–43 Leeds, Chapel Allerton; 1943–47 HMF Chaplain; 1947–52 Leeds, Brunswick; 1952–55 Cambridge; 1955–60 Missionary Society; 1962–67 York Wesley; 1967–71 Cambridge.
Publications: Editor *Man's Religious Quest* (Croom Helm, 1977).

FRANCIS, David Noel, 5 Downleaze, Bristol BS9 1NB. (0272 684286)–MA(Cantab). *b. 13 July 1904, Hampstead, London NW. m. 18 Jan 1936: 1d., 1s.*
Education: –1915 Essendine Elem. Sch., Paddington; 1915–20 William Ellis Sch., Hampstead; 1925–28 Peterhouse, Cambridge; 1928–30 Wesley House. *Appointments:* 1930–33 MMS; 1933–41 India (Hyderabad); 1941–42 MMS (Dept.); 1942–45 Newcastle-u-Lyme; 1945–49 Westbury Park, Bristol; 1949–56 Boscombe (St. George's); 1956–58 South Norwood; 1958–67 Local Preachers Dept.
Connexional Committees: 1958–67 Local Preachers.
Publications: No Risk No Fun (Sermons); *But Above All* (Sermons); *About Prayer; Treasures of Darkness; ABC of Preaching; Let Us Worship* (Ed.).
Special Interests: Reading and Writing. *Hobbies and Recreations:* Gardening and D.I.Y. Jobs.

FRANCOM, Alan Albert, Wesley Manse, 34 Fore Street, Beacony, Camborne, Cornwall TR14 7SR. (0209 713049) *b. 16 April 1936, Wirral, Cheshire. m. 14 June 1958: 3d., 2s.*
Education: 1940–41 Barnston Prim. Sch.; 1942–51 Heswall County Council Sch.; 1952–55 Birkenhead, Laird Sch. of Art; 1960–63 Hartley Victoria. *Appointments:* 1964–67 Jamaica Dt; 1967–69 Caribbean Conf.; 1969–76 Hyde and Denton, Manchester; 1976–82 Birmingham Mission; 1982– Camborne.
Special Interests: Religion, Healing, Personal Growth and Relationships.
Hobbies and Recreations: Golf, Reading.

FRANKLIN, Arthur Bernard, 1251 Wimborne Rd., Redhill, Bournemouth, Dorset BH10 7BW. (0202 525808)–BA(Lond.). *b. 28 Jan 1916, North Kensington, London. m. 26 July 1947: 1d., 1s.*
Education: 1924–34 Haberdashers Aske's, Hampstead; 1955–60 London Univ., External Student; 1945–47 Handsworth. *Appointments:* 1947–51 French West Africa; 1952–55 Camborne; 1955–60 Newquay; 1960–66 Falmouth; 1966–73 Truro; 1973–80 Chairman Cornwall District.
Connexional Committees: 1953–59 Overseas Missions; 1973–80 Home Mission; 1973–80 General Purposes: 1973–80 Stationing; 1977– Trustees for Methodist Church Purposes.
Hobbies and Recreations: Music, Reading, Gardening, Golf.

FRANKLIN, Edward Curtiss, 8 Yewtree Close, Wimborne, Dorset BH21 1LL. (0202 884181) *b. 21 Sept 1902, London. m. 1. 16 Oct 1931, 2. 22 April 1967: 2s.*
Education: 1913–16 Latymer Upper Sch.; 1916–19 Kent Coll., Canterbury; Handsworth. *Appointments:* 1926–

29, 1929–32 Wuchang Dt; 1932–36 Hupeh Dt; 1936–40 Hull, Coltman St.; 1940–45 Portsmouth; 1945–47 Sheffield; 1947–49 Sierra Leone; 1949–53 Salisbury; 1953–58 Woking; 1958–61 Frome; 1961–67 Devizes.
Connexional Committees: Overseas Missions.
Hobbies and Recreations: Reading, Gardening, D.I.Y.

FREELAND, David Lionel, Browning Lodge, Kent College, Pembury, Tunbridge Wells, Kent TN2 4AU. (089 282 3870)–BA(Cantab), BSc(Liverpool). *b. 20 Oct 1940, London. m. 5 April 1966: 2s.*
Education: 1952–59 Sir George Monoux Grammar Sch., Walthamstow; 1959–63 Liverpool Univ., 1963–64 Westminster Coll., Oxford; 1971–73 Cambridge Univ.; 1971–73 Wesley House.
Appointments: 1973–78 Hastings, Bexhill and Rye; 1978 Chaplain at Kent Coll., Pembury.
Hobbies and Recreations: Gardening.

FREEMAN, Arthur, Herbert, 128 Matlock Crescent, Cheam, Sutton, Surrey SM3 9SZ. (01 644 6199) *b. 13 April 1916, Croxley Green, Herts. m. 30 Nov 1940: 1d., 1s.*
Education: Elem., Croxley Green, St. Albans. *Appointments:* 1952–55 Brigg; 1955–62 High Wycombe; 1962–67 Grays; 1967–74 Waltham Abbey and Hertford; 1974–81 Leigh-on-Sea.
Connexional Committees: 1968–74 Youth Committee.
Hobbies and Recreations: Cricket, Garden.

FREEMAN, George Sydney, The Garbutt, Stratton Rd., Holcombe, Bath BA3 5ED. (0761 232493) *b. 18 March 1908, Birmingham. m. 1 Aug 1934: 2s.*
Education: 1913–22 Leigh Rd. Council Sch., Birmingham; 1922–28 Evening Institute, Private Study; Victoria Park. *Appointments:* 1928–29 Great Yarmouth; 1932–37 Llantrisant and Bridgend; 1937–41 Neath and Port Talbot; 1941–46 Halifax North; 1946–53 Halifax St. Johns; 1953–59 Bristol East; 1959–66 Sheffield, Brunswick; 1966–69 Staveley; 1969–73 Bristol Frome Valley.
Special Interests: English Literature, Arts, Countryside, Sports. *Hobbies and Recreations:* Painting, Photography, Walking, Gardening.

FREEMAN, Roy Howard, 23 Chiltern Rd., Hitchin, Herts. SG4 9PJ. (0462 2627)–BA(Lond.). *b. 24 Sept 1914, Leicester. m. 8 Feb 1941: 2s.*
Education: 1919–24 Mantle Rd., Leicester; 1924–33 Wyggeston Grammar Sch. for Boys, Leicester; 1933–36 Univ. Coll., Nottingham; 1946–47 Richmond. *Appointments:* 1955–56 H.M. Committee; 1956–58 Ticehurst; 1958–64 Epworth and Crowle; 1964–68 Doncaster Dt, Coalfield Mission; 1968–72 Doncaster West; 1972–77 Bridlington; 1977 Letchworth.
Special Interests: Worship and Preaching, Teaching. *Hobbies and Recreations:* Walking, Music, Books.

FREEMAN, Roy Sydney, 4 Primrose Drive, Ripon, N. Yorks. HG4 1EY. (0765 3375)–BD(Lond.). *b. 18 Feb 1931, Leicester. m. 25 Aug 1956: 2d., 1s.*
Education: 1941–49 Loughborough Grammar Sch.; 1952–55 Richmond.
Appointments: 1955–56 Home Mission Caravans; 1956–58 Ticehurst; 1958–64 Epworth and Crowle; 1964–72 Doncaster District Coalfields Mission/Doncaster West; 1972–80 Bridlington; 1980– Ripon and Masham.
Connexional Committees: 1979– General Purposes.

FREEMAN, William, 106A Broadwater Rd., Worthing, Sussex BN14 8HL. (0903 39536) *b. 4 June 1903, Redditch, Worcs. m. 10 Aug 1932: 2s.*
Education: Elem. Schs., Redditch; 1926–29 Didsbury. *Appointments:* 1925–26 Ludlow; 1926–29 Didsbury; 1929–31 Tamworth and Lichfield; 1931–32 West Bromwich Hill Top; 1932–34 Worthing; 1934–38 Dorking and Horsham; 1938–40 Nottingham West; 1940–42 H.M. Chaplain; 1942–46 Salisbury Church St.; 1946–49 Weymouth; 1949–54 Sittingbourne; 1954–58 Leicester South; 1958–64 Ormskirk; 1964–68 Neath.
Special Interests: Preaching, Pastoral Visitation. *Hobbies and Recreations:* Reading, Walking.

FRENCH, Cyril Aldom, 12 Northfield Rd., Broughton Pastures, Aylesbury, Bucks HP20 1PB. (0296 83142)–BA(B'ham). *b. 10 Dec 1899, Manchester. m. 29 July 1926: 1s.*
Education: 1911–14 Kingswood; 1919–22 Birmingham Univ.; 1919–22 Handsworth. *Appointments:* 1923–24 Newport Mon.; 1924–26 Pickering; 1926–27 Portsmouth Mission; 1927–30 Newport and Cowes; 1930–33 Sydenham; 1933–36 Mostyn Road; 1936–44 Aylesbury; 1944–49 Orpington; 1949–53 Barnet; 1953–56 Cross Hills, Silsden and Cowling; 1956–62 Whitstable and Herne Bay; 1962–65 Bingley.
Special Interests: Church Union.

FRETWELL, Alfred, Parkside, 65 Main Rd., Romford, Essex RM2 5EH.–BA(Lond.). *b. 22 June 1894, Hull, North Humberside. m. 8 May 1965.*
Education: 1904–10 Choir Sch. Hull; 1921–22 Didsbury, Manchester.
Appointments: 1919–21 Bury St. Edmunds; 1922–25 Ely (Cambs.); 1925–28 Buckingham; 1928–31 Lincoln High St.; 1931–34 Otley; 1934–37 South Devon Mission; 1937–41 Cheltenham; 1941–45 Farnworth, Bolton, Lancs.; 1945–48 Lincoln, Aldersgate; 1948–53 Sandbach; 1953–58 Sudbury, Suffolk.
Special Interests: Music.

FRITH, Donald, 61 John F. Kennedy Estate, Washington, Tyne and Wear NE38 7AJ.
Education: 1960–63 Univ. of Bristol; 1970–71 Univ. of York; 1959–63 Didsbury. *Appointments:* 1963–65 Whitehaven; 1965–69 Church of

South India; 1969–70 Sowerby Bridge; 1970–78 Resigned; 1978– Gateshead and Jarrow.

FRITH, Stephen, Westfield, Sandstone Walk, Heswall, Wirral, Merseyside L60 0BX. (051 342 6568) *b. 19 Jan 1903, Hondslough, Kingswood, Frodsham, Warrington. m. 19 Oct 1948.*
Education: Delamere Sch.; Epworth Coll.; 1927 Cliff Coll.; 1929–30 Richmond; 1930–32 Headingley.
Appointments: 1933–36 Chester St. John St.; 1935–38 Peek, Athol St., Isle of Man; 1938–41 Rhosymedre and Chirk; 1941–44 Nantwich and Burland; 1944–48 Runcorn; 1948–52 New Mills; 1952–59 Oxford; 1959–69 Oswestry; 1969–75 East Dereham; 1975–78 Frodsham.
Special Interests: Making Friends.
Hobbies and Recreations: Tennis, Cricket, Snooker, Bowls.

FROST, Robert William, 16 Denham Crescent, Mitcham, Surrey CR4 4LZ. (01 648 8666)–BA(Manch.). *b. 27 April 1950, Halifax. m. 28 June 1975: 1s.*
Education: 1961–65 Plymouth Coll.; 1965–66 King Edward's Sch.; 1971–74 Manchester Univ.; 1974–75 Manchester Poly.; 1971–75 Hartley Victoria. *Appointments:* 1975–78 Pontefract; 1978– London Mission, Tooting.
Connexional Committees: 1979–81 Cliff Coll. Committee; 1981– Commission on Evangelism (Home Missions).
Publications: Home Mission; Methods of Mission; Evangelism in a Pop Culture.
Special Interests: Leader and Founder of the 'Gospel Roadshow' which has toured the U.S.A., Spain, Britain and Ireland. *Hobbies and Recreations:* Drama, Theatre, Sailing, Writing.

FROST, Ronald William, 244 Mount Pleasant Rd., Tottenham, London N17 6EZ. (01 808 4937)–BD(Lond.). *b. 19 Oct 1920, Vauxhall, London N1Y 6EZ. m. 25 June 1949, (died 2 Sept 1980): 1s.*
Education: 1925–26 Lawn Lane, Vauxhall; 1926–31 Athelney St., Lewisham; 1931–36 Catford Central Commercial Institute; 1947–49 Univ. of London; 1947–49 Richmond.
Appointments: 1945–47 Chipping Norton and Stow; 1949–52 Sowerby Bridge; 1952–59 Burslem Mission; 1959–65 Plymouth and Devonport Mission; 1965–77 Birmingham Mission; 1977– London (Tottenham).
Connexional Committees: 1963–74 Home Mission Committee; Sub-Committees, Central Missions Committee, Commission on Evangelism.
Local Council Committees: Birmingham Temperance Society, President 1966–77, Treasurer 1977–; Midland Band of Hope Union, President 1975–.
Publications: Leckie Lecture 1973, *Varieties of Mission;* Malins Memorial Lecture 1976, *A Puritan in the Permissive Age.*
Special Interests: Evangelism *A Plea for the Central Hall* (1963), Youth Leadership Training (Member of Scout Leadership Training Team 1954–77).
Hobbies and Recreations: Member of the Magic Circle.

FROST, Terence Clifford, 2 Eastwood Ave., High Lane, Tunstall, Stoke on Trent. (046 834 88106) *b. 18 March 1928, Tipton Staffs. m. 1956: 1d., 2s.*
Education: Elem.; 1948–49 Cliff Coll.; 1952–54 Handsworth.
Appointments: 1954–55 Pontypridd; 1955–58 Wigan Wesley–Standishgate; 1958–62 Leigh; 1962–66 Hull Mission; 1966–72 London Mission (Hackney); 1972–80 Preston (Lune St.); 1981– Tunstall.
Council Member: 1972–81 Community Relations Council.
Special Interests: Homeless single young people, Community Relations Council.

FROUD, J. Frank, 13 Elvaston Rd., Hexham, Northumberland NE46 2HA. (0434 604692) *b. 15 April 1901, Newcastle upon Tyne. m. 7 Aug 1933.*
Education: Todd's Nook, Newcastle; Blue Coat, Durham City; Dukes Sch., Alnwick; 1918–20 Durham; 1922–25 Richmond. *Appointments:* 1925–29 Burma Dt; 1929–31 East Cornwall Mission; 1931–33 Redcar, Satburn and Guisborough; 1933–34 Downham Market, Wesley; 1934–36 Allendale; 1936–40 East Suffolk; 1940–41 Stonley; 1941–42 Chaplain H.M.F.; 1942–45 Leeds, Armley; 1945–51 Gateshead East; 1951–56 Hexham; 1956–57 Hull Jubilee and Trinity; 1957–59 Otley; 1964–67 Amble.
Special Interests: Cars, Horses, Riding.
Hobbies and Recreations: Model Engineering.

FRY, Peter Anthony, 10 Linden Close, Radstock, Bath, Avon BA3 3EJ. (0761 32236) *b. 23 April 1930, Cardiff. m. 23 March 1957: 1d., 1s.*
Education: 1953–56 Richmond.
Appointments: 1952–53 Home Mission Caravan; 1956–57 Madeley and Dawley; 1958–61 Doncaster District Coalfields Mission; 1962–66 Walton on Thames; 1967–71 Wimborne; 1972–78 Aldershot, Farnborough and Camberley; 1979– Midsomer Norton.

FULTON, William, 29 Alkrington Green, Middleton, Manchester M24 1ED. (061 643 3285) *b. 9 March 1930, Sunderland. m. 17 Oct 1959: 2d., 1s.*
Education: 1935–41 St. Helen's CE Sch., Wheathampstead, Herts.; 1941–42 West Southwick Elem. Sch., Sunderland; 1943–45 Sunderland Jun. Technical Sch.; 1953–56 Headingley. *Appointments:* 1952–53 East Cornwall; 1956–58 Cowbridge and St Athan; 1958–61 Blyth and Seaton Delaval; 1961–68 Barry; 1968–74 South London Mission; 1974–78 Macclesfield; 1978– Manchester North and Middleton.
Local Council Committees: 1970–74 Lambeth Borough Youth Committee; 1968–74 Lambeth C.R.C.
Hobbies and Recreations; Bowls, Watching Cricket, Exploring Britain.

GALLIERS, Brian James Newby, 4 Manor Cresc., Hornchurch, Essex RM11 2EH. (040-24-50146)–MA(Leeds), BD, Mth(London). *b. 30 April 1931, London. m. 1956: 1d., 1s.*

Education: 1942–47 St. Albans Sch.; 1951–54 Headingley. *Appointments:* 1954–55 Romford; 1955–57 Wesley Coll., Headingley, Asst. Tu.; 1957–64 Redhill; 1964–67 Croydon (South Norwood); 1967–72 Newcastle upon Tyne (Brunswick Central); 1972–80 Wesley Deaconess Order (Warden); 1980–82 Birmingham (Sutton Park); 1982– London North East District (Chairman). *Connexional Committees:* 1967–72 Local Preachers. *Publications: Something To Declare* (1969). *Hobbies and Recreations:* Walking, Music, Reading, Most Sports.

GAMBLE, David, 31 Chestnut Ave., York YO3 0BR. (0904-22886)–LL.B, MA. *b. 21 May 1947, Gravesend, Kent.*
Education: 1952–53 Cuxton Prim. Sch.; 1954–58 Wakeley Rd. Jun. Sch., (Rainham, Kent); 1958–61 Gillingham Grammar Sch.; 1961–65 Lawrence Sheriff Sch. for Boys (Rugby); 1965–68 Hull Univ.; 1971–74 Wesley House. *Appointments:* 1974–81 Tadcaster; 1981– York South.
Connexional Committees: 1976–82 Connexional Childrens Committee. *Special Interests:* Music, Canals, Cats. *Hobbies and Recreations:* City Opera Group, York, Narrow-Boating, Squash.

GAMESON, Brian John, 481 Clayhill Rd., Vange, Basildon, Essex SS16 4NN. (0268-553066) *b. 28 June 1934, Tredegar, Monmouthshire. m. 8 Aug 1959: 1s.*
Education: 1945–48 Handsworth Grammar Sch., Birmingham; 1948–51 Bournemouth Sch., Bournemouth; 1955–56 Cliff Coll.; 1956–59 Richmond. *Appointments:* 1959–62 Bude; 1962–66 Normanton; 1966–73 Leigh-on-Sea; 1973– Basildon.
Special Interests: Boys' Brigade, Borstal (Girls). *Hobbies and Recreations:* Singing, Curator at Wesley's House, Reading, Visiting Ancient Sites and Houses.

GARD, Albert Ivor, The Manse, Clarence Place, Pontypool, Gwent NP4 8AY. (049 55 2861) *b. 15 June 1920, Crediton, Devon. m. 21 Dec 1946: 1d., 1s.*
Education: East Worlington; 1946–47 Cliff College; 1956–58 Didsbury, Bristol. *Appointments:* 1951–56 Wye Valley; 1958–64 West Indies Dt (Jamaica); 1964–69 Crewkerne; 1969–72 Guyana Dt; 1972–75 Wellington (Som); 1975–81 MCCA (Jamaica); 1981– Pontypool.
Special Interests: Evangelism. *Hobbies and Recreations:* Gardening.

GARDINER, Christopher Herbert, 48 Lane End Drive, Knaphill, Woking, Surrey GU21 2QG. (04867-2524) *b. 15 Mar 1946, Southall, Middlesex. m. 2d., 1s.*
Education: 1967–71 Wesley, Bristol. *Appointments:* 1971–72 Coventry Mission; 1972–76 Castleford; 1976–80 Andover; 1980– Woking and Walton-on-Thames.
Special Interests: Cosmology. *Hobbies and Recreations:* Railways, Music, Model Engineering, Motor Mechanics, Woodwork.

GARDINER, Denis Egerton, 50 Mount Vernon Rd., Barnsley, South Yorks S70 4DW. (0226-203711) *b. 16 Nov 1928, Abergavenny, Gwent. m. 11 Aug 1956: 1d., 2s.*
Education: 1935–39 Hereford Rd. Elem., Abergavenny; 1939–42 Shirley Elem., Southampton; 1953–56 Didsbury, Bristol. *Appointments:* 1956–61 St. Austell; 1961–65 Gravesend and Dartford; 1965–70 Medway Towns; 1970–79 Loughborough; 1979 Barnsley.
Connexional Committees: 1965–70 Connexional Youth Council; 1974–83 Home Missions Team Ministry Sub-Committee (Sec); 1974–79 Methodist Day Schools Committee; 1974–77 Connexional Candidates Committee; 1980–82 DRS Healing & Pastoral Committee. *Council Member:* 1972–79 Leicestershire County Council.
Special Interests: Team Ministry, Counselling. *Hobbies and Recreations:* Sport, Reading, Music.

GARDINER, Gerald Charles, 27 Princes Gdns., Ealing, London W5 1SD. (01-998-1962)–BA(Open). *b. 18 Jan 1938, Shanklin, Isle of Wight. m. 13 July 1963: 2s.*
Education: 1949–54 Northgate Grammar Sch., Ipswich; 1960–63 Richmond. *Appointments:* 1964–70 Nigeria Dt; 1970–73 Huddersfield (West); 1973–79 Bedford (South); 1979– Ealing and Acton.
Connexional Committees: 1970–73 MMS Home Committee.
Special Interests: Peace Groups, World Development. *Hobbies and Recreations:* Gardening, Reading, Stamp Collecting.

GARDNER, Colin Stanley, 10 Springfield Rd., Halesowen, West Midlands B62 8JY. (021-422-2934) *b. 27 April 1942, Sutton Coldfield, West Midlands. m. 6 April 1968: 3s.*
Education: 1953–58 Bishop Vesey's Grammar Sch., Sutton Coldfield; 1959–60 South Staffordshire Coll. of Commerce; 1965–69 Wesley, Bristol. *Appointments:* 1969–74 Forest of Dean Circuit; 1974–81 Liskeard and Looe Circuit; 1981– Blackheath (Birmingham).
Connexional Committees: 1982– Div. Board of Education and Youth. *Publications: One and All* (A Book of Cornish Christian Stories for Children 1979).
Special Interests: The Work of the Church Among Children and Young People, Social Responsibility Matters, Methodist History. *Hobbies and Recreations:* Travel, Photography, Philately, Gardening.

GARDNER, Helen Diana, The Manse, Huntingfield, Addington, Croydon, Surrey CR0 9BA. (0689-42381) *b. 15 Nov 1939, England. s.*
Education: 1944 St. Vincent's Convent, Acton; 1948 Harvington Sch., Ealing; 1954 Kent Coll., Pembury; 1957 Chiswick Poly.; 1958 Central Sch. of Speech and Drama; 1978–80 Wesley, Bristol. *Appointments:* 1980– Croydon
Special Interests: People, Prisons. *Hobbies and Recreations:* Music, Sport, Puzzling, Books.

GARDNER, Ronald, 5 Woodfield Drive, Bradley, Keighley, West Yorkshire BD20 9EN. (0535 33598) *b. 3 Feb 1910, Ebbw Vale. m. 1 Aug 1938: 1d., 2s.*

Education: Willowtown, Ebbw Vale; 1932–5 Didsbury.
Appointments: 1931–32 Marlborough Mission; 1935–37 President's List; 1937–40 Attleborough; 1940–45 Neath and Port Talbot; 1945–49 Bridgend; 1949–52 Swansea; 1952–57 Harrogate; 1957–62 Bradford (Manningham); 1962–66 Leeds (Brunswick); 1966–71 Leeds (South); 1971–75 Retford.
Hobbies and Recreations: Reading, Gardening, Art (Painting and Drawing).

GARFOOT, John, 41 Cley Rd., Swaffham, Norfolk PE37 7NP. (0760-21493)–BA(Lond.). *b. 15 June 1916, Sutton Bridge. m. 6 Aug 1945: 2s.*
Education: 1926–34 Spalding G.S.; 1934–38 Univ. Coll., Nottingham; 1945–46 Richmond. *Appointments:* 1946–50 Weardale; 1950–57 Wisbech; 1957–64 King's Lynn; 1964–71 Wymondham, Attleborough and Watton; 1971–81 Ely; 1981 Dereham and Swaffham; 1967–75 East Anglia Synod Secretary.
Connexional Committees: 1969–82 Church in Rural Life; 1969–82 Travel and Allowances.
Special Interests: Rural Methodism. *Hobbies and Recreations:* Music, Gardening.

GARFOOT, Raymond Francis, 159 Sleaford Rd., Boston, Lincs. PE21 7PF. (0205-63372)–MA(Oxon), BA(Cantab.). *b. 22 May 1946, Sutton Bridge, Lincs. m. 11 Aug 1971: 2d., 1s.*
Education: 1951–53 Norwich Rd. Inf.; 1953–57 Ramnoth Rd. C.P. Boys, Wisbech; 1957–64 King Edward VII G.S. for Boys, King's Lynn; 1964–67 Oriel Coll., Oxford; 1967–68 Keswick Hull Coll. of Education, Norwich; 1970–73 Wesley House. *Appointments:* 1973–74 Netherton; 1974–75 Leeds (North East); 1975–80 Leeds; 1980 Boston.
Connexional Committees: 1982 Rural Life Committee.
Special Interests: Peace Movement, Ancient Religions. *Hobbies and Recreations:* Poetry, Music, Philately, Walking, Gardening.

GARFORTH, James Lawson, 3 Beach End Rd., Uphill, Weston-super-Mare, Avon BS23 4YD. (0934-413025) *b. 7 Sept 1912, Trincomalee, Ceylon. m. 18 Oct 1953: 1d., 2s.*
Education: 1923–29 Kingswood Sch., Bath; 1934–37 Handsworth.
Appointments: 1937–47 Hyderabad, India; 1947–61 Church of South India, Dornakal Diocese; 1961–65 Hull (West) Circuit; 1965–71 Birmingham (South West); 1971–76 Southport; 1976–81 Darwen; 1981–82 St. Annes-on-Sea, Lancs.
Connexional Committees: 1961–65 Methodist Missionary Society General Committee; 1961–71 M.M.S. Eastern Committee.
Special Interests: Overseas Missions, Third World. *Hobbies and Recreations:* Reading, Ornithology, Geology, Walking, Gardening, Philately.

GARLICK, Kenneth Benjamin, Wesley House, 1 Chester Road, Wanstead, London E11 2JR. (01-530-2589) *b. 6 Jan 1923, Leicester. m. 13 Aug 1955: 1d., 2s.*
Education: 1928–34 Prim. and Jun. Sch., Leicester; 1934–39 Green Lane Secondary Sch., Leicester; 1960–63 Durham Univ.; 1968–70 London Univ.; 1950–53 Headingley.
Appointments: 1948–50 Cwm and Kingston; 1950–53 Headingley Coll.; 1953–55 Bradford Mission; 1955–57 Bishop Auckland; 1957–60 Leeds Mission; 1960–67 Newcastle upon Tyne Mission; 1967–74 Walton-on-Thames; 1974 London, Leytonstone and Forest Gate; 1978– District Property Committee Secretary, London NE; 1979– District Grants Committee (H.M. and L.M.).
Connexional Committees: 1969–74 Registrar W.H.S.; 1974– Librarian W.H.S.; 1978– Archives and History Committee; 1977– Property Board; 1978– London Mission Committee; 1979– Trustee Wesley's Chapel, London; 1979– Leysion Mission Committee; 1978– N.A.B.C. Religious Advisory Committee. *Publications:* Editor *Hill's Arrangement* (1971–); *Wesley College, Headingley* (1973); *Mr Wesley's Preachers* (1977); Various Articles W.H.S. Proceedings since 1969; *Garlick's Methodist Registry* (1982).
Special Interests: Methodist History, Methodist Statistics, Wesleyana, Ministerial Training. *Hobbies and Recreations:* Reading, especially History and Biography, Writing and Research on Methodist History, Cricket.

GARNER, Joseph Stanley, Meadow Garth, Drayton, Banbury, Oxon OX15 6EH. (029 573 226) *b. 22 Mar 1903, Lowfield House Farm, Wigton, Cumberland. m. 8 Aug 1935: 2d., 1s.*
Education: 1908–15 Bishop Goodwin Memorial Sch., Carlisle; 1927–30 Handsworth.
Appointments: 1926–27 Kirkoswald; 1930–33 Jersey (Wesley); 1933–38 Guernsey (English); 1938–45 Banbury; 1945–50 London (Brixton Hill); 1950–56 Lincoln (Wesley); 1956–61 Louth; 1961–66 Scunthorpe; 1966–71 Wellingborough; 1958–65 Lincoln District Synod Secretary.
Connexional Committees: 1930–38 Young Methodism; 1940–45 Youth; 1946–50 Overseas Mission; 1963–70 Building Schemes (Convener); 1965–71 Chapel; 1947–82 Finance.
Special Interests: History, Literature, Environment. *Hobbies and Recreations:* Gardening, Golf.

GARNER, Keith Vincent, The Ministers Flat, Methodist Central Hall, Eastlake St., Drake Circus, Plymouth, Devon PL1 1BA. (0752–660393) *b. 4 Jan 1955, Lancashire. m. 19 Aug 1978: 1s.*
Education: 1967-72 Wardley Grammar Sch.; 1972–74 Eccles 6th Form Coll.; 1974–76 Cliff Coll.; 1977–80 Wesley, Bristol.
Appointments: 1980– Plymouth and Devonport Mission.
Connexional Committees: Home Mission Commission on Evangelism.
Special Interests: Evangelism, Church Growth and Youth Work. *Hobbies and Recreations:* Sport, especially Cricket and Association Football.

GARRITT, Charles Eric, 46 Lustrells Cresc., Saltdean, Brighton, East Sussex BN2 8FJ. (0273-31474) *b. 22 March 1900, Doncaster. m. 13*

Aug 1932: 1d.
Education: 1904–13 Wadworth National; 1913–16 Doncaster Technical; 1921 Cliff College; 1924–27 Handsworth. *Appointments:* 1927–29 Ludlow; 1929–31 Belper; 1931–33 Chertsey and Walton; 1933–36 Manchester (Victoria); 1936–40 Neath and Port Talbot; 1940–44 South Devon Mission; 1944–49 Mansfield; 1949–53 London, Leytonstone and Forest Gate; 1953–59 Caerphilly; 1959–66 Hungerford; 1945–49 District Secretary (Nottingham District) of Christian Citizenship Dept.
Connexional Committees: 1945–53 Christian Citizenship; 1949–53 London Mission & Extension Committee. *District Committees:* 1944–53 District Christian Citizenship; 1945–49 District Home Mission Committee; 1945–49 Candidates Committee. *Local Council Committees:* 1943–44 President of Kingsbridge, Salcombe and District Free Church Federal Council; 1956–57 President Caerphilly Free Church Federal Council. *Publications:* Numerous Articles, Sermons etc., in Periodicals and Magazines, English and Canadian 1934–80.
Special Interests: Philately. *Hobbies and Recreations:* Oil Painting, Gardening.

GARTSIDE, James, 36 Cross Flatts Ave., Leeds, West Yorkshire LS11 7BG. (0532-705756) *b. 11 Mar 1927, Chadderton, Oldham. m. 16 Aug 1958: 3d.*
Education: 1955–58 Hartley Victoria. *Appointments.* 1958–61 Stockport South; 1961–65 Pontefract; 1965–71 Bradford (Woodehouse Grove); 1971–78 Pontefract; 1978–82 Southport; 1982– Leeds South.

GASKELL, James, 1029 Melton Rd., Syston, Leicester LE7 8BE. (0533-693129) *b. 10 June 1909, Oldham. m. 1. Deceased. 2. 17 Aug 1977: 2d.*
Education: Elem., Oldham; 1932–35 Headingley. *Appointments:* 1931–32 Teignmouth; 1932–35 Headingley Coll.; 1935–36 President's List; 1936–38 Leominster; 1938–40 Sheffield Mission; 1940–45 Glasgow, Claremont St.; 1945–49 Haslingden, Manchester Rd.; 1949–54 Leicester, King Richard's Rd.; 1954–57 Leicester North; 1957–60 Coalville; 1960–64 North of Scotland Mission; 1964–69 Otley; 1969–72 Normanton; 1972–74 Peel, I.O.M.; 1974–75 Barnsley.
Special Interests: Previously Reading and Gardening. *Hobbies and Recreations:* Restricted due to Blindness, time given to Learning to Read Braille.

GATEHOUSE, Maurice Douglas, 20 Applerigg, Kendal, Cumbria LA9 6EA. (0539-20513)–BD(Lond.). *b. 14 Nov 1917, Darlington. m. 24 July 1946: 2d., 2s.*
Education: 1925–28 Oldfield Lodge Sch., Bath; 1928–35 Queen's Coll., Taunton; 1939–41 Richmond; 1941–43 Headingley. *Appointments:* 1943–45 London, East Ham Mission; 1945–49 Colchester; 1949–54 Southend-on-Sea; 1954–59 Tonypandy; 1959–66 Kilburn and Hampstead; 1966–72 Exmouth; 1972–79 Weston-super-Mare; 1979– Kendal.
Hobbies and Recreations: Handicrafts, Clock Repairs, Golf, Fly Fishing.

GATES, Bryan Paul, 113 Henleaze Rd., Westbury-on-Trym, Bristol. (0272-622797) *b. 30 July 1953, Southport, Merseyside. m. 4 June 1977.*
Education: 1964–68 Birkdale Secondary Sch.; 1980 Wesley, Bristol.
Hobbies and Recreations: Cricket.

GATWARD, Gordon John, Wesley House, Hawes, N. Yorks DL8 3NT. (096 97 268)–BD(Lond.). *b. 12 Dec 1947, Kimpton, Herts. m. 3 April 1971: 3s.*
Education: 1952–59 Kimpton CP Sch.; 1959–66 Hatfield Technical; 1969–72 Richmond; 1972–73 Wesley, Bristol. *Appointments:* 1973–75 Dursley and Stonehouse; 1975–81 Cirencester (Prev. Stroud & Cirencester); 1981– Wensleydale.
Connexional Committees: 1976– Home Missions Church in Rural Life Committee.
Special Interests: Rural Life, Agriculture. *Hobbies and Recreations:* Caving, Fell Walking, Canoeing, Shooting, Land Rovers.

GAWTHROP, Alan, The Manse, Kirkoswald, Penrith, Cumbria CA10 1EW. (076-883-257) *m.*
Education: 1964–66 Hartley Victoria. *Appointments:* 1966–70 Loftus and Staithes; 1970–77 Redcar Saltburn and Guisborough; 1977–82 Whitehaven; 1982– Kirkoswald.

GENT, Edward Barry, 6 Park Hill Drive, Leicester LE2 8HR. (0533-832765)–BA(Birm.), MA(Camb.). *b. 28 April 1936, Rugby, Warwickshire. m. 23 June 1962: 1d., 1s.*
Education: 1941–45 Mill Rd. CE, Oundle; 1945–47 Paddox Jun., Rugby; 1947–54 Lawrence Sheriff Sch., Rugby; 1954–57 Univ. of Birmingham; 1960–62 Univ. of Cambridge; 1960–62 Wesley House.
Appointments: 1962–67 Chaplain, Meantsipim Sch., Cape Coast, Ghana; 1967–71 Malton; 1971–78 Driffield; 1978– Leicester South East.

GEORGE, Alfred Raymond, 40 Knole Lane, Bristol BS10 6SS. (0272-503698)–MA, BD(Oxon), MA(Cantab.). *b. 26 Nov 1912, Gloucester.*
Education: 1923–31 Crypt Sch., Gloucester; 1931–35 Balliol Coll., Oxford; 1935–37 Fitzwilliam House, Cambridge; 1937–38 Marburg Univ.; 1935–37 Wesley House.
Appointments: 1938–40 Assistant Tutor Handsworth Coll.; 1940–42 Assistant Tutor Hartley Victoria Coll.; 1942–46 Manchester, Great Western St.; 1946–67 Wesley Coll., Headingley, Leeds (Principal 1961–67); 1967–68 Permitted to work in Univ. of Leeds, also in charge of Coll. property of Wesley College, Headingley; 1968–72 Richmond Coll., (Principal); 1972–81 Wesley Coll., Bristol; 1982– Warden, New Room, Bristol, 1975 President of Conference.
Connexional Committees: At present Doctrinal Committee (Conference); History of Methodism; World Methodist Council (British Committee, Chairman); Building Schemes and Co-operation with

other Communions; 1982– Archive and History; Ecumenical, John Wesley's Chapel; In the past at various times Church Membership; Transfer of Autonomy and Overseas Districts; Faith and Order. *Publications: Communion with God in the New Testament* (Fernley-Hartley Lecture) 1953; Joint Editor, *A History of the Methodist Church in Great Britain* (Volume II 1978). *Special Interests:* Liturgy, Ecumenism, Free Church Federal Council Ministers, 1979, Chairman of Executive Committee, 1980–, Representative of BBC Assembly 1981–, Faith and Order Commission of WCC, 1961–75, Member WCC 5th Assembly 1975, Joint Liturgical Group, 1963–, International Consultation in English Texts, 1969, World Methodist Council, 1956–, Executive 1961–76, 1981–, International conversations with Roman Catholics 1971–.

GIBBINS, Albert Edward, 6 Barnet Rd., Sheffield S11 7RP. (0742-308171)–TD. *b. 16 Mar 1916, Sunderland. m. 6 Jan 1944: 2s. Education:* 1921–26 Ford (South Hylton); 1926–29 Barnes (Sunderland); 1929–31 Sunderland Jun. Technical; 1931–32 Sunderland Technical Coll.; 1938–40 Didsbury; 1940–41 Hartley. *Appointments:* 1941–43 Cheadle (Staffs); 1943–51 Chaplain HM Forces; 1951–56 Newcastle N.W.; 1956–63 Sheffield (Carver St.); 1963–67 Jersey; 1967–72 Belper; 1972–77 Wombwell and Hoyland; 1977–81 Rochdale. *Special Interests:* Scouting. *Hobbies and Recreations:* Gardening, Music.

GIBBON, Joseph Anthony, 27 Oundle Drive, Wollaton Park, Nottingham NG8 1BN. (0602 786423)–BD(Lond.). *b. 9 Dec 1932, Witton Park, Bishop Auckland, Co. Durham. m. 10 Aug 1957: 2d., 1s. Education:* 1937–40 Witton Park Council; 1940–43 Escomb Council; 1943–50 King James 1st Grammar, Bishop Auckland; 1951–53 Royal Air Force Regiment; 1954–57 Leeds Univ.; 1954–57 Headingley. *Appointments:* 1957–60 Rugby (Lutterworth); 1960–65 Northampton; 1965–72 Oxford, Wesley; 1972–80 Doncaster (Priory Place); 1980– Nottingham Mission. *Connexional Committees:* 1972–80 Social Responsibility; 1974– World Development. *Special Interests:* Community Relations, World Development. *Hobbies and Recreations:* Family and Travel, Walking and Westerns.

GIBBINS, Ronald Charles, 49 City Rd., London EC1Y 1AU. (01-253-2262)–BSc(Lond.), D.Min(Eden St. Louis, U.S.A.). *b. 19 Sept 1922, London. m. 7 Aug 1949: 2d., 1s. Education:* 1945–48 Didsbury, Bristol; 1965–69 Goldsmiths Coll., London Univ.; 1969–71 London North East Poly.; 1976–79 Eden Theol. Seminary, St. Louis, U.S.A. *Appointments:* 1948–49 Bradford Mission; 1949–50 Spennymoor; 1950–57 Middlesbrough; 1957–64 Basildon New Town; 1964–78 London East End Mission; 1978– London Wesley's Chapel; *Connexional Committees:* 1964–68 London Mission; 1976– Home Mission Board. *Publications: The Undeserving Poor* (Beckley Lecture 1977); *Mission for the Secular City* (1976). *Hobbies and Recreations:* Travel.

GIBBS, Albert George, 22 Langford Rd., Heaton Chapel, Stockport, Cheshire SK4 5BR. (061-432-7795) *b. 8 Mar 1893, York. m. 1. 1922 Deceased. 2. 1958: 2d. Education:* 1903–06 Liverpool Institute; 1906–09 Glasgow High Sch.; 1914–15, 1919–21 Didsbury. *Appointments:* 1915–19 HM Forces; 1919–21 Didsbury; 1921–22 Ryedale; 1922–25 Wensleydale; 1925–29 Todmorden; 1929–32 Blackburn Mission; 1932–36 Clitheroe; 1936–42 Blackburn Wilpshire; 1942–45 Glasgow; 1945–51 Alston; 1951–56 Southport; 1956–59 Lichfield; 1959–63 Manchester S.E.; 1963–69 Stoke on Trent, Tunstall. *Special Interests:* Travel, Music, History. *Hobbies and Recreations:* Gardening, Woodwork.

GIBBS, Ian Christopher Stockdale, 13 Broadway, Rodbourne Cheney, Swindon, Wilts SN2 3BN. (0793-34314) *m. Education:* Handsworth. *Appointments:* 1972–74 Bridlington; 1974–79 Workington; 1979–82 Gloucester; 1982– Swindon.

GIBBS, Irene Marion, Wesley House, 633 High Rd., Benfleet, Essex SS7 5SF. (037 45 3313) *b. 26 Oct 1925. s. Education:* 1930–36 Norlington Rd. Elem. Sch., Leytonstone; 1936–39 Loughton High Sch.; 1939–41 Reigate County Sch.; 1955–57 Deaconess Coll., Ilkley; 1973–74 Wesley, Bristol. *Appointments:* 1974–79 Todmorden; 1979– Leigh on Sea. *Connexional Committees:* 1975–79 Division of Ministries. *Special Interests:* Children and People. *Hobbies and Recreations:* Reading and Excursions into Family Life, Enjoyment of Drama, Musical Appreciation.

GIBSON, George Scott, 31 Crawford Close, Lillington, Leamington Spa CV32 7HA. (0926-312-195) *b. 23 Sept 1914, Newcastle upon Tyne. m. 26 Dec 1940: 1s. Education:* Sandyford Rd Sch.; West Jesmond Sch.; Heaton Technical Coll., Newcastle upon Tyne; 1946–48 Handsworth. *Appointments:* 1968–70 Rhondda; 1970–75 Frodsham; 1975–62 Sunderland West; 1962–67 Leicester West; 1967–74 Staple Hill and Fishponds; 1974–82 Kimberley. *Publications:* Occasional Articles and Sermons over the Years in *Joyful News* (series of Bible Studies and Devotional), *Christian World Pulpit, Expository Times.*

GIBSON, Harold Arthur, 103 Hough Lane, Wombwell, Barnsley, South Yorkshire S73 0EG. (0226-752259)–BA(Leeds). *b. 12 Feb 1919, Port of Spain, Trinidad, West Indies. m. 26 Jan 1945: 1d., 1s. Education:* 1928–30 Wetherby Council Sch., Yorkshire; 1930–31 Tadcaster Grammar Sch., Yorkshire; 1931–35 King James' Grammar Sch., Knaresborough, Yorkshire; 1938–42 Leeds Univ.; 1938–42 Headingley.

Appointments: 1943–50 Western Nigeria and the Gambia, West Africa; 1950–62 Sussex Mission (East); 1962–68 Staines and Feltham; 1968–74 Higham Ferrers; 1974–79 Teddington; 1982– Wombwell and Hoyland.
Connexional Committees: 1950–55 Western Committee at Mission House.
Hobbies and Recreations: No longer actively but still interested in most forms of sport, particularly Cricket, Tennis, Football, Badminton and Swimming.

GIBSON, James Stanley, The Manse, 19 Ridley Ave., Blyth Northumberland NE24 3BA. (06-706-2097) *b. 13 July 1919, Newcastle upon Tyne. m. 26 Dec 1945: 1s.*
Education: 1924–30 Sandyford Elem. Sch., West Jesmond Elem. Sch.; 1930–36 Heaton Secondary Grammar Sch., Newcastle upon Tyne; 1956–57 Headingley.
Appointments: 1957–60 Rhondda (Ely Valley); 1960–63 Durham; 1963–67 Redcar, Saltburn and Guisbrough; 1967–71 Leeds (Richmond Hill); 1971–77 Ebbw Vale; 1977–82 Buckley and Deeside; 1982– Blyth Valley.
Connexional Committees: 1972–77 Board of Division of Social Responsibility (as Cardiff and Swansea District Ministerial S.R. Secretary.
Special Interests: Church and Social History, especially the History of Methodism, Homiletics. *Hobbies and Recreations:* Reading, Travel, Cricket and Football.

GIFFARD, Raymond Roy, 48 Station Rd, Wigston Rd, Leicester LE8 2DJ. (0533 888444) *b. 6 Dec 1935, Sark, Channel Islands. m. 15 Aug 1964: 2s.*
Education: Educated on the Island of Sark; 1961–64 Didsbury, Bristol.
Appointments: 1964–67 Knighton; 1967–75 Stourvale; 1975–79 Rugby; 1979– Leicester South East.
Hobbies and Recreations: Stamp Collecting, Photography.

GIFFORD, Anna Margaret, The Manse, Colebrookvale, Nantyglo, Brynmawr, Gwent. (0495-290355) *b. 12 Nov 1931. s.*
Education: 1942–45 Colston's Girl's Sch., Bristol; 1945–49 Bridgwater Girls' Sch., Somerset; 1949–53 Northern Sch. of Music, Manchester; 1975–77 Wesley House.
Appointments: 1977–82 Forest of Dean; 1982– Abertillery.
Special Interests: Pastoral Counselling, Ecumenical Relationships. *Hobbies and Recreations:* Swimming, Stamps, Cooking, Cats.

GILBERT, Charles Robert Wolsey, 3 Vale Rd., Ash Vale, Aldershot, Hants GU12 5HH. (0252-24887)–DipTheol(Lond.). *b. 22 Sept 1922, Christchurch, Camb. m. 18 July 1953: 3d., 1s.*
Education: St. Peter's, Upwell, Camb.; 1950–53 Richmond. *Appointments:* 1949–45 Attleborough; 1953–77 Forces Chaplain (Army); 1977– Secretary Royal Navy, Army and Royal Air Force Board; 1978– Chaplain to Household Cavalry.
Connexional Committees: 1977– HM Com.
Hobbies and Recreations: DIY, Gardening, Helping at Detention Centre, Chaplain to Dunkirk Veterans Ass., Housing Trusts.

GILCHRIST, Eileen, 32 Broadway, Worsley, Manchester M28 4EA. (061-790-3558) *b. 6 Oct 1943, Edinburgh. s.*
Education: 1954–59 Newark High Sch.; 1959–61 North Kelvinside Senior Sch.; 1965–66 Teeside Poly., Child Care Course; 1972–76 Queens.
Appointments: 1976–81 Gateshead and Jarrow; 1981– Worsley.
Special Interests: Human Relations Training, Group Work within the Church, Place of Quietness and Silence within Spirituality. *Hobbies and Recreations:* Gardening, Swimming, Walking, Classical Music, Reading.

GILL, Kenneth Edward (Bishop), 83 Kenton Rd., Newcastle upon Tyne NE3 4NL. (0632-851502) *b. 22 May 1932, Birstwith. m. 20 April 1957: 2d., 1s.*
Education: 1937–44 Birstwith Prim. Sch.; 1944–48 Harrogate Grammar Sch.; 1954–57 Hartley Victoria.
Appointments: 1957–80 Church of South India; 1980– Assistant Bishop of Newcastle.
Connexional Committees: 1980–82 MCOD Central Committee.
Publications: Meditations in The Holy Spirit (C.L.S. Madras 1979).
Special Interests: Gardening.

GILLESPIE, Harry W., 22 Maltby Rd., Mapperley, Nottingham NG3 5QZ. (0602-267146) *b. 3 Oct 1922. m. 1954: 2d.*
Education: 1948–50 Headingley.
Appointments: 1947–48 Cowbridge and St Atham; 1950–53 Attleborough; 1953–58 Castleford; 1958–61 Salisbury; 1961–68 Dewsbury; 1968–75 Leicester West; 1975– Nottingham Central.
Connexional Committees: 1972– Membership Committee; 1979– General Committee N.C.H.

GILLMAN, David John, 114 Lunsford Lane, Larkfield, Maidstone, Kent ME20 6HS. (0732 842019)–BD(Lond.). *b. 1 April 1957, London. m. 9 April 1977: 1d.*
Education: Minchenden Sch., Southgate, London; 1977–80 Wesley, Bristol. *Appointments:* 1980– Maidstone.

GILSON, Nigel Langley, 53 York Ave., Wolverhampton, W. Midlands WV3 9BX. (0902-24430)–DFC, MA. *b. 11 April 1922, Holcombe, Nr. Bath, Somerset. m. 31 July 1951: 4d.*
Education: Holcombe Methodist Day Sch.; Midsomer Norton County Secondary Sch.; 1940–41, 1945–47 St. Catherine's Society, Oxford; 1947–50 Fitzwilliam House, Cambridge, 1947–50 Wesley House.
Appointments: 1950–52 Camelford and Wadebridge; 1952–58 Newark; 1958–67 Rhodesia; 1967–71 Filey (Chaplain Hunmanby Hall); 1971–75 Oxford, Wesley; 1975– Chairman Wolverhampton and Shrewsbury District.
Connexional Committees: Overseas Division (Overseas Service, GP,

Home and Central Committee); Home Missions; Various Working Parties; GP Committee; Ministers in Other Appointments (Chairman); Community Development Group (Chairman); Stationing Committee; Ministers' Housing Society. *Publications:* Sundry Articles, Reviews in *Methodist Recorder,* other Methodist Publications, Various Lectures in Church and Educational Context.
Special Interests: Community Relations (Oxford Council for Racial Equality, Wolverhampton Council for Race Relations), World Development, Peace Movement (W.D.C.), Ecumenical Relations (Many and Various). *Hobbies and Recreations:* Family Activities of all Kinds, Gardening, Walking (gentle), Theatre (when possible).

GILYEAD, John Anthony, 33 Carlyn Drive, Chandler's Ford, Eastleigh, Hants SO5 2DJ. (0703-68803) *b. 10 July 1936, Pocklington, East Yorkshire. m. 11 Aug 1962: 2d., 2s.*
Education: 1941–51 County Prim. and Pocklington Secondary Modern; 1957–58 Cliff College; 1958–62 Headingley. *Appointments:* 1962–64 Shrewsbury; 1964–66 Craven Arms and Church Streton; 1966–71 Cannock Chase; 1971–77 Birmingham (Moseley Rd. and Sparkhill); 1977– Eastleigh.
Connexional Committees: 1969–71, 1980– Division of Education and Youth.
Special Interests: Worship, Preaching, Local Radio, Youth Work. *Hobbies and Recreations:* Walking, Theatre, Reading.

GILYEAD, Michael John, 64 Woodthorpe Rd., Ashford, Middlesex TW15 2RU. (07842-52559)–BA. *b. 4 Nov 1928, Headingley, Leeds. m. 22 Oct 1960: 1d., 1s.*
Education: Bembridge Sch., I.O.W.; 1953–56 Manchester Univ.; 1953–57 Hartley Victoria. *Appointments:* 1957–59 Bolton (Wesley); 1959–63 Pontefract; 1963–68 Whitstable and Herne Bay; 1968–73 Harlow Mission; 1973–79 London (Shooters Hill); 1979– Staines and Feltham.

GIRT, Gillian, 28 Courtenay Rd., Splott, Cardiff CF2 2JQ. (0222-26946)–BA(Lond.). *b. 11 Nov 1946, Doncaster, England. s.*
Education: 1951–54 Enfield Inf. and Jun. Sch.; 1955 Hexthorpe Jun. Sch, Doncaster; 1956–58 Tang Hall Jun. Sch., York; 1958–65 Mill Mount Grammar Sch., York; 1965–68 Royal Holloway Coll., London Univ.; 1971–73 Birmingham Univ.; 1970–73 Queens. *Appointments:* 1973–76 Ebbw Vale; 1976–81 Cardiff.
Special Interests: Music, Nature Conservation. Hobbies and Recreations: Singing, Piano, Philately, Needlework.

GITTNER, George Edward, 17 Staincross Common, Mapplewell, Barnsley, South Yorkshire ST5 6JD. (0226-382318)–BA(Birm.). *b. 14 Oct 1938, Kingston-upon-Hull. m. 4 July 1964: 3s.*
Education: 1949–57 Hull Grammar Sch.; 1957–61 Queens Coll., St. Andrews Univ.; 1963–66 Birmingham Univ.; 1963–66 Handsworth Coll.
Appointments: 1966–72 Bury; 1972–77 Tunstall; 1977– Barnsley.
Connexional Committees: 1978– Education and Youth.
Special Interests: Christian Education, Childrens Youth Work, Scouting.
Hobbies and Recreations: Mathematics, Calligraphy.

GLASSON, Thomas Francis, 29 Bear Cross Ave., Bournemouth, Dorset BH11 9NU. (02016-5001)–BD, BD(Hons), MA, DD(Lond.). *b. 8 Oct 1906, Derby. m. 29 July 1937: 1d.*
Education: 1911–17 Clarence Rd. Prim. Sch., Derby; 1917–1921 Derby Municipal Secondary Sch.; 1930–33 Richmond. *Appointments:* 1933–36 Manchester and Salford Mission; 1936–39 Bradford Mission; 1939–44 Newcastle-under-Lyne; 1944–48 Windsor and Maidenhead; 1948–51 Richmond and Barnes; 1951–52 Supply; 1952–56 Redhill; 1956–60 London, Brixton Hill; 1960–72 New College, London, Lecturer in New Testament Studies and Biblical Theology.
Connexional Committees: 1946–72 Various Ministerial Training Committees (Probationers, Board of Studies, Richmond College Executive, Candidates). *Council Member:* Member of Studiorum Novi Testamenti Societas; 1975–81 Member of the Court of Southampton Univ. *Publications: Thomas Glasson: Lay Preacher* (1943), *The Second Advent: The Origin of the NT Doctrine* 1945 (3rd ed. 1963), *His Appearing and His Kingdom: The Christian Hope in the Light of its History* (1953), *Greek Influence in Jewish Eschatology* (1961), *Moses in the Fourth Gospel* (1963), *The Revelation of John* (1965), *Jesus and the End of the World* (1980), Drew Lecture (1968) *Human Destiny: Has Christian Teaching Changed?*
Special Interests: Eschatology. *Hobbies and Recreations:* Music.

GLEDHILL, Anthony Harry, Wesley Lodge, 17 Austin St., Hunstanton, Norfolk PE36 6AJ. (04853-2193) *b. 20 Dec 1921, Mansfield, Notts. m. 30 June 1951: 1d., 2s.*
Education: 1926–31 Prim. Sch., Crossgates, Leeds; 1931-39 Roundhay Sch., Leeds; 1947–49 Didsbury, Bristol. *Appointments:* 1946–47 Minehead; 1949–51 Ibiaku—Eastern Nigeria; 1951–56 Wye Valley Mission; 1956–60 Louth; 1960–65 Barton-on-Humber; 1965–72 Aberdare; 1972–78 Spalding; 1978– Hunstanton.
Special Interests: Hymnology, Liturgy. *Hobbies and Recreations:* Gardening, Wood Carving, Walking.

GLENDINNING, Kenneth Newton, 20 Wallwood Rd., Leytonstone, London E11 1DF. (01-539-4109)–BA(Manchester). *b. 24 Dec 1941, Aberdeen. m. 1 May 1982.*
Education: 1952–58 Spennymoor Grammar Sch., Co. Durham; 1962–67 Manchester Univ.; 1962–67 Hartley Victoria. *Appointments:* 1967–75 Leeds North East; 1975–81 Senior Community Relations Officer, Leeds; 1981– London Mission, Hackney.
Connexional Committees: 1982– Division of Social Responsibility.
Special Interests: Police, Community Relations. *Hobbies and Recreations:* Philately, Cricket, Ice Hockey.

GLOVER, Dorothy Joan (nee Moyle), Fernleigh, Agar Rd., Truro, Cornwall TR1 1JU. (0872-2914) *b. 13 Aug 1932, Higher Pentire, Helston, Cornwall. m. 8 Sept 1982.* *Education:* 1937–40 Gumwalloe Elem.; 1940–43 Mrs. Cox's Private Sch.; 1943–46 Helston Grammar Sch.; 1946–48 Edgehill Coll., Bideford; 1957–59 Wesley Deaconess Coll., Ilkley; 1970 Kingsmead, Selly Oak; 1974–75 Wesley House. *Appointments:* 1975–79 Hunstanton; 1979–80 Belize and Honduras Dt; 1980– Truro. *Connexional Committees:* 1981– Overseas Division Cornwall District Ministerial Secretary (present). *Special Interests:* Missionary Concern, Travel, Country Life. *Hobbies and Recreations:* Reading, Walking, Cooking and Housewifery.

GOADBY, Raymond, 2 Main Rd., Long Hanborough, Oxford OX7 2BE. (0993-882693) *b. 17 May 1932, Alfreton, Derbyshire. 3s.* *Education:* 1937–43 Ridgeway Jun. Sch.; 1943–44 Heage Secondary Modern Sch.; 1944–49 Herbert Strutt Grammar Sch., Belper; Currently Student of Open Univ.; 1957–60 Handsworth. *Appointments:* 1960–63 South Molton; 1963–68 Sheffield, Carver St.; 1968–71 Bishop Auckland; 1971–72 Halifax; 1972–77 Ulverston; 1977–80 Cannock Chase; 1980–82 President's List; 1982– Witney and Faringdon. *Special Interests:* Liturgy, Spirituality, Political Theology. *Hobbies and Recreations:* Drama, Cricket, Reading, Listening to Classical Music.

GOATLEY, John, 12 Glen Rd., Fleet, Aldershot, Hants GU13 9QR. (02514-7698)–BSc(Glasgow), BD(Lond.). *b. 3 June 1929, Saltash, Cornwall. m. 7 Oct 1957: 2d., 1s.* *Education:* 1938–43 Royal Merchant Navy Sch., Wokingham; 1943–47 Plymouth Coll.; 1951–55 Glasgow Univ.; 1958–61 Richmond. *Appointments:* 1961–71 Methodist Church, Sierra Leone; 1971–76 Exmouth and Budleigh Salterton; 1976– Aldershot, Farnborough and Camberley. *Connexional Committees:* 1972–76, 1978– M.C.O.D. Central Committee. *Special Interests:* World Mission, Christian Education. *Hobbies and Recreations:* Bee-Keeping, Walking, Cycling, Gardening, Singing in Choir.

GODDEN, Leonard Charles Willoughby, 28 Westover Rd., Westbury-on-Trym, Bristol BS9 3LZ. (0272-500548) *b. 3 Feb 1909, Weymouth, Dorset. m.: 1d.* *Education:* Weymouth Central Sch.; 1932–35 Didsbury. *Appointments:* 1931–32 East Cornwall Mission; 1932–35 Didsbury Coll.; 1935–37 Stoke-on-Trent (Stoke); 1937–40 Sheffield Mission; 1940–45 Huddersfield (High St.); 1945–47 Nottingham North; 1947–52 Somerset Mission; 1952–55 Helston; 1955–62 Bristol South; 1962–66 Bristol (Clifton and Redland). *Special Interests:* Mental Handicap (Chaplain at Brentry Hospital for Mentally Handicapped, Bristol).

GODDEN, Vernon John, 120 Hucclecote Rd., Gloucester GL3 3SB. (0452-66118) *b. 16 March 1938, Devizes, Wilts. m. 10 Aug 1963: 1d., 1s.* *Education:* 1946–53 Dauntsey's Sch., West Lavington, Wilts; 1956–68 Culham Coll.; 1962–65 Richmond. *Appointments:* 1965–68 Wellingborough; 1968–73 Winchester; 1973–81 Bristol (South); 1981– Gloucester. *Connexional Committees:* 1968– Prison Committee; 1981– Home Mission Board. *Special Interests:* Prison After-Care, Langley House Trust. *Hobbies and Recreations:* Gardening, Music.

GODFREY, Francis Charles, 138 Plymouth Rd., Redditch B97 4PA. (0527-41243)–BSc, BD. *b. 29 Nov 1926, Middlesbrough. m. 28 July 1956: 1d., 2s.* *Education:* 1937–41 Acklam Hall, Middlesbrough; 1942–23 Malet Lambert, Hull; 1944–47, 1949 Hull Univ.; 1951–53 Headingley. *Appointments:* 1954–55 Ashby de la Zouche; 1956–61 Burton on Trent; 1962–66 Nottingham South; 1967–74 Redhill and Reigate; 1975– Redditch. *Connexional Committees:* Joint Church Buildings Committee. *Local Council Committees:* 1971–72 Education Committee (Crawley). *Publications:* Epworth Review. *Special Interests:* Counselling and Group Work. *Hobbies and Recreations:* Piano, Painting, Wine Making, Sport—when younger.

GOLDHAWK, Norman Panter, Nestor, Norfolk Rd., South Holmwood, Dorking, Surrey RH5 4LA. (0306-67165)–BA(Lond.), MA(Cantab.). *b. 1 Oct 1909, Wealdstone, Harrow, Middlesex. m. 29 July 1935: 2d., 1s.* *Education:* 1916–20 Quainton Hall, Harrow; 1920–26 The John Lyon Sch., Harrow; 1926–30 Univ. Coll., London; 1933–34 Marburg Univ., Germany; 1944–47 New Coll., Edinburgh; 1930–33 Wesley House. *Appointments:* 1934–37 Edinburgh, Nicholson Sq.; 1937–42 Edinburgh Mission; 1942–47 Higham Ferrers; 1947–52 London, Kilburn and Hampstead; 1952–71 Richmond Coll., Tutor Church History and History of Christian Doctrine. *Connexional Committees:* Methodist Catechism (Junior 1951; Senior 1952); 1952–71 Ministerial Training; 1952–71 Board of Studies; 1966–69 Hymns and Songs (Convener); 1955– History of Methodism; 1968– Methodist Church Music Society (Chairman); 1947–71 Wesley House Governors; 1952–71 Richmond. *Publications: Communism, Capitalism and Christianity* (Brunner, E., Eng. Trans. 1949); *Two Types of Faith* (Buber, M., Eng. Trans. 1951); *John Wesley, A Theological Biography* (Schmidt, M., Eng. Trans. Vol.I 1962, Vol.II PtI 1966); *The Church in an Approach to Christian Doctrine* (Ed. Lewis 1954); *An Outline of Church History* in *The Preacher's Handbook* (Vol.V 1957, Vol.VI 1959, Vol.VII 1961); Articles in *The London Quarterly & Holborn Review* and in *The Hymn Society of Great Britain and Ireland Bulletin*; *Die Freikirchliche Tradition in England* in *Die*

Sammlung (Dec. 1954); *The Methodist People in the Early Victorian Age* in *A History of the Methodist Church in Great Britain* (Vol.II 1978); *William Paley: or The Eighteenth Century Revisited* in *Providence* (Ed. M. Wiles 1979); *On Hymns and Hymn-Books* (1979). *Special Interests:* Theology, Music. *Hobbies and Recreations:* Radio 3, Playing and Listening to Piano and Organ.

GOLDING, Edward R., 172 Northwich Rd., Weaverham, Northwich, Ches. CW8 3AY. (0606-852329)–BA(Manchester). *b. 24 Aug 1920, Darlington, Co. Durham. m. 11 March 1950: 2s.*
Education: 1925–31 Corporation Rd., Darlington; 1932–39 Queen Elizabeth Grammar Sch., Darlington; 1947–50 Manchester Univ.; 1947–50 Hartley Victoria. *Appointments:* 1946–47 Motherwell; 1950–53 Dudley; 1954 Manchester (Wythenshawe); 1955–56 Manchester and Salford Mission; 1957–64 Penrith; 1965–69 Barnard Castle; 1970–76 Newcastle-upon-Tyne (Heaton and Wallsend); 1977–81 Hull (West); 1982– Northwich.
Connexional Committees: 1961–64 Local Preachers.
Special Interests: Lake District Fell Walking. *Hobbies and Recreations:* Photography, Gardening, Woodwork.

GOLLINS, Robert William, 1 Prospect Villas, Whitehill Rd., Halifax, W. Yorks HX2 9SS. (0422-244418) *b. 5 Jan 1939, Bromborough, Cheshire. m. 22 Aug 1964: 1d., 3s.*
Education: Ashville Coll., Harrogate; Withernsea High Sch., Holderness; Salford Grammar Sch.; Hartley Victoria. *Appointments:* 1965–67 Holyhead; 1967–72 Wrexham; 1972–77 Sandbach and Alsager; 1977– Halifax.
Connexional Committees: 1981– Social Responsibility, Politics and Economics Committee.
Special Interests: Education (Schools), Local Authority Health Care, Social Responsibility, Youth Work. *Hobbies and Recreations:* Walking, Music, Camping, Fishing, Art.

GOOCH, Colin Norman, 14 New Rd., Ilminster, Somerset TA19 9AE. (046-05-2839) *b. 1 June 1943, Luton, Bedfordshire. m. 2 Sept 1967: 2d., 2s.*
Education: 1954–59 Luton Grammar Sch.; 1966–69 Richmond.
Appointments: 1969–72 Craven Arms and Church Stretton; 1972–76 Barnstaple; 1976–79 Tavistock; 1979– South Petherton and Crewkerne.

GOODALL, Guy Robin, 21 Gloucester Ave., Chelmsford, Essex CM2 9DP. (0245-56766) *b. 16 March 1948, Bromley. m. June 1970: 2d.*
Education: Judd Sch., Tonbridge; 1968 Cliff College; 1969–72 Wesley, Bristol. *Appointments:* 1972–75 Preston (Lune St. & Orchard); 1975–79 Great Harwood; 1979– Chelmsford.
Connexional Committees: Division of Education and Youth Training and Resources Advisory Group.
Special Interests: Broadcasting, Church Growth. *Hobbies and Recreations:* Gardening, Ornithology, Sport (general).

GOODBURN, John Raymond, 23 South Canterbury Rd., Canterbury, Kent CT1 3LH. (0227-63180)–BA(Leeds), BA(Cantab.). *b. 25 Sept 1940, Burnley, Lancashire. m. 14 Aug 1965: 3d.*
Education: 1946–52 Cockton Hill Prim. Sch., Bishop Auckland; 1952–59 King James First Grammar Sch., Bishop Auckland; 1959–62 Leeds Univ.; 1962–65 Wesley House.
Appointments: 1965–67 Assistant Tutor, Handsworth Coll.; 1967–72 Birmingham South West; 1972–75 Maidstone; 1975– Canterbury and Faversham.
Connexional Committees: 1973–75 Board of Division of Ministries.
Special Interests: Chaplaincy in Higher Education. *Hobbies and Recreations:* Photography, Music, Sport.

GOODE, Raymond John, 83 Dog Kennel Lane, Oldbury, Warley, West Midlands B68 9LZ. (021-552-2145) *b. 10 March 1944, Blackheath, Birmingham. m. 21 Aug 1971: 1d.*
Education: 1949–54 Beeches Rd. Prim./Jun. Sch.; 1954–59 Britannia Rd. Secondary Sch.; Blackheath, Birmingham; 1968–72 Hartley Victoria. *Appointments:* 1972–76 Hunts Mission; 1976– Oldbury.
Hobbies and Recreations: Reading.

GOODRIDGE, Ernest Noel, Fieldings, 15 Oaklands Gate, Northwood, Middlesex HA6 3AA. (092-74-21034)–MA(Cantab.). *b. 24 Dec 1921, Thrapston, Northants. m. 16 Aug 1948: 1d., 2s.*
Education: 1933–41 Kingswood Sch., Bath; 1946–49 Emmanuel Coll., Cambridge; 1948–49 Wesley House. *Appointments:* 1949–53 Walls, Shetland; 1953–59 Banbury; 1959–63 Bicester; 1963–70 Croydon (S. Norwood); 1970–77 Bournemouth; 1977– Harrow.
Local Council Committees: 1965–70 Croydon Education Committee, Religious Advisory Sub Committee; 1964–70 Secretary Croydon Council of Churches; 1971–77 Secretary Bournemouth Council of Churches.
Publications: Experiment in Unity (Mowbrays 1968) with Neville B. Cryer.
Special Interests: Ecumenical Relations, Church and Community Relations. *Hobbies and Recreations:* Carpentry, Photography.

GOODRIDGE, Joseph, 73B London Rd., Peterborough, Cambridgeshire PE2 9BS. (0733-54514) *b. 11 Sept 1933, Northampton. m. 16 Aug 1979.*
Education: 1954–56 Cliff Coll.; 1956–60 Hartley Victoria.
Appointments: 1960–61 Liverpool Linacre Mission; 1961–62 Snaith; 1962–74 Church of South India; 1974–78 Kettering and Corby; 1978– Peterborough.
Special Interests: Indian Art, Poetry, Customs. *Hobbies and Recreations:* Walking, Climbing, Tennis, Photography.

GOODWIN, Rowland, 30 Daresbury Rd., Chorlton-Cum-Hardy, Manchester M21 1WA. (061-881-6799)—BA(Manchester), BD(Lond.). *b. 1 Sept 1929, Rixton, Nr. Warrington. m. 11 Aug 1956: 2d., 1s.*
Education: 1935–40 Hollins Green CE Sch.; 1940–48 Urmston Grammar Sch.; 1951–54 Manchester Univ.; 1954–56 London Univ. (External); 1951–54 Hartley Victoria.
Appointments: 1950–51 Carlisle, Cecil St.; 1954–56 Linacre Mission; 1956–60 Staple Hill and Fishponds; 1960–65 Motherwell and Wishaw; 1965–80 Industrial Chaplain Darlington District; 1980– Industrial Chaplain Manchester and Stockport District.
Connexional Committees: 1966–79 Team Ministries; 1965–72, 1980– Church in Industry. *Local Council Committees:* 1969–74 Darlington Borough Council Careers Committee; 1976–80 Durham County Manpower Committee. *Publications: Stress at Work* (1976); Luton Industrial Coll. Foundation Lecture (1976); *The Micro Revolution* (1978); *Micros and Men* (1979); *Employment Technology and Work* (1981).
Special Interests: Mission in Relation to Industry, Employment and The Future for Work. *Hobbies and Recreations:* Gardening, Reading, Camping, Music, Dog Breeding, Watching TV, Manchester United.

GORDON, Geoffrey Douglas, 5 St. Davids Way, Marlborough, Wilts SN8 1DH. (0672-52457)—BA, BD(Manchester). *b. 19 July 1937, Sutton, Surrey. m. 25 June 1960: 1d., 1s.*
Education: 1947–55 Trinity Sch. of John Whitgift, Croydon; 1955–60 Manchester Univ.; 1958–60 Hartley Victoria. *Appointments:* 1960–65 Antigua; 1966–71 Dominica; 1971–79 Hinckley; 1979– Marlborough.
Connexional Committees: 1973–79 Overseas Division.
Hobbies and Recreations: Gardening, Transport, Philately.

GOSS, Brian William, 46 Lyndhurst Gdns., Barking, Essex IG11 9YB. (01-594-3552)—MA(Cantab.), BA(Reading). *b. 15 Oct 1931, Reading. m. 4 Aug 1962: 2s.*
Education: 1936–39 Alfred Sutton Sch., Reading; 1939–50 Reading Sch.; 1950–53 Univ. of Reading; 1953–55 Wesley House.
Appointments: 1955–58 Poole; 1958–64 Bury; 1964–69 Ipswich; 1969–76 Harrow; 1976–81 Romford; 1981– London Mission (East Ham).
Connexional Committees: 1974–79 D.S.R. World Development Committee; 1979– D.S.R. Healing & Pastoral Ministry Committee.
Special Interests: Suicide Prevention, Counselling.

HE & WIFE & 2 SONS KILLED IN ROAD ACCIDENT

GOUGH, Samuel Frederick, 105 Dale Rd., Rawmarsh, Rotherham. *b. 19 Sept 1939, Dudleston Heath, Ellesmere, Salop. m. 9 Aug 1969: 4s.* YOUNGER SURVIVING SON – TIM GOUGH (G.P.)
Education: 5–11 yrs. Chriftins Ellesmere Secondary Modern; 1965–66 Cliff Coll.; 1966–70 Hartley Victoria. *Appointments:* 1970–72 Bridlington; 1972–75 York North; 1975–82 Pickering; 1982– Rotherham.
Special Interests: Charismatic Renewal, Cliff Coll., Encouraging Evangelicals to be concerned about social matters; Chairman of Local Peace Movement at Pickering.
Hobbies and Recreations: Photography, Bird Watching, Any kind of Sports (excluding Blood Sports), Light Reading.

GOWLAND, William, Luton Industrial Coll., Chapel St., Luton LU1 2SE. (052-29374) *b. 3 Oct 1911, Richmond, Yorks. m. 17 Aug 1939: 1d., 3s.*
Education: 1916–26 Cleasby and Blackwells Schs.; 1926–32 Darlington Technical Coll.; 1932–35 Hartley Victoria. *Appointments:* 1935–39 Castletown, Isle of Man; 1939–48 Tilehurst; 1948–54 Manchester and Salford Mission, Albert Hall; 1954 Luton Industrial Coll., Principal, 1979, President of the Conference.
Publications: Militant and Triumphant (1954) Re-printed Australia (1956) and U.S.A. (1958); *The Glide Lecture* (U.S.A.); The Beckley Lecture.
Hobbies and Recreations: Gardening, Photography, Fishing.

GOWMAN, Douglas Harold, 119 Melton Rd., West Bridgford, Nottingham NG2 6FG. (0602-233292)—BD. *b. 20 Dec 1920, Paignton, Devon. m. 20 Aug 1949: 2d.*
Education: Townhill Sch., Swansea; Dynevor Secondary Sch., Swansea; 1945–48 Hartley Victoria.
Appointments: 1948–50 Hanley; 1950–53 Rhondda; 1953–60 Chelmsford; 1960–67 Torquay and Paignton; 1967–78 Gravesend; 1978– Nottingham South.

GOY, Leslie R., Belwood, 28 Ashgarth Court, Rossett Green, Harrogate HG2 9LE. (0423-870150) *b. 7 June 1912, Old Brumby, Scunthorpe, Lincs. m. 17 Aug 1940: 1d., 2s.*
Education: Scunthorpe Central Sch.; 1933–37 Hartley Victoria.
Appointments: 1937–39 Hull, Anlaby Rd.; 1939–40 Leeds, Chapel Allerton; 1940–43 Hull, Waltham St.; 1943–45 Leeds Chapel, Allerton; 1945–52 Harrogate; 1952–56 London Westminster; 1956–61 Birmingham Mission; 1961–68 London, Kilburn; 1968–74 Dunstable; 1974 Harrogate.
Connexional Committees: 1942–52 Methodist Youth; 1954–61 Home Missions. *Publications: Club Prayers & Club Fellowship* (M.Y.D.).
Special Interests: TV (1957–69 Adviser ITV). *Hobbies and Recreations:* Gardening, Painting.

GRAHAM, Douglas, 32 Bower Mount Rd., Maidstone, Kent ME16 8AU. (0622-58801) *b. 19 March 1933, Bacup, Lancashire. m. 12 Aug 1961: 3s.*
Education: Prim., Secondary, Education at Local State Schs. in Bacup; 1945–48 Accrington Technical Sch.; 1948–54 Burnley Municipal Coll., Further Education; 1957–61 Handsworth.
Appointments: 1961–66 Fleetwood; 1966–70 Leighton Buzzard; 1970–75 Doncaster; 1975–80 High Wycombe; 1980– Maidstone.

Local Council Committees: 1971–74 Doncaster Education Committee. *Special Interests:* Member of Methodist Revival Fellowship, Conservative Evangelicals in Methodism. *Hobbies and Recreations:* Electronics, Photography.

GRAHAM, George, Four Acres, 122 Lancaster Rd., Cabus, Garstang, Preston, Lancs PR3 1JE. (09952-3261).
Education: 1951–54 Headingley. *Appointments:* 1950–51 Hartlepool; 1954–60 Wishaw; 1960–65 Rotherham; 1965–66 Dewsbury; 1966–70 Thetford; 1970–73 Merthyr Tydfil; 1973–81 Grassington; 1981– Garstang.

GRAHAM, Ian Thomas Falcus, 122 Leigh Rd., Eastleigh, Hants SO5 4DU. (0703-612871) *b. 21 March 1928, Wallsend on Tyne. m. 2 Aug 1952: 1d., 1s.*
Education: Newcastle Royal Grammar Sch.; 1949–52 Hartley Victoria. *Appointments:* 1952–58 Church of South India; 1958–62 Wye Valley Mission; 1962–69 Cannock Chase; 1969–73 Cradley Heath; 1973–81 Exeter; 1981– Eastleigh.
Hobbies and Recreations: Music, Photography.

GRAHAM, James Neil, 10 Harrogate Rd., Ripon, North Yorkshire HE4 1SR. (0765-2439) *b. 4 July 1929, Birmingham. m. 21 July 1956: 1s.*
Education: 1934–37 Hyssington (Montgomery); 1937–40 Thirsk (Yorks), British and Foreign; 1940–44 Topcliffe (Yorks.); 1944–45 Ashville Coll.; 1951–52 Cliff Coll.; 1952–55 Headingley. *Appointments:* 1951–52 Ledbury; 1955–57 Pateley Bridge; 1957–62 Wensleydale; 1962–69 Sleaford; 1969–76 Ryedale; 1976– Ripon and Masham.
Special Interests: Rural Methodism.
Hobbies and Recreations: Walking.

GRAHAM, John George, 8 West Mead Court, Standens Barn, Northampton NN3 3TF. (0604-413177) *b. 27 Jan 1943, Penrith; m. 14 April 1973: 1d.*
Education: 1947–53 Sutton-on-Sea; 1953–60 Alford Grammar; 1966–67 Cliff Coll.; 1969–70 Handsworth; 1970–73 Queens. *Appointments:* 1973–76 London Mission (West); 1976– Northampton.
Hobbies and Recreations: Restoring Old Furniture, Re-Making Old Cycles, Gardening, Photography, Swimming, Golf, Squash.

GRANT, Alan Henry, 50 Carter St., Sandown, Isle of Wight PO36 8DQ. (0983-405157) *b. 2 Sept 1910, Cleethorpes, Lincs. m. 8 Aug 1942: 2d.*
Education: 1934–38 Hartley Victoria. *Appointments:* 1938–40 Gateshead West; 1940 Newcastle Central and Sandyford; 1941–43 Manchester, Oldham St., Blackburn Mission; 1943–48 Sunderland North; 1948–52 London, Finchley and Hendon; 1952–57 London, Wanstead and Woodford; 1957–60 Shetland; 1960–68 Lincoln North; 1968–73 Leeds North East.
Connexional Committees: 1957–60 Stationing Committee.
Special Interests: History, Music.
Hobbies and Recreations: Gardening, Walking.

GRANT, John Reid, 9 Helmsley Close, Shiney Row, Tyne and Wear DH4 7ND. (038-579-852778)–BA(Birmingham). *b. 8 Aug 1937, Newburn-on-Tyne. s.*
Education: 1948–56 Tynemouth High Sch.; 1959–62 Birmingham Univ.; 1963–64 Pittsburgh Theological Seminary (USA); 1958 Cliff Coll.; 1959–63 Handsworth. *Appointments:* 1964–65 Marlborough; 1965–68 Bradford, Great Horton; 1968–71 Stockton-on-Tees; 1971–74 Weardale; 1974–76 Birmingham, Elmdon; 1976– Houghton-le-Spring.

GRASBY, Derek, Bestwood Park Church Flat, Beckhampton Rd., Bestwood Park, Nottingham NG5 5NG. (0602-264486)–BA(Bristol), MA(Bristol). *b. 20 March 1956, Leeds. s.*
Education: 1965–68 St. Vincents R.C. Sch. (for blind and partially sighted), Liverpool; 1968–74 Exhall Grange Sch. (partially sighted and physically handicapped), Coventry; 1974–76 Southport Technical Coll., Merseyside; 1977–81 Bristol Univ.; Wesley, Bristol. *Appointments:* 1981– Nottingham Central.
Special Interests: New Testament Studies, Christian Social Responsibility. *Hobbies and Recreations:* Walking, Photography, Theatre and Concert Going, Reading.

GRAVES, Peter Charles, 29 West Hill Ave., Epsom, Surrey KT19 8LE. (20521)–ThM, DMin. *b. 23 March 1943, Bromley, Kent. m. 17 July 1976: 2s.*
Education: 1948–54 Sherrington Rd. Prim., London SE7; 1954–56 Eltham Central Sch., London SE9; 1956–61 Eltham Green Sch. (Comprehensive) SE9; 1967–68, 1973–74 Union Theological Seminary, Virginia, USA; 1975–76 London Univ., Garnet Coll.; 1963–67 Handsworth. *Appointments:* 1966–68 Guest Staff Minister, Shiloh Church, Dayton, Ohio, USA; 1968–69 Enfield; 1969–72 Highgate; 1972–76 Chaplain and Lecturer, Middlesex Poly.; 1976–77 Chaplain and Senior Lecturer in Religious Studies; 1977–79 Head of Student Welfare; 1979– Sutton.
Connexional Committees: Former member of Healing and Pastoral Ministry; Sector Ministry; Student Work; Central Committee MCOD; Overseas Service Committee MCOD and Pastoral Oversight Committee of Wesley House, Cambridge; No present membership of any Connexional Committee.
Special Interests: Pastoral Ministry, Evangelism. *Hobbies and Recreations:* Travel, Theatre.

GRAY, John Richard, 24 St. Edmunds Rd., Felixstowe, Suffolk IP11 8DJ. (03942-72312)–BA(Leeds), MA(Leeds). *b. 26 Nov 1915, Buxton, Derbyshire. m. 1 Jan 1945: 1d., 1s.*
Education: 1921–26 Kents Bank Rd. Sch., Buxton; 1926–31 Buxton Coll.; 1938–41 Leeds Univ.; 1938–41 Headingley. *Appointments:* 1941–45 London (Shepherds Bush); 1945–51

Norton-on-Tees; 1951–59 Darlington; 1959–64 Glossop; 1964–71 Ipswich; 1971–77 Swansea; 1977–81 Cardiff.
Special Interests: C. Wesley, J. S. Bach. *Hobbies and Recreations:* Horticulture, Oenology.

GRAY, John Thomas, 8 St. Andrews Lane, Titchmarsh, Kettering, Northants NN14 3DN. (08012-3267) *b. 29 Aug 1896, Titchmarsh. m. 22 March 1954.*
Education: 1900–10 Titchmarsh CE Sch.; 1926–27 Cliff Coll.
Appointments: 1929–32 Southall and Uxbridge Mission; 1932–36 Bury St. Edmunds and Sudbury; 1936–42 Liverpool, Grove St. and Woolton; 1942–49 Birmingham, Sutton Park; 1949–55 Blackheath; 1955–62 Birmingham, Smethwick; 1962–67 Coventry.
Connexional Committees: 1945–56 Home Missions.
Hobbies and Recreations: Gardening.

GRAY, Peter Raymond, 91 Birch Rd., Berry Brow, Huddersfield HD4 7LP. (0484-661473) *b. 16 Mar 1943, Nottingham. m. 25 July 1978.*
Education: 1948–50 Fairweather Green Inf., Bradford; 1950–54 Daisy Hill Jun., Bradford; 1954–59 Bradford Grammar Sch.; 1962–63 Cliff Coll.; 1965–68 Richmond. *Appointments:* 1968–69 Ipswich; 1969–72 Bradford (Trinity); 1972–77 Ilkley; 1977– Huddersfield (Pennine).
Hobbies and Recreations: Actively involved with Historic Commercial Vehicle Club (I am the owner of two preserved buses).

GRAYSTON, Kenneth, 11 Rockleaze Ave., Bristol BS9 1NG. (0272-683872)—MA(Oxon), MA(Cantab.). *b. 8 July 1914, Sheffield. m. 1942.*
Education: 1925–33 Colfe's Grammar Sch., Lewisham, London; 1933–37 Univ. of Oxford; 1937–41 Univ. of Cambridge; 1937–41 Wesley House. *Appointments:* 1941–42 Highgate; 1942–44 Royal Ordnance Factory Chaplain, Cumberland; 1944–49 Assistant Head of Religious Broadcasting, BBC, London; 1949–65 Tutor in New Testament Language and Literature, Didsbury Coll., Bristol; 1965–79 Professor of Theology, Univ. of Bristol; 1973–75 Dean of Faculty of Arts; 1976–79 Pro-Vice-Chancellor.
Connexional Committees: 1949–66 Ministerial Training Committee; 1955–65 Secretary of Studiorum Novi Testamenti Societas; 1960– Member of Joint Committee on Translation of New English Bible; 1971–76 Chairman Christian Aid Scholarships Committee.
Publications: Epistles to Galatians and Philippians (1957); *Epistles to Philippians and Thessalonians* (1967); A Large Number of Lectures, Articles in Various Journals.
Special Interests: New Testament Studies. *Hobbies and Recreations:* Walking, Travel.

GREAVES, Henry, 7 Hackness Drive, Scarborough, N. Yorks YO12 5SB. (0723-62306)—LLB.
Education: 1939–40 Didsbury.
Appointments: 1940–43 Hurst and Hyde; 1943–46 Rawtenstall; 1946–49 Cadishead; 1949–54 Manchester, Pendleton; 1954–62 Gateshead West and Blaydon; 1962–67 Sheffield, Ecclesall; 1967–72 Macclesfield.

GREEN, Frederick Pratt, 96 Hillcrest Rd., Thorpe, St. Andrew, Norwich NR7 0JR. Hon DHL Emory Univ., Atlanta, Georgia, U.S.A. *b. 2 Sept 1903, Liverpool. m. 6 Aug 1931.*
Education: 1910–13 Huyton High Sch.; 1913–17 Wallasey Grammar Sch.; 1917–20 Rydal Sch., Colwyn Bay, 1925–28 Didsbury.
Appointments: 1924 Severn Valley Mission, 1928–31 Filey; 1931–34 Otley; 1934–39 Manningham, Bradford; 1939–44 Ilford, London; 1944–47 Finsbury Park, London; 1947–52 South Norwood, London; 1952–57 The Dome Mission, Brighton; 1957–64 Chairman of York and Hull District; 1964–69 Sutton, Surrey.
Connexional Committees: 1957–64 General Purposes Committee, Stationing Committee. *Publications:* Poetry: *This Unlikely Earth* (1952); *The Skating Parson* (1965); *The Old Couple* (1976); Hymns: *26 Hymns* (1971); *Hymns and Ballads* (1982); Rep. in most contemporary Hymn Books.
Special Interests: General Literature, Music.

GREEN, Peter Geoffrey, 20 Wharf Rd., Higham Ferrers, Wellingborough, Northants NN9 8BQ. (0933-312230) *b. 23 Oct 1943, Leicester. m. 1. 16 Aug 1969 (deceased) 2. 24 July 1982: 2d.*
Education: 1955–60 Rushey Mead Boys, Leicester; 1960–62 Wyggeston Boys Grammar, Leicester; 1968–69 National Youth Leaders Training Coll.; 1964–65 Cliff Coll.; 1965–69 Richmond. *Appointments:* 1969–76 Oswestry, Ellesmere and Chirk; 1976–82 Kidderminster and Stourport; 1982– Higham Ferrers; 1977–81 Education and Youth District Secretary (Wolverhampton and Shrewsbury District); 1971–76 Free Church Chaplain Chirk Hospital.
Connexional Committees: 1977–79 Board of Division of Education and Youth. *Publications:* Article: The Preacher at His Prayers in *Worship and Preaching* (Methodist Publishing House October 1975); Article: Pulled by a Bishop in *The Expository Times* (T&T Clark, Edinburgh August 1981).
Special Interests: Methodist Children's Work, Ministry of Healing, Christian Literature for Lay People.
Hobbies and Recreations: Classical Music, Detective Fiction, Lawn Tennis, Walking.

GREEN, Walter Francis, 7 Heol Fargoed, Bargoed, Mid-Glamorgan CF8 8PP. *b. 5 Oct 1913, Ferndale, Rhondda, Glamorgan, South Wales. m. 6 Jan 1945: 2d, 4s*
Education: 1917–27 Ferndale Inf. and Jun.; 1938–40 Handsworth; 1940–41 Hartley Victoria; 1941–42 St. Austell; 1942–43 Marazion; 1943–45 Bury St. Edmunds; 1945–48 Thetford; 1948–51 Dalecroft; 1951–55 Forest of Dean; 1955–60 Brynmour; 1960–65 Bridgend; 1965–78 Rhymney Valley.
Hobbies and Recreations: Gardening.

GREEN, Wilfred, 28 Northcliffe, Great Harwood, Blackburn BB6 7PJ. (0254-886128).
Education: 1951–54 Hartley Victoria. *Appointments:* 1954–55 Knighton; 1955–57 Watford; 1957–61 Liverpool South; 1961–67 Liverpool North; 1967–70 Carlisle; 1970–79 Fleetwood; 1979– Great Harwood.

GREENAWAY, Guy Ernest, 5 Raley Rd., Locks Heath, Nr. Southampton, Hants SO3 6PA. (04895-2036) *b. 28 Jan 1916, Stroud, Glos. m. 1. 8 Aug 1944 (deceased) 2. 4 Dec 1957: 2s.*
Education: 1930 Stroud Inf., Castle St., Stroud Elem. Boys, Brick Row; 1934–35 Cliff Coll.; 1936–39 Handsworth. *Appointments:* 1939–42 Cowbridge and St. Athan; 1942–44 London, Finchley and Hendon; 1944–46 Ilford; 1947–59 Chaplain HMF; 1959–62 Stroud and Cirencester; 1962–69 Bristol South; 1969–74 Bristol Clifton and Redland; 1974–80 Swindon.
Hobbies and Recreations: Tennis, Swimming, Gardening, Camping and Caravanning.

GREET, Brian Aubrey, 37 Sutton Passeys Cresc., Wollaton Park, Nottingham NG8 1BX. (0602-787598)–BA(Birmingham), BD(Manchester), STM(Drew).*b. 12 June 1922, Bristol. m. 3 July 1954: 1d., 1s.*
Education: 1927–33 Sefton Park Prim.; 1933–38 Fairfield Grammar; 1947–51 Univ. of Birmingham; 1951–52 Drew Univ. (NJ, USA); 1954–58 Univ. of Manchester; 1947–51 Handsworth. *Appointments:* 1945 Burnley Fulledge; 1945–47 South Devon Mission; 1952–54 Mansfield Central; 1954–58 Manchester and Salford Mission; 1958–63 Wallasey; 1963–69 Birmingham, Elmdon; 1969–73 Guildford; 1973– Chairman Nottingham and Derby District.
Connexional Committees: 1958–63 MYD; 1973–81 District Chairman; 1979– City Centre; 1977–80 Joint Buildings; 1979–82 Presidents Council; 1979–82 Home Mission Exec. *Publications: To Communion With Confidence* (Published in USA as *Broken Bread in a Broken World*); *What Makes a Minister?* (1979); Contributions to symposia *In Church* and *Preachers Handbook Number II.*
Special Interests: History of Art. *Hobbies and Recreations:* Gardening, Travel, Piano, DIY.

GREET, Kenneth Gerald, 16 Orchard Ave., Shirley, Croydon, Surrey CR0 8UA. (01-777-5376)–DD. *b. 17 Nov 1918, Bristol. m. 26 July 1947: 2s., 1s.*
Education: 1930–35 Cotham Grammar Sch., Bristol; 1945–47 Handsworth. *Appointments:*1943–45 Bridgend; 1945–47 Handsworth Coll.; 1947–54 Rhondda; 1954–71 Secretary Department of Christian Citizenship; 1971– Secretary of Conference; 1980– President of the Conference.
Connexional Committees: All Connexional Committees.
Publications: The Mutual Society (1962); *Man and Wife Together* (1962); *Large Petitions* (1964); *Guide to Loving* (1965); *The Debate about Drink* (1969); *The Sunday Question* (1970); *The Art of Moral Judgement* (1970); *When the Spirit Moves* (1975); *Lion from a Thicket* (1979); *The Big Sin* (1982).
Hobbies and Recreations: Tennis, Photography.

GREETHAM, Eddie, 7 Lynmouth Close, North Hykeham, Lincoln LN6 8UJ. (0522-693177) *b. 22 Aug 1916, West Pinchbeck, Lincolnshire. m. 1 Jan 1943: 2d.*
Education: 1936–39 Richmond. *Appointments:* 1939–44 Bristol South; 1944–49 Lincoln (Aldersgate); 1949–54 Hull (Coltman St.); 1954–59 Guernsey; 1959–65 Sheffield (Ecclesall); 1965–70 Chesterfield; 1970–76 Norwich (Calvert St.); 1976–81 Reading.
Connexional Committees: 1958–59 Methodist Association of Youth Clubs, President; 1959–67 Youth; 1975–81 Methodist Homes for the Aged (Board of Management).

GREEVES, Denise M., 32 Kingswood Ave., London NW6 6LR. (01-969-4004)–BD. *w.*
Education: Wesley Deaconess Coll., Ilkley, Kingsmead Selly Oak, Wesley House. *Appointments:* 1975–78 Liverpool, Crosby; 1978– London Mission (North West).
Connexional Committees: 1971–79 Team Ministries; 1979– Social Responsibility, Social Questions. *Council Member:* Paddington Christian Council, Chairman.

GREEVES, Derrick Amphlet, Red Barn, Langwathby, Penrith, Cumbria CA10 1LW. (076-881-707)–MA. *b. 29 June 1913, Bowden, Cheshire. m. 19 July 1942, 3d., 1s.*
Education: 1923–25 Bolton Sch.; 1925–30 Preston Grammar Sch.; 1931–34 Manchester Univ.; 1934–37 Cambridge Univ.; 1934–37 Wesley House. *Appointments:*1937–38 President's List; 1938–39 London, Barnet; 1939–43 Bristol, Redland; 1943–47 Chaplain HMF; 1947–52 London, South Norwood; 1952–55 London, Finsbury Park; 1955–64 London, Westminster; 1964–69 Guildford; 1969–74 Worcester; 1974–78 Salisbury.
Connexional Committees: Overseas; Church Membership; General Purposes, President's Council, Kingswood Sch.; Trinity Hall Sch. *Council Member:* Central Religious Advisory Council; Religious Adviser Television and Rediffusion.
Publications: Christ in Me (1962); *A Word in Your Ear* (1970); *Preaching Through St. Paul* (1980).
Special Interests: Biography and Family Life. *Hobbies and Recreations:* Gardening, Water Colour Painting.

GREEVES, Frederic, 1 Westmorland House, Durdham Park, Bristol BS6 6XH. (0272-741594)–BA(Manchester), MA(Camb.), Hon LLD(Bristol). *b. 1 June 1903, Sidcup. m. 29 Nov 1929: 1d., 1s.*
Education: 1911–14 Wallasey Grammar; 1914–19 Merchant Taylors' Sch. (Crosby); 1921–24 Manchester Univ.; 1930–31 Cambridge Univ.; 1923–24 Didsbury. *Appointments:* 1924–27 Assistant Tutor (Didsbury College); 1928–30 Cheltenham; 1930–33 Cambridge; 1933–39 Sutton, Surrey; 1939–46 Oxford; 1946–66 Didsbury Coll., Bristol, Tutor; 1949–66 Principal.

Publications: Jesus the Son of God (1939 and 1947); *The Christian Way* (1945 and 1965); Fernley-Hartley Lecture: *The Meaning of Sin* (1956); Cato Lecture: *Theology and the Cure of Souls* (1960).

GREGORY, Arthur Stephen, 4 Appelrigg, Kendal, Cumbria LA9 6EA. (0539-22072)–MA(Oxon). *b. 21 Jan 1895, Bedford. m. 6 Aug 1926: 2d., 1s.*
Education: 1906–14 Kingswood; 1914–15, 1919–21 Trinity College, Oxford. *Appointments:* 1922–23 Marlborough Mission; 1923–24 Withernsea; 1924–26 Handsworth Coll. (A.T.); 1926–27 Jersey (Eng.); 1927–30 Macclesfield; 1930–33 Sutton, Sy.; 1933–36 Southport (South); 1936–39 Bradford (Manningham); 1939–42 Letchworth; 1942–46 Leeds (Headingley); 1946–50 Kendal; 1950–55 Nantwich; 1955–58 Halifax (Fairfield); 1958–62 St. Leonards and Bexhill.
Connexional Committees: 1931 Candidates (July) Committee; 1930–33 New Methodist Hymn Book.
Publications: The Church Which is His Body (1931); *Hymns and the Faith* (1934); *Psalms and Chanting* (1946); *Praises with Understanding* (1936, 1949, 1972).
Special Interests: Music, Hymnology.
Hobbies and Recreations: Pianoforte—Study and Practice, Gardening, Fell Walking.

GREGORY, David Ronald, Wesley Coll., Henbury Rd., Westbury-on-Trym, Bristol BS10 7QD. *b. 24 Dec 1942, North Tamerton, Cornwall. m. 4 Sept 1965.*
Education: Tamar Sch. for Boys, Plymouth; 1961–62 Co-Operative Training Coll.; 1981– Wesley, Bristol.
Special Interests: Youth Work (especially Boys' Brigade and Girls' Brigade). *Hobbies and Recreations:* DIY, Sport.

GREGORY, H. Michael, Woodlands, 543 Clydach Rd., Ynystawe, Swansea, West Glamorgan SA6 5AA. (0792-842550)–BA(Bristol). *b. 8 Nov 1936, Pontypool. m. 5 Aug 1963: 2s.*
Education: 1947–55 Jones' West Monmouth Grammar Sch., Pontypool; 1955–58 Univ. of Bristol; 1958–59 Univ. of Exeter; 1965–66 Univ. of Nottingham; 1978–80 Wesley, Bristol. *Appointments:* 1980–82 Swansea and Gower; 1982– Abergavenny.

GREGORY, Leslie David, Rydal Mount, Halifax Rd., Brighouse, West Yorks HD6 2QJ. (0484-714854) *b. 18 Dec 1919, Brentford End, Middlesex. m. 4 Nov 1954: 2s.*
Education: 1931–36 Isleworth County Grammar Sch.; 1945–47 Hartley Victoria. *Appointments:* 1947–49 Wishaw; 1949–50 Stanley; 1950–57 Carlisle; 1957–62 Ashington; 1962–66 Weston-super-Mare; 1966–71 Ashington; 1971–74 Shildon; 1974–79 Kendal; 1979– Brighouse.

GREWCOCK, Trevor, The Manse, Howden Rd., Barlby, Selby, North Yorks YO8 7HG. (0757-702223) *b. 4 Dec 1939, Ratby, Leicestershire. m. 20 Aug 1967: 2d.*
Education: Ratby Prim./Jun.; King Edward VII Grammar Sch., Coalville, Leics.; 1965–66 Cliff Coll.; 1967–70 Wesley, Bristol. *Appointments:* 1970–73 Thirsk; 1973–77 Thirsk and Boroughbridge; 1977–80 Burton-on-Trent; 1980– Snaith and Selby.

GREWER, Kenneth Stanley, 22 Highcroft Ave., Bispham, Blackpool FY2 0BJ. (0253-56018) *b. 3 June 1915, York. m. 27 July 1946: 2d., 1s.*
Education: 1920–29 Scarcroft Sch.; 1929–32 Commercial Coll.; 1939–40 Didsbury; 1940–42 Hartley Victoria. *Appointments:* 1942–44 Ill Health; 1944–46 Upwell and Manea; 1946–47 Cromer, Sheringham and Holt; 1947–49 North Walsham; 1949–52 Bolton; 1952–55 Huddersfield (Gledholt); 1955–62 Scarborough; 1962–68 Blackpool North; 1968–72 Sidmouth and Bridport; 1972–76 Peterborough; 1976–81 Wymondham, Attleborough and Watton.

Special Interests: Clinical Psychology and Sociology. *Hobbies and Recreations:* Gardening, Cricket.

GRIBBEN, Robert William, 23 Minster Yard, Lincoln LN2 1PY. (0522-25443)–BA(Melbourne), MA(Cantab.), Theol M(Melbourne Coll. of Divinity). *b. 7 March 1943, Mooroopna, Victoria, Australia. m. 29 June 1968: 1d., 1s.*
Education: 1954–60 Shepparton High Sch., Shepparton, Victoria, Australia; 1961–65 Queen's Coll., Univ. of Melbourne; 1970–75 Melbourne Coll. of Divinity; 1966–69 Wesley House. *Appointments:* 1970–74 Portland, Victoria; 1974–76 Key, Victoria; 1975–76 Chaplain, Epworth Hospital, Melbourne; 1977–80 Chaplain, Ormond Coll., Univ. of Melbourne; 1980– Ecumenical Lecturer, Lincoln Theol. Coll. (U.K.).
Connexional Committees: 1974–77 Faith and Order Committee (Victoria and Tasmania Conference) Convener; 1981– Local Preachers' Examinations Board (U.K.). *Publications: The Portland Bay Methodists* (1972); *Communion in Australian Churches* (Editor, Author 1979); *Music in Worship: the Set Liturgies* (1980); *Liturgical Dance Movement* (introductory essay 1982).
Special Interests: Liturgy, Ecumenics.
Hobbies and Recreations: Hunting Mediaeval Churches.

GRICE, Geoffrey, Meadow Cottage, South Park Cresc., Gerrards Cross, Bucks SL9 8HJ. (028-13-84193) *b. 22 July 1920, Derby. m. 24 Dec 1951: 2s.*
Education: 1932–34 Rotherham Grammar Sch.; 1934–37 Sheffield High Storrs Grammar Sch.; 1948–50 Richmond. *Appointments:* 1946–48 Walton-on-Thames; 1950–51 Shooters Hill; 1951–54 West Hartlepool, 1954–59 Skipton; 1959–66 Sheffield, Ecclesall; 1966–74 Guernsey, Elizabeth Coll., Guernsey; 1974– Hillingdon.
Special Interests: Church History, Religious Art. *Hobbies and Recreations:* Oil Painting, Photography.

GRICE, John Herbert, 21 Victoria St., Cambridge CB1 1JP. (0223-354468)–MA(Cantab.), BA(Bristol). *b. 31 Dec 1934, Grimsby, Lincs. m. 2 Jan 1965: 1d., 1s.* *Education:* 1945–53 Wintringham Grammar Sch., Grimsby; 1955–58 St. Catherine's Coll., Cambridge; 1959–62 Didsbury, Bristol. *Appointments:* 1962–76 Sri Lanka; 1962–63 Colombo South; 1963–66 Moratuwa-Rawatawatta; 1966–67 Colombo South; 1968–72 UVA; 1973–76 Matara-Tangalla; 1977–79 Study Leave; 1979– Chaplain, Robinson Coll., Cambridge. *Connexional Committees:* 1969–72, 1974–76 (Sri Lanka) Training Committee. *Publications:* Contributor to *A History of Methodism in Ceylon 1814–1964* (1971). *Special Interests:* Comparative Religion, Inter-Faith Dialogue. *Hobbies and Recreations:* Music and Travel.

GRIFFIN, John Wesley, 39 Brook Rd., Bomere Heath, Shrewsbury, Shropshire SY4 3QA. (0939-290630) *b. 19 July 1907, Talke Pits, Stoke-on-Trent, Staffs. m. 15 Aug 1936: 1d., 3s.* *Education:* 1912–16 Talke Pits Mission Sch.; 1916–21 Talke Council Sch.; 1927–28 Cliff Coll.; 1930–33 Didsbury. *Appointments:* 1929–30 Knighton; 1933–35 Severn Valley Mission; 1935–36 North of Scotland Mission; 1936–38 Forest of Dean Mission; 1938–41 Raunds; 1941–46 Sheffield North; 1946–50 Chester (St John's); 1950–55 Cannock Chase; 1955–62 Salisbury; 1962–66 Buxton; 1966–69 Shrewsbury; 1969–72 Craven Arms and Church Stretton.

GRIFFIN, Kenneth, Church Bungalow, Thistle Way, Ty-Sign, Risca, Gwent NP1 6PL. (0633-612652)–BD(Lond.). *b. 6 Dec 1920, Bristol. m. 2 Aug 1950: 2d., 1s.* *Education:* 1925 St. Johns LA Council Sch.; 1926–32 Knowle Council Sch., School Rd., Bristol; 1932–37 Cotham Secondary Sch., Bristol; 1947–49 Handsworth. *Appointments:* 1945 Cheadle (Staffs); 1945–46 Sleaford; 1946 Bellingham; 1946–47 Harpenden; 1949–51 Towcester; 1951–53 Shipley; 1953–56 Helston; 1956–60 Bilston; 1960–63 Sale; 1963–68 Manchester, Cheetham Hill and Prestwich; 1968–73 Warrington; 1973–78 Merthyr Tydfil and Brecon; 1978– Risca and Cross Keys. *Connexional Committees:* 1954–55, 1957–60 Christian Citizenship. *Special Interests:* Hospital Chaplaincies, 1965–68 Crumpsall, 1968–73 Merthyr Tydfil Marriage Guidance; Student Oversight, 1968–73 Padgate Coll., Overseas Students and Residents. *Hobbies and Recreations:* Walking, Swimming, Photography, Gardening.

GRIFFITH, Gruffydd Morris, Angorfa, 7 Redwood Drive, Rhyl, Clwyd LL18 3RU. (0745-31055) *b. 18 Aug 1911, Blaenau Ffestiniog, Gwynedd. m. 4 June 1941: 2d., 2s.* *Education:* 1916–18 Inf. and Boys Jun.; 1918–1924 Maenofferen Sch.; 1924–31 Grammar Sch., Blaenau Ffestiniog; 1932–35 Handsworth. *Appointments:* 1931–32 Mold (Welsh); 1935–39 Bangor do; 1939–40 Caernarvon do; 1940–41 Holywell do; 1941–42 Liverpool, Mt. Zion do; 1942–43 Ferndale do; 1943–45 Glamorgan Mission do; 1945–50 Holywell do; 1950–55 Cefn Mowr do; 1955–65 Llangollen do; 1965–70 Bagillt do; 1970–77 Cefn Mowr do. *Connexional Committees:* District Secretary; First N. Wales; Sunday School Work; Secretary Loans and Grants; District Chapel Committee; District Treasurer of Ministerial Travelling Fund; Secretary of Home Mission Affairs of the District. *Local Council Committees:* 1981–83 Present President of Rhyl Free Church Council. *Special Interests:* Travelling, Camping and Caravanning. *Hobbies and Recreations:* Gardening.

GRIFFITHS, David John, 20 Burton Rd., Meajham, Burton-on-Trent, Staffs DE12 7NH. (0530-70501) *b. 13 Mar 1940, Ruabon. m. 25 Mar 1967: 2s.* *Education:* 1951–59 Sir John Deane's Grammar Sch., Northwich, Cheshire; 1961–62 Cliff Coll.; 1962–67 Handsworth. *Appointments:* 1968–78 Methodist Church, Sierra Leone; 1978– Ashby-de-la-Zouch. *Connexional Committees:* 1980–82 MCOD Central Committee. *Special Interests:* 3rd World Concerns, Racial Harmony. *Hobbies and Recreations:* Photography, General Interest in Music and Singing.

GRIFFITHS, Dennis, Llys-y-Mor, 11 Walthew Ave., Holyhead, Anglesey, Gwynedd LL65 1AF. (0407-2482) *b. 15 Dec 1941, Mancott, Hawarden, Flintshire. m. 29 July 1972: 1s.* *Education:* 1947–53 Lixwm CP; 1954–57 Basingwerk Secondary, Holywell; 1957–60 Ysgol Glan Clwyd Yrhyl; 1960–62 Bala Preparatory Coll.; 1962–66 Hartley Victoria. *Appointments:* 1966–67 Pwllheli; 1967–69 Machynlleth; 1969–70 Llanrhaeadr; 1970–74 Corwen; 1974– Ynys Mon. *Connexional Committees:* 1978– Overseas Committee.

GRIFFITHS, Edward Henry, 25 Highfield Park, Rhyl, Clwyd LL18 3N4. (0745 53595)–BA(Birmingham), BD(Wales). *b. 23 July 1919, Ysceifog, Holywell, Flintshire. m. 24 July 1948: 2d., 2s.* *Education:* 1924–31 Ysceifiog; 1931–39 Holywell County Sch.; 1939–43 Birmingham Univ.; 1943–46 Bangor Univ. Coll.; 1939–43 Handsworth. *Appointments:* 1943–44 Tregarth (Welsh); 1944–45 Bangor do; 1945–46 Tregarth do; 1946–48 Llanfaircaereuon do; 1948–50 Ystumtuen do; 1950–55 Liverpool (Oakfield) do; 1955–60 Llanrhaeadr do; 1960–65 Conwy do; Llanrwset do; 1970–75 Caernarfon do; 1975–82 Dyffrynclwyd do. *Connexional Committees:* Education and Youth, Division of Ministries. *Publications: Life and Work of D. R. Hughes* (1965); *Life and Work of George M. L. L. Davies* (2 Vols., 1967, 1968); Essays: *Ysgrifau Cemdes* (1971), *O Dydd i Ddydd* (1966); Several Translations.

Special Interests: History, Biography. *Hobbies and Recreations:* Gardening, Travelling.

GRIFFITHS, John Henry, Gwyndy, Llangynfelyn, Machynlleth, Powys 5Y20 8PU. (097086-474)—BA(Lond.) 1952. *b. 25 Aug 1915. m. July 1946: 1d., 1s.*
Education: Ystumtuew Council Sch.; Univ. of London; 1936–39 Handsworth Coll. *Appointments:* 1940–45 Lampeter; 1945–47 Swansea (Welsh); 1947–50 Brynmawr; 1950–55 Aberystwith (Welsh); 1955–57 Machynlleth; 1957–63 Cardiff (Welsh); 1963–70 Llanidleos; 1970–75 Llandeilo; 1977–80 Aberystwith (Welsh).
Connexional Committees: 1963–74 Chairman South Wales District.
Council Member: 1977–80 President Free Church Council of Wales.
Local Council Committees: 1972–74 Llandeilo Town Council.
Publications: Yr Eglwys yw y Testament Newydd (1953); *Ar Nodyn Ysgafor* (1981); *Wesleyanism in Cardiganshire,* Historical Society Lecture 1971.
Hobbies and Recreations: Gardening.

GRIFFITHS, Leslie John, 12 Brook Rd., Loughton, Essex IG10 1BW. (01-508-1834)—BA(Wales), MA(Camb.). *b. 15 Feb 1942, Burry Port, Carmarthenshire. m. 26 July 1969: 1d., 2s.*
Education: 1953–60 Llanelli Grammar Sch.; 1960–64 Univ. of Wales, Cardiff; 1967–69 Fitzwilliam Coll., Cambridge; 1967–70 Wesley House. *Appointments:* 1970–71 Petit-Goâve, Haiti; 1971–74 Port-au-Prince, Haiti; 1974–77 Reading; 1977–80 Cap Haitien, Haiti; 1980– Woodford and Wanstead.
Publications: The Great Tradition—Gerald Manley Hopkins, Church Quarterly (July 1971).
Special Interests: History, Sport, Literature/Theology, The Caribbean Novel, Local Education. *Hobbies and Recreations:* Laughter and Fellowship spiced with occasional Moments of Solitude.

GRIFFITHS, William George, Charnwood, 34 Mendip Drive, Frome, Somerset BA11 2HT. (0373-63519) *b. 6 Oct 1902, Tanyfron, Nr. Wrexham, Clwyd, N. Wales. m. 8 Aug 1936: 1d.*
Education: 1907–14 Rhos (Nr. Wrexham) Prim., Jun., and Intermediate; 1914–19 Ruabon (Nr. Wrexham) Grammar Sch.; 1929–32 Handsworth. *Appointments:* 1927–29 Lampeter (Welsh); 1932–33 Airdrie and Coatbridge; 1933–36 Leominster; 1936–40 Llanelly and Carmarten; 1940–45 Congleton; 1945–50 Swansea; 1950–55 Great Barr and Kingstanding; 1955–62 Loughborough; 1962–68 Redruth.
Special Interests: The Pastoral Work of the Ministry. *Hobbies and Recreations:* Gardening.

GRIGG, Norman Alfred, 17 Nelson Ave., Stoke, Plymouth, Devon PL1 5RL. (0752–53062)—BD. *b. 11 Feb 1945, Gosport, Hants. m. 25 Aug 1972: 1d., 3s.*
Education: 1950–56 Leesland CE County Prim.; 1956–62 Gosport County Grammar Sch.; 1963–64 Cliff Coll.; 1965–67 Didsbury, Bristol; 1967–69 Wesley, Bristol.
Appointments: 1969–71 Ripley; 1971–76 Derby Mission; 1976– Plymouth and Devonport Mission.
Special Interests: Broadcasting, Local Radio, Regional TV, Children's Programmes. *Hobbies and Recreations:* Music, Family.

GRILLS, Malcolm John, 1 Claremont Lane, Trull Rd., Taunton, Somerset TA1 4QX. (0823-87058)—BA(Bristol). *b. 11 Feb 1949, Macclesfield. m. 28 Sept 1974: 1d.*
Education: 1960–67 King's Sch., Macclesfield; 1971–74 Bristol Univ.; 1977–78 Liverpool Coll. of Higher Education; 1971–74 Wesley, Bristol.
Appointments: 1974–75 Bristol South; 1975–78 St. Helens and Prescot; 1978– Chaplain to Queen's Coll., Taunton.
Special Interests: Life, The Universe and Everything. *Hobbies and Recreations:* Photography, Canoeing, Computer, Programming, Motor Cycling.

GRINTER, David Arthur, 40 Kirby Rd., North End, Portsmouth PO2 0PB. (0705-661043)—MA BSc. *b. 20 July 1943, Bristol. m.*
Education: 1961–64 Imperial Coll., London Univ.; 1965–67 Wesley House. *Appointments:* 1967–70 Eccles; 1970–75 Midsomer Norton; 1975 Portsmouth.

GROSE, Peter Varcoe, 24 Dennis Rd., Padstow, Cornwall PL28 8DE. (0841-532424)—BA(Bristol). *b. 18 Aug 1926, Gorran, Cornwall. m. 20 Aug 1955: 1d., 1s.*
Education: 1931–37 Gorran; 1937–44 St. Austell County Sch.; 1950–53 Bristol Univ.; 1950–53 Didsbury, Bristol. *Appointments:* 1949–50 Nantwich; 1953–55 Andover; 1955–60 Helston; 1960–65 Falmouth; 1965–71 Exmouth and Budleigh Salterton; 1971–78 Bodmin; 1978– St. Columb and Padstow.
Hobbies and Recreations: Bird Watching.

GROVES, George Arthur, Upper Flat, Burnside, Ewhurst Rd., Cranleigh, Surrey GU6 7EF. (048-66-2970) *b. 1907, Manchester. m.: 1d.*
Education: Rivington Rd., Manchester; Richmond.
Appointments: 1945–46 Home Missions; 1946–48 London Mission East Ham; 1948–51 Hartlepools Central Mission; 1951–54 Lancaster Sulyard St.; 1954–59 Preston Lune St.; 1959–65 London Ilford; 1965–71 Grays.

GROVES, Leslie J., Priesthaus, East Rd., Maidenhead, Berks SL6 1PH. (0628 26668) *b. 9 April 1922, London. m. 13 Aug 1952: 1s.*
Education: Raine's Foundation Sch., London E1; 1946–48 Univ. of London; 1946–48 Richmond. *Appointments:* 1948–52 South Petherton; 1952–56 Ilfracombe; 1956–63 Medway Towns; 1963–69 Woking; 1969–76 Andover; 1976– Windsor and Maidenhead.
Connexional Committees: 1953–1961 Connexional Youth Council.
Special Interests: Ecumenical Work, Peace, Total Abstinence. *Hobbies and Recreations:* Photography, Motoring.

GROVES, Martin Leslie, 10 Pyatt St., Meadows, Nottingham NG2 2LF. (0602-864264)–MTheol(St. Andrews), ThM(Princeton). *b. 14 July 1953, Barnstable, N. Devon. m. 13 Aug 1977: 1s.*
Education: 1963–66 Priors Court; 1966–72 Kingswood; 1972–76 St. Andrews; 1976–77 Princeton Theological Seminary, N.J., U.S.A.; 1977–80 Oxford Univ.; 1980–82 Wesley, Bristol. *Appointments:* 1982– Nottingham Mission.
Special Interests: Xian Social Ethics.

GUEST, Paul Thomas, 13B Heath Rd., Petersfield, Hants GU31 4JE. (0730-3317) *b. 15 June 1929, Beeston, Nottingham. m. 11 Aug 1956: 3d.*
Education: 1942–50 The St. Thomas A'Becket Grammar Sch. (RC), West Bridgeford, Nottingham; 1953–56 Headingley. *Appointments:* 1952–53 Shepton Mallet; 1953–56 Headingley Coll.; 1956–60 East Suffolk; 1960–65 South Derbyshire; 1965–70 Uttoxeter and Dove Valley; 1970–78 Camberley and Aldershot; 1978– Petersfield, Liphook and Haslemere.
Special Interests: Ecumenical Movement, Forces Chaplaincies.
Hobbies and Recreations: Ornithology, Art.

GULLIFORD, Eric, 21 Mountview Rd., Clacton-on-Sea, Essex CO15 6LW. (0255-425949)–BD(Lond.). *b. 2 Dec 1912, Manchester. m. 17 April 1943: 1d., 1s.*
Education: 1936–39 Richmond. *Appointments:* 1939–42 London (Forest Gate); 1942 Buckingham and Brackley; 1943–47 Swindon (Bath Rd.); 1947–55 Portsmouth and Southsea; 1955–61 London (Ilford); 1961–68 Clacton-on-Sea; 1968–75 Northampton; 1975–77 North Walsham.

GUNSTONE, William Roy, 36 Orchard Paddock, Haxby, York YO3 8DD. (0904-768326)–BD(Lond.). *b. 19 March 1925, Chadderton, Lancashire. m. 28 July 1951: 1d., 1s.*
Education: 1930–36 Mills Hill Inf. Sch., Chadderton; 1936–40 Holt Grammar Sch., Liverpool; 1948–50 Richmond. *Appointments:* 1947–48 Plymouth; 1950–53 Westfield St., St. Helens; 1953–60 Bishop Auckland; 1960–70 Shildon; 1970–75 Bristol North; 1975– York North.
Connexional Committees: 1955–61 Overseas Mission; 1972–75 Ministerial Training; 1976–81 Probationers Oversight.
Hobbies and Recreations: Gardening.

GUY, Cecil Frederick, 50A Blenheim Ave., Highfield, Southampton SO2 1DU. (0703-553335)–MA(Camb.). *b. 9 June 1909, Muswell Hill. m. 15 Aug 1936: 2s.*
Education: 1917–25 Tollington Sch.; 1930–33 Wesley House. *Appointments:* 1929–30 Slough; 1933–36 Ripon; 1934 Cardiff (Roath); 1936–39 Newbury; 1939–42 Leeds (West); 1942–46 Knaresborough; 1946–50 High Wycombe; 1950–54 Rushden; 1954–59 Paulton; 1959–66 Camberley; 1966–74 Bromsgrove.
Special Interests: Chamber Music.
Hobbies and Recreations: Violin, Viola.

GWYTHER, Cyril Edward, Wesley Villa, Victoria Rd., Pembroke Dock, Dyfed SA72 6XX. (68-5188)–MA(Liverpool), PhD(Sheffield). *b. 14 Aug 1903, Marylebone, London. m. 1. Aug 1947 deceased 2. Aug 1978: 1d.*
Education: St. Thomas, London; Chamberlayne Wood Rd. Sch.; 1956–61 Liverpool Univ. (part time); 1962–67 Sheffield Univ.; 1924–27 Handsworth. *Appointments:* 1927–31 Oxford; 1931–35 London, Ilford; 1935–47 Tonypandy Mission; 1947–51 Cardiff, Roath; 1951–56 London, Tooting Mission; 1956–68 Liverpool Mission; 1968–82 Tenby.
Connexional Committees: 1944–47 Secretary of Home Mission Committee in Cardiff and Swansea District, and on Many Synod Committees. *Council Member:* Served as Chaplain to Students in London and Cardiff; Served as Prison Chaplain in Cardiff; Served on various Committees for Social Service.
Publications: The Valley Shall Be Exalted (1949); Articles to Various Magazines, Religious and Political.
Special Interests: Social Service, Community Life. *Hobbies and Recreations:* Sport of most forms, especially Cricket, played in various grades.

GYNES, David James, 110 Peveril Rise, Livingston, West Lothian EH54 6NX. (0506-413631)–BA. *b. 12 Nov 1940, Oxford. m. 22 Dec 1959: 2s.*
Education: 1945–49 East Oxford County Prim.; 1949–51 Marston County Prim.; 1951–56 City of Oxford High Sch. for Boys; 1972–75 Manchester Univ.; 1971–75 Hartley Victoria. *Appointments:* 1975–80 Hemel Hempstead and Berkhamstead; 1980– Edinburgh and Forth.
Special Interests: Ecumenical Integration. *Hobbies and Recreations:* Family History (Genealogy), Brass Rubbing, Guide Dog Puppy Walking.

HADFIELD, Edward, 12 Whitcroft Rd., Pershore, Worcs WR10 1EN. (0386 552970) *b. 9 March 1901, Edale, Derbyshire. m. 23 May 1934: 2d.*
Education: Chesterfield Grammar Sch.; 1919–20 Midland Agricultural Coll.; 1924–25 Cliff Coll.; 1927–30 Didsbury. *Appointments:* 1926–27 Pateley Bridge; 1930–34 Hyderabad (S. India); 1934–36 Belper; 1936–39 Nuneaton; 1939–46 Stafford; 1946–49 Leek; 1949–53 Ashbourne; 1953–57 Castle Donington; 1957–61 Witney; 1961–66 Market Drayton.
Connexional Committees: Overseas Missions.
Special Interests: Agriculture, Cricket. *Hobbies and Recreations:* Gardening, Cricket, Golf.

HAILE, Ian, 42 Falmouth Rd., Truro, Cornwall TR1 2HX. (0872-72514)–B/Met(Sheff.). *b. 10 Feb 1934, Ashbourne. m. 29 April 1961: 2d.*
Education: 1945–51 Monmouth Sch.; 1952–56 Sheffield Univ.; 1956–59 Handsworth. *Appointments:* 1959–60 Home Mission Caravan; 1960–64 Redruth; 1964–69 Truro; 1969–76 Stafford; 1976–80 Bloxwich and Willenhall; 1980– Chairman

Cornwall District.
Connexional Committees: 1971–72 Education and Youth; 1980– General Purposes; 1980– Home Missions; 1975–80 Conference Scrutineers' Secretary.
Hobbies and Recreations: Gardening.

HAILEY, Donald Stanley, St. Paul's Manse, 56 Woodfield Rd., Northgate, Crawley, West Sussex RH10 2ER. (0293-21456) *b. 26 Sept 1924, Manchester. s.*
Education: 1928–35 Victoria Park Council Sch.; 1935–40 Stretford Grammar Sch.; 1950–52 Hartley Victoria. *Appointments:* 1949–50 Leominster; 1950–52 Hartley Victoria Coll.; 1952–54 Tunstall (Jubilee); 1954–57 London East Ham Mission; 1957–63 Dorking and Horsham, 1963–68 Teddington; 1968–74 Ealing and Acton; 1974–75 Supernumerary; 1975– Crawley.
Connexional Committees: 1959–72 Methodist Committee on Healing and Pastoral Ministry.
Special Interests: Psychology, Healing. *Hobbies and Recreations:* Music, Painting, Table Tennis, Badminton, Billiards and Snooker.

HAINE, Alan, 2 Gullon Walk, Withywood, Bristol BS13 8NG. (0272-640557)–MA(Cantab.). *b. 11 Nov 1950, Epping, Essex. s.*
Education: 1956–62 Staples Rd. Inf. and Jun. Schs., Loughton, Essex; 1962–69 Buckhurst Hill County High Sch., Chigwell, Essex; 1970–76 Jesus Coll., Cambridge; 1973–76 Wesley House. *Appointments:* 1976–78 Edinburgh (Nicolson Sq.); 1978– Bristol (Bedminster).
Special Interests: Church History, Bible Study, Church Music. *Hobbies and Recreations:* Choral Singing, Listening to Music, Collecting Gramophone Records

HAINSWORTH, Gerald Moody, 8 Bursdon Close, Leicester LE3 6PG. (0533-874859)–MA(Cantab.), BSc(Dunelm), BD(Lond.). *b. 2 June 1936, East Retford, Notts. m. 31 December 1977: 2d., 2s.*
Education: 1947–50 Newton-le-Willows Grammar Sch.; 1950–52 Rochdale High Sch. for Boys; 1959–62 Univ. of Newcastle; 1962–64 Univ. of Cambridge; 1962–64 Wesley House. *Appointments:* 1964–69 Newcastle, Brunswick Central; 1969–74 Cheltenham; 1974–76 Basildon; 1976–81 Kettering and Corby; 1981– Leicester West; 1980– Synod Secretary of Oxford and Leicester District.
Connexional Committees: 1978–80 Board of Division of Ministries; 1982 Memorials Committee.
Publications: Methodism and Adult Education (M.Ed, Dissertation, Leicester, 1982).
Special Interests: Adult and Further Education. *Hobbies and Recreations:* Male Voice Choir, Hill Walking.

HAINSWORTH, John, 64 Penrose Ave., Blackpool. (0253-63146)–BA, BD(Lond.), MA(Lancaster). *b. 29 Oct 1937, Leeds, England. m. 2 July 1960: 2d., 2s.*
Education: 1948–53 Roundhay Grammar; 1953–55 Leeds Coll. of Technology; 1966–67 St. Martin's Coll., Lancaster; 1972–78 Open Univ.; 1979–80 Lancaster Univ.; 1962–65 Hartley Victoria.
Appointments: 1965–68 Lancaster; 1968–74 Burnley; 1974– Blackpool.
Special Interests: Social and Personal Psychology, Church Organisation, Ministerial Training. *Hobbies and Recreations:* DIY, Car Maintenance, Further Studies.

HALDEN, Kingsley, 56 Redston Rd., London N8 7HE. (01-340-1859)–BA(Bristol). *b. 23 Jan 1930, Jamaica, West Indies. m. 1959: 1d., 1s.*
Education: 1937–49 Elemen. and Private Secondary Education in Kingston, Jamaica; 1967–70 Bristol Univ. *Appointments:* 1970–73 Camborne; 1975–78 Hartlepool; 1978– Finsbury Park and Southgate.
Connexional Committees: 1973–82 DSR Sub-Committee for Healing and Pastoral Ministry; 1980– DSR Sub-Committee for Community Relations; 1978– NCH Central Committee; 1980– Overseas Division Central Committee; 1982– DSR Board.
Special Interests: Church's Contact with Committee and Koynonya for Contact among Church Congregations. *Hobbies and Recreations:* Music, Visiting New Places.

HALE, Alan Marcel, Hawthorns, Eastertown, Lympsham, Somerset BS24 0HY. (093-472-488) *b. 11 Dec 1923, Bristol. m. 21 Aug 1953.*
Education: 1927–33 Stoke Bishop (Bristol) Prim. Sch.; 1933–37 Greenbank (Bristol) Boys' Sch; 1937–41 South Bristol Central Sch.; 1965–67 Portsmouth Coll. of Education; 1948–51 Handsworth.
Appointments: 1947–48 Frome; 1951–53 Brighton (Dome Mission); 1953–56 Nottingham Mission; 1956–60 Portsmouth and Southsea; 1960–63 Salisbury; 1963–64 Bristol South; 1964–75 Hartcliffe Sch., Bristol; 1975– Deputy-Head of Broadoak Sixth Form Centre, Weston-super-Mare.
Special Interests: Youth Work.
Hobbies and Recreations: Gardening, Micro Computers.

HALL, Alfred Daemond, 29 Stocks Lane, Chester CH3 5TE. (0244-25736) *b. 14 Mar 1923, Waterloo, Liverpool. m. 1. 18 March 1950, 2. 15 June 1976.*
Education: 1933–39 Merchant Taylors' Crosby; 1947–49 Hartley Victoria. *Appointments:* 1945–47 Supply; 1949–52 Forest of Dean; 1952–57 Ormskirk; 1957–60 Blackpool South; 1960–65 Wem; 1965–70 East Dereham; 1965–70 Officiating Chaplain to RAF, Swanton Morley; 1970–74 Hull North; 1974–79 Rhyl and Prestatyn; 1979– Chester.
Connexional Committees: 1968–75 Hartley Victoria Coll. Committee; 1964–74 Secretary HVC Old Students' Association.
Special Interests: American Methodism (4 visits), Driving (Member Institute of Advanced Motorists), Compiling Audio-Visual Slide Travel Programmes. *Hobbies and Recreations:* Photography, Furniture Repair, DIY, Study of Antiques.

HALL, Arthur James, 151 Yew Tree Lane, Harrogate, N. Yorks HG2 9JX. (0423-872635)–BD, BEd. *b. 26*

Sept 1929, Astbury, Nr. Congleton, Cheshire. m. 10 Aug 1957: 2d., 1s. *Education:* Smallwood CE Prim. Sch.; Senior Boys Secondary Sch., Congleton, Cheshire; 1964–68 London; 1973–74 Sussex; 1976–78 Manchester; 1953–57 Hartley Victoria. *Appointments:* 1957–59 Ripley, Derby; 1959–60 British Guiana Dt; 1960–64 Ipswich; 1964–68 London Mission, Tooting; 1968–74 Wimbledon (Garth Sch.); 1974–82 Northwich (Tarporley High Sch.); 1982– Chaplain Ashville Coll. *Connexional Committees:* 1977–82 Day Schs. Committee. *Council Member:* Education and Youth, Ministries; Secretary of Formal Education Committee. *Local Council Committees:* Vale Royal Education Advisory Committee. *Publications: Merton Mode III* (Syllabus in Religious Education CEM). *Hobbies and Recreations:* Gardening, Tennis, Walking, Cycling, Music.

HALL, Bernard, 54 Chaucer Rd., Brixton, London SE24 0NU. (01-274-4823)–MA. *b. 11 May 1924. m. 1950: 2d., 1s.* *Education:* 1932–35 Devonshire Rd. Prim. Sch., Blackpool; 1935–38 Blackpool Grammar Sch.; 1938–42 Royal Grammar Sch., Newcastle upon Tyne; 1942–44 St. Johns Coll., Cambridge; 1947–50 Wesley House. *Appointments:* 1950–55 Kent Coll., Canterbury; 1955–59 Gravesend and Dartford; 1959–64 East Nigeria Dt; 1964–67 Hastings; 1967–74 Bristol East; 1974–78 London, Islington; 1978–80 London Mission, Hackney; 1980–82 Methodist International House; 1982– London Mission, Broomwood and Clapham.

HALL, David Ralph, 133 Radbourne St., Derby DE3 3BW. (0332-44942)–BA(Birmingham). *b. 10 March 1951, Bishop Auckland, Co. Durham. m. 14 July 1976: 2s.* *Education:* 1956–62 Sedgefield Inf. Sch.; 1962–69 Bede Hall Grammar Sch., Billingham; 1976–79 Birmingham Univ. *Appointments:* 1980– Derby Derwent Mission. *Hobbies and Recreations:* Gardening.

HALL, David Roland, 18 Ferryhill Place, Aberdeen AB1 2SE. (0224-25798)–MA(Oxon), BA(Cantab.), MTh(Serampore). *b. 8 April 1933, Wakefield. m. 24 April 1967: 1d., 1s.* *Education:* 1945–51 Kingswood Sch.; 1951–55 Oriel Coll., Oxford; 1957–59 Wesley House. *Appointments:* 1959–60 Cliff Coll.; 1960–62 Barton-on-Humber; 1962–77 Church of South India; 1979– North of Scotland Mission. *Hobbies and Recreations:* Chess, Badminton.

HALL, George David, 2 Fairfield, Broadgate Lane, Horsforth, Leeds LS18 5AD. (0532-582448)–MA(Liverpool), BD(Lond.), Cert Ed(Edge Hill). *b. 3 Nov 1941, Blackburn, Lancashire. m. 30 July 1976: 1d., 1s.* *Education:* Queen Elizabeth's Grammar Sch., Blackburn; Edge Hill Coll., Ormskirk; Univ. of Liverpool; 1963–66 Hartley Victoria. *Appointments:* 1966–68 Leigh-on-Sea; 1968–70 London, Highgate; 1970–74 Hindley; 1974–77 Wimbledon; 1977–81 Harrogate, Ashville Coll.; 1981– Leeds, Horsforth and Bramley. *Special Interests:* Church History, Modern Social History; Education. *Hobbies and Recreations:* Reading, TV and Films, Swimming, Transport History.

HALL, Gilbert Sydney, 5 Widecombe Ave., Weeping Cross, Stafford ST17 0HX. (0785-661369) *b. 5 March 1934, Basford, Stoke-on-Trent. m. 23 July 1960: 1d., 1s.* *Education:* Ryecroft Jun.; 1945–50 Eversleigh House Secondary; 1955–56 Cliff Coll.; 1959–60 St. Andrews, Selly Oak, Coll.; 1958–59 Hartley Victoria. *Appointments:* 1959–60 Missionary Training; 1960–62 Eccles; 1962–63 West Nigeria Dt; 1963–67 Nigeria Conf.; 1967–74 Rochdale North; 1974–75 Sierra Leone Dt; 1975–80 Shrewsbury; 1980– Stafford. *Connexional Committees:* 1968–71 Bolton/Rochdale District Ministerial Secretary. *Local Council Committees:* 1981–82 Chairman of the Council of Churches. *Special Interests:* 1978– Treasurer of the Methodist Revival Fellowship. *Hobbies and Recreations:* Support of Family (Sports, Events).

HALL, Ian Gareth, 87 Chester Rd., Middlewich, Cheshire CW10 9EU. (060684 3184)–BA(Bristol), MPS, PhC. *b. 2 Sept 1933, Morley, Yorkshire. m. 20 July 1957: 2s.* *Education:* 1944–51 Batley Grammar Sch.; 1953–55 Bradford Technical Coll.; 1955–58 Univ. of Bristol; 1955–58 Didsbury, Bristol. *Appointments:* 1958–61 Blyth and Seaton Delaval; 1961–65 Blaydon; 1981– Middlewich. *Local Council Committees:* 1958–61 Youth Advisory Committee (Blyth); 1982– Mayor's Charity Committee (Middlewich). *Publications: Sixty Years of Methodism in Seghill* (April 1961). *Special Interests:* Training of Preachers, Pharmacy, Japan, Nuclear Disarmament. *Hobbies and Recreations:* Cricket, Gardening.

HALL, Margaret Mary, 43 James St., Stoke-on-Trent ST4 5HB. (0782-47489)–MA. *b. 22 Oct 1934, Longsdon, Stoke-on-Trent. s.* *Education:* 1939–43 West End Prep. Sch.; 1943–53 Leed Westwood Hall Girls High Sch.; 1953–56 Univ. of London (Bedford Coll.); 1956–57 Univ. of London (Institute of Education); 1974–76 Wesley House. *Appointments:* 1976–81 Hyde and Denton; 1981– Stoke-on-Trent South. *Hobbies and Recreations:* Yoga, Reading.

HALL, Robert John, Woodstock, Manor Brow, Keswick, Cumbria CA12 4AW. (0596-73983) *b. 24 Sept 1900, Southwark, London. m. 30 June 1937: 1d.* *Education:* West Sq. Central Sch.; 1913–16 Borough Poly.; 1918–21 Regent St. Poly.; 1925–28 Victoria Park. *Appointments:* 1924–25 Gateshead; 1928–30 Stafford; 1930 Shanklin; 1931–36 Winchester; 1936–39 Wakefield; 1939–45 Louth; 1945–50 Sheffield, Ecclesall; 1950–55 Peak; 1955–62 Alford; 1962–66

Wisbech.
Local Council Committees: 1933–36 Winchester Education Committee.

HALL, Stanley, 26 Denbydale Way, Royton OL2 5TJ. (061-624-5264)–BA(Manchester). *b. 26 Jan 1927, Bacup, Lancs. m. 16 Aug 1954: 3d.*
Education: 1930–37 Western Council Sch.; 1937–42 Bacup-Rawtenstall Grammar Sch.; 1948–51 Manchester Univ.; 1979–80 Hartley Victoria. *Appointments:* 1980– Shaw and Royton.
Publications: Accounting Principles and Practice (Pergamon 1963).
Special Interests: Business, Ethics.
Hobbies and Recreations: Cricket, Tennis, Chess, Walking.

HALL, Thomas, 8 Heaton Ave., Cleckheaton, West Yorkshire BD19 3ET. (0274-873717) *m.: 2d.*
Education: Westhill Coll., Birmingham; 1949–51 Hartley Victoria. *Appointments:* 1948–49 Preston Clubland; 1948–50 Hartley Victoria Coll.; 1951–53 Edinburgh Nicholson Sq.; 1953–58 Liverpool North; 1958–64 London Mission East Ham; 1964–71 Durham Coast and Peterlee; 1971–78 Wednesday Mission; 1978– Spen Valley.

HALLAM, Rex, 18 Albert Rd., Wellington, Telford, Shropshire TF1 3AR. (0952-3237)–BA(Open Univ.). *b. 20 Sept 1919, Clowne, m. 11 July 1947: 1s., 1d.*
Education: 1924–29 Crosland Moor C.E. Sch.; 1929–36 Royds Hall Grammar Sch.; 1941–42 Kingsmead Coll.; 1945–47 Handsworth.
Appointments: 1940–41 Longton and Fenton; 1942–45 London East Ham Mission; 1947–49 E. Nigeria Dt; 1949–52 Helmsley; 1952–58 B. Guiana; 1958–63 Northwich; 1963–68 Walsall; 1968– Wellington (Shropshire).
Connexional Committees: 1975–78 Candidates Committee.
Special Interests: Music (LRAM, ARCM, LTCL). *Hobbies and Recreations:* Playing the Piano and Conducting Choral Groups, Drama.

HALLIDAY, Peter J., 3 St. Matthews Terrace, Leyburn, N. Yorks DL8 5EL. (0960-22138) *b. 6 Aug 1929, Coventry. m. June 1965: 1d., 1s.*
Education: 1934–45 Local Schs. in Coventry; 1951–54 Headingley.
Appointments: 1950–51 Presteigne and Kington; 1954–56 Wombwell and Hoyland; 1956–62 Seamen's Mission; 1962–63 Quinton; 1963–67 Birmingham, Islington and Quinton; 1967–70 Sheffield North; 1970–74 The Peak; 1974–80 Manningtree and Harwich; 1980– Wensleydale.

HALSTEAD, Barbara, 99 The Fairway, Banbury, Oxon OX16 0RS. (0295-51959) *b. 7 May 1935, Nelson, Lancashire. s.*
Education: Nelson Grammar Sch.; City of Coventry and City of Birmingham Training Colls; 1969–70 Handsworth; 1970–72 Queens.
Appointments: 1972–78 East Ham Mission (Dagenham); 1978– Banbury.
Connexional Committees: 1979– President NCH General Committee; 1979– President Home Missions Church in Rural Life Sub-Committee.
Hobbies and Recreations: Philately, Bird Watching, Model Making, Reading, Cacti and Flowering Plants.

HALSTEAD, David, 50 Burnley Rd., Ainsdale, Southport PR8 3LR. (0704-77406)–BD(Lond.), ThM(Lexington). *b. 19 April 1942, Preston, Lancs. m. 19 June 1965: 2d.*
Education: 1947–53 St. Stephens CE Prim., Preston; 1953–60 Preston Grammar Sch.; 1966–67 Lexington Theol. Seminary; 1962–66 Richmond; 1969 Kingsmead. *Appointments:* 1967–69 Mansfield; 1970–72 United Church of Zambia; 1972–80 Manchester and Salford; 1980– Southport.
Connexional Committees: 1972–82 Central Committee Overseas Division; 1975–82 General Purposes.
Special Interests: Church Growth, Overseas Missions, Community Work, New Forms of Worship.
Hobbies and Recreations: Boat Building, Golf.

HALSTEAD, Ernest John, 1 Wells Court, Springfield, Chelmsford, Essex CM1 5ND. (0245-58187) *b. 5 April 1905, Newark, Notts. m. 26 Sept 1934: 1s.*
Education: Magnus Grammar Sch., Newark; 1928–31 Handsworth Coll.
Appointments: 1928–31 Handsworth; 1931–33 Blackwell; 1933–36 Birmingham Mission; 1936–39 Glasgow, Claremont St.; 1939–44 Retford, Grove St.; 1944–48 Doncaster, Priory Place; 1948–51 Tadcaster; 1951–57 Huddersfield Hillhouse and North East; 1957–61 Marple; 1961–66 Sheffield South; 1966–69 Manchester and Salford Mission.
Hobbies and Recreations: Reading, Gardening.

HAMBLIN, Roland Stuart, 49 Barton Lane, Barton on Sea, Hants BH25 7PJ. (0425-613757) *b. 21 June 1907, Bristol. m. 15 Aug 1936: 1d.*
Education: 1917–22 St. George Grammar Sch., Bristol; 1930–33 Handsworth. *Appointments:* 1929–30 Stroud and Cirencester; 1933–38 Bournemouth; 1938–39 London East Ham Mission; 1939–62 Chaplain HMF; 1962–70 Secretary RN, Army and RAF Board.
Connexional Committees: 1950–52, 1958–79 Royal Navy, Army, RAF Board.
Special Interests: Cricket, RSPB.
Hobbies and Recreations: Bowls, Biographical Reading, Classical Music, Gardening.

HAMBLY, Cyril Grey, Bourne House, Trimpley, Ellesmere, Salop SY12 0BE. (069-171-2274)–BMus. *b. 6 Jan 1931, Cardiff. m. 31 Oct 1957: 2s.*
Education: 1940–47 Howard Gardens High Sch., Cardiff; 1969–71 Univ. of Wales; 1951–54 Hartley Victoria. *Appointments:* 1954–56 Llandrindod Wells; 1956–57 Newport; 1957–60 Willenhall (Staffs); 1960–66 Abergavenny; 1967–69 Mold; 1969–71 Bangor; 1974–81 Dereham and Swaffam; 1981– Ellesmere.
Publications: Contributor to *Partners in Praise* (9 Hymns) also

Sing New Songs (N.C.E.C. 13 Hymns); also *A Hymn for the Lectionary* 70 Hymns and Tunes by C. G. Hambly (Caedmon).
Special Interests: Music, Poetry.

HAMER, Tom, 14 Normandy Way, Dorchester DT1 2PP. (0305-5301)—HCF. *b. 10 Aug 1910, Farnworth, Lancs. m. 21 March 1941: 3d., 1s.*
Education: 1915–24 St. Michaels, Great Lever; 1933–36 Hartley Victoria. *Appointments:* 1936–47 Mysore District; 1947–59 Church of South India; 1959–66 Truro; 1966–71 East Grinstead; 1971–78 Diss; 1978– Crewkerne and S. Petherton.
Connexional Committees: 1966–71 OM Eastern Committee.
Hobbies and Recreations: Woodwork, Gardening.

HAMER, Vernon, 10 Rockley Ave., Radcliffe-on-Trent, Nottingham NG12 1AR. (06073-2509) *b. 3 April 1925, Bardsley, Ashton-under-Lyne, Lancs. m. 15 Aug 1953: 2s.*
Education: 1936–39 Hyde County Grammar; 1949–52 Headingley.
Appointments: 1947–49 Chipping Norton and Stow; 1952–53 Birstall and Birkenshaw; 1953–58 Spen Valley; 1958–63 Hazel Grove and Poynton; 1963–72 Guernsey (Victoria) and Sark; 1972– Nottingham South.
Special Interests: English Language.
Hobbies and Recreations: Music, Badminton.

HAMFLETT, David Gordon, The Manse, St. Anns Chapel, Gunnislake, Cornwall PL18 9HW. (0822-832462)—BA(B'ham). *b. 24 May 1954, Sale. m. 27 June 1975: 1s.*
Education: 1965–66 Solihull Sch.; 1966–72 Brentwood Sch.; 1972–75 Bristol Univ.; 1975–78 Queen's Coll., Birmingham. *Appointments:* 1978–82 Callington and Gunnislake; 1982– Northampton.
Hobbies and Recreations: Photography, Reading, Music, Watching Rugby, Football.

HAMMOND, Ernest Leslie, The Manse, 27 Station Rd., Nailsea, Bristol BS19 2PD. (0272-852473)—Dip Theol(Bristol). *b. 8 Jan 1931, Greenwich, London. m. 2 Aug 1958: 2s.*
Education: 1936–41 Hughes Field Sch., Deptford; 1941-45 Creek Rd. Sch., Deptford; 1945–49 Brixton Sch. of Building; 1953–56 Didsbury, Bristol. *Appointments:* 1952–53 Oundle; 1953–56 College; 1956–58 Loftus and Staithes; 1958–63 Durham Coast and Peterlee; 1963–68 Enfield; 1968–76 Clifton and Redland; 1976– Bedminster.
Special Interests: Pastoral/Social Counselling, Hospital Chaplaincy, Radio Broadcasting. *Hobbies and Recreations:* All Sports, Gardening, Cine Films.

HAMMOND, Harold, The Manse, Langwathby, Penrith, Cumbria CA10 1NB. (076-881-277) *b. Kingston upon Hull. m. 5 Jan 1943: 1d., 2s.*
Education: 1932–35 Cliff Coll.; 1936–39 Handsworth.
Appointments: 1939–40 Leicester, Humberston Rd.; 1940–42 Oundle; 1942–46 Ripley; 1946–50 Northampton, Kettering Rd.; 1950–56 Hull Mission; 1956–64 Glasgow Mission; 1964–68 Huddersfield Mission; 1968–76 Great Yarmouth Central Hall; 1976–81 Scarborough, Queen St.
Connexional Committees: 1960–64 Church of Scotland, Church and Industry Committee.

HANCOCK, Alan Peter, 31 The Avenue, St. George, Bristol BS5 8HL. (0272-557507)—BA. *b. 29 Nov 1955, Stoke-on-Trent. m. 11 Aug 1979; 1d.*
Education: 1960–67 Chell Inf. and Jun.; 1967–72 Hanley High Sch.; 1972–74 S-o-T Sixth Form Coll.; 1975–79 Birmingham Univ.; 1978–79 Queen's. *Appointments:* 1980–81 Old Hill; 1981– Bristol, Kingswood.
Connexional Committees: 1979–80 Ministerial Training Committee.
Special Interests: Foreign Languages.
Hobbies and Recreations: All Sport.

HANCOCK, Christopher, The Manse, Oakridge Centre, Vivian Rd., Basingstoke, Hants RG21 2LG. (0256 23590) *b. 23 Feb 1914, Thornhill, Derbyshire. m. 7 Oct 1961: 1d., 2s.*
Education: 1919–25 Bamford Jun. Sch.; 1925–30 New Mills County Secondary Sch.; 1947–48 Brincliffe Emergency Coll., Sheffield; 1961–63 Durham Univ., Newcastle upon Tyne; 1970–71 Swansea Univ.
Appointments: 1961–64 Hexham; 1964–66 Rhodesia; 1966–77 Zambia; 1977– Basingstoke.
Special Interests: Pastoral Counselling. *Hobbies and Recreations:* Gardening, Walking.

HANCOCK, Derek, Wesley House, 22 Chestnut Ave., Wetherby, W. Yorks, Leeds LS22 4SG. (0937-62854)—Dip Theol(Lond.). *b. 14 Dec 1939, Longton, Stoke-on-Trent. m. 22 Aug 1965: 2d.*
Education: 1945–55 Meir Secondary Modern; 1961–65 Richmond.
Appointments: 1965–67 Hungerford; 1967–72 Mansfield West; 1972–79 Leeds N/East; 1979– Tadcaster.
Connexional Committees: 1976–78 Division of Education and Youth.
Special Interests: Clinical Theology, Pastoral Counselling. *Hobbies and Recreations:* Philately, Squash, Swimming, Gardening.

HANCOCK, Reginald, 39 Laundry Lane, Thorpe St. Andrew, Norwich NR7 0XG. (0603 33936) *b. 5 Dec 1932, Dunbar. m. 14 Dec 1957: 1d., 1s.*
Education: 1937–50 Dunbar Secondary Sch.; 1955–58 Hartley Victoria. *Appointments:* 1958–61 Thornley; 1961–65 Berwick; 1965–67 Penrith; 1967–72 Doncaster North East; 1972–79 Chelmsford; 1979– Norwich.

HANCOCK, Trevor Lewis, Gordon House, 46 London Rd., Kirton, Boston, Lincs PE20 1JA. (0205-722303) *b. 8 Sept 1936, Lincoln, m. 24 June 1961: 2d.*
Education: 1940–47 Boultham Park, Lincoln; 1948–51 King Alfred Sch., Plön, Germany; 1951–53 High Storrs Grammar, Sheffield; 1961–62 St. Andrew's, Selly Oak; 1958–61 Handsworth. *Appointments:* 1962–63 Clitheroe; 1963–72 South East Asia Conf.; 1972– Boston.
Connexional Committees: 1974–76 Overseas Missions; 1980–82 Education and Youth.

Special Interests: Radio Broadcaster, formerly overseas with Radio Malaysia, BBC World Service, F.E.B.C., now contributor to BBC Radio Lincolnshire. *Hobbies and Recreations:* Photography, Gardening, Watching Sport, Reading.

HANCOCK, Walter Cyril, 16 Higher Tristram, Polzeath, Wadebridge, Cornwall PL27 6TF. (020-886-3544)–BSc(Lond.), BD(Manchester). *b. 22 Feb 1912, Lincoln. m. 7 Dec 1939: 1d., 1s.*
Education: 1922–28 City Sch., Lincoln; 1930–32 Nottingham Univ. Coll.; 1933–36 Manchester Univ.; 1933–36 Didsbury. *Appointments:* 1936–45 China (Hupeh Dt); 1948–51 Bodmin; 1951–55 Bude; 1955–58 Minehead; 1958–74 Resigned (Teaching); 1974–78 Newquay, Perranporth and St. Agnes.
Hobbies and Recreations: Gardening, Swimming, Lapidary.

HANDSCOMB, Keith Farnsworth, 11 Swannington St., Burton upon Trent DE13 0RT. (0823-64439) *b. 20 Dec 1932, Bedford. m. 30 June 1962: 1d., 1s.*
Education: 1943–49 Bedford Modern Sch.; 1958–62 Handsworth. *Appointments:* 1962–64 East Dereham; 1964–68 Nottingham West; 1968–74 Lincoln North; 1974– Burton on Trent.
Special Interests: Engineering. *Hobbies and Recreations:* Walking, DIY.

HANKS, Peter Hardie, 35 Quarry Rd., Ryde, Isle of Wight PO33 2TY. *b. 27 July 1917, Cwmaman, Aberdare, South Wales. m. 23 Oct 1948: 1d.*
Education: 1921–25 Clarence St. Inf., Miskin, Mountain Ash; 1925–30 York St. Jun., Miskin, Mountain Ash; 1930–31 Central Sch., Miskin, Mountain Ash; 1946–48 Handsworth. *Appointments:* 1948–49 HM Committee; 1949–52 Bishop's Castle and Clun; 1952–56 Leominster; 1956–62 Burslem (Hill Top); 1962–69 West Wight; 1969–75 Southampton; 1975– East Wight. *Connexional Committees:* 1973–76 Board of Property.

HANSON, John Charles, 18 Berwick Rd., Shrewsbury, Shropshire SY1 2LN. (0743-4141) *b. 6 March 1940, Pontefract, Yorkshire. m. 30 July 1966: 2s.*
Education: Wakefield Tutorial Sch.; King Sch., Pontefract; 1959–61 Kesteven Training Coll., Lincolnshire; 1963–66 Richmond. *Appointments:* 1966–74 Honduras and Belize; 1974–80 Neath; 1980– Shrewsbury.
Connexional Committees: 1976–79 Division Education and Youth.
Special Interests: Senior Instructor British Canoe Union, involved currently in Mental Health/Pastoral Work. *Hobbies and Recreations:* Outdoor Pursuits.

HARBEY, Albert William, The Methodist Manse, 103 Chapel St., Kilburn, Derby DE5 0PB. (0332-880183) *b. 12 April 1935, Derby. m. 29 June 1957: 2s.*
Education: 1940–45 Brailsford CE; 1945–51 Queen Elizabeths Grammar Sch., Ashbourne; 1981– East Midlands Ministerial Training Course, Nottingham Univ. *Appointments:* 1981– Belper.
Special Interests: Awarded Associate Membership of Institute of the Motor Industry (A.M.I.M.I.). *Hobbies and Recreations:* Motor Sport, Sport in general.

HARBOUR, Keith David, 12 Hall Drive, Torrisholme, Morecambe, Lancashire LA4 6SX. (0524-410072) *b. 30 April 1945, Gateshead, Co. Durham. m. 15 Aug 1970: 2d.*
Education: 1950–52 Sheriff Hill Co. Prim.; 1952–56 Glynwood Co. Jun.; 1956–61 Whitehall Rd., Secondary Technical Sch.; 1968–72 Hartley Victoria. *Appointments:* 1972–74 Blackpool North; 1974–79 Preston, Lune St. and Orchard; 1979 Morecambe and Heysham.

HARDING, David J., 77 Felixtowe Rd., Abbey Wood Estate, London SE2 9QQ. (01-310-9330)–BSc, BD(Lond.). *b. 5 June 1935, Pensilva, Cornwall. m. 1958: 1d., 1s.*
Education: 1946–48 Liskeard Grammar Sch.; 1948–54 Hele's Sch., Exeter; 1954–57 Univ. Coll., London; 1959–61 Richmond. *Appointments:* 1961–65 Ashton under Lyne; 1965–69 Whitehaven; 1969–76 General Secretary of Fellowship of Reconciliation; 1976–82 Director of United Nations Association; 1982– Plumstead Mission.
Connexional Committees: 1982– Secretary Methodist Peace Fellowship. *Publications: Now Let Us Sing* (1968); *Peace Without Defeat* (1971); *For Christmas* (1971); *Now We Must Sing* (1971); *Now Let Me Think* (1972); *Love In Conflict* (1974); *UNO It Works* (1977); *Why the UN is Important* (1979).
Special Interests: The Politics of Peace. *Hobbies and Recreations:* Music, Art, Poetry, the Countryside.

HARDWICK, James William, The Manse, St. Keverne, Nr. Helston, Cornwall TR12 6NE. (0326 280399)–BA(Rhodes Univ., South Africa). *b. 6 Nov 1922, Rochdale, Lancs. m. 8 Aug 1953.*
Education: 1927–30 St. Thomas CE Sch.; 1930–38 Castlemere Boys Central Sch.; 1947–48 Cliff Coll.; 1950–53 Rhodes Univ., Gramarstown. *Appointments:* 1949–52 Powpoland East (South Africa); 1952–53 Windhoek do; 1953–55 Kimberley do; 1955–60 Waterberg Mission do; 1960–61 New Mills; 1961–63 Peel; 1963–70 Wolstanton and Audley; 1970–75 Colchester; 1975–80 Ulverston; 1980– Helston.
Connexional Committees: 1960–63 Overseas Mission. *Local Council Committees:* 1965–70 Newcastle (Staffs) Local Schools Committee.
Special Interests: 1962–72 Football Referee, 1972– Assessor County FA; Vice President Colchester Refs Society, 1965– Cricket Umpire.
Hobbies and Recreation: Gardening.

HARDWICK, Ralph Leonard, 28 Cliff Ave., Nettleham, Lincoln LN2 2PU. (0522-751587) *b. 2 April 1904, Mavis Bank, Jamaica. m. 22 May 1935 (w.): 3d.*
Education: 1914–20 Kingswood Sch., Bath; 1931 Mt. Allison, U.

Sackville, N.B. Canada; 1931–35 Pine Hill Divinity Hall, Halifax, N.S. Canada. *Appointments:* 1943–46 Canadian Army Chaplain Service; 1930–46 United Church of Canada; 1946–50 Stowmarket; 1950–53 King's Lynn; 1953–58 Pocklington; 1958–65 Pickering; 1965–70 Scunthorpe.
Special Interests: Bible Study, Fellowship Groups, Youth Work. *Hobbies and Recreations:* Colour Photography, Walking.

HARDY, Clifford Ernest, 5 Harding Ave., Eastbourne, East Sussex BN22 8PH. (0323-24545) *b. 20 Nov 1917, Goodmayes, Essex. m. 25 Oct 1944: 3d., 1s.*
Education: 1927–33 Wallasey Grammar Sch.; 1938–41 Hartley Victoria. *Appointments:* 1941–44 Tipton; 1944–50 Leeward Islands; 1950–54 Spalding; 1954–62 Melton Mowbray; 1962–69 Birmingham (Sutton Park); 1969–76 Helston; 1976–83 Eastbourne.
Special Interests: Council of Churches, Bible Society. *Hobbies and Recreations:* Gardening, Music.

HARDY, David Alan, 99 Higham Lane, Nuneaton CV11 6AL. (0203 384303)–BSc, BA, PhD. *b. 10 Oct 1944, Exeter. m. 20 May 1972: 3d.*
Education: 1956–63 Hele's Grammar, Exeter; 1963–69 Birmingham Univ.; 1972–74 Wesley House. *Appointments:* 1974–80 York North; 1980– Nuneaton and Allerstone.
Publications: Various Scientific Papers 1969–72.
Hobbies and Recreations: Railways.

HARDY, Ernest, Pentire, 23 St. Anne's Gdns., Llanrhos, Llandudno, Gwynedd LL30 1SD. (0492-81765) *b. 25 Nov 1901, Salford, Lancashire. m. 7 Sept 1967: 2s.*
Education: 1905–13 St. Clement's, Ordsall, Salford; 1913–16 Salford Grammar Sch.; 1922–25 Victoria Park, Manchester. *Appointments:* 1925–27 Castleford; 1927–28 Huddersfield (Shepley); 1928–34 Ashton-under-Lyne; 1934–39 Sheffield (Brunswick); 1939–45 Norwich; 1945–51 Ashton-under-Lyne; 1951–57 Bramhall; Chairman of District, 1949–51 Manchester First, 1951–57 Stockport, 1957–65 Cumbria.
Connexional Committees: 1949–65 Home Mission; 1949–65 Stationing; 1949–65 General Purposes. *Local Council Committees:* 1972–74 Llandudno Council of Churches, President. *Publications: God and Comrade Norvic* Jointly with Baptist Minister, Rev. Stanley A. Baker (1943).
Special Interests: Evangelism.
Hobbies and Recreations: Reading, Sport.

HARE, David Jeromy, Jasmine Cottage, Caspidge, Pikes Pool Lane, Bromsgrove, Worcs B60 1LH. (0527-33907)–BA(B'ham), ThM(Austin, USA) ALAM. *b. 31 Jan 1937, Lincoln. s.*
Education: 1947–55 The Lincoln Sch.; 1958–61 The Univ. of Birmingham; 1961–62 Austin Presbyterian Theol. Seminary, USA; 1977–78 Birmingham Poly. C.T.E.T.; 1958–61 Handsworth.
Appointments: 1962–64 Bradford (Woodhouse Grove); 1964–69 Shipley; 1969–77 Redditch; 1978– Minister in another appointment (Waseley Hills High Sch., Rubery, Head of Religious Education).
Special Interests: Education, Ecumenism. *Hobbies and Recreations:* Drama, Theatre Arts.

HARGREAVES, Frank Whittaker, 4 Eversley Close, Rhyl, Clwyd LL18 4US. (0745-31824) *b. 13 Oct 1909, Padiham, Lancs. m. 30 July 1938 (w.).*
Education: Accrington Grammar; 1932–35 Richmond. *Appointments:* 1936–38 Tonbridge; 1938–40 Canterbury; 1940–45 St. Leonards and Bexhill; 1945–48 London East End Mission; 1948–52 West Wight; 1952–58 Nottingham (West); 1958–63 Leicester (South); 1963–69 Buckingham and Brackley; 1969–74 Wrexham.

HARKER, George F., The Priory, Hudswell, Richmond, N. Yorkshire DL11 6BL. (0748-4137) *b. 16 Dec 1917, Richmond, N. Yorks. m. 20 July 1949: 1d., 1s.*
Education: 1930–35 Richmond Sch., Yorks,; 1938–39 Cliff Coll.; 1940–42 Headingley. *Appointments:* 1939–40 Oundle; 1942–43 Church Eresley; 1943–65 Royal Army Chaplains Department; 1965–70 Wensleydale; 1970–76 Richmond, Yorks.
Hobbies and Recreations: Carpentry.

HARKER, Maurice, 2 Nugent Rd., Southbourne, Bournemouth BH6 4ET. (0202-423161) *b. 12 June 1904, Wakefield. m. 12 Aug 1936: 1d., 1s.*
Education: 1916–19 Morley Grammar Sch.; 1930–33 Didsbury. *Appointments:* 1929–30 Whitehaven; 1930–33 Didsbury Coll.; 1933–38 Ambleside; 1938–45 Ormskirk; 1945–52 Southport; 1952–59 Bournemouth; 1959–66 Plymouth, King St.; 1966–73 Bournemouth.
Connexional Committees: 1952–59 Overseas.
Special Interests: Care of Terminally Ill.

HARLAND, Frederick William, 16 Northgate Rd., Linthorpe, Middlesbrough, Cleveland. (0642-818735) *b. 17 Sept 1917, Darlington. m.: 1d., 4s.*
Education: 1939–42 Hartley Victoria. *Appointments:* 1946–47 H.M. Comm.; 1947–48 Greenock; 1948–49 Peak; 1949–52 New Zealand Conf.; 1952–53 Swindon, Prospect Place.

HARLAND, Richard Michael, 285 North Rd., Hull HU4 6BZ. (0482-51017).
Education: 1963–66 Headingley. *Appointments:* 1966–69 Peak; 1969–74 Sheffield South; 1974– Hull.

HARLING, William Allan, 39 Sea Lane Gdns., Ferring, Worthing. *b. 9 Sept 1909. m.: 2d., 1s.*
Education: Elementary; Headingley. *Appointments:* 1930–31 Bradford, Kirkgate; 1934–35 President's List; 1935–37 HM Comm.; 1937–39 London, Highgate; 1939–40 St. Ives (Cornwall); 1940–41 Welton and Rocklands; 1941–43 London Mission

NW; 1943–48 London Mission North; 1948–49 Chorley; 1949–55 Bedford South; 1955–63 Malden; 1963–70 Chichester and Bognor; 1970–72 President's List.
Council Member: Maldon Borough Council (Essex) 6 Years.
Special Interests: Opposing the Ecumenical Heresy. *Hobbies and Recreations:* Gardening, Salmon Fishing.

HARPER, Donald David Hart, 33 Lady Rd., Edinburgh EH16 5PA. (031-667-1465)—BA(Lond.). *b. 2 Nov 1919, Dalkeith, Midlothian. m. 23 July 1949: 2d., 2s.*
Education: 1928–36 Bromley County Sch.; 1945–48 Handsworth.
Appointments: 1948–49 Dorchester; 1949–52 Ilfracombe; 1952–56 Cardiff Wesley; 1956–59 Royal Air Force (Chaplain); 1959–66 Newcastle, Central and Sandyford; 1966–73 Burton-on-Trent; 1973–79 Castle Donington; 1979– Edinburgh and Forth (Nicholson Square).
Special Interests: Industrial Archeology (especially Transport), Heraldry, Linguistics, Military History, Music, Travel. *Hobbies and Recreations:* National Tramway Museum, Strathspey Railway Association, Amateur Dramatics, Car-driving.

HARPER, Frank, Engelberg, Ash Hill, Compton Rd W., Wolverhampton WV3 9DS. (0902-24947) *b. 20 June 1897, Wolverhampton. m. 20 Oct 1925: 1d.*
Education: National Sch., Wolverhampton; 1922–25 Hartley Victoria. *Appointments:* 1925–27 Huddersfield; 1927–28 North Devon; 1928–32 Halifax North; 1932–37 Bradford SE/Low Moor; 1937–40 Cannock Chase; 1940–47 Manchester Patricroft; 1947–53 Birmingham Washwood Heath; 1953–59 Manchester Withington; 1959–62 Nottingham Central; 1962–66 Burslem Clowes.
Special Interests: Administration, Rebuilding and New Churches.
Hobbies and Recreations: Engineering, Motor, Gardening.

HARRIS, Albert Frederick, 194 Henver Rd., Newquay, Cornwall TR7 3EH. (06373-3516) *b. 10 Oct 1895, Launceston. m. 31 July 1928: 1s.*
Education: Secondary.
Appointments: 1924–26 Diss; 1926–28 East Dereham; 1928–33 Camborne; 1933–34 Huddersfield High St.; 1934–38 Okehampton; 1938–43 Truro (St. Marys); 1943–50 St. Columb and Padstow; 1950–56 St. Austell; 1956–61 Bodmin.
Hobbies and Recreations: Bowling.

HARRIS, Arthur, Hillcroft, 18 Selborne Drive, Douglas, Isle of Man. (0624-21004) *b. 14 Jan 1928, Marham, King's Lynn, Norfolk. m. 14 Aug 1954: 1d., 1s.*
Education: 1946–48 Cliff Coll., Sheffield; 1949–51 Richmond.
Appointments: 1948–49 Pontypridd, 1951–54 Ashby-de-la-Zouch; 1954–59 Ashbourne; 1959–64 Leeds Armley; 1964–71 Aireborough; 1971–76 Castletown (IOM); 1973–74 Colorado, USA; 1976– Douglas and Peel (IOM); 1981- District Chairman (IOM).
Connexional Committees: 1975–78 Ministries; 1972–75 Overseas Home Committee; 1981– Home Missions.
Special Interests: Preaching, Pastoral Care, Administration.

HARRIS, Herbert William, 165 Wokingham Rd., Reading, Berkshire RG6 1LS. (0734-61765)—BA(Lond.), MA(Camb.). *b. 2 Feb 1920, Barnstaple, Devon. m. 16 June 1949: 1d., 1s.*
Education: 1930–37 Barnstaple Grammar Sch.; 1937–40 Univ. Coll., Exeter; 1947–49 Fitzwilliam House, Cambridge, 1947–49 Wesley House.
Appointments: 1950–54 Durham; 1954–58 Middlesbrough; 1958–63 London (Finchley and Hendon); 1963–67 Filey (Chaplain of Hunmanby Hall); 1967–74 Harpenden (also Chaplain to the National Children's Home Branches); 1974–78 Wimbledon; 1978– Reading (Chaplain to Reading Univ.); 1959–63 District Secretary for Home Missions, London, N.W. District, Precentor to the Synods of London N.W. and Southampton Districts.
Publications: Articles on the Hymns of Charles Wesley.
Special Interests: Study of the Works of the Wesleys (especially the hymns of Charles), The Works of Karl Barth, Theology in General. *Hobbies and Recreations:* Singing, Writing Hymns, Poetry, Reading, Gardening.

HARRIS, Jeffrey Wallace, 21 Beadon Rd., Bromley, Kent BR2 9AS. (01-460-2915)—MA(Manchester), BD(Lond.). *b. 30 July 1924, Tynemouth, Northumberland. m. 9 Aug 1952: 3s.*
Education: 1935–40 Tynemouth High Sch.; 1956–58 Manchester Univ.; 1956–58 Hartley Victoria.
Appointments: 1946–48 Nantwich (Hospital St.); 1951–53 Sale; 1953–56 Oldham East; 1956–61 Manchester (Gravel Lane); 1961–67 Buxton; 1967–71 Bramhall, 1971– Secretary Home Mission Division.
Connexional Committees: 1971– Home Mission Division.
Publications: Counting to Some Purpose (with P. Jarvis); *Can British Methodist Grow Again?; A Profile of Methodism; Concern for Each Inner City; The Church in the Council Housing Estate* (with P. Jarvis).

HARRIS, John, 67 Broadway, Morecambe LA4 5XX. (0524-411642)—BA(Open Univ.). *b. 14 May 1930, Hesket-New-Market, Cumbria. m. 27 July 1957: 1s.*
Education: 1935–41 Hesket-New-Market Jun. Sch.; 1941–48 Nelson Grammar Sch., Wigton; 1952–55 Hartley Victoria. *Appointments:* 1951–52 Swinton and Pendlebury; 1955–57 Sale; 1957–62 Connah's Quay and Hawarden; 1962–70 Blackpool North; 1970–73 Altrincham; 1973–81 Southport; 1981– Morecambe and Heysham.
Special Interests: Religious Journalism. *Hobbies and Recreations:* Music.

HARRIS, Robert Geoffrey, 19 Hickton Rd., Swanwick, Derby DE55 1AF. (0773–602994)—BA(Warwick), BD(Lond.), PhD(St. Andrews). *b. 12 July 1948, London, England. m. 20 July 1974: 1s.*
Education: 1959–66 Buckhurst Hill

County High Sch.; 1967–70 Warwick Univ.; 1972–75 St. Andrews Univ.; 1978–81 Wesley, Bristol.
Appointments: 1981– Ripley.
Publications: Bergson and Catholic Thought, Article in *The Month* (Dec 1976); *Copleston and Chevalier on French Metaphysics,* Article in *Downside Review* (Jan 1976).
Special Interests: Methodist Study Centre, Tutor in Greek Studies, MAYC Youth Worker's Certificate.
Hobbies and Recreations: Sport, Music.

HARRIS, Terence Reginald, 20 Whipton Lane, Exeter EX1 3DS. (0392-56716) *b. 15 March 1935, Gloucester. m. 15 Aug 1964: 1d., 1s.*
Education: 1940–42 Derby Rd. Inf. Sch., Gloucester; 1942–46 Widden St. Jun. Sch., Gloucester; 1946–52 Sir Thomas Rich's (Bluecoat) Sch., Gloucester; 1952–55 Gloucestershire Royal Infirmary, Department of Pathology; 1956–58 Institute of Pathology and Tropical Medicine, RAF Halton, RAF Wroughton; 1958–62 Didsbury.
Appointments: 1962–64 Marlborough; 1964–69 Biggleswade; 1969–74 Reading; 1974–80 Gloucester; 1980– Exeter.
Special Interests: Looking After a Family, Fulfilling a Ministry, Keeping a House and Garden Going. *Hobbies and Recreations:* Philately, Piano, Chess, Swimming.

HARRIS, William Butcher, 37 Glenville Rd., Rustington, West Sussex BN16 2EA. (09062-3712)– MA(Oxford), BA(Camb.), LT(Madras), HonDD(Serampore). *b. 14 March 1913, Charlbury, Oxford. m. 1. July 1942, 2. 17 May 1961.*
Education: 1918–23 Charlbury Elemen. Sch.; 1923–32 City of Oxford High Sch.; 1932–36 Wadham Coll., Oxford; 1943–44 Meston Training Coll., Madres; 1936–39 Wesley House. *Appointments:* 1939–40 Pocklington; 1940–41 Sheffield Ecclesall; 1943–47 Madras District; 1947–51 Church of South India, Madras Diocese; 1951–69 Tinnevelly Diocese; 1969–77 Madurai Diocese.
Publications: Commentaries on I Corinthians (Christian Students Library 1950); *Romans CSL* (1964); *Unity in Christ* (Commentary on Ephesians 1966); *Thessalonians Preachers Caum* (1968).

HARRISON, Edward, 48 Warwick Place, Leamington Spa, Warwickshire CV32 5DF. (0926-26084) *b. 3 Feb 1928, Bear Park, Co. Durham. m. 16 July 1956: 2d.*
Education: A. J. Dawson, Wellfield, Co. Durham; 1952–55 Headingley.
Appointments: 1951–52 Norwich (St. Peters); 1955–57 Glasgow (Parkhead and Burnbank); 1957–62 Edinburgh Mission; 1962–69 Sunderland (South); 1969–76 Birmingham (Moseley Rd. and Sparkhill); 1976– Leamington Spa.
Hobbies and Recreations: Bird-Watching, Gardening.

HARRISON, Gordon William, The Manse, Mercer Rd., Gorton, Manchester M18 8LL. (061-223-8668)–BA(Birmingham). *b. 12 Oct 1943, Kidderminster, Worchestershire. m. 9 Aug 1975: 1s.*
Education: 1956–60 Soham Grammar Sch., Cambridgeshire; 1960–62 Lowestoft Grammar Sch.; 1962–65 Westminster Coll., Oxford; 1971–75 Univ. of Birmingham; 1971–75 Queens. *Appointments:* 1975–78 Harpenden; 1978– Manchester and Salford Mission.

HARRISON, Richard Andrew, *4 Chapel Hill Rd., Pocklington, York– MA, LLB. b. 19 April 1939, Grimsby. m. 5 Aug 1967: 1d., 2s.*
Education: 1950–53 Wintringham Grammar Sch., Grimsby; 1954–57 King Edward VI Grammar Sch., Louth; 1957–60 Leeds Univ.; 1965–67 Cambridge Univ.; 1977–78 Sheffield Univ.; 1965–67 Wesley, House. *Appointments:* 1967–70 Derby East; 1970–75 Sheffield Norfolk; 1975–78 Sheffield Brunswick; 1978– Pocklington, Commission for Local Administration.
Connexional Committees: 1975– Law and Polity. *Council Member:* 1982 Pocklington Town Council.

HARRISON, Robert Sefton, 38 Bretton Rd., Ravenshead, Nottingham NG15 9DB. (06234-3747) *b. 25 Feb 1907, Chadderton, Lancs. m. 22 April 1935: 1d., 1s.* d 2001
Education: 1927–30 Handsworth.
Appointments: 1926 President's List (Supply, Spilsbury); 1930–46 Hunon District, China; 1946–49 Penarth and Barry; 1949–54 Newport, Stow Hill; 1954–59 Birmingham, Belmont Row; 1959–62 Greenock; 1962–67 Driffield; 1967–69 Kirby Stephen, Appleby and Teboy.
Connexional Committees: 1949–54 Overseas Missions. *Council Member:* 1973–82 South Lakeland District Council; 1976–82 South East Cumbria Community Health Council (1980–81 Chairman); 1971–79 Clerk, Armside Parish Council.
Local Council Committees: S. Lakesland District Council, Planning, Environmental Health (1981–82 Chairman), Public Works, Policy and Resources, Manual Workers' Coordination.
Special Interests: Chinese Concerns, Local Government. *Hobbies and Recreations:* Gardening, Strolls in the Country, Reading, History, Poetry, Novels.

HARRISON, Thomas William, Alpenrose, 34 Hillside Ave., Sutton-on-Sea, Lincs LN12 2JH. (0521-41039) *b. 5 July 1910, Edlington, Nr. Woodhall Spa, Lincs. m. 1. 28 July 1938, 2. 8 Aug 1981: 1d., 1s.*
Education: 1917–21 Monks Rd. Council Sch., Lincoln; 1921–25 Technical Institute, Grantham; 1925–26 Lincoln Technical Coll.; 1928–29 Cliff Coll.; 1932–35 Headingley.
Appointments: 1931–32 Liverpool Mission; 1935–38 President's List (1935 Worksop, 1936 Longton, 1937 Leek, 1938 Littleborough); 1938–41 Tipton (Park Lane); 1941–45 Kidderminster; 1946–51 Alford; 1951–56 Skegness and Wainfleet; 1956–60 Ely; 1960–67 Lowestoft; 1967–73 Cleethorpes; 1973–82 Alford.
Connexional Committees: 1941–44 Dept of Social Welfare.
Special Interests: Housing. *Hobbies and Recreations:* Travel, Gardening, Christian Art.

HARRISON, Will, 95 McKinnell Cresc., Rugby, Warwickshire CV21 4AU. (0788-3793) *b. 26 Oct 1907, Stockton-on-Tees. m. 24 July 1937. Education:* 1920–23 Leicester Technical Sch.; 1931–34 Wesley, Headingley. *Appointments:* 1934–47 Northern Rhodesia; 1947–49 Rugby; 1949–53 Kenya District; 1953–56 Glasgow (Parkhead); 1956–1962 North of Scotland Mission; 1962–65 Falkirk; 1965–70 Rugby; 1970–74 Chipping Norton.

HARROD, John Anthony, 9 Stour Rd., Tyldesley, Manchester M29 7HH. (0942-882160)–MA(Camb.), BSc(Lond.), PhD(Manchester). *b. 26 March 1947, Lincoln. m. 6 July 1974: 1d., 1s.*
Education: 1958–65 Lincoln Sch.; 1965–68 Univ. of London; 1968–71 Fitzwilliam Coll., Cambridge; 1972–75 Univ. of Manchester; 1968–71 Wesley House. *Appointments:* 1971–73 Assistant Tutor, Hartley Victoria Coll.; 1973–75 Tutor in Philosophy and Theology, Hartley Victoria Coll.; 1975–81 Bolton; 1981– Leigh; 1973– Lecturer (Part Time) in Department of Philosophy of Religion, Univ. of Manchester; 1978 Served as Lecturer, Department of Extra Mural Studies, Manchester Univ.; 1976 Appointed to Faculty Board, Theology Faculty, Univ. of Manchester.
Connexional Committees: 1973– Connexional Probationers' Oversight Committee; 1979–82 Connexional Doctrinal Committee; 1978– Connexional General Purposes Committee; 1980– Appointed Member of Committee of Oxford Institute of Methodist Theological Studies; 1981– Faith and Order Committee; 1979– Served on Team Leading Annual Ordinands' Retreat prior to Methodist Conference; 1981–82 Served on Division of Social Responsibility Working Party on Marriage and Family. *Local Council Committees:* 1975– Secretary of Hartley Victoria Executive Committee; 1981– Appointed to Governing Body of Fred Longworth Comprehensive Sch., Tyldesley, Lancs.; 1982– Appointed Chairman of Governors, Bedford Butts Methodist Sch., Leigh, Lancs.; Probationers Secretary, Bolton and Rochdale District. *Publications:* 1981 Fernley Hartley Lecturer, Methodist Conference; Book Reviews in *Epworth Review.*
Special Interests: Philosophical, Theology and Ethics. *Hobbies and Recreations:* Gardening, Carpentry, Picture Framing, General DIY, Music, Reading.

HART, Harry, 21 Sandhurst Close, Leicester LE3 6RD. (0533-858880) *b. 17 May 1915, London. m. 1942: 1s.*
Appointments: 1951–52 Rhymney Valley; 1952–56 North Walsham; 1956–61 Peterborough; 1961–65 Newport, Mon.; 1965–70 Chelmsford; 1970–75 Grays; 1975–81 Leicester West.

HART, Herbert Maurice, Beechwood, Sandymere Rd., Northam, Bideford, Devon EX39 1EY. (023-72-4623) *b. 16 May 1904, Blackheath, London. m. 2. 3 Jan 1956: 1d.*
Education: 1914–20 Aske's Haberdasher's, Hatcham, London; 1925–28 Richmond. *Appointments:* 1928–31 Otley; 1931–35 South Norwood; 1935–40 London Mission East; 1940–41 Southampton; 1941–42 Home Mission Committee; 1942–48 East Cornwall Mission; 1948–56 Wellington, Shropshire; 1956–68 Doncaster District, Coalfields Mission.
Connexional Committees: 1957–68 Home Mission.
Special Interests: Methodist Guild Holidays Director from 1933, Local Men's Forum. *Hobbies and Recreations:* Reading, Writing, Gardening.

HARVEY, Alan Edward Davidson, 725 Parkfield Rd., Wolverhampton WV4 6EE. (0902-332631)–BA(Bristol), BSc(Birmingham). *b. 3 June 1946, Oxford. m. 31 July 1971: 1d., 1s.*
Education: 1957–64 Hele's Grammar Sch., Exeter; 1964–69 Birmingham Univ.; 1969–73 Bristol Univ.; 1969–73 Wesley, Bristol. *Appointments:* 1973–74 Bradford Mission (Univ. Chaplain); 1974–79 Sheffield South; 1979– Wolverhampton (Darlington St.).
Connexional Committees: 1980– Team Ministries Committee.
Publications: Biochemical Journal **108**, (1968), 101–106; *Clinica Chimica Acta* 21 (1968), 85–90.
Special Interests: Race Relations, Alliance of Radical Methodists, Collaborative Ministry. *Hobbies and Recreations:* Music, Walking, Books, Winemaking.

HARVEY, Albert, Hawsacre, Thorpe Lane, Robin Hoods Bay, Whitby, North Yorks YO22 4RN. (0947 880358) *b. 4 July 1900, Barton-on-Humber, Lincs. m. 20 Aug 1930: 1d.*
Education: Barton Wes. Sch.; 1924–27 Didsbury. *Appointments:* 1923–24 Epworth; 1927–30 Withernsea; 1930–33 Paisley Mission; 1933–34 Manchester, Oldham Rd.; 1934–38 Otley; 1938–44 Cheddar Valley; 1944–49 Bridlington Quay; 1949–52 Pickering; 1952–55 Filey Eb; 1955–60 Redcar and Saltburn; 1960–63 Sheffield, Carver St.; 1963–66 Chester-Le-St.

HARVEY, Roy James, 11 Newlands, Elmsett, Ipswich IP7 6NZ. (047333-655) *b. 29 July 1914, Saxtead, Sussex. m. 15 Aug 1946: 1d.*
Education: 1919–29 Framlingham Elemen.; 1938–39 Cliff Coll.; 1939–42 Hartley Victoria. *Appointments:* 1942–43 New Forest Mission; 1943–45 Hurst and Hyde; 1945–46 Dursley and Stonehouse; 1946–48 Newton and Hyde; 1948–52 Batley (Hick Lane); 1952–56 Somerset Mission; 1956–63 Weston-super-Mare; 1963–68 Yeovil; 1968–80 Clacton-on-Sea.

HARVEY, Vivian Arthur, 7 Temple Rd., Stowmarket, Suffolk IP14 1AX (0449-612619) *b. 27 Nov 1927, Ellingham, Norfolk. m. 15 Aug 1953: 1d., 2s.*
Education: 1932–39 Ellingham Elemen.; 1939–46 Bungay Grammar; 1950–51 Richmond. *Appointments:* 1948–49 Leominster; 1951–52 Upwell and Manea; 1952–53 Liverpool Central; 1953–54 Sheffield

North; 1961–64 Peterborough; 1964–73 Kettering; 1973–76 Manningtree and Harwich; 1976–81 Downham Market; 1981– Stowmarket.
Special Interests: Liturgy and Worship. *Hobbies and Recreations:* East Anglian Windmill Studies, World War Two Modelling.

HASLAM, David Arthur, 134 Wrottesley Rd., Harlesden, London NW10 5XR. (01-965-7454)–BSc, BA. *b. 24 Nov 1942, Lancashire. m. 6 Aug 1966: 1d., 1s.*
Education: 1953–57 King George 5th Sch., Southport; 1957–61 Manchester Grammar Sch.; 1961–64 Birmingham Univ.; 1965–69 Birmingham Univ.; 1965–69 Handsworth. *Appointments:* 1969–71 Coventry Mission; 1971–74 Southampton; 1974– London, Harlesden.
Connexional Committees: 1973–76 Board of Social Responsibility; 1974–80 DSR World Development Committee; 1975–79 Central Finance Board. *Council Member:* War on Want (Vice Chairperson); Christian Concern for Southern Africa; End Loans to Southern Africa (Secretary).
Publications: Unto the Least of These (1970); *Go Sell* (1975); *Agenda for Prophets* (Editor 1980).
Special Interests: World Development, Anti Racism, Southern Africa, Transnational Corporations.
Hobbies and Recreations: Fell Walking, Music, Reading, My Family.

HASLAM, Graham Thomas, 39 Clayton Rd., Jesmond, Newcastle-upon-Tyne NE2 4RQ. (0632-813417)–MA, BSc. *b. 31 March 1936, Dinnington, Sheffield. m. 12 Aug 1961: 1d., 1s.*
Education: 1947–54 Maltby Grammar Sch.; 1954–57 Leeds Univ.; 1957–58 Sheffield Univ.; 1958–61 Didsbury, Bristol.
Appointments: 1961–66 Coventry; 1966–69 Leeds (Headingley); 1969–75 Hillingdon; 1975–82 Shebbear College; 1982– Newcastle Student Chaplaincy.

HASLER, Murray John, 18 Gledholt Rd., Gledholt, Huddersfield, West Yorkshire HD1 4HP. (0484-36332) *b. 27 Dec 1936, Hounslow, Middlesex. m. 3 Aug 1963: 2s.*
Education: 1961–65 Handsworth.
Appointments: 1965–67 Dorchester; 1967–69 Dunstable; 1969–77 Huddersfield South; 1977– Huddersfield Pennine.
Special Interests: Politics. *Hobbies and Recreations:* Printing, Cricket.

HASWELL, John Hirst Winn, Berakiel, 13 Henley Rd., Exmouth, Devon EX8 2LX. (03952-4527)–BA(Manchester). *b. 5 Oct 1898, Birkenhead, Cheshire. m. 1. May 1926 2. 23 Aug 1958: 1d.*
Education: 1903 St. Luke's Sch., Birkenhead; 1912 Birkenhead Institute; 1920–23 Manchester Univ.; 1923–26 London Univ.; 1920–23 Hartley Victoria. *Appointments:* 1919–20 East London Mission; 1920–23 Hartley College; 1923–26 East London Mission; 1926–28 West Africa; 1928–30 Manchester IX; 1930–33 London, Shooters Hill; 1933–36 Castletown, Isle of Man; 1936–56 Chaplain, RAF; 1956–58 Nantwich; 1958–60 Attleborough, Norfolk.
Publications: Various, *Introduction to the Holy Land* (Duckworth 1969); *20th Century Sky Pilot.*
Special Interests: Royal Air Force, Toc H, Christian Aid, Help the Aged Charity.

HATCHER, Stephen George, 15 Trent Holme Drive, The Mount, York YO2 2DF. (0904-22858)–BD(Lond.). *b. 28 Oct 1943, Walpole St. Andrew, Norfolk. m. 12 Aug 1978: 1d.*
Education: 1965–68 Richmond.
Appointments: 1968–71 Holmfirth; 1971–76 Birstall and Birkenshaw; 1976–81 Glasgow (St. Johns); 1981– York (South).

HATTERSLEY, John Chandler, Wesley Manse, 1 Chequett's Close, Callington, Cornwall PL17 7HQ. (057-93-3274) *b. 2 July 1920, Willesden, London. m. 23 July 1949: 1d., 2s.*
Education: 1925–31 Harrow CP Greenhill; 1931–34 Alpha Preparatory Sch., Harrow; 1934–36 Westminster Technical Coll.; 1946–49 Richmond. *Appointments:* 1949–63 Kenya District; 1963–69 Truro; 1969–75 Perranporth; 1975–80 Redruth; 1980– Callington.
Connexional Committees: 1963–69 Overseas Division.

HAWKES, David Graham, 9 New Zealand Ave., Salisbury, Wilts SP2 7JX. (0722-4833) *b. 21 Nov 1940, Romford, Essex. m. 1 April 1967: 1d.*
Education: 1952–57 Royal Liberty Grammar Sch., Romford; 1963–67 Didsbury, Bristol. *Appointments:* 1967–71 East Wight; 1971–74 Bournemouth; 1974–77 National Christian Education Council; 1977–82 Petersfield, Liphook and Haslemere; 1982– Salisbury.
Connexional Committees: 1974–79 Divisional Board of Education and Youth; 1975–79 Connexional Children's Committee.
Special Interests: Children's Work, Family Worship, Christian Education.
Hobbies and Recreations: Inland Waterways, Photography.

HAWKES, Frazer John, 14 Warde-Aldam Cresc., Wickersley, Rotherham, S. Yorkshire S66 0HN. (0709-542721) *b. 23 Oct 1948, Shoeburyness, Essex. m. 8 Sept 1973: 2s.*
Education: 1953–60 Richmond Ave. Inf. and Jun. Sch., Shoeburyness, Essex; 1960–65 Southend Grammar Sch. for Boys, Essex; 1972–76 Wesley, Bristol. *Appointments:* 1976–79 South Petherton and Crewkerne; 1979– Rotherham.
Hobbies and Recreations: Walking, Gardening, Tropical Fish, Freshwater Fish.

HAWKES, Herbert George, 11 Saltersbrook Rd., Darfield, Barnsley, South Yorkshire S73 9AU. (0226-753356) *b. 6 Jan 1918, Littleport, Ely, Cambridgeshire. m.*
Education: 1947–48 Didsbury, Bristol. *Appointments:* 1946–47 Evesham; 1947–48 Didsbury; 1948–49 Pickering, Hungate; 1949–50

Jersey, Wesley Grove; 1950–51 Hunstanton and Docking; 1951–54 Rotherham; 1954–56 Cannock Chase; 1956–59 West Wight; 1959–63 Bradford, Manningham; 1963–66 Huddersfield North East; 1966–69 Masham.

HAWKINS, Kenneth, 10 Woodhall Rd., Penn, Wolverhampton, West Midlands WV4 4DJ. (0902-331198)–BD(Lond.). *b. 11 Dec 1937, York. m. 17 Aug 1963: 1d., 2s.* *Education:* 1942–49 Acomb CP, York; 1949–56 Nunthorpe Sch., York; 1958–60 College of the Venerable Bede, Durham; 1962–65 Hartley Victoria. *Appointments:* 1965–68 Cheadle (Staffs); 1968–74 Chester; 1974– Wolverhampton (Trinity); 1975–76 MAYC President. *Special Interests:* Childrens and Youth Work, Hospital Chaplaincy. *Hobbies and Recreations:* Numismatics, Sailing, Hockey, Reading, Watching TV.

HAWKRIDGE, Geoffrey Bertie Leedham, 108 Eastmoor Pk., Harpenden, Herts AL5 1BP. (058-27-3773) *b. 26 Oct 1925, Leicester. m. 15 Aug 1953: 1s., 1d.* *Education:* 1936–41 City Boys Sch., 1949–51 Hartley Victoria. *Appointments:* 1947–49 Clitheroe; 1951–53 North of Scotland Mission; 1953–57 Glasgow West; 1957–62 Worksop; 1962–67 Hinckley; 1967–74 Birmingham (Elmdon); 1974–78 Kettering; 1978– Harpenden. *Hobbies and Recreations:* Archaeology, History, Music, Nature, Conservation.

HAWTHORNE, Raymond Albert, 97 Kingsmead Ave., Worcester Park, Surrey KT4 8UT. (01-337-2348) *b. 7 May 1927, Birmingham. m. 13 April 1957: 1d., 1s.* *Education:* 1934–43 Pitmaston Rd., Birmingham; 1953–54 Cliff Coll.; 1955–58 Hartley Victoria. *Appointments:* 1958–60 Kirkoswald; 1960–64 Hindley; 1964–67 Douglas; 1967–74 Stourbridge and Brierley Hill; 1974–80 Lytham St. Annes; 1980– Wimbledon. *Connexional Committees:* 1971–74, 1975– Property. *Special Interests:* Travel, Wesleyana. *Hobbies and Recreations:* Garden, Motoring.

HAWTON, Edward George, The Yews, 7 Victoria Rd., Tamworth, Staffs B79 7HS. (0827-62456)–BSc(Lond.), BD(Lond.). *b. 28 June 1930, Ashford, Middlesex. m. 24 April 1954: 1d., 2s.* *Education:* 1941–48 Strodes, Egham, Surrey; 1948–51 Kings, London; 1955–56 Kings, London; 1961–63 Handsworth. *Appointments:* 1963–66 Spennymoor and Ferryhill; 1967–68 Karoi, Zimbabwe; 1969–71 Kwenda, Zimbabwe; 1973–75 Moleli, Zimbabwe; 1976–82 Birmingham, Elmdon; 1982– Tamworth. *Connexional Committees:* 1980– Board of Division of Ministries. *Publications:* Editor *Bulletin of the Fellowship of the Kingdom* (1977–82).

HAYES, Colin Frederick, Sion Methodist Manse, La Grande Route De St. Jean, Sion, St. John, Jersey. (0534-62497) *b. 27 Nov 1928, Catford, London. m. 5 July 1958: 3s.* *Education:* 1939–44 Bromley Grammar Sch.; 1946–47 R.N. Metereological Training Sch.; Ealing Coll.; Bristol Univ.; 1953–57 Didsbury, Bristol. *Appointments:* 1957–59 Trowbridge; 1959–64 Devon and Dorset Mission; 1964–66 Sheffield Mission; 1966–71 Chesterfield; 1972–77 Bristol Frome Valley; 1982 Birmingham, Asbury; 1977–82 Jersey C.I.; 1978–82 Secretary of Jersey District Synod; 1982 Birmingham, Asbury. *Special Interests:* The Circuit Ministry, Communication in all its forms. *Hobbies and Recreations:* Photography, still and cine, Electronics, Music, Drawing, Design.

HAYES, Leslie Webster, The Manse, 7 Gibraltar Terrace, St. Mawes, Truro TR2 5BQ.–BA. *b. 6 March 1910, West Hartlepool, Durham. m. 17 Aug 1943: 2d., 2s.* *Education:* 1915–22 Elwick Rd. Sch., West Hartlepool; 1922–23 Technical Coll.; 1923–27 Harrogate Grammar Sch.; 1932–35 Birmingham Univ.; 1932–35 Handsworth. *Appointments:* 1931–32 Thirsk; 1935–40 South Shields; 1940–43 Wye Valley Mission; 1943–46 Cardiff (Roath); 1946–51 St. Just; 1960–68 South Devon Mission; 1968–79 Roseland. *Publications:* Articles on Modern Poetry, Wesley and Watts in *Methodist Recorder* and *London Quarterly.* *Special Interests:* English Literature, History, Archaeology, Natural History. *Hobbies and Recreations:* Walking, Swimming.

HAYES, Wilfred, 17 Relton Terrace, Whitley Bay, Tyne and Wear NE25 8DZ. (0632-530450) *b. 17 Aug 1913, Warrington, Lancs. m. 4 Sept 1937: 1d., 1s.* *Education:* 1918–32 Oakwood Ave. Council Sch., Warrington; 1947–48 Wesley, Headingley. *Appointments:* 1939–40 Pontypool (Eastern Valley), Home Mission; 1940–42 Wakefield; 1942–43 Sheffield North; 1943–44 London Seaman's Mission; 1944–45 Colchester; 1945–47 Chelmsford; 1947–50 Leeds Mission; 1950–56 Newcastle West; 1956–61 Newcastle North West; 1961–68 Newcastle, Brunswick; 1968–78 North Shields and Whitley Bay. *Council Member:* 1951–56 District MAYC Organiser and Secretary. *Special Interests:* Methodist History. *Hobbies and Recreations:* Oil Painting.

HAYMAN, Michael Arthur, 39 New Town Rd., Colchester, Essex CO1 2EF. (0206-73888)–BD(Lond.). *b. 5 Feb 1932, St. Marylebone, London. m. 22 June 1957: 2d., 1s.* *Education:* 1937–43 Essendine Rd. Elemen. Sch.; 1943–50 St. Marylebone Grammar Sch.; 1955–58 Headingley. *Appointments:* 1958–61 Ticehurst; 1961–64 Linacre Mission; 1964–68 London (Highgate); 1968–75 Norwich (Calvert St.); 1975–82 Colchester; 1982– London, Finsbury Park and Southgate. *Connexional Committees:* 1967–68, 1972–75 BSR Board. *Local Council Committees:* 1964–65 St. Pancras Education Committee. *Special Interests:* Social

Responsibility Matters, Ministry. *Hobbies and Recreations:* Reading, Tapestry Work, Writing Poetry.

HAYMAN, Peter George, Dunford House, Midhurst, Sussex GU29 0DG. (073-081-2381) *b. 17 Aug 1926, Birmingham. w: 2d.*
Education: 1931–39 Eastlands Boys Sch., Rugby; 1939–41 Rugby Coll. of Further Education; 1949–52 Hartley Victoria. *Appointments:* 1948–49 Stamford; 1952–54 Penzance (Newlyn); 1954–59 South Shields; 1959–62 Manchester and Salford Mission; 1962–66 Secretary Manchester YMCA; 1966–69 Tutor Wolfson Coll., Cambridge; 1969– Principal, Dunford House, Midhurst.

HAYWARD, Lewis James, 186 Dales Rd., Ipswich, Suffolk IP1 4JY. (0473-41189) *b. 20 Sept 1913, Brackley, Northants. m. 30 Aug 1939: 3d.*
Education: 1916–26 Brackley CE Sch.; 1926–32 Magdalen Coll. Sch., Brackley; 1935–37 Cliff Coll. *Appointments:* 1950–53 Chorley; 1953–57 East Suffolk; 1957–62 Hitchin; 1962–65 Llanelly and Carmarthen; 1965–70 Peterborough; 1970–73 Dove Valley; 1973–78 Malton, Yorks.
Special Interests: People. *Hobbies and Recreations:* Gardening, Reading, Caravanning.

HAYWOOD, Peter Graham, 1 Whiteside Way, Cleveleys, Blackpool FY5 2BA. (0253-852909)—BSc(Econ)(Lond.), BD(Manchester). *b. 11 Nov 1939, Bolton, Lancs. m. 27 Nov 1976: 2d., 2s.*
Education: Hayward High Sch.; 1972–74 Manchester Univ.; 1965–66 Bolton Coll. of Education; 1971–74 Hartley Victoria. *Appointments:* 1974–79 Lytham St. Annes; 1979– Fleetwood.
Special Interests: Overseas Aid. *Hobbies and Recreations:* Walking, Reading.

HAZLEHURST, Harry, Wesley Manse, Walls, Shetland ZE2 9PF. (059-571-210)—BA(Sheffield). *b. 13 Feb 1918, Hope, Derbyshire. m. 11 Aug 1945: 4s.* d. 24.12.99
Education: Nether Edge Secondary Sch., Sheffield; 1936–39 Sheffield Univ.; 1939–40 Sheffield Univ. Education Dept. *Appointments:* 1943–45 Brynmawr; 1945–52 Ripley and South Normanton; 1952–57 Ashby-de-la-Zouch; 1957–63 Ulverston; 1963–69 Millom; 1971–79 Thornley; 1979– Walls.
Connexional Committees: 1955–57 Social Responsibility.
Special Interests: Politics, Social Affairs. *Hobbies and Recreations:* Gardening, Rugmaking, All Sport.

HEAD, Leonard David, 2 East Mount, North Ferriby, North Humberside HU14 3BX. (0482-634451) *b. 12 April 1915, Pirton, Nr. Hitchin, Hertfordshire. m. 20 April 1943: 1d., 1s.*
Education: 1920–29 Elemen. Education, Pirton Village Sch.; Cliff Coll. *Appointments:* 1964–67 Hull North; 1967–80 Bishop Auckland.
Special Interests: Gardening, Reading, Car Riding.

HEAFFORD, Frank Barrie, 47 King Edward Ave., Aylesbury, Bucks HP21 7JE. (0296-23363)—BA. *b. 18 Oct 1934, East Bridgeford, Notts. m. 16 Aug 1958: 3s.* d 04.02.14
Education: 1945–52 West Bridford Grammar Sch.; 1954–57 Birmingham Univ; 1968 Institute of Education (London Univ.); 1954–58 Handsworth. *Appointments:* 1958–61 Barnsley East; 1961–66 Colchester; 1966–72 Chislehurst; 1972–79 Watford; 1979– Aylesbury.
Connexional Committees: 1970– Sector Committee (Now Advisory Committee for Ministers in Other Appointments); 1969– Community Development Committee (Was with Lay Training, now Divisional Ministry).
Special Interests: Community Development, Occasional Assistant AVEC, Founder Member Aylesbury Peace Campaign. *Hobbies and Recreations:* Cabinet Making, Sport, Music, Gardening.

HEALEY, George Charles Wilson, 7 Firtree Rd., Hastings, East Sussex. (0424-427374) *b. 19 March 1916, Hastings.*
Education: 1946–47 Handsworth. *Appointments:* 1947–48 Barton-on-Humber; 1948–71 Chaplain HMF (RN); 1971–73 London Mission, North West; 1973–81 London Mission, Hackney.

HEALEY, John Bartlett, 8 Brooks Close, Staplehurst, Kent TN12 0PP. (0580-891631) *b. 2 Oct 1915, Empingham, Nr. Oakham. m. 18 Jan 1944: 1d., 1s.*
Education: 1920–27 Empingham CE Sch.; 1927–34 Oakham Sch.; 1937–41 Richmond. *Appointments:* 1941–44 Guildford; 1944–47 Farnworth; 1947–50 Hitchin; 1950–54 Northampton (Kettering Rd.); 1954–59 St. Austell; 1959–63 Launceston; 1963–69 Helston; 1969–73 Camelford and Wadebridge; 1973–77 Ashford (Kent); 1977–79 Hunts Mission.

HEAP, Charles Edward, 4 Radcot Close, Maidenhead, Berks SL6 7UJ. (0628-36803)—BA(Leeds), MA(Cantab.). *b. 1 Mar 1911, Burley-in-Wharfedale, Yorks. m. 7 Dec 1957: 2d., 1s.*
Education: 1920–30 Bradford Grammar; 1930–34 Leeds Univ.; 1935–38 Cambridge; 1935–38 Wesley House. *Appointments:* 1938–40 North of Scotland Mission; 1940–42 Edinburgh, Nicholas Square; 1942–46 Chaplain RAF; 1946–49 Goole; 1949–54 Skipton; 1955–1960 Blackburn; 1960–66 Hillingdon; 1966–76 Windsor and Maidenhead.

HEAP, Donald Neville, Jagtial, 194A Upper Rd., Kennington, Oxford OX1 5LR. (0865 736200) *b. 13 April 1918, Leeds, Yorkshire. m. 12 April 1950: 4s.*
Education: 1923–24 Derby Rd., Heaton Moor, Stockport; 1925–27 Victoria Rd., Council Sch., Chester; 1927–28 Love Lane Central Sch., Chester; 1928–33 Kingswood Sch., Bath; 1946–48 Headingley.
Appointments: 1945–46 Oundle; 1948–61 Church of South India; 1961–65 Evesham; 1965–70 London, Wanstead and Woodford; 1970–77 Holsworthy; 1977–82 Isles of Scilly.
Connexional Committees: 1961–70 Eastern Committee (MMS).

Special Interests: Ecumenism, Pacifism, Bible Society, Missionary Work, India, Church of South India, Countryside. *Hobbies and Recreations:* Sport (Cricket, Football, Tennis), Photography, Writing, Travel.

HEAP, James Arthur, The Manse, 189 Pendleton Rd., Darlington, Co. Durham DL1 2EP. (0325-64916) *b. 16 May 1934, Manchester. m. 14 July 1962: 1d., 3s.* *Education:* Various Jun.; 1945–51 Audenshaw Grammar Sch.; 1961–62 Westhill Coll., Birmingham; 1958–61 Richmond. *Appointments:* 1962–64 Ripley; 1964–69 Worsley; 1969–75 Leeds (South); 1975– Darlington.

HEARLE, Antony Mervyn, 29 Lacy Drive, Wimborne, Dorset BH21 1AY. (0202-883461)–MA(Cantab.). *b. 9 June 1922, Frampton Cotterell, Bristol. m. 26 June 1953: 3s.* *Education:* 1932–41 Kingswood; 1947–50 Wesley House. *Appointments:* 1945–47 Shepton Mallet; 1950–58 Ivory Coast and West Africa; 1959–63 Newark-on-Trent; 1963–69 Harrogate; 1969–77 Chester; 1977–82 Guildford; 1982– Wimbourne. *Connexional Committees:* 1969–77 Overseas Missions.

HEARLE, Dennis Claude, 7 Pinewood Rd., Poole, Dorset BH13 6JP. (0202-764661)–BA(Lond.), BD(Lond.), MA(Lond.). *b. 20 April 1920, Frampton Cotterell, Gloucestershire. m. 21 April 1951: 2d., 2s.* *Education:* 1930–36 Kingswood Sch., Bath; 1937–38 Bristol Univ.; 1939–40 Handsworth; 1940–41 Richmond; 1941–42 Headingley. *Appointments:* 1942–43 Swansea; 1943–44 Abergavenny; 1944–75 Royal Air Force Chaplaincy; 1975– Bournemouth; 1974–75 Honorary Chaplain to H.M. the Queen. *Connexional Committees:* 1977– Royal Navy, Army and Royal Force Board. *Special Interests:* Local History, Legend. *Hobbies and Recreations:* Photography.

HEARN, Kenneth Victor, 34 Park Rd., Birstall, Leicester LE4 3AU. (0533-674117) *b. 26 Aug 1929, London. m. 11 Aug 1962: 2d.* *Education:* 1940–45 Brockley County Grammar Sch.; 1949–51 Wm. Booth Memorial Training Sch.; 1956–59 Didsbury, Bristol. *Appointments:* 1959–62 Bristol (South); 1962–67 Nottingham (East); 1967–72 Birmingham (Elmdon); 1972–77 Taunton; 1977–82 Exeter; 1977–81 Chaplain HM Prison, Exeter; 1982– Leicester (North). *Connexional Committees:* 1968–72 Local Preachers.

HEATH, Stephen Noel, 68 Vicarage Rd., Leyton, London E10 5EA. (01-539-3369) *b. 24 Dec 1954, Kirkbymoorside, North Riding, Yorkshire. m. 18 Oct 1975: 1d., 2s.* *Education:* 1966–63 Lady Cumleys Grammar Sch., Pickering, N. Yorks, 1973–74 Cliff Coll.; 1982– Wesley, Bristol. *Appointments:* 1981–82 Leytonstone and Forest Gate. *Local Council Committees:* 1979–82 London Borough of Waltham Forest Youth Committee. *Hobbies and Recreations:* Cycling, Gardening.

HEATHCOTE, Arthur Weston, 4 Manderley Sea Rd., Milford-on-Sea, Hants SO4 0PG. (059069-5792)–BSc(Birm. and Lond.), MSc, MTh(Lond.), MA(Cantab.), PhD(Lond.). *b. 12 April 1916, Dursley, Glos. m. 15 April 1947.* *Education:* 1929–32 Prince Henry's G.S., Evesham; 1932–34 Dudley G.S.; 1934–37 Birmingham Univ.; 1937–40 Wesley House. *Appointments:* 1940–45 High Wycombe; 1945–48 Skipton; 1948–49 Grassington; 1949–52 Brecon; 1952–55 Tenby; 1955–57 Divinity Master, King Edward VI G.C., Retford; 1957–62 Head of Divinity Department, Avery Hill Coll., Eltham; 1962–67 Senior Lecturer in Historical Theology, Univ. of Keele; 1967–76 Principal Lecturer and Head of Department of Religious Studies, Redland Coll., Bristol. *Publications: Israel in the Time of Solomon* (1960); *From the Death of Solomon to the Capture of Judah* (1959); *From the Exile to Herod the Great* (1964); *Introduction to the Letters of St. Paul* (1963); Translation, Editing and Production of English Editions of the following: *Theology of the Old Testament* (E. Jacob 1958); *A Dictionary of Life in Bible Times* (W. Corswant 1960); *The First Epistle of St. Paul to the Corinthians* (J. Héring 1961); *Grace and Guilt* (P. Tournier 1962); *The Second Epistle of St. Paul to the Corinthians* (J. Héring 1967); *Commentary on the Epistle to the Hebrews* (J. Héring 1970); *The Epistle of St. Paul to the Philippians* (J.-F. Collange 1979). *Special Interests:* Enjoyment and Study of Nature, The Sciences, Music, Art.

HEAVEN, Joseph, 28 Blackmore Rd., Stalbridge, Sturminster Newton, Dorset DT10 2NT. (0963-62032) *b. 3 Dec 1908, London. m. 31 July 1937: 1d., 1s.* *Education:* 1931–34 Richmond. *Appointments:* 1930–31 Market Harborough; 1931–34 Richmond Coll.; 1934–36 London City Rd. (Wesley's Chapel); 1936–40 Hitchin; 1940–42 Bedford St. Pauls; 1942–46 HMF Chaplain; 1946–51 Oxford; 1951–56 Penarth; 1956–64 Salisbury; 1964–70 Portland, Dorset; 1970–73 Southport.

HENMAN, Cyril Ernest James, Linden Garth, 17 Wheatley Ave., Ilkley, W. Yorks LS29 8PT. (0943-609084) *b. 7 Aug 1908, Lewisham, London. m. 10 Aug 1938: 1s.* *Education:* 1920–24 East Anglian Sch., Bury St. Edmunds, Suffolk; 1931–34 Handsworth. *Appointments:* 1934–36 President's List; 1936–38 Manchester, Gravel Lane; 1938–41 Cadishead; 1941–44 Widnes; 1944–48 Eccles; 1948–51 Manchester, Chorlton and Moss Side; 1951–54 Huddersfield, Gledhott; 1954–55 Huddersfield, West; 1955–60 Halifax, Ebenezer; 1960–65 Skipton; 1965–68 Bradford, Manningham; 1968–73 Bingley.

HENSON, Evelyn Winfred, 16 Newton Rd., Faversham, Kent ME13 8DY. (079582-2461)–BA(Bristol). *b. 18 Sept 1947, Wiesbaden, Germany. s.*
Education: 1959–66 Palmer's Girls' Sch., Grays, Essex; 1966–69 Kenton Lodge Coll. of Education, Newcastle upon Tyne; 1973–77 Univ. of Bristol; 1977–78 Univ. of Birmingham; 1973–76 Wesley, Bristol; 1977–78 Queen's. *Appointments:* 1978– Canterbury and Faversham. *Connexional Committees:* 1978–81 Methodist Stewardship Organisaiton; 1982– Conference Committee of Appeal. *Local Council Committees:* 1981–82 Chairman, Faversham Council of Churches.
Special Interests: Counselling (Marriage Guidance Counsellor), Education, Training. *Hobbies and Recreations:* Tropical Fish, Photography, Travel, Wine-Making.

HERRIOTT-ING, Patricia Elinor, 69 Tilehurst Rd., Reading, Berks RG3 2JL. (0734-581004)–BA, MDiv. *b. 2 Feb 1953, Harvard, Illinois, USA. m. 16 Aug 1980.*
Education: Harvard, Illinois Community Sch., finishing at Harvard High Sch. in June 1971; 1971–75 Cornell Coll., Mt. Vernon, Iowa, USA; 1975–76 Iliff Theol. Seminary, Denver, Colorado, USA; 1976–79 Garrett-Evangelical Theol. Seminary, Evanston, Illinois, USA.
Appointments: 1979–80 Hunstanton; 1980–82 Minister Without Appointment, Petersfield, Haslemere and Liphook; 1982– Reading and Silchester.
Special Interests: Music, Innovative Worship, The Changing Role of Women in Church and Society.
Hobbies and Recreations: Singing, Needlework, Walking, Travelling, Cooking, Letter-writing, Reading.

HEROD, Frederick George, 4 The Hermitage, Eliot Hill, London SE13 7EH. (01-852-7080)–BA. *b. 10 June 1906, Haslingden. w: 2d.*
Education: Sir John Deane's Grammar Sch., Northwich; Manchester Grammar Sch.; 1930–34 Manchester Univ.; 1929–34 Hartley.
Appointments: 1934–36 President's List; 1936–37 Thornley; 1937–40 Bolton, Moor Lane; 1940–42 Ticehurst; 1942–47 Gravesend.
Publications: What Men Believe (1968); *World Religions* (1970); *Who Cares?* (1972); *The Gospels—A First Commentary* (1976); *Challenge* (1980).

HEWISON, William, 20 Tower Rd., Orpington, Kent BR6 0SQ. (0689-25129) *b. 14 March 1933, Chester-le-Street, Co. Durham. m. 11 Aug 1956: 2d., 1s.*
Education: 1938–44 West Pelton Prim./Jun.; 1944–49 Chester-le-Street Grammar; 1953–56 Handsworth.
Appointments: 1956–60 Normanton; 1960–66 Leeds Mission; 1966–71 Marple; 1971–75 Derby (Queens Hall) Mission; 1975–76 Collegate United Methodist Church, Iowa, USA; 1976– Orpington.
Connexional Committees: 1968–71 Social Responsibility. *Local Council Committees:* 1976– Gypsy Liaison Group.
Hobbies and Recreations: Growing Camellias, Painting, Sport.

HEWITT, David Arthur, 29 Lacy Drive, Wimborne, Dorset BH21 1AY. (0202-883461) *b. 26 Jan 1925, Palmers Green, London. m. 27 Oct 1953: 1d., 1s.*
Education: 1937–41 Owens Sch., Islington; 1949–52 Handsworth.
Appointments: 1947–49 Newmarket Mission; 1952–54 Cheltenham; 1954–58 Gloucester; 1958–62 Manchester and Salford Mission; 1962–67 Hereford; 1967–74 Birmingham (Sutton Park); 1974–82 Wimborne; 1957–58 Prison Chaplain (Gloucester); 1958–62 Prison Chaplain (Manchester).
Connexional Committees: 1956–58, 1968–74 Education and Youth; 1980–82 Social Responsibility; 1972–74 Candidates; 1976–82 Candidates (Group Secretary); 1967–69 Conference Working Party on Church Membership.
Special Interests: Christian Stewardship. *Hobbies and Recreations:* Music, Walking.

HEWITT, Howard Reginald, Brookside, Carlton Rd., Manby, Louth, Lincs LN11 8HH. (050-782-220) *b. 3 Dec 1906, Stow, Nr. Lincoln. m. 5 Oct 1943: 1d.*
Education: 1912–21 Sturton by Stow Council Sch.; 1926–27 Cliff Coll.; 1932–35 Handsworth.
Appointments: 1931–32 Lowestoft; 1935–36 Evangelist Exeter District; 1936–40 Camelford and Wadebridge; 1940–41 Newmarket; 1941–45 Pembroke; 1945–49 Neath and Port Talbot; 1949–52 Grantham; 1952–57 Downham Market; 1957–63 Chatteris; 1963–67 Madeley and Dawley; 1967–71 Brigg; 1944–45 Chaplain to Mayor of Pembroke.
Hobbies and Recreations: Gardening.

HEXT, Kenneth Samuel James, 30 Devon Sq., Newton Abbot, South Devon TQ12 2HH. (0626 3387)–MA(Cantab.). *b. 7 June 1940, Princetown. m. 19 Aug 1967: 2d.*
Education: 1945–71 Princetown CPS; 1951–52 Tavistock Grammar Sch.; 1952–58 Queen Elizabeth Sch., Crediton; 1959–63 Fitzwilliam Coll., Cambridge; 1959–63 Wesley House.
Appointments: 1963–67 Assistant Tutor, Hartley Victoria Coll., Manchester; 1967–70 Middleton; 1970–71 Bideford; 1971–81 Chaplain, Edgehill Coll.; 1981– Newton Abbot.
Special Interests: Education, N.T. Studies. *Hobbies and Recreations:* Railways, Walking, Gardening, Avoiding Committees.

HEY, Robert Graham, 1 Linden Ave., Woodseats, Sheffield S8 0GA. (0742-745449) *b. 16 July 1947, Leeds. m. 24 July 1947: 2d.*
Education: 1952–58 Lower Wortley Prim. and Jun. Sch.; 1958–62 Harrington High Sch.; 1967–68 Cliff Coll.; 1969–70 Handsworth; 1970–73 Queen's. *Appointments:* 1973–79 Barnsley; 1979– Sheffield (Brunswick).
Special Interests: Preaching, Methodist History. *Hobbies and Recreations:* Gardening, English Literature, Music.

HEYES, Edward, 138 Hednesford Rd., Brownhills, Walsall, West Midlands WS8 7NA. (0543-375904)–BD. *b. 24 Dec 1928, Coventry. m. 21 July 1955: 3d.*
Education: 1939–44 Bablake Sch., Coventry; 1944–49 Coventry Technical Coll.; 1949–52 Hartley Victoria. *Appointments:* 1952–55 Stamford; 1955–60 London Mission (Poplar and Bow); 1960–65 London Mission (East Ham); 1965–68 London, Finsbury Park and Southgate; 1968–72 Walsall Mission; 1972– Probation Officer.

HEYES, James Alexander, 84 Ambleside, Bartley Green, Birmingham B32 3HY. (021-426-5493) *b. 28 Dec 1908, Wigan, Lancs. m. 9 April 1940: 2d., 1s.*
Education: 1930–31 Cliff Coll.; 1931–34 Didsbury. *Appointments:* 1934–36 President's List; 1936–39 Northampton, Gold St.; 1939–42 Deal; 1942–47 Chaplain HMF; 1947–51 Nottingham East; 1951–55 Nottingham Central; 1955–60 Wallasey; 1960–63 Northampton; 1963–67 Wrexham; 1967–72 Nelson, Lancs; 1972–77 Rochdale South.
Connexional Committees: 1951–55 Overseas Missions.
Special Interests: Hospital Visitation, Old People's Welfare.

HIBBERTS, John Michael, 63 Brownedge Lane, Bamber Bridge, Preston, Lancs PR5 6TA. (0772-35184)–BA(Open), Dip Theol(Lond.), Dip/A/Ed(Manchester). *b. 9 July 1943, Stoke on Trent. m. 15 April 1968: 2d., 2s.*
Education: 1948–54 Abbey Hulton Prim. Sch.; 1954–59 Carmountside Secondary Sch.; 1962–63 Stoke on Trent Technical Coll.; 1963–64 Cliff Coll.; 1963–68 Hartley Victoria.
Appointments: 1968–73 Rochdale North; 1973–83 Preston Trinity; 1983– Burslem Mission.
Special Interests: Current Affairs.
Hobbies and Recreations: Photography, Woodwork, Tennis.

HICKS, Joseph Ronald, 34 New Rd., Brownhills, Walsall WS8 6AT. (05433 2151).
Education: 1953–57 Didsbury.
Appointments: 1957–59 Dorchester; 1959–65 Witney; 1965–68 Buckfastleigh; 1968–77 Cannock Chase; 1977– Brownhills and Pelsall.
Hobbies and Recreations: Morris Dancing, Stamp Collecting, Gardening, Folk Singing, Hiking.

HIGGINSON, Robert Orpe, Whitecroft, 92 Wimborne Rd., Poole, Dorset BH15 2DA. (0202-674715)–BA(B'Ham). *b. 23 March 1921, Stratford-upon-Avon. m. 3 Aug 1950: 1d., 2s.*
Education: 1926–31 Warwickshire CC Sch., Broad St., Stratford-upon-Avon;1931–39 King Edward VI Sch., Stratford-upon-Avon; 1947–50 Birmingham Univ.; 1947–50 Handsworth. *Appointments:* 1946–47 Belper; 1950–53 East Suffolk; 1953–56 Leek; 1956–60 Horncastle; 1960–64 Wetton and Longnor; 1964–70 Chipping Norton; 1970–75 North Walsham and Aylsham; 1975–81 Stour Valley; 1981– Poole; 1975–81 Officiating Chaplain to Forces at Blandford Camp.
Connexional Committees: 1972–76 Youth Camps. *Council Member:* 1978–80 Chaplain to Mayor and Blandford Forum Town Council.
Hobbies and Recreations: Gardening.

ARTHUR
HIGHFIELD, Robert A., 7 Crampton Close, Sutton-in-Ashfield, Notts NG17 2HP. (0623-516822).
Education: 1930–33 Didsbury.
Appointments: 1929–30 Kirbymoorside; 1933–36 Kendal; 1936–40 Liverpool (Brunswick); 1940–45 Birkenhead South, Bebington; 1945–48 Littleborough; 1948–53 Mansfield (Bridge St.); 1953–58 Nottingham (North); 1958–66 St. Columb and Padstow; 1966–72 S. Petherton and Crewkerne.
b 30.7.07 d. 18.6.91

HIGMAN, Ernest, 1 Leverton Court, Melton Rd., West Bridgford, Nottingham NG2 6FL. (0602-233951) *b. 8 June 1895, Washaway, Cornwall. w: 1d., 1s.*
Education: 1900–06 Washaway; 1906–10 Bodmin County; 1919–20 Cliff Coll.; 1921–24 Richmond.
Appointments: 1920–21 Hunts Mission; 1924–29 British Guiana; 1930–33 North India; 1934–45 British Guiana; 1946–51 St. Vincent, West Indies; 1951–54 S. Petherton and Crewkerne; 1954–58 Pembroke; 1958–63 Knighton.
Special Interests: Farming. *Hobbies and Recreations:* Walking.

HILDRED, Linda, 118 Watch House Lane, Doncaster DN5 9LT. (0302-783980)–BD, AKC(Lond.). *b. 2 May 1955, Mansfield, Notts. s.*
Education: 1967–73 Manor Grammar Sch., Mansfield, Woodhouse; 1973–77 Univ. of London, King's Coll.; 1977–80 Wesley, Bristol. *Appointments:* 1980– Doncaster.

HILL, David Roger, Asbury House, Merrey Rd., Rising Brook, Stafford ST17 9LX. (0785-42097)–BD(Lond.). *b. 2 June 1941, Ramsey, Hunts. m. 25 June 1966: 2d., 1s.*
Education: 1946–52 Bevios Town Jun., Southampton; 1952–60 Taunton Sch., Southampton; 1961 Cliff Coll.; 1962–66 London Univ.; 1962–66 Richmond. *Appointments:* 1966–67 Rochdale Mission; 1967–70 Ashington (Northumberland); 1970–73 Tana River (Kenya); 1973–78 Sunderland South; 1978–82 Stourbridge.
Connexional Committees: 1975–78, 1981– M.C.O.D. Central Committee.
Special Interests: Rock Music, Football, Writing Musicals. *Hobbies and Recreations:* Rock Guitarist, Snooker.

HILL, Michael Wilson, 9 The Beeches, Bower Lane, Rugeley, Staffs WS15 2QY. (088-94-2356) *b. 17 July 1936, Morley, Nr. Leeds, W. Yorks. m. 25 Feb 1967: 2s.*
Education: 1940–47 Westerton Prim. Sch.; 1947–49 Batley Grammar Sch., 1949–52 Cockburn High Sch. (Leeds); 1956–60 Hartley Victoria.
Appointments: 1960–62 Bridgend; 1962–67 Sandbach and Alsager; 1967–72 Nantwich; 1972–82 Telford North; 1982– Cannock Chase; 1963–71 Assistant Secretary, Chester and Stoke on Trent District; 1980–

Secretary to Wolverhampton and Shrewsbury Synod. *Local Council Committees:* 1972–82 Cemetary Committee of Newport (Shropshire) Town Council. *Special Interests:* Work Amongst the Elderly. *Hobbies and Recreations:* Classical Music.

HILL, Thomas Rowland, The Forum, 83 Roman Way, Tudor Park, Ross-on-Wye, Herefordshire HR9 5UY. (0989-65624) *b. 26 Dec 1918, Tredegar, Gwent. w: 1d.* *Education:* 1929–38 Tredegar County Sch.; 1938–41 Hartley Victoria. *Appointments:* 1941–44 Grays and Tilbury; 1944–45 Llandrindod Wells; 1945–48 Pontypool (Eastern Valley); 1948–51 Cardiff (Roath); 1951–52 Evesham; 1952–55 Nuneaton and Atherstone; 1955–61 Witney; 1961–66 West Wight; 1966–73 Evesham; 1973–79 West Wight; 1979–82 Chippenham and Brinkworth.

HILL, Wilfred James, 23 Whitehall Gdns, Canterbury, Kent CT2 8BD. (0227-61197)–MC, BSc(Wales). *b. 30 Mar 1903, Abercarn, Gwent. m. 14 Aug 1934: 1s.* *Education:* 1907–15 Crosskeys Elemen.; 1915–17 Pontywaun County Sch.; 1923–26 Univ. Coll.of Wales, Cardiff; 1929–31 Didsbury. *Appointments:* 1931–33 Ledbury; 1933–36 Barton-on-Humber Wesley; 1936–40 Clacton on Sea; 1940–42 Cambourne; 1942–46 Chaplain HMF; 1946–52 Chorley; 1952–54 Bolton Wesley; 1954–60 Medway Towns; 1960–65 Llanglly and Carmarthen; 1965–69 Brownhills.

HILLS, Harold Stanley, 3 Newlands Drive, Ripon, North Yorkshire HG4 2JY. (0765-5389) *b. 9 May 1915, Leeds. m. 9 Jan 1947.* *Education:* Bishop Monkton CE; Harrogate Technical Coll.; Richmond. *Appointments:* 1941–43 London (Sydenham and Forest Hill); 1943–47 Chaplain HMF; 1947–50 Bury, Lancs.; 1950–54 Bolton, Bridge St.; 1954–58 Burnley; 1958–69 St. Just, Cornwall; 1969–77 Sedbergh; 1977–80 Stour Vale. *Connexional Committees:* 1972–76 Local Preachers. *Local Council Committees:* 1948–50 Bury Youth Committee; 1959–69 Schools Manager, St. Buryan etc.; 1969–77 Sedbergh W.R.C.C. *Publications:* Contributions to Various Publications. *Hobbies and Recreations:* Golf.

HIMSWORTH, Frank, 1 Fairdale Gdns., Hayes, Middx. UB3 3JA. (01-573-3116)–BA(B'Ham), BD(Lond.). *b. 14 Oct 1934, Doncaster. m. 11 July 1959: 3d.* *Education:* 1946–53 Percy Jackson Grammar Sch.; 1953–56 Birmingham Univ.; 1956–59 Richmond. *Appointments:* 1959–68 Sierra Leone District; 1968–78 Wandsworth and Fulham/Richmond and Hounslow; 1978– Hillingdon. *Local Council Committees:* 1981 Hillingdon Education Committee. *Special Interests:* Samaritans. *Hobbies and Recreations:* Gardening, Badminton, Touring, Sport.

HINCH, Raymond William, 44 Mellowdew Rd., Wyken, Coventry CV2 5GN. (0203-444062) *b. 27 July 1946, Market Harborough, Leicestershire. m. 17 July 1976: 2d.* *Education:* 1951–57 Caldecott Prim. Sch., Rutland; 1957–64 Stamford Sch., Stamford, Lincs.; 1975–76 Westhill Coll. of Education, Selly Oak, Birmingham; 1972–76 Queen's. *Appointments:* 1976–79 West Bromwich; 1979– Coventry. *Special Interests:* Home and Family. *Hobbies and Recreations:* Walking, Photography.

HINES, Edgar Herbert, 3 Furzehat Park Rd., Plymstock, Plymouth PL9 8LE. (0752-42512) *b. 5 Oct 1891, Aston, Birmingham. m. 1 Nov 1918: 1d.* *Education:* King Edward Grammar, Birmingham; 1913–15 Didsbury. *Appointments:* 1915–18 Edinburgh, Nicholson Sq.; 1918–19 Chaplain HMF; 1919–21 London, Clapton; 1921–24 London, Lewisham; 1924–31 Manchester and Salford Mission; 1931–35 Hull Mission; 1935–40 Devonport Garrison; 1940–47 Chairman Scotland District; 1947–52 Plymouth, King St.; 1952–55 Minehead and Dunster. *Connexional Committees:* Home Mission; General Purposes; Education, BBC Religious Advisory. *Hobbies and Recreations:* Games.

HINSON, David Francis, The Manse, 14 Nodes Drive, Stevenage, Herts SG2 8AL. (0438-62536)–BA(Leeds), CertEd. *b. 9 Feb 1930, Tufnell Park, London N19. m. 5 Sept 1956: 1d., 1s.* *Education:* 1935–41 Burghley Rd. Sch., Tufnell Park, London; 1941–48 Holloway Grammar Sch., London; 1951–54 Leeds Univ.; 1954–55 London Univ., Institute of Education; 1951–54 Wesley, Headingley. *Appointments:* 1950–51 Market Harborough; 1955–69 Educational Missionary, Northern Rhodesia/Zambia; 1969–75 Hemel Hempstead and Berkhamstead; 1975–80 St. Albans; 1980– Stevenage; 1979– Secretary Methodist Study Centre, p/t. *Connexional Committees:* 1969–75 MMS Central Committee; 1975– Executive and Board, Division of Ministries; Board of Division of Education and Youth (various dates). *Local Council Committees:* Founder Member and First Chairman Apsley District Action Group, Hemel Hempstead. *Publications:* Key Book No20 *Faith is the Key* (USCL) (SPCK); Theological Education Fund Study Guides No7 *History of Israel* (1973); No10 *The Books of the Old Testament* (1974); No15 *Theology of the Old Testament* (1976). *Special Interests:* Bible Study, Especially Old Testament, Adult Education in Church Context, Established Areas of New Town Work. *Hobbies:* Family History Research, Collection of Early Postcards Illustrative of Areas in which Families Lived.

HINTON, Alan, 61 Broadway, Droylsden, Manchester M36 6FE. (061-370-1831)–BSc. *b. 3 June 1949, Middlesbrough. s.* *Education:* 1960–64 Ayresome Secondary Modern Sch.; 1964–66 Longlands Coll. of Further Education; 1978–80 Univ. of Birmingham; 1978–81 Queen's. *Appointments:*

1981– Droylsdon and Oppenshaw. *Connexional Committees:* Youth and Community Committee. *Council Member:* 1970–72 Local Officer of ASTMS.
Hobbies and Recreations: Massage, Hedonism, Gadgets, Science Fiction.

HIRST, Donald Kirkham, Wesley House, 19 London Rd., Biggleswade, Bedfordshire SG18 8ED. (0767-312156).
Education: 1946–47 Richmond.
Appointments: 1946–47 Richmond; 1947–49 Salisbury, Dews Rd.; 1949–51 Bournemouth; 1951–53 Stoke-on-Trent, Hanley Trinity; 1953–57 Warrington; 1957–62 Burnley Brunswick; 1962–68 Whaley Bridge; 1968–73 Bolton, Park St.; 1973– Biggleswade.

HIRST, John Barrie, 13 Southwood Lane, Grassington, Skipton, North Yorkshire BD23 5NA. (0756-752309) *b. 8 Jan 1933, St. Luke's Hospital, Halifax, Yorks. m. 28 May 1960: 3s.*
Education: 1937–40 Roe Lee Park Council Sch., Brownhill, Blackburn; 1940–44 St. Bartholomew's CE Jun. Sch., Great Harwood; 1944–51 The Royal Grammar Sch., Clitheroe; 1954–57 Handsworth.
Appointments: 1957–60 Stamford; 1960–64 New Mills; 1964–71 Stour Valley; 1971–76 Weymouth; 1976–81 Portsmouth and Southsea; 1981– Grassington.
Special Interests: Prison Chaplaincy Work, Rural Life, Gardening, Beekeeping, Samaritan Work with Special Emphasis upon Work Amongst Alcoholics, Musical Appreciation, Literature and Poetry, Photography, Dialects. *Hobbies and Recreations:* Cumyxophily, Numismatism, Calligraphy.

HISCOCK, Peggy A. Priscilla, 43 Collier Rd., Hastings, E. Sussex TN34 3JR. (0424-423274) *b. 24 Dec 1922, Redhampton, Havant, Hants. s.*
Education: Havant CE and Council Sch.; Waldron House Secretarial Coll.; 1957–58 Kingsmead; 1948–50 Deaconess Coll. *Appointments:* 1968–75 United Church of Zambia; 1975–78 International House, London (Warden); 1978– Hastings, Bexhill and Rye.
Connexional Committees: Overseas Committee (now retired); Still serving on the Africa Advisory Committee.

HOAR, Philip Charles, 9 Clarkefields, Bayston Hill, Shrewsbury. (074372-3826)–MA. *b. 15 June 1953, Torquay. s.*
Education: Westhill County Prim. Sch., 1964–77 Torquay Boys Grammar; 1971–74 Exeter Coll., Oxford; 1974–77 Wesley House.
Appointments: 1977–81 Oxford; 1981– Shrewsbury.

HOAR, Ronald William Cecil, 15 Woodlands Rd., Handforth, Wilmslow, Cheshire SK9 3AW. (0625-523480)–BD(Lond.). *b. 31 Oct 1931, Shedfield, Hampshire. m. 14 July 1956: 2d., 3s.*
Education: 1936–42 Shedfield CE Inf. and Jun.; 1942–47 Prices Sch., Fareham; 1952–55 Univ. of London; 1952–55 Richmond. *Appointments:* 1955–58 Shepton Mallet; 1958–62 South London Mission; 1962–67 London (Westminster); 1967–76 Bristol Mission; 1976–79 Great Yarmouth and Gorleston; 1979– Manchester and Stockport District Chairman.
Connexional Committees: 1967–72 Home Mission; 1975–78 Central Missions; 1973– Panel for Nomination of Chairmen; 1979– Property; 1979– Home Mission; 1979– Stationing; 1979– G.P.C.; 1980– Medical; 1980– Building in Co-operation with Other Communion; 1979– History and Archives; 1981– Deaconess.
Special Interests: Church Publicity, Church Growth, Community Relations, Evangelism. *Hobbies and Recreations:* Oil Painting, DIY Pursuits, Sport, Gardening.

HOARE, Brian Richard, Ridgeway, Cliff Lane, Curbar, Sheffield S30 1XD. (024-688-3196)–BD(Lond.), CertEd(Lond.). *b. 9 Dec 1935, Upminster, Essex. m. 24 Mar 1962: 1d., 1s.*
Education: 1941–46 Southwell Methodist Sch., (Notts); 1946–54 Southwell Minster Grammar Sch.; 1956–59 Westminster Coll., London; 1968–71 Richmond. *Appointments:* 1971–74 Chaplain, Hunmanby Hall, Filey; 1974–77 Hull Mission; 1977– New Testament Tutor, Cliff Coll.
Connexional Committees: 1975– Home Mission Board; 1979– Main Committee for the New Hymnbook; 1982– Conference Committee on Appeal. *Council Member:* 1980–82 Chairman, Conservative Evangelicals in Methodism. *Publications:* Notes on Book of Revelation for *Discovering the Bible* (I.B.R.A. 1980); Editor: *Methods of Mission* (Methodist Publishing House, for Home Mission Division 1979); Regular Contributor to *Methodist Recorder;* Occasional Articles in *Epworth Review, Third Way, CEIM Newsletter, Spectrum, In Touch, Christian Graduate* etc; Hymn Tune in *Partners in Praise*, and 4 Tunes and a Hymn in New Hymnbook *(Hymns and Psalms).*
Hobbies and Recreations: Music, Conductor of Curbar and District Churches United Choir, Cliff Coll. Choir, Accompanist and Composer of Title Track on 'Together', a Cassette Produced by Profile Recordings, 1980.

HOCKLEY, Ronald James, 77 Harewood Ave., Newark, Notts NG24 4AN. (0636-704959) *b. 18 June 1931, Madura, S. India. m. 5 July 1958: 2s.*
Education: 1941–48 Kingswood; 1954–58 Didsbury. *Appointments:* 1958–60 Hemel Hempstead; 1960–63 Dornakal Diocese CSI; 1963–68 Consett; 1968–74 Sunderland South; 1971–81 Bingham; 1981– Newark.
Connexional Committees: 1964–67 OM. *Local Council Committees:* 1975–81 Sch. Managements; 1977 Mayors Chaplain.
Special Interests: Service as RAF Chaplain, Hospital Chaplain, Prison Chaplain. *Hobbies and Recreations:* Propinquity.

HODGINSON, John Leonard, 55 Fog Lane, Manchester M20 0AR. (061-445-7791)–MA. *b. 1931. m. 1956: 1d., 1s.*

Education: 1952–55 London Univ.; 1971–73 Cambridge Univ., Fitzwilliam Coll.; 1952–55 Richmond; 1971–73 Wesley House. *Appointments:* 1955–56 Cowbridge and St. Athan; 1956–57 Missionary Training; 1957–77 South East Asia Dt; 1977–78 Mission House; 1978– Chinese Work in Manchester. *Connexional Committees:* 1977–80 Transfer of Authority to Overseas Districts; 1980– Central Committee. *Special Interests:* China and the Chinese.

HODGKINSON, Raymond John, 5 King's Ave., Chichester, W. Sussex PO19 2EA. (0243-783128)–BD(Lond.). *b. 14 March 1926, Derby. m. 26 July 1952: 2s.*
Education: 1936–41 Bemrose Grammar Sch., Derby; 1948–51 Richmond. *Appointments:* 1946–48 Plymouth East; 1951–54 Camelford and Wadebridge; 1954–59 Oldham West; 1959–64 Kingswood, Bristol; 1964–71 Leicester East; 1971–78 Witney and Faringdon; 1978– Chichester and Bognor Regis. *Connexional Committees:* 1960–64 Christian Citizenship Committee.

HODGKINSON, Reginald, 253 Brindle Rd., Bamber Bridge, Preston, Lancashire PR5 6YL. (0772-35523) *b. 4 Oct 1905, Derby. m. 8 Aug 1934: 3d.*
Education: Elem.; 1927–30 Hartley. *Appointments:* 1930–34 Wisbech; 1934–36 Sheffield Mission; 1936–37 Pocklington; 1937–44 Silsden; 1944–48 Oldham (Wesley); 1948–55 Altrincham; 1955–62 Southport. *Special Interests:* Prayer and the Spiritual Life. *Hobbies and Recreations:* Music—Piano, Art—Painting.

HODGKISS, Elizabeth Daphne, The Manse, Tebay, Penrith, Cumbria CA10 3UY. (058-74-275)–BD(Lond.). *b. 21 March 1936, Salford, Lancs. s.*
Education: 1941–54 Pendelton High Sch. for Girls, Salford; 1954–56 Bingley Teacher Training Coll.; 1961–63 Wesley Deaconess Coll., Ilkley. *Appointments:* 1963–66 Home Mission Caravan; 1967–75 Walls, Shetland; 1975– Kirkby Stephen, Appleby and Tebay. *Connexional Committees:* 1967–75 Education and Youth. *Special Interests:* Evangelism, Local Preachers' Training. *Hobbies and Recreations:* Knitting, Reading, Natural History.

HODGSON, Keith, 60 Longsight, Harwood, Bolton, Lancs BL2 3HX. (0204-51805) *b. 23 Mar 1942, Darlington. m. 23 Aug 1968: 1d., 1s.*
Education: 1966–67 Headingley; 1967–69 Wesley, Bristol. *Appointments:* 1969–72 Todmorden; 1972–77 Trowbridge; 1977– Bolton. *Special Interests:* Third World Concerns. *Hobbies and Recreations:* Walking, Badminton, Gardening.

HODGSON, Peter William, 2 Llanfair Rd., Penygraig, Tonypandy, Mid Glam CF40 1TA. (0443-432343) *b. 4 May 1930, Bradford, Yorkshire. m. 2 June 1959: 3d.*
Education: 1935–38 Cooper Lane Inf., Bradford; 1938–41 Horton Bank Top Jun., Bradford; 1941–46 Grange High Sch. for Boys; 1978–81 Wesley, Bristol. *Appointments:* 1981– Mid Glamorgan Mission. *Connexional Committees:* 1980– Div. of Min. Publicity Committee. *Special Interests:* The Healing Church. *Hobbies and Recreations:* Gardening, Photography.

HODSMAN, Kenneth Ernest, 6 New Rd., Brackley, Northants NN13 6AH. (0280-702088) *b. 12 Nov 1909, Withernsea, N. Yorks. m. 20 July 1940 (w.).*
Education: Withernsea Prim.; Hymers Coll., Hull; 1933–36 Headingley. *Appointments:* 1936–37 Longton Zion; 1937–38 Hay; 1938–42 Cheddar Valley; 1942–45 Bridgend; 1945–48 Cardiff (Roath); 1948–52 Bebington; 1952–55 Manchester, Harpurley; 1955–58 Middlesbrough; 1958–63 Oxford; 1963–69 Thame and Watlington; 1969–74 Stoke Wesley and South. *Hobbies and Recreations:* Singing.

HODSON, Ernest Kingsley, 18 New Farm Rd., Alresford, Hants SO24 9QP. (096-273-4203)–BD(Lond.). *b. 6 Feb 1908, Leicester. m. 1 Aug 1938: 1d., 1s.*
Education: 1918–24 Wyggeston Grammar, Leicester; 1931–35 Richmond. *Appointments:* 1936–49 Haiti (West Indies); 1949–52 Jamaica (West Indies); 1952–56 London, Lewisham and Peckham; 1956–62 Shooters Hill; 1962–74 N. Rhodesia and Zambia; 1974–76 Sherborne. *Special Interests:* The Church Overseas. *Hobbies and Recreations:*Travel, Photography, Tape Recording, Stamps.

HODSON, George Leonard, 6 Wheatacres, Thetford, Norfolk IP24 1AQ. *b. 23 June 1906, Lincoln. m. 2 Aug 1934: 2s.*
Education: Lincoln Technical Sch.; 1927–30 Didsbury. *Appointments:* 1930–34 Newmarket and Mildenhall; 1934–36 N. Derbyshire; 1936–39 Bradford, Greenhill; 1934–44 Louth; 1944–47 Castle Donington; 1947–51 Sheffield NE; 1951–55 Marple; 1955–58 Louth; 1958–65 Thetford; 1965–66 Barnsley East; 1966–70 King's Lynn.

HOE, Derek, 54 Rooley Ave., Bradford, West Yorkshire BD6 1DA. (0274-720253) *b. 17 Oct 1937, Derby. m. 10 April 1965: 1d., 1s.*
Education: 1942–50 Littleover CE; 1950–51 Pastures Hill Secondary Modern; 1951–54 Bemrose Grammar Sch.; 1964–67 Richmond. *Appointments:* 1967–70 Hungerford; 1970–75 Bilston; 1975– Bradford Trinity. *Connexional Committees:* 1974–79 Church in Industry. *Special Interests:* Aircraft Industry. *Hobbies and Recreations:* Gardening, Support of National Trust; Aircraft Kit Construction.

HOLBROOK, Arthur Sanders, 5 St. Wilfrid's St., Calverley, Pudsey, West Yorkshire LS28 5RQ. (0532-555658) *b. 28 Aug 1900, Swallownest, Nr. Rotherham, S. Yorks. m. 6 July 1932: 2d.*
Education: 1905–13 Woodhouse Elem. Sch., Sheffield; 1926–28

Hartley. *Appointments:* 1928–32 East London Mission; 1932–36 Leicester II; 1936–41 Hinckley (Stockwell Head); 1941–45 Sheffield (Ecclesall); 1945–48 Ashton under Lyne; 1948–52 Sheffield (North); 1952–56 Peak and Bradwell; 1956–62 Alderley Edge and Knutsford; 1962–67 Ilkeston.
Connexional Committees: 1932–41 Youth. *Publications: John Wesley and the German Hymn* Translation of Dr John Nuelsen's *John Wesley und das Deutsche Kirchenlied* (Parry Moore & Holbrook 1972).
Special Interests: Hymnody and Hymn Tunes. *Hobbies and Recreations:* Chiefly Work and Making Things Needed—Apart from Reading.

HOLDEN, Leslie Norman, Outspan, Primrose Hill, Blackwell, Derby DE55 5JF. (0773-810924) *b. 1 May 1903, Bilston, Staffordshire. m. 31 Dec 1930: 1d., 2s.*
Education: 1908–13 Bilston Wesley Day Sch.; 1913–19 Wolverhampton Grammar Sch.; 1924–25 Handsworth; 1925–27 Richmond. *Appointments:* 1927–32 Transvaal District; 1932–49 S. African Conference; 1949–54 Week St. Mary; 1954–59 Rotherham; 1959–65 Staveley; 1965–69 The Peak.

HOLDEN, Tony, 146 Windsor Rd., London E7. (01-472-2276)–MA. *b. 24 Aug 1940, Nelson, Lancs. m.*
Education: 1961–63 Wesley House, Cambridge. *Appointments:* 1963–66 Aberdare; 1966–71 Accrington; 1971–76 Bilston; 1976– London Mission, Bow.

HOLDEN, William Alfred, 1 St. Dunstans Close, Glastonbury, Somerset BA6 9AR. (0458-31286)–MA(B'Ham), BD(Lond.). *b. 6 April 1910, Southport, Lancashire. m. 18 Nov 1937 (w.): 1s.*
Education: 1921–26 King George V Grammar Sch., Southport; 1931–34 Birmingham Univ.; 1960–64 Post Graduate Birmingham Univ.; 1931–34 Handsworth. *Appointments:* 1930–31 Millom; 1934–47 Burma Dt; 1947–50 Accrington; 1950–54 Burma Dt; 1954–60 London, Finsbury Park; 1954–60 London, Highgate; 1964–73 Basildon; 1976– Somerset Mission.
Connexional Committees: 1956–68 Eastern Committee (MMS).
Publications: Commentary *Epistle to the Romans* (Burmese); Have Contributed to I.B.R.A.
Special Interests: Early Church History, Comparative Study of Religion, Philology, Tutor Methodist Study Centre. *Hobbies and Recreations:* Painting, Walking.

HOLDER, John Richard, The Links, Moreton St., Prees, Whitchurch, Shropshire SY13 2EQ. (0948-840) *b. 16 July 1899, Brambling Fields, Malton, Yorks. m. 4 July 1928: 1d., 2s.*
Education: 1904–5 Norton Council Sch.; 1906–12 Old Malton Council Sch.; 1924–25 Hartley.
Appointments: 1922–23 Hay on Wye; 1926–27 Richmond, Yorks; 1927–28 Hamilton; 1928–29 Weobley; 1929–31 East Dereham; 1932–35 Manea; 1936–37 Bury St. Edmunds; 1938–44 Barnsley West; 1945–47 Connah's Quay and Hawarden; 1948–50 Bolsover; 1951–55 Stour Vale; 1956–58 Tamworth; 1959–61 Nantwich; 1962–66 Howden.
Hobbies and Recreations: Gardening, Cycling.

HOLDING, Leslie George, Glen-Tregar, 5 Highfield Ave., Dovercourt, Harwich, Essex CO12 4DP. (025-55-7474) *b. 15 June 1909, Ebbw Vale, Gwent. m. 28 July 1938: 1d., 2s.*
Education: Pontygof, Ebbw Vale; 1932–36 Richmond. *Appointments:* 1931–32 Chipping Norton and Stow-on-the-Wold; 1936–40 Stoke-on-Trent (Hanley); 1940–45 Montrose; 1945–50 South Shields; 1950–56 Leicester (North); 1956–60 Letchworth; 1960–68 Leighton Buzzard; 1968–74 Manningtree and Harwich.

HOLDSWORTH, George Leslie, 4 Westwood Ave., Ipswich, Suffolk IP1 4EQ. (0473-54206)–BD(Lond.). *b. 26 June 1919, Leeds. m. 7 Dec 1978: 1d.*
Education: –1930 St. Michael's CE Sch.; 1930–35 Leeds Modern Sch.; 1939–43 London External Student; 1939–40 Didsbury; 1940–42 Hartley Victoria. *Appointments:* 1942–43 Luton A; 1943–46 Wolverton and Bletchley; 1946–50 Harpenden; 1950–57 St. Albans; 1957–59 York (Wesley); 1959–63 Filey Trinity; 1963–70 Brighton and Hove; 1970–77 Redhill and East Grinstead; 1977–78 Mid-Sussex; 1978– Ipswich.
Connexional Committees: 1957–58 Connexional Candidates; 1956–75 Local Preachers' Connexional Committee Studies Board.
Publications: Junior Minister (Epworth 1951); Various Articles in the *Preachers' Quarterly,* 1957–63.
Hobbies and Recreations: Sketching, Photography, Tapestry.

HOLGATE, Charles Dixon, Wesley Manse, Station Rd., Totnes, Devon TQ9 5HW. (0803-862350)–BA(Leeds). *b. 30 Sept 1925, Crewe, Ches. m. 3 Sept. 1953: 1d., 1s.*
Education: 1936–42 Nantwich and Acton Grammar Sch.; 1950–53 Wesley, Headingley. *Appointments:* 1953–55 Lerwick and N. Isles; 1955–61 Birmingham, Smethwick; 1961–64 Resigned (Teacher); 1967–75 Plymouth, King St.; 1975– Totnes.
Connexional Committees: Social Responsibility c.70's.

HOLLAND, Albert, 34 Ida Rd., Skegness, Lincolnshire PE25 2AU. (0754-3182) *b. 30 March 1927, Burslem, Stoke-on-Trent, Staffs. m.*
Appointments: 1952–53 Leighton Buzzard; 1953–56 Hartley Victoria; 1956–57 Kirby Moorside; 1957–58 Camelford and Wadebridge; 1958–61 Camborne; 1961–62 Chesterfield, Salters Gate; 1962–63 Supernumerary; 1963–66 Shaw and Royton; 1966–69 New Mills; 1969–74 Tarporley; 1974–79 Rossendale; 1979– Skegness and Wainfleet.

HOLLAND, Bernard George, Overleigh, Trennick Lane, Truro, Cornwall TR1 1SU. (0872-2110)–MA(Oxon), BD, MTh, PhD(Lond.). *b. 6 Jan 1934, Manipay, Sri Lanka. m. 23 Aug 1958: 1d., 2s.*

Education: 1944–53 Kingswood Sch., Bath; 1953–56 Oxford, St. Peter's Coll.; 1956–59 Richmond Coll. *Appointments:* 1959–62 North of Scotland Mission; 1962–68 Romford; 1968–73 Harrow; 1973– Chaplain, Truro Sch.
Connexional Committees: Lectionary Committee, Services and Baptism. *Publications: Baptism in Early Methodism* (Epworth Press 1970); *Fernley-Hartley Lecturer* (1970 Conference); *The Doctrine of Infant Baptism in Non-Wesleyan Methodism*; Occasional Publications, *Wesley Historical Society,* 1970.
Special Interests: Methodism, Religious Education. *Hobbies and Recreations:* Sailing, Wind-Surfing, Mountain Walking.

HOLLAND, David Brian, 13 Sudbrooke Rd., London SW12. (01-673-2645)—MA(Cantab.), BD(Manchester). *b. 6 June 1932, Cheam, Surrey. m. 10 Aug 1957: 1d., 1s.*
Education: 1943–50 Whitgift Sch., Croydon; 1952–55 Queens Coll., Cambridge; 1955–57 Hartley Victoria. *Appointments:* 1957–59 Hemel Hempstead; 1959–62 Whitby; 1962–67 Swindon; 1967–70 Woking; 1970–76 Croydon; 1976– London Mission, Broomwood and Clapham.
Connexional Committees: 1981– London Mission Committee. *Local Council Committees:* 1971–76 Croydon Sch. Sub-Committee; School Governor.
Special Interests: Education, Social Democratic Party, 1982– Member Wandsworth Area Steering Committee. *Hobbies and Recreations:* Chairman Railton Youth Club, Tennis, Walking.

HOLLIDAY, Dorothea Mary, The Farncombe Community, 5 Wolseley Rd., Farncombe, Godalming, Surrey GU7 3DX. (048-68-7253) *b. 24 March 1923, Kingsnorton, Birmingham. s.*
Education: 1928–34 Kindergarten, High Sch., Jun. Sch., Welwyn Garden City; 1934–41 Hitchin Girls' Grammar Sch.; 1942–44 Homerton Coll., Cambridge; 1947–49 Wesley Deaconess Coll.; 1973–74 Wesley House. *Appointments:* 1974–77 Glossop; 1977– Guildford (Farncombe Community).
Connexional Committees: GL (1948) and YMA (1960) Committees; 1964–66 Women's Work and Overseas Committees. *Council Member:* 1976–81 World Methodist Council, Worship Committee and British Committee.
Special Interests: Methodist Retreat Group (Convenor), Association for Promoting Retreats (Council and Committees), Julian Meetings, National Centre for Christian Communities and Networks (Management Committee), Ecumenical Work, Prayer, Education.
Hobbies and Recreations: Art, Poetry, Travel, Gardening, Writing.

HOLLIS, Stanley Victor, 1 Colaton Terrace, Cotmaton Rd., Sidmouth, Devon EX10 8QU. (03955-6398) *b. 18 Dec 1901, Great Yarmouth, Norfolk. m. 1 May 1931 (w.): 1s.*
Education: Queen's Park Board Sch., Bedford; 1922–23 Cliff Coll.; 1925–28 Handsworth.
Appointments: 1924–25 Blandford; 1928–35 Mysore District, S. India; 1935–38 St. Just, Cornwall; 1938–41 Bilston Wesley; 1941–46 Chaplain RAF; 1956–62 Georgetown, Guyana, West Indies; 1962–67 Home Missions Dept. (Committee on Migration).
Connexional Committees: 1962–69 MMS Western Committee. *Council Member:* Municipal Council, Hassan, Mysore, S. India. *Publications: The Immigrant and the Community* (Epworth Press 1964); *I was a Stranger* (Home Mission Dept. 1967); Articles in various magazines.

HOLLMAN, Henry Wybert, 46 Osmaston Rd., Stourbridge, West Midlands DY8 2AL. (038-43-5204) *b. 12 Oct 1913, Birkenhead. m. 1 Feb 1946: 1d., 1s.*
Education: 1918–26 Longmoor Lane Council Sch., Aintree, Liverpool; 1926–30 Alsop High Sch., Walton, Liverpool; 1938–40 Didsbury; 1940–41 Hartley Victoria. *Appointments:* 1941–47 Hunan District, China; 1947 Bodmin; 1948–49 Hunan District, China; 1949–53 Rochdale; 1953–57 Walsall; 1957–63 Leicester North; 1963–69 Ashton-under-Lyne; 1969–75 Cheetham Hill and Prestwich; 1975–80 Malvern and Ledbury.
Connexional Committees: 1955–57, 1961–63 Overseas Missions. *Local Council Committees:* 1965–69 Ashton under Lyne Education.

HOLLY, John, 12 Springfield Gdns., Banwell, Avon BS24 6HW. (0934-823861) *b. 18 Jan 1909, Tredegar, Gwent. m. 12 Aug 1939: 1s.*
Education: 1920– Municipal Secondary Sch.; 1931–34 Hartley Victoria. *Appointments:* 1934–37 Stratford upon Avon; 1938–41 Chatham Central Hall Naval Port Mission; 1941–46 Maidstone; 1946–51 Chatham; 1951–57 Luton; 1957–64 London, Streatham and Dulwich; 1964–70 Tiverton; 1970–75 Wadhurst.
Hobbies and Recreations: Reading, Gardening, Rugger.

HOLMAN, Kenneth A., 11 Campbell St., Wishaw, Strathclyde. (0698-373114) *b. 29 Nov 1919, Taunton, Somerset. m. 3 April 1954: 3s.*
Education: 1923–32 Askwith Prim. and Jun; 1933–36 Taunton; 1961–63 Headingley. *Appointments:* 1961–62 Bingley; 1963–68 Holmfirth; 1968–74 Bingley; 1974–80 Huddersfield; 1980– Motherwell and Wishaw.
Special Interests: Home Mission, Hymns, Methodist History. *Hobbies and Recreations:* Member Methodist Philatelic Society, General Philately.

HOLME, Edward, 47 Kings Ave., Clacton-on-Sea, Essex CO15 5ER. (0255-814021) *b. 23 May 1910, Millom, Cumberland. m. 19 July 1940: 1d., 1s.*
Education: 1922–26 Millom Grammar Sch.; 1931–22 Cliff Coll.; 1933–36 Hartley Victoria.
Appointments: 1936–39 Ilford; 1939–43 Leigh-on-Sea; 1943–47 Sheffield, Carver St.; 1947–50 Blackburn, Trinity; 1950–52 Blackpool North; 1952–55 London East End Mission; 1955–61 Ilford; 1961–65 Manningtree and Harwich; 1965–70 Clacton-on-Sea; 1970–75 Daventry.

Connexional Committees: 1952 Necessitous LP Fund (Member and Trustee).
Hobbies and Recreations: Painting.

HOLMES, Arthur James, 31 St. Monica Court, St Monica Home, Westbury-on-Trym, Bristol BS3 9UN. (0272-624031) *b. 3 July 1910, Cowes, IoW. m. 17 Nov 1937: 3d., 1s.*
Education: –1922 Boscombe Council Sch., Bournemouth; 1922–27 Parkstone High Sch., Dorset; 1930–34 Handsworth. *Appointments:* 1934–40 Burma; 1941–42 Yeovil; 1942–45 Skegness; 1945–47 Trowbridge; 1947–57 Bolton (Park St.); 1951–53 Bolton (Farnworth); 1953–56 Doncaster North-East; 1956–61 Stoke-on-Trent (Longton and Fenton); 1961–65 Withernsea; 1965–69 Rhosymedre and Chirk; 1969–74 Coningsby; 1974–77 Farnborough.
Special Interests: New Testament Studies. *Hobbies and Recreations:* Walking, Scrabble.

HOLMES, George William, Somerby House, Audley, Stoke-on-Trent. (0782-721390) *b. Knaresborough, Yorkshire. m. 1 Sept 1945: 1d., 1s.*
Education: Knaresborough Council Sch., Elem.; 1929–31 Cliff Coll. *Appointments:* 1963–68 Nuneaton and Atherstone; 1968–72 Worksop; 1972–75 Wolstanton and Audley.

HOLMES, Leslie, 16 Kingswood Gdns, Leeds LS8 2BT. (0532-662066) *b. 25 Feb 1932, Normanton, Yorkshire. m. 21 Aug 1957: 1d., 1s.*
Education: 1944–49 Keighley Grammar Sch.; 1952–53 Cliff Coll.; 1954–57 Wesley, Headingley; 1957–58 St. Andrews. *Appointments:* 1958–67 Ghana Dt, 1967–74 Pudsey and Farsley; 1974– Leeds North East; 1978– Leeds Synod Secretary.
Connexional Committees: 1968–71, 1972–75, 1981– Overseas Division.
Special Interests: Clinical Theology.
Hobbies and Recreations: Sport, Cricket, Football, Golf.

HOLMES, Ralph E. C., 13 Queens Rd., Fairfield, Buxton, Derbys. (0298-2491) *b. 12 June 1929, Washington, Co. Durham. m. 9 April 1955: 3s.*
Education: 1949–54 Cliff Coll.; 1960–62 Headingley. *Appointments:* 1962–67 Bingley; 1967–70 Hull Mission; 1970– Buxton.

HOLMES, Stuart, 9 Old Rd., Stanningley, Pudsey LS28 6BG. (0532-574770) *b. 15 Aug 1929, Keighley, Yorkshire. m. 3 Aug 1957: 3s.*
Education: 1935–39 Pelsall Lane Jun. Sch., Rushall, Walsall; 1939–40 Aldridge Senior Sch., Walsall; 1940–43 Eastwood Sch., Keighley; 1954–58 Headingley. *Appointments:* 1958–63 Batley; 1963–69 Grimsby; 1969–74 Harrogate; 1974–79 Leeds, Richmond Hill; 1979– Pudsey.
Special Interests: Wesley Historical Society. *Hobbies and Recreations:* Woodwork, especially Woodturning.

HOLLINGHURST, George Frederick, Mallyan Hale, Fording Bridge, Hampshire SP6 2NH. (0725-21117)—BA, BD, DPhil. *b. 26 July 1911, Northenden, Cheshire. m. 4 July 1940: 2s.*
Education: 1917–20 Cheadle Hulme (Prim. Sch.); 1921–23 Derby Rd., Long Eaton (Jun. Sch.); 1924–28 Bournemouth Sch.; 1933–36 Univ. of Birmingham; 1936–39 Univ. of London; 1949–54 Univ. of Oxford (St. Catherine's Society); 1933–37 Handsworth. *Appointments:* 1932–33 Dorchester; 1937–38 Stamford; 1938–40 Filey; 1940–41 Northallerton; 1941–45 Weston-super-Mare; 1945–49 Harrow, 1949–53 Oxford; 1953–58 Ilford; 1958–63 Croydon; 1963–69 Blackheath and Lee; 1969–72 Bristol (South).
Local Council Committees: 1946–48 Agreed Syllabus of Religious Instruction (for Middlesex County Council) Drafting Committee.

HOLT, Harold, The Haven, 8 Wardman Cresc., Redcar, Cleveland TS10 2DQ. (0642-470557) *b. 11 March 1909, Rochdale, Lancashire. m. 14 Aug 1935: 1s.*
Education: 1914–15 Belfield Inf., Rochdale; 1915–19 Newbold Council, Rochdale; 1919–23 Fleece St. Central, Rochdale; 1950–51 Hartley Victoria. *Appointments:* 1950–51 Heywood; 1951–54 Radcliffe; 1954–58 Chorley; 1958–62 Durham; 1962–70 Redcar, Saltburn and Guisborough.
Special Interests: General Reading.
Hobbies and Recreations: Walking, Gardening, DIY.

HOLT, Kenneth James, 4 Greenbanks Close, Milford-on-Sea, Lymington, Hants SO4 0SQ. (059-069-3414)—BD. *b. 28 Oct 1908, Halifax, Yorks. m.: 2d., 1s.*
Education: 1914–17 Private Sch.; 1917–21 Heath Grammar Sch., Halifax; 1921–26 Rydal Sch., Colwyn Bay; 1932–37 London Univ.; 1932–37 Richmond. *Appointments:* 1937–42 New Forest Mission; 1942–47 Chaplain HMF; 1947–52 Wimborne; 1952–66 Chaplain HMF; 1966–69 West Wight.
Special Interests: Travel. *Hobbies and Recreations:* Woodwork, Golf.

HOLT, Sidney Robert, 20 Luffenham Close, Stamford, Lincs PE9 2SE. (0780-4335) *b. 22 May 1905, Leicester. m. 3 Oct 1932: 1d., 1s.*
Education: 1916–22 Wyggeston Grammar, Leicester; 1926–29 Didsbury. *Appointments:* 1929–44 Lucknow and Benares District, N. India; 1944–50 Melton Mowbray; 1950–55 Banbury; 1955–61 Stamford; 1961–64 Hunstanton and Docking; 1966–70 Wantage and Abingdon.
Connexional Committees: 1945–50 Overseas Mission; 1955–61 Ministers Children's Fund.
Hobbies and Recreations: Reading, Music.

HOLTOM, Derek George, 193 Ashby Rd., Scunthorpe, South Humberside DN16 2AQ. (0724-843053) *b. 16 June 1932, Colombo. m. 19 July 1958: 1d., 1s.*
Education: 1941–44 Ashville Coll.; 1944–45 West Bromwich Grammar Sch.; 1945–49 Haberdashers Askes Boys Sch., New Cross, London; 1956–59 Richmond. *Appointments:* 1959–62 Cheadle (Staffs.); 1962–66

Wath and Mexborough; 1966–73 Kettering; 1973–76 Northampton; 1976– Scunthorpe.
Special Interests: Ecumenical Work, Hospital Chaplaincy Work, Rotary.
Hobbies and Recreations: Fishing, Photography, Ornithology.

HOLTOM, Randolph William, Kodai, 43 Vernon Cresc., Ravenshead, Nottingham NG15 9BP. (06234-2991)–BSc(Birmingham). *b. 18 Dec 1904, Sparkhill, Birmingham. m. 25 July 1930: 1d., 1s.* d. 4.1.93.
Education: 1911–16 Hall Green Council Sch.; 1916–21 Central Secondary Sch.; 1921–25 Birmingham Univ.; 1926–28 Didsbury. *Appointments:* 1925–26 Tipton; 1928–35 Batticaloa Central Coll., Ceylon; 1935–37 Gateshead; 1937–44 Birmingham Mission; 1945 West Bromwich; 1945 Resigned Ministry; 1970– Returned Supernumerary.
Hobbies and Recreations: Looking on at other people's interests.

HOLWELL, David Woodford, 8 Rosamund Ave., Pickering, North Yorkshire YO18 7HF. (0751-72714) *b. 13 Nov 1908, Kirkby Underwood, Lincolnshire. m. 23 Aug 1951 (w.): 2s.*
Education: 1913–17 Kirkby Underwood; 1917–22 Grantham, Jun. and Central; 1933–36 Wesley, Headingley. *Appointments:* 1936–48 Hyderabad, South India; 1948–51 Andover; 1951–54 Louth; 1954–57 Higham Ferrers; 1957–62 Oundle; 1962–66 Melton Mowbray; 1966–73 Pickering.

HOMER, Ivan Raymond, 4 Spinneyside, Groby, Leicester LE6 0GX. (0533-876035)–BA(Leeds). *b. 14 April 1928, Dudley, Worcs. m.*
Education: 1953–55 Wesley, Headingley. *Appointments:* 1955–65 Burma; 1965–70 Stourbridge; 1970–79 Walsall; 1979 Leicester (West).

HOMER, Reginald William, 33 Brownlow St., York YO3 7LW. (0904-26251)–BA(Manch.), BD(Lond.). *b. 13 May 1933, Hednesford, Staffs. m.: 1d., 1s.*
Education: 1938–40 Station Rd. Inf., Hednesford; 1940–44 West Hill Jun., Hednesford; 1945–50 Rugeley Grammar; 1955–58 Manchester; 1955–59 Hartley Victoria.
Appointments: 1959–61 Tiverton; 1961–65 Guyana, West Indies; 1965–70 Bloxwich; 1970–76 Plymouth; 1976–79 Barry.
Connexional Committees: 1966–70 Overseas; 1972–75 July Committee.
Hobbies and Recreations: Walking, Reading, Sport.

HOOD, Peter Maurice Gordon, North Manse, 24 Market St., Spilsby, Lincs PE23 5JX. (0790-52411) *b. 12 May 1928, Longton, Stoke-on-Trent. m. 21 Aug 1971.*
Education: 1930–35 Chaucer House Sch., Longton; 1935–39 Newcastle-under-Lyne High Sch.; 1955–58 Handsworth. *Appointments:* 1958–63 Nantwich; 1963–67 Buckley and Mold; 1967–69 Wellington (Salop); 1969–73 Wigton; 1973–76 Clitheroe; 1976–81 Derby South; 1981 Spilsby.
Special Interests: Antique Pottery, House, Garden. *Hobbies and Recreations:* Antique Collecting, Canoeing, Horse Riding, Reading.

HOPE, John Laurence, 39 Sharps Lane, Ruislip, Middx HA4 7JG. (08956-32507)–BD(Lond.). *b. 30 May 1937, Erith, Kent. m. Aug 1961: 4s.*
Education: 1948–53 Shooters Hill Grammar Sch.; 1958–61 Richmond.
Appointments: 1961–66 Derby Mission; 1966–71 Derby South; 1971–77 Kingston-on-Thames; 1977– Harrow.
Connexional Committees: 1965–82 Division of Education and Youth.
Special Interests: Religious Broadcasting, Youth Work. *Hobbies and Recreations:* Golf.

HOPE, John Surtees, 460 Ridgacre Rd. West Quinton, Birmingham B32 1AX. (021-422-2534) *b. 22 Feb 1937, New Brancepeth, Nr. Durham City, Co. Durham. m. 9 April 1966: 2d.*
Education: 1942–48 Ushaw Moor Council Sch.; 1948–53 Johnston Grammar Sch., Durham City; 1962–66 Didsbury, Bristol. *Appointments:* 1966–68 Blackheath; 1968–71 Nuneaton; 1971–78 Birmingham South West; 1978– Birmingham West.
Local Council Committees: 1980– Parent Govenor of Four Dwellings Prim. and Secondary Schs., on Governing Body. *Publications:* Article No.7, *Biblical Theme of The People of God,* in Preachers Handbook, No.11 (Epworth Press 1969).
Special Interests: Correspondence Tutor for Connexional Local Preachers Examinations. *Hobbies and Recreations:* Painting, Photography, Walking.

HOPGOOD, Cecil Robert, 60 Ringwood Rd., Eastbourne, E. Sussex BN22 8TB. (0323-30046)–BA(Manch.), BD(Manch.). *b. 1 Jan 1908, Andover, Hants. m. 27 Dec 1939: 2d.*
Education: 1913–19 Village Sch.; 1919–25 Andover Grammar Sch.; 1929–34 Manchester Univ.; 1934–35 London Sch. of Oriental Studies; 1929–34 Hartley; 1934–35 Richmond. *Appointments:* 1935–60 Northern Rhodesia Dt; 1960–65 Bingley; 1965–68 North of Scotland Mission; 1968–71 Falkirk, Wallacestone and Stirling; 1971–77 United Church of Zambia Ministerial Training Coll.
Publications: Tonga Grammar (1940); *Practical Introduction to Tonga* (1948); Contribution to *African Ideas of God* (Symposium Ed. E. W. Smith); Chief Translator of Tonga Bible; Sundry Other Books in Tonga.
Special Interests: Language, Literature, Nature Lover. *Hobbies and Recreations:* Country Walking, Gardening.

HOPKINS, Arthur William, 1 The Garlands, Scarborough, N. Yorks YO11 2SO. (0723-68870)–BA. *b. 8 May 1908, London. m. 1 Feb 1962.*
Education: 1920–28 Elliott Secondary Sch., London; 1949–52 Univ. of Reading; 1929–32 Didsbury.
Appointments: 1932–38 Southall and Uxbridge Mission; 1938–62 Chaplain HMF; 1962–69 Chaplain, The Leys Sch., Cambridge; 1969–74

Scarborough.
Connexional Committees: 1974– Methodist Education Committee.
Council Member: 1979– Independent Member Scarborough Borough Council. *Local Council Committees:* Housing, Planning, Leisure and Amenities, Chairman of Governors, Scarborough Sixth Form Coll.
Special Interests: Education, Welfare.
Hobbies and Recreations: Golf, Music.

HOPKINS, Edgar James, Half Path Cottage, 7 The Dell, Kingsclere, Nr. Newbury, Berks. *b. 21 Oct 1910, Kingsclere. m. 20 Feb 1941: 2s.*
Education: 1929–32 Handsworth.
Appointments: 1932–34 Peterborough; 1935–37 Leicester (Bishop St.); 1938–40 London (Sydenham and Forest Hill); 1941–44 Leicester (Clarendon Park); 1945–47 Hyderabad Dt., India; 1948–53 Ceylon Dt; 1954–63 Hong Kong Dt; 1964–73 London (Streatham and Dulwich).
Hobbies and Recreations: Travel, Photography, Painting, Tennis.

HOPKINS, Gordon Richard, 24 Scott Lane, Riddlesden, Keighley, West Yorkshire BD20 5BT. (0535-603929) *b. 24 Nov 1933, Walthamstowe, London E17. m. 24 Aug 1963: 3d.*
Education: 1938–41 Walthamstowe; 1941–46 Weeley, Essex; 1946–48 Clacton-on-Sea Secondary Modern; 1961–64 Didsbury, Bristol.
Appointments: 1964–67 Woking, Surrey; 1967–72 London Mission, Tooting; 1972–80 Halifax; 1980– Keighley and Worth Valley.
Local Council Committees. 1974–80 Youth and Community Advisory Committee, Calderdale, Halifax.
Special Interests: Youth Work and Fellowships, Church, Family, Conferences. *Hobbies and Recreations:* Photography.

HOPKINS, William Herbert, 11 The Close, Olton, Solihull, West Midlands B92 8AP. (021-706-5618)–BA(Open Univ.). *b. 28 March 1923, Newchurch, Rossendale, Lancs. m. 11 Aug 1951: 2s.*
Education: 1933–41 Kingswood Sch.; 1958–59 Westhill; 1973–81 Open Univ.; 1946–48 Handsworth.
Appointments: 1948–51 Wye Valley Mission; 1951–54 Eccles; 1954–57 Rawtenstall; 1957–62 Bolton Wesley; 1962–67 Forest of Dean; 1967–68 Ross and Monmouth; 1968–71 Teacher of Religious Education, Sheldon Heath, Birmingham; 1971–75 Head of RE, Sharman's Cross, Solihull; 1975– Head of Community Studies, Highgate Sch., Birmingham.
Connexional Committees: 1957–62 Connexional Youth Council.
Publications: Methodist Youth in Uniform (1957); *The First Promise* (1968).
Special Interests: World Faiths, Council of Churches, Using the Community as a Resource for Learning. *Hobbies and Recreations:* DIY.

HOPWOOD, Alfred, 5 Dedale Rd., Sherwood, Nottingham NG8 3GL. (0602-267680) *b. 4 Nov 1908, Hanley, Staffordshire. m. 1 Aug 1936: 2d., 1s.*
Education: 1915–19 Prim. Schs.; 1919–27 Orme Boys' Sch., Newcastle-under-Lyme; 1928–31 Hartley. *Appointments:* 1931–33 Folkestone and Dover; 1933–35 Hay; 1935–37 Wye Valley Mission; 1937–40 Leith and Tranent; 1940–44 Chorley; 1944–49 Jarrow; 1949–56 Nottingham North; 1956–61 Nottingham West (including University Chaplaincy); 1961–64 Harwood; 1964–66 Burnley.
Special Interests: Mathematics, Classical Music, 17th, 18th, 19th Century English Literature, Cricket, Biblical Studies.

HOPWOOD, Douglas Richard, 13 Southdown Way, Storrington, Pulborough, W. Sussex RH20 3NS. (090-66-4984) *b. Finchley, N. London. m.*
Education. 1971–75 Queen's
Appointments: 1975–81 Chelmsford; 1981– Worthing.

HORNER, Alan Philip, 7 Rowanlea Drive, Giffnock, Glasgow G46 6BS. (041-633-1434)–BA, BD(Manch.). *b. 8 March 1934, Northallerton. m. 28 July 1956: 2d.*
Education: 1945–49 Stockton Grammar Sch.; 1950–52 King James I Grammar Sch., Bishop Auckland; 1952–55 Durham Univ.; 1955–58 Manchester Univ.; 1955–58 Hartley Victoria. *Appointments:* 1958–62 Kendal; 1962–68 Harlow Mission; 1968–77 Warrington; 1977–82 Chester; 1982– Chairman of the Methodist Synod in Scotland.
Connexional Committees: 1959–62 Youth; 1978– General Purposes; 1982– Home Mission Board; 1982– President's Council.
Hobbies and Recreations: Walking, Photography, Swimming, Music, Poetry.

HORNER, John, 59 Morrab Rd., Penzance, Cornwall TR18 4EP. (0736-3052)–MA(Newcastle-on-Tyne), BD(Lond.). *b. 31 March 1928, Lucknow, India. m. 14 May 1960: 1d., 2s.*
Education: 1938–46 Prior's Court and Kingswood; 1950–53 Richmond.
Appointments: 1955–59 Berwick-on-Tweed; 1959–62 Penzance; 1962–65 Wanstead and Woodford; 1965–71 Hexham; 1971–80 Nottingham Mission; 1980– Penzance.
Publications: The Wind to Blow a Play for Pentecost (Stainer & Bell 1979).
Special Interests: Classical Music, Watercolour Painting, Mediaeval Architecture.

HORSWILL, David, 103 Weirwood Ave., Garrowhill Ballieston, Glasgow G69 6LQ. (041-771-0280)–BSc(Glasgow). *b. 22 April 1936, Plymouth. m. 23 June 1961: 1d., 1s.*
Education: 1946–48 Staveley Grammar Sch., Derbyshire; 1948–55 Kingswood Sch., Bath, Somerset; 1955–58 Glasgow Univ.; 1958–61 Handsworth. *Appointments:* 1961–66 Sunderland North; 1966–70 Gateshead South West; 1970–77 Hexham; 1977–81 Morpeth; 1981– Glasgow St. John's.
Connexional Committees: 1967–73, 1976–79 Education and Youth.
Special Interests: Children's and Youth Work, Education in the Church, Pastoral Mission, Team Ministry, Charismatic Movement,

Church Growth. *Hobbies and Recreations:* Jogging, Golf, Badminton, Chess, Interests in all Sports, Caravanning/Camping, Boating/Fishing, Fell Walking, Gardening, Home Decorating.

HORSWILL, M. Wilson, 9 Portal Close, Royal Circus, West Norwood, London SE27. (01-761-1471) *b. 21 Aug 1903, Stanley, Co. Durham. m. 25 July 1934: 1d., 1s.*
Education: 1908–17 Annfield Plain Jun., South Moor Council, Annfield Plain Senior; 1918–24 Evening School, Tanfield Lea Secondary Sch., (Mining Engineering); 1928–30 Victoria and Hartley. *Appointments:* 1928–30 Hurst and Hyde; 1931 Whitehaven; 1931–33 Roker Ave., Sunderland; 1933–37 Middlesbrough; 1937–41 Darlington; 1941–42 Ripon; 1942–47 RAF Chaplain; 1947–52 Ealing and Acton; 1952–57 Kineton; 1957–65 Sittingbourne; 1965–70 Maidstone.
Connexional Committees: 1965–70 Chapel Dept.; 1960–73 Christian Stewardship.
Special Interests: Travel, Party Leader of Groups to European Countries and Holy Land.

HORTON, David, Chelsea Methodist Church, 155A King's Rd., London SW3 5TX. (01-352-9305) *b. 19 Dec 1943, London. m. 18 June 1966: 1d., 1s.*
Education: 1948–52 Trebanos Jun. Sch.; 1952–54 Mumbles Jun. Mixed; 1954–62 Swansea Technical Sch.; 1963–64 Cliff Coll.; 1964–68 Didsbury, Bristol. *Appointments:* 1968–71 Cleckheaton and Heckmondwike; 1971–73 London, Westminster; 1973– Victoria and Chelsea.
Connexional Committees: 1981– Healing and Pastoral Ministry Committee.
Special Interests: Counselling.
Hobbies and Recreations: Photography.

HORTON, William David, 6 The Drive, Sevenoaks, Kent TN13 3AE. (0732-452870)–BA(Lond.), MA(Cantab.). *b. 12 Nov 1928, Tottenham, London. m. 11 Aug 1956: 3d., 1s.*
Education: 1940–47 Southgate County Grammar; 1947–51 Kings Coll., London Univ.; 1951–53 Wesley House. *Appointments:* 1953–56 Bury St. Edmunds; 1956–60 London Mission (Central); 1960–66 Guernsey and Alderney; 1966–76 Bury St. Edmunds; 1976– Sevenoaks; 1979– Candidates Secretary.
Connexional Committees: 1979– Candidates Committee. *Publications: The Story of Methodism in Sevenoaks* (Lecture 1979).
Special Interests: Wesley Historical Society, Pastoral Concerns. *Hobbies and Recreations:* Gardening, Walking, Needlecraft.

HOSKINS, William Arthur, 3 Hadrians Walk, Alcester, Warwickshire B49. (0789-3354)–MA(Cantab.). *b. 24 Sept 1917, Truro, Cornwall. m. 18 Jan 1947: 2d., 1s.*
Education: 1926–36 Redruth County; 1936–39 St. Catherine's, Cambridge; 1939–42 Wesley House. *Appointments:* 1943–44 Tamworth; 1945–73 Zimbabwe; 1973–77 Wolstanton and Audley; 1977–82 Stratford-upon-Avon.
Connexional Committees: 1974–82 Overseas Division Central Committee.
Hobbies and Recreations: Walking.

HOUGH, Colin, West Lea, Route des Quennevais, St. Brelade, Jersey. (0534-43933)–BD. *b. 27 Mar 1934, Stoke-on-Trent. m. 5 July 1958: 3d.*
Education: 1940–45 Milton (Stoke-on-Trent) Inf. and Jun.; 1945–50 Hanley High Sch.; 1954–58 Hartley Victoria. *Appointments:* 1958–61 Kimberley; 1961–65 Guyana Dt; 1965–70 Gainsborough; 1970–79 Guernsey and Alderney; 1979– Jersey.
Connexional Committees: 1966–70, 1971–77 MMS Central Committee; 1979– Education and Youth. *Local Council Committees:* 1973–79 States of Guernsey Mediators Panel; 1979– States of Jersey Religious Education Advisory Council.
Special Interests: Religious Education, Further Education, Prison Chaplaincy, Community Relations, Ecumenical Affairs. *Hobbies and Recreations:* Travel, Tennis, Badminton, Squash, Swimming, Cycling, Drama, Music, Gardening, Painting and Decorating, Food and Wine.

HOUGHTON, Edward, 15 Elsee Rd., Rugby, Warwicks CV21 3BA. (0788-3253) *b. 8 Feb 1916, Stockport. m. 1 Aug 1944: 2s.*
Education: 1928–34 County Sch., Hyde; 1937–40 Handsworth.
Appointments: 1940–44 Towcester; 1944–47 Peterborough; 1947–50 Higham Ferrers; 1950–53 Spennymoor; 1953–59 Witney; 1959–65 Leicester South; 1965–68 Norwich St. Peters; 1968–74 Frodsham; 1974–82 Brownhills and Pelsall.
Connexional Committees: 1981–82 Hymnbook (text).
Special Interests: Hymnology (especially Wesley Hymns), Member Hymn Society of GB and Ireland, Contributor to Bulletin.

HOWARD, Basil Nowell, 78 Oakfields, Burnopfield, Newcastle-upon-Tyne NE16 6PQ. (0207-70238)–BD(Lond.). *b. 18 Sept 1918, Runcorn, Cheshire. m. 10 Aug 1949: 1d., 1s.*
Education: 1929–36 Kingswood Sch.; 1939–42 London Univ.; 1939–42 Wesley, Headingley.
Appointments: 1942–44 Knighton (West St.); 1944–45 Newbury; 1945–46 Kendal; 1946–49 Whitehaven; 1949–54 Haslingden; 1954–59 Darlington (South); 1959–63 St. Helens; 1963–68 Ulverston; 1968–75 Stretford and Urmston; 1975–80 Manchester (Cheetham Hill and Prestwich); 1980– Gateshead (South West).
Connexional Committees: 1961–63 Education; 1973–78 Board of Property.
Hobbies and Recreations: Listening to and Making Music.

HOWARD, Harry Bramwell, 37 Manor Orchard, Taunton, Somerset TA1 4SN. (0823-77860) *b. 5 Sept 1913, London E5. m. 20 July 1940: 3d., 1s.*
Education: 1924–29 Watford

Grammar Sch.; 1933–37 Richmond. *Appointments:* 1937–39 President's List; 1939–42 Brighton and Hove; 1942–49 East Wight; 1949–54 Brentford and Hounslow; 1954–56 West Wight; 1956–60 Stockport South; 1960–68 Free Church Federal Council; 1968–76 Ealing and Acton. *Publications: Onward with Christ* (NNSU 1956).

HOWARD, Peter James, 10 Hartmann St., Accrington, Lancs BB5 1TB. (0254-33387) *b. 6 March 1949, Clacton-on-Sea, Essex. m. 10 July 1976: 2s.*
Education: 1954–56 St. Osyth Rd. Prim. Sch.; 1956–60 Alton Park Jun. Sch.; 1960–65 Clacton County Secondary Sch. for Boys; 1972–76 Queen's. *Appointments:* 1976–78 Bridlington; 1978– Accrington and Haslingden.
Special Interests: Worship, Biblical Studies, Prayer and Devotional Life, Ecumenism. *Hobbies and Recreations:* Photography, German.

HOWARTH, Arthur Stanley, 9 Shirley Rd., Wallington, Surrey SM6 9QB. (01-647-5808) *b. 8 July 1905, Liverpool. s.*
Education: 1918–21 Ramsgate County; 1921–22 Swindon; 1923 Helston; 1927–30 Richmond.
Appointments: 1926–27 Wimborne; 1930–33 Ely; 1933–36 Hitchin; 1936–42 Melton Mowbray; 1942–46 Chelmsford; 1946–53 London, Lewisham; 1953–58 London, Leytonstone and Forest Gate; 1958–63 Sheerness; 1963–67 London, Greenwich.
Hobbies and Recreations: Cycling, Gardening.

HOWARTH, Carl, 33 Bushey Mill Lane, Watford, Herts WD2 4QU. (0923-21872) *b. 1 April 1943, Harpurhey, Manchester. m. 5 Aug 1967: 1d., 2s.*
Education: 1946–54 Moston Fields County Prim.; 1954–60 North Manchester Grammar Sch. for Boys; 1965–69 Richmond. *Appointments:* 1969–70 Lowestoft; 1970–74 Thetford; 1974–79 Stoke-on-Trent (South); 1979– Watford.
Connexional Committees: 1975–79 Education and Youth. *Council Member:* 1972–74 Brandon Parish Council.
Special Interests: Preachers and Personalities of the 18th, 19th Century. *Hobbies and Recreations:* Gardening, Football.

HOWARTH, Deryck Nordan, 140 Blackwell Lane, Darlington, Co. Durham DL3 8QQ. (0325-64968) *b. 30 Nov 1923, Bristol. m. 29 July 1950: 1d., 2s.*
Education: 1936–42 Rydal; 1947–49 Handsworth. *Appointments:* 1949–51 High Wycombe; 1951–56 Cardiff (Roath); 1956–62 Cannock; 1962–70 Wolverhampton (Darlington St.); 1970–74 Peterborough; 1974– Darlington.
Hobbies and Recreations: Fishing, Oil Painting.

HOWE, Keith, Wesley Manse, 73 Hill Top, Bolsover, Chesterfield, Derbyshire S44 6NG. (0246-823180) *b. 18 Dec 1933, Horsley Woodhouse, Derbyshire. m. 5 April 1958: 1d.*
Education: 1940–48 Smalley Boys Endowed Sch.; 1957–60 Hartley Victoria. *Appointments:* 1960–63 Peak; 1963–67 Peel (Isle of Man); 1967–73 Saltash and St. Germans; 1973– Bolsover and Staveley.
Connexional Committees: 1963–67 Church Membership.
Special Interests: Healing, Church Unity. *Hobbies and Recreations:* Printing (Letterpress).

HOWELL, Arthur Hetherington, 51 Bayham Rd., Bristol BS4 2DR. (0272-776714) *b. 16 Feb 1919, Barrow-in-Furness, Cumbria. m. 4 July 1953: 3d.*
Education: 1945–48 Wesley, Headingley. *Appointments:* 1948–50 Ledbury; 1950–53 Walkden; 1953–57 Worksop; 1957–61 Padiham; 1961–66 Kidderminster and Stourport; 1966–73 Ledbury; 1973–78 Sittingbourne; 1978– Bristol South.
Hobbies and Recreations: Golf.

HOWELL, Bernard Harold, 5 Castle Grove, Newbury, Berks RG13 1PS. (0635-40014) *b. 22 July 1927, West Ealing, London. m. 23 July 1955: 4s.*
Education: 1932–38 Northfields Jun. Sch.; 1938–42 Ealing Modern Sch.; 1942–48 Southall Technical Coll.; 1952–55 Handsworth.
Appointments: 1950–52 Allendale; 1955–58 Leeds (Richmond Hill); 1958–62 Birmingham (Sutton Park); 1962–68 Birmingham (South West); 1968–74 Wimborne; 1974–77 Mid Wilts (Devizes); 1977– Newbury and Hungerford.
Connexional Committees: 1966–68 Youth Committee.
Special Interests: Ecumenism.
Hobbies and Recreations: Cine Photograpy, Group Travel (Holy Land etc), Sailing, Reading.

HOWLING, Renée, Harleigh, 64 Station St., Misterton, Doncaster, S. Yorkshire DN10 4DE. (0427-890282) *b. 14 May 1925, Hyde, Cheshire. w, 10 Nov 1956: 1d., 3s.*
Education: 1930–39 St. Marys CE Sch., Haughton Green, Denton, Manchester; 1953–55 Wesley Deaconess Coll. *Appointments:* 1981– Gainsborough.
Special Interests: Work Amongst Young People (MAYC), Sociology.
Hobbies and Recreations: Reading, Motoring, Walking.

HOWSON, Peter James, c/o Rev. C. W. R. Gilbert, RN Army RAF Committee, 1 Central Buildings, Westminster, London SW1H 9NH.– BSc(Lond.), MA(Cantab.). *b. 16 May 1947, Hackney, London. m. 4 July 1975: 2s.*
Education: 1952–58 Stamford Hill Inf. and Jun. Sch.; 1958–65 Tottenham County Sch.; 1965–68 London Sch. of Economics and Political Science; 1972–74 Univ. of Cambridge; 1972–75 Wesley House.
Appointments: 1975–77 London Mission West (Hinde St.); 1977– Chaplain HMF.
Publications: A Short History of Karonga (Published by Malawi Government Department of Antiquities 1968).
Hobbies and Recreations: Computers, Theatre.

HOYLES, James Arthur, 73 The Oval, North Anston, Sheffield S31 7BX. (0909-566261)–BA(Open Univ.). *b. 23 Aug 1908, Cranswick, Driffield, N. Humberside. w. 6 Aug 1935: 2d., 2s.*
Education: 1912–22 Cranswich Elem.; 1927–28 Cliff Coll.; 1976–80 Open Univ.; 1982– Sheffield Univ., Post Graduate Research; 1928–30 Richmond; 1930–31 Headingley.
Appointments: 1931–35 Tiverton; 1935–37 Holsworthy; 1937–41 Falmouth; 1941–45 Swansea; 1945–51 Paisley Mission; 1951–58 Wolstanton and Audley; 1958–64 Stockport; 1964–68 Buckingham and Brackley; 1968–76 Secretary Home Mission Division.
Connexional Committees: 1952–76 Social Responsibility; 1968–76 Home Missions; 1968–76 NCH; 1961–82 Free Church Council; 1968–72 British Council of Churches.
Publications: Treatment of the Young Delinquent (1952); *Religion in Prison* (1954); *The Pastor's Dilemma* (1956); *The Church and the Criminal* (1964); *Christ Alive in Prison* (1971); *Sent to Prison* (1980).
Special Interests: Prison Chaplaincy, Penal Policy. *Hobbies and Recreations:* Golf, Oil Painting.

HUBBALL, Ronald William, 13 Draycott Rd., Upper Tean, Stoke-on-Trent ST10 4JF. (0538-722260) *b. 16 Sept 1924, Davenham, Northwich, Cheshire. m. 12 June 1954.*
Education: 1929–35 Davenham CE Sch.; 1935–41 Sir John Deane's Grammar Sch., Northwich; 1945–46 Univ. of Manchester; 1979–81 Hartley Victoria. *Appointments:* 1980– Cheadle.
Connexional Committees: 1964–77 Local Preachers Committee.
Hobbies and Recreations: Photography, Walking, Music (Choral).

HUBBARD, Harold Charles, 6 Waverley Rd., Bognor Regis, West Sussex PO21 5NB. (0243-822505) *b. 7 July 1905, Ipswich, Suffolk. m. 2 (w.): 1d., 1s.*
Education: 1908–21 Elem.; 1921–23 Ipswich Central.
Appointments: 1949–51 Hastings; 1951–55 Rotherham; 1955–60 Hastings; 1960–66 Worksop; 1966–67 Tiverton; 1967–70 Bolton.
Special Interests: Padre Local Branch TOCH, Helping Serve Meals for Lonely People, Member of Committee on Council, Elderly Folk, Pastoral Work, Preaching.
Hobbies and Recreations: Bowls.

HUBBUCK, Albert Reginald, 18 Wordsworth Rd., Abingdon, Oxon OX14 5NY. (0235-25144)–BA(Manch.), BD(Glasgow), PhD(Edinburgh). *b. 31 Dec 1903, Prudhoe-on-Tyne. m. 25 July 1936: 1d., 2s.*
Education: Elizabeth Grammar Sch., Hexham; Manchester Univ.; Glasgow Univ.; Edinburgh Univ.; 1929–32 Hartley. *Appointments:* 1932–38 Glasgow II (Parkhead); 1938–42 Paisley Mission; 1942–46 Edinburgh Mission; 1946–49 Newcastle-upon-Tyne, Heaton and Wallsend; 1949–54 Stockport, Tiviot Dale; 1954–57 Stockport, Hazel Grove and Poynton; 1957–58 Per., USA; 1958–60 Stockport, Hazel Grove and Poynton; 1960–66 Swansea; 1966–71 Birkenhead.
Connexional Committees: Youth.

HUBERY, Douglas Stanley, 268 Rugeley Rd., Cannock, Staffs SW12 5QW. (052438-76264) *b. 2 Aug 1916, Cheslyn Hay, Staffs. m. 6 Jan 1944: 2s.*
Education: 1927–32 Elmore Green Central Sch., Bloxwich; 1932–35 Queen Mary's Grammar Sch., Walsall; 1936–37 Cliff Coll.; 1937–40 Handsworth. *Appointments:* 1940–44 London Missions, East Ham; 1944–49 London Missions, Tooting; 1949–53 Sunderland Mission; 1953–60 Westhill Coll. of Education; 1960–70 Methodist Youth Department; 1970–73 Methodist Education Department; 1973–78 Division of Education and Youth.
Connexional Committees: 1960–78 All Connexional Committees as representing MYD, MEC, DEY.
Publications: The Emancipations of Youth (Beckley Lecture 1963); *Teaching the Christian Faith Today* (1965); *Christian Education and the Bible* (1967); *The Teaching Methods of Jesus* (1970); *Christian Education in State and Church* (1972); *The Methodist Contribution to Education in England* (1977).
Special Interests: Probus Club, Music.
Hobbies and Recreations: Sports, Driving Cars.

HUCKER, Michael Frederick, Assistant Principal Chaplain, RAF Strike Command, c/o RAF Northwood, Middx HA6 3EP. (01-65-26161 Ext. 7266)–M.B.E., MA(Bristol), BD(Lond.). *b. 1 May 1933, Bath. m. 13 May 1961: 1d., 1s.*
Education: 1944–49 City of Bath Boys Sch.; 1955–59 Didsbury, Bristol.
Appointments: 1959–62 Uxbridge, Hayes and Yiewesley; 1962– Chaplain Royal Air Force.
Hobbies and Recreations: Gardening, Reading, Music.

HUCKNALL, John Neville, 28 Durnsford Way, Cranleigh, Surrey GU6 7LW. (04-866-2522) *b. 15 Jan 1944, Newark, Notts. m. 21 Oct 1970: 1d., 2s.*
Education: 1949–55 Sutton-on-Trent County Primary Sch.; 1955–62 Southwell Minster Grammar Sch.; 1974–77 Wesley, Bristol.
Appointments: 1977–82 Trowbridge and Bradford-on-Avon; 1982– Guildford.
Hobbies and Recreations: Walking, Music, Photography.

HUDSON, John Dean, 1 Overstrand Close, Arnold, Nottingham NG5 6PT. (0602-201992)–BEd(Nottingham). *b. 15 July 1947, Birmingham. m. 23 Aug 1970: 1d., 1s.*
Education: 1958–65 Central Grammar Sch., Birmingham; 1965–69 Loughborough Coll. of Education; 1972–75 Queens. *Appointments:* 1975–80 Bromley and Chaplain at Farrington's Sch.; 1980– Nottingham Central.
Special Interests: Inter-faith Dialogue.
Hobbies and Recreations: Woodwork, Squash, Home-Made Wines.

HUDSON, John James Birchall, 12 Oaklands Ave., Romford, Essex RM1 4DB. (0708-40474)—BA(Manch.), MA(Cantab.). *b. 17 Nov 1918, Nelson, Lancashire. m. 1 July 1948: 2s.*
Education: 1931–36 Kingswood Sch., Bath; 1936–42 Univ. of Manchester; 1946–47 Wesley House.
Appointments: 1940–43 National Service; 1943–45 Fleetwood; 1945–46 Presteigne and Kington; 1946–47 Wesley House; 1947–51 Chorley; 1951–55 Radcliffe; 1955–60 Coventry; 1960–65 Nottingham South; 1965–72 Coalville; 1972–77 Leicester South East; 1977– Romford.

HUDSON, Peter, 32 Cranbrook Rise, Cranbrook, Ilford, Essex IG1 3QN. (01-554-4949) *b. 1 July 1934, Didsbury, Manchester. m. 27 July 1964: 3d., 1s.*
Education: 1945–61 Hulme Hall Coll.; 1951–52 Stockport Coll.; 1957–58 Cliff Coll.; 1960–63 Didsbury, Bristol; 1963–64 West Hill Coll., Birmingham.
Appointments: 1964–66 Tunbridge Wells; 1966–71 Penarth; 1971– London, Ilford.
Connexional Committees: 1974–80 Board of Education; 1967–70 Youth and Community Committee; 1971– NCH General Committee. *Local Council Committees:* 1979– London Borough of Redbridge Communal Homes 'Independent Person'.
Special Interests: Community Development, Ecumenical, Youth Work, Multi Faith Understanding.
Hobbies and Recreations: Visiting Historical Places, The Countryside, The Secondhand Trade.

HUDSON, Peter Neville, 3 Merton Rd., Slough, Berks SL1 1QW. (0753-20742) *b. 31 Jan 1929, Spennymoor, Co. Durham. m. 23 July 1955: 2d.*
Education: King St., Spennymoor; Nevilles Cross High Sch., Durham; 1952–55 Headingley. *Appointments:* 1955–58 Beccles, Loddon and Bungay; 1958–62 Scarborough; 1962–66 Hull (Trinity); 1966–71 Sheffield (Eccleshall); 1971–73 London, Highgate; 1973–76 Caerphilly; 1976–81 Hull (West); 1981– Slough.
Connexional Committees: 1963–66 Youth; 1969–70 National President MAYC.
Special Interests: Opera. *Hobbies and Recreations:* Hiking, Travel.

HUGHES, Allan James, 20 Grove Rd., Millhouses, Sheffield S7 2GZ. (0742-363419) *b. 7 March 1930, Cleethorpes, Lincolnshire. m. 7 April 1958: 1s.*
Education: 1954–57 Hartley Victoria.
Appointments: 1957–60 Luton Industrial Mission; 1960–63 Wath and Mexborough; 1963–73 Grimsby Mission; 1973–81 Tunstall (Stoke-on-Trent); 1981– Sheffield Mission.
Connexional Committees: 1966–72 Home Mission Division.
Hobbies and Recreations: Music, Opera, Travel.

HUGHES, Edward, Rosalind, 87 Badminton Rd., Downend, Bristol BS16 6BU. (0272-570329) *b. 3 May 1899, Llangollen, Clwyd. m. 1 June 1925: 1d.*
Education: Elem.; 1921 Cliff Coll.
Appointments: 1956–58 Great Yarmouth Temple; 1958–59 Brynmawr; 1959–63 Wombwell and Hoyland; 1963–66 Wolverhampton, Darlington St.
Special Interests: Gardening, Bowls.
Hobbies and Recreations: Books and Bowling.

HUGHES, George Wynne, 1 Ashburton Rd., West Kirby, Wirral, Merseyside L48 4ER. (051-625-7740)—BA(Wales), MA(Cantab.), PhD(Edinburgh). *b. 26 Nov 1897, Treuddyn, Clwyd. m. 20 Aug 1930 (w.): 2s.*
Education: 1912– Elem.; 1922–25 Bangor; 1925–28 Cambridge; 1933–37 Edinburgh, 1925–28 Wesley House. *Appointments:* 1928–30 Bangor, Welsh; 1930– Coolbridge; 1933–37 Edinburgh Mission; 1937–46 Hoylake; 1946–55 Llandudno, 1955–61 Leeds, Headingley; 1961–64 Preston, Trinity.
Publications: Articles 1939, 1930, 1930.
Special Interests: Preaching, Pastoral Ministry. *Hobbies and Recreations:* Golf, Gardening, Indoor Plants.

HUGHES, Henry Trevor, 102 New Rd., Hethersett, Norwich NR9 3HQ. (0603-811038)—MA(Cantab.), MA(Oxon). *b. 27 Feb 1910, Wallasey. m. 10 Aug 1946: 1d., 1s.*
Education: 1921–26 Perse Sch., Cambridge; 1932–35 Wesley House.
Appointments: 1935–41 Chaplain Culford Sch.; 1941–45 Chaplain Royal Air Force; 1945–46 Assistant Minister Westminster Central Hall; 1945–46 Chaplain Westminster Coll.; 1946–53 Vice Principal; 1953–69 Principal; 1969–75 Wymondham, Attleborough and Watton; 1965 First Methodist Select Preacher, Univ. Oxford.
Connexional Committees: 1946–53 Education. *Local Council Committees:* 1974–81 Norfolk Education Committee; 1975– Chairman of Governors, Wymondham Coll., Norfolk.
Publications: Prophetic Prayer (1947); *Teaching the Bible to Seniors* (1948); *Teaching the Bible to Juniors* (1949); *Why We Believe* (1950); *The Piety of Jeremy Taylor* (1960); *Faith and Life* (1962); *Life Worth Living* (1965); *A Progress of Pilgrims* (1979).
Special Interests: Education. *Hobbies and Recreations:* Painting.

HUGHES, John, Gregynog, Newtown, Powys SY16 3PN. (0868-687-295) *b. 3 March 1891, Tregarth, Gwynedd. m. 1919 (w.): 1s.*
Education: 1898–1905 Tregarth National Sch.; 1912–13 Clynnog Private Grammar Sch.; 1914–16 Handsworth. *Appointments:* 1916–17 St. Davids; 1917–20 Chaplain HMF; 1920–21 Pontypridd; 1921–24 Llandeilo; 1924–28 Machynlleth; 1928–31 Brynmaws; 1931–34 Newtown; 1934–37 Towyn; 1937–34 Liverpool; 1939–41 Manchester; 1941–45 Llanfyllin; 1945–46 Caernarfon; 1946–49 Rhyl; 1949–53 Ruthin; 1953–58 Bagillt; 1958–59 Supernumerary, 1959–60 Chester, Welsh.
Connexional Committees: 1956–57 President Welsh Assembly; 1934–55 Secretary Welsh Assembly; 1930–33 Assistant Secretary; 1922–30 Journal Secretary. *Publications: Yr Addoliad Cyhoeddus* (Yr Eurgrawn 1956).

HUGHES, William Edward, 48 Ashkirk, Dudley, Cramlington, Northumberland NE23 7DG. (0632-500448) *b. 29 July 1915, Birkenhead, Cheshire. m. 15 Sept 1945.*
Education: Hemmingford St. and Pilgrim St. Prim. Sch.; 1919–23 Bidston Ave. Council Sch.; 1923–26 Brassey St. Elem. Sch.; 1926–29 Birkenhead. *Appointments:* 1951–52 Rhymney Valley; 1952–55 Todmorden; 1955–59 Sunderland West; 1959–62 Hull (Trinity); 1962–67 Consett; 1967–71 Driffield; 1971–76 Chester-le-Street; 1976–80 Buckley and Deeside.
Publications: The World in My Prayers (Epilogues); *The Place of Prayer, The Door is Open* (Books of Prayers); *Someone's There, The Smashed Rainbow, The Stray Shepherd* (Poetry).
Special Interests: Social Reponsibility. *Hobbies and Recreations:* Article and Poetry Writing.

HUGHES, William Thomas, Arthog, 22 Linden Drive, Cae Del, Mold, Clwyd CH7 1QT. (0352-4869) *b. 30 March 1916, Leeswood, Nr. Mold.*
Education: 1921–32 Leeswood Council Sch.; 1932–37 Mold Alun Grammar Sch.; 1939–42 Wesley, Headingley. *Appointments:* 1942–45 Machynlleth; 1945–46 Corwen; 1946–49 Dinas Mawddwy; 1949–50 Llanfyllin; 1950–51 Ferndale; 1951–55 Llanfaircaereinion; 1955–64 Llanidloes; 1964–69 Lampeter; 1969–75 Llanasa; 1975– 79 Machynlleth; 1979–80 Rhyl; 1980–81 De Gwynedd.
Special Interests: Reading, Birds. *Hobbies and Recreations:* Gardening, Cricket.

HUGMAN, Edward John, 74 Bushey Wood Rd., Totley Rise, Sheffield, South Yorks S17 3QB. (0742-364016)–BA(Manch.), BD(Manch.). *b. 4 Jan 1917, Hull. m. 6 Jan 1945: 1d., 2s.*
Education: 1922–28 Sidmouth St. Elem. Sch., Hull; 1928–32 Boulevard Municipal Secondary Sch., Hull; 1938–43 Manchester Univ.; 1938–43 Hartley Victoria. *Appointments:* 1943–45 Andover and Hurstbourne; 1945–51 Selby; 1951–53 Tadcaster; 1953–57 Sheffield North; 1957–60 Bolton (Bridge St.); 1960–66 Burton-on-Trent (Parker St.); 1966 contd. Religious Education at City Sch., Sheffield.
Connexional Committees: 1980– Day Schools Committee of Division of Education and Youth.

HUGMAN, G. Rodney, 90 Windsor Rd., Hull, Horth Humberside HU5 4HQ. (0482-59196)–BSc(Lond.). *b. 28 March 1918, Hull. m. 23 July 1949: 4s.*
Education: 1923–29 Sidmouth St. Sch., Hull; 1929–35 Hull Municipal Technical Coll.; 1947–49 Handsworth. *Appointments:* 1946–47 Salisbury (Dews Rd.); 1949–52 Chorley; 1952–56 Bingley; 1956–59 Stour Valley Mission; 1959–62 Liverpool (South East); 1962–66 Shebbear; 1966–73 Ashford (Kent); 1973–79 Keighley; 1979–80 Shipley and Bingley; 1980– Hull (West).
Special Interests: Astronomy, Cartography, Mathematics, Community Relations Council.
Hobbies and Recreations: Peace Movement, Overseas Students, Walking.

HULME, Paul, 43 Manor Rd., Taunton, Somerset. (72734)–BA. *b. 14 May 1942, Sheffield. m. 1 May 1976: 2s.*
Education: 1951–58 Hadfield House, Sheffield; 1962–64 Cliff Coll.; 1964–68 Didsbury, Bristol. *Appointments:* 1968–70 Beccles, Loddon and Bungay; 1970–75 Brighton, Dome Mission; 1975–79 Newquay Wesley; 1979– Taunton.
Connexional Committees: Home Mission Committee.
Hobbies and Recreations: Home.

HUMPHREYS, Trevor, Bradford House, Ruthin Rd., Bwlchweyn, Wrexham, Clwyd LL11 5UT. *b. 28 March 1911, Maerdy, Mid Glam. m. 16 July 1958.*
Education: Abergynolwyn Council Sch., Merioneth; 1939–42 Headingley. *Appointments:* 1942–49 Beaumaris; 1949–50 Llandudno; 1950–55 Bangor; 1955–60 Llandudno; 1960–65 Holywell; 1965–70 Portmadog; 1970–76 Llangollen.
Hobbies and Recreations: Gardening, Motoring.

HUNT, Alan William, 44 Windsor Rd., Hailsham, East Sussex BN27 3HL. (0323-841199) *b. 21 June 1927, Anstey, Leicestershire. m. 19 July 1958: 1d., 2s.*
Education: 1931–38 Anstey; 1938–43 Loughborough Coll. Sch.; 1955–58 Didsbury, Bristol. *Appointments:* 1958–61 Shepton Mallett; 1961–66 Coalville; 1966–73 Portsmouth and Southsea; 1973–79 Yeovil; 1979– Eastbourne.
Publications: A Study of the Cow Plain Methodist/Anglican Ecumenical Experiment, and the Lessons which may be drawn from it (St. George's House, Windsor January 1973).
Special Interests: Ecumenism, Education, Chaplaincy and Care of the Sick. *Hobbies and Recreations:* Philately, Gardening, Football, Cricket.

HUNT, G. Clifford, 38 Raphael Rd., Hove, E. Sussex BN3 5QQ. (0273-732536) *b. 5 Nov 1920, South Wigston, Leicester. m. 19 Aug 1950: 1d., 1s.*
Education: 1925–32 South Wigston; 1932–36 Alderman Newton Sch., Leicester; 1947–49 Hartley Victoria. *Appointments:* 1946–47 Hunts Mission; 1949–50 Dursley and Stonehouse; 1950–53 Leeds (Bramley and Farsley); 1953–57 West Bromwich (Hill Top); 1957–65 Leamington Spa; 1965–73 Northampton; 1973–81 Christchurch and Lymington; 1981– Brighton and Hove.
District Committees: 1968–73 Property Secretary (Oxford and Leicester District); 1974–80 Home Mission Secretary (Southampton District).
Hobbies and Recreations: County Cricket.

HUNT, James Royden, Wesley Manse, Warwick Rd., Kineton, Warwick CV35 0HN. (0926-640385) *b. 9 Dec 1929, Guildford, Surrey.*

m. 14 July 1956: 1d., 1s.
Education: 1941–48 Royal Grammar Sch., Guildford; 1952–55 Handsworth. *Appointments:* 1955–58 Worcester; 1958–63 Ransey; 1963–68 Shaftesbury; 1968–76 Silchester; 1976 Kineton.
Connexional Committees: 1959–62 Christian Citizenship; 1970–73 Youth; 1970– Nadea Member Uniformed Organisations Sub-Committee.
Special Interests: Rural Life. *Hobbies and Recreations:* Scouting, Camping.

HUNTER, Geoffrey William, 13 Bradshaw Close, Steeple Aston, Oxford OX5 3SA. (47092)–BA(Open). *b. 3 Oct 1939, Liverpool. m. 22 April 1967: 2d.*
Education: 1951–59 Colwyn Bay Grammar Sch.; 1959–62 Nottingham Univ.; 1981–82 Westminster Coll., Oxford; 1963–66 Richmond.
Appointments: 1966–68 Normanton; 1968–74 Louth; 1974–81 Oxford.

HUNTER, Ronald, 44 Waugron Rd., Llandaff, Cardiff CF5 2JL. (0222-562395) *b. 12 Dec 1938, Dublin.*
Education: 1943–55 St. Andrews National Sch., Dublin; 1955–58 Clogher Rd. Technical Coll., Dublin; 1967–68 Cliff Coll.; 1975–77 Wesley, Bristol. *Appointments:* 1977– Cardiff.
Parliamentary Service: Non Political Agent to Speaker of House of Commons 1979 Election.
Special Interests: Religious Advisory Group Chairman to Cardiff Broadcasting Company. *Hobbies and Recreations:* Sailing, Theatre.

HURST, Terence, 46 Ancaster Rd., Whickham, Newcastle upon Tyne NE16 5BQ. (0632-887794) *b. 25 June 1941, Derby. m: 1d., 2s.*
Education: 1952–57 Derby Grammar Sch.; 1962–66 Handsworth.
Appointments: 1966–68 Corby; 1968–73 Northampton; 1973–80 Gateshead and Jarrow; 1980 Gateshead South West.
Special Interests: Music, Reading, Poetry, Local Radio. *Hobbies and Recreations:* Gardening, Squash, Swimming, Writing.

HURT, N. Keith, 2 Chester House, Pages Lane, London N10 1PR. (01-444-9845)–MA, BD, STM.
Education: 1954–57 London Univ.; 1959–61 Wesley, Headingley; 1967–68 Andover Newton, USA.
Appointments: 1961–65 Stockton; 1965–68 Per. USA; 1968 Hull East; 1968–78 Nottingham Coll. of Education; 1978– Secretary Division of Education and Youth.

HUTCHENS, William Nicholas James, 9 Tudor Cresc., Wolverhampton WV2 4PX. (0902-341794) *b. 14 July 1925, Mullion, Cornwall. m. 7 June 1950: 2d.*
Education: 1930–35 Mullion; 1935–40 Heslton Grammar Sch.; 1958–60 Didsbury, Bristol. *Appointments:* 1960–61 Castletown (Isle of Man); 1961–66 Bromsgrove; 1966–72 Taunton; 1972–80 Lichfield, 1980– Wolverhampton Trinity.
Special Interests: Pastoral Counselling, The Work of Housing Societies. *Hobbies and Recreations:* Used to Play Cricket, Gardening.

HUTCHINGS, Francis Owen, St. Andrews Church, RAF Wildenrath, BFPO 42.–BA(Leeds), BA(Open). *b. 16 May 1935, Leicester. m. 18 Aug 1962: 1d., 2s.*
Education: 1947–51 Leicester City Boys Grammar; 1958–62 Headingley; 1959–62 Leeds Univ.; 1971–78 Open Univ. *Appointments:* 1962–64 Wakefield; 1964–66 Wesley House, Berlin; 1966– Chaplain HMF.
Special Interests: Motor Cars, Dinghy Sailing, Windsurfing, Cocker Spaniels, Reading, Walking.

HUTCHINGS, Peter Herbert, 12 Lemington Gdns., Fenham, Newcastle-upon-Tyne NE5 2EN. (0632-748303) *b. 15 April 1929, Portsmouth. m. 23 June 1962: 1d., 1s.*
Education: 1936–39 Portsmouth Grammar Sch.; 1940–45 Purbrook Park County High Sch.; 1959–62 Didsbury, Bristol. *Appointments:* 1962–66 Dudley; 1966–70 Bilston; 1970– Newcastle-upon-Tyne (West) Industrial Chaplain.
Connexional Committees: 1980– Team Ministries Committee.
Special Interests: Industry, Industrial Relations, New Technology. *Hobbies and Recreations:* Drawing, Painting, Model Engineering, Radio, Music.

HUTCHINGS, Roger Courtenay Gerrard, 56 Shaw Rd., Heaton Moor, Stockport SK4 4PX. (061-442-9202)–BA. *b. 4 Nov 1942, Bristol. m. 13 May 1978: 2s.*
Education: 1949–61 Bristol Grammar Sch.; 1961–64 Hatfield Coll., Univ. of Durham; 1964–65 Univ. of Newcastle upon Tyne; 1966–69 Univ. of Bristol; 1966–69 Wesley, Bristol. *Appointments:* 1969–74 Liverpool South East (as Chaplain to Liverpool Univ. and Colls.); 1974–76 National Officer, one for Christian Renewal; 1976–79 Barnsley; 1979– BBC Religious Broadcasting Dept.
Connexional Committees: 1976– Radio and TV Committee.
Hobbies and Recreations: Music (Organ Playing), Photography, Model Railways.

HUXTABLE, Anthony Graham, Oaklands, 88 Westway, Wimbotsham, King's Lynn, Norfolk PE34 3QB. (0366-382120)–BA. *b. 19 Aug 1947, Barnstaple. m. 16 July 1977: 2d.*
Education: 1959–62 South Molton Secondary Modern; 1964–65 Devon Coll. of Agriculture, Bicton; 1975–79 St. Johns Coll., Nottingham; 1976–79 Nottingham Univ.; 1973–74 Cliff Coll.; 1979–81 Wesley, Bristol.
Appointments: 1981– Downham Market.

HYMER, Kenneth, 8 Orwell Ave., Denton, Manchester M34 2LR. (061-336-2367) *b. 3 March 1932, York. m. 4 Aug 1960: 2s.*
Education: Headingley 1955–58.
Appointments: 1958–60 Loftus and Staithes; 1960–65 Knaresborough; 1965–72 Stokesley; 1972–75 Staines and Feltham; 1975–80 Ashton-u-Lyne; 1980– Denton.
Hobbies and Recreations: Caravanning, Walking, Gardening.

IGWE, G. Egemba, 5 Heath Rd., Hale, Altrincham, Cheshire WA14 2UJ. (061 928 0533)–BA,

MA(Cantab), PhD(Lond.). *b. 28 Dec 1925, Umuda Isingwu, Umuahia, Nigeria. m. 24 July 1954: 1d., 3s. Education:* 1930–35 Methodist Central Sch., Umuda Isingwu, Umuahia, Nigeria; 1936–37 Methodist Sch., Mission Hill, Umuahia, Nigeria; 1938–48 Uzuakoli Coll.; 1950–55 Cambridge Univ.; 1950–55 Wesley House; 1970–73 London Univ. *Appointments:* 1955–63 East Nigeria Dt; 1963–77 Nigerian Conf.; 1977–78 Manchester and Salford Mission; 1978– Altrincham. *Connexional Committees:* 1959–61 Standing Committee (and others) Eastern Nigeria District Synod; 1962–66 All Committees of Methodist Church Nigeria; 1959–66 Nigeria Church Union Committee; 1959–66 Christian Council of Nigeria;1978– World Development Action Committee (DSR); 1980– DSR Board; 1980– Central Committee (MOD). *Publications: New Testament in Idoma* (1970); *IGBO Book of Worship* (1965); *A Descriptive Grammar of Igbo* (1963); *A Short Grammar of Igbo* (1964); *Igbo Language Course* (1967); *Introductory Igbo Language Course for Non-Igbo Speakers* (1966 MMS); *Four Sermons in Assoziationen, Band 7* (1979 Radius/ Germany). *Hobbies and Recreations:* Stamp Collecting, Gardening.

INGER, Frank Henry, 1 Bedford Rd., St. Ives, Cornwall, TR26 1SP. (0736 795633) *b, 17 March 1921, Nottingham. m. 11 Aug 1949: 2d. Education:* 1932–37 High Pavement Secondary Sch., Nottingham; 1946–47 Didsbury, Bristol. *Appointments:* 1947–49 Blackburn Mission; 1949–51 Kingston upon Hull; 1951–54 London Mission East; 1955–60 London, Finsbury Park and Southgate; 1960–64 Peterlee; 1964–67 Keighley; 1967–70 Daventry; 1970–76 Lincoln Central; 1976–81 Newquay; 1981–St. Ives, Cornwall. *Connexional Committees;* 1949–51 Connexional Christian Citizenship Committee; 1957– Connexional Ministers Retirement Fund Committee; 1978–82 Connexional Division of Ministries Board. *Local Council Committees:* 1951–54 Bethnal Green Borough Youth Committee; 1955–60 Edmonton Borough Youth Committee; 1964–67 Keighley Borough Youth Committee; 1964–67 Keighley Borough Social Services Committee. *Publications: Demobilisation Crusade* (1946); *New Hymns for Special Occasions and Dedication Services* (1972); *'Action Services' for Harvest Festivals and Christmas* (1973). *Special Interests:* Hymns, Hymn Writers and Hymn-Writing. *Hobbies and Recreations:* Hymn Writing, T.V. Electronics.

INGHAM, James Herbert William, 30 Beaconsfield Rd., Clacton-on-Sea, Essex CO15 6BU. (0255 420774) *b. 17 Aug 1909, Lower Sydenham, London SE26. m. 29 July 1939: 1d., 2s. Education:* 1914–26 Haseltine Rd., L.C.C. Elem. Sch.; 1926–29 Poplar Sch. of Engineering; 1933–37 Handsworth. *Appointments:* 1932–33 Kirkby-Lonsdale; 1937–38 Gateshead; 1938–39 Wishaw; 1939–42 Armadale; 1942–45 Wigton, 1945–48 Burnley; 1948–51 Portland; 1951–56 Windsor; 1956–61 Lewisham; 1961–66 Southampton; 1966–72 Medway Towns; 1972–76 Darlaston. *Special Interests:* Chairman Local Branch of Arthritis Care, Secretary of Clacton Ministers' Fraternal. *Hobbies and Recreations:* Model Making, Reading, Watching Football, Gardening.

INGLE, Handley Cecil, 3 Elm Grove, Teignmouth, Devon TQ14 8SA. (06267 3968) *20 Nov 1901, Birmingham. m. 29 Jan 1933: 2d., 2s. Education:* 1910–17 Truro Sch.; 1922–25 Handsworth. *Appointments:* 1925–37 Madras District; 1938–66 Per B.F.B.S. *Special Interests:* Institute of Religion and Medicine.

INGYON, Bernard John, 39 Clayton Rd., Jesmond, Newcastle upon Tyne NE2 4RQ. (0632 813417)– BA(Newcastle), BD, MA(Manch). *b. 23 Jan 1946, Finedon, Northants. m. 27 July 1968; 1d., 1s. Education:* 1951–57 Higham Ferrers County Prim.; 1957–64 Wellingborough Grammar Sch.; 1964-67 Univ. of Newcastle-upon-Tyne; 1968–71 Hartley Victoria; 1971–72 Perkins Sch. of Theol., Southern Methodist Univ. Dallas, Texas, U.S.A. *Appointments:* 1972–76 Shildon (Newton Aycliffe New Town); 1976– Newcastle Brunswick Central–Chaplain to Newcastle Univ. and Newcastle Poly. *Special Interests:* Christian Social Ethics. *Hobbies and Recreations:* Squash, Listening to Music.

ION, William Wharton, 36 Thorold Street, Boston, Lincs. PE12 6PH. (0205 61928) *b. 11 May 1903, Doncaster. m. 9 July 1931: 4d. Education;* Elem. Doncaster. 1926–28 Hartley. *Appointments:* 1924–26 Market Rasen and Caistor; 1928–30 Horncastle; 1930–33 Brigg; 1933–38 Louth; 1938–41 Bacup and Ravenstall; 1941–45 Manchester (Hr. Openshaw); 1945–50 Sheffield (Surrey St.); 1950–55 West Bromwich; 1955–59 Blackheath (Birmingham Rd.); 1959–66 Cradley Heath; 1966–70 Manchester (Droylsden and Openshaw).

IRELAND, James Campbell, Avondale, Alston, Cumbria CA9 3TH. (0498 81302) *b. 22 Dec 1929, Gosport, Hampshire. m. 12 May 1951: 1d., 1s. Education:* 1935–40 Leesland Jun. Sch., Gosport; 1940–41 Evacuation; 1941–44 Gosport Central Sch.; 1944–47 Boys Training Sch. Royal Corps of Signals, Catterick Camp; 1970–72 Hartley Victoria. *Appointments:* 1972–79 Ormskirk; 1979– Alston. *Hobbies and Recreations:* Dabbling in Electronics, All Sports.

IRELAND, Pearson Renney, 28 Beacon Hill, London N7 9LY. (01 607 2155) *b. 13 March 1939, Little Broughton, Cockermouth, Cumberland. m. 7 Jan 1961: 2d., 3s. Education:* 1950–55 Cockermouth Grammar Sch.; 1963–67 Hartley Victoria. *Appointments:* 1967–69

Beverley; 1969–75 Ripon and Masham; 1975–81 Huddersfield (West); 1981– London (North and Central) Mission.
Hobbies and Recreations: Sport, Buses.

ISHERWOOD, Edward, Fernleigh, 77 The Mount, Shrewsbury, Shropshire. (53767) *b. 25 Feb 1897, Blackbury, Lancs. m. 1924: 2d.*
Education: 1915–16 Evening Continuation Sch.; 1916–18 Blackburn Commercial Coll.
Appointments: 1928–30 Darlington; 1930–32 Sunderland; 1933–36 Chesterfield; 1936–38 Downham Market; 1938–44 Huddersfield Lindley; 1944–48 Weardale; 1948–52 Hobeoch; 1952–55 Bridport; 1955–60 Tewkesbury; 1960–67 Shrewsbury.
Special Interests: Horology, Theology.

ISHERWOOD, Terence, 9 Berrow Rd., Burnham-on-Sea, Somerset TA8 2ET. (782306) *b. 7 June 1942, Helmshore, Rossendale, Lancs. m. 2 July 1966: 1d., 2s.*
Education: Helmshore and Haslingden Schs.; 1962–66 Hartley Victoria. *Appointments:* 1966–68 Stafford; 1968–71 Cradley Heath; 1971–76 Zimbabwe Conf.; 1976– Weston-super-Mare.
Connexional Committees: 1978– Overseas.

IVATT, William Henry, 10 Pinewood Close, Bourne, Lincs PE10 9RH. (07782 2587) *b. 26 Nov 1902, Weston Hills, Spalding, Lincs. m. 20 April 1963: 1d.*
Education: Deeping St. Nicholas, Tongue End; Willesby Sch., Spalding; 1925–26 Cliff Coll.; 1929–32 Hartley Victoria. *Appointments:* 1932–36 Bradford, Woodhouse Grove; 1936–39 Tamworth and Lichfield; 1939–45 Brandon and Deerness Valley; 1945–51 Durham; 1951–56 Gainsborough; 1956–62 Louth; 1962–67 Brigg; 1967–70 Bury St. Edmunds.
Connexional Committees: 1946–51 Temperance and Social Welfare; 1957–62 Church Membership.
Special Interests: Bible Society British and Foreign, Free Church Council, Council of Churches, F.K. Hospital Visiting and Chaplaincies.
Hobbies and Recreations: Gardening, Reading.

IZZETT, David Stewart Thomas, 7 Barberry Rd., Hemel Hempstead, Herts. HP1 1SD. (0442 51497)–MA(Cantab), BA(Lond.)., AKC. *b. 19 July 1910, Croydon. m. 1. 1945 (w.), 2. 1978: 1d., 3s.*
Education: 1917–28 Croydon High Sch.; 1928–32 Finch Travelling Scholar, Berlin Univ.; 1934–37 Wesley House. *Appointments:* 1938–43 Ceylon Dt; 1940–43 Principal, Wesley Coll., Colombo; 1943–66 Chaplain H.M.F.; 1962–66 Assistant Chaplain-General; 1966–72 Watford; 1972–75 London, Finsbury Park and Southgate.
Connexional Committees: 1966–74 Methodist Missionary Society; 1981 New Testament Examiner, Methodist Study Centre; 1952–82 Bible Lands Society (Chairman 1982); 1967 Garden Tomb, Jerusalem, Trustee; Near and Middle East Committee (BCC), (Member). *Local Council Committees:* 1971–72 Mayor's Chaplain, Watford; 1970–72 President, Watford Council of Churches. *Publications: If Any Man* (Play 1948); *Leading Tours to the Holy Land* (1962–82); *In the Steps of St. Paul. Hobbies and Recreations:* Member Royal Philatelic Soc., Archaeology.

JACKSON, Alan, 50 Elm Drive, Market Drayton, Shropshire TF9 3HE. (0630 2067) *b. 30 Jan 1915, Ashby, Scunthorpe, Lincs. m. 1 Jan 1944: 2d., 3s.*
Education: 1922–25 South Coates Lane, Hull; 1925–26 Rosemary St., Elem., Mansfield; 1926–31 Brunts Sch., Mansfield.; 1937–40 Handsworth. *Appointments:* 1940–53 E. Nigeria Dt; 1953–57 Blackburn, Clayton St.; 1957–61 Preston, Lune St.; 1961–66 Oldbury Wesley; 1966–73 Market Drayton; 1973–80 Leeds, Rothwell.
Hobbies and Recreations: Fuchsias, Fishing, Bowls.

JACKSON, Graeme Clark, 10 Handel Close, Edgware, Middx. HA8 7QZ. (01 952 3688)–MA. *b. 17 Feb 1929, Kandy, Sri Lanka. m. 7 Sept 1956: 1d., 1s.*
Education: Various in Sri Lanka (Richmond and Kingswood), South India (Hebron); 1942–44 L.P.C.I., Toronto, Canada: 1944–47 Kingswood; 1952–55 Didsbury, Bristol. *Appointments:* 1953–64 Ceylon Dt; 1964–66 Ceylon Conf.; 1966–74 World Council of Churches; 1974– Secretary Overseas Division.
Connexional Committees: 1974– Overseas Missions; 1977–82 Stationing Committee.
Hobbies and Recreations: Bird Watching, Weather Watching, Playing Violin.

JACKSON, Harry, 27 Napier St., Hyde, Cheshire. (061 366 0263) *b. 30 May 1908, Normanton, Yorks. m. 8 June 1935: 1d.*
Education: Normanton Grammar Sch. *Appointments:* 1964–65 Walsall; 1965–68 Whitehaven; 1968–73 Eston and South Bank; 1973–77 Sleaford.
Local Council Committees: Parish Councillor, Metheringham, Lincoln.
Publications: Every Heart a Crib (Nativity play published by Epworth Press).
Special Interests: Fuchsia cultivation.
Hobbies and Recreations: Gardening.

JACKSON, James, Flat 3, Seafield House, 23 Seafield Rd., Lytham St. Annes, Lancs. FY8 5PY. (739903) *b. 28 Nov 1901, Willington, Co. Durham. m. 6 Aug 1928: 1d., 1s.*
Education: 1906–14 Willington Council Sch.; 1921–24 Hartley; 1924–25 Livingstone Coll, London.
Appointments: 1925–28 East Africa Dt.; 1928–33 Newcastle-upon-Tyne Central; 1933–39 Newcastle-upon-Tyne, Gloucester St. and Heaton and Wallsend; 1940–46 Chaplain H.M.F.; 1945–50 Stoke-on-Trent, Hanley; 1950–56 Nottingham South; 1956–63 Eastern Nigeria District (Chairman); 1963–68 Nottingham South.
Connexional Committees: 1945–56 Finance; 1946–56 Property; 1960–63 West African Council.

Special Interests: Anthropology, Literature. *Hobbies and Recreations:* Sports.

JACKSON, John Dawson, 13 Hallfields, Radford Semele, Leamington Spa, Warwicks CV31 1TS. (0926 25113)–BA, BD(Manch). *b. 9 Nov 1914, Burslem, Stoke-on-Trent, Staffs. m. 25 April 1946: 1d.* *Education:* 1920–26 Park Rd. Jun./Senior Sch., Burslem; 1926–33 Newcastle-under-Lyme High Sch.; 1933–38 Manchester Univ.; 1933–38 Hartley Victoria. *Appointments:* 1938–39 Oldham; 1939–45 Ningpo, China; 1946–50 Stafford; 1950–56 Cambridge; 1956–60 Birmingham, Sparkhill; 1960–64 Gt. Yarmouth; 1965–70 Cambridge; 1970–76 Hackney Mission.

JACKSON, John Frederick, 34 Colews Ave., Alford, Lincs. LN13 0AH. (05212 6125) *b. 13 Mar 1913, Kingston upon Hull. m. 3 June 1942: 3d., 1s.* *Education:* Hull Grammar Sch.; 1935–39 Headingley. *Appointments:* 1939–42 Pickering; 1942-46 Chaplain H.M.F.; 1946–49 Nottingham North; 1949–52 Nottingham Cent.; 1952–61 Gibraltar; 1961–65 Corley; 1965–72 Worksop; 1972–75 Oakham; 1975–79 Berlin, Germany.

JACKSON, John Richard, 2 Wallington Rd., Billingham, Cleveland TS23 3UL. (0642 562046)–BA(Cantab), BSc(Nott.), PhD(Newcastle-upon-Tyne). *b. 10 Feb 1947, Nottingham. m. 22 July 1972: 1d., 1s.* *Education:* 1958–61 Gibraltar Grammar Sch.; 1961–65 Corby Grammar Sch.; 1965–68 Univ. of Nottingham; 1968–71 Univ. of Newcastle-upon-Tyne; 1971–74 Univ. Coll., Cardiff; 1974–76 Univ. of Cambridge; 1974–77 Wesley House. *Appointments:* 1977–80 Durham and Deerness Valley; 1980– Stockton.

JACKSON, Richard, 9 Eden Grove, Horfield, Bristol BS7 0PQ. (0272 691056) *b. 9 Feb 1940, Retford, Notts. m. 16 September, 1967: 1d., 1s.* *Education:* 1943–51 Drummond Rd. Inf./Green Lane Prim., Bradford; 1951–53 Belle Vue Grammar Sch., Bradford, Yorks; 1953–56 Queen Elizabeth Grammar Sch., Darlington; 1965–67 Headingley; 1967–68 Wesley, Bristol; 1968–69 Kingsmead. *Appointments:* 1969–79 Methodist Church Sierra Leone; 1979– Overseas Division. *Special Interests:* Mission, Church Growth, Renewal. *Hobbies and Recreations:* Photography, Squash.

JACKSON, Robert Paul, 5 Tower Close, Brown Lees, Biddulph, Stoke-on-Trent, Staffordshire ST8 6NQ. (0782 513246) *b. 31 March 1954, Penrith, Cumbria. m. 15 Sept 1979.* *Education:* 1959–63 Reagill, Nr. Penrith; 1963–65 Crosby Ravensworth, Nr. Penrith; 1965–72 Appleby Grammar, Cumbria (Comprehensive); 1979–82 Wesley, Bristol. *Appointments:* 1982– Biddulph and Mow Cop. *Special Interests:* Right-Wing Politics, History, Economics, Argriculture, Travel. *Hobbies and Recreations:* Chess, Cross-Country Running, Trains, Listening to Music esp. Sacred/Bluegrass and Classical Pianists.

JACKSON, Stanley, 33 Church Rd., Shoeburyness, Essex SS3 9EU. (2712) *10 Oct 1954, Darlington, Co. Durham. m. 9 July 1977.* *Education:* 1960–66 Beaumont St. Inf. and Jun. Sch.; 1966–71 Queen Elizabeth Grammar Sch., Darlington; 1972–73 Darlington Coll. of Further Education; 1977–80 Wesley, Bristol. *Appointments:* 1980– Southend-on-Sea. *Hobbies and Recreations:* Squash, Other Sports, Reading.

JAGGARD, Derek William Wesley, 58 Station Rd., Soham, Ely, Cambridge CB7 5DY. (0353 720347) *b. 24 May 1938, Gt. Bentley, Essex. m. 4 April 1968: 1d., 1s.* *Education:* 1949–54 Colchester Royal Grammar; 1978–80 Wesley, Bristol. *Appointments:* 1980– Newmarket. *Special Interests:* Rural Methodism. *Hobbies and Recreations:* Tropical Fish.

JAMES, David Stanley, 26 St. Johns Drive, Hooe, Plymouth PL9 9SB. (0752 43879)–BD(Lond.). *b. 7 May 1940, Buxton, Derbyshire. m. 18 July 1964: 3s.* *Education:* 1951–58 Ealing Grammar Sch. for Boys; 1960–64 Hartley Victoria. *Appointments:* 1964–66 Poole; 1966–73 Christchurch and Lymington; 1973– Chaplain H.M.F. *Special Interests:* Broadcasting Media, 18th Century Church History; Concept of Nationhood; Methodist Spirituality. *Hobbies and Recreations:* Lawn Tennis, Cricket.

JAMES, David Walter, 21 Eaglehurst, Eagle Rd., Branksome, Poole, Dorset BH12 1AP. (0202 764651)–BA(Manchester), MA(Cambridge). *b. 7 May 1913, Weston-super-Mare. m. 5 Oct 1939: 1d., 2s.* *Education:* 1919–24 Local Schs. in Cardiff and Bournemouth; 1924–31 Kingswood Sch., Bath; 1931–34 Univ. of Manchester; 1934–37 Fitzwilliam House, Univ. of Cambridge; 1934–37 Welsey House. *Appointments:* 1937–51 Lucknow and Banares District, India; 1951–57 Swindon; 1957–62 London, Brixton Hill; 1962–67 St. Leonards and Bexhill; 1967–73 East Grinstead; 1973–78 Petersfield. *Connexional Committees:* 1958–70 Methodist Missionary Society's Eastern Committee: 1958–78 Overseas Missions Pastoral Committee; 1960–73 Church Membership Committees. *Publications: Fellowship of The Kingdom Bulletin* (Editor 1954–61); *Brothers in Ministry, The Story of Walter and Francis Bertram James.* *Special Interests:* Christian Peace-Making, British and Foreign Bible Society, Charismatic Renewal. *Hobbies and Recreations:* Amateur Photography, Reading especially Political and Religious Biography, Light Fiction, Travel.

JAMES, Gordon, 128 Hednesford Rd., Cannock, Staffordshire WS11 2BS. (054 35 71714) *b. 26 Oct 1935, Bayston Hill, Shropshire. m. April 1961: 1s.* *Education:* 1943–47 Kingswood Coll., Grahamstown, South Africa;

1947–48 Priory Sch. for Boys, Shrewsbury; 1948–55 Kingswood Sch., Bath; 1961–62 Academic, De Horst, Driebergen, Netherlands; 1957–61 Headingley. *Appointments:* 1962–64 St. Martin, Leeward Islands; 1964–67 St. Eustatius, Leeward Islands; 1968–71 Antigua; 1971–77 Blackburn; 1977–83 Cannock Chase.

JAMES, James Leslie, Windover, Beacon Oak Rd., Tenterden, Kent TN30 6SA. (2315) *b. 26 Sept 1918, Penzance. m. 23 July 1947: 1d.* *Education:* 1946–47 Hartley Victoria. *Appointments:* 1947–52 St. Austell, Zion; 1952–59 London, Brentford and Hounslow; 1959–64 Harrow; 1964–70 High Wycombe; 1970–77 Dover; 1977– Ashford, Kent. *Special Interests:* History. *Hobbies and Recreations:* Gardening.

JAMES, John Orial, Wesley Manse, Castle Street, Winchcombe, Cheltenham, Glos. GL54 5JA. (0242 602380)–BA. *b. 7 April 1946, Bristol. m. 9 Sept 1972: 1d., 1s.* *Education:* 1951–52 Eastville Inf., Bristol; 1952–54 Glenfrome Inf. and Jun., Bristol; 1954–57 Bristol Grammar Prep Sch.; 1957–64 Bristol Grammar Sch.; 1971–74 Bristol Univ.; 1971–74 Wesley, Bristol. *Appointments:* 1974–76 Leeds Mission; 1976– Cheltenham. *Connexional Committees:* 1978– Divisional Board of Education and Youth.
Special Interests: The Peace Movement. *Hobbies and Recreations:* Music, Movies, Theatre, Walking, Bristol Rovers Football Club, Piano.

JAMES, Leonard Glyn, 42 Firs Ave., Felpham, Bognor Regis, Sussex PO22 8QA. (969 3622) *b. 27 Oct 1901, Swansea, Glamorgan. m. 15 July 1931: 2s.* *Education:* 1906–11 St. Helens Council Sch., Swansea; 1911–15 Municipal Secondary Sch., Swansea; 1923–26 Hartley. *Appointments:* 1922–24 Launceston; 1928–30 Cheslyn Hay; 1933–39 Sheffield; 1939–42 Newcastle under Lyme; 1942–46 Northwich; 1946–51 Kingswood, Bristol; 1951–56 Andover; 1956–63 Chichester; 1963–67 Cheddar.
Connexional Committees: 1956–63 Rural Travel Committee.
Special Interests: Methodist Homes for the Aged, Pastoral Visitation, Reading. *Hobbies and Recreations:* Gardening, Decorating, Carpentry, Golf.

JAMES, Martin Peter, Treviscoe, 6 Tavistock Rd., Launceston, Cornwall PL15 9EZ. (0566 3171)–BA(Reading), MA(Cantab.). *b. 12 Jan 1942, Azamghar, India. m. 24 July 1965: 2s.* *Education:* 1946–51 Woodstock Sch., Landour, India; 1952–60 Kingswood.; 1960–63 Reading Univ.; 1963–65 Wesley House. *Appointments:* 1965–68 Skelmersdale; 1968–73 Warrington; 1973–78 Leicester North; 1978–82 Telford South; 1982– Launceston. *Hobbies and Recreations:* Cooking, Golf, Cricket, John Wesley.

JARVIS, Keith Fenton, 13 Beverley Rd., Market Weighton, York YO4 3JN. (0696 73407)–BD(Lond.). *b. 17 April 1941, Heywood, Lancs. m. 7 Aug 1965: 1d., 1s.* *Education:* 1944–52 St. Lukes Prim. Sch.; 1952–57 Rochdale Secondary Technical Sch. for Boys; 1960–61 Cliff Coll.; 1961–65 Hartley Victoria. *Appointments:* 1965–68 Birmingham, Moseley Rd. and Sparkhill; 1968–74 Whaley Bridge; 1974–79 Coalville; 1979– Market Weighton.
Special Interests: Evangelism, Revival, direct contact with Ruanda Mission (C.M.S.) and with Southwold Holiday Conference associated with Ruanda Revival. *Hobbies and Recreations.* Walking, Wildlife Painting (watercolour).

JARVIS, Peter George, 19 Witan Way, Wantage, Oxon OX12 9EU. (02357)–BD(Lond.). *b. 2 Aug 1925, London. m. 15 Aug 1967.* *Education:* 1930–34 Hollies Private Sch., Southgate N14; 1934–41 King's Sch., Macclesfield; 1950–54 Handsworth. *Appointments:* 1949–50 Walton-on-Thames; 1954–57 Dudley; 1957–61 Leighton Buzzard; 1961–67 Harrow; 1967–72 Reading; 1972–78 London, Tooting Mission; 1978– Wantage and Abingdon.
Connexional Committees: 1968–78 Local Preachers' Committee.
Publications: Sermons in *Expository Times* (1960–66); Article in *Expository Times* (April 1966); Article in *Epworth Review* (May 1978); Book *Come to Terms* (Epworth Press May 1979).
Special Interests: Preaching, History, English Literature. Hobbies and Recreations: Bird-Watching, Walking, Reading, Music.

JARVIS, Robert Edward, 61 Ingleside Rd., North Shields, Tyne and Wear NE29 9PB. (0632 573781) *b. 25 May 1920, Whitley Bay, Northumberland. m. 8 Nov 1941: 1d.* *Education:* –1936 Wallsend Grammar Sch. *Appointments:* 1980 North Shields and Whitley Bay. *Special Interests:* The Theatre. *Hobbies and Recreations:* Music.

JEFFERIES, Keith Roy, 76 Meadow Rise, Billericay, Essex. (54748)–MA, BD. *b. 31 Aug 1928, Southend-on-Sea. m. 7 Aug 1954: 1d., 1s.* *Education:* 1949–52 Richmond; 1974–76 Kings Coll., Univ. of London. *Appointments:* 1948–49 Leigh, Lancs.; 1952–54 St. Albans; 1954–57 Chaplain H.M.F.; 1957–61 Colchester; 1961–66 Leigh-on-Sea; 1966–74 Wesley House, Gibraltar; 1976–81 Teacher in RE Seven Kings High Sch.; 1981– Head of RE Appleton Sch., Benfleet.
Special Interests: Political and Social Studies. *Hobbies and Recreations:* Reading, Walking.

JEFFERIES, Paul, 83 Trap Lane, Brent Green, Sheffield S11 7RF. (0742 304664)–BA(Dunelm), MA(Cantab.). *b. 7 Oct 1915, Littleborough, Lancashire. m. 26 May 1948: 3d., 1s.* *Education:* 1926–28 Sir George Monoux Grammar Sch., Walthamstow, London; 1928–33 Heaton Secondary, Newcastle-upon-Tyne; 1933–37 Armstrong Coll., Newcastle-upon-Tyne; 1939–42 Wesley House. *Appointments:* 1942–

51 Hunan District, China; 1951–53 Coventry; 1953–66 Hong Kong District (Chinese); 1966–72 Glasgow (Cathcart Rd. and Pollokshaws); 1972–80 Lincoln South.
Connexional Committees: 1968–72 Central Committee MCOD; Asia Committee MCOD.
Special Interests: Art, Things Chinese. *Hobbies and Recreations:* Painting, Gardening, Walking.

JEFFERSON, Derek Henry, 8 Canterbury Avenue, Sheffield S10 3RT. (0742 301531)–BA(Bristol), BD(Lond.). *5 Feb 1923, Enfield, Middlesex. m. 12 Aug 1952: 2d., 1s.*
Education: 1928–34 Raglan Elem., Edmonton; 1934–40 Latymer's, Edmonton; 1940–41 Univ. Coll., London; 1947–50 Bristol Univ.; 1947–50 Didsbury, Bristol.
Appointments: 1945–47 Cowbridge and St. Athan; 1950–52 Sutton, Surrey; 1952–55 Market Rasen and Caiston; 1955–58 Lincoln North; 1958–63 Sheffield North East; 1963–68 Worcester; 1968–74 Redditch; 1974–80 Barnsley; 1980– Sheffield, Carver St.
Connexional Committees: 1960–73 Ministerial Training Committee; 1972–73 Home Mission Department.
Local Council Committees: 1964–68 City of Worcester Education Committee (co-opted member).
Special Interests: Ecumenism, Church and Society, Labour Party. *Hobbies and Recreations:* Walking, Reading, Music.

JENKINS, David Glyn, 96 Park Lane, Tilehurst, Reading, Berks RG3 5DT. (0734 27128)–BA(B'ham.). *b. 15 May 1949, Heacham, Norfolk. m. 1 Jan 1972: 1d., 1s.*
Education: 1954–60 Heacham Inf. and Jun. Schs.; 1960–67 King Edward VII Grammar Sch., King's Lynn; 1968–71 St. Paul's Coll., Cheltenham; 1973–76 Birmingham Univ.; 1973–77 Queen's. *Appointments:* 1977–82 Salisbury; 1982– Reading and Silchester.
Special Interests: Musical Composition (composer of 'Fish Man Jazz' musical). *Hobbies and Recreations:* Reading esp. English Literature, Piano and Singing; Sport esp. Long Distance Running.

JENKINS, Ewart Dudley, 1 Connaught Rd., East Cowes, I.W. PO32 6DR. (0983 296857) *b. 17 April 1921, East Peckham, Tonbridge, Kent. m. 28 July 1951: 1d., 1s.*
Education: 1933–38 Judd Sch., Tonbridge; 1948–50 Didsbury, Bristol. *Appointments:* 1947–48 Cardiff, Canton; 1950–52 Aberdare; 1952–55 Cardiff, Canton; 1955–59 Penzance, Chapel St.; 1959–66 Swindon; 1966–73 Bude; 1973–80 Christchurch and Lymington; 1980– West Wight.

JENKINS, Jack Frederick, 14 Kingsley Park, Whitchurch, Hants RG28 7HA. (2202 025682) *b. 28 Oct 1925, Bristol. m. 1 Feb 1950: 2s.*
Education: 1934–36 Dr. Bell's, Fishponds, Bristol; 1936–39 Mangotsfield, Bristol. *Appointments:* 1981– Andover.

JENKINS, John Wallace Carruthers, The Manse, Bridle Stile, Mosborough, Sheffield S19 5BR. (0742 486225)–BA(Lond.), BD(Lond.). *b. 28 Dec 1920, Benares, N. India. m. 25 May 1946: 2d., 2s.*
Education: Brighton Rd. Inf., St. Helier, Jersey, C.I.; Clarence St. Junior, Swindon; Kingswood Sch., Bath; 1939–42 Univ. Coll., London; 1948–50 Richmond. *Appointments:* 1946–48 Douglas, I.O.M.; 1950–55 Tonbridge (with Chaplaincy at Kent Coll. for Girls, Pembury); 1955–60 Purley; 1960–65 London Miss., Broomwood and Clapham; 1965–71 Kingston-on-Thames; 1971–79 Amersham; 1971– Sheffield South.
Connexional Committees: c.1960 Church Membership; 1965–67 Candidates.
Special Interests: Youth Work, Group Leadership Training, Fellowship of the Kingdom (Gen. Sec. 1982–).
Hobbies and Recreations: Sport (Football, Tennis, Swimming), Photography, Gardening.

JENKINS, Wilfrid John, 17 Halsdon Ave., Exmouth, Devon EX8 3DW. (71302)–MA(Bristol) *b. 10 Jan 1897, Chester. m. 29 July 1925 (w.): 1d., 2s.*
Education: 1906–09 Wesleyan Higher Grade, Chester; 1909–12 City and County Sch., Chester; Manchester Univ.; Bristol Univ.; 1919–22 Didsbury. *Appointments:* 1918–19 H.M. Forces; 1922–25 Newton Abbot; 1925–27 Torrington; 1927–30 Sherborne.
Council Member: 1942–49 Bath City Council; 1949–69 J.P.
Publications: William Wilberforce (1932); *The Way of World History* (1961); *Her Majesty's Government* (1967); *Local Government in Britain* (1967); *The Courts of Justice* (1967).
Special Interests: History. *Hobbies and Recreations:* Reading, Gardening.

JENKINSON, Thomas Reginald, Flat 1, Atlantic House, 57 Sandylands Promenade, Morecambe, Lancs. LA3 1DW. (0524 410934) *b. 9 May 1913, Buckley, Clwyd, North Wales. m. 28 July 1948: 2d., 1s.*
Education: 1916–24 Buckley Council Sch.; 1925–28 Mold Alan Grammar; 1946–48 Headingley.
Appointments: 1945–46 Wensleydale; 1948–53 Nelson, Lancs.; 1953–58 Morecambe and Heysham; 1958–59 Blackpool, North; 1959–68 Preston, Lune St.; 1968–78 Liverpool Mission.
Connexional Committees: 1973–76 Home Missions.
Special Interests: Music, British Countryside, Reading. *Hobbies and Recreations:* Jogging, Walking, Swimming, Tennis, Caravanning.

JENNER, Brian Robert, 18 Victoria Rd., Barnsley, S. Yorkshire S70 2BB. (0226 203557)–MA(Manchester), BA(Open), BD(Lond.). *b. 11 May 1943, Glossop, Derbyshire. m. 28 Dec 1971: 2s.*
Education: 1954–59 Lowestoft Grammar Sch.; 1964–69 Handsworth; 1972–77 The Open Univ.; 1979–80 Univ. of Manchester. *Appointments:* 1969–71 Stockton-on-Tees; 1971–74 Darlington; 1974–79 York

(Centenary); 1980– Barnsley. *Connexional Committees:* 1975–81 D.S.R. Healing and Pastoral Ministries Committee; 1979– D.S.R. Politics and Economics Committee: 1981– D.S.R. Working Party on Disarmament, International Security and Peace; *Publications:* Numerous Journal Articles. *Special Interests:* Member of Alliance of Radical Methodists, Vice-chairman of Urban Theology Unit, Theological Interests, Theology and Social Theory. *Hobbies and Recreations:* Mountain Walking, Model Boats, Model Railways, Home Winemaking.

JENNINGS, Derek William, 5 Charleston Rd., Eastbourne, East Sussex BN21 1SE. (0323 32569) *b. 30 July 1936, Harrow, Middlesex. m. 6 April 1963: 2d., 1s. Education;* 1941–47 Roxeth Hill Prim., Harrow; 1947–49 Lascekkes Secondary Modern, Harrow; 1949–51 Ealing Technical Coll.; 1957–59 Cliff Coll.; 1959–63 Didsbury, Bristol. *Appointments:* 1963–67 Ipswich; 1967–70 Luton North; 1970–75 Glasgow West; 1975–80 Hull West; 1980– Eastbourne. *Hobbies and Recreations:* Photography.

JENNINGS, John Richard, 10 Kingsway, Wembley, Middx. HA9 7QR. (01 902 1426) *25 April 1936, Reddingmuirhead, Scotland. m. 4 Aug 1962: 1d., 2s. Education:* 1947–55 Kingswood Sch.; 1959–62 Didsbury, Bristol. *Appointments:* 1963–70 Carribbean; 1971–75 Lincoln; 1975–81 Chapness Hall, Rochdale, 1981– Wembley, *Special Interests:* Art, Music.

JENNINGS, Peter, Whitechapel Mission, 212 Whitechapel Rd., London E1 1BJ. (01 247 8666)–MA(Oxon and Manchester) *b. 9 Oct 1937, Sale, Cheshire, m. 28 Dec 1963: 2s. Education;* 1942–49 Urban Rd., County Prim. Sch.; 1949–56 The Manchester Grammar Sch.; 1956–60 Keble Coll., Oxford; 1960–63 Manchester Univ.; 1960–63 Hartley Victoria. *Appointments:* 1963–67 Swansea; 1967–74 London Mission (East); 1974–81 General Secretary, Council of Christians and Jews; 1981–82 Walthamstow and Chingford; 1982– Whitechapel Mission. *Connexional Committees:* 1978–81 Advisory Committee on Ministerial Appointments; 1976–81 Connexional Standing Committee on Community Relations. *Publications:* Regular Contributor to Journals, Lecturer on Jewish-Christian Relations and Middle-Eastern Affairs. *Special Interests:* Inter-Faith Relations in General and Jewish-Christian Relations in particular. *Hobbies and Recreations:* Squash, Photography.

JENNINGS, Stuart Brian, 76 Redcatch Rd., Knowle, Bristol BS4 2EY. (0272 776165) *b. 6 Sept 1957, Leicester. m. 31 July 1979: 1d. Education:* 1968–72 Anstey Martin High; 1972–74 Longslade Upper; 1978–79 Charles Keen Coll.; 1979–80 Cliff Coll.; 1980– Wesley, Bristol. *Special Interests:* Egyptology. *Hobbies and Recreations:* Stamp Collecting and Walking.

JEWELL, Albert John, 167 Otley Rd., Leeds LS6 3QG. (0532 752323)–MA(Oxon), BA(Cantab), MPhil(Lond.). *b. 28 Dec 1936, St. Albans, Herts. m. 10 Aug 1962: 1d., 1s. Education:* 1947–55 St. Albans Sch.; 1957–60 Oriel Coll., Oxford; 1960–62 Fitzwilliam Coll., Cambridge; 1960–62 Wesley House; 1970–76 King's Coll., London. *Appointments:* 1962–64 Assistant Tutor, Didsbury Coll., Bristol; 1964–69 Cheltenham; 1969–73 London, Sydenham and Forest Hill; 1973–77 Chaplain, Ashville Coll., Harrogate; 1977– Leeds Mission, Chaplain to Leeds Univ. and Poly. *Connexional Committees:* 1977– Connexional Candidates Committee. *Publications: Prayers for all the Family* (Epworth 1968); Contributor to *Partners in Learning* (1982–83). *Special Interests:* National Vice-Chairman of The Samaritans. *Hobbies and Recreations:* Member of Choral Society, Member of Wesley Historical Society.

JINKS, Kenneth Ernest, West Winds, 61 Penrhyn Beach West, Penrhyn Bay, Llandudno, Gwynedd LL30 2NB. (Colwyn Bay 46923)–MA(Manchester). *b. 4 Dec 1910, Birmingham. m. 29 July 1939: 1d. Education:* 1915–23 Highfield Rd. Council Sch., Saltley, B'ham; 1923–28 King Edward VI's Grammar Sch., Aston, B'ham.; 1933–36 London Univ.; 1933–37 Richmond; 1946–54 Manchester Univ. *Appointments:* 1937–38 President's List; 1938–42 Holyhead; 1942–47 Warrington; 1947–53 Alderley Edge; 1953–55 Liverpool Mission; 1955–59 Swansea; 1959–67 Macclesfield; 1967–73 Blackpool North; 1973–78 Walsall. *Publications:* Articles in various newspapers and periodicals. *Special Interests:* Psychology, Child Psychology, Psychology and Healing. *Hobbies and Recreations:* Bird Watching, Painting, Writing, Sport, Cricket, Tennis, Table Tennis, Billiards, Snooker.

JOB, John Brian, Ataraxia, Cliff Lane, Claver, Sheffield S30 1XD. (024 688 3241)–MA(Oxon), BD(Lond.). *b. 9 June 1932, Ipswich. m. 7 April 1962: 1d., 3s. Education:* 1939–45 Ipswich Sch.; 1945–51 Kingswood Sch.; 1951–58 Merton Coll., Oxford; 1960–62 Headingley. *Appointments:* 1962–63 Westminster Coll., Chaplain; 1963–66 Rydal Sch., Chaplain; 1966–69 Aireborough; 1969–75 Immanuel Coll., Ibadan, 1975 Cliff Coll. Tutor (O.T.). *Connexional Committees:* 1977–79 Candidates Committee; 1982 Faith and Order Committee; 1982 Fernley-Hartly Trust; 1970–75 Connexional Secretary for Ministerial Training, Methodist Church Nigeria. *Publications:* Editor *Towards a United Church* (1964); Editor *Studying God's Ward* (1971– IVP); *Where is my Father?* (Epworth 1978); Revised Scripture Index for Gesenins-Kantschz *Hebrew Grammar* (OUP 1980); *Annual Lecture for Conservative*

Evangelicals in Methodism (1981); *The Covenant of Marriage. Special Interests:* Hebrew Prophets. *Hobbies and Recreations:* Tennis, Gardening.

JOBLING, Ronald, 29 Regent Drive, Fulwood, Preston PR2 3JB. (0772 719254) *b. 28 July 1915, Sheffield. m. 27 May 1944: 1d.*
Education: Merrywood Secondary Sch., Bristol; 1938–41 Hartley Victoria. *Appointments:* 1941–44 Bolton Wesley; 1944–46 Chaplain H.M.F.; 1946–50 Brigg and Scotter; 1950–53 Whitehaven; 1953–57 Doncaster Coalfields Mission; 1957–63 Preston Trinity; 1963–68 Clitheroe; 1968–70 Newcastle-on-Tyne, Brunswick Central; 1970–80 Bolton and Rochdale District Chairman.
Connexional Committees: Prior to 1980 President's Council, G.P., H.M., Property, Church Membership, Ministries; 1976– Ministers' Medical Committee.
Special Interests: Gardening, All Sports, People. *Hobbies and Recreations:* Reading, Pastoral Persuits.

JOHNS, Alfred Thomas, 47 Beech Ave., Keyworth, Nottingham NG12 5DE. (06077 2601)–BD(Lond.). *b. 21 Sept 1902, Croydon. m. 1. 14 Aug 1930; 2. 14 Nov 1981: 2s.*
Education: 1907–12 Private Prep. Sch.; 1912–18 Whitgift Middle Sch.; 1920–23 Kings Coll., London; 1923–27 Richmond. *Appointments:* 1927–30 Teignmouth; 1930–33 Kingston-on-Thames; 1933–36 Guildford; 1936–39 Biggleswade; 1939–40 Sheffield, Brunswick; 1940–48 Torquay and Paignton; 1948–52 Teignmouth; 1952–58 Bristol, King Street; 1958–62 Minehead and Dunster; 1962–65 Taunton; 1965–68 Sutton.
Hobbies and Recreations: Model Railways.

JOHNS, Godfrey Spencer, 61 Barton Rd., Dover, Kent CT16 2NE. (0304 206613) *b. 21 Jan 1927, Varteg, Gwent. m. 18 Aug 1956: 2d., 1s.*
Education: 1951–54 Hartley Victoria.
Appointments: 1950–51 Bridgend; 1954–56 East Dereham; 1956–58 Cardiff, Roath; 1958–62 Spilsby; 1962–72 West Indies Dt; 1972 Dover and Deal.
Connexional Committees: 1974–82 Overseas Division Central Committee. *Local Council Committees:* Many School Governorships; 1974– Local Advisory Body for Education.

JOHNSON, Arnold Samuel, 16 The Grove, Moordown, Bournemouth BH9 2TR. (0202 513630)–BD. *b. 16 Feb 1932, Keyingham, Nr. Hull. m. 3 Aug 1957: 1d., 2s.*
Education: 1940–43 Pickering Rd., Prim. Jun. Sch., Hull; 1943–48 Kingston High Sch., Hull; 1954–57 Headingley. *Appointments:* 1957–60 Durham City; 1960–65 Hexham; 1965–72 Newcastle on Tyne, North West; 1972–79 Hull East; 1979– Bournemouth.
Connexional Committees: 1975–79 Board of Education and Youth.
Special Interests: Broadcasting, Christian Aid, work among Mentally Handicapped. *Hobbies and Recreations:* Art, Natural History, Drama, General Sport.

JOHNSON, Arthur Sidwell, Karur, Lower Park Street, Stow-on-the-Wold, Cheltenham, Glos. GL54 1AH. (0451 30348)–BA(B'ham). *b. 16 Nov 1899, Brightlingsea. m. 17 Dec 1926.*
Education: 1909–1911 Woodhouse Grove; 1911–1915 Kingswood Sch.; 1915–16 Lincoln Technical Sch.; 1920–24 Handsworth.
Appointments: 1918–19 Derbyshire Mission; 1919–24 Sittingbourne; 1924–30 South India Dt; 1930–33 London, Clapham; 1933–36 Stoke-on-Trent, Burslem; 1936–48 South India Dt; 1948–55 Wiltshire Mission; 1955–61 Manningtree and Harwich.

JOHNSON, Clifford Dixon, Crescent Lodge, Crescent Rd., Truro TR1 3EP. (0872 72608)–BA(Manch.) *b. Fishburn, Co. Durham. m. 1d., 1s.*
Education: Stockton Grammar Sch.; Manchester Univ.; Hartley Victoria.
Appointments: 1952–54 Leicester West; 1954–58 Wolverhampton; 1958–64 South London Mission; 1964–71 Richmond and Barnes; 1971–81 Worthing; 1981– Truro.
Connexional Committees: Commission on Evangelism.
Special Interests: Psychotherapy, Healing and Counselling, Meditation and Prayer, Sociology of Mission and Community Development, Fellowships and Church Growth.
Hobbies and Recreations: Golf, Foreign Travel, Gospel Music, Visiting Churches.

JOHNSON, David Ivor, 104 Dingwall Drive, Greasby, Wirral L49 1SQ. (051 677 1736) *b. 23 March 1943, Doncaster, Yorkshire. m.*
Education: 1955–61 Doncaster Technical High Sch.; 1962–63 Cliff Coll.; 1966–70 Didsbury and Wesley, Bristol. *Appointments:* 1970–72 Preston, Lune St.; 1972–79 Morecambe and Heysham; 1979– Hoylake and West Kirby.
Connexional Committees: 1972–78 Education and Youth–Youth Community; 1977–78 Education and Youth–Editorial Committee.
Special Interests: Church Growth, Christian Communication. *Hobbies and Recreations:* Music, Railways, Sport.

JOHNSON, David Michael, 9 Valley Drive, Sevenoaks, Kent TN13 1EG. (0732 458725)–BA, MA. *b. 29 May 1935, Bradford, Yorks. m. 29 July 1961: 1d., 1s.*
Education: 1945–52 Bradford G.S.; 1956–59 St. Catherine's Coll., Cambridge Univ.; 1959–62 Headingley; 1962–63 Institute of Education, London Univ.; 1968 Sch. of Oriental and African Studies, London Univ. *Appointments:* 1963–74 S.E. Asia Dt (Sarawak); 1974– Master and Head of Library, Sevenoaks Sch., Kent.
Special Interests: Education. *Hobbies and Recreations:* Cricket, Sailing, Music, Books.

JOHNSON, Derek, 2 Marian Rd., Boston, Lincs. PE21 9HA. (0205 62933)–BD(Lond.). *b. 19 May 1926. m. 20 Aug 1955: 1d., 1s.*

Education: 1931–37 Queen St. Prim., Fenton, Stoke on Trent; 1937–39 Queen St. Prim., Senior Boys, Stoke on Trent; 1939–41 Junior Technical Sch., Burslem; 1950–53 Headingley. *Appointments:* 1953–55 Barton on Humber; 1955–58 Driffield; 1958–61 Gainsborough; 1961–64 Bishop Auckland; 1964–67 Shildon; 1967–69 Great Harwood; 1969–74 Blackburn; 1974 Boston.

JOHNSON, George Edwin, Flat No. 2, Lyndhurst, Bent Lane, Sutton in Craven, Keighley, Yorks. BD20 7AL. *b. 20 Nov 1890, Preston, Nr Hull, E. Yorks. m. 25 June 1918: 1d., 1s.*
Education: Preston Council; 1911–12 Cliff Coll.; 1912–14 Handsworth. *Appointments:* 1915–17 H.M. Forces; 1917–19 Chaplain H.M.F.; 1919–20 N. Derbys Mission; 1920–21 Doncaster Oxford Place; 1921–24 Sheffield Park; 1924–27 Nottingham, Wesley; 1927–29 Stockton on Tees; 1929–34 Middlesbrough Mission; 1934–36 Barnsley E.; 1936–40 Sheffield Mission; 1940–47 York Clifton; 1947–50 Knaresboro; 1950–54 Shildon Wesley; 1954–56 Wath on Dearne.
Connexional Committees: 1937–39 Home Mission Committee.

JOHNSON, Gordon Kitching, 16 Mendham Close, High Heworth, Gateshead, Tyne and Wear NE10 9BJ. (0632 381628) *b. 22 Feb 1919, Darlington, County Durham. m. 27 Sept 1943: 1d., 1s.*
Education: Queen Elizabeth Grammar Sch., Darlington, Co. Durham; 1950–53 Richmond. *Appointments:* 1953–58 Chester-le-Street; 1958–61 Wensleydale; 1961–67 Thornley; 1967–75 Bedale; 1975–80 Barnard Castle; 1980– Gateshead and Jarrow.
Special Interests: Psychology and Engineering

JOHNSON, Harry, 53 Shiphay Park Rd., Torquay, S. Devon TQ2 7DG. (0803 64177)—BD, PhD(Lond.). *b. 28 Oct 1925, Warrington, Lancs. m. 20 Aug 1949: 1d., 4s.*
Education: Boteler Grammar Sch., Warrington; London Univ.; 1948–50 Headingley. *Appointments:* 1946–47 Snaith; 1947–48 Retford; 1950–54 Durham; 1954–61 Leeds, Chapel Allerton; 1961–69 Sutton, Surrey; 1969–79 Kingston upon Thames; 1979– Torbay.
Publications: The Humanity of The Savior (Epworth Press 1962).
Special Interests: Extra Mural Lecturer at London Univ. in Philosophy. *Hobbies and Recreations:* Music.

JOHNSON, Harry, 9 Waudby Garth Rd., Keyingham, E. Yorks. (09644 3940) *b. 17 Nov 1894, Middleton-on-the-Wolds, E. Yorks. m. 17 June 1924: 1d.*
Education: Carnaby Village; 1918–20 Hartley. *Appointments:* 1920–21 Supply; 1921–24 Edinburgh; 1924–25 Hoyland; 1925–28 North Shields; 1928–33 South Shields; 1933–38 Grimsby; 1938–41 Isle of Man, Castletown; 1941–46 Douglas; 1946–50 Silsden; 1950–54 Hoyland and Wombwell; 1954–60 Beverley.
Connexional Committees: 1930–54 Temperance and Social Welfare; Methodist Relief Fund.
Special Interests: Outdoor Games, Football etc. *Hobbies and Recreations:* Gardening, Television.

JOHNSON, Harry Carter, 2 Brent Way, Finchley, London N3 1AL. (01 349 0912) *b. 20 May 1898, Tibshelf, Derbyshire. m. 10 Aug 1929: 2d., 3s.*
Education: Tibshelf Colliery Elem.; Staveley Grammar Sch.; 1922–25 Richmond. *Appointments:* 1925–27 Helston; 1927–29 Ripley; 1929–32 Peterborough; 1932–33 Helston; 1933–37 Ipswich, Museum St.; 1937–40 Manchester, Gravel Lane; 1940–45 Leeds, Bramley; 1945–49 Blackheath; 1949–51 Camborne; 1951–55 Leeds, Bramley and Horsforth; 1955–59 Peterborough; 1959–62 Blackheath.
Special Interests: Methodist and other Friendships, Family Wellbeing. *Hobbies and Recreations:* Reading, Gardening, Sport.

JOHNSON, Ian David, 16 Grafson Place, Droitwich, Worcs. WR9 8NQ. (0905 775282) *b. 5 Mar 1939, York. m. 1 April 1967: 2s.*
Education: 1946–50 Lower Wortley C.P. Sch., Leeds; 1950–55 West Leeds High Sch.; 1965–68 Didsbury, Bristol; 1968–69 William Temple Coll., Rugby. *Appointments:* 1969–76 Birmingham, Moseley Rd. and Sparkhill (Team Ministry); 1976–82 Keighley and Worth Valley; 1982– Worcester.
Connexional Committees: 1974–76 H.M. Inner City Committee; 1976–79 Connexional Candidates Committee.
Publications: Can You Help in the Vestry (Vestry Prayers, Joint 1981).
Special Interests: Community Work. *Hobbies and Recreations:* Gardening, Ornithology.

JOHNSON, John, 53 Camdon Hurst, Milford-on-Sea, Lymington, Hants.—MA. *b. 18 Nov 1906, Newcastle-on-Tyne. m. 10 July 1935: 3d.*
Education: 1912–18 Gateshead Grammar; 1918–22 Durham Univ.; 1929–33 Didsbury. *Appointments:* 1933–35 Manchester and Salford Mission; 1935–38 H.M. Committee: 1938–40 Gloucester; 1940–61 Chaplain H.M.F.; 1961–71 Aylesbury.

JOHNSON, John, 41 Magnolia Way, Pilgrims Hatch, Brentwood, Essex CM15 9QV. (215346)—LTCL, AMusLCM. *b. 28 July 1942, Coalville, Leicestershire. m. 16 June 1966: 1d., 1s.*
Education: 1947–53 Bardon-Hill Prim. Sch.; 1953–61 Wellington Grammar Sch., Salop; 1962–66 Headingley; 1971–72 Northern Sch. of Music; 1973–74 Leeds Univ., Bretton Hall Coll. *Appointments:* 1966–68 Bolton, Farnworth; 1968–70 Bishops Castle and Clun; 1970–73 Sowerby Bridge; 1974–77 Music Teacher Nicholas Sch., Basildon; 1978–83 Romford, 1977– Head of Music Hainault High Sch
Special Interests: Music especially Choral, District MCMS Executive, Organist, Circuit Youth Ministerial Sec. *Hobbies and Recreations:* Scouter, Tennis Player, Circuit and District and Local Choirs.

JOHNSON, Keith Mitchell, Astbury, Bragmans Lane, Sarratt, Richmansworth, Herts. WD3 4NP. (Kings Langley 63024)–BA(Lond.), BD(Lond.). *b. 14 Nov 1932, Hull, Yorks. m. 3 March 1962: 1d.*
Education: 1937–43 Eastfield Rd. Inf. and Jun., Hull; 1943–50 Kingston High, Hull; 1950–53 Univ. Coll., London; 1955–57 Wesley, Headingley; 1957–58 Ecumenical Institute, Bossey, and Univ. of Geneva. *Appointments:* 1958–60 Colchester; 1960–64 London, Leytonstone and Forest Gate; 1964–70 Kilburn and Hampstead; 1967–74 Harlesden; 1974–78 Resigned; 1978– London, Horlesden, O.Appt.
Local Council Committees: 1970–75 Brent Social Services Committee, co-opted member. *Publications: Race–What Can The Churches Do?* (1979).
Special Interests: Race Relations, All Branches of Ethics; The Arts–except Ballet, Travel, World Poverty.
Hobbies and Recreations: Music–Classical, Cricket, Soccer, Gardening, Indiscriminate Reading, Writing Letters.

JOHNSON, Maurice Bernard, 11 Forest Rd., Lydney, Gloucestershire GL15 5LD. (0594 42262) *b. 24 June 1948, Southport, Lancashire. m. 24 July 1971.*
Education: 1959–66 King George V Sch. for Boys, Southport; 1966–69 Dudley Coll. of Education; 1976–79 Queen's. *Appointments:* 1979– Forest of Dean.
Hobbies and Recreations: Festiniog Railway Society, Nederlandse Vereniging van Belangstellenden In Het Spoor–En Tramwegwezen, Music, Isle of Man.

JOHNSON, Owen Russell, 88 London Rd., Guildford, Surrey GU1 1SS. (0483 67890) *b. 17 Feb 1910, Reading, Berks. m. 6 Aug 1939: 1d., 1s.*
Education: 1915–25 Elem.; 1930–31 Cliff Coll.; 1933–36 Richmond.
Appointments: 1932–33 Chipping Norton and Stow; 1937–41 Bridgend; 1941–45 Blyth and Seaton; 1945–48 Doncaster, Oxford Place; 1948–52 Weston Super Mare; 1952–57 Torquay; 1957–62 Southend-on-Sea; 1962–69 Leytonstone and Forest Gate; 1969–72 Stoke-on-Trent, South; 1972–76 Normanton.
Hobbies and Recreations: Music.

JOHNSON, Raymond Ackerley, 8 Lowside Close, Calver, Derbyshire, Nr. Sheffield S30 1WZ. (0433 30297) *b. 21 May 1907, Patricroft, Eccles, Manchester. m. 4 Jan 1941: 1d., 1s.*
Education: 1911–18 Peel Green Jun. Sch.; 1918–23 Eccles Secondary Sch.; 1929–32 Victoria Park.
Appointments: 1932–56 Sierra Leone Dt; 1956–62 Ludlow; 1962–66 Marple; 1966–72 Sierra Leone Dt.
Special Interests: Literacy in the Third World, B.B.B.S. Work, Christian Aid. *Hobbies and Recreations:* Carpentry, Gardening, Exploring the Peak National Park.

JOHNSON, Stanley, 35 Somerset Avenue, Wilpshire, Blackburn, Lancs. BB1 9JD. (0254 48212)–BA. *b. 7 May 1930, Manchester. m. 10 Aug 1956: 3d., 3s.*
Education: 1941–45 North Manchester High Sch.; 1952–55 Birmingham Univ.; 1952–55 Handsworth. *Appointments:* 1951–52 Motherwell and Wishaw; 1955–57 Durham; 1957–62 Liverpool South East; 1962–67 Birmingham, Sutton Park; 1967–78 Stoke-on-Trent, Longton Mission; 1978– Blackburn.
Connexional Committees: 1970s Connexional Home Mission Committee.
Hobbies and Recreations: Gardening, Camping.

JOHNSON, Thomas, The Leysian Mission, 112 City Rd., London EC1V 2NB. (01 253 3683) *b. 23 Nov 1930, Clydebank, Scotland. m. 14 July 1956: 1d., 2s.*
Education; 1941–46 Gateshead High Sch.; 1946–51 Gateshead Central Polytechnic; 1952–55 Handsworth. *Appointments:* 1955–58 Snaith; 1958–64 Leeward Islands Dt; 1964–70 Scarborough; 1970–76 York, Wesley; 1976– London, Leysian Mission.
Special Interests: Boys' Brigade, Mental Welfare. *Hobbies and Recreations:* Camping and Caravanning.

JOHNSON, Thomas Kingsley, 29 White House Drive, Sedgefield, Stockton-on-Tees, Cleveland TS21 3BX. (0740 20962) *b. 17 Sept 1923. m. 31 May 1952: 1d., 1s.*
Education: 1934–37 Billingham Secondary Modern; 1938–42 Stockton Technical; 1947–48 Cliff Coll.; 1948–50 Hartley Victoria.
Appointments: 1951–63 East Nigeria Dt; 1963–70 Nigeria Conf.; 1970–71 CTS Killingworth, Brunswick; 1971–78 Gateshead and Jarrow; 1978–80 Middlesborough; 1980–82 Redcar, Saltburn and Guisborough; 1982– Spennymoor, Ferryhill.
Connexional Committees: 1976–78 M.C.O.D. Home Committee.
Special Interests: Personal Relationships, Church Growth, Ecumenical Co-operation. *Hobbies and Recreations:* Walking, Tennis, Swimming, Golf, Reading.

JOHNSTON, John Donaldson, 16 Peard Rd., Tiverton, Devon EX16 4LG. *b. 29 Aug 1908, Seaham Harbour, Co. Durham. m. 31 July 1939.*
Education: Seaham Upper Standard. 1932–34 Victoria Park, Manchester; 1934–35 Hartley Victoria, Manchester. *Appointments:* 1936–39 Bodmin; 1939–42 Walls, Shetland; 1942–46 Burton-on-Trent; 1947–64 Southern Rhodesia; 1964–67 Apleby, Westmorland; 1967–70 Pinetown, Natal; 1970–71 Radstock; 1971–73 Walls, Shetland; 1973– Tiverton.

JOINER, Rowland George, 423 Springfield Rd., Chelmsford, Essex CM2 6AP. (0245 57712)–BA(Birmingham), LTh(Paris). *9 May 1930, Leigh-on-Sea, Essex. m. 22 Oct 1955: 3d., 1s.*
Education: 1941–48 Wescliff High Sch.; 1951–54 Birmingham; 1951–54 Handsworth; 1954–55 Faculte Libre de Theologie Protestante and La Sorbonne. *Appointments:* 1955–57 French W. Africa Dt; 1957–62 Ivory Coast Dt, West Africa; 1962–64 Univ. D'Abidjan; 1964–69 Southampton; 1969–80 London East

Ham Mission; 1980– Chelmsford. *Special Interests:* Counselling (M.G.C.), Church Growth, Consultant at Chelmsford Cathedral Centre for Research and Training. *Hobbies and Recreations:* Sport, Gardening, Camping.

JOLLEY, Arthur William, 75 Wellington Rd., Mablethorpe, Lincolnshire. (05213 3474) *b. 1 Nov 1931, Loughborough, Leicestershire. m. 20 July 1957: 1d., 2s.*
Education: 1943–47 Loughborough Coll. Sch.; 1950–51 Cliff Coll.; 1951–54 Handsworth. *Appointments:* 1954–57 Bridgend; 1957–60 Newcastle Mission; 1960–62 Brynmawr; 1962–67 Resigned (Mental Health Work); 1967–71 Hinckley; 1971–75 Derby South; 1975–80 Holyhead; 1980– Alford. *Local Council Committees:* 1978–80 Llangefni Town Council. *Special Interests:* Mental Health, Languages.

JOLLIE, Leslie, 10 Mercia Court, Larkhill, Bexhill-on-Sea, East Sussex TN40 1TY. (0424 221831)–BD, MTh(Lond.). *b. 6 April 1905, Harrogate, Yorkshire. m. 29 July 1933.*
Education: Grove Rd., Harrogate; 1927–30 Didsbury; 1945–50 London Univ. (External). *Appointments:* 1926–27 Chipping Norton; 1930–33 Bradford Mission; 1933–36 Ticehurst; 1936–40 Gateshead Mission; 1940–46 Sheffield, Carver St.; 1946–52 Ealing and Acton; 1952–56 St. Leonards and Bexhill; 1956–57 Bombay District, India; 1957–64 South Norwood; 1964–67 Chislehurst, 1967–70 Harrow. *Connexional Committees:* 1946– Spiritual Healing; 1950– Class Leaders; 1954– Candidates. *Publications: The Life of the World to Come* (E.P. 1952). *Special Interests:* Bird Watching, Astronomy, Healing, Church Architecture. *Hobbies and Recreations:* Pursuit of the above!

JONES, Albert Wynne, Wesley Manse, 32 Edgehill Rd., Aberystwyth, Dyfed SY23 1LZ. (0970 617227) *b. 12 March 1927, Mynytho, Nr. Pwllheli, Gwynedd, North Wales. m. 11 Aug 1970.*
Education: 1932–42 Foel Gron Prim. Sch., Mynytho; 1952–55 Handsworth. *Appointments:* 1955–57 Lampeter; 1957–59 Llanfair; 1959–65 Machynlleth; 1965–70 Ystumtuen; 1970–75 Llanfyllin; 1975–80 Arfon; 1980 Aberystwyth. *Connexional Committees:* Division of Social Responsibility Board. *Special Interests:* Literature, Music, Poetry. *Hobbies and Recreations:* Gardening.

JONES, Anthony Ward, 43 Bath Rd., Wootton Bassett, Swindon, Wiltshire SN4 7DF. (0793 853197)–BA(Lond.), BA(Cambridge), MA(Cambridge). *b. 6 Aug 1950, Sedgley, Staffordshire. m. 30 Aug 1975: 1s.*
Education: 1961–67 High Arcal Grammar Sch., Sedgley, Staffs.; 1968–71 Wolverhampton Poly./London Univ.; 1972–73 Univ. Coll. of Wales, Aberystwyth; 1973–75 Fitzwilliam Coll., Cambridge; 1973–76 Wesley House. *Appointments:* 1976–81 Clitheroe; 1981– Chippenham and Brinkworth. *Local Council Committees:* 1981– Wooton Bassett Town Council Unemployment Committee. *Special Interests:* Education, Family Worship, Ecumenical Activities, Study of Liturgy, Methodist History. *Hobbies and Recreations:* Gardening, Philately, Sport, My Family!

JONES, Arnold Brackley, 9 Parkside Close, Park Ave., Hull, North Humberside HU5 3EZ. (0482 41076) *b. 4 Sept. 1908, Ilford, Essex. m. 5 Dec 1934: 1d., 1s.*
Education: 1922-26 The Leys Sch., Cambridge; 1932–35 Richmond. *Appointments:* 1935–38 President's List, 1938–41 Matlock; 1941–44 Middlesbrough; 1944–48 Whitby; 1948–53 Heswall; 1953–58 Solihull; 1958–63 Malvern; 1963–68 Hull North; 1968–73 Wolaston and Audley. *Special Interests:* Music, Reading, Cricket.

JONES, Arthur Eric Glendower, 6 Grove Close, Norwood, Beverley, North Humberside HU17 9JT. (0482 863510) *b. 21 Sept 1911, Carlisle. m. 2 Dec 1944: 1s.*
Education: Hanson, Bradford, W.Yorks.; 1939–41 Richmond; 1941–42 Headingley. *Appointments:* 1942–47 Western Nigeria District; 1947–49 Sierra Leone District; 1949–52 Sheffield, Norfolk; 1952–56 Sheffield, Carver St.; 1956–60 Scunthorpe; 1960–64 High Wycombe; 1964–67 Kiveton Park; 1967–72 Chislehurst; 1972–76 Whitstable and Herne Bay. *Special Interests:* Psychology. *Hobbies and Recreations:* Gardening.

JONES, Arthur Geoffrey, 9 Rye View, High Wycombe, Bucks HP13 6HL. (0494 26747)–BA, BD. *b. 10 Sept 1920, Sheffield, Yorks. m. 19 Dec 1951: 2d., 1s.*
Education: 1928–31 Queen Elizabeth Grammar Sch., Blackburn, Lancs.; 1931–33 Bolton Sch.; 1933–36 Sibford; 1946–49 Univ. of Manchester; 1946–49 Hartley Victoria. *Appointments:* 1949–50 South-West China Dt; 1950–52 S. China Dt; 1953–70 Rhodesia District; 1970–75 Bury and Heywood; 1975–82 Harrogate; 1982– High Wycombe.

JONES, Arthur Gordon, 21 Empress Ave., Woodford Green, Essex. (01 504 3233)–BD(Lond.). *b. 21 Nov 1914, Surbiton. m: 2d.*
Education: 1927–31 Haberdashers Askes Hatcham; London Univ.; 1934–38 Richmond. *Appointments:* 1938–40 Leominster, 1940–44 Birmingham Mission; 1944–48 London, Broomwood and Stockwell; 1948–54 Ghana Dt; 1954–57 Kent Mission; 1957–63 Shooter's Hill; 1963–68 Purley; 1968–72 Exeter; 1972–73 London, Hackney Mission; 1973–79 The Richmond Fellowship. *Publications: Bridge of Friendship* (Cargate Press 1954); *While He Was Yet Young* (Methodist Book Depot Cape Coast 1954); *What Did Jesus Teach?* (N.C.E.C. 1969). *Special Interests:* Music, Contributing to I.B.R.A. *Hobbies and Recreations:* Music.

JONES, Arthur Leslie, 14 Newfields, Sporle, King's Lynn, Norfolk PE32 2UA. (0760 22314) *b. 24 Sept 1907, Leicester. m. 1. (d. 1954), 26 March 1932; 2. 4 Oct 1955: 3d., 2s.* *Education:* St. Saviour's CE, Leicester; Wyggeston Grammar Sch., Leicester. *Appointments:* 1951–53 Oldham; 1953–57 Wellington, Shrops.; 1957–62 Nantwich; 1962–68 Aylsham; 1968–72 Sheffield N.; 1972–76 Acle.
Special Interests: Social Responsibility, Homes for Aged. *Hobbies and Recreations:* Gardening, Reading, Cooking.

JONES, Arthur Stanley, 6 Oaklands Close, Attleborough, Norfolk NR17 2LT. (0953 453693)–BA. *7 Dec 1912; Codsall, Nr Wolverhampton, Staffs. m. 20 Jan 1942: 1d., 1s.* *Education:* 1917–24 Codsall CE Sch.; 1924–31 Wolverhampton Grammar Sch; 1934–37 Birmingham Univ.; 1934–37 Handsworth. *Appointments:* 1937–58 Bengal Dt, India; 1959–63 Belper; 1963–67 Derby Derwent; 1967–72 Kimberley; 1972–77 Doncaster; Lowestoft and East Suffolk.
Connexional Committees: 1958–65 Overseas Missions. *Publications: Londonderry March of Events* (1971); *The Lotus Pool* (1944). *Special Interests:* Life and Thought of India, Pastoral Practice. *Hobbies and Recreations:* Apiculture, Gardening.

JONES, Bernard Ewart, 39 Stour Lodge, Fulwood, Preston PR2 3EY. (0772 717311)–MA, BD(Manchester), BA(Liverpool), PhD(Leeds). *b. 25 July 1916, Liverpool. m. 10 Aug 1943: 2d.* *Education:* 1927–32 Liverpool Collegiate Sch.; 1935–38 Liverpool Univ.; 1938–41 Manchester Univ.; 1938–41 Hartley Victoria. *Appointments:* 1941–43 Manchester, Pendleton; 1943–48 Liverpool, Grove St. and Woolton; 1948–54 Hoylake and West Kirby; 1954–57 Manchester, Prestwich; 1957–67 Hartley Victoria Coll.; 1967–73 Wesley Coll., Bristol; 1973–81 Bramhall.
Connexional Committees: 1962–Church Membership Committee; 1968–80 Church Membership Secretary; 1973–79 General Purposes Committee; 1973–80 Division of Ministries. *Publications: Honest to Goodness* (1964); *Earnest Enquirers after Truth* (1970); *Belonging* (1973); *What is a Christian?* (1975).
Special Interests: Philosophy of Religion, Church Membership. *Hobbies and Recreations:* Director of Methodist Holiday Homes Ltd. (1969–).

JONES, Brian Stanley, 33 Churchfield Rd., Rothwell, Leeds, W.Yorks. LS26 0EJ. (0532 822132) *b. 12 Nov 1932, Wolverhampton, W. Midlands. m. 11 June 1960: 2s.* *Education:* 1945 Technical High, Wolverhampton; 1953 Fircroft Coll., Selly Oak, B'ham.; 1954 Cliff Coll.; 1955 Hartley Victoria. *Appointments:* 1960–63 Walls, Shetland; 1963–68 Bishops Castle and Clun; 1968–72 Louth; 1972–77 Wakefield; 1977–80 Leicester North; 1980 Leeds, Rothwell; 1968–72 RAF Chaplaincy. *Local Council Committees:* 1977–80 Manager of Education Board (Sileby Prim. Sch.).
Special Interests: Prayer, Evangelism, Social Activities, Hospital and Prison Work, Ecumenical Activities, Charismatic Movement. *Hobbies and Recreations:* Yoga, Playing the Piano, Reading, Walking, Cycling, Birdwatching, Swimming.

JONES, Christine, 3 Heather Drive, Kinver, Stourbridge, West Midlands DJ7 6DR. (038483 2540)–BA(Nottingham), MA(Manchester), MPhil(Nottingham). *b. 25 Oct 1950, Liverpool. m. 19 June 1977: 1s.* *Education:* 1962–69 Aigburth Vale High Sch., Liverpool; 1969–73 Nottingham Univ.; 1973–74 Glasgow Univ.; 1975–77 Manchester Univ. full time, –1980 part time; 1975–77 Hartley Victoria. *Appointments:* 1977–82 Stoke-on-Trent, Hanley; 1982– Stourbridge and Brierley Hill. *Hobbies and Recreations:* Reading, Hiking, Squash, Swimming, Canoeing, Music, Playing Piano and Guitar.

JONES, David Booth, 280 Liverpool Rd. South, Burscough, Ormskirk, Lancs. L40 7TD. (0704 893230)–BSc. *b. 11 Jan 1945, Cheadle Hulme. m. 13 April 1968: 2d., 2s.* *Education:* 1957–64 Mosley Hall Grammar; 1964–67 Manchester Univ. Faculty of Technology; 1969–70 Didsbury Coll. of Education; 1976–78 Wesley, Bristol. *Appointments:* 1978– Ormskirk. *Connexional Committees:* 1981–83 Education. *Local Council Committees:* 1981–83 Liverpool District Education and Youth (Ministerial Secretary).
Special Interests: Youth Work, Renewal. *Hobbies and Recreations:* Astronomy, Bird Watching, Gardening.

JONES, David Clifford, 12 Carlton Court, Carlton Rd., Harpenden, Herts AL5 4SY. (058 27 3881) *b. 30 May 1926, Swansea, Glam. m. 28 July 1951: 2d., 1s.* *Education:* 1937–43 Swansea Grammar Sch.; 1948–51 Hartley Victoria. *Appointments:* 1951–62 Burma Dt; 1962–67 Tavistock; 1967–72 Port Talbot; 1972–78 St. Columb and Padstow; 1978– Harpenden.
Connexional Committees: 1964–67, 1970–72 Overseas Missions. *Special Interests:* National Childrens Home. *Hobbies and Recreation:* Reading, Travel, Indian Classical Music.

JONES, David Leslie, 2 Mount Pleasant Rd., Pudsey, West Yorkshire LS28 7DY. (0532 570707) *b. 22 Aug 1952, Harrogate, Yorkshire. m. 18 Aug 1973: 1d., 1s.* *Education:* 1963–68 Marlowe Hall, Newton Aycliffe, Co. Durham; 1970–72 Cliff Coll.; 1974–78 Queen's Coll. *Appointments:* 1978– Pudsey and Farsley.
Hobbies and Recreations: Fell Walking, Photography, Art (Painting).

JONES, Douglas Roger, 19 Estcourt Rd., Gloucester GL1 3LU. (0452 22594) *b. 18 Nov 1922, Liverpool. m. 3 Aug 1950: 1s.* *Education:* 1934–39 Liverpool

Institute High Sch.; 1945–48 Richmond. *Appointments:* 1948–52 Derby South; 1952–56 Cadishead; 1956–61 Longton Mission; 1961–68 Bristol East; 1968–75 Bristol North; 1975 Gloucester.
Special Interests: Marriage Guidance Counselling, Youth Counselling.
Hobbies and Recreations: Gardening, Walking.

JONES, Eric, Epworth Lodge, Field Rd., Stroud, Glos. GL5 2HZ. (045 36 4818)–BD(Lond.). *b. 2 March 1918, Manchester. m. 14 April 1952: 1d., 2s.*
Education: 1929–33 Chorlton Grammar Sch., Manchester; 1940–42 Headingley. *Appointments:* 1939–40 Bradford Mission; 1940–43 Headingley Coll.; 1943–46 Pontypridd; 1946–51 Bradford Shipley; 1951–58 Glasgow, Cathcart Rd.; 1958–63 Wolstanton and Audley; 1963–71 Cheltenham; 1971–76 Somerset Mission; 1976– Stroud and Dursley.

JONES, Ernest, 5 Ingestre Court, Ingestre Rd., Oxton, Birkenhead L43 5UY. (051 653 8122)–BA(Birmingham) *b. 2 Sept 1898, Madeley, Shropshire. m. 8 Oct 1953.*
Education: 1903–11 Madeley Wesleyan; 1911–15 Coalbrookdale County Sch.; 1921–24 Birmingham Univ.; 1921–24 Handsworth.
Appointments: 1920–21 Edinburgh Mission; 1924–28 Gold Coast, Kumasi; 1928–31 London, Leytonstone and Forest Gate; 1931–36 Leeds Mission; 1936–39 Nottingham South; 1939–49 Wigan Mission; 1949–55 Leeds, Headingley; 1955–61 Birkenhead; 1961–64 Preston, Lune St.
Connexional Committees: 1964–67 International House.
Hobbies and Recreations: Football, Walking.

JONES, Geoffrey, 555 Broadway, Chadderton, Oldham, Lancashire OL1 2JH. (061 681 3891) *b. 15 May 1930, Bury, Lancashire. m. 28 March 1953: 1d., 2s.*
Education: 1945–47 Bury Technical Sch.; 1959–62 Hartley Victoria. *Appointments:* 1962–67 Rochdale South; 1968–82 Oldham; 1982– Radcliffe.
Connexional Committees: 1977–82 Home Missions; 1977–79 Cliff Coll.
Special Interests: Church Growth, Evangelism. *Hobbies and Recreations:* Sport, Bird Watching.

JONES, Ivor Harold, 17 Northover Rd., Bristol BS9 3LN. (0272 502903)–MA(Oxon), BA(Cantab), MLitt(Bristol), PhD(Bristol), FRCO. *b. 31 Jan 1934, Bradford, Yorkshire. m. 12 Aug 1961: 1d., 1s.*
Education: King Edward VII Sch., Sheffield; Brasenose Coll., Oxford; 1960–61 Heidelberg Univ., West Germany; Wesley House.
Appointments: 1961–64 Handsworth Coll., Assistant Tutor; 1964–66 London Highgate; 1966–73 Hartley Victoria Coll. Tutor; 1973 Wesley Coll., Bristol Tutor, N.T. Studies.
Connexional Committees: Secretary of Hymns and Songs Committee; Convener of Hymns and Psalms Committee.

JONES, John, 7 Prices Ave., Cliftonville, Margate, Kent CT9 2NS. (0843 20123) *b. 10 Jan 1933, Coventry. m.*
Education: Didsbury. *Appointments:* 1959–60 Missionary Training; 1960–67 Leeward Islands, West Indies; 1967–70 Caribbean Conference; 1970–76 Birmingham Elmdon; 1976–82 Leamington; 1982– Margate.

JONES, John Bryn, Erw Lâs, 1 Ffordd Hengoed, Bryn Coch Uchaf, Yr Wyddgrug, Clwyd CH7 1QD. (0352 2340)–BA(Open Univ.). *b. 9 Nov 1924, Dolgellau, Merionnydd. m. 27 July 1955: 2d., 2s.*
Education: 1928–39 Corris Prim. Sch.; 1974–78 Open Univ.; 1940–49 Cliff Coll.; 1950–53 Handsworth.
Appointments: 1949–50 Corwen (Drudion), 1953–55 Pwllheli; 1955–57 Ystumtuen; 1957–60 Treffynnon; 1960–66 Caergybi and Amlwch; 1966–68 Yr Wyddgrug; 1975– Minister in other appointment.
Connexional Committees: 1966–68 Connexional Youth Committee.
Local Council Committees: 1962–66 Aberffraw Parish Council.
Special Interests: Reading, Writing, Politics, Theology, Liturgy, Welsh History and Literature. *Hobbies and Recreations:* Walking, Gardening, Philately, Caravanning.

JONES, John Frederick, 1 St. James' Ave., Bolton, Lancs. BL2 6HY. (0204 21147) *b. 17 Feb 1918, Birkenhead. m. 14 Aug 1946: 1d., 1s.*
Education; Burscough, Lancs.; 1940–41 London Univ.; 1939–40 Handsworth; 1940–41 Richmond; 1941–42 Headingley. *Appointments:* 1942–46 Grimsby, George St.; 1946–50 Halifax North; 1950–53 Barnsley East; 1953–57 Burnley, Brunswick; 1957–64 Mansfield Bridge St.; 1964–69 Market Rasen and Caistor; 1969–75 Launceston, Cornwall; 1975–80 Ripon and Masham, 1980– Bolton, Lancs.
Local Council Committees: 1955 President Burnley F.C. Council; 1978–79 Ripon Council of Churches.
Special Interests: Reading Historical and Biographical Works; Study of Old Churches. *Hobbies and Recreations:* Bowls, Snooker, Driving (motor cars), Walking, Gardening.

JONES, Marian Jean, 6 Langdale Ave., Oldham, Lancs. OL8 4DL. (061 624 5933).
Education: Ysgol Gynradd, Llanfyllin; Ysgol Uwchradd, Llanfyllin; Queen's Coll.; Wesley, Bristol. *Appointments:* 1976–77 Dyffryn, Conwy; 1977–78 Dyffryn, Clwyd; 1979– Oldham and Saddleworth.

JONES, Nichola Grace, The Manse, 44a Bolingbroke Rd., Farley Hill, Luton, Bedfordshire, LU1 5JE. (0582 27902) BA. *1 Nov 1957, Sheffield.*
Education: Bidston Ave. Jun. Sch., Birkenhead; 1969–76 Manchester High Sch. for Girls; 1976–79 Manchester Univ.; 1979–82 Univ. of Cambridge; 1979–82 Wesley House.
Appointments: 1982– Luton South.
Special Interests: Photography.
Hobbies and Recreations: Sports, Music, Reading.

JONES, Peter Trefor, Epworth, North Rd., Aberystwyth, Dyfed SY23 2EE. (0970 617296)–BSc(Wales), BD(Manchester). *b. 12 June 1938), Leeds, Yorkshire. m. 9 Aug 1961: 1d., 1s.*
Education: 1942–44 Furnace Inf. Sch., LLanelli; 1944–46 Moortown Prim. Sch., Leeds; 1946–56 Leeds Grammar Sch.; 1956–59 Univ. Coll. of Wales, Aberystwyth; 1959–61 Univ. Coll. of Wales, Aberystwyth (Post Grad. Research); 1961–64 Univ. of Manchester; 1961–64 Hartley Victoria. *Appointments:* 1964–69 Middlesbrough, 1969–76 Darlington; 1976– Aberystwyth. *Special Interests:* Student Chaplaincy. *Hobbies and Recreations:* Classical Music (records and books), Walking, Reading History, Armchair Follower of Most Sports, Reading Thrillers.

JONES, Raymond Lionel, 88 Coach Rd., Sleights, Whitby, North Yorkshire YO22 5EQ. (0947 810587) *b. 22 Feb 1934, West Hartlepool. m. 27 July 1957: 1d., 2s.*
Education; 1939–44 Dawley C.P.; 1944–45 Wellington Grammar, Salop; 1945–49 Ashby-de-la-Zouch Boys Grammar; 1949–52 Wolstanton County Grammar; 1962–64 Edge Hill Teachers Training Coll., Ormskirk; 1954–57 Richmond. *Appointments:* 1957–59 Lerwick and North Isle; 1959–60 Wakefield; 1960–61 Bingley; 1971–78 Whitchurch, Salop; 1978– Whitby. *Special Interests:* Education (especially place of Music in School); School/Governor/Parent Relationships. *Hobbies and Recreations:* Sailing, Music (Singing, Recorder), Model Railway, Painting.

JONES, Reginald Lloyd, 8 Oakley Close, Teignmouth, Devon TQ14 8RX. (06267 6140)–DipTh(Lond.). *b. 3 June 1909, Reading, Berkshire. m. 14 Aug 1940: 1d., 1s.*
Education: 1914–24 Wilson Sch., Reading; 1932–36 Richmond. *Appointments:* 1931–32 South Hants. Mission; 1936–38 Birmingham, Moseley Rd.; 1938–40 Birmingham, Islington; 1940–42 Chelmsford; 1942–46 Chaplain H.M.F.; 1946–51 Coventry; 1951–54 Sheffield; 1954–59 Norwich; 1959–63 Bournemouth; 1963–69 Okehampton; 1969–74 Teignmouth. *Connexional Committees:* 1956–59 Youth.
Hobbies and Recreations: Gardening, Music, Clarinet.

JONES, Richard David Clarke, 168A Seagrave Rd., Sileby, Loughborough, Leics. LE12 7TS. (0509 81 2302) *b. 21 Aug 1942, Swansea. m. 15 Aug 1970: 1d., 1s.*
Education: 1954–59 Bishop Gore Grammar Sch.; 1966–70 Handsworth. *Appointments:* 1970–75 Lancaster; 1975–81 Burnley; 1981– Loughborough.

JONES, Richard Granville, 8 St. Andrews Close, Holt, Norfolk NR25 6EL. (026 371 2181)–MA(Cantab), BD(Manch.). *b. 26 July 1926, Dursley, Glos. m. 1955: 3d.*
Education: 1936–44 Truro Sch.; 1944–47 St. Johns Coll., Cambridge; 1950–53 Manchester Univ.; 1950–53 Hartley Victoria. *Appointments:* 1949–50 Plymouth East; 1953–55 Area Secretary SCM; 1955–59 Sheffield North; 1959–64 Sheffield Carver; 1964–69 Birkenhead; 1969–73 Hartley Victoria Coll. (Tutor), 1973–78 (Senior Tutor), 1978–82 (Principal); 1982– Fakenham and Wells.
Connexional Committees: 1968–79, 1981– Faith and Order; 1959–67 Church Membership; 1973–82 Division of Ministries; 1982– Division of Social Responsibility; 1979– Hymn Book. *Publications: Worship for Today* (Ed. 1968); *Towards a Radical Church* (Joint 1969); *How Goes Christian Marriage?* (1978); *Groundwork of Worship and Preaching* (1980); *A. S. Peake Memorial Lecture* (1980).

JONES, Robert Lynton, 77 Clockhouse Lane, Collier Row, Romford, Essex RM5 3QP. (0708 25544)–BSc. *b. 30 April 1949, Wrexham. m. 18 Aug 1973: 2s.*
Education: 1960–67 John Bright Grammer Sch., Llandudno; 1967–70 Univ. of Nottingham; 1978–81 Wesley House. *Appointments:* 1981– Romford.

JONES, Tecwyn, 21 Bryn Moryd, Valley, Gwynedd LL65 3BG. (0407 740668) *b. 21 Feb 1909, Porthmadog, Gwynedd. m.: 4d.*
Education: –1923 Talsarnau, Meirionethshire and Porthmadog Elem. Schs.; 1929–30 Richmond; 1930–32 Headingley. *Appointments:* 1932–34 Dinas Mawddwy; 1934–36 Holyhead and Amlwch; 1936–38 Tregarth; 1938–39 Brynmawr; 1939–45 Holyhead and Amlwch; 1945–50 Llanrheadr-ym-Mochnant; 1950–51 Llanfaircaereinion; 1951–55 Coedpoeth; 1955–60 London, Welsh; 1960–74 Holyhead and Amlwch.
Connexional Committees: 1952–55 Local Preachers Connexional Committee.
Special Interests: Welsh Literature, Nature Study. *Hobbies and Recreations:* Poetry Writing, Bird Watching.

JONES, William Eric, Wesley House, 10 Mainwaring Rd., Lincoln LN2 4BL. (0522 25625) *b. 23 March 1920, Liverpool. m. 23 July 1947: 1d., 1s.*
Education: 1925–26 Penryn St. Elem. Sch., Liverpool; 1927–37 Collegiate Sch., Liverpool; 1946–47 Handsworth. *Appointments:* 1942–45 RAF Chaplain; 1947–51 Peterborough; 1951–55 Nottingham Central; 1955–60 Stockport, Tiviot Dale; 1960–65 Wallasey; 1965–71 Birmingham, Moseley Rd. and Sparkhill; 1971–73 Birmingham, Islington and Quinton; 1973– Chairman of the Lincoln District. *Connexional Committees:* 1973– M.Y.D. Home Missions, General Purposes, Church in Rural Life; Connexional Advance Fund, Stationing, President's Council. *Hobbies and Recreations:* Music, Sport of all kinds, Gardening.

JONES, William Henry, Bwthyn, 3 Belmont Rd., Bangor, Gwynedd LL57 2LL. (0248 2976)–BD(Lond.). *b. 12 Oct 1938, Tetcott, Holsworthy, Devon. m. 16 Aug 1959: 1s.*
Education: 1943–49 Clawton Prim. Sch.; 1949–58 Shebbear Coll.; 1960–63 London Univ., Richmond; 1963–64 Southampton Univ.; 1960–63 Richmond. *Appointments:* 1964–66

Southampton; 1966–71 Burslem; 1971–78 Frodsham; 1978– Bangor and Holyhead.
Special Interests: World Disarmament. *Hobbies and Recreations:* Gardening, Swimming.

JOSELIN, Eric Sidney, The Manse, 93 Spencer Rd., Wigan, Lancs. WM1 2QL. (0942 48644) *b. 13 Sept 1923, London. m. 18 Aug 1949: 1d., 2s.*
Education: 1934–39 Manor House Sch., Clapham; 1939–40 Highfield Sch., Wandsworth Common; 1940–41 Kingston Technical Coll.; 1947–49 Westhill, Selly Oak, Birmingham; 1959–61 Didsbury, Bristol.
Appointments: 1961–66 Bury; 1966–73 Clitheroe; 1973–78 Blackpool North; 1978– Wigan.
Connexional Committees: 1962–66 Education and Youth; 1970–73 Education and Youth (District Youth Sec.); 1978– Ministries (Sec.).
Council Member: 1970–73 Parish councillor, Whalley Parish Council; 1970–73 Chaplain to Chairman of Clitheroe District Council.
Special Interests: Evangelical and Charismatic Renewal, The Furthering of Ecumenical Relationships, Evangelistic Outreach. *Hobbies and Recreations:* Philately, Water-Colour and Oil Painting, Fell Walking etc.

JOSEY, John Victor, Oak House, High St., Partridge Green, Horsham, W.Sussex RH13 8HX. (0403 710722)–DipTheol(Lond.). *b. 20 May 1905, Reading. m. 25 July 1936: 3d.*
Education: Petersfield Elem.; 1926–27 Cliff Coll.; 1930–33 Richmond.
Appointments: 1929–30 H.M. Comm.; 1933–35 Ipswich; 1935–37 Canterbury; 1937–40 Sheerness; 1940–45 Chaplain H.M.F.; 1945–48 South London Mission; 1948–51 Market Rasen; 1951–55 Alford; 1955–61 Market Harboro; 1961–63 Witney; 1966–70 Tewkesbury.
Local Council Committees: 1953–55 Mablethorpe; Post Flood.
Special Interests: Youth Work.
Hobbies and Recreations: Gardening.

JOWETT, Raymond Bernard, 29 Windermere Rd., Haydock, St. Helens, Merseyside WA11 0ES. (0744 23606) *b. 26 July 1923, Long Eaton, Derbyshire. m.: 1d., 1s.*
Education: Long Eaton Grammar Sch.; 1945–49 Headingley.
Appointments: 1944–45 H.M. Forces; 1949–59 Sierra Leone Dt.; 1959–64 Loughborough; 1964–70 Leicester West; 1970–78 Mansfield: 1978– Makerfield.
Connexional Committees: 1961–65 Overseas Missions Committee.
Special Interests: Chaplain to Forces (Army Cadet Force). *Hobbies and Recreations:* Gardening, Walking, Host at Guild Holidays.

JOYCE, Walter James, 7 Moreton Park Rd., Bideford, Devon EX39 3AU. (02372 2733) *b. 13 March 1914, Finedon, Northamptonshire. m. June 1946: 1d., 2s.*
Education: 1924–28 Welling Sch.; 1938–39 Cliff Coll.; 1939–40 Handsworth; 1940–41 Richmond; 1941–42 Headingley. *Appointments:* 1946–51 Nottingham South; 1951–55 London, Enfield; 1955–60 Nottingham South; 1960–69 Exeter; 1969–77 Bideford; 1977–79 Shaftesbury.
Local Council Committees: 1972–77 School Governor.
Special Interests: Education, Mental Health, Crime and Punishment.
Hobbies and Recreations: Gardening, Sport, Painting.

JOYNSON, William Thomas, 142 Cheriton Rd., Folkestone, Kent CT19 5JR. (0303 53403)–BA(Open Univ.). *b. 11 Feb 1920, Congleton, Cheshire. m. 9 Jan 1943: 2d., 1s.*
Education: 1925–34 St. James' Sch., Congleton, Cheshire; 1974–77 Open Univ.; 1949–51 Richmond Coll. *Appointments:* 1947–49 Bournemouth; 1951–52 St. Albans; 1952–55 Holywell Cross and Staveley, Chesterfield, 1955–65 Dover; 1965–70 St. Leonards and Bexhill; 1970–75 Darlington, Bondgate; 1975–81 London, Finsbury Park and Southgate; 1981– Folkestone.
Local Council Committees: 1981 Local Advisory Body for Education, Folkestone.
Special Interests: Christian Ethics, Sport. *Hobbies and Recreations:* Woodwork, Gardening.

JUBY, Leonard Ward, Norwood, 14 Park Rd., Ipswich, Suffolk IP1 3ST. (0473 211261) *b. 3 Aug 1893, Ipswich. m. 1. 1922; 2. 9 June 1961: 2d., 1s.*
Education: Ipswich Secondary Sch.; 1919–20 Didsbury; 1920–21 Richmond. *Appointments:* 1921–33 Sierre Leone; 1933–34 Newport and Cowes; 1934–37 West Wight; 1937–42 Eccles; 1942–43 Ipswich, Museum St.; 1945–51 Sierre Leone Dt; 1951–52 Colville; 1952–55 Rugby; 1955–59 Sierre Leone Dt.; Chairman of District for Sierre Leone.
Connexional Committees: General Committee for M.M.S.; Western Committee for M.M.S.
Special Interests: 1935–37 The Mende Language from 1935–37; Taught Post-graduate students at Oxford Univ. the Mende Language one day a week in term time.

JUDD, George Leslie, 46 Whitehorse Square, Hereford HR4 0HD. (0432 267344)–MEd(Ohio) *b. 16 March 1944, Senghenydd, S. Wales. m. 10 Aug 1974: 1d., 1s.*
Education: 1955–59 Birchfield Rd. Secondary Modern, Birmingham; 1967–70 Richmond Coll.; 1970–71 Methodist Theological Sch. in Ohio, Delaware, U.S.A. *Appointments:* 1971–73 Dursley, Stonehouse; 1973–74 Barnsley; 1974–76 North Dakota Conference, U.S.A.; 1976–81 Gateshead and Jarrow; 1981– Hereford.

JUDKINS, Robert Richard, 357 Fox Hill Rd., Sheffield S6 1HH. (0742 313518) *b. 19 June 1923, London. m. 9 Aug 1952: 1d., 1s.*
Education: 1951–52 St. Andrew's, Selly Oak; 1949–52 Handsworth.
Appointments: 1953–61 E. Nigeria Dt; 1961–66 Wolverton and Bletchley; 1966–73 Birmingham, Wesley; 1973–78 Birmingham, Elmden; 1978– Sheffield North.
Connexional Committees: 1962–66 Overseas; 1967–70 Overseas; 1979– Overseas.

Special Interests: Peace and Reconciliation. *Hobbies and Recreations:* Walking, Camping, Cycling, Music, Home and Family, Gardening.

KAYE, Richard Lewis John, 89 Ashgrove, Killay, Swansea SA2 7QZ. (0792 296049) *b. 1 Nov 1915, Preston, Lancs. m. 14 Aug 1945: 1d., 1s.*
Education: 1920–26 Llansannan Prim.; 1926–31 Denbigh Grammar; 1938–41 Didsbury. *Appointments:* 1941–45 Knaresborough; 1945–50 Salisbury; 1950–56 Sutton, Surrey; 1956–61 Liverpool North; 1961–67 London, Finsbury Park and Southgate; 1967–74 High Wycombe; 1974–80 Chairman London N.W. District; 1980–81 Watford.
Connexional Committees: 1946–50 Youth Department; 1974–80 Home Missions; 1974–80 Property; 1974–80 General Purposes; 1974–80 London Mission.
Special Interests: Sunday Sch., Youth Work. *Hobbies and Recreations:* Photography, Gardening, Cookery.

KEDWARD, Neville Fedrick, 80 Parton Rd., Churchdown, Glos. GL3 2AY. (0452 855925) *b. 1 June 1908, Hertford. m. 22 May 1982: 2s.*
Education: 1921–28 Kingswood. *Appointments:* 1938–41 London Mission West; 1941–42 H.M. Committee; 1942–43 South Yorks Coalfield Mission; 1943–63 Chaplain H.M.F.
Hobbies and Recreations: Golf, Cricket, Rugby Football.

KEEN, Richard, 24A Kew Rd., Southport, Merseyside PR8 4HN. (0704 64976) *b. 16 May 1918, London N2. m. 9 May 1946: 3d.*
Education: 1923–29 Long Lane Prim.; 1929–34 Christ's Coll.; 1939–41 Richmond; 1941–42 Headingley. *Appointments:* 1942–43 Sunderland North; 1943–46 Ceylon North District; 1946–50 Douglas, I.O.M.; 1950–56 Liverpool North; 1956–61 Wigan Mission; 1961–66 Southport South; 1966–70 Hoylake and West Kirby; 1970–76 Liverpool North; 1976–77 St. Helens and Prescot. *Connexional Committees:* 1948–70 O.M. for varied periods.

KEEP, David John, Heatherdene, Woodbury, Exeter EX5 1NR. (0395 32318)–MA(Oxon), BA(Cantab), PhD(Sheffield). *b. 4 Dec 1936, Bedford, m. 1 Aug 1962: 1d., 1s.*
Education: 1942–44 Queen's Park CPS; 1945–55 Bedford Modern Sch.; 1957–60 New Coll., Oxford; 1960–62 Fitzwilliam House, Cambridge; 1962–63 Univ. of Zurich; 1964–71 Univ. of Sheffield; 1960–62 Wesley House. *Appointment:* 1963–64 Coalville; 1964–66 Belper; 1966–71 Pilgrim Sch., Bedford; 1971– Rolle Coll., Exmouth.
Local Council Committees: 1975–80 Devon Standing Conf. on RE.
Publications: History Through Stamps (1975); *St. Boniface and His World* (1979); Articles in *Zwingliana* (1963/75/77); *Epworth Review* (1966/74); *Studies in Church History* (1975/82); *Henry Bullinger* (1975); *Evangelical Quarterly* (1975/81); *National Trust Yearbook* (1976); *Bedfordshire Mag.* (1976); *TR. Devon Assoc.* (1977).
Special Interests: L.R.C. Parole Board Exeter, Univ. London Schs. Exams Committee. *Hobbies and Recreations:* Stamp Collecting, Choral Singing.

KEIGHLEY, David Alan, 135 Fairfax Ave., Hull HU5 4QZ. (0482 42097)–MA(Cantab), BD(Lond.). *b. 15 April 1926, Shipley, Yorkshire. m. 10 April 1950: 1d., 1s.*
Education: 1938–44 Bradford Grammar Sch.; 1944–45 Emmanuel Coll., Cambridge; 1951–53 Richmond Coll. *Appointments:* 1953–56 London Mission, Hackney Mission; 1956–63 British Council of Churches, Executive. 1963–70 Rome, Italian Methodist Conference and Methodist Conference Representative in Italy; 1970–75 Sheffield North; 1975–80 Wakefield; 1980–81 Research Fellow, the Queen's Coll., Birmingham; 1981– Hull West.
Connexional Committees: 1963–70 C.C. Dept Standing Committee on International Releations; 1970–72 Chairman, Joint Standing Committee of MMS and Dept of C.C. *Council Member:* 1963–70 Official Observer at UNFAO (HQ in Rome) for the Commission of the Churches on International Affairs of the WCC; 1963–65 Permanent Deputy Methodist Observer, Second Vatican Council, Sessions 2–4; 1972–80 Member, Board of Directors, Christian Aid. *Local Council Committees:* 1971–74 Chairman, Sheffield Christian Aid Committee; 1978–80 Chairman, Wakefield Council of Churches. *Publications: Pursuing the Roman Catholic-Methodist Dialogue* (Epworth Review Sept 1977); *A Note on Mixed Marriages* (Epworth Review May 1978); Awarded *George Eayrs Essay Price 1981–82* (unpublished). *Special Interests:* English Church History 1688–1750 especially the theological background of John Wesley as a young man. *Hobbies and Recreations:* Gardening, Music.

KELLEY, Frank Musson, 14 Birdhurst Court, Woodcote Rd., Wallington, Surrey SM6 0PG. (01 669 2380) *b. 23 Aug 1894, Froghall, Staffs. m. 30 June 1920. 1d.*
Education: 1908–13 West Leeds High Sch.; 1914–15 Manchester Univ.; 1914–17 Hartley.
Appointments: 1917–20 Brighton; 1920–21 Clay Cross; 1921–24 Laxey, Isle of Man; 1924–29 Forest Hill; 1929–32 Weston-super-Mare; 1932–36 Bournemouth; 1936–45 Kingston-upon-Thames; 1945–49 Cardiff Wesley; 1949–56 London, Kilburn and Hampstead; 1956–61 Kingston-upon-Thames.

KELLINGTON, Derek Clifford, 43 Toll End Rd., Tipton, West Midlands DY4 0HE. (021 557 1323) *b. 25 Feb 1935, Misterton, Nottinghamshire. m. 15 Aug 1959: 1d., 3s.*
Education: 1940–45 Misterton County Prim. Sch.; 1945–53 Gainsborough Grammar Sch.; 1956–59 Headingley. *Appointments:* 1959–62 East Dereham; 1962–67 March and Chatteris; 1967–72 Boston; 1972–79 Wolverhampton,

Darlington St.; 1979– Tipton. *Connexional Committees:* Youth Committee.

KELLY, Frank Henry, 5 Elmhurst Drive, South Woodford, London E18 1BP. (01 989 1473)–BD(Lond.). *b. 24 July 1921, Liverpool. m. 27 July 1949: 1d., 1s.*
Education: 1926–32 Parkhill CE Elem.; 1932–37 Holt High Sch.; 1974–75 London Univ., Institute of Education (P.G.C.E.); 1979 London Univ. Sch. of Oriental and African Studies, Teacher Fellowship Summer Term, 1947–49 Richmond. *Appointments:* 1945–46 Presteigne and Kington; 1946–47 Wimborne; 1949–50 Bury St. Edmunds; 1950–55 Oldham West; 1955–58 Manchester, Harpurley; 1958–62 Great Barn and Kingstanding; 1962–69 Hillingdon; 1969–74 (M.M.S.) Kenya Conference; 1975– Rokeby Boys Comprehensive Sch., Newham.
Connexional Committees: 1960–69 Christian Citizenship; 1963–69 Church in Industry Committee; 1964–69 Joint Overseas Christian Citizenship; 1969–73 Kenya Conf., Ministerial Training; 1971–73 Committee Secretary. *Local Council Committees:* 1964–69 London Borough of Hillingdon Education Committee. *Publications:* Articles in the *Christian Citizen* (1968–70); *M.M.U. Bulletin.*
Special Interests: Ministry and Ministries, Education, International Affairs. *Hobbies and Recreations:* Gardening.

KEMP, Ernest Ronald, 3 Temple Terrace, Louth, Lincs. LN11 0EP. (0507 603402)–BD(Lond.). *b. 18 May 1928, Manchester. m. 6 Aug 1960: 2d., 1s.*
Education: 1934 Lambourn, Berks. Inf. and Jun. Sch.; 1937 Beechgrove Jun. Sch., Wigan; 1939 Mundella Secondary Sch., Nottingham; 1942 Rochdale High Sch.; 1944 Firth Park Grammar Sch., Sheffield. 1950–53 Headingley. *Appointments:* 1949–50 Bedale; 1950–53 Headingley Coll.; 1953–58 Durham; 1958–61 Oldbury Wesley; 1961–66 Lowestoft; 1966–75 Medway Towns; 1975– Louth.
Hobbies and Recreations: Astronomy.

KEMP, Geoffrey, 2 Edinburgh Drive, Darlington, Co. Durham DL3 8AW. (0325 68119) *b. 7 July 1921, Kingston-upon-Hull. m. 30 May 1942: 2d., 2s.*
Education: 1932–36 Riley High Sch., Hull; 1948–50 Headingley. *Appointments:* 1950–54 Stanley; 1954–58 Stoke-on-Trent, Hanley Trinity; 1958–61 Howden Caves; 1961–68 Durham; 1968–74 Gateshead East, Gateshead and Jarrow; 1974–79 Scarborough; 1979– Chairman, Darlington District.
Connexional Committees: 1975– Home Mission; 1977– General Purposes; 1977– Trustees for Methodist Church Purposes; 1980– Property Board. *Local Council Committees:* 1979– North Yorkshire County Council Education Committee; 1979– Schs. Sub-Committee.
Hobbies and Recreations: Reading, Gardening.

KEMP, Ronald, 39 Westcroft, Leominster, Herefordshire HR6 8HF. (0568 5368) *b. 1 March 1914, Handsworth, Birmingham. m. 7 April 1947.*
Education: 1919–1931 Handsworth County Sch.; 1931–33 Handsworth Technical Sch.; 1933–39 Handsworth Technical Coll.; 1961–63 Handsworth. *Appointments:* 1958 MAYC V-Pres.; 1961–63 Handsworth Coll.; 1963–66 Salisbury; 1966–71 Aldershot and Farnborough; 1971–76 Sheffield North; 1976–81 Nuneaton and Atherstone.
Connexional Committees: Full-time Methodist Youth Workers Pastoral Oversight Committee (Past); 1958 M.A.Y.C. President. *Council Member:* Connexional Youth Council.
Special Interests: Work amongst young people. *Hobbies and Recreations:* Bird Watching; Music, Singing, Reading, Walking, Gardening, Photography, Tape-Recording, Writing Poetry.

KEMP, Ronald Frederick, 60 Gordon Field, Market Rasen, Lincs. LN8 3AF. (0673 843362) *b. 8 Feb 1921, Framfield, East Sussex. m. 18 Aug 1950: 1d., 1s.*
Education: 1931–37 Lewes County Sch. for Boys; 1945–47 Hartley Victoria. *Appointments:* 1947–51 Uttoxeter and Ramsor; 1951–55 Longton and Fenton; 1955–58 Newcastle, Staffs.; 1958–61 Nottingham West; 1961–65 Rotherham; 1965–69 Gateshead East; 1969–74 Nuneaton and Atherstone; 1974–79 Castletown, Isle of Man; 1979– Market Rasen and Caistor.

KENDALL, Richard Elliot, 3 Northwood Ave., Purley, Surrey CR2 2ER. (01 660 1964)–MA(Lambeth). *b. 19 Dec 1915, Manchester. m. Oct 1943: 1d., 1s.*
Education: 1927–33 Pates Grammar Sch., Cheltenham, Glos. 1936–39 Handsworth. *Appointments:* 1939–52 S.W. China Dt; 1952–57 Doncaster South; 1957–67 Kenya Dt, East Africa; 1967–76 Conference of British Miss. Societies; 1976–81 British Council of Churches.
Connexional Committees: 1975–81 Division of Social Responsibility; 1975– Division of Finance; 1952–57, 1968– Overseas Division. *Council Member:* 1967–81 British Council of Churches, Staff Member; 1967–75 Conference of British Missionary Societies. *Publications: Beyond the Clouds* (1945); *Eyes of the Earth* (1953); *The End of an Era* (1978); *Charles New and the East Africa Mission* (1978); Beckly Lecture, Plymouth Conference *Christianity and Race* (1982).
Special Interests: World Mission, Race Relations, Africa, China, History, International Relations, Social Affairs. *Hobbies and Recreations:* Gardening, Carpentry.

KENDREW, Gordon Blenkiron, 45 Kingsway, Lytham St. Annes FY8 1AB. (0253 736396) *b. 30 June 1917, Southport. m. 26 Nov 1947: 1d., 1s.*
Education: 1922–27 Southport Coll.; 1927–34 King George V Sch., Southport; 1938–42 Headingley.

Appointments: 1942–46 Whitehaven; 1946–48 Barrow-in-Furness; 1948–51 Ilkley; 1951–56 Frodsham; 1956–63 Clitheroe; 1963–70 Wigton; 1970–76 Carlisle; 1976–82 Lytham St. Annes.
Connexional Committees: 1977–82 Connexional Property Boards.

KENDRICK, Derek, 67 Gathurst Lane, Shevington, Wigan, Lancs. WN6 8HW. (025 75 2510) *b. 7 Feb 1933, Wigan. m. 27 Sept 1980: 1d., 1s.*
Education: 1937–40 St. Lukes Inf.; 1940–44 St. Marks Jun.; 1944–47 Pemberton Senior; 1956–57 Cliff Coll.; 1957–60 Hartley Victoria.
Appointments: 1960–65 Winsford; 1965–73 Nottingham Mission; 1973 Wigan O.Appt.

KENNEDY, John Douglas, 25 Danesdale Rd., London E9 5DB. (01 533 3106)–BD. *23 Aug 1940, Glasgow. m.*
Education: 1972–73 Birmingham Univ.; 1966–69 Richmond.
Appointments: 1969–72 Worthing; 1972–73 Birmingham Univ.; 1973–78 Sri Lanka; 1978– London, Bow Mission.
Connexional Committees: Division of Social Responsibility, International Committee.
Special Interests: All-Age Worship, Theology of the Family.

KENT, Wyndham Henry, The Manse, School Rd., Terrington St. John, Wisbech, Cambs. (094 582 512) *b. 3 Oct 1926, Basingstoke, Hants. m. 27 Dec 1948: 1d.*
Education: 1981–82 Wesley House.
Appointments: 1980– Wisbech.

KENYON, Godfrey, 2 Crich Ave., Littleover, Derby DE3 6ES. (0332 46715) *b. 12 Aug 1926, Wolstanton, Stoke-on-Trent. m. 30 Aug 1956: 1d., 1s.*
Education: 1931–37 Hob Hill Jun. Sch., Dukinfield; 1937–44 Hyde Grammar Sch.; 1949–51 Hartley Victoria. *Appointments:* 1951–55 Clitheroe; 1955–62 Frodsham; 1962–69 Douglas, Isle of Man; 1969–79 Birkenhead; 1979– Derby Derwent Mission, Queens Hall.
Connexional Committees: 1964–67 Central Missions. *Council Member:* 1977–79 President of Manx Labour Party; Management Committee of Birkenhead Labour Party.
Special Interests: Politics, Inner City Deprivation. *Hobbies and Recreations:* Music.

KERRIDGE, Peter Avon, 2 Dane Drive, Wilmslow, Cheshire SK9 2AH. (0625 528718) *b. 5 Aug 1920, Gt. Yarmouth, Norfolk. m. 28 June 1947: 2d., 1s.*
Education: 1925–31 Edward Worledge Jun.; 1931–37 Gt. Yarmouth Grammar Sch.; 1945–47 Handsworth. *Appointments:* 1943–44 President's List (Farnham and Alton); 1944–45 Sussex Mission; 1947–51 Hexham; 1951–57 Doncaster North East; 1957–62 St. Albans; 1962–70 Hull, Trinity/North/West; 1970–75 York and Hull District Chairman; 1975–79 Secretarty, Property Division; 1979– General Secretary, Property Division.

KETTELL, Ronald, 169 Barrowby Rd., Grantham, Lincs. NG31 8AJ. (0476 75893) *b. 9 April 1920, Butt Lane, Stoke-on-Trent. m. 26 July 1947: 1d., 1s.*
Education: 1923–30 Reginald Mitchell Prim. Sch., Butt Lane, Staffs.; 1930–31 Kidsgrove Senior Boys; 1931–35 Stoke-on-Trent Technical Coll., Burslem; 1945–48 Headingley.
Appointments: 1940–45 H.M. Forces; 1945–48 Headingley Coll.; 1948–52 Cheadle, Staffs.; 1952–55 Macclesfield; 1955–60 Long Eaton; 1960–63 Melton Mowbray; 1963–67 Stoke-on-Trent, Burslem Hill Top; 1967–72 Wolstanton and Audley; 1972–78 Wem and Prees Green; 1978–81 Dudley, West Midlands; 1981– Grantham; 1960–63 P.M.U.B. Chaplain (officiating) H.M. Prison, Ashwell; 1960–63 P.M.U.B. Chaplain (officiating) R.A.F. Cottesmore.
Special Interests: Local History.
Hobbies and Recreations: Gardening.

KILNER, Roy, 6 Wesley Ave., London NW10 7BN. (01 961 4946) *b. 28 Jan 1929, Barnsley, Yorkshire. m. 8 July 1953: 1d., 1s.*
Education: 1934–40 Barugh Green Elem.; 1940–42 Secondary; 1942–44 Technical; 1971–75 London Univ. Extra Mural Dept. (part time); 1950–53 Hartley Victoria. *Appointments:* 1953–54 Leith and Tranent; 1954–58 Burnley; 1958–61 Garstang; 1961–67 Hull West; 1967–70 Bradford;1970–77 London, Hammersmith; 1979– Minister in other appointments; Assistant Prison Chaplain.
Connexional committees: 1977–82 Home Missions Prison Committee.
Special Interests: Penal Reform and Methodist Contribution to present Chaplaincy Service in H.M. Prisons.
Hobbies and Recreations: Photography, Gardening, Walking, Travel.

KIME, George Walter, 22 Netheroyd Hill Rd., Fixby, Huddersfield, W.Yorks. HD2 2ZP. (0484 46549)–BEd *b. 3 July 1927, Thurnscoe, Yorks. m. 1. 2. 12 Aug 1972: 2d., 2s.*
Education: 1941–46 Barnsley Tech. Coll.; 1964–65 Kings Coll., London; 1966–70 Keswick Hall Coll. of Ed., Cambridge Inst. of Ed.; 1980– Leeds Univ.; 1968 Exchange Univ. Connecticut; 1949–51 Handsworth.
Appointments: 1948–49 Retford; 1949–51 Handsworth Coll.; 1951–52 Pontypridd; 1953–56 Chatham Mission; 1956–59 Doncaster Priory Place; 1959–63 Skegness and Wainfleet; 1964–65 London, Tottenham; 1965–80 Resigned (Teacher); 1980– Halifax.
Publications: Served on Committees for Publishing of *Agreed Syllabus in Rel. Ed. for Norfolk and Norwich* (L.E.A. 1977–79).
Special Interests: Photography, Chairman Norfolk and Norwich Photographic Society 1978. *Hobbies and Recreations:* Mountaineering, Tennis, L.T.A. Coach.

KINCH, Anthony George, 42 Newbridge Crescent , Wolverhampton, West Midlands WV6 0LH. (0902 752213) *b. 25 March 1940, Stokenchurch, Buckinghamshire. m. 20 Aug 1966:1d., 1s.*
Education: 1944–53 Stokenchurch C.P. and C.M.; 1953–58 High

Wycombe Technical Sch.; 1959–61 Newland Park Teachers' Training Coll.; 1963–66 Richmond Coll. *Appointments:* 1966–70 Netherton; 1970–81 Telford South; 1981– Wolverhampton, Darlington St. *Local Council Committees:* 1975–78 Member Salop Community Health Council; 1972–81 Member and Chairman, Age Concern, Wrekin. *Publications:* Internal papers include *The Methodist Church in Relation to Telford* (1977); *Staffing Arrangements and Circuit Boundaries in Telford* (1981). *Special Interests:* The Church in relation to community development, The Care of the Elderly, The Church in the Inner City. *Hobbies and Recreations:* Former Football Referee, Public Transport System of the United Kingdom, Social and Economic History.

KINCHIN, Frederick Alexander, Cople, Casterton Close, Mill Rd., Market Rasen, Lincs. LN8 3BP. (0673 842699) *b. 20 April 1902, West Kensington. m. 23 Nov 1940.* *Education:* 1913–18 Latymer Upper Sch., Hammersmith, London W6; 1930–33 Handsworth Coll. *Appointments:* 1933–42 Burma District; 1942–46 Helston; 1946–57 Burma District; 1957–65 Settle; 1965–69 Ryedale; 1969–74 Market Rasen and Caistor. *Hobbies and Recreations:* Bowls.

KINDLEYSIDES, Peter, The Manse, Derby Rd., Wirksworth, Derby DE4 4AQ. (062 982 2456) *b. 31 Aug 1933, Stockton-on-Tees, Co. Durham. m. 2 June 1956. 2d., 1s.* *Education:* 1970 72 Manchester Univ.; 1976–78 Open Univ.; 1969–72 Hartley Victoria. *Appointments:* 1972–78 Hazel Grove and Poynton; 1978– Wirksworth. *Special Interests:* Healing Ministry and Community Service. *Hobbies and Recreations:* Reading, Photography, Music, Walking.

KING, David, The Manse, 60 High St., Stotfold, Hitchin, Herts. SG5 4LD. (0462 732054) *b. 2 March 1951, Bridlington. m. 16 Aug 1980.* *Education:* –1966 Headlands Sch., Bridlington; 1970–72 Askham Bryan Coll. of Agriculture and Horticulture, York.; 1975–78 Wesley Coll., Bristol. *Appointments:* 1978– Hitchin and Letchworth; 1982– Free Church Chaplain, Fairfield (Psychiatric) Hospital. *Special Interests:* Youth Work. *Hobbies and Recreations:* Gardening, Restoration of Furniture.

KING, Fred, The Manse, St. Andrew's Rd., Sheringham, Norfolk NR26 8SA. (0263 822485) *b. 30 Aug 1921, Queensbury, Bradford. m. 27 July 1950: 2d., 1s.* *Education:* 1926–33 Brougham St. Elem., Skipton; 1933–36 Ermysted's Grammar Sch., Skipton; 1936–38 Doncaster Grammar Sch.; 1947–49 Hartley Victoria. *Appointments:* 1949 Tipton, Park Lane, 1950–56 Eastern Nigeria Dt; 1956–59 Maryport; 1959–65 Leeds South; 1965–70 Guernsey and Alderney; 1970–79 Bury St. Edmunds; 1979– Cromer and Sheringham; 1972–77 East Anglia District Property Secretary; 1981–82 President, Hartley Victoria Old Students Association. *Connexional Committees:* 1972–77 Property Board. *Special interests:* World Disarmament. *Hobbies and Recreations:* Classical Music, Gardening, Walking, Caravanning.

KING, Kenneth Ernest, 140 Shirehampton Rd., Sea Mills, Bristol. (0272 682304) *m.: 1d., 2s.* *Education:* 1950–52 Hartley Victoria. *Appointments:* 1948 Lerwick, Shetland; 1952–55 Barnsley East; 1955–58 Nottingham East; 1958–64 Wisbech; 1964–69 Derby South; 1969 74 Blackpool South; 1974 82 Preston, Lune St.; 1977–82 Leicester South-East, 1982 Bristol, Clifton and Redland. *Special Interests:* Travel in the Middle East in the Steps of Jesus, St. Paul and the Apostles, with illustrated lectures. *Hobbies and Recreations:* Photography, Archaeology of the Middle East.

KING, Martin John, c/o Secretary Royal Navy, Arm and Royal Air Force Board, 1 Central Building, Westminster, London SW1H 9NH. MA, BSc. *b. 28 March 1951, Buckinghamshire. m. 6 Sept 1975: 2s.* *Education:* 1962–69 Wolverhampton Grammar Sch.; 1969–72 Southampton Univ.; 1973–76 Wesley House. *Appointments:* 1976–80 Shaw and Royton; 1980– Chaplain H.M.F. *Special Interests:* Science and Religion, Audio Visual Aids. *Hobbies and Recreations:* Swimming, Walking, Cycling, Caravanning.

KING, Paul Rigby, 37 Tattenham Way, Burgh Heath, Tadworth, Surrey KT20 5LX. (07373 51575)–BA(Leeds and Bristol). *b. 18 July 1939, Stockport. m.* *Education:* 1944–46 Poynton County Prim.; 1946–57 Stockport Grammar Sch.; 1957–60 Leeds Univ.; 1960–61 London Univ. (Institute of Education); 1965–68 Bristol Univ.; 1965–67 Didsbury, Bristol; 1967–68 Wesley, Bristol. *Appointments:* 1968–70 Lancaster; 1970–75 Longton Mission; 1975– Sutton, Surrey. *Connexional Committees:* 1975– Local Preachers' Studies Board. *Special Interests:* Adult Education, Pastoral Counselling. *Hobbies and Recreations:* Music, Sport, Gardening, Travel, Rambling, Politics.

KINGSNORTH, Stephen Leslie, 5 Comforts Farm Ave., Hurst Green, Oxted, Surrey RH8 9DH. (08833 4143) MA. *b. 3 May 1952, Bromley, Kent. m. 24 Oct 1981: 1s.* *Education:* 1963–65 Askes Haberdashers, Hatcham; 1965–70 Heles G.S. Exeter; 1971–74 Fitzwilliam Coll., Cambridge; 1974–76 Wesley House. *Appointments:* 1976–77 Derby Mission; 1977–80 Derby Derwent Mission; 1980– Purley.

KIRBY, Ralph, Silver Birches, Sch. Lane, Burghfield Common, Reading, Berks. RG7 3LB. (073529 2930) *b. 22 Aug 1909, Wigston, Leicester. m. 22 Aug 1936: 1d., 1s.*

Education: Wigston Magna, Wyggeston Grammar Sch., Leicester; 1929–33 Richmond. *Appointments:* 1933–34 Canterbury; 1934–36 Bloxwich; 1936–39 Woolwich; 1939–46 Medway Towns; 1946–51 Kilburn and Hampstead; 1951–58 Ealing; 1958–66 Windsor and Maidenhead; 1966–74 Farnham and Alton.
Publications: One Hundred Great Bible Stories; The Bible in Pictures; Pilgrim's Progress in Pictures; The Bible Story with Living Pictures; The Methodist Bedside Book.

KIRK, Alan, 62 Randsfield Ave., Brough, North Humberside HU15 1BG. (0482 668404) *b. 11 Sept 1942, Wolverhampton. m. 31 Dec 1966: 2s.*
Education: 1954–59 King Edward VI Grammar Sch., Aston, Birmingham; 1964–68 Hartley Victoria.
Appointments: 1968–70 Stamford; 1970–75 Peterborough; 1975–82 Darlington; 1982– Hull West.
Special Interests: Member of Fellowship of Reconciliation.
Hobbies and Recreations: Golf, Philately (GB), Model Railways.

KIRK, Maurice W., April Cottage, Manor Way, Verwood, Wimborne, Dorset BH21 6HF. (0202 822321)–DipTheol(Lond.). *b. 11 June 1914, Bilston, Staffs. m. 18 Aug 1944: 2d.*
Education: 1923–24 Walsall Grammar; 1925–29 Dudley Grammar; 1937–40 Richmond.
Appointments: 1940–44 Wimborne; 1944–47 Newcastle, Staffs. (Eben); 1947–52 Bristol East; 1952–57 Cheddar Valley; 1957–61 Camelford; 1961–66 St. Austell; 1956–62 Romsey.
Connexional Committees: 1957–63 Church Membership.
Hobbies and Recreations: Photography, Tape-Recording, Walking, Philately.

KIRKMAN, Arthur, 72 Wells Rd., Fakenham, Norfolk NR21 9HH. (0328 2174) *b. 16 April 1927, Moulton-Seas-End, Lincs. m. 2 April 1956: 1d., 1s.*
Education: 1932–38 Mablethorpe Jun.; 1938–43 Alford Grammar Sch.; 1950–53 Handsworth.
Appointments: 1953–56 Uttoxeter and Ramsor; 1956–59 Staveley; 1959–65 Barnsley East; 1965–71 Beccles, Loddon and Bungay; 1971–76 Wisbech; 1976– Fakenham and Wells.
Local Council Committees: 1972–76 Probation After-Care Committee.
Special Interests: Church History.
Hobbies and Recreations: Walking, Collecting Walking Sticks, Charles Dickens.

KIRKPATRICK, Harold Brian, 19 Woodland Grove, Burslem, Stoke-on-Trent, Staffs. ST6 7EB. (0782 87815)–MA(Manchester), BD(Lond.). *b. 16 Dec 1928, Belfast, N.I. m. 14 March 1959 (w.): 1d., 1s.*
Education: 1935–39 St. George's Prim. Sch., Belfast; 1939–44 Southwell Sch. for Boys, Downpatrick, N.I.; 1944–49 Belfast Technical Coll.; 1966–70 Manchester; 1973–76 Leeds; 1954–58 Hartley Victoria. *Appointments:* 1958–60 Castletown, I.O.M.; 1960–66 Crewe; 1966–72 Headingley; 1972–83 Burslem Mission; 1983– Blackpool South.
Connexional Committees: 1968–72 Social Responsibility. *Local Council Committees:* 1975–83 Education Committee, Staffs. County Council.
Special Interests: Education, Evanglism, Youth Groups. *Hobbies and Recreations:* Athletics, Stamp Collecting, House Building.

KIRKWOOD, Alexander Cameron, 9 The Mead, Darlington, Co. Durham DL1 1EU. (0325 62769) *b. 21 March 1952, Scarborough, North Yorkshire. m.*
Education: 1957–63 Barrowcliff Jun. Sch., Scarborough; 1963–68 Scalby County Secondary Modern, Scarborough; 1968–70 Scarborough Coll. of Technical Education; 1975–76 Cliff Coll.; 1977–80 Wesley Coll., Bristol. *Appointments:* 1981– Darlington.
Special Interests: European Methodism, World Development.
Hobbies and Recreations: Reading, Walking, Badminton, Travelling.

KISSACK, Reginald, Borodaill, Glen Mooar, Kirk Michael, Isle of Man. (0624 87298)–MA, BD. *b. 4 Sept 1910, Liverpool. m. 29 July 1938: 1d., 1s.*
Education: 1921–29 Liverpool Collegiate Sch.; 1929–33 Trinity Hall, Cambs.; 1933–35 Richmond.
Appointments: 1935–38 Chaplain, Westminster Coll.; 1938–41 Bolton, Wesley; 1941–46 Chaplain H.M.F.; 1946–52 Oxford; 1952–55 Leeds, Brunswick; 1955–63 Italy Dt; 1963–65 Colwyn Bay; 1965–75 Chairman Liverpool District.
Connexional Committees: 1939–41 Youth; 1947–63 World Methodism; 1965–75 Home Missions, Education, Property. *Publications: The Clue to Rome* (1959); *Spotlight on John Wesley* (1962); *Church or no Church* (1964); *Methodists in Italy* (1961).
Special Interests: Methodist History.
Hobbies and Recreations: Genealogy.

KITCHING, Robert Jackson, 23 Almond Brook Rd., Standish, Near Wigan, WN6 0TB. (0257 421299)–MA(B'ham.), BA(Manchester). *b. 10 July 1944, Fulwood, Preston, Lancashire. m. 28 June 1969: 2s.*
Education: 1949–55 Fulwood and Cadley Co. Prim. Sch.; 1955–62 Hutton Grammar Sch.; 1962–65 Didsbury Coll. of Education; 1971–74 Manchester Univ.; 1974–76 Birmingham Univ.; 1971–74 Hartley Victoria. *Appointments:* 1974–79 Tipton; 1979– Wigan.
Special Interests: Methodist History.
Hobbies and Recreations: Gardening, Walking, Philately.

KNAPP, Gresham S. B., Langholem, Arwenack Ave., Falmouth, Cornwall TR11 3LD. (0326 311134) *b. 1 Jan 1903, Otley, Yorkshire. m. 17 Aug 1933.*
Education: 1913–19 Kingswood Sch., Bath; 1921–24 Birmingham Univ.; 1919–20 Cliff Coll.; 1921–24 Handsworth. *Appointments:* 1920–24 Darwen; 1924–28 Marlborough; 1928–30 Watford; 1930–32 Oxford; 1932–35 Shepton Mallet; 1935–39 Wilts Mission; 1939–42 Chesterfield; 1942–46 Chaplain H.M.F.; 1946–51

Sirhowy Valley; 1951–53 Swinton; 1953–57 Wimborne; 1957–62 Aylsham; 1962–65 Rhymney Valley.

KNIGHTON, Donald George, 110 Langleys Rd., Selly Oak, Birmingham B29 6HT. (021 472 0960)–BA(Oxford), MA(Oxford), BA(Cambridge). *b. 20 June 1932, Penarth, South Glamorgan. m. 23 July 1960: 1d., 2s.*
Education: Victoria Prim. Sch., Penarth; Westbourne House Sch., Penarth; Penarth County Grammar Sch.; Kingswood Sch., Bath; 1952–55 Oriel Coll., Univ. of Oxford; 1957–59 Fitzwilliam House, Univ. of Cambridge; 1957–59 Wesley House.
Appointments: 1959–63 Oxford (assistant at Wesley Memorial Church) and Student Christian Movement Staff Secretary; 1963–68 Worcester; 1968–74 Wimbledon; 1974– Birmingham South West.
Connexional Committees: 1971– Connexional Candidates' Committee as Member and Group Secretary.
Local Council Committees: School Managership and Governorships; Chairman and Member of Selly Oak Redevelopment Group; Member of West Midlands Rent Assessment Panel.
Special Interests: Church History, Pastoral Theology, Community Development. *Hobbies and Recreations:* Reading, Walking, Gardening.

KNOTT, Wilfred Charles, 47 Polwithen Drive, Carbis Bay, St. Ives, Cornwall TR26 2SP. (0736 797017) *b. 15 Aug 1897, Copenhagen. m. 25 Jan 1922 (w.): 1d., 1s.*
Appointments; 1957–58 Bristol, South Gloucester; 1958–62 Sleaford; 1962–63 St. Columb and Padstow.

KNOWLES, George William Sudell, 28 Lower Greenfield, Ingol, Preston, Lancs. PR2 3ZU. (0772 733496)–MA(Oxon), MA(Cantab). *b. 5 Oct 1927. Lea, Preston. m. 23 July 1956: 1d., 1s.*
Education: 1938–45 Kirkham Grammar Sch.; 1948–51 St. John's Coll.; 1954–55 Göttingen Univ.; 1951–54 Wesley House.
Appointments: 1955–56 West Bromwich, Wesley; 1956–62 Church of South India; 1962–68 Blackburn, Trinity; 1968–73 Blackpool North; 1973–74 Ivory Coast Dist.; 1974–76 Benin Dist.; 1976–80 Clitheroe; 1980– North Lancs. District, Chairman.
Connexional Committees; 1965–70 Central Committee of MMS; 1980– General Purposes: 1980– Home Mission Board; 1980– Stationing Committee.
Special Interests: The World Church, European Languages and Culture.
Hobbies and Recreations: Gardening.

KNOWLES, S. Dugdale, 49 Queen St., Peterhead, Aberdeenshire AB4 6TU. (0779 3671) *b. Hellifield, Yorkshire. m. 8 Aug 1956: 2d.*
Education: Sawley, Nr. Clitheroe Council Sch.; Ribblesdale Senior Sch., Clitheroe, Lancs.; 1949–50 Cliff Coll., Derbyshire; 1951–54 Hartley Victoria, Manchester.
Appointments: 1950–51 Buckingham and Brackley; 1954–55 Ledbury; 1955–56 Whitehaven; 1956–59 Haworth and Oakworth; 1959–63 Derby, Derwent; 1963–66 Macclesfield; 1966–71 South Craven; 1971–74 Southport; 1974–78 Spen Valley; 1978– North of Scotland Mission.

KNOWLES-BERRY, Janet Myra, 71 Meadway St., St. Austell, Cornwall PL25 5AE. (0726 3858) *b. Stockport, Cheshire. m. 2s.*
Education: Wesley Coll., Bristol.
Appointments: 1981– St. Austell.
Hobbies and Recreations. Dog Breeding and Showing.

KRESCHNAK, Helmut Frieder, The Manse, Moorland View, Newton Abbot, Devon TQ12 4EW. (0626 66744) *b. 8 July 1952, Chemnitz, East Germany. m. 31 July 1975.*
Education: 1959–63 Pestalozzi Schule; 1963–72 Helmholtz-Gymnasium; 1972–80 Heidelberg Univ.; 1980–81 Wesley House, Cambridge. *Appointments:* 1981– Newton Abbot.
Hobbies and Recreations: Basketball, Writing Letters, Reading.

KYNASTON, David, 7 Marlborough Rd., Parkstone, Poole BH14 0HJ. (0202 741479) *b. 4 May 1926, Manchester, Lancashire. m. 25 March 1950: 2d., 2s.*
Education: 1931–38 Primary, Abbey Hey, Gorton, Manchester; 1939–44 Secondary, Ardwick Central, Manchester; 1956–59 Hartley Victoria. *Appointments:* 1959–65 Zimbabwe; 1965–70 Manchester, Chorlton and Moss Side; 1970–73 Sale; 1973–80 Oxford; 1980– Poole.
Connexional Committees: 1966–70 Overseas Division, General Committee.
Hobbies and Recreations: Music and Handicrafts.

LACY, Harold Edward, 53 Cocknage Rd., Longton ST3 4NZ. (0782 319106)–BA. *b. 25 July 1936, York. m. 16 April 1960: 1d., 1s.*
Education: 1941–45 Knavesmire Prim., York; 1945–54 Archbishop Holgates Grammar, York; 1973–77 Open Univ.; 1958–62 Headingley.
Appointments: 1962–67 Selby; 1967–70 Midsomer Norton; 1970–78 Redhill and East Grinstead; 1978– Longton Mission.
Connexional Committees: 1980– Home Missions Board. *Council Member:* 1963–66 Derwent R.D.C.
Special Interests: Wesley Church Growth. *Hobbies and Recreations:* Walking, Gardening, Philately.

LACY, John Cyril, 14 Green Lane, Leeds, W. Yorkshire LS16 7LP. (0532 677508)–BA(Leeds). *b. 4 July 1943, York. m. 7 Aug 1965: 2d., 1s.*
Education: –1962 St. Peter's Sch., York; Tang Hall county Prim. Sch., York; 1963–66 Leeds Univ.; 1968–69 San Francisco Theol. Seminary, San Anselmo, California, U.S.A.; 1966–68 Richmond Coll. *Appointments:* 1969–72 Wakefield; 1972–79 Sheffield N.E.; 1980– Leeds, Headingley.
Special Interests: Psychotherapy, Counselling. *Hobbies and Recreations:* Sport, Music, Camping, Walking.

LADLOW, Clifford Oswald, 14 Ashdown Close, Sticker, St. Austell, Cornwall PL26 7EU. (0726 63056)

b. 16 June 1906, Lincoln. m. 8 Aug 1934: 1d., 2s.
Education: 1918–22 Firth Park Grammar Sch., Sheffield; 1928–31 Didsbury. *Appointments:* 1927–28 Helston; 1931–34 London Mission, Poplar and Bow; 1934–37 London Mission, Tooting; 1937–46 Liverpool Mission; 1946–54 Plymouth and Devonport Mission; 1954–58 Rotherham, Eastwood Mission; 1958–63 Blackpool South; 1963–68 Newquay; 1968–73 Bideford.
Connexional Committees: Home Mission, General Purposes, Stationing, during the 2 years when Chairman of Plymouth District 1952–54.
Special Interests: Recording for Cornwall Tapes for the Handicapped Association.

LAIDLER, Robert David, 15 Wortley Rd., Highcliffe, Christchurch, Dorset BH23 5DR. (042 52 72796) *b. 2 June 1942, Gillsand, Cumberland. m. 21 June 1969: 2d., 1s.*
Education: 1947–53 Pendower Prim./Jun., Newcastle upon Tyne; 1953–58 Rutherford Grammar, Newcastle upon Tyne; 1965–69 Handsworth. *Appointments:* 1969–71 Bradford Mission; 1971–76 Newbury and Hungerford; 1976–81 Poole; 1981– Christchurch and Lymington.
Connexional Committees: 1976–80 Division Board, Division of Education and Youth. *Council Member:* 1972–75 Aldbourne Parish Council.
Hobbies and Recreations; Walking, Swimming, General Reading, Decorating Manses.

LAIRD, Ian, 1 Pleydell Crescent, Sturry, Nr. Canterbury, Kent. (0227 711329) *b. 24 Oct 1938, Middlesbrough. m. 16 June 1962: 2d., 1s.*
Education: 1950–55 Middlesbrough High Sch.; 1973–75 Christ Church College, Canterbury; 1965–67 Headingley; 1967–68 Bristol.
Appointments: 1968–73 Canterbury and Faversham; 1973–78 Resigned; 1978–82 Teacher, Sturry C.E. Prim. Sch.; 1982– Head of English Herme CE Prim. Sch.
Special Interests: Education and Youth Work. *Hobbies and Recreations:* Archery, Music, Children's Drama.

LAKE, Ronald Frederick, 14 Park Rd., Alverstoke, Gosport, Hants. PO12 1HH. (07017 26376) *b. 13 Dec 1910, Ryde, Isle of Wight. m. 9 Jan 1936: 3d.*
Education: –1925 Ryde Senior Council; 1945–47 Handsworth.
Appointments: 1947–52 St. Columb and Padstow; 1952–60 Basingstoke; 1960–69 Gosport and Fareham; 1969–76 Eastleigh.
Hobbies and Recreations: Walking, Cycling, Gardening.

LAKE, William Colin Wallace, Wesley Manse, Middleton Rd., Pickering, N. Yorks. YO18 8AL. (0751 72810)–MA(Oxon), BD(Lond.). *b. 4 July 1932, Sidborough, Nr. Tiverton, Devon. m. 26 July 1958: 1d., 1s.*
Education: 1943–44 Exmouth Grammar; 1944–50 Queen Elizabeth's, Crediton; 1952–55 Exeter Coll., Oxford Univ.; 1955–58 Richmond Coll. *Appointments:* 1958–61 Helmsley; 1961–66 Otley; 1966–73 Hull East; 1973– Pickering.
Special Interests: Church History, Politics, Renewal. *Hobbies and Recreations:* Gardening, Walking.

LAKE, William Henry, 12 Riversway, Gargrave, Skipton, North Yorkshire BD23 3NR. (075 678366) *b. 8 June 1908, Hull. Education:* 1928–29 Cliff Coll.; 1931–34 Headingley. *Appointments:* 1930–31 Ledbury; 1934–38 Nottingham, Tennyson St. and Central; 1938–41 Gainsborough; 1941–45 Worksop; 1945–50 Bolton Mission; 1950–56 Walsall Mission; 1956–66 Hull Mission; 1966–74 Bolton Mission; 1974–78 Skipton.
Connexional Committees: Home Mission General; Home Mission Executive; Central Missions Com.

LAKIN, John A., 87 Queens Rd., Ashford, Kent TN24 8HD. (0233 21216) *b. 15 Nov 1925. m.*
Education: 1950–53 Handsworth.
Appointments: 1953–57 Gold Coast Dt; 1957–61 Ghana Dt; 1961–65 Oswestry; 1965–70 Walsall; 1970–72 Tavistock; 1972–81 Week St. Mary; 1981 Ashford, Kent.

LAKING, John Evans, Ashton House, 4 West St., Ryde, I.O.W. PO33 2NN. *b. 12 Nov 1902, Morecambe. w: 1s.*
Education: 1924–27 Hartley.
Appointments: 1927–31 Bottesford; 1931–34 Loughborough; 1934–35 Nottingham, Mayfield Grove; 1935–38 Nottingham South; 1938–42 Sheffield, Brunswick; 1942–50 Macclesfield; 1950–55 Birmingham, Smethwick; 1955–60 Fleetwood; 1960–68 Middleton.
Local Council Committees: 1953–55 Smethwick Education Committee.

LAMBRICK, Lawrence Richard, 12 Highfield Rd., Bollington, Nr. Macclesfield, Cheshire SK10 5LR. (0625 72259)–BSc. *b. 29 Jan 1933, Germiston, South Africa. m. 5 April 1958: 3d., 1s.*
Education: 1946–50 Mansfield High Sch., Durban, South Africa; 1952–54 Univ. of Natal, South Africa; 1976–78 Wesley Coll., Bristol. *Appointments:* 1978– Macclesfield.
Special Interests: Crisis Counselling, Experience-centred Education.
Hobbies and Recreations: Art.

LAMMING, Stanley Kenton, 25 Marine Rd., Penrhyn Bay, Llandudno, Gwynedd LL30 3NA. (0782 49825)–BA(B'ham). *b. 21 Sept 1897, York. m. 26 Oct 1930: 1d.*
Education: 1902–10 York Priory St. Wesleyan Sch.; 1910–14 Archbishop Holgate's Grammar Sch.; 1923–26 Birmingham Univ.; 1923–26 Handsworth. *Appointments:* 1926–35 China, Hunan and Hupeh Dt; 1935–38 Weardale; 1938–44 Sheffield, Norfolk; 1944–50 North Shields; 1950–55 Stoke on Trent; 1955–59 Helston; 1959–63 Stockport, Tivot Wale.
Local Council Committees: 1945–50 Northumberland Education Committee.
Special Interests: The Ecumenical Movement. *Hobbies and Recreations:* Reading, Bowls.

LAMPARD, John Stuart, 4 Gorse Avenue, Worthing, W. Sussex BN14 9PG. (0903 60356)—BA, MTh. *b. 24 June 1942, London. m. 3 Aug 1968: 1d., 1s.*
Education: 1955–60 The Leys Sch.; 1966–69 Bristol; 1969–70 Phillips, Okla, U.S.A.; Didsbury, Bristol.
Appointments: 1970–76 Leeds, Headingley; 1976–81 Lytham St. Annes; 1981– Worthing.
Publications: Look at Your Church (Epworth 1975).

LANCASTER, Peter Fred Lawson, 33 Firth Park Ave., Firth Park, Sheffield S5 6HF. (0742 386202)—BA(Leeds). *b. 26 Jan 1934, York. m. 12 June 1982.*
Education: 1947–53 Easingwold Grammar Sch.; 1956–60 Leeds Univ.; 1956–60 Headingley.
Appointments: 1960–65 Birstall and Birkenshaw; 1965–69 Bacup; 1969–72 Morecambe; 1972–79 Wakefield; 1979– Sheffield North East; Chaplain to 7 Mayors in various appointments; 1972–79 Chaplain to H.M. Prison, Wakefield; Member of Managing Bodies of Local Schs., inc. Chairman of Chaplain BB/GB 1979–. *Council Member:* 1962–65 Secretary, Bradford F.K.; 1966–69 President of Whitworth Valley Council of Churches; 1972–78 Wakefield Council of Churches; 1979– Firth Park Council of Churches, President Designate. *Local Council Committees:* 1974–79 Member of Radio Leeds, Religious Broadcasting Team; 1965–69 Secretary, Ministers Fraternal, Bacup.
Special Interests: Evangelism, Youth Work, Work Amongst Elderly.
Hobbies and Recreations: Sport.

LANDER, Derrick Rodney, 37 Ivy Rd., Poynton, Stockport, Cheshire SK12 1PE. (0625 872378) *b. 1 Nov 1948, Sheffield. m. 4 Dec 1971: 1d., 1s.*
Education: 1969–71 Cliff Coll.; 1974–78 Wesley, Bristol.
Appointments: 1978– Hazel Grove and Poynton.
Special Interests: Social Studies, Politics, Music. *Hobbies and Recreations:* Sport, Squash, Football, Cricket, Drama.

LANE, Peter Gerald, The Farmhouse, Rue du Catillon, St. Peters, Guernsey, Channel Islands. (0481 65100)—BA. *b. 6 July 1935, Gloucester. m. 29 July 1961: 2d., 1s.*
Education: 1940–43 Longlevens County Prim. Sch., Gloucester; 1943–54 Crypt Grammar Sch., Gloucester; 1954–58 Sheffield Univ.; 1958–61 Bristol Univ.; 1958–61 Didsbury, Bristol., *Appointments:* 1961–63 Dursley and Stonehouse; 1963–69 Stafford; 1969–71 Wantage and Abingdon; 1971–80 Chaplain and Housemaster at Elizabeth Coll., Guernsey; 1980– Headmaster, St. Peter Port Secondary Sch., Guernsey.
Connexional Committees: 1963–65 Connexional Local Preachers; 1965–69 Connexional Youth Committee; 1971– Connexional Committee for Formal Education.
Special Interests: Education. *Hobbies and Recreations:* Hockey, Tennis.

LANE, Stephen Lawrence, 11 Collins Ave., North Shore, Blackpool FY2 0NS. (0253 591119) *b. 20 Feb 1901, Sporle, Norfolk. m. 1 July 1926: 1d.*
Education: Hammonds Grammar Sch., Swaffham; 1921–23 Hartley Victoria. *Appointments:* 1920–21 Wisbech; 1923–24 Enfield; 1924–26 Chesterfield; 1926–29 Morley; 1929–32 Rhondda; 1932–35 Newport; 1935–38 Burnley; 1938–48 Kineton; 1948–51 Pendlebury; 1951–58 Southport Bank and Hesketh Bank; 1958–67 Stour Valley Mission.
Hobbies and Recreations: Gardening, Walking.

LANG, Derek, 11 High St., Metheringham, Lincoln LN4 3EA. (0526 20280)—BSc(Lond.), MA(Cantab) *b. 2 March 1950, Wheatley Hill, Durham. m. 14 Aug 1971: 2d.*
Education: 1961–66 Luton County Secondary Technical; 1966–68 Luton Sixth Form Coll.; 1968–72 Luton Coll. of Technology; 1975–78 Wesley House. *Appointments:* 1978 Sleaford.
Hobbies and Recreations: Model Boats.

LANGHAM, Harold Winston, 22 22 Coxwell St., Faringdon, Oxon SN7 7HA. (0367 21318) *b. 20 May 1911, Fardingdon. m. 3 Aug 1940: 1s.*
Education: 1919–23 Faringdon Council Sch.; 1923–28 King Alfred's Sch., Wantage; 1933–37 Headingley.
Appointments: 1937–39 York Wesley; 1939–42 Cardiff, Wesley; 1942–46 R.A.F. Chaplain; 1946–49 Helmsley; 1949–56 Leicester South; 1956–64 Leicester North; 1964–76 Ormskirk, Lancs.; 1976–79 Banbury; 1956–63 Secretary of Oxford and Leicester District.
Connexional Committees: 1952–56 Local Preachers. *Council Member:* 1954–62 Leicester Christian Industrial Council; 1967–72 Liverpool District Redevelopment Committee. *Local Council Committees:* 1957–58 President Leicester F.E.C.; 1958 Lord Mayor's Chaplain; 1971–76 Chairman U.N.A., Ormskirk.
Special Interests: Environmental Problems, CND, National Society for Abolition of Factory Farming.
Hobbies and Recreations: Gardening, Cycling, Walking, Climbing.

LANGLEY, Michael, 23 Broomfield Lane, Palmers Green, London N13 4HB. (01 886 0978)—BD(Lond.), ThM(Austin, U.S.A.). *b. 19 March 1940, Irthlingborough, Northamptonshire. m. 23 July 1966: 1d., 3s.*
Education: Wellingborough G.S.; 1963–64 World Council of Churches Scholarship to Austin Theological Seminary, Austin, U.S.A.; 1960–63 Richmond. *Appointments:* 1963–64 Austin, U.S.A.; 1964–66 Leigh-on-Sea; 1966–69 Leicester North; 1969–74 Cardiff, Roath; 1974–82 Reading; 1982– London, Finsbury Park and Southgate.
Connexional Committees: 1971–74 Property Board.
Hobbies and Recreations: Philately, Sport.

LANNIGAN, Henry Charles Carver, 12 Meadowhead Rd., Plains, Airdrie, Lanarkshire ML6 7JF. (0236 842702)—MC, TD, MA, BD. *b. 27 Nov 1916, Wishaw, Lanarkshire. m.*

19 Sept 1945: 3s.
Education: 1922–29 Wishaw Academy; 1929–35 Wishaw High; 1935–39 Glasgow Univ.; 1939–42 Manchester Univ.; 1939–42 Hartley Victoria. *Appointments:* 1942–47 Chaplain H.M.F.; 1947–51 Stoke-on-Trent, Stoke; 1951–57 Coatbridge and Airdrie; 1957–63 Grimsby Mission; 1963–69 Sheffield, Carver St.; 1969–74 Sale; 1974–81 Airdrie and Armdale.
Connexional Committees: Royal Navy, Army and Air Force Board.
Council Member: 1981– Secretary Plains Community Council.
Special Interests: Community Affairs, 1947–68 Territorial Army. *Hobbies and Recreations:* Gardening, Cooking.

LANSDOWN, Dennis Frank, Chelwood, Grenadier Rd., Ash Vale, Surrey GU12 5DT. (0252 319340) *b. 23 May 1904, Bristol. m. 19 July 1931: 1d., 2s.*
Education: 1915–19 St. George Secondary; 1924–27 Handsworth.
Appointments: 1927–48 Sri Lanka; 1948–51 Shepton Mallet; 1951–60 Birmingham, Islington; 1960–67 Coventry.

LANSLEY, Douglas, 27 Park Lane, Cottingham, N. Humberside HU16 5RH. (0482 844716)—BA(Lond.). *b. 5 Sept 1910, London. m. 21 April 1938: 1d., 1s.*
Education: 1921–28 Univ. Coll. Sch., Hampstead; 1928–31 King's Coll., London; 1932–35 Richmond.
Appointments: 1931–32 Bodmin; 1935–37 Hull Kingston; 1937–39 Blackheath, London; 1939–40 Liverpool, Brunswick; 1940–45 Littleborough; 1945–49 London, Walthamstow; 1949–55 Hinckley; 1955–61 Cleethorpes, Trinity; 1961–67 Teddington; 1967–71 Rotherham; 1971–75 Ripon.
Connexional Committees: 1950–61 Connexional Youth Council.

LANSLEY, Raymond Alan Herbert, 14 Ramsey Close, Shepherd's Way, Brookmans Park, Hatfield, Herts. AL9 6NP. (0707 58380)—BD. *b. 20 Jan 1936, Wanstead, Essex. m. 8 July 1961: 2s.*
Education: 1947–55 Kingswood Sch., Bath; 1958–62 London Univ.; 1970–71 Westminster Coll., Oxford; 1979–81 Sch. of Education, Univ. of Bristol; 1958–62 Richmond.
Appointments: 1962–64 Nottingham West; 1964–67 Birmingham, Smethwick; 1967–71 Aylesbury; 1972–75 Head of Religious Studies at the Grange County Secondary Sch., Aylesbury; 1975–82 Chaplain and Head of Religious Studies at City of Bath Technical Coll.; 1982– Chaplain and Head of Religious Studies at Queenswood Sch., Brookmans Park, Hatfield.

LAPWORTH, David Clifford, 39 Wormald St., Almondbury, Huddersfield, W. Yorks. HD5 8NQ. (0484 23574) *b. 28 June 1939, Birmingham. m. 23 June 1962: 1d., 1s.*
Education: 1951–55 Handsworth Technical Sch.; 1960–64 Didsbury, Bristol. *Appointments:* 1964–66 Canterbury and Faversham; 1966–73 Medway Towns; 1973–80 Richmond and Hounslow; 1980– Huddersfield E.
Connexional Committees: 1968–72 Social Responsibility.

LARKINSON, Roger Charles, 2 Belle Vue Rd., Cinderford, Glos. GL14 2AB. (0594 22229)—MA(Cantab) *b. 25 July 1945, Bedford. m. 8 Aug 1970: 1d., 2s.*
Education: 1950–56 Benson Prim Sch., Shirley, Croydon; 1956–63 Trinity Sch. of John Whitgift, Croydon; 1964–67 St. Catharine's Coll., Cambridge; 1967–70 Wesley House. *Appointments:* 1970–73 Birkenhead; 1973–77 Leeds West; 1977–81 Sierra Leone Dt; 1981– Forest of Dean.
Publications: (Forthcoming) Two articles in the NT introductory section of a forthcoming African Bible Commentary, i. *The Background to the NT in the Graeco-Roman World,* ii. *The NT and Pagan Religious Movements; Paper on The Church's Contribution to National Development; Biblical Aspects 1982.*
Special Interests: Languages, NT Study, Worship. *Hobbies and Recreations:* Photography, Listening to Music, Cycling in course of duties.

LARTER, Laurence, Woodbank, Hollybank Rd., Hook Heath, Woking, Surrey GU22 0JP. (04862-73404) *b. 22 Sept 1901, Hull. m. 4 July 1931: 2d., 1s.*
Education: 1924–27 Hartley Coll.
Appointments: 1927–31 London Mission East; 1931–33 York; 1933–36 Helmsley; 1936–40 Thirsk; 1940–45 Batley; 1945–49 Leeds, Rothwell and Normanton; 1949–55 Leeds, Richmond Hill; 1955–63 Pately Bridge; 1963–68 Northallerton.
Connexional Committees: 1940 Local Preachers.
Special Interests: Colour Problem, Missionary Overseas.

LAUNDER, George Henry, Langholme Methodist Home for the Aged, Arwenack Ave., Falmouth, Cornwall TR11 3LD. (0326 311134). *b. 13 March 1908, Redruth, Cornwall.*
Education: 1931–34 Headingley.
Appointments: 1934–48 Trichinopoly Dt., India; 1948–78 Church of South India.

LAVENDER, David Frank, 9 The Peth, Durham DH1 4PZ. (0385 48755)—MA(Oxon and Cantab). *b. 18 Oct 1951. m. 31 July 1976: 1d.*
Education: Great Yarmouth Grammar Sch.; 1970–74 University Coll., Oxford; 1974–77 Wesley House. *Appointments:* 1977–81 Bilston; 1981– Durham and Deerness Valley; 1981– Methodist Chaplain for Univ. of Durham; 1981– Chaplain St. Mary's Coll., Univ. of Durham.
Connexional committees: 1982 Board of Division of Education and Youth.

LAWRENCE, David, 9 Spindle Close, Kidderminster DY11 5DX. (0562 3300) *b. 15 May 1924, Watford, Herts. m. 8 Aug 1953; 2s.*
Education: 1934–41 Watford Grammar Sch.; 1946–47 Cliff Coll.; 1947–49 Hartley Victoria.
Appointments: 1949–51 Huntingdon Mission; 1951–57 Nigeria and Fernando Poo; 1957–61 East Wight;

1961–68 Newmarket; 1968–73 Diss; 1973–79 Norwich; 1979– Kidderminster.
Connexional Committees: 1962–69, 1975–79 Overseas Missions.
Special Interests: Church Growth, Holy Spirit Renewal. *Hobbies and Recreations:* Photography, Caravan Club.

LAWRENCE, George Edward, Westbury, Upper Rd., Pillowell, Nr. Lydney, Glos. GL15 4QZ. *b. 15 Jan 1903, York. m. 27 Aug 1936: 2s.*
Education: Haughton Sch., St. Saviourgate, York; 1922 Cliff Coll.; 1924–27 Didsbury. *Appointments:* 1927–29 Cinderford; 1929–36 Leeward Islands, Nevis and Anguilla; 1936–46 Montserrat; 1946–50 Smethwick, Regent St.; 1950–56 Chichester and Bognor; 1956–62 Budleigh Salterton; 1962–68 Bristol, Bedminster.
Connexional Committees: 1955 M.M.S. Western Committee.
Publications: Wesley of the West Indies (1938); *Thomas O'Garra–West Indian Local Preacher* (1956); Several Pamphlets, Typescripts *Netherlands and Methodism; Montserrat its Methodism* (1967); *Anguilla Methodist Caribbeana; Hartwell of Haiti; Circles of Opportunity* (1977); *Faith and Works of Van Gogh* (1975); *Methodism of Vincent Van Gogh* (1979).
Hobbies and Recreations: Methodist History, Art.

LAWRENCE, Henry Jesse, Tegwani, 6B Lancaster Gardens, Beltinge, Herne Bay, Kent CT6 6PU. (022 73 3308)–BD. *b. 16 Nov 1902, Banbury. m. 1. 19 Aug 1931 (died); 2. 25 May 1972: 3d.*
Education: Tewkesbury; 1925–28 Handsworth Coll. *Appointments:* 1924–25 Evesham; 1925–28 Handsworth Coll.; 1928–31 Calcutta English; 1931–33 Ticehurst; 1933–37 London, Clapton; 1937–39 Manningtree and Harwich; 1939–45 Chaplain H.M.F.; 1945–49 East Wight; 1949–53 Colchester; 1953–65 Chairman General Superintendent, Southern Rhodesia District; 1965–66 Glasgow, Cathcart Rd.

Connexional Committees: 1953–68 Methodist Missionary Society; General Committee.
Hobbies and Recreations: Photography, Gardening.

LAWRENCE, Walter, 10 Lyndhurst, Bent Lane, Sutton-in-Craven, Keighley, W. Yorks. BD20 7AL. (0535 32767) *b. 27 June 1916, Kirkby in Lonsdale. m. 21 Sept 1939: 1d., 1s.*
Education: 1921–26 Grayrigg, Westmorland; 1926–30 Kendal Green Elem. Sch.; 1935–36 Cliff Coll.; 1949–51 Headingley.
Appointments: 1951–53 Thornley; 1953–58 Rochdale North; 1958–63 Manchester Mission; 1963–70 Portsmouth Mission, Eastney Central Hall and Chaplain to the Royal Marines; 1970–77 Loftus and Staithes; 1977–81 Ryton and Prudhoe.

LAWRY, Stanley Kenneth, Grosvenor Manse, Grosvenor St., Mold, Clwyd CH7 1EJ. (0352 3051)–MA(Cantab). *b. 26 April 1922, Plymouth. m. 10 Aug 1950: 3d., 2s.*
Education; 1927–30 Gunnerside Sch., Plymouth; 1930–41 Plymouth Coll., 1941–2, 1945–47 Emmanuel Coll., Cambridge; 1947–48 Cambridge Department of Education; 1948–49 Univ. of North Carolina, U.S.A.; 1979–80 Hartley Victoria.
Appointments: 1979– Buckley and Deeside.
Special Interests: Education, Child Care, Politics. *Hobbies and Recreations:* Reading, Gardening, Sport, Choral Singing, Travel.

LAWSON, Alfred, 28 Broomfield Grove, Rotherham S60 2SY. (0709 2306)–Dip Theol(Lond.). *b. 11 March 1927, Chester. m. 6 April 1957: 3d., 2s.*
Education: 1932–38 Hoole and Newton, Chester; 1938–41 Love St. Central Sch., Chester; 1948–49 Cliff Coll.; 1951–54 Richmond Coll.; 1954–55 Selly Oak, St. Andrews Missionary Coll. *Appointments:* 1955–61 Agbani, Eastern Nigeria; 1961–66 Elland; 1966–71 Hull Mission; 1971–78 Hillingdon; 1978– Rotherham.

Special Interests: Wesleyana. *Hobbies and Recreations:* People, Soul Winning.

LAWSON, John, 229 Exwick Rd., Exeter, Devon EX4 2AT. (0392 58908)–BSc(Lond.), MA(Cantab), BD(Cantab). *b. 16 July 1909, Leeds. m. 30 July 1936: 1d., 1s.*
Education: 1921–26 Nottingham High Sch.; 1927–30 Midland Agricultural Coll., Sutton Bonington; 1932–35 Wesley House.
Appointments: 1931–32 Belper; 1936–38 H.M.Comm.; 1938–40 Liverpool, Anfield; 1940–45 Grantham; 1945–48 Lincoln, Wesley; 1948–50 Liverpool, Waterloo; 1950–55 Downham Market; 1955–76 Candler Sch. of Theol., Emory Univ., Atlanta, Georgia, U.S.A.
Connexional Committees: 1940–55 Connexional Local Preachers' Committee. *Publications: Green and Pleasant Land* (S.C.M. 1955); *Contribution to History of the Methodist Church in Great Britain, vol. 1* (Epworth 1967); *Historical and Theological Introduction to the Apostolic Fathers* (Macmillan U.S. 1961); *Christian Year with Charles Wesley* (Epworth 1967); *Comprehensive Handbook of Christian Doctrine* (Prentice-Hall 1967); *An Evangelical Faith for Today* (Abingdon 1972); *Vote Labour, Why?* (Gollancz 1945); *Notes on Wesley's 44 Sermons* (Epworth 1946); *Biblical Theology of S. Irenaeus* (Epworth 1948); *Who Joins the Glorious Host?* (Epworth 1950); *What Do We Believe?* (S.P.C.K. 1951); *Full Communion with the Church of England* (S.P.C.K. 1951); *Study Notes on Christian Doctrine* (with A. Dale) (Epworth 1952); *Methodism and Catholicism* (S.P.C.K. 1954), *Selections from Wesley's Notes on New Testament* (Epworth 1955); *Man and his Needs* (Edinburgh House 1955).
Special Interests: Methodist History. *Hobbies and Recreations:* Gardening.

LAWTON, Arthur John, 54 Coventry Rd., Market Harborough, Leics. LE16 9BZ. (0858 62889)–

BD(Lond.). *b. 19 June 1926, Wolstanton, Staffordshire. m. 29 March 1952: 2s.*
Education: 1937–44 Newcastle-under-Lyme High Sch.; 1948–51 Headingley. *Appointments:* 1951–52 Kimberley; 1952–57 Nottingham South; 1957–62 Bradford, Manningham; 1962–68 Rhyl and Prestatyn; 1968–73 Colwyn Bay and Llandudno; 1973–78 Truro; 1978– Market Harborough.'
Special Interests: Bible Studies. *Hobbies and Recreations:* Literature, Sport.

LAWTON, James Kenneth, Arbits, 17 Old Oak Ave., Chipstead, Coulsdon, Surrey CR3 3PG. (073 75 53429) *b. 13 Aug 1918, Moston, Manchester. m. 31 July 1949: 1d., 1s.*
Education: 1929–33 Cheadle Hulme Sch.; 1946–49 Headingley.
Appointments: 1945–46 Hurst and Hyde; 1946–49 Headingley Coll.; 1949–52 Cardiff, Wesley; 1952–54 Ashton under Lyme; 1954–61 Bolton, Bridge St.; 1961–63 Walsall Mission; 1963–68 British Council of Churches; 1968–71 Huddersfield Mission; 1971–76 Romiley; 1976–77 Liverpool North; 1977 Gen Sec. Churches Council on Alcohol and Drugs.
Connexional Committees: 1958–82 Christian Citizenship Dept.–Division of Social Responsibility; 1950 Methodist Peace Fellowship Executive; 1975–82 M.H.A. Housing Association. *Council Member:* 1963–68 British Council of Churches Staff Member; 1979–82 Free Church Federal Council–Consultant Member. *Local Council Committees:* 1961–63 Local Education Committee, Walsall; 1968–71 Huddersfield community Relations Council; 1970–71 Chairman; 1974–76 Stockport Community Health Council.
Publications: Mark '71 (1971); *The Sober Truth* (1979).
Special Interests: Ecumenical Mission and Outreach in the World Church, All Church and Society Issues–Housing, Penal Affairs, Health Matters, Social Psychology, Politics and Economics–Family Life, Social Psychiatry and Counselling. *Hobbies and Recreations:* Travel, Photography, Drama, Magic, Rotarian.

LAZENBY, Leslie, 24 Chamber Rd., Shaw, Oldham OL2 7AR. (0706 847393)–DFM. *b. 26 Feb 1921, Leeds. m. 5 Feb 1944: 1d., 1s.*
Education: 1955–57 Hartley Victoria. *Appointments:* 1957–60 Kirkby Stephen, Appleby and Tebay; 1960–63 Hastings; 1963–69 Bromley; 1969–74 Gravesend and Dartford; 1974–79 Jun. Supernumerary; 1979–82 St. Austell; 1982– Shaw and Royton.
Connexional Committees: 1961–66 Youth; 1966–74 London Mission. *Local Council Committees:* 1970–74 Gravesend Community Relations.
Special Interests: Mission, Healing. *Hobbies and Recreations:* Art, Sport.

LEACH, J. Derrick, 3 Cheltenham Drive, Sale, Cheshire M33 2DQ. (061 973 3613) *b. Bolton. m: 2d.*
Education: Tonge Fold Council Sch., Bolton; St. John's, Accrington; Accrington Grammar Sch.; Blackpool Grammar Sch.; 1953–56 Hartley Victoria. *Appointments:* 1956–59 Matlock; 1959–66 Ashfield; 1966–73 Preston, Trinity: 1973–80 Colwyn Bay; 1980– Sale.
Hobbies and Recreations: Photography, Walking, Books.

LEAH, Edward Barrie, Ivydene North Street, Barrow-upon-Humber, South Humberside. (0469 30264) *b. Church Accrington, Lancs. m. 11 July 1970: 1d., 1s.*
Education: 1947–55 Central Prep., Accrington; 1955–59 Padiham Secondary Technical, Sch.; 1959–62 Accrington Coll. of Further Education; 1962–63 Burnley Technical Coll.; 1966–67 Hartley Victoria. *Appointments:* 1970– Barton-upon-Humber.
Connexional Committees: Division of Ministries. *Council Member:* Barrow-on-Humber Parish Council. *Hobbies and Recreations:* Lapidary.

LEAR, Geoffrey James, 6 Chatsworth Rd., Morecambe, Lancashire LA4 4JQ. (0524 411879) *b. 7 July 1930, Stockport. m. 21 July 1956.*
Education: 1935–41 Alexandra Park Council Sch., Stockport; 1941–46 Stockport Sch.; 1950–53 Headingley. *Appointments:* 1953–56 Saddleworth; 1956–60 Shaw and Royton; 1960–67 Blyth and Seaton Delaval; 1967–75 North Shields and Whitley Bay; 1975– Morecambe and Heysham.
Connexional Committees: 1974– Connexional Probation's Oversight Committee; 1979– Division of Ministries Board.
Special Interests: Political History, Railways. *Hobbies and Recreations:* Railway Modelling.

LEARY, William, 52 St. Peter's Way, Mickle Trafford, Chester CH2 4EJ. (0244 300031)–BA(Manch.). *b. 5 Nov 1917, Tetney, Lincolnshire. m. 29 July 1948: 2s.*
Education: Humberston, Lincs.; 1962–64 Lincoln Diocesan Training Coll.; 1973–76 Open Univ.; 1945–47 Hartley Victoria. *Appointments:* 1947–48 South Petherton; 1948–52 Wath on Dearne; 1952–58 Sheffield North East; 1958–62 Lincoln North. *Connexional Committees:* 1952–58 Christian Citizenship; 1974–78 Education and Youth; 1968– Archives (1978– Connexional Archivist).
Publications: History of Methodism in Lincoln (1969); *History of Methodism in Boston* (1972); *History of Methodism in Louth* (1981); Many local centenary histories (1964–80); 4 George Eayrs History Prize Essays.
Special Interests: Methodist History, Stamp Collecting. *Hobbies and Recreations:* Snooker.

LEATHWOOD, Ronald Frederick, 5 Over Hall Drive, Winsford, Cheshire CW7 1EY. (060 65 3335) *b. 17 May 1934, Middlewich, Cheshire. m. 22 Dec 1962: 1d., 1s.*
Education: 1956–67 Cliff Coll.; 1959–63 Hartley Victoria.
Appointments: 1963–65 Cheadle, Staffs.; 1965–71 Whitchurch; 1971–74 Ilkeston; 1974–78 Buckley and Deeside; 1978– Winsford.
Hobbies and Recreations: Reading, Music, Photography, Railways.

LEDGARD, John Christopher, 2 Broad St., Bampton, Oxon OX8 2LS. (0993 850302)–BA(Open Univ.). *b. 3 June 1941, Huddersfield. m. 28 June 1965: 1 foster d., 3s.*
Education: 1945–52 Swainton CE Prim. Sch.; 1952–59 Scarborough High Sch. for Boys; 1972–76 (external) Open Univ.; 1979– (external) Univ. Coll. of Wales, Cardiff, Faculty of Theol.; 1963–67 Headingley. *Appointments:* 1967–70 Lerwick, North Roe and North Isles; 1970– Chaplain, Royal Air Force. *Connexional Committees:* 1967–70 Youth Committee. *Publications: History of the Sherburn Methodist Circuit* (1969).
Special Interests: Working on Chaplaincy subject for MTh Degree, Methodist History. *Hobbies and Recreations:* Gardening, Railways.

LEE, Donald Rathbone, 12 Marshalswick Rd., St. Albans, Herts.–MBE, BD(Lond.). *b. 28 March 1911, Stockport, Cheshire. m. 11 June 1940: 3d., 2s.*
Education: 1916–22 Cheadle Heath Council Sch., Stockport; 1922–27 Stockport Grammar Sch.; 1934–38 External Student, London Univ.; 1931–35 Handsworth.
Appointments: 1935–36 Greenock, 1936–37 Runcorn, 1937–40 Edinburgh; 1940–42 Perth; 1942–47 Royal Army Chaplains' Department; 1947 Romford; 1947–51 Stockport, Trinity; 1951 Romford; 1952–57 Oxford; 1957–64 Worcester; 1964–68 Birmingham, Sutton Park; 1968–77 Chairman, Southampton District; 1977–82 Jersey; 1973–74 President of the Methodist Conference; 1975–76 Moderator, Free Church Federal Council.
Connexional Committees: 1968–74 Committee for Chapel Affairs, and as President-Designate, President, and Ex-President, all Connexional Committees; Former Member, Southlands Coll. Governing Body. *Council Member:* Free Church Federal Council; 1977–82 Jersey Council of Churches; 1978–80 President of same. *Local Council Committees:* 1935–82 apart from years as Army Chaplain and as Dist. Chairman, a member of all local Circuit and Church Committees.
Special Interests: All Ecumenical concerns and ventures, Church Music, Youth Work, member of Methodist Sacramental Fellowship and Methodist Church Music Society. *Hobbies and Recreations:* Music, Gardening, Ecumenical Travel.

LEE, Geoffrey, 14 Howard Rd., Yardley, Birmingham B25 8AL. (021 706 1004)–BSc, MSc. *b. 1 July 1928, Cleckheaton, West Yorkshire. m. 31 May 1952: 4d.*
Education: 1939–46 Whitcliffe Mount Grammar Sch., Cleckheaton; 1946–51 Univ. of Manchester; 1980–81 Wesley House, Cambridge.
Appointments: 1981– Birmingham, Elmdon.
Connexional Committees: 1952–55 and 1961–65 Independent Methodist Church, Connexional Committee Member. *Local Council Committees:* 1963–65 President, Cleckheaton Council of Churches.
Special Interests: Politics, Education, Social Implications of the Gospel and Ministry in Multi-Racial/Inner City Areas. *Hobbies and Recreations;* Gardening, Walking, Sport, Camping.

LEE, Kathleen Bertha (Mrs.), 12 Park Rd., Harlesden, London NW10 8TB. (01 965 4624) *b. 26 Oct 1918, London. m. 23 July 1975 (w.).*
Education: Craven Park Private Sch.; Clarks Coll.; 1944–46 Wesley Deaconess. *Appointments:* 1973–75 Harpenden; 1975–78 Leeds; 1978–82 Bolton.
Connexional Committees: 1975 Team Ministries; 1977– Medical Sub-Committee; 1979– Panel for Nomination of Chairmen of Districts.

LEECH, John, 29 Burlington Rd., Altrincham, Cheshire WA14 1HR. (061 928 2429)–BA(Hons.)(B'ham). *b. 16 Feb 1935, Chesterton, North Staffs. m. 4 Aug 1967: 1d., 1s.*
Education: 1940–44 Chesterton Prim. and Jun.; 1944–53 Newcastle, Staffs., High Sch.; 1956–59 Birmingham Univ.; 1955–59 Handsworth. *Appointments:* 1959–61 Camelford and Wadebridge; 1961–67 Nottingham North; 1967–75 Hastings, Bexhill and Rye; 1975– Altrincham.
Special Interests: Politics, Methodist History. *Hobbies and Recreations:* Cricket, Chess, Drama.

LEEDHAM, Walter, 24 Cottesmore Rd., Stamford, Lincolnshire PE9 2SQ. (0780 62282) *b. 13 June 1928, Grimsby, Lincolnshire. s.*
Education: Healing Jun. and Secondary Modern Schs.; Cleethorpes High Sch. of Commerce; 1953–55 Cliff Coll.; 1957–61 Hartley Victoria. *Appointments:* 1961–63 Dorchester; 1963–66 Driffield; 1966–73 Salisbury; 1973–76 St. Ives; 1976– Stamford; 1981–82 Exchange to New Zealand.
Special Interests: Foreign Travel, International Relationships, Handicapped Groups. *Hobbies and Recreations:* Sport, Music, Theatre, Art.

LEES, Eric David, 79 Saxon Way, Sawehall Rd., Chester CH1 5JL. *b. 6 June 1909, Shrewsbury. m. 16 Sept 1948 (w.).*
Education: 1916–17 Rivington Rd.; 1917–19 St. Helens North St.; 1919–26 Cowley Grammar; 1934–36 Birmingham Univ. *Appointments:* 1950–53 North Isles; 1953–55 Ashton-under-Lyme, Stamford St.; 1955–59 Sandbach and Alsager; 1959–62 Whitchurch, St. John's; 1962–65 Glasgow West; 1965–67 Bingley; 1967–69 Huddersfield South; 1969–72 South Derbyshire; 1972–74 Glossop.

LEIGHTON, David Hargreaves, c/o RN, Army and RAF Board, 1 Central Buildings, Tothill St., London SW1H 9NH. *b. 20 Aug 1943, Solihull.*
Education: 1955–62 Tudor Grange Grammar Sch., Solihull, 1964–68 Richmond. *Appointments:* 1968–72 Brinkworth; 1972–75 Winsford; 1975– Chaplain HMF.

LEMMON, Herbert Gordon, 374 Main Road, Dovercourt, Harwich, Essex CO12 4DD. (025 55 2054)–MA(Cantab). *b. 30 March 1933, Downham Market, Norfolk. m. 1*

Aug 1960: 1s.
Education: 1939–43 Willesby Jun. Boys Sch., Spalding, Lincs.; 1943–51 Culford Sch., Bury St. Edmunds, Suffolk; 1953–56 Fitzwilliam House, Cambridge; 1953–56 Wesley House.
Appointments: 1956–58 Liverpool, Linacre Mission; 1958–59 Thetford; 1959–60 Cromer, Sheringham and Holt; 1960–66 Pontypool, Eastern Valley; 1966–73 London, Sydenham and Forest Hill; 1973–80 Cambridge; 1980– Manningtree and Harwich.
Connexional Committees: Synod Appointments: 1962–66 District Youth Secretary, Cardiff and Swansea District; 1973–77 District Social Responsbility Secretary, London N.E. District; 1977–80 Assistant Secretary; 1980– Synod Secretary, London N.E. District; 1962–66 Connexional Youth Council; 1982– Connexional Panel for Nomination of Chairmen of Districts. *Local Council Committees:* 1967–73 Lewisham Borough Youth Committee (1969–73 Vice-Chairman); 1969–73 London Youth Committee.
Hobbies and Recreations: Sports, Theatre, Television.

LE MOIGNAN, Edward Frank, 51 Hightown Rd., Ringwood, Hants. BH24 1NQ. (042 54 78609) *b. 17 March 1912, Portsmouth. m. 15 April 1939. 2d.*
Education: 1924–28 St. Johns College, Southsea; 1945–47 Handsworth. *Appointments:* 1947–48 London, Blackheath and Lee; 1948–50 Rawtenstall; 1950–54 Sherborne; 1954–60 Salisbury; 1960–66 Bristol, Bedminster; 1966–72 Dorchester; 1972–77 Yeovil.

LENTON, Raymond, 63 Herbert St., Hemel Hempstead, Herts. HP2 5HP. (0442 69068) *b. 25 March 1908, Downham Market. m. 6 Oct 1948: 1d., 1s.*
Education: 1915–21 Holbeach, St. Marks CE; 1928–29 Cliff Coll.
Appointments: 1940–43 King's Lynn; 1943–44 Fenland; 1944–47 Lerwick/North Roe; 1947–51 Dover; 1951–57 Shooters Hill; 1957–63 Maidenhead and Windsor; 1963–70 Milton Keynes; 1970–76 Hemel Hempstead/Berkhamsted; 1929–32 Cliff Evangelist.
Connexional Committees: 1947–52 Youth; 1974–81 Division of Ministries; M.S.C.
Special Interests: 1937–82 Travel Leader (45 years). *Hobbies and Recreations:* Football Association Referee (30 years).

LE POIDEVIN, David Wilfred, 26 Doniford Rd., Watchet, Somerset TA23 0TE. (0984 31714) *b. 17 Oct 1940, Brislington, Bristol. m. 13 Aug 1966: 2d., 1s.*
Education: 1945–52 Vale Inf. and Jun. Sch., Guernsey; 1952–59 Guernsey Grammar School for Boys; 1962–66 Didsbury, Bristol.
Appointments: 1966–68 Bridgend; 1968–72 Risca and Cross Keys; 1972–77 Reading; 1977– West Somerset.
Publications: How to Trace Your Ancestors in Guernsey (1978).
Special Interests: Channel Island Affairs, Politics, Sport, Music, History, National Trust, International Friendships. *Hobbies and Recreations:* Gardening, Family History, Family Walks.

LE POIDEVIN, Pamela Reta, Carlton House, Exeter Rd., Braunton, N. Devon EX33 2BN. (0271 812137) *b. 3 Nov 1933, Guernsey.*
Education: 1938–44 Forest Parish Sch.; 1944–47 Guernsey States Intermediate Sch. for Girls; 1955–57 Wesley Deaconess. *Appointments:* 1976– Barnstaple.
Special Interests: The Countryside. *Hobbies and Recreations:* Gardening, Housework, Cooking.

LE SEELLEUR, Charles David, 1 Cedar Rd., Balby, Doncaster, S. Yorks. DN4 9DT. (0302 852024) *b. 23 May 1927, St. Martins, Jersey, C.I. m. 19 Dec 1956: 1d., 1s.*
Education: 1933–36 Springside Sch.; 1936–41 St. Martins Collegiate Sch.; 1941–44 Victoria Coll.; 1945–46 Cliff Coll.; 1949–51 Richmond.
Appointments: 1951–53 Kirkoswald; 1953–54 Gainsborough; 1954–58 Spilsby; 1958–62 Wolverhampton, Darlington St.; 1962–67 Runcorn; 1967–74 Northwich; 1974–79 Chippenham; 1979– Doncaster.
Special Interests; Youth Fellowships; House Groups; Methodist Doct. of Holiness. *Hobbies and Recreations:* Sport, Gardening, Walking.

LESTER, William Kinsley, 11 Wimbrick Hey, Moreton, Wirral, Merseyside L46 9RU. (051 678 6449) *b. 18 Sept 1909, Biddulph, Stoke-on-Trent. m. 29 May 1944.*
Education: Biddulph Elem. Sch.; 1933–36 Handsworth.
Appointments: 1936–44 Leeward Islands Dt; 1944–47 Camborne; 1947–48 Birmingham, Belmont Row; 1948–51 Wellington, Salop; 1951–55 Widnes; 1955–58 Liverpool, Crosby; 1958–63 Kimberley; 1963–64 Stockport Tiviot Dale; 1964–67 Manchester, Withington; 1967–71 Stretford and Urmanston; 1971–74 Garstang.
Special Interests: Literature. *Hobbies and Recreations:* Bowling and Gardening.

LE SUEUR, Frederic Oliver, 15 Ash Tree Rd., Burnham-on-Sea, Somerset TA8 2LD. (0278 783858)–BA. *b. 3 June 1897, Jersey. w: 1d., 1s.*
Education: Keighley Grammar Sch.; 1919–21 Birmingham Univ.; 1919 Richmond; 1919–21 Handsworth.
Appointments: 1921–24 Kent Mission; 1924–25 Mid Norfolk Mission; 1925–28 Hunts Mission; 1928–32 Rochdale Mission; 1932–37 Birstal; 1937–41 Dewsbury; 1941–47 Grimsby George St.; 1947–52 Gainsborough; 1952–62 Chairman Lincoln District.
Connexional Committees: 1953–59 Overseas Missions; 1952–62 Home Missions; 1952–62 General Purposes; 1957–77 Rural Travel; 1952–62 Stationing Committee; Convener of Conference Commissions–a. Rural Methodism, b. Rural Travel, c. Local Administration of Small Churches, d. Deployment of the Ministry. *Council Member:* 1952–63 Lindsey, Lincs. Education Committee.

LE SUEUR, John Philip, 18 Victoria Rd., Acocks Green, Birmingham B27 7YA. (021 706 1731)–BA(Leeds). *b. 12 Aug 1928, St. Ives, Hunts. m. 27 July 1954: 3d., 1s.*

Education: Elementary Schs.– Gomersall, W. Yorks, Mirfield, W. Yorks.; 1938–41 Mirfield Grammar Sch.; 1941–46 Winteringham Grammar Sch., Grimsby; 1949–51 Leeds Univ.; 1949–51 Headingley. *Appointments:* 1951–53 Retford; 1953–54 Wath-on-Dearne; 1954–70 Lucknow and Banaras Dt; 1968–70 Chairman; 1970–72 Church of N.India; 1972–78 Stroud and Cirencester; 1978– Birmingham, Elmdon.
Hobbies and Recreations: Music, Photography.

LETCH, Ralph Arthur, 97 Allithwaite Rd., Flookburgh, Grange-over-Sands, Cumbria LA11 7VR. (044 853 229)–BSc, PhD(Lond.), BD(Manc.). *b. 1909, Shenley, Hertfordshire. m. 1938.*
Education: 1914–21 Shenley Prim. Sch.; 1921–28 Queen Elizabeth's Grammar Sch., Barnet; 1928–33 Royal Coll. of Science, Imperial Coll., Univ. London; 1933–35 Univ. of Manchester; 1933–35 Hartley. *Appointments:* 1935–38 Bolton, Wesley; 1938–41 Heywood; 1941–46 Rochdale South; 1946–52 Lytham St. Annes; 1952–57 Preston, Lune St.; 1957–62 Blackpool North; 1962–66 Luton West; 1966–71 Grimsby West; 1971–74 Littleborough.
Connexional Committees: 1960–66 Ministerial Training. *Local Council Committees:* 1949–52 Lytham St. Annes Education Committee; 1956–57 Preston Education Committee.
Publications: Temptation and Freedom.
Special Interests: Relationship of Psychology and Theology. *Hobbies and Recreations:* Gardening, Natural History.

LEVER, Clifford, Guelder Cottage, Uplands Rd., Denmead, Hants. PO7 6HE. (07014 55984) *b. 21 Dec 1899, Farnworth, Lancs. m. 5 Aug 1930: 2d.*
Education: 1911–14 Farnworth Grammar Sch.; 1918–20 Manchester Coll. of Technology1924–26 Handsworth. *Appointments:* 1926–29 Bombay Dt, India; 1929–30 Wolverhampton, Darlington St.; 1930–33 Truro; 1933–35 St. Ives, Cornwall; 1935–40 London Mission West; 1940–46 Chaplain H.M.F.; 1946–47 Southall Mission; 1947–52 Jersey Wesley Grove; 1952–57 Truro St. Mary's; 1957–61 Plymouth King St.; 1961–67 Ipswich.
Publications: 'On My Heart Too', Epic of Calais (Epworth Press).
Special Interests: Writing, Painting, Music.

LEWIS, Albert Stacey, 2 Rowan Drive, Lutterworth, Leics. LE17 4SP. (045 55 2364) *b. 21 Aug 1920, Lincoln. m. 2 Sept 1952.*
Education; 1931–37 Lincoln Sch.; 1946–48 Richmond. *Appointments:* 1948–50 Higham Ferrers; 1950–54 Louth; 1954–58 Spalding; 1958–63 Brighton and Hove; 1963–69 Biggleswade; 1969–75 Horncastle and Bardney; 1975–80 Nuneaton and Atherstone; 1980– Rugby and Daventry.

LEWIS, Brian, 18 Viking Rd., Bridlington, North Humberside YO16 5TW. (0262 72471)–BA(B'ham). *b. 27 Sept 1936, Northampton. m. 30 June 1960: 1d., 1s.*
Education: 1948–52 Warwick Sch.; 1952–53 Northampton Grammar Sch.; 1959–62 Birmingham Univ.; 1958–62 Handsworth.
Appointments: 1962–64 Beverley; 1964–70 Melton Mowbray; 1970–75 Sierra Leone; 1975–80 Leicester South East; 1980– Bridlington.
Connexional Committees: 1981–82 DSR Board (as District Representative).
Special Interests: Disarmanent, Development and World mission, Local Radio, Hospital Chaplaincy.
Hobbies and Recreations: Reading, Photography, D.I.Y.

LEWIS, Christopher John Solven, 50 Cyprus Rd., Titchfield Common, Fareham, Hants. PO14 4LB. (04895 83983)–MA(Oxon), BD(Manchester). *b. 3 Sept 1932, Swindon, Wilts. m. 21 June 1958: 1d., 1s.*
Education: 1944–51 Commonweal C.S.G., Swindon; 1953–56 Wadham Coll., Oxford; 1956–59 Hartley Victoria. *Appointments:* 1959–61 Maryport; 1961–69 Dahomey-Togo District (Schs. Chaplain and Cotonou); 1969–73 Southampton; 1973–78 Christian Aid Area Secretary, S. Hants.; 1978–82 Birmingham Moseley Rd. and Sparkhill.
Connexional Committees: 1977–83 Overseas Division, Central Committee.
Special Interests: Race, Inner City, Third World. *Hobbies and Recreations:* Petanque.

LEWIS, D. Albert, Rydal Mount, 16 Churton Rd., Rhyl LL18 3ND.–BA(Wales). *b. 1 Dec 1901, Cletwr Cottage, Trerddol, Cards. m. 12 Aug 1936: 1s.*
Education: 1906–12 Taliesin Prim. Sch., Cards; 1901–13 Aberdovey Prim. Sch., Merioneth; 1921–26 Preparatory Sch., Carmarthen; Univ. Coll., Bangor, North Wales; 1932–34 Richmond Coll. *Appointments:* 1929–30 Denbigh; 1932–33 Tregarth; 1933–36 Bagillt; 1936–37 Manchester Welsh; 1937–39 Ystumtuen; 1939–42 Newtown; 1942–45 Llanhaeadr; 1945–50 Llanrwst; 1950–55 Abercynon; 1960–65 Mold; 1965–69 Portmadoc.
Connexional Committees: 1950–55 Ministerial Training Fund.
Hobbies and Recreations: Golf.

LEWIS, Ewart Walter, 63 Winchester Way, Willingdon, Eastbourne, Sussex BN22 0JU. (0323 54580)–BA(B'ham). *b. 8 Nov 1903, Staines, Middlesex. m. 15 May 1967.*
Education: Ashford County Secondary Sch.; 1925–28 Birmingham Univ.; 1925–28 Handsworth. *Appointments:* 1928–34 Burma Dt; 1934–37 Reading; 1937–41 Lincoln, High St.; 1941–46 Manchester and Salford Mission; 1946–51 Glasgow Mission; 1951–59 Plymouth and Devonport Mission; 1959–62 Southall Mission; 1962–68 Romford.
Hobbies and Recreations: Bowls, Walking, Photography.

LEWIS, Greville Robert, 67 Allport Rd., Bromborough, Wirral L62 6AA. (051 334 1772) *b. 21 Aug 1921,*

Walsall. m. 28 July 1950: 2d.
Education: 1933–39 Kingswood Sch.; 1945–47 Richmond.
Appointments: 1947–50 Southampton; 1950–53 Farnham; 1953–58 Great Barr and Kingstanding; 1958–64 Eastbourne; 1964–72 Worthing; 1972–78 Leamington Spa; 1978– South Wirral.
Hobbies and Recreations: Bird Watching.

LEWIS, Hywel Meilir Pennant, Llys Myfyr, Llanrwst, Gwynedd LL26 0DB. (0492 640600)–BA, BD. *4 May 1919, Meifod, Powys. m. 14 Aug 1947: 2d.*
Education: Llanfyllin Elem. Sch.; Llanfyllin County Sch.; Dolgellau Grammar Sch.; 1937–43 Univ. of Manchester; 1937–43 Hartley Victoria. *Appointments:* 1943–45 Corwen Welsh; 1945–50 Llanasa Welsh; 1950–55 Holywell Welsh; 1955–60 Bangor Welsh; 1960–65 Beaumaris Welsh; 1965–70 Caernarvon Welsh; 1970– Dyffryn Conway Welsh; 1962–64 District Secretary of Second North Wales District; 1962– Chairman of Historical Society of Methodist Church in Wales.
Connexional Committees: 1952–62 Ministerial training Committee; 1974– Church in Rural Life Committee; 1948–74 Member of the Welsh Assembly. *Council Member:* Member of North Wales Area Executive Committee of W.E.A.; Member of North Wales Area Council of W.E.A. *Publications:* Contributor to *Bywgraffiadur Cymreig,* (Welsh National Biography); Articles published in *Yr Eurgrawn* (Welsh Methodist Quarterly); Convener of Group which published study *Second Homes in Wales* (H. Mission Publication 1974).
Special Interests: Historical Studies, Ecumenical Activities, Adult Education, Lecturer W.E.A. and Extra Mural Department (Univ. Coll. of N. Wales, Bangor). *Hobbies and Recreations:* Mountaineering, Youth Work, Celtic Studies, Travelling, Contacts with Methodists in Europe.

LEWIS, Ian William, 8 Cecil Ave., Baildon, Shipley, Bradford BD17 5LH. (0274 581128)–OBE. *b. 23 Jan 1927, Bristol. m. 6 Sept 1952: 2s.*
Education: 1932–41 Frampton Cotterell Council Sch.; 1947–50 Handsworth Coll. *Appointments:* 1950–59 Kenya Dt; 1959–72 Halifax Wesley; 1972–80 Brighton and Hove; 1980– Shipley and Bingley; 1960–72 Chaplain, Halifax General Hospital. *Connexional Committees:* Connexional O.M. Committee. *Local Council Committees:* 1960–72 Youth Executive of Halifax Education Committee. *Publications: St. Andrews*–Occasional Paper (Home Mission Dept 1968).
Special Interests: Community Care (Samaritans/Alcoholics Clubs etc.), Counselling, Worship as Celebration, Ecumenism. *Hobbies and Recreations:* Reading, Light Music, Gardening Sport, Walking.

LEWIS, Lionel Elton George, The Manse, Shebbear, Beaworthy, Devon EX21 5SH. (040 928 262) *b. 15 July 1926, Poole, Dorset. m. 17 July 1954: 1d.*
Education: 1931–40 Elem.; 1947–48 Cliff Coll.; 1950–53 Didsbury, Bristol.
Appointments: 1949–50 Cheddar Valley; 1953–54 Dorchester; 1954–59 Wakefield; 1959–64 Falmouth; 1964–70 Gloucester; 1970– Shebbear.
Hobbies and Recreations: Gardening, Woodwork, Music, D.I.Y.

LEWIS, Michael John, 6 Ashberry Drive, Messingham, Scunthorpe, South Humberside DN17 3QS. (0724 762305) *b. 2 March 1954, Holbeach, Lincolnshire. m. 21 Aug 1976: 2s.*
Education: 1959–65 Pinchbeck Prim. Sch.; 1965–70 Spalding Gleed Sch.; 1970–72 Boston Coll. of Further Education; 1975–76 Cliff Coll.; 1978–81 Queens. *Appointments:* 1981– Scunthorpe.
Hobbies and Recreations: Science Fiction, Childrens and Adults Board Games, Local Church History.

LEYLAND, Arthur Stanley, 79 Church Hill Rd., Sutton, Surrey SM3 8LL. (01 644 8528)–MA, MPhil, DD. *b. 25 Nov 1901, St. Georges, Salop. m. 17 July 1926.*
Education: Priors Lee Elem.; Private Tutor; Univ. of Leeds; Univ. of London; 1924–26 Hartley Victoria.
Appointments: 1922–24 Pocklington; 1926–28 Abertillery; 1928–31 Wolverhampton; 1931–34 Mioddlesbrough; 1934–42 Darlington; 1942–45 Bristol, Redland; 1945–51 London, Highgate; 1951–58 Barnet; 1958–67 Brixton Hill.
Connexional Committees: Annual Conference, British Methodism, 1940–44 Assistant Record Secretary, 1944–45 Record Secretary, 1945–57 Assistant Secretary, Member of the Stationing Committee, Member of the General Purposes Committee, Convener of the two year Commission which established M.Y.D., Convener of the Commiittee which transferred ownership of Manse Furnishings from Circuits to Ministers; 1969–78 Secretary for the Interchange of Preachers between the British Council of Churches and the National Council of the Churches of Christ in the USA; Joint Leader with RC Priest and Anglican Bishop of Ecumenical Cruises; Organiser and Leader of Groups touring European Countries, Soviet Russia, Holy Land; 1947 Pioneered Exchange of Pastorates, UK-USA; 1948– Secretary Conference Committee Exchange of Pastorates; Associate Director, Exchange of Pastorates, World Methodist Council.
Publications: Wrote weekly *Adventure Page in Methodist Recorder* (London).
Hobbies and Recreations: Golf.

LIGHTFOOT, Archibald, 11 Warrenhurst, Montpellier Crescent, Wallasey, Merseyside L45 9JZ. (051 638 4816) *b. 18 Dec 1887, Togston, Northumberland. m. 30 Oct 1963.*
Education: Amble Public; 1911–14 Didsbury. *Appointments:* 1914–15 Midsomer Norton; 1915–17 Wye Valley Mission; 1917–18 Herefordshire Mission; 1918–21 East Durham; 1921–24 Boston; 1924–27 Rochdale; 1927–30 Blyth; 1930–33 Maldon; 1933–37 Castle

Donington; 1937–40 Newark. *Connexional Committees:* 1936–41 Membership Committee.

LIGHTFOOT, Edward Malcolm, 15 Station Rd., Aspatria, Carlisle CA5 2AJ. (0965 20302) *b. 13 Jan 1916, Warrington. m. 16 Aug 1950: 2d.*
Education; Beach Rd. Boys Sch.; Boottle Technical Coll.
Appointments: 1964–65 Wantage and Abingdon; 1965–69 Berwick; 1969–72 Hetton-le-Hole; 1972–76 Hartlepool; 1976–81 Wigton.
Hobbies and Recreations: Gardening.

LILLIE, William, 18 Newlands Drive, Ripon, N. Yorks. HG4 2JY. (0765 5955) *b. 28 April 1913, Middlesbrough. m. 11 Jan 1947: 2d.*
Education: 1918 1929 Hugh Bell Central Sch.; 1938–41 Headingley.
Appointments: 1941–47 Trichinopoly District, South India; 1947–59 Trichinopoly-Tanjore Diocese, Church of South India; 1959–62 Pocklington; 1962–67 Hunts Mission; 1967–75 Leytonstone and Forest Gate; 1975–81 Makerfield.
Publications: Some Customers and Ceremonies of The Karur and Dharapuram Areas (Trichy 1956); *A Christian Catechism* (Tamil 1957); Into to *O.T. Prophets* (1969); *Critical Commentary on Job* (1971); Articles in *A Theological Word Book* (1963) and in a one-vol. *Bible Commentary* (1972)–all published by C.L.S., Madras.
Hobbies and Recreations: Music, Drawing, Gardening.

LINTON, Lawrence, 32 Kensington Place, Brighton, Sussex BN1 4EJ. (0273 684937). *b. 24 July 1903, Leeds. m. 18 Sept 1936: 1s.*
Education: 1908–16 Park Lane Council Sch., Leeds, 1931–34 Richmond. *Appointments:* 1934–42 Bombay and Punjab, India; 1942–44 Burma; 1944–47 Bombay and Punjab, India; 1947–49 Manchester, Pendleton; 1949–52 Worthing; 1952–56 Calcutta, India; 1956–63 Hunts Mission. *Local Council Committees:* 1960–63 County Education Committee, Huntingdonshire.
Special Interests: International Goodwill Contacts, The Anglo-Indian.
Hobbies and Recreations: Numismatics, Roman Bronze.

LISTER, Alan Glynn, 17 Stephenson Terrace, Wylam, Northumberland NE41 8DZ. (06614 2143) *b. 22 Oct 1945, Bradford on Avon, Wiltshire. m. 23 July 1966: 1d., 1s.*
Education; 1957–62 Commonweal G.S., Swindon; 1965–67 Didsbury, Bristol; 1967–69 Wesley Coll., Bristol. *Appointments:* 1969–71 West Somerset; 1971–75 Clevedon; 1975– Hexham.
Connexional Committees; 1980– Board, Dey; 1980– Dey CCRD; 1979– Church in Rural Life Committee. *Council Member:* 1979– Wylam Parish Council. *Local Council Committees:* 1981– Chairman Ovingham Joint Burial Committee.
Special Interests: Rural Sociology, Christian Education. *Hobbies and Recreations:* Cricket, Choral Singing, Playing the Bassoon.

LISTER, Gordon Herbert, 7 Armley Grange Drive, Leeds LS12 3QH. (0532 637613) *b. 24 April 1930, Heckmondwike, Yorkshire. m. 13 July 1957: 2d.*
Education: 1935–43 Norristhorpe Council Sch., Liversedge; 1943–45 Batley Technical Coll., Batley; 1954–55 Cliff Coll.; 1955–58 Handsworth.
Appointments: 1958–61 Rochdale North; 1961–64 Littleborough; 1964–69 Bedale; 1969–72 Sleaford; 1972–78 Pudsey and Farsley, 1978– Leeds West; 1969–72 Officiating Chaplain RAF Digby; 1973– Hospital Chaplain, The General Infirmary, Leeds, 1972 75 Industrial Chaplain, part-time.
Connexional Committees. 1967 Chairman, Conference Music Committee. *Local Council Committees:* 1973–78 West Riding C.C., Sch. Manager Pudsey; 1978–80 Leeds City Council, Sch. Governor.
Publications: Articles on Music and Children–*Methodist Magazine;* Short Stories–Radio Leeds.
Special Interests: Church Music, Liturgy, Wesleyanna, Methodist History, Clinical Theology, Hospital Chaplaincy. *Hobbies and Recreations:* Music, Art, Drama, Literature, Cricket, Writing, Wesleyanna, Member of Elgar and Barbirolli Societies.

LISTER, Harry, 40 Churchill Ave., Southport, Merseyside PR9 9PS. *b. 28 Nov 1914, Stacksteads, Nr. Bacup, Lancs. m. 27 Dec 1944: 2d.*
Education: –1925 Lord St. Council Sch., Fleetwood; 1925–31 Baines Grammar Sch., Poulton-le-Fylde; 1949–51 Hartley Victoria.
Appointments: 1951–53 London Mission, Hackney; 1953–57 Bacup; 1957–61 Bury; 1961–65 Alston; 1965–74 Southport, Banks and Hesketh Bank; 1974–79 Gornal and Sedgley.
Special Interests: Methodism, its origins and place in the Evangelical Faith, The 18th Century and other Revivals, Reading, Biography, Theology. *Hobbies and Recreations:* Certain Sports (Football, Cricket etc.), Walking, Odd Jobs, Gardening.

LITHERLAND, Geoffrey, 2 Stroud Rd., Bisley, Stroud, Glos. GL6 7BQ. (045 277 400)–BA(Cantab), MA(Cantab.), BD(Lond.). *b. 9 Jan 1911, Knutsford, Ches. m. 14 Aug 1942: 1d., 2s.*
Education; 1921–29 Altrincham Grammar Sch.; 1929–32 St. John's, Cambridge; 1934–37 Headingley.
Appointments: 1937–38 President's List; 1938–42 Swansea; 1942–46 London, Wandsworth; 1946–51 Petersfield; 1951–53 Bournemouth; 1953 56 Manchester, Droylsden and Openshaw; 1956–59 Liverpool South; 1959–64 West Indies Dt; Principal Queen's Coll., Nassau; 1964–72 Warden, Wesley Deaconess Order.
Connexional Committees: Various.

LITTLE, Wilfrid James, 5 Leyton Villas, Redland, Bristol BS6 6JF. (0272 836726) *b. 31 Dec 1901, Kington Langley, Wilts. m. 4 Aug 1937: 1d.*
Education: Kington Langley; Chippenham Secondary; 1928–30 Hartley. *Appointments:* 1926–28

Colnbrook and Chertsey; 1930–33 Shaftesbury; 1933–35 Shaftesbury and Mere; 1935–37 West Monmouth Mission; 1937–40 Chelmsford; 1940–46 Brinkworth; 1946–50 Paulton; 1950–52 Driffield; 1952–57 Lincoln, Aldersgate; 1957–62 Woolstanton and Audley; 1962–70 Nantwich. *Connexional Committees:* 1935– Methodist Church Music Society. *Publications: John Wesley's Chapel 1930–1980* (Bristol). *Special Interests:* Pastoral Psychology, Church Music, Hymnology. *Hobbies and Recreations:* Gardening.

LIVINGSTONE, Cynthia Joyce Ethelwyn (maiden name Brook), 119 Rein Road, Tingley, Wakefield, West Yorkshire WF3 1JQ. (0532 533485)–MA(Edinbrugh), BD(Edinbrugh). *b. 10 April 1923, Brentford Middlesex. m. 26 June 1954: 1d., 2s.* *Education:* 1928–29 Private Sch., Brentford; 1929–32 Private Sch., Highgate; 1932–34 Aske's Haberdashers, New Cross; 1934–37 Eastbourne High Sch.; 1937–40 Bolton Sch., Chorley New Rd., Bolton; 1941–43 Southlands Training Coll.; 1947–50 Edinburgh Univ.; 1950–53 Bradford Coll., Emm Lane. *Appointments:* 1978–79 Leigh; 1979– Morley. *Special Interests:* Preaching the Gospel, Helping People to Grow in Christian Faith.

LLOYD, Albert Kingsley, 13 High St., Orwell, Royston, Herts. SG8 5QN. *b. 2 Nov 1903, Dudley. m.* *Education:* 1916–20 Kingswood Sch.; 1922–26 Richmond. *Appointments:* 1926–29 London, Harrow; 1929–31 London, Kilburn and Hampstead; 1931–36 Bedford; 1936–39 London, Finsbury Park; 1939–44 Biggleswade; 1944–47 Cambridge; 1947–52 London, Enfield; 1952–69 Dept. of Connexional Funds; 1964 President of the Conference.

LLOYD, Cyril, Heulfryn, Barmouth Road, Dolgellau, Gwynedd LL40 2YT. (0341 422524) *b. 15 May 1923, Ffynnongroyw, Flintshire. m. 17 Oct 1951: 1d.* *Education:* 1926–37 Ffynnongroyw Prim. Sch.; 1947–50 Headingley. *Appointments:* 1945–47 Ystumtuen; 195;–52 Pwllheli; 1952–55 Brynmawr and Tredegar; 1955–60 Mold; 1960–65 Llanfair; 1965–70 Caernarfon; 1970– Glannau Meirion A Dyfi. *Special Interests:* Methodist and Local History. *Hobbies and Recreations:* Walking.

LLOYD, Edward William Robert, Wesley Manse, 87 Old Coach Rd., Kelsall, Tarporley, Cheshire CW6 0RA. (0829 51276) *b. 24 Dec 1917, Wrexham, N. Wales. m. 28 Aug 1948: 1d., 1s.* *Education;* 1934–37 Grove Park Grammar Sch., Wrexham; 1945–47 Hartley Victoria. *Appointments:* 1947–54 Kent Mission; 1954–63 Chester, George St. and Chester; 1963–72 Wallasey; 1972–77 Leeds, Headingley; 1977– Kelsall and Tarporely. *Hobbies and Recreations:* Fishing (fly), Music.

LOADES, A. Alfred, 232 Reepham Rd., Norwich NR6 5SW. (0603 45038) *b. 29 Jan 1934, Holt, Norfolk. m. 10 Aug 1960: 2s.* *Education;* 1945–52 Fakenham Grammar Sch.; 1956–57 Cliff Coll.; 1957–60 Richmond. *Appointments:* 1960–61 Sheffield Industrial Mission; 1961–63 Port Talbot, Industrial Chaplain; 1963–65 Ely; 1965–72 Chaplain H.M.F.; 1972–80 Lowestoft; 1980– Norwich. *Connexional Committees:* 1960–63 Church in Industry; 1975–80 Board of Social Responsibility. *Special Interests:* Member Royal Norfolk Agricultural Show, Education (Schools). *Hobbies and Recreations:* Natural History, Water Colour Painting, Tennis.

LOCKE, Eric James, Val d'Or, Ewyas Harold, Herefordshire HR2 0JB. (0432 240257)–BA, BD. *b. 13 Nov 1934, Leicester. m. 22 Aug 1959: 2d., 1s.* *Education:* 1945–53 Thornbury Grammar Sch.; 1953–56 Durham Univ.; 1956–59 Richmond. *Appointments:* 1959–61 Glasgow, Parkhead; 1961–66 Darlaston; 1966–73 Kidderminster; 1973–82 Doncaster; 1982– Cwm and Kingstone. *Special Interests:* Telling Stories. *Hobbies and Recreations:* Walking, Theatre, Music.

LOCKHART, Grahame, 89 Grange Rd., Belmont, Durham DH1 1AQ. (0385 42771)–BA. *b. 29 Sept 1949, Glasgow. m. 3 Dec 1971: 1d., 2s.* *Education:* 1961–66 Shawlands Academy, Glasgow; 1976–77 Langside Coll., Glasgow; 1978–81 Manchester Univ.; 1978–81 Hartley Victoria. *Appointments:* 1981– Durham and Deerness Valley. *Hobbies and Recreations:* Reading, Sport.

LOCKING, Graham Robert, 65 Station Rd., Woodhouse, Sheffield S13 7RA. (0742 693148) *b. 22 April 1953, Grimsby, Lincolnshire. m. 20 Dec. 1975: 1d., 2s.* *Education:* 1971–72 Cliff Coll., 1972–74 Luton Industrial Coll.; 1974–78 Wesley, Bristol. *Appointments:* 1978–80 London, East End Mission; 1980– Sheffield Mission. *Special Interests:* Alcoholism. *Hobbies and Recreations:* Golf, Bird-watching, Music.

LOCKWOOD, Trevor, 27 Shafter Rd., Dagenham, Essex RM10 8AJ. (01 593 9840) *b. 1 July 1940, Christchurch, Nr Wisbech, Cambs. m. 6 Aug 1966: 1d., 1s.* *Education:* 1945–51 Christchurch Prim. Sch.; 1951–56 Wisbech Grammar Sch.; 1961–62 Cliff Coll.; 1962–66 Handsworth. *Appointments:* 1966–70 Coalville; 1970– London Mission, East Ham. *Connexional Committees:* 1979–81 and 1982– Division of Ministries Executive Committee. *Publications:* Booklet *The Formation of the Dagenham Pastoral Unit and Team Ministry* (1978). *Special Interests:* Church (Shared and Lay Ministry developed through Team Ministry). *Hobbies and*

Recreations: Sport, Reading, Gardening, Astronomy, Music, Piano, Family Man.

LOCKYER, John Kenneth, 10 Romilly Park, Barry, South Glamorgan CF6 8RP. (0446 735839) *b. 25 Feb 1917, Castleford, Yorkshire. m. 24 Oct 1945: 1d.*
Education: 1922–31 Pontefract Rd. Boys Sch., Castleford; 1934–38 Leeds Univ.; 1946–48 London; 1946–48 Richmond Coll. *Appointments:* 1940–43 Thame and Watlington; 1943–45 Dursley and Stonehouse; 1945–46 Faringdon; 1948–50 Walsall; 1950–53 Bridgend; 1953–57 Yeovil; 1957–60 Antigua, West Indies Dt; 1960–66 Week St. Mary; 1966–72 Plymouth; 1972–78 Weymouth; 1978– Barry; 1953–57 Officiating Chaplain to Forces; 1957–60 Missionary Chaplain to Leper Colony and H.M. Prison, Antigua, W.I.
Connexional Committees: 1967–72 and 1981– Overseas Missions Central Committee; 1967–72 District O.M. Secretary, Plymouth and Exeter; 1981– Cardiff and Swansea.
Special Interests: Mechanics, Do It Yourself Projects, Home Printing. *Hobbies and Recreations:* Travel, Motoring, Swimming.

LOGAN, Michael John, White Gables, Swinstead Rd., Corby Glen, Grantham, Lincolnshire NG33 4NU. (047684 618) *b. 10 July 1917, Groby, Nr. Leicester. m. 28 Nov 1946: 2d.*
Education: 1948–49 Handsworth. *Appointments;* 1949–52 Ticehurst; 1952–54 Glossop, 1954–59 Southend-on-Sea; 1959–62 St. Neots, Hunts.; 1962–68 Mid-Sussex; 1968–71 Wem and Prees Green; 1971–76 Sheffield, Carver St.; 1976–82 Sleaford.
Special Interests. Wesleyana, Hymnology, Hagiology. *Hobbies and Recreations:* Country Life, Life Member National Trust Life Fellow; R.S.P.B. Life Member; Leicestershire County Cricket Club.

LOFTHOUSE, George Arthur, 31 Holmfield, Burbage, Buxton, Derbyshire SK17 9DF. (0298 2152) *b. 24 Aug 1901, Brotton, North Yorkshire. m. 1. 9 July 1932; 2. 8 April 1967: 1d., 1 step-daughter, 1 step-son.*
Education; 1906–15 Brotton CE Sch.; 1915–17 Guisborough Grammar Sch.; 1921–22 Cliff Coll.; 1926–28 Hartley. *Appointments:* 1928–30 Portland; 1930–32 Eyemouth; 1932–36 Shotley Bridge; 1936–38 Crook; 1938–42 Sutton and Kirkby; 1942–47 Hartlepools; 1947–53 South Bank, Eston; 1953–57 Stokesley; 1957–62 Shildon; 1962–67 Skelmersdale.
Connexional Committees: 1956–65 Conference Elected Member of the Church Membership Committee.
Local Council Committees: Last Mayor's Chaplain at Buxton.
Hobbies and Recreations: Gardening, Photography.

LOMAX, Robert Ronald, 31 Holly Bank Rd., Huddersfield HD3 3LX. (0484 651539) *b. 31 Oct 1925, Manchester. m. 19 Sept 1953: 3s.*
Education: Elem. Sch. only; 1929–36 St. Thomas, Lower Crumpsall, Manchester; 1936–39 Heath St., Cheetham Hill, Manchester; 1949–51 Headingley; 1951–52 St. Andrews, Selly Oak. *Appointments:* 1947–48 Wye Valley Mission; 1948–49 Brynmawr; 1952–58 Barbados and Trinidad District; 1958–62 Keighley; 1962–68 Warrington; 1968–75 Northwich; 1975–82 Halifax; 1982– Huddersfield.
Hobbies and Recreations: Walking, Gardening.

LONG, George Ernest, 15 Trinity Drive, Holme, Carnforth, Lancs LA6 1QL. (0524 781667)–BA(Liverpool), MA(Cantab). *b. 10 April 1910, Southport, Lancs. m. 10 June 1967: 1d., 1s., 1 step-daughter, 2 step-sons.*
Education: 1920–28 King George V Sch., Southport; 1928–31 Liverpool Univ.; 1931–34 Cambridge Univ.; 1931–34 Wesley House.
Appointments: 1934–47 Hyderabad District, S. India; 1947–50 Medak Diocese Church of S. India; 1950–51 Dornakal Diocese (C.S.I.); 1951–53 Droylsden and Openshaw; 1953–70 Handsworth Coll., Tutor Ch.Hist.; 1970–75 Liverpool North.
Connexional Committees: 1953–70 Ministerial Training; 1953–70 Candidates; 1953–70 Probationers.
Local Council Committees: 1951–53 Manchester District Overseas Missions; 1953–70 Birmingham Dist. Probationers Committee; 1965–70 Birmingham District General Purposes.
Special Interests: Church History, Overseas, Missions. *Hobbies and Recreations:* Walking.

LONLEY, Frank Hollis, 11 Melbourne Rd., Royston, Herts SG8 7DG. (0763 42332)–MBE(1960). *b. 20 July 1907, Arlesey, Beds. m. 1 Aug 1935.*
Education: 1912–19 Pixmore Letchworth, Herts.; 1919–24 Hitching Grammar Sch.; 1928–30 Richmond; 1930–31 Headingley.
Appointments: 1931–63 W. Nigeria; 1963–65 Fakenham and Wells; 1965–69 Northern Nigeria; 1969–72 Mansfield.
Special Interests: Africa and Her People, Particularly of Nigeria.
Hobbies and Recreations: All the practical activities involved in a lifetime of Missionary Work, Travel, Gardening, Reading, Early years Sport.

LORD, Leonard Vincent, 5 Heather Ave., Shaw, Oldham OL2 8HL. (0706 849398) *b. 4 Jan 1934, Manchester. m. 6 Aug 1960: 1d., 1s.*
Education: 1976–78 Huddersfield Polytechnic; 1954–56 Cliff Coll.; 1956–60 Handsworth Coll.
Appointments: 1960–62 Normanton; 1962–66 Bradford, Low Moor and West Bowling; 1966–71 Manchester, Shaw and Royton; 1977–O.A. Manchester North and Middleton.
Special Interests: Student Counsellor.
Hobbies and Recreations: Music, Photography, Badminton

LORIMER, Malcolm George, 5 Hartburn Lane, Stockton-on-Tees, Cleveland TS18 3QJ. (0642 66985) *b. 12 June 1951, Haworth. m. 31 July 1977.*
Education: 1962–67 Keighley Secondary Technical Sch.; 1973–77 Queens, Birmingham.

Appointments: 1977– Stockton. *Hobbies and Recreations:* Collecting Cricket Books, Walking.

LOVELL, George, 7 Reddons Rd., Beckenham, Kent BR3 2LY. (01 659 0270)–BD, PhD(Univ. of Lond.). *b. 7 July 1929, Rishton, Lancashire. m. 16 February 1952: 1d., 1s.* *Education:* 1932–42 Rishton, Lancs. Wesleyan Day Sch.; 1942–44 Accrington, Lancs. Jun. Technical Sch.; 1955–58 Univ. of London; 1968–73 Univ. of London (part-time); 1955–58 Richmond Coll. *Appointments:* 1958–62 Llanelli and Carmarthen; 1962–66 London, Sydenham and Forest Hill; 1966–72 Croydon, South Norwood; 1970–75, 1972–76 Director of Project; 1976– Director of Avec–A Service Agency for Church and Community Work. *Connexional Committees:* 1963–70 Methodist Division of Education and Youth; 1966–79 Methodist Board of Lay Training. *Publications: Ten Days in Hospital* (Epworth Press 1963); *The Youth Worker as a First-Aid Counsellor in Impromptu Situations* (Chester House Publications 1971); *Church and Community Development–An Introduction* (Grail and Chester House Publications 1972); *Churches and Communities–An Approach to Development in the Local Church,* Joint author with C. Widdicombe (Search Press 1978); *Diagrammatic Modelling: An Aid to Theological Reflection in Church and Community Work* (The William Temple Foundation Occasional Paper No. 4, 1980); *Human and Religious Factors in Church and Community Work*–The Beckley Social Service Lecture 1981 (Grail Publications 1982). *Special Interests:* Church and Community Development Work, Adult Education. *Hobbies and Recreations:* Swimming, Walking, Gardening, DIY, Theatre, Reading.

LOVELL, Lewis Frederick, Count House Cottage, Townshend, Hayle, Cornwall TR27 6AQ. (0736 85 586)–BA(Lond.), BD(Lond.), BD(Manchester). *b. 16 June 1921, Bromley, Kent. m. 6 Aug 1949: 1d., 1s.* *Education:* 1929–39 Eltham Coll., Lond.; 1939–41 Birkbeck Coll., London; 1947–49 Hartley Victoria. *Appointments:* 1945–47 Chelmsford; 1949–51 Sandbach; 1951–55 Berwick on Tweed; 1955–58 Helmsley; 1958–63 Ormskirk; 1963–69 Hunts Mission; 1969–75 Hayle; 1975–78 Marazion. *Special Interests:* Bible Study/Teaching, M.S.C. (Greek). *Hobbies and Recreations:* Gardening, Railway Modelling.

LOVELL, Terence Robert, 1 Borrowdale Close, Penylan, Cardiff CF2 5LQ. (0222 499352) *b. 19 May 1928, Barry, South Glamorgan. m. 23 July 1955: 1d.* *Education:* Holton Boys Secondary, Barry; 1950–53 Handsworth. *Appointments:* 1949–50 Newport, Hill St.; 1953–55 Wye Valley Mission; 1955–60 Neath and Port Talbot; 1960–63 Bath, Avon; 1963–68 Birmingham, Wesley; 1968–75 Haverfordwest and Milford Haven; 1975–82 Plymouth, Devonport; 1982– Cardiff. *Local Council Committees:* Milford Haven, Pembs., Chairman's Chaplain. *Special Interests:* Book Collecting, Reading, British History 1914–48. *Hobbies and Recreations:* Bird Watching, Study of Natural History, Music, Listening and Study of its History.

LOWE, Roger Eric, 6 Salcombe Gardens, Mill Hill, London NW7 2NT. (01 959 1995) *b. 6 Sept 1941, Axminster, Devon. m. 7 Sept 1963: 2d., 1s.* *Education:* 1953–58 Woking County Grammar Sch.; 1975–79 Queens. *Appointments:* 1975–77 Birmingham, Blackheath; 1979– London, Finchley and Hendon. *Special Interests:* Almost Everything. *Hobbies and Recreations:* Walking, Camping, Computing, Reading, Listening to Music.

LOWERY, Ralph, 22 Grove Lane, Knottingley, W. Yorkshire WF11 8ES. (0977 82198)–BD(Lond.). *b. 5 July 1913, Hetton-le-Hole, Co. Durham. m. 4 April 1942: 1d.* *Education:* 1918–27 Hetton-le-Hole, CE Elem.; 1938–39 Manchester Univ.; 1935–39 Hartley Victoria. *Appointments:* 1938–39 Hartley Victoria Coll.; 1939–40 Middlesborough; 1940–46 Hartlepools; 1946–47 E. Nigeria Dt, West Africa; 1947–50 Sunderland W.; 1950–51 Newcastle-upon-Tyne, N.W.; 1951–56 Pontefract, Micklegate; 1956–60 Keighley; 1960–66 Pontefract; 1966–73 Newcastle-upon-Tyne, Heaton and Wallsend; 1973–74 Blackpool; 1974–79 Pontefract. *Connexional Committees:* 1958–60 General O.M. Committee. *Publications:* Occasional Articles in *Proceedings Wesley Historical Soc.;* Article in *From Mow Cop to Peake* (1982); Lecture (1982) N.E. Branch, Centenary of *Dr Robert F. Wearmouth of Oxhill, Social Historian.* *Special Interests:* As Above, Besides M.S.C. Correspondence of Ministerial Candidates. *Hobbies and Recreations:* Music with particular reference to Elgar's works.

LOY, Frederick William, 28B Beeston Rd., Sheringham, Norfolk NR26 8EH. (0263 3691) *b. 14 Nov 1907, Sheffield. m. 25 July 1936: 2d., 1s.* *Education:* Council Sch., Sheffield; 1930–32 Hartley. *Appointments:* 1932–33 Cardiff; 1933–36 Penge and Bromley; 1936–37 Hay; 1937–39 Luton; 1939–42 Beccles, Loddon and Bungay; 1942–45 Kings Lynn; 1945–49 Leicester, Hinckley Rd.; 1949–55 Cromer; 1955–63 Norwich, St. Peters. *Connexional Committees:* Ministers Retirement Fund; Junior Catechism Committee. *Publications:* Newspaper Articles. *Hobbies and Recreations:* Tennis, Golf.

LUCAS, Beryl Elizabeth, 28 Evelyn Rd., Barnet, Herts EN 9JT. (01 449 6033) *b. North London.* *Education:* The Skinners' Company's Sch., Stamford Hill, London N16; Rhyl County Sch., North Wales;

1973–76 Wesley, Bristol. *Appointments:* 1976–81 Nottingham West; 1981– Barnet. *Connexional Committees:* 1974– Connexional Candidates Committee; 1977–81 Connexional Candidates Examination Committee.

LUCAS, Jack, Valley Farm Cottage, Fimber, Driffield, N. Humberside YO25 9LY. (0377 86698)—BSc, BD, MSc. *b. 18 June 1935, Moor Row, Cumberland. m. 20 June 1959: 1d., 2s.* *Education:* 1945–53 Whitehaven Grammar Sch.; 1953–56 Leeds Univ.; 1956–59 Manchester Univ.; 1973–74 Univ. Coll., North Wales; 1956–59 Hartley Victoria. *Appointments:* 1959–62 Upwell and Manea; 1962–65 Sheffield Mission; 1965–69 Leominster; 1969–73 Selby; 1974– Bishop Burton Coll. of Agriculture.

LUCKCOCK, Francis Laurence Saunders, The Manse, 9 Willow Avenue, Stapleford, Nottingham NG9 7FZ. (0602 392182)—BA. *b. 20 April 1939, Madras, South India. m. 26 Oct 1968: 3d., 2s.* *Education:* 1950–52 Priors Court Sch.; 1952–58 Kingswood Sch., Bath; 1958–60 St. Peter Coll. of Education, Saltley, Birmingham; 1960–61 Sunderland Coll. of Education; 1966–67 Institute of Education, Univ. of London; 1972–75 Univ. of Manchester; 1972–75 Hartley Victoria. *Appointments:* 1975–81 South Derbyshire; 1981– Long Eaton; 1975– Industrial Chaplain to the Coal Industry. *Connexional Committees:* 1982 Representative to Board of Social Responsbility; 1980–82 Representative to DSR Standing committee for Family Life; 1982– Representative to DSR Standing Committee for Family, Healing and Personal Concerns. *Special Interests:* Life Member National Trust, Life F.R.G.S., Life Member of London Huguenot Society, Hon. Member N.U.M. and Power Group, Member Industrial Mission Association (Midlands Region), Member C.E.I.M., Member C.N.D.

LUKCOCK, Stuart Sydney, Longford, 71 Runton Rd., Cromer, Norfolk NR27 9AU. (0263 513563) *b. 28 May 1908, Muswell Hill, London. m. 2 April 1938: 2d., 2s.* *Education:* Alexandra Park Prim. Sch.; Glendale County Secondary Sch., Wood Green, London N22; 1929–30 Didsbury; 1930–32 Headingley. *Appointments:* 1932–44 Madras Dt, India; 1944–45 Forest of Dean Mission; 1945–48 Madras Dt, India; 1948–53 Church of South India; 1953–56 Bath; 1956–61 Buckfastleigh; 1961–65 Church of South India; 1965–70 Hartlepools; 1970–74 Church of South India. *Publications:* Missionary Deputation Addresses, Travel Lectures. *Special Interests:* Mission Promotion, Local Preacher Training, Class Leading, Preaching, Peace Group Work. *Hobbies and Recreations:* Gardening, Photography.

LUCRAFT, Ian Gilchrist, 8 Andover St., Sheffield S3 9EG. (0742 737800)—BA. *b. 25 Sept 1946, Epsom, Surrey. m. 20 March 1976: 1s.* *Education:* 1951–57 Pound Lane County Prim. and Jun. Schs., Epsom; 1957–65 Kingston on Thames Grammar Sch.; 1966–69 Univ. Coll., Univ. of Durham; 1969–72 Birmingham Univ.; 1972–74 Leeds Univ.; 1982– Sheffield Univ.; 1969–70 Handsworth; 1970–72 Queen's. *Appointments:* 1972–74 Leeds North-East; 1974 Sheffield Inner City Ecumenical Mission. *Connexional Committees:* 1976– DSR Community and Race Relations Sub-Committee. *Special Interests:* Community Action and Race. *Hobbies and Recreations:* Computing, Genealogy, U.S. Political History, Squash, Carpentry.

LUDLOW, Shirley 15 Hollins Lane, Hampsthwaite, Harrogate HG3 2EJ. (0423 770396) *b. 22 March 1935, Leeds, Yorkshire* *Education:* 1977–79 Wesley, Bristol. *Appointments:* 1979– Harrogate.

LUKE, Richard Hubert, Boulders, St. Breward, Bodmin, Cornwall PL30 4NX. (0208 850653) *b. 22 Sept 1908, Camborne, Cornwall. m. 1. 9 Aug 1937, 2. 15 Sept 1960: 1s.* *Education:* 1919–25 Redruth Grammar; 1931–34 Richmond Coll. *Appointments:* 1930–31 Wellington, Salop; 1934–37 London Mission, Hackney; 1937–46 London Mission, East Ham; 1946–52 Helston; 1952–55 St. Ives; 1955–62 Camborne; 1962–63 Newquay; 1963–73 Chairman Cornwall District; 1956–63 Secretary Cornwall District Synod. *Connexional Committees:* 1958–73 Home Missions; 1963–73 Education and Youth; 1945–57 Christian Citizenship; 1972–73 Presidents Council; 1959–73 Faith and Order; 1967–73 Chapel Committee; 1963–73 Stationing; 1963–73 General Purposes. *Local Council Committees:* 1963–73 Cornwall County Council Education: 1963–74 Ministry of Labour West Cornwall Youth Employment, 1960–74 Chairman. *Publications:* 1982 Charles Coulson Lecture. *Special Interests:* Reading, Sport. *Hobbies and Recreations:* Woodwork, Gardening, Painting.

LUKE, Stanley, 3 Church Rd., Shortlands, Bromley, Kent BR2 0HP. (01 460 7006) *b. 22 July 1899, Truro, Cornwall. w: 1d.* *Education:* Devon County Sch.; 1921–24 Hartley. *Appointments:* 1924–26 London, Forest Hill; 1926–30 Burnley; 1930–33 Sheffield, Psalter Lane; 1933–36 Littleborough; 1936–39 Cardiff, Roath; 1939–45 Penzance, Chapel St.; 1945–48 Newquay; 1948–52 St. Just; 1952–56 Redruth, Wesley; 1956–61 Southend-on-Sea; 1961–66 Hertford. *Connexional Committees:* 1945–56 Secretary Cornwall Synod.

LUND, Derek Calvert, 49 Station Rd., Altofts, Normanton, West Yorkshire WF6 2NB. (0924 893193) *b. 27 Oct 1934, Halifax. m. 25 March 1961: 2d., 1s.* *Education.* 1939–45 Bradshaw Prim./Jun. Sch.; 1945–48 Ovenden Secondary Modern Sch.; 1948–50 Halifax Jun. Technical Sch.; 1962–65 Headingley. *Appointments:* 1965–68 Brighouse; 1968–71 Wensleydale; 1971–76 Driffield; 1976–80 Ossett and Horbury; 1980– Pontefract and

Normanton.
Special Interests: Counselling People. *Hobbies and Recreations:* Music, Football, Gardening.

LUNN, Ian Carmichael, 110 West Town Lane, Bristol BS4 5DT. (0272 779369)–BSc(Dunelm), MA(Cantab). *b. 9 March 1928, Gosforth. m. 11 Aug 1956: 2d., 2s.* *Education:* 1938–45 Worksop Coll.; 1945–49 King's Coll., Univ. of Durham, Newcastle; 1951–53 Wesley House. *Appointments:* 1953–56 Forest of Dean; 1956–61 Wiltshire Mission; 1961–68 Bristol South; 1968–75 Sutton, Surrey; 1975– Bristol District Chairman.

LUNN, Jennifer Barbara, The Manse, Station Rd., Bentham, Lancaster LA2 7LF. (0468 61257)– BD. *b. Huddersfield.*
Education: Eastburn Prim. Sch., Keighley Girls' Grammar Sch.; Leeds College of Commerce; Wesley Deaconess; 1973–74 Wesley, Bristol. *Appointments:* 1974–79 Barnsley; 1979– Settle.
Connexional Committees: Conservative Evangelicals in Methodism.

LUNT, Raymond, 93 Dunelm South, Sunderland, Tyne and Wear SR2 7QX. (0783 42218)–FCA. *b. 27 April 1941, Winsford, Cheshire. m. 29 Aug 1964: 1d.*
Education: 1952–58 Winsford Verdin Grammar Sch.; 1980–82 Manchester Univ.; 1980–82 Hartley Victoria. *Appointments:* 1982– Sunderland South.
Connexional committees: 1975–80 Connexional Home Missions Board. *Council Member:* 1967–73 Winsford Urban District Council; 1973–76 Vale Royal District Council (Chairman and Mayor 1972); 1973–76 Winsford Town Council, Finance Chairman. *Local Council Committees:* Member of Steering Committee; Planning, Management, Amenities, Housing, Finance. *Publications:* Occasional Newspaper Articles.
Special Interests: Drama in Worship, Evangelism, Play-Writing, Christian Stewardship. *Hobbies and Recreations:* Crown Green Bowls, Walking, Spectator at Cricket and Football, Music, Gardening.

LUSCOMBE, Philip, 37 Eversley Rd., Upper Norwood, London SE19 3PY. (01 653 4902)–MA(Oxon). *Appointments:* 1976–79 London Mission South; 1979 London, Sydenham and Forest Hill.

LUSTY, John Richard, 28 The Croft, Sudbury, Suffolk CO10 6HW. (0787 72738) *b. 23 Oct 1932, London. m. 11 Aug 1956: 3s.* *Education:* Billericay Sch.; 1953–56 Didsbury Coll., Bristol.
Appointments: 1956–57 Sheffield, Surrey St.; 1957–58 Gower; 1959–62 Ely; 1963–68 Bedford South; 1969–75 Gt. Yarmouth and Gorleston; 1976–81 Bury St. Edmunds; 1982– Plymouth.
Special Interests: Stewardship. *Hobbies and Recreations:* Photography, Gardening.

LYDDON, Hedley Percival, 29 Poplar Rd., Merton Park, London SW19 3JR. (01 542 4758)–BD. *b. 18 Jan 1927, Chagford, Devon. m. 26 July 1956: 2d.*
Education: 1931–37 Chagford Prim.; 1937–44 Queen Elizabeth's Grammar Sch., Crediton, Devon; 1951–54 Richmond. *Appointments:* 1954–57 Deal; 1957–61 Kent Mission; 1961–66 Chislehurst; 1966–73 Kingston-upon-Thames; 1973–78 London, Tooting Mission; 1978– Wimbledon. *Connexional committees:* 1976–81 Prison Committee; Penal Affairs (sub committee) D.S.R. *Local Council Committees:* 1973–76, 1979– Merton Education Committee.
Special Interests: Penal Reform. *Hobbies and Recreations:* Cricket, Philately.

LYNN, William McLarnon, 27 Egerton Rd., Birkenhead, Merseyside L43 1UJ. (051 652 5458)–STM. *b. 15 Dec 1944, Sunderland, Co. Durham. m. 20 July 1968: 2s.* *Education:* Southmoor Technical Sch., Sunderland; 1969–72 Univ. of Birmingham; 1973–74 Univ. of Dubuque, USA, Theological Seminary; 1965–69 Hartley Victoria. *Appointments:* 1969–73 Wolverhampton, Darlington St.; 1973–74 World Council of Churches Scholarship, USA; 1974–79 Stourbridge and Brierley; 1979– Birkenhead.

LYON, Keith Frederick, The Manse, 19 Queen Anne's Gardens, Ealing, London W5 5QD. (01 567 2992). *Education:* 1947–50 Hartley Victoria. *Appointments:* 1950–53 Higham Ferrers; 1953–57 Stroud and Cirencester; 1957–61 Brinkworth; 1961–66 Ashford, Kent; 1966–69 St. Leonard's and Bexhill; 1969–76 Dunstable; 1976– Ealing and Acton.

MACADAM, John Fullerton, Chaplain's Office, 8 Regiment Rct, BFPO 17. (010-49-251-273798) *b. 1 Nov 1935, Glasgow. m. 19 August 1961: 3d.*
Education: 1940–45 Angus Oval Prim. Sch., Glasgow; 1945–47 Cardonald Jun. Sch., Glasgow; 1947–50 Bellahouston Academy, Glasgow; 1957–61 Wesley, Headingley.
Appointments: 1961–64 Ryton and Prudhoe; 1964–69 Gateshead East; 1969–74 Bedale; 1974– HM Forces Chaplain.
Connexional Committees: 1966–67 MAYC Committee. *Local Council Committees:* 1967 Gateshead Youth Council.
Special Interests: Hymnology, Church Music. *Hobbies and Recreations:* Drama, Philately, Football Referee, Music, Reading, Photography.

MACDONALD, David Hills, 15 Lynnwood Ave., Newcastle upon Tyne NE4 6XB. (0632-733503) *b. 18 Aug 1932, Askern, Nr. Doncaster, South Yorkshire. m. 15 April 1961: 1d., 1s.*
Education: 1936–43 Askern Moss Rd. Inf.; 1943–45 Sutton Rd. Secondary Modern Sch.; 1945–47 Doncaster Technical High Sch.; 1956–57 St. Andrews, Selly Oak; 1953–56 Handsworth.
Appointments: 1957–61 S.E. Asia (Sarawak); 1961–66 Doncaster South; 1966–73 Newcastle upon Tyne, North West; 1973–78 Newcastle/Tyne Heaton and

Wallsend; 1978– Newcastle West. *Connexional Committees:* 1963–68 Overseas Missions Central Committee; 1968–74 Eastern Committee and Successor (Asia Committee).
Special Interests: China (History and Peace). *Hobbies and Recreations:* Music (Listening to Classical), Playing Northumbrian Pipes.

MACK, James, 63 High St., Eston, Middlesbrough, Cleveland TS6 9EH. (0642-464399)–BD. *b. 8 May 1918, Glasgow. m. 28 June 1945: 3d.*
Education: 1923–26 Springfield Rd. Sch.; 1926–29 Ramshorn Sch.; 1930–35 Whitehill Sch.; 1939–42 Headingley. *Appointments:* 1942–44 Glasgow, Cathcart Rd.; 1944–47 Chaplain HMF; 1947–53 Stockton; 1953–59 Edinburgh Mission; 1955–59 District Youth Secretary Scotland; 1959–66 Darlington; 1961–64 Secretary of Darlington District Synod; 1966–76 Glasgow West; 1977–81 Paisley Mission;
Connexional Committees: 1955–59 Youth Committee; Early 1960's Faith and Order.
Special Interests: Industrial Mission. *Hobbies and Recreations:* Walking, Gardening, Golf.

MACKENZIE, Andrew Garnet, 21 Castle Hill, Duffield, Derby DE6 4EA. (0332-841167)–BD(Lond.). *b. 9 April 1937, Barrow-in-Furness. m. 26 Sept 1959: 3d.*
Education: 1948–53 Hamond's Grammar Sch., Swaffham, Norfolk; 1964–67, 1971–72 Richmond; 1967 Kingsmead. *Appointments:* 1968–79 Kenya Conference; 1979– Belper; 1982– Synod Secretary, Notts and Derby District; 1981–82 District JMA Secretary.
Special Interests: The World. *Hobbies and Recreations:* Black Fives.

MACKENZIE, Kenneth, 45A Rhos Rd., Colwyn Bay, Clwyd LL28 4RS. (4092-48925) *b. 19 March 1912, Wallasey, Cheshire. m. 26 July 1939: 2d., 2s.*
Education: 1917–23 Riverside Council Sch., Wallasey; 1923–28 Oldershaw Grammar Sch., Wallasey; 1932–55 Wesley, Headingley.
Appointments: 1935–37 Sunderland South East; 1937–41 Southport South; 1941–46 Chaplain HMF; 1947 Ilfracombe; 1947–52 Southport North; 1952–57 York Wesley; 1957–64 Bolton Mission; 1964–69 Morecambe and Heysham; 1969–77 Kirkby Stephen, Appleby and Tebay.
Connexional Committees: Convenor Church Benevolence Committee; President's Council; Pastoral Sub-committee.
Special Interests: Ecumenical Follies, Psychiatry. *Hobbies and Recreations:* Woodwork, Printing.

MACKINDER, Janet Aileen, 41 Tatefield Grove, Kippax, Leeds LS25 7LA. (862780) *b. 25 Sept 1935, Bromley, Kent. m. 24 May 1980.*
Education: 1947–50 Swanley County Secondary Sch.; 1960–62 Wesley, Deaconess Coll.; 1967–68 Kingsmead. Appointments: 1980– Castleford.
Hobbies and Recreations: Walking, Sewing, Gardening.

MACLENNAN, Duncan Alexander Fraser, Walsoken House, St. Peters St., Stamford, Lincs PE9 2PQ. (0780-4195)–BD(Lond.). *b. 6 May 1934, Glasgow. m. 17 Dec 1960: 2d., 1s.*
Education: 1941–48 Shawlands Academy; 1948–52 Latymers Grammar Sch.; 1956–57 Cliff Coll.; 1958–62 Richmond.*Appointments:* 1952–58 Bow Mission; 1962–64 Bedale; 1964– Chaplain HMF (RAF).
Special Interests: Pastoral Counselling and Education. *Hobbies and Recreations:* Cycling.

MADDRAN, James Ronald, 23 Cold Overton Rd., Oakham, Rutland, Leics LE15 6NT. (2239) *b. 18 April 1925, Liverpool. m. 18 April 1964: 1s.*
Education: 1930–38 Morrisson; 1938–41 Old Swan Technical Coll.; 1954–57 Hartley Victoria
Appointments: 1957–63 Leeward Islands Dt; 1963–66 Brigg; 1966–70 Newton-le-Willows; 1970–74 Huddersfield West; 1974–77 Ipswich; 1977–82 Hull West; 1982– Melton Mowbray.
Connexional Committees: 1964–66 MMS Central; 1972–74 MMS Central.
Hobbies and Recreations: Bonsai.

MAGOR, Glanville Thomas, 9 Godolphin Rd., Helston, Cornwall TR13 8PX. (032-65-2303)–BD(Hons)(Lond.). *b. 5 May 1925, Rotherham, Yorkshire. m. 17 July 1954: 1d., 1s.*
Education: 1936–40 Loughborough Coll. Sch.; 1941–44 Loughborough Coll. (Aeronautical Dept.); 1953–54 Theological Faculty, Montpellier, France; 1949–53 Handsworth.
Appointments: 1954–56 Porto Novo Seminary, Dahomey; 1957–58 Sierra Leone District; 1959–69 Milton Margai Teachers Coll., Freetown, Sierra Leone; 1969–76 Glasgow (St. Johns) (Univ. Chaplain); 1976– Helston.
Connexional Committees. 1973–74 OM.
Special Interests: Science, Religion, Radical Theology. *Hobbies and Recreations:* Puppetry, Early Railway History.

MAGUIRE, Andrew Philip, 206 Lowestoft Rd., Gorleston, Great Yarmouth, Norfolk NR31 6JQ. (0493-61469)–MA, BD. *b. 15 March 1954, Carshalton, Surrey. m. 12 Aug 1978: 1s.*
Education: 1964–71 Raynes Park Grammar Sch.; 1972–76 Worcester Coll., Oxford; 1978–81 Hartley Victoria. *Appointments:* 1981– Great Yarmouth and Gorleston.
Publications: What is the Significance of Utilitarianism for Contemporary Christian Ethics? (1979 Univ. of Manchester *Papers in Religion and Politics*).
Special Interests: The Ecumenical Movement. *Hobbies and Recreations:* Music, Gardening.

MAKEY, John Alan, 2 Saxon's Drive, Maidstone, Kent ME14 5HS. (0622-52895)–BA(Birmingham). *b. 7 May 1934, Dover, Kent. m. 4 April 1959: 3s.*
Education: 1945–52 Dover County Grammar Sch. for Boys; 1954–58 Handsworth. *Appointments:* 1958–59 Cowbridge and St. Athan; 1959–69 Corozal, Belize, Central America;

1969–75 Gateshead and Jarrow; 1975–81 Tonbridge; 1981– Maidstone.
Connexional Committees: 1970–75 Overseas Division Central Committee.
Hobbies and Recreations: Music, Basketball, Cricket, Football, Squash, Tennis.

MALE, Donald, 37 Rivermead Ave., Exmouth, Devon EX8 3BR. (75939) *b. 26 Sept 1914, Halesowen, Worcestershire. m. 20 July 1940: 2s.*
Education: 1926–33 Halesowen Grammar Sch.; 1933–35 Manchester Univ.; 1933–34 Victoria Park; 1934–37 Hartley Victoria. *Appointments:* 1937–44 Yeovil; 1944–49 Sidmouth; 1949–54 Bristol (Horfield); 1954–60 Bournemouth; 1960–66 West Kirby; 1966–72 Harrow; 1972–74 Exmouth; 1957–60 Synod Secretary Southampton District.
Connexional Committees: 1957–60 General Purposes.
Hobbies and Recreations: Rugby, Football, Cricket, Gardening (especially Sweet Peas).

MALLETT, Reginald, Byvale, Sandy Lane Rd., Charlton Kings, Cheltenham GL53 9DB. (0242-518519)–BD(Lond.), MB, CHB(Birmingham), MFCM(Royal Coll. of Physicians of the United Kingdom). *b. 27 Aug 1929, Warrington, Lancashire. m. 7 Aug 1956: 1d., 1s.*
Education: 1940–46 Boteler Grammar Sch.; 1946–48 Wigan Coll. of Mining and Technology; 1952–55 London Univ.; 1964–70 Birmingham Univ.; 1952–55 Richmond Coll.
Appointments: 1951–52 Sheffield Mission; 1955–56 London Mission, Poplar and Bow; 1956–59 London, Westminster; 1959–64 Manchester and Salford Mission; 1971–75 General Medical Practitioner; 1976–79 Registrar and Senior Registrar in Community Medicine; 1979–82 Consultant in Community Medicine; 1982– District Medical Officer, Cheltenham District Health Authority.
Connexional Committees: 1977– Ministers Medical Sub Committee; 1979– Committee for Further Training for the Ministry.
Publications: 1978– Articles on Perinatal Mortality in Medical Journals.
Special Interests: Medical Ethics, English and American History, Gardening. *Hobbies and Recreations:* Music, Walking.

MALTAS, Clement, Charis, Primrose Hill, Blackwell, Derbys DE5 5JF. (812563) *b. 8 Nov 1904, Roberttown, Liversedge, Yorkshire. w.*
Education: 1909–14 Knowle Mirfield, Yorkshire; 1914–18 Norristhorpe, Liversedge, Yorkshire; 1931–33 Cliff Coll. *Appointments:* 1964–67 Grays; 1967–70 Hindley.
Hobbies and Recreations: Music, Cricket, Football.

MANKIN, Kenneth, 25 Hoodcote Gdns, Winchmore Hill, London N21 2NG. (01-360-1459)–BA(Open). *b. 22 July 1939, Jarrow on Tyne. m. 14 Aug 1975: 2s.*
Education: Cliff Coll.; 1962–66 Hartley Victoria. *Appointments:* 1966–68 Portsmouth and Southsea; 1968–72 Sunderland South; 1972–77 Fleetwood; 1977– London, Finsbury Park and Southgate.
Connexional Committees: 1975– Board of Division of Education Youth; 1977– Connexional Uniformed Organisation's Committee. *Council Member:* District Secretary Education Training; District Secretary Education and Youth; 1980– District General Purposes Secretary; 1981– Assistant Secretary of Synod. *Local Council Committees:* 1972–77 Secondary Sch. Governor; Member of Education Committee, London Borough Enfield.
Publications: Contribution to *Celebration* and *Getting it all Together,* 4 monthly worship publications of United Church of Canada; Report with others on Bishop of Durham's Commission on Church in Urban Community; Report for Council of Social Services *Teenage problems with reference to delinquency.*
Special Interests: Member of Methodist Pastoral Support Team to Northern Ireland; Education and Youth Work, Boys Brigade. *Hobbies and Recreations:* Gardening, Home, Family, Photography, Touring.

MANLEY, Arthur, 33 Saunders Close, Kettering NN16 0AP. (519921) *b. 14 Dec 1903, Paulton, Somerset. w.: 2s.*
Education: Wesleyan Sch., Paulton; 1925 Cliff Coll.; 1928–31 Handsworth. *Appointments:* 1927–28 Retford; 1931–34 London, Tottenham; 1934–37 Newmarket; 1937-41 Cambridge; 1941–45 Chaplain HMF; 1945–48 Wolverton and Bletchley; 1948–53 Hull, Coltman St.; 1953–59 Sheffield, Ecclesall; 1959–68 Kettering.
Special Interests: Music, Classical, Pastoral, Hospitals, Travel. *Hobbies and Recreations:* Gardening, Motoring, Reading, TV, Radio.

MANN, Cecil Palmer, 1 Springbank Ave., Endon, Stoke-on-Trent, Staffordshire ST9 9EL. (0782-503228)–BA. *b. 15 July 1930, Gosford, New South Wales, Australia.*
Education: 1940–48 Rock Ferry High Sch., Birkenhead; 1948–52 Liverpool Univ.; 1970–72 Manchester Univ.; 1970–72 Hartley Victoria.
Appointments: 1972–76 Belper; 1976– Leek.
Special Interests: Geographical and Historical Studies, Mission in Rural Areas, Work Among Young People.
Hobbies and Recreations: Gardening, Photography, Walking, Reading, Stamp Collecting.

MANN, David, 45 Southam Rd., Hall Green, Birmingham B28 8DQ. (021-777-1945)–BD(Lond.). *b. 29 Aug 1930, Silkstone Common, Nr. Barnsley, Yorkshire. m. 11 Oct 1969: 2d.*
Education: 1941–49 Wath-upon-Dearne Grammar Sch.; 1951–52 Cliff Coll.; 1953–57 Hartley Victoria.
Appointments: 1952–53 Banbury; 1957–58 Wirksworth; 1958–62 Newcastle (Staffs); 1962–64 London Mission (South); 1964–69 Mid-Wales Mission; 1969–74 Sheffield Mission; 1974–82 Cannock Chase; 1982– Birmingham, Moseley Rd. and

Sparkhill.
Hobbies and Recreations: Tennis, Theatre, Travel.

MANN, David Douglas, 5 Southmayne Rd., High Barnes, Sunderland, Tyne and Wear SR4 8NF. (0783-285215) *b. 11 Mar 1938, South Shields. m. 1 June 1953: 2s.*
Education: 1943–46 Ingleton Inf.; 1946–49 Mortimer Rd. (South Shields); 1949–54 South Shields High Sch.; 1958–59 Durham Sch. of Agriculture; 1970–72 Queen's.
Appointments: 1972–76 Ryton and Prudhoe; 1976–79 Radcliffe; 1979– Sunderland South.
Special Interests: Wildlife Conservation. *Hobbies and Recreations:* Bird Watching.

MANTLE, William Eric, 32 The Drive, Orpington, Kent BR6 9AP. (26368)–MA. *b. 16 May 1917, Claybanger, Devon. m. 22 June 1949: 1d., 2s.*
Education: 1927–35 Tiverton Sch.; 1935–36 Seale-Hayne Coll.; 1960–65 Bristol Univ.; 1938–41 Richmond.
Appointments: 1941–43 Tamworth and Lichfield; 1943–73 Chaplain HMF; 1973–82 Christian Aid.
Connexional Committees: R. Navy, Army, RAF Board. *Publications:* Thesis for Bristol Univ. *The Theological Significance of the PMUB Church of the RAF and its Contribution to the Reunion of the Churches.*
Special Interests: Royal Air Force History, John Wesley and Wesleyana.
Hobbies and Recreations: Aircraft and Flying, Horses and Polo, Gardening and Landscaping.

MANUELL, Frederick George, 19 Black Oak Rd., Cyncoed, Cardiff CF2 6QT. (0222-752477)–BA(Leeds). *b. 12 July 1930, Portsmouth. m. 4 March 1956: 4s.*
Education: 1935–38 Burnham-on-Crouch, Essex; 1938–39 Selsey, Sussex; 1939–41 Prim. Port Isaac, N. Cornwall; 1941–46 Sir James Smiths Grammar Sch., Camelford, Cornwall; 1946–48 Chichester High Sch., Sussex; 1948–50 Brighton Technical Coll.; 1951–54 Leeds Univ.; 1951–54 Headingley.
Appointments: 1954–57 Uxbridge, Hayes and Yiewsley; 1957–64 Slough; 1964–72 London, Finsbury Park and Southgate; 1972–78 Leigh-on-Sea; 1978– Cardiff.
Connexional Committees: 1963–72 Christian Citizenship.
Hobbies and Recreations: Woodwork, Gardening, Sketching, Sailing, Chess, Car Maintenance.

MARES, Stephen Robert, 56 Crescent Drive North, Woodingdean, Brighton BN2 6SN. (0273-34825)–MA(Cantab.), BSc(Birm.). *b. 8 Sept 1951, Cardiff. m. 18 July 1981.*
Education: 1956–63 Roath Park Inf. and Jun. Schs., Cardiff; 1963–70 The Stationers' Company's Sch., London; 1970–73 Birmingham Univ.; 1973–74 Westminster Coll., Oxford; 1976–79 Wesley House. *Appointments:* 1979– Brighton (Dome Mission).
Local Council Committees: 1979– Free Church Council Rep., East Sussex Education Committee.
Special Interests: Education, Youth Work, MAYC, Boys' Brigade. *Hobbies and Recreations:* Travel, especially Trains, Sport, Walking, Music.

MARK, Timothy John, 15 Fieldhouse Rd., Doncaster DN5 7RN. (0302-853022)–BA, MLitt, MEd(Bristol), PhD(Leeds). *b. 4 Feb 1934, Penarth. m. 20 Sept 1975: 1d., 1s.*
Education: 1945–50 Purley County Grammar Sch. for Boys; 1954–58, 1969–70 Univ. of Bristol; 1974–79 Univ. of Leeds; 1954–58 Didsbury, Bristol. *Appointments:* 1959–69 Church of South India; 1970–73 Head of Religious Education, Passmores Comprehensive Sch., Harlow, Essex; 1973–76 Lecture in Religious Studies, Doncaster Coll. of Education; 1976–78 Senior Lecturer in Education, Doncaster Metropolitan Institute of Higher Education; 1978– Principal Lecturer, Social and Personal Studies.
Publications: The Church of South India: its doctrine of the Church as embodied in its Church Order, MLitt, Bristol, dissertation, 1968; *The performance of a sample of eleven year old pupils on creativity tests in a comprehensive school given in a timed and in an untimed situation,* MEd Bristol, dissertation, 1971; *The Relevances of Education* by Jerome S. Bruner, Review, *Journal of Moral Education,* Vol. 3, 2, February 1974; *A study of cognitive and affective elements in the religious development of adolescent,* PhD (Leeds), dissertation, 1979; *Compassionate attitudes in two comprehensive school, Journal of Moral Education,* Vol. 11, No. 2, 1982; *Negative attitudes and the adolescent's understanding of religion: an impetus for curriculum change, Digest,* Journal of the Association of Christian Teachers, Vol. 8, 2, 1982; Ed. J. H. Peatling: *Annual Review of Research: Religious Education,* Vol. 2, 1981, contributor, Character Research Press, USA; Ed. J. Sutcliffe: *Dictionary of Religious Education,* SCM Press, 1983, contributor, forthcoming; *Measuring self-esteem and religious behaviour: some problems and connections,* Working Paper read to the Research Group, International Seminar on Religious Education and Values, at Driebergen, Holland, 30th June 1982.
Special Interests: Religious development of adolescents. *Hobbies and Recreations:* Child-rearing, Badminton.

MARKHAM, Thomas William, 76 Gunthorpe Rd., Peterborough PE4 6TP. (0733-73147) *b. 4 July 1924, Great Limber, Lincolnshire. m. 13 Aug 1953: 1d., 2s.*
Education: 1929–38 Brocklesby Park CE Sch.; 1948–51 Headingley.
Appointments: 1947–48 Cheadle; 1951–53 Market Weighton; 1953–56 Epworth and Crowle; 1956–62 Halifax (West); 1962–69 Nottingham (North); 1969–75 Grimsby (West); 1975– Peterborough.
Hobbies and Recreations: Photography, Gardening.

MARR, Stephen John, 11 Warfield Ave., Waterlooville, Portsmouth, Hants PO7 7JN. (07014-2291) *b. 21 Nov 1939, Harrow, Middlesex. m. 15 June 1968: 1d., 1s.*
Education: 1950–56 Lower Sch. of

John Lyon, Harrow; 1964–68 Wesley, Bristol . *Appointments:* 1968–71 North of Scotland Mission; 1971–78 Scunthorpe; 1978– Portsmouth. *Special Interests:* Ecumenical Work. *Hobbies and Recreations:* Music, Cricket.

MARRAT, Francis Dixon, 22 Clover Rd., Eaton Socon, Huntingdon, Cambs PE19 3HD. (0480-212774) *b. 9 Sept 1902, Birmingham. m. 14 July 1949: 1d., 1s. (w.).*
Education: Rydal Sch., Colwyn Bay; 1927–30 Didsbury. *Appointments:* 1926 Halifax and Bradford, Chairman's Assistant; 1930–34 Stoke Newington; 1934–36 Kilburn and Hampstead; 1936–38 Bedford; 1938–44 Southall and Uxbridge; 1944–47 Woking; 1947–48 French West Africa; 1948–49 Mexborough; 1949–52 Twickenham; 1952–57 Slough Mission; 1957–60 French West Africa; 1960–68 Sierra Leone.

MARRIOTT, Edward Meuris, 20 Hartington Rd., Millhouses, Sheffield S7 2LE. (0742-361546)–BD. *b. 31 March 1925, Daventry. m. 14 Aug 1954: 1d., 2s.*
Education: 1936–41 Lawrence Sherrif Sch., Rugby; 1941–43 Rugby Technical Coll.; 1949–52 Headingley. *Appointments:* 1948–49 Cheadle (Staffs); 1952–54 Kimberley; 1954–58 Mansfield (Nottingham Rd.); 1958–61 Liverpool North; 1961–68 North Shields and Whitley Bay; 1968–75 Tadcaster; 1975– Sheffield (Ecclesall).
Hobbies and Recreations: Walking, Photography, DIY.

MARSDEN, Harold, 3 Tivydale Drive, Darton, Barnsley, South Yorkshire S75 5PG. (0226-382931) *b. 26 Nov 1907, Morley, Leeds, West Yorkshire. m. 26 July 1938: 2s.*
Education: 1911–19 Cross Hall Elem. Sch.; 1919–23 Morley Grammar Sch.; 1932–36 Didsbury. *Appointments:* 1931–32 Daventry; 1936–37 Wath-upon-Dearne; 1937–40 Longton and Fenton; 1940–42 Wye Valley Mission; 1942–44 Barrow-in-Furness; 1944–48 Great Harwood; 1948–53 Bacup; 1953–58 Halifax, St. John's; 1958 Halifax, Fairfield; 1959–63 Halifax, Wesley; 1963–69 Huddersfield South; 1969–75 Hebden Bridge.
Special Interests: English History and Literature, Money (coin collecting). *Hobbies and Recreations:* Painting, Walking.

MARSDEN, Keith, The Manse, Chulmleigh Rd., Merchard Bishop, Crediton, Devon EX17 6NZ. (03637-281) *b. 27 Sept 1939. m.: 2s.*
Education: 1964–65 Cliff Coll.; 1969–70 Westhill Coll. of Education; 1966–69 Handsworth.
Appointments: 1970–72 Halifax; 1972–76 Sheffield, Ecclesall; 1976–81 Knaresborough; 1981– Ringsash.
Special Interests: Relevant and Progressive Evangelism, Youth Work, Christ's Ministry through the Church to the Complete Person in Community. *Hobbies and Recreations:* Family Life and Interests, Gardening, Board Games.

MARSH, Herbert George, 27 Elwy Rd., Colwyn Bay, Clwyd LL28 4SB. (0492-48584)–MA(Cantab.), DD(Manchester). *b. 17 Aug 1889, Cambridge. m. 28 Aug 1922: 1d., 2s.*
Education: Cambridge, Perse Grammar Sch.; St. Catherine's, Cambridge; Manchester Univ.; Hartley Victoria. *Appointments:* 1913–14 Burnley; 1914–15 Horwich; 1915–16 Cambridge; 1916–23 Oldham (Royton); 1923–30 Blackpool; 1930–35 Oldham (Hollingwood); 1935–41 Manchester (Culcheth); 1941–46 Derby (King St.); 1946–53 Cradley Heath.
Connexional Committees: 1927–41 Ministerial Training Committee.
Publications: Origin and Significance of the New Testament Baptism (Manchester 1941).

MARSH, Leslie Joseph, Wesley Manse, Drews Holloway, Halesowen, W. Midlands B63 2AQ. (0384-66040)–MA(Cantab.), BA(Bristol). *b. 2 July 1930, Davenham, Cheshire. m. 23 Nov 1968: 2d.*
Education: 1935–40 Brookdale Park, Newton Heath, Manchester; 1940–49 Kingswood Sch.; 1950–53 St. Catherines Coll., Cambridge; 1958–69 St. Andrews Coll., Selly Oak; 1955–58 Didsbury.
Appointments: 1959–61 Howden Caves; 1961–66 Hanley (Trinity); 1966–73 Bolton; 1973–76 Cardiff; 1976–80 Cwmbran.
Connexional Committees: 1972–82 Drama Committee.
Hobbies and Recreations: Music.

MARSH, Vernon, The Manse, Approach Rd., London E2. (01-980-5278)–BA.*b. 20 April 1949, St. Albans. m. 4 Oct 1980.*
Education: Summerbee Inf., Summerbee Jun., Bournemouth; Bournemouth Sch.; 1967–70 Downing Coll.; 1972–73 Tŭbingen Univ.; 1970–72 Wesley House.
Appointments: 1973–74 Newcastle, Brunswick; 1974–80 Gateshead and Jarrow; 1980– London Mission (East).
Hobbies and Recreations: The Countryside, Listening to Music.

MARSHALL, Horace Charles, 66 Wildbrook, Port Talbot, West Glamorgan SA13 2UN. (0639-883920) *b. 3 Nov 1919, Grimsby, Lincs. m. 26 June 1947: 1d., 1s.*
Education: Elem.; Secondary; 1945–47 Hartley Victoria. *Appointments:* 1947–50 Stafford; 1950–54 Woodville and Swadlincote; 1954 Louth; 1959–64 Gainsborough; 1964–69 Liverpool, Crosby; 1969–74 Berwick upon Tweed; 1974–79 Market Rasen; 1979 Port Talbot.
Parliamentary Service: 1939–45 HM Forces.

MARSHALL, I. Howard, 132 Deeside Gdns, Aberdeen AB1 7PX. (0224-35259)–MA, BD, PhD(Aberdeen), BA(Cantab.). *b. 12 Jan 1934, Carlisle. m. 25 March 1961: 3d., 1s.*
Education: 1946–51 Aberdeen Grammar Sch.; 1951–57 Aberdeen Univ.; 1957–59 Cambridge Univ.; 1959–60 Gottingen; 1957–59 Wesley House. *Appointments:* 1960–62 Assistant Tutor, Didsbury Coll.; 1962–64 Darlington South; 1964– Lecturer, subsequently Professor, Univ. of Aberdeen (New Testament Exegesis).

MARSLAND, Derrick Ronald, 2 The Mount, Malton, North Yorkshire YO17 0ND. (0653-2173) *b. 24 Mar 1923, Cleckheaton, Yorkshire. m. 22 Dec 1958: 2s.*
Education: 1928–34 Whitcliffe Rd. Jun. Sch., Cleckheaton; 1934–39 Heath Grammar Sch., Halifax; 1954–55 Cliff Coll.; 1956–58 Rhodes Univ., Grahamstown, South Africa.
Appointments: 1959–66 South Africa Conf.; 1966–71 Swansea and Gower; 1971–76 Crewe; 1976– Malton.
Local Council Committees: 1976–82 Clerk to Governor, Malton CP Sch.; 1978– Governor at Malton Sch.
Hobbies and Recreations: Sport, Music.

MARSTON, Charles Denis Graham, 35 Hill Cliffe Rd., Walton, Warrington WA4 6PA. (0925-63612) BA(Manchester). *b. 30 July 1921, Birkenhead, Cheshire. m. 28 July 1952: 2s.*
Education: 1926–32 Port Sunlight Elem. Sch.; 1932–38 Wirral Grammar Sch.; 1949–52 Hartley Victoria.
Appointments: 1952–65 North Rhodesia Dt; 1965–66 Zambia United Church; 1966–73 Hillingdon; 1973–80 Shildon; 1980– Warrington.
Connexional Committees: 1977– Home Missions Board.
Hobbies and Recreations: Gardening, Walking, Camping.

MARTIN, David Peter, 18 The Park, Onchan, Isle of Man. (0624-4464)–BA(Manchester), BA(Bristol). *b. 4 Oct 1952, Biggleswade, Bedfordshire. m. 14 July 1979.*
Education: 1964–71 Pilgrim Sch., Bedford; 1971–75 Lanchester Poly., Coventry; 1977–80; Univ. of Bristol; 1977–80 Wesley, Bristol.
Appointments: 1980– Douglas and Peel, IOM.
Hobbies and Recreations: Running.

MARTIN, Denman Kempthorne, 18 Abbey Hill Rd., Winchester, Hants SO23 7AT. (0962-4292)–BD(Lond.). *b. 2 Aug 1920, Cheshunt, Herts. m. 26 July 1947: 1d., 2s.*
Education: 1931–33 Plymouth Coll.; 1933–34 Sutton Secondary Sch., Plymouth; 1935–36 Poole Grammar Sch.; 1936–37 Kingswood Sch., Bath; 1946–47 Richmond.
Appointments: 1947–50 Camborne; 1950–54 Harpenden; 1954–58 Oxford; 1958–65 Croydon (South Norwood); 1965–70 Bideford (Chaplain, Edgehill Coll.); 1970–76 Blackpool (South); 1976–81 Swanage; 1981– Winchester.
Connexional Committees: Connexional Candidates Committee.
Special Interests: Drama, Entertainment. *Hobbies and Recreations:* Sailing, Photography.

MARTIN, Keith William, Bramlea, High Ridge Way, Bramhope, Leeds LS16 9AP. (0532-678355) *b. 27 Aug 1940, Esher, Surrey.*
Education: 1951–58 Poole Grammar Sch., Poole, Dorset; 1963–67 Richmond. *Appointments:* 1967–69 Colchester; 1969–74 Ilfracombe; 1974–77 Salisbury; 1977– Otley (Otley and Aireborough since 1981).

MARTIN, Kenneth A. J., 1 Wesley Villas, Frome BA11 1HP. (0373-62092).
Education: 1950–53 Handsworth.
Appointments: 1953–54 President's List (Newark-Leigh); 1954–55 East Cornwall Mission; 1955–56 South Devon Mission; 1965–60 Redruth; 1960–66 Bishop Auckland; 1966–71 Teesdale; 1971–77 Hatherleigh; 1977– Frome and Shepton Mallett.
Connexional Committees: 1958–60 Youth Council; 1980– Day Sch. Committee.

MARTIN, Sidney John, 75 Springfield Rd., Southwell, Notts NG25 0BS. (0636 814225)–BA(Cantab.), BSc(Bristol). *b. 28 June 1904, Winchcombe, Glos. m. 10 Aug 1935: 2s.*
Education: 1914–22 Cheltenham Grammar Sch.; 1922–25 Bristol Univ.; 1929–30 Marburg and Berlin; 1926–29 Wesley House.
Appointments: 1930–33 Edinburgh; 1933–37 Wellington (Salop); 1937–41 Penarth and Barry; 1941–46 Cardiff (Roath Park); 1946–51 Headingley, Leeds; 1951–55 Belper; 1955–59 Colwyn Bay and Llandudno; 1959–65 Clevedon (Somerset); 1965–72 Skegness.
Publications: Hidden Treasures, (Epworth Press, Talks to Young People 1956).
Special Interests: Spiritual Healing.
Hobbies and Recreations: Walking, Reading, Sport, Music.

MARTIN, Victor Henry, 23 Frayne Rd., Ashton Gate, Bristol BS3 1RU. (0272-663671) *b. 29 Nov 1918, Enfield, Middlesex. m. 9 Aug 1949: 2s.*
Education: 1923–29 George Spicer Inf. and Jun. Sch.; 1929–35 Enfield Grammar Sch.; 1947–49 Didsbury, Bristol. *Appointments:* 1946–47 Jersey; 1949–52 Abergavenny; 1952–55 Sleaford; 1955–60 Skegness; 1960–67 Shrewsbury; 1967–74 Market Harborough; 1974–79 Bromsgrove; 1979– Bristol (Bedminster).
Connexional Committees: 1958–64 Education Committee.
Special Interests: Prison Work, Langley Trust. *Hobbies and Recreations:* Chess, Stamp Collecting, Golf.

MARTLEW, George, 8 Staple Close, West Quantoxhead, Taunton, Somerset TA4 4DF. (0984-32752)–MA(Liverpool), BSc(Liverpool), DipEd(Liverpool). *b. 10 May 1907, Wigan, Lancs. m. 30 July 1935: 1d., 1s.*
Education: 1912–18 Manor CE Sch., Earlestown, Newton-le-Willows, Lancs.; 1918–24 Ashton-in-Makerfield, Grammar Sch.; 1924–28 Liverpool Univ.; 1932–35 Didsbury.
Appointments: 1935–37 Nigeria; 1937–50 Kenya; 1950–55 Looe; 1955–62 Harrow; 1962–69 Enfield; 1969–72 Trowbridge and Bradford-on-Avon.
Connexional Committees: 1951–55, 1956–62 Overseas Missions, General Committee; 1963–69 Western Committee.
Special Interests: Preaching, African Affairs. *Hobbies and Recreations:* Gardening, Carpentry.

MARTYN, William Joseph, 11 Carr Rd., Calverley, Pudsey, West Yorkshire LS28 5RT. (0274-612606)–BD. *b. 1 Aug 1919, Looe,*

Cornwall. m. 9 Aug 1949: 1d., 1s.
Education: 1924–26 Private; 1926–29 Looe Council Sch.; 1929–37 Liskeard Grammar; 1939–41 Richmond; 1941–43 Headingley.
Appointments: 1943–44 Brixham and Dartmouth; 1944–46 Plymouth; 1946–49 Bishop's Castle and Clun; 1949–54 Ashbourne; 1954–59 Liverpool South; 1959–66 Blackburn (Clayton St.); 1966–71 Bilston; 1971–77 Ellesmere Port/South Wirral; 1977– Bradford (Woodhouse Grove).
Hobbies and Recreations: Music, Photography.

MASKELL, George Henry, Holly Bank, 8 Chapel Rd., Rowledge, Farnham, Surrey GU10 4AP. (025125-4101) *b. 15 April 1911, Westborough, Dewsbury, Yorks. m. 2 Aug 1939: 1s.*
Education: Waverley Grammar Sch., Birmingham; 1933–36 Richmond.
Appointments: 1936–37 President's List; 1938–39 London, Tooting; 1939–41 London, Broomwood and Stockwell; 1941–42 Barnstaple; 1942–46 Redditch; 1946–51 Birmingham, Moseley Rd.; 1951–55 Coventry; 1955–61 London, Finchley and Hendon; 1961–68 Bedford North; 1968–75 Malvern.

MASON, Bill, The Manse, 96A Kingsway, Wellingborough, Northants NN8 2PD. (0933-222357) *b. 22 Oct 1932, Farnborough, Hants. m. 28 March 1964: 1d., 1s.*
Education: 1937–47 Queens Rd. Council Sch., Farnborough; 1972–74 Wesley, Bristol. *Appointments:* 1974–76 Fenland; 1976–79 Wisbech; 1979– Wellingborough.
Special Interests: Prison Chaplaincy.
Hobbies and Recreations: Gardening, Walking, Natural History, Music, Reading.

MASON, David, East End Mission, 583 Commercial Rd., Stepney, London E1 0HH. (01-790-1926)–OBE, BD(Lond.), STM(Boston). *b. 22 May 1926, London. m. 27 July 1957: 2d., 1s.*
Education: 1937–44 Mercers' Sch.; 1944–47 Univ. Coll. Hospital; 1956–57 Boston Univ.; 1949–52 Richmond.
Appointments: 1952–54 London Mission (East Ham); 1955–56 London, Finsbury Park; 1957–60 Longton and Fenton; 1960–72 West London Mission and Notting Hill; 1972–76 Director, Hammersmith CDP; 1976–78 Deputy Director, International Defence Aid; 1979–81 General Secretary, Voluntary Action Lewisham; 1981– London East End Mission.
Parliamentary Service: Parliamentary Candidate, February and October 1974, May 1979. *Connexional Committees:* 1968–72 Community Relations. *Council Member:* 1973–77 Greater London Council; 1971–73 Royal Borough of Kensington and Chelsea. *Local Council Committees:* 1973–77 Vice-Chairman, Planning Committee, GLC; 1973–77 Chairman, Green Belt Panel, GLC; 1976–77 Chairman, West Area Transport Committee, GLC. *Publications: Christianity and The Neighbourhood* (1970); *The Case for Christian Pacifism* (1964); *News From Notting Hill* (1968).
Special Interests: Politics, Community Work, Race Relations.
Hobbies and Recreations: Reading, Cinema, Walking.

MASON, Edward Donald, 7 St. Peter's Close, Westmeads, Bognor Regis, West Sussex PO21 5QA. (0243-864605) *b. 3 Dec 1914, Sedbergh, Yorkshire. m. 16 Aug 1939: 2d., 1s.*
Education: Tebay Elem., Westmoreland; 1934–37 Cliff Coll.
Appointments: 1937–43 London, Deptford and Greenwich Mission; 1943–47 Tadcaster; 1947–50 Droxford; 1950–56 Walsall; 1956–68 Portchester; 1968–75 Reading; 1975–80 Windsor and Maidenhead.
Special Interests: Evangelism.
Hobbies and Recreations: Drawing and Sketching, Ornithology.

MASON, Eileen Joyce SRN. *b. 28 Dec 1928, Stoke Newington, London.*
Education: 1939–42 Southgate County Secondary Sch., London N13; Wolsey Hall, Oxford; 1953–55 Wesley Deaconess; 1961–62 Kingsmead. *Appointments:* 1981–82 Lerwick and North Roe; 1982– Douglas and Peel, IOM.
Hobbies and Recreations: Bird Watching.

MASON, Harold, Arcadia, Furnham Rd., Chard, Somerset TA20 1AE. (046-06-3289)–MA, BSc. *m. 1s.*
Education: 1955–58 Headingley.
Appointments: 1958–59 Newcastle (Brunswick); 1959–63 Colne; 1963–66 Morecambe and Heysham; 1966–72 Bolton; 1972–77 Skegness and Wainfleet; 1977– Sidmouth and Bridport.

MASON, Ian, 25 Carlton Ave., Batley, West Yorks WF17 7AJ. (0924-473907)–BD(Lond.). *b. 20 Nov 1937, Tottington, Bury, Lancs. m. Lomas, 24 June 1961: 1d., 2s.*
Education: 1949–53 Stand Grammar Sch., Whitefield; 1960–64 Wesley, Headingley. *Appointments:* 1964–69 Northallerton; 1969–73 Sleaford; 1973–80 Sleaford County Secondary Sch., Head of Religious Education; 1980 Batley.
Hobbies and Recreations: Photography, Classical Guitar-Playing.

MASON, John Henry, 16 Station Rd., Crewkerne, Somerset TA18 8AJ. *b. 3 May 1937, Wednesbury, South Staffs.*
Education: Kings Hill Sch.; Woodland Grange Sch.; Wolverhampton Coll. of Art; 1961–65 Handsworth.
Appointments: 1965–70 Rawtenstall; 1970–75 Camborne; 1975–80 Bude; 1980– South Petherton and Crewkerne.
Hobbies and Recreations: Painting, Photography, Music.

MASON, William Wallace, 89 Elmsleigh Drive, Leigh-on-Sea, Essex SS9 3D5. *b. 30 June 1916, Henshaw, Northumberland. m. 9 Aug 1947: 1s.*
Education: Henshaw, Northumberland; Haltwhistle, Northumberland; 1938–39 Cliff Coll.; 1945–47 Hartley Victoria.
Appointments: 1943–46 Leith and Tranent; 1947–50 Wensleydale; 1950–56 London Mission, Plumstead; 1956–73 London Mission, Poplar;

1973–82 Leigh-on-Sea.
Hobbies and Recreations: Walking, Reading, Gardening.

MATTERS, Ronald Henry, 28 Rolleston Drive, Lenton, Nottingham NG7 1JT. (0602-417096) *b. 29 May 1924, Forest Gate, London E7. m. 2 Jan 1954: 1d., 1s.* d. 19.08.00
Education: 1929–35 Sandringham Rd., Forest Gate Inf. and Jun.; 1935–37 Manor Park Secondary; 1937–39 Milton High Sch.; 1967–68 Birmingham Univ.; 1946–47 Cliff Coll.; 1948–51 Wesley, Headingley. *Appointments:* 1947–48 Edinburgh (Nicolson Sq.); 1951–53 Coventry Mission; 1953–55 Pontypool (Eastern Valley); 1955–67 Kenya Dt., East Africa; 1968–72 Grenada, West Indies; 1972–77 Tunstall, Stoke on Trent; 1977– Nottingham West.
Special Interests: World Development, Peace and Disarmament, Community Relations, Politics. *Hobbies and Recreations:* Reading, Ball Sports, Films, Drama.

MATTHEWMAN, Frank, 15 Kingston Sq., Norwich NR4 7PF. (0603-54675) *b. 3 Feb 1911, Leeds. m. 17 Aug 1939: 1d., 1s.*
Education: 1923–27 Leeds Central High; 1932–35 Handsworth Coll., Birmingham. *Appointments:* 1931–32 Evesham; 1935–36 Glasgow (East Mission); 1936–39 Manchester (Grosvenor St.); 1939–41 Manchester (City Rd.); 1941–45 Leigh (King St.); 1945–49 Carlisle (Fisher St.); 1949–53 Newport (Stow Hill); 1953–59 Bloxwich; 1959–62 Sunderland (West); 1962–68 Birmingham (Smethwick); 1968–71 Hinckley; 1971–77 Nottingham (North).

MATTHEWS, David John Tristram, Stepaloft, Smithy Lane, Hixon, Stafford ST18 0PS. (0889-270902)—MA(Cantab.), BA(Birmingham). *b. 4 Sept 1915, Birmingham.*
Education: 1927–34 King Edward VI Grammar Sch., Camp Hill, Birmingham; 1934–39 Univ. of Birmingham; 1939–41 Univ. of Cambridge; 1939–41 Wesley House *Appointments:* 1946–51 West Bromwich; 1951–56 Sheffield North; 1956–61 London (Wanstead and Woodford); 1961–67 Birmingham (Elmdon); 1967–74 Cannock; 1974–79 Shrewsbury.

MATTHEWS, John Henry, The Spinney, 64 Boston Rd., Spilsby, Lincs PE23 5HH. (0790-52497) *b. 24 Sept 1912, Haltway, Nr. Sheffield. m. 26 Dec 1938: 1d., 1s.*
Education: Elem. Sch., Halfway, Nr. Sheffield; 1933–34 Cliff Coll.
Appointments: 1950–51 Bradford, Gt. Horton Wesley; 1951–55 Birmingham, Smethwick; 1955–61 Skegness and Wainfleet; 1961–66 Grantham; 1971–77 Lincoln, Wesley; 1977–82 Spilsby.
Special Interests: Rural Methodism. *Hobbies and Recreations:* Gardening, Reading.

MAVERS, Robert Brian, 65 Victoria Rd., Runcorn, Cheshire WA7 5BE. (092-85-72570) *b. 17 March 1938, Liverpool. m. 23 Oct 1965: 1d., 2s.*
Education: 1961–64 Hartley Victoria. *Appointments:* 1964–66 Ripley; 1966–69 Ilkeston; 1969–76 Notttingham East; 1976– Runcorn.

MAW, Douglas, The Manse, Prince Imperial Rd., Chislehurst, Kent BR7 5LX. (01-467-3359)—BA(Lond.), MA(Cantab.). *b. 12 June 1927, Ryhill, W. Wakefield, W. Yorks. m. 23 March 1963: 1d.*
Education: 1938–45 Elland Grammar Sch.; 1945–49 Westminster Coll. and Kings Coll., London Univ.; 1953–54 Protestant Faculty of Theology, Montpellier, France; 1951–53 Wesley House. *Appointments:* 1954–61 Ivory Coast; 1962–63 Paris; 1963–74 Benin (Porto Novo Theol. Coll.); 1974–80 Leicester SE; 1980– Chislehurst.
Connexional Committees: 1977–80 Overseas Division.
Special Interests: Overseas Church, Ecumenical Relationships, Ministerial Recruitment and Training. *Hobbies and Recreations:* Travel, Photography, Music.

MAWDITT (nee Jobling), Helen Mary, 31 Station Rd., Borrowash, Derby BD7 3LG. (0332-670587)—BA(Nottingham and Bristol). *b. 11 March 1954, Preston. m. 18 Aug 1979.*
Education: 1965–66 Burnley High Sch.; 1966–72 Carlisle and County High Sch.; 1972–75 Nottingham Univ.; 1975–78 Bristol Univ.; 1975–78 Wesley, Bristol. *Appointments:* 1978–80 Derby Derwent Mission; 1980– Derby East.
Special Interests: Ancient Monuments, Methodist History, Disarmament, Life Style. *Hobbies and Recreations:* Walking, Knitting, Sewing, Craft, Reading, German Classes.

MAY, Donald Wilfred Edwin, 49 Acresfield Rd., Salford, Greater Manchester M6 7GE. (061-736-1920)—BD. *b. 11 March 1922, Winson Green, Birmingham. m. 5 Aug 1950: 2d.*
Education: 1927–34 Sir Josiah Mason's Sch., Erdington, Birmingham; 1934–38 King Edward's Grammar Sch., Aston, Birmingham; 1946–49 Headingley. *Appointments:* 1949–55 Fleetwood; 1955–61 Bebington; 1961–71 Liverpool (South); 1971–78 Altrincham; 1978– Manchester and Salford Mission.
Connexional Committees: 1975– Home Mission Board and its Executive. *Local Council Committees:* 1980– Salford City Education Committee.
Special Interests: Inner Cities, Community Development, Community Relations, Education. *Hobbies and Recreations:* Golf.

MAY, Francis Vernon, 1 The Drive, Coulsdon, Surrey CR3 2BL. (01 660 0601)—MA(Oxon), BA(Cantab.). *b. 8 Nov 1929, Yunnan, SW China. m. 8 Aug 1957: 2s., 1s.*
Education: –1940 Private Tuition and Prim. Sch.; 1940–42 Prior's Court (Kingswood Prep.); 1942–48 Kingswood Sch.; 1949–52 St. John's Coll., Oxford; 1952–54 Wesley House. *Appointments:* 1954–57 Trowbridge and Bradford-on-Avon; 1957–62 Leytonstone and Forest Gate; 1962–68 Kent Coll. (Chaplain); 1968–75 Blackheath and Lewisham; 1975– Purley.
Local Council Committees: 1976–79

Croydon Education Dept., Schools Sub-Committee representing Free Churches.
Special Interests: Methodist-Roman Catholic Relationships, Local Councils of Churches and Ecumenism. *Hobbies and Recreations:* Oil Painting, Walking, Bird and Animal Watching, Horses, Home Wine-Making, Poetry, Trees, Physiognomy, Figure Studying.

MAYALL, John William Morritt, 69 Stoneleigh Ave., Earlsdon, Coventry CV5 6DA. (0203-712364) *b. 26 Jan 1901, Castleford, Yorkshire. m. (1) 1931, (2) 1964, (3) 1970, 1d., 1s.*
Education: 1924–27 Didsbury.
Appointments: 1927–30 Jersey; 1930–36 Gainsborough; 1936–40 Oldham; 1940–45 Stalybridge; 1945–52 Eccles; 1952–56 Middlesbrough; 1956–64 Liverpool; 1964–69 Newcastle-upon-Tyne North West.
Connexional Committees: Women and the Ministry. *Publications:* Various papers to several Publications.
Special Interests: Psychological Treatment of Mental/Emotional Traumatic Conditions.

MAYES, Elizabeth Emily, 1 Knowle Close, Redditch, Worcs B98 6JN. (0527-60860) *b. 12 Nov 1938, Lisburn, Co. Antrim, N. Ireland.*
Education: 1944–50 Wallace High Sch., Lisburn, Prep. Dept.; 1950–56 Grammar Sch.; 1956–60 Stranmillis Training Coll., Belfast; 1962–63 Kingsmead Coll., Selly Oak; 1971–73 Queens. *Appointments:* 1973–77 Leominster, Presteigne and Kington; 1977– Redditch.
Connexional Committees: 1976–77 Rural Life Committee; 1980–83 Connexional Candidate Examination Committee.

MAYLOR, James Derek, Riversmead, Lynton Ave., Boston Spa, Wetherby, W. Yorks LS23 6BL. (0937-842156)–BA. *b. 6 Aug 1928, Mellor, Derbyshire. m. 20 Aug 1955: 4d.*
Education: Wolverhampton Municipal Secondary Sch.; 1950–53 Leeds Univ.; 1950–53 Headingley.
Appointments: 1949–50 Knighton; 1953–55 Douglas Victoria; 1955–59 Sunderland; 1959–64 Haydon Bridge; 1964–69 Middlesbrough; 1969 Nottingham; 1976– Boston Spa.

MAYNARD, Eric Frederick, 98 Albany Rd., Sittingbourne, Kent ME10 1EL. (0795-24261) *b. 7 April 1927, Hornsey, London. m. 2 June 1951: 1d., 2s.*
Education: 1932–38 North Harringay Prim. and Jun. Sch.; 1938–43 Stationers' Company Sch.; 1956–58 Richmond. *Appointments:* 1958–62 Holsworthy; 1962–66 Clifton and Redland; 1966–71 Bedminster; 1971–78 London, Ealing and Acton; 1978– Sittingbourne and Sheerness.
Hobbies and Recreations: Classical Music, Sport of all Kind.

MAYNE, John, 35 Grove Rd., Selsey, Chichester, West Sussex PO20 0AS. (0243-603155) *b. 3 Dec 1901, Stoke, Devonport, Plymouth, Devon. m. 9 Aug 1930 (w.).*
Education: 1905–17 Elem. Sch.; 1926–28 Hartley Victoria.
Appointments: 1928–32 Kilkhampton; 1932–37 Halifax, Hanover (Elland, Bethesda); 1937–39 Leeds (Armley); 1939–44 London, Ealing and Acton; 1944–47 Tooting; 1947–50 Bristol East; 1950–54 Hull (Bourne); 1954–59 Barnsley East; 1959–67 Gravesend and Dartford.
Connexional Committees: 1951–54 Temperance and Social Welfare.
Council Member: President of Council of Christian Churches at Bristol, Hull, Barnsley and Barnsley Evangelical Crusade, and at Dartford.
Special Interests: Evangelism, Preaching, Pastoral Work, Youth Work, Music and Choral, Elocution.
Hobbies and Recreations: Reading, Music, Sport.

McAVOY, Roger, 12 Lakes Rd., Dukinfield, Cheshire Sk16 4TP. (061-330-2795)–BSc(Cardiff), BA(Birmingham). *b. 23 Aug 1943, Leeds, Yorkshire. m. 12 Aug 1972: 3d., 1s.*
Education: 1948–54 Stanley Grove Jun. Sch., Nr. Wakefield; 1954–59 Rothwell Grammar Sch., Nr. Wakefield; 1964–68 Univ. of S. Wales (Cardiff); 1970–73 Univ. of Birmingham; 1970–73 Queens.
Appointments: 1973–75 Malvern and Ledbury; 1975–80 Barnsley; 1980– Ashton under Lyne.
Special Interests: Hospital Chaplaincy work. *Hobbies and Recreations:* Fell Walking, Deltiology.

McBAIN, Robert George, 9 Rectory Rd., Wokingham, Berkshire RG1 1DJ. (0734-781756)–DipTheol(Lond.), FE Teachers Cert(1972). *b. 22 Feb 1944, Welford-on-Avon, Nr. Stratford-upon-Avon. m. 24 June 1967: 1d., 1s.*
Education: 1948–55 Broad St. County Prim. Sch., Stratford-upon-Avon; 1955–62 King Edward VI Grammar Sch., Stratford-upon-Avon; 1970–72 The Elms Technical Coll., Stoke-on-Trent; 1964–68 Hartley Victoria. *Appointments:* 1968–70 South Molton; 1970–73 Tunstall; 1973–81 Nottingham North; 1981– Reading.
Connexional Committees: 1971–73 Connexional Youth Board; 1974– MDEY Board; 1974– Executive and Finance Committee of MDEY. *Local Council Committees:* 1974–80 Rep of Voluntary Organisations on Nottingham City Council Community Facilities Committee.
Special Interests: Education/Youth.
Hobbies and Recreations: Gardening, Sport, Reading, Walking.

McCARTHY, John Brian, 337 Pontefract Rd., Featherstone, Pontefract, West Yorks WF7 5AD. (0977-791538)–BD(Lond.). *b. 31 July 1936, Broughton, Wrexham, m. 22 Aug 1963: 1d., 1s.*
Education: 1947–55 Kings Sch., Pontefract; 1955–58 Hull Univ.; 1960–63 London Univ.; 1960–63 Richmond. *Appointments:* 1963–69 Castleford; 1969– Pontefract.
Connexional Committees: 1966–72 Connexional Education and Youth.
Special Interests: Community Service.
Hobbies and Recreations: Badminton, General Sport.

McCLUSKEY, Patrick Alan, Trinity Manse, Tower Rd., Felixstowe IP11 7PR. (03942-2023) *b. 9 May 1939,*

Croydon, Surrey. m. 9 April 1966: 2d., 1s.
Education: 1950–54 Tavistock Secondary Modern Boys Sch., Croydon; 1963–67 Didsbury, Bristol. *Appointments:* 1967–69 Blackburn; 1969–71 Derby Mission; 1971–76 Ashfield; 1976–81 Great Yarmouth and Gorleston; 1981– Ipswich.
Special Interests: Church Growth. *Hobbies and Recreations:* German Shepherd Dogs, Offset Printing, Ventriloquism. d 2002.

McINERNEY, Thomas, 7 Modecombe Grove, Henbury, Bristol. (0272-505039) *b. 2 Aug 1940, Salford, Lancs. m. 5 Sept 1964: 1d., 1s.*
Education: 1947–55 Halton Bank, Salford; 1958–61 Worsley Technical Coll.; 1961–64 Bolton Technical Coll.; 1975–76 Bolton Coll. of Education (Technical); 1981– Wesley, Bristol.
Special Interests: Church Growth, Methodist Revival Fellowships, C.E.I.M. Member. *Hobbies and Recreations:* Rambling, Caravanning.

McINTOSH, Graham, The Manse, 72 Lidgett Lane, Dinnington, Sheffield S31 7QD. (0909-562410)–LRAM. *b. 10 Sept 1936, Halifax, West Yorkshire. m. 12 Sept 1964: 1s.*
Education: 1946–51 Royston Secondary Modern (S. Yorks.); 1951–54 Barnsley Technical Coll.; 1975–78 Manchester Univ.; 1975–78 Hartley Victoria. *Appointments:* 1978–80 Horncastle and Bardney; 1980– Worksop and Kiveton.
Publications: The Romantic Tradition in Keyboard Music (1978); *The Development of Country Music* (1980).
Special Interests: Classical Music, Young People. *Hobbies and Recreations:* Travel, Walking, Tennis.

McKAY, Peter Alexander, 27 Meadow Gdns, Beccles, Suffolk NR34 9PA (0502-712281) *b. 6 Jan 1942, Stourbridge, Worcestershire. m. 17 Aug 1968: 2s.*
Education: 1947–53 Cradley CE Prim.; 1953–59 Halesowen Grammar; 1959–60 Cliff Coll.; 1965–67 Headingley; 1967–69 Wesley, Bristol. *Appointments:* 1969–71 Blackburn; 1971–74 Tipton; 1974–77 Tamworth; 1977–80 Leominster, Presteigne and Kington; 1980– Lowestoft and East Suffolk.
Special Interests: Long-term Planning, especially in Relating Buildings to the Needs of the Church, The Strategy of Mission, Ministry in Personal Crisis. *Hobbies and Recreations:* Music.

McKEATING, Henry, 339 Wollaton Rd., Wollaton Park, Nottingham NG8 1FQ. (0602-282343)–MTh, PhD(Lond.). *b. 15 Jan 1932, Eaglesfield, Cumberland. m. 1957: 3d., 1s.*
Education: 1942–49 County Grammar Sch., Cockermouth, Cumberland; 1955–56 Univ. of Strasbourg, France; 1951–55 Handsworth. *Appointments:* 1956–57 Thetford; 1957–59 Hunstanton and Docking; 1959– Lecturer in Theology, Univ. of Nottingham.
Connexional Committees: Education and Youth. *Publications: Living with Guilt* (SCM 1970); *Cambridge Bible, Amos, Hosee, Micah* (1971); *God and the Future* (SCM 1974); *Studying the Old Testament* (Epworth 1979); Plus numerous articles in various journals.
Special Interests: Old Testament Study, Christian Education. *Hobbies and Recreations:* Walking, Flower Photography.

McKEE, Henry Alford, 325 Ainsworth Rd., Bury, Lancs BL8 2LU. (061-764-4214) *b. 16 June 1921, Londonderry, Co. Londonderry. m. 9 Jan 1945: 1s.*
Education: 1932–38 Carlisle Grammar Sch., Carlisle; 1947–49 Hartley Victoria. *Appointments:* 1949–51 Wallasey; 1951–54 Bury.

McKEE, Wilfrid, 77 Sunnybank Rd., Bolton le Sands, Carnforth, Lancs LA5 8HG. (0524-823041) *b. 15 Dec 1908, Salford, Lancs. m. 21 Sept 1935: 1d., 1s.*
Education: Salford Secondary Sch. Boys; 1930–31 Marburg, Germany; 1927–30 Richmond. *Appointments:* 1931–33 King's Lynn; 1933–35 Peel; 1935–37 Clitheroe; 1937–40 Accrington; 1940–45 Morecambe and Heysham; 1945–48 Bolton Park St.; 1948–52 Bolton Wesley; 1952–55 Blackburn Mission; 1955–61 Oldham East; 1961–66 Manchester, Cheetham Hill and Prestwich; 1966–71 Oldham West; 1971–74 Cadishead.
Connexional Committees: 1940–45 Temperance and Social Welfare.

McKENZIE, Graham Maurice, The Boulders, Binstead, Isle of Wight. (0983-62460).
Education: 1949–51 Didsbury.
Appointments: 1951–54 Wellingborough; 1954–56 Bingley; 1956–60 Worksop; 1960–78 Chaplain HMF.

McKENZIE, Ian Donald, 33 Walshaw Ave., Colwyn Bay, Clwyd LL29 7UY. (0492-31864)–MA, BSc. *b. 4 Aug 1934, London. m. 13 Aug 1966: 1d., 1s.*
Education: 1943–51 Roan Sch., London SE3; 1951–54 Queen Mary Coll., Univ. of London; 1961–64 Wesley House. *Appointments:* 1964–66 Assistant Chaplain at Kingswood Sch., Bath; 1966–72 Gloucester; 1972–78 Bristol (Clifton and Redland); 1978– Chaplain at Rydal Sch., Colwyn Bay.
Local Council Committees: 1969–72 Gloucestershire County Education Committee.
Hobbies and Recreations: Theatre, Music, Reading, Gardening, Walking, Tennis, Squash.

McLURE, Robert, Dormarky, Glasgow Rd., Kilsyth, Glasgow G65 9AE. (0236-823135) *b. 17 Jan 1921, Glasgow. m. 23 July 1949: 1s.*
Education: 1933–38 Whitehill Secondary, Glasgow; 1945–48 Hartley Victoria. *Appointments:* 1948–49 Glasgow Paisley Rd.; 1949–52 Sunderland West; 1952–58 Glasgow West; 1958–61 Redcar, Saltburn and Guisborough; 1961–74 Glasgow East; 1974–82 Edinburgh and Forth; 1982– Kilsyth.

McQUEENEY, Joyce, 19 Belle Vue Grove, Middlesbrough, Cleveland TS4 2PU. (0642-823575) *b. 24*

March 1936, Salford, Lancs. s.
Education: 1947–52 Pendleton High Sch.; 1952–54 Royal Technical Coll., Salford; 1954–60 Manchester Coll. of Science and Technology; 1976–78 Wesley Bristol; 1978–79 Trinity Theol. Coll., Singapore. *Appointments:* 1979– Middlesbrough and Eston. *Special Interests:* Christian Aid, 1967–76 Area Secretary; Girl Guides Association. *Hobbies and Recreations:* Girl Guides, Travel, Photography.

McRAE SPENCER, Ian Angus, The Manse, Molemead, North Moleton, N. Devon. *b. 29 May 1943, Edinburgh: 1d., 1s.*
Education: 1955–62 The Grammar Sch., Plympton, S. Devon; 1962–65 St. Lukes Coll., Exeter; 1980–82 Wesley, Bristol. *Appointments:* 1982– South Molton.

McWADE, James Alexander, 11 Bayr Grianagh, Castletown, Isle of Man. (0624-822541) *b. 8 Feb 1937, Glasgow. m. 30 June 1962: 2s.*
Education: 1958–59 Cliff Coll.; 1971–72 Lanchester Poly./Coventry Cathedral, Centre for Urban Studies; 1960–64 Hartley Victoria. *Appointments:* 1964–66 Presteigne and Kington; 1966–71 Birmingham, Smethwick; 1972–79 Bilston; 1979– Castleton.
Connexional Committees: 1979– Division of Social Responsibility. *Local Council Committees:* Social Responsibility.

MEACHEM, David Thomas, 86a Walsall Rd., Darlaston, Wednesbury, West Midlands WS10 9JT. (021-526-2373) *b. 2 May 1949, Jersey C.I. m. 5 July 1975: 1s.*
Education: 1960–67 Queen's Coll., Taunton, Somerset; 1969–72 Alsager Coll. of Education; 1979–82 Wesley, Bristol. *Appointments:* 1978–79 Buckley and Deeside; 1982– Walsall and Darlaston.

MEADLEY, Thomas Donald, 159 Old Bath Rd., Cheltenham, Glos GL53 7DW. (0242-512251)–BA(Lond.), BD(Manchester). *b. 29 Dec 1909, Longdown, New Forest, Hants. m. 1 Aug 1939: 1d., 2s.*
Education: 1916–19 Wintringham, Grimsby; 1920 Buxton Grammar; 1921–28 Epworth Coll., Rhyl; 1928–30 Leicester Univ. Coll.; 1930–34 Manchester Univ.; 1930–34 Hartley Victoria. *Appointments:* 1934–36 Tunstall; 1936–40 Nantwich; 1940–44 Northampton; 1944–49 Hull; 1949–52 Bristol, Kingswood; 1952–57 Leeds Mission; 1957–65 Cliff Coll. Principal; 1965–74 Newton Abbot.
Connexional Committees: –1974 Faith and Order; 1957–65 Home Missions; 1957–65 Anglican/Methodist Conversations.
Publications: Conducting a Service (1957); *Attending a Service* (1963); *Route to the Cross* (1969); *Top Level Talks: Christian Summit Meeting* (1969); *How the Cross Heals* (1967).
Special Interests: Peter Taylor Forsyth's Theology, Primitive Methodism. *Hobbies and Recreations:* Football, Cricket, Walking.

MEAKIN, Margaret Amy Elizabeth, Wesley Manse, Upwell, Wisbech, Cambs PE16 6JB. (0945-772456) *b. 3 March 1930, Hemel Hempstead, Herts. w.*
Education: 1957–59 Wesley, Deaconess Coll. *Appointments:* 1976– Fenland.
Connexional Committees: 1975–78 Women's Fellowship.

MEARS, Paul Arthur, c/o Royal Navy, Army and RAF Board, 1 Central Buildings, London SW1H 9NH. *b. 19 Jan 1936, Croydon. m. 5 Aug 1961: 2d.*
Education: 1947–52 Norbury Manor Boys Sch.; 1957–58 Cliff Coll.; 1958–61 Handsworth. *Appointments:* 1961–65 Wensleydale; 1965– Chaplain HMF.
Special Interests: Pastoral Counselling. *Hobbies and Recreations:* Football, Travel.

MEECH, Michael, 125 Meadowview Rd., West Ewell, Epsom, Surrey KT19 9TT. (01-393-2841) *b. 29 Sept 1932, East Coker, Somerset. m. 4 Aug 1956: 1d., 1s.*
Education: 1942–50 Yeovil; 1952–55 Leeds Univ.; 1952–55 Wesley, Headingley. *Appointments:* 1955–58 Minehead and Dunster; 1958–63 Bridgwater; 1963–68 Manchester Mission; 1968–75 Sutton (Surrey); 1975–78 BBC; 1978– Broadcaster and Writer.
Connexional Committees: 1958–80 Radio and TV Committee; 1971–78 Board of Division of Social Responsibility; 1975– National Children's Home General Committee. *Publications:* Editor British Council of Churches Magazine *Vision One*; Sundry Articles, Radio Talks, Interviews, Documentaries; Listed in Foyles List of Lecturers and After-Dinner Speakers.
Special Interests: Humanity, God, Sport, Music. *Hobbies and Recreations:* Gardening, Good Food, Good Company, Good Conversation.

MEIR, John Kenneth, 9 Hollis Rd., Up Hatherley, Cheltenham GL51 6SL. (0242-510529)–BA, PhD. *b. 1 July 1914, Nottingham. m. 28 July 1941: 1d., 1s.*
Education: 1924–29 Rastrick Grammar Sch.; 1929–33 Ashville Coll.; 1938–39 West Hill; 1934–38 Hartley Victoria. *Appointments:* 1939–40 Sunday Sch. Dept.; 1940–42 Letchworth; 1942–46 Sheffield, Ecclesall; 1946–50 Edinburgh Mission; 1950–51 Walthamstow; 1951–60 Methodist Youth Dept.; 1960–63 Purley; 1963–69 Leigh on Sea; 1969–74 Eltham; 1974–79 Bath.
Connexional Committees: Methodist Yth. Dpt. *Council Member:* World Council of Christian Education. *Publications: The Child in the Midst* (with E. H. Hayes 1953); *Junior Worship* (with E. H. Hayes 1956); *Teach and Learn* (1956); *Coming to Church* (1962); *Labour of Love* (1971); Two Robert Raikes Lectures.

MELLOR, I. G. Howard, 8 Elgin Rd., Croydon, Surrey CR0 6AX. (01-654-2845)–BD(Lond.). *b. 28 Jan 1949, Huddersfield. m. 5 April 1975.*
Education: Royds Hall Secondary

Sch., Paddock, Huddersfield; 1969–72 London Univ.; 1974–76 London Univ.; 1967–68 Cliff Coll.; 1969–72 Richmond; 1972–73 Wesley, Bristol; 1974–76 Heythrop Coll.
Appointments: 1973–76 London NE Mission; 1976– Croydon.
Local Council Committees: 1977–80 Youth Sub Committee. *Publications: Ways to Worship with Young People* (MDEY).
Special Interests: AVEC, a service agency for church and community development.

MELLOR, John, Coatham House, 13 Rectory Lane, Wolsingham, Bishop Auckland, Co. Durham DL13 3AJ. (095-65-7403)–MA(Camb.), BA(Camb.), BD(Lond.). *b. 14 June 1915, Ladismith, Cape Province, South Africa. m. 7 April 1942: 1d., 2s.*
Education: 1928–33 Rydal Sch., Colwyn Bay, N. Wales; 1933–36 Queens Coll., Cambridge; 1936–37 Westminster Coll., London Univ.; 1937–40 Richmond. *Appointments:* 1942–45 Hull; 1945–48 Blackburn; 1948–52 Whitley Bay; 1952–57 Warrington; 1957–59 Swindon; 1959–61 Rhondda; 1961–67 Head of Dept., Bede Grammar Sch. for Boys; 1967–80 Head of Dept. Wolsingham Grammar Sch.
Special Interests: 1945–64 Youth Clubs, 1965– Examiner, Cambridge Board, Manchester JMB. *Hobbies and Recreations:* Rugby, Football, Tennis.

MELLOR, Thomas Farrall, 3 Queens Park, Colwyn Bay, Clwyd LL29 7BG. (0492-2739) *b. 4 Jan 1901, Kingsley, North Staffs. m. 5 Dec 1931: 1d.*
Education: 1906–13 Kingsley Endowed; 1914–15 Leek High Sch.; 1921–22 Cliff Coll.; 1924–27 Handsworth. *Appointments:* 1923–24 Marlborough Mission; 1927–54 Mysore District, India; 1954–56 Manchester, Chorlton and Moss Side; 1957–59 Leigh-on-Sea; 1960–62 London Mission, Camden Town and Kings Cross; 1963–67 Pontypool.
Connexional Committees: 1959–61 Methodist Missionary Society.
Special Interests: Pastoral Visitation. *Hobbies and Recreations:* Gardening, Radio, TV.

MERRIMAN, Richard Albert, 18 Green Lane, Whitstable, Kent CT5 4JE. (0227-265569) *b. 26 May 1908, London. m.*
Education: Ben Jonson, London; 1932–36 Handsworth.
Appointments: 1931–32 Chelmsford; 1936–38 President's List; 1938–40 Stamford; 1940–41 Maryport; 1941–46 Chaplain HMF; 1946–50 Wisbech; 1950-53 Chelmsford; 1953–56 Bishop Auckland; 1956–61 Newmarket; 1961–66 Stewkley; 1966–71 Ampthill; 1971–73 Newmarket.

MERRITT, Arthur, 12 Mount Pleasant Ave, Radipole, Weymouth, Dorset DT3 5JS. (0305-783049) *b. 29 July 1923, Hanham, Bristol. m. 19 Aug 1950: 2d., 1s.*
Education: 1934–39 Kingswood Grammar Sch.; 1945–49 Didsbury, Bristol. *Appointments:* 1949–51 Bridgwater; 1951–57 Portland; 1957–62 Harrogate; 1962–68 Northampton; 1968–78 Leicester; 1978– Weymouth.
Hobbies and Recreations: Painting.

MIDDLEHURST, Arthur Penlington, 11 Park Rd., Worsley, Manchester M28 5DU. *b. 9 June 1918, Nutgrove, Thato Heath, St. Helens, Lancs. m. 11 Feb 1946: 3s.*
Education: 1923–27 Nutgrove, (St. Helens) Methodist Prim. and Jun.; 1927–29 Rice Lane, (Liverpool) Jun.; 1929–33 Evered Ave. Selective Central Sch.; 1939–40 Didsbury; 1940–42 Hartley Victoria.
Appointments: 1942–49 Ceylon; 1949–52 Runcorn; 1952–56 Middlewich; 1956–61 Droylsden and Openshaw; 1961-65 Widnes; 1965–68 Redruth; 1968–73 Birkenhead; 1973–76 Newquay; 1976–79 Not Stationed; 1979– Worsley.
Special Interests: Natural History, Local History, Musical Appreciation. *Hobbies and Recreations:* Pottery, Gardening, Glass Cutting, Decorating.

MIDDLEMIST, George, 256 Lichfield Rd., New Invention, Willenhall, West Midlands. (0922-76431) *b. 23 Feb 1948, Stanley, Co. Durham. m. April 1975: 2s.*
Education: 1959–64 Consett Grammar Sch.; 1969–73 Wesley, Bristol. *Appointments:* 1973–75 Bristol (Kingswood); 1975–78 Liverpool South; 1978– Bloxwich and Willenhall.
Special Interests: Ecumenical Involvements. *Hobbies and Recreations:* Reading, Music.

MIDDLETON, George Bert, 9 Smithson Drive, Mattishall, Dereham, Norfolk NR20 3QH. (0362-858153)-BD(Lond.). *b. 22 Oct 1914, Stoke Poges, Bucks. m. 9 Aug 1941: 2d., 2s.*
Education: 1925–33 Northgate Sch., Ipswich, 1934–38 Richmond.
Appointments: 1938–42 E. Dereham; 1942–46 Watton; 1946–50 King's Lynn; 1950–54 High Wycombe; 1954–56 Market Rasen; 1956–60 Huddersfield West; 1960–65 Manchester SE; 1965–70 Manchester NE; 1970–75 New Mills; 1975–79 Oldham.
Connexional Committees: 1946–49 Education; 1959–62 Candidates' Examination.

MIDDLETON, John Clifford, Clint House, Armathwaite, Carlisle, Cumbria CA4 9PB. *b. 25 Jan 1909, Nelson, Lancs. m. Aug 1936: 1d.*
Education: Keighley Trade and Grammar Sch., Keighley, Yorks.; 1929–32 Hartley. *Appointments:* 1932–33 Market Rasen; 1933–34 London, Balham; 1934–36 Rhosymedre and Chirk; 1936–42 Sedbergh; 1942–45 Preston; 1945–50 Dudley; 1950–53 Selby; 1953–56 Brighouse; 1956–59 Halifax; 1959–64 Maryport; 1964–69 Haltwhistle; 1969–75 Sherburn.

MILES, William, The Bungalow, Daddyhole Plan, Torquay. (0803-26703) *b. 7 Dec 1903, Ebbw Vale. m. 21 Sept 1933: 3s.*
Education: Willowtown Elem. EV; 1926–29 Handsworth.
Appointments: 1929–31 Jeppe Johannesburg, SA; 1950–51

Maidenhead; 1952–57 Darwen; 1957–64 Wellington, Som.; 1964–68 Bideford.
Hobbies and Recreations: Walking, Philately.

MILLS, Arthur E., 158 Wilderspool Causeway, Warrington WA4 6QA. (0925-35548) *b. 17 Aug 1899, Swindon, Wilts. m. 21 July 1949.*
Education: 1924–27 Hartley.
Appointments: 1923–24 London, Stratford; 1927–28 Scotter; 1928–29 Docking; 1929–30 Abergavenny; 1930–31 Bristol V; 1931–33 Winterton; 1933–34 South Shields; 1934–36 Halifax North; 1936–37 Middleton-on-Tees; 1937–40 Nottingham North; 1940–44 Clay Cross; 1944–47 Newcastle, Staffs.; 1947–49 Melton Mowbray; 1949–52 Chesterfield, Saltersgate; 1952–58 Tipton, Bell St.; 1958–63 Stour Vale; 1963–65 Stoke-on-Trent, Longton; 1965–67 Darwin; 1967–68 Warrington.

MILLS, Harry, 62 Grosvenor Rd., Solihull, West Midlands B91 3PU. (021-705-8941) *b. 27 April 1928, Oldham, Lancs. m. 25 July 1956: 2d., 1s.*
Education: 1939–43 Chadderton Grammar Sch., Oldham; 1943–44 Colwyn Bay Grammar Sch.; 1944–45 Chadderton Grammar Sch.; 1945–47 St. Johns Coll., York; 1951–55 Handsworth.*Appointments:* 1955–61 Kenya District; 1961–63 St. Pauls United Theol. Coll.; 1963–67 Lavington Church, Nairobi, Kenya; 1967–70 Great Barr and Kingstanding; 1970– Myton Sch., Warwick.
Hobbies and Recreations: Photography, Gilbert and Sullivan, Genealogy.

MILLS, James, 294 Victoria Rd. West, Thornton, Cleveleys, Blackpool, Lancs FY5 3QD. (0253-852284)–BD(Lond.). *b. 14 May 1920, Bacup, Lancashire. m. 28 June 1947: 2s.*
Education: 1924–31 Sharneyford Elem.; 1931–34 Bacup Central; 1939 Cliff Coll.; 1946–48 Hartley Victoria. *Appointments:* 1948–53 South Shields; 1953–61 York (Clifton); 1961–64 Scarborough; 1964–69 Brighton and Hove; 1969–75 Woking; 1975–80 Wakefield; 1980– Fleetwood; 1957–64 Secretary York and Hull District Synod.
Special Interests: Methodist Guild Holidays. *Hobbies and Recreations:* Fell Walking.

MILSON, Frederick William, 1 Kestrel Grove, Bournville, Birmingham B30 1TQ. (021-472-8131)–MA(Leeds), BD(Lond.), PhD(Birmingham). *b. 25 Dec 1912, Sheffield. m. 3 Sept 1939: 1d., 1s.*
Education: 1912–21 Burngreeve Rd., Sheffield; 1921–24 Ripley Council; 1924–26 Swanwich Hale Secondary; 1946–50 Hull Univ. Coll.; 1955–58 Leeds Univ.; 1962–66 Birmingham Univ.; 1932–36 Wesley, Headingley. *Appointments:* 1936–38 Manchester Mission; 1938–41 Southall and Uxbridge Mission; 1941–46 Sheffield Mission; 1946–50 Hull Mission; 1950–54 Longton Mission; 1955–60 Leeds, Brunswick; 1960–77 Westhill Coll.
Publications: Youth and Community Work (RKP 1970); *Youth in a Changing Society* (RKP 1972); *An Introduction to Compliment Skill* (RKP 1973); *An Introduction to Community Work* (RKP 1974); and 15 other books.
Special Interests: Sociology, Group Work, Political Education. *Hobbies and Recreations:* Cricket Watching, Travel, Reading.

MINOR, John Edward, 6 Church St., Caistor, Lincolnshire LN7 6UG. (0472-851287)–BA(Manchester), MA(Manchester). *b. 1942, Manchester.*
Education: 1953–57 Manchester Central Grammar Sch.; 1957–60 Baines' Grammar Sch., Poulton-le-Fylde; 1970–74 Univ. of Manchester; 1970–74 Hartley Victoria.
Appointments: 1974–78 Horncastle and Bardney; 1978– Market Rasen and Caistor. *Connexional Committees:* 1980– Methodist/ Roman Catholic Committee.
Publications: 1980 Lecture to Lincolnshire Methodist History Society *Primitive Methodism and Pentecostalism*; Many other lectures of a less public sort.
Special Interests: Lay Training, Ecumenical Matters, Church in Rural Life. *Hobbies and Recreations:* Hill Walking, Photography, Tramways and Narrow Gauge Railways.

MINSHULL, Eric Lincoln, 10 Seedfield Croft, Cheylesmore, Coventry, West Midlands CV3 5HU. (0203-501260)–BA(Lond.). *b. 24 Feb 1913, Congleton, Cheshire. m. 2s.*
Education: Wagg St. Wesleyan Sch., Congleton; New St. County Sch.; London Univ.; 1936–39 Didsbury.
Appointments: 1939–44 Manchester and Salford Mission; 1944–48 Liverpool (South); 1948–52 Manchester and Salford Mission; 1952–61 Coventry Mission; 1961–68 Manchester and Salford Mission; 1968–79 Chairman Darlington District.
Connexional Committees: 1952–59, 1961–79 Connexional Home Missions Committee; 1968–79 Connexional General Purposes; 1968–76 Church in Industry; 1969–79 Sector Ministries; 1975–78 President's Council.

MIRRILEES, Alexander, Lochranza, Kirkhead Rd., Grange-over-Sands, Cumbria LA11 7DD. (04484-2366) *b. 1 Oct 1911, Glasgow. m. 4 Feb 1942: 1d.*
Education: 1916–22 Dundas Vale Sch., Glasgow; 1922–28 Woodside Secondary Sch., Glasgow; 1935–38 Wesley, Headingley. *Appointments:* 1938–42 Barton-on-Humber; 1942–43 Coatbridge and Airdrie; 1943–46 Glasgow, Parkhead; 1946–49 North of Scotland Mission; 1949–53 Leek; 1953–58 Worcester; 1958–63 Harrogate; 1963–68 Birmingham, Great Barr and Kingstanding; 1968–75 Ulverston.
Special Interests: Methodist Guild Guest Houses as Host and also as Hosting Secretary.

MITCHELL, Edward John, Talana, St. Ives Rd., Carbis Bay, St. Ives, Cornwall. (0736-88-796393) *b. 30 July 1916, Redruth, Cornwall. m. 13 Aug 1955: 2d., 1s.*
Education: 1920–34 Secondary.

Appointments: 1953–56 Redruth; 1956–61 Chester; 1961–65 Camelford and Wadebridge; 1965–68 British and Foreign Bible Society (District Secretary) Cumbria; 1968–71 West Midlands; 1971–75 Devon and Cornwall; 1975–81 Wellington (Somerset); 1981– St. Ives (Cornwall).
Special Interests: Evangelism.
Hobbies and Recreations: Gardening.

MITCHELL, Frank N., 44 Palace Ave., Paignton, Devon. (0803-558780) *b. 5 Jan 1897, Lincoln. m. 8 Aug 1923: 2d.*
Education: –1913 Lincoln Sch.; 1919–22 Didsbury. *Appointments:* 1922–25 Shepton Mallett; 1925–28 Buxton; 1928–31 Manchester, Pendleton; 1931–36 Eccles; 1936–42 London, Kilburn and Hampstead; 1942–48 Harrow; 1948–55 Torquay and Paignton; 1955–62 Redhill.
Hobbies and Recreations: Music, Reading.

MITCHELL, John Gordon, 8 Ancroft Way, Fawdon, Newcastle upon Tyne NE3 2BX. (0632-854163) *b. 3 July 1929, Greenock, Renfrewshire. m. 15 Aug 1956: 2d.*
Education: 1934–40 Highlanders Academy, Greenock; 1940–42 The Mount, Greenock; 1950–53 Wesley, Headingley. *Appointments:* 1953–56 North of Scotland Mission; 1956–62 Haltwhistle; 1962–68 Sunderland North; 1968–73 Newcastle Mission; 1973–80 Consett; 1980- Chairman of District (Newcastle-upon-Tyne).
Connexional Committees: 1967–74 Connexional Youth Council; 1980– General Purposes; 1980– Home Missions; 1980– Property; 1981– President's Council; 1980– Stationing Committee.

MITCHELL, John Lumley, 220 Green Lane, Norbury, London SW16 3BL. (01-764-2039)–BD(Lond.), BA(Lond.), MTh(Lond.). *b. 26 July 1927, Keighley, Yorkshire. m. 28 July 1956: 3d.*
Education: –1941 Highfield, Keighley; 1969–73 Birkbeck, Univ. of London; 1979–81 Kings, Univ. of London; 1950–53 Wesley, Headingley. *Appointments:* 1949–50 Bradford Mission; 1953–55 Kirkoswald; 1955–58 Manchester and Salford Mission; 1958–63 Hastings; 1963–66 Croydon; 1966– West London Institute of Higher Education.
Local Council Committees: 1960–63 Hastings Lea Youth Sub-Committee.

MITCHELL, Leslie, 17 Grundale, Kirkella, North Humberside HU10 7LA. (0482-657572) *b. 9 April 1913, Hull. m. 16 May 1980: 1d.*
Education: 1936–39 Headingley.
Appointments: 1939–42 Bury St. Edmunds; 1942–46 Chaplain HMF; 1946–49 Nuneaton; 1949–53 Birmingham, Great Barr; 1953–57 Sheffield, Brunswick; 1957–62 Stockport, Tiviot Dale; 1962–68 Colwyn Bay; 1968–73 Nottingham South; 1973–78 Sheffield, Carver St.

MITCHELL, Reginald James, 41 Annandale Ave., Bognor Regis, W. Sussex PO21 2ES. (0243-823895) *b. 4 Dec 1924, Blaenafon, Gwent. m. 23 July 1949: 2s.*
Education: 1947–49 Handsworth.
Appointments: 1949–50 Brighton (Dome Mission); 1950–53 Derby (South); 1953–56 Bridgend; 1956–61 Cadishead and Irlam; 1961–66 Mid-Wiltshire; 1966–71 Bath; 1971–74 Manchester (South East); 1974–79 Salisbury; 1979– Weardale.
Special Interests: Ecumenics, Ministerial Training, Served Southampton District as Probationers' Secretary and Ecumenical Secretary and Darlington District as Ecumenical Secretary.
Hobbies and Recreations: Photography, Music, Model Railways.

MITCHELL, Reginald Thomas George, 141 Cleeve Drive, Ivybridge, Devon PL21 9DB. (07-554-3188) *b. 25 Feb 1917, Edinburgh. m. 12 April 1945: 1d., 1s.*
Education: 1922–26 Park Rd., Rosyth, Scotland; 1926–28 Hyde Pard Rd., Plymouth; 1928–33 Sutton High Sch., Plymouth; 1933–37 Plymouth Sch. of Pharmacy; 1938–40 Handsworth; 1940–41 Hartley Victoria. *Appointments:* 1941–45 Port-of-Spain, Trinidad; 1945–48 Kingstown, St. Vincent; 1949–66 British Guiana Dt; 1966–70 Guyana Dt; 1970–71 Turks and Caicos Islands, West Indies; 1971–81 Plymouth.
Connexional Committees: 1972–75 Home Committee (MMS). *Council Member:* 1966–70 Mackenzie Local Authority, Guyana, Nominated Member. *Local Council Committees:* 1970–71 Turks and Caicos Islands Education Committee.
Special Interests: The World Church, especially as it affects the Third World, The Economic Situation and Social Conditions of Third World.
Hobbies and Recreations: Music, Singing, Swimming, Walking.

MITTON, Charles Leslie, 14 Cranbrook Rd., Handsworth, Birmingham B21 8PJ. (021-554-7892)–BA(Manchester), BD, MTh, PhD(Lond.), Hon DD(Aberdeen). *b. 13 Feb 1907, Liverpool. m. 1937: 1d., 1s.*
Education: 1917–25 Kingswood Sch., Bath; 1925–28 Manchester Univ.; 1928–30 Didsbury.
Appointments: 1930–33 Headingley Coll., Assistant Tutor; 1933–36 Dunbar; 1936–39 Keighley; 1939–45 Scunthorpe; 1945–51 Nottingham, Sherwood; 1951–70 Handsworth Coll., 1956–70 Principal.
Connexional Committees: 1947–70 Ministerial Training Committee.
Publications: Clue to Wesley's Sermon (Epworth 1943); *Epistle to Ephesians, Origin and Purpose* (OUP 1951); *Pauline Corpus of Letters* (Epworth 1955); Commentary on St. Mark (Epworth 1957), *The Good News* (Lutterworth 1961); *Epistle of James* (Eardmans USA and M.M. & Scott 1966); *Jesus, Fact Behind the Faith* (Mowbrays 1973); *Commentary on Ephesians* (M.M. & Scott 1976); *Your Kingdom Come* (Eardmans & Mowbrays 1976).

MOFFAT, Leslie, 20 Goldwine Lane, Monmouth, Gwent NP5 3ES. (0600-3392) *b. 24 Aug 1906, Brigham, Cockermouth, Cumberland. m. 3 Sept 1934: 1d., 1s.*
Education: Rawlingson St., Barrow-

in-Furness; Barrow Technical Sch.; Cliff Coll.; 1928–30 Didsbury; 1930–31 Headingley. *Appointments:* 1927–28 Severn Valley Mission; 1931–36 Barbados Dt; 1936–39 Birstall; 1939–45 Ilkeston; 1945–51 Skegness and Wainfleet; 1951–53 Thirsk; 1953–59 Horncastle; 1959–65 Rugby; 1965–70 Monmouth and Ross.
Hobbies and Recreations: Choral Singing, Old Time and Modern Dancing.

MOLE, John, 12 Pretoria Ave., Morpeth, Northumberland. (0670-519137)–BA, BD, PhD. *b. Hetton-le-Hole, Durham.*
Education: Manchester Univ.; London Univ.; Leeds; 1950–53 Headingley. *Appointments:* 1953–55 Bradford Woodhouse Grove; 1955–60 Bradford East; 1960–64 Truro Sch. (Chaplain); 1964–81 Northumberland Training Coll.; 1981–82 President's List.

MONKHOUSE, John Palmer, Woodcroft, Langwathby, Penrith, Cumbria CA10 1NB. (076-881-400) *b. 15 Feb 1910, Langwathby. m. 19 Oct 1949: 1d., 1s.*
Education: 1914–22 Langwathby CE; 1922–28 Penrith Queen Elizabeth Grammar; 1945–47 Hartley Victoria. *Appointments:* 1947–48 Carlisle (Cecil St.); 1948–49 Blackburn (Trinity); 1949–52 Maryport; 1952–54 Carlisle (Fisher St.); 1959–64 Sedbergh; 1964–69 Leeds (Richmond Hill) Cross Gates; 1969–74 Stockton; 1951–61 Carlisle District, Secretary of Synod.
Publications: Currock, Carlisle Jubilee Booklet; Garsdale Centenary Brochure (Sedbergh CCT); Fell End Centenary Brochure (Sedbergh CCT).
Special Interests: Methodist History, Hymns and Tunes. *Hobbies and Recreations:* Most Sports, Philately.

MONKTON, David, Wesley Manse, 9 Hillhead, Lerwick, Shetland ZE1 0ED. (0595-2874) *b. 13 Feb 1932, Netherntraw, Dudley, West Midlands. m. 20 Aug 1960: 2d., 1s.*
Education: 1943–48 Dudley Grammar Sch.; 1949–52 Birmingham Coll. of Technology; 1954–58 Didsbury, Bristol. *Appointments:* 1958–60 Coventry Mission; 1960–65 London Mission (Bow); 1965–71 Bishops Stortford; 1971–77 Lincoln North; 1977– Lerwick, North Roe and North Isles; 1977– Chairman Shetland District.
Connexional Committees: 1977–82 General Purposes; 1977–82 Home Missions; 1977–82 Stationing. *Local Council Committees:* 1977–82 Shetland Islands Council, Education Committee; 1979–81 Chairman, Shetland Churches Council.
Publications: Articles in *Preachers Quarterly* (1969) and *Worship and Preaching* (1970–71) on *Understanding Media;* Religious Feature Writer, *East Anglian Daily Times* 1969–78.
Special Interests: Studies in 19th Century Rural Mission, Religious News Broadcaster and Interviewer, BBC Radio Shetland 1978–82.
Hobbies and Recreations: Member of Lerwick Orchestra, Painting, Drawing, Gardening, Model Making out of Waste Materials.

MOODY, Gordon Edward, Cotleigh, Main Rd., Salcombe, Devon TQ8 8AD. (054-884-2811)–MBE, MA. *b. 5 Dec 1912, London. m. 28 April 1942: 1d., 1s.*
Education: 1917–24 Downhills Elem. Sch., Tottenham; 1924–28 Tottenham County Sch.; 1935–39 Didsbury. *Appointments:* 1939–42 Ashby-de-la-Zouch; 1942–45 Ashbourne; 1945–48 Macclesfield; 1948–52 South Devon Mission; 1952–58 Chaplain HMF; 1958–78 Secretary, The Churches' Council on Gambling.
Connexional Committees: 1959–74 The Christian Citizenship Department; 1974–78 Division of Social Responsibility. *Council Member:* 1951–57 Cookham Parish Council (Berkshire). *Publications: The Facts about the Money Factory* (Churches Council on Gambling 1972); *Social Control of Gambling* (Churches Council on Gambling 1974).
Special Interests: Formation in Britain of Gamblers Anonymous and G.A. General Services Board, Formation of Society for Study of Gambling and Gordon House Association, Hostels for Single, Homeless Compulsive Gamblers. *Hobbies and Recreations:* Kitchen Gardening, Boating, Bread Making, Home Brewing.

MOORE, David John, 25 Campbell Rd., Bow, London E3 4DS. (01-980-2583) *b. 7 May 1937, Bath. m. 1962: 1d., 1s.*
Education: 1961–63 Richmond. *Appointments:* 1963–66 Port Talbot; 1966–73 London Mission East; 1973– London Mission, Bow.
Special Interests: Care of the Homeless and Alcoholics. *Hobbies and Recreations:* Association Football.

MOORE, Gerald Hedley, 13 House Farm Rd., Gosport, Hants PO12 3TE. (07017-83038) *b. 18 June 1947, Exeter, Devon. m. 27 Aug 1973: 2s.*
Education: 1959–63 Hele's Sch., Exeter; John Stocker Jun. Sch., Exeter; Union St. Inf. Sch., Exeter; 1970–71 Cliff Coll.; 1972–75 Wesley, Bristol. *Appointments:* 1974–75 PRA; 1975–78 Swansea; 1978– Gosport and Fareham.
Special Interests: Broadcasting Radio. *Hobbies and Recreations:* Electronics, Computers.

MOORE, Harold Ernest, 41 Springbank, The Broadway, South Chadderton, Oldham O19 9JB. (061-678-8704: *b. 7 Dec 1931, Crook, County Durham. m. 5 Aug 1960: 2s.*
Education: Peases West Elem. Sch., Billy Row, Crook; 1951–53 Cliff Coll.; 1955–59 Hartley Victoria. *Appointments:* 1959–61 Home Missions; 1961–64 Walsall; 1964–70 Blackpool South; 1970–76 Walthamstow and Chingford; 1976–82 Derby South; 1982– Oldham (South).
Council Member: Committee of the Conservation Evangelicals in Methodism.
Special Interests: Evangelism, Church Growth, Healing and Occultism

(Counselling). *Hobbies and Recreations:* Recorded Music, Photography.

MOORE, Isaac Ramsay, 16 Madeira Park, Tunbridge Wells, Kent TN2 5SX. (0892-26824) *b. 18 June 1925, Langside, Glasgow. m. 25 July 1953: 1d., 1s.*
Education: 1930–36 Battlefield Jun. Sch.; 1936–41 Queen's Park Senior Secondary; 1947–49 Hartley Victoria; 1952–53 St. Andrew's, Selly Oak.
Appointments: 1949–52 Kendal; 1953–58 Leeward Islands; 1958–61 Falkirk, Wallacestone and Stirling; 1961–66 Barrow-in-Furness; 1966–71 Bristol (Staple Hill); 1971–79 Finchley and Hendon; 1979– Tunbridge Wells.
Connexional Committees: 1975–78 Home Committee (Overseas Division).
Special Interests: Overseas Mission, Youth Work, Ecumenical Affairs.
Hobbies and Recreations: Swimming, Walking, Reading.

MOORE, Philip Samuel, 107 Abbey Rd., Westbury-on-Trym, Bristol BS9 3QJ. (0272-621473)–BA(Manchester), BD(Manchester). *b. 9 June 1930, Havercroft, Nr. Wakefield, Yorkshire. m. 20 April 1957: 1d.*
Education: 1935–38 Havercroft Inf. Sch.; 1938–41 Ryhill Jun. Sch.; 1941–43 South Hiendly and Ryhill Secondary Modern Sch.; 1943–49 Hemsworth Grammar Sch.; 1953–59 Manchester Univ.; 1953–56 Hartley Victoria. *Appointments:* 1956–59 Saddleworth; 1959–66 Manchester (Harpurhey); 1966–68 Southport South; 1968–71 Southport; 1971–78 Nottingham (South); 1978– Bristol (Clifton and Redland).
Connexional Committees. 1967–74 Kingswood and Trinity Hall Sch. Management Committee, 1967– Ministers Childrens Fund Committee; 1974–78 Division of Ministries, 1981– Connexional Candidates Examination Committee; 1981– Connexional Probationers Oversight Committee.
Special Interests: World Development, World Peace, Christian Aid, Ministerial Further Training.
Hobbies and Recreations: Reading, Walking, DIY, Model Railways.

MOORE, Robert, Locksley Hithe, 18 The Sycamores, Bramhope, Leeds LS16 9JR. (0532-678141)–MA. *b. 8 Aug 1933, Newcastle upon Tyne. m. 16 Dec 1961: 1d., 2s.*
Education: 1946–51 Gateshead Grammar Sch.; 1968–69 Univ. of Newcastle upon Tyne; 1973 National Institute for Social Work Training; 1974–76 Shaw Univ. Carolina, USA; 1981–82 Bradford Univ.; 1959–62 Headingley. *Appointments:* 1962–64 Wigan; 1964–66 Berwick upon Tweed; 1966–68 Housemaster, Red Bank Approved Sch.; 1969–73 Deputy Superintendent at Harrogate Branch of National Children's Home; 1973–81 Regional Director of Social Work, Caribbean Region of NCH; 1981– Otley and Aireborough (NCH).
Special Interests: Sport, Outdoor Life, Ethnic Minorities.

MOORE, Roger Lionel, 77 May Lane, Hollywood, Birmingham B47 5PA. (0564-822151) *b. 5 Dec 1940, Bristol. m. 5 Aug 1972: 1d., 1s.*
Education: 1952–58 Kingswood Grammar Sch.; 1968–71 Wesley, Bristol. *Appointments:* 1971–76 Ilkeston; 1976–79 Nottingham South; 1979– Birmingham, Moseley Rd and Sparkhill.
Connexional Committees: 1977– Childrens Committee; 1977– Uniformed Organisations Committee.
Special Interests: Education and Youth, especially Children's Work, Work with the Unemployed, West Indian Communities, Music. *Hobbies and Recreations:* Photography, Stamp Collecting, Music.

MORALEE, George Douglas, 15 Wycomb Grove, Melton Mowbray LE13 1EQ. (0664-67473) *b. 7 Sept 1908, South Shields, Co. Durham. m. (2) 8 Aug 1951: 1d., 2s.*
Education: 1913–21 Westoe Rd. Elem. Sch., South Shields; Hartley Victoria. *Appointments:* 1934–36 Liverpool Trinity; 1936–39 Hartlepool; 1939–44 Bridlington Quay; 1944–47 Leeds Mission; 1947–51 Perth and Dundee; 1951–58 Liverpool North; 1958–67 Bebington; 1967–75 Wolverhampton Trinity.
Connexional Committees: 1955–67 Chapel Committee, Manchester.
Special Interests: Reading Theology and Philosophy. *Hobbies and Recreations:* All forms of Sport, Music, Opera, President of Gilbert and Sullivan Society 12 Years.

MORGAN, Gwylfa Hugh, Awelfryn, 4 Idris Villas, Tywyn, Gwynedd. (0654-710902)–MA. *b. 13 Sept 1910, Llanfyllin, Montgomeryshire. m. 9 April 1941: 1d., 2s.*
Education: Prim. and County Sch., Llanfyllin; Bangor Univ. Coll.; 1935–38 Wesley House. *Appointments:* 1938 Portmadoc; 1939–40 Criccieth; 1940–41 Dinas Mawddwy; 1941–46 Chaplain HMF; 1946–50 Tywyn; 1950–55 Newtown; 1955–60 Barmouth; 1960–65 Newtown; 1965–75 Llanrhaeadr.
Special Interests: Old Testament Studies. *Hobbies and Recreations:* Walking and Gardening.

MORGAN, Irvonwy, 12 Heathdene Rd., Wallington, Surrey SM6 0TD. (01-647-9481)–MA, BD, PhD. *b. 11 April 1907, Trefuglwys, Powys, Wales. m. 19 March 1942: 2d (Deceased).*
Education: 1918–26 Kingswood Sch.; 1929–32 Cambridge Univ.; 1932–33 Guildhall Sch. of Music; 1929–32 Wesley House.
Appointments: 1928–29 Bath; 1932–35 London Mission, Poplar and Bow; 1935–36 Withdrew; 1936–37 President's List; 1937–51 London Mission, Poplar and Bow; 1951–79 Secretary London Mission Committee; President of the Conference 1967
Connexional Committees: 1953–56 Methodist Chapel Aid; 1951–79 Property Board; 1951–79 Home Mission Board; 1956–82 Trustee Westminster Central Hall; 1954–82 Wesley's Chapel. *Council Member:* 1972 Moderator of Free Church Federal Council; 1972–73 President Kingswood Association; 1976–77 President Bible Lands Society; 1956–79 Chairman Greater London Council

Churches Committee. *Publications: Twixt the Mount and the Multitude; The Non-Conformity of Richard Baxter* (1946); *Prince Charles' Puritan Chaplain* (1957); *The Godly Preachers of the Elizabethan Church* (1965); *Puritan Spirituality* (1973); *A Rent for Love* (1973); *Moonflight* (1978).
Hobbies and Recreations: Rugby Football, former player Cambridge Univ. and London Welsh.

MORGAN, John, 5 The Forge, Bridge St., Hungerford, Berks RG17 0EG. (0488-2412) *b. 21 Dec 1919, Treharris, Glamorgan. m. 3 July 1947: 2d.*
Education: 1931–36 Quakers Yard Secondary Sch., Merthyr Tydfil; 1939–42 Richmond; 1942–43 Headingley. *Appointments:* 1943–44 Peel; 1944–47 Chaplain HMF; 1947–51 Newport, Mon.; 1951–56 Swansea; 1956–62 Birmingham, Sutton Park; 1962–67 Harrogate; 1967–75 London, Walthamstow and Chingford; 1975–81 London, Hammersmith and Fulham; 1981– Newbury and Hungerford.
Hobbies and Recreations: Gardening, Sport.

MORGAN, John Jeffrey, 266 Western Ave., Port Talbot, West Glamorgan SA12 7NF. (0639-883649) *b. 12 Nov 1939, Gorseinon. m. 22 May 1960: 1d., 2s.*
Education: 1950–56 Gowerton Grammar; 1967–70 Wesley, Bristol. *Appointments:* 1970–73 Malvern; 1973–77 Birmingham, Asbury; 1977– Port Talbot.
Hobbies and Recreations: Swansea City FC Supporter.

MORGAN, John Wilfred, 333 Lyndon Rd., Solihull, West Midlands B92 7QS. (021-742-5583) *b. 18 July 1945, Sutton Coldfield. m. 15 June 1968: 1d., 1s.*
Education: 1950–60 Boldmere Sutton Coldfield; 1967–70 Handsworth; 1970–71 Queens. *Appointments:* 1971–74 Dewsbury; 1974–82 Worcester; 1982– Birmingham, Elmdon.
Special Interests: World Development, Justice, Peace, Broadcasting, Poetry. *Hobbies and Recreations:* Sport, Cookery.

MORGAN, William Islwyn, 15 King Edward Rd., Brynmawr, Gwent NP3 4SD. (0495-310422) *b. 15 Sept 1909, Hirwaun, Nr Aberdare, Mid Glamorgan. m. 19 Aug 1942.*
Education: 1914–23 Hirwaun Elem.; 1935–39 Handsworth Coll.
Appointments: 1939–42 Llandilo, Welsh; 1942–43 Abercynon, Welsh; 1943–46 Brynmawr, Welsh; 1946–55 Llandiloes, Welsh; 1955–74 Brynmawr, Welsh.
Connexional Committees: 1948–56 Secretary South Wales District Home Mission Committee; 1956–63 Sec. S.W. District Chapel Committee; 1957–62 Assistant Secretary Welsh Methodist Assembly; 1962–63 Secretary of Welsh Methodist Assembly; 1963–72 Secretary South Wales District Synod; 1972– President of Welsh Methodist Assembly. *Publications:* Numerous articles in Welsh Methodist Magazine *Yr Eurgrawn* and *Bathafarn* Welsh Methodist Historical Journal.
Special Interests: Methodist History.

MORLEY, William Peter Douglas, 226 Stockton Lane, York YO3 0BR. (0904-54568)–BD. *b. 7 Aug 1917, London. m. 2s.*
Education: 1930–35 Kingswood; 1936–37 Kings Coll., Westminster Coll., London Univ.; 1937–40 Richmond. *Appointments:* 1940–41 Waltham Abbey and Hertford; 1941–47 Culford Sch. (Chaplain); 1947–54 London, Bermondsey Settlement; 1954–59 Longton Mission; 1959–66 Bristol, Clifton and Redland; 1966–70 Scarborough; 1970–76 York Centenary; 1976–81 York Wesley; 1981–82 Sherburn.
Connexional Committees: Candidates (Twice); MAYC (Vice President 1954); Children's Committee (MYD); Uniformed Organisations (Chairman, MYD). *Local Council Committees:* 1949–54 London County Council Youth Committee; 1949–54 Bermondsey Borough Council Youth Committee.
Special Interests: The Scout Movement, Feed the Minds, Local Radio.

MORRELL, John Horwood, 20 Youldon Way, Hurrabridge, Yelverton, Devon PL20 7SN. (0822-853860)–BD(Lond.). *b. 7 Nov 1933, Plymouth. m. 12 Aug 1967.*
Education: 1955–59 Univ. of London; 1955–59 Richmond. *Appointments:* 1959–62 Newcastle-upon-Tyne (Brunswick); 1962–66 Carlisle; 1966–69 Rotherham; 1969–74 Weston-super-Mare; 1974–79 West Somerset; 1979– Tavistock.
Connexional Committees: 1976–82 Division of Ministries Board. *Local Council Committees:* 1966 Carlisle County Borough Education Committee.
Hobbies and Recreations: Drama, Walking, Photography.

MORREY, William R., 36 Victoria Rd., Sheffield S10 2DL. (0742-662187)–BA(Birmingham). *b. 24 March 1953, Stoke-on-Trent. m. 4 Jan 1976: 2s.*
Education: 1964–70 Stanfields Technical High Sch.; 1970–71 City of Stoke-on-Trent Sixth Form Coll.; 1971–74 Birmingham Univ.; 1973–76 Queens. *Appointments:* 1976–79 Bideford; 1979– Sheffield (Ecclesall).

MORRIS, Arnold C., Upper Flat, Mill Lodge, 85 Reigate Rd., Reigate, Surrey RH2 0RE. (0737-66326)–BD(Lond.). *b. 27 Jan 1914, Caerphilly, Glamorgan. m. 11 April 1942: 1s.*
Education: Leeds Modern; 1935–39 Handsworth. *Appointments:* 1939–42 Manchester Mission; 1942–47 Stockport, Mount Tabor; 1947–52 Newcastle, Staffs.; 1952–55 Colwyn Bay; 1955–62 Cambridge; 1962–69 Purley; 1969–75 Penarth; 1975–79 Edinburgh, Nicolson Square; 1979–82 Bristol, Clifton and Redland.
Hobbies and Recreations: Cricket, and other games.

MORRIS, Bert Alfred Reginald, Trinity Manse, Histons Hill, Codsall WV8 2ER. (090-74-2256) *b. 22 Jan 1929, Putney, London. m. 10 Aug*

1957: 2d., 1s.
Education: Cheam Central Boys Sch.; 1952–54 Hartley Victoria.
Appointments: 1951–52 President's List; 1955–57 London Poly.; 1957–62 London, Finchley and Hendon; 1962–63 Penzance; 1965–70 London Mission East Ham; 1970–81 Wanstead and Woodford; 1981– Wolverhampton Trinity.
Connexional Committees: 1978– Minsters Retirement Fund.

MORRIS, Raymond George, 4 Seafield Close, Barton-on-Sea, New Milton, Hants BH25 7HR. (0425-612165)–BA(Lond.), BD(Lond.). *b. 3 Oct 1911, Bridgwater, Somerset. m. (2), 1963: 3s.*
Education: 1923–30 Dr. Morgan's Sch., Bridgwater; 1931–34 Birkbeck Coll., Univ. of London; 1934–35 Dept. of Education, Univ. of Bristol; 1946–47 Richmond. *Appointments:* 1945–46 Stroud and Cirencester; 1947 Louth; 1951 Dorking and Horsham; 1956 London, East Ham Mission; 1959 Southend-on-Sea; 1964 Bristol North; 1969 Cheddar Valley; 1972–76 Forest-of-Dean; 1968–76 Bristol District Synod Secretary.

MORROW, Irene, 7 Coniston Rd., Blackpool FY4 2BY. (0253-41017)
Education: 1950–52 Wesley Deaconess Coll.; 1954–55 Kingsmead. *Appointments:* 1973–74 Airdrie; 1974–79 Accrington; 1979– Blackpool.

MORTIMER, Edward Thomas, 206 North Ave., Southend-on-Sea, Essex SS2 4EU. (0702-65175) *b. 3 Oct 1906, Bow, East London. m. 10 Aug 1939: 3s.*
Education: 1910 LCC; 1917 Bow Central Schs.; 1931–34 Hartley Victoria. *Appointments:* 1934–37 President's List; 1937–39 Salisbury, Dews Rd., 1939–41 London Mission, Plumstead; 1941–44 Stockton, Brunswick; 1944–45 Downham Market; 1945–48 London Mission, South East; 1948–50 Derby South; 1956–62 Watford; 1962–67 London, Waltham Abbey and Hertford; 1967–74 Fenland.

MORTLOCK, Albert Charles, 170A London Rd. West, Batheaston, Bath BA1 7QU. (0225-859190)–BD. *b. 17 Nov 1909, Colchester, Essex. m. 2d.*
Education: 1921–25 Hamilton Rd., Colchester; 1933–36 Richmond.
Appointments: 1932–33 Okehampton; 1936–37 President's List; 1936–37 Walsall Mission; 1941–42 Bristol East; 1942–46 Bromley Common and Orpington; 1951–52 Chesterfield Holy Cross; 1952–56 Coalville; 1956–61 London Wimbledon; 1961–64 Watton and Rocklands; 1964–71 Southend-on-Sea; 1971–75 London, Finsbury Park and Southgate.
Special Interests: Travel, Music, Hymns, Family.

MORTLOCK, Peter Barclay, 89 Wentworth Rd., Harborne, Birmingham B17 9ST. (021-427-1747)–BA(Open Univ.). *b. 11 March 1945, Colchester. m. 9 Aug 1969: 3s.*
Education: 1950–63 Endsleigh Sch., Colchester, Essex; 1966–70 Richmond. *Appointments:* 1970–74 Goole; 1974–78 Aylesbury; 1978- Birmingham South West.
Connexional Committees: 1981– Division of Social Responsibility Board Member; 1982– Methodist Homes for the Aged Board.
Special Interests: Chairman Woodgate Valley City Farm Trust, Social Work Theory, Access to Health Resources. *Hobbies and Recreations:* Philately, Music, Sport.

MORTON, Harry Osborne, 34B Campbell Rd., Bow, London E3 4DT. (01 980-9460)–MA. *b. 28 June 1925, Wales, Nr. Sheffield, South Yorkshire. m.7 Aug 1954: 2d., 2s.*
Education: 1936–43 The King's Sch., Pontefract; 1943–45 King's Coll., Cambridge; 1949–52 Hartley Victoria. *Appointments:* 1952–54 Yorkshire Traveller, SCM of GB&I; 1954–58 Study Secretary, SCM of India, Pakistan and Ceylon; 1958–59 Presbyter-in-charge, Egmore, Madras; 1960–63 Scholarship Secretary, WCC, Geneva; 1963–72 Secretary for East and Central Africa, MMS; 1972–73 Gen. Sec. MMS; 1973–80 Gen. Secretary British Council of Churches; 1980–81 London Mission (East Ham); President of the Conference 1972.
Hobbies and Recreations: Music.

MORTON, John Gardner, The Martins, Vinefields, Bury St. Edmunds, Suffolk IP33 1YA. *b. 22 June 1897, Perth, Scotland. (w): 1d.*
Education: 1907–13 Kingswood Sch., Bath; 1921–24 Richmond.
Appointments: 1924–26 Kirkoswald; 1926–28 Mid-Norfolk Mission; 1928–31 Hinckley; 1931–34 Birmingham, Smethwick; 1934–37 Cheltenham; 1937–46 Jamaica Dt; 1946–51 St. Neots; 1951–55 Kirkoswald; 1955–59 Wymondham.

MORTON, Joseph Clifford, Walden, 11 Manley Rd., Frodsham, via Warrington WA6 7RU. (0928-85-33163) *13 March 1894, St. Helens. m. (2) 1971: 2s.*
Education: Porth Secondary Sch.; 1928–30 Hartley Victoria.
Appointments: 1930–32 Wishaw; 1932–34 Bolton; 1934–39 Rochdale; 1939–41 Morecambe; 1941–46 Chaplain HMF; 1946–49 Worksop; 1949–54 Sheffield (Brunswick); 1954–59 Didsbury (St. Pauls); 1959–65 Kelsall.
Publications: Sermons in the *Expository Times* from 1946–54.
Special Interests: Reading, Study.
Hobbies and Recreations: Golf.

MORTON, Neville, Epworth, 101 Mundesley Rd., North Walsham, Norfolk NR28 0DB. (0692-403312) *b. 24 Dec 1918, Outwell.*
Education: 1924–30 Outwell (Elem.); 1930–36 Wisbech Grammar Sch.; 1938–39 Cliff Coll.; 1945–47 Hartley Victoria. *Appointments:* 1947–49 Spilsby; 1949–56 Barnsley West; 1956–62 Barnsley East; 1962–69 Lincoln Central; 1969–77 Brownhills and Pelsall; 1977– North Walsham.
Special Interests: Cliff Coll., Evangelism, Bible Society, Youth Work, Rural Life. *Hobbies and Recreations:* Ornithology, Agriculture, Horticulture.

MORTON, Robert Graham, 5 Drumry Rd., Clydebank, Dumbartonshire G81 2LJ. (041-952-1772) *b. 1 March 1948, Bathgate. Education:* 1953–63 Armadale Jun. Secondary Sch.; 1970–72 Cliff Coll.; 1975–78 Manchester Univ.; 1975–78 Hartley Victoria. *Appointments:* 1978– Glasgow West. *Special Interests:* Mission and Evangelism. *Hobbies and Recreations:* Music, Photography, Travel.

MORTON-GEORGE, Paul E., 14 Drive Mead, Coulsdon, Surrey CR3 2BD. (01-668-3880)–BA(Lond.), MA(Cantab.). *b. 10 March 1910, Chingford, Essex. m. 27 Aug 1938: 1d., 1s.*
Education: 1920–28 Bancrofts, Woodford, Essex; 1931–34 Wesley House. *Appointments:* 1934–37 Waltham and Hertford Mission; 1937–43 Birmingham, Wesley; 1943–46 Chaplain HMF; 1946–52 St. Leonards and Bexhill; 1952–59 Harrow; 1959–65 Sutton, Surrey; 1965–75 National Christian Education Council (Editorial Dept.). *Connexional Committees:* Church Membership, TV and Drama. *Publication: Adolphus Tompkinson, Do You See* and other talks for Children; *For Heaven's Sake* and other plays. *Special Interests:* Amateur Drama, Heraldry, Stamp Collecting. *Hobbies and Recreations:* Gardening.

MOSLEY, Albert Watson, 7 Woodway Cresc., Harrow, Middlesex HA1 2NH. (01-907-5981)–MA(Cantab.), PhD(Leeds). *b. 7 June 1926, Farnhill, Keighley, Yorks. m. 2 Aug 1952: 4d.*
Education: 1931–77 Glusburn Council Sch.; 1937–44 Keighley Boys' Grammar Sch.; 1944–47 Trinity Coll., Cambridge; 1951–52 Univ. of Göttingen, Germany; 1964–68 Leeds Univ. (part time); 1949–51 Wesley House. *Appointments:*1952–63 Rhodesia Dt; 1963–69 Keighley; 1969–77 Kingsmead Coll., Selly Oak, Birmingham; 1977– Overseas Division, General Secretary. *Connexional Committees:* 1965– Central Committee Overseas Division; 1978– President's Council; 1978– Connexional GP; 1978– Law and Polity; 1978– Ecumenical; World Methodist Council British Committee; Div of Finance; General, Central Finance Board, Central Finance Board Council; Mission and Service Fund Budget Committee. *Publications: Jesus Audiences in the Gospels of St. Mark and St. Luke* N.T. St. 10 (1963–64), 139–49; *Historical Reporting in the Ancient World* N.T. St. 12 (1965–66), 10–26; and Various Articles in Overseas Division Publications. *Special Interests:* New Testament Exposition, Theology of Mission, African Literature, Learning from other Cultures, Languages. *Hobbies and Recreations:* Camping, Classical Music, Gardening, Photography.

MOSTON, John Russell, 28 The Croft, Sudbury, Suffolk CO10 6HW. (0787-72738) *b. 24 Oct 1929, Burslem, Stoke-on-Trent, Staff. m. 9 Aug 1958: 1d., 1s.*
Education: 1953–56 Headingley. *Appointments:* 1952–53 Wolverhampton Trinity; 1956–58 Pendlebury and Pendleton; 1958–62 Leeds (Brunswick); 1962–69 Coventry; 1969–74 Birmingham (Elmdon); 1974–82 Cromer and Sheringham; 1982– Bury St. Edmunds. *Special Interests:* Prayer and Divine Healing, Church History. *Hobbies and Recreations:* Oil Painting, Photography.

MOSTYN, James, Holmegarth, Cardrona Rd., Grange-over-Sands, Cumbria LA11 7EW. (044-84-3631)–BA(Leeds). *b. 13 Mar 1914, Salford, Leeds. m. 17 Mar 1945: 1d., 1s.*
Education: 1926–32 King George V Sch., Southport; 1938–42 Headingley. *Appointments:* 1942–45 Barton-on-Humber; 1945–48 Cardiff (Roath); 1948–51 Castletown (IOM); 1951–56 Gateshead (South); 1956–62 Swansea; 1962–66 Newport; 1966–71 Swansea; 1971–76 Bloxwich; 1976–79 Abergavenny.

MOTSON, William, 2 Upton Rd., West Tarring, Worthing, Sussex BN13 1BU. (0903-66738) *b. 17 May 1914, Swineshead, Nr. Boston, Lincs. m. 21 Oct 1943: 1s.*
Education: 1919–23 Swineshead Jun. Sch.; 1923–28 Swineshead Elem. Sch.; 1937–40 Didsbury. *Appointments:* 1940–44 St. Helens; 1944–46 Cadishead; 1946–50 London, Plumstead; 1950–57 Greenwich and Deptford; 1957–64 London, East End Mission; 1964–70 Barnet; 1970–75 Brighton; 1975–79 Worthing. *Connexional Committees:* 1952–72 London Mission Committee; 1972–74 Home Missions; 1973–80 Methodist Homes for the Aged; 1952–72 Social Responsibility. *Special Interests:* Methodist History, Musical Appreciation. *Hobbies and Recreations:* Reading, Football, Television.

MOTTASHED, Arthur William, 5 Ullswater Rd., Blackpool, Lancs FY4 2BZ. (0253–42391) *b. 3 Mar 1929, Leicester. m. 7 Dec 1955: 1d., 1s.*
Education: 1941–47 West Bridgford Grammar; 1951–54 Richmond. *Appointments:* 1954–56 Huntingdon; 1956–60 Bridgend; 1960–63 Pontypool; 1963–69 Cardiff Roath; 1969–76 Coventry; 1976– Blackpool South. *Connexional Committees:* 1965–69 Church Membership. *Special Interests:* Exploring Inner Space, Marriage Counselling, Psycho-Sexual Therapy, Writing Poetry. *Hobbies and Recreations:* Music, Badminton.

MOUNTFORD, John Oulsnam, 33 New Rd., Stourbridge, West Midlands DY8 1PA. (038-43-5053) *b. 16 May 1920, Lancaster. m. 7 Jan 1944: 1d., 1s.*
Education: 1931–35 Clee Grammar, Cleethorpes, Lincs.; 1935–39 Newport High, Newport, Gwent; 1939–40 Univ. of Wales; 1945–47 Handsworth. *Appointments:* 1947–58 Church of South India; 1958–61 Cardiff, Roath; 1961–69 Church South India; 1969–74 London Mission, North and Central; 1974–80 Bournemouth; 1980– Stourbridge and Brierley Hill. *Connexional Committees:* 1974–79

MMS Central Committee.
Special Interests: Music, Art. *Hobbies and Recreations:* Golf, Photography.

MOUNTFORD, William Herbert, Westbury, 11 Chase Ave., King's Lynn, Norfolk PE30 5QY. (0553-2357) *b. 13 March 1925, Sunderland, Co. Durham. m. 9 Aug 1952: 2s.*
Education: 1930–36 Redby Sch., Sunderland; 1936–43 Bede Collegiate Boys Sch.; 1943–44 Queens Coll., Cambridge; 1948–50 Handsworth.
Appointments: 1947–48 Pickering Hungate; 1950–52 Glasgow East Mission; 1952–55 Crook; 1955–60 Bingham; 1960–65 Ossett and Horbury; 1965–68 Leeds Armley; 1968–75 Peterborough; 1975–80 London (Walthamstow and Chingford); 1980– King's Lynn.
Connexional Committee: 1965–70 Connexional Youth Council. *Local Council Committees:* 1975–80 Waltham Forest Education Committee.
Special Interests: Geography FRGS (1962), Home Missions, Church Growth. *Hobbies and Recreations:* Study of Maritime Matters, Pedigree Dogs.

MOUNTNEY, John Royston, 125 Park Cresc., Abergavenny, Gwent NP7 5TN. (0875-3097)–BA(Manchester). *b. 20 June 1921, Wolverhampton. m. Aug 1971.*
Education: 1926–32 Wednesfield CE; 1932–35 Bilston Central; 1935–40 Wednesebury Boys High; 1947–50 Manchester Univ.; 1947–50 Hartley Victoria. *Appointments:* 1945–47 Stour Valley Mission; 1950–51 Ashby-de-la-Zouch; 1951–55 Wellington (Shropshire); 1955–58 Forest of Dean; 1958–61 Clevedon; 1961–65 Spilsby; 1965-67 Forest of Dean; 1967–68 Supernumerary; 1968–71 Darwen; 1971–79 Sheffield (South); 1979–82 Abergavenny.
Special Interests: Travel, Music. *Hobbies and Recreations:* Singing.

MOWL, Kenneth Leslie, 26 Linden Drive, Hasland, Chesterfield, Derbyshire S41 0NQ. (0246-70588) *b. 26 Aug 1909, Exning, Newmarket. m. 23 November 1940.*
Education: 1920–26 Newmarket Secondary Sch. *Appointments:* 1945–48 Thetford; 1948–53 King's Lynn; 1953–57 Sheffield (Norfolk); 1957–62 Sheffield (North); 1962–69 Chesterfield; 1969–74 Staveley.
Publications: Part Author of *Meditations for Private Devotion* Compiled by Staff of King's Lynn Circuit in 1949.
Special Interests: 1967–69 Founder and President of Jack o'Diamonds Motor Cycle Club in Chesterfield, Twinning with Church in Germany. *Hobbies and Recreations:* Reading, Sports.

MUFF, Peter, 109 Stroud Rd., Gloucester Gl1 5AH. (0452-22002)–BSc(Manchester). *b. 29 Dec 1931, Halifax, Yorkshire. m. 24 July 1954: 2d., 2s.*
Education: 1942–49 Sowerby Bridge Grammar Sch.; 1949–52 Manchester Univ.; 1973–75 Wesley, Bristol.
Appointments: 1975–80 Swindon; 1980– Gloucester.
Publications: A Cross-Field Photomultiplier with Sub-Nanosecond Risetime Suitable for Nuclear Studies IEEE Trans Nuclear Science Vol. NS15 No.1 Feb. 1968, (Jointly with J. A. Lodge, R. B. Owen and D. Smout).
Special Interests: The Relationship of Science with Christianity. *Hobbies and Recreations:* Reading, Photography.

MULLINS, David Harold, West London Mission, 19 Thayer St., London W1M 5LJ. (01-935-2551)–BSc, BA. *b. 15 Oct 1951, Cardiff.*
Education: 1958–63 Ton-yr-ywen Inf. and Prim. Sch.; 1963–70 Howardian High Sch., Cardiff; 1970–73 Sch. of Environmental Studies, Univ. Coll., London; 1978–80 Fitzwilliam Coll., Cambridge; 1977–80 Wesley House. *Appointments:* 1980–81 Harpenden; 1981–82 West London Mission, President's Assistant; 1982– Hull East.
Hobbies and Recreations: Guitar, Music, Sketching, Walking.

MUNCEY, Harold Crowson, 11 Arthur Kennedy Close, Boughton-under-Blean, Faversham, Kent ME13 9BQ. (0227-751231) *b. 21 Jan 1897, Bromley, Kent. m. 26 Aug 1926 (w.): 1d.*
Education: Bromley (Kent) National Sch.; 1919–22 Didsbury.
Appointments: 1922–25 Blackpool; 1925–26 Liverpool, Linacre Mission; 1926–29 Glasgow, Claremont St.; 1930–35 London, Peckham; 1936–42 London, Finsbury Park; 1942–48 London, Blackheath; 1948–54 Sevenoaks; 1954–57 Kent Mission; 1957–63 Deal; 1963–68 Ramsgate.
Connexional Committees: 1951–56 Home Missions.

MUNDY, Peter Henry, 38 Old Deer Park Gdns., Richmond, Surrey TW9 2TL. (01-940-0866) *b. 27 April 1922, Bowes Park, London N22. m. 1950: 1d., 1s.*
Education: 1933–38 Southgate County Grammar Sch.; 1949–52 Univ. of London; 1949–52 Richmond.
Appointments: 1948–49 Wymondham; 1952–53 Kirkby Stephen, Appleby and Tebay; 1953–55 Tunstall; 1955–59 London, Tottenham and Stoke Newington; 1959–64 Southend-on-Sea; 1964–68 Great Yarmouth and Gorleston; 1968–73 Teddington; 1973–79 London Mission, North West; 1979– Richmond and Hounslow.
Connexional Committees: 1963 Manse Furniture; 1957 National Children's Home.
Special Interests: Social Responsibility.

MURPHY, William, 25 Sondes Place Drive, Dorking, Surrey RH4 3ED. (0306-882967) *b. 25 Jan 1930, Liverpool. m. 14 Sept 1963: 1s., 3d.*
Education: 1941–46 Liverpol Collegiate Grammar Sch.; 1961–62 Westhill Coll., Selly Oak, Birmingham; 1958–61 Didsbury, Bristol.
Appointments: 1962–68 Basingstoke; 1968–75 London (Wandsworth Rd. Mission); 1975– Dorking and Horsham.
Special Interests: Community and Youth Work, Ecumenical Affairs. *Hobbies and Recreations:* Squash, Tennis, Gardening.

MURRAY, Eric William, 74 The Ridgeway, Chingford, London E4 6PU. (01-529-1756)–BD(Lond.). *b. 24 Nov 1932, Portsmouth. m. 12 Dec 1959: 2s.*
Education: 1942–50 Elizabeth Coll. (Guernsey); London Univ.; 1961–62 Southampton Univ.; 1958–62 Richmond. *Appointments:* 1962–65 London, Whitechapel Mission; 1965–69 London Mission, North and Central; 1969–72 Home Mission Dept.; 1972–80 Religious Films Ltd and CTVC; 1980– London, Walthamstow and Chingford.
Special Interests: Counselling.
Hobbies and Recreations: Painting.

MURRISH, Robert Cyril, 1 Clifden Terrace, Lostwithiel, Cornwall PL22 0AW. (0208-872212) *b. 11 Jan 1932, Flint, Michigan, USA. m. 18 July 1959: 2d., 1s.*
Education: 1937–44 Cape Cornwall, (St. Just-in-Penwith) County Prim. Sch.; 1944–49 Humphrey Davy Grammar Sch., Penzance; 1956–59 London Univ.; 1956–59 Richmond.
Appointments: 1959–60 South Molton; 1960–65 Tamworth; 1965–70 Falmouth; 1970–80 St. Austell; 1980 Bodmin.
Connexional Committees: 1980– Divisional Board Education and Youth. *Publications: A History of Mevagissey Methodists 1752–1980.*
Special Interests: Education and Youth, Overseas Missions, National Children's Home, Christians Behind the Iron Curtain, Northern Ireland.
Hobbies and Recreations: Photography, Philately, Travel, Reading, Television, Sports.

MUSGRAVE, James Desmond, 35 Cove Rd., Silverdale, Carnforth, Lancs LA5 0RR. (0524-701148) *b. 25 Sept 1914, Storth, Milnthorpe. m. 26 Oct 1944: 1d., 1s.*
Education: 1919–24 West End Council Sch., Morecambe; 1925–30 Morecambe Grammar Sch.; 1937–40 Hartley Victoria. *Appointments:* 1940–47 North Rhodesia Dt; 1947–49 Preston (Fylde Rd.); 1949–52 Wath-on-Dearne; 1952–56 Weston-super-Mare; 1956–60 Nottingham N; 1960–65 Kidderminster; 1965–69 Stoke-on-Trent.
Special Interests: Local History.
Hobbies and Recreations: Walking, Gardening, Woodwork.

MYER, John, 56 London Rd., Daventry, Northants NN11 4EA. (032-72-2431) *b. 3 Jan 1919, London. m. 3 June 1961: 3s.*
Education: 1930–35 Battersea Grammar Sch.; 1951–53 Handsworth.
Appointments: 1950–51 Plymouth (King St.); 1953–58 Bournemouth; 1958–64 London, Walthamstow; 1964-67 Redhill; 1967–72 Kenya Dt; 1972–75 Hull West; 1975– Rugby and Daventry.
Special Interests: World Development, Disarmament, Education and Youth. *Hobbies and Recreations:* Walking, Music, Gardening.

MYERS, George Robinson, Tri Saeth, Penmaen Park, Llanfairfechan, Gwynedd LL33 0RN. (0248-681069)–BD(Lond.), BA(Lond.). *b. 7 April 1909, Liverpool, Litherland. m. 4 Sept 1935 (w.): 1d., 1s.*
Education: 1914 Ancona Rd. Council Sch., Plumstead; 1914–16 Private Sch., (Prep) at Huddersfield; 1916–19 Huddersfield Grammar Sch.; 1919–26 Kingswood Sch., Bath; 1928–32 Richmond. *Appointments:* 1932–34 Mission, Sheffield; 1934–37 Dome Mission, Brighton; 1937–41 Manchester Mission; 1941–46 Buxton; 1946–52 Hoylake; 1952–57 Southport; 1957–71 Bangor; 1952–57 Secretary to Governors, Trinity Hall Sch., Southport; Chaplain to Methodist Univ. and Coll. Students, 1937–41 Manchester, 1957–71 Bangor.
Connexional Committees: –1971 A Founder Member of Methodist Conference Drama Committee; 1952–57 Member of Schools Management Committee.
Publications: Several Plays, mainly Religious, including *Amor Christi* (1935), *Adeste Fideles* (1937), *Joseph* (1939), *Miracle* (1945); *Bitter Heart* (1958), *King of All Kings* (1961), all Epworth Press; Comedies include *Sugar for the Inspector* (MYD 1954); *Jeremiah's Christmas* (Samuel French), under Pen Name of Malcolm Kay.
Special Interests: Religious Drama, Theatre, Music, Travel, Walking.
Hobbies and Recreations: Since Retirement in 1971, Listening to Music, Walking, Cooking and Baking, Gardening, Dramatic Society.

NAPIER, Robert Grant West, 1 Hydes Rd., Wednesbury, W. Midlands WS10 9SX. (021-556-0420) *b. 7 June 1935, Edinburgh. m. 7 July 1962: 1d.*
Education: 1940–43 James Gillespie's Boys Sch., Edinburgh; 1943–51 George Heriot's Sch., Edinburgh; London Univ.; 1959–63 Richmond. *Appointments:* 1963–65 Luton; 1965–70 Bristol Mission; 1970–78 Gainsborough; 1978– Wednesbury Mission.
Connexional Committees: Mid 1970's Social Responsibility; 1982– Press Service Committee.
Special Interests: Has been a Member of the Methodist Recorder Reporting Team for the Methodist Conference every year since 1963.

NASH, William J. R., 48 Fairlea Rd., Emsworth Rd., Emsworth, Hants PO10 7SX. (024-34-3153) *b. 14 Jan 1903, Portsmouth. m. (2), 24 Jan 1981: 1s.*
Education: Elem. and Secondary Sch.; 1926–29 Richmond.
Appointments: 1929–31 Bridport; 1931–33 Hastings; 1933–35 Woolwich; 1935–38 Macclesfield; 1938–42 Tunstall; 1942–48 Truro (St. Mary's); 1948–51 Perranporth; 1951–56 Falmouth; 1956–60 Andover; 1960–68 Silchester.

NAYLOR, Thomas Bayles, 1/13 Holbeck Rd., Scarborough, North Yorkshire YO11 2XF. (0723-66306)–BA(Birmingham). *b. 24 Nov 1907, Guildford, Surrey. m. 11 July 1936.*
Education: 1917–21 Newcastle-upon-Tyne Royal Grammar Sch.; 1921–25 Kingswood Sch., Bath; 1930–33 Birmingham Univ.; 1929–33 Handsworth. *Appointments:* 1928–29 Stainland; 1933–36 London Mission, East Ham; 1936–39 S. Yorks Coalfields Mission; 1939–45 Bradford, Woodhouse Grove; 1945–50 Lincoln Wesley; 1950–55 York Wesley; 1955–60 Sheffield, Ecclesall;

1960–67 Redcar; 1967–72 Whitby; 1945–50 Lecturer in R.E. at Lincoln Training Coll.; 1950–55 Officiating Chaplain to RAF Rufforth; 1967–72 Fylingdales.
Connexional Committees: 1938–39 As District for Christian Citizenship; 1942–50 Youth; 1952–55, 1961–66 Chapel Affairs; 1958–61 Candidates Examination. *Publications: At the Beginning of the Way* (MYD 1942).
Special Interests: Eastern Europe, Music and Hymns. *Hobbies and Recreations:* Walking, Piano and Organ, Car Maintenance and Workshops.

NEAL, William James, Mirembe, Claygate Rd., Laddingford, Yalding, Maidstone, Kent. (089-273-263)*b. 22 Sept 1889, Dorchester. m. 21 Aug 1924.*
Education: Dorchester Boys Sch.; 1912–14 Richmond.
*Appointments:*1914–15 Supply; 1915–17 Ledbury; 1917–20 Wiltshire Mission; 1920–21 Cinderford; 1921–24 Stourbridge; 1924–27 West Monmouth Mission; 1927–30 London Mission East; 1930–33 London Mission West Ham; 1933–36 Portsmouth; 1936–39 Presteigne; 1939–41 Birmingham, Moseley Rd.; 1941–51 Lentwardine; 1951–54 Dursley.
Special Interests: Bunyon and Hardy, Preaching.

NEEDHAM, Gerald Day, 7 Wood End, Bramhall, Cheshire SK7 3LN. (061-439-9977)–MA(Oxon and Cantab.). *b. 11 Dec 1918, Stone, Staffs. m. (2), 8 Dec 1979: 2d., 1s.*
Education: 1923–29 Christ Church, Stone; 1929–37 Alleyne's Grammar Sch., Stone; 1937–39 St. Catherine's Oxford; 1946–48 Fitzwilliam, Cambridge; 1946–48 Wesley House.
Appointments: 1945–46 Darlington and Leeds (South); 1948–50 Tutor, Seminaire Protestant Porto Novo, Dahomey; 1950–52 Leeds (South); 1952–56 Mansfield (Bridge St.); 1956–61 Liverpool (Crosby); 1961–69 Chaplain, Kingswood Sch.; 1969–77 Colchester; 1977 Cheadle Hulme Sch.; 1973– Awarder, O Level Religious Studies, Oxford and Cambridge Schools Examination Board.
Connexional Committees: 1974– Connexional Probationers' Oversight Committee. *Publications: Les Béatitudes* (in French 1949); *Plays, The Dream* (1960); *The Judgement of Jesus* (1962); *Crisis* (1967).
Special Interests: Education, Classical Music, Theatre. *Hobbies and Recreations:* Photography, Sea Fishing, Caravanning, Walking, Reading Whodunits.

NEEDHAM, James, 2 Somerset Ave., Clitheroe, Lancs BB7 2BE. (0200-23229)–BD. *b. 20 Jan 1934, Rushton Spencer, Staffordshire. m. 7 Sept 1957: 1d., 2s.*
Education: 1939–44 Bosley CE Prim.; 1944–49 Leek High Sch.; 1959–63 Hartley Victoria.
Appointments: 1963–65 Tarporley; 1965–69 Chester; 1969–80 Sandbach and Alsager; 1980– Clitheroe.
Connexional Committees: 1970–74 Youth. *Local Council Committees:*1974–80 Cheshire Youth Service Advisory Sub Committee.

NELSON, Arthur, Epworth, 38 Fairfield Rd., Widnes, Cheshire WA8 6SG. (051-424-2494)–MA, BD. *b. 1926, m.*
Education: 1948–51 Queens Coll., Cambridge; 1951–54 Hartley Victoria. Appointments: 1954–56 Glasgow (Cathcart Rd. and Pollokshaws); 1956–61 Whitehaven; 1961–64 Manchester, Cheetham Hill and Prestwich; 1964–69 Stockport; 1969–74 New Mills; 1974– Widnes.

NEVILLE, Alan Joseph, 3 Drimsynie Court, Lochgoilhead, by Cairndow Argyll. (030-13-286). *b. 28 June 1911, Stockton-on-Tees. m. 25 Feb 1939: 2s.*
Education: 1922–27 King James Grammar Sch., Bishop Auckland.
Appointments: 1969–74 Haworth and Oakworth; 1974–79 Chepstow and Caldicot.
Connexional Committees: 1970–73 Membership; 1978–79 Overseas Division. *Publications: Motoring in North-East England* (1967);*Heritage of the North I & II* (1970, 1972).
Special Interests: Landscape. *Hobbies and Recreations:* Painting, Woodwork, Cricket, Hockey.

NEW, Charles Thomas Frank, The Manse, Maryland Lane, Moreton, Wirral, Merseyside L46 7TT. (051-677-6127) *b. 29 Aug 1941, Bromley, Kent. m. 17 Mar 1962: 3d.*
Education: 1954–58 Cray Valley Technical High Sch.; 1965–69 Handsworth. *Appointments:* 1969–73 Manchester, Swinton; 1973–82 Wallasey; 1982– Birkenhead.
Special Interests: Part Time Member of Training Staff of AVEC. *Hobbies and Recreations:* Sailing, Walking.

NEWBOLD, Brian, The Manse, Broad Lane, Holmfirth, Huddersfield HD7 1LS. (048-489-3415) *b. 25 April 1931, Loughborough, Leics. m. 30 Mar 1957: 3s.*
Education: 1942–47 Loughborough Grammar Sch.; 1953–56 Handsworth.
Appointments: 1956–59 Raunds; 1959–63 Barnsley (West); 1963–64 Wath and Mexborough; 1964–68 Skegness and Wainfleet; 1968–74 Rugby; 1974–79 Chester.
Connexional Committees: 1972–74 C. Youth Council.
Special Interests: Nature Conservation, Amnesty International.
Hobbies and Recreations: Ornithology, Apiculture.

NEWBY, Walter, 26 Rokesly Ave., London N8 8NR. (01-340-6581)–BA. *b. 11 Dec 1914, Hoyland Common, Nr. Barnsley, Yorks. m. 30 Dec 1944: 2d., 1s.*
Education: 1919–28 Hoyland Common; 1937–38 Cliff Coll.; 1938–41 Hartley Victoria. *Appointments:* 1941–46 Chatham Mission; 1946–49 London, East Ham Mission; 1949–54 Gt. Yarmouth (Temple); 1954–59 Pontefract, Horsefair; 1959–64 Bridgend; 1964–67 London, Lewisham and Peckham; 1967–72 London Mission (Hackney); 1972–75 Rochdale (Champness Hall); 1975–81 London Mission (Lambeth).
Special Interests: Evangelism.
Hobbies and Recreations: Football, Cricket.

NEWELL, Roy David, 6 Blackheath Rise, London SE13 7PN. (01-852-0227)–BA, BD(Manch.). *b. 17 March 1935, Farnworth, Lancs. m. 26 June 1960: 2d., 2s.*
Education: 1940–46 All Saints Prim. Sch., Farnworth; 1946–54 The Bolton Sch.; 1954–57 Manchester Univ.; 1958–61 Hartley Victoria.
Appointments: 1961–63 Wombwell and Hoyland; 1963–72 CSI Diocese of Madras; 1972–74 London Mission East Ham; 1974–81 London Mission East; 1981– London Mission South East.
Connexional Committees: 1973– MCOD Asia Advisory Group; 1976– MCOD Pastoral Committee; 1973–79 MCOD Overseas Service Committee; 1976– Member CSI Council in Great Britain. *Local Council Committees:* 1978–81 Area Youth Committee (City of London and Tower Hamlets); 1981– Area Youth Committee (Greenwich).
Special Interests: Industrial and Urban Mission, Youth Work. *Hobbies and Recreations:* Motor Mechanics, Canoeing, Camping, DIY.

NEWELL, Roy Norman, 21 Moor Drive, Leeds LS6 4BY. (0532-752428)–MA(Oxon), BA(Cantab.). *b. 23 May 1936, Birmingham. m. 25 Aug 1965: 1d., 1s.*
Education: 1947–55 King Edward VI Sch., Five Ways, Birmingham; 1957–60 The Queen's Coll., Oxford; 1961–64 Wesley House.
Appointments: 1964–65 Sutton (Surrey); 1965–70 Stevenage; 1970–75 Wakefield; 1975–82 Batley; 1982– Leeds, Headingley.
Connexional Committees: 1972–74 Candidates Examination Committee; 1973–75 Divisional Board, Social Responsibility (Leeds District SR Secretary).
Special Interests: Hospital Chaplaincy Work, The Caring of the Terminally Ill (Hospice Movement), Prayer and Spirituality. *Hobbies and Recreations:* Cricket, Rugby Union (Referee, County Panel Standard, Retired from First-Class Rugby in 1976), Steam Railways.

NEWLAND, Rowland Frederick, 18 Bournemouth Park Rd., Southend-on-Sea, Essex SS2 5LN. (0702-66571)–BD(Lond.). *b. 10 Aug 1914, St. Leonards-on-Sea, Sussex. m. 9 Jan 1943: 2s.*
Education: 1920–26 St. Mary Magdalen's Sch.; 1926–30 Hastings Grammar Sch.; 1960–61 Birkbeck Coll.; 1936–40 Richmond.
Appointments: 1940–43 London East Ham Mission; 1943–47 London Finsbury Park; 1947–53 Margate; 1953–57 London Brixton Hill; 1957–79 Resigned; 1979– Southend-on-Sea.
Connexional Committees: 1951–53 Temperance and Social Welfare Dept. *Council Member:* 1952 President Margate Free Church Federal Council.
Hobbies and Recreations: All Forms of Transport, Gardening.

NEWMAN, Leslie Arthur, 141 Surrenden Rd., Brighton, Sussex 3N1 6ZA. (0273-507564)–BA(Dunelm), PhD(Dunelm). *b. 15 Aug 1904, Maulden, Beds. w: 1s.*
Education: Bedford; London Univ.; Durham Univ.; 1924–28 Richmond.
Appointments: 1928–31 London, Ilford; 1931–35 Leicester, King Richard's Rd.; 1935–39 Harrogate; 1939–44 Scarborough, Queen St.; 1944–53 Newcastle-upon-Tyne, Brunswick; 1953–67 Brighton Dome Mission.
Publications: Highways in the Byways (1944); *News from the North* (1954); *Pathway to the Danw* (1946); *Gypsy Tells Her Story* (1955); *The Master Enters* (1945).
Special Interests: Psychiatry.

NEWMAN, Martyn Alan, 79 Chester Rd., Whitby, South Wirral L65 6SB. (051-355-1294)–BA. *b. 13 Sept 1944, Swindon, Wilts. m. 5 Aug 1966: 1d., 1s.*
Education: 1949–55 Even Swindon Prim. Sch.; 1955–62 Headlands Grammar Sch., Swindon; 1962–66 Univ. of Exeter; 1966–69 Univ. of Birmingham; 1966–69 Handsworth.
Appointments: 1969–71 Canterbury, Kent Coll. (Chaplain); 1971–73 Cadishead; 1973–76 Cadishead and Eccles; 1976– South Wirral.

NEWMAN, Michael, National Children's Home, 85 Highbury Park, London N5 1UD. (01-226-2033)–MA, FRSA. *b. 28 Dec 1929, Warsop, Notts. m. 16 Aug 1957: 3d., 2s.*
Education: 1939–48 Ashville; 1950–53 St. John's, Oxford; 1953–56 Wesley House. *Appointments:* 1956–58 Richmond Coll. Assistant Tutor; 1958–62 Tavistock; 1962–67 Colwyn Bay; 1967–77 London, Finsbury Park and Southgate; 1977– National Children's Home.
Council Member: 1971–80 Association for Promotion of Retreats, St. George's House, Windsor.
Special Interests: Retreats. *Hobbies and Recreations:* Looking, Being Quiet, Growing Sweet Peas.

NEWTON, Gordon Dennis, 30 York Rd., Broadstone, Dorset BH18 8ET. (0202-693662) *b. 19 Dec 1944, Tunbridge Wells, Kent. m. 3 Aug 1968: 1d., 1s.*
Education: 1950–51 St. Mark's, Tunbridge Wells; 1951–52 Bosham, CP (W. Sussex); 1952–56 Fishbourne CE; 1956–61 Chichester High Sch. for Boys; 1964–67 Didsbury, Bristol; 1967–68 Wesley, Bristol.
Appointments: 1968–70 Wellingborough; 1970–75 Bradford (Trinity); 1975–78 Bolton; 1978– Poole; 1971–75 Secretary of the Bradford Churches' Industrial Training Centre; 1980– Secretary of the Southampotn District Methodist Synod.
Hobbies and Recreations: Music, Gardening, Walking.

NEWTON, John Anthony, 36 Priory Ave., Bedford Park, Chiswick, London W4 1TY. (01-994-5147)–BA(Lond.), MA(Cantab.), PhD(Lond.), HonDLit(Hull). *b. 28 Sept 1930, Grantham, Lincs. m. 28 Dec 1963: 4s.*
Education: 1935–42 Carlton Rd. Prim. Sch., Boston; 1942–49 Boston Grammar Sch.; 1949–53 Univ. Coll., Hull; 1953–55 The Institute of Historical Research, Univ. of London; 1956–58 Wesley House.
Appointments: 1955–56 Chaplain, Kent Coll., Canterbury; 1958–61 Assistant Tutor, Richmond Coll.; 1961–64 Louth; 1964–65 Stockton-

on-Tees; 1965–67 Tutor, Didsbury Coll., Bristol; 1967–72 Wesley Coll., Bristol; 1972–73 Tutor, St. Paul.s United Theol. Coll., Limuru, Kenya; 1973–78 Principal, Wesley Coll., Bristol; 1978– West London Mission; President of the Conference 1981.
Connexional Committees: 1973–78 Connexional Probationer's Oversight Committee; 1973–78, 1980– Stationing Committee; 1980– President's Council; 1978– Overseas Division, Overseas Service Committee; 1965–72, 1973–78 Connexional Candidates' Committee.
Publications: Methodism and the Puritans (Dr. Williams's Library Lecture 1964); *Susanna Wesley and the Puritan Tradition in Methodism* (1969); *The Palestine Problem* (1971); *Edward King: Search for a Saint* (1977); *The Fruit of the Spirit in the Lives of Great Christians* (1979).
Special Interests: Spirituality, 19th Century Church History. *Hobbies and Recreations:* Gardening, Walking, Music, Tennis, Reading.

NEWTON, John Colwell, 4 Hollywood Way, Woodford Green, Essex IG8 9LQ. (01-527-1182)– BA(Bristol), BSc(Southampton). *b. 27 March 1935, Fawley, Hants. m. 25 June 1960: 2d., 1s.*
Education: 1945–53 Yeovil Sch.; 1953–56 Southampton Univ.; 1957–60 Didsbury, Bristol. *Appointments:* 1960–62 Canterbury and Faversham; 1962–66 Huddersfield (West); 1966–71 Goole; 1971–76 Mid-Sussex; 1976–82 Ealing and Acton; 1982– London (Walthamstow and Chingford).
Connexional Committees. 1974–80 Board of Division of Ministries; 1976–80 Executive Committee of Division of Ministries. *Local Council Committees:* 1977–81 Ealing Borough Education Committee.
Hobbies and Recreations. Music, Stamp Collecting.

NEWTON, John Joseph, 11 Meadow Vale, Ripon, N. Yorks HG4 2PN. (0765-6188) *b. 12 Sept 1909, Hull, Humberside. m. 18 July 1942: 2d., 1s.*
Education: Elem. and Hull Municipal Technical Coll.; 1932–33 Cliff Coll.; 1952–53 Headingley (Non-residential). *Appointments:* 1952–55 Pocklington; 1955–58 Manchester and Salford Mission; 1958–62 Malton; 1962–66 Masham; 1966–71 Thirsk; 1971–74 Alford; 1974–76 Coningsby.
Special Interests: Evangelism, Total Abstinence, Music. *Hobbies and Recreations:* Woodwork, Allotment Holder, Gardening.

NICHOLAS, Thomas Stephen, The Manse, La Croix-au-Lion, St. Peter, Jersey, Channel Islands. (0534-81479) *b. 25 Nov 1928, Redruth, Cornwall. m. 27 March 1954: 1d., 1s.*
Education: 1933–39 East End Prim. Sch., Redruth; 1939–41 Trewirgie Secondary Sch.; 1941–46 Redruth County Sch.; 1956–58 Didsbury, Bristol. *Appointments:* 1958–62 Bristol, S. Gloster; 1962–67 Saltash and St. Germans; 1967–72 Penzance; 1972–77 Plymouth (King St.); 1977– Jersey.
Connexional Committees: 1978– Property Board.

NICHOLAS, William Maurice, 75 Caithness Rd., Stamford, Lincs PE9 2TD. (0780-52694) *b. 5 Aug 1915, Epworth. m. 28 Dec 1942: 1d., 1s.*
Education: 1926–27 Ashton-under-Lyne Grammar Sch.; 1927–30 Hereford High Sch.; 1930–33 West-Monmouth Sch.; 1933–35 Monmouthshire Training Coll., Caerleon; 1939–41 Richmond; 1941–42 Headingley. *Appointments:* 1942–43 Sherbourne; 1943–46 Chaplain HMF; 1946–48 Rugby; 1948–51 Peterborough; 1951–53 Stourbridge; 1953–55 Stour Vale; 1955–61 Martham; 1961–66 Witney; 1966–72 Ashby-de-la-Zouch; 1972–75 Derby, Derwent; 1977-80 Worksop and Kweton.
Hobbies and Recreations: Arts and Crafts, Sport in General, Football, Cricket.

NICHOLSON, David William, 18 Marne Ave., Welling, Kent DA16 2EY. (01-303-1452) *b. 5 March 1941, Dewsbury, Yorkshire. m. 31 Dec 1966: 1d., 1s.*
Education: Earlsheaton Secondary Modern Sch., Dewsbury; 1966–67 Headingley; 1967–68 Wesley, Bristol.
Appointments: 1968–72 Maidstone; 1972–79 Chislehurst; 1979– Shooters Hill.
Connexional Committees: 1979– Division of Social Responsibility Board; 1980– Chairman Connexional Family Life Committee.
Special Interests: Psychotherapist, Analytical Psychology. *Hobbies and Recreations:* Music, Golf, Badminton.

NICHOLSON, Edgar Harold, 1 Cumberland Ave., Chilwell, Beeston, Nottingham NG9 4DH. (0602-254451) *b. 3 April 1923, Newport, Mon., Gwent. m. 26 Sept 1949: 1d., 1s.*
Education: 1928–34 Durham Rd. Inf. and Prim., Newport; 1934–40 Bassaleg Secondary Sch.; 1946–47 Richmond. *Appointments:* 1947–59 Burma Dt; 1959–65 Bloxwich; 1965–72 Wem and Prees Green; 1972–79 Melton Mowbray; 1979– Nottingham West.
Connexional Committees: 1967–69 Overseas Mission General and Eastern Committees
Special Interests: Biblical Exposition. *Hobbies and Recreations:* Photography, Philately, Horticulture, Watching Cricket.

NICHOLSON, Kenneth David, 21 Dovedale Rd., Wallasey, Merseyside L45 0LP. (051-639-2001) *b. 16 Jan 1916, Leek, Staffs. m. 23 March 1956: 1d.*
Education: 1926–32 Kingswood; 1932–33 Woodhouse Grove; 1946–48 Handsworth. *Appointments:* 1945–46 Sierra Leone Dt; 1948-51 Mission House Education Dept.; 1951–62 Sierra Leone Dt; 1962–66 Channock Chase; 1966–70 Birkenhead; 1970–78 Warrington, 1978– Wallasey.
Connexional Committees: 1964–69 OM. *Publications:* Audio-Visual Acts of Worship *Think on These Things* and *How Great Thou Art* published by Concordia Films.
Special Interests: Audio-Visual Worship. *Hobbies and Recreations:* Photography, Painting.

NIXON, Ernald Clay, 60 Welland Lodge Rd., Cheltenham, Glos GL52 3HQ. (0242-514922) *b. 6 April 1915, Norton in the Moors, Staffs. m. 1 Jan 1946: 1d., 1s.*
Education: 1939–42 Hartley Victoria.
Appointments: 1942–43 Belper; 1943–45 Matlock; 1945–49 Liverpool Mission; 1949–52 Pocklington; 1952–59 Pickering; 1959–64 Kirkby, Stephen, Appleby and Tebay; 1964–69 Sedbergh; 1969–75 Paulton; 1975– Tewkesbury; 1960–65 Secretary of the Carlisle District Synod.

NIXON, Isaac Blenkinsop, 7 Woodland Ave., Nantwich, Cheshire CW5 6JE. (0270-625606) *b. 17 Mar 1925, Renwick, Cumbria. m. 8 Oct 1955: 1d., 1s.*
Education: 1949–51 Hartley Victoria.
Appointments: 1948–49 Bridgwater (Som.); 1951–54 Bedale; 1954–60 South Derbyshire; 1960–66 Chesterfield; 1966–72 Doncaster West; 1972–77 Burnley; 1977– Nantwich.
Connexional Committees: 1980– Property.

NOBLE, John Trevor, 32 Burton Rd., Ashby-de-la-Zouch, Leicestershire LE6 5LL. (0530-412298) *b. 23 Dec 1920, Huddersfield. m. 8 July 1944: 1d., 2s.*
Education: –1933 Jun. Sch.; 1933–36 Central Sch.; 1937–42 Huddersfield Technical Coll., Part Time; 1971–72 Hartley Victoria. *Appointments:* 1972–77 Todmorden; 1977–82 Doncaster; 1982– Ashby-de-la-Zouch.
Special Interests: Property Maintenance. *Hobbies and Recreations:* Car Maintenance, Gardening, Methodist Guild Holidays.

NOCK, Peter, 11 Kingsley Rd., Kingsbridge, Devon TQ7 1EY. (0548-2073) *b. 19 Nov 1935, Dudley, West Midlands. m. 15 Oct 1960: 1s.*
Education: 1939–50 General Education (numerous schools); 1958–62 Wolverhampton Poly.; 1953 Cliff Coll.; 1972–74 Queens.
Appointments: 1974–77 Chipping Norton and Stow-on-the-Wold; 1977-82 Northampton; 1982– Kingsbridge and Salcombe.
Connexional Committees: 1982– General Purposes (Ministerial Allowances Sub-Committee).
Publications: Methodist Conference Public Meetings, 1980 and 1981; Article *Management Review and Digest* (BIM) *Can Churches Manage* (Oct 1980); Oxford and Leicester District Survey Report on Pastoral Care of The Ministry (1978).
Special Interests: Ex-Management Consultant Inbucon (Past Chairman of British Institute of Management Churches Cttee.), Church Management and Mission. *Hobbies and Recreations:* Music, Walking.

NOEL, Bertrand, The Bungalow, Downs Rd., East Studdal, Dover, Kent CT15 5BX. (03045-64120) *b. 2 April 1908, Dover. m. 18 Aug 1937: 1d., 1s.*
Education: 1915–23 St. Martin's Boys' Council Sch., Dover; 1930–33 Hartley Victoria. *Appointments:* 1933–35 Leicester, Hinckley Rd.; 1935–37 Minehead and Dunster; 1937–41 Teignmouth; 1941–45 Cardiff, Roath; 1945–48 Newport (Mon.); 1948–49 Wesley House, Hamburg; 1949–53 Brighton; 1953 Blackheath and Lee; 1958–64 Lewisham and Peckham; 1964–69 Hemel Hempstead; 1969–74 Ringsash.
Hobbies and Recreations: Gardening.

NORGATE, Raymond Henry, 192 City Way, Rochester, Kent ME1 2AU. (0634-44035)–BA. *b. 1 Feb 1934, London. m: 2d., 1s.*
Education: 1944–46 John Bright Grammar Sch., Llandudno; 1946–52 Emanuel Sch., London; 1957–60 Birmingham Univ.; 1960–61 Princeton Theol. Seminary NJ, USA; 1957–60 Handsworth.
Appointments: 1961–63 London, Enfield; 1963–68 London Mission (North and Central); 1968–73 Worcester; 1973– Medway Towns.

NORGETT, Gilbert William, 17 Springdale Close, Brixham, Devon TQ5 9RL. (08045-7446) *b. 24 March 1915, Brentford, Middx. m. 2 Dec 1939: 2d.*
Education: 1920–22 Brentford Inf. Sch.; 1922–26 Rothschild Sch., Brentford; 1926–31 Isleworth County Sch.; 1945–47 Richmond.
Appointments: 1947–49 Holbeach; 1949–54 Lincoln, Aldersgate; 1954–58 Reading; 1958–65 Staines and Felton; 1965–69 London Mission, Rivercourt; 1969–74 Falmouth; 1970–80 Newquay, Perranporth and St. Agnes.
Hobbies and Recreations: Gardening and all Sports.

NORTHEY, Robert, Sunnydale, Bristol Rd., Langford, Nr. Bristol, Avon BS18 7JE. (0934-144) *b. 5 March 1912, Bentinck, Newcastle-upon-Tyne. m. 4 Sept 1943 (w.): 1d., 3s.*
Education: 1917–26 Mill Lane, Council Sch.; 1937–37 Salvation Army Training Coll., Denmark Hill, London. *Appointments:* 1964–65 Whitehaven; 1965–67 Jarrow; 1967–70 Berwick-on-Tweed; 1970–73 Pontypool; 1973–75 Rhondda and Ely Valley.
Special Interests: Reading, especially Classics, History, Methodist Beginnings. *Hobbies and Recreations:* Rug Making, Decorating, Sport, Cricket, Football, Bowls.

NOWELL, Charles Geoffrey Hulme, 1 Pebble Lane, Budleigh Salterton, Devon EX9 6NN. (03954-3199)–BA(Open Univ.). *b. 27 Aug 1926, Wilmslow, Cheshire. m. 16 July 1958: 2d., 1s.*
Education: –1942 King's, Macclesfield; 1950–53 Wesley, Headingley. *Appointments:* 1949–50 Colchester; 1953–55 Holyhead; 1955–60 Crewe (Trinity); 1960–67 Darlaston; 1967–76 Jersey; 1976– Exmouth and Budleigh Salterton.

NOWELL, Colin Raymond, 309 Preston Old, Blackburn BB2 2TX. (0254-21109) *b. 27 Nov 1928, Wilmslow, Cheshire. m. 12 Aug 1961: 2d., 1s.*
Education: 1941–46 Manchester Grammar Sch.; 1957–60 Handsworth.
Appointments: 1960–66 Madeley and Dawley; 1966–69 Sowerby

Bridge; 1969–73 Mansfield West; 1973–78 Bolsover and Staveley; 1978– Blackburn.
Special Interests: Founder of the Institute of Church Renewal which promotes and co-ordinates Lay Witness Missions in the UK. *Hobbies and Recreations:* Caravanning.

NOWELL, Terence Michael, The Manse, Bradwell, Sheffield S30 2JL. (0433-20470)–BA. *b. 2 March 1948, Pontefract, West Yorkshire. m. 1969: 2s.*
Education: 1959–64 King's Sch.; 1970–74 Hartley Victoria.
Appointments: 1974– Peak.

NUNNERLEY, George Richard, 29 Waterside, Evesham, Worcs WR11 6BU. (0386-2380) *b. 10 Nov 1920, Crewe, Cheshire. m. 29 July 1950: 1d., 1s.*
Education: 1946–48 Headingley.
Appointments: 1948–50 Pateley Bridge; 1950–53 Darwen; 1953–58 Ludlow; 1958–61 Buxton; 1961–67 Martham; 1967–72 Acle; 1972–78 Hunstanton; 1978– Evesham.

NURSE, Claude Arthur, Stour Valley House, Fairfield Rd., Blandford Forum, Dorset. (0258-53236)–BD. *b. 20 April 1929, Terrington, Norfolk. m: 3d., 1s.*
Education: 1951–54 Handsworth.
Appointments: 1957–64 Burma Dt; 1964–68 Stainland and Greetland, 1968–74 Ely; 1974–81 Higham Ferrers; 1981– Stour Valley.

ODELL, Alan John, 120 Stainbeck Lane, Leeds LS7 3QS. (0532-681757)–BA(Manch.). *b. 23 Sept 1929, Marston Moretaine, Bedford. m. 2d.*
Education: 1934–40 Marston Moretaine CP Sch.; 1940–47 Bedford Modern Sch.; 1949–52 Manchester Univ.; 1949–52 Hartley Victoria.
Appointments: 1952–55 Cromer, Sheringham and Holt; 1955–61 Norwich (Calvert St.); 1961–66 Penarth; 1966–75 Leeds Mission and Headingley; 1975– Leeds (North East).
Connexional Committees: 1963–65 Education; 1974–78 Ministries; 1973–75 Candidates. *Local Council Committees:* 1970– Chairman Leeds Supplementary Benefit Appeal Tribunal.
Special Interests: Pastoral Theology.
Hobbies and Recreations: Photography, Reading, Exploring the Countryside.

OGLE, Alan Dawson, The Manse, Spa View Place, Hackenthorpe, Sheffield S12 4HD. (0742-484824) *m: 1d., 1s.*
Education: Ecclesfield Grammar Sch.; Didsbury, Bristol.
Appointments: 1948–50 Kimberley; 1950–51 Kidderminster; 1951–55 Halifax (Ebenezer); 1955–59 Huddersfield (West); 1959–64 Peak; 1964–69 Loughborough; 1969–75 Sheffield (Brunswick); 1975–82 Chesterfield; 1982– Sheffield (South).
Publications: Several Hymns and Short Articles.

O'GORMAN, Brian Stapleton, 9 Trysull Gdns, Wolverhampton WV3 7LD. (0902-762167) *b. 4 March 1910, Hale, Cheshire. m. 16 Aug 1939: 2d.*
Education: 1920–26 Bowdon Coll., Cheshire; 1932–35 Handsworth.
Appointments: 1931–32 Minehead and Dunster; 1935–40 Manchester Mission; 1940–43 London, Islington Mission (London); 1943–50 Longton Mission; 1950–57 Sheffield Mission; 1957–75 Chairman Wolverhampton and Shrewsbury District; President of the Conference 1969.
Local Council Committees: 1979– Wolverhampton Art Gallery and Public Library Sub-Committee; 1975– Supplementary Benefit Appeal Tribunal Wolverhampton.

OLDHAM, Rex, 1 The Firs, Lynn Rd., Downham Market, Norfolk PE38 9SJ. (0366-383231)–BA(Open Univ.). *b. 13 Dec 1928, New Balderton, Nottinghamshire. m. 11 Aug 1955: 3s.*
Education: 1939–46 Magnus Grammar Sch., Newark; 1949– 52 Handsworth. *Appointments:* 1952–55 Bristol (South Gloucestershire); 1955–58 West Bromwich (Wesley); 1958–63 Leominster; 1963–68 Gainsborough; 1968–75 Cheddar Valley; 1975– Downham Market.

OLDS, Alfred, 21 Josephs Court, Perranporth, Cornwall TR6 0DN. (087-257-3487) *b. 12 March 1908, Newbridge, Nr. Penzance, Cornwall. m. 7 Aug 1935: 2d.*
Education: 1912–22 Newbridge Board Sch.; 1928–31 Victoria Park.
Appointments: 1931–33 Swansea; 1933–38 Caldicot; 1938–41 Falmouth; 1941–47 St. Dennis; 1947–51 London, Deptford; 1951–62 Shebbear; 1962–67 Tadley; 1967–71 Chepstow.
Special Interests: Reading, Writing.
Hobbies and Recreations: Tennis, Golf.

OLIVER, Frederick John, 55 Fisher Ave , Rugby, Warwickshire CV22 5HW. (0788-2954) *b. 15 July 1908, Weston-super-Mare, Avon. m. 7 Aug 1939: 1d.*
Education: 1912–21 Locking Rd. Council Sch.; Weston-s-Mare.
Appointments: 1961–65 Ryedale; 1965–70 Ashfield; 1970–73 Rugby.
Hobbies and Recreations: Gardening, Toymaking, Listening to Classical Music.

OLIVER, Leonard, 121 Beccles Rd., Bungay, Suffolk NR35 1HX. (0986-2296) *b. 13 Dec 1915, Gillingham, Kent. m. 11 May 1940: 3s.*
Education: 1920–25 Wesleyan Sch., Gillingham; 1925–30 Catterick Camp. Garrison; 1931–32 Richmond, Yorks., Grammar. *Appointments:* 1967–71 Shildon; 1971–76 Downham Market; 1976–82 Ipswich.
Special Interests: Education and Youth, Training. *Hobbies and Recreations:* Photography, Gardening, Walking.

OLIVER, Richard, 32 Peel Rd., Gosport, Hants PO12 1JT. (07017-26054)–MA. *b. 23 Nov 1901, Durham. m. 29 July 1933: 1d.*
Education: 1941–47 Manchester Univ.; 1925–26 Cliff Coll.; 1930–32 Hartley; Blue Coat Boys Sch., Durham.
Appointments: 1928–30

Kingsbridge; 1930–32 Hurst and Hyde; 1932–33 North Shields; 1933–36 Alnwick; 1936–41 Farsley and Pudsey; 1941–47 Manchester, Oxford Rd. and South East; 1947–48 Stockport, Mount Tabor; 1948–51 Bristol, Bishopston; 1951–57 Stockton; 1957–62 Cannock Chase; 1962–66 Saddleworth.
Special Interests: Psychology and Theology. *Hobbies and Recreations:* Music, Electronics.

ONYETT, Frank, 141 York Rd., Acomb, York YO2 5LP. *b. 9 Nov 1911, Keyworth, Notts. m. 4 April 1935: 1d., 1s.*
Education: 1916–23 Keyworth Prim. Sch.; 1923–25 British Boys' Sch., Melton Mowbray, Leics.; 1945–47 Handsworth. *Appointments:* 1947–52 Newark; 1952–58 York Wesley; 1958–63 St. Albans; 1963–69 Harrogate; 1969–76 Ripon.
Hobbies and Recreations: Photography and Gardening.

ORMEROD, Peter Metcalf, 29 Rosemede Ave., Kendal, Cumbria LA9 6DH. (0539-21450)–BD. *b. 1 Feb 1938, Rochdale. m. 19 June 1965: 1d., 2s.*
Education: 1943–49 Greenbank Prim. and Jun. Sch.; 1949–54 Rochdale Grammar Sch. for Boys; 1963–67 Headingley. *Appointments:* 1967–69 Nottingham (Central); 1969–74 Matlock; 1974–79 South Shields; 1979– Kendal.
Special Interests: Cyprus Affairs. *Hobbies and Recreations:* Walking, Sport, Philately, Reading, Music.

ORMESHER, Robert, 155 Coldhill Lane, Newby, Scarborough, North Yorkshire YO12 6SD. (0723-72266) *b. 25 May 1943, Manchester, England. m. 22 July 1972: 2d., 1s.*
Education: 1948–53 St. Pauls Peel Inf., Little Hulton, Manchester; 1953–58 Birch Rd. Secondary Modern, Walkden, Manchester; 1963–64 Cliff Coll.; 1970–73 Hartley Victoria.
Appointments: 1973–76 Thirsk and Boroughbridge; 1976–81 Nottingham Central; 1981– Scarborough.

ORTON, Frances Mary Ruth, 57 Ilkeston Rd., Heanor, Derbys DE7 7BP. (07737-5896)–BA(Sheffield). *b. 19 May 1932, Sheffield.*
Education: 1943–50 High Storrs Grammar Sch., Sheffield; 1950–54 Sheffield Univ.; 1960–62 Wesley Deaconess Coll., Ilkley.
Appointments: 1974–81 High Wycombe; 1981– Ilkeston.

OSBORN, Lionel Edwin (Leo), 38 The Drive, Bury, Lancs BL9 5OG. (061-764-4447) *b. 6 May 1952, Handsworth, Birmingham. m. 10 Dec 1977.*
Education: 1956–59 The Laurels Preparatory Sch.; 1959–61 Handsworth Preparatory Sch.; 1961–63 Cherry Orchard Jun. Sch.; 1963–70 King Edward's Five Ways Grammar Sch.; 1972–76 Wesley, Bristol.
Appointments: 1976–81 Ripley; 1981– Bury and Heywood.
Special Interests: Church History, Youth Work, Football, Chaplaincy.
Hobbies and Recreations: Playing, Watching and Refereeing Football, Football Programme Collecting, Music, Cricket.

OSBORNE, Alfred Francis, 3 Stroud Rd., Bisley, Stroud, Glos GL6 7BQ. (045277-496) *b. 25 Feb 1916, Leamington Spa. m. 7 Aug 1948: 1d., 2s.*
Education: Campion Sch., Leamington Spa; 1945–48 Handsworth. *Appointments:* 1944–46 Hastings; 1948–51 Coventry; 1951–54 Sheffield NE; 1954–58 Hartlepools; 1958–62 St. Columb and Padstow; 1962–67 Stroud and Cirencester; 1967–75 Mid-Wilts; 1975–80 Southend-on-Sea.
Council Member: President of Chippenham Council of Churches.
Publications: An Account of Grange Road Methodist Church, West Hartlepool (Written for 50th Anniversary of the Building 1954); *Methodism in the Village of Bisley, in Gloucestershire* (A Local History Project given as W.H.S. Lecture, Bristol, March 1982).
Special Interests: Geology, Fossils, Local History, Philosophy. *Hobbies and Recreations:* Reading, Gardening, Exploring the Past, Microscopy.

OSBORNE, Harold H., 7 Cloverley Rd., Bridlington YO16 5UH. (0262-601645) *b. 2 Jan 1906, Derby. m. 11 Aug 1940: 1d., 2s.*
Appointments: 1927–28 Weardale; 1928–31 Handsworth Coll.; 1931–34 Dorchester; 1934–37 Presteigne; 1937–40 Batley; 1940–45 Morley; 1945–48 Brighouse; 1948–51 Bridlington; 1951–56 Hull Mission; 1956–62 Redruth; 1962–68 Newcastle Mission; 1968–73 Nottingham Central.
Connexional Committees: Finance and Property, 10 yrs and 9 yrs; Citizen and DSR, 19 yrs.
Hobbies and Recreations: Cricket, Tennis, Photography.

OSBORNE, Roger James, 170 Fort Austin Ave., Crownhill, Plymouth, Devon PL6 5NS. (0752-772037)–BA(Birmingham). *7 Feb 1951, St. Ives, Cornwall. m. 21 July 1973: 3d.*
Education: 1956–62 Halestown CP; 1962–70 The Humphry Davy Grammar; 1972–75 Univ. of Birmingham; 1975–76 Univ. of Birmingham Sch. of Education; 1972–76 Queens. *Appointments:* 1976–79 Newbury and Hungerford; 1979–82 Reading; 1982– Plymouth Central.
Special Interests: Cornish Methodism, Religious Education. *Hobbies and Recreations:* Cycling, Squash, Cooking, Gardening, Genealogy.

OWEN, Norman Percy, Trinity Manse, 17 Shrewsbury Rd., Shifnal, Shropshire TF11 8AQ. (0952-460681) *b. 5 Sept 1927, Netherton, Dudley, Worcs. m. 13 Aug 1955: 1s.*
Education: 1938–40 Northfield Rd. Sen. Sch., Netherton; 1942–47 Dudley Technical Coll.; 1948–49 Cliff Coll.; 1952–55 Hartley Victoria.
Appointments: 1951–52 Kington and Presteigne; 1955–57 Ashington; 1957–70 Oakengates and Shifnal; 1970– Telford South.
Special Interests: Ministry in New Towns, Ecumenical Projects. *Hobbies and Recreations:* Hi Fi (Tape Recording), Tennis, Football.

OWEN, Rex, Springfield Manse, 86 Bolton Rd., Addingham, Ilkley LS29 0JA. (0943-830228)—BA(Open Univ.). *b. 27 Aug 1937, Manchester. m. 23 July 1964: 1d., 2s.*
Education: 1948–55 Prince Henry's Grammar Sch., Otley, Yorkshire; 1960–64 Hartley Victoria.
Appointments: 1964– Bahamas Dt, West Indies and MCCA; 1975– Leek.
Special Interests: Psycho-therapy, Drama. *Hobbies and Recreations:* Electronics, Watch and Clock Repair.

OWENS, David Stanley, 49 King Edward Rd., Bath, Avon BA2 3PB. (0225-25230). *b. 30 Jan 1925, Weybridge, Surrey. m. 11 Aug 1951: 2s.*
Education: 1935–41 City of London Freemen's Sch.; 1943 Herriot Watt Coll. of Engineering (Edinburgh Univ.); 1949–51 Didsbury, Bristol.
Appointments: 1947–48 Portsmouth Mission; 1948–49 Saddleworth; 1951–53 Bury St. Edmunds; 1953–59 Wolverton and Bletchley; 1959–65 Chesham and Chalfont St. Giles; 1965–70 Dover; 1970–79 Tunbridge Wells; 1979– Bath.
Connexional Committees: 1974–76 Connexional Church Membership Committee; 1976–79 Division of Ministries Board.
Special Interests: Samaritans, Care for Homeless Ex-Prisoners. *Hobbies and Recreations:* Photography, Car Maintenance, Country Walks.

PACEY, Albert Leslie, Ilkley, West Yorkshire LS29 8EP. (0943-609198) *b. 14 September 1910, Whittlesey m. 1 Aug 1936: 2s.*
Education: 1915–1921 Spalding Council Sch.; 1921–28 Spalding Grammar Sch.; 1930–33 Victoria Park. *Appointments:* 1933–39 S.W. China Dt; 1939–42 Skegness; 1942–47 Bedale; 1947–51 Ripon; 1951–57 Hitchin; 1957–63 Elland; 1963–66 Barnoldswick; 1966–71 Romiley; 1971–75 Shaw.

PADGEN, Frank Thomas, 49 Westway, Garforth, Leeds LS25 1DA. (0532- 863352) *b. 4 Oct 1930, London. m. 11 Aug 1956: 2d., 1s.*
Education: 1942–46 Eastbourne Grammar Sch.; 1953–56 Richmond.
Appointments: 1956–59 Stoke-on-Trent, Tunstall; 1959–64 Ellesmere Port; 1964–67 Southport South; 1967–70 Leeds, Richmond Hill; 1970– Appointed to BBC as Radio Producer with responsbility for Religious Broadcasting, Radio Leeds.
Connexional Committees: 1959–64 Church Membership Committee; 1976–82 Radio and TV Committee.
Special Interests: Writing for Teletext. *Hobbies and Recreations:* Gardening, The Family.

PADLEY, Walter Henry, 7 Church Lane, Bardney, Lincoln LN3 5TZ. (0526- 398267) *b. 22 Dec 1915, New England, Peterborough, Northamptonshire. m. 25 March, 1940: 2s.*
Education: 1920–22 Lincoln Rd. Infants Sch., New England, Peterborough; 1922–25 Lincoln Rd. Boys Sch., New England, Peterborough; 1925–31 King Edward VIth Grammar Sch., Spilsby, Lincolnshire. *Appointments:* 1953–60 Sowerby Bridge; 1960–66 Nottingham North; 1966–73 Long Eaton; 1973–81 Loughborough; 1962–73 Assistant Synod Secretary, Nottingham and Derby District.
Special Interests: International Relationships. *Hobbies and Recreations:* Sport, Gardening, Reading, Scrabble.

PAGE, Edward, 23 Paddock Close, Castle Donington, Derby DE7 2JW. (0332- 810384)—MTh(Lond.). *b. 20 June 1903, Bristol. m. 16 Aug 1967.*
Education: 1925–28 Handsworth.
Appointments: 1928–30 Barnstaple; 1930–33 Ripley; 1933–37 Rotherham; 1937–42 Barrow-in-Furness; 1942–46 Darwen; 1946–58 Paisley Mission; 1950–57 Glasgow, Cathcart Rd.; 1957–63 Dudley; 1963–69 Long Eaton.

PAGE, Saumuel Kenneth, 37 Leicester Rd., Sapcote, Leicestershire. (045- 526 3628)—BD. *b. 12 Aug 1907, London. m. 29 Dec 1943: 2d.*
Education: 1921–28 Elem. schs., Cathedral High Sch., Bombay; 1933–37 Leonard Coll., Jubbuzpur, India;
Appointments: 1942–54 U.S.A. Conference; 1954–55 Durham; 1955–57 Camelford and Wadebridge; 1957–60 Mansfield Central and West; 1960–63 Grimsby Centenary; 1963–66 Wombwell and Hoyland; 1966–69 Manchester Chelteham Hill and Prestwich; 1969–73 Birmingham Mission.
Special Interests: Biblical history, Textual Criticism, Indian Missions.
Hobbies and Recreations: Stamp Collecting, English Bibles.

PAILIN, David Arthur, 1 Horhsam Ave., Hazel Grove, Stockport, Cheshire SK7 5HW. (061-483-2924)—MA(Cantab), MA, PhD(Manchester). *b. 19 April 1936, Stockport. m. 27 July 1961: 1d., 1s.*
Education: 1947–54 Bancroft's Sch., Woodford Wells, Essex; 1954–58 Trinity Coll., Cambridge; 1958–59 Perkins Sch. of Theology, Southern Methodist Univ., Dallas, Texas; 1959–61 Univ. of Manchester; 1959–61 Hartley Victoria. *Appointments:* 1961–62 Romiley and Hempshaw; 1962–66 Romiley and Windlehurst; 1966– Assistant Lecturer, then Lecturer, then Senior Lecturer in Philosophy of Religion at the Univ. of Manchester (Dean of Faculty of Theology, 1978 and 1979).
Connexional Committees: 1970–79 Faith and Order Committee; Doctrinal Committee of Appeal.
Publications: Way to Faith (1969); contributions to symposia and articles in learned journals.
Special Interests: The study of faith and reason in the modern age and the contribution of process philosophy to theological understanding. *Hobbies and Recreations:* Climbing, Collecting 17th & 18th Century Books.

PALMER, George Edward, 39 Melling Rd., Southport, Merseyside PR9 9DU. (0704-32305) *b. 12 March 1942, Liverpool. m. 14 Dec 1963: 3d., 1s.*
Education: 1947–57 Listre Drive Sch., Liverpool; 1960–61 Cliff Coll.; 1966–70 Hartley Victoria.
Appointments: 1970–76 Leigh; 1976– Southport.

Special Interests: Life of John Wesley. *Hobbies and Recreations:* Swimming, Walking.

PALMER, John Arthur, 23 Spring Lane, Hemel Hempstead, Herts. HP1 3QH. (0442-52642) *b. 12 July 1939, Battersea. m. 4 July 1964: 2d., 1s.*
Education: 1962–66 Didsbury, Bristol. *Appointments:* 1966–68 Bromsgrove; 1968–75 Bury and Heywood; 1975– Hemel Hempstead and Berkhamsted. *Connexional Committees:* 1971–73 Christian Citizenship; 1977–82 Board of Social Responsibility.
Special Interests: Church Growth. *Hobbies and Recreations:* Reading, Philosophy.

PALMER, John Bernard, 22 Hillcrest, Great Clacton, Essex CO15 4HU. (0255-421336) *b. 23 Feb 1913, Clapton, London. m. (2) 1972: 1s.*
Education: Canterbury Rd., Leyton; Leyton County High for Boys; 1947–49 Richmond. *Appointments:* 1946–47 Tamworth; 1949–51 Thornley; 1951–55 Aldershot and Farnborough; 1955–57 Liverpool North; 1957–65 London Mission, Tooting; 1965–68 Manningtree and Harwich; 1968–74 Supernumerary; 1974–76 London Mission South; 1976–82 London, Blackheath and Lewisham.
Publications: Cricket Book Reviews: *Cricket Society Journal.*
Special Interests: Local History; Philately. *Hobbies and Recreations:* Cricket, Reading, Music.

PALMER, John Edward, 30b Cock Rd., Kingswood, Bristol BS15 2SH. (0272- 673877) *b. 15 Aug 1935, Derby. m. 26 March 1960: 2d.*
Education: Herbert Strutt Grammar Sch., Derby; 1979–81 Wesley, Bristol. *Appointments:* 1981– Bristol, Kingswood.
Special Interests: Music. *Hobbies and Recreations:* Organs, Military History.

PALMER, William Andrew John, 8 Kings Rd., Camborne, Cornwall TR14 8LT. (0209-714178)–BSc. *b. 25 March 1948, St. Kitts Nevis, West Indies. m. 21 Oct 1972: 1d.*
Education: Penzance Grammar Sch.; 1968–70 Univ. of Manchester Institute of Science and Technology; 1977–80 Wesley, Bristol.
Appointments: 1980– Camborne.
Special Interests: Youth Work.
Hobbies and Recreations: Computers, Painting and Sketching.

PALMER, William John, 11 Greenway Avenue, Woodford, Plympton, Plymouth PL7 4RR. *b. 7 Nov 1915, Peel, Isle of Man. m. 23 May 1942: 3 d., 1s.*
Education: 1919–26 Clothworkers Sch., Peel; 1926–32 Douglas High Sch., for Boys; 1935–39 Didsbury Coll., Manchester. *Appointments:* 1939–42 Dursley and Stonehouse; 1942–44 Halifax St. John's; 1944–50 Leeward Islands, West Indies; 1950–55 Birmingham Mission; 1955–60 Smethwick; 1960–63 Penzance Central; 1963–67 Penzance; 1967–72 St. Columb and Padstow; 1972–74 Kimberley; 1974–80 Penzance.
Special Interests: Ministry of Healing. *Hobbies and Recreations:* Weaving, Painting, Music.

PANTON, Norman Claude, 39 Wannock Lane, Willingdon, Eastbourne, East Sussex BN20 9SD. (03212-3915)–BA. *b. 17 Jan 1908, Woodford, Essex. m. 10 Aug 1935: 2d.*
Education: 1919–26 St. Olave's Grammar Sch., London; 1928–31 Birmingham Univ.; 1928–31 Handsworth. *Appointments:* 1931–33 Devonport; 1933–35 Huntingdon Mission; 1935–39 Chichester and Bognor; 1939–46 Chaplain H.M.F.; 1946–51 Chichester and Bognor; 1951–54 Brighton and Hove; 1954–60 Northampton, Kettering Rd. and Northampton; 1960–66 Watford; 1966–67 Scunthorpe; 1971–74 Gainsborough.

PAPE, Walter Roy, 264 Duffield Rd., Derby DE3 1EP. (0332-557320)–BA(Lond.), BD(Lond.), STM(Yale). *b. 21 June 1935,* Bulwell *Nottingham, England. m. 13 Aug 1960: 1d., 1s.*
Education: 1940–46 Ockbrook Prim Sch., Nr Derby; 1946–48 Spondon House Secondary Modern Sch., Nr. Derby; 1948–54 Long Eaton Grammar Sch.; 1954–57 Queen Mary Coll., London Univ.; 1957–60 London Univ.; 1960–61 Yale Univ. Divinity Sch., U.S.A.; 1957–60 Richmond Coll.
Appointments: 1961–62 East Cornwall Mission; 1962–65 Church of South India; 1965–72 Lecturer in Biblical Studies and Theology, United Theological Coll., Bangalore, S. India; 1972–76 Assistant Professor in Theology, United Theological Coll.; 1976–77 Newark; 1981– Derby Derwent Mission; 1978– Part-time Lecturer in Christian Doctrine, East Midlands Ministry Training Course, Univ. of Nottingham Adult Education Dept.
Connexional Committees: 1978–80 Methodist Church Overseas Division, Central Committee; 1978–81 Asia Advisory Committee; 1979– Methodist Church, Faith and Order Committee; 1979– Methodist Church, Doctrinal Committee; 1979–81 (Inter-Divisional) Methodist Church, Working Party on Multi-Faith Society. *Council Member:* 1965–75 Church of South India Central Mysore Diocese: Committee to Advise Bishop on Liturgical Matters; 1971–73 Executive Committee; 1971–75 Ministerial Committee; 1978– British Council of Churches: Committee for Relations with People of Other Faiths, (Vice-Chairman from 1981); 1978– C.R.P.O.F., Theological Issues Consultative Group, Secretary of; 1981–83 Triennium, Member of General Assembly. *Publications:* Articles in *Theology, Bangalore Theological Forum, Indian Journal of Theology, Religion and Society, Laity;* Visiting Lecturer to Papal Seminary, Pontifical Athenaeum, Poona, India in January 1975, *Indian Christologies.*
Special Interests: Indian Christian Theology, Inter-Faith Dialogue. *Hobbies and Recreations:* Hill Walking, Philately, Archaeology of Roman Britain.

PARKER, Frederick, Asbury House, Merrey Rd., Rising Brook, Stafford ST17 9LX. (0785-42097) *b. 24 Sept 1925, Liverpool.*

Education: 1938–40 Alsop High Sch., Liverpool; 1949–51 Handsworth. *Appointments:* 1948–49 Belper; 1951–54 Ripley; 1954–56 Accrington; 1956–61 Coalville; 1961–67 Bebington; 1967–70 Shrewsbury; 1970–73 Droyslden and Openshaw; 1973–76 Oldham; 1976–67 Littleborough; 1977–80 South Normanton; 1980–82 Stafford; 1982– Old Hill.
Hobbies and Recreations: Walking, Classical Music.

PARKES, John Harold, 12 Claremont Rd., Bridport, Dorset DT6 3AY. (0308 23564)–BA, BD. *9 April 1900, Hucknall, Notts. m. 22 April 1930: 1d., 1s.*
Education; 1912–15 Nottingham High Sch.; 1923–26 Victoria Park. *Appointments:* 1922–23 Crosshills; 1926–28 Nottingham Central; 1928–30 Manchester; 1930–34 Derby, Dairyhouse Rd.; 1934–39 London, Thornton Heath; 1939–45 Rochdale North; 1945–49 Burnley, Brunswick; 1949–55 Bridgwater; 1955–58 Dunstable, Victoria St.; 1958–65 London, Tottenham.
Connexional Committees: Overseas Missions; Candidates Committee. *Council Member:* Various Local Committees; National Free Church Federal Council.

PARKES, William, The Manse, Gunn St., Biddulph, Stoke-on-Trent ST8 6AY. (0782-513246)–DD(Asbury, Kentucky). *b. 22 April 1933, Dudley, Worcestershire. m. 18 Aug 1956: 1d., 3s.*
Education: Jesson CE Jun., Dudley; Grammar Sch., Dudley; 1970–74 London Univ. (Diploma in Criminology); 1953–56 Hartley Victoria; 1963 Candler Sch. of Theol., Emory Univ., Atlanta (W.M.C. Scholarship). *Appointments:* 1956–59 Barnsley West; 1959–65 Sheffield, Brunswick; 1965–71 Whitechapel Mission, London; 1971–78 Blackburn; 1978–80 General Evangelist, United Methodist Church, U.S.A.; 1980– Biddulph and Mow Cop.
Connexional Committees: 1965–72 Archives; 1966–73 Achives and History (British Section, W.M.C.); 1964–73 Prison Committee (H.M.). *Council Member:* 1980– Governor, Biddulph High Sch. *Local Council Committees:* 1966–72 Free Church Federal Council, Central Committee on Prison Affairs. *Publications:* Articles on Methodist History in *London Quarterly & Holborn Review, Proceedings of W.H.S. 1966; Thomas Bryant: Independent Methodist;* Articles: *Postal History, American Philatelist, The Confederate Philatelist, The Philatelist* (London); Sermonic material in *The Preachers Magazine;* Tapes: Some 25 in *American Expository Library.*
Special Interests: Preaching. Wesleyan Theology, Evangelism and Mission, Role of Church with Delinquents, Postal History (American Civil War specialist). *Hobbies and Recreations:* Methodist Pottery, Methodist History.

PARKHOUSE, Gordon, 23 Marlborough Drive, Tytherington, Macclesfield, Cheshire SK10 2JY. (0625-26051)–BD(Lond.). *b. 11 May 1920, Grimsby. m. 18 Dec 1948: 1s.*
Education: 1925–30 Barnsole Rd., Gillingham, Kent; 1930–37 County Sch. for Boys, Gillingham; 1946–49 London; 1949 Gottingen; 1946–49 Richmond. *Appointments:* 1949–53 Leeds, Armley; 1953–60 Cleethorpes, Mill Rd.; 1960–65 Birmingham, Moseley Rd. and Sparkhill; 1965–70 Manchester, Chorlton and Moss Side; 1970–78 Lytham St. Annes; 1978– Macclesfield.
Connexional Committees: 1962– Ministers' Retirement Fund; 1959–61 Candidates' Exmination Committee, and co-opted on two other occasions; 1979– Panel for nomination of Chairmen of Districts.
Special Interests: Early Church Worship and Modern Experimental Worship. *Hobbies and Recreations:* Music, Bird Watching.

PARKIN, Benjamin, Flat 1, Lyndhurst, Bent Lane, Sutton-in-Craven, Keighley BD20 7AL. (0535-34080) *b. 28 April 1906, Sheffield. m. 1929: 1d., 2s.*
Education: 1911–18 Pye Bank Council, Sheffield; 1918–22 Central Secondary Sch., Sheffield. *Appointments:* 1946–53 Sheffield, Norfolk; 1953–58 Barnsley East; 1958–66 Wakefield; 1966–71 Bradford, Gt. Horton; 1971–76 South Craven; 1958–66 Methodist Chaplain, Wakefield Prison and Detention Centre; 1955–75 Social Responsibility. *Local Council Committees:* 1967–71 Free Church Council Secretary, Bradford.
Special Interests: Governor–Rogers Almshouses, Marriage Guidance Counsellor 1961–71, Class 1 Football Referee, Most Sports. *Hobbies and Recreations:* Gardening, Walking.

PARKINS, Jesse, 33 Church St., Burbage, Hinckley, Leics. LE10 2DA. (0455-632220) *b. 9 May 1908, Dunstable Beds. m. 28 Aug 1937: 3s.*
Education: 1911–15 Burr St. Inf., Dunstable; 1915–23 Britain St. Council Sch., Dunstable; 1931–34 Handsworth. *Appointments:* 1930–31 Brecon; 1934–37 Presidents List; 1937–40 Stockton on Tees, North Terrace; 1940–43 West Bromwich Wesley; 1943–46 Sheffield Mission; 1946–51 Gateshead Mission; 1951–58 Glasgow East Mission; 1958–65 Hinckley, Stockwell Head; 1965–73 Tottenham. *Connexional Committees:* 1944–46 Temp. and Social Welfare Dist Repres.
Hobbies and Recreations: DIY, Gardening.

PARKINSON, James, 44 Green Drive, Southall, Middlesex UB1 3AZ. (01 574 3553) *b. 3 Nov 1925, Trimdon Grange, Co. Durham. m. 1 Aug 1953: 1d., 1s.*
Education: 1930–33 Cold Heselden, Merton, Council Sch.; 1933–39 Blackhall Colliery Council Sch., Co. Durham; 1953–54 St. Andrews, Selly Oak; 1947–49 Hartley Victoria. *Appointments:* 1949–52 Sheffield North East; 1952–53 Rotherham; 1954–62 Bengal Dt, India; 1963–70 Bradford, Great Horton, Wesley; 1970–74 Skipton; 1974– London, Southall Mission.
Connexional Committees: 1968–73 M.M.S. Central Committee.

Special Interests: Inter-Faith and Community Relations. *Hobbies and Recreations:* D.I.Y., Camping.

PARRINDER, Edward Geoffrey, 31 Charterhouse Rd., Orpington, Kent BR6 9EJ. (0689-23887)–MA, DD, PhD(Lond.), HonDLitt (Lancaster). *b. 30 April 1910, New Barnet, Herts. m. 25 July 1936: 1d., 2s.*
Education: 1918–26 Leigh Hall Coll.; 1932–33 Faculté, libre de théologie protestante, Montpellier; 1929–32 Richmond. *Appointments:* 1933–40 French West Africa; 1940–43 Redruth; 1943–46 French West Africa; 1946–49 Guernsey French; 1949–58 Univ. Coll., Ibadan, Nigeria; 1958–77 King's Coll. London Univ.; 1977–78 International Christian Univ., Tokyo; 1978–82 Univ. of Surrey; 1960–72 Hon. Sec. British Association for History of Religions; 1980–82 President London Society for Study of Religions; 1981– President London Society for Jews and Christians. *Publications: West African Religion* (1949); *West African Psychology* (1951); *Religion in an African City* (1953); *Witchcraft* (1958); *Worship in the World's Religions* (1961); *Comparative Religion* (1962); *Upanishads Gita and Bible* (1962); *What World Religions Teach* (1963); *The Christian Debate* (1964); *The World's Living Religions* (1965); *Jesus in the Qur'an* (1965); *African Mythology* (1967); *Religion in Africa* (1969); *Avatar and Incarnation* (1970); *Dictionary of Non-Christian Religions* (1971); *The Indestructible Soul* (1973); *The Bhagavad Gita* (1974); *The Wisdom of the Forest* (1975); *Mysticism in the World's Religions* (1976); *The Wisdom of the Early Buddhists* (1977); *Sex in the World's Religions* (1980); Wilde Lectures in *Natural and Comparative Religion,* Oxford 1966–69; *Charles Strong (Australian Church)* 1964; *Teape Lectures,* Delhi and Madras 1973; *Lily Montagu Lecture* 1982.
Hobbies and Recreations: Travel, Gardening, Literature.

PARROTT, Michael John, 327 Padgate Lane, Padgate, Warrington, Cheshire WA1 3JU. (0925-813254)–BA.Theol(Manchester). *b. 3 Jan 1948, Stockport. m. 29 July 1972: 1d., 1s.*
Education: Banks Lane Prim. and Jun.; Dial Stone Lane Secondary Modern; 1967–69 Stockport Coll. of Technology; 1969–71 Manchester Polytechnic; 1972–75 Manchester Univ.; 1972–76 Hartley Victoria.
Appointments: 1976–81 Newcastle, Staffs.; 1981– Warrington.
Special Interests: Mission and Youth Work. *Hobbies and Recreations:* Swimming, Badminton, Squash, Music.

PARRY, Daniel Bramwell Booth, The Manse, Lower St., Cleobury Mortimer, via Kidderminster DY14 8AE. (0299-270407) *b. 18 Jan 1937, Newcastle-on-Tyne. m. 22 June 1968: 1d., 1s.*
Education: 1948–53 King Edward VI Grammar Sch., Morpeth, Northumberland; 1961 St. Andrew's Coll., Selly Oak; 1961 Univ. of London Sch. of Oriental and African Studies; 1956–60 Headingley. *Appointments:* 1961–70 Ivory Coast District; 1970–78 Telford South; 1978– Shropshire South.
Connexional Committees: 1979– Board of the Division of Property (District Rep. Wolverhampton and Shrewsbury District), District Property Secretary.
Special Interests: Rural Work, Clinical Theology. *Hobbies and Recreations:* Gardening, Bird Watching.

PARRY, Geraint Wynne, 1 Cleveland Ave., Tywyn, Gwynedd. (0654-710568) *b. 27 Sept 1916, Caernarfon. m. 30 April 1953: 1d.*
Education: 1928–32 Caernarfon Secondary; 1947–49 Hartley Victoria.
Appointments: 1949–51 Dinas Mawddwy; 1951–53 Cefnmawr; 1953–60 Llandilo; 1960–65 Portmadoc; 1965–81 Glannau Meirion and Dyfi.
Publications: 4 Welsh Novels (1965, 1970, 1974, 1978); TV Play (1977).
Special Interests: Literature. *Hobbies and Recreations:* Walking, Gardening.

PARSONS, Donald Arthur, 10 Braid Ave., Edinburgh EH10 6DR. (031-447-6359)–BA, BD. *b. 8 Jan 1935, Redditch, Worcestershire. m. 13 Aug 1960: 2d., 1s.*
Education: 1940–45 Bridge St. Inf. and Boys Jun.; 1945–52 Redditch County High Sch.; 1952–55 Bristol Univ.; 1955–58 Richmond.
Appointments: 1958–65 Madeley and Dawley; 1965–74 Lancaster; 1974–78 Edinburgh Mission; 1978– Edinburgh and Forth.
Connexional Committees: c.1970 Board of Dey; 1965–71 Student Work Committee; 1976–82 HM Central Churches Committee.
Council Member: 1980– Tollcross Community Council, Edinburgh, 1982– Chairman. *Publications: Ecumenism in Lancaster in the Early '70s* (1973 for Clergy Course, St. Georges House, Windsor).
Special Interests: Ecumenical and Mission Work, Relations between Church and Community, Religious Drama. *Hobbies and Recreations:* Tennis, Table Tennis, Golf, Cinema, Theatre, Music, Travel.

PARSONS, John Hamblin, 71 Dennis Rd., East Molesey, Surrey KT8 9EE. (01-979-3846) *b. 9 June 1888, Radstock, Somerset. m. Aug 1920 (w.): 1d., 1s.*
Education: Wellow Inf.; 1909–13 Highbridge, Somerset; 1913–14 Bath City Technical Sch.; 1911–14 Headingley. *Appointments:* 1914–17 Bristol, Clifton; 1917–19 Chaplain H.M.F.; 1919–22 Shepton Mallet; 1922–25 Wiltshire Mission; 1925–29 Cheltenham; 1929–36 Gloucester; 1936–45 Oxford; 1945–50 Reading; 1950–57 Oxford District Missionary.
Special Interests: Walking in the Country, Railway Service. *Hobbies and Recreations:* Music (piano).

PARSONS, Norman Charles, 1 Hales Rd., Sittingbourne, Kent ME10 1SR. *b. 27 Oct 1905, St. Leonards-on-Sea. m. 11 Aug 1937: 1d., 1s.*
Education: 1912–18 Sittingbourne Council Sch.; 1918–20 Borden Grammar Sch., Sittingbourne; 1931–34 Handsworth. *Appointments:* 1930–31 Devonport; 1934–36

Birmingham, Belmont Row; 1936–37 Ripon; 1937–39 Birmingham Mission; 1939–40 Rhyl; 1940–44 Birmingham Mission; 1944–49 Birmingham, Moseley Rd.; 1949–56 Wolverhampton, Trinity; 1956–62 London, Finsbury Park; 1962–66 Doncaster, Priory Place; 1966–70 Chairman, Bolton and Rochdale District; 1951–69 Exchange Preacher USA; 1972 Special Assignment, Malta.
Connexional Committees: General Purposes, Home Missions, Finance Board, Social Responsibility, Stationing, Property, Overseas Missions. *Local Council Committees:* 1962–66 Doncaster Education Committee.
Hobbies and Recreations: Music, Photography, Travel, Reading.

PARSONS, Philip Kenneth, 6 Brook Furlong, Bembridge, Isle of Wight PO35 5QR. (0983-872043) *b. 17 Sept 1916, Chaotung, Yunnan, China. m. 21 Nov 1945: 1d., 1s.*
Education: 1926–28 Bristol, Bishops Rd.; 1928–29 Ventnor Jun.; 1929–35 Sandown County Secondary; 1937–40 Didsbury. *Appointments:* 1940–46 Hupeh Central China District; 1946–50 South West China District; 1950–53 Bideford; 1953–65 Kenya, East Africa; 1965–71 Nottingham South; 1971–80 East Wight; 1968–71 Secretary Nottingham and Derby District.
Special Interests: Classical Music, The History, Customs and Language of the Hau Miao Tribe of S.W. China. *Hobbies and Recreations:* Golf, Building, Bridge.

PARSONS, Reginald George, Flat Two, Tennyson View, Alum Bay New Rd., Totland Bay, Isle of Wight PO39 0ES. *b. 1 April 1916, Birmingham. m. 17 Sept 1938: 1d., 1s.*
Education: 1921–27 Stratford Rd. Council Sch., Sparkbrook, Birmingham; 1927–30 Moseley Secondary Sch., Wake Green Rd., Moseley, Birmingham; 1950–51 Hartley Victoria (Non-resident). *Appointments:* 1950–52 Todmorden; 1952–56 Newmarket Mission; 1956–61 West Wight; 1961–68 Andover; 1968–75 Stour Valley; 1975–81 Blackheath, Birmingham.
Special Interests: Care and Concern for Elderly, Evangelism outside the accepted four walls of the Church. *Hobbies and Recreations:* Gardening, Walking, Cricket, Reading.

PARSONS, Richard Keith, 3 St. Paul's Crescent, Torquay, Devon TQ1 3QN. (0803-33012)–BSc, BD. *b. 17 Sept 1916, Chautung, Yunnan, SW China. m. 22 Aug 1942: 1d.*
Education; 1929–35 County Secondary Sch., Sandown, I.O.W.; 1935–36 Univ. Coll. of the South West of England, Exeter; 1940–42 Kingsmead; 1937–40 Hartley Victoria. *Appointments:* 1942–50 Hupea Dt, China; 1950–52 Bristol, Redland; 1952–53 Birmingham, Bristol Rd. and St. Paul's, 1953–58 Education Secretary, United Christian Council, Sierra Leone Dt.; 1958–65 Northlew; 1965–69 Barnstaple; 1969–74, 1974–80 London Hammersmith and Fulham, Chinese Chaplaincy.
Connexional Committees: 1964–66 Overseas Missions. *Publications: Souls for your Hire* (1972). *A history of the Northlew Circuit.*
Special Interests: Local Methodist History. *Hobbies and Recreations:* Choral Singing.

PARSONS, Roger John, 30 Vineway, Brentwood, Essex CM14 4UU. (0277-215709)–BA(Hull). *b. 19 July 1940, Rhyl, N. Wales. m. 7 Aug 1965: 1d., 2s.*
Education: 1950–58 Kingswood; 1950–53 Priors Court; 1959–62 Hull Univ.; 1962–65 Headingley. *Appointments:* 1965–67 Leeds, Richmond Hill; 1967–70 Morley; 1970–75 Ipswich; 1979–81 Ramsgate; 1981– Romford.
Special Interests: Drama, Worship and Preaching, Social Responsibility, Literature (esp. Poetry). *Hobbies and Recreations:* Amateur Drama, Cooking, Reading (Novels, Poetry, The *Guardian*).

PARSONS, Stanley Eric, Shawcroft, Brookfield Drive, Teignmouth TQ14 8QQ. (06267-4595) *b. 23 Mar 1918, Dudley, West Midlands. m. 18 Aug 1946: 1d., 1s.*
Education: Dudley Intermediate School; 1939–40 Didsbury; 1940–42 Hartley Victoria. *Appointments:* 1942–44 Manchester, Grosvenor St.; 1944–46 Poynter, Manchester; 1946–49 Manchester Mission; 1949–53 London Mission, East Ham; 1953–58 Bristol South; 1958–61 Bude; 1961–62 Manchester Mission; 1962–66 Plymouth and Devonport; 1966–74 Hull Mission; 1974–82 Teignmouth.
Connexional Committees: 1952–55 Division of Social Responsibility.

PARTNER, Ernest, 8 Kennett Close, Norwich, Norfolk NR4 7JA. (0603-53534) *b. 17 Jan 1908, Portslade, Sussex. m. 4 Jan 1945.*
Education: 1913–20 St. Andrews, Portslade; 1920–24 Brighton, Hove and Sussex Grammar Sch.; 1928–31 Handsworth. *Appointments:* 1931–49 French West Africa; 1949–52 Oldham; 1952–57 Norwich; 1957–63 King's Lynn; 1963–68 Truro; 1968–73 Matlock.
Connexional Committees: Overseas' Missions.

PASSMORE, William Redpath, 11 Ruskin Drive, Wootton Bassett, Swindon, Wiltshire SN4 8JL. (0793-850445) *b. 5 May 1911, Hemsworth, Nr. Wakefield, Yorkshire. m. 14 Aug 1940: 1d., 1s.*
Education: 1923–28 Scarborough Boy's High Sch.; 1933–36 Hartley Victoria. *Appointments:* 1936–37 Leicester, King Richard's Rd.; 1937–38 Faversham; 1938–40 Glossop; 1940–43 Kirbymoorside, 1943–48 Malton; 1948–53 York; 1953–59 Leeds Mission; 1959–62 Gateshead Mission; 1962–68 Newcastle-upon-Tyne West; 1968–74 Corby.

PATCHETT, David N. S., 3 Westward Ho!, Grimsby, South Humberside DN34 5AF. (0472-70443) *b. 4 Feb 1929, Bradford, Yorks. m. 15 Dec 1956: 1d., 1s.*
Education: 1940–45 Grange Grammar Sch., Bradford; 1952–55 Handsworth. *Appointments:* 1951–52 Oldbury; 1955–57 Kimberley; 1957–60 Littleborough; 1960–66

London Mission, Hackney; 1966–71 Tonypandy Mission; 1971–74 Grimsby West; 1974– (Supernumerary).

PATERSON, Daniel James Reid, 13 Mansionhouse Rd., Paisley, Renfrewshire PA1 3RG. (041-889-2827) *b. 23 Feb 1944, Winchburgh, West Lothian, Scotland. m. 2 Aug 1969: 1d., 1s.*
Education: 1956–62 Trinity Academy, Edinburgh; 1974–77 Wesley, Bristol. *Appointments:* 1977– Paisley Mission.
Hobbies and Recreations: Music, Walking, Golf.

PATTISON, R. Clifford C., 2 Nutley Close, Goring by Sea, Worthing, Sussex BN12 4JZ. (0903-501876) *b. 5 May 1907, Forest Gate, London. m. 24 Feb 1938: 3s.*
Education: Leyton High Sch.; 1928–31 Victoria Park. *Appointments:* 1931–36 Plymouth; 1936–46 London, Forest Gate; 1946–51 Stoke on Trent, Wolstanton; 1951–55 Cheadle, Stoke on Trent; 1955–62 Luton; 1962–71 Worthing.

PATRICK, Graham Arthur, 9 Fairview Ave., Alsager, Stoke-on-Trent ST7 2NW. (093-63-2243)–BA, BD, PhD. *b. 28 Sept 1939, London. m. 7 Aug 1965: 1d., 1s.*
Education: 1944–51 Bungay, Suffolk County Prim. Sch.; 1951–58 Bungay, Suffolk Grammar Sch.; 1958–61 Durham Univ.; 1961–62 Westminster Coll., Oxford; 1964–67 Handsworth.
Appointments: 1967–70 Assistant Tutor, Handsworth Coll.; 1970–75 Bristol North; 1975–80 Liverpool South-East; 1980– Sandbach and Alsager.
Connexional Committees: 1975–78 Doctrinal Committee of Appeal.
Publications: F. J. A. Hart–A Neglected Theologian (Expository Times, Dec 1978); *A Modern Prophet (Alexander Solzhenitsyn) (Epworth Review,* May 1980); *1881–1981: The Centenary of the Westcott and Hart text* (*Expository Times,* Sept 1981); *The Pastor and His Family* (*Expository Times,* Sept 1982).
Special Interests: Victorian Religion, New Testament, Christian Spirituality, English Literature.
Hobbies and Recreations: Reading, Music, Ornithology, Badminton.

PATTERN, Marcus Alwyn, 14 Hollingwood Drive, Bradford, West Yorks BD7 4DH. (0274-571341) *b. 17 May 1933, Long Sutton, Lincs. m. 5 April 1958: 3s.*
Education: 1938–44 Long Sutton Prim. and Jun.; 1944–50 Sir John Gleed Sch., Spalding; 1955–58 Handsworth. *Appointments:* 1958–61 Brigg; 1961–65 South Shields; 1965–70 High Wycombe; 1970–75 Hatfield, Herts.; 1975–81 Halifax; 1981– Bradford, Great Horton.
Hobbies and Recreations: Music, Walking and Photography.

PAWLETT, Kathryn Elaine, Shephalah, 92 Portsmouth Way, Basingstoke, Hants. RG22 6HG. (0256-3836)–BA. *b. 27 Sept 1953, Kendal. m. 15 Aug 1981.*
Education: 1965–72 Rutherford, Newcastle; 1972–75 Birmingham Univ.; 1976–79 Wesley, Bristol.
Appointments: 1979–81 Selby; 1981– Basingstoke.

PAYLER, Albert Martin, 9 Burnham Gardens, Bognor Regis, West Sussex PO21 2LA. (0243-863842) *b. 30 July 1906, London. m. 13 Oct 1936: 3d., 1s.*
Education: Elem. and Pitman's Coll.; 1930–33 Didsbury. *Appointments:* 1933–47 Madras District, South India; 1947–53 Church of South India; 1953–61 Wiltshire Mission; 1961–64 Church South India; 1964–68 Frome and Shepton Mallett; 1968–70 Crook; 1970–71 Church of North India.
Connexional Committees: 1967–68 O.M. Pastoral; 1967, 1968, 1969 Transfer of Authority.
Special Interests: Transfer of MMS Property to C.S.I. and C.N.I.; Methodist Homes for the Aged.

PAYNE, Arthur George, 38 Duporth Bay, St. Austell PL26 6AQ. (0726-5590) *b. 14 Feb 1901, Eastbourne. m. 31 July 1937: 3d., 1s.*
Education: –1911 St. Philips, Eastbourne Elem.; 1911–14 Polegate Elem.; 1925–28 Richmond.
Appointments: 1924–25 Llandrindod and Brecon; 1928–30 Hereford; 1930 Monmouth, Wye Valley Mission; 1931–34 Midsomer Norton; 1934–37 St. Austell and Mevagissey; 1937–40 Perranporth and St. Agnes; 1940–45 Chaplain H.M.F.; 1945–46 Kent Mission; 1946–57 Mysore Dt India and S. India Church; 1957–63 Liphook and North Hants.; 1963–68 Sherborne.
Hobbies and Recreations: Gardening, Football, Tennis.

PAYNE, John Frederick William, 54 Leicester Rd., Shepshed, Loughborough, Leics. LE12 9DQ. (05095-3286) *b. 27 July 1953, Port Talbot, W. Glam. m. 25 June 1978: 1d.*
Education: 1976–80 Wesley, Bristol.
Appointments: 1980– Loughborough.

PAYNE, Kenneth James, 53 Davian Way, Walton, Chesterfield, Derbys S40 3JE. (0246 202411) *b. 8 Dec 1913, Chadwell Heath, Essex. m. 6 Oct 1943: 3s.*
Education: 1937–40 Richmond.
Appointments: 1940–60 Barbados and Trinidad District, West Indies and Guyana; 1960–63 Wetherby; 1963–72 Castleford; 1972–77 Coalville; 1977–82 Peterborough.
Hobbies and Recreations: Woodwork, Music.

PAYNE, Trevor Henry, 236 Bristol Rd., Gloucester GL1 5TA. (0452-422324)–MA.
Education: 1956–59 Wesley House.
Appointments: 1959–61 London, Regent St. Polytechnic; 1961–65 Hunstanton and Docking; 1965–72 Leicester South; 1972–79 Gloucester; 1979– Education Department H.M. Prison, Gloucester.

PEACOCK, Fred, The East End Mission, 583 Commercial Rd., Stepney, London E1 0HJ. (01-790-1120) *b. 27 March 1909, North Ormesby, Middlesbrough, Cleveland. m. Aug 1941 (w.).*
Education: 1912–15 North Ormesby Mixed Inf.; 1915–18 Jun. Sch.; 1918–21 Sen. Sch.; 1921–25 Middlesbrough High Sch.; 1933–37 Didsbury.

Appointments: 1932–33 Brixham and Dartmouth; 1937–39 South Molton; 1939–58 London Central Mission; 1958–65 Aberdare; 1965–74 Llanelli; 1974–77 London East End Mission.

PEACOCK, John, 26 Rosehill Rd., Burnley, Lancs. BB11 2JS. (0282-24663) *b. 20 May 1931, Chop Gate, Middlesbrough, Yorks. m. 30 Oct 1957: 3s.*
Education: 1936–42 Chop Gate; 1942–47 Yarm Grammar Sch.; 1952–55 Handsworth. *Appointments:* 1955–58 Knighton; 1958–63 Accrington; 1963–68 Preston, Trinity; 1968–78 Dudley; 1978– Burnley.
Special Interests: Sport.

PEACOCK, Royston Leslie Hines, 5 Stanley Rd., Deal, Kent CT14 7BT. (03045-4435) *b. 14 May 1929, Plymouth. m. 2 Aug 1956: 2d.*
Education: 1940–41 Canton High Sch., Boys, Cardiff; 1941–47 Weston-s-Mare Grammar Sch., Boys; 1951–54 Richmond. *Appointments:* 1950–51 Radstock and Coleford; 1954–56 Home Mission, Caravan Mission; 1956–60 Stourbridge and Brierley Hill; 1960–65 Southampton; 1965–72 Devonport; 1972–77 Sittingbourne and Sheerness; 1977– Dover and Deal.
Special Interests: Christian Aid, Race Relations, Nuclear Disarmament, National Children's Home. *Hobbies and Recreations:* Rotarian, Sailing, Photography, Travel.

PEADEN, William Roger, 28 St. James's Rd., Dudley DY1 3JB. (0384-52918)—BA, MLitt, PhD. *b. 10 Feb 1930, Yorkshire. m. 1958: 1d., 2s.*
Education; Archbishop Holgates Grammar Sch., York; 1953–56 Bristol; 1953–56 Didsbury, Bristol.
Appointments: 1957–73 Zimbabwe Dt; 1973–78 Wolverhampton, Trinity; 1978– Dudley.
Connexional Committees: 1975–81 DSR Standing Committee for Community Relations; 1977– District Rep. to Divisional Board of Ministries. *Local Council Committees:* 1978– Dudley Education Committee.
Publications: Monograph entitled *Missionary Attitudes to Shona Culture;* Articles in the following books, *Christianity South of the Zambesi* and *Themes in the Christian History of Central Africa.*
Special Interests: Missionary History, Community Relations, World Development. *Hobbies and Recreations:* Sailing, Painting, Walking.

PEAKE, Leslie Sillman, 20 Langdale Rd., Cheltenham GL51 5LY. (0242-26458)—MA(Oxon), BLitt(Oxon). *b. 4 April 1900, Manchester. m. 5 June 1939: 2d.*
Education; 1911–12 Hulme Grammar, Manchester; 1912–18 Merchant Taylors, Crosby; 1919–22 New Coll., Oxford; 1922–25 Mansfield Coll., Oxford.
Appointments: 1925–31 Middlesbrough; 1931–34 Birmingham; 1934–38 Preston, Wesley; 1938–46 Penrith; 1946–51 Edinburgh, Nicholson Square; 1951–56 Falkirk; 1956–61 St. Ives, Bedford Rd.; 1961–65 Wye Valley Mission.
Publications: Arthur Samuel Peake A Memoir (1930); Reviews for *Times Literary Supplement* (1934–45).
Special Interests: History, Literature, Psychology. *Hobbies and Recreations:* Theatre.

PEARCE, Baden Albert Reeve, 11 Church Crescent, Whetstone, London N20 0JR. (01-368-3021)—BD(Lond.), JP. *b. 15 Dec 1927, Edgware, Middx. m. 24 Sept 1955: 1d., 2s.*
Education: 1932–39 Camrose Council Sch.; 1939–44 Christ's Coll., Finchley, 1956–59 Handsworth. *Appointments:* 1959–60 Selly Oak Coll.; 1960–62 Manchester, Chorlton and Moss Side; 1963–66 London, Harrow; 1966–68 Leeds North-East; 1968–78 Richmond and Hounslow, 1978– London, Highgate.
Connexional Committees: 1982 (Designated) Division of Social Responsibility. *Council Member:* 1971–78 Labour Councillor, London Borough of Hounslow; 1977–78 Mayor. *Local Council Committees:* 1971–78 Social Services: 1971–74 Health; 1974–78 Housing; 1974–78 Area Health Authority, Ealing, Hammersmith and Hounslow.
Special Interests: Politics, Magistracy (JP 1976–). *Hobbies and Recreations:* Gardening, Walking.

PEARCE, Keith Reginald, 210 Malvern Rd., St. John's, Worcester WR2 4LL. (0905-422180)—BA(Manchester). *b. 11 Feb 1951, Coventry. m. 4 Aug 1973: 1d., 1s.*
Education: 1962–69 King Henry VIII Grammar Sch., Coventry; 1971–75 Manchester Univ.; 1971–75 Hartley Victoria. *Appointments:* 1975–78 Bloxwich and Willenhall; 1978– Worcester. *Connexional Committees:* 1981– MAYC Editorial Group.
Special Interests: Local Radio, Youth Work, Gospel Music. *Hobbies and Recreations:* Outdoor Pursuits, Canoeing and Mountaineering, Gospel Rock Music.

PEARCE, Raymond John, 11 Pearce Rd., Llandaff, Cardiff CF5 2AF. (0222- 562619) *b. 18 May 1922, Tredegar, Gwent. m. 16 Aug 1951: 2d., 1s.*
Education: Tredegar County Grammar Sch.; 1946–49 Hartley Victoria. *Appointments:* 1945–46 Tamworth and Lichfield; 1949–50 Overseas Mission Div.; 1950–52 Newport; 1952–56 Neath and Port Talbot; 1956–60 Grimsby, George St.; 1960–66 Portsmouth and Southsea; 1966–67 Old Hill; 1967–74 Torquay and Paignton; 1974–81 Cannock Chase; 1981– Cardiff.
Connexional Committees: Church Membership.
Hobbies and Recreations: Music, Gardening.

PEARSON, Albert, 15 Harbour View Crescent, Penzance, Cornwall TR18 2AZ. (0736-3560) *b. 16 April 1882, Lye, Stourbridge. m. 1915: 1d.*
Education: 1887–1894 Wollescoat Board Sch.; 1908–11 Hartley.
Appointments: 1911–13 Farringdon; 1913–14 Cardiff II; 1914–15 Monmouth; 1915–20 Penzance; 1920–23 Ramsor; 1923–27 Burton-on-Trent; 1927–35 Middleton; 1935–

41 Manchester, Higher Openshaw; 1941–46 Chorley; 1946–51 Penzance, Mount St.

PEARSON, Philip Chisholm, 16 Brook Rd., Lymm, Ches. WA13 9AH. (092575- 2373)–BA, BD, MA(Manchester). *b. 16 April 1926, Shaoyang, Paoking, China. m. 18 Feb 1966: 2d., 1s.*
Education: 1936–44 Kingsmoor Sch., Glossop; 1948–53 Wigan and District Mining and Technical Coll., Manchester Univ.; 1950–53 Hartley Victoria. *Appointments:* 1953–56 Manchester, Stretford and Urmston; 1956–60 New Mills; 1960–65 Macclesfield; 1965–73 Zambia; 1973–78 Ashby-de-la-Zouch; 1978– Warrington.
Special Interests: Church History. *Hobbies and Recreations:* Cycling, Painting.

PEARSON, Raymond, 71 Village Rd., Garden Village, Hull, N. Humberside HU8 8QS. (0482-20564)–BD(Lond.). *b. 8 Nov 1922, Carlin How, Saltburn-by-Sea, Yorkshire. m. 6 Aug 1949: 2s.*
Education: 1926–33 Carlin How Jun. Sch.; 1933–40 Guisborough Grammar Sch.; 1947–49 Richmond Coll. *Appointments:* 1949–51 Thetford; 1951–54 Fakenham and Wells; 1954–59 Downham Market; 1959–63 Driffield; 1963–68 Tadcaster; 1968–77 Northallerton; 1977– Hull East.
Special Interests: Gilbert and Sullivan Operas. *Hobbies and Recreations:* Walking, Theatre, Crosswords.

PEARSON, Trevor, 43 Langdon Fields, Galmpton, Brixham, Devon TQ5 0PL. (0803-845225) *b. 20 June 1917, Congleton, Cheshire. m. 12 April 1944: 1d., 1s.*
Education: 1922–26 Wagg St. Wesleyan Day Sch.; 1926–29 Congleton Council Sch.; 1929–33 Macclesfield Grammar Sch.; 1937–40 Handsworth. *Appointments:* 1940–44 Bridgend; 1944–48 Wye Valley Mission; 1948–53 Hereford; 1953–60 Derby East; 1960–65 Birmingham, Islington; 1965–74 Kidderminster; 1974–79 Callington.

PEART, Ross, 18 Menlowe Gardens, North Liverpool L18 2EJ. (051-722-4565)–BA(Dunelm), MA(Cantab). *b. 12 Feb 1944, Bishop Auckland, Co. Durham. m. 1964. 2d.*
Education: Wolsingham Grammar Sch.; 1962–64 Durham Univ.; 1967–69 Cambridge Univ.; 1967–69 Wesley House. *Appointments:* 1969–74 Pudsey and Farsley; 1974–78 Liverpool South; 1978– Liverpool, Central Hall.
Council Member: 1976 World Methodist Council, Dublin; 1981 Honolulu, Hawaii. *Publications:* Home Missions Occasional Paper *The Charismatic Movement and Methodism* (1973); *An A.B.C. of Holy Spirit Bukwal* (1974); *For the People in the Pew* (Understanding the Charismatic Movement 1980).
Special Interests: Evangelism, Healing, Charismatic Renewal. *Hobbies and Recreations:* Geology, Travel, Gardening, Doing Phd Research into Forward Movement in Methodism.

PECK, Norman Harold, 7 Clabon Third Close, Norwich, Norfolk NR3 4HH. (0603-45658) *b. 10 Dec 1935, Ipswich. m. 3 April 1967: 2s.*
Education: 1940–44 Nacton Rd. Prim. Sch., Ipswich; 1944–45 Cliff Lane Prim. Sch., Ipswich; 1945–52 Northgate Grammar Sch., Ipswich; 1964–68 Westhill, Coll., Birmingham; 1961–64 Handsworth.
Appointments: 1965–69 Wolverhampton, Trinity; 1969–76 Loughborough; (Hospital Chaplain 7 years, Industrial Chaplain, Rolls Royce); 1976– Norwich (Industrial Chaplain, RAF Padre).
Special Interests: Industrial Mission, Youth Work. *Hobbies and Recreations:* Sport, Gardening.

PEDDIE, Geoffrey, 18 Goodshaw Ave., Blackburn, LAncs. BB1 8PF. (0254-61437) *b. 2 Jan 1939, Hanley, Stoke-on-Trent. m. 22 July 1919: 2d., 1s.*
Education: 1968–70 Hartley Victoria. *Appointments:* 1970–75 Leek; 1975–81 Grimsby West; 1981– Blackburn. *Connexional Committees:* 1977–79 Social Responsibility.
Special Interests: Social Studies. *Hobbies and Recreations:* Variety of Sports.

PENBERTHY, Clarence Irving, 29 Downside St., Somerset BA16 0DL. (0458- 42313) *b. 28 Oct 1930, Camborne, Cornwall. m. 28 July 1956: 1d., 1s.*
Education: 1935–37 Beacon Infants' Sch.; 1937–41 Roskear Jun. Boys Sch.; 1941–48 Redruth County Grammar Sch.; 1952–55 Didsbury, Bristol. *Appointments:* 1955–58 Aberdare; 1958–63 Cardiff, Roath; 1963–70 Merthyr Tydfil; 1970–78 Hastings, Bexhill and Rye; 1978– Somerset Mission.
Connexional Committees: 1971–75 Connexional Childrens' Committee.
Special Interests: Music. *Hobbies and Recreations;* Electrónics, Car Mechanics.

PENDLEBURY, William Arnold, 36 Whitfield Ave., Pickering, N. Yorks YO18 7HY. (0751-74917) *b. 5 Dec 1903, Bolton, Lancashire. m. 3 May 1933: 1d., 1s.*
Education: 1908–15 Victoria Wesleyan; 1915–1918 Bolton Municipal Secondary; 1918–19 Bolton Technical; 1925–29 Richmond. *Appointments:* 1929–31 Pickering; 1931–32 Northallerton; 1932–33 Kirby Moorside; 1933–38 Tadcaster; 1938–42 Bingley; 1942–47 York, Centenary; 1947–53 Halifax West; 1953–60 Bristol, Bedminster; 1960–65 Newton Abbot; 1965–69 Derby, Derwent.
Special Interests: Church Work, Visitation. *Hobbies and Recreations:* Poster Work, Choir, Walking, Theological Reading.

PENNA, John, Court House, North St., Haverfordwest, Dyfed SA61 2JE. (0437-2740) *b. 19 April 1922, Snaith, Yorkshire. m. 31 July 1951: 2s.*
Education; 1932–36 Hemsworth Grammar Sch.; 1934–36 Woodhouse Grove Sch.; 1949–51 Hartley Victoria. *Appointments:* 1948–49 Pontypridd; 1951–52 Retford; 1952–55 Camelford and Wadebridge; 1955–61 Holsworthy; 1961–66 Trowbridge; 1966–71 Sirhowy Valley; 1971–74

Preston, Lune St.; 1974–82 Ashbourne; 1982– Haverfordwest and Milford Haven.
Hobbies and Recreations: Gardening, Music, Photography.

PEPPER, Anthony Thomas, 20 Bankpark Crescent, Tranent, East Lothian EH33 1AS. (0875-610388)–MA(Cantab). *b. 13 April 1921, Balham, London. m. 16 July 1948: 3d., 1s.*
Education: 1926–29 Wimbledon High Sch. for Girls, Kindergarten; 1929–34 Kings Coll. Jun. Sch., Wimbledon; 1934–35 KCS Wimbledon; 1935–39 The Leys Sch., Cambridge; 1942–45 War Service Lt. Royal Artillery; 1946–48 Cambridge Univ.; 1946–48 Wesley House. *Appointments:* 1948–53 District Synod Sec., Burma District; 1954–62 Chaplain, the Leys Sch., Cambridge; 1962–67 Woodhouse Grove, 1967–72 Wimbledon; 1972–79 Sunderland South; 1979– Edinburgh and Forth.
Publications: Commentaries on Amos and Hosea (1952 in Burmese); *Prayers and Services* with Donald Whittle, James Bates and Kenneth Underwood (1962).
Special Interests: Christianity and Buddhism, Ecumenical Relations.
Hobbies and Recreations: Most Sports particularly Cricket and Rugby, Reading, Gardening.

PERKINS, John Arthur, 418 Stenson Rd., Littleover, Derby DE3 7HD. (0332-760987) *b. 19 March 1937, Leicester. m. 22 Aug 1964: 4s.*
Education: 1942–48 Abbey Park Rd. Jun. Sch., Leicester; 1948–53 City Boys Grammar Sch., Leicester, 1960–64 Headingley. *Appointments:* 1964–69 Staveley; 1969–76 Long Eaton; 1976– Derby South.
Connexional Committees: 1975–82 Synod Sec., Notts/Derby District.
Hobbies and Recreations: Gardening, Stamp Collecting, Railways.

PEROWNE, Peter John, 28 Combe Park, Bath BA1 3NR. (0225-21343)–BA(B'ham.). *b. 15 Oct 1934, Hackney. m. 8 Aug 1959: 1d., 2s.*
Education: 1945–52 Royal Liberty Sch., Romford; 1956–59 Birmingham Univ.; 1956–59 Handsworth.
Appointments: 1959–64 Bocas Del Toro; 1965–68 Panama; 1968–72 Peak; 1972–77 Sheffield, Ecclesall; 1977– Bath.
Special Interests: Member of the Sheffield Sch. of Christian Psychotherapy. *Hobbies and Recreations:* Growing Cacti.

PERRY, Cyril E., 23A Heathside Rd., Woking, Surrey GU22 7EY. (04862-63256) *b. 4 Oct 1914, Rhymney, Mon. m. 3 Aug 1946: 3s.*
Education: –1929 Rhymney Secondary Sch.; 1939–40 Handsworth; 1940–41 Richmond; 1941–42 Headingley. *Appointments:* 1942–44 Kidderminster; 1944–46 Saddleworth; 1946–52 Cardiff Roath; 1952–58 Halifax, St. John's; 1958–63 Cardiff, Wesley; 1963–69 Birmingham, Islington and Quinton; 1969–75 Cardiff, Canton; 1975–77 Cardiff; 1977–82 Swansea.
Connexional Committees: 1960–69 Connexional Property Committee.
Special Interests: English Literature.
Hobbies and Recreations: Gardening, Bowls, Golf.

PETERS, John Maskell, Capstone, 14 Devonshire Rd.. Douglas, Isle of Man. (0624-21-968)–BA(Manchester). *b. 10 June 1947, Rawtenstall, Lancashire. m. 19 Aug 1972: 2d.*
Education: 1952–58 St. Mary's CE, Rawtenstall; 1958–63 Haslingden County Secondary Sch.; 1963–65 Bacup and Rawtenstall Grammar Sch.; 1969–72 Manchester Univ.; 1968–72 Hartley Victoria.
Appointments: 1972–78 Nantwich; 1978–81 Ramsey, Isle of Man; 1981– Douglas, Isle of Man; 1982– Synod Secretary, Isle of Man District.
Connexional Committees: 1978–79 Division of Social Responsibility; 1979–81 Division of Education and Youth; 1981–82 Overseas Division.
Special Interests: Member of The Evangelical Alliance, The Methodist Revival Fellowship, Conservative Evangelicals in Methodism. *Hobbies and Recreations:* Soccer, Railways.

PETTET, Herbert Edward Clayton, 37 Coningsby Rd., High Wycombe, Bucks. HP13 5NX. (0494-37288) *b. 2 April 1902, Southampton. m. 23 Sept 1931: 2s.*
Education: 1908–12 Elem. Sch., Southampton; 1912–14 Taunton Secondary Sch., Southampton; 1914–19 Scholarship to Christs Hospital, Horsham, Sussex; 1919–23 Higher Technical Course Certificate in Shipbuilding and Naval Architecture, Univ. Coll. of Southampton; 1925–28 Richmond. *Appointments:* 1928–47 Madras District; 1947–62 Church of South India; 1962–69 Risca and Cross Keys; 1973–79 Free Church Chaplain, High Wycombe General Hospital.
Connexional Committees: 1962–69 District Secretary for Missions, Cardiff and Swansea Dist.; 1962–69 Member of General Committee of Methodist Missionary Society.
Special Interests: Pastoral Visitation.
Hobbies and Recreations: Gardening, Tennis.

PHILIPSON, Peter Brian, 104 Mount Wise, Newquay, Cornwall TR7 1QP. (063-73-3325)–MPS. *b. 19 Dec 1924, West Hartlepool, Co Durham. m. 7 Sept 1953: 1d., 1s.*
Education; 1931–36 Elwick Rd. Elem. Sch., West Hartlepool; 1936–41 West Hartlepool Secondary Sch.; 1944–46 Sunderland Technical Coll.; 1947–49 Handsworth.
Appointments: 1949–52 South China Dt; 1952–56 Hong Kong Dt; 1956–59 Bombay Dt; 1959–63 Redcar Saltburn and Guisborough; 1963–66 Swindon; 1966–71 Bath; 1971–76 Weston-super-Mare; 1976–81 Forest of Dean; 1981– Newquay, Perranporth and St. Agnes.
Connexional Committees: 1964–70 General Committee of the Methodist Missionary Society.
Hobbies and Recreations: Stamp Collecting, Recorded Music.

PHILLIPS, Brian Douglas, 7 Cromford Drive, Staveley, Chesterfield, Derbys. S43 3TB. (0246-472488)–BSc(Adelaide U.), DipEd(Adelaide U.), BD(Melbourne Coll. Divinity). *b. 8 Nov 1938, Adelaide, South Australia. m. 11 May 1963: 2s.*
Education: 1951–55 Adelaide Technical High Sch.; 1956–60

Adelaide Univ.; 1957–60 Lincoln Coll., Adelaide Univ.; 1966–69 Melbourne Coll. of Divinity; 1970 Flinders Univ., Adelaide; 1978–79 Australian National Univ., Camberra; Wesley Coll., Adelaide.
Appointments: 1970–80 Australian Methodist Church; 1980– Balsover and Staveley.
Publications: Let's Study Prayer and Meditation, (Platypus Cassettes, Melbourne, 10 half hour lectures 1977); *Worship as Anamnesis* (St. Mark's Review 1976); *Historical Hero as Mythical Messiah (the Jesus of St. Mark),* Wesley Lecture, Camberra 1977; *The Poor of Yahweh; Foundation for a Revolution and the Hope of the Earth,* Wesley Lecture, Camberra, (St. Mark's Review 1979).
Special Interests: Doing Theology in the Local Church, Biblical Story Telling. *Hobbies and Recreations:* Model Railways.

PHILLIPS, Colin Richard, Avalon, 59 Woodhill Rd., Portishead, Bristol BS20 9EY. (0272-847217)–BA(Open Univ.). *b. 7 Oct 1940, Wednesfield, Staffs. m. 17 April 1965: 2s.*
Education: 1951–56 Bilston Grammar Sch., Staffs.; 1960–61 Cliff Coll.; 1964–65 Westhill Coll., Birmingham; 1961–64 Hartley Victoria. *Appointments:* 1965–70 Swansea; 1970–76 Cannock Chase (1970–72 Nether Stowe Sch.; 1972–74 Chase Terrace Sch.); 1976–79 Clifton and Redland, Lawrence Weston Sch.; 1979– Clevedon, Lawrence Weston Sch.
Connexional Committees: 1969–71 Drama Committee.
Special Interests: Education, Drama.
Hobbies and Recreations: Sport, Tennis, Badminton, Football.

PHILLIPS, Cyril James, 37 Queenswood Ave., Boothville, Northampton NN3 1JT. (0604-45802) *b. 24 Aug 1904, Hornsey, London. m. 7 Jan 1939: 2d., 1s.*
Education: Campsbourne Elem. Sch., Hornsey; 1928–31 Richmond.
Appointments: 1931–51 Leeward Islands Dt; 1951–58 Leicester, Saxby St. and East; 1958–62 Wigan, Standishgate; 1962–67 Newcastle-under-Lyme; 1967–70 Nottingham North.

PHILLIPSON, William Oliver, 106 Trull Rd., Taunton, Somerset TA1 4QF. (0823-81497)–MA(Bristol). *b. 24 April 1904, Sandwich, Kent. w: 1d., 2s.*
Education: Kingswood, Bath; 1934–37 Bristol Univ.; 1924–27 Handsworth. *Appointments:* 1927–31 Bristol, Bedminster; 1931–34 Newport, Stow Hill; 1934–40 Bristol, King Street; 1940–50 Bristol, Bedminster South; 1950–52 Stoke-on-Trent District Missionary; 1952–66 Secretary Chapel Committee.
Hobbies and Recreations: Fishing.

PHIPPEN, Charles Dennis, 11 Selden Rd., Worthing, West Sussex BN11 2LL. MA(Cantab). *b. 9 May 1921, Bristol. m.: 3s.*
Education: 1932–38 Bristol Cathedral Sch.; 1948–50 Wesley House. *Appointments:* 1951–61 Medak Diocese, C.S.I. (Hyderabad District, India); 1961–67 Staines and Feltham; 1967–74 Reading; 1974–79 Torbay; 1979– Worthing.
Connexional Committees: 1972–73 Chairman of Home Committee, Overseas Division.
Special Interests: Music, Photography, Travel–tour leader for Raymond Cook etc.

PHIPPS, Keith Malcolm, 222 Rutland Ave., High Wycombe, Bucks HP12 3LN. (0494-22643) *b. 7 Oct 1952, London. m. 25 July 1981.*
Education: Roundwood Park Secondary Sch., Harpenden, Herts.; Grove Sch., St. Leonards-on-Sea, Sussex; Sutton Coldfield Coll. of Further Education, West Midlands; 1973–74 Cliff Coll.; 1976–80 Wesley, Bristol. *Appointments:* 1978– High Wycombe.

PICKARD, Albert Evan, 30 Wychwood Ave., Knowle, Solihull, West Midlands B93 9DG. (056-45-3057) *b. 18 Sept 1889, Cowbridge, Glamorgan, S. Wales. m. 31 Oct 1944.* d. 1984
Education: 1901–1907 Cowbridge Grammar Sch.; 1909–12 Headingley.
Appointments: 1912–15 Wye Valley Mission; 1915–16 Shorncliff Camp.; 1916–17 Deal; 1917–19 Chaplain H.M.F., 1919–23 Birmingham Mission; 1923–27 Birmingham, Islington; 1927–30 Birmingham, Moseley Rd. and Sparkhill; 1930–33 Birmingham, Bristol Rd.; 1933–40 London, Highgate; 1940–48 London, Finchley and Hendon; 1948–52 London, Finsbury Park; 1952–54 London, Kilburn and Hampstead.
Connexional Committees: 1931 Elected to the Wesleyan Legal Conference, last surviving member.

PICKARD, Donald Alfred, 11 St. Quintin Ave., London W10 6NX. (01-969-0892)–BA, BSc. *b. 20 Jan 1941, Sunderland. m.*
Appointments: 1966–67 Per, Germany; 1967–69 Peterborough; 1969–75 Nigeria Conf.; 1975– London Mission, Notting Hill.

PICKARD, Stephen, Epworth House, Eastfield Road, Pickering, N. Yorks. YO18 7HU. (0751 72895).
Education: 1913–16 Headingley.
Appointments: 1916–18 Epworth; 1918–20 Withensea; 1920–22 Pickering; 1922–23 Wolsingham and Weardale; 1923–26 Doncaster, Oxford Place; 1926–29 Hexham; 1929–32 Hebden Bridge; 1932–36 Macclesfield; 1936–37 Bradford, Low Moor; 1937–40 Redcar and Saltburn; 1940–43 Worksop, Wesley; 1943–46 Derby, Derwent; 1946–51 Ripley; 1951–53 North Walsham.
b. 29.10.1888. d. 1989

PICKERING, Jeffrey Norman, Nab Gate, Cornbirthwaite Rd., Windermere, Cumbria LA23 1DJ. (096-62-3766)–BD(Lond.). *b. 19 Feb 1926, Dinnington, Nr. Sheffield, Yorks. m. 7 Aug 1952: 2d., 1s.*
Education: 1931–34 Retford, Grove St., Wesleyan Inf. Sch.; 1934–37 Worksop, Newcastle Ave. Jun. Sch.; King Edward VI Grammar Sch., Retford; 1948–51 Handsworth.
Appointments: 1947–48 Castletown, Isle of Man; 1951–53 Bournemouth; 1953–60 Torquay and Paignton; 1960–67 Redhill, Surrey; 1967–74 London, Finsbury Park; 1974–80 Birmingham, Sutton Park; 1980– Chairman of Cumbria District: 1968–

80 Precentor of Methodist Conference; 1976–80 Correspondence Secretary of Methodist Conference.
Connexional Committees: 1980– Connexional General Purposes Committee; 1980–81 President's Council; 1980– Home Mission Divisional Board; 1980– Stationing Committee.
Hobbies and Recreations: Music, Philately, Model Railways, Bird-Watching, Gardening.

PICKETT, Brian Laurence, 2 Grove Rd., Merrow, Guildford, Surrey GU1 2HP. (0483-60140)– BA(Reading), BA(B'ham.), MA(B'ham.). *b. 17 June 1948, Ilford, Essex. m. 27 July 1973: 2d.*
Education: 1953–60 Earls Hall Jun. Sch., 1960–65 Westcliff High Sch., 1966–70 Univ. of Reading; 1968–69 Rheinische Friedrich-Wilhelms Universität, Bonn; 1970–73 Univ. of Birmingham; 1970–73 Queen's Coll.
Appointments: 1973–78 Southampton; 1978– Guildford.
Special Interests: Germany–East and West, Welsh, Orthodox Liturgy, The Psalms, Plainsong, Retreat Work.
Hobbies and Recreations: Choral and Solo Singing.

PIGOTT, Daniel Albert, Fairholme, Penybont Rd., Knighton, Powys. LD7 1HB. (0547 528418)– BA(Lond.), MEd(Leicester), PhD(B'ham.).
Appointments: 1981– Knighton and Leintwardine.

PIKE, David, 101 Bare Lane, Morecambe, Lancs. LA4 6RP. MA, BD. *b. 13 Oct 1911, Suffield, Nortwalsham. m. 29 July 1939: 2s.*
Education: 1922–27 Colby and Paston Grammar Sch., North Walsham, 1933–36 Richmond.
Appointments: 1936–38 Brownhills; 1938–40 Chelmsford; 1940–46 Chaplain HMF; 1946–50 Bolton, Wesley; 1950–55 Bradford, Woodhouse Grove; 1955–60 Aireborough; 1960–65 Hull Trinity; 1965–75 Louth.

PILE, Robert Wilfrid, 15 Lester Close, Higher Compton, Plymouth PL3 6PX. (0752-772695)– BD(Lond.). *b. 13 Mar 1915, Plymouth. m. 28 Dec 1944: 4d.*
Education: 1925–31 Plymouth Coll.; 1938–42 Richmond; 1942–43 Wesley House. *Appointments:* 1943–45 London Mission, East Ham; 1945–52 Hunan Dt, China; 1952–58 Ceylon; 1958–65 Secretary Home Organisation; 1958–73 Secretary, Missionary Society; 1965–73 Secretary, Asia Organisation; 1973–80 Cheltenham; Chaplain, Wesley Coll., Secretary of Synod, Study Secretary, National Christian Council.
Connexional Committees: 1958–74, 1975–81 Missionary Society; 1973–79 Law and Polity; 1977–80 Candidates.
Special Interests. China, International Affairs, S.D.P. *Hobbies and Recreations:* Times Crossword, Gardening.

PILLINGER, Stanley M., 20 Tadworthy Rd., Northam, Bideford, N. Devon EX39 1JN. (023-72-5164) *b. 19 Oct 1914, Bath. m. 5 Jan 1945: 1d.*
Education: 1925–29 Walcot Senior Sch. 1937–40 Handsworth.
Appointments: 1940–42 Builth Wells; 1942–43 Cardiff Wesley; 1943–45 Faringdon; 1945–50 Bideford; 1950–52 Bolton Wesley; 1952–55 Kettering; 1955–59 Derby, Derwent; 1959–65 Plymouth East; 1965–68 Buckfastleigh; 1968–73 Newcastle West; 1973–80 Cradley Heath.
Connexional Committees: 1960–66 Church Membership Committee.
Special Interests: Methodist Healing Fellowship. *Hobbies and Recreations:* Bird Watching, Gardening, Sketching and Painting, Folk Dancing.

PILLOW, Edward Ronald, 38 Lynford Ave, Winchester, Hants. SO22 6BN. (0962-61172)– BD(Lond.). *b. 4 April 1909, London. m. 22 Dec 1941: 1d., 1s.*
Education: 1919–26 Whitgift, Croydon; 1931–34 Didsbury.
Appointments: 1934–51 Hupeh District, China; 1951–54 Petersfield and Haslemere; 1954–58 Winchester; 1958–63 Southampton; 1963–68 Pateley Bridge; 1968–74 Huddersfield West.
Connexional Committees: 1951–57, 1959–62 Overseas Missions.

PINCHES, Roy Samuel, 13 Sybil Rd., Leicester LE3 2EX. (0533-891470) *b. 28 June 1942, Widnes, Cheshire. m. 23 Aug 1969: 1d., 1s.*
Education: 1954–58 Arnot St. Sch., Liverpool; 1966–70 Handsworth.
Appointments: 1970–72 South Molton; 1972–73 Oswestry, Ellesmere and Chirk; 1973–78 Buckley and Deeside; 1978– Leicester West.
Special Interests: Family Life, Pastoral.
Hobbies and Recreations: Reading, Walking, Caravanning, Gardening, Model Making, Model Railways.

PINDER, George Geoffrey, Woodside Cottage, Cross Lane, Minshull Vernon, Crewe, Ches. CW1 4RG. (027-071-675) *b. 18 Aug 1905, Penrith, Cumbria. m. 16 Aug 1933: 1d., 1s.*
Education: 1910–17 Penrith Elem. Sch.; 1917–20 Queen Elizabeth Grammar Sch., Penrith; 1923–24 Cumbria Agricultural Coll.; 1927–30 Didsbury. *Appointments:* 1926–27 Wellington, Salop; 1930–33 Manchester and Salford Mission; 1933–36 Willenhall, Union St.; 1936–40 Cheltenham; 1940–47 Sunderland North; 1947–52 Newcastle upon Tyne (Brunswick); 1952–58 Stockport, Tiviot Dale; 1958–63 Lytham St. Annes; 1963–65 Walsall.
Local Council Committees: 1977–80 Church Minshull Parish Council.
Special Interests: Preaching and Hospital Visitation. *Hobbies and Recreations:* Walking, Gardening.

PINE, Norman, 63 Assheton Rd., Clayton Bridge, Manchester M10 6NJ. (061-681-1646)– BEng(Liverpool). *b. 7 Nov 1933, Liverpool. m. 19 March 1960: 2s.*
Education: 1946–52 Liverpool Institute High Sch. for Boys; 1953–56 Liverpool Univ.; 1975–77 Wesley House. *Appointments:* 1981–

Manchester North and Middleton. *Hobbies and Recreations:* Painting, Gardening, Tennis, Table Tennis.

PITTAM, William Henay, 92 Henhurst Hill, Burton-on-Trent, Staffs., DE13 9TA. (0283-68512)–BD.
Education: 1948–51 Handsworth. *Appointments:* 1947–48 St. Neots; 1948–51 Handsworth Coll.; 1951–53 Stafford; 1953–60 Peel; 1960–65 Sherburn; 1965–73 Withernsea; 1973– Burton-on-Trent.

PITTOCK, David William, 27 Carlton Rd., Lowestoft, Suffolk NR33 0RU. (0502-65573)–BA. *b. 15 June 1944. s.*
Education: 1972–76 Queens. *Appointments:* 1976–81 Ilkeston; 1981– Lowestoft and East Suffolk.

PITTS, Hubert Allan, 11 Gleve Rd., St. George, Bristol BS5 8JJ. (0272-556911)–BD(Lond.). *b. 23 Sept 1920, Exeter, Devon. m. 19 July 1947: 1d., 2s.*
Education: 1932–38 Hele's Sch., Exeter; 1946–49 Univ. of London; 1946–49 Richmond. *Appointments:* 1949–65 Church of South India, Mysore Diocese; 1965–70 Folkestone; 1970–74 Marlborough; 1974–80 Bristol South; 1980– Bristol, Kingswood.
Connexional Committees: 1974–80, 1981–82 MCOD (formerly MMS); 1980–82 Div. of Ministries.
Special Interests: Wild Flowers.

PLANT, Richard James, 29 Victoria Ave., Bloxwich, Walsall WS3 3HS. (0922-75083)–MA(Oxon), BA(Cantab). *b. 6 July 1928, London. m. 17 Jan 1959: 2s.*
Education: 1938–46 Emanuel; 1948–52 Jesus, Oxford; 1952–53 Westminster, London; 1953–55 Wesley House. *Appointments:* 1955–58 Coventry Mission; 1958–62 Swinton, Pendlebury and Pendleton; 1962–65 Wimbledon; 1967–70 Leigh, Lancs.; 1970–75 Manchester and Salford Mission; 1975–80 Doncaster; 1980– Bloxwich and Willenhall.
Publications: Arabic Coins and how to read them (BA Seaby Ltd. 1973); *Greek Semitic and Asiatic Coins and how to read them* (Scorpion Publishers 1979); *Greek Coin types and their identification* (BA Seaby Ltd 1979).

PLATT, William James, Flat 8, 147 Lent Rise Rd., Burnham, Bucks. SL1 7BN. (06-286-63594)–DD(Knox Coll., Toronto Univ., Canada). *b. 2 May 1893, Horwich, Bolton. m. 8 June 1921: 1d.*
Education: 1910–18 Rivington and Blackrod Grammar Sch.; 1914–16 Didsbury. *Appointments:* 1916–24 Lagos Dt, West Africa; 1924–30 French West Africa Dt; 1924–30 Chairman and General Superintendent of French West African District, Abidjan, Ivory Coast; 1949–61 General Secretary of British and Foreign Bible Society, London.
Connexional Committees: 1930–61 Overseas Division General Committee and Various sub-Committees. *Publications: Three Women in Central Asia* (1964); *From Fetish to Faith* (1935); *An African Prophet* (1934); *Whose World* (1940).
Special Interests: World Missionary Affairs, Royal Commonwealth Society. *Hobbies and Recreations:* Tennis.

PLATTEN, James, 1 Springfield Crescent, Seaham, Co. Durham SR7 7SU. (0783-813339) *b. 18 Nov 1932, Meadowfield, Co. Durham. m. 16 Aug 1958: 1d., 1s.*
Education: 1937–45 Brandon County Sch., Co. Durham; 1946–47 Durham Commercial Coll.; 1955–59 Hartley Victoria. *Appointments:* 1959–61 Tipton, Park Lane; 1961–67 London Mission, Poplar; 1967–72 Blaydon; 1972–82 Seaham, 1982– Loftus and Staithes.
Connexional Committees: 1968–74 Connexional Children's Work Committee. *Publications: The Use of Premises* (Div. of Education and Youth, Occasional Paper c1973).
Hobbies and Recreations: Soccer, Cricket, Philately, Photography, Music.

PLATTS, John Hebden, 28 Eddleston Ave., Kenton Park, Newcastle upon Tyne NE3 4SJ. (0632-852423)–MA, BD. *b. 8 July 1937, Guisborough, Yorks. m. 26 Sept 1964: 1d., 1s.*
Education: 1941–48 Linthorpe Prim. Sch., Middesbrough; 1948–49 Acklam Hall Grammar Sch., Middlesbrough; 1949–55 Queen Elizabeth Grammar Sch., Darlington; 1957–60 Trinity Coll., Cambridge; 1961–64 Headingley. *Appointments:* 1964–65 Bristol South; 1965–68 Glossop; 1968–73 Sheffield, Carver St.; 1973–78 Middlesbrough; 1978– Newcastle upon Tyne, Brunswick Central.
Hobbies and Recreations: Tennis, Squash, Walking.

PLATTS, William, 10 Northcote, Whickham, Newcastle upon Tyne NE16 5RU. (0632 882888)–BD(Lond.). *b. 17 Nov 1909, Birdwell, Nr Barnsley, Yorks. m. 24 Aug 1938: 2s.*
Education: 1931–34 Hartley. *Appointments:* 1934–35 President's List, Newcastle upon Tyne District; 1935–38 Gateshead, W. (Chairman's Asst.); 1938–40 Berwick on Tweed; 1940–42 Edinburgh (Leith Ec); 1942–46 Gateshead W.; 1946–49 Hull, St. George's Rd.; 1949–54 Gateshead E.; 1954–59 N. Shields and Cullercoats; 1959–65 Newcastle upon Tyne, Heaton and Wallsend; 1965–70 Whickham; 1970–75 Gateshead S.W.

PLUMB, Joyce Freda, 33 College Rd., Ringwood, Hants. BH24 1NV. (042 54 3407). *b. 1 May 1930, London. s.*
Education: 1941–46 Bridgwater Grammar Sch.; 1954–57 Wesley Deaconess Coll. *Appointments:* 1975–76 Newark; 1976–83 Wimborne.
Special Interests: Healing Ministry.
Hobbies and Recreations: Sewing, Embroidery, Knitting, Swimming.

POCKLINGTON, Lloyd Edward, 16 Manor Rd., Bexhill-on-Sea, E. Sussex TN40 1SP. (0424-213935) *b. 11 Feb 1910, Louth, Lincolnshire. m. 27 Oct 1936. 2d.*

Education: King Edward VI Grammar Sch., Louth, Lincs.; Queen Elizabeth Grammar Sch., Alford, Lincs. 1930–33 Headingley.
Appointments: 1933–52 Bengal Dt; 1956–59 Manchester South; 1959–62 Eccles; 1962–72 Lucknow and Benares Dt; 1972–75 London International House, Warden.

POLLARD, George, 44 Vernon Rd., Sheffield S17 3QE. (0742 368562) *b. 4 Dec 1902, Fleetwood, Lancs. m. 18 Aug 1932: 4s.*
Education: Elem. Sch. and Baines Grammar Sch., Poulton-le-Fylde; 1925–28 Didsbury. *Appointments:* 1924–25 Cinderford; 1928–31 Clitheroe; 1931–32 Loftus and Cleveland; 1932–36 Bacup, Market Place; 1936–40 Manchester and Salford Mission; 1940–46 Derby Mission; 1946–52 Coventry Mission; 1952–59 London Mission, East Ham; 1959–60 Romford; 1960–68 Sheffield Mission.
Connexional Committees: Home Missions, Cliff Coll., Rural Travel.
Special Interests: Central Missions.
Hobbies and Recreations: Reading, Gardening, Sport.

POMERY, Ernest Peter George, 36 North Rd., Midsomer Norton, Bath BA3 2ZQ. (0761-412137)–BD. *b. 18 May 1932, St. Just-in-Roseland. m. 1963: 3d.*
Education: 1958–62 Richmond.
Appointments: 1962–64 Wirksworth; 1964–72 Scunthorpe; 1972–75 Chesterfield; 1975– Midsomer Norton.

POOLE, Derek Gordon, 6 Goddington Rd., Strood, Rochester, Kent ME2 3DD. (0634-77485) *b. 9 Feb 1941, Southport, Lancs. m. 28 May 1977: 1d., 2s.*
Education: 1952–60 Culford Sch., Bury St. Edmunds; 1961–65 Headingley. *Appointments:* 1965–67 Leeward Islands Dt; 1967–74 Caribbean Conf.; 1974– Medway Towns.
Hobbies and Recreations: Carpentry, Motor Mechanics, Household Maintenance, Bee Keeping.

POPE, John Russell, 11 Lime Grove, Exmouth, Devon EX8 5NN. (039-52-78438) *b. 15 Aug 1909, Barry, Glamorgan. m. 27 July 1939: 1d., 1s.*
Education: 1920–25 Canton High Sch., Cardiff; 1925– Technical Coll.; 1931–32 Cliff Coll.; 1932–36 Handsworth. *Appointments:* 1936–39 Manchester and Salford Mission; 1939–44 Liverpool South; 1944–48 Manchester and Salford Mission; 1948–57 Bristol Mission; 1957–59 Nottingham Mission; 1959–76 Chairman Plymouth and Exeter District; 1974 President of the Conference; 1976–79 Ilfracombe.
Connexional Committees: Home Mission, General Purposes, Stationing, etc. as Chairman; 1973–76 All Committees as President Designate, President and ex President.
Special Interests: Preaching Tours–1953 S. Africa, 1959 New South Wales, 1962 Bahamas; 1966 New England; 1964 and 1969 2 Visits to Holy Land; 1969 Audience with the Pope, 1976 Hong Kong. *Hobbies and Recreations:* Gardening, Politics, Travel.

POVEY, Norman, 10 Dimbles Lane, Lichfield, Staffs. WS13 7HW. (05432-22989) *b. 21 Feb 1903, Wrexham. m. 8 Aug 1934: 4s.*
Education: Council Sch., Brynteg; Secondary Sch., Grove Park; 1928–31 Didsbury. *Appointments:* 1931–34 S. Hants. Mission; 1934–36 Manchester, Grosvenor St.; 1936–39 Glossop, Wesley; 1939–44 Halifax, St. John's; 1944–46 Northampton, Park Ave.; 1946–49 Ipswich, Museum St.; 1949–55 Southend-on-Sea, Park Rd.; 1955–57 East Ham, Barking; 1958–64 Chelmsford; 1964–68 Gt. Yarmouth.
Connexional Committees: 1955–65 Home Missions. *Local Council Committees:* 1955–58 Barking Education Committee.
Publications: Associated with Prayers, contributed to *A Prayer at Hand* (Ed. F. G. Doubleday 1967); *To God in Prayer* (Ed. F. G. Doubleday 1970).
Special Interests: Music. *Hobbies and Recreations:* Crosswords, Folk Lore.

POWELL, Edward George Williams, Flat D, Brockmere, 43 Wray Park Rd., Reigate, Surrey RH2 0EG. (073724-8777)–BA(Lond.), MA(Lond.). *b. 6 Jan 1909, Swalwell, Newcastle-on-Tyne, Co. Durham. m. 27 July 1935: 1d., 3s.*
Education: 1914–19 Swalwell Sch.; 1919–26 Blaydon Secondary Sch.; 1 year at Swalwell Sch., learning to teach; 1927–31 Westminster Coll.; 1929–31 King's Coll., London Univ.
Appointments: 1939–43 Leigh; 1943–46 Worksop; 1946–53 Retford; 1953–61 Sheffield North; 1961–65 Leeds North East; 1968–75 Newcastle, Staffs.; 1975– Redhill and East Grinstead.

POWELL, Eric George, 3 Larch Rd., Glasgow G41 5DA. (041-427-1331) *b. 21 Jan 1920, Stalybridge, Cheshire. m. 5 Aug 1949: 1s.*
Education: 1925–30 St. John's Stalybridge; 1930–34 Westhill, Stalybridge; 1945–47 Hartley Victoria. *Appointments:* 1947–49 Leith and Tranent; 1949–50 North of Scotland Mission; 1951–55 Haworth and Oakworth; 1955–59 York Centenary; 1959–62 Liverpool South; 1962–69 Castletown, Isle of Man; 1969 Glasgow South.
Connexional Committees: 1979 Property Board; 1962–66 Connexional Youth Committee; 1966–69 Overseas Mission Committee.
Hobbies and Recreations: Reading, Music.

POWERS, Alan George, 65 Lewisham Rd., River, Dover, Kent CT17 0QG. (030-47-3085)–MDiv. *b. 18 Dec 1940, Birmingham. m. 9 July 1966: 2s.*
Education: 1943–51 Severne Rd. Jun. Sch.; 1951–54 Pitmaston Secondary Modern; 1954–57 Bordesley Green County Technical; 1957–61 Brooklyn Technical, Birmingham; 1966–67 Christian Theological Seminary, U.S.A. World Council of Churches Scholarship; 1962–66 Richmond Coll.; 1973–74 Queen's. *Appointments:* 1966–67 Per. U.S.A.; 1967–70 Redcar, Saltburn and Guisborough; 1970–73 London Mission South; 1974–82 Leeds,

Headingley; 1982– Dover and Deal. *Connexional Committees:* 1977–82 Board of Social Responsibility; 1977–82 Community Relations Committee; 1979–82 Multi-Racial Projects Committee.
Special Interests: The Theologies of R. Bultmann and K. Barth. *Hobbies and Recreations:* Collecting and Studying Works of D. H. Lawrence, Member of D. H. Lawrence Society.

POWIS, John Charles, 61 Whitsbury Rd., Fordingbridge, Hants. SP6 1LB. (0425 53134)–BD(Lond.). *b. 30 July 1937, London. m. 27 June 1964: 1d., 2s.*
Education: 1948–50 North Haringey Secondary Modern; 1950–53 Enfield Technical Sch.; 1962–66 Hartley Victoria Coll. *Appointments:* 1966–69 Rotherham; 1969–75 Blaydon; 1975–80 Gateshead South West; 1980– Salisbury.
Special Interests: Clinical Theology.

POWLEY, Brian George, 73 Arundel Way, Ipswich, Suffolk IP3 8QG. (0473-717522)–MA(Oxon), BA(Cantab), PhD(Glasgow). *b. 14 Nov 1939, Gt. Yarmouth, Norfolk. m. 30 July 1966: 1s.*
Education: 1951–59 Gt. Yarmouth Grammar Sch.; 1959–62 Exeter Coll., Oxford; 1962–65 Wesley House. *Appointments:* 1965–67 Assistant Tutor, Didsbury Coll., Bristol; 1967–71 Motherwell and Wishaw; 1971–75 Sheffield, Carver St.; 1975–81 Methodist Chaplain, Birmingham Univ.; 1981 Ipswich. *Connexional Committees:* 1982– Member of the Studies Board of the Local Preachers' Department. *Publications:* Articles, Sermons and Book Reviews in *Expository Times, Epworth Review, Worship and Preaching* and other journals.
Special Interests: The history of the Interpretation of the New Testament. *Hobbies and Recreations:* Classical Music.

PRATT, Alfred George, 112 Stroud Green Drive, Bognor Regis, West Sussex PO21 5SZ. (0243 822852) *b. 19 Oct 1913, Richmond, Surrey. m. 23 June 1943: 1s.*
Education: 1918–27 Holy Trinity and St. Mary's CE Schs., Richmond; 1935–38 Handsworth.
Appointments: 1938–50 South West China Dt; 1950–55 Sittingbourne; 1955–59 Pontefract; 1959–64 Ripley; 1964–67 Leytonstone and Forest Gate; 1967–70 Grimsby West; 1970–73 Rothwell; 1973–78 Gateshead.
Special Interests: Railways, History, 18th Century Literature.

PRATT, Geoffrey Charles, 2 Dial Park Road, Great Moor, Stockport SK2 7LS. (061-483-3706) *b. 2 April 1937, Leeds. m. 4 July 1964: 2s.*
Education: 1941–50 Rowland Rd., Leeds 11; 1950–52 Bentley Lane, Leeds 7; 1960–61 Cliff Coll.; 1961–65 Hartley Victoria. *Appointments:* 1965–67 Downham Market; 1967–71 Tiverton; 1971–79 Manchester, Stretford and Urmston; 1979– Hazel Grove and Poynton.
Connexional Committees: 1981– Board of Property.
Special Interests: Youth Work.
Hobbies and Recreations: Bowls, Music, Books.

PRATT, Norman, 23 Chestnut Drive, Bare, Morecambe LA4 6HZ. (0524-420411) *b. 3 Sept 1913, Bacup, Lancs. m. 27 May 1944: 1d.*
Education: Local Sch., Pilning, Lancs.; 1936–39 Hartley Victoria. 1939–44 Hunan Dt, China; 1944–47 Market Rasen and Caistor; 1947–49 Grimsby, George St.; 1949–55 Jamaica Dt; 1955–65 Bahama Dt; 1965–70 Nottingham West, 1970–74 Stockton; 1974–79 Preston Trinity; 1979–82 Lancaster.
Hobbies and Recreations: Gardening.

PRESCOTT, Malcolm Crosby, Dumplings Hill, Boxford, Colchester CO6 5JW. (0787-210378)–MA. *b. 15 Dec 1918, Tetbury, Gloucestershire. m. 4 March 1945 (w.): 2d., 2s.*
Education: 1927–32 Tetbury Grammar Sch.; 1932–37 Kingswood Sch., Bath; 1937–40 Univ. Coll., London Univ.; 1940–43 Fitzwilliam House, Cambridge; 1940–43 Wesley House. *Appointments:* 1943–73 Chaplain HMF; 1966–73 Assistant Chaplain General; 1969–73 Hon. Chaplain to the Queen; 1976–80 Research Fellow and Tutor, Queen's Coll., Birmingham.
Parliamentary Service: President Liberal Association South Suffolk; Approved Parliamentary Candidate, Liberal Party; Member Liberal Parliamentary Association; Liberal International and Association of Liberal Councillors; all from 1981.
Connexional Committees: 1967–71 R.N., Army and RAF Board. *Council Member:* 1982 Babersh District Council, Suffolk. *Local Council Committees:* 1974–76 West Suffolk Area Health Authority; 1982 Planning, Development Control and Personnel Committees, Babersh District Council. *Publications:* Articles and Reports *RAChD Journal* and some other Journals.
Special Interests: Professional Associate Clinical Theology Association, Political Scene, International Affairs, Human Behaviour.

PRICE, Antony Howard, 68 Golden Cross Lane, Catshill, Bromsgrove, Worcs. B61 0LG. *(0527-76405) 27 July 1932, Gloucester. m. 12 June 1954: 2d., 1s.*
Education: Crypt Grammar, Gloucester; 1979–81 Wesley Coll., Bristol. *Appointments:* 1981– Bromsgrove.
Special Interests: Church History.
Hobbies and Recreations: Gardening.

PRICE, David Leonard, 64 Chelston Ave., Yeovil, Somerset BA21 4PU. (0935-4545) *b. 14 May 1942, Wolverhampton. m. 14 July 1973: 2s.*
Education: 1947–49 Tettenhall Inf. Sch., Wolverhampton; 1949–53 Red Cross St. Jun. Sch., Wolverhampton; 1953–58 Wolverhampton Grammar Sch.; 1958–63 Wolverhampton and Staffordshire Coll. of Technology; 1966–69 Hartley Victoria; 1969–70 Garrett Methodist Seminary, Evanston, Illinois, U.S.A.
Appointments: 1970–72 Burton upon Trent; 1972–79 Barnsley; 1979– Yeovil.
Special Interests: Pastoral Care of the Dying, Hospital Chaplaincy,

School Governor. *Hobbies and Recreations:* Collecting Miniature Historical Vehicles, Sport, Reading.

PRICE, Harold Edward, 6 The Homes, Langford, Bristol BS18 7HU. *b. 17 May 1900, Birmingham.* *Education:* 1908–13 Tindal St. Boys Sch.; 1913–16 Central Technical Sch.; 1924–27 Didsbury. *Appointments:* 1923–24 N. Scotland Mission; 1927–28 Mid Gloucester Mission; 1928–31 London Mission East; 1931–34 London, Ilford; 1934–35 Sheffield Mission; 1935–37 London Mission, Hackney; 1937–40 East Durham; 1940–44 The Hartlepools; 1944–48 Downham Market; 1948–52 Scunthorpe Trinity; 1952–56 Sherborne; 1956–59 South Petherton and Crewkerne; 1959–62 Risca and Cross Keys; 1962–66 South Normanton.

PRICE, James Herbert, Handsworth, West Rd., Bowdon, Cheshire WA14 2LF. (061-928-3034)–MA. *b. 29 Dec 1890, Birmingham. m. 29 July 1918: 2d. 1s.* *Education:* Birmingham Technical; 1944 Manchester Univ.; 1911–14 Richmond. *Appointments:* 1914–16 London Hackney and Victoria Park; 1916–17 London Mission East; 1917–19 Southall Mission; 1919–22 Stafford; 1922–25 Wolverhampton, Darlington St.; 1925–28 Hull, Queen's Rd.; 1928–32 Leeds, Bramley; 1932–37 Burnley Wesley; 1937–41 Oldham, Manchester St.; 1941–45 Manchester, Wesley; 1945–50 Manchester Gravel Lane; 1950–51 Altringham; 1951–57 Manchester District missionary; 1957–59 Chairman Manchester and Stockport. *Connexional Committees;* 1947 Stationing; 1959 General Purposes: 1950–61 Law and Polity; 1947–59 Home Missions: 1947–60 General Chapel. *Publications:* 1940 *Adolescent Psychology.* *Hobbies and Recreations,* Radio, Cricket, Football.

PRICE, John Arthur, 1 Beech Court, Pocklington, York YO4 2NE. (07592-3354).

Education: 1959–62 Headingley. *Appointments:* 1962–64 Pontypridd; 1964–69 Bingham; 1969–76 Knaresborough; 1976–81 York Wesley; 1981– Pocklington.

PRICE, Kenneth Victor, 411 Brentwood Rd., Gidea Park, Romford, Essex RM2 6DD. (040-24-46101) *b. 13 Dec 1918, Derby. m. 2 Aug 1947: 1s.* *Education:* Kedleston Rd. Sch. and Bemrose Sch., Derby; 1938–39 Cliff Coll.; 1946–47 Handsworth. *Appointments:* 1947–50 Oakengates; 1950–55 Sunderland West; 1955–63 London, Enfield; 1963–68 London, Kilburn and Hampstead; 1968–75 Southend-on-Sea; 1975– Romford. *Connexional Committees:* 1964–74 Member Committee on Healing and Pastoral Ministry. *Special Interests:* Diaries and Diarists.

PRICE, Peter Owen, Principal Chaplain C.S.F.C., Ministry of Defence, Lacon House, Theobolds Rd., London WC1 X8RY. (01-430-6842)–QHC, BA(Open Univ.). *b. 18 April 1930, Swansea. m. (2) 1982: 3d (by first marriage).* *Education:* Wyggeston Sch., Leicester; 1954–57 Didsbury, Bristol. *Appointments:* 1957–60 Birmingham Mission; 1960– Chaplain HMF.

PRICHARD, Eric Clifford, 361 Cannock Rd., Hightown, Cannock WS11 2TD. (05438 2464)–MA, BD. *b. 29 June 1928, Liverpool. m. 31 Aug 1963: 1d., 2s.* *Education:* 1940–46 Holt Sch., Liverpool; 1948–52 Univ. Coll., N. Wales, Bangor. *Appointments:* 1981 Cannock Chase. *Local Council Committees:* 1978–79 Education Committee Wolverhampton Borough Council. *Publications:* Articles on R.E. in School.

PRIEST, Charles Reginald, 62 Church Court, Midsomer Norton, Bath BA3 2JA. (0761-415823) *b. 17 July 1908, Stechford, Birmingham. m. 26 April 1933: 1d., 1s.* *Education:* 1913–21 Stetchford Council Sch., Birmingham; 1921–24 Aston Commercial Sch., Birmingham. *Appointments:* 1963–67 Castleford; 1967–70 Camelford and Wadebridge; 1970–73 Swansea; 1950–59 Additional Superintendent Registrar, Birmingham. *Special Interests:* Music (ex-Principal, Rubery Academy of Music). *Hobbies and Recreations:* Music, Reading, Walking.

PRIEST, Paul Nicholas, 11 Browning Ave., Boscombe, Bournemouth BH5 1NR. (0202-34622) *b. 6 Nov 1944, Birmingham. m. 10 Aug 1968: 2d.* *Education:* Bishop Vesey's Grammar Sch.; Sutton Coldfield, Warwickshire; 1981–82 Union Theological Seminary, Richmond, Virginia 23227, USA; 1965–69 Didsbury/Wesley Coll., Bristol. *Appointments:* 1969–74 Romford; 1974–81 Birkenhead; 1981–82 World Council of Churches Scholar; 1982– Bournemouth. *Hobbies and Recreations:* Photography, Badminton, Member of British Magical Society.

PRIESTLEY, Edward, 20 Lowdale Lane, Heights, Whitby, N. Yorks YO22 5BU. (0947-810458) *b. 2 Oct 1902, West Hartlepool. m. 1. 8 July 1931; 2. 26 July 1976 (w.).* *Education:* 1925–28 Didsbury. *Appointments:* 1924–25 Epworth; 1928–31 Driffield; 1931–32 Spalding; 1932–36 Sunderland, Durham Rd. and West; 1936–39 Gateshead East; 1939–44 Leeds, Headingley; 1944–50 Stockton, Brunswick; 1950–55 Newcastle North West; 1955–61 Whitby; 1961–64 Morley. *Publications:* Articles in the Methodist Press and British Weekly; sermons in the *Christian World Pulpit* (1932–56).

PRIESTLEY, Ronald David, 22 Barrington Gate, Holbeach, Spalding, Lincs. PE12 7LB. (0406-23270) *b. 21 March 1925, Lincoln. m. 18 Aug 1954: 2s.* *Education:* 1935–41 City Sch., Lincoln; 1949–51 Headingley. *Appointments:* 1947–49 Garstang; 1951–54 Spilsby; 1954–59

Scunthorpe; 1959–63 Louth; 1963–68 Alford; 1968–73 Gainsborough; 1973– Holbeach.

PRIESTNALL, David Andrew, The Manse, Noblett Rd., Sneyd Green, Stoke-on-Trent ST1 6HR. (0782-21818)–MA(Oxon. and Cantab.). *b. 4 June 1948. m: 2d.*
Education: 1972–75 Wesley House. *Appointments:* 1975–77 Newcastle upon Tyne, Brunswick Central; 1977–82 Stockport; 1982– Stoke-on-Trent, Burslem Mission.

PRINCE, William, The Manse, 16A Church Lane, Chessington, Surrey KT9 2DJ. (01-397-3046) *b. 29 Nov 1943, Crewe. m. 28 June 1969: 1d., 1s.*
Education: 1948–54 Edleston Rd. Prim. Sch.; 1954–59 Bedford St. Boys Sch.; 1966–70 Hartley Victoria. *Appointments:* 1970–72 Stamford; 1972–77 Hinckley; 1977– Kingston-upon-Thames.

PRITCHARD, Frederick Smith, 1E Lewis St., Bilston, West Midlands WV14 7LZ. (0902-42052)–BA(B'ham.), BDHons(Lond.). *b. 2 April 1924, Wolverhampton. m. 2 Aug 1951: 2s.*
Education: 1929–33 Neachell Lane Prim.; 1933–42 Wolverhampton Grammar; 1942–43 and 1946–48 Birmingham Univ.; 1946–50 Handsworth. *Appointments:* 1950–52 Gainsborough; 1952–56 Horncastle; 1956–59 Birmingham Islington; 1959–65 Cardiff Wesley; 1965–70 Sirhowy Valley; 1970–76 Newport, Gwent; 1976– Bilston, W. Midlands.
Connexional Committees: 1966–72 Christian Citizenship, District Sec.
Special Interests: Charismatic Renewal, Healing particularly Inner Healing. *Hobbies and Recreations:* Reading.

PRITCHARD, John Ralph, 6 Westlands Grove, Portchester, Hants. PO16 9AA. (0705-375818)–BA(Bristol), BA(Cambridge). *b. 15 April 1941, Bradford, Yorkshire. m. 3 July 1965: 1d., 1s.*
Education: 1952–54 Wade Deacon Grammar Sch., Widnes, Lancs.; 1954–59 The Manchester Grammar Sch.; 1959–62 The Univ. of Bristol; 1963–65 The Univ. of Cambridge; 1963–65 Wesley House. *Appointments:* 1965–75 Ivory Coast District; 1965–67 Paris; 1967–75 Port and Industrial Chaplain, Abidjan; 1975–80 Sheffield, Carver St.; 1980– Gosport and Fareham.
Connexional Committees: 1975– Transfer of Authority to Overseas District; 1977– Overseas Division Africa Advisory Group. *Publications:* Editor *Urban Africa and L'Afrique Urbaine* (1972–74); various Journal articles, *Travelling Along* (with John Simmonds, SCM 1982).
Special Interests: Ministerial Further Training (10 year course Leader, 1979–), Urban Theology Unit (vice chairman 1977–80), Alliance of Radical Methodists. *Hobbies and Recreations:* Walking, Stamp-Collecting.

PRITCHARD, Ralph John, 34 Hunters Chase, Herne Bay, Kent CT6 7BD. (022-73-3682)–BA(B'ham.). *9 Aug 1913, Watford, Herts. m. 2 Aug 1939 (w.): 1d., 3s.*
Education: 1920–30 Watford Grammar Sch.; 1932–36 Handsworth. *Appointments:* 1936–38 President's List (Stockport, Tiviot Dale); 1938–41 Bradford, Ottley Rd.; 1941–45 Bradford, Manningham; 1945–49 Mansfield, Bridge St.; 1949–54 Widnes; 1954–60 Sale; 1960–66 Altrincham; 1966–72 Saddleworth and Lees; 1972–77 Shropshire South.
Connexional Committees: 1956–66 Overseas Missions.
Special Interests: The World Church, Christian Aid etc. *Hobbies and Recreations:* Gardening, Philately.

PROWTING, Michael John Patrick, The Manse, Greville Way, Newton Aycliffe, Co. Durham DL5 5EX. (0325-313508)–MA(Cantab), BD(Lond.). *b. 17 March 1943, Louth, Lincs. m. 25 July 1970: 3d.*
Education: 1954–62 Louth Grammar Sch.; 1962–65 Christ's Coll. Cambridge; 1965–68 Richmond Coll. *Appointments:* 1968–71 Liverpool South; 1971–75 Wakefield; 1975–80 Bury and Heywood; 1980– Shildon.
Connexional Committees: 1974– Connexional Children's Committee; 1976– Board Education and Youth. *Local Council Committees:* 1980– Governor Woodham Comprehensive Sch.
Hobbies and Recreations: Camping, Reading Thrillers.

PUDNER, Anthony W., c/o Revd. C. R. Wolsey Gilbert, Royal Navy, Army and Royal Air Force Board, 1 Central Buildings, Tothill St., London SW1H 9NH.
Education: 1956–60 Wesley, Bristol. *Appointments:* 1960–64 Isles of Scilly; 1964–69 Falmouth; 1969–71 Porthleven; 1971– Chaplain HMF.

PUGH, Reginald Evans, 2 Pendre Ave., Prestatyn, Clwyd, N. Wales LL19 95L. (074-56-6637)–BD(Lond.). *b. 1908, Longwood, Huddersfield. m. 1940.*
Education: Spark Hall Sch.; Goitfield Sch.; Huddersfield Coll.; London Univ.; 1931–34 Headingley. *Appointments:* 1930–31 Wells-Next-The-Sea; 1934–37 Kingston-on-Thames; 1937–40 Liverpool, Anfield and St. Domingo; 1940–45 Burnley, Brunswick; 1945–48 Oldham, Manchester St; 1948–51 Swansea Brunswick; 1951–55 Leigh, King St.; 1955–58 Birmingham, Belmont Row; 1958–64 Ashton-under-Lyne; 1964–67 Pudsey and Pudsey and Farsley; 1967–73 Darwen.
Special Interests: Church History, History of Christian Doctrine. *Hobbies and Recreations:* Gardening.

PULLAN, Michael John, 46 Baugh Gardens, Downend, Bristol BS16 6PP. (0272-561926)–BEd(Leeds), BD(Manchester). *b. 7 Aug 1946, Bramley, Leeds. m. 17 Aug 1974: 1s.*
Education: 1957–64 West Leeds Boys High Sch.; 1964–67 City of Leeds and Carnegie Coll. of Ed.; 1968 Leeds Univ.; 1971–74 Manchester Univ.; 1971–74 Hartley Victoria Coll.
Appointments: 1974–79 Goole;

1979– Bristol Frome Valley. *Connexional Committees:* MDEY–Advisory Committee Full-time Youth and Community Posts. *Local Council Committees:* 1975–78 Chairman of School Managers/Governors, Old Goole 1st Sch. *Hobbies and Recreations:* Jogging, Collecting Stamps, Ecology.

PURSEHOUSE, Gerald Frederick Henry, 14 Beech Crescent, Townville, Castleford, West Yorkshire WF10 3RJ. (0977-552140)–BA(Bristol), BSc(Lond.). *b. 27 April 1926, Redgrave. Suffolk. m. 20 Aug 1960: 3s.*
Education: 1931–37 Diss Church Sch.; 1937–39 Diss Grammar Sch.; 1939–43 Sebright Sch., Wolverley, Nr Kidderminster; 1943–45 Queen Mary Coll., London Univ.; 1955–58 Didsbury, Bristol. *Appointments:* 1958–60 Knighton; 1960–65 Bloxwich; 1965–69 South Derbyshire; 1969–74 Nottingham North; 1974–79 Louth; 1979– Castleford.
Special Interests: Music. *Hobbies and Recreations:* Reading, Walking, Gardening, Watching all kinds of Sport.

PURVS, Richard, 34 Fox and Hounds Rd., Newcastle-upon-Tyne, Tyne and Wear NE5 2EL. (0632-744129) *b. 13 July 1928, Hexham, Northumberland. m. 30 March 1957: 1d., 1s.*
Education: 1933–39 Hexham Prim.; 1939–42 Queen Elizabeth High Sch.; 1953–56 Hartley Victoria. *Appointments:* 1956–59 Amble and Anwick, 1959–65 Huddersfield West; 1965–70 Keighley; 1970–76 Edinburgh, Nicholson Square; 1976– Newcastle West.
Connexional Committees: 1965–70 Christian Citizenship; 1980– Social Responsibility. *Local Council Committees.* 1967–70 Chairman Keighley Community Relations Council.
Special Interests: Scouting, Christian Endeavour, Community Relations, Christian Aid, Temperance and Alcohol Abuse. *Hobbies and Recreations:* Walking, Gardening, Stamp Collecting.

PUTNAM, Eric Royston, 127 Lynton Rd., West Acton, London W3 9HN. (01-992-2494) *b. 6 Aug 1931, Andover, Hants. m. 6 Aug 1966: 1d., 1s.*
Education: 1935–42 Naunton Park, Cheltenham; 1942–47 Cheltenham Grammar Sch.; 1947–48 North Glos. Tech. Coll.; 1948–53 Luton Technical Coll.; 1963–66 Hartley Victoria. *Appointments:* 1966–71 Romiley, Stockport; 1971–73 Derby South; 1973– London Industrial Chaplaincy.
Connexional Committees: Development and Training, Div. of Ministries.
Special Interests: Applications of New Technology, Apprentice Training and Development, Engineering Design. *Hobbies and Recreations:* Cycling, Swimming, Gardening, Country Walks.

PYE, Jonathan Howard, The Manse, 19 Burnside, Amble, Northumberland NE65 0HB. (0665-710285)–BA(Dunelm), MA(Dunelm). *b. 3 June 1956, St. Helens, Merseyside. m. 4 Aug 1979.*
Education: 1967–74 The Cowley Sch.; 1974–79 St. John's Coll., Univ. of Durham; 1977–80 Wesley House. *Appointments:* 1980– Morpeth; 1980– Methodist Chaplain, H.M.P. Acklington and H.M.P. Castington. *Publications: A Bibliography of the Published Works of Ian Thomas Ramsey* (Abbey House Publications 1979).
Special Interests: Member of The Society for the Study of Theology, Member of The Christian Philosphers' Group, Member of The Durham Union Society. *Hobbies and Recreations:* Rugby Union, The Arts, Two Cats.

QUENET, Joaquin Thomas, 147 Regent Farm Rd., Gosforth, Newcastle-upon-Tyne NE3 3HD. (0632-852349) *b. 8 July 1953, Cabra, Cordoba, Spain. m. 6 Sept 1975: 2s.*
Education: 1960–65 Spring Gardens Jun. Sch., North Shields; 1965–69 Ralph Gardner High Sch., North Shields; 1969–70 Marden High Sch, North Shields; 1976– Kingsmead; 1973–76 Wesley, Bristol. *Appointments:* 1977–79 Caribbean and The Americas Conference; 1979–82 Leeward Islands Dt, M.C.C.A.; 1982– Newcastle-upon-Tyne, Brunswick Central.
Special Interests: Overseas Missions and Development, Ecumenical Affairs. *Hobbies and Recreations:* Antique Porcelain/China Collecting, Stamp Collecting, Radio Listening, Astronomy.

QUERIPEL, Roy Henry, 174 Station Rd., Hatton, Derby DE6 5EH. (0283-812265) *b. 24 Nov 1929, Guernsey. m. 6 Aug 1957: 1d., 1s.*
Education: 1936–37 St. Peter's Inf. Sch.; 1937–41 Forest Jun. Sch.; 1941–45 Elizabeth Coll.; 1954–57 Richmond Coll.
Appointments: 1957–59 Epworth and Crowle; 1959–64 Haworth and Oakworth; 1964–67 Holmfirth; 1967–72 Ryedale; 1972–75 Knighton and Leintwardine; 1975–80 Keighley; 1980– Dove Valley.

QUICK, Melvin Walter, 12 Oxford Rd., St. John's, Wakefield, Yorkshire WF1 3LB. (0924-375681) *b. 16 Dec 1921, London, Ontario, Canada. m. 25 Nov 1942: 1d., 2s.*
Education: 1926–40 Elem. Schs. and High Sch.; 1947–50 Veterans' Special Coll., Ontario, Nazerene Coll. *Appointments:* 1952–63 Church of Nazerene, 1963–67 Leeds Mission and Leeds Central; 1967–71 London, Kilburn and Hampstead; 1971–76 London, Finchley and Hendon; 1976–79 South Craven; 1976– Wakefield.
Connexional Committees: 1971–73 Church in Industry.
Special Interests: Industrial Chaplaincy. *Hobbies and Recreations:* Fresh Water Fishing,

Do-it-Yourself, Wood Carving, Water Colour Painting, Languages.

QUICK, Sydney, 17 Barton Close, Heamoor, Penzance, Cornwall TR18 3JA. (0736-68119) *b. 16 Oct 1911, Drift, Penzance. m. 28 July 1937.*
Education: –1919 Lescudjack CS; –1925 Commercial Coll. (Private); 1931–34 Victoria Park.
Appointments: 1934–36 President's List; 1936–39 Shebbear; 1939–40 Barnstaple; 1940–45 St. Columb and Padstow; 1945–48 London, Sydenham and Forest Hill; 1948–52 Penzance, Chapel St.; 1952–56 Camborne; 1956–60 Plymouth, King St.; 1960–63 Penzance; 1967–71 St. Just; 1971–76 Stoke-on-Trent, Hanley.
Special Interests: Choral Singing, Sport.

QUINE, Frederick James Bushby, Montclare, Liskey Hill Crescent, Perranporth, Cornwall. (087-257-3189) *b. 12 April 1904, Birkenhead. m. 18 Aug 1931: 1d., 2s.*
Education: 1924–27 Handsworth.
Appointments: 1927–30 Church of South India; 1931–36 Teddington; 1936–42 Reading; 1942–47 Gloucester; 1947–52 Tunbridge Wells; 1952–56 Cheltenham; 1956–61 Wellington, Salop; 1961–69 Perranporth.
Special Interests: The Blind. *Hobbies and Recreations:* Writing, Gardening, Travel.

RACE, Leonard, 27 Brookside, St. Austell, Cornwall PL25 4HL. (0726-65294) *b. 24 April 1916, Arthington, Wharfedale, Yorks. m. 21 Dec 1945: 2d., 2s.*
Education: 1920–30 Burley Rd. Elem., Leeds; 1939–42 Hartley Victoria. *Appointments:* 1942–43 Bury St. Edmunds; 1943–46 South Petherton; 1946–49 Roseland; 1949–53 Leeward Islands Dt; 1953–58 Roseland; 1958–59 Cwm and Kingstone; 1959–62 Blackpool North; 1962–69 South Molton; 1969–76 St. Austell.
Special Interests: Travelling and Driving. *Hobbies and Recreations:* Reading, Music.

RACK, Henry Denman, 15 Gildridge Rd., Manchester M16 8PS. (061-881-4305)–MA(Oxon), BA(Cantab). *b. 24 Aug 1931, Bishop Auckland. m. 29 July 1964: 2d., 1s.*
Education: 1944–50 Kingswood Sch., Bath; 1952–55 Magdalen Coll., Oxford; 1955–58 Fitzwilliam Coll., Cambridge; 1958–59 Univ. of Tübingen; 1955–58 Wesley House. *Appointments:* 1959–60 Walton on Thames; 1960–62 Brighton (Dome); 1962–63 Wells and Fakenham; 1963–64 President's Assistant, Didsbury Coll.; 1964–65 Ipswich; 1965–70 Hartley Victoria Coll.; 1970– Lecturer in Ecclesiastical History, Univ. of Manchester.
Connexional Committees: Ministerial Training; 1976– Faith and Order; 1982– Archives and History Committee. *Publications: The Future of John Wesley's Methodism* (1965); *Twentieth Century Spirituality* (1969).
Special Interests: Modern Church History. *Hobbies and Recreations:* Walking, Painting, Music.

RAINE, Alan Gowland, 17 Woodland Grove, Burslem, Stoke on Trent ST6 7EB. (0782-88251)–BA. *27 July 1940, Bishop Auckland. m. 29 Oct 1960: 2d., 2s.*
Education: 1951–55 King James 1st Grammar Sch., Bishop Auckland; 1971–74 Manchester Univ.; 1971–74 Hartley Victoria. *Appointments:* 1974–80 Stockton; 1980– Stoke on Trent, Burslem.
Hobbies and Recreations: Joinery, Walking.

RAINE, Frederick Hutton, 125 Dudley Rd., Plympton, Plymouth PL7 3RZ. (0752-339067) *b. 27 Aug 1916, Gateshead, Co. Durham, 3 March 1942: 2s.*
Education: 1927–32 Gateshead Secondary; 1935–39 Didsbury.
Appointments: 1939–42 Leeds Mission; 1942–44 Batley, Zion; 1944–47 Leeds, Headingley; 1947–50 Settle; 1950–54 North Shields and Cullercoats; 1954–56 Norton and Radstock; 1956–59 Sheffield North; 1959–64 Newquay; 1964–67 Bridgend; 1967–73 Penzance; 1973–76 North Hill; 1976-81 Camelford and Wadebridge.
Hobbies and Recreations: Philately.

RAINE, William Whitfield, 31 Quarry Hill, Sowerby Bridge, West Yorkshire HX6 3BQ. (0422-831109) *b. 21 Sept 1920, Newcastle-on-Tyne. m. 1. 29 July 1951; 2. 6 Dec 1969: 5d., 1s.*
Education: 1925–31 Westgate Hill Inf. Jun. and Senior Elem. Sch.; 1931–36 Royal Grammar Sch., Newcastle-on-Tyne; 1945–48 Hartley Victoria. *Appointments:* 1948–51 London, East Ham Mission; 1951–57 Gateshead East; 1957–67 Doncaster N.E.; 1967–68 Doncaster South; 1968–72 Doncaster West; 1972–74 Bridgwater; 1974– Sowerby Bridge.
Local Council Committees: 1970–71 Doncaster Education Committee.
Hobbies and Recreations: Photography, Bread Baking, Theatre, Music.

RAMSEY, Sidney Frederick James, 87 Aviemore Rd., Hemlington, Middlesbrough, Cleveland TS8 9JA. (0642-591328). *b. 13 Sept 1915, Hoxton, Shoreditch, London. m. 26 July 1947: 2s.*
Education: 1920–29 St. John's L.C.C. Sch.; 1936–39 Cliff Coll.; 1945–47 Handsworth. *Appointments:* 1947–50 Birmingham Mission; 1950–55 Newquay; 1955–58 Shipley; 1958–63 Middlesbrough; 1963–72 Resigned; 1972–80 Stoke-on-Trent, Burslem.
Council Member: City of Stoke on Trent.
Special Interests: Politics. *Hobbies and Recreations:* Fishing, Walking.

RANSOME, Cyril Rowntree, 29 Carr Manor Ave., Leeds LS17 5BJ. (0532-684225) *b. 8 July 1899, Scagglethorpe, Malton, Yorkshire. m. 18 Aug 1928: 1d.*
Education: 1902–13 Quarry Mount and Belle Vue Prim., Leeds; 1913–17 Boy's Central High; 1924–26 Hartley.
Appointments: 1923–24 Colchester; 1926–40 Eastern Nigeria District,

West Africa; 1940–48 Hexham; 1948–56 Bedale; 1956–61 Brownhills and Pelsall; 1961–66 Ryedale; Precentor, College and Eastern Nigera Synod; Board of Modern School Governors, Brownhills and Ryedale; Chaplaincies, Hexham (Army), Bedale (R.A.F.), Brownhills (Urban District Council), Ryedale (Hospital); Methodist Stewardship Organisation, Ryedale, 1963. Pilot scheme to explore feasibility of a campaign in a tough rural circuit on a circuit level; 1941–76 Methodist Guild Holidays, Host.
Connexional Committees: 1953–56 Central Committee of the Overseas Division. *Council Member:* 1946–48 Haydon Bridge, Northumberland, Parish Council; Parish Councillor.
Special Interests: Preaching, Reading, Classical Music, The Countryside, Sport.

RATCLIFFE, Philip David, 80 Leckhampton Rd., Cheltenham, Glos. GL53 0BN. (0242-24889)–BA(B'ham.). *b. 11 May 1932, Sheffield, Yorks. m.*
Education: 1943–50 Sheffield City Grammar Sch.; 1954–57 Birmingham Univ.; 1953–57 Handsworth.
Appointments: 1957–60 Consett; 1960–65 Doncaster District Coalfields Mission; 1965–72 Redcar Saltburn and Guisborough; 1972–76 Newbury and Hungerford; 1977–80 Teacher of Religious Studies Southampton and Ringwood; 1980 Cheltenham.
Special Interests: Ministerial Further Training, Bible Study and Teaching Methods, Spirituality, Counselling, Encounter and 'T' Groups, Education.
Hobbies and Recreations: Walking, Music, TV Sport.

RATTENBURY, Harold Morley, 24 Rumple Croft, Otley, W.Yorks. LS21 2RE. (0943-465117)–MA(Oxon), MA(Cantab). *b. 23 Aug 1915, Kuling, China. m. 8 April 1942: 1d., 3s.*
Education: 1924–26 Clarence Sch., Weston-super-Mare; 1926–34 Kingswood Sch., Bath; 1934–37 Oriel Coll., Oxford; 1937–40 Wesley House. *Appointments:* 1940–42 Newcastle, Brunswick; 1942–46 Chaplain H.M.F.; 1946–50 Watford; 1950–54 Leamington; 1954–67 Wesley Coll., Headingley, Tutor in Church History and History of Doctrine; 1967–75 Hoylake and West Kirby; 1975–80 Ossett and Horbury.
Connexional Committees: General Purposes, Church Membership, Overseas Missions, Ministerial Training, Connexional Schs.
Publications: A Sketch of Church History (1962); *Lively Oracles* (1976). d _ 06.05.

RAWLINGS, Ronald S., 17 Hillside Gardens, Barnet, Herts. EN5 2NG. (01-449-8386) *b. 26 Sept 1919, London. m. 1 Aug 1946: 1d., 2s.*
Education: 1930–36 Willesden County Grammar; 1939–42 Didsbury. *Appointments:* 1942–46 Yeovil; 1946–49 Sedbergh; 1949–55 Staines and Feltham; 1955–60 St. Leonards and Bexhill; 1960–67 Ealing and Acton; 1967–75 Dorking and Horsham; 1975– Barnet; 1962–75 Synod Secretary, London South West District.
Connexional Committees: 1962–75 Central Finance Board; 1965– Ministers Retirement Fund Com.
Hobbies and Recreations: Clock Repair and Overhaul.

RAYMONT, A. John, Silverdale, Woodside Close, Pembury, Tunbridge Wells TN2 4BQ. (089-282-2387) *b. 27 Dec 1894, Budleigh Salterton, Devon. m. 3 Aug 1922: 1d., 1s.*
Education: 1915–16 Handsworth; 1919–21 Handsworth.
Appointments: 1921–22 Trowbridge; 1922–24 Frome; 1924–27 Redruth; 1927–30 Stourbridge; 1930–34 Birmingham, Mosley Rd.; 1934–38 Finchley and Hendon; 1938–45 Ipswich; 1945–49 Liverpool, Anfield; 1949–55 Birkenhead; 1955–59 Leeds, Brunswick.

RAYNES, Ernest Charles, 5 Ashleigh Drive, Chellaston, Derby DE7 1RG. (0332 701851) *b. 1888, Derby. m. 1921: 2s.*
Education: Heanor Grammar; 1915–17 Richmond. *Appointments:* 1917–24 Leeward Islands Dt; 1924–27 Wiltshire Mission; 1924–27 Gloucester; 1927–31 Rotherham; 1931–35 Lincoln, Wesley; 1945–50 London, Finchley and Hendon; 1950–55 London, Wandsworth.

RAYNOR, George Herbert, 299 Church Rd., St. Annes-on-Sea, Lytham St. Annes, Lancs. FY8 3NP. (0253-727890) *b. 10 Nov 1914, Southport. m. 9 Feb 1942 (w.): 2d.*
Education: 1922–28 Southport Coll.; 1928–32 Kingswood Sch.; 1935–38 Didsbury. *Appointments:* 1938–42 Hoylake and Kirby; 1942–45 Barnsley West; 1945–50 Scunthorpe Trinity; 1950–56 Blackburn, Clayton St.; 1956–61 Blackpool N.; 1961–66 Lytham St. Annes; 1966–69 Blackburn; 1969–80 North Lancashire District Chairman.
Connexional Committees: Overseas Missions, Home Mission, Education, General Purposes, Presidents Council, Property Board. *Local Council Committees:* 1969–80 Lancashire County Education Committee; 1970–80 Lancaster Univ. Council; 1969–80 Nothern Church Leaders.

READ, David John, The Manse, Middlefield Rd., Hoddesdon, Herts. EN11 9ED. (09924-62881) *b. 10 July 1937, King's Lynn, Norfolk. m. 26 June 1968: 3d.*
Education: 1948–52 Gaywood Park Secondary Sch., King's Lynn; 1952–53 King's Lynn Technical Coll.; 1961–65 Richmond. *Appointments:* 1965–67 Colchester; 1967–70 Hunts. Mission, Huntingdon; 1970–75 Bloxwich and Willenhall; 1975–82 Southport; 1982– Waltham Abbey and Hertford.

READ, David William, The Manse, St. Andrew's Church Centre, Pike Drive, Chelmsley Wood, Birmingham B37 7US. (021-770-4219)–BA(Manch.), MA(Cantab). *b. 18 Sept 1942, Southport, Lancs. m. 1 Aug 1968: 1d., 1s.*
Education: 1951–61 St. Dunstan's Coll., Catford; 1962–65 Manchester Univ.; 1965–67 Cambridge Univ.; 1969–70 Birmingham Univ.; 1965–67 Wesley House. *Appointments:*

1967–69 Romford; 1970–75 Carlisle; 1975– Birmingham, Elmdon. *Connexional Committees:* 1972–81 Connexional Youth Council/Board of Education and Youth and Executive Committee. *Publications:* One contribution to *Stories Round the Year* (NCEC 1977). *Hobbies and Recreations:* Home and Family.

READSHAW, Robert Anthony, 16 Lock Lane, Partington, Nr. Urmston, Manchester M31 4PX. (061-775-3842) *b. 2 May 1949, Wisbech, Cambridgeshire. m. 1 May 1982.* *Education:* 1960–65 Queens Boys Secondary Modern Sch., Wisbech; 1970–71 Cliff Coll.; 1972–76 Wesley, Bristol. *Appointments:* 1976–81 Wensleydale; 1981– Sale.

REAM, William, George Bertram, 60 Lowther Rd., Norwich NR4 6QW. (0603-52877)–MA. *b. 30 July 1912, Manchester. m. 5 July 1952: 1d., 1s.* *Education:* 1922–24 Brentwood Grammar Sch.; 1924–31 City of London Sch.; 1931–34 Jesus Coll., Cambridge; 1934–36 Wesley House. *Appointments:* 1936–38 Assistant Tutor, Handsworth Coll.; 1938–50 South China Dt; 1950–51 Research in UK; 1951–57 Sierra Leone Dt; 1957–62 Newcastle, Staffs.; 1962–67 High Wycombe; 1967–71 Birkenhead; 1971–74 Sidmouth and Bridport; 1974–78 Norwich. *Connexional Committees:* 1958–62 Methodist Missionary Society Cttee. *Publications: The Support of the Clergy in the First Five Centuries A.D.* (Articles published by the International Review of Missions 1954). *Special Interests:* International Affairs especially China, Councils of Churches, Amnesty International. *Hobbies and Recreations:* Gardening, Stamp Collecting, Walking.

REASBECK, Peter Allen, 43 Ash Grove, Leeds LS6 6AX. (0532-751292)–BA(Dunelm.), MA(Cantab). *b. 21 Aug 1933, Doncaster. m. 28 July 1962 (w.): 1d., 2s.* *Education:* 1945–52 Doncaster Grammar; 1952–55 Univ. Coll., Durham; 1955–58 Wesley House. *Appointments:* 1958–60 H.M. Department; 1960–63 Durham Coast and Peterlee; 1963–68 Middlesbrough; 1968–75 Stockton; 1975– Leeds, Headingley.

REDDINGTON, (nee Stoyle), Eleanor Mary Esther, 51 Wern Rd., Skewen, Neath, West Glamorgan SA10 6DL. (0792-812389)–BA. *6 July 1953, Cheltenham. m. 31 July 1980.* *Education:* 1958–64 Jun. Sch.; 1964–66 Houghton-le-Spring Grammar; 1966–71 Newquay Grammar; 1971–74 Univ. of Exeter; 1978–80 Queens Coll. *Appointments:* 1980– Neath. *Hobbies and Recreations:* Walking, Swimming, Bird Watching.

REDDISH, David Brian, 135 Mill Lane, Dorridge, Solihull, West Midlands B93 8NY. (05645-3885)–BSc(Manchester), BD(Manchester). *b. 23 Oct 1937, Oldham, Lancs. m. 1 Aug 1962: 2d.* *Education:* Freehold Inf./Jun. Sch., Oldham; 1949–55 Manchester Grammar Sch.; 1955–58 Manchester Univ., Institute of Science and Technology; 1960–63 Manchester Univ., Theology Faculty; 1960–63 Hartley Victoria. *Appointments:* 1963–68 Trowbridge and Bradford-on-Avon; 1968–74 Birmingham, Elmdon; 1974–79 Hoylake and West Kirby; 1979– Birmingham, Elmdon. *Connexional Committees:* 1976–80 Chairman of Youth and Community Committee in D.E.Y.; 1976– Member of Board and Executive, M.D.E.Y. *Local Council Committees:* 1982– Solihull District Health Authority.

REDHEAD, Bernard William, 10 Beechwood Ave., Romiley, Cheshire SK6 4DL. (061-430-3679). *b. 28 Sept 1915, Gainsborough, Lincs. m. 30 Oct 1945: 1d., 1s.* *Education:* 1926–32 Lincoln Sch.; 1938–40 Didsbury; 1941–42 Hartley Victoria. *Appointments:* 1943–49 China, Hupeh Dt; 1949–52 Market Rasen and Caistor; 1952–56 Batley; 1956–59 Sheringham and Cromer; 1959–62 Bradford, West Houghton; 1962–65 Doncaster; 1965–68 Stanley; 1968–72 Skegness and Wainfleet; 1972–77 Peak; 1977–82 Hyde and Denton. *Hobbies and Recreations:* Photography, Gardening.

REDMAN, Ronald Douglas, 237 Holland Rd., Clacton-on-Sea, Essex CO15 6NL. (0255-812143) *b. 23 Dec 1918, London. m. 5 Sept 1942: 1d., 1s.* *Education:* 1947–49 Richmond. *Appointments:* 1946–47 Withernsea; 1949–50 Bradford, Woodhouse Grove; 1950–53 Doncaster, Priory Place; 1953–58 London Mission, Hammersmith; 1958–63 Teddington; 1963–67 Shooters Hill; 1967–72 Newark; 1972–73 London Mission, East Ham; 1973– Clacton-on-Sea. *Hobbies and Recreations:* Painting, Music.

REED, Bryan Holwell, 7 FForddlas, Prestatyn, Clwyd LL19 9SG. (074–56–5382)–BD(Lond.). *b. 26 Jan 1905, Okehampton, Devon. m. 16 June 1931: 3d., 1s.* *Education:* 1918–20 St. Dunstan's Coll., Catford; 1920–23 Shebbear Coll., N. Devon.; 1923–26 Victoria Park. *Appointments:* 1926–28 Hudderfield. High St.; 1928–35 Southend-on-Sea; 1935–42 Walthamstow; 1942–46 Rhyl and Prestatyn; 1946–52 Westhill Coll., Selly Oak; 1952–53 Birmingham, Kings Heath; 1953–61 Methodist Youth Dept.; 1961–68 Finchley and Hendon; 1968–75 American United Methodist Church, New Hampshire Conference. *Connexional Committees:* 1945–65 Youth Department; 1952–61 Overseas Missions; 1953–61 Education. *Publications:* Ed. with Dr. Scott Lidgett *Methodists Growing up in the Church* (1956); *In the Modern World* (1929); *Eighty Thousand Adolescents* (1950). *Hobbies and Recreations:* Gardening.

REED, Denis, 10 Worgret Rd., Fleets Bridge Parr, Poole, Dorset BH15 3EN. (0202-676006) *b. 30 Nov 1904, Stroud, Nr. Petersfield, Hampshire. m. 10 Oct 1933: 1d., 1s.*

Education: 1909–14 Hythe, Hants., Broonenhurst, Thorney Hill; 1914–17 Branksome Heath, Parkstone, Dorset; 1917–22 Poole Secondary; 1923–24 Winchester Teacher Training Coll.; 1926–30 Richmond. *Appointments:* 1930–66 Burma Dt; 1966–69 High Wycombe. *Connexional Committees:* 1966–74 Eastern, Overseas Division. *Publications:* Burmese Translation work for Burma Church. *Special Interests:* History, Theology, Study of Religions, Cricket. *Hobbies and Recreations:* Gardening, Bird Watching.

REED, Keith Andrew, 3 The Avenue, Clifton, York YO3 6AS. (0904-23881)–BA(Bristol). *b. 26 July 1939, Yeadon, Nr. Leeds. m. 7 July 1962: 1s., 2d.* *Education:* 1944–47 Froebelian Sch., Horsforth; 1947–56 Bradford Grammar Sch.; 1959–62 Bristol Univ.; 1959–63 Didsbury, Bristol. *Appointments:* 1963–65 Dursley and Stonehouse; 1965–71 Huddersfield West; 1971–80 Leeds, Headingley; 1980– York North. *Hobbies and Recreations:* Music, Walking.

REEDMAN, Frank Edward, 52 Mead Vale, Weston-super-Mare, Avon BS22 8RR. (0934-28059) *b. 28 April 1904, Elton, Huntingdonshire. m. 21 Sept 1937: 1d.* *Education:* 1909–19 Elton CE Sch., Hunts.; 1928–31 Didsbury. *Appointments:* 1927–28 Daventry; 1931–35 Whitehaven; 1935–42 Hunts. Mission, 1942–47 Blackburn, Clayton St.; 1947–54 London, Finsbury Park; 1954–61 Ealing and Acton; 1961–66 Southend-on-Sea; 1966–71 Gloucester. *Connexional Committees:* 1956–59 London Mission Committee. *Special Interests:* Music. *Hobbies and Recreations:* Cricket.

REEP, David John, 30 Prince of Wales Rd., Dorchester, Dorset DT1 1PP. (0305-62421)–BA(Lond.), BA(B'ham). *30 Dec 1932, Stoke Climsland, Cornwall. m. 10 Aug 1957: 1d., 3s.* *Education:* 1944–51 Callington Grammar Sch.; 1951–54 Univ. Coll. of the South West, Exeter; 1954–57 Handsworth. *Appointments:* 1957–61 Port Talbot; 1961–67 Neath; 1967–74 Hemel Hempstead and Berkhamsted; 1974–81 Worthing; 1981– Dorchester. *Connexional Committees:* 1964–66 and 1968–70 Christian Citizenship Dept. *Special Interests:* Ecumenical Work, BFBS. *Hobbies and Recreations:* Music, Walking.

REES, Edward Morgan, Rosebank Villa, Victoria St., Blairgowrie, Perthshire PH10 7AG. (0250-3416) *b. 16 July 1907, Beccles, Suffolk. m. 10 Aug 1935 (w.): 1d., 2s.* *Education:* 1915–19 Woodhouse Grove, Apperley Bridge; 1919–22 Kingswood, Bath; 1922–24 Harwich County High; 1929–30 Didsbury; 1930–32 Headingley. *Appointments:* 1928–29 Reeth; 1932–36 Bedale; 1936–37 Amble; 1937–42 Newcastle upon Tyne, Heaton and Wallsend; 1942–47 Hexham; 1947–50 Whitehaven; 1950–56 Gateshead West; 1956–61 Gateshead East; 1961–67 Ryton and Prudhoe; 1967–72 Brampton.

REES, Islwyn Howard, 46 Western Ave., Newport, Gwent NPT 3SN. (0633-63473)–BA(Leeds). *b. 14 April 1925, Bargoed, Mid-Glamorgan, South Wales. m. 17 June 1950: 1d.* *Education:* 1937–42 Lewis' Grammar Sch., Pengam, Glamorgan; 1955–58 Leeds Univ.; 1955–58 Headingley. *Appointments:* 1958–62 Aberdare; 1962–67 Swansea; 1967–70 Neath; 1970–78 Cardiff; 1978–82 West Bromwich; 1982– Newport. *Connexional Committees:* 1959–62 Youth Committee District Representative; 1966–69 Education Committee District Representative. *Local Council Committees:* Community Health Council, Cardiff, 1974–78 Representative of the Free Churches. *Publications: Christianity and Marxism* (Lecture given to Students Union of Cardiff 1966); *Meditation and Spiritual Maturity* (Extra-Mural Department of Swansea Univ. 1973). *Special Interests:* Psychotherapy, Counselling, Alternative Healing Therapies, Eastern Mysticism, Yoga, Metaphysics. *Hobbies and Recreations:* Reading, Meditation, Music, Walking, Fishing, Cliff-Climbing, Swimming.

REES, Philip Anthony, 1 Teesgate, Thornaby, Stockton-on-Tees, Cleveland TS17 9AN. (0642-66989)–BA(B'ham). *b. 31 July 1950, West Bromwich, Staffordshire. m. 4 Sept 1971: 2s.* *Education:* 1961–65 West Bromwich Technical-Grammar Sch.; 1965–67 West Bromwich Technical Coll.; 1968– West Bromwich Coll. of Commerce and Technology; 1973–76 Birmingham Univ.; 1970 Cliff Coll.; 1972–76 Queens. *Appointments:* 1976–81 Stoke-on-Trent, Hanley; 1981– Stockton-on-Tees. *Special Interests:* Hospital Chaplaincy, Church Growth, Church Management. *Hobbies and Recreations:* Sport, Reading, Listening to Records, Cirplanology.

REID, Geoffrey Charles, 18 Victoria Rd., Barnsley, South Yorks. S70 2BB. (0226-203557)–MA. *b. 5 Sept 1946, Newcastle upon Tyne. m. 10 Dec 1971: 1d., 1s.* *Education:* 1958–65 Heaton GS, Newcastle upon Tyne; 1965–68 Newcastle upon Tyne, Univ.; 1968–71 Wesley House. *Appointments:* 1971–73 Newcastle upon Tyne, Heaton and Wallsend; 1973–79 Rotherham; 1979– Barnsley. *Parliamentary Service:* Oct 1974 Liberal Candidate, Rother Valley; Prospective Liberal Candidate, Barnsley/Barnsley Central. *Publications: We shall not full direction need—a beginner's guide to the Methodist Conference* (1979). *Special Interests:* 1978–82 Secretary, Alliance of Radical Methodists, 1980– Member Victoria Rd. Manse Community. *Hobbies and Recreations:* Liberal Party Politics, Home Brewing, C.N.D.

RENDER, John Clifford, 46 Thanet St., Clay Cross, Chesterfield, Derbyshire S45 9JT. (0246-862330).
Education: 1946–48 Richmond.
Appointments: 1948–50 Hupeh Dt, China; 1951–56 Mysore Dt, India; 1957–61 Thornley; 1961–67 Walls; 1967–72 Boston; 1972–77 Ashby-de-la-Zouch; 1977– Clay Cross.

RENOUF, Eric John, The Manse, 2 Castle Hill, Carisbrooke, Newport, Isle of Wight PO30 1XX. (0983-522538)–BD. *b. 22 April 1932, Guernsey, Channel Islands. m. 3 April 1956: 2d., 1s.*
Education: 1943–47 Guernsey Intermediate Sch. for Boys; 1954–55 St. Andrew's Coll., Selly Oak; 1971–72 Westminster Pastoral Foundation; 1951–54 Richmond. *Appointments:* 1954–55 Miss. Training; 1955–65 Jamaica Dt; 1965–70 Frome and Shepton Mallet; 1970–79 Swindon; 1979– West Wight.
Council Member: 1967–70 Shepton Mallet Urban District Council.
Special Interests: Pastoral Counselling. *Hobbies and Recreations:* Gardening, Photography.

RENOUF, Francis John, Williams House, Furlong Way, Shrewton, Salisbury, Wilts SP3 4DY. (0980-620338) *b. 11 Jan 1907, Les Gouies. m. 22 April 1931: 3s.*
Education: 1912–20 St. Andrews' Sch., Guernsey, C.I. *Appointments:* 1966–71 Driffield; 1971–75 Radstock.
Parliamentary Service: 1963–66 People's Deputy in Court of Chief Pleas, Sark, C.I.; Member of various Island Committees.
Hobbies and Recreations: Gardening.

RENOUF, Kenneth Basil, 43 The Park, Yeovil, Somerset BA20 1DE. (0935-4542) *b. 3 May 1933, Guernsey, Channel Islands. m. 17 Aug 1957: 2s.*
Education: 1938–40 St. Andrews, Guernsey, Prim. Sch.; 1940–44 Schools in St. Helens, Brighouse; 1944–45 Guernsey Grammar Sch., Oldham; 1945–49 Guernsey Grammar Sch., Guernsey, C.I.; 1953–56 London Univ.; 1953–56 Richmond. *Appointments:* 1956–59 Ipswich; 1959–62 Glossop; 1962–67 Stroud and Cirencester; 1967–72 Bristol North; 1972–75 Liverpool South East; 1975– Yeovil.
Parliamentary Service: 1949–53 British Railways, Southern Region, Guernsey.
Special Interests: Pastoral and Ecumenical Work. *Hobbies and Recreations:* Reading, Watching Sport.

RENSHAW, Norman, 20 St. Gregory's Ave., Salisbury, Wilts. SP2 7JP. (0722-28736) *b. 28 June 1909, Sale, Cheshire. m. 12 Aug 1939. 2d.*
Education: Central Sch., Sale; 1932–35 Hartley. *Appointments:* 1935–38 High Wycombe; 1938–39 Forest of Dean; 1939–42 Buckingham and Brackley; 1942–45 Keighley; 1945–46 Driffield; 1946–49 Helston; 1949–50 Nuneaton; 1950–54 Shaftesbury and Gillingham; 1954–57 Plymouth East; 1957–60 Redditch; 1960–63 Daventry; 1963–64 Abertillery; 1964–65 Rhosymedre and Chirk; 1965–68 Oldbury; 1968–71 Cadishead; 1971–74 Garstang.

REVETT, Geoffrey William, 17 Hoof Close, Littleport, Ely, Cambridge CB6 1HU. (0353-860389) *b. 15 April 1940, Eight Ash Green, Colchester, Essex. m. 25 June 1966: 2d., 1s.*
Education: 1945–51 Eight Ash Green Prim.; 1951–60 Colchester Royal Grammar Sch.; 1962–66 Didsbury, Bristol. *Appointments:* 1966–68 Bude; 1968–70 Barnoldswick; 1970–76 Barnsley; 1976– Ely.
Special Interests: Christian Aid.
Hobbies and Recreations: Cycling, Gardening.

REYNOLDS, Bernard, 26 Orchard Way, Flitwick, Beds. MK45 1LF. (0525-713468) *b. 3 May 1929, Gt. Yarmouth, Norfolk. m. 7 July 1956: 2d.*
Education: Northgate Jun., Gt. Yarmouth; Hospital Boy's Senior Sch., Gt. Yarmouth; 1953–56 Richmond. *Appointments:* 1956–59 Wombwell and Hoyland; 1959–62 Barnsley, Wesley; 1962–69 London, Waltham Abbey; 1969–73 Gosport and Fareham; 1973– Bedford South and Ampthill.
Special Interests: Counselling.
Hobbies and Recreations: Photography, Swimming, Walking, Reading.

REYNOLDS, Dennis George, 72 Cranmore Lane, Aldershot, Hants. GU11 3BB. (0252-23575).
Appointments: 1976–80 Ashford Kent,; 1979– Aldershot, Farnborough and Camberley.

RHODES, John Stuart. 593 Crewe Rd., Wistaston, Crewe, Cheshire CW2 6PX. (0270-68720)–MA. *b. 28 Oct 1932, Batley, Yorkshire. m. 13 Aug 1960: 1d., 1s.*
Education: 1937–43 Birstall County Prim.; 1943–50 Batley Grammar; 1950–54 Univ. Coll., Durham; 1955–57 Fitzwilliam House, Cambridge; 1955–57 Wesley House.
Appointments: 1957–60 Liverpool, Crosby; 1960–65 Tonbridge; 1965–70 Orpington; 1970–75 Durham; 1975–80 Oxford; 1980– Chairman, Chester and Stoke District.
Connexional Committees: Connexional Candidates Connexional Probationers' Oversight, Student Work, Further Training, Property Board, Home Mission Board, GP. *Local Council Committees:* Cheshire County Education Committee.
Special Interests: Education, Music.
Hobbies and Recreations: Rotary.

RIACH, Joseph, 12 High West Lane, Hawthorn, Seaham, Co. Durham SR7 8RY. (0783-270-332)–BD. *b. 11 Nov 1906, Buckie, Scotland. m. 5 Aug 1935: 1d., 1s.*
Education: 1917–23 Buckie Higher Grade; 1928–29 Handsworth; 1929–32 Headingley. *Appointments:* 1932–36 Newbury; 1936–39 London, Ealing and Acton; 1939–44 Wigan; 1944–48 Huddersfield, Lindley; 1942–54 Grimsby, George St.; 1954–58 London, Finsbury Park; 1958–63 Biggleswade; 1963–68 Bridport; 1968–70 Caerphilly.

RICE, David John, 13 Enmore Rd., London SW15 6LL. (01-788-1219) *b. 14 Nov 1945.*
Education: 1970–73 Queen's.
Appointments: 1973–78 Warrington; 1978– Richmond and Hounslow.

RICH, Ronald H., 199 Wilton Rd., Shirley, Southampton SO1 5JA. (0703-771515) *b. 15 Dec 1921, London. m. 3 Aug 1950: 1d., 1s.*
Education: 1946–48 Wesley, Bristol.
Appointments: 1948–51 Brighton and Hove; 1951–55 Birmingham Mission; 1955–62 Colwyn Bay and Llandudno; 1962–69 Lytham St. Annes; 1969–77 Birmingham, Solihull; 1977– Southampton.
Connexional Committees: 1956–68 Social Responsibility; 1973–77 Birmingham District, Synod Secretary.
Special Interests: Christian Drama, Writing for Stage.

RICHARDS, Edgar, 40 Penhallow Rd., Newquay, Cornwall TR7 3DA. (06373–6515)–BA, BD, PhD(Lond.). *b. 17 Sept 1912, Delabole, Cornwall. m. 26 Sept 1939: 1s.*
Education: 1917–24 Tintagel Council Sch.; 1924–29 Sir James Smith Grammar Sch., Camelford; 1930–34 Wolsey Hall, Oxford; 1934–37 Richmond. *Appointments:* 1937–40 Newton Abbot; 1940–45 Chaplain H.M.F.; 1945–46 Bristol, Clifton; 1946–50 Newquay; 1950–54 Bristol South; 1954–59 Launceston; 1959–63 East Wight; 1963–68 Reading; 1968–72 Camelford and Wadebridge; 1972–76 Southampton.
Connexional Committees: 1947–50 Youth Committee: 1968–72 Education Committee.
Special Interests: Youth, Education, Ecumenical Affairs. *Hobbies and Recreations:* Gardening, Tennis, Swimming, Walking.

RICHARDS, Leslie Eric Pearson, 71 Waterloo Rd., Wellington, Somerset TA21 8JF. (082347 2724) *b. 5 Aug 1939, Redditch, Worcestershire. m. 7 Aug 1965: 2d., 1s.*
Education: 1944–50 Headless Cross Sch.; 1950–56 Redditch County High Sch.; 1961–65 Richmond.
Appointments: 1965–67 Bury St. Edmunds and Sudbury; 1967–72 Sheffield North East; 1972–81 Lowestoft and East Suffolk; 1981– Wellington, Somerset.
Special Interests: Christian Unity. *Hobbies and Recreations:* Tennis, Gardening, Listening to Music, The Countryside.

RICHARDS, Malcolm Ernest, Sunny Cottage, 68 Monmouth Rd., Westonzoyland, Bridgwater, Somerset TA7 0HG. (0278-69-287) *b. 27 June 1940, Edgware, Middlesex. m. 12 Oct 1974: 1s.*
Education: 1953–59 Torquay Boy's Grammar Sch.; 1975–77 Portsmouth Polytechnic; 1965–69 Handsworth.
Appointments: 1969–70 Newark; 1970–71 Camelford and Wadebridge; 1971–74 West Somerset; 1974 Bridgwater (O.A.).
Special Interests: Marriage Guidance Council Member. *Hobbies and Recreations:* Sport, D.I.Y.

RICHARDS, Robert Andrew, 15 Churchgate Way, Terrington St. Clement, Kings Lynn, Norfolk PE34 4PG. (0553-828344)–BA(Bristol). *b. 2 May 1945, Salisbury, Wilts. m. 1 June 1968: 2d., 1s.*
Education: 1956–61 Chingford County High Sch.; 1969–72 Brentwood Coll. of Education; 1978–81 Bristol Univ.; 1978–81 Wesley, Bristol. *Appointments:* 1981–Kings Lynn.
Special Interests: History. *Hobbies and Recreations:* Golf, Photography.

RICHARDSON, Harvey Stuart, 31 Kempton Close, Lordswood, Chatham, Kent ME5 8PW. (0634-660149)–BA. *b. 8 Aug 1946, Bushey, Herts. m. 27 July 1974: 1d., 1s.*
Education: 1953–57 Kingsfield Preparatory Sch., Oxhey, Herts.; 1957–64 John Lyon Sch., Harrow; 1964–66 Royal Academy of Music, London; 1971–74 Birmingham Univ.; 1971–75 Queen's.
Appointments: 1975–78 Winsford, Cheshire; 1978– Medway Towns.
Connexional Committees: 1982– Candidates Committee.
Special Interests: Ecumenical Growth in the Churches, Encourage those preparing and training for the Ministry. *Hobbies and Recreations:* Violin, Piano, Reading.

RICHARDSON, John E., 11 Wellesley Rd., Chiswick, London W4 4BS. (01-994-8970)–BA(Leicester), BA(Leeds). *b. 21 Jan 1942, Wigan. m. 12 Aug 1964: 2d.*
Education: 1947–53 St. James' Rd. County Prim. Sch., Orrell; 1953–60 Up Holland Grammar Sch.; 1960–64 Univ. of Leicester; 1964–67 Univ. of Leeds; 1964–67 Headingley; 1980 Methodist Theological Seminary, Seoul, South Korea. *Appointments:* 1967–69 Assistant Tutor, Wesley Coll., Bristol; 1969–74 Bristol South; 1974–76 Streatham and Dulwich; 1976– West London Mission, Hinde St.
Connexional Committees: 1974– Convener of Connexional exumenical Committee; M.C.O.D. Central, G.P. and Asia Committees.
Special Interests: Ecumenical Movement. *Hobbies and Recreations:* Reading, Sport, Gardening.

RICHARDSON, John Fletcher Winter, 5 Roundbarn, Roman Rd., Turton, Bolton. (0204-852981)–BA. *20 May 1934, Newcastle upon Tyne. m. 23 July 1961: 1d., 1s.*
Education: 1947–51 Greener's Academy; 1951–52 Cliff Coll.; 1957–60 Manchester Univ.; 1957–61 Hartley Victoria. *Appointments:* 1961–63 Preston; 1963–66 Accrington; 1966–69 Manchester Mission; 1969–71 Blackburn Mission; 1971 Bolton Mission (B.B.C.).
Council Member: 1973–76 Community Health Councillor.

RICHARDSON, Kathleen Margaret (Mrs), 10 New Lane, Skelmanthorpe, Huddersfield, W. Yorks HD8 9EH. (0484-862572) *b. 24 Feb 1938, Chesterfield. m. 26 Dec 1964: 3d.*
Education: 1942–49 Calow CE; 1949–56 Chesterfield, St. Helena; 1956–58 Stockwell Coll.; 1961–63 Wesley Deaconess Coll.; 1977–79 Wesley House. *Appointments:* 1973–77 Stevenage; 1979– Denby Dale and Clayton West.
Connexional Committees: 1975–77

Building Schemes and Co-op with other Communions; 1980– Doctrinal Committee.

RICHARDSON, Keith, 65 Birchway Ave., Blackpool FY3 8EZ. (0253-32720)–BA. *b. 17 Jan 1943, Bedford. m. 24 June 1972: 1d.*
Education: 1948–54 Thornborough County Prim. Sch.; 1954–58 Buckingham County Secondary Modern; 1970 Cliff Coll.; 1971–74 Hartley Victoria. *Appointments:* 1974–77 Blackburn; 1977– Blackpool North.
Special Interests: Local Radio. *Hobbies and Recreations:* Tropical Fish Keeping.

RICHARDSON, Neil Graham, 64 Brantingham Rd., Whalley Range, Manchester M16 8HQ. (061-226-3616)–MA(Oxon), BA(Cantab), MLitt(Bristol). *b. 2 Dec 1943, Horsforth, West Riding. m. 28 Oct 1972: 2s.*
Education: 1948–55 Westfield County Prim. Sch., Yeadon, Yorks.; 1955–63 Bradford Grammar Sch.; 1963–67 The Queen's Coll., Oxford; 1969–71 Fitzwilliam Coll., Cambridge; 1969–71 Wesley House. *Appointments:* 1971–73 Assistant Tutor, Wesley Coll., Bristol; 1973–77 Oxford; 1977–81 Ecumenical Lecturer, Lincoln Theological Coll., Lincoln; 1981 Manchester and Salford Mission.
Connexional Committees: 1979– Local Preachers' Board of Studies; 1981– Roman Catholic-Methodist Committee. *Publications: Was Jesus Divine?* (Epworth 1979); *The Panorama of Luke* (Epworth/SCM 1982); *Boundaries in the New Testament* (Article, *Epworth Review* Jan 82).
Special Interests: New Testament Studies, Theological Education, Ecumenical Relations. *Hobbies and Recreations:* Cross Country Running, Piano Playing, Gardening.

RICHARDSON, Norman John, The Wilderness, 39 Shirley Church Rd., Shirley, Croydon CR0 5EF. (01-656-2220) *b. 24 Sept 1927, Luton, Beds. (w.): 1d.*
Education: 1938–43 Luton Grammar Sch.; 1951–54 Handsworth. *Appointments:* 1954–57 Bloxwich; 1957–61 Chorley; 1961–62 London Mission East; 1962–67 Fakenham and Wells; 1967–72 Leicester West; 1972–78 Fleetwood; 1978– Division of Social Responsibility, Secretary.
Connexional Committees: 1973–75 Division of Ministries Board; 1974–77 Connexional General Purposes Committee; 1978 Division of Social Responsibility Board.
Special Interests: Current Affairs, Brass Bands.

RICHARDSON, Sidney Yearsley, 22 Garton Rd., Loughborough, Leics. LE11 2DY. (0509-213209)–BA, BD, BSc. *b. 3 June 1910, Woodchurch, Cheshire. m. 27 July 1935: 2s.*
Education: 1915–22 Laird St. Elem. Sch., Birkenhead; 1922–28 Birkenhead Institute; Liverpool Univ. *Appointments:* 1974–77 London, Harrow.
Publications: Article in *From Mow Cop to Peake* on John Skevington 1982 Yorkshire Branch of the Wesley Historical Society.
Special Interests: Methodist History, Offset Litho Printing. *Hobbies and Recreations:* Gardening, Woodwork.

RICHARDSON, Taylor, 6 Ramshill Rd., Scarborough, N. Yorks YO11 2QE. (0723-66369) *b. 13 Sept 1902, Newcastle upon Tyne. m. 9 March 1933: 2d.*
Education: LEA Sch.; Private Studies; 1925–28 Didsbury. *Appointments:* 1924–25 Bedale; 1928–31 Bedale; 1931–33 Spilsby; 1933–37 Stourbridge; 1937–41 Birmingham, Sutton Park; 1941–44 Birmingham, Wesley; 1944–48 Burnley, Fulledge; 1948–53 Sheffield, Norfolk; 1953–58 Worksop; 1958–63 Swanage; 1963–67 Liphook.
Hobbies and Recreations: Reading, Motoring.

RICHES, Colin Edwin, 47 Walcot Rise, Diss, Norfolk IP22 3PD. (0379-2791) *b. 6 Feb 1929, Norwich, Norfolk. m. 19 July 1956: 1d., 1s.*
Education: 1934–39 Hellesdon Jun. Sch.; 1939–41 Hellesdon Central Sch.; 1941–45 Bracondale Sch., Norwich; 1952–55 Headingley.
Appointments: 1951–52 Midhurst; 1955–57 Leeds, Armley; 1957–62 Wymondham and Attleborough; 1962–67 Edinburgh Mission; 1967–76 Martham; 1976– Diss.
Publications: Dew Yew Lissen Hare (1975); *Orl Bewtiful An New* (1978); *Recordings on Home mission Cassettes* (1981, 1982).
Special Interests: Dialect Readings. *Hobbies and Recreations:* Local Radio.

RIDDELL, Robert Gordon, 68 Vicarage Rd., Leyton, London E10 5EA. (01-539-3369)–BSc. *b. 9 May 1946, Glasgow. m. 13 March 1971: 2s.*
Education: 1958–64 Ellon Academy; 1964–68 Aberdeen Univ.; 1980–82 Wesley, Bristol. *Appointments:* 1982– London, Leytonstone and Forest Gate.
Publications: British Patent 1 483 441 (17 Aug 1977).

RIDGE, George Louis William, Meyrick Lodge, 36B Bodorgan Rd., Bournemouth BH2 6NL. (0202-26688) *b. 16 June 1903, Fulham, London. m. 2 April 1938: 2d., 1s.*
Education: Mitcham, Links Rd.; 1932–34 Hartley (External).
Appointments: 1929–31 Shrewsbury; 1932–34 Manchester IV; 1934–37 Southeast London Mission; 1937–44 Radcliffe; 1944–49 Southampton; 1949–54 London, Bayswater; 1954–60 Bournemouth; 1960–67 West Wight; 1967–73 Shaftesbury and Gillingham.
Special Interests: Preaching, Old People's Clubs.

RIDGWAY, Harold Seward, 39 St. Michaels Rd., Pembroke, Dyfed SA71 5JQ. (0646-686040) *b. 17 Jan 1915, Stoke on Trent. m. 14 Aug 1947: 1d.*
Education: –1929 Church Lawton CE, Cheshire; 1938–39 Cliff Coll.; 1939–42 Hartley Victoria.
Appointments: 1942–44 Madeley; 1944–46 Church Stretton; 1946–47 Oakengates; 1947–50 Woodville and Swadlincote; 1950–54 Burnley; 1954–57 Ashton-u-Lyne; 1957–62 Frodsham; 1962–67 Golborne; 1967–70 Bury; 1970–76 Pembroke;

1976–81 Llanelli and Carmarthen. *Hobbies and Recreations:* Photography, Art.

RIDHOLLS, Joseph Alfred David, St. Johns, 22 Liskey Hill, Perranporth, Cornwall TR6 0ET. (087257-2223)–BA(Bristol) *b. 16 Jan 1924, Plymouth. m. 26 May 1953: 4d., 1s.* *Education:* 1929–34 Oxford St. C.P., Plymouth; 1934–35 Public Central Sch., Plymouth; 1935–40 Plymouth Coll.; 1949–52 Bristol Univ.; 1949–52 Didsbury. *Appointments:* 1955–57 Derby South; 1957–62 Perranporth and St. Agnes; 1962–67 Cambridge; 1967–70 Pontefract; 1974–75 Sheffield Inner City Ecumenical Mission; 1975–80 Camborne; 1980– Newquay, Perranporth and St. Agnes. *Publications: Spirit of the Desert* (Epworth 1968); *Spark of Grace* (1978); *Romany Revival (Gypsies for Christ)* (1980). *Special Interests:* Gypsy Evangelism, Youth Work. *Hobbies and Recreations:* Romany Studies.

RIGBY, Jon, Marien Lyst, 26 Cardan Drive, Ben Rhydding, Ilkley, West Yorks. LS29 8PH. (0943-600701) *b. 3 Nov 1914, Atherton, Nr. Manchester. m. 28 July 1945 (w.): 2s.* *Education:* 1920–25 Lee St., Atherton; 1925–28 Central Boys, Scarborough, Yorks; 1928–29 Friarage Boys, Scarborough, Yorks; 1949–53 Hartley Victoria. *Appointments:* 1940–43 Stour Valley Mission, Dorset; 1943–45 Leighton Buzzard, Bedfordshire; 1945–49 Bodmin, Cornwall; 1949–56 Rochdale North, Lancs.; 1956–61 Parkhead and Burnbank, Glasgow; 1961–64 Withington, Manchester; 1964–69 Bradford, Great Horton; 1969–75 Shipley, Yorks.; 1975–78 Motherwell and Wishaw. *Hobbies and Recreations:* Poetry, Astronomy, Drawing, Line.

RIGBY, Philip, Wesley Manse, Christ's Pieces, Cambridge CB1 1LG. (0223-350200)–BA(Nottingham), BA, MA(Cambridge). *b. 27 July 1937, Blackpool, Lancs. m.* *Education:* 1948–55 Arnold Sch., Blackpool; 1957–60 Univ. of Nottingham; 1960–62 Wesley House. *Appointments:* 1962–64 West London Mission, Hinde St.; 1964–67 Burton-on-Trent; 1967–73 Oxford; 1967–73 Assistant Chaplain for Students in Oxford; 1973–80 Hull, West, CCT and Chaplain for Hull Univ.; 1980– Cambridge CCT and Univ. Chaplaincy. *Connexional Committees:* 1976– Board of Ministries Division; 1980– Executive.

RIMMER, Nicholas, 19 Spital Terrace, Gainsborough, Lincs. DN21 2HD. (0427-2714)–MA(Cantab.). *b. 10 April 1928, Hesketh Bank, Nr. Preston, Lancs. m. 29 July 1953: 1d., 1s.* *Education:* 1932–39 Hesketh Bank Prim. C.E. Sch.; 1939–46 Hutton Grammar Sch., Nr. Preston, Lancs.; 1949–52 Cambridge Univ., Fitzwilliam Coll.; 1949–52 Wesley House. *Appointments:* 1948–49 Market Weighton; 1952–53 Presteigne and Kington; 1953–57 Otley; 1957–62 Leeds, Horsforth and Kirkstall; 1962–68 Scunthorpe; 1968–72 Skegness; 1968–78 Synod Secretary of Lincoln District; 1972–79 Grimsby West; 1979– Gainsborough. *Connexional Committees:* 1975–76 Connexional General Purposes Committee: 1979– Budget Committee of mission and Service Fund. *Publication: Is It True* (articles in Methodist Magazine, June-Nov 1968). *Hobbies and Recreations:* Sport, Cricket, Bowls.

ROBB, Frank Everard, 99a Manchester Rd., Southport, Merseyside PR9 9BB. (0704-38286) *b. 10 June 1909, London. m. 17 July 1941: 1d., 1s.* *Education:* 1914–19 Townsend St. Elem. Sch.; 1919–23 Bermondsey Central Sch.; 1933–34 Cliff Coll. *Appointments:* 1950–53 Peak and Bradwell; 1953–57 Melton Mowbray; 1957–60 Northwich; 1960–63 Radcliffe; 1963–68 Bolton; 1968–75 Burnley. *Local Council Committees:* 1964–68 Member of the Lancashire Division of Education No. 12 and Vice Chairman of the Welfare Committee. *Hobbies and Recreations:* Music, Woodwork, Sport.

ROBBINS, Richard Frank, Inverleith, 14 Offley Rd., Sandbach, Cheshire CW11 9AY. (09367-3483)–DipTheol(Lond.). *b. 12 May 1915, Warmington, Warwicks. m. 7 Aug 1954.* *Education:* 1920–21 Warmington Council Sch.; 1921–30 Horton Council, Oxon; 1946–49 London Univ.; 1946–49 Richmond. *Appointments:* 1949–54 Harrow; 1954–57 Fakenham and Wells; 1957–62 Wellingborough; 1962–68 Harpenden; 1968–73 Letchworth; 1973–80 Penrith, Cumbria; 1980– Hospital Chaplain, Grange Hall Hospital, Cheshire. *Connexional Committees:* 1970, 1971, 1972 Candidates. *Special Interests:* Youth Work, House Groups. *Hobbies and Recreations:* Farming, Gardening, Music, Walking.

ROBERTS, Alec Malcolm, St. Helens, Rocky Park Rd., Plymstock, Plymouth, Devon PL9 7DQ. (0752-43270)–BD. *6 Dec 1935, Bristol. m. 13 Aug 1960: 1s.* *Education:* 1946–52 St. George Grammar Sch., Bristol; 1957–60 Richmond. *Appointments:* 1960–63 Llandrindod Wells; 1963–68 Risca and Crosskeys; 1968–75 Buckfastleigh; 1975– Plymouth. *Connexional Committees:* 1966–68 Education and Youth; 1973–76 Division of Ministries Board; 1982– General Purposes: 1976– Synod Secretary. *Hobbies and Recreations:* Reading, Carpentry, Art, Photography, Sport, Philately.

ROBERTS, David, 31 All Saints Rd., Bromsgrove, Worcs. B61 0AG. (0527-73765)–BA(B'ham.) *b. 26 Oct 1934, Lyme Regis. m. 9 Sept 1958: 1d., 2s.* *Education:* Worcester Royal Grammar Sch.; 1955–58 Univ. of Birmingham; 1955–58 Handsworth.

Appointments: 1958–59 Miss. Training; 1959–62 E. Nigeria District; 1962–65 M.L.T.C. Umuahia, Principal; 1965–67 Port Harcourt; 1968–72 Amble; 1972–79 Bolton; 1979– Bromsgrove.
Connexional Committees: 1973–76 Overseas Division Central Committee; 1976– Connexional G.P. *Publications: Ghana Bulletin of Theology* (1962); *Bulletin of the Society for West African Church History; Separatist Churches in Umuahia.*
Special Interests: Aladura Churches in West Africa. *Hobbies and Recreations:* Membership Secretary Jawa CZ Motorcycle Owners Club, Carpentry, Camping, Cycling, Trees, Walking.

ROBERTS, David Kenneth, 9 Boulsworth Rd., Preston Grange, North Shields, Tyne and Wear NE29 9EN. (0632-573776)–BD(Lond.), DipTh(Lond.). *b. 6 Feb 1939, Salford, Lancs. m. 2 July 1966: 2s.*
Education: 1945–50 Cromwell Rd. Prim., Swinton, Lancs.; 1950–55 Leigh Grammar Sch., Leigh, Lancs.; 1962–64 Bible Training Institute, Glasgow; 1964–67 Headingley.
Appointments: 1967–70 Consett; 1970–75 N Shields and Whitley Bay; 1975–80 Harrogate; 1980– Extension Secretary, N.E. England, British and Foreign Bible Society.
Connexional Committees: 1976–82 Local Preachers Connexional Committee.
Special Interests: Bible (Translation, Publication and Distribution), Expository Preaching, Evangelism and Evangelical Witness, Church History. *Hobbies and Recreations:* Cricket and Sport in General, Reading, Music, Photography.

ROBERTS, Edward Alan, 34 Lowbank Court, Willowdale, Ontario, Canada M2M 3A4. (416-225-6758) *b. 17 Feb 1927, Melton Mowbray. m. 7 April 1956: 1d., 1s.*
Education: –1941 Melton Mowbray; 1942–45 Melton Mowbray Technical Coll.; 1966–68 Ryerson Polytechnical Institute, Toronto; 1949–50 Cliff Coll.; 1950–53 Hartley Victoria Coll.; 1953–54 Selly Oak Coll.
Appointments: 1954–61 East Nigeria Dt; 1961–66 Bolton; 1969–74 Kenya Conference; 1974–81 South Derbyshire; 1981– United Church of Canada.
Special Interests: Radio, TV and Film Production (in Kenya). *Hobbies and Recreations:* Philately, Photography.

ROBERTS, Eric Desmond, The Manse, 2 Highercroft Rd., Lower Darwen, Darwen, Lancashire BB3 0QR. (0254-51289) *b. 27 Nov 1916, Lambeth, London. m. 12 Aug 1950: 1d., 1s.*
Education: 1921–27 Erconwald St. Elem. Sch., London W12; 1927–31 North Kensington Central Sch., North Kensington, London W11; 1938–39 Cliff Coll., 1946–49 Hartley Victoria. *Appointments:* 1945–46 Hull North; 1949–50 Garstang; 1950–54 Settle; 1954–59 Bradford, Westbrook; 1959–64 Pudsey; 1964–69 Nuneaton; 1969–74 Sowerby Bridge; 1974–81 Garstang; 1981– Darwen.
Special Interests: Home Missions, Visiting. *Hobbies and Recreations:* Reading, Walking.

ROBERTS, George C., Whitecote, 4 Winchester Rd., Burnham-on-Sea, Somerset TA8 1HZ. (0278-784819)–BA(Leeds), DipEd(Leeds). *b. 16 Sept 1910, Carlton, Nr. Selby, Yorks. m. 25 July 1910: 1d., 2s.*
Education: 1922–29 Goole Grammar Sch.; 1929–33 Univ. of Leeds.
Appointments: 1962–63 Shebbear; 1963–69 Leeds, Bramley, West Leeds and Horsforth; 1969–72 Birmingham, Blackheath.
Connexional Committees: 1958–62 Member of Connexional Education Committee.
Special Interests: Music.

ROBERTS, Harold, 32 Byng Rd., Tunbridge Wells, Kent TN4 8EJ. (0892-21945)–MA(Bangor), PhD(Cambridge), HonDD(Trinity Coll., Dublin). *b. Sept 1896, Ashley, Manchester, Cheshire. m. (1), (2) 4 May 1972.*
Education: Hulme Grammar Sch., Manchester; 1918 Bangor Univ.; 1921–26 Jesus Coll., Cambridge Univ.; 1921–33 Wesley House.
Appointments: 1918–19 Beaumaris, Welsh; 1923–24 Altrincham; 1924–26 Cambridge A.T.; 1926–29 Liverpool, Waterloo; 1929–34 Oxford, Wesley Memorial; 1934–40 Headingley Coll., Tut. Theol.; 1940–41 Richmond Coll. Tut. Theol.; 1941–46 Ipswich, Museum St.; 1946–68 Richmond Coll., Tut. Theol.; 1955–68 Principal; 1957 President of the Conference.
Connexional Committees: President World Methodist Council, 1967 Joint Chairman, Anglian Methodist Unity Commision. *Publications:* Part-author *The Doctrine of the Holy Spirit* (1938); *The Message and Mission of Methodism* (Ed. 1945); *Jesus and The Kingdom of God* (1955); *Anglican-Methodist Conversations* (1963).

ROBERTS, James Edgar, Moresk, 22 Treassowe Rd., Penzance, Cornwall TR18 2AU. (0736-68351) *b. 27 June 1913, Troon, Cornwall. m. 1 Aug 1947: 1d., 1s.*
Education: 1918–27 Carnkie Council. *Appointments:* 1950–51 Wiltshire Mission; 1951–53 Tunstall Jubilee; 1953–56 South Devon Mission; 1956–60 Falmouth; 1960–63 Swansea; 1963–70 St. Columb and Padstow; 1970–74 Redruth; 1974–77 Ringsash; 1977–78 Pontypridd.
Special Interests: New Testament, Church History, Preaching, Pastoral Visitation. *Hobbies and Recreations:* Music, Piano.

ROBERTS, John, Alexandra House, Marine Parade, Dovercourt, Essex CO12 3JY. *b. 27 Oct 1900, Oldham, Lancs. m.: 2d.*
Education: Sutton-in-Ashfield, Wigan and London: Southlands: 1926–29 Didsbury. *Appointments:* 1925–26 Rochdale; 1929–33 Birmingham Mission; 1933–36 Oxford, Wesley Memorial; 1936–40 Boston Central; 1940–45 Mansfield; 1945–48 Wigan; 1948–57 London Mission East; 1957–63 Castleford; 1963–66 Leeds, Bramley and Horsforth.

ROBERTS, John Alun, Cartrefle, Rhydyfoel, Abergele, Clwyd. (0492-56849) *b. 13 Sept 1911, Llanllechid Gwynedd. m. 31 July 1940: 1d., 1s.* *Education:* 1915–25 Llanllechid; 1925–26 Cefnfaes; 1932–33 Ysgol Bethesda; 1934–37 Handsworth. *Appointments:* 1933–34 Ystumtuen; 1937–39 Pwllheli; 1939–40 Dinas Mawddwy; 1940–45 Caergybi ac Amlwch; 1940–45 Llanrwst; 1948–50 Caergybi ac Amlwch; 1950–55 Llangefni; 1955–60 Conwy; 1960–65 Caernarfon; 1965–70 Llandudno; 1070–75 Abergele; 1975–76 Llanrwst.
Publications: 1980 Cofio'r Gorffennol.
Special Interests: Welsh Methodism, Sport, Labour Party. *Hobbies and Recreations:* Any form of manual work.

ROBERTS, John Hugh, Wesley House, Cross Rd., Idle, Bradford BD10 9RU. (0274-613150)–BA(Leeds). *b. 6 Dec 1926, Holyhead. m. July 1954: 3d., 1s.* *Education:* 1939–45 Holyhead Grammar Sch.; 1949–52 Leeds Univ.; 1949–52 Headingley. *Appointments:* 1948–49 Newbury; 1952–54 Beverley; 1954–69 Zimbabwe; 1969–76 Middlesbrough; 1976– Bradford Woodhouse Grove. *Connexional Committees:* 1977–82 Division of Property.
Special Interests: Politics. *Hobbies and Recreations:* Sports, Reading.

ROBERTS, John Roger, 15 Maelgwyn Rd., Llandudno, Gwynedd. (0492-76690)–BA(Wales). *b. 23 Oct 1935, Ruabon. m. 27 Nov 1962: 2d., 1s.* *Education:* 1947–54 John Brigh Grammar Sch., Llandudno; 1954–57 Univ. Coll., Bangor; 1958–60 Handsworth. *Appointments:* 1957–58 Pwllheli Welsh; 1960–63 Pwllheli; 1963–65 Abergele; 1965–70 Llangollen; 1970–81 Dyffryn Conwy; 1981– Arfon.
Parliamentary Service: 1979 Liberal Candidate, Conwy; Prospective Candidate; 1980– President Welsh Liberal Party. *Connexional Committees:* Social Responsibility; Methodist Relief Fund. *Council Member:* 1976– Aberconwy Borough Council. *Local Council Committees:* 1982– Chairman, Environmental Health Committee; Policy and Finance Committee. *Publications:* Editor *Cyhoeddwr* (1970–81); Author *Llandudno–A Resort and its Churches.*

ROBERTS, Robert Arfon, 7A Woodlands Ave., Rhos-on-Sea, Colwyn Bay, Clwyd LL28 4RU. (0492-40082) *b. 10 April 1906, Caernarfon, North Wales. m. 3 Oct 1932: 2d.*
Education: 1913–17 Caernarfon Council; 1917–24 Caernarfon County; 1924–25 Univ. Coll. of N. Wales, Bangor; 1925–28 Handsworth. *Appointments:* 1928–52 Bengal Dt, N. India; 1952–56 Market Drayton; 1956–60 Pontypool, Park Terrace; 1960–66 Tipton, Park Lane; 1966–71 London, Tottenham.

ROBERTS, Robin Edward, 1 Chapel Cottages, Main St., Beckley, Nr. Rye, East Sussex TN31 6RN. (079-726-517) *b. 15 Dec 1939, Sussex. s.*
Education: 1945–51 Northam County Prim. Sch.; 1951–55 Rye County Secondary Sch.; 1970–72 Bible Training Institute, Glasgow; 1972–75 Wesley, Bristol.
Appointments: 1975– Biddulph and Mow Cop.
Hobbies and Recreations: Photography, Record Collecting.

ROBERTSHAW, Norman, 26 Barnes Rd., Darlington, Co. Durham DL3 9BL. (0325 63546) *b. 9 Jan 1922, Stourbridge, Worcs. s.*
Education: 1948–50 Hartley Victoria. *Appointments:* 1947–48 Presteigne and Kington; 1950–52 Liverpool Central; 1952–57 Wigan Wesley; 1957–62 Earlstown; 1962–67 Liverpool North East; 1967–70 Warrington; 1970–76 Edinburgh Mission; 1976– Darlington.

ROBINSON, Arthur, Ebenezer Cottage, Pamber Rd., Silchester, Reading, Berks. RG7 2NY. (0734-700289) *b. 16 June 1921, Liverpool, Lancashire. m. 17 Aug 1950: 1s.* *Education:* 1926–35 Major Lester Council Sch.; 1945–48 Headingley. *Appointments:* 1948–51 Ripley; 1951–58 Burton-on-Trent, George St./Trinity; 1958–64 Workington; 1964–71 Kendal; 1971–76 Abergavenny; 1976–82 Silchester; 1982– Reading and Silchester. *Connexional Committees:* 1961–68 Social Responsibility.
Special Interests: Pastoral Work, Bible Studies. *Hobbies and Recreations:* Music.

ROBINSON, Donald, 2 Croft Cottages, Sunderland St., Tickhill, Doncaster DN11 9QH. *b. 2 Oct 1918, Lancaster. m. 19 Feb 1976: 1d., 1s.*
Education: Darwen Grammar: 1941–42 Hartley Victoria; 1942–43 Headingley; 1943–44 Wesley House; 1944 St. Andrews, Selly Oak. *Appointments:* 1939–40 South Devon Mission; 1940–41 Uttoxeter; 1944–45 Miss. Cttee.; 1945–48 N. China Dt; 1948–49 S.W. China Dt; 1949–58 S. Rhodesia Dt; 1958–63 Bradford, Manningham; 1963–68 Doncaster N.E.; 1968–72 Snaith; 1972–79 Castleford.
Hobbies and Recreations: Gardening, Model Railways.

ROBINSON, Esward, 1 Heathcliffe, Redhills Rd., Arnside, Carnforth, Lancs LA5 0AT. (0524-761768) *b. 21 April 1909, Brotton, Saltburn, Yorks. m. 2 Aug 1937: 1d.* *Education:* 1914–19 Brotton Prim; 1919–20 Loftus Senior; 1920–26 Guisborough Grammar Sch.; 1930–33 Hartley. *Appointments:* 1933–34 Assistant to Chairman of District, Newcastle on Tyne; 1934–37 Newcastle, Central and Sandyford, 1937–39 Glasgow, Alexandra Parade; 1939–43 Glasgow, Parkhead and Burnbank; 1943–45 Loftus and Staithes, 1939–43 Glasgow, Parkhead and Bunrbank; 1943–45 Loftus and Staithes; 1945–50 Redcar, Guisborough and Saltburn; 1950–55 Newcastle on Tyne West; 1955–60 Gateshead East; 1960–63 Bishop Auckland; 1963–67 Kimberley; 1967–71 Derby East; 1971–74 Ashfield.
Hobbies and Recreations: Walking, Reading.

ROBINSON, John Donald, Willows, Anningson Lane, New Waltham, Grimsby, South Humberside DN36 4LQ. (0472-814566)–JP. *b. 3 Sept 1936, Moreton, Cheshire. m. 8 July 1961: 1d., 1s. Education:* 1947–52 Park High Sch., Birkenhead; 1958–62 Hartley Victoria. *Appointments:* 1962–64 Lowestoft; 1964–68 Swinton and Pendlebury; 1068–73 Gt. Yarmouth and Gorleston; 1973– Cleethorpes; 1979– Secretary of Lincoln District Synod.
Connexional Committees: 1982 Suggestion and Memorials. *Council Member:* Justice of the Peace. *Local Council Committees:* 1969–73 Great Yarmouth Education Committee; 1969–73, 1974–78, 1981– Schs, Governor.
Special Interests: Justice of the Peace, Rotary. *Hobbies and Recreations:* Angling, Postcards, Music, Gardening.

ROBINSON, John Walter Richard, The Manse, 2 Richmond Drive, Clacton on Sea, Essex CO15 2PQ. (0255-427874)–DipTheol(Lond.). *b. 6 Dec 1938, Braintree, Essex. m. 17 Aug 1963: 1d., 1s.*
Education: 1943–49 Manor St. Sch., Braintree; 1949–54 County High Sch., Braintree; 1955–58 Coll. of Further Education, Chelmsford; 1959–63 Richmond. *Appointments:* 1963–65 Ipswich; 1965–72 Gt. Yarmouth; 1972– Clacton.
Special Interests: Methodist history, Hymnology, Communication in the Free Church Tradition. *Hobbies and Recreations:* Lecturing on Topographical Detail History of Popular Music, Camping, Vehicle Maintenance, Member National Accordion Organisation.

ROBINSON, Lawrence, Engelberg, Ash Hill, Compton, Wolverhampton, West Midlands. (0902-24947) *b. 21 April 1888, Hull. m. 1919 (w.): 2s. Education:* 1898 Waverley Rd., Higher Grade, Birmingham; 1910–13 Hartley. *Appointments:* 1913–17 Selby; 1917–20 Shipley; 1920–23 Pocklington; 1923–27 Hull VII; 1927–32 Hull I; 1932–36 Old Hill; 1936–41 Darlaston, Slater St.; 1941–45 Blackheath; 1945–50 Birmingham, Smethwick; 1950–54 Walsall, Stafford St. and Walsall.
Connexional Committees: 1927–32 Secretary, Hull District (P.M. Church).
Hobbies and Recreations: Football, Swimming.

ROBINSON, Norman Montague, La Petite Jaomiere, Rue de la Lande, Albecq, Guernsey, C.I. (0481-57274) *b. 12 July 1908, Rotherham. m. 10 Sept 1940 (w.): 3s.*
Education: 1920–26 Rotherham Grammar Sch.; 1931–34 Richmond. *Appointments:* 1934–48 Lucknow Dt., India, 1948–50 Yeovil; 1950–54 Winchester; 1954–59 Medway Towns; 1959–63 Peterborough; 1963–66 Leeds, South; 1966–69 Tipton; 1969–74 Maryport.
Connexional Committees: 1971–74 Central Committee O.M.
Hobbies and Recreations: Wood Carving, Walking, Classical Music.

ROBINSON, Peter W., 11 Spalding Rd., Gosberton, Spalding, Lincs. PE11 4NP. (0775-840323)–BA(Manchester). *b. 11 May 1942, Kidderminster, Worcestershire. m. 24 July 1971.*
Education: 1953–57 Sladen CE Secondary Sch., Kidderminster; 1969–72 Manchester Univ.; 1966–67 Cliff Coll.; 1968–72 Hartley Victoria. *Appointments:* 1972–77 Louth; 1977–82 Lincoln North; 1982– Spalding.
Connexional Committees: 1976–79 Education and Youth Divisional Board.
Special Interests: Methodist History. *Hobbies and Recreations:* Badminton.

ROBINSON, Wilfred H., 8 Aspin View, Knaresborough, N. Yorkshire HG5 8HN. (0423-864380)–MA(Cantab.). *b. 1912, Burton-on-Trent. m. 1939: 2s.*
Education: 1922–31 Burton Grammar Sch.; 1931–34 Cambridge, Fitzwilliam; 1934–37 Manchester; 1934–37 Hartley Victoria.
Appointments: 1937–39 Student Christian Movement; 1939–40 Bury and Ramsbottom; 1940–43 Gen. Sec. Christian Auxiliary Movement; 1943–46 King's Lynn; 1946–50 Ryton and Prudhoe; 1950–53 Hexham; 1953–59 London, Leysian Mission; 1959–64 London, Walthamstow; 1964–71 London, Ilford; 1971–75 Knaresborough.
Connexional Committees: 1945–64 Education: 1946–64 Christian Citizenship (Exec 1947–64). *Council Member:* 1940–42 Commission of the Churches for Int. Friendship and Social Resp.; 1943 Foundation Member British Council of Churches; 1947–62 Free Church Federal Council; Exec. 1953–62. *Local Council Committees:* 1966–70 London Borough of Redbridge Educ. Cttee. *Publications:* Editor *Community* (1940–43).
Special Interests: People, Ecumenism, Hospital Chaplaincy. *Hobbies and Recreations.* Philately.

ROBSON, Aubrey, 33 Eastwood Drive, Rainham, Essex RM13 9HH. (04027-52031)–(M.I.Mech. E.). *b. 1 April 1925, Newcastle-upon-Tyne. m. 18 June 1949: 1d., 2s.*
Education: 1930–36 Elem. Sch.; 1937–39 Junior Technical Sch., Newcastle-upon-Tyne; 1940–48 Rutherford Coll. of Technology, Newcastle-upon-Tyne; 1972–74 Hartley Victoria. *Appointments:* 1974–78 Industrial Chaplain, Barking Council of Churches; 1978– London Mission, East Ham.
Special Interests: Work Among the Mentally Handicapped. *Hobbies and Recreations:* Music.

ROBSON, William Joseph, 18 Baring Rd., Southbourne, Bournemouth, Dorset BH6 4DS. (0202-424401) *b. 6 June 1910, Waskerley, Co. Durham. m. (1) 3 Sept 1939 (died 1960); (2) 10 June 1961: 1d., 1s.*
Education: 1915–20 Reid St., Darlington; 1920–24 Central Commercial Sch, Darlington; 1932–35 Hartley Victoria. *Appointments:* 1935–36 Supply, Bellingham; 1936–38 Allendale; 1938–41 Carlisle, Cecil St.; 1941–47 Perth; 1947–52 Shipley, Bradford; 1952–58 Finchley and Hendon; 1958–61 Guildford; 1961–68 Walton-on-Thames; 1968–

73 Ashford, Kent; 1973–76 Camberley.
Connexional Committees: 1953–58 Secretary of London N.W. Synod; 1951–76 Correspondence, Daily Record, Journal; Secretary of the Conference; Trustee and Chairman of the Methodist Ministers Annuitant Society; Member of the Board of Management and Executive of Methodist Homes for the Aged.
Publications: Methodist Recorder, Conference Reports, Book Reviews and Devotional Columns.
Special Interests: Care of Elderly, Samaritans, School Governor, Political History. *Hobbies and Recreations:* Golf , Cars, Gardening.

ROCHESTER, Albert, Dene Holm, The Green, Upper Poppleton, York YO2 6DP. (0904-794626) *b. 29 Sept 1936, Sunderland. m. 30 July 1971: 3d.*
Education: 1947–52 Monkwearmouth Grammar Sch., Sunderland; 1963–66 Headingley.
Appointments: 1967–68 Aberdare; 1968–73 Withernsea; 1974–81 Shipley and Bingley; 1981– York South.
Hobbies and Recreations: Gardening.

RODD, Cyril Stanley, 43 Higher Drive, Banstead, Surrey SM7 1PL. (01-393-1909)–MA, MSocSc, PhD. *b. 10 Oct 1928, Portsmouth.*
Education: 1940–47 Portsmouth Grammar Sch.; 1949–54 Wesley House. *Appointments:* 1948–49 Poole, 1954–56 Somerset Mission; 1956–67 Handsworth Coll., Tutor; 1967–69 Research Associate, Univ. of Kent at Canterbury; 1969– Southlands Coll., Lecturer and Roehampton Institute of Higher Education.
Connexional Committees: 1956–67 Ministerial Training Committee (in rotation as Handsworth Staff Representative). *Publications: The Psalms* (2 Vols. Epworth Press 1963, 1965); *Kingship and the Cult* (LQHR 1959, 21–26); *Modern Issues in Biblical Study: Rediscovered Hebrew Meanings* (ET71, 1959–60, 131–134); *Spirit or Finger* (ET72, 1960–61, 157–158); *The Basis of Christian Ethics* (ET 75, 1963–64, 16–19); *Is there a specifically Christian Ethic?* (ET 77, 1965–66, 147–49); *The Christian Faith in a Secular Society* (ET 78, 166–67, 179–82); *The Family in the Old Testament* Bible Translator, 18, 167, 19–26); *Some Aspects of the Sociology of Religion* (LQHR 1967, 128–137); *Church Affiliation and Denominational Values* (Sociology 2, 1968, 79–90); *Are the Ethics of Jesus Situation Ethics?* (ET 79, 1967–68, 167–170); *Can the Churches be Opinion Leaders?* (New Directions 5.19, 25–29); *What happens to the Ordinand?* (Theology LXXII. 591, 408–412); *Learning from the Social Sciences: Part II. XI: Implications of the Sociological Study of Religion* (ET 83, 1971–72, 68–73); *Shall not the Judge of all the Earth do what is Just? (Gen 18:25)* (ET 83, 171–72, 137–139); *Religiosity and its Correlates: Hall Green, Birmingham* (in *Religion in the Birmingham Area,* ed. Alan Bryman, Univ. of Birmingham, 1976); *Some Further Studies in St. Mark's Gospel* (ET 87, 175–76, 297–301); *Max Weber and Ancient Judaism* (SJTh 32, 1979, 457–469); *The Synoptic Problem* (Roehampton Monograph Series, 2, 1979); *On Applying a Sociological Theory to Biblical Studies* (JSOT19, 1981, 95–106); *Man, Metaphor and Mediation* (Peake Memorial Lecture 1982, unpublished); *Salvation Proclaimed: XI. Colossians 2:8–15* (ET94, 1982–83, 36–41); Editor, *The Expository Times* (since 1976).
Hobbies and Recreations: Music.

RODGERS, Peter Warwick, 63 Valentine Rd., Kings Heath, Birmingham B14 7AJ. 021 444-2367)–BD(Lond.). *b. 29 Sept 1929, Liverpool. m. 10 Aug 1956: 2s.*
Education: 1939–46 Holt High Sch.; London Univ.; 1951–54 Richmond.
Appointments: 1950–51 Kirby Moorside; 1954–55 Home Mission Caravan Mission, Oxford and Gloucester District; 1955–59 Barton-on-Humber; 1959–64 Hull West; 1964–69 Ellesmere Port; 1969–78 Birmingham, Islington and Quinton; 1978– Birmingham, Moseley Rd. and Sparkhill.
Connexional Committees: 1967–68, 1970–81 Church Membership; 1974–79 Board of Ministries.
Special Interests: Property Matters.
Hobbies and Recreations: Painting in Watercolours and in Pastels.

RODGERS, Stanley, 62 Kendal Green, Kendal, Cumbria LA9 5PT. (0539-23229) *b. 18 Dec 1907, Beighton, N.E. Derbyshire. m. 28 July 1938.*
Education: 1932–34 Headingley.
Appointments: 1931 Wellington Salop; 1934–35 President's List; 1935–36 Darlington North; 1937–40 Brighton, Dome Mission; 1940–45 Chaplain H.M.F.; 1945–47 Sowerby Bridge; 1947–52 Wellington, Salop; 1952–56 London, Ealing; 1956–61 Otley; 1961–67 Bedale; 1967–73 Saltburn, Redcar and Guisborough
Connexional Committees: 1966–72 General Chapel Committee, Manchester.

ROEBUCK, Albert, The Watchorn Manse, Derby Rd., Alfreton, Derbyshire DE5 7AQ. (0773-832063) *b. 28 July 1929, Mexborough, Yorkshire. m. 13 March 1952: 1d., 2s.*
Education: 1942–47 Mexborough Grammar Sch.; 1949–50 Cliff Coll.; 1961–63 Headingley. *Appointments:* 1963–67 Glasgow West; 1967–72 Gornal and Sedgley; 1972–81 Macclesfield; 1981– Alfreton, Watchorn.

ROEBUCK, Arthur, 79 Vernon Rd., Worsbrough, Barnsley, South Yorkshire S70 5HH. (0226-84798) *b. 19 Oct 1907, Salford, Manchester. m. 1936: 1s.*
Education: 1912–21 Shepley Council; 1922–28 Huddersfield Technical (part-time); 1932–34 Hartley Victoria. *Appointments:* 1931–32 Swansea; 1934–38 Bideford; 1938–41 Bridgwater; 1941–45 Ifracombe; 1945–52 Barnsley West; 1952–59 South Normanton; 1959–66 Wirksworth; 1966–73 Barnsley.
Special Interests: Christian Aid,

Temperance, Free Church Council. *Hobbies and Recreations:* Gardening.

ROEBUCK, Stuart Walton, The Manse, Culford Sch., Culford, Bury St. Edmunds, Suffolk IP28 6TU. (028-484-576)–BD(Lond.). *b. 28 June 1939, Huddersfield. m. 12 Oct 1963: 1d., 1s.*
Education: 1944–50 Berry Brow Prim. Sch., Huddersfield; 1950–55 Almondbury Grammar Sch., Huddersfield; 1974–77 London Univ. (External); 1974–77 Wesley, Bristol. *Appointments:* 1977–82 Guildford; 1982– Culford Sch., Bury St. Edmunds, Chaplain. *Local Council Committees:* 1979–82 Surrey Council of Churches, Local Radio Committee.
Special Interests: Marshall Scholarship in 1980, Fellow of the Chartered Insurance Institute.

ROGAN, John, 26 Mayfield Rd., St. Annes-on-Sea, Lancs. FY8 2DP. (0253-711717) ***b. 24 June 1914, Whitehaven, Cumbria. m.** 9 Jan 1946: 2s.*
1939–42 Hartley Victoria.
Appointments: 1942–43 Stoke-on-Trent, Hanley; 1943–48 Cheadle, Staffs; 1948–51 Manchester, Denton; 1951–55 Buxton; 1955–62 Whaley Bridge; 1962–67 Brampton; 1967–74 Glossop; 1974–77 Nottingham East; 1977–80 Fleetwood.

ROGERS, Brian William, 14 Well St., Bury St. Edmunds, Suffolk IP33 1EQ. (0284 4574)–BA(B'ham.). *b. 10 May 1932, Slough Buckinghamshire. m. 12 April 1958: 1d., 2s.*
Education: 1937–42 Farnham Royal Prim. Sch.; 1942–50 Sir William Borlase Sch., Marlow, Bucks; 1953–56 Birmingham Univ.; 1956–57 The Biblical Seminary in New York; 1953–56 Handsworth.
Appointments: 1956–57 Travelling Scholar; 1957–59 Brighton, Dome Mission; 1959–63 Goole; 1963–67 Durham; 1967–72 St. Albans; 1972–79 Wallasey; 1979– Bury St. Edmunds; 1968–72 H.M. Secretary, London, North West; 1973–75 Property Secretary, Liverpool; 1975–79 Synod Secretary, Liverpool. *Connexional Committees:* 1964–67 H.M. Department Prison sub-Committee; 1973–79 Board of Property Division.

ROGERS, Donald Guy, 1 Emanuel Rd., Langdon Hills, Basildon, Essex SS16 6EX. (0268-42079)–BA(Bristol), BD(Lond.), MTh(Lond.). *b. 30 May 1937, Clapham, London. m. 9 Aug 1961; 1d., 2s.*
Education: 1942–43 Wimbledon Park Sch.; 1943–48 London Rd., Burgess Hill; 1948–55 Brighton Hove and Sussex Grammar Sch.; 1955–58 Univ. of Bristol; 1958–61 Richmond. *Appointments:* 1961–66 Mansfield West; 1966–68 London Mission East; 1968–71 London, Leytonstone and Forest Gate; 1971–76 Wisbech; 1976–77 The Hengrave Community (O.A.); 1977–82 Cwm and Kingstone; 1982– Basildon. *Connexional Committees;* 1973–74 President's Commission on Spirituality; 1975–82 Faith and Order. *Publications: Catholic Growth in Methodism* (with C.N.R. Wallwork 1971); M.Th. Dissertation Serialised in the *Bulletin of the Methodist Sacramental Fellowship* (1972).
Special Interests: 1974– Chairman of the Methodist Sacramental Fellowship. *Hobbies and Recreations:* Singing, Drawing.

ROGERS, Edward, 49 Fernhurst Rd., Croydon, Surrey CR0 7DJ. (01-656-1729)–MA, BD. *4 Jan 1909, Fleetwood, Lancashire. m. (1) 21 Aug 1937; (2) 3 Oct 1979.*
Education: 1919–27 Baines, Poulton-le-Fylde Grammar Sch.; 1927–33 Manchester Univ.; 1930–33 Hartley. *Appointments;* 1933–37 East London Mission; 1937–39 Bakewell; 1939–47 Birmingham, Sutton Park; 1947–50 Southport North; 1950–75 Secretary Dept. of Christian Citizenship, Social Responsibility Div.; President of the Methodist Conference 1960.
Connexional Committees: 1950–75 Home Mission, Overseas, Education and Youth, Social Responsibility.
Council Member: 1950–80 British Council of Churches; 1953– Free Church Federal Council; 1956–70 W.C.C. (C.C.I.A.). *Publications:* Numerous (see *Who's Who*).
Special Interests: Theology, Science, History, Social Questions. *Hobbies and Recreations:* Country Walks, Miscellaneous Reading.

ROGERS, William Garth, Central Hall, Oldham St., Manchester M1 1JT. (061-236-5141)–BA. *b. 23 Feb 1939, Cardiff. m. 21 July 1962: 1d., 3s.*
Education: 1949–54 Abertillery Grammar; 1958–62 Handsworth.
Appointments: 1962–64 Coventry Mission; 1964–70 South London Mission; 1970–72 Medway Towns; 1972–77 Croydon; 1977– Manchester and Salford Mission.
Connexional Committees: 1978–82 Candidates Committee; 1978–82 Inner City Committee. *Local Council Committees:* 1965–70 Inner London Education Authority; 1970–72 Kent Education and Youth Committee; 1972–77 Croydon Youth Committee.
Special Interests: Mission, Youth Work. *Hobbies and Recreations:* Golf, Music.

ROGERSON, Gilbert Eric, Upper Flat, 7 Hurst Rd., Eastbourne, East Sussex, BN21 2PJ. (0323-639506) *b. 5 Nov 1913, Ashton-under-Lyne. m. 29 Dec 1942: 1d.*
Appointments: 1964–66 Andover; 1966–69 Mid Wiltshire; 1969–74 Sittingbourne and Sheerness; 1974–76 Stoke-on-Trent, Burslem; 1976–78 President's List.
Special Interests: Family Life, Preaching Appointments, Bible Reading, Sermon Preparation, General Reading, Favourite Authors G. Campbell Morgan, Martin Lloyd-Jones, R. H. Hudson. *Hobbies and Recreations:* Woodwork, Television Programmes dealing with Wildlife, Music.

ROGERSON, Ralph, 72 Highmoor Rd., Caversham, Reading RG4 7BG. (0734-472223)–BA(Open). *b. 24 Feb 1923, Widnes, Lancashire. m. 15 Aug 1953: 1d., 1s.*
Education: 1927–34 Farnworth, Widnes, CE; 1934–38 Widnes Central; 1948–50 Handsworth.

Appointments: 1947–48 Belper; 1950–51 Wolverton/Dunstable; 1951–53 Stretford and Urmston; 1953–57 Runcorn; 1957–62 Warrington; 1962–68 Douglas, Isle of Man; 1968–73 Manchester Mission; 1973–77 Birkenhead; 1977– Reading.
Connexional Committees: 1982– Invalid Ministers Rest Fund. *Local Council Committees:* 1974–77 School Governor, Wirral; 1982– School Governor, Caversham.
Special Interests: Drama, Politics, Sport, Travel (inc. USSR and USA). *Hobbies and Recreations:* Sport, Reading, Theatre.

ROLPH, Geoffrey Albert, 30 Napier Ave., Fulham, London SW6 3PT. (01-736-4537) *b. 7 Dec 1927, Clapton, London. m. 17 July 1954 (w.): 1d., 1s.*
Education: 1932–38 Chapelend and Winn's Ave., Walthamstow; 1938–43 South West Essex Technical Coll. and Sch. of Art; 1949–51 Handsworth. *Appointments:* 1948–49 Liverpool, Central; 1951–54 Towcester; 1954–59 Colne; 1959–63 Huddersfield, Fartown Trinity; 1963–68 Spalding; 1968–73 Norwich, St. Peters; 1973–81 Tottenham; 1981– London Mission, Hammersmith and Fulham. *Special Interests:* Ecumenism, Justice and Peace. *Hobbies and Recreations:* Sports, Stamps, Camping.

ROONEY, William John Wesley, 40 The Broadway, Minster, Sheerness, Kent ME12 2SB. *b. 28 June 1937, Enniskillen, N. Ireland. m. 20 June 1964: 1d.*
Education: 1942–50 Lisblake, 1950 51 Jone's Memorial; 1951–54 Enniskillen Technical Coll.; 1960–64 Hartley Victoria. *Appointments:* 1964–66 Leominster; 1966–71 Abergavenny; 1971–77 Newport, Gwent; 1977– Sittingbourne. *Hobbies and Recreations:* Bird Watching, Carpentry.

ROOS, Charles Edward, 6 Woodcock Hill, Kenton, Harrow, Middx. HA3 0JG. (01-907-3042)–BD(Lond.). *30 April 1931, London. m. 23 Aug 1958: 2s.*
Education: 1942–47 Strode's Sch., Egham, Surrey; 1950–53 Loughborough Coll., Leicestershire (Teaching Certificate and Diploma of Loughborough Coll.); 1955–58 Richmond. *Appointments;* 1958–61 Holyhead; 1961–67 Ipswich; 1967–76 Dorking and Horsham; 1976– Harrow.
Connexional Committees: 1970–80 Education and Youth.
Special Interests: Music. *Hobbies and Recreations:* Sport, Gardening.

ROPER, Ronald, 34 Westville Oval, Harrogate, N. Yorkshire HG1 3JW. (0423-504158)–BA. *b. 9 June 1928, Bedlington, Northumberland. m. 14 Aug 1958.*
Education: 1933–37 Bedlington Council Inf./Jun. Sch.; 1937–39 Ormalington C.P. Sch.; 1939–46 Blyth Grammar Sch.; 1947–49 St. John's Coll., York; 1955–58 Didsbury, Bristol. *Appointments:* 1958–62 Jarrow; 1962–65 Haltwhistle; 1965–69 Sheffield South; 1962–72 Staveley; 1972–77 Sheffield, Brunswick; 1977–80 Durham Coast and Peterlee; 1980– Harrogate.

ROSAMOND, Cyril Clifford, 20 Rufford Ave., New Ollerton, Newark, Notts. NG22 9PN. (0623-860354)–BA. *b. 31 Jan 1926. m. 24 July 1953: 3d., 1s.*
Education: 1949–52 Wesley, Bristol. *Appointments:* 1948–49 Ambleside and Uxbridge, Hayes and Yiewsley; 1954–57 Edinburgh Mission; 1957–60 Bloxwich; 1960–65 Blackburn, Trinity; 1965–70 Bedford North; 1970–73 South Craven; 1973–78 York, Wesley; 1978– Mansfield, Bridge St.

ROSE, Donald, 26 Coombe Rise, Findon Valley, Worthing, West Sussex BN14 0ED. (090671-2350)–MA. *b. 7 May 1909, Sheffield, Yorkshire. m. 20 April 1937: 1d., 1s.*
Education: Sheffield Central Secondary Sch.; 1933–36 Manchester Univ.; 1940–42 Birmingham Univ.; 1930–34 Victoria Park.
Appointments: 1934–38 Oldham, Union St.; 1938–42 Birmingham, Tyseley; 1942–48 Bristol East; 1948–52 Cambridge, Wesley; 1952–64 Worthing; 1964–71 Oxford, Wesley Memorial; 1971–75 Gloucester.
Connexional Committees: 1948–52 Governor, Southlands Coll.; 1965–71 Governor, Westminster Coll.
Publications: The Man Who Broke History in Two (1948); *Hints on Being a Methodist* (1953).

ROSE, John Ashley, 10 Park Rd., Chipping Norton, Oxon OX7 5PA. (0608 3966)–BA(B'ham.), BD(Manchester). *b. 8 Feb 1911, Knighton, Powys. m. 25 April 1939 (w.): 1d., 1s.*
Education: 1916–22 Prim.; 1922–28 Priory County Sch., Shrewsbury; 1928–32 Birmingham Univ.; 1932–35 Manchester Univ.; 1932–35 Hartley Victoria. *Appointments:* 1935–36 Jamaica District; 1936–37 Oundle; 1937–44 Western Nigeria Dt; 1944–47 East Suffolk; 1947–51 Peterborough; 1951–56 Dudley; 1956–61 Birmingham Wesley; 1961–66 Evesham; 1966–72 Knighton, Powys; 1972–75 Shropshire South.

ROSE, Michael Benjamin Colton, The Manse, Manor Hall Rd., Southwick, Brighton BN4 4NA. (0273-593467)–BSc. *31 March 1925, London. m. 25 Aug 1951: 2d.*
Education: Bromley County Sch.; Lincoln City Sch.; Leeds Univ.; 1949–51 Didsbury. *Appointments:* 1947–51 Glasgow, Parkhead; 1951–53 Edinburgh, Leith; 1953–56 Pocklington; 1956–57 Jamaica Dt, W.I.; 1957–61 North Allerton; 1961–66 Hull, Trinity; 1966–71 Retford; 1971–76 Pontefract; 1976–81 South Craven; 1981 Brighton and Hove.
Special Interests: Living. *Hobbies and Recreations:* 19th Century illustrated books.

ROSE, Ronald Harry, 15 Bearstead Rise, Crofton Park, London SE4 1RQ. (01-699-6352)–BD(Lond.). *b. 7 Dec 1913, Wandsworth, London. m. 29 Nov 1941; 3d., 1s.*
Education: 1919–27 Honeywell Rd., Battersea, London S.W.11, Infs. and Elem.; 1927–31 BEC Secondary Sch., Beechcroft Rd., Tooting, London; 1931–32 Regent St. Polytechnic, London; 1946–48 Richmond. *Appointments:* 1948–56 Sunderland North; 1956–61 Durham;

1961–66 Kilburn and Hampstead; 1966–69 Watford; 1969–79 Free Church Federal Council, Secretary to Hospital Chaplaincy Board. *Connexional Committees:* 1964–66 Candidates Committee. *Special Interests:* Music, Peace Movement Activities. *Hobbies and Recreations:* Pianoforte, Reading, Bowls.

ROSE, Walter Stanley, 281 Otley Rd., Leeds LS16 5LN. (0532-785546)–BD(Lond.). *b. 6 July 1923, Willenhall, Staffs. m. 29 July 1950 (w.): 1d., 1s.*
Education: 1928–31 Normanby, Eston, Prim.; 1931–33 Holmfirth Prim.; 1933–42 Kingswood Sch.; 1942–46 War Service, Royal Marines; 1946–49 Headingley. *Appointments:* 1949–55 Chaplain, Culford and East Anglian Sch.; 1955-58 Barnsley East; 1958–64 Leeds, Headingley; 1964–71 Knaresborough; 1971–78 Otley; 1978– Chairman of Leeds District; 1962–78 Secretary of Synod, Leeds. *Connexional Committees:* 1956–58 Youth Council; 1955–58 SS Committee: 1957–58 MAYC Committee; 1958–74 Ministerial Training; 1958– Probationers Oversight; 1970– General Purposes; 1978– Home Mission; 1974– Ministers Retirement Fund; 1966–67 and 1978– Stationing; 1972–77 WHS and IWHS; 1978 Archives and History. *Local Council Committees:* 1979–83 Moderator, Leeds Free Church Federal Council.
Publications: 1961 Sesquicentenary Story.
Special Interests: Rugby Football, Headingley FC and Yorkshire Referees Society. *Hobbies and Recreations:* Philately MPS, Music MCMS, PSV Circle, Registration Information Services.

ROSKILLY, Margaret Lilian, 46 Station Rd., Findochty, Buckie, Banffshire AB5 2PJ. *b. 26 Oct 1947, Roseworthy, Cornwall. s.*
Education: 1953 Connor Downs Prim.; 1954–59 Kehelland Prim.; 1959–62 Treswithian Secondary; 1963–66 Cornwall Technical Coll.; 1966–69 Furzedown Coll. of Education, London; 1972–73 Kingsmead; 1978–80 Wesley, Bristol. *Appointments:* 1980– North Scotland Mission.

ROSS, William M., 38 Compton Rd., Heaton, Newcastle-upon-Tyne NE6 5QL. (0632-655907) *1 April 1926, London. m. 5 Aug 1950: 4s.*
Education: 1948–50 Richmond.
Appointments: 1946–47 H.M. Forces; 1947–48 Bristol, Kingswood; 1950–62 Bahamas Dt, West Indies; 1962–65 Liverpool South East; 1965–66 Jamaica Dt; 1966–72 Maryport; 1972–78 Hetton; 1978– Newcastle-upon-Tyne, Heaton and Wallsend.

ROSSITER, Henry Sydney Frederic, Gaston Cottage, Tisburn, Salisbury, Wiltshire SP3 6LG. (0747-870604) *b. 15 Oct 1896, Reading, Berkshire. m. 15 Oct 1926: 1d., 2s.*
Education: Reading Higher Elem.; 1921–23 Richmond. *Appointments:* 1923–27 South China Dt; 1927–33 Bahamas Dt; 1933–39 South Rhodesia Dt; 1939–42 Leamington, Dale St.; 1942–45 Redditch; 1945–47 Stockport, Trinity; 1947–50 Swindon, Bath Rd.; 1950–52 Thame and Watlington; 1952–55 West Bromwich, Hill Top; 1955–58 South Derbyshire; 1958–61 Stoke-on-Trent, Hanley Trinity; 1961–65 Peterborough.

ROTHWELL, Frank, 12 Goodrington Rd., Paignton, Devon TQ4 7LG. (0803-843691) *b. 30 Dec 1920, Manchester. m. 12 Aug 1950: 2d., 1s.*
Education: 1925–27 Seymour Rd. Prim.; 1927–31 Carrington Jun.; 1931–35 Cadishead Secondary Modern; 1948–50 Headingley.
Appointments: 1946–48 Raunds; 1950–56 Bristol, King St.; 1956–61 Newark; 1961–68 Hoylake and W. Kirby; 1968–74 Exeter; 1974– Torbay.
Connexional Committees: 1956–61 Probationers; 1968–74 Home Mission.
Hobbies and Recreations: Sports.

ROTHWELL, Malcolm Arthur, 7 Albany Terrace, Dundee DD3 6HQ. (0382-23059)–BSc(Lond.), BD(Manch.), PhD(Edin.). *b. 17 Sept 1943, Eccles, Lancs. m. 20 Aug 1970: 1d., 2s.*
Education: 1955–62 Bolton Sch., Lancs; 1963–67 and 1968–69 Goldsmiths Coll., Univ. of London; 1970–72 Univ. of Edinburgh; 1969–72 Hartley Victoria. *Appointments:* 1972–74 Edinburgh Mission; 1974–77 Nottingham Central; 1977–81 Chaplain, Hunmanby Hall; 1981– Dundee, Perth and Blairgowrie.
Connexional Committees: 1977–79 Connexional working party on election of Ministerial Candidates.
Special Interests: Selection of Ministerial Candidates: Marriage Counselling, Religious Education.
Hobbies and Recreations: Tropical Fish, Gardening.

ROUTH, Stanley, 5 Raines Meadows, Grassington, Skipton, N. Yorks. BD23 5NB. (0756-752647) *b. 29 Nov 1914, Winteringham, South Humberside. m. 7 March 1953: 1d., 1s.*
Education: 1919–29 Winteringham; 1935–36 Cliff Coll.; 1938–40 Handsworth; 1940–41 Headingley.
Appointments: 1941–45 Presteigne and Kingston; 1945–49 Grantham; 1949–54 Bridgend; 1954–57 Guernsey; 1957–60 Hull East; 1960–63 Preston, Trinity; 1963–66 Colne; 1966–72 Jersey; 1972–75 Appleby; 1975–80 Sunderland, North.
Special Interests: Church History.
Hobbies and Recreations: Bee Keeping, Fly Keeping, Water Colour.

ROUTLEDGE, Norman Thurston, 7 Selby Terrace, Maryport, Cumbria CA15 6NF. (090081-2614).
Education: 1954–57 Headingley.
Appointments: 1957–60 Shildon; 1960–67 The Hartlepools; 1967–74 Hull East; 1974– Maryport.

ROWE, Arthur. *b. 14 Sept 1930, Walthamstow. m. 1964: 2s.*
Education: 1935–41 Walthamstow, Chapel End Sch.; 1941–47 South West Essex Technical Coll., Walthamstow; 1954–57 Didsbury, Bristol. *Appointments:* 1957–60 Devonport; 1960–64 Sunderland North; 1964–68 Ryton and Prudhoe; 1968–79 Leicester South East; 1979–

Aldershot, Farnborough and Camberley.
Special Interests: Community Church. *Hobbies and Recreations:* Photography, D.I.Y., Art, Music, Sport.

ROWE, Colin Gordon, 76 Coombe Lane West, Kingston upon Thames, Surrey KT2 7DA. (01-949-3340) *b. 29 Sept 1927, Hull. m. 25 Aug 1954: 1d., 1s.*
Education: Hymers Coll., Hull; 1949–52 Headingley. *Appointments:* 1948–49 Barton on Humber; 1952–54 Wymondham; 1954-58 Hornsea, Trinity; 1958–64 Birmingham Mission; 1964–72 Aldershot and Farnborough; 1972–80 Wimbledon; 1980–81 Slough; 1981– Chairman, London, South West District.

ROWE, Trevor Taylor, 29 Briar Rd., Kenton, Harrow, Middx. HA3 0DP. (01-907-3530)–BSc(Lond.), MA(Cantab.), BD(Hull). *b. 17 Dec 1929, Hull. m. 30 July 1955: 2d.*
Education: 1938–48 Hymers, College, Hull; 1948–51 Univ. Coll. of Hull; 1951–53 Univ. of Cambridge; 1954–58 Univ. of Hull; 1951–53 Wesley House. *Appointments:* 1953–55 Market Weighton; 1955–60 Hull East; 1960–65 Southport South; 1965–70 Birmingham, Moseley Rd. and Sparkhill; 1970–79 Queen's Coll., Lecturer in Pastoral Theology, Senior Methodist Tutor, Acting Principal; 1979– General Secretary, Division of Ministries. *Publications:* ed. *Queen's Sermons* (Epworth 1973); *St. Augustine, Pastoral Theologian* (Fernley Hartley Lecture) (Epworth 1974); *Wholeness, Body, Mind and Spirit–One Man* (Epworth 1976); *The Communication Process* (Epworth 1978).

ROWLAND, Edward John, 53 Chestnut Ave., Ewell, Epsom, Surrey KT19 0SY. (01-393-2322) *b. 24 May 1933, Didcot, Oxon. m. 30 March 1959: 1d., 1s.*
Education: 1938–44 Old Didcot Jun. Sch.; 1944–49 Wallingford Grammar Sch.; 1956–60 Didsbury, Bristol. *Appointments:* 1960–62 Bristol, Clifton and Redland; 1962–66 Hillingdon; 1966–71 Ashfield; 1971–79 Eastbourne; 1979– Wimbledon. *Connexional Committees:* 1980– Division of Ministries Board.

ROWLAND, Raymond G., 117 Dedworth Rd., Windsor, Berks. SL4 5BB. (075-35-64783)–BEng(Sheffield), BA(Manchester). *23 July 1924, Ashford, Derbyshire. m. 1 Aug 1951: 3s.*
Education: 1929–35 Bakewell Methodist Jun. Sch.; 1935–42 Lady Manners Sch., Bakewell; 1942–45 Sheffield Univ.; 1948–51 Manchester Univ.; 1948–51 Hartley Victoria. *Appointments:* 1946–47 Aylesbury; 1947–48 Kidderminster; 1951–58 Nigeria Dt; 1958–64 Peterborough; 1964–73 Cambridge; 1973–80 Harrow; 1980– Windsor. *Connexional Committees:* 1967–73 Central Committee Overseas Division
Special Interests: Genealogy. *Hobbies and Recreations:* Gardening, Photography, Saxon Churches.

ROWLANDS, Hugh, Bod Gwynant, Gele Ave., Abergele, Clwyd LL22 7BB. (0745-822761) *b. 17 Feb 1917, Menai Bridge, Anglesey. m. 28 July 1947: 1d., 1s.*
Education: Menai Bridge Elem.; Beaumaris Grammar; 1939–40 Handsworth; 1940–42 Hartley Victoria. *Appointments:* 1942–44 Llanrhareadr, Welsh; 1944–50 Bagillt, Welsh; 1950–55 Portmadoc, Welsh; 1955–60 Denbigh, Welsh; 1960–65 Llandudno, Welsh; 1965–75 Tregarth, Welsh; 1975–82 Dyffryn, Clwyd, Welsh, Chairman Cymru District; 1974 President Welsh Assembly.
Council Member: Council of Church for Wales, (vice President 1980–82).
Hobbies and Recreations: Walking.

ROWLEY, Leonard, 2 St. Maeburne, 15 Marine Parade, Penarth, South Glamorgan CF6 2BG (0222-707037) *b. 24 June 1905, Audley, Stoke-on-Trent. m. 2 June 1930: 1d.*
Education: 1926–27 Cliff Coll.
Appointments: 1950 Bilston; 1955–60 Canton, Cardiff; 1960–67 Wye Valley Mission; 1967–70 Pontypool.

ROYALL, Arthur Frederick, 34 Vicarage Rd., Henley-on-Thames, Oxon RG9 1HW. (04912-2087) *b. 10 Dec 1914, Stockwell, London SW. m. 21 Aug 1948: 2d.*
Education: 1919– Elem.; 1919– Central; Burton-on-Trent Technical Coll. *Appointments:* 1950–52 Wigton; 1952–55 Chelmsford; 1955–58 Bishops Castle and Clun; 1958–63 Stourbridge; 1963–68 Redditch; 1968–75 Andover; 1975–79 Southampton.
Hobbies and Recreations: Amateur Radio.

RUDDICK, Paul, 16 Orlando Drive, Carlton, Nottingham NG4 3FL. (0602-248166) *b. 3 Dec 1945, Oakley, Basingstoke, Hampshire. m. 29 Aug 1970: 2s.*
Education: 1950–53 Hemsworth Prim. Sch.; 1953–57 Swindon, Oxford St. Jun. Sch.; 1957–60 Malmesbury Grammar Sch.; 1960–64 Taunton's Sch., Southampton; 1966–69 Richmond. *Appointments:* 1970–74 United Church of Papua New Guinea and the Solomon Islands; 1975–80 Derby East; 1980– Nottingham East. *Connexional Committees:* 1977–82 Central Committee, Overseas Division; 1978–84 Overseas Service Committee.
Special Interests: Pastoral Counselling, Hospital Chaplaincy, Overseas, Social Responsibility.
Hobbies and Recreations: Reading.

RUDMAN, Stanley, 31 Eldorado Rd., Cheltenham. (0242-517868)–MA(Oxon), MLitt(Dunelm), BA(Cantab.). *b. 24 Jan 1934, Rochdale. m. 22 Aug 1959: 2d., 1s.*
Education: 1945–52 Rochdale Grammar Sch.; 1952–56 Oriel Coll., Oxford; 1964–65 Birmingham Univ.; 1956–59 Wesley House.
Appointments: 1959–60 Orsmkirk; 1960–64 N. Shields and W. Bay; 1965–66 Shipley; 1966–68 W Midlands Coll. of Education; 1968–71 Doncaster Coll. of Education, 1971– Coll. of St. Mary and St. Pauls.
Local Council Committees: 1976–81 Gloucestershire Education Committee. *Publications:* Translations from German and Swedish.

Special Interests: Christian Ethics. *Hobbies and Recreations:* Gardening, Walking, Travelling.

RUPP, Ernest Gordon, 42 Malcolm Place, King St., Cambridge CB1 1LS. (0223-68365)—FBA, MA, DD, DTheol. *b. 7 Jan 1910, London. m. 6 Aug 1938: 1s.*
Education: Owen's Sch., Islington, London; 1928–31 King's Coll., London; 1931–32 London Institute of Education; 1933–37 Univ. Cambridge; 1937–38 Univ. of Strasbourg; 1937–38 Univ. of Basle; 1933–37 Wesley House.
Appointments: 1937–38 Home Mission Committee; 1938–46 Chislehurst; 1946–47 Wesley House, President's Assistant; 1947–52 Richmond Coll. Tutor, Church History; 1952–56 Cambridge Univ.; 1956–67 Manchester Univ.; 1967–74 Wesley House Principal; 1968–77 Dixie Professor of Ecclesiastical History and Fellow of Emmanuel Coll., Cambridge; 1968 President of the Methodist Conference.
Connexional Committees: 1964– Faith and Order Committee of Conversations with the Church of England and Roman Catholics, World Council of Churches; 1947–74 Ministerial Training. *Publications: The Righteousness of God* (1953 Birbeck Lectures); *Patterns of Reformation* (Fernley Hartley Lecture); *Luther's Progress to the Diet of Worms, Thomas Jackson* (Wesley Historical Society Lecture); *Just Men, Sir Thomas More, Old and New Reformation* (Cato Lecture).

RUSH, Pamela Elsie, 1 Larkspur Ave., Chasetown, Walsall WS7 8SR. (05436-2277)—BEd(Lond.). *b. 23 Jan 1933, Reading.*
Education: 1944–49 Kendrick Grammar Sch., Reading; 1965–68 Eaton Hall Coll. of Education, Retford; 1973–75 Brentwood Coll. of FE; 1978–80 Hartley Victoria.
Appointments: 1980– Cannock Chase.
Special Interests: The Developing World, Ecumenism. *Hobbies and Recreations:* Walking, Cycling, Photography, Music, Painting, Pottery, Gardening.

RUSHTON, David, 42 Essex Gardens, Gateshead, Tyne and Wear NE9 5BB. (0632-771689) *b. 1 Aug 1939, Wakefield, Yorks. m. 27 Aug 1966: 1d., 1s.*
Education; 1950–57 Thornes House Grammar; 1957–59 Westminster Coll.; 1967–68 Birmingham Univ.; 1964–68 Handsworth;
Appointments: 1968–70 Amble and Alnwick; 1970–75 Stanley; 1975–78 Banbury; 1978– Gateshead South West.
Hobbies and Recreations: Photography.

RUSHTON, Geoffrey Hulse, 35 Davison Ave., Whitley Bay, Tyne and Wear NE26 1SQ. MA(Cantab.), BD(Lond.). *b. 19 April 1928, Middlesbrough. m. Aug 1955: 2s.*
Education: 1938–47 Kingswood Sch.; 1950–53 Wesley House.
Appointments: 1949–50 Newmarket Mission; 1953–55 Coventry; 1955–59 Sheffield, Brunswick; 1959–65 Bilston; 1965–71 Sheffield, Ecclesall; 1971–78 Middlesbrough; 1978– North Shields and Whitley Bay.
Connexional Committees: 1963–65 Connexional Youth Council; 1975–78 Board of the Division of Ministries; 1975–77 Central Missions Committee. *Publications: I Peter* (Small Epworth pamphlet, 1968).
Special Interests: Ecumenical Activities. *Hobbies and Recreations:* Calligraphy, Woodwork.

RUSSELL, Adrian A., 34 Fore St., Beacon, Camborne, Cornwall TR14 7SO.
Appointments: 1977–82 Camborne; 1982– Brighouse.

RUSSELL, Fred, 22 Colchester Ave., Penylan, Cardiff CF3 7BP. (0222-487189)—BA(Wales), BD(Manchester). *b. 25 Sept 1919, Abertillery. m. 27 July 1949: 1d., 1s.*
Education: 1931–38 Abertillery County Sch.; 1938-42 Univ. Coll. of North Wales, Bangor; 1947–49 Hartley Victoria. *Appointments:* 1945–46 Guildford; 1946–47 Glasgow, Paisley Rd.; 1949–54 Risca and Crosskeys; 1954–61 Swansea; 1961–68 Nottingham West; 1968–75 Cardiff, Roath; 1975 Cardiff.
Connexional Committees: 1952–58 Christian Citizenship.
Special Interests: Temperance Work, Methodist Chaplain at Cardiff Prison since 1968. *Hobbies and Recreations:* Gardening.

RUSSELL, Peter William, Kingsmead Coll., 997 Bristol Rd., Selly Oak, Birmingham B29 6LP. (021-472-0013)—MA(Oxon), BA(Cantab.). *b. 7 March 1929, Swindon. m. 8 Aug 1958: 3s.*
Education: 1934–39 Quinton CE Prim. Sch., Birmingham; 1939–47 Kingswood Sch.; 1949–54 Oriel Coll., Oxford; 1957–58 Lund Univ., Sweden; 1973–74 Birmingham Univ.; 1954–57 Wesley House, Cambridge. *Appointments:* 1958–61 Shooters Hill; 1961–65 Plymouth, King St.; 1966–67 Trinity Coll., Umuahia, Nigeria; 1968 Tutor in New Testament, Wesley Coll.; 1968–73 Extra Tutor, Epworth Theological Coll., Zimbabwe; 1974–77 Leeds Mission; 1977– Univ. and Poly. Chaplain; Kingsmead Coll., Selly Oak, Principal.
Connexional Committees: 1975– Overseas Division Central Committee; 1977– Overseas Service and Pastoral Committees.
Publications: Method in the Theology and Philosophy of Religion of Anders Nygren in the Modern Churchman, vol. III, No.3 June 1960; *The Limitations of Theology in Epworth Review,* vol. 2, No.2 May 1975.
Special Interests: New Testament, Philosophy of Religion, Adult Education and Training Methods, Missiology. *Hobbies and Recreations:* Music, Cricket, Rugby, Squash, Swimming, Repairing Things.

RUSSELL, Thomas, Fairlawns, Ham Street, Ashford, Kent TN26 2HG. (023373 2771) *b. West Bromwich, Staffs. m.: 1d.*
Education: London Univ.; 1928–30 Richmond; 1930–31 Headingley.
Appointments: 1927–28 Knighton;

1931–35 Margate; 1935–37 Tamworth and Lichfield; 1937–41 Selby; 1941–46 Chaplain HMF; 1946–49 Southport North; 1949–53 St. Leonards and Bexhill; 1953–59 Sussex Mission; 1959–64 Birmingham Sutton Park; 1964–70 Epworth and Crowle.
Connexional Committee: July Committee.
Special Interests: A wide variety of interests. *Hobbies and Recreations:* Water Colour Painting.

RYAN, Donald Holt, The Manse, 20 Roumania Drive, Craig Y Don, Llandudno, Gwynnedd LL30 1UL. (0492-76080) *b. 2 Jan 1932, Tottington. m. 21 March 1959: 2d.*
Education: 1937 Tottington Sch.; 1945 Bury Technical Coll.; 1956–57 Cliff Coll.; 1957–60 Hartley Victoria. *Appointments:* 1960–65 Whitehaven; 1965–71 Barrow in Furness; 1971–81 Wolverhampton, Darlington St.; 1981 Colwyn Bay and Llandudno.
Connexional Committees: 1966 Youth Commitee; 1971–76 Education and Youth Committee; 1979 Archives and History Committee. *Local Council Committees:* 1966–71 Barrow in Furness Youth Committee.
Special Interests: Methodist Commemorative Pottery. *Hobbies and Recreations:* Photography, History, Mountain Walking.

RYDER, Gordon, 12 Magna Grove, Sandal, Wakefield WF2 7NG. (0924-255363) *b. 20 June 1936, Bradford, Yorkshire. m. 30 June 1962: 3d.*
Education: 1947–52 Belle Vue Grammar Sch., Bradford; 1958–62 Hartley Victoria. *Appointments:* 1962–64 Wymondham and Attleborough; 1964–69 Bristol, Clifton and Redland; 1969–75 Brighton and Hove; 1975–80 Bristol North; 1980– Wakefield.
Connexional Committees: 1976–80 Division of Ministries Board.
Special Interests: Hospital Chaplaincy Work. *Hobbies and Recreations:* Gardening, Swimming, Music.

RYELAND, Joan Alberta, 29 Castlemead Drive, Saltash, Cornwall PL12 4LQ. (075-55-4169) *b. 28 May 1928, Plymouth, Devon. s.*
Education: 1933–38 Salisbury Rd. Prim. and Jun. Sch.; 1938–44 Plymouth High Sch. for Girls; 1949–51 Wesley Deaconess Coll., Ilkley; 1957–58 Kingsmead. *Appointments:* 1951–52 H.M. Sellyoak, Caravan, Hull District; 1952–53 H.M. Caravan, Lincoln District; 1953–57 Mission House, HQ Overseas Div. YMA Secretary; 1958–60 Laymens Training Institute, Shagamu, Nigeria; 1961–62 HM Caravan, Carlisle District; 1962–63 HM Caravan, Shetland; 1963–66 South Moulton; 1966–71 Chaplains Assistant, BAOR; 1971–73 Islington Community Project; 1973–80, Livingston New Town Ecumenical Team, Scotland; 1980– Saltash and St. Germans Circuit.
Connexional Committees: 1974–76 General Purposes, 1953–57 OM General Committee. *Council Member:* 1976–81 World Methodist Council; 1975–79 British Rep on Diakonia World Executive. *Local Council Committees:* 1973–80 Treasurer Dedridge Community Council.
Special Interests: Prison Welfare, Church and Community Involvement. *Hobbies and Recreations:* Photography, Gardening, Knitting, Walking.

SADLER, John, 1 Oxford Villas, Guiseley, Leeds LS20 9AD. (0943-73152) *b. 31 Jan 1943, Wolverhampton. m. 2s.*
Education: 1964–67 Didsbury; 1967–68 Wesley, Bristol.
Appointments: 1968–70 Leeds Headingley; 1970–76 Pontefract; 1976– Otley and Aireborough.
Connexional Committees: 1981– General Purposes.

SAILS, Andrew William, 7 Rutherford Rd., Liverpool L18 0HJ. (051-722-1395)—BA(Sussex), MA(Cantab.). *b. 22 Jan 1949, Reading, Berks. m. 10 July 1971: 1d., 1s.*
Education: 1956–59 Bristol Grammar Sch.; 1959–67 Nottingham High Sch.; 1967–70 Sussex Univ.; 1970–72 Cambridge Univ.; 1970–72 Wesley House. *Appointments:* 1972–75 West London Mission (Hinde St.); 1975–79 Brighton, Dome Mission; 1979– Liverpool SE.
Connexional Committees: 1979–80 MDEY Board; 1977– City Centre Committee; 1980– Student Work Committee. *Local Council Committees:* 1976–79 East Sussex County Council Education Committee.
Special Interests: Student Chaplaincy, World Development. *Hobbies and Recreations:* Modern Novel, Fell Walking, Astronomy.

SALMON, Albert Edward David, 80 Linden Ave., Herne Bay, Kent CT6 8TZ. (02273-5707) *b. 22 Jan 1916, Rotherhithe, London. m. 23 Sept 1944: 2d., 1s.*
Education: 1921–27 Albion St. Boys Sch., London SE16; 1927–31 Monnow Rd. Central Sch.; 1937–39 Cliff Coll.; 1961–62 Hartley Victoria.
Appointments: 1961–64 Manchester, Stretford and Urmston; 1964–69 Manchester, Droylsden and Openshaw; 1969–71 Castleford; 1971–76 Nuneaton; 1976–81 Gateshead and Jarrow.
Hobbies and Recreations: Gardening, Fuchsias, Reading.

SALMON, Dennis John Edward, 44 Sompting Rd., Lancing, Sussex BN15 9JX. (0903-753039) *b. 29 Dec 1929, Addiscombe, Surrey. m. (1) 21 Jan 1961 (died) (2) 10 June 1972: 2d., 2s.*
Education: 1936–39 Ashburton Sch., Croydon, Surrey; 1940–42 Purley County Sch., Old Coulsdon, Surrey; 1942–46 Caterham Sch., Surrey; 1951–54 Didsbury, Bristol; 1954–55 St. Andrews Coll.
Appointments: 1955–71 Rhodesia Dt; 1964–67 Tutor in Old Umtali Biblical Institute and Epworth Theol. Coll.; 1971–76 Richmond and Hounslow; 1976–81 Bristol, Frome Valley.
Connexional Committees: 1971–76 London South West District Overseas Committee; 1976–81 Bristol District Overseas Committee.
Special Interests: World Affairs, especially Africa, Care of Housebound

and Disabled, My Family and Their Interests. *Hobbies and Recreations:* Sketching, Painting, Travel, Gardening, Swimming, Tennis.

SALMON, George Brynmor, Tammie Norie, Bay Rd., Trevone, Padstow, Cornwall PL28 8QZ. (0841-520060)–BA(Open). *b. 21 July 1911, Briton Ferry, Neath, S. Wales. m. 29 July 1939: 2d., 2s.* *Education:* 1919–22 Stationers' Company Sch., Hornsey; 1922–28 Kingswood Sch., Bath; 1932–36 Handsworth. *Appointments:* 1936–41 Manchester and Salford Mission; 1941–43 Bristol, Bishopston; 1943–46 Chaplain HMF; 1946–50 Nottingham, South; 1950–54 London, Wanstead and Woodford; 1954–58 London, Chingford; 1958–64 Birmingham, Sutton Park; 1964–71 London, Finchley and Hendon; 1971–76 London, Croydon. *Connexional Committees:* 1948–50 Youth Committee; 1952–54 Church Membership; 1956–58 Temperance and Social Welfare; 1961–64 General Committee of Missionary Society. *Hobbies and Recreations:* Stamps with a direct association with Christianity and with Church History, Close-up Photography, Gardening, Recording Classical Music.

SALMON, Robert William, 8 Duncan Drive, Guildford, Surrey GU1 2NR. (0483-573826) *b. 22 May 1915, Harrow, Middlesex. m. 11 Jan 1945: 1d., 1s.* *Education:* 1926–32 Kingswood Sch., Bath; 1938–41 Headingley. *Appointments:* 1941–44 Diss; 1944–45 Bromley Common and Orpington; 1945–49 Wakefield; 1949–52 Mansfield (Bridge St.); 1952–59 Norwich (St. Peters); 1959–65 Bristol (East); 1965–71 Ilford; 1971–76 Aldershot and Farnborough; 1976–81 Brighton and Hove. *Hobbies and Recreations:* Gardening and Painting.

REV. & MRS. SALMON CALLED AT HILL 21.8.91.

SAMPSOM, Donald John, 68 Love Lane, Pinner, Middlesex HA5 2EX. (01-866-1743) *b. 27 June 1934, Kingsbridge, S. Devon. m. 10 Aug 1968: 1d., 1s.* *Education:* Kingsbridge Grammar; 1959–63 Didsbury, Bristol. *Appointments:* 1963–68 London (Enfield); 1968–75 Liverpool South East; 1975–80 Bristol South; 1980– Harrow. *Connexional Committees:* 1974– Stewardship; 1982–83 Board of Education and Youth. *Publications: The Pastoral Care of the Ordained Ministry* (July 1976); *Coping with Methodism's Itinerant Ministerial System* (1980). *Special Interests:* Pastoral Theology. *Hobbies and Recreations:* Cricket, Football, Gardening.

SAMPSON, Trenwith John Wallis, 70 Sweetbriar Lane, Exeter EX1 3AQ. (0392-75070)–BA(Bristol), BD(Lond.), DSc(Strasbourg) *b. 3 Aug 1934, Gulval, Nr. Penzance, Cornwall. m. 25 June 1960: 1d., 2s.* *Education:* 1939–45 Gulval Prim.; 1945–52 Penzance Grammar Sch.; 1952–55 Bristol Univ.; 1959–61 London Univ.; 1967–68 Strasbourg Univ.; 1968–70 In Absentia Strasbourg Univ.; 1955–58 Handsworth. *Appointments:* 1958–59 Home Missions (Caravan Missions); 1959–63 Swindon; 1963–67 Romford; 1967–68 Research at Strasbourg Univ.; 1968–75 Plymouth, King St.; 1975–82 Coventry; 1977–81 Part-Time Tutor (Open Univ.); 1982– Exeter (Univ. Chaplain). *Connexional Committees:* 1979–82 The President's Council; 1981– Connexional Candidates Committee. *Council Member:* 1975–82, Coventry, Member of Joint Council of Chapel of Unity. *Publications: The Scriptures in St. Augustine's Writings up to the Confessions* (1970). *Special Interests:* Inter-Religious Dialogue. *Hobbies and Recreations:* Music, Drama, Walking, Exploring France.

SAMS, David Christopher, Rugenbarg 251, Lurup, 2000 Hamburg 53, W. Germany. (010-4940-834212) *b. 28 March 1947, Bristol. m. 17 July 1981: 1d.* *Education:* 1958–64 Bedminster Down Secondary Sch., Bristol; 1973–77 Wesley, Bristol. *Appointments:* 1977–78 London Mission Poplar; 1978–82 Chaplain HMF; 1982– Chaplain, British Sailors Society. *Special Interests:* Electronics (Micro-Miniaturisation and Data Processing). *Hobbies and Recreations:* Squash, Reading, Horse Riding, Jogging, Cooking.

SANDBACH, Joseph Ernest OBE. 8 Seal Rd., Selsey, Chichester, West Sussex PO20 0HW. (0245-602307) *b. 24 Nov 1898, Shurlach, Northwich, Cheshire. m. 2 Aug 1926: 1d., 2s.* *Education:* 1905–12 Victoria Rd., Northwich; 1920–23 Victoria Park. *Appointments:* 1923–26 Huddersfield; 1926–31 Leeds; 1931–35 West and South-West China; 1935–37 St. Austell, Zion; 1937–52 South West China Dt; 1952–62 Hong Kong Dt Eng. *Publications:* The Story of the Japanese Occupation of Hong Kong, on tapes in MMS for Imperial War Museum. *Special Interests:* Far Eastern Affairs.

SANDERS, Arthur David, 278 Cumberworth Lane, Denby Dale, Huddersfield HD8 8QS. (0484-862338)–BA, BSc, Special Diploma (Social Studies), MSc. *Education:* 1946–54 Kingswood Sch., Bath; Oxford (Balliol Coll.); Manchester (Dept. Management Sciences); 1960–63 Didsbury, Bristol. *Appointments:* 1963–66 South Molton; 1966–71 Manchester S.E./Hyde and Denton; 1971–74 Hazel Grove and Poynton; 1974–77 Hindley; 1977–81 President's List (incl. Somerset Mission and Tiverton); 1981– Denby Dale and Clayton West. *Parliamentary Service:* 1974 and 1979 Parliamentary Candidate; 1979 European Parliamentary Candidate. *Connexional Committees:* 1971–74 Education and Youth; 1975–77 Social Responsibility. *Council Member:* Founder and First Chairman Hazel Grove Community Council. *Special Interests:* Finance, Property, Politics.

SANDERS, Dennis Douglas, 18 Exe Hill, Shiphay, Torquay TQ2 7NF. (0803-63591) *b. 28 Sept 1929,*

Birmingham. m. 21 July 1956: 1d., 2s.
Education: 1934–40 Cowper St. Jun., Birmingham; 1940–43 Gower St. Senior Boys; 1950 Cliff Coll.; 1951–54 Handsworth.
Appointments: 1954–57 Stafford; 1957–62 Huddersfield North East; 1962–69 Coventry; 1969–77 Leamington Spa; 1977– Torbay.
Council Member: 1975–77 South Warwickshire Community Health Council, Vice Chairman.
Special Interests: Mental Health, Founder Chairman South Warwickshire Group Homes and Dale Street Day Centre, 1971–77.
Hobbies and Recreations: Gardening, Books.

SANDERS, Hubert Guy, 6 Wavel Grove, Wakefield, West Yorkshire WF2 6JW. (0924-256521)–MA, BD(Manchester). *b. 5 Nov 1913, Ramsbottom, Lancashire. m. (1) 7 Oct 1943 (2) 14 Aug 1975: 1d.*
Education: 1924–27 Haslingden Secondary Sch.; 1927–31 Warrington Secondary Sch.; 1931–37 Manchester Univ.; 1934–37 Didsbury.
Appointments: 1937–49 South Ceylon District; 1949–52 London (Ilford); 1952–56 Colchester; 1956–61 Clacton-on-Sea; 1961-65 Darlington (South); 1965–70 Tadcaster; 1970–75 Wakefield; 1975–80 Batley.
Connexional Committees: 1972–80 Chapel Affairs/Board of Property; Various Synod and District Secretaryships; Mission House Committees and Connexional Ad Hoc Committees and Sub-Committees
Special Interests: Biblical Studies, Hymnology, Ecumenical Affairs.
Hobbies and Recreations: Railways.

SANDERS, Keith Sidney James, 54 Kingsfield Ave., North Harrow, Middlesex HA2 6AT. (01-427-7979) *b. 22 Aug 1935, Wellington, Somerset. m. 7 July 1962: 1d., 2s.*
Education: 1946–52 Wellington Sch.; 1959–62 Didsbury, Bristol.
Appointments: 1962–65 Ashby-de-la-Zouch; 1965–70 Doncaster, Priory Place; 1970–74 Bolton; 1974–80 Exeter; 1980– Harrow.
Connexional Committees: 1980– Methodist Stewardship Organisation.
Hobbies and Recreations: Philately, Gardening.

SANDERS, Thomas William, 28 Arundel Way, Newquay, Cornwall TR7 3AG. (06375-4317) *b. 20 Nov 1908, Shildon, Co. Durham. m. 17 Aug 1938: 1d.*
Education: 1913–24 Timothy Hacworth, Shildon; 1931–34 Hartley Victoria. *Appointments:* 1934–38 President's List; 1938–41 Camelford and Wadebridge; 1941–44 Southampton; 1944–51 Gateshead South; 1951–55 Liverpool, Grove St.; 1955–59 London, Walthamstow; 1959–68 London, Leysian Mission; 1968–70 Redruth; 1970–74 Bradford, Great Horton.
Connexional Committees: Youth Committee.
Special Interests: Youth Work.
Hobbies and Recreations. Bowls, President Local Probus Club.

SANDERSON, Frank, 9 Broadwood Close, Penwortham, Preston, Lancs PR1 0XU. (0772-745252) *b. 28 Aug 1931, Blackburn. m. 21 June 1958: 2s.*
Education: 1936 St. Phillips CE, Blackburn; 1942–45 Blakey Moor Secondary Modern, Blackburn; 1953–55 Cliff Coll.; 1956–59 Hartley Victoria. *Appointments:* 1959–64 Accrington; 1964–70 Morecambe and Heysham; 1970–73 Portsmouth Mission; 1973–76 Bingley; 1976–77 Paisley Mission; 1977– Preston, Lune St. and Orchard.
Local Council Committees: 1978– Secretary, Preston Free Church Federal Council.
Special Interests: Army Cadet Force, Lancashire. *Hobbies and Recreations:* Gardening.

SANKEY, James, 33 Churchill Cresc., Marple, Stockport, Cheshire SK6 6HL. (061-427-2620)–MA(Cantab.), BSc(Reading). *b. 31 Jan 1909, Abbey Village, Nr. Chorley, Lancs. m. 29 Oct 1943: 2d., 2s.*
Education: 1922–28 Leigh Grammar Sch.; 1928–32 Reading Univ.; 1938–40 Wesley House. *Appointments:* 1939–44 Trichinopoly Dt, India; 1944–46 St. Austell, St. James; 1946–48 Trichinopoly Dt, India; 1948–52 S. India Church; 1952–57 Falmouth; 1957–61 Kent Mission; 1961–66 London, Finsbury Park and Southgate; 1966–71 Somerset Mission; 1971–74 Leek; 1974–77 Radyr.

SAPSFORD, Donald Victor, 21 Wigton Rd., Carlisle, Cumbria CA2 7BB. (0228-24450) *b. 29 Dec 1921, Hackney Wick, London. m. 24 Sept 1949: 2s.*
Education: Vange Council Sch.; Craylands Secondary Sch.; Leeds Coll. of Technology; 1961–63 Richmond. *Appointments:* 1963–68 Bolton Bridge Street; 1968–75 Douglas, Isle of Man; 1975– Carlisle.
Connexional Committees: 1971–75 Youth and Education; 1976–82 Ministries.
Special Interests: History, Literature.
Hobbies and Recreations. Gardening, DIY

SARGANT, Norman Carr, 75 Lower Redland Rd., Bristol BS6 6SP. (0272-730497)–BA(Birmingham). *b. 3 Jan 1909, Highgage, London N6. m. 19 Feb 1935: 4d.*
Education: 1919–22 St. Wilfred's Sch., Seaford; 1922–27 The Leys Sch., Cambridge; 1928–31 Birmingham Univ.; Handsworth.
Appointments: 1931–47 Mysare District; 1947-72 Mysore Diocese CST (Bishop 1951–72); 1974–81 Honorary Canon, Bristol Cathedral; 1981– Canon Emeritus; 1979– Honorary Archivist.
Publications: The Dispersion of the Tamil Church (1940, 1912); (with A. M. Ward) *W. E. Tomlinson* (1952); *The Lingayats* (1963); *Mary Carpenter and India* (1977); *From Mission to Church in Karnataka* (1979).
Special Interests: Indian Church History. *Hobbies and Recreations:* Photography

SARGENT, Raymond Edward, The Manse, Parkway Methodist Church, Conduit Place, Bristol BS2 9RU. (0272-554545) *b. 4 Feb 1925, London, Lambeth. m. 7 Aug 1954: 2d., 1s.*
Education: 1939 Orpington Central

Sch.; 1950–53 Didsbury, Bristol. *Appointments:* 1949–50 Deal; 1953–55 Barbados; 1955–57 Grenada; 1957–61 Wombwell and Hoyland; 1961–62 Manchester, Withington; 1962–65 Manchester, Drylsden; 1965–67 Eccles; 1967–74 Luton North; 1974–78 Maidenhead; 1978– Bristol North.
Connexional Committees: 1963–67 Overseas Missions.
Special Interests: Hospital Chaplain.
Hobbies and Recreations: Gardening, Walking.

SAUNDERS, Arthur William, 3 The Link, Leasingham, Sleaford, Lincolnshire NG34 8JX. (0529-302376) *b. 11 May 1906, Egham, Surrey. m. 19 Aug 1937: 2d.*
Education: 1911–19 Egham Hythe Board Sch.; 1919–24 Strode's Sch., Egham; 1924–26 Univ. Coll., London; 1931–34 Manchester Univ.; 1931–34 Hartley; 1934–35 Hartley Victoria.
Appointments: 1935–37 Belize, British Honduras; 1937–42 Stanncreek, British Honduras; 1942–46 Belize; 1947–50 Savanna-la-Mar, Jamaica; 1950–52 St. Ann's Bay; 1953–58 Lucea; 1959–67 Bombay, India; 1968–71 Area Secretary (in UK) The Leprosy Mission.
Council Member: 1972–82 South Asia Church Aid Association; 1978– Modern Churchmen's Union; 1971– Sleaford and District Council of Churches (Secretary 73–75).
Special Interests: Liturgy. *Hobbies and Recreations:* Heraldry.

SAUNDERS, Denys John, Selly Oak Colls., Birmingham B29 6LQ. (021-472-4231) *b. 16 Jan 1921, Hendon, Middx. m. 28 Dec 1946: 1d., 3s.*
Education: 1931–37 Royal Grammar Sch., Guildford, Surrey; 1945–48 Richmond. *Appointments:* 1948–49 MMS Education Dept.; 1949–60 Church of South India; 1960–72 MMS HQ, A-V Dept.; 1972– Selly Oak Colls.
Publications: Filmstrip Handbook for India (1955); *Visual Aids for Village Workers* (1960); *Visual Communication Handbook* (1973).
Special Interests: Cross-Cultural Communication, Learning in Groups.
Hobbies and Recreations: Photography, Gardening, Squash.

SAVAGE, Hamer Hollings, 63 Gilbert Rd., Cambridge CB4 3NZ. (0223-356047) *b. 15 Aug 1929, Leeds, Yorkshire. m. 2 April 1966: 2d.*
Education: 1934–38 Cookridge Council Sch., Cookridge, Leeds; 1938–47 Leeds Grammar Sch.; 1964–67 Hartley Victoria.
Appointments: 1967–71 Crewe; 1971–75 Bishop Auckland; 1975–80 Northwich; 1980– Cambridge.
Special Interests: Church Growth.
Hobbies and Recreations: Geneology.

SAVAGE, Kevin Gordin, 18 Rowton Grange Rd., Chapel-en-le-Frith, Stockport, Cheshire SK12 6LD. (0298-812774) *b. 11 Feb 1954, Whitehaven, Cumbria. m. 21 July 1973: 2d.*
Education: 1965–72 Whitehaven County Grammar Sch.; 1975–79 Wesley, Bristol. *Appointments:* 1979– Whaley Bridge.
Hobbies and Recreations: Motorcycling, Fell-Walking, Athletics, Reading.

SAVIDGE, Charles, Green Pastures, 234 Queen Edith's Way, Cambridge CB1 4NL. (0223-248883) *b. 16 Sept 1905, Cambridge.*
Education: 1931–34 Hartley Victoria.
Appointments: 1934–37 President's List; 1937–40 Bristol, Kingswood; 1940–43 Wiltshire Mission; 1943–46 Ipswich, Rope Walk; 1946–49 Lowton; 1949–52 Rhondda, Ely Valley; 1952–55 East Cornwall Mission; 1955–59 Haworth and Oakworth; 1959–71 Llanymynech; 1971–73 Netherton.
Hobbies and Recreations: Rowing, Cycling.

SAVILL, Douglas Frank, The Manse, Cross Green, Otley, West Yorkshire LS21 1HE. (0943-462308) *b. 12 Sept 1932, Langley, near Saffron Walden, Essex. m. 6 May 1967: 3s.*
Education: 1937–46 Langley CE Sch.; 1962–63 Cliff Coll.; 1963–66 Handsworth. *Appointments:* 1966–71 Weardale; 1971–77 Stockton-on-Tees; 1977– Otley.
Connexional Committees: 1970–72 Home Committee of Overseas Missions; 1982– Division of Social Responsibility.
Special Interests: Local Radio.
Hobbies and Recreations: Cricket, Stamps and Coins.

SAVILLE, John Brown, 5 Oxford Rd., Halifax HX1 2QJ. (0422-65434) *b. 1 March 1940, Horsforth, Yorkshire. m. 4 Sept 1965: 1d., 2s.*
Education: 1945–51 St. Margaret's CE Sch.; 1951–56 Prince Henrys Grammar Sch.; 1976–79 Manchester Univ.; 1976–79 Hartley Victoria.
Appointments: 1979– Coalville.
Special Interests: Music in Worship.
Hobbies and Recreations: Music, Electronics.

SAWYER, Ernest, Willersley House, 85 Main St., Willerby, Hull HU10 6BY. (0482-657408) *b. 12 Dec 1907, Hull. m. 8 Oct 1936: 1d., 1s.*
Education: –1922 Hull Municipal Technical Coll.; 1929–32 Richmond.
Appointments: 1932–53 Gold Coast Dt; 1954–55 Newton Abbot; 1955–56 Supernumerary; 1956–57 Missionary Committee; 1957–58 Leeds, Richmond Hill; 1958–71 Leprosy Mission (Supernumerary).
Council Member: Kumasi Town Council, Ghana 1947.
Special Interests: Leprosy Mission and MMS Deputation, Sport.

SAXBY, Alan, 135 Park Grove, Barnsley, South Yorks S70 1QG. (0226-203029)–BA(Bristol), BA(Lond.). *b. 28 Feb 1937, Sheffield. m.*
Education: 1948–53 High Storrs, Sheffield; 1960–64 Bristol Univ.; 1960–64 Didsbury, Bristol.
Appointments: 1964–66 Coalville; 1966–72 Barnsley (East) and Barnsley; 1972– Coll. Counsellor, Coll. of Techology, Barnsley.
Hobbies and Recreations: Rock Climbing.

SCARLETT, Geoffrey William, The Manse, 122 Lincoln Rd., Tuxford, Newark, Notts NG22 0HS. (0777-870257)–MA.

Education: 1964–68 Didsbury, Bristol. *Appointments:* 1968–70 Bridgend; 1970–73 Crewe; 1973–74 Canterbury and Faversham; 1974–79 Sunderland South; 1979– Retford. *Special Interests:* Lay Training—at present, Circuit Homiletics Tutor and a Tutor involved in Methodist Study Centre Work, Hymn Writing. *Hobbies and Recreations:* Visiting Castles, Crosswords, Similar Puzzles.

SCOTT, Edward T., 2 Linhurst Newtown, Blackwell, Bromsgrove, Worcs B60 1BP. (021-445-1022). *Education:* 1936–39 Richmond. *Appointments:* 1939–44 SW China; 1944–46 Brigg and Scotter; 1946–51 Sevenoaks; 1951–55 Gravesend and Dartford; 1955–59 Cambridge; 1959–64 London, Kilburn and Hampstead; 1964–70 London, Harrow; 1970–75 Devonport; 1975–80 Ambleside and Windermere.

SCOTT, John Henry, 104 Malsis Rd., Keighley, West Yorkshire BD21 1JQ. (0535-602599)–BD(Lond.). *b. 15 Dec 1942, Hanley, Stoke-on-Trent. m. 15 June 1968: 2d.* *Education:* 1947–50 Northwood Inf.; 1950–54 Northwood County Jun.; 1954–61 Hanley High Sch.; 1961–64 Northern Sch. of Music, Manchester; 1964–68 Hartley Victoria. *Appointments:* 1968–72 Stafford; 1972–78 Darlaston; 1978– Keighley and Worth Valley. *Special Interests:* Chaplaincies, Prison (Open), Hospital (Small General Hospital), Industry (Engineering Works). *Hobbies and Recreations:* Music, Walking, Photography.

SCOTT, Percy, 53 Alexandra Rd. South, Manchester M16 8GH. (061-226-7311)–BD, DTheol. *b. 14 Nov 1910, South Clifton, Nr. Newark, Notts. m. 17 July 1937: 2d., 1s.* *Education:* 1922–28 Lincoln Municipal Technical; 1935–37 Marburg, Germany; 1931–35 Richmond. *Appointments:* 1930–31 Peel, Isle of Man; 1937–39 Exeter; 1939–45 Stockton-on-Tees; 1945–47 Leeds (Chapel Allerton); 1947–73 Hartley Victoria Coll., 1959–73 Principal. *Connexional Committees:* Ministerial Training Committee. *Publications:* Doctorate Thesis 1939. *Special Interests:* The Church and Her Ministry, Sport, Rotary. *Hobbies and Recreations:* Sport.

SEARLE, John Derek, 621 Wellingborough Rd., Northampton NN3 3HR. (0604-401157)–BA(Birmingham), BD(Lond.). *b. 15 May 1932, Bury St. Edmund's, Suffolk. m. 10 Aug 1957: 3d.* *Education:* 1940–50 Culford; 1952–55 Birmingham Univ.; 1952–55 Handsworth. *Appointments:* 1955–57 Coventry; 1957–62 Stockton-on-Tees; 1962–68 Higham Ferrers; 1968–72 Liverpool South East; 1972–77 Chelmsford; 1977– Northampton. *Connexional Committee;* 1971–72 Childrens Committee. *Publications: Look and Listen* (Chester House 1968); *Look and Listen Through the Year* (St. Andrew Press 1974); *Twentieth Century Christians* 12 Mini-Biographies (St. Andrew Press 1977); *On the Right Track* Christians in Sport (awaiting publication); and Contributions to Various Anthologies of Prayer. *Special Interests:* Marriage Guidance. *Hobbies and Recreations:* Sailing, DIY.

SEARLES, Robin Victor, 61 Bexhill Close, Pontefract, West Yorkshire WF8 2LE. (0977-702673) *b. 27 Nov 1946, Birmingham. m. 30 Oct 1971: 2d., 1s.* *Education:* 1957–62 Lordswood Technical Sch.; 1970–71 Cliff Coll.; 1972–75 Wesley, Bristol. *Appointments:* 1971–72 Hackney Mission; 1971–72 Malton; 1975–78 Dursley and Stonehouse; 1978– Pontefract and Normanton.

SEDDON, William Peter, 26 Brunel St., Burnley, Lancs BB12 8AE. *b. 25 Nov 1930, Mexborough, South Yorkshire. m. 22 June 1957: 2d., 3s.* *Education:* 1934–41 Roman Terrace Inf./Jun.; 1941–43 Dolcliffe Rd. Secondary; 1943–49 Mexborough Grammar Sch.; 1954–57 Hartley Victoria. *Appointments:* 1957–60 Coningsby; 1960–67 Manchester North East; 1967–72 Blackpool South; 1972–77 Stoke-on-Trent, Hanley; 1977– Burnley. *Hobbies and Recreations:* Sport, Walking, Music.

SELMAN, Ivan James, 2 Bayswater Ave., Westbury Park, Bristol BS6 7NS. (0272-44952)–BA(Bristol), BD(Manch.). *b. 7 June 1932, Warmley, Gloucestershire. m. 11 Aug 1956: 1d., 3s.* *Education:* 1942–50 Kingswood Grammar Sch.; 1950–53 Bristol Univ.; 1953–56 Manchester Univ.; 1953–56 Hartley Victoria. *Appointments:* 1956–58 Yeovil; 1958–64 Eastleigh; 1964–69 East Wight; 1969–76 Swindon; 1976– Bristol, Clifton and Redland. *Connexional Committees:* Committee for Joint Building Schemes and Cooperation with other Communions; Community Relations Standing Committee. *Publications: Bristol Handbook for Local Ecumenical Projects* (with Canon James Free 1979). *Special Interests:* Ecumenism, Community Relations, Teaching. *Hobbies and Recreations:* Music, Painting, Photography, Gardening, Walking.

SENIOR, Geoffrey Roy, 55 Trelawny Rd., Plympton, Plymouth PL7 4LJ. (0852-337727)–BD(Lond.). *b. 18 Oct 1927, Dewsbury. m. 20 April 1957: 1d., 1s.* *Education:* Local Primary Sch.; 1939–47 Dewsbury and Leeds Technical Colls.; 1960–62 London Univ. (External Student); 1954–57 Hartley Victoria. *Appointments:* 1957–67 S.E. Asia Dt; Principal Methodist Theol. Sch., Medan; 1966 Acting General Secretary, Malaya and Singapore Christian Council; 1967–74 Leith; 1974–81 Hong Kong—Methodist Schs. Chaplain and Supervisor; 1981– Plymouth. *Connexional Committees,* 1981 Central Committee Overseas Division; 1981– Asia Advisory Committee. *Special Interests:* China and Chinese Culture. *Hobbies and Recreations:* Chinese Stamps, Ships, Walking.

SERCOMBE, Eglon, 10 Auckland Rd., Retford, Notts DN22 7XZ. (0777-701072) *b. 23 Dec 1923, Teignmouth, Devon. m. 20 Aug 1955: 1s.*
Education: 1927–31 Teignmouth Prim.; 1931–34 Ashburton Jun.; 1934–38 Ashburton Grammar; 1938–40 King Edward VI Grammar, Totnes; 1950–53 Didsbury, Bristol.
Appointments: 1953–55 Cowbridge and St. Athan; 1955–61 Selby; 1961–67 Thirsk; 1967–72 Carlisle; 1972–82 Retford.
Special Interests: Prison Work, Blind Welfare, President of Guild of Methodist Braillists, Guide Dogs for the Blind Association (Guide Dog Owner). *Hobbies and Recreations:* Music, Sport.

SEXTON, David George Sylvester, 14 Monkton Hill, Chippenham, Wilts SN15 1EP. (0249-2001) *b. 7 May 1933, Birchington-on-Sea, Kent. m. 2 Aug 1967: 1d., 1s.*
Education: Birchington on Sea CE Prim. Sch.; Goldington Rd. Elem. Sch., Bedford; Harpur Secondary Modern Sch., Bedford; 1958–62 Handsworth. *Appointments:* 1962–64 Devonport; 1964–69 Porthleven; 1969–75 Keighley; 1975–79 Mid Wiltshire; 1979– Chippenham and Brinkworth.
Connexional Committees: 1973–75 Education and Youth.
Special Interests: Youth Work, Social Issues. *Hobbies and Recreations:* Sport, Participating and Watching.

SEYMOUR, William Frederick, 3 Selkirk Rd., Curzon Park, Chester CH4 8AH. (0244-674734)–BA. *b. 9 Aug 1935, Hackney. m. 31 July 1965: 1d.*
Education: 1946–53 Sir George Monoux Grammar Sch., Walthamstow; 1955–58 Shoreditch Coll., Egham, Surrey; 1962–65 Bristol Univ.; 1962–65 Didsbury, Bristol.
Appointments: 1965–67 Barry; 1967–71 London Mission Poplar; 1971–77 Colchester; 1977– Chester.
Publications: So You Want a Church Wedding (MPH 1977).
Special Interests: Correspondence Tutor for Local Preachers (Worship and Preaching, Student Chaplaincy, Chester. *Hobbies and Recreations:* Photography, Handicrafts.

SHADDICK, Ronald, 948 Atherton Rd., Hindley Green, Wigan WN2 4TA. (0942-59605) *b. 21 Jan 1931, Epsom, Surrey. m. 28 June 1958: 2s.*
Education: New Malden Coll., High Harrogate Coll., Coopers' Company Sch., Bow EC; 1955–58 Handsworth.
Appointments: 1958–63 Bishop's Castle and Clun; 1963–64 Stoke-on-Trent, Hanley Trinity; 1964–71 Eastbourne; 1971–76 London Mission, Broomwood and Clapham; 1976–79 Dorking and Horsham; 1979– Hindley.
Hobbies and Recreations: Photography, Audio/Visual.

SHANNAHAN, Alf, 12 Leahurst Close, Hoole, Chester CH2 3NS. (0244-21950) *b. 22 July 1929, Barrow-in-Furness. m. 28 Dec 1957: 2s.*
Education: 1956–57 Cliff Coll.; 1957–60 Hartley Victoria.
Appointments: 1960–65 Guisborough; 1965–67 Billingham; 1967–72 Liverpool South East; 1972–77 Northampton; 1977– Chester.
Connexional Committees: 1972–77 Ministries. *Local Council Committees:* 1968–72 Huyton (Liverpool) Education Committee; 1968–72 School Governor (Court Hey, Liverpool).
Special Interests: Wild Life, Conservation. *Hobbies and Recreations:* Photography, Caravanning, Philately.

SHARP, Alan, 47 Thurncroft Rd., Wibsey, Bradford BO6 3ER. (0274-676946) *b. 26 Aug 1940, New Silksworth, Co. Durham. m. 2 April 1966: 1d., 1s.*
Education: 1951–56 Ryhope Grammar Sch.; 1960–63 Cliff Coll.; 1963–67 Handsworth.
Appointments: 1968–72 Jamaica; 1972–77 Dewsbury; 1977– Bradford, Great Horton.
Connexional Committees: 1979– MCOD Central Committee.
Hobbies and Recreations: Photography, Walking.

SHARP, Christopher John, 14 Tangmere, Spennymoor, Co. Durham DL16 6TY. (0388-815198)–BA(Manch.). *b. 3 March 1944, Sowerby, Thirsk, Yorkshire. m. 1 July 1967: 1d., 2s.*
Education: 1955–56 City of Norwich Sch.; 1956–60 St. Bartholomew's Grammar Sch., Newbury; 1976–79 Univ. of Manchester; 1976–79 Hartley Victoria. *Appointments:* 1979– Spennymoor and Ferryhill.
Special Interests: Christian Adult Education; Renewal and Faith Sharing Groups. *Hobbies and Recreations:* Sport (Tennis), The Countryside, Nature, Conservation, Bird Watching.

SHARP, David George, 34 Wellington Rd., Nantwich, Cheshire CW5 7BX. (0270-625278)–MA(Cantab.), CertEd(Camb.), BD(Manch.)–*m. 30 July 1966: 2d.*
Education: 1943–46 St. Johns CE Prim. Sch., Ainsdale; 1946–49 Dalmain Rd. Prim. Sch., London SE23; 1949–57 Dulwich Coll.; 1959–62 Gonville and Caius Coll., Cambridge; 1962–63 Cambridge Univ. Dept. of Education; 1966–69 Manchester Univ.; 1966–69 Hartley Victoria. *Appointments:* 1969–75 New Testament Tutor, Cliff Coll.; 1975–78 Chaplain, Woodhouse Grove Sch.; 1978– Nantwich.
Connexional Committees: 1970–76 Wesley Deaconess Order, General Committee; 1975–77 Connexional Candidates Committee; 1976– Faith and Order Committee (1982–Executive). *Publications: No Stained Glass Window Saints* (Epworth 1976); *The Evangelical's Use of Scripture* (CEIM Lecture 1979); *Discovering the Bible, Part III* (with others, IBRA 1981).
Special Interests: Developing Team (Lay and Ordained) Ministry, Worship, Evangelism, Bible Teaching. *Hobbies and Recreations:* Music, DIY, History Books.

SHARP, John Richard, 3 Heather Rd., Lowestoft NR32 4PG. (0502-81921) *b. 2 April 1911, Grimsby. m. 27 Aug 1938: 1d., 1s.*
Education: Grimsby Municipal Coll.; 1928–29 Cliff Coll.; 1936–37 Selly Oak, Westhill; 1932–36 Richmond.
Appointments: 1936–38 Sheffield; 1938–40 Northallerton; 1940–44 Thirsk; 1944–47 Darwen; 1947–51 Leeds, Armley; 1951–55 Norwich, St. Peters; 1956–60 Newbury; 1960–67 Cromer; 1967–73 Lowestoft; 1973–76 Diss.
Special Interests: Natural History.
Hobbies and Recreations: Painting, Gardening.

SHARP, Lawrence Ewart, 179 Smithy Bridge Rd., Littleborough, Lancs OL15 0DB. (0706-73095) *b. 24 Feb 1935, Derby. m. 2 April 1960. 1d., 1s.*
Education: 1940–42 Clarence Rd. Prim. Sch.; 1942–43 Hasting St. Jun. Sch.,; 1943–46 Derby Diocesan Sch.; 1946–51 Derby Grammar Sch.; 1966–68 Handsworth.
Appointments: 1968–71 Leeds West; 1971–77 Liverpool North; 1977– Littleborough.
Special Interests: The Circuit Ministry.

SHARPLES, David Miles, 132 Crow Lane East, Newton-le-Willows, Merseyside WA12 9UA. (09252-6169)—BD. *b. 25 June 1939, Leigh, Lancashire. m. 11 May 1963: 2d., 1s.*
Education: 1944–50 King St. Methodist Inf. and Prim., Leigh; 1950–51 Windermere County Secondary Sch., Leigh; 1951–55 Bridgwater Sch. for Boys, Worsley; 1965–69 Hartley Victoria.
Appointments: 1969–71 Holyhead; 1971–76 Newcastle, Staffs.; 1976–81 Newark; 1981– Makerfield.
Connexional Committees: Overseas Division; 1974–76 Home Committee; 1976–81 Connexional Day Sch. Committee.
Hobbies and Recreations: Table Tennis, Badminton, Birdwatching.

SHARPLES, Victor, 42 Sandy Way, Walton on Thames, Surrey KT12 1BN. (093-22-20858) *b. 19 Oct 1926, Mellor, Nr. Blackburn, Lancs. m. 6 Aug 1955: 3s.* d. 1997
Education: 1931–40 St. Mary's, Mellor, Nr. Blackburn, Lancs.; 1941–48 Blackburn Municipal Technical Coll.; 1950–53 Headingley.
Appointments: 1953–55 Pateley Bridge; 1955–58 Knaresborough; 1958–64 Chingford; 1964–70 The Peak; 1970–77 Chester; 1977– Woking and Walton on Thames.
Special Interests: Hospital Chaplaincy Work, American Exchanges, Minnesota 1975, Idaho 1980.
Hobbies and Recreations: Travel, Golf, Gardening.

SHARROCK, Malcolm Joseph, 3 Molinnis Rd., Bugle, St. Austell, Cornwall PL26 8QJ. (0726-850222)—BA(Birmingham). *b. 31 Jan 1947, Stockport, Cheshire. m. 19 Feb 1972: 1d., 2s.*
Education: 1952–58 Cale Green, Prim. and Jun.; 1958–60 Dial Stone Secondary Modern; 1960–63 Stockport Sch.; 1974–77 Birmingham Univ.; 1974–78 Queens.
Appointments: 1978– Bodmin.
Hobbies and Recreations: Drawing and Pastel Painting, Reading.

SHARROCKS, Peter, 228 Green Lane, Norbury, London SW16 3BL. (01-764-6707) *b. 1 July 1940, Stockton-on-Tees. m. 14 Aug 1965: 2s.*
Education: 1951–56 Stockton Grammar Sch.; 1963–66 Handsworth.
Appointments: 1966–68 Dudley; 1968–71 Bilston; 1971–77 Wellington, Salop; 1977– Croydon.
Connexional Committees: 1973–78 Div. Education and Youth, MAYC Youth and Community; 1975–82 Regional Development Committee; 1970–82 Div. Education and Youth, Executive and Finance. *Local Council Committees:* 1972–77 Telford Youth Council; 1978–82 Croydon Youth Sub Committee, 1978–82 Croydon Youth Training Council.
Special Interests: Youth and Community Work, The Church and Community Development Practice, Race Relations. *Hobbies and Recreations:* Music, Folk Songs, Writer and Singer of Contemporary Christian Songs, Sport, Squash, Tennis, Soccer, Family Life.

SHAW, Bernard Arthur, 4 Bekingham Close, Crewe, Cheshire CW8 8JE. (0270-68484)—HonDV(Keele). *b. 12 Sept 1914, Wakefield, Yorkshire. m. 19 Feb 1944 (w.): 1d., 2s.*
Education: 1919–26 Outwood Elem.; 1926–27 Queen Elizabeth GS, Wakefield; 1927–31 Lancaster Royal GS; 1938–41 Richmond.
Appointments: 1941–42 Bristol (King St.); 1942–46 RAF (Chaplain); 1946–51 Stoke on Trent (Longton Mission); 1951–57 West London Mission (Hinde St.); 1957–62 Leeds Mission; 1962–80 Chairman, Chester and Stoke on Trent; 1977–78 President of Conference.
Hobbies and Recreations: Walking, Reading.

SHAW, Derek Leslie Francis, 56 Grosvenor Drive, Whitley Bay, Tyne and Wear NE26 2JS. (0632-521655)—BD(Lond.). *b. 13 Feb 1942, Salisbury, Rhodesia/now Harare, Zimbabwe. m. 31 July 1965: 1d., 1s.*
Education: 1955–60 Prince Edward; 1967–68 William Temple Coll.; 1964–67 Richmond. *Appointments:* 1968–70 Bolton; 1970–74 Ukuu Circuit, Meru District, Kenya; 1974– North Shields and Whitley Bay.
Connexional Committees: 1979–82 Overseas Division Central Committee.

SHAW, Thomas, Kynewas, 14 Lanmoore Estate, Lanner, Redruth, Cornwall. (0209-212104) *b. 25 April 1916, Manchester. m. 2 Jan 1945: 1d., 1s.*
Education: 1921–30 All Saints, Chorlton-cum-Hardy, and Chapel St., Levenshulme, Elem. Sch., Manchester; 1938–40 Handsworth; 1940–41 Headingley. *Appointments:* 1941–44 Camelford and Wadebridge; 1945–48 Holbeach, 1948–51 Rotherham; 1951–55 Holsworthy; 1955–58 Camborne; 1958–63 Truro, 1968–73 Helston.
Publications: The Bible Christians 1815–1907 (Epworth Press 1965); *A History of Cornish Methodism*

(Truro 1967); *The Menhinick Family* (priv. pub. Rotherham 1950); *John Wesley and Methodism, A Guide for Schools* (Wesley Historical Society 1971); *Methodism in the Camelford and Wadebridge Circuit 1743–63,* and many Cornish Methodist local histories, privately published.
Special Interests: Methodist History and Cornish subjects. *Hobbies and Recreations:* Genealogy.

SHEARD, Michael Rowland, 25 Marylebone Rd., London NW1 5JR. (01-935-2541)–BA, PhD. *b. 4 Aug 1942, Scunthorpe, Lincs. m. 20 March 1982.*
Education: 1953–60 Scunthorpe Grammar Sch.; 1960–63 Kings Coll., London; 1963–64 Westminster Coll., Oxford; 1970–74 Hartley Victoria. *Appointments:* 1974–78 North Shields and Whitley Bay; 1978– Connexional World Affairs Youth Secretary Overseas Division. *Connexional Committees:* 1978– MCOD Central Committee; 1978– MDEY Board; 1981– DSR Board. *Publications: Origins and Development of Primitive Methodism in Manchester to 1830* (WHS Occasional Papers 1979).
Special Interests: History of Methodism with particular reference to 19th century, World Development and Peace Education. *Hobbies and Recreations:* Skin-diving, Gardening, Reading.

SHEARER, William Russell, 32 Layton Lane, Shaftesbury, Dorset SP7 8EY. (0747-2678)–MA(Cantab.). *b. 12 Oct 1898, Luffenham, Rutland. m. 2 Aug 1934.*
Education: 1910–16 Harrogate Grammar; 1916–21 Leeds; 1921–23 Wesley House. *Appointments:* 1923–28 Stoke-on-Trent (Tunstall); 1928–33 Manchester and Salford Mission; 1933–39 London (Highgate); 1939–40 Sutton (Surrey); 1940–45 Stoke-on-Trent (Bethesda, Hanley); 1943–50 Chairman Stoke and Macclesfield Dt; 1950–63 Chairman Birmingham Dt; President of the Conference 1954.
Connexional Committees: 1942–52 Church Membership; 1948–63 Chapel Committee; 1954–69 Overseas Missions. *Publications:* Fernley-Hartley Lecture 1965.

SHEPPARD, Frederick Orum, 53 Glanwern Ave., Newport, Gwent NPT 9DH. (0633-277976) *b. 6 March 1904, Streatham, London. m. 16 April 1938: 1d., 1s.*
Education: 1909 Council, London; 1910–18 Council, Swindon; 1930–32 Hartley Victoria. *Appointments:* 1928–30 Margate; 1932–34 Clitheroe; 1934–37 Cheltenham; 1937–39 Faringdon; 1939–42 Rochdale; 1942–51 Chaplain HMF; 1951–54 Bristol (Clifton and Redland); 1954–61 Newport, Stow Hill; 1961–70 Devonport.
Hobbies and Recreations: Football, Tennis, Golf, Gardening.

SHERIFF, David Henry Kingsley, East End Mission, 583 Commercial Rd., London E1 0RJ. (01-790-3366)–BD. *b. 22 Jan 1929, Gainsborough, Lincs. m. 13 Aug 1955: 1s.*
Education: 1940–46 Kingswood; 1947–49 Univ. Coll., London; 1952 Cliff Coll.; 1952–55 Richmond.
Appointments: 1955–56 Cromer, Sheringham and Holt; 1957–61 Turks and Caicos Is.; 1962–67 Kingston, Jamaica; 1967–72 Leigh-on-Sea; 1972–78 London, Hackney Mission; 1978– London, East End Mission.
Connexional Committees: 1967–70 Overseas Division; 1975–78 DSR.
Special Interests: Qualified Teacher and Youth Worker (ILEA), Lecturer (Part Time) Sociology and Religious Studies. *Hobbies and Recreations:* Photography, Gardening, Ballet.

SHERIFF, Horace Kinfaun, 20 Dunraven Rd., Little Neston, South Wirral, Cheshire L64 9QU. *b. 28 Oct 1899, Devonport. m. 29 July 1933: 1d.*
Education: 1904–14 Liskeard (Cornwall) Council Sch.; 1926–27 Hartley Victoria. *Appointments:* 1927–29 Oldham, Union St.; 1929–31 Plymouth, Greenbank; 1931–37 Taunton; 1937–42 Cardiff, Roath; 1942–47 Dudley, Wesley; 1947–52 Jersey, Aquila Rd.; 1952–56 Longton and Fenton; 1956–60 Penzance, Chapel St.; 1960–65 Manchester, Newton Heath.
Connexional Committees: 1932–35 Y. People and S.S.; 1947–52 Temperance and Social Welfare. *Hobbies and Recreations:* Tennis, Bowls.

SHERRATT, George, 36 Merrow Lane, Guildford, Surrey GU4 7LQ. (0483-34696) *b. 3 April 1908, Wolverhampton, Staffordshire. m. 23 July 1938: 2d., 1s.*
Education: 1913–18 Brickkiln St., Wolverhampton, Jun.; 1918–23 Higher Grade Sch., Wolverhampton; 1932–35 Didsbury. *Appointments:* 1931–32 Knighton; 1935–38 Darlington; 1938–40 Oldham; 1940–47 Sunderland (St. John's); 1947–52 Warrington; 1952–55 Liverpool (Crosby); 1955–59 London Mission (Archway Central Hall); 1959–69 London Mission, Deptford Central Hall; 1969–73 Sutton (Surrey).
Connexional Committees: 1955–57 Temperance and Social Welfare; 1960–69 London Mission.
Special Interests: Honorary Chaplain to Forces, 1930–40, 1940–47, 1947–52 Army, 1940–52 Airforce, 1947–52 Navy, 1955–69 Hospitals. *Hobbies and Recreations:* Visiting.

SHERRINGTON, John Brian, c/o The Secretary, Royal Navy, Army and Air Force Board, 1 Central Buildings, London SW1.–BA(Lond.), BD(Lond.). *b. 6 July 1938, Wigan. m. 2 Sept 1961: 3s.*
Education: 1949–58 Wigan Grammar Sch.; 1958–60 London Univ.; 1963–66 Hartley Victoria. *Appointments:* 1966–69 Cannock Chase; 1969–72 Liverpool, Crosby; 1972– Chaplain HMF.
Special Interests: Education, Religious Education in a Secular Society. *Hobbies and Recreations:* Gardening, Fly-Fishing, Philately.

SHILLING, Peter William, 80 Warbreck Hill Rd., Blackpool, Lancs FY2 9UW. (0253-51556)–BD(Lond.). *b. 8 Oct 1943, London. m. 13 Aug 1966: 1d., 1s.*
Education: Swaffield Rd. Inf. Sch., Wandsworth, London; Dulwich Coll. Prep. Sch.; Coombe House Private

Sch.; 1969–72 Richmond.
Appointments: 1972–78 Coventry Mission; 1978– Blackpool North.
Special Interests: Mission Work, Being with My Wife and family.

SHORT, Raymond Arthur, 6 Longfield Drive, Amersham, Bucks HP6 5HD. (024-03-3653)–MA(Cantab.). *b. 15 June 1925, Merton Park, London SW19. m. 30 July 1953: 1d., 2s.*
Education: 1940–43 Kingswood Sch., Bath; 1943–44 Liverpool Univ., Sch. of Architecture; 1948–51 Cambridge Univ.; 1948–51 Wesley House. *Appointments:* 1947–48 Stoke Newington and Mildmay Park; 1951–53 Hunts Mission; 1953–57 South Shields; 1957–61 Durham; 1961–64 BBC Religious Broadcasting Dept., Radio Producer, Manchester; 1964–70 TV Producer, Manchester; 1970– Executive TV Producer, BBC TV London.
Connexional Committees: 1961– TV Committee; 1973–76 Division of Ministries; 1971– Ministers in other Appointments.
Special Interests: Art, Exhibiting member of Chiltern Painters, Philosophy of Religion. *Hobbies and Recreations:* Golf.

SHREEVE, Christopher John, 19 Park View Ave., Branston, Lincoln LN4 1NU. (0522-791476) *b. 18 May 1948, Norwich, Norfolk. s.*
Education: 1959–64 City of Norwich Grammar Sch.; 1977–79 Wesley, Bristol. *Appointments:* 1979– Lincoln Central.
Special Interests: Holy Spirit Renewal, Evangelism, Children's Work, Teaching. *Hobbies and Recreations:* Art, Model Making, Music, Outdoor Activities.

SHREWSBURY, John Lionel Cheverton, 6 Mossbank Close, Hadfield, Hyde SK14 8EH. (04574-61089)–MA(Oxon), BA(Cantab.). *b 26 Dec 1918, Great Grimsby. m. 3 Aug 1950: 2s.*
Education: 1929–37 Boteler Grammar Sch., Warrington; 1937–40 Jesus Coll., Oxford; 1940–42 Fitzwilliam House, Cambridge; 1940–42 Wesley House. *Appointments:* 1942–44 Crosby; 1944–45 Scilly Isles; 1945–48 Rotherham; 1948–51 Worksop; 1951-52 Bradford East; 1952–55 Penarth and Barry; 1955–58 Birmingham Wesley; 1958–61 Bolton; 1961–64 Aberystwyth; 1964–69 Cheetham Hill and Prestwich; 1969–72 Douglas IOM; 1972–75 Worksop; 1975–77 Stretford; 1977– Glossop.
Special Interests: Ecumenism.
Hobbies and Recreations: Mountain Walking, Travel, Languages.

SHRIMPTON, Anthony, 5 Penarth Ave., Portsmouth PO6 2AJ. (0705-376057) *b. 18 Aug 1935, Shanghai. m. 20 Mar 1965: 1d., 1s.*
Education: 1948–54 Haberdasher's Askes; 1959–63 Handsworth.
Appointments: 1965–68 Hull West; 1968–74 Oxford; 1974–80 Salisbury; 1980– Portsmouth.
Council Member: 1967–68 Brough (Yorks) Council.
Hobbies and Recreations: BAAB Senior Coach, Marathon and Cross Country, BAAB Club Coach, Middle Distance, Gold Medal England Cross-Country Team, World Championships, 1979, 1981.

SHUTTER, Derek, 2 Park Lane, Oswaldtwistle, Accrington, Lancs BB5 3AF. (0254-33843)–BSc(Lond.), BA(Bristol). *b. 10 Dec 1929, Epsom. m. 18 Aug 1956: 1d., 3s.*
Education: 1940–48 City of London Freemen's Sch., Ashtead; 1949–53 Regent St. Poly., London; 1953–56 Didsbury, Bristol. *Appointments:* 1956–60 Boston; 1960–66 Sheffield (Carver St.); 1966–71 Bradford (Woodhouse Grove); 1971–76 Lytham St. Annes; 1976– Accrington and Haslingden.

SIDDLE, James Robert, 24 Eldon Rd., Winton, Bournemouth, Dorset BH9 2RT. (0202-526287) *b. 26 Dec 1913, Liverpool. m. 16 April 1938: 2s.*
Education: 1919–23 Blenheim Council Sch., Leeds; 1923–25 Francis Ave. Council Sch., Southsea, Portsmouth; 1925–27 Meanwood Rd. Council Sch., Leeds; 1958–59 Hartley Victoria; 1972–73 Kingsmead. *Appointments:* 1959–64 Market Rasen and Caistor Circuit; 1964–68 Staveley; 1968–72 Retford; 1973 Honduras District MCCA; 1973–76 Bahamas District MCCA; 1976–81 Poole.
Hobbies and Recreations: Gardening, Music.

SIDDONS, John Basil, The Manse, 6 Chapel Hill, Hayle, Cornwall TR27 4JU. (0736-753325) *b. 3 July 1933, Rawmarsh, Nr. Rotherham. m. 22 Sept 1956: 1d., 1s.*
Education: Fitzwilliam Inf. and Jun. Sch., Swinton, Yorks.; Mexborough Schofield Technical Sch., Yorks.; 1963–65 Headingley. *Appointments:* 1965–66 Uttoxeter; 1966–71 Ilkeston; 1971–74 Sheffield North; 1974–80 Bridlington; 1980– St. Ives and Hayle.
Special Interests: Gardening, Interior Decorating, Church in Industry Affairs. *Hobbies and Recreations:* Various Sports, including Cricket, Tennis, Football, Walking, Motoring.

SIGSWORTH, John Harold, 136 Cottingham Rd., Hull HU6 7RY. (0482-43055)–BA(Oxon), BA(Cantab.), DipEd(Leeds). *b. 24 March 1937, Normanby, Middlesbrough. m. 26 Aug 1961: 4s.*
Education: 1942–47 Normanby Prim. and Jun.; 1947–55 Sir William Turners Grammar Sch., Redcar; 1955–58 Keble Coll., Oxford; 1958–59 Leeds Univ., Dept. of Education; 1959–61 Wesley House.
Appointments: 1961–65 Hexham; 1965–70 Stanley; 1970–74 Fenland; 1974–82 Bury St. Edmunds (Chaplain Culford Sch.); 1982– Hull West.

SILVANUS, David Gethin, 27 Pollen Close, Figheldean, Salisbury, Wilts SP4 8JP. (098-07-365)–DipTheol. *b. 15 May 1922, Aberdare, Glamorgan. m. 24 Aug 1946: 1d., 2s.*
Education. 1935–41 Aberdare Boys Grammar Sch.; 1947–50 United Theological Coll., Univ. of Wales, Aberystwyth. *Appointments:* 1950–54 Presbyterian Church of Wales, Tredegar, Gwent; 1954–76 Chaplain, Royal Air Force; 1976–78 Education

Welfare Service, Wilts C.C.; 1978– Salisbury.
Special Interests: Ecumenical Movement, Social Reponsibility, Sharing Groups. Hobbies and Recreations: Watching Rugby Football, Musical Appreciation, Reading, Political Biographies.

SIMMONDS, John Malcolm, 530 Manchester Rd., Crosspool, Sheffield S10 5PQ. (0742-305676)– BD(Lond.). *b. 30 July 1941, Chesterfield, Derbyshire. m.25 July 1964: 2s.*
Education: 1946–52 Old Hall Prim., Chesterfield; 1952–59 Chesterfield Sch.; 1964–67 London Univ. (External Student); 1961–65 Handsworth. *Appointments:* 1965–67 Lerwick, North Roe and Northern Isles (Shetland); 1967–71 Birmingham (Sutton Park); 1971–76 Cannock Chase; 1976– Sheffield (Carver St.).
Connexional Committees: 1981– Church Membership. *Publications: Travelling Along* (SCM 1982) with John Pritchard.
Special Interests: In-Service Training for Ministry, Contemporary Theology, Shared Ministry, Peace Movement. *Hobbies and Recreations:* Photography, Fell-Walking, Gardening, DIY, Cars and Motoring, Travel.

SIMMONDS, Trevor Glyn, 1 St. Julian's Ave., Newport, Gwent NPT 7JT. (0633-58150) *b. 23 June 1929, Neath, Glamorganshire. m. 22 June 1957: 1d., 1s.*
Education: 1954–57 Handsworth. *Appointments:* 1957–60 Darlaston; 1960–65 Willenhall; 1965–72 Cardiff Wesley; 1972–78 Hereford; 1978– Newport (Gwent).

SIMMONS, Arthur, 1 Hummersknott Ave., Darlington, Co. Durham DL3 8JX. (0325-68412)–BA. *b. 24 Sept 1895, Stafford. m. (2) 1955:1d., 1s.*
Education: Stafford Grammar Sch., 1913 Stafford Pupil Teaching; 1914 Rugeley Pupil Teaching; 1919–21 Birmingham Univ.; 1915 Richmond; 1919–21 Handsworth.
Appointments: 1921–24 Ledbury; 1924–27 Snaith; 1927–30 Sheffield Park; 1930–35 Leeds, Headingley; 1935–39 Stockport, Trinity; 1939–44 Bradford, Manningham; 1944–49 Sutton, Surrey; 1949–53 Darlington; 1953–57 Chairman, Darlington and Middlesbrough District; 1954–57 Shildon.
Connexional Committees: All Chairman's Committees. *Local Council Committees:* Newton Aycliffe Commission. *Publications: The Measure of a Christian* (1935); *The Meaning of Love* (1938); Plays: *The Master's Cup* (1935–59); *The Other Carpenter* (1939); *Whom God Chose* (1936); *The Mustard Seed* (1957).
Special Interests: Council of Churches, United Nations, Citizen's Advice Bureau. *Hobbies and Recreations:* Woodworking, Gardening, Golf, Walking.

SIMMONS, Gordon Frederick, 30 Passmore, Tinkers Ridge, Milton Keynes MK6 3DZ. (0908-670332)– BA, BD(Manch.). *b. 8 July 1921, Finchley, London. m. 27 July 1950: 2s.*
Education: 1926– Gordon House, Finchley; 1930– Finchley High Sch.; 1934–37 Univ. Coll. Sch., Hampstead; 1948–51 Hartley Victoria.
Appointments: 1946–48 Barnstaple (Boutport); 1951–54 Patricroft and Eccles; 1954 Eccles (Wesley); 1955–59 Eccles; 1959–63 Brentford and Hounslow; 1963–66 Bath; 1966–72 Barnoldswick; 1972–55 Nelson; 1975 PRA (USA); 1976– Milton Keynes.
Connexional Committees: 1967– LP Studies Board; 1979– LP Connexional Committee; 1972–75, 1978– Connexional Candidates; 1978– Property Board.
Special Interests: Reflected in Connexional Committees, Ecumenical. *Hobbies and Recreations:* Gardening, Reading.

SIMONS, George William, 6 Saxon Rd., Hoylake, Wirral, Merseyside L47 3AE. (051-632-4850) *b. 4 Nov 1923, Sheffield. m. 12 Aug 1950: 1d., 1s.*
Education: 1928–34 Brightside, Sheffield; 1934–38 Owler Lane, Sheffield; 1948–50 Headingley.
Appointments: 1947–48 Kirkoswald; 1950–51 Liverpool, Crosby; 1951–55 Goole; 1955–61 Lowestoft; 1961–66 Birmingham, Elmdon; 1966–73 Birkenhead; 1973–79 Nottingham (West); 1979– Hoylake and West Kirby.
Connexional Committees: 1970–73 Church Membership. *Local Council Committees:* 1957–61 Lowestoft Education Committee.

SIMPSON, Bertram Louvain, 26 Orchard Cresc., Wolverhampton, West Midlands WV3 8DS. (0902-763110) *b. 10 Dec 1914, Sunderland. m. 13 July 1946: 1d., 3s.*
Education: 1919–27 Barnes; 1927–30 Jun. Technical Sch.; 1938–40 Didsbury; 1940–41 Hartley Victoria.
Appointments: 1941–44 Wellingborough; 1944–45 Oundle; 1945–48 Thornley and Co. Durham Coast; 1948–54 Kirkby Stephen; 1954–57 Penrith; 1957–62 Brompton; 1962–67 Gornal and Sedgley; 1967–73 Old Hill; 1973–79 Netherton.
Connexional Committees: 1950–52 Temperance and Social Welfare.
Special Interests: General Reading. *Hobbies and Recreations:* Music, Painting.

SIMPSON, George Hudson, 53 Harewood Cresc., Oakworth, Keighley, West Yorks BD22 7NH. (0535-65263) *b. 1 April 1911, York. m. 20 Aug 1938: 2s.*
Education: –1925 Park Grove, York; 1925–27 York Commercial Sch.; 1931–34 Hartley Victoria.
Appointments: 1934–35 Wetton and Lengnor; 1935–36 Heckmondwike (Batley Rd.); 1937–39 Motherwell; 1939–41 Parkheath, Glasgow; 1941–42 Snaith; 1942–45 Driffield; 1945–48 Halifax (Ebenezer); 1948–52 Camborne; 1952–55 Penzance (Chapel St.); 1955–60 Hitchin; 1960–67 Halifax North; 1967–69 St. Austell; 1969–72 Wombwell and Hoyland; 1972–76 Haworth and Oakworth.

SIMPSON, James, 33 Breadcroft lane, Barrow on Soar, Loughborough, Leics LE12 8HW. (0509-43556) *b. 10 March 1904, Langley,*

Macclesfield, Cheshire. m. 1 Aug 1934: 1d.
Education: St. James Jun. Sch., Sutton, Macclesfield; Henry VII Grammar Sch., Macclesfield; 1928–31 Handsworth. *Appointments:* 1927–28 Liverpool Mission; 1931–33 Redditch; 1933–36 Evesham; 1936–41 Longton, Stoke on Trent; 1941–46 Leek; 1946–50 Bideford; 1950–52 Kettering; 1952–60 Bolsover; 1960–65 Coalville; 1965–72 Accrington; 1972– Loughborough.
Hobbies and Recreations: Gardening, Reading, Cricket (watching only).

SIMPSON, Wilfred Robinson, 8 Oban Ave., Maybury Rd., Hull HU9 3NJ. (0482-797145) *b. 23 Aug 1906, Hull. m. 10 Oct 1933: 1d.*
Education: 1927–30 Didsbury.
Appointments: 1930–46 Hupeh Dt, Central China; 1946–49 Driffield; 1949–53 Bridlington; 1953–58 Hull (West); 1958–64 South Shields; 1964–69 Sunderland North; 1969–71 Shildon.
Connexional Committees: 1954–58 Overseas Missions: Representing the Hull District; 1960–66 Representing the Newcastle District.
Special Interests: Overseas Missions.
Hobbies and Recreations: Photography.

SINCOCK, John Sydney, The Jays, 39 Parkside, Little Paxton, Huntingdon, Cambs PE19 4NN. (0480-74933) *b. 5 March 1911, Fulham, London. m. 8 Sept 1939: 1d., 2s.*
Education: Millbank (London); Cliff Coll. *Appointments:* 1946–50 N.T.H.; 1955–57 Shetland; 1957–60 Cardiff Coloured Mission; 1960–63 Swinton; 1963–65 London Mission, North and Central; 1965–70 Hunts Mission; 1970–73 St. Neots.
Hobbies and Recreations: Gardening, Reading.

SINFIELD, Herbert Mortimer, Fox Hollow, Parsons Way, Winscombe, Avon BS25 1BT. (093484-2073) *b. 22 Nov 1900, Scarborough, Yorkshire. m. 9 Aug 1938: 2d.*
Education: Falsgrave Sch., Scarborough; 1911–16 Scarborough Municipal Sch.; 1919 Queens Coll., Taunton; 1915 Scarborough Art Sch., Night Student; 1916–19 Salford Technical Coll.; 1921–24 Didsbury.
Appointments: 1924–27 Tow Law; 1927–30 Oldbury; 1930–35 Hull (Coltman St.); 1935–39 London, Ilford; 1939–42 Derby (South); 1942–49 Wolverhampton (Trinity); 1949–54 Birmingham (Mosley Rd.); 1954–59 Wembley; 1959–65 Weston-super-Mare.
Publications: The Only Way (1929); *Jesus and Our Questions* (1932); *God and My Life* (1937); *Methodism's Message in Modern Terms* (1945); *Golden Chains* (1947).
Special Interests: Art, Natural History.
Hobbies and Recreations: Painting, Gardening, Walking.

SKERRATT, Cyril, 12 Philip Rd., Blandford Forum, Dorset DT11 7NR. (0258 53921) *b. 19 July 1915, Alsager, Stoke-on-Trent. m. 18 Sept 1943: 1d.*
Education: 1920–26 Alsager CE; 1926–33 Crewe County Grammar; 1946–47 Richmond. *Appointments:* 1947–53 Market Rasen and Caistor; 1953–58 Gainsborough; 1958–63 Alford; 1963–68 Ellesmere; 1968–76 Kettering; 1976–80 Banbury.
Connexional Committees: 1960–63 Education.
Special Interests: Peace Movement, Third World Development. *Hobbies and Recreations:* Gardening, Music, Cricket, Reading.

SKIDMORE, John, 42 Charles Ashmore Rd., Sheffield S8 8GJ. (0742-746126)–BA(Leeds). *b. 3 July 1915, Normanton, Yorkshire. m. 14 Aug 1945: 2s.*
Education: 1918–27 Normanton Woodhouse Council Sch., 1927–34 Normanton Grammar Sch.; 1939–42 Leeds Univ.; 1938–42 Headingley.
Appointments: 1942–45 Cowbridge and St. Athan; 1945–50 London Mission (Rivercourt and Shepherds Bush Road); 1950–55 Hebden Bridge; 1955–62 Sheffield (Ecclesall); 1962–69 Barnsley (East); 1969–76 Newcastle upon Tyne (West); 1976–81 York (Centenary).
Local Council Committees: 1967–69 Barnsley Education Committee.

SKINNER, Francis Edward, Willersley House, 85 Main St., Willerby, Hull HU10 6BY. (0842-653353) *b. 11 Jan 1894, Beverley, East Yorkshire. m. 20 Feb 1920: 1d., 2s.*
Education: 1905–09 Beverley Grammar; 1912–13 Cliff Coll.; 1913–15 Headingley. *Appointments:* 1915–16 Supply; 1916–30 Burma Dt; 1930–33 Birmingham Islington; 1933–37 Stourbridge; 1937–41 Huddersfield, Brunswick St.; 1941–46 Bradford Manningham; 1946–51 Buxton; 1951–54 Morpeth; 1954–56 Hebden Bridge.
Publications: Manual of Church Membership (Burmese); *The Greatest Among Them* (Play); *Vestry Prayers* (2 Editions).

SKINNER, Howard Lansdown, 67 South Ave., Gillingham, Kent ME8 6EE. (0634-364705) *b. 14 Feb 1926, Highams Park, London. m. 23 July 1953: 3d., 1s.*
Education: 1931–33 Highams Park Private Sch.; 1933–37 Selwyn Ave. Jun. Sch., Highams Park; 1937–39 William Morris Central Sch., Walthamstow; 1939–41 Barnstaple Grammar Sch.; 1941–42 Surbiton County Sch.; 1949–51 Handsworth.
Appointments: 1947–49 Cardiff (Wesley); 1951–56 Coventry; 1956–61 Chislehurst; 1961–68 London, Lewisham and Peckham; 1968–75 Whitstable and Herne Bay; 1975– Medway Towns.
Connexional Committees: 1976– Church Membership Committee.
Hobbies and Recreations: Historic Buildings, Cathedrals and Parish Churches, Brass Rubbing, Photography, Camping and Walking, Member of the Camping Club of Great Britain, Friend of the Iona Community.

SKINNER, Leslie F., 47 Eastdean Ave., Epsom, Surrey KT18 7SW. (03727-25467)–TD. *b. 26 Nov 1911, York. m. 23 July 1941: 1d., 2s.*
Education: 1923–27 Elmfield Coll., York; 1934–37 Hartley Victoria.
Appointments: 1937–38 Lucknow and Benares, N. India; 1938–41 N. Derbyshire Mission; 1941–46 HMF

Chaplain; 1946–50 Manchester (Gravel Lane); 1950–54 Altrincham; 1954–59 London Mission, Stockwell; 1959–65 Kingston on Thames; 1968–77 Walton on Thames and Woking; 1947–66 Territorial Army Chaplaincy Service; 1958–66 Senior Chaplain 56th London Division; 1963–66 DACG (TA) London District.
Connexional Committees: 1950–52, 1957–62 Overseas Missions; 1959–62 Chairman HOD Committee; 1957–69 Royal Navy, Army and Royal Air Force Board. *Local Council Committees:* 1948–50 Salford Youth; 1949–54 Manchester Council Social Service; 1956–59 Lambeth Youth Committee; 1962–64 Chairman Kingston Council of Churches; 1966–68 Ecumenical Committee Corby Development Corporation; 1966–68 Methodist Rep. Peterborough Diocesan Ecumenical Experiment Committee.
Publications: Methodism in Walton on Thames (1979).
Special Interests: Reading, Church Music, History, Buildings. *Hobbies and Recreations:* Gardening, Cricket, Football, Swimming, Travel.

SKINNER, Michael James, 152 Victoria Park Rd., Leicester. (0533-705342)–MA(Cantab.). *b. 23 Feb 1919, Cambridge. m. 17 Mar 1954: 1d., 3s.*
Education: 1927–32 St. Faith's Prep. Sch., Cambridge; 1932–38 The Leys Sch., Cambridge; 1938–41 Jesus Coll., Cambridge; 1941–43 Wesley House. *Appointments:* 1943–46 Ambleside and Windermere; 1946–47 President's Assistant; 1947–51 Handsworth Coll., Assistant Tutor; 1951–57 Durham; 1957–59 Filey; 1959–74 Tutor Wesley House, Cambridge; 1974–80 Principal Wesley House; 1980– Leicester South East.
Connexional Committees: 1950's Church Membership; 1957–80 Ministerial Training. *Publications: This is Christianity* (1966); *House Groups* (1969); *The Sermon on the Mount* (1966).
Special Interests: Ecclesiology and Christian Doctrine in General. *Hobbies and Recreations:* Music, Golf.

SKINNER, Norman Ralph, 92 St. Andrews Rd., Bridport, Dorset DT6 3BL. (0308-22766)–BA(Lond.), BD(Lond.). *b. 27 Aug 1933, Ludlow, Shropshire. m. 14 Aug 1959: 1d., 1s.*
Education: 1939–45 Lancasterian Sch., Shrewsbury; 1945–52 Priory Sch. for Boys, Shrewsbury; 1952–56 Univ. Coll., London; 1956–59 Handsworth. *Appointments:* 1959–63 Preston (Lune St.); 1963–68 Manchester and Salford Mission; 1968–73 Bristol South; 1973– Sidmouth and Bridport.
Connexional Committees: Methodist/United Reformed Church Liaison Committee. *Local Council Committees:* 1965–68 City of Salford Education Committee; 1974– West Dorset Area Youth Committee.
Publications: On Choral Music, *A Wesley Overture* (1979); Variations on Purcell's *Westminster Abbey* (1973); Variations on a Folk Tune (1981–82).
Special Interests: Youth and Education, Christian Unity, Organ Recitalist, Conductor of Youth Orchestra and District Orchestra; Composing and Arranging Orchestral Music, Music Criticism and Adjudication. *Hobbies and Recreations:* Journalism, Local History, Table Tennis, Chess.

SKUTT, Brian William George, 19 Mill Rise, Bourton, Gillingham, Dorset SP8 5DH. (0747-840635) *b. 18 April 1939, Salisbury, Wiltshire. m. 3 July 1965: 1s.*
Education: 1950–57 Bishop Wordsworth Sch., Salisbury; 1961–65 Didsbury, Bristol. *Appointments:* 1965–67 Swindon; 1967–74 Liskeard; 1974–75 Ashton-under-Lyne; 1975–80 Radstock; 1980– Shaftesbury and Gillingham.
Hobbies and Recreations: Stamp Collecting, Music, Gardening.

SLATER, Stanley James, 10 Littledale, Pickering, North Yorkshire YO18 8PS. (0751-73936) *b. 16 Feb 1914, Rotherham. m: 1s.*
Education: 1935–38 Headingley. *Appointments:* 1938–39 Market Drayton; 1939–42 Wishaw; 1942–45 Walls; 1945–49 Chesterfield; 1949–55 Otley; 1955–63 The Peak; 1963–69 Elland; 1969–73 Eccles; 1973– Macclesfield.

SLEATH, Victor William, 9 Harvest Hill Close, Sydenham, Leamington Spa, Warwicks CV31 1RB. (0926-34648) *b. 2 Oct 1908, London. m. 3 Sept 1936: 2s.*
Education: 1914–20 Gladstone Park, Dollis Hill, London; 1920–22 Furness Rd., Harlesden; 1930–33 Victoria Park. *Appointments:* 1933–40 Kenya Dt; 1940–44 South Africa; 1944–46 Weardale; 1946–48 Doncaster; 1948–49 London, Broomwood and Stockwell; 1949–52 Newmarket; 1952–56 Guernsey; 1956–59 Retford; 1959–62 Sheffield NE; 1962–67 Burton-on-Trent; 1967–70 Rugby; 1970–73 Ripley.
Special Interests: Scout Movement.

SMITH, Alan Armstead, 26 Ridgeway Drive, Lydiate, Maghull, Liverpool L31 0DE. (051-526-2836)–BD(Lond.). *b. 24 May 1936, Blackburn, Lancs. m. 13 July 1963: 2d.*
Education: 1940–47 Audley Prim., Blackburn; 1947–53 Queen Elizabeth Grammar Sch., Blackburn; 1959–63 Handsworth. *Appointments:* 1963–67 St. Ives, Wesley; 1967–72 Nottingham East; 1972–75 South Wirral; 1975–77 First Church Rockingham, North Carolina, USA; 1977 Liverpool North.
Special Interests: Politics. *Hobbies and Recreations:* Philately, Sport, Music.

SMITH, Anthony John, Wesley Manse, Church St., Chipping Norton, Oxon OX7 5NT. (0608-2631)–BA(Bristol), FCA. *b. 26 Nov 1937, Northampton. m. 3 April 1965: 1d., 1s.*
Education: 1949–54 Northampton Grammar Sch.; 1963–66 Bristol Univ.; 1967 Kingsmead Coll.; 1963–67 Didsbury, Bristol. *Appointments:* 1967–68 Grenada; 1968–71 Barbados, Bethel; 1971–76 Cradley Heath; 1976–82 Witney and Faringdon; 1982– Chipping Norton

and Stow.
Special Interests: Computers.
Hobbies and Recreations: Chess, DIY, Music.

SMITH, Arthur Leslie, 20 Cowper Cresc., Bengeo, Hertford, Herts SG14 3DY. (0992-51179)—BA. *b. 2 Jan 1927, Southport. m. 25 Sept 1954: 1s.*
Education: 1937–43 King George V Grammar Sch., Southport; 1948–51 Univ. of Leeds; 1948–51 Headingley. *Appointments:* 1948–49 Saddleworth; 1951–53 Castletown IOM; 1953–59 Stafford; 1959–63 Leeds Mission; 1963–82 Balls Park Coll./Hertfordshire Coll. of Higher Education.

SMITH, Charles H, Wesley Villa, 10 Salthouse Rd., Millom, Cumbria LA18 5AD. (0657/2581) *b. 12 Aug 1922, Nr. Sprotborough, Doncaster. m. 24 May 1947: 2d., 1s.*
Education: Cliff Coll. *Appointments:* 1964–68 Wath and Mexborough; 1968–72 Clowne; 1972–76 Bromborough; 1976–77 Newtown, Powys; 1977–82 Buckley and Deeside.
Special Interests: Colliery and Prison Chaplaincy. *Hobbies and Recreations:* Map Reading, Gardening.

SMITH, Christopher Hughes, 36 Amesbury Rd., Moseley, Birmingham B13 8LE. (021-449-0131)—MA. *b. 30 Nov 1929, Nottingham. m. 3s.*
Education: 1935–39 St. Silas, Blackburn; 1939–48 Bolton Sch.; Emmanuel Coll., Cambridge; 1953–55 Wesley House. *Appointments:* 1955–58 East Midlands Intercollegiate Secretary, Student Christian Movement; 1958–65 Leicester (South); 1965–74 Birmingham (South-West); 1974– Chairman, Birmingham District.
Connexional Committees: Divisional Boards of Education and Youth; Home Missions; Property; Ministries; Student Work Committee; Board of Management Methodist Residential Schools, (various dates).
Publications: Andrew Ndhlela Lecture, Zimbabwe Methodist Conference 1979.
Hobbies and Recreations: Gardening, Music, Books.

SMITH, Christopher Hulse, Parkwood, Hall Rd., Wallington, Surrey SM6 0RT. (01-647-1550)—MA(Cantab.). *b. 3 Jan 1923, Hipperholme, Yorks. m. 28 July 1951: 1d., 2s.*
Education: 1933–42 Kingswood Sch.; 1942 Emmanuel Coll., Cambridge; 1946–48 Wesley House. *Appointments:* 1948–51 SW China District; 1951–54 Methodist Missionary Society; 1954–64 Trinity Theol. Coll., Singapore; 1964–69 Wesley Church, Singapore; 1970–75 Trinity Methodist Church, Singapore; 1975– Sutton (Surrey).
Connexional Committees: 1977–80 Overseas Division Central Committee.
Special Interests: The Church in Asia, Pastoral Counselling, Samaritans.
Hobbies and Recreations: Birdwatching, Photography.

SMITH, Clarence Raymond, 149 Gravelly Hill, Birmingham B23 7NR. (021-373-3204) *b. 30 Aug 1927, Tonypandy, Rhondda, S. Wales. m. 6 June 1954: 1d., 2s.*
Education: Prim. Tai Sch., Penygraig, Rhondda; Secondary, Porth County Grammar; 1949–51 Handsworth.
Appointments: 1947–48 Rhondda; 1948–49 Forest of Dean; 1951–55 Manchester Mission; 1955–58 Newcastle (Brunswick); 1958–64 Darlington; 1964–69 Birmingham Mission, as Industrial Chaplain; 1969 Birmingham Sutton Park (Industrial Chaplain).
Connexional Committees: 1959–64 Christian Citizenship (Social Responsibility); 1964–79 Church in Industry Committee. *Publications:* Various Lectures mainly via Luton Industrial Coll.
Special Interests: History and Present Role of Trade Unions. *Hobbies and Recreations:* Rugby Union.

SMITH, David Howard, Old Schoolhouse, Bodinnick-by-Fowey, Cornwall PL23 1LX. (072687-367)—BD(Lond.), BA. *b. 7 June 1900, Gt. Harwood, Lancs. m. (2) 3 March 1977: 3d. (By 1st m.)*
Education: 1905–10 Gt. Harwood British (Elem.) Sch.; 1910–17 Accrington Grammar Sch.; 1923–24 Univ. of Manchester; 1953–66 Lecturer in Comparative Religion Univ. of Manch.; 1920–24 Victoria Park. *Appointments:* 1925–31 N. China District; 1932–33 Wuchang Theol. Seminary (Hupeh District); 1933–46 Chairman of N. China District; 1948–50 Padiham; 1950–53 Bath; 1953–56 Manchester Univ.
Connexional Committees: 1950–53 Methodist Missionary Committee.
Publications: The Pattern in the Mount (Epworth Press 1947); *Chinese Religions* (Weidenfeld & Nicholson 1968); *Confucius* (Temple Smith Ltd 1973); *The Wisdom of the Taoist Mystics* (Sheldon Press 1980); Sectional Editor for China and Japan in Dictionary of Comparative Religion (Ed. S. G. F. Brandon) (Weidenfeld & Nicholson 1970); Chapters contributed to the following books: *The Saviour God* (Manchester Univ. Press 1963) Chapter on *Saviour Gods in Chinese Religion; Ancient Empires Vol. I* (Weidenfeld & Nicholson 1970) Chapter on *Building of the Great Wall of China; Man and His Salvation* (Manchester Univ. Press 1973) Chapter on *Conflicting Ideas of Salvation in AD 5th C. China;* Articles published at various times in the following journals: *Numen; Bulletin of John Rylands Library; History of Religions (Chicago); Journal of the Royal Asiatic Society; London Quarterly; Modern Churchmen; Expository Times; Political Quaterly; Epworth Review;* Lecturer in Comparative Religion for the Adult Education Depts. of Manchester, Liverpool and Newcastle Univ. Visiting lecturer on Chinese Buddhism at Lancaster Univ. (1967–75); 1965–80 Adviser for Encyclopedia Britannica on Chinese Philosophy and Religion.
Special Interests: Chinese Philosophy and Religion, The Church's Missionary Policy and Outreach.
Hobbies and Recreations: Chess, Chinese Literature and Culture.

SMITH, David Paul Christopher, Peveril, 1 Brenda Cresc., Thornton, Liverpool L23 4TY. (051-924-5106) *b. 21 Dec 1948, Bradford, Yorkshire. m. 4 Sept 1971: 3s.*
Education: 1960–65 Rhodesway Secondary Modern Sch., Bradford; 1968–69 Cliff Coll.; 1969–71 London Bible Coll.; 1971–74 Wesley, Bristol. *Appointments:* 1974–77 Durham and Deerness Valley; 1977–82 Gornal and Sedgley; 1982– Liverpool (Linacre Mission).
Special Interests: Evangelism and Church Growth. *Hobbies and Recreations:* Gardening, Photography, Car Mechanics, Model Railways.

SMITH, David Walter, 24 Alexandra Drive, Surbiton, Surrey KT5 9AB. (01-399-0377) *b. 2 Aug 1933, Leicester. m. 3 Aug 1968: 1d., 1s.*
Education: 1945–50 Wyggeston Grammar Sch.; 1963–64 Lancaster Theol. Seminary; 1959–63 Handsworth. *Appointments:* 1963–64 Per Canada; 1964–65 Edinburgh Mission; 1965–68 West London, Mission; 1968–75 Streatham and Dulwich; 1975–79 Wellingborough; 1979– Kingston-on-Thames.
Special Interests: Prison Work, Pastoralia, Ministry of Healing, Local Preachers' Affairs. *Hobbies and Recreations:* Music, Piano, Golf.

SMITH, Elsie J. W., 11 Low Cudworth Green, Cudworth, Barnsley, S. Yorks S72 8EL. (0226-710338) *b. 11 June 1922, Edinburgh. s.*
Education: 1927–33 Broughton Prim. Sch.; 1933–39 Broughton Secondary Sch.; 1949–51 Deaconess Coll., Ilkley. *Appointments:* 1973–80 Newcastle (Staffs.); 1980– Barnsley.
Special Interests: Pastoral Work, New Church Building. *Hobbies and Recreations:* Reading, Television, Music, Countryside.

SMITH, Eric John Douglas, 24 Upper Way, Farnham, Surrey. (0252-723674) *b. 29 Dec 1917, Exeter, Devon. m. (2) 1 Jan 1981: 1d.*
Education: 1920's Swaffield Rd., Wandsworth, London; 1930–32 Wandsworth Technical Institute, London. *Appointments:* 1967–70 Wombwell and Hoyland; 1970–73 Bradford (Manningham); 1973–76 Banbury; 1976–82 Basildon.
Publications: Various Research Papers, viz *Jour. Inst. Fuel* Vol. 29, No. 185 1956; *Trans. Brit. Ceramic Soc., A Symposium,* 1953, also Vol. 58 No. 5, 1959; Ibid Vol. 62 No. 10 1963.
Special Interests: Organ Music of J. S. Bach, N. T. Greek, Metallurgical Science. *Hobbies and Recreations:* Oil Painting, Turning, Gardening, Car Maintenance.

SMITH, Frank, Epworth House, Hollington Rd., Raunds, Wellingborough, Northants NN9 6NH. (0933-622137) *b. 12 March 1924, Wakefield, West Yorkshire. m. 18 Aug 1956.*
Education: 1929–32, 1932–35 Snapethorpe, Inf., Jun., Wakefield; 1935–39 Ings Rd. Central, Wakefield; 1952–55 Hartley Victoria.
Appointments: 1955–56 Northallerton; 1956–59 Halifax (North); 1959–66 Skipton; 1966–74 Brighouse; 1974–79 Shipley; 1979 Raunds; 1963–74 Synod Secretary (West Yorkshire District); 1969–74 Scrutineers Secretary (Conference); 1975 Assistant Secretary of the Conference.
Connexional Committees: 1970–74 Home Mission; 1971– GP; 1974– Law and Polity.
Hobbies and Recreations: Model Railways, Gardening.

SMITH, Frank William, 61 Skellingthorpe Rd., Lincoln LN6 7QT. (0522-680122) *b. 1 Jan 1928, Walthamstow. m. 11 Aug 1956: 2d., 1s.*
Education: 1950–53 Handsworth. *Appointments:* 1953–56 Ipswich; 1956–61 Downham Market; 1961–66 Folkestone; 1966–71 Gravesend and Dartford; 1971–80 Croydon; 1980– Lincoln South.

SMITH, Fraser Douglas, 12 Kinloch Drive, Heaton, Bolton, Greater Manchester BL1 4LZ. (0204-41619)– BD(Lond.), MA(Cantab.). *b. 9 Oct 1947, Coventry. m. 11 Aug 1973: 2d.*
Education: 1955–66 King Henry VIII, Coventry; 1966–69 Kings Coll., London Univ.; 1971–73 Wesley House. *Appointments:* 1973–75 Douglas IOM; 1975–82 Nottingham Mission; 1982– Bolton Mission.
Publications: Glory to God in the High St. (1982).
Special Interests: Religious Broadcasting. *Hobbies and Recreations:* Family Life, Keeping Fit, Enjoying the Countryside, Sports, Music, Watching Tropical Fish.

SMITH, George Henry Bryan, The Laurels, 36 Westbury Rd., Edington, Westbury, Wilts B13 4QF. (0380-830224) *b. 28 Jan 1919, Cayton, Nr. Scarborough. m. 18 Aug 1962: 2d., 1s.*
Education: Cayton Sch.; Gladstone Rd. Sch., Scarborough; 1957–62 Cliff Coll.; 1962–63 Richmond.
Appointments: 1963–65 Uttoxeter; 1965–68 Downham Market; 1968–71 Ripley; 1971–75 East Dereham; 1975–81 Ringsash.
Special Interests: Evangelism. *Hobbies and Recreations:* Gardening.

SMITH, Gordon F., 34 Whitburn, Skelmersdale, Lancs WN8 8HQ. (0695-22134) *b. 23 April 1930, Tipton, Staffs. m. 11 July 1959: 3d.*
Education: 1934–37 Park Lane Prim.; 1937–41 Tipton Green Jun.; 1941–46 Tipton Central High Sch.; 1951–54 Hartley Victoria.
Appointments: 1954–57 Cheadle (Staffs.); 1957–62 Stoke-on-Trent (Longton and Fenton); 1962–67 Ormskirk; 1967–76 Orrell and Lamberhead Green; 1976– Skelmersdale.
Special Interests: Music. *Hobbies and Recreations:* Music, Gardening, Swimming.

SMITH, Graham Roy, 23 Plessey Cresc., Whitley Bay, Tyne and Wear NE25 8QB. (0632-520928) *b. 17 Sept 1945, Liverpool. m. 25 July 1970: 2d., 1s.*
Education: 1950–56 Kingsthorne Rd. CP Sch.; 1956–61 Gateacre Comprehensive Sch.; 1961–66

Riversdale Technical Coll.; 1966–68 Liverpool Regional Coll. of Technology; 1970–71 Cliff Coll.; 1971–73 Edgehill; 1973–75 Wesley, Bristol. *Appointments:* 1975–78 Epworth and Crowle; 1978– N. Shields and Whitley Bay. *Hobbies and Recreations:* Railways.

SMITH, Graham S., 29 Heald Close, Rochdale, Lancashire OL12 7HJ. (0706-46566) *b. 3 Jan 1949, Huddersfield. m. 19 Aug 1978: 1d.* *Education:* 1960–68 Huddersfield New Coll.; 1968–72 Bradford Technical Coll.; 1974–78 Queens. *Appointments:* 1978– Rochdale. *Special Interests:* Church Growth. *Hobbies and Recreations:* Printing, Handicrafts.

SMITH, Harold Walter, 59 The Firs, Elworth St., Sandbach, Cheshire CW11 9BA. *b. 11 Aug 1901, Hurley, Berks. m.* *Education:* 1914 Maidenhead; 1924–26 Victoria Park. *Appointments:* 1924–25 Camelford and Wadebridge; 1925–26 S. Yorkshire Mission; 1926–28 Victoria Park Coll.; 1928–30 Worksop; 1930–31 Dewsbury; 1931–35 Hull, Stepney; 1935–38 Portsmouth; 1938–40 Ashton under Lyne; 1940–46 Chaplain HMF; 1946–52 Sandbach Providence; 1952–57 Bromhall; 1957–62 Bury St. Edmunds; 1962–66 Bolton Bridge St. *Special Interests:* History.

SMITH, Hubert Adrian James, 8 Eastgate Gdns., Guildford, Surrey GU1 4AZ. (0483-75432)–FRGS. *b. Derby. m. 1967: 2d* *Education:* 1951–58 Kingswood Sch., Bath; 1958–60 Cliff Coll.; 1960–63 Univ. of London; 1960–63 Richmond. *Appointments:* 1963–65 Launceston; 1965–70 Stoke-on-Trent (South); 1970–75 King's Lynn, 1975–82 Dorking and Horsham. *Special Interests:* Preaching, History, English Literature. *Hobbies and Recreations:* Antiques and Restoration of Old Furniture, Classic Motor Cars, Music (Piano and Organ), Swimming, Jogging.

SMITH, James Colin, 24 Bank St., Brierley Hill, West Midlands DY5 3DA. (0384-77160)–BA(Dublin), MA(Cantab.). *b. 16 May 1947, Isleworth, Middlesex. m. July 1971: 2s.* *Education:* 1957–65 Rydal Sch.; 1966–68 Magee Univ. Coll.; 1968–70 Trinity Coll., Dublin; 1971–73 Fitzwilliam Coll., Cambridge Univ.; 1971–74 Wesley House. *Appointments:* 1974–79 Lincoln Central; 1979– Stourbridge and Brierley Hill.

SMITH, John William, Wesley House, 12 King's Rd., Spalding, Lincs PE11 1QB. (0775-2629) *b. 17 Nov 1931, Worcester. m. 11 June 1955: 1d., 1s.* *Education:* 1936–40 British Sch., Worcester; 1940–44 St. Martin's Sch., Worcester; 1944–47 Worcester Technical Coll.; 1964–67 Didsbury, Bristol. *Appointments:* 1967–69 Gainsborough; 1969–73 Brigg; 1973–78 St. Just in Penwith; 1978– Spalding. *Special Interests:* Local History and Methodist History. *Hobbies and Recreations:* Tennis, Cricket, Reading, Gardening.

SMITH, Kenneth Charles George, 45 Broomleaf Rd., Farnham, Surrey GU9 8DQ. (0252-714192) *b. 17 May 1928, Bristol. m. 13 Aug 1954: 3s.* *Education:* 1932–39 Filton Ave. Elem. Sch., Bristol; 1939–44 Cotham Grammar Sch., Bristol; 1949–51 Handsworth. *Appointments:* 1948 Trowbridge and Bradford; 1951–54 Llandrindod Wells; 1954–60 Pontypool (Eastern Valley); 1960–66 Sheffield, Brunswick; 1966–71 Penarth; 1971–80 Long Eaton; 1980– Farnham and Alton. *Special Interests:* Healing Ministry, The Charismatic Movement. *Hobbies and Recreations:* Gardening, Caravanning, Woodwork.

SMITH, Peter, 10 Ridgeway, Lanchester, Durham DH7 0PT. (0207-52085) *b. 10 April 1913, Camelon, Falkirk, Scotland. m. 24 Jan 1939: 1d., 1s.* *Education:* Camelon, Inf., Jun., Senior. *Appointments:* 1962–66 Gateshead South West; 1966–73 Houghton Le Spring; 1973–78 Consett.

SMITH, Peter David, 1a Hillside Rd., Stratford-upon-Avon, Warwickshire CV37 9EB. (0789-67971)–BA(Open). *b. 26 April 1938, New Haw, Weybridge, Surrey. m. 2 Oct 1965: 1d., 1s.* *Education:* 1951–55 The Grammar Sch. for Boys, Farnham; 1955–60 Guildford County Technical Coll; 1963–64 Westhill Training Coll.; 1960–63 Richmond. *Appointments:* 1964–65 Liverpool, Linacre Mission; 1965–71 Sheffield, Carver St.; 1971–76 Bradford, Woodhouse Grove; 1976–82 Birmingham, Elmdon; 1982– Stratford-upon-Avon. *Connexional Committees:* 1977–82 Education and Youth. *Publications: Faith, Folk and Clarity; Faith, Folk and Nativity; Faith, Folk and Festivity; Jesus Folk; New Orbit;* Stories in *Theme Work;* Involvement and Songs in *Partners in Praise* and *One World Songs.* *Special Interests:* Folk Guitar, Classical Piano, I am a Field Worker for PHAB, and Chairman of Lydon Amnesty International Group also interests in Local Community Action Groups. *Hobbies and Recreations:* Music, Sport, Reading.

SMITH, Raymond, The Manse, New Rd., Minsterley, Shrewsbury, Shropshire SY5 0HS. (074-374-267). *m: 2s.* *Education:* 1959–63 Handsworth. *Appointments:* 1963–65 Retford; 1965–69 Bolsover; 1969–75 Barnsley; 1975–80 Nottingham Central; 1980– Minsterley.

SMITH, Raymond Vernon, 4 St. Maeburne, 15 Marine Parade, Penarth, South Glamorgan CF6 2BG. (0222-707037) *b. 6 June 1908, Aberkenfig, Glamorgan, South Wales. m. 27 Dec 1937: 1s.* *Education:* 1913–22 Tondu Boys Sch.; 1932–33 Cliff Coll. *Appointments:* 1937–43 Wye Valley Mission; 1943–45 Tenby; 1945–48 Wednesbury; 1948–51 Aldershot; 1951–56 Neath; 1956–62 London,

Sydenham and Forest Hill; 1962–69 Medway Towns; 1969–73 Cardiff Wesley.
Hobbies and Recreations: Reading, Sport, Railways.

SMITH, Reginald Arthur, 4 Ros Lyn, Carbis Bay, St. Ives, Cornwall TR26 2QE. (Carbis Bay 797650) *b. 14 Dec 1907, London. m. October 1938: 2d., 1s.*
Education: St. Johns Sch., Holloway, N. London; 1932–35 Handsworth.
Appointments: 1931–32 Manningtree; 1935–38 President's List; 1938–40 London, Brixton Hill; 1940–45 London Mission, Tooting; 1945–50 London Mission, Waltham; 1950–53 Bristol, Bedminster; 1953–56 Birmingham, Sutton Park; 1956–59 Camborne; 1959–64 Derby South; 1964–69 Mansfield West; 1969–72 Manchester, Cheetham Hill and Prestwich.
Connexional Committees: Youth Committee. *Publications: Odd Men Out* (Pamphlet 1944); Social Services Course (Walthamstow Coll.).
Special Interests: Scanveyo, Scouts, London and National Rotary, Mixed Clubs—Boys Brigade and Girls Brigade. *Hobbies and Recreations:* Reading, Writing, Travel.

SMITH, Reginald Charles North, 48 Poldhu Rd., Liskeard, Cornwall PL14 3BX. (0579-46050) *b. 29 April 1905, Leeds. m. 16 Aug 1933: 1d., 1s.*
Education: 1910–17 Harehills, Leeds; 1917–20 Central High, Leeds; 1927–30 Didsbury. *Appointments:* 1926–27 Mid-Glos; 1930–33 Marazion; 1933–35 East Suffolk; 1935–36 Leeds Mission; 1936–38 Malton; 1938–42 Market Rasen; 1942–45 Silsden; 1945–48 Kelsall; 1948–50 Doncaster; 1950–52 Brinkworth; 1952–55 Kirby Moorside; 1955–58 Ebbw Vale; 1958–61 Forest of Dean; 1961–67 Liskeard; 1967–68 Barnstaple; 1968–70 Thirsk.
Connexional Committees: Temperance and Social Welfare; Local Preachers.

SMITH, Roger Harrison, 28 Stoke Rd., Methwold, Thetford, Norfolk. (0366-728252)–MA(Cantab). *b. 6 Sept 1923, Luton. m. 29 Sept 1964: 1d., 2s.*
Education: 1943–53 Warwick Sch.; 1953–56 Peterhouse, Cambridge; 1956–58 London; 1958–59 Leeds; 1980– Open; 1956–59 Headingley.
Appointments: 1959–72 Sierra Leone Dt; 1972–77 Wellington (Salop); 1977–82 Spalding.
Publications: Notes on Preaching (Pamphlet on Preaching Method for English Speaking Teachers in Sierra Leone), 1973.
Special Interests: Local Preacher Training (Tutor and Doctrine).
Hobbies and Recreations: Painting, Birdwatching, Choir Singing.

SMITH, Stanley B., 15 Branksome Grove, Stockton-on-Tees, Cleveland TS18 5DD. (0642–583182) *b. 9 Sept 1901, Grimsby. m. 20 Aug 1931.*
Education: 1906–15 South Parade Elem., Grimsby; 1922–23 Cliff Coll.; 1925–28 Didsbury. *Appointments:* 1924–25 Loftus and Staithes; 1928–31 Wolverton; 1931–32 Kendal; 1932–36 Bridlington; 1936–40 Haworth and Oakworth; 1940–46 Dewsbury; 1946–52 Brighouse; 1952–57 Marple; 1957–62 Bolton, Bridge St.; 1962–66 Chester-le-Street.

SMITH, Stanley Walter, 10 Hall Close, Worthing, W. Sussex BN14 9BQ. (0903-64912) *b. 14 March 1911, Doncaster, Yorks. m. 13 May 1939: 1d.*
Education: 1922–29 Doncaster Grammar Sch.; 1929–31 Nottingham Univ.; 1934–36 Handsworth.
Appointments: 1937–51 Eastern Nigeria, West Africa; 1952-55 Hastings; 1955–59 Huddersfield NE; 1959–62 Bradford, Woodhouse Grove; 1962–66 Manchester and Salford Mission; 1966–72 Hungerford; 1972–76 Salisbury.
Local Council Committees: 1953–55 Hastings Education Committee; 1963–66 Salford Education Committee.
Special Interests: Refugees, Social Responsibility Matters, Africa, Apartheid, Creative Writing. *Hobbies and Recreations:* Walking, Gardening, Bookbinding.

SMITH, Terry John, 24 Kedale Rd., Seaford, E. Sussex BN25 2BX. (0323-892720)–BA.
Education: 1964–68 Hartley Victoria.
Appointments: 1968–75 Bridgend; 1975– Mid-Sussex.

SMITH, Thomas Laurence, Roydon, 52 Whitchurch Rd., Tavistock, Devon PL19 9BD. (0822-2840)–BA(Bristol). *b. 31 Mar 1926, Usk, Gwent. m. 4 Aug 1955: 1d., 1s.*
Education: Usk Council Sch.; West Monmouth Sch., Pontypool; 1950–53 Bristol Univ.; 1950–53 Didsbury, Bristol. *Appointments:* 1949–50 Bristol (Fishponds); 1953–55 Shepton Mallet; 1955–59 Witney; 1959–66 Petersfield and Haslemere; 1966–73 Plymouth (King St.); 1973–80 Barnstaple; 1980– Tavistock.
Connexional Committees: 1977–81 Property Division Board.
Special Interests: Prison Chaplaincy.
Hobbies and Recreations: Photography.

SMITH, Thomas Mervyn, 18 Bescot Drive, Pleck, Walsall, West Midlands WS2 9DF. (0922-23926) *b. 1 Dec 1939, Coventry. m. 23 Dec 1967: 3d.*
Education: 1951–54 Coventry Technical Sch.; 1954–56 Woodlands Sch., Coventry; 1956–60 Coventry Technical Coll.; 1960–62 Lanchester Coll., Coventry; 1965–67 Headingley; 1967–69 Wesley, Bristol.
Appointments: 1969–73 Milton Keynes; 1973–78 Bristol, Kingswood; 1978–81 Darlaston; 1981– Walsall and Darlaston.
Special Interests: Philosophy of Religion, New Testament Studies, Liturgy. *Hobbies and Recreations:* Motoring, Photography, most Outdoor Sports, but especially Cricket and Golf.

SMITH, William Beddard, 17 Horton Rd., Middleton Cheney, Banbury, Oxon OX17 2LE. (0295-710962) *b. Stourbridge, West Midlands. m. 28 May 1935: 1s.*
Education: 1928–31 Victoria Park.

Appointments: 1931–34 Hanley; 1934–36 Tipton; 1936–44 South West China Dt; 1944–49 Gainsborough; 1949–54 Reading; 1954–55 Dunstable; 1955–58 Teaching Appointment, Luton Boys Sch.; 1958–63 Hetton-le-Hole; 1963–70 Raunds; 1970–75 Wantage and Abingdon; 1975–78 Buckingham and Brackley.
Special Interests: Chinese Language and Culture. *Hobbies and Recreations:* Gardening, Music.

SMITHSON, David Wiles, 148 Slade Lane, Manchester M19 2AQ. (061-2244-4586)–BD. *b. 4 Oct 1929, Kempston, Bedford. m. 7 Oct 1955: 1d., 2s.*
Education: 1939–42 Newmarket Secondary Sch.; 1942–46 Bedford Modern Sch.; 1949–53 Handsworth. *Appointments:* 1953–69 Lucknow, Benares Dt, North India; 1969–76 Eccles Manchester; 1976– Manchester Withington.
Special Interests: Indian Religions and Culture. *Hobbies and Recreations:* Indian Cooking.

SNAITH, John Graham, 8 Knights Way, Milton, Cambridge CB4 4DE. (0223-860182)–MA(Oxon), BD(Lond.). *b. 10 Jan 1934, Durham. m. 6 Aug 1960: 1d., 1s.*
Education: 1945–47 Leeds Grammar Sch.; 1947–53 Kingswood Sch., Bath; 1953–57 Pembroke Coll., Oxford Univ.; 1957–58 Hebrew Univ. of Jerusalem; 1958–60 Richmond. *Appointments:* 1960–61 Wymondham and Attleborough; 1961–63 Univ. of Ibadan, W. Africa; 1963–66 Clarendon Press, Univ. of Oxford; 1966–71 Dept. of Theol., Univ. of Nottingham; 1971– Faculty of Oriental Studies.
Connexional Committees: 1977– Faith and Order Committee.
Publications: Ecclesiasticus (Cambridge Bible Commentary on New English Bible 1974); *The Importance of Ecclesiasticus—Expository Times* 75 (1963) 66–69; *Biblical Quotations in the Hebrew of Ecclesiasticus—Journal of Theological Studies* 18 (1967) 1–12; *Literary and Historical Investigation in Jeremiah* Ch. 46—*Journal of Semitic Studies* 16 (1971) 15–32; 6 Articles on *The Preacher's Use of the Old Testament* in *Worship and Preaching* 3 (1973) Feb–Dec; 6 Articles on *Investigating Some Old Testament Passages* in *Worship and Preaching* 4 (1974) Feb–Dec; *Ben Sira's Supposed Love of Liturgy* in *Vetus Testamentum* 25 (1975) 167–174; Reviews for *Vetus Testamentum, Journal of Theological Studies, Epworth Review, Methodist Recorder, Journal of Semitic Studies.*
Hobbies and Recreations: Pianos, Music.

SNEDDON, Robert, 21 Manley Rd., Sudden, Rochdale, Lancashire OL11 3NJ. (0706-40834)–BSc(Birmg.), BA(Cantab.). *b. 14 Feb 1954, Dover, Kent. m. 23 Feb 1980.*
Education: 1965–72 Dover Grammar Sch. for Boys; 1972–77 Birmingham Univ.; 1977–79 Cambridge Univ.; 1977–81 Wesley House; 1980–81 Finch Scholar. *Appointments:* 1981– Rochdale.
Special Interests: Hinduism, Comparative Religion, World Development, Liturgy. *Hobbies and Recreations:* Gardening.

SNOOK, Barrie David, Wesley House, 17A Leigh Rd., Havant, Hants PO9 2ET. (0705-475797) *b. 4 Oct 1938, Poole. m. 21 January 1961: 2d.*
Education: 1979–81 Wesley, Bristol. *Appointments:* 1981– Portsmouth.

SOFTLEY, Derek, The Manse, 9 Westhead Rd., Croston, Preston, Lancashire PR5 7RQ. (0772-600213) *b. 24 May 1937, Morpeth, Northumberland. m. 21 March 1959: 2d.*
Education: 1948–54 King Henry VIII, Coventry; 1962–65 Hartley Victoria. *Appointments:* 1965–70 Turks and Calcos Islands; 1970–74 Wesley, Kingston Jamaica; 1974–79 Hinckley; 1979– Ormskirk.
Hobbies and Recreations: Sailing, Tennis, DIY.

SOLLITT, James Alfred, 3 High Mill Drive, Scarborough YO12 6RN. (0723-74902) *b. 8 July 1901, London. m. 10 May 1980.*
Education: 1905–16 Loftus Senior; 1926–28 Hartley Victoria; 1928–29 Kingsmead. *Appointments:* 1924–26 Enfield; 1929–48 E. Nigeria; 1948–49 Prestwich; 1949–54 Holmfirth; 1954–59 Brighouse.
Connexional Committees: 1962–77 Methodist Homes for the Aged.
Hobbies and Recreations: Music—Records—Classical, Carpentry, Gardening.

SOPER, Donald Oliver, Hinde St., Methodist Church, W1. (01-935-6179)–MA(Cantab.), PhD(Lond.). *b. 31 Jan 1903, Wandsworth. m. 3 Aug 1927: 4d.*
Education: 1915–20 Askes Haberdashers; 1921–24 Cambridge Univ.; 1924–26 Wesley House.
Appointments: 1926–29 S. London Mission; London Mission; 1936–78 West London Mission.
Parliamentary Service: 1963– Peerage. *Connexional Committees:* 1953 President of Conference.
Local Council Committees: 1960–63 LCC.
Hobbies and Recreations: Games, Music.

SORRELL, Frank Maurice, 580 Newmarket Rd., Cambridge CB5 8LL. (02205-4229) *b. 22 Sept 1914, Bradfield, Essex. m: 2s.*
Education: 1925–31 Harwich County High; 1939–42 Hartley Victoria. *Appointments:* 1942–44 Bottesford; 1944–46 Withernsea; 1946–50 Pocklington; 1950–55 Ipswich (Rope-Walk) and Ipswich; 1955–59 Holbeach; 1959–65 Bishop's Stortford; 1965–72 Downham Market; 1972–79 Whitby.
Connexional Committees: General Chapel Committee.

SOULSBY, Thomas, 3 Epworth Mount, Ocker Hill, Randwick, Stroud, Glos GL6 6HY. (04536-5646) *b. 8 April 1916, Hetton-le-Hole, County Durham. m. 26 Dec 1945.*
Education: 1921–27 CE Sch., Hetton-le-Hole; 1927–30 Hetton-le-Hole Secondary; 1939–42 Hartley Victoria.
Appointments: 1942–45 East Cornwall Mission; 1945–46 Blackburn Mission; 1946–50 Crook;

1950–54 Stafford; 1954–57 Isle of Man, Douglas; 1957–64 Stourvale; 1964–71 Halesowen; 1971–76 Stamford; 1976–81 Epworth. *Connexional Committees:* 1950–54 Christian Citizenship. *Hobbies and Recreations:* Gardening, Photography.

SOUTH, Jeffrey Hubert, 71 Jackson St., Coalville, Leicestershire LE6 2NP. (0530-812020)—BA(Open). *b. 11 June 1940, Jersey CI. m. 17 Aug 1968: 1s.*
Education: 1947–51 Victoria Coll. Prep.; 1951–52 Dartford Secondary Modern; 1952–55 Langford Secondary Modern, Feltham; 1955–58 Chiswick Poly.; 1961–62 Cliff Coll.; 1963–67 London Univ.; 1963–67 Richmond. *Appointments:* 1967–71 Doncaster Coalfields Mission/Doncaster West; 1971–74 Rossendale; 1974–79 Chesterfield; 1979–82 Nottingham North; 1982– Coalville.
Special Interests: Family Church and Family Worship. *Hobbies and Recreations:* Reading, Spending Time with Family.

SOWDEN, Andrew David, The Manse, Tinhay, Lifton, Devon PY6 0AJ. (056684-257) *b. 8 Oct 1947, Plymouth. s.*
Education: 1959–63 Burleigh Secondary Modern, Plymouth; 1978–81 Wesley, Bristol. *Appointments:* 1981 Launceston.

SOWLER, Peter, 24 Priory Rd., Milford Haven, Dyfed SA73 2DT. (06462-3407) *b. 9 Sept 1950, Leicester. m. 6 May 1972: 1d., 1s.*
Education: 1962–67 Alderman Newton's Boys Grammar Sch.; 1976–79 Queen's. *Appointments:* 1979– Haverfordwest and Milford Haven. *Hobbies and Recreations:* Music, Piano, Guitar.

SPEED, Arthur Joseph, 28 Ingleside Cresc., South Lancing, West Sussex BN15 8EN. (0903-761646) *b. 22 Sept 1920, Birkenhead, Merseyside.*
Education: 1945–47 Hartley Victoria. *Appointments:* 1947–49 High Wycombe; 1949–50 Llandrindod Wells; 1950–53 President's List; 1953–55 Nottingham East; 1955–59 Ipswich; 1959–65 Nowich St. Peter's; 1965–70 Ipswich; 1970–74 London, Harrow.

SPENCER, Brian, 53 Oxford Rd., Kidlington, Oxford OX5 2BP. (08675-3958).
Education: 1972–76 Wesley, Bristol. *Appointments:* 1976–80 St. Austell; 1980– Oxford.

SPENCER, Jeffrey, 14 Cypress Cresc., Blyth, Northumberland NE24 2NB. (06706-61674) *b. 24 Jan 1912, Hawes, Yorks. m. 10 Aug 1939: 1d., 1s.*
Education: 1917–19 Hawes Inf. Sch.; 1919–26 Sedbergh British Sch.; 1926–29 Sedbergh Public Sch.; 1932–35 Headingley. *Appointments:* 1935–36 Whitby; 1936–39 Snaith; 1939–42 Worcester; 1942–47 Liverpool, Grove St. and Woolton; 1947–50 Bebington; 1950–55 Newcastle Mission; 1955–62 Newcastle West; 1962–69 Blyth; 1969–75 Aireborough.
Hobbies and Recreations: Bird Watching.

SPENCER, Leslie Finemore, 11 Rutland Cresc., Ulverstone, Cumbria LA12 9LX. (0229-53759) *b. 30 May 1897, Redditch. m. 23 April 1935 (w.): 1d.*
Education: Wesleyan Sch., Redditch; 1923–26 Didsbury. *Appointments:* 1922–23 Luton, Chapel St.; 1926–29 Hitchin; 1929–33 Lincoln, Wesley; 1933–36 Yeadon; 1936–40 Castleford; 1940–46 Leeds, Armley; 1946–52 Scunthorpe; 1952–57 Leicester East; 1957–65 Ulverston. *Special Interests:* Methodist History. *Hobbies and Recreations:* Gardening.

SPENCER, Terence, The Manse, Sherburn, Durham, County Durham DH6 1DN. (0385-720233)—BA.Theol.(Birmingham). *b. 3 March 1948, Keighley, Yorkshire. m. 11 Aug 1979.*
Education: 1953–59 Long Lee Prim. Sch., Keighley; 1959–65 Eastwood Secondary Sch., Keighley; 1965–67 Leeds Technical Coll.; 1967–71 Leeds Poly.; 1976–80 Queen's. *Appointments:* 1980– Durham and Deerness Valley.
Special Interests: Youth Work, Current Affairs, Systematic Theology, Mission, Renewal. *Hobbies and Recreations:* Walking, Travelling, Reading, Gardening.

SPENCER, William Arthur, 188 Warwick Ave., Derby DE3 6HP. (0332-767589)—BA, BD(Lond.). *b. 14 Jan 1935, Mansfield, Woodhouse, Notts. m. 23 Aug 1958: 2d.*
Education: 1940–45 Oxclose Lane, Prim. and Jun. Mixed, Mansfield, Woodhouse, Notts.; 1945–53 Brunts Grammar Sch., Mansfield; 1953–56 Univ. Coll., London; 1956–58 Richmond. *Appointments:* 1958–61 Beverley; 1961–69 Long Eaton; 1969– Derby South.
Special Interests: Ancient History, Archaeology, Astronomy, Caravanning, Continental Travel, Football, Languages. *Hobbies and Recreations:* Gardening, Philately, Snooker.

SPERRING, Ivor Keith, Woodstock, Landkey, Barnstaple, Devon EX32 0JU. (0271-83-214) *b. 23 Feb 1940, Kingstanding, Birmingham. m. 2 Oct 1965: 1d., 1s.*
Education: 1951–55 Brownhills Secondary Modern Boys; 1959–61 Cliff Coll.; 1961–65 Handsworth. *Appointments:* 1965–67 London, East Ham; 1967–70 Birmingham, Islington Quinton; 1970–78 Leominster, Malvern and Ledbury; 1978– Barnstaple.
Publications: Hymn *The Carpenter* (1965).
Special Interests: Chaplaincy to Technical Colls. and Agricultural Industry. *Hobbies and Recreations:* Fishing, Photography, Gardening.

SPINNEY, Bryan Frank, 17 First Ave., St. Anne's Park, Bristol BS4 4DU. (0272-778131) *b. 20 Nov 1930, Southampton. m. 26 Aug 1958: 1d., 1s.*
Education: Prim. Schs.; Taunton's Sch., Southampton; 1953–56 Richmond. *Appointments:* 1956–58 Brighton and Hove; 1958–59 Stour Valley Mission; 1959–63 Shaftesbury and Gillingham; 1963–68

Winchester; 1968–71 Sevenoaks; 1971–74 Orpington; 1974–80 Aldershot, Farnborough and Camberley; 1980– Bristol South. *Connexional Committees:* 1964–68 Local Preachers; 1977– Ministries. *Publications:* Methodist Hymn-Book Revision 1904 and 1933 (1980); Reprint of Wesley's *Foundery Tune-Book* with added notes (1981). *Special Interests:* Church Music and Hymnology. *Hobbies and Recreations:* Music, Household DIY, Gardening.

SPIVEY, Ronald Vincent, 2 The Close, Seafield Rd., Sidmouth, Devon EX10 8HE. (03955-3603)–MA(Cantab.), DD(Temple Univ., Philadelphia). *b. 7 July 1906, Wolverton, Bucks. m. 2 Aug 1933: 1s.*
Education: 1919–24 Elmfield Coll., York.; 1925–30 Trinity Coll., Cambridge; 1928–30 Wesley House. *Appointments:* 1930–32 Worthing; 1932–33 Hull; 1933–35 Birmingham; 1935–36 President's List; 1936–39 Southport; 1939–42 Bristol East; 1942–48 Cambridge; 1948–58 London, Wesley's Chapel; 1958–60 Rhodesia; 1960–66 United Theol. Coll., Bangalore; 1966–67 St. Paul's Coll., Limuru, Kenya; 1967–70 London, Hinde Street. *Connexional Committees:* 1942–58 Education; 1948–58 Church Membership; 1968–80 Healing and Pastoral Ministry; 1967–70 Overseas. *Publications:* 1942–65 Various Pamphlets for Students; *Preaching The Word* (Indian Students Library 1965).

SPYBEY, George, 23A Parson's Lane, Alford, Lincs LM13 9BE. (05212-2200) *b. 21 Oct 1917, Beeston, Notts. m. 12 April 1947: 1d., 2s.*
Education. Derby Rd., Long Eaton, 1938–39 Cliff Coll.; 1947–48 Westhill Training Coll., Birmingham; 1955–56 Hartley Victoria. *Appointments:* 1956–61 Oldham East; 1961–63 Ashton-under-Lyne; 1963–66 Manchester, Swinton; 1966–70 Sheffield South; 1970–73 Barnard Castle; 1973–78 Shildon; 1978– Alford.

Hobbies and Recreations: One time Football Referee and Table Tennis Player, now Spectator.

SQUIRE, William Hugo, The Manse, Wellington Rd., St. Dennis, St. Austell, Cornwall PL26 8BN. *b. 19 Aug 1937, Bray, County Wicklow, Eire. m. 30 July 1969: 2d., 1s.*
Education: 1941–44 Killiney National Sch.; 1944–49 Avoca Secondary Sch.; 1949–54 Wesley Coll., Dublin; 1954–57 Trinity Coll., Dublin; Edgehill Coll., Belfast. *Appointments:* 1960–61 Moy; 1961-62 Fivemiletown; 1965–67 Waterford City, Eire; 1967–68 Lisburn; 1968–70 Clones; 1970–73 Kildare, Eire; 1973–74 Ballintra, Eire; 1974–76 Rochdale; 1976–81 Clifton; 1981– St. Dennis, Cornwall. *Special Interests:* Gardening. *Hobbies and Recreations:* Historical Novels.

STACEY, Arnold John, 19 Doveleat, Chinnor, Oxford OX9 4DW. (0844-52276) *b. 27 March 1932, Swindon, Wilts. m. 30 June 1956 (w.): 2d., 2s.*
Education: 1943–50 Marlborough Grammar Sch.; 1966–68 City of Birmingham Coll. of Commerce; 1952–55 Richmond. *Appointments:* 1955–58 Romford; 1958–64 Thame and Watlington; 1964–66 Looe; 1968–74 Child Care Officer and Social Work Team Leader, Gloucestershire County Council; 1974– Assistant Area Officer, Buckinghamshire County Council. *Connexional Committees:* 1982– Advisory Committee on Ministerial Appointments. *Special Interests:* Social Work, Rural Circuits. *Hobbies and Recreations:* Gardening, Walking, Motoring.

STACY-MARKS, John Anthony, Flexbury Manse, Flexbury Park Rd., Bude, Cornwall (0288-2367) *b. 21 Feb 1946, Eastbourne.*
Education: Dolfins, Ascham, Eastbourne Coll.; 1967–70 Richmond. *Appointments:* 1970–71 Luton Industrial Coll. and Community Centre; 1971–73 Bideford; 1973–80 Nottingham Mission; 1980– Bude.

Special Interests: Youth Work. *Hobbies and Recreations:* Music, Horticulture, Countryside.

STADEN, David Alexander, 67 Station Rd., Stanley, Co. Durham DH9 0JP. (0207-34347) *b. 2 May 1939, Carlisle. m. 8 Aug 1970.*
Education: 1951–57 Kingswood Sch., Bath; 1962–63 Cliff Coll.; 1963–67 Didsbury, Bristol. *Appointments:* 1967–69 Hartlepool; 1969–72 Saddleworth and Lees; 1972–77 Burton-on-Trent; 1977–80 London, Walthamstow and Chingford; 1981– Stanley. *Hobbies and Recreations:* Railways, Music.

STAFFORD, Alan, 44 Belmont Rd., Bushey, Herts WD2 2JP. (0923-23906) *b. 29 Aug 1920, Newcastle-on-Tyne, m. 10 Aug 1950: 2d., 1s.*
Education: 1945–48 Richmond. *Appointments:* 1948–50 Andover; 1950–52 Castleford; 1950–58 Newcastle (Brunswick); 1958–65 Bedford (North); 1965–71 Amersham; 1971–79 Aylesbury; 1979– Watford.

STAFFORD, Hector R., 5 Holly Gdns., Lowfell, Gateshead, Tyne and Wear NE9 5TP. (0632-873553) *b. 7 May 1908, Newcastle upon Tyne. m. 4 Aug 1934: 2d.*
Education: 1927–30 Didsbury. *Appointments:* 1930–32 Wolsingham and Weardale; 1932–36 St. Albans; 1936–39 Harrow; 1939–44 London, Ilford; 1944–48 Barnet; 1948–54 Darlington (South); 1954–61 Bishop Auckland; 1961–68 Gateshead (East); 1968–73 London Mission (North West).

STAGG, Lawrence Jack, 26 Love Lane, Andover, Hants SP10 2AB. (0264-65604)–BA(Birmingham). *b. 13 Sept 1902, Andover. m. 25 July 1960.*
Education: Andover Council Sch.; Andover Grammar Sch.; 1923–26 Handsworth. *Appointments:* 1926–29 Aldershot and Farnham; 1929–31 Walton and Egham; 1931–34 Manchester (Gravel Lane); 1934–39 Brighton and Hove; 1939–45 Cleethorpes (Trinity); 1945–50 Kilburn (Quex Rd.); 1950–54 Luton

1954–61 Scunthorpe; 1961–66 Louth.
Hobbies and Recreations: Gardening.

STAINER-SMITH, W. Norman, Fernlea, Barns Lane, Burford, Oxon OX8 4NE. (099382-2365) *b. 29 Dec 1915, London. m. 6 Jan 1945: 2d., 1s.*
Education: Strand, Rutlish; 1938–40 Handsworth; 1940–42 Headingley.
Appointments: 1942–45 Thetford; 1945–48 Chatteris; 1948–53 Truro; 1953–57 Bristol Ebenezer; 1957–63 Birmingham, Moseley Road and Sparkhill; 1963–68 Wolstanton and Audley; 1968–75 Maidstone, Witney and Faringdon.
Connexional Committees: 1946–65 Connexional Youth Council; 1947–48 MAYC President (National).
Local Council Committees: 1970–75 Chairman of Leeds North Sch. Governors (8 schools).
Special Interests: Education, Youth, Local Government, World Methodism, Music. *Hobbies and Recreations:* Foreign Travel (For 38 years have arranged Tours for taking Methodists and others to many different Countries, including USA, Russia, Canada, Holy Land, Egypt, Scandinavia, Italy).

STANBURY, Albert John, 24 Park Rd., Southport, Merseyside PR9 9LA. (0704-38253)–BA(Lond.). *b. 13 Feb 1904, Millbrook, Cornwall. m. 1 Sept 1936: 3s.*
Education: 1916–19 Devonport High Sch.; 1929–32 Richmond.
Appointments: 1928–29 Llandrindrod; 1932–35 Bude and Kilhampton; 1935–36 Worksop; 1936–39 Liverpool, Grove St. and Woolton; 1939–42 Ellesmere Port; 1942–47 Birkenhead and Bebington; 1947–53 Leigh-on-Sea; 1953–58 Maidstone; 1958–63 Ramsgate; 1963–69 Nottingham West; 1969–71 Southport.

STANBURY, F. John, 7 Abbotts Ann Rd., Harestock, Winchester, Hants SO22 6ND. (0962-881139)–BA(Cantab.), MA(Cantab.). *b. 18 Sept 1945, Launceston, Cornwall. m. 19 Aug 1971: 1d.*
Education: 1956–63 Shebbear Coll.; 1969–72 Fitzwilliam Coll., Cambridge; 1969–72 Wesley House.
Appointments: 1972–75 Stamford; 1975–78 Carlisle; 1978– Winchester.
Special Interests: The Ecumenical Movement, Liturgy. *Hobbies and Recreations:* Music.

STANDHAFT, Edward Charles Patrick, 2 Silecroft Rd., Bexleyheath, Kent DA7 5BL. (01-303-8801)–MA. *b. 20 July 1944, Malvern, Worcs. m. 23 Aug 1969.*
Education: 1958–62 Queen's Coll., Taunton; 1963–66 Bristol Univ.; 1966–69 Wesley House.
Appointments: 1969–70 Bury St. Edmunds; 1970–76 Zimbabwe Dt; 1976– Shotters Hill.
Connexional Committees: 1980– Disarmament International Security and Peace.
Hobbies and Recreations: Running, Drama, Photography, Writing for radio/TV.

STANDING, William Arnold, White Gates, 92 Nyewood Lane, Bognor Regis, West Sussex PO21 2TT. (0243-825348) *b. 29 July 1913, Bolton, Lancs. m. 5 Oct 1940: 2s.*
Education: 1918–27 Walmesley CE; 1939–40 Cliff Coll.; 1950–51 Richmond. *Appointments:* 1951–56 Greenwich and Deptford; 1956–64 London, Walthamstow; 1964–71 London, Ilford; 1971–76 Grays; 1976–81 Lincoln Central.
Special Interests: Council for Music in Hospitals. *Hobbies and Recreations:* Gardening, Stamp, Shell and Various Collections.

STANFIELD, John Edward, 68 Melbourn Rd., Royston, Herts SG8 7DG. (0763-43445)–MA(Cantab.). *b. 6 April 1920, Hankow, China. m. 4 June 1959: 2d., 1s.*
Education: 1931–39 Kingswood Sch., Bath; 1946–50 Trinity Coll., Cambridge; 1948–50 Wesley House.
Appointments: 1950–57 Gambia Dt, West Africa; 1957–61 Ryton and Prudhoe; 1961–66 Taunton; 1966–71 Bromley; 1971–76 Southend; 1976–81 Swindon; 1981– Cambridge.

STANFORD, Percival Guy, 139 Woodside Rd., Amersham, Bucks HP6 6NJ. (02403-3504) *b. 13 July 1926, Stoke-on-Trent, Staffs. m. 13 Aug 1955: 2d., 1s.*
Education: 1931–37 Priesthead Sch., Kenton, Middx.; 1937– 43 Harrow County Sch. for Boys, Harrow; 1950–53 Handsworth.
Appointments: 1949–50 Wolverton and Bletchley; 1953–55 High Wycombe; 1955–60 Wantage and Wallingford; 1960–65 London, Bayswater; 1965–72 Chichester and Bognor; 1972–79 Witney and Faringdon; 1979– Amersham.
Special Interests: DIY, Gardening, Reading.

STANIFORTH, Trevor, 37 Southcliff Park, Clacton-on-Sea, Essex CO15 6HH. (0255-423640)–BSc, BD. *b. 27 Aug 1932, Oughtibridge, Nr. Sheffield. m. 1962: 1d., 1s.*
Education: 1937–43 Oughtibridge Council Sch.; 1943–51 Penistone Grammar Sch.; 1951–54, 1957–60 Manchester Univ.; 1957–60 Hartley Victoria. *Appointments:* 1960–62 Retford; 1962–68 Lincoln (North); 1968–75 Derby (South); 1975–80 Luton (North); 1980– Clacton-on-Sea.
Special Interests: President, Southport Methodist Holiness Convention; 1971–77 Chairman Methodist Revival Fellowship.
Hobbies and Recreations: Walking, Gardening, Furniture Restoration.

STANLAKE, Renhilda Margery, 20 Wynford Way, Low Moor, Bradford BD12 0PQ. (0274-675370) *b. 1 Oct 1928, Luxulyan, Cornwall. s.*
Education: 1933–42 Bugle Council Mixed Sch.; 1942–43 Newquay Commercial Sch.; 1954–56 Wesley, Deaconess Coll. *Appointments:* 1974–80 Biddulph and Mow Cop; 1980– Bradford (Trinity).

STANLEY, Peter Michael, 2 Applegarth Close, Basingstoke, Hants RG21. (0256-23103)–MA(Oxon). *b. 2 March 1931, Nottingham. m. 11*

Aug 1956: 1d., 3s.
Education: 1940–50 Nottingham High Sch.; 1950–54 Wadham Coll., Oxford; 1954–56 Handsworth.
Appointments: 1956–59 Hungerford; 1959–63 Peterborough; 1963–68 Leicester (North); 1968–74 Hoylake and W. Kirby; 1974–80 Redhill and E. Grinstead; 1980– Basingstoke.
Connexional Committees: 1972– Chapel Dept. and Property Board.
Publications: The Forgetful Saint (Lutterworth Press 1968).
Special Interests: Sport, Politics.
Hobbies and Recreations: Golf, Tennis, Table-Tennis, Gardening.

STANTON, Philip John Fraser, The Manse, L'Aumone, Câtel, Guernsey, CI. (0481-57232)–BA(Birmingham), MA(Exeter). *b. 26 Dec 1951, Caracas. m. 28 July 1980: 1d.*
Education: 1963–71 Queen Elizabeth Grammar Sch., Surrey; 1973–76 Birmingham Univ.; 1973–77 Queen's. *Appointments:* 1977–80 Plymouth Central Hall; 1980– Guernsey C.I.

STANWORTH, Margaret Morgan, Wesley Manse, Pentwyn Rd., Blackwood, Gwent NP2 1HN. (0495-225296) *b. 29 Jan 1926, Birmingham. s.*
Education: 1931–37 St. Michael's Inf. Sch.; 1937–39 Grove Lane Secondary; 1939–43 Soho Coll.; 1949–51 Wesley, Deaconess Coll.
Appointments: 1978– Sirholoy Valley.
Connexional Committees: 1971–74 Board of Division of Ministries; 1972–75 Board of Division of Property; 1971–77 Church Membership Committee; 1973–76 Wesley Deaconess Order Committee; 1972–73 Vice President of Deaconess Order; 1982– Connexional Candidates Committee.
Hobbies and Recreations: Walking, Photography, Painting, Natural History, Reading.

STARK, Christopher, 24 Emerson Ave., Middlesbrough, Cleveland TS5 7QH. (0642-817297)–BA. *b. 13 March 1936, Birmingham. m. 14 Aug 1965: 3d.*
Education: 1941–47 George Dixon Jun. Sch.; 1947–55 George Dixon Grammar Sch.; 1955–59 Sheffield Univ.; 1959–61 Wesley House.
Appointments: 1961–64 Woking; 1964–69 Sleaford; 1969–75 Chaplain HMF; 1975–78 Alford; 1979– Middlesbrough and Eston.
Special Interests: Fostering, Family Welfare, Rural Work, Youth Work.
Hobbies and Recreations: Photography, Music, Sport.

STATON, John Edward, 40 Hepscott Terrace, South Shields, Tyne and Wear NE33 4TH. (0632-552048)–BA. *b. 11 Oct 1953, Kettering. m. 17 July 1982.*
Education: 1965–72 Abbeydale Boys Grammar Sch.; 1972–76 Univ. of Sheffield; 1978–79 Univ. of Bristol; 1978–81 Wesley, Bristol.
Appointments: 1981– South Shields.
Special Interests: Football, Drama, Music, Literature. *Hobbies and Recreations:* Watching Sport, Playing Organ, Visiting Historical Buildings.

STATON, Maurice William, 10 West View, Blackhill, Consett, Co. Durham DH8 0AJ. (0207-502121)–BA(Dunelm), MA(Newcastle upon Tyne), BD(Manc.), MPhil(Notts.). *b. 2 May 1942, Darlington, Co. Durham. m. 16 Aug 1969: 2s.*
Education: 1953–60 Queen Elizabeth Grammar Sch., Darlington; Kings Coll., Newcastle (Durham Univ.); Manchester Univ.; 1964–67 Hartley Victoria. *Appointments:* 1967–69 Ripley; 1969–74 Nottingham Central; 1974– Consett.
Connexional Committees: 1977 Church Membership Sub-Committee; 1979– EC of Ibid; 1980– Board of Ministries.
Special Interests: Practical Theology and Pastoral Care, especially among the unemployed and also hospital chaplaincy. *Hobbies and Recreations:* Natural History, Fell Walking, Railways, Fellow of the Royal Geographical Society.

STEARS, Alan, Wesley House, Bond St., Newcastle upon Tyne NE4 8BA. (0632-731747)–MA, BSc.
Education: 1978–80 Hartley Victoria.
Appointments: 1980– Newcastle West.
Hobbies and Recreations: Industrial Chaplaincy.

STEDEFORD, Laurance Raymond, The Manse, Washfield Lane, Treeton, Rotherham, S. Yorkshire S60 5PU. (0742-697754)–BA(Lond.), DipEd. *b. 18 Feb 1923, Stoke Mandeville, Bucks. m. 1 Jan 1949: 4d., 1s.*
Education: 1933–36 Northwood Prep. Sch.; 1936–40 Merchant Taylors Sch. (Herts.); 1947–48 Westminster Coll.; 1961–62 Richmond. *Appointments:* 1953–61 British and Foreign Bible Society, N. Africa; 1962–68 Wem and Prees Green; 1968–77 Oswestry, Ellesmere and Chirk; 1977– Rotherham.
Local Council Committees: 1966–77 NE and NW Shropshire Youth Committees; 1980– Rotherham Cemeteries and Crematorium Liaison Committee.
Special Interests: Music, Israel Past and Present.

STEDMAN, Frederick William John, 10 Linnet Drive, Barton Seagrave, Kettering, Northants NN15 6SA. (0536-72-3240) *b. 3 March 1915, Oswestry, Shropshire. m. 1 Aug 1945.*
Education: 1920–24 Albert Rd., Oswestry; 1924–32 Technical Institute, Oswestry; 1938–40 Handsworth; 1940–41 Headingley.
Appointments: 1941–45 South Devon Mission; 1945–48 Plymouth (King St.); 1948–51 Newton Abbot; 1951–55 Darlaston (Pinfold St.) and Darlaston; 1955–60 Kettering; 1960–66 Ringsash; 1966–70 West Bromwich (Wesley); 1970–72 Liphook; 1972–74 Stour Vale; 1974–77 South Normanton; 1977–80 Birmingham (Smethwick).
Connexional Committees: 1962–68 Connexional Chapel Committee.
Special Interests: Theology, History.
Hobbies and Recreations: Reading, Listening to Records and Tapes.

STEEL, Charles Machan, 32 Eton Rd., Stratford upon Avon, Warwicks CV37 7ER. (0789-205200) *b. 1 Aug 1912, Greasbrough, Yorks. m. 15 May 1941: 2d.*
Education: Greasbrough Jun.;

Rotherham Grammar Sch.; 1934–37 Handsworth. *Appointments:* 1937–49 Yunnan, SW China; 1950–54 Louth; 1954–59 Driffield; 1959–67 Stratford upon Avon; 1967–73 Keswick; 1973–77 Kelsall.

STEPHENS, Alan, 84 Slewins Lane, Hornchurch, Essex RM11 2BU. (04024-791293) *b. 1 July 1928, Annfield Plain, Co. Durham. m. 19 Feb 1957: 2d., 1s.*
Education: 1939–42 Annfield Plain Intermediate Sch.; 1951–54 Hartley Victoria. *Appointments:* 1954–69 Bengal Dt; 1969–72 Enfield; 1972–77 Romford; 1977– Springboard Housing Association Ltd.
Connexional Committees: 1970–75 Overseas Missions.
Special Interests: Community Relations, House Groups, Housing, World Development. *Hobbies and Recreations:* Gardening, Woodwork, Theatre, Camping.

STEPHENS, Arthur Rosevear, Spindrift, Tregenna Court, Camborne, Cornwall TR14 7QU. (0209-712958) *b. 26 Oct 1908, Plymouth. m. 28 July 1937: 1d.*
Education: 1919–22 Devonport High Sch.; 1931–32 Handsworth. *Appointments:* 1930–31 South Devon Mission; 1934–35 Derby District (Chairman's Assistant); 1935–36 Sunderland District (Director of Social Welfare Dept.); 1936–38 Plymouth (Ebenezer and Greenbank); 1938–40 Devonport; 1940–43 Porthleven; 1943–46 Chaplain HMF; 1946–47 Brinkworth; 1947–54 Gloucester; 1954–57 Walkden and Worlsey; 1957–62 Bolton (Park St.); 1962–69 Camborne; 1969–73 Looe; 1951–54 Secretary Gloucester Council of Churches; 1947–54 Officiating Chaplain to Gloucester Regiment Depot; 1950–54 Part Time Teacher at Gloucester Technical Coll. *Local Council Committees:* 1962–69 Hospital Committee, Camborne.
Special Interests: Several Years as Supervisor of Probationer Ministers' Studies. *Hobbies and Recreations:* Rugby Union Referee, 1949–54 Gloucester Society, 1954–58 Manchester Society, Music.

STEPHENS, Geoffrey Nickolls, 13 Capper Close, Newton Poppleford, Sidmouth, Devon EX10 0HD. *b. 28 May 1903, Malden, Essex. m. 21 Aug 1938 (w.): 1s.*
Education: Various Jun. Schs.; 1913 Charles Church Sch., Plymouth; 1930–33 Richmond. *Appointments:* 1933–36 Marazion; 1936–39 Dorchester; 1939–44 Hayle; 1944–50 Launceston; 1950–54 St. Austell; 1954–57 Devonport; 1957–60 Coventry; 1960–65 Bristol East; 1965–69 Andover; 1969–72 Salisbury.
Special Interests: Music (singing), Garden. *Hobbies and Recreations:* Woodwork, General Handicrafts, Hospital and Social Visiting.

STEPHENS, John Spratt, 13 White Knights Rd., Earley, Reading. (0734-64634) *b. 14 June 1930, Thornbury, Gloucestershire. m. 22 April 1957.*
Education: 1941–47 Kingswood Grammar Sch., Bristol; 1953–56 Handsworth. *Appointments:* 1956–58 Beverley; 1958–62 Bridlington; 1962–67 Hinckley; 1967–71 Reading; 1971–77 Eastleigh; 1977–82 Bournemouth; 1982– Reading; 1980– Chairman Radio and TV Sub-Committee.
Connexional Committees: 1964–67, 1968–73 Division of Social Responsibility; 1973–79 Secretary of Synod, Southampton District.
Special Interests: Local Radio. *Hobbies and Recreations:* Sport, Natural History.

STEPHENS, Joseph, 86 Middleton Hall Rd., Kings Norton, Birmingham B30 1DG. (021-458-1059)—MA, BD. *b. 23 Jan 1933, Pilning, Glos. m. 14 Aug 1954: 2d.*
Education: 1931–36 Pilning Jun. Sch.; 1936–37 Staple Hill Sen. Sch.; 1937–44 Kingswood Grammar Sch.; 1951–54 Edinburgh Univ.; 1954–55 Moray House Training Coll., Edinburgh; 1957–59 Hartley Victoria. *Appointments:* 1949–50 Poole; 1959–61 Cowbridge and St. Athan; 1961–64 Rhondda; 1964–70 Darlington; 1970–78 Birmingham (Moseley Rd. and Sparkhill); 1978– Birmingham (South West).
Connexional Committees: 1975–80 C. Probationers Oversight Committee; 1977– Deaconess Pastoral Oversight Committee; 1980– Conn. Candidates Committee.
Special Interests: Inter-Faith Dialogue, Community Relations, Human Rights. *Hobbies and Recreations:* Literature.

STEPHENS, William Peter, The Queen's Coll., Somerset Rd., Birmingham B15 2QH. (021-454-8171)—MA(Camb.), BD(Camb.), DSR(Strasbourg). *b. Penzance.*
Education: 1939–45 Lescudjack Sch.; 1945–52 Truro Sch.; 1952–55 Clare Coll., Cambridge; 1957–58 Univ. of Lund, Sweden; 1965–67 Univ. of Strasbourg, France; 1966–67 Univ. of Muenster, Germany; 1955–57 Wesley House; 1980–81 Queen's, Research Fellow. *Appointments:* 1958–61 Hartley Victoria, Assistant Tutor; 1961–65 Nottingham (West) and Univ. Chaplain; 1967–71 Croydon; 1971–73 Hartley Victoria, Tutor; 1973–80 Wesley, Tutor; 1981– Queen's, Tutor.
Connexional Committees: 1962–65 Local Preachers; 1972– European Relations; 1973– World Methodist (British Committee); 1980– Faith and Order; 1972–80 Roman Catholic-Methodist Commission; 1982– Overseas Division. *Council Member:* 1976– Bristol City Council. *Local Council Committees:* 1968–71 Croydon, Education (Schools Sub-Committee); 1976–78 Bristol, Housing; 1977–80 Arts and Leisure; 1979–80 Open Spaces and Amenities; 1979 Public Works. *Publications:* Co-Translator Luther's Works Vol 41 (1966); *The Holy Spirit in the Theology of Martin Bucer* (1970); *Faith and Love* (1971); *The Holy Spirit* (Edited Don Kirkpatrick 1974); *Christians Conferring* (1978); *Our Churches* (1978); *Methodism in Europe* (1980).
Special Interests: Politics, Theology of the Reformation, European Affairs. *Hobbies and Recreations:* Squash, Skiing, Mountain Walking, Swimming, Theatre, Opera.

STEVENSON, Raymond George Gregory, Runnymede, Fernleigh Rd., Wadebridge, Cornwall PL27 7AZ. (020881-2887) *b. 16 Oct 1929, Plymouth. m. 11 Aug 1958: 2d., 2s.*
Education: 1940–45 Devonport High Sch.; 1945–50 Plymouth Art Coll.; 1952–55 Bristol.
Appointments: 1955–58 Penzance Central; 1958–63 Leeds South; 1963–71 Swindon; 1971–81 Bristol, Kingswood; 1981– Camelford and Wadebridge.
Connexional Committees: 1982– Property Division.
Special Interests: Architecture, Music. *Hobbies and Recreations:* Woodwind Ensemble Playing and Teaching, Beach and Rock Fishing.

STEWART, George Edward, Epworth House, 35 Carr Rd., Nelson, Lancashire BB9 7JS. (0282-65716)–BA(Lond. and Open Univ.). *b. 20 July 1927, Belfast, Northern Ireland. m. 21 Jan 1953: 2d.*
Education: 1936–42 Graymount, Belfast; 1943–45 Belfast Coll. of Technology; 1947–50 Hurlet Coll., Glasgow; 1960 Langside Coll., Glasgow; 1963–67 Handsworth.
Appointments: 1967–74 Accrington; 1974–77 Garstang; 1974–77 Assistant Secretary North Lancs. Synod; 1977–82 Loftus and Staithes; 1982– Nelson.
Council Member: 1981–82 Chaplain to Mayor of Langborough (Cleveland). *Local Council Committees:* 1971–74 Official Free Church Chaplain, Accrington, Victoria Hospital.
Special Interests: Church History, Methodist History, Social Studies, Boy's Brigade. *Hobbies and Recreations:* Metalcraft, Reading, Veteran Motor Car Rebuilding, Driving.

STILLWELL, Martin John, 39 Broomfield Ave., Hasland, Chesterfield, Derbyshire S41 4LU. (0246-73416) *b. Chichester, West Sussex. m. 31 March 1975: 2d.*
Education: 1963–70 Chichester High Sch. for Boys; 1975–79 Wesley, Bristol. *Appointments:* 1979– Chesterfield.
Special Interests: Prayer (Theology and Practice). *Hobbies and Recreations:* Guitar, Writing (Poetry and Meditations), Feature Films.

STOCKER, Clifford Oswald, 16 Brynwood Drive, Newtown, Powys SY16 2EG. (0686-25949) *b. 12 March 1905, Cardiff.*
Education: 1917–20 Howard Gardens Secondary, Cardiff; 1929–32 Handsworth. *Appointments:* 1928–29 Wadebridge and Camelford; 1932–34 Frome; 1934–37 Wellington (Shropshire); 1937–39 Knighton; 1939–42 West Monmouth; 1942–45 Bodmin; 1945–49 Shaftesbury; 1949–53 Weymouth; 1953–56 Northampton; 1956–62 Ripley; 1962–67 Wigan; 1967–70 Halifax.
Connexional Committees: 1945–54 Temperance and Social Welfare.

STOCKS, Brian, 34 Manor Rd., Woolton, Liverpool L25 8QG. (051-428-2298)–BA. *b. 11 Jan 1935, South Normanton, Derbyshire. m. 25th June 1958: 4d.*
Education: 1957–61 Wesley, Bristol.
Appointments: 1961–62 Missionary Training; 1962–65 North Rhodesia Dt; 1965–69 United Church of Zambia; 1969–77 Stockport; 1977– Liverpool South East.
Connexional Committees: 1979–82 Overseas Division.
Hobbies and Recreations: Photograpy, Angling.

STONE, Geoffrey, 5 Hill Side, Bolton BL1 5DT. (0204-43302)–BD. *m: 1d., 1s.*
Education: 1951–54 Richmond.
Appointments: 1954–55 Sutton, Surrey; 1955–57 Newcastle upon Tyne (Brunswick); 1957–62 Preston (Trinity); 1962–67 Morecambe and Heysham; 1967–76 Newcastle upon Tyne (Brunswick Central); 1976–80 Newcastle upon Tyne (West); 1980– Chairman, Bolton and Rochdale District.

STONE, Kenneth, 31 Bradwall Rd., Sandbach, Cheshire CW11 9AG. (09367-2074)–BSc. *b. 6 Aug 1929, Stoke on Trent. m. 6 Aug 1960: 1d., 1s.*
Education: 1940–48 Newcastle (Staffs.) High Sch.; 1949–54 Sheffield Univ.; 1955–58 Handsworth.
Appointments: 1958–59 Newbury; 1959–60 Newport (Hill St.); 1960–64 Rhondda; 1964–69 Burslem (Hill Top); 1969–77 Whitehaven; 1977– Sandbach and Alsager.
Connexional Committees: 1976– General Purposes.

STONE, Robert, 212 River Green, Clifton Estate, Nottingham NG11 8AU. (0602-212158) *b. 5 June 1910, Stoke-on-Trent. m. 5 June 1937 (w.): 3d.*
Education: Elem. Education and Private Tuition; 1953–54 Hartley Victoria. *Appointments:* 1953–54 Todmorden; 1954–58 Littleborough; 1958–63 Rochdale South; 1963–68 Preston, Lune St.; 1968–75 Poole, Dorset; 1975–77 Matlock.
Special Interests: Guild Holidays (Host). *Hobbies and Recreations:* Football, Gardening, Reading, Classical Music.

STONES, Vernon, 10 Pinewood Rd., Midsomer Norton, Bath BA3 2RG. (0761-414053) *b. 16 Oct 1912, Bradford, Yorks. m. 15 May 1941: 1d., 2s.*
Education: 1918–23 Thornbury, Bradford, Prim. Sch.; 1923–30 Bradford Grammar Sch.; 1934–37 Hartley Victoria. *Appointments:* 1937–52 SW China Dt; 1952–57 Bristol (Kingswood Zion); 1957–60 Midsomer Norton; 1960–68 Methodist Missionary Society, Chinese in London; 1968–72 Trowbridge and Bradford on Avon; 1972–76 Tavistock.
Connexional Committees: 1960–70 MMS General Committee.
Special Interests: China. *Hobbies and Recreations:* Gardening, Painting, Travel.

STONES, William Anthony, 3 Bentinck Rd., Fairfield, Stockton on Tees, Cleveland TS19 7PU. (0642-584225) *b. 9 July 1934, Nottingham. m. 6 Aug 1960: 2d., 1s.*
Education: Sycamore Rd. Inf., Nottingham; St. Annswell Rd. Jun. Sch.; Morley Sch., Wells Rd., Nottingham; 1956–60 Handsworth.

Appointments: 1960–63 Crook; 1963–68 Thornley; 1968–75 Leeds Richmond Hill; 1975– Stockton.

STONHAM, Reginald Charles, The Old Hall, Portesham, Weymouth, Dorset DT3 4EZ. (030-587-252) *b. 15 Nov 1903, Broadstairs, Kent. m. 29 July 1931: 2d., 1s.*
Education: St. Peter's Sch., Broadstairs; 1924–27 Handsworth.
Appointments: 1927–29 Llanelli and Carmarthen; 1929–32 Cardiff (Roath Rd.); 1932–36 Liverpool (Linacre Mission); 1936–41 Stockport (Trinity); 1941–46 Newcastle, Staffs (Brunswick); 1946–52 Reading; 1952–57 East Wight; 1957–68 Chairman, Portsmouth District.
Connexional Committees: 1942–48 Youth Department; 1942–56 Clubs etc., and MAYC Committee.
Special Interests: Hymns, Methodist History, Liturgy, Member of FK from 1924 and of MSF since formation in 1935. *Hobbies and Recreations:* Gardening.

STOPFORD, Michael, 21 Helmsley Way, Northallerton, North Yorkshire DL7 8TA. (0609-2647) *b. 15 July 1947, Halifax, West Yorkshire. m. 4 Jan 1969: 1d., 1s.*
Education: 1952–58 Holy Trinity (Inf. and Jun.) Church Sch., Halifax; 1958–63 Grace Ramsden's Grammar Sch., Elland, Yorkshire; 1978–81 Wesley, Bristol. *Appointments:* 1981 Northallerton.
Special Interests: The Work of Christ in Prisons (Chaplain at HM Prison, Northallerton). *Hobbies and Recreations:* Family, Walking.

STOTT, Albert, 11 Lavender Lane, Cirencester, Glos GL7 1PP. (0285-61536) *b. 13 March 1906, Batley, Yorks. m. 1 July 1935: 1d.*
Education: Several L/A Elem. Schs.; 1927–30 Victoria Park.
Appointments: 1926–27 Farsley, Pudsey and Yeadon; 1930–40 Sierra Leone Dt., W. Africa; 1940–43 Redruth; 1943–46 Chaplain HMF; 1946–56 Stroud, Cirencester; 1956–57 Berkhamsted; 1957–65 Hereford; 1965–66 Alfreton; 1966–72 Trowbridge and Bradford on Avon.
Special Interests: Social History, Toc H Branch Affairs.

STOYLE, Percy Vivian Gwynfryn, Parka Vean, St. Columb Rd., St. Columb, Cornwall TR9 6PG. (0726-860382) *b. 16 Feb 1913, Ferndale, Glamorgan. m. (2) 6 Aug 1956: 1d., 1sd., 2s.*
Education: 1920–27 Prim. Sch., Ferndale; 1938–39 Cliff Coll.
Appointments: 1962–63 Whitehaven; 1963–66 Houghton-le-Spring; 1966–74 St. Columb and Padstow; 1974–77 Camelford and Wadebridge.
Hobbies and Recreations: Gardening, Photography, Reading, Walking, Bird Watching, Music.

STRATFORD, Stanley Thomas, 5 Exchange Rd., West Bridgford, Nottingham NG2 6BX. (0602-816808) *b. 20 May 1902, Faversham, Kent. m. 25 Dec 1926: 2s.*
Education: 1906–16 Elem. Sch.; 1924–26 Handsworth.
Appointments: 1923–24 Coatbridge and Airdrie; 1927–29 Supply; 1929–32 Torrington; 1932–36 Stainland and Greetland; 1936–40 Glasgow South; 1940–43 Southport South; 1943–56 RAF Chaplain; 1956–61 Grantham; 1961–66 Lancaster; 1966–69 Rhyl and Prestatyn.
Special Interests: Music.

STRATTON, Joseph Arthur, 7 The Avenue, Newton Abbot, Devon TQ12 2BZ. (0626-60861)–BD(Lond.). *b. 22 Jan 1917. m. 9 Aug 1947: 1d., 1s.*
Education: All Saints Prim. Sch., London; Silver St. Prim. Sch., London; Latymer Grammar Sch., London; 1945–47 Handsworth.
Appointments: 1943–45 Newmarket Mission; 1947–50 Faringdon; 1950–55 Watford; 1955–61 Ilford; 1961–74 Worthing; 1974–81 Newton Abbot.
Connexional Committees: 1958 Connexional Youth Committee; 1960 Radio and Television Committee. *Publications: What Would You Do If* (1962).
Special Interests: Germany, Deputy Director of Community Education for the Young European, 1965–72 Marriage Guidance Counsellor.
Hobbies and Recreations: Film Making, Tape Recording, Aircraft History, Stamp Collecting, Broadcasting.

STRAWBRIDGE, Harold, Flat 7, 23 Seafield Rd., Lytham, Lytham St Annes, Lancs FY8 5PY. (0253-730206) *b. 23 Sept 1901, Salford, Lancs. m. 14 Aug 1929: 1d.*
Education: 1906–13 Woodbine St., Higher Grade Sch.; 1913–19 Salford Grammar Sch.; 1922–25 Handsworth.
Appointments: 1925–27 Diss; 1927–29 Belper; 1929–30 Appleby; 1930–33 Bishop Auckland; 1933–37 Darlington; 1937–40 Portsmouth; 1940–44 Manchester (Regent Rd.); 1944–47 Blackburn; 1947–52 London, Southall; 1952–54 Oldham; 1954–57 North Hill; 1957–62 Manchester (Walkden); 1962–64 Accrington.
Special Interests: History. *Hobbies and Recreations:* Walking.

STRAWSON, William, Handsworth, 32 Northorpe, Bourne, Lincolnshire PE10 0HJ. (077-82-2518)–MTh, PhD. *b. 20 Sept 1916, Gainsborough, Lincolnshire. m. 27 Aug 1944: 1s.*
Education: 1928–32 Stamford; London Univ.; Cambridge Univ.; 1940–41 Richmond; 1941–42 Hartley Victoria; 1942–43 Headingley; 1943–44 Wesley House.
Appointments: 1939–40 Rochdale N; 1944–46 Chaplain HMF; 1946–52 London, Finchley and Hendon; 1952–54 South Norwood; 1954–55 Birmingham, Sutton Park; 1955–70 Handsworth Coll., (Tutor Systematic Theol. and Philosophy of Religion); 1970–75 Queen's Coll., (Senior Methodist Tutor).
Connexional Committees: Faith and Order, Healing, Ministerial Training, World Methodism, Candidates, Doctrinal, Appeal (Convenor).
Publications: Jesus and Future Life (1959, 2nd Ed. 1972); *Teachers and New Theology* (1969); *Christian Approach to Humanist* (1963); Joint Editor *A Shorter Bible* (Rev.); Contributor to *A Christian in Modern World* (ed. D. Hubery); *Religion and Medicine* (ed. J. Crowlesmith); *Queen's Sermons* (ed. I. Rowe);

Mental Health and Church (ed. D.S.R.); Chapter on Methodist Theology 1850–1950 in *History of Methodist Church* (Vol. III).

STREET, Francis Robert, 3 Bryn Newydd East, Prestatyn, Clwyd LL19 9ES. (07456-2527)–OBE. *b. 3 Aug 1915, Southsea, Hants. m. 21 Aug 1946: 1d., 2s.*
Education: 1927–34 Gillingham (Kent) County High Sch.; 1934–38 Westminster Coll., London; 1938–41 Richmond. *Appointments:* 1941–43 Uttoxeter; 1944–70 Chaplain HMF (RN); 1970–78 Rhyl and Prestatyn; 1978–80 Lytham St. Annes.
Connexional Committees: RN, Army and RAF Board.

STREET, Kenneth Edwin, 22 Vauxhall, St. Helier, Jersey, Channel Islands. (0534-22763)–BA(Nottingham), MA(Camb.). *b. 8 Nov 1940, Keynsham, Somerset. m. 4 July 1964: 1d., 2s.*
Education: 1945–51 Keynsham Prim. and Jun. Sch.; 1951–59 City of Bath Boys Grammar Sch.; 1959–62 Univ. of Nottingham; 1962–64 Univ. of Cambridge; 1962–64 Wesley House. *Appointments:* 1964–67 Coventry Mission; 1967–72 Birmingham (Sutton Park); 1972–82 Guernsey; 1982– Jersey.
Connexional Committees: 1975–79 Channel Islands Synod Secretary; 1979– Channel Islands District Chairman; Stationing Committee; General Purposes; Home Mission.*Council Member:* 1974– Free Church Advisor To Channel Television. *Local Council Committees:* 1979–82 Guernsey Welfare Service Chairman; 1979–82 Friends of St. Julian Chairman; 1978–82 Guernsey Industrial Tribunal Panel Member
Special Interests: TV and Media Work. *Hobbies and Recreations:* Gardening, Woodwork, Sailing.

STRINGER, Paul Robert, 15 Dawlish Ave., Droylsden, Manchester M35 6WA. (061-370-2306).
Education: 1972–76 Bristol.
Appointments: 1976–78 Manchester and Salford Mission; 1978– Manchester Droylsden and Openshaw.

STRINGER, Peter John Hubert, Pinehurst, Wansbeck Rd., Ashington, Northumberland. (0670-812137) *b. 14 April 1945, Burnley, Lancashire. m. 19 Feb 1965: 1d., 2s.*
Appointments: 1975–79 Manchester and Salford Mission; 1979–80 Manchester, Droyldsen and Openshaw; 1980– Ashington and Newbiggin.

STRINGFELLOW, James Edwin, 41 Emlyn Rd., London W12 9TF. (01-743-9962)–BD(Lond.). *b. 10 Feb 1927, Bolsover, Derbyshire. m. 17 July 1954: 4d.*
Education: 1938–45 Chesterfield Grammar; 1949–51 Richmond.
Appointments: 1948–49 Chatham Garrison and Naval Port Mission; 1951–54 Berwick upon Tweed; 1954–63 East Nigeria District; 1963–68 Derby East; 1968–74 Harrogate; 1974–79 Doncaster; 1979– London Mission, Hammersmith and Fulham.
Connexional Committees: 1964–68 Social Responsibility; 1975–82 Division of Ministries Board; 1977–82 Executive, Further Training Committee, Ministerial Training Committee; 1977– Ministerial Further Training Secretary (PT).
Local Council Committees: 1976–78 Doncaster Education Commitee.
Special Interests: Training, Growth.
Hobbies and Recreations: Birdwatching, Genealogies, Gardening.

STUBBINGS, Roger, 15 Galloway Rd., Fleetwood, Lancashire FY7 7BD. (03917-2176)–BA(Notts), BA(Bristol). *b. 14 Nov 1946, Huddersfield, Yorkshire. s.*
Education: 1957–65 Huddersfield New Coll., 1965–68 Nottingham Univ.; 1974–77 Bristol Univ.; 1974–77 Wesley, Bristol. *Appointments:* 1977–79 Preston (Lune St. and Orchard); 1979– Fleetwood.
Connexional Committees: 1981– British Roman Catholic, Methodist Conversations.
Hobbies and Recreations: Classical Music, Foreign Travel, Rugby League, Walking, Cookery.

STUBBS, William, O., 48 Bideford Way, Cannock, Staffs WS11 1QA. (05435-3366) *b. 6 June 1925, Kelsall, Chester. m. 15 Aug 1953: 1d., 1s.*
Education: Kelsall Village Sch.; 1945–47 Cliff Coll.; Hartley Victoria.
Appointments: 1949–51 London, Poplar and Bow; 1951–54 Kirbymoorside; 1954–59 Easingwold; 1959–66 Doncaster (South); 1973–81 Wolverhampton (Darlington St.); 1981– Cannock Chase.
Connexional Committees: 1968–72 Church Membership.
Special Interests: Methodist Local Histories, Local History, The Churches Evangelical Work and Witness. *Hobbies and Recreations:* Photography, Gardening, Country Walks.

STUCKEY, Thomas James, 70 Sweetbriar Lane, Exeter EX1 3AQ. (0392-75070)–BSc, BD, MTh. *b. 10 May 1940, Kingsbury Episcopi, Martock, Somerset. m. 16 July 1966: 1d., 2s.*
Education: 1951–56 Yeovil Grammar Sch.; 1958–63 City Univ. London; 1967 London Univ.; 1973 Edinburgh Univ.; 1965–67 Richmond.
Appointments: 1967–81 Exeter; 1981– Hartley Victoria Coll., Tutor in Theology and Philosophy.
Connexional Committees: Home Missions, Commission on Evangelism.
Publications: Various in Engineering Magazines; May 1982 *Epworth Review.*
Special Interests: Preaching, Spirituality, Theology, Envangelical Renewal. *Hobbies and Recreations:* Music, Cars, Motorbikes.

STYLES, Richard Michael, Hillside Manse, Parke Rd., Brinscall, Nr. Chorley, Lancs PR6 8PU. (0254-8303-74) *b. 6 Dec 1951. m.*
Education: 1977–81 Wesley, Bristol.
Appointments: 1981– Chorley.

SUCH, Royston Jeffery, Wesley Manse, 8 Park Ave., St. Ives, Cambs PE17 4JW. (0480-62293)–LLB. *b. 3 May 1946, London. m. 28 Dec 1972: 2d., 1s.*
Education: 1957–64 Brentwood Sch.; 1964–67 Univ. Coll., London Univ.; 1967–68 The Coll. of Law; 1978–80 Wesley House.
Appointments: 1980– Hunts Mission.
Special Interests: Law, Dogs. *Hobbies and Recreations:* Camping, Relishing Country Life.

SUGDEN, Leonard Herbert, 2 High St., Loddon, Norwich NR14 6AH. (0508-20246)–BA(B.ham), BD(Lond.), MPS. *b. 13 Jan 1915, Garforth, Yorks. m.22 Dec 1945: 1d., 3s.*
Education: 1920–25 Garforth Council; 1926–27 Castleford Grammar; 1927–31 West Leeds High; 1931–34 Leeds Technical Coll.; 1935–36 Leeds Univ.; 1939–43 Birmingham Univ.; 1939–43 Handsworth. *Appointments:* 1943–45 Salisbury; 1945–46 Walton on Thames; 1946–49 Staines and Feltham; 1949–57 Wakefield; 1957–62 Fakenham and Wells; 1962–65 Norwich, Calvert St.
Connexional Committees: 1959–63 Youth Council; 1976–81 Ministries.
Special Interests: Pharmacist, Drama.
Hobbies and Recreations: Photography.

SULLY, George Henry, Flat 1, 55 Musters Rd., West Bridgford, Nottingham NG2 7PQ. (0602-816095)– MA(Leeds), BD(Lond.). *b. 28 April 1909, London. m. 14, Aug 1937 (w.): 1d., 2s.*
Education: 1914–22 St. Lukes Parochial Sch.; 1922–25 St. Clement Danes, Holborn Estate Grammar Sch.; 1931–35 Richmond.
Appointments: 1930–31 Aldershot; 1935–37 President's List; 1937–39 Leeds East; 1939–41 Bradford, Shipley; 1941–46 Chaplain HMF; 1946–49 Farsley; 1949–50 Aireborough; 1950–56 Leeds, Headingley; 1956–63 Nottingham South; 1963–68 Derby South; 1968–74 Leeds, Horsforth and Bromley.

SULSTON, Peter George, The Manse, 41 Back Lane, Wymondham, Norfolk NR18 0LB. (0953–602194)–BA(Cantab.), MA(Cantab.). *b. 2 June 1942, Edinburgh. m. 5 Aug 1967: 1d., 2s.*
Education: 1953–60 Haberdashers' Aske's Sch., Hampstead; 1960–63 Magdalene Coll., Cambridge; 1964–67 Wesley House. *Appointments:* 1967–69 Bristol (Clifton and Redland); 1969–74 Bolton; 1974–81 Watford; 1981– Wymondham, Attleborough and Watton.
Connexional Committees: 1977–81 Board of Division of Education and Youth; 1979– Connexional Probationers' Oversight Committee; 1977– Secretary, Wesley House Oversight Committee. *Publications: Theology and Biblical Studies, A Guide to First Degree Courses in UK Universities* (Careers Research and Advisory Centre 1967); Contributor *Partners in Learning* 1982.
Special Interests: The Modern Novel, Adult Christian Education. *Hobbies and Recreations:* Long-distance Running, Hill-Walking, Drama, Reading.

SUMMERS, Peter Leslie, 153 Wilmslow Rd., Handforth, Wilmslow, Cheshire SK9 3JL. (0625-525354)–BA. *b. 16 July 1942, East Runton, Norfolk. m. 1964: 1d., 1s.*
Education: 1946–51 East Runton Jun.; 1951–52 St. Peters St., Stapen Hill; 1952–55 Burton-on-Trent Technical High; 1955–58 Handsworth Grammar; 1958–61 Drax Grammar; 1962–65 Headington Technical, Oxford; 1966–70 Hull Coll. of Technology; 1977–80 Manchester Univ.; 1977–80 Hartley Victoria. *Appointments:* 1980– Bramhall.

SUMMERSBY, Tom, 1 Fernhill Gdns, Kingston upon Thames, Surrey KT2 5DL. (01-546-1441) *b. 29 Sept 1926, Ealing. m. 22 Dec 1951: 1d., 1s.*
Education: 1937–43 Bromley County Grammar Sch.; 1964–66 Didsbury. *Appointments:* 1966–69 Hatherleigh; 1969–76 Bristol, Frome Valley; 1976–82 Bedford South and Ampthill; 1982– Kingston upon Thames; Also Chaplain at HM Remand Centre, Latchmere House, Ham Common, Richmond.
Publications: Youth and the Rural Scene (1975).
Special Interests: Church Growth, The Healing Role of the Church.
Hobbies and Recreations: Gardening, Concertina.

SUMNER, Ian, 2 Ash St., Southport, Merseyside PR8 6JH. (0704-40130) *b. 6 May 1939, Preston, Lancashire. m.: 1d., 1s.*
Education: 1944–52 Cadley Jun. Sch.; 1952–55 Fulwood High Sch.; 1962–66 Hartley Victoria.
Appointments: 1966–69 Spennymoor and Ferryhill; 1969–71 Oldbury; 1971–77 Chester-le-Street; 1977–82 South West Cumbria; 1982– Southport.
Special Interests: Wesley Historical Society. *Hobbies and Recreations:* Secondhand Books, Collect British Stamps.

SUTCH, Leonard Ernest, Hilbre, The Mount, Heswall, Wirral, Merseyside L60 4RE. (051-342-6324) *b. 15 Sept 1923, Chelsea, London. m. 18 Aug 1956: 2d.*
Education: 1932–37 Hazelrigge Rd., Clapham; 1949–50 Cliff Coll.; 1950–53 Handsworth. *Appointments:* 1953–56 Nottingham West; 1956–61 Cliff Coll.; 1961–64 Dudley (Gornal); 1964–69 Darlington St., Wolverhampton; 1969–81 Crosby; 1981– Heswall.
Connexional Committees: 1976–79 Ministries Committee.
Special Interests: Swimming, Hiking, Walking, Climbing, International Relations.

SUTCLIFFE, Derek, 2 Crown Drive, Inverness IV2 3NL. (0463-31170)–*BA(Leeds). b. 13 Feb 1935, Havercroft, Yorkshire. m. 9 Aug 1961: 1d., 2s.*
Education: 1939–46 South Hiendley Prim. Sch.; 1946–53 Hemsworth Grammar Sch.; 1955–58 Leeds Univ.; 1955–58 Headingley.
Appointments: 1958–61 Edinburgh (Nicholson Sq.); 1961–68 Arbroath

and Montrose; 1968–76 Paisley Mission; 1976– Inverness.
Connexional Committees: 1970–74 Education and Youth.
Special Interests: Finance, Politics.
Hobbies and Recreations: Sport.

SUTCLIFFE, John Gordon, 19 Derby Rd., Poulton-le-Fylde, Blackpool, Lancs FY6 7AF. (0253-882796) *b. 12 March 1928, Hoghton, Lancashire. m. 17 Dec 1955: 1d., 1s.*
Education: 1939–44 Hutton Grammar Sch., Preston; 1947–48 Cliff Coll.; 1952–55 Didsbury, Bristol.
Appointments: 1951–52 Newbury; 1955–57 Blackburn Mission; 1957–63 Manchester and Salford Methodist Mission; 1963¡70 London, Harrow; 1970– Blackpool North; Have held Chaplaincies in Colleges, HM Prison, ATC; A British Council of Churches Representative to observe the EEC prior to Britain's entry into the Community; BCC Representative on an Anglo-German Committee to formulate youth exchange programmes.
Connexional Committees: 1960–78 Cliff Coll. Committee.
Special Interests: Evangelism and Church Growth, World Mission and World Methodism. *Hobbies and Recreations:* Photography, Fell-Walking, Do-it-Yourself Projects.

SUTCLIFFE, Peter Wilkinson, 20 Beadon Rd., Bromley, Kent BR2 9AT. (01-464-2540)–BA(Leeds). *b. 15 Jan 1932, Wakefield, Yorks. m. 11 Aug 1961: 1d., 2s.*
Education: 1942–50 Hemsworth Grammar Sch., Yorks WR; 1952–55 Leeds Univ.; 1952–55 Headingley.
Appointments: 1955–58 Edinburgh (Nicholson Sq.); 1958–61 Glasgow (Cathcart Rd. and Pollokshaws); 1961–69 Stockton on Tees; 1969–75 Darlington; 1975–80 Stokesley; 1980– London South East District Chairman.
Connexional Committees: 1974–77 President's Council; 1973–76 and 1977– General Purposes Committee; 1980– Home Mission Division.
Local Council Committees: 1968–69 Chairman Egglescliffe Parish Council (Co. Durham); 1965–69 Parish Council.
Hobbies and Recreations: Sport, Philately.

SUTCLIFFE, Thomas George Antony, 200 Turner St., Hanley, Stoke-on-Trent ST1 6LT. (0782-22781) *b. 6 Sept 1931, Uttoxeter, Staffs. m. 5 Aug 1957: 1d., 1s.*
Education: 1943–46 Uttoxeter Grammar Sch.; 1946–48 Kent Coll., Canterbury; 1954–57 Richmond.
Appointments: 1957–60 Doncaster (Priory Place); 1960–64 The Peak; 1964–69 Grimsby (West); 1969–76 Burslem Mission; 1976– Stoke-on-Trent, Hawley.
Special Interests: Church History, Hymnology, English History. *Hobbies and Recreations:* Music, Choral Singing.

SUTTIE, Ian, 22 St. Ninian's Rd., Upperby, Carlisle, Cumbria CA2 4LT. (0228-22455)–BA. *b. 18 Sept 1956, Cambridge. s.*
Education: 1961–63 St.Ives (Huntingdon) Prim. Sch.; 1963–68 St. Ives (Huntingdon) Jun. Sch.; 1968–75 Ramsey Abbey Sch.; 1975–78 Univ. of York; 1978–81 Wesley House. *Appointments:* 1981– Carlisle.

SUTTON, Edwin Wrate, 1 Springfield Terrace, Seaham, Co. Durham SR7 7SU. (0783-813339)–BD(Lond.). *b. 28 Feb 1921, West Walton, Norfolk. m. 20 May 1950: 2d.*
Education: 1926–35 West Walton; 1959–61 Hartley Victoria (External).
Appointments: 1958–61 Rawtenstall; 1961–69 Morley; 1969–74 Waltham Abbey and Hertford; 1974–77 Ipswich; 1977–82 Higham Ferrers; 1982– Seaham.
Hobbies and Recreations: Gardening, Walking.

SUTTON, Frank Herbert, 8 Byland Close, Simonstone, Burnley, Lancs BB12 7QA. (0282-75645)–MA(Oxon), BA(Cantab.). *b. 30 May 1908, Great Harwood, Blackburn, Lancs. m. 27 Sept 1944: 1s.*
Education: 1916–19 Queen Elizabeth's Grammar Sch., Blackburn; 1919–26 Rydal; 1926–29 Jesus Coll., Oxford; 1930–32 Wesley House. *Appointments:* 1932–39 Mysore District, South India; 1941–43 Bristol South; 1943–47 Ramsey, Isle of Man; 1947–51 Plymouth, King St.; 1951–56 Stoke on Trent; 1956–64 Leek; 1964–69 Nantwich; 1969–73 Brandon and Deerness Valley.
Connexional Committees: 1944–47, 1953–56 Overseas Missions.
Special Interests: Correspondence Tutor, Local Preachers, Religious Movements. *Hobbies and Recreations:* Car Maintenance, Carpentry etc., Cricket, Tennis.

SUTTON, Gerald Andrew, Beaumont, Stockenill Rd., Leominster HR6 8PP. (0568-2406) *b. 24 Oct 1932, Pontypridd, S. Wales. m. 2 April 1960: 2d., 1s.*
Education: 1960–61 Selly Oak; 1957–60 Didsbury, Bristol.
Appointments: 1961–72 Zimbabwe; 1972–76 St. Austell; 1976 Leominster, Presteigne and Kingston.

SUTTON, Harry, 148 North Rd., Clacton-on-Sea, Essex CO15 4EP. (0255-422886) *b. 23 May 1915, Old Colwyn, Clwyd. m. 17 Oct 1946: 1d., 1s.*
Education: 1920 Dr. Walsh's Preparatory Sch., Rhyl; 1921–26 Clwyd St. Prim. Sch., Rhyl; 1926 Streetly, West Midlands, Prim. Sch.; 1926–31 Queen Mary's Grammar Sch., Walsall, West Midlands; 1939–41 Richmond; 1941–42 Headingley.
Appointments: 1942–44 Bradford, Green Hill; 1944–45 London, East Ham Mission; 1945–48 Wakefield; 1948–53 Colchester; 1953–62 Clacton-on-Sea; 1962–67 Manningtree and Harwich; 1967–74 Beverley; 1974–80 Melton Mowbray.

SWAIN, Raymond John, Wesley House, 1 Clive Rd., Market Drayton, Shropshire TF9 3DJ. (0630-2631)–BA(Birmingham). *b. 8 Dec 1936, Fulham, London. m. 23 July 1966.*
Education: 1941–48 Prim. (Various); 1948 Latymer Upper; 1949–55 Leyton County High Sch. for Boys;

1957–59 Westminster Coll.; 1962–65 Birmingham Univ.; 1962–66 Handsworth. *Appointments:* 1966–68 Romford; 1968–73 Manningtree and Harwich; 1973–79 Stafford; 1979– Market Drayton.
Connexional Committees: 1977–79 Property; 1978–79 Methodist/URC Liaison Group.
Special Interests: Local Broadcasting. *Hobbies and Recreations:* Drama, Music.

SWALES, Frederick John, Arnmore, Arnside, Carnforth, Lancs LA5 0AQ. (0524-761397) *b. 20 June 1938, Marston, Bedfordshire. m. 23 June 1962: 1s.*
Education: 1943–48 Marston Shelton Jun. Sch.; 1948–53 Stewartby Secondary Sch.; 1955–56 Cliff Coll.; 1959–63 Hartley Victoria.
Appointments: 1963–65 Cromer, Sheringham and Holt; 1965–70 Bloxwich; 1970–76 Skipton; 1976– Kendal.
Connexional Committees: 1977– Division of Education and Youth.
Special Interests: Youth Work.
Hobbies and Recreations: Ships, Oceanography.

SWINGLEHURST, Peter Briggs, The Manse, Chapel Rd., Alderley Edge, Cheshire SK9 7DU. (0625-583337) *b. 25 Aug 1929, Sale, Cheshire. m. 10 Feb 1956: 1d., 1s.*
Education: 1934–36 Northenden Prim. Sch.; 1936–39 Brownley Green Jun. Sch.; 1939–45 Yew Tree Secondary Sch.; 1950–51 Cliff Coll.; 1951–54 Handsworth.
Appointments: 1954–76 West Indies (Jamaica); 1976–81 Glossop; 1981– Alderley Edge and Knutsford.
Hobbies and Recreations: Gardening, Woodwork, Sport.

SYDENHAM, Frederick Reginald, 4 Cressy Rd., Alfreton, Derby DE5 7BR. (0773-833259)–BA(Open Univ.). *b. 28 April 1916, Plymouth. m. 25 July 1949: 3d., 1s.*
Education: 1923–27 Linwood, Bournemouth; 1927–32 Grammar Sch., Bournemouth; 1970–74 Open Univ.; 1974–76 Exeter Univ. (External); 1945–47 Handsworth.
Appointments: 1947–50 Leeds (South); 1950-56 Mansfield (West); 1956–60 Rugby; 1960–63 Hull (West); 1963–64 Ripley; 1964–68 Ilkeston; 1968–74 Penzance; 1974–80 Bodmin; 1980– South Normanton; 1976–80 District DSR Secretary, Cornwall.
Connexional Committees: 1977–80 DSR. *Publications: Healing Ministry of Wesley* in *Quarterly Review of Churches' Fellowship for Physical and Spiritual Studies* (Nos. 100/101 1979).
Special Interests: Healing Ministry of Holy Spirit of God. *Hobbies and Recreations:* Family Outings, Travel.

SYKES, Frank Elmer, 12 Churchill Close, Watton, Thetford, Norfolk IP25 6BB. (0953-881438) *b. 28 March 1935, Bradford, Yorkshire. m. 18 May 1959: 1d., 1s.*
Education: Lorne St. Jun. Sch., Bradford; Westgate Hill Jun. Sch., Bradford; Highfield Secondary Modern; 1955–56 Cliff Coll.; 1970–72 Queens. *Appointments:* 1972–75 Birmingham, Blackheath; 1975–81 Kings Lynn; 1981– Wymondham, Attleborough and Watton.
Hobbies and Recreations: Photography, Walking.

TABARN, William Francis, 68 Brantingham Rd., Whalley Range, Manchester M16 8QH. (061-881-5080) *b. 13 April 1934, Ormskirk, Lancs. m: 1d., 4s.*
Education: 1938–46 Skelmersdale Jun. Prim.; 1946–49 Wigan Technical Coll.; 1952–54 Church Army Training Coll.; 1957–58 Hartley Victoria.
Appointments: 1958–60 Swinton and Pendlebury; 1960–63 Todmorden; 1963–69 Blackburn, Clayton St.; 1969–72 Dudley; (1972–75 Resigned; 1975–79 National Association of Youth Clubs;) 1979– Manchester and Salford Mission.
Connexional Committees: 1977–79 Education and Youth; 1979– Youth and Community; 1979– Connexional Co-ordinator and Secretary J.M.M.
Special Interests: All youth work, European Exchanges. *Hobbies and Recreations:* Cars, Fishing, Enamelling.

TAIT, Ronald A., 121 Main St., Ashfordby, Melton Mowbray, Leicestershire LE14 3TS. (0664-812275)–BA. *b. Marylebone, London. m. Aug 1959: 1d., 1s.*
Education: Marling Sch., Stroud, Gloucestershire; 1953–56 Bristol Univ.; 1953–57 Didsbury, Bristol.
Appointments: 1957–59 Sale; 1959–64 Ashton-u-Lyne; 1964–69 Stockport; 1969–75 Nottingham Central; 1975 Melton Mowbray.

TANSLEY, Ernest William, 3 The Chine, Saltbury-by-Sea; Cleveland TS12 1QL. (0287-23667)–BD(Lond.). *b. 9 May 1904, Tooting, London. m. 10 Aug 1939: 1d.*
Education: 1920–21 Teacher Training Sch., Hucknall, Notts.; 1930–34 Handsworth.
Appointments: 1929–30 Brixham and Dartmouth; 1934–36 President's List; 1936–39 Loftus and Cleveland; 1939–44 South Shields; 1944–51 Durham; 1951–55 London, Ilford; 1955–60 London, Ealing and Acton; 1960–66 Kingston-on-Thames; 1966–69 London Mission, East Ham; 1969–72 Buckingham and Brockley.
Hobbies and Recreations: Travel, Gardening.

TAPLIN, Alan, 60 Wellingborough Rd., Rushden, Northants NN10 9YN. (0933-312778) *b. 12 July 1932, Manchester. m. 11 Sept 1954: 3s.*
Education: 1937–43 Blackley Jun. and Sen. Sch., Manchester; 1943–48 North Manchester Grammar Sch.; 1957–59 Hartley Victoria.
Appointments: 1959–63 Holbeach; 1963–69 Leeds South; 1969–75 Batley; 1975–81 Gloucester; 1981– Higham Ferrers.
Special Interests: District Property Secretary 1982—Local Radio.
Hobbies and Recreations: Tape Recording, Painting.

TAYLOR, Charles, Karibuni, 73 Bridlington St., Hunmanby, Filey, N.Yorks. YO14 0LP. (0723-890567)–BA, BD(Manch.), MA(Cantab.). *b. 16 Nov 1906, Prestwich, Manchester. m. 2 Oct 1937: 2d., 1s.*
Education: 1917–25 Farnworth Grammar Sch.; 1925–30 Manchester Univ.; 1933–36 Wesley House.

Appointments: 1936–38 Filey; 1938–44 Headmaster, Fulneck Boys Sch.; 1944–49 Eccles; 1949–54 Sale; 1954–61 Bristol South; 1961–66 Nottingham East; 1966–70 Bradford, Woodhouse Grove; 1970–75 Cambridge.
Connexional Committees: Education; 1957–70 Ministerial Training.

TAYLOR, Donald Spark, The Manse, Chapel Lane, Mickleton, Chipping Campden, Glos. GL55 6SD. (03-8677-278)—MC, MA(Cantab.). *b. 2 Oct 1922, Leeds. m. 15 Aug 1953: 1d., 1s.*
Education: 1934–40 Stationers Company; 1940–41 Kingswood Sch.; 1941–42, 1945–47 Peterhouse, Cambridge; 1947–48 Wesley House. *Appointments:* 1948–49 Oldbury; 1949–50 Worcester; 1950–56 Smethwick; 1956–61 Hull North; 1961–66 Leeds, Chapel Allerton; 1966–72 Leeds, Richmond Hill; 1972–77 Stratford upon Avon; 1977– Evesham.
Connexional Committees: 1959–72 Church Membership.

TAYLOR, H. Gregory, Westing, Coombe Rd., Saltash, Cornwall PL12 4ER. (075-55-3630) *b. 8 April 1897, Faringdon, Berkshire. m. 2 July 1926 (w.): 1s.*
Education: Bishop Wordsworth's Sch., Salisbury, Wilts.; 1921–23 Hartley. *Appointments:* 1920–21 Filey; 1923–25 Bournemouth; 1925–26 Portland; 1926–32 Weymouth; 1932–37 Weston-super-Mare; 1937–49 Clacton-on-Sea; 1949–56 Cleethorpes; 1956–62 Banbury.
Local Council Committees: 1928–32 Weymouth Education Committee; 1940–49 Clacton-on-Sea Sea Defence Committee; Library Committee; Clacton Representative on North East Essex Education Committee.
Hobbies and Recreations: 1941–42 President of the Rotary Club, Clacton-on-Sea.

TAYLOR, Joseph Michael, The Manse, Threemilestone, Truro, Cornwall TR3 6DP. (0872-77698)—BD(Lond.), BA(Open Univ.). *b. 3 Dec 1943, Sunderland, Tyne and Wear. m. 17 Aug 1970: 1s.*
Education: 1956–60 Southmoor Technical Sch., Sunderland; 1964–68 Hartley Victoria. *Appointments:* 1968–71 St. Helens and Prescot; 1971–76 Blaydon; 1976–82 Keswick Cockermouth; 1982 Truro.
Special Interests: Church Growth, Biblical Studies. *Hobbies and Recreations:* Photography, Fell Walking.

TAYLOR, Norman, 1 Broxholm Rd., Heaton, Newcastle upon Tyne NE6 5RL. (0632-655713) *b. 10 Jan 1924, Bedworth, Warks. m. 24 July 1952: 1d., 2s.*
Education: Fitton St. Sch., Nuneaton; 1948–51 Handsworth.
Appointments: 1947–48 East Dereham; 1951–56 Bradford, Great Horton; 1956–61 Grimsby, Flottergate; 1961–67 Birmingham, Sutton Park; 1967–73 Coventry; 1973– Newcastle upon Tyne, Heaton and Wallsend.
Connexional Committees: 1978–80, 1981– Division of Property.
Special Interests: 1968–79 Chairman of Albert Cape House, Sutton Coldfield, Birmingham (Abbeyfield Erdington Society). *Hobbies and Recreations:* Bowls, Gardening.

TAYLOR, Paul, 30 Queens Rd., Blackburn, Lancashire BB1 1QG. (0254-57365)—BA. *b. 22 Oct 1947, Preston. m. 16 Aug 1975: 2s.*
Education: 1959–65 Balshaw's Grammar, Leyland, Lancashire, 1971–75 Wesley, Bristol.
Appointments: 1975–77 Coatbridge, Airdrie and Armadale; 1977– Blackburn.
Special Interests: Hospital Chaplaincy, Community Relations, Blackburn and District Council for the Disabled. *Hobbies and Recreations:* Photography, Walking, Fishing, Gardening, Reading.

TAYLOR, Ralph Frederick Gordon, The Manse, 29 Mill Rd., Loddon, Norwich, Norfolk NR14 6DR. (0508-20219)—BA(Bristol). *b. 12 Sept 1927, Ottawa. m. 9 Dec 1955: 1d., 4s.*
Education: 1938–45 Minehead Grammar Sch.; 1951–54 Bristol; 1951–54 Didsbury, Bristol.
Appointments: 1950–51 Newbury; 1954–66 S. India Church; 1966–72 Grimsby Mission; 1972–79 Swindon; 1979–Loddon.

TAYLOR, Ronald, 34 Groveway, Stockwell, London SW9 0AR. (01-735-6009)—BA, BD. *b. 2 Dec 1936, Shirebrook, Derbyshire. m. 10 Aug 1963: 2d., 1s.*
Education: Caxton Lane Jun., Shirebrook; 1947–55 Chesterfield Grammar Sch.; 1955–61 Manchester Univ.; 1957–61 Hartley Victoria.
Appointments: 1961–63 Bury St. Edmunds; 1963–67 Boston; 1967–73 Bedford North; 1973–76 Derby South; 1976–81 Chelmsford; 1981– London Mission, Wandsworth Rd.
Special Interests: Radio, Education.
Hobbies and Recreations: Music, Photography.

TAYLOR, Stanley, 27 Sandy Lane, Melton Mowbray, Leicestershire LE13 0AN. (0664-64384) *b. Ulverston, Cumbria. m. 23 Nov 1941: 1d.*
Education: St. Paul's, Manchester; Loreburn Coll., Manchester; Southport Coll., Lancashire Technical. *Appointments:* 1968–74 Consett; 1974–80 Lancaster; 1980– Melton Mowbray.

TEARE, William, 6 Kingsway, Banbury, Oxon OX16 9NT. (0295-62602) *b. 23 Jan 1924, New Silksworth, Sunderland, Tyne and Wear. m. 25 July 1953: 1d., 1s.*
Education: New Silksworth Intermediate; 1948–51 Richmond.
Appointments: 1948 Chester-le-Street; 1951–53 Morpeth and Bedlington; 1953–57 Hetton-le-Hole; 1957–62 Carlisle; 1962–67 Blaydon; 1967–72 Sheffield, Ecclesall; 1972–80 Boston, Lincs.; 1980– Banbury.
Connexional Committees: 1970–80 Healing and Pastoral Committee; 1975 Working Party on Exorcism.
Special Interests: Relationship of Christianity to 'Paranormal' and 'Occult', Spiritual Healing, Meditation, Member of C.F.P.S.S. *Hobbies and Recreations:* Photography, Walking, Map Reading.

TEASDALE, Robert, 107 Welholme Ave., Grimsby, South Humberside DN32 0BP. (0472-77644) *b. 1 Aug 1933, Rossendale, Lancs. m. 6 Aug 1960: 1d., 1s.*
Education: 1954–55 Cliff Coll.; 1956–60 Hartley Victoria. *Appointments:* 1960–62 Birmingham Mission; 1962–67 Worsley; 1967–73 Derby Derwent; 1973–74 P.R.A.; 1974–81 Blackburn; 1981– Grimsby.

TEASDALE, Thomas, 4 Burrill Rd., Bedale, North Yorkshire DL8 1ET. (067-722638) *b. 10 Dec 1923, Felling-on-Tyne. m. 18 Dec 1954: 2s.*
Education: 1928–33 Felling Prim.; 1933–37 Dunston Board; 1949–50 Cliff Coll.; 1951–54 Hartley Victoria. *Appointments:* 1954–60 Abergavenny; 1960–62 Sheffield Mission; 1962–67 Holsworthy; 1967–75 Harrogate; 1975– Bedale.

TEBBUTT, Brian Neal, 19 All Saints Villas Rd., Cheltenham, Glos. GL52 2HB. (0242-512271)–LLB, BD. *b. 28 April 1936, Birmingham. m. 4 Aug 1961: 1d., 1s.*
Education: Warmington County Prim., Northants; Hall Green County Prim. and Jun., Birmingham; King Edward VI Grammar, Camp Hill, Birmingham; 1954–57 Univ. of Birmingham; 1957–58 Univ. of Birmingham Institute of Education, Saltley Teachers Training Coll.; 1958–62 Univ. of London; 1958–61 Richmond. *Appointments:* 1961–63 South Normanton; 1963–66 Stoke on Trent, Stoke; 1966–71 Sheffield, Carver St.; 1971–78 London, Finsbury Park and Southgate; 1978–83 Cheltenham.
Connexional Committees: 1970 Board of Property; 1968 Law and Polity. *Publications:* Lecturer, Bristol Univ., Extramural Dept. (1979–83). *Special Interests:* Pastoral Care and Counselling, Group Work in the Church, Church Architecture. *Hobbies and Recreations:* Art, Architecture, Music, Ornithology, Natural History, Topography, Railways, Literature.

TEDCASTLE, Rupert Gerald Marjoribanks, 255 Bramley Rd., Southgate, London N14 4UY. (01-363-4393). *b. 11 June 1933. s.*
Education: 1957–61 Didsbury, Bristol. *Appointments:* 1961–66 Birkenhead; 1966–71 London, Highgate; 1971–73 London Wesley's Chapel; 1973–80 London Leysian Mission; 1980– London, Finsbury Park and Southgate.
Council Member: Freeman of the City of London; 1982– Member of the Guild of Freemen.

TEMPLE, Arthur, 40 The Avenue, Linthorpe, Middlesbrough, Cleveland TS5 6PD. (0642-817331)–SRN, RMN. *b. 19 Feb 1930, Detroit, Michigan, U.S.A. m. 7 March 1951: 1d., 1s.*
Education: 1935–41 Various Prim. and Jun. Sch. in Newcastle upon Tyne and North West Durham; 1941–47 Rutherford Grammar Sch., Newcastle upon Tyne; 1950–53 St. Nicholas (Psychiatric) Hospital, Gosforth, Newcastle upon Tyne; 1954–56 Royal Victoria Infirmary, Newcastle upon Tyne; 1957–59 Headingley. *Appointments:* 1959–64 Middlesbrough; 1964–70 Newcastle, Brunswick Central; 1970–73 Seahouses; 1973–78 Hastings, Bexhill and Rye; 1978 Middlesbrough and Eston.
Connexional Committees: 1971–82 D.S.R. Standing Committee on Healing and Pastoral Ministry (and its predecessors). *Publications:* Various Articles in Healing Publications.
Special Interests: Hospital Chaplaincies. *Hobbies and Recreations:* Sport, Music.

TEMPLE, James Hope, Epworth, 1a Radegund Rd., Cambridge CB1 3RH. (0223-245898)–MA(Cantab.). *b. 4 July 1921, Hong Kong. m. 1 July 1949: 2d.*
Education: 1931–35 Earnseat, Arnside; 1935–40 The Leys, Cambridge; 1947–49 Wesley House. *Appointments:* 1945–46 Market Weighton; 1946–47 Uttoxeter; 1949–50 Tunstall; 1950–55 Romford; 1955–57 Manchester Mission; 1957–64 Northern Rhodesia Dt; 1964–69 Paulton; 1969–74 Sidmouth and Bridport; 1974–77 Redditch; 1977 Cambridge.
Publications: 1972 The Mighty Oak.
Special Interests: Fellowship of the Kingdom Bible Society. *Hobbies and Recreations:* Knitting, Grandchildren.

TEMPLE, Richard James, 15 Ravendale Rd., Gainsborough, Lincs. DN21 1XD. (0427-2618) *b. 19 Sept 1946, Bedfont, Middlesex. m. 17 July 1971: 1d.*
Education: 1958–63 Longford Secondary Sch., Feltham; 1970–73 Wesley Coll., Bristol. *Appointments:* 1973–75 Loddon and Bungay; 1975–78 Retford; 1978– Gainsborough.
Special Interests: Prison and Industrial Chaplaincy Work. *Hobbies and Recreations:* Gardening, Swimming, Walking, Railway Modelling.

TENNENT, Henry Waddow, 40 Inverewe Ave., Thornliebank, Glasgow G46 8TA. (041-638-4512) *b. 13 Dec 1916, Tollcross, Glasgow. m. 5 June 1946: 1d., 2s.*
Education: 1921–28 Wellshot Public Sch.; 1928–31 Eastbank Academy; 1938–40 Handsworth Coll.; 1940–41 Headingley. *Appointments:* 1941–43 Snaith; 1943–44 Retford, Gro. St.; 1944–46 Chaplain H.M.F.; 1946–47 Spalding; 1947–51 Trowbridge; 1951–55 Bristol, Kingswood Zion; 1955–62 Glasgow, Claremont St. and Glasgow West; 1962–68 Motherwell; 1968–69 Greenock; 1969–82 Chairman Scotland District; 1962–69 Secretary Scotland District; 1969–82 Scottish Churches Council; 1976–82 Church and State Forum in Scotland; 1964–68 Scottish Churches Multilateral Conversations; 1972–82 Vice-Chairman of Conversations.
Connexional Committees: 1956–62 Overseas Missions; 1969–82 General Purposes; 1969–82 Home Missions; 1969–82 Stationing Committee; 1972–82 Ecumenical Committee.
Special Interests: Wesley Hymns. *Hobbies and Recreations:* Music, Travel.

TERRY, William Snowdon, 17 Oldchurch Rd., Axbridge, Somerset BS26 2BE. (0934-732795) *b. 14 May 1898, Gillingham, Kent. m. 2 July 1925: 1d., 1s.*
Education: 1909–13 Mathematical Sch., Rochester, Kent; 1936–38 London Sch. of Economics; 1919–21 Hartley. *Appointments:* 1919–20 Banbury; 1922–25 London, East; 1925–28 Hull III; 1933–38 London, Standstead Rd.; 1934 London, Brixton Hill; 1938–46 Reading; 1946–49 Birmingham, Wesley; 1949–55 Birmingham, Belmont Row; 1955–59 Morecambe and Heysham; 1959–63 Eastleigh.
Special Interests: Psychiatric, Social Work. *Hobbies and Recreations:* Gardening.

TEWKESBURY, Keith, 18 Birchfield Drive, Stourport-on-Severn, Worcesterhire DY13 8UE. (02993 6641)—BA(Open), BD(Manchester). *b. 21 June 1944, London Borough of Merton. m. 26 July 1969: 2d.*
Education: Pelham Boys' Sch.; 1964–67 Westminster Coll. of Education; 1969–72 Open Univ.; 1974–77 Manchester Univ.; 1964–67 Westminster Coll. *Appointments:* 1977–82 Dudley; 1982– Stourport-on-Severn.
Connexional Committees: 1982– Div. of Education and Youth.
Special Interests: Community and Race Relations, Pastoral Counselling. *Hobbies and Recreations:* Squash, Running, Swimming, Occasional Horse Riding, Classical Music.

THEWLIS, Frank, 347 Redmires Rd., Sheffield S10 4LD. (0742-307966) *b. 13 Sept 1917, Huddersfield. m. 10 Sept 1943.*
Education: 1930–36 King George V Sch., Southport; 1938–41 Headingley. *Appointments:* 1941–43 Liverpool Mission; 1943–46 Chaplain HMF; 1946–50 London Mission, East; 1950–55 Birmingham, Great Barr and Kingstanding; 1955–59 Keighley; 1959–64 Huddersfield Mission; 1964–67 Bradford Mission; 1967–75 Brighton, Dome Mission; 1975–81 Sheffield Mission.
Connexional Committees: Home Mission Committee. *Local Council Committees:* Huddersfield and Bradford Education Committees.
Publications: Think Again (paperback 1978).
Special Interests: Regular Broadcaster, Chaplain to St. John Ambulance (Order of St. John).

THEXTON, Thomas Leslie, 12 Winyards View, Crewkerne, Somerset TA18 8HZ. (0460-73639) *b. 25 March 1911, Pinner, Middlesex. m. 2 Feb 1939.*
Education: 1922–24 Kingston Grammar Sch.; 1924–27 Surbiton County Sch.; 1932–36 Richmond. *Appointments:* 1936–50 S.W. China District; 1949–50 Chairman S.W. China District; 1950–54 Birmingham, Belmont Row; 1954–58 Huddersfield West; 1958–63 London, Leytonstone and Forest Gate; 1963–68 Huddersfield West; 1968–74 Birmingham, Elmdon.
Connexional Committees: 1954–58 Overseas Mission.
Special Interests: Peace Movements. *Hobbies and Recreations:* Gardening, Walking, Marquetry, Reading.

THOMAS, Arthur Sylvester, 63 Bempton Oval, Bridlington YE16 5HW. *b. 2 May 1916, Rawdon. m. 24 Aug 1963: 1d., 1s.*
Education: 1922–25 Aireborough Grammar Sch.; 1961–63 Headingley. *Appointments:* 1963–66 Ryedale; 1966–67 Resigned; 1967–70 Huddersfield West; 1970–73 Horncastle and Bardney; 1973–76 North Walsham; 1976–81 Northallerton.

THOMAS, Edgar Frank, 4a Elm Ave., Ashton-on-Ribble, Preston PR2 1SR. (0772-729565) *b. 15 Jan 1893, Bath, Somerset. m. 25 July 1928: 2d.*
Education: Bath, 1919–22 Richmond. *Appointments:* 1918–19 HMF; 1922–26 Mid Somerset Mission; 1926–29 Devon and Dorset Mission; 1929–33 Sheffield, Burngrove Rd.; 1933–38 Carlisle, Fisher St.; 1938–44 St. Helens and Prescott; 1944–50 Bolton, Bridge St.; 1950–53 Fleetwood; 1953–57 Halifax North; 1957–62 Haworth.

THOMAS, George Jeff, 8 Paris Rd., Paignton, South Devon TQ3 2PH. (0803-522969)—BA(Manch.). *b. 29 June 1942, Gateshead, Co. Durham, Tyne and Wear. m. 6 Nov 1965: 1d., 1s.*
Education: Low Fell Secondary Modern, Gateshead; 1972–75 Manchester Univ.; 1971–75 Hartley Victoria. *Appointments:* 1975–79 Welwyn; 1979– Torbay.

THOMAS, Hugh Ernest, 67 Meadway, London N14 6NJ. (01-886-8222)—BA(Lond.), BD(Lond.). *b. 7 June 1915, Stevenage, Herts. m. 14 April 1943: 1d.*
Education: 1925–33 Alleyne's Grammar Sch., Stevenage; 1933–36 Univ. of London, Kings Coll.; 1933–37 Westminster Coll., London; 1946–48 Richmond. *Appointments:* 1939–46 Fourah Bay Coll., Sierra Leone; 1948–49 Methodist Boys High Sch., Gambia; 1949–50, 1951–55 Wesley Coll., Kumasi, Ghana; 1950–51, 1955–67 Trinity Coll., Ghana; 1967–77 Secretary, Overseas Division; 1977–81 Sierra Leone Theol. Hall and Church Training Centre.
Connexional Committees: 1967–77 Central Committee, M.C.O.D.; 1974–76 Div. of Ministries Board.
Publications: Our Methodist Faith (Methodist Book Depot, Ghana 1961).
Special Interests: African Church History, Worship. *Hobbies and Recreations:* Gardening, Music, Writing Verse.

THOMAS, Owen George, 608 Chepstow Rd., Newport, Gwent NPT 9BZ. (0633-272066)—BA(Wales). *b. 6 May 1919, Hankow, China. m. 7 Aug 1946: 2d., 2s.*
Education: 1931–33 Hymers Coll., Hull; 1933–36 Kingswood Sch., Bath; Wales, Univ. Coll. of South Wales and Monmouthshire.
Appointments: 1941–46 Wye Valley Mission; 1946–49 St Just, 1949–51 Clay Cross; 1951–56 Manchester S.E.; 1956–61 Barry; 1961–66 Pembroke; 1966–72 Waltham Abbey and Hertford; 1972–78 Shooters Hill; 1978– Newport.
Connexional Committees: 1979 Appeals Committee.

Special Interests: Industrial Chaplaincy including Dry Docks, Flour Mill, Woollen Mill.

THOMAS, Ronald Lang, 5 Channel View, Sketty, Swansea, West Glamorgan SA2 8LY. (0792-206793) *b. 17 Dec 1928, Port Talbot, West Glamorgan. m. 6 April 1957: 2d., 1s.*
Education: Port Talbot Prim. and Jun. Mountain Sch.; 1953–56 Hartley Victoria. *Appointments:* 1952–53 Aberdare; 1956–58 Stockport South; 1958–61 Shipley; 1961–66 Alford; 1966–69 Stratford-upon-Avon; 1969–75 Coventry; 1975–82 Cardiff; 1982 Swansea Circuit.
Connexional Committees: 1979– Methodist Property Board, Manchester.
Special Interests: Pastoral Psychology, Trained Hypnotist and Use of Hypnotherapy. *Hobbies and Recreations:* Reading, Walking.

THOMAS, Stanley Theodore, The Manse, Station Lane, Hedon, Hull, North Humberside HU12 8JY. (0482-896121)–BA(Bristol). *b. 5 Aug 1925, Kuling, Central China. m. 13 Aug 1952: 1d.*
Education: 1936–44 Kingswood Sch.; 1944–46 Bristol Univ.; 1947–49 Didsbury, Bristol. *Appointments:* 1949–52 Stour Valley Mission; 1952–56 Sheffield, Surrey St.; 1956–60 Sheffield, North; 1960–63 Port Talbot; 1963–68 Northwich; 1968–69 Barnsley West; 1969–74 Sheffield Mission; 1974–76 Guernsey, Alderney and Sark; 1976–79 Bailiwick of Guernsey; 1976–79 Chairman of Channel Islands.
Connexional Committees: 1976–79 Home Missions; 1976–79 General Purposes; 1976–79 Stationing Committee.
Hobbies and Recreations: Entomology, Genealogy.

THOMAS, Trevor Mechain, Epworth, 47 Myrddin Crescent, Carmarthen, Dyfed. (0267-6004) *b. 21 July 1921, Oswestry. m. 24 July 1954: 3s. (1 deceased).*
Education: 1926–34 Oswestry Elem. Sch.; 1934–36 Oswestry Technical Sch.; 1945–47 Handsworth. *Appointments:* 1942–43, 1943–45 Rhosymedre and Chirk, Welsh; 1945–46 Llandeilo, Welsh; 1946–47 Handsworth, Welsh; 1947–48 Llandeilo, Welsh; 1948–50 Lampeter, Welsh; 1950–55 Llanidloes, Welsh; 1955–60 TreorchyWelsh; 1960–70 Llandeilo, Welsh; 1970–72 Swansea, Welsh; 1972–81 Sirhowy Valley, Welsh; 1981– Llanelli and Carmarthen, Welsh.

THOMAS, William Owen, Yr Wylfa, 6 Victoria Rd., Oswestry, Salop SY11 2BP. (0691-2925) *b. 28 Jan 1924, Y Felinheli, Arfon. m. 12 Aug 1953: 2d.*
Education: 1948–50 Hartley Victoria. *Appointments:* 1946–48 Cerrigydrnchin; 1950–52 Bogillt; 1953–55 Caergybi; 1955–60 Blaenau Ffestiniog; 1960–65 Llanfyllin; 1965–70 Rhyl and Prestatyn; 1970– Llanrhaeadr (Chairman Cymru District).

THOMPSON, Alan Macey, 14 Woodbank, Egremont, Cumbria CA22 2RL. (0946-820232) *b. 22 Aug 1928, Cracoe, Skipton, N.Yorks. m. 20 May 1959: 1d., 1s.*
Education: 1932–39 Cracoe Prim. Sch.; 1939–46 Ermysted's Grammar Sch., Skipton; 1951–54 Headingley. *Appointments:* 1954–57 Berwick upon Tweed; 1957–60 Blyth and Seaton Deleval; 1960–65 Denby Dale and Clayton West; 1965–71 Otley; 1971–80 Penrith; 1980– Whitehaven.
Hobbies and Recreations: Model Railway, Model Making, Fell Walking.

THOMPSON, Christopher, Almora, 20 Dawley Rd., Wellington, Telford, Salop TF1 2HR. (0952-44730) *b. 21 April 1901, Aldbrough, North Humberside. m. (w. 7 Oct 1977), 30 June 1931: 1d.*
Education: 1906–10 Patrington; 1910–15 Hull; 1922–23 Cliff Coll.; 1924–27 Hartley. *Appointments:* 1927–28 Dover and Folkestone; 1928–31 Banbury; 1931–32 Kingstone; 1932–37 Leintwardine; 1937–42 Ashbourne; 1942–46 Hungerford; 1946–49 North Cave; 1949–54 Dawley and Madeley; 1954–59 Wirksworth; 1959–66 Minsterley.
Special Interests: Gardening.

THOMPSON, Edwin, The Manse, Clun, Craven Arms, Shropshire SY7 8LE. (058-84-255) *b. 12 April 1916, Newcastle upon Tyne. m. 28 July 1945: 1d.*
Education: 1924–34 Dame Allan's Sch., Newcastle upon Tyne: 1938–41 Hartley Victoria. *Appointments:* 1941–45 Walton on Thames; 1945–50 Skegness and Wainfleet; 1950–55 Gateshead South West; 1955–61 Newcastle, Brunswick; 1961–68 Gateshead South West; 1968–76 Chester le Street; 1976–81 Barnoldswick.
Connexional Committees: 1954–61 Church Membership. *Publications: This Remarkable Family–A Study of the Barratt Family; Welsh Border Heritage* (both given as W.H.S. Lectures).
Special Interests: Church History–Methodist in particular, Rotarian. *Hobbies and Recreations:* Fell Walking and Exploring, Reading.

THOMPSON, Harold, 3 Providence Crescent, Oakworth, Keighley, West Yorks. BD22 7QU. (0535-44032) *b. 30 Dec 1905, Liverpool. m. 14 Aug 1937: 1d., 1s.*
Education: 1911–19 Boaler St., Council Sch., Liverpool; 1931–34 Didsbury. *Appointments:* 1930-31 Thirsk (Chairman's Asst.); 1934–37 Coventry; 1937–40 Lichfield, Army Work; 1940–47 West Bromwich, Hill Top; 1947–51 Stourbridge and Brierley Hill; 1951–55 Birmingham, Moseley Rd. and Sparkhill; 1955–60 Radcliffe; 1960–65 Shaw and Royton; 1965–70 Keighley; 1970–74 Brighouse.

THOMPSON, John, Methodist Manse, Barmoor, Ryton, Tyne and Wear NE40 3TS. (089422-2494).
Education: 1951–54 Hartley Victoria. *Appointments:* 1954–55 Missionary Training; 1955–63 East Nigeria Dt; 1963–73 Nigeria Conf.; 1973–76 Goole; 1976–81 Wigton; 1981–

Ryton and Prudhoe.
Connexional Committees: 1982 Overseas Division.

THOMPSON, Leslie Malcolm, 97 Teg Down Meads, Winchester, Hants. SO22 5NG. (0962-63947) *b. 30 April 1905, Thornton Heath, London. m. 25 July 1936: 2d., 1s.* *Education:* 1911–17 Pixmore, Letchworth; 1917–21 Hitchin Grammar Sch.; 1930–33 Richmond. *Appointments:* 1929–30 South London Mission; 1933–34 Presidents' List; 1934–35 Armadale; 1935–36 President's List; 1936–37 Middlesbrough; 1937–39 Sunderland; 1939–42 East Cornwall Mission; 1942–47 Launceston; 1947–50 St. Austell; 1950–55 East Wight; 1955–59 Lostwithiel; 1959–67 Bury; 1967–70 Congleton.
Hobbies and Recreations: General Reading, Recorded Music, Walking, T.V. Sports Programmes, Gardening, Stamp Collecting.

THOMPSON, Michael Edward Wesley, The Methodist Church, Wesley St., Hazel Grove, Stockport, Cheshire SK7 4VQ. (061-483-8969)–MA(Wales), BD(Lond.), PhD(Sheffield). *b. 14 Nov 1940, Loughborough, Leicestershire. m. 6 Jan 1970: 2d.*
Education: 1948–59 Loughborough Grammar Sch.; 1967–68 Univ. Coll. of North Wales, Univ. of Wales; 1964–68 Richmond. *Appointments:* 1968–70 London Mission, Rivercourt and Hammersmith; 1970–75 Manchester and Salford Mission; 1975–79 Trinity Coll., Legon, Ghana; 1979– Hazel Grove and Poynton. *Connexional Committees:* 1973–75 Connexional Probationers Oversight Committee. *Publications:* Book, *Situation and Theology. Old Testament Interpretations of the Syro-Ephraimite War* (forthcoming); Articles forthcoming, *Isiah's Sign of Immanuel* in *Expository Times* and *Isiah's Ideal King (Journal for the Study of the Old Testament).*
Special Interests: The Old Testament.
Hobbies and Recreations: Railways, Travel.

THOMPSON, Raymond William, Ruskin Glen, 10 Madeira Rd., Ventnor, Isle of Wight PO38 1QP. (0983-852295) *b. 17 Oct 1928, Bromley, Kent. m. 11 Aug 1956: 1d., 2s.* *Education:* 1939–45 Bromley County Grammar Sch.; 1951–54 Didsbury, Bristol. *Appointments:* 1954–57 Marlborough; 1957–60 Faversham; 1960–63 Jersey; 1963–69 Sittingbourne and Sheerness; 1969–79 Clacton-on-Sea; 1979– East Wight.
Local Council Committees: 1981 Chaplain to Chairman of Isle of Wight County Council.

THOMPSON, Richard William, 10 Thornton Rd., Bebington, Wirral, Merseyside L63 5PS. (051-608-5665)–MA, BSc. *b. 11 Oct 1942, Stockport, Cheshire. m. 5 Aug 1967: 1d., 1s.*
Education: 1953–60 The Manchester Grammar Sch.; 1960–63 Univ. of Bristol; 1965–67 Wesley House. *Appointments:* 1967–70 Redcar Saltburn and Guisborough; 1970–76 Sierra Leone Dt; 1976–80 Birmingham, Smethwick; 1980–81 Birmingham, West; 1981 Birkenhead.

THOMPSON, Robert, *Fairhaven, Bishops Tawton, Barnstaple, N. Devon YO17 0MG. (0271-75432) b. 2 March 1912, Lealholm, Whitby, N. Yorks. m. 18 April 1953.* *Education:* 1917–26 Lealholm; 1935–36 (Non-residential) Cliff Coll.; 1960–62 Hartley Victoria. *Appointments:* 1960–62 Birstall; 1962–67 Malton; 1967–76 Barnstaple.
Hobbies and Recreations: Gardening, Reading, Pastoral Work.

THOMPSON, William Arthur, Iona, Course Lane, Newburgh, Wigan, Lancs. WN8 7UB. (02576-2403) *b. 22 March 1939, Liverpool m. 18 Aug 1966: 2s.*
Education: 1951–57 Upholland Grammar Sch., Lancs., 1958–61 Manchester Univ., Medical Sch.; 1963–67 Headingley. *Appointments:* 1967–71 Downham Market; 1971– Probation Officer, Ormskirk.
Connexional Committees: 1981– DSR–Penal Affairs Group.
Special Interests: Nation Vice-Chairman of Nat. Assoc. of Probation Officers (NAPO)–Trade Union and Profess. Assoc.

THOMSON, John William, 18 Greystones Grange Rd., Sheffield S11 7JJ. (0742-660837) *b. 17 May 1905, Waltham Abbey, Essex. m. (2) 20 March 1982: 1d., 1s.*
Education: 1910–15 Welsford's Academy, Waltham Cross; 1915–19 Poole Grammar Sch.; 1919–23 Queen's Coll., Taunton; 1927–30 Richmond. *Appointments:* 1926–27 Supply; 1930–38 Lucknow Dt., India; 1938–39 Blackpool; 1939–43 Derby, Derwent; 1943–44 Chaplain H.M.F.; 1946–53 Sheffield, Ecclesall; 1953–58 Leamington; 1958–64 Colchester; 1964–69 Redditch; 1969–72 Stratford on Avon.
Special Interests: All Sports.

THORNBER, Allan, 12 Wynstay Rd., Hoylake, Wirral, Merseyside L47 5AR. (051-632-1655)–BD(Lond.), BA(Open). *b. 3 Jan 1906, Padiham, Lancs. w. 1d.*
Education: HE Wallasey; 1928–31 Didsbury. *Appointments:* 1927–28 Matlock; 1931–34 Clitheroe; 1934–37 Uppermill; 1937–41 Leigh; 1941–42 Ashton-u-Lyne; 1942–44 Chaplain HMF; 1944–45 Ashbourne; 1945–48 Preston; 1948–53 Leith; 1953–57 Nottingham; 1957–60 Ilford; 1960–65 St. Leonards/Bexhill; 1965–68 Cadishead; 1968–71 Manchester, Shaw and Royton.

THORNTON, Andrew, 13 Branksome Grove, Stockton-on Tees, Cleveland TS18 5DD. (0642-583183) *b. 26 Aug 1903, Berwick upon Tweed. m. 14 Aug 1930.*
Education: 1914–20 Berwick Grammar Sch.; 1923–26 Hartley. *Appointments:* 1926–30 Staithes; 1930–33 Grimsby I; 1933–37 Ferry Hill; 1937–44 Middlesbrough; 1944–49 Sunderland West; 1949–54 Scarborough; 1954–61 Darlington South; 1961–66 Ilkley.
Connexional Committees: 1938–44 Youth Committee; 1944–49 Local Preachers Committee; 1961–66 District Representative, Deaconess

Committee. *Local Council Committees:* 1973–76 Cleveland Education Committee.
Special Interests: Education, Music, Drama, Samaritans, History. *Hobbies and Recreations:* Theatre, Concerts, Billiards, Travel.

THORNTON, Arthur, 24 Park Rd., Southport, Merseyside PR9 9LA. (0704-34195) *b. 29 Nov 1906, Hull. m. 11 Aug 1938: 1d., 2s.*
Education: Elem.; 1932–35 Headingley. *Appointments:* 1931–32 Severn Valley Mission; 1935–36 Sheffield Dist. Special Youth Work; 1936–39 Southport North, Chairman's Ass.; 1939–42 Kettering; 1942–47 Nottingham South; 1947–50 Sunderland South; 1950–56 Liverpool Crosby; 1956–59 Leicester South; 1959–64 Higham Ferrers; 1964–67 Preston Trinity; 1967–72 Peel, I.O.M.
Special Interests: Methodist History. *Hobbies and Recreations:* Reading, Gardening, Woodwork.

THORNTON, Kenneth Gordon, 18 Carr Lane, Shipley, West Yorkshire BD18 2JS. (0274-583480)–BA(McMaster Univ.), BD(Pine Hill Divinity Hall). *b. 9 June 1942, Brampton, Ontario, Canada. s.*
Education: 1948–55 S.S. No 15 Chinguacousy Prim. Sch.; 1955–60 Brampton High Sch., Brampton, Ontario, Canada; 1960–63 McMaster Univ., Hamilton, Ontario, Canada; 1963–66 Pine Hill Divinity Hall, Halifax, Nova Scotia, Canada; 1966–68 Glasgow Univ. *Appointments:* 1968–70 Canterbury/Richmond Charge (United Church of Canada); 1970–75 Coatbridge, Airdrie and Armadale; 1975–80 Bishop Auckland; 1980– Shipley and Bingley.
Hobbies and Recreations: Books, Music, Walking.

THORNTON, Sam, 6 Tiverton Ave., Sale, Cheshire M33 4RJ. (061-973-5259) *b. 27 Nov 1921, Brighouse. m. 11 Aug 1951: 2d., 1s.*
Education: 1931–35 St. Martin's CE; 1935–38 Brighouse Technical; 1948–50 Hartley Victoria.
Appointments: 1947–48 Abergavenny; 1950–52 Saddleworth; 1952–54 Cheadle; 1954–60 Manchester, Chorlton and Moss Side; 1960–66 Alderley Edge and Knutsford; 1966–74 Stockport; 1974 Sale.
Special Interests: Scouting. *Hobbies and Recreations:* Gardening.

THORNTON-SMITH, Dennis George, 12 Queen's Rd., Wisbech, Cambs. PE13 2PB. (0945-583870) *b. 6 March 1982, Rotherhithe, Bermondsey, London. m. 28 July 1951: 1d., 2s.*
Education: 1926–32 Goodmayes Council Sch.; 1932–37 Leyton County High for Boys; 1946–47 Cliff Coll.; 1947–49 Handsworth.
Appointments: 1949–55 East Cornwall Mission; 1955–60 Cradley Heath; 1960–65 Kidderminster; 1965–71 Cambridge; 1971–77 North Walsham and Aylsham; 1977–79 Fenland; 1979– Wisbech.
Connexional Committees: 1978– Member of Property Division as East Anglia Property Secretary.
Special Interests: Healing Ministry.
Hobbies and Recreations: Ornithology, Car Maintenance, Gardening.

THORP, Edgar Bentley, 8 Ffordd Onnen, Prestatyn, Clwyd LL19 9HY. (07456-2494)–MA(Oxon and Cantab.). *b. 25 July 1905, Mysore City, S. India. m. 13 Jan 1934.*
Education: 1913–17 Nottingham High Sch.; 1917–23 Kingswood Sch.; 1923–27 Brasenose Coll., Oxford; 1927–30 Wesley House.
Appointments: 1930–47 Trichinopoloy District, S. India; 1947–63 Tiruchirapalli and Tanjore Diocese, Church of South India.

THORP, James Eric, Trelawn, Middlesykes Lane, Grimoldby, Louth, Lincs. LN11 8TE. (050782-518) *b. 20 July 1907, Devonport. m. 24 July 1937: 2s.*
Education: Council Schs., Coventry, Torquay, Whitechapel Foundation Grammar (London); Bourne Coll.; 1930–33 Hartley. *Appointments:* 1933–35 Wishaw; 1935–38 East Dereham; 1938–39 Ledbury; 1939–42 Kings Lynn; 1942–44 Reading; 1944–48 Pontefract, Micklegate; 1948–51 Huddersfield; 1951–55 Dover; 1955–58 Willenhall; 1958–62 Oswestry; 1962–68 Louth; 1968–72 Canterbury and Faversham.
Special Interests: Youth. *Hobbies and Recreations:* Hi Fi, Woodwork, Model Engineering, Caravanning, Reading.

THORPE, Derek, 26 Woodlands Drive, Harrogate, North Yorkshire HG2 7AX. (0423-887701)–BA(B'ham.). *b. 28 Dec 1932, Batley, West Yorkshire. m. 27 July 1957: 2d., 2s.*
Education: 1936–43 Carlinghow Sch., Batley; 1943–50 Batley Grammar Sch.; 1954–57 Birmingham Univ.; 1953–57 Handsworth.
Appointments: 1957–62 Bradford, Great Horton; 1962–65 Sheffield South; 1965–75 York, Wesley; 1975–81 Scarborough; 1981– Harrogate.
Connexional Committees: 1975–81 Property Board.
Special Interests: Ecumenism, Christian Aid, Work among handicapped (physical and mental).
Hobbies and Recreations: Cricket, Gardening, Walking in Yorkshire Dales and Lake District.

THORPE, Geoffrey Raymond, 3 Endwood Court Rd., Handsworth Wood, Birmingham B20 2RX. (021-554-8121) *b. 17 Feb 1939, Sheffield. m. 16 July 1966: 1d., 1s.*
Education: Abbeydale Secondary Modern, Sheffield; 1962–66 Handsworth; 1965–66 Birmingham Univ. *Appointments:* 1966–68 Forest of Dean; 1968–70 Swindon; 1970–79 Bristol, Kingswood; 1979– Birmingham, Asbury.
Special Interests: The Renewal of the Church for Mission, Church Growth, The Counselling and Healing Ministry. *Hobbies and Recreations:* Colour Slide Photography, Winemaking.

THURMAN, Philip, 15 Wakefield Close, Colchester, Essex CO1 2SD. (0206-865527) *b. 4 March 1903, Cotgrave, Notts. m. 17 July 1935 (w.): 1d., 1s.*
Education: 1908–15 Cotgrave; 1916–19 Ashville Coll., Harrogate; 1925–26 Cliff Coll.; 1927–30 Victoria

Park. *Appointments:* 1926–27 Sherringham and Holt; 1930–32 St. Columb; 1932–34 Ilkestone; 1934–37 Manchester and Salford Mission; 1937–40 Bodmin; 1940–45 Shaftesbury and Gillingham; 1945–50 The Peak; 1950–54 Frodsham; 1954–57 Chatteris; 1957–63 Hornsea, Trinity; 1963–66 Filey, Ebenezer; 1966–69 Chipping Norton and Stow.
Publications: Centenary Booklet, Chipping Norton, Oxon (1968).
Special Interests: Pastoral Visitation.
Hobbies and Recreations: Bowls, Gardening.

THYNE, Walter, 24 Newlands Park Grove, Scarborough, N.Yorks. (0723-64570) *b. 16 Feb 1901, Darlington, Co. Durham. m. 5 April 1930 (w.): 1d., 1s.*
Education: 1923–26 Hartley.
Appointments: 1926–28 Thetford; 1928–29 Richmond, Yorks; 1929–33 Brynmawr; 1933–36 Church Stretton; 1936–40 Holmfirth; 1940–46 Doncaster, Oxford Place; 1946–52 Crook; 1952–57 Haltwhistle; 1957–62 York, Clifton; 1962–66 Scarborough.
Hobbies and Recreations: Gardening.

TIBBETTS, Brian Paul, 19 Carlton Ave.; Barrow-in-Furness, Cumbria LA13 9AT. (0229-22047)–BA(Bristol), MA(Cantab). *b. 21 Feb 1932, Stourbridge. m. 20 April 1963: 2s.*
Education: 1941–49 King Edward VI Sch., Stourbridge; 1949–52 Bristol Univ.; 1954–57 Cambridge Univ.; 1954–57 Wesley House.
Appointments: 1957–59 Whitehaven; 1959–64 Middlesbrough; 1964–70 Swansea; 1970–75 Portsmouth and Southsea; 1975– Barrow-in-Furness.
Connexional Committees. 1972 Education Committee; 1973–80, 1981– Education and Youth Board.
Hobbies and Recreations: Philately, Tennis, Badminton.

TIBBETTS, Kenneth, Stavelea, Birchliffe Rd., Hebden Bridge, West Yorkshire HX7 8DB. (0422-843203).
Education: 1947–50 Headingley.
Appointments: 1945 Supply; 1946–47 Kirkbymoorside; 1950–51 Berwick-upon-Tweed; 1951–53 Hyde and Denton; 1953–57 Wensleydale; 1957–61 Cross Mills; 1961–65 Winsford; 1965–72 Haworth and Oakworth; 1972–82 Saddleworth; 1976 Oldham and Saddleworth.

TIGG, Frederick, 21 Maricroft, Wem, Shrewsbury SY4 5AN. (0939-32870) *b. 1901, Kennington, London. m. (2) April 1950: 3d.*
Education: 1924–27 Handsworth.
Appointments: 1927–29 Tipton; 1929–31 Matlock; 1931–35 Walls; 1935–40 Derby, Derwent; 1940–42 Castleford, Carlton St.; 1942–46 Newcastle on Tyne, Ryton; 1946–49 Clayton West; 1949–52 Halifax, St. Johns; 1952–56 Wigan, King St.; 1955–60 Middleton; 1960–63 Wensleydale; 1963–68 Loftus and Staithes.

TILSLEY, Gwilym Richard, Estyn, 5 Ffordd Pendyffryn, Pestatyn, Clwyd LL19 5RU. (07456-7876)–BA(Wales), MA(Cantab.). *b. 26 May 1911, Ty-Llwyd, Llanidlows, Mont. m. 16 Aug 1945: 1s.*
Education: 1917–23 Manledd Council Sch.; 1923–29 Llanidloes County Sch.; 1931–34 Univ. Coll. of Wales, Aberstwyth; 1934–37 Univ. of Cambridge, Fitzwilliam House; 1934–37 Wesley House.
Appointments: 1937–40 Ystumtuen, Welsh; 1940–45 Machynlleth, Welsh; 1945–50 Aberdare, Welsh; 1950–55 Conwy, Welsh; 1955–60 Llanrwst, Welsh; 1960–65 Caernarfon, Welsh; 1965–70 Rhyl, Welsh; 1970–75 Coedpoeth, Welsh; 1971–74 Chairman, First N.Wales District. 1968–71 Synod Secretary, First N. Wales District. *Council Member:* 1970–75 Chairman of Welsh Religious Advisory Council of B.B.C. *Local Council Committees:* Secretary and President of various local Fraternals and Committees.
Publications: Y Glöwr a Cherddi Eraill (collection of poems 1958); *Crefydd y Beirdd* (1977); Editor of *Yr Eurgrawn* (Welsh Methodist Quarterly 1966–).
Special Interests: Welsh Poetry, Winner of Bardic Chair, Welsh Royal National Eisteddfod 1950 and 1957. *Hobbies and Recreations:* Arch-Druid of Wales 1969–72, Member of Yr Academi Gymreig (Welsh Literary Society).

TILSLEY, William T., 15 Greenways, Beckham, Kent BR3 3NG. (01-650-3004) *b. 4 Jan 1892, Pontypridd, Glam. m. (2): 1d., 1s.*
Education: Pontypridd County Sch.; 1913–15 Handsworth.
Appointments: 1915–16 Market Harborough; 1916–19 Pontypridd; 1919–21 Cowbridge; 1921–24 Aberdare; 1924–28 Glasgow, Claremont St.; 1928–31 Birmingham, Smethwick; 1931–35 Nottingham, Wesley; 1935–36 Nottingham Central; 1936–42 Glasgow, Claremont St.; 1942–47 Glasgow St. Thomas; 1947–52 Glasgow, Paisley Rd.; 1952–57 Bangor.

TIMMINS, Leslie James Maxwell, CTVC Hillside, Merry Hill Rd., Bushey, Herts. WD2 1DR. (01-950-4426) *b. 11 July 1919, Sunderland, Co. Durham. m. 1947: 2s.*
Education: Bede Sch., Sunderland; 1946–47 Bristol. *Appointments:* 1947–51 Hull East; 1951–58 London Mission South; 1958–62 Portsmouth Mission; 1962–67 Bristol Mission; 1967–70 London, Streatham and Dulwich; 1970– Director Foundation for Christian Communication.
Connexional Committees: H.M. Div. Ministries, Social Responsibility.
Publication: Vision On (Epworth Press 1965); *Thank God It's Friday* (Chapman 1975); *Truth to Tell* (Beckley Lecture); *YMCA Lectures* (1968); Journalism, Book Reviews etc.
Special Interests: Broadcasting, both TV and Radio, Writing and Journalism, IBA Adviser for 12 years. *Hobbies and Recreations:* Reading, Cricket, Rugby.

TIMMS, Peter, 15 Richmond Rd., Dalston, London E8. (01-254-4800) *b. 30 Oct 1929, Mapplewell, Barnsley, S. Yorkshire. m. 16 Feb 1949: 2d., 1s.*
Education: 1933–40 Prim.; –1943

Secondary Modern; Prison Service Coll.; 1978–81 Southwark Ordination Course. *Appointments:* 1981– London Mission, Hackney. *Council Member:* B.C.C. Penal Affairs; Life Member of the Society of Civil and Public Servants, for distinguished service. *Publications:* Numerous Lecture and Articles on Penal Affairs and Social Issues; recently published valuable evidence to Lord Scarman on the Brixton Disturbances. *Special Interests:* Multiple Sclerosis Society Chairman, ex. Chairman Prison Christian Fellowship (England and Wales), Member Koestler Trust, Prison Reform Trust, Oxford House Trust. *Hobbies and Recreations:* Writing, D.I.Y., Politics, Management and Organisational Studies.

TITTERINGTON, Graham, Carlton House, 6 Southey St., Keswick, Cumbria CA12 4EF. (0596-73646) *14 Aug 1910, Workington. m. 6 Aug 1938: 1d., 2s.*
Education: 1921–25 Workington Grammar; 1931–34 Hartley. *Appointments:* 1934–35 President's List; 1935–38 Wymondham; 1938–40 Coventry; 1940–42 Haltwhistle; 1942–46 Chaplain H.M. Forces; 1946–50 Newcastle West; 1950–54 Penrith; 1954–58 Alston; 1958–62 Chester-le-Street; 1962–68 Greenock; 1968–72 Inverness; 1972–75 Millom.

TODD, Geoffrey S., 9 Sunnyside Rd., Clevedon, Avon BS21 7TE. (0272-872580)–MA.
Education: 1947–50 Manchester Univ.; 1950–53 Wesley House. *Appointments:* 1953–54 Hunts Mission; 1954–58 Blyth and Seaton Deleval; 1958–62 West Africa Dt; 1962–65 Cardiff, Roath Park; 1965–70 Chester; 1970–76 Bristol, Clifton and Redland; 1976– Clevedon.

TOINTON, Ronald, 6 Moor Terrace, Millom, Cumbria LA18 5EN. (0657-2070) *b. 19 Feb 1908, Lincoln. m. 13 Aug 1938: 1d., 2s.*
Education: 1918–25 Lincoln Sch., Grammar; 1932–35 Headingley. *Appointments:* 1931–32 Bardney; 1935–36 Presidents' List; 1936–38 Cromer, Sheringham and Holt; 1938–40 Spilsby; 1940–46 Berwick-on-Tweed; 1946–49 Norwich, Calvert St.; 1949–52 Houghton-le-Spring; 1952–56 Cromer, Sheringham and Holt; 1956–60 Millom; 1960–67 Barrow-in-Furness; 1967–73 Ambleside and Windermere. *Special Interests:* Linguistics, The Wesley Hymns. *Hobbies and Recreations:* Golf, Gardening.

TOMLINSON, Christopher Charles, c/o Reverend C. R. W. Gilbert, 1 Central Buildings, Westminster, London SW1. 25 May 1935, Plymouth, Devon. m. 5 Jan 1962: 2s.
Education: 1946–51 Shebbear Coll.; 1951–53 Sheffield Coll. of Art; 1958–61 Handsworth; 1961–62 Selly Oak. *Appointments:* 1961–71 South East Asia Dt; 1972– Chaplain H.M.F. *Hobbies and Recreations:* Cricket, Sailing.

TOMLINSON, Harold, 53 Bushey Wood Rd., Dore, Sheffield S17 3QA. (0742-368340) *b. 20 May 1904, Leeds, Yorkshire. m. 22 Oct 1946: 1d., 2s.*
Education: 1909–15 Cross Flatts Council Sch., Leeds; 1915–19 Cockburn High Sch., Leeds; 1924–27 Victoria Park. *Appointments:* 1927–46 Ningpo, China; 1941–43 Australian Meth. Church, Goulburn, N.S.W.; 1944–45 Australian Meth. Church, Bathurst, N.S.W.; 1946–48 Plymouth; 1948–55 Sheffield Ecclesall; 1955–60 Oxford; 1960–69 Devon and Dorset Mission. *Connexional Committees:* 1946–48 Methodist Overseas Missions Committee.
Special Interests: Yorkshire Dialect, Member of Yorkshire Dialect Society. *Hobbies and Recreations:* Cricket–Yorkshire, Test Cricket, Gardening, Sweet Pea Culture.

TOMPKINS, Winifred Betty, 213 Scar Lane, Golcar, Huddersfield HD7 4AU. (0484-654569) *b. 18 Feb 1929, Sheffield. s.*
Education: 1934–40 Hunters Bar Jun., Sheffield; 1940–46 High Storrs Grammar, Sheffield; 1955–57 Wesley Deaconess. *Appointments:* 1976–78 Durham Coast and Peterlee; 1978–80 Motherwell and Wishaw; 1980– Huddersfield Pennine.

TONG, Joseph William, 41 Cedar Ave., Sutton Weaver, Runcorn, Cheshire WA7 3ET. (092-86-676) *b. 6 March 1915, Hedon, Near Hull, North Humberside. m. 26 Dec 1945: 2d.*
Education: Hedon Council Sch.; 1939–40 Didsbury; 1940–42 Hartley Victoria. *Appointments:* 1942–46 Carlisle, Cecil St.; 1946–51 Berwick-on-Tweed; 1951–55 Crosshills; 1955–62 Marple; 1962–69 Eccles; 1969–74 Congleton; 1974–81 Frodsham.

TONG, Sidney, 34 Hoodcote Gardens, Winchmore Hill, London N21 2NE. (01-360-4502) *b. 18 June 1920, Hedon, E.Yorkshire. m. 22 Aug 1946: 1d.*
Education: Hedon Council Sch.; 1945–47 Hartley Victoria. *Appointments;* 1947–49 Lerwick and North Roe; 1949–53 Whitehaven; 1953–59 Liverpool, Grove St. and Woolton; 1959–62 Shipley; 1962–68 Bebington; 1968–73 Cheadle, Staffs.; 1973–81 Folkestone; 1981 London, Finsbury Park and Southgate. *Connexional Committees:* 1968–75 Church in Rural Life (Home Missions), Secretary; 1979– Ministers Retirement Fund.

TONG, William Lewis Vaughan, Hillside, Paddockhall Rd., Haywards Heath, West Sussex RH16 1HQ. (0444-413498)–MA(Cantab.). *b. 9 March 1942, Slough. m. 3 July 1965: 1d., 1s.*
Education: 1955–61 Slough Grammar Sch.; 1962–65 Wesley House, Cambridge. *Appointments:* 1965–67 Derby East; 1967–68 Leeds Mission; 1968–74 Watford; 1974–78 Bramhall; 1978– Mid-Sussex.
Special Interests: Adult Education in Church. *Hobbies and Recreations:* Fishing, Walking, Philately, Music.

TONKIN, Herbert Seymour, The Manse, Hartland, Bideford, Devon EX39 6DG. (02374-271) *b. 18 March 1918, Norbury, London. m.*

27 Sept 1949: 2s.
Education: 1930–37 Private Schs. and Truro Sch.; 1938–40 Didsbury; 1940–41 Hartley Victoria.
Appointments: 1941–42 Hyderabad Dt, India; 1942–44 Indian Army; 1944–47 Chaplain H.M.F. ; 1947–51 Reading; 1951–56 Oxford; 1956–60 Devonport; 1960–63 London, Brixton Hill; 1963–68 Purley; 1968–76 Portsmouth and Southsea; 1976– Bude.

TOOLEY, Wilfred, 37 Twyford Ave., East Finchley, London N2 9NU. (01-883-3027)–MA, BD. *b. 10 June 1930, South Shields, Co Durham. m. 1956: 2d.*
Education: 1951–54 Bristol Univ.; 1954–56 London Univ.; 1951–54 Didsbury, Bristol. *Appointments:* 1954–57 Wolverton and Bletchley; 1957–61 Manchester, Droylsden and Openshaw; 1961–66 Bramhall; 1966–69 Weston-super-Mare; 1969–78 Queens Coll., Taunton, Chaplain; 1978– Secretary, Division of Education and Youth.

TOPPING, Clifford, 11 Kingsway, Crewe, Cheshire CW2 7NB. (0270-60003) *b. 20 June 1926, Preston, Lancs. m. 8 May 1948: 1d., 1s.*
Education: 1932–38 Emmanuel CE Sch., Preston; 1938–41 Fulwood and Cadley County Secondary Sch.; 1941–46 Preston Technical Coll.; 1959–62 Church of South Africa; 1962–1963 Handsworth.
Appointments: 1963–66 Longton and Fenton; 1966–71 Durham Coast and Peterlee; 1971–77 Otley, Colliery Chaplain; 1977– Crewe.
Connexional Committees: 1978–81 Board of Property.
Hobbies and Recreations: Gardening, Walking, Painting.

TOPPING, Frank, 12 Margetts Place, Lower Upnor, Rochester, Kent. (0634-725411) *b. 30 March 1937, Birkenhead. m. Berry, June, 1958: 1d., 2s.*
Education: St. Annes RC Jun., Rock Ferry; St. Anselm's Coll., Birkenhead; North West Sch. of Speech and Drama, Southport; 1964–67 Bristol, Didsbury. *Appointments:* 1967–70 Brighton, Dome Mission; 1970– British Broacasting Corporation (Producer), Radio and Television.
Publications: Lord of the Morning (1977); *Lord of the Evening* (1979); *Lord of My Days* (1980); *Working at Prayer* (1981); *Lord of Life* (1982).
Special Interests: Writing Songs, Offshore Sailing, R.Y.A. Yacht Master.

TOWN, Keith Ernest, 186 Heywood Rd., Prestwich, Manchester M25 5LD. (061-773–1601)–BA(Manchester). *b. 1 Nov 1944, Bradford, Yorkshire. m. 12 Oct 1966: 3d.*
Education: 1947–51 Whetley Lane Inf.; 1951–55 Lilycroft Jun.; 1955–61 Bradford Grammar Sch.; 1978–81 Manchester Univ.; 1978–81 Hartley Victoria. *Appointments:* 1981– Cheetham Hill and Prestwich.
Local Council Committees: Education Authority Representative Governor of Parrenthorn High Sch.

TOWNLEY, Frank Henry, 35 Park Lane, Castle Donington, Derby DE7 2JF. (0332-810284)–DipTheol(Lond.). *b. 18 March 1916, South London. m. 20 Aug 1938 (w.): 1d.*
Education: L.C.C. Kennington, South London; 1958–60 Richmond.
Appointments: 1960–62 Ilkeston; 1962–68 Watford; 1968–74 Shaftesbury; 1974–79 Bournemouth; 1979– Castle Donington.

TOWNSEND, Michael Jonathan, 196 Roils Head Rd., Halifax, West Yorkshire HX2 0NH. (0422-61448)–BA(Leicester), MPhil(Leicester), BD(Manchester). *b. 10 Aug 1947, Barnstaple, North Devon. s.*
Education: 1962–66 Barnstaple Grammar Sch.; 1966–69 Univ. of Leicester; 1969–72 Univ. of Manchester; 1972–73 Institute Oecumenique Bossey; 1969–73 Hartley Victoria. *Appointments:* 1973–79 Selby; 1979– Halifax.
Connexional Committees: 1981– Committee for European Affairs; 1981– Board of Studies Division of Ministries; 1981– Connexional Probationers Oversight Committee; 1982– Doctrinal Committee.
Publications: Worship-its nature and function, Worship and Preaching (1974); *The Preachers Use of the Bible, Worship and Preaching* (1975); *James 4:1-4, A Warning against Zealotry?, Expository Times* (1976); *Who needs Theology Anyway?, Worship and Preaching* (1976) *Twentieth-Century Christian Poetry, Epworth Review* (1977); *God in the After Silence: Introduction to the Poetry of R.S. Thomas, Encounter USA* (1978); *Exit the Agape?, Expository Times* (1979); *Our Tradition of Faith, Epworth Press* (1980); *Christ, Community and Salvation in the Epistle of James, Evangelical Quarterly* (1981); Numerous book reviews.
Special Interests: The Relationship between literature and theology, Liturgy, The nineteenth century novel. *Hobbies and Recreations:* Listening to music, Reading, Exploring Scotland.

TOZE, Stephen James, 3 Millersdale, Harlow, Essex CM19 4QD. (0279-23602)–BA(B'ham.). *b. 25 June 1951, Worsley. m. 28 July 1979.*
Education: 1962–69 Bolton Sch.; 1976–79 Birmingham Univ.; 1976–80 Queens Coll. *Appointments:* 1980– Harlow Mission.
Hobbies and Recreations: Painting, Photography.

TREMBATH, Peter Westbury, The Manse, Delancey Lane, St. Sampson's, Guernsey, C.I. (0481 44123) *b. 13 Jan 1934, Trewellard, West Cornwall. m. 25 July 1959: 2d., 1s.*
Education: 1939–45 Carnyorth Prim. Sch.; 1945–52 Penzance County Grammar Sch.; 1955–59 Didsbury, Bristol. *Appointments:* 1959–61 Wolverton and Bletchley; 1961–65 Stour Vale; 1965–71 Kidderminster; 1971–77 Bath; 1977–82 Redditch; 1982 Balliwick of Guernsey.
Publications: Occasional *In Fellowship series of articles for Methodist Recorder* (1969–81).
Special Interests: Anything Cornish.

Hobbies and Recreations: Sport—particularly Cricket, Music, Reading, Embroidery.

TREVITHICK, Anythong George, 28 St. Kenelm's Ave., Halesowen, West Midlands B63 1DW. (021-550-1461) *b. 19 Jan 1937, Airdrie, Coatbridge, Lanarkshire, Scotland. m. 21 Aug 1964: 2d.*
Education: 1942–45 George Dixon Sch., Birmingham; 1945–58 Maidenhall Rd., Luton; 1948–55 Kingswood Sch., Bath; 1957–60 Richmond. *Appointments:* 1960–62 Walton on Thames; 1962–63 Wellington; 1963–67 Rhymney Valley; 1967–72 Hereford; 1972–77 Stafford; 1977– Halesowen.

TREVITHICK, John Edward, Maison La Corderie, Green St., St. Helier, Jersey, Channel Islands. (0534-74226) *b. 1902, Gillingham, Kent. m.*
Education: 1923–25 Victoria Park. *Appointments:* 1922–23 Faversham; 1925–26 Bolton; 1926–27 Barnstaple; 1927–28 Burton-on-Trent; 1928–30 Carlisle; 1930–34 Grimsby Central; 1934–37 Torquay and Paignton; 1937–40 London, Ilford; 1940–44 Gloucester; 1944–51 Plymouth and Devonport Mission; 1951–57 Great Yarmouth Central Mission; 1957–66 Chatham Mission.

TREW, Malcolm Frederick, 68 Berridale Ave., Cathcart, Glasgow G44 3AE. (041-637-1810) *b. 24 Nov 1934, Tottenham, London N17. m. 12 Aug 1961: 2d.*
Education: 1946–52 Tottenham Grammar Sch.; 1976–78 Glasgow Univ.; 1955–59 Hartley Victoria. *Appointments:* 1959–61 Barnsley West; 1961–64 Sheffield Mission; 1964–69 Retford; 1969–79 Glasgow South; 1979– Paisley Mission. *Connexional Committees:* 1970–76 Social Responsibility.
Special Interests: Social Work, Group Work. *Hobbies and Recreations:* Music, D.I.Y., Photography.

TREZISE, Raymond Henry, 28 The Green, Acomb, York YO2 5LR. (0904-798284) *b. 5 June 1934, Hessle, North Humberside. m. 17 Aug 1963: 2d.*
Education: 1945–51 Beverley Grammar Sch.; 1957–61 Headingley. *Appointments:* 1961–63 Pateley Bridge; 1963–68 Batley; 1968–78 Dewsbury; 1978– York South. *Connexional Committees:* 1974– Methodist Stewardship Organisation (Secretary since 1979. *Hobbies and Recreations:* Bird Watching, Drawing, Gardening.

TRIFFITT, Alan James, 4 Russell Ave., Wyke Rd., Weymouth, Dorset DT4 9RA. (0305-784140) *b. 9 March 1924, Larkhill Camp, Nr. Salisbury, Wilts. m. 6 Aug 1955: 2s.*
Education: Amesbury Inf. Sch.; Amesbury CE Jun. and Sen. Sch.; Bishop Wordsworth's Sch., Salisbury; 1948–50 Didsbury, Bristol.
Appointments: 1945–48 Forest of Dean; 1950–52 Southampton; 1952–54 Sutton, Surrey; 1954–57 Leeds, Richmond Hill; 1957–62 Stroud and Cirencester; 1962–70 West Wight; 1970–76 Portland.
Special Interests: Social Responsibility Questions, Penal Matters and the Treatment of Prisoners, The Bible Society, History of Methodism.
Hobbies and Recreations: Gardening, Stamp Collecting, Listening to Music, The Use and Origin of Words, Listening to the Radio, Watching Sport on TV.

TRIPP, David Howard, 15 Lampton Park Rd., Hounslow, Middlesex TW3 4HS. (01–570-0200)–BA(Cantab.), MA(Leeds). *b. 4 March 1940, Lambeth. m. 1966: 1d., 1s.*
Education: 1951–59 Owen's; 1959–63 Univ of Cambridge; 1963–65 Univ. of Leeds; 1965–66 Univ. of Heidelberg; 1963–65 Wesley Coll., Headingley. *Appointments:* 1966–68 Liverpool South; 1968–73 Bebington; 1973–81 Manchester, Cheetham Hill; 1981– London, Richmond and Hounslow.
Connexional Committees: 1978– Faith and Order; 1970, 1978 elected to Conference; 1982–84 Conference, elected rep.; 1978– Churches' Council for Covenanting; 1978–81 Manchester Diocesan Worship Committee; 1975– Secretary, Henry Bradshaw Society. *Local Council Committees:* 1981 London Borough of Hounslow, Community Education Advisory Committee. *Publications: Books: The Renewal of the Covenant* (1969); ed. *E.C. Ratcliff, Liturgial Studies* (1976); *E.C. Ratcliff Papers on Liturgical Revision* (1980); Contributor to *SCM Dictionary of Liturgy and Worship; The Study of Liturgy; Yale Dictionary of the Middle Ages; The Sacrifice of Praise* (Couratin Festschrift 1981); *Liturgy Reshaped* (Cuming Festschrift 1982); Articles in: *London Quarterly* and *Holborn Review, Preacher's Quarterly, Church Review, Scottish Journal of Theology, Modern Churchman, Expository Times, Epworth Review.*
Special Interests: Liturgy. *Hobbies and Recreations:* Railways.

TRUELOVE, Harry, Carn Brea, 4 Cambrian Drive, Prestatyn, Clwyd LL19 9RL. (074-56-4039) *b. 11 July 1896, Chapeltown, Sheffield. m. 27 Aug 1923: 1d., 1s. (deceased).*
Education: Elem., Owler Lane, Sheffield; Tinsley, Sheffield; 1919–21 Victoria Park. *Appointments:* 1921–23 Huddersfield; 1923–27 Wenchow Dt, China; 1927–31 Redruth; 1931–33 Connah's Quay; 1933–38 Rhyl and Prestatyn; 1938–42 Sheffield North; 1942–45 Norwich, Calvert St.; 1945–48 Boston Central; 1948–55 Rhyl and Prestatyn; 1955–59 Newcastle upon Tyne Central; 1959–62 Leeds, Rothwell; 1933–38 Secretary, Chester and Warrington District; 1948–55 Secretary, Chester and Stoke-on-Trent District.
Local Council Committees: 1933–38, 1948–55 Secretary, Chester and Warrington Synod.

TRUELOVE, Leslie, 25 Rushbed Drive, Reedsholme, Rossendale, Lancs BB4 8NQ. (0706-220994) *b. 4 July 1916, Mapplewell, Yorks. m. 1 Jan 1945: 2s.*
Education: 1928–35 Normanton Grammar Sch.; 1938–40 Didsbury; 1940–41 Hartley Victoria.
Appointments: 1941–44 Home Mission Department; 1944–46 Chaplain, H.M.F.; 1947–52 Colombo English Circuit; 1952–71 Chaplain,

H.M.F.; 1971–81 Hastings, Bexhill and Rye.
Hobbies and Recreations: Sport, Sailing, Carpentry, Music, Photography.

TUCKER, Frederick George, 34 Penhallow Rd., Newquay, Cornwall TR7 3DA. (063-73-6895)– MA(Oxon). *b. 14 Oct 1893, Launceston, Cornwall. m. 9 Nov 1939 (w.).*
Education: Launceston Board Sch.; Horwell Grammar Sch., Launceston; 1920–23 Lincoln Coll., Oxford; Kingsmead Coll., Birmingham.
Appointments: 1924–25 Supply; 1925–58 Sierra Leone Dt, West Africa.
Hobbies and Recreations: Bowls, Indoor and Outdoor.

TUCKER, John Edwin, 21 Ashcroft Rd., Cirencester, Glos. G7 1RA. (0285-3655) *b. 22 Oct 1923, Dymock, Glos. m. 16 Aug 1947: 2d., 2s.*
Education: 1928–32 Dymock; 1932–34 Chipping Campden Jun.; Chipping Campden Grammar Sch.; 1950–52 Handsworth. *Appointments:* 1952–54 Frome; 1954–58 Ashton-under-Lyne; 1958–63 Paulton; 1963–71 Weston-super-Mare; 1971–81 Brinkworth; 1981– Cirencester.
Special Interests: Rural Methodism.
Hobbies and Recreations: Sport, Hockey, Tennis, Gardening.

TUCKER, William John Ronald, 349 Bramhall Lane, Stockport, Cheshire SK3 8TP. (061 456 3601) *b. 3 Nov 1907, Tillhouse Farm, Broadclyst, Devon. m. 17 June 1937: 2d.*
Education: 1912–18 St. Peters, Southborough, Kent; 1918–24 Sir Andrew Judd, Tonbridge; 1943–45 Durham Univ.; 1926–27 Cliff Coll.; 1930–33 Richmond. *Appointments:* 1933–38 Liverpool Mission; 1938–39 Newcastle West; 1939–45 South Shields; 1945–51 Luton; 1951–57 Derby South; 1957–64 Leicester West; 1964–73 Manchester, Withington.
Special Interests: United Nations, Local Government, Youth Clubs.
Hobbies and Recreations: Gardening.

TUDOR, Charles Leonard, 54 Abington Park Crescent, Northampton NN3 3AL. (0604-406990) *b. 2 April 1898, St. Georges, Telford, Shropshire. w. 10 Sept 1924: 1d., 1s.*
Education: 1903–12 St. Georges CE Sch.; 1912–19 Oakengates Technical Coll.; 1921–23 Hartley.
Appointments: 1919–21 Nantwich; 1923–26 Derby, Kedleston St.; 1926–35 Northampton, Kettering Rd.; 1935–40 Harrogate; 1940–45 Cleethorpes, Mill Rd.; 1945–48 London, Highgate; 1948–60 Secretary of Home Mission Division; 1960–65 General Secretary of Home Mission Division.
Connexional Committees: 1947–65 Home Mission Division; 1948–65 Property Division; 1950–65 Finance Division. *Local Council Committees:* 1960–65 British Council of Churches; Christian Endeavour Unions and Sunday Sch. Unions.
Special Interests: Evangelism in Mens' Movements, General Literature. *Hobbies and Recreations:* Gardening.

TUDOR, Richard John, Central Hall, Westminster, London SW1 9NU. (01-222-8553/8754)– BA(Manch.), DD(Honorary–Texas Wesleyan Coll., Fort Worth, Texas, U.S.A.). *b. 8 Feb 1930, Northampton. m. 21 July 1956: 1d., 1s.*
Education: 1940–45 Clee Grammar Sch., Cleethorpes, Lincs.; 1945–48 Queen Elizabeth's Boy's Sch., Barnet; 1951–54 Manchester Univ.; 1981 Texas Wesleyan Coll.; 1951–54 Hartley Victoria. *Appointments:* 1954–57 London, East Ham Mission; 1957–60 Fleetwood; 1960–71 Derby Mission; 1971–75 Coventry Mission; 1975–81 Brighton Dome Mission; 1981– London, Westminster.
Connexional Committees: 1967–70 Home Mission; 1962–70 Central Missions.
Special Interests: Making Friends, Preaching. *Hobbies and Recreations:* Cooking, Letting my wife do the garden, Motoring, Travelling Abroad.

TULEY, Arthur, 3 Killerton Rd., Bude, Cornwall EX23 8EL. (0288-2404).
Education: 1939–42 Headingley.
Appointments: 1942–43 Sussex Mission; 1943–48 Chaplain, HMF; 1948–52 Newcastle, Heaton and Wallsend; 1952–58 Weston-super-Mare; 1958–63 London, Ealing and Acton; 1963–68 Bath; 1968–73 Cheltenham; 1973– Bude.

TUNNICLIFFE, Michael, 73 Canberra Crescent, Meir Park, Stoke on Trent ST3 7RA. (07818-4958)– BA(B'ham.), MA(B'ham.). *b. 20 June 1954, Boney Hay, Walsall, Staffs. m. 28 July 1979.*
Education: 1959–65 Chase Terrace Inf./Jun.; 1965–72 Chase Terrace Comprehensive; 1972–77 Birmingham Univ.; 1978–81 Wesley House. *Appointments:* 1981– Stoke-on-Trent South.
Publications: Hebrew Glossary–For Texts in J. H. Eaton's *First Studies in Biblical Hebrew* and *Readings in Biblical Hebrew I and II* (Univ. of Birmingham 1980).
Special Interests: Old Testament.
Hobbies and Recreations: Genealogy.

TURK, Francis Dowdeswell, 24 Park Rd., Southport, Merseyside PR9 9LA (0704-815780) *b. 30 Oct 1914, Aberdare, S.Wales. m. 19 Aug 1944: 1d., 2s.*
Education: 1920–26 Park Sch., Elem.; 1926–28 Central Secondary: 1936–37 Cliff Coll.; 1937–40 Headingley. *Appointments:* 1940–42 Blackburn Trinity; 1942–44 Liverpool North; 1944–47 Manchester Mission; 1947–53 Manchester, Harpurhey; 1953–57 Uxbridge and Hayes; 1957–63 Dudley; 1963–68 Brentford and Hounslow; 1968–73 Reading; 1973–78 Gosport.
Special Interests: Ministry of Healing.
Hobbies and Recreations: Reading, Gardening, Snooker, Televiewing, Football.

TURNER, Alfred Kingsley, 48 Park Rise, Harpenden, Herts. AL5 3AL. (05827-5484)–MA(Cantab.), BA(Oxon). *b. 19 July 1909, Radstock, Somerset. m. 19 Aug 1936: 1d., 1s.*
Education: 1919–28 Kingswood Sch.; 1928–31 Hertford Coll., Oxford; 1931–33 Wesley House.
Appointments: 1933–35 President's List; 1934 Guernsey and Sark, French; 1936–39 Frome; 1939–44 Barnet; 1944–50 Ealing and Acton; 1950–55 Finchley and Hendon; 1955–61 Harpenden; 1961–62 Amersham; 1962–74 Chairman London N.W. District.
Connexional Committees: 1955–82 N.C.H.; 1959–64 Admission of Women to the Ministry (Secretary).
Special Interests: Order of Christian Witness. *Hobbies and Recreations:* Chess, Bird Watching.

TURNER, Edwin Jordon, 4 South Lane, Norham, Berwick-upon-Tweed TD15 2LR. (0289-82470)–BD(Lond.). *b. 15 April 1915, Heddon-on-the-Wall, Northumberland. m. 22 July 1944: 1d., 1s.*
Education: 1920–26 Stansfield Street, Sunderland; 1926–30 Monkwearmouth Central, Sunderland; 1937–40 Headingley.
Appointments: 1940–46 Devonport; 1946–53 Walsall, Wesley; 1953–62 Paisley Mission, Barrhead; 1962–67 Edinburgh, Leith; 1967–71 Blaydon; 1971–76 Scarborough; 1976–80 Bishop Auckland.
Connexional Committees: 1950–53 Division of Education and Youth; 1971–75 Commission on Evangelism.
Council Member: 1963–67 Scottish Churches Council.
Special Interests: Ecumenical Relations. *Hobbies and Recreations:* Gardening, Woodwork, Golf, Walking.

TURNER, George Herbert, Epworth, 82B Cliff Rd., Hornsea, North Humberside HU18 1HX. (04012-2297)–BA(Leeds). *b. 14 March 1924, Market Weighton. m. 13 Aug 1952: 1d., 2s.*
Education: 1930–35 Market Weighton CE Sch.; 1935–42 Pocklington Sch.; 1948–51 Leeds Univ.; 1948–51 Headingley.
Appointments: 1946–48 Upwell and Manea; 1951–53 Withernsea; 1953–56 Leeds, Bramley and Farsley; 1956–61 Goole; 1961–65 Bridlington; 1965–70 Skipton; 1970–74 Hull West; 1974–80 Bolsover and Staveley; 1980– Hornsea.

TURNER, Gordon, 12 Anderson Rd., Bishopdown, Salisbury SP1 3DX. (0722-24134) *b. 26 Nov 1923, Sunderland, Co. Durham. m. 2 Aug 1951: 2d., 3s.*
Education: 1928–34 Stansfield St., Roker, Sunderland; 1934–40 Monkwearmouth Central Sch., Sunderland; 1946–48 Headingley.
Appointments: 1948–51 Glasgow, Claremont St.; 1951–55 Greenock; 1955–58 Hinckley, Stockwell Head; 1958–66 Leicester East; 1966–69 London, Kilburn and Hampstead; 1969–72 Secretary, Methodist Youth Dept.; 1972–78 Secretary, Division of Education and Youth; 1978– Salisbury.
Connexional Committees: 1958–69 M.V.D. Council and Executive. *Local Council Committees:* 1960–65 Youth Committee, Leicester; 1981 Youth and community Service, Salisbury. *Publications: Methodist Concise Guides* (1955–69); *Partners in Learning* (1969–78); *Partners in Leadership* (1970); *Experiental Teaching* (Lima, Peru 1971); *The Place of the Sunday School in the Christian Community* (Montreaux 1973).
Special Interests: History, Zen. *Hobbies and Recreations:* Japanese Gardens and Flower Arranging, Painting, Reading.

TURNER, Gordon Alfred, 41 Fairways, Frodsham, Warrington, Cheshire WA6 7RU. (0928-33180) *b. 15 Aug 1927, Runcorn. m. 14 Aug 1954: 1d., 2s.*
Education: 1931–34 Holy Trinity; 1934–38 Weston Point; 1938–41 Balfour Rd. Boys Sch.; 1952–55 Headingley. *Appointments:* 1951–52 Market Drayton; 1955–60 Halifax; 1960–64 Luddenden; 1964–69 Redditch; 1969–74 Kingsbridge and Salcombe; 1974–81 Dewsbury; 1981– Frodsham.
Hobbies and Recreations: Horology.

TURNER, James Thomas, 28 Atholl Bank Drive, Perth PH1 1NF. (0738-24007) *b. 19 April 1935, Bolton, Lancashire. m. 21 March 1967: 1s.*
Education; 1940–46 Tonge Moor Prim., Bolton; 1946–48 Castle Hill Secondary, Bolton; 1948–50 Bolton Technical Coll.; 1964–68 Cliff Coll.; 1965–67 Headingley; 1967–68 Wesley Coll., Bristol; 1968–69 Kingsmead, Selly Oak, Birmingham.
Appointments: 1969–74 Bahamas District; 1974–81 Northwich; 1981– Dundee, Perth and Blairgowrie.
Special Interests: Caribbean Methodism. *Hobbies and Recreations:* Caravanning, Stamp Collecting.

TURNER, Joan Margaret, Methodist Church Flat, Tithe Laithe, Hoyland, Barnsley, South Yorkshire S74 9DQ. (0226-742360)–BA. *b. 2 May 1948, Sheffield.*
Education: 1953–59 Ridgeway County Prim. Sch., Derbyshire; 1959–66 Westfield Comprehensive Sch., Mosborough, Nr. Sheffield; 1966–69 Liverpool Coll. of Commerce; 1969–70 Manchester Univ.; 1972–73 Birmingham Univ.; 1979–81 Wesley, Bristol.
Appointments: 1981–82 Wombwell and Hoyland; 1982– Barnsley.

TURNER, John, 19 Selcroft Rd., Purley, Surrey CR2 1AG. (01-660-0033)–BA(Manch.), BA(B'ham.). *b. 14 Feb 1931, Burnley. m. 13 Sept 1958: 4d.*
Education: 1942–49 Burnley Grammar Sch.; 1949–52 Manchester Univ.; 1955–59 Birmingham Univ.; 1955–59 Handsworth.
Appointments: 1959–65 Ivory Coast District, W. Africa; 1965–70 Durham; 1970–75 St. Helens and Prescot; 1975– Purley.
Connexional Committees: 1965–70 Education and Youth Comm.; 1965–70 Methodist Day Schools Comm.; 1973–75 Overseas Division, Central Committee; 1980– Social Responsibility.
Special Interests: Politics, Peace

Movement etc.; Languages. *Hobbies and Recreations:* Music, Reading, Gardening, Fell Walking and Climbing, Camping, Travel.

TURNER, John Munsey, 37 Rothwell Rd., Halifax, W.Yorks. HX1 2HA. (0422-53827)–MA(Cantab.), MA(Bristol). *b. 15 Feb 1930, Wolverhampton. m. 16 Feb 1965: 1d.*
Education: 1935–39 Woodfield Ave. Sch., Penn, Wolverhampton; 1939–49 Wolverhampton Grammar Sch.; 1949–52 St. Catharine's Coll., Cambridge; 1953–56 Didsbury, Bristol. *Appointments:* 1956–58 Colchester; 1958–62 Burton on Trent, Trinity; 1962–68 Sheffield, Norfolk; 1968–70 Leeds Mission; 1970–81 Queen's Coll., Tutor Church History; 1981– Halifax.
Connexional Committees: 1968–78 Faith and Order; 1973–78 Doctrinal Committee of Appeal; 1980– History of Methodism; 1968–71 Connexional Candidates; 1982– Fernley Hartley Trust. *Publications: Introducing Theology* (1975); ed. *Queen's Essays* (1980); Chapters in *History of Methodism* (Davies, Rupp and George, Vol.II, Vol.III etc.
Special Interests: 19th and 20th Century Church History. *Hobbies and Recreations:* Local History, League Football.

TURNER, Laurence John, 5 Kingsley Rd., Luton Beds. LU3 2LS. (0582-51023)–BA(Bristol), ThM(Richmond, U.S.A.). *b. 26 April 1935, Barnet, Herts. m. 12 July 1980.*
Education: 1946–52 Enfield Grammar Sch.; Bristol Univ.; 1967–68 Union Theological Seminary, Richmond, VA., U.S.A.; 1964–67 Didsbury, Bristol. *Appointments:* 1968–73 Leeds West; 1973–80 Castleford; 1980– Luton North.
Connexional Committees: 1971–74 Local Preachers' Committee; 1974–77 Board of Division of Ministries; 1969– Local Preachers' Studies Board.
Hobbies and Recreations: Architecture, Local History, Windmills.

TURNER, Martin Hugh, Ashfield, 37 Rawson Ave., Halifax, W.Yorks. HX3 0LR. (0422-54610) *b. 13 July 1948, Leyton, London. m. 11 Dec 1976: 1d., 1s.*
Education: 1959–66 Buckhurst Hill County High Sch.; 1966–69 Brentwood Coll. of Education; 1976–77 West Hill Coll. of Education; 1974–76 Wesley Coll., Bristol.
Appointments: 1977–80 Bradford Mission; 1980– Halifax, St. Andrews.
Connexional Committees: 1982–83 Education and Youth.
Special Interests: Evangelism, Youth Work, Moral Theology. *Hobbies and Recreations:* Fishing, Antique Restoration, Gardening, Sport.

TURNER, Raymond Charles, 100 Weymoor Rd., Harborne, Birmingham B17 0RU. (021-427-5571) *b. 2 March 1911, Tipton, Staffs. m. 18 Aug 1938: 1d.*
Education: 1916–25 Council Sch.; 1931–35 Didsbury. *Appointments:* 1935–37 London, Whitechapel Mission; 1937–38 Carlisle, Wigton Rd.; 1938–41 Willenhall, Union St.; 1941–46 Bilston, Wesley; 1946–50 Burton-on-Trent, Station St.; 1950–58 West Bromwich, Wesley; 1958–65 Birmingham South West; 1965–72 Lichfield; 1972–77 Stratford-on-Avon.
Connexional Committees: 1966–72 Chapel/Property Committee.
Hobbies and Recreations: Reading.

TURNEY, Theodore Lloyd, Cynfal, Menai Ave., Bangor, Gwynedd LL57 2HH. (0248-53365) *b. 3 May 1899, Liscard, Wallasey. m. (1), (2) 27 July 1927.*
Education: 1921–24 Handsworth.
Appointments: 1920–21 Severn Valley Mission; 1924–25 Wye Valley Mission; 1925–27 Bristol, Clifton; 1927–28 Bangor; 1928–31 Preston, Wesley; 1931–35 Blackburn; 1935–38 Liverpool, Waterloo; 1938–41 Wallasey; 1941–48 Portsmouth Mission; 1948–51 Barrow in Furness; 1951–54 Sheffield, Carver St.; 1954–57 Leicester West; 1957–63 Whitchurch, St. John's.
Connexional Committees: Connexional General Purposes Committee; 1927–32 Methodist Union Committee.
Special Interests: Preaching, Member of Constituency of Executive Committee (Conservative).

TÜSCHER, Otto, 28 St. Lawrene Ave., Eastwood, Nottingham NG16 3LD. (07-737-2994) *b. 26 July 1925, Sissach (Blld)., Switzerland. m. 27 Aug 1955: 1d., 1s.*
Education: 1932–41/1943–45 Educated in Switzerland; 1945– obtained Swiss National Diploma in Horticulture; 1949–50 Cliff Coll.; 1950–52 Theological Training Coll., St. Chrischona, Nr. Basel; 1955–56 Theological Faculty, Paris; 1953–55 Richmond. *Appointments:* 1956–64 Dahomey, Togo District, West Africa; 1964–70 Barton upon Humber; 1970–82 Scunthorpe; 1982– Kimberly.
Connexional Committees: 1975–82 Central Committee, Overseas Division; 1976–81 European Relations Committee. *Council Member:* 1978–80 Mayor of Scunthorpe.
Special Interests: Promotion of Work Overseas, Hospital Chaplaincy Work; 1970–82 Hospital Chaplain; 1975–82 Member of Area and Regional Chaplaincy Advisory Committees.*Hobbies and Recreations:* Lapidary, Growing of Bonsai Trees; Home Wine Making, Photography.

TWIDDY, David George Vashon, Methodist Manse, Shield Hill Rd., Reddingmuirhead, Falkirk, Stirlingshire FK2 0DT. (0324-715852)–BD(Lond.). *b. 3 March 1926, Ludlow, Shropshire. m. 22 June 1957: 3s.*
Education: 1934–42 Ludlow Grammar Sch.; 1951–54 London Univ. (External Student); 1950–53 Hartley Victoria. *Appointments:* 1949–50 Glasgow, East Mission; 1953–55 Edinburgh, Nicholson Square; 1955–60 Liverpool North; 1960–65 Lancaster; 1965–70 Shrewsbury; 1970–75 Paisley Mission; 1975– Falkirk, Wallacestone and Stirling.
Connexional Committees: 1973–79 Overseas. *Council Member:* Chairman of Reddingmuirhead and

Wallastone Community Council.
Hobbies and Recreations: Gardening, Cricket.

TWINN, Rowland James, 9 Carmarthen Close, Winsford, Cheshire CW7 1LP. (06065-54153) *b. 18 Sept 1921, London. m. Jan 1943: 3d.*
Education: Leyton Secondary Sch. for Boys; 1940–42 London S.W. Polytec; Cooper's Hill Coll.
Appointments: 1979– Winsford.
Hobbies and Recreations: Drama, Gardening.

UNDERHILL, Stanley Edward Albert, Lappa, 23 Penare Rd., Penzance, Cornwall TR18 3AJ. (0736-61630) *b. 19 Jan 1914, Bristol. m. 23 June 1940: 1d.*
Education: 1917–28 St. Simon's CE Elem. Sch., Bristol. *Appointments:* 1950–51 Daventry; 1951–55 Macclesfield; 1955–58 Risca and Cross Keys; 1958–63 Redruth; 1963–67 Truro; 1967–74 Penzance; 1974–79 Redruth.
Council Member: Probus Parish Council, Cornwall.
Special Interests: Christian Aid, Bible Society. *Hobbies and Recreations:* Gardening, Reading, Walking, Radio and Television.

UNSWORTH, Gordon, 21 Station Rd., Hemsworth, Pontefract, West Yorks. WF9 4JW. (0977-610526) *b. 26 June 1936, Consett, Co. Durham. m. 2 Nov 1963: 1d., 1s.*
Education: 1948–54 Stanley Grammar Sch., Stanley, Co. Durham; 1978–80 Queen's Coll.
Appointments: 1980– Barnsley.
Hobbies and Recreations: Singing, Garden.

UPRIGHT, Norman, 4 Crescent Rise, Truro, Cornwall TR1 3ER. (0872-76362)–MA, BD(Manch.). *b. 21 Aug 1907, Seacombe, Cheshire. m. 15 Aug 1942: 1s.*
Education: 1919–26 City and County Sch., Chester; 1926–31 Manchester Univ.; 1926–31 Hartley.
Appointments: 1931–34 Coventry; 1934–38 Birmingham, Islington; 1938–42 Colwyn Bay; 1942–46 Warrington; 1946–51 Bournemouth; 1951–56 London, Ilford; 1956–62 Leicester North; 1962–68 Barnet; 1968–73 Truro.
Connexional Committees: 1934–38 Candidates; 1942–46 Probationers; 1947–54 Christian Citizenship; 1955–81 Homes for Aged.

UPTON, Ronald Leslie, 42 Chatfield Rd., Woodseats, Sheffield, S. Yorks. S8 0HE. (0742 749088) *b. 25 May 1903, Burton-on-Trent, Staffs. (w.).*
Education: Local Higher Elem., Bloxwich, Staffs.; 1925–28 Didsbury.
Appointments: 1928–41 China, Hupeh Dt; 1941–45 Falmouth; 1945–48 Wellington, Salop; 1948–53 Leeds, Rothwell; 1953–59 Chesterfield, Holywell Cross and Staveley; 1959–64 Kiveton; 1964–68 Caerphilly.
Connexional Committees: 1953–56 Missionary Society Committee.
Hobbies and Recreations: Art, Music, Gardening, Reading.

VALE, David Graham, 18 Prince Andrew Drive, Dersingham, Kings Lynn, Nortfolk PE31 6JW. (0485-40634) *b. 20 Feb 1953, Buxton, Derbyshire. s.*
*Education:*1964–71 Buxton Coll.; 1975–76 Cliff Coll.; 1976–80 Wesley, Bristol. *Appointments:* 1980– Hunstanton.
Hobbies and Recreations: Photography, Theatre.

VALENDER, Frederick Willmott, 1 The Peppergarth, Northallerton, N. Yorks. DL7 8NP. (0609-779334)–BA(Leeds). *b. 9 June 1916, Pebworth, Nr. Starford-upon-Avon. m. 4 April 1949: 2s.*
Education: Prince Henry's Grammar Sch., Evesham, Worcs.; 1938–41 Leeds Univ.; 1938–41 Headingley.
Appointments: 1941–47 Kenya District; 1947–51 Thirsk; 1951–66 Kenya District; 1966–70 Stokesley; 1971–75 Methodist Church in Kenya; 1975–78 Haverfordwest; 1978–81 Pocklington.
Special Interests: Africa, Christian Stewardship. *Hobbies and Recreations:* Gardening, Writing.

VALLE, Arthur Sydney, 11 Norfolk St., Beverley, North Humberside HU17 7DN. (0482-867792)–MA(Oxon), MA(Cantab.). *b. 1918, Wallington, Surrey. m. 1959.*
Education: 1929–36 Whitgift Sch., Croydon; 1936–39 Christ Church, Oxford; 1939–41 Wesley House.
Appointments: 1941–43 Edinburgh Mission; 1943–45 Coatbridge and Airdrie; 1945–48 Tunstall, Jubilee; 1948–54 Bristol East; 1954–59 Buckingham and Brackley; 1959–62 Newcastle, Staffs.; 1962–67 Cambridge; 1967–74 Wrexham; 1974–79 Beverley.

VALLEY, Norman Wilson, Freshwater Court, Freshwater, Isle of Wight PO40 9NU. (0983-752174) *b. 9 March 1917, Saxilby, Lincs. w. 25 Oct 1952: 1d.*
Education; 1929–34 City Sch., Lincoln; 1946–48 Handsworth.
Appointments: 1948–51 Manchester Mission; 1951–55 New Mills; 1955–59 Hull East; 1959–74 Methodist Youth Camps; 1964–66 Leeds, Ladylane Mission, Gipton.
Connexional Committees: 1961–64 Youth. *Council Member:* 1963–74 Mudesley Parish, Norfolk; 1975–79 Totland Parish, Isle of Wight.
Special Interests: Youth and Prison Reform, Voice of Methodism. *Hobbies and Recreations:* Piano, Organ.

VENN, Charles Herbert, 228 Limpsfield Rd., Sanderstead, South Croydon, Surrey CR2 9DA. (01-657-6435) *b. 22 April 1917, Islington, London. m. 7 Oct 1939.*
Education: 1947–50 Richmond.
Appointments: 1950 Guildford; 1953–56 London Mission South; 1956–61 London Mission, Plumstead; 1961–68 London, Blackheath and Lee; 1968–75 Purley; 1975–82 Margate.
Connexional Committees: 1974– Minister's Retirement Fund.
Special Interests: Pastoral Psychology, World Peace Movement.
Hobbies and Recreations: Music, Literature, Drama.

VENNER, Basil Henry, 21 Kingshill Rd., Dursley, Glos. GL11 4DQ. (0453-2565) *b. 16 March 1923, Chichester,*

Sussex. *m. 28 Aug 1945: 1d., 1s.* *Appointments:* 1952–70 Methodist Church, South Africa; 1970–72 London Mission, East Ham; 1978– Stroud and Dursley.

VERE, Colin, 7 Park Rd., Harrogate, North Yorkshire HE2 9AZ. (0423-503551)–BA(Dunelm), BD(Manchester). *b. 18 March 1942, Boston, Lincolnshire. m. 12 April 1965: 1d., 1s.*
Education: 1947–53 Park County Jun. Sch., Boston; 1953–61 Boston Grammar Sch.; 1961–64 Hatfield Coll., Univ. of Durham; 1966–69 Univ. of Manchester; 1969–70 United Theol. Coll., Bangalore, Univ. of Serampore; 1966–69 Hartley Victoria. *Appointments:* 1970–75 Bury and Heywood; 1975–80 Bramhall; 1980– Harrogate.
Connexional Committees: 1977–80 Division of Education and Youth Board.
Hobbies and Recreations: Cricket.

VERNON, Godfrey, 21 Llandegveth Close, Croesyceiliog, Cwmbran, Gwent NP44 2PE. (06333-4680) *b. 18 March 1904, Manchester. m. 11 July 1933: 1s.*
Education: 1909–18 Moston Fields Sch.; 1926–29 Hartley Victoria; 1927–28 Victoria Park.
Appointments: 1925–26 Worksop; 1929–30 Mevagissey; 1930–31 Diss; 1931–33 Newport; 1933–34 Chichester; 1934–38 Sheffield, Brunswick; 1938–44 Stockport; 1944–47 Nottingham North; 1947–50 Ashton-under-Lyne; 1950–52 Darlaston; 1952–55 Preston, Trinity; 1955–59 Manchester, Droylsden and Openshaw; 1959–64 Retford; 1964–68 Garstang.
Connexional Committees: 1945–46 Overseas Missions. *Local Council Committees.* 1966–68 Garstang Council, Road Safety; 1968–73 Cwmbran Newtown Citizens Advice Bureau (unpaid).
Special Interests: The Preservation and Spiritual Renewal of Methodism. *Hobbies and Recreations:* Writing Poetry.

d. 09.08.82

VERRINDER, Wilfred John, April Rise, 35 Lodge Rd., Leatherhead, Surrey KT22 9QY. (0372-373921)–BD(Lond.) *b. 12 Oct 1919, Swindon, Wilts. m. 23 July 1949: 2s., 1d.*
Education: 1931–36 Grammar Sch., Swindon; 1947–50 Richmond.
Appointments: 1950–56 Halifax, Ebenezer; 1956–60 Ashfield, Notts.; 1960–64 Banbury; 1964–76 Trowbridge (as Sector Minister); 1976 Dorking.
Special Interests: Music.

VICKERS, Donald Frank, Maranatha, Croft Lane, Wainfleet, All Saints, Skegness, Lincs. PE24 4PA. (0754-880-746)–BA(Lond.), BD(Lond.). *b. 13 Sept 1917, Boultham, Lincoln. m. 3 April 1943: 1s.*
Education: 1928–34 Scunthorpe Grammar Sch.; 1934–38 Kings Coll., London; 1938–39 Hull; 1948–50 Headingley. *Appointments:* 1947 Belper; 1950–52 Glasgow Parkhead and Burbank; 1953–56 Witney; 1956–60 Leeds, Armley; 1960–62 Birstall and Birkenshaw; 1962–75 Warrington; 1975–78 Whaley Bridge; 1978–82 Grimsby West.
Special Interests: Cricket, Classics, French. *Hobbies and Recreations:* Stamps, Coins, D.I.Y., Painting.

VIDAMOUR, Thomas Nicholas Moullin, 2 Elms Close Terrace, Newlyn, Penzance, Cornwall TR18 5AU. (0736-3594) *b. 8 Jan 1932, Guernsey. m. 25 Aug 1959: 2s.*
Education: 1955–59 Didsbury, Bristol. *Appointments:* 1959–64 Forest of Dean; 1964–69 Haworth and Oakworth; 1969–73 Liskeard; 1973–80 Helston; 1980 Penzance.

VINCENT, Irvin James, Pendower, Shells Lane, Shepton Beauchamp, Ilminster, Somerset TA19 0LX. (0460-40394)–BA. *b. 22 July 1932, Mitcham, Surrey. m. 18 July 1959: 2d., 1s.*
Education: 1943–48 Mitcham Grammar Sch.; 1955–59 Didsbury, Bristol. *Appointments:* 1959–61 Dursley and Stonehouse; 1961– Chaplain H.M.F.

Special Interests: Sport, Soccer, Cricket. *Hobbies and Recreations:* Music, Table-Tennis.

VINCENT, John James, 239 Abbeyfield Rd., Sheffield S4 7AW. (0742–386688)–BD(Lond.), S.T.M. Drew, Dr Theol, Basel. *b. 29 Dec 1929, Sunderland. m. 4 Dec 1958: 1d., 2s.*
Education: 1942–47 Manchester Grammar Sch.; 1954–55 Drew Univ., U.S.A.; 1955–56 Basel Univ., Switzerland; 1951–54 Richmond.
Appointments: 1950–51 Ledbury; 1956–62 Manchester and Salford Mission; 1962–69 Rochdale Mission; 1969–70 Visiting Professor, Boston Univ. and New York Theological Seminary; 1970– Sheffield Inner City Ecumenical Mission.
Connexional Committees: 1962–67 G.P.; 1964–70 H.M. *Publications: Christ In a Nuclear World (1962); Christian Nuclear Perspective* (1963); *Christ and Methodism* (1965); *Here I Stand* (1967); *Secular Christ* (1968); *The Race Race* (1970); *The Jesus Thing* (1973); *Alternative Church* (1976); *Stirrings* (1976); *Starting All Over Again* (1981); *Into the City* (1982); *A Worker's Mark's Gospel* (1983).
Special Interests: Theology, Bible Study, City Mission, Theological Education. *Hobbies and Recreations:* Jogging, Writing.

VINCENT, Stanley Varcoe, 63 Church Court, Midsomer Norton, Bath BA3 2JA. (0761 416294) BA. *b. 6 Sept 1905, Devonport. m. 10 Oct 1933: 1d., 2s.*
Education: Haberdashers' Askes Hampstead Sch.; 1927–30 Birmingham; 1927–30 Handsworth.
Appointments: 1930–42 Burma Dt; 1942–44 Mysore Dt, India; 1945–46 Burma Dt; 1947–52 Falmouth; 1952–54 Penzance; 1954–64 Burma Dt; 1965–69 Hong Kong Dt; 1956–64 British and Foreign Bible Society, Rangoon; 1964–69 Hong Kong.
Connexional Committees: Overseas Asia Committee; Overseas General Committee.

VINE, Victor Edward, 19 Bushy Park Gardens, Teddington, Middx., TW11 0LQ. (01-977-3527) *b. 17 July 1926, Edmonton, N. London. m. (2) 1 Aug 1974: 1d., 1s.* *Education:* 1931–36 Prim., Egham; 1936–39 Secondary, Hayes; 1948–50 Handsworth. *Appointments:* 1950–52 Banbury; 1952–56 Selby; 1956–59 Liverpool N.E.; 1959–64 Walkden and Worsley; 1964–69 Devon and Dorset Mission; 1969–74 Okehampton; 1974–79 Romford; 1979 Teddington. *Connexional Committees:* 1960–75 Connexional Youth Council/Board of Education and Youth. *Publications: Episcopé in Methodism* (Proc. WHS, Dec 1956, Vol. XXX pt8); *Episcopacy in Our System* (*Ep. Review,* Sept 1979, Vol. 6, No. 3).

VIVIAN, Walter George Flaxman, South London Mission, Bermondsey Central Hall, Bermondsey St., London SE1 3UJ. (01-407-2014) *b. 31 May 1921, U.K. m. 8 Nov 1947: 1d., 1s.* *Education:* 1932–35 The Central Sch., Winchester; 1945–46 Cliff Coll.; 1950–52 Headingley. *Appointments:* 1948–49 East Suffolk; 1949–50 Snaith, Yorks.; 1952–53 Barbados, Bethel; 1953–58 Barbados, James St.; 1958–59 Furlough; 1959 St. Lucia; 1960–65 Louth; 1965–69 Dunstable; 1969–77 Hunts. Mission; 1977– South London Mission. *Connexional Committees:* 1962–65 Overseas Missions, 1970– New Constitution. *Hobbies and Recreations:* Swimming, Photography.

WADDINGTON, George, 69 Norton Rd., Heysham, Morecambe Lancs LA3 1PF. (0524-51432) *b. 20 July 1919, Longwood, Huddersfield, Yorks. m. 21 Aug 1948: 1d., 1s.* *Education:* 1930–34 Royds Hall Grammar Sch., Huddersfield; 1935–39 Huddersfield Technical Coll.; 1945–47 Hartley Victoria. *Appointments:* 1947–48 Kimberley; 1948–49 Chorley; 1949–52 Liverpool Mission; 1952–57 Shrewsbury; 1957–64 Wolverhampton Trinity; 1964–72 Isles of Scilly; 1972–77 Paisley Mission; 1977– Morecambe and Heysham. *Connexional Committees:* 1967–76 Methodist Homes for the Aged. *Local Council Committees:* Isles of Scilly Council, Education; Welfare; Old People's Home; Library. *Special Interests:* The Lifeboat Service, Hon. Chaplain since 1964, at present also Station Committee Chairman (Morecambe). *Hobbies and Recreations:* Carpentry, Greenhouse, Gardening, Boating.

WADDY, John Leonard, 3 Southlands Court, South Terrace, Littlehampton, West Sussex BN17 5NX. (09064-5024) *b. 21 March 1906, Wakefield, Yorkshire. m. 7 Aug 1935: 3d.* *Education:* 1911–14 Coatbridge; 1914–18 Greenock Academy; 1918–22 Kingswood Sch.; 1922–24 Todmorden Secondary Sch.; 1928–29 Birmingham; 1928–31 Handsworth. *Appointments:* 1931–35 Chichester and Bognor; 1935–38 Gainsborough; 1938–41 Worksop (Wesley); 1941–46 North of Scotland Mission; 1946–50 Huddersfield (Buxton Rd.); 1950–56 Cardiff (Canton); 1956–63 Gravesend; 1963–68 Cardiff (Roath); 1968–72 Stafford; 1950–56 Free Church Chaplain to Rookwood Hospital, Cardiff; 1963–68 Chaplain Cardiff Prison; 1968–72 Stafford Prison; Member of Parole Board at Stafford Prison. *Connexional Committees:* 1947–50, 1953–56; 1960–63 Local Preachers. *Publications: The Bitter Sacred Cup (The Wednesday Riots of 1743–44)* (1976); *The Waddy Family* (1982). *Special Interests:* History, Genealogy. *Hobbies and Recreations:* Modern Languages (French, German, Norwegian), Hockey, Swimming.

WADE, Cyril George, 13 Ancaster Ave., Scartho, Grimsby, South Humberside DN33 3LH. (0472-73477) *b. 29 Oct 1913, Stamford, Lincolnshire. m. 28 Nov 1942: 1s.* *Education:* Stamford Blue Coats Sch., Love Lane Boys, Pontefract, Yorks; 1953–55 Handsworth. *Appointments:* 1953–55 Cradley Heath Christ Church, 1955–59 Ely; 1959–64 Scunthorpe; 1964–71 Ashton under Lyne; 1971–74 Cleethorpes; 1974–79 Alford. *Hobbies and Recreations:* Photography, Numismatics.

WADE, Garfield, 70 Flambard Ave., Christchurch, Dorset BH23 2NF. (0202-486875)–MA(Leeds). *b. 1 Sept 1911, Burnley, Lancs. m. 14 Aug 1939: 1d., 1s.* *Education:* 1919–22 Stoneyholme, Burnley; 1922–26 Todmorden Rd. Central, Burnley; 1942–45 Leeds Univ.; 1933–37 Headingley. *Appointments:* 1932–33 Matlock; 1937–39 Leeds, Headingley; 1939–46 Bradford, Woodhouse Grove; 1946–50 Liverpool Central; 1950–56 Leigh-on-Sea; 1956–63 Bournemouth; 1963–68 Exeter; 1968–76 Birmingham, Sutton Park. *Connexional Committees:* 1953–66 Local Preachers; Wesleyan Methodist Preachers Annuitant Society. *Hobbies and Recreations:* Gardening, Bees.

WADE, Kenneth Allan, 36 Woods Ave., Hatfield, Herts AL10 8NA. (07072-64929) *b. 21 Oct 1914, Boroughbridge, Yorks. m. 27 Dec 1937: 2d.* *Education:* Boroughbridge Jun. and Sen. Sch. *Appointments:* 1952–56 Holmfirth; 1956–62 Sunderland North; 1962–67 Jarrow; 1967–74 Durham; 1974–80 Danby. *Special Interests:* History, Biography. *Hobbies and Recreations:* Reading, Photography, Watching Sport, especially Cricket, Football.

WAGGETT, Ralph, 30 Manor Way, Beckenham, Kent BR3 3LJ. (01-658-6484)–MA. *b. 31 May 1921, Sunderland. m. 8 Aug 1952: 1d., 2s.* *Education:* 1926–32 Redby Sch.; 1932–39 Bede Grammar Sch.; 1939–42 Leeds Univ.; 1948–51 Cambridge; 1948–51 Wesley House. *Appointments:* 1946–48 Glasgow (Claremont St.); 1951–52 Coatbridge and Airdrie; 1952–55 Bedale; 1955–60 Hartlepool; 1960–65 Scunthorpe; 1965–68 Sunderland South; 1968–73 Holbeach; 1973–81 London, Forest Hill and Sydenham; 1981– Bromley.

Connexional Committees: Board of Property.
Hobbies and Recreations: Music, Gardening.

WAIGHTS, Kenneth Laws, 40 St. James, Shaftesbury, Dorset. (0747-3223) *b. 15 May 1909, Bournemouth. m. 1 Aug 1935.*
Education: George Watsons Coll., Edinburgh; 1928–31 Handsworth.
Appointments: 1931–33 Exeter; 1933–36 HM Comm.; 1936–40 Hastings; 1940–41 Liverpool, Brunswick; 1941–44 Liverpool Mission; 1944–48 Scarborough, Queen St.; 1948–57 Nottingham Mission; 1957–62 Bristol Mission; 1962–66 Sunderland South; 1966–74 Chairman Newcastle upon Tyne District; 1974–77 Shaftesbury and Gillingham, 1971 President of the Conference.
Local Council Committees: 1982–83 Mayor of Shaftesbury.

WAINE, William Ronald, 68 Goodison Boulevard, Gantley, Doncaster DN4 6DG. (0602-292581)–BD(Lond.). *b. 22 June 1933, Chilton, Co. Durham. m. 15 Feb 1958: 1d.*
Education: 1938–44 Chilton Prim. Sch., Co. Durham; 1944–49 Alderman Wraith Grammar Sch., Spennymoor; 1959–62 Headingley. *Appointments:* 1962–65 Amble and Alnwick; 1965–70 Ashington; 1970–82 Nottingham Mission; 1982– Doncaster.
Connexional Committees: 1965– Local Preachers' Studies Board.
Council Member: 1981–82 Chaplain to Nottinghamshire County Council.
Publications: Introducing the Old Testament (1974).
Special Interests: Old Testament Studies, Local Preachers' Training, Prison Chaplaincy. *Hobbies and Recreations:* Football, Golf, Gardening, Reading.

WAINWRIGHT, Cyril, 1 Home Park Rd., Wimbledon Park, London SW19 7HL. (01-946-1258)–BA, BD(Lond.). *b. 23 Sept 1905, Poynton, Cheshire. m. 1 Aug 1938: 1d., 1s.*
Education: 1909–17 St. George's CE; 1917–19 Stockport Commercial Sch.; 1929–32 Victoria Park.
Appointments: 1928–29 Peterborough; 1932–34 Sheffield, South St.; 1934–36 West Hartlepool; 1936–38 Tipton, Park Lane; 1938–44 Mansfield (A); 1944–49 Nottingham East; 1949–62 Tooting Mission; 1962–66 Chairman of W. Yorkshire District; 1965–76 Chairman, London South West District.
Connexional Committees: 1958–79 Property Board; 1958–82 Trustees for Methodist Church Purposes; 1957–62 Christian Citizenship; 1962–76 Home Mission; 1962–76 General Purposes; 1966–76 Ministerial Training; 1973–76 President's Council.
Special Interests: Secretary United Methodist Ministers' Annuitant Society. *Hobbies and Recreations:* Golf.

WAINWRIGHT, Thomas Haydn, Shalom, 3 Pinewood Place, Aberdeen AB1 8LT. (0224-324378) *b. 22 Jan 1915, Barry, South Wales. m. 30 Dec 1944: 2d.*
Education: 1920–30 Barry County Sch.; 1935–36 Cliff Coll.; 1938–40 Didsbury. *Appointments:* 1940–44 Newbury; 1944–45 Berwick-on-Tweed; 1945–46 Pickering; 1946–49 South Shields; 1949–54 Montrose; 1954–56 Glasgow (Shettleston); 1956–66 Falkirk; 1966–70 Edinburgh (Nicholson Sq.); 1970–77 North of Scotland (Aberdeen).
Local Council Committees: 1957–58 President Aberdeen Council of Churches. *Hobbies and Recreations:* Gardening.

WAINWRIGHT, William Malcolm, 2 Tanza Rd., Hampstead, London NW3 2UB. (01-435-6036)–MA(Oxon), BA(Cantab.). *b. 12 Feb 1931, Leeds. m. 17 Jan 1959: 2d., 2s.*
Education: 1935–41 Cross Featts Sch., Beeston, Leeds; 1941–50 Leeds Grammar Sch.; 1950–54 Pembroke Coll., Oxford; 1954–56 Wesley House. *Appointments:* 1957–62 Western Nigeria District; 1962–68 Immanuel Coll., Ibadan; 1968–72 Market Rasen and Caistor; 1972–79 Redcar, Saltburn and Guisborough; 1979– London Mission (North West).
Publications: Living Together (USCL Key Book).
Special Interests: More of a GP than a specialist. *Hobbies and Recreations:* Reading.

WAITE, William Morley, 20 Genesta Rd., Westcliff on Sea, Essex. (0702–353257) *b. 14 Oct 1902, Reading, Berks. m. 27 Oct 1932: 1d.*
Education: 1907–17 George Palmer Central Sch.; 1927–30 Richmond.
Appointments: 1926–27 Bishop's Stortford; 1930–34 British Guiana Dt.; 1934–35 Canterbury; 1935–36 Llandrindod Wells; 1936–39 Diss; 1939–42 Pontypool, Ely Valley; 1942–46 Sirhowy Valley; 1946–50 Downham Market; 1950–55 Ipswich, Museum St.; 1955–60 Marlborough; 1960–65 East Sussex Mission; 1965–80 Fakenham.
Connexional Committees: Overseas Mission.
Hobbies and Recreations: Painting and Other Art.

WAKEFIELD, George Greener, 2B Park Rd., Eccles, Manchester M30 9JJ. (061-789-1869) *b. 5 Sept 1928, Swalwell, Co. Durham. m. 15 Dec 1956: 1d., 2s.*
Education: Durston Hill Council Sch.; 1953–56 Hartley Victoria; 1956–57 St. Andrews, Selly Oak.
Appointments: 1957–63 Eastern Nigeria Dt; 1963–71 Oldham West; 1971–76 Hyde and Denton; 1976– Cadishead and Eccles.
Special Interests: Overseas Missions and Related Subjects, Pacifism.
Hobbies and Recreations: Orchestral Concerts, Choral Concerts.

WAKEFIELD, Gordon Stevens, The Queen's Coll., Edgbaston, Birmingham B15 2QH. (021-454-1527)–MA, M.Litt. *b. 15 Jan 1921, Crewe, Cheshire. m. 2 July 1948: 3d., 1s.*
Education: 1931 Elem. Sch. in Crewe; 1931–39 Crewe County Secondary Sch.; 1941 Univ. of Manchester; 1946–49 Univ. of Cambridge; 1946–49 Wesley House.
Appointments: 1944–46 London (Finchley and Hendon); 1949–52 Oxford; 1952–57 Stockport (South);

1957–61 Newcastle upon Tyne (Brunswick); 1961–63 Bristol (Ebenezer) 1963–72 Connexional Editor; 1971–79 Chairman, Manchester and Stockport District; 1979– Principal, The Queen's Coll., Birmingham.
Connexional Committees: 1962–76, 1981– Faith and Order; 1971–79 Home Mission; 1964–79 General Purposes; 1976– Ministerial Training; 1972–75 President's Council. *Local Council Committees:* 1974–79 City of Manchester Education Committee. *Publications: Puritan Devotion* (1957); *Methodist Devotion* (1966); *Unity at the Local Level* (with Hetley Price 1966); *On the Edge of the Mystery* (1969); *The Life of the Spirit in the World of Today* (1969); *Robert Newton Flew* (1971); *Fire of Love* (1979); *Crucifixion-Resurrection* by Hoskyns and Davey (Edited with Biographical, Introduction and Epilogue).
Special Interests: Spirituality, Liturgy, History of Ideas, Biography. *Hobbies and Recreations:* Watching and Thinking Cricket, Cathedrals and Churches.

WAKEFIELD, Harry, 103 Radnor Drive, Southport PR9 9QF. (0704-25722) *b. 4 Sept 1894, Audley, Staffs. m. 26 Aug 1925: 1d.*
Education: 1898–1906 Kidsgrove Elem. Sch.; 1922–23 Livingston Medical Coll.; 1920–23 Hartley.
Appointments: 1919–20 Gloucester and Cheltenham; 1923–34 Eastern Nigeria; 1934–37 Penrith; 1937–41 Liverpool, Everton Rd.; 1941–45 Liverpool Mission; 1945–50 Liverpool South; 1950–54 Blackpool South; 1954–60 Chairman Gambia District.
Connexional Committees: 1923–50 Missionary Committee.
Special Interests: Reading, Biography.

WAKEFIELD, Robert Gilhespie, 52 The Avenue, Durham DH1 4EB. (0385-47950) *b. 5 Sept 1928, Swalwell, Tyne and Wear. m. 24 Dec 1955: 2d., 1s.*
Education: 1933–34 Swalwell County Inf.; 1934–40 Dunston Hill County Jun.; 1940–45 Blaydon Grammar Sch.; 1952–55 Hartley Victoria. *Appointments:* 1951–52 St. Ives, Cornwall, Wesley; 1955–57 Kirkoswald; 1957–59 Port of Spain, Trinidad; 1959–62 Saint Lucia; 1964–67 Georgetown, Guyana; 1967–73 Consett; 1973–80 Redcar, Saltburn and Guisborough; 1980– Durham and Deerness Valley.
Connexional Committees: 1981–82 Overseas Division Central Committee.
Special Interests: Church Growth, The Ecumenical Movement. *Hobbies and Recreations:* Long Distance Walking, Gardening, Photography, Rotary.

WAKELING, Norman William, The Manse, Cockfield, Bishop Auckland, County Durham. BA(Manch.). *b. 27 May 1945, Paddington, London. m. 8 April 1972: 2d., 1s.*
Education: 1956–64 Owens Grammar Sch., Islington, London.; 1964–67 Westminster Coll., Oxford; 1972–75 Manchester Univ.
Appointments: 1975–80 Widnes; 1980– Bishop Auckland.
Special Interests: Church History and the Church Growth Movement.

WALES, Ian Harry, 3 Oakfield Rd. North., Ormesby, Middlesbrough, Cleveland TS3 6EL. (0642-245989) *b. 26 June 1952, Gosforth, Newcastle upon Tyne. s.*
Education: 1957–63 Newlands Preparatory Sch., Gosforth; 1963–68 Skerry's Coll. and Grammar Sch., Newcastle on Tyne; 1968–70 Gosforth Grammar Sch.; 1970–71 Cliff Coll.; 1975–79 Wesley Coll. Bristol. *Appointments:* 1979–81 Tipton; 1981– Middlesbrough and Eston.
Local Council Committees: 1980–81 Board of Governors of Mount Pleasant Jun./Infs. Sch., Coseley.
Special Interests: Use of Music/Drama in Church etc. *Hobbies and Recreations:* Music, Photography, Travel.

WALKER, Eric M., Fairmount, Wellington Rd., St. Saviour, Jersey C.I. *b. 13 Feb 1907, Newquay, Cornwall. m. 29 July 1938: 2d., 2s.*
Education: 1917–18 Hoe Grammar Sch., Plymouth; 1918–21 Truro Sch.; 1921–23 Victoria Coll., Jersey; 1930–31 Livingstone Coll., Leyton; 1927–30 Richmond. *Appointments:* 1931–38 Andros Bahamas; 1939–42 North Eleuthera, Bahamas; 1942–45 South Eleuthera, Bahamas; 1945–50 Jersey French; 1950–54 Tavistock; 1954–58 Penzance; 1958–63 Cheddar Valley; 1963–66 Ledbury; 1966–70 Jersey.
Connexional Committees: 1967–70 Home Missions.
Special Interests: Watercolour Painting, Walking.

WALKER, John Dennis, 10 Waltham Rd., Boscombe East, Bournemouth, Dorset BH7 6PE. (0202-424085)–BA(Leeds), MA(Manchester). *b. 9 March 1944, Swindon, Wilts. m. 8 Aug 1970: 2d.*
Education: 1954–57 Lewes County Grammar Sch. for Boys, Sussex; 1957–58 King Alfred's Grammar Sch., Wantage, Oxon; 1958–62 Weymouth Grammar Sch., Dorset; 1962–65 Leeds Univ.; 1965–67 Manchester Univ.; 1967–68 Austin Presbyterian Seminary, Texas; 1981 St. George's House, Windsor; 1965–67 Hartley Victoria. *Appointments:* 1967–68 World Council of Churches Exchange Student, Austin, Texas, U.S.A.; 1968–70 Southampton; 1970–75 Bramhall; 1975–81 Guildford; 1981– Bournemouth.
Connexional Committees: 1972–73 Secretary of President's Commission on Spirituality; 1974–81 Faith and Order; 1978–81 Hymnody; 1978–81 Transfer of Authority to Other Conferences; 1980– Ecumenical Committee; 1979– Vice-Chairman of Methodist Retreat Group. *Council Member:* 1977–81 Surrey Consultative Council of Churches; 1978–81 Member of Board, Wey Institute of Religious Studies. *Local Council Committees:* 1977–78 Chairman, Godalming Council of Churches. *Publications:* Article on Spirituality in *Epworth Review* (Jan 1974).
Special Interests: Retreat Conducting, Ministry of Healing, Industrial Chaplaincy. *Hobbies and Recreations:* Music–Organ Recitalist, Gardening.

WALKER, Michael Bryan, 71 Church St., Louth, Lincolnshire. (0507-603635)–BSc(Manch.), BD(Lond.). *b. 10 May 1934, Marple, Cheshire. m. 1960: 1d., 1s.* *Education:* 1939–45 Romley Council Prim.; 1945–52 Manchester Grammar; 1952–57 Manchester Univ.; 1957–60 Handsworth; 1960–61 St. Andrews. *Appointments:* 1961–62 Attleborough; 1962–66 Church of South India; 1966–67 Further Study; 1967–69 Stockport; 1969–72 Widnes; 1972–76 London Mission (Bow); 1976–80 London (Walthamstow and Chingford); 1980–82 Northwich; 1982– Louth. *Local Council Committees:* 1969–72 Youth Club Management; 1976–80 School Governors. *Publications:* Sundry articles especially in Indian publications (periodicals and journals), also in *Expository Times* and *Now*—all 1962–66. *Special Interests:* Social Concerns, Buildings, Education, Arts, Media, Politics and Economics, World Affairs. *Hobbies and Recreations:* Gardening, Walking, Photography, Art, Music, Cars, Nature, Modelling.

WALL, John Ambrose, 1 Oberon Close, Hartford, Huntingdon, Cambs PE18 7TB. (0480-53857) *b. 23 April 1921, London. m: 4d.* *Education:* Elem. and Grammar Schs., London. *Appointments:* 1952–57 Preston (Trinity); 1957–62 Lincoln (South); 1962–70 Hitchin; 1970–75 Banbury; 1975–79 London (Leytonstone and Forest Gate); 1979– Hunts Mission.

WALL, John H., 61 Cheviot View, Ponteland, Newcastle-upon-Tyne NE20 9BH. (0661-22057)–BSc(Dunelm). *b. 20 April 1933, Darlington, Co. Durham. m. 28 April 1962: 2d., 3s.* *Education:* 1941–51 Darlington Queen Elizabeth Grammar; 1951–55 Kings Coll., Newcastle Univ. of Durham; 1955–56 Leeds Univ.; 1963–65 Headingley. *Appointments:* 1959–63 Beccles, Loddon and Bungay; 1965–66 Norwich, St. Peter's; 1966–72 Bolsover and Staveley; 1972–77 Stockton; 1977–82 Newcastle West; 1982– Religious Broadcasting Producer, Radio; 1979–82 Tees. *Connexional Committees:* 1980– Radio and TV Standing Committee. *Special Interests:* Local Radio. *Hobbies and Recreations:* Electronics, Sailing.

WALLACE, Gilbert, 27 East Rd., Navenby, Lincoln LN5 0EP. (0522-810343) *b. 6 Aug 1906, Sheffield. m. 17 Aug 1932 (w.): 1d.* *Education:* 1918–22 Central Secondary Sch., Sheffield; 1926–29 Victoria Park. *Appointments:* 1929–31 Hicks Hill; 1931–32 Diss; 1932–33 Framlingham; 1933–35 Ipswich, Museum St.; 1935–39 Leeds West; 1939–41 Leeds, Brunswick; 1941–46 Chaplain HMF; 1946–50 Spilsby; 1950–54 Lincoln Wesley; 1954–60 Sleaford; 1960–65 Gainsborough; 1965–69 Barton-on-Humber. *Local Council Committees:* 1954–60 Lincolnshire (parts of Kesteven) Education Committee.

WALLBANK, William, 180 Bolton Rd., Kearsley, Bolton BL4 9BU. (0204-73598)–BA(Liverpool), BD(Manch.). *b. 1 Dec 1933, Southport. m. 25 July 1959: 1d.* *Education:* 1939–43 St. Stephens CE Sch., Banks, Southport; 1943–45 Churchtown Council Sch., Southport; 1945–52 Hutton Grammar Sch.; 1952–55 Liverpool Univ.; 1955–59 Manchester Univ.; 1955–59 Hartley Victoria. *Appointments:* 1959–61 Barnstaple; 1961–64 Liverpool North; 1964–70 St. Helens and Prescot; 1970–75 Altrincham; 1975–78 Manchester North and Middleton; 1978– Farnworth. *Connexional Committees:* 1972–75 Social Responsibility. *Special Interests:* Music, Organ, Piano, Singing, Local History. *Hobbies and Recreations:* The Countryside.

WALLER, Ralph, Chaplain's House, Westminster Coll., North Hinksey, Oxford OX2 9AT. (0865-240253)–MTh. *b. 11 Dec 1945, Scunthorpe, Lincolnshire. m. 28 Dec 1968.* *Education:* 1964 John Leggott Grammar Sch.; 1964–67 Westminster Coll.; 1973–75 Univ. of Nottingham (Part Time); 1978–81 Univ. of Durham (Member of Staff); 1979 King's Coll., Univ. of London; 1969–72 Richmond. *Appointments:* 1972–75 Melton Mowbray; 1975–81 Durham; 1978–81 Chaplain to St. Mary's and St. Aidan's Colls., Univ. of Durham; 1981– Chaplain of Westminster Coll. *Connexional Committees:* 1975–81 Divisional Board of Education and Youth; 1982– Family, Healing and Personal Concerns Committee (DSR); 1976– Student Work Committee. *Special Interests:* Nineteenth Century Church History, English and German Religious Thought. *Hobbies and Recreations:* Swimming, Walking, Reading.

WALLING, Michael John, 19 Petts Wood Rd., Orpington, Kent BR5 1JT. (0689-21956) *b. 6 May 1937, Bournemouth. m. 17 April 1965: 1d., 1s.* *Education:* 1948–53 Bournemouth Sch.; 1962–66 Didsbury, Bristol. *Appointments:* 1966–68 Poole; 1968–73 Southampton; 1973–78 Portsmouth and Southsea; 1978– Orpington. *Connexional Committees:* 1977– Ecumenical; 1970–80 DSR Politics and Economics Standing Committee; 1981– DSR Board; 1982– DSR Management Group. *Special Interests:* Graphic Arts, Natural History, Politics. *Hobbies and Recreations:* Watercolour Painting, Fishing, Walking.

WALLIS, Arthur Richard Ernest, Seaspray, 29 Walls Rd., Bembridge, IOW PO35 5RD. (098 387 2253) *b. 31 Aug 1902, Portsmouth, Hants. m. 6 Nov 1931: 1d., 2s.* *Education:* 1915–18 Portsmouth Secondary Sch. *Appointments:* 1957–67 S. India Church; 1942–46 Served with the Royal Indian Navy as Lt. Commander (Madras). *Connexional Committees:* 1957–65 Diocesan Treasurer, Tiruchy Dt; 1958 Ordained as Senior Candidate. *Council Member:* 1960–62 Moderator's Commissary for Tiruchy Dt, Church of South India. *Special Interests:* Music. *Hobbies and Recreations:* Gardening.

WALLWORK, Charles Norman Robert, 22 Melville Rd., Barnes, London SW13 9RJ. (01-748-4779) *b. 5 Jan 1946, Edinburgh. m. 27 July 1968: 1s.*
Education: 1957–64 Queen Elizabeth Grammar Sch., Penrith, Cumbria; 1964–67 Sunderland Coll. of Education; 1971–73 Birmingham Univ.; 1971–74 The Queen's Coll., Birmingham. *Appointments:* 1974–78 Frodsham; 1978– Richmond and Hounslow.
Connexional Committees: 1982– Methodist Ministers' Childrens' Committee. *Publications: Catholic Growth in Methodism* (1970 Ed); *A Book of Vestry Prayers* (1976); *Methodists at Prayer* (Ed 1981, 1982).
Special Interests: Methodist History, Liturgy and Worship, Methodist Sacramental Fellowship, Ecumenical Society of the Blessed Virgin Mary.
Hobbies and Recreations: Round Table, Travel, Queen's–Handsworth Association.

WALTON, Norman Dawson, 16 Kentwood Rd., Kendal, Cumbria LA9 5JX. (0539-32476) *b. 18 Oct 1911, North Walsham, Norfolk. m. 11 June 1946: 2d.*
Education: 1919–25 Norwich High Sch. for Boys; 1925–29 Winton Sch., Norwich; 1931–34 Handsworth.
Appointments: 1934–36 President's List; 1936–38 Ripley, Wesley; 1938–43 Bournemouth; 1943–46 Pontypool, Eastern Valley; 1946–52 Norwich, St. Peter's; 1952–55 Luton; 1955–58 Alford; 1958–68 Carlisle; 1968–76 Clitheroe.
Connexional Committees: 1970–74 Local Preachers' Committee.
Hobbies and Recreations: Walking, Wild Flowers, Parish Churches.

WALTON, Roger Leonard, 20 Kenton Rd., Halewood, Liverpool L26 9TS. (051-486-1204)–BA, BSc. *b. 5 April 1953, Otley, Yorkshire. m. 27 July 1975: 1d.*
Education: 1960–64 Francis St. Jun. Sch.; 1964–69 Priesthope Sch.; 1969–71 Salt Grammar Sch.; 1971–74 Univ. of Newcastle-upon-Tyne; 1974–77 Univ. of Birmingham; 1974–78 Queen's. *Appointments:* 1979– Liverpool (South).
Special Interests: Youth Work in all Forms, Theological Thinking.
Hobbies and Recreations: Table Tennis, Wine Making, Reading, Films.

WARBURTON, Geoffrey James, 85 Victoria Rd., Fulwood, Preston PR2 4NL. (0772-719144) *b. 9 July 1930, Poynton, Cheshire. m. 28 March 1959: 1d., 1s.*
Education: 1941–48 Stockport Sch.; 1955–59 Hartley Victoria.
Appointments: 1954–55 Home Mission Caravans; 1959–63 Morpeth and Bedlington; 1963–68 Wigan, Standishgate; 1968–74 Leeds, Richmond Hill; 1974–81 Harrogate; 1981– Preston, Trinity.
Special Interests: Churches Ministry of Healing. *Hobbies and Recreations:* Numismatics, Gardening, Photography.

WARD, Frank, Royal House, Gill, Dalston, Carlisle, Cumbria CA5 7JP. (0228-710598) *b. 3 April 1898, Darfield, Yorks. m. 19 June 1928: 2s.*
Education: Darfield Council; 1923–25 Hartley. *Appointments:* 1921–23 Appleby; 1925–27 Crowle; 1927–28 Brough; 1928–31 Goole; 1931–35 Bristol, Eastville; 1935–38 Doncaster, Spring Gardens; 1938–42 Ryton and Prudhoe; 1942–47 Consett; 1947–50 Newcastle West; 1950–55 Penrith; 1955–58 Ashington; 1958–64 Carlisle.

WARD, Harold William, 28 Hibbert Close, Rugby, Warwicks CV22 6DS. (0788-76929) *b. 29 Sept 1922, Rotherham, Yorks. m. 20 Aug 1949: 1d.*
Education: 1934–39 Rotherham Grammar Sch.; 1947–49 Handsworth.
Appointments: 1949–61 Bahamas Dt; 1961–64 Loughborough; 1964–71 Bahamas Dt; 1971–77 High Wycombe; 1977– Rugby and Daventry.
Special Interests: Methodist Revival Fellowship. *Hobbies and Recreations:* Philately.

WARD, John Henry, Arrabona, 225 Nottingham Rd., Mansfield, Nottinghamshire NG18 4SE. (0623-21494) *b. 11 Aug 1937, York. m. 4 April 1964: 2d., 2s.*
Education: 1942–49 New Earswick Jun. Sch., York; 1949–50 Archbishop Holgate's Grammar Sch., York; 1950–54 Nunthorpe Grammar Sch., York; 1954–56 York Coll. of Art (Part-time); 1956–58 Lincoln Coll. of Art (Part-time); 1958–59 York Coll. of Art (Part-time); 1960–64 Hartley Victoria. *Appointments:* 1964–68 Derby Mission; 1968–71 London, Finsbury Park and Southgate; 1971–78 Blackburn (Central Mission); 1978–82 Mansfield (West); 1982– Mansfield Mission.
Council Member: 1982–83 Chaplain to the Chairman of Mansfield District Council. *Local Council Committees:* 1978– School Governor, High Oakham Middle Sch., Mansfield.
Special Interests: Renewal in the Church, Revival in the Nation.
Hobbies and Recreations: Art, Architecture, Railway History, Scenic Modelling (Model Railways), Gardening, Walking/Hiking.

WARD, John Michael, 22 Windsor Sq., Exmouth, Devon EX8 1JY. (03952-3550) *b. 1 June 1933, Hastings. m. 4 July 1962: 2d., 2s.*
Education: The Leys, Cambridge; 1958–62 Didsbury, Bristol.
Appointments: 1962–64 Bude; 1964–69 Ilfracombe; 1969–76 Birmingham Wesley and Astbury; 1976– Exmouth, Budleigh Salterton.
Connexional Committees: 1966–69 DSR.
Special Interests: Community Relations, Pastoral Psychology.
Hobbies and Recreations: Badminton, Swimming, Sailing, Numismatics, DIY.

WARD, Joseph Neville, 66 Mount Rd., Canterbury, Kent CT1 1YF. (0227-61125)–MA, BD. *b. 17 April 1915, Oxenhope, Yorkshire. m. 24 Jan 1942: 2s.*
Education: 1927–34 Kingswood, Bath; 1934–37 Exeter Coll., Oxford; 1937–40 Manchester Univ.; 1937–40 Hartley Victoria. *Appointments:* 1940–41 Bradford, Greenhill; 1941–

43 Kendal; 1943–44 Scarborough Jubilee; 1944–47 Morcambe and Heysham; 1947–50 Blackburn, Clayton St.; 1950–58 Bromley, Kent; 1956–62 Purley; 1962–67 London Mission, Hinde St.; 1967–74 Bath; 1974–78 Canterbury.
Publications: The Use of Praying; Five for Sorrow Two for Joy; Friday Afternoon; The Following Plough; Beyond Tomorrow; Contributor: *Doing Theology.*
Hobbies and Recreations: Music Gardening.

WARD, William Robert, The Mount, Sturminster Newton, Dorset DT10 2DG. (0258-72385) *b. 25 May 1924, High House, Firbank, Nr. Kendal, Cumbria. m. 25 July 1953: 2d., 1s.*
Education: 1929–38 Lowgill Sch.; 1948–51 Hartley Victoria.
Appointments: 1947–48 South Devon Mission; 1951–53 Cardiff (Canton); 1953–55 Whitehaven; 1955–58 Ramsey (IOM); 1958–61 Chorley; 1961–64 Ilfracombe; 1972–76 Helston; 1976–82 Stour Valley (Dorset).
Hobbies and Recreations: Gardening, Listening to Music, Reading, Walking.

WARDEN, Rodney Edward, The Manse, 15 Portland St., Whitwell, Worksop, Notts S80 4RJ. (0909-720494) *b. 5 Feb 1944, Dulwich, London SE. m. 7 Aug 1971: 4s.*
Education: 1947–52 Oliver Goldsmiths County Inf. Sch.; 1952–55 St. Pauls Wood Hill County Prim. Sch.; 1955–57 Alma Rd. County Secondary Sch.; 1957–60 East Lane County Secondary Sch.; 1966–67 Cliff Coll.; 1968–71 Richmond.
Appointments: 1972 Brinkworth; 1974–78 Lincoln North; 1978–81 Pateley Bridge; 1981– Worksop and Kiveton.
Special Interests: Hospital Chaplaincy, Rural Area Ministries.
Hobbies and Recreations: Tropical Fish.

WAREING, Thomas Roy, 9 Gypsy Lane, Warminster, Wilts BA12 9LR. (0985-213707)–BD(Lond.). *b. 20 June 1923, Rochdale, Lancs. m. 14 Aug 1954: 2s.*
Education: 1934–40 Manchester Grammar Sch.; 1940–42 Rochdale Technical Coll.; 1942–43 Manchester Coll. of Technology; 1950–53 Handsworth. *Appointments:* 1949–50 Stone (HM); 1953–54 Leominster; 1954–57 Tamworth; 1957–62 Harpenden; 1962–69 Windsor and Maidenhead; 1969–74 Purley; 1974–82 Weston-super-Mare; 1982– Trowbridge (Meth/URC).
Connexional Committees: 1959–62 Christian Citizenship; 1980–82 Social Responsibility.
Special Interests: Church Order, Christian Leadership. *Hobbies and Recreations:* Photography, Gardening.

WARING, Ernest James, Anglezark, 34 Greenover Rd., Brixham, S. Devon TQ5 9NA. (080-45-3555) *b. 6 April 1900, Chester. m. 6 April 1942: 2d., 1s.*
Education: All Saints Hoole and Love Street, Chester; 1924–26 Hartley Victoria. *Appointments:* 1926–29 Bishop Auckland; 1929–30 Chesterfield I; 1930–32 Hull IV; 1932–33 Bradford II and Great Horton; 1934–37 Cleckheaton; 1937–40 Bradford Woodhouse Grove; 1940–41 Bradford, Low Moor; 1941–46 Newmarket Mission; 1946–50 Bloxwich Pinfold; 1950–54 Calne; 1954–59 Liverpool Central and NE; 1959–61 Walkden; 1961–64 Worsley; 1964–65 Great Harwood.
Hobbies and Recreations: Motoring, Reading.

WARMAN, Noel Leslie Philip, 14 Garfield Rd., Ryde, Isle of Wight PO33 2PT. (0983-62029)–BA, RIBA. *m. 1960: 1d., 1s.*
Education: Kingston Sch. of Art; Bristol Univ.; 1952–55 Didsbury, Bristol. *Appointments:* 1951–52 Cheltenham; 1955–64 Ghana Dt; 1964–69 Newark; 1969–73 Rhodesia Dt; 1973–80 Sheffield, Carver St.; 1980– East Wight.
Connexional Committees: 1964–69, 1974–80 Overseas Division Central Committee; 1966–69 Property Division Central Committee; 1982– MHA General Committee.

WARNE, Harry, 40 Pennine Way, Chesterfield, Derbyshire S40 4NF. (0246-74481)–BD(Lond.) *b. 15 April 1923, Darlington, Co. Durham. m. 11 Aug 1951: 3s.*
Education: 1937–41 Darlington Technical Coll.; 1945–49 Headingley.
Appointments: 1949–51 Manchester (Pendleton); 1951–56 Manchester (South East); 1956–62 Douglas (Victoria); 1962–67 Bramhall; 1967–72 Brighton and Hove; 1972–77 Worthing; 1977–82 Mansfield (Bridge St.); 1982– Chesterfield.
Connexional Committees: 1957–61 Memorials Committee; 1971–72 Division of Education and Youth Working Party 'Commitment Amongst Children' which finally issued the report adopted by Conference; 1973 'Children and the Holy Communion'. *Publications:* Contributions to *Partners in Learning* within the following themes: *We Explore God's World* (Jnrs 1974–75); *God's Chosen People; Mission To and From the Caribbean* (YP); *Wonderful Creation* (J 1975–76); *Adventurous Living* (Seniors 1976–77); *Community of Faith* (1978 Snrs).
Special Interests: International and Political Affairs, Mission, Theology, Preaching, Science and Evolution, Christian Education. *Hobbies and Recreations:* Film Making and Photography, Foreign Travel, Cricket.

WARNER, Raymond, 3 St. David's Ave., Romiley, Cheshire SK6 3JT. (061-494-8263) *b. 12 July 1916, Berkeley, Gloucestershire. m. 9 June 1956: 1s.*
Education: 1924–32 Cliftonville Coll., Margate; 1940–41 Richmond; 1941–42 Hartley Victoria; 1942–43 Headingley. *Appointments:* 1943–55 Leeward Islands Dt (West Indies); 1955–56 Methodist International House, Bayswater, London; 1956–61 Leeds, Headingley; 1961–66 Norwich (St. Peters); 1966–73 Sandbach and Alsager; 1973–78 Manchester, Withington; 1978–82 Romiley.

WARRELL, Alan, 24 Sedlescombe Rd. South, St. Leonards on Sea, East Sussex TN38 0TA. (0424-423408)–

03.06.13

BA(Lond.), MA(Camb.). *b. 3 July 1930, Streatham, London SW2. m. 1 Jan 1959: 1d., 2s.*
Education: 1942–49 Tiffin Boys, Kingston upon Thames; 1949–54 Univ. Coll., Leicester; 1954–56 Wesley House. *Appointments:* 1957–63 Eastern Nigeria Dt; 1963–68 Didsbury South; 1968–73 Wolverhampton Trinity; 1973–78 Kent Coll., Pembury, Chaplain; 1978– Hastings, Bexhill and Rye.
Connexional Committees: 1979– Board of Division of Education and Youth. *Publications: IBRA Bible Notes.*
Special Interests: Children's Work.
Hobbies and Recreations: Philately, Gardening.

WARREN, Clifford William, 2 Beacon Close, Park Gate, Southampton SO3 7AR. (048-95-84060)—AIB. *b. 25 April 1935, Luton, Beds. m. 20 June 1959: 1d., 2s.*
Education: 1945–52 Luton Grammar Sch.; 1967–69 Richmond.
Appointments: 1969–73 Loughborough; 1973–78 Southampton; 1978– Area Secretary (Southampton) Christian Aid.
Connexional Committees: 1982 Division of Social Responsibility's Committee on International Relief and Development Affairs. *Local Council Committees:* 1966–67 Chairman, Southampton Council of Churches.
Special Interests: World Development, Human Rights.
Hobbies and Recreations: Sport, Golf, Tennis, Walking, Reading.

WARREN, Ernest Edward, 1 Mount Pleasant, The Rise, Kingsdown, Deal, Kent CT14 8BE. (03045-4948) *b. 20 Sept 1916, Potton, Bedfordshire. m. 15 Aug 1942: 2s.*
Education: 1919–30 Pottom, Bedfordshire; 1938–39 Cliff Coll.; 1945–47 Richmond. *Appointments:* 1947–50 Hunstanton and Docking; 1950–54 London Mission South East; 1954–59 London Mission East; 1959–64 London, Wanstead and Forest Gate; 1964–69 London, Walthamstow; 1969–76 London Mission, Plumstead; 1976–81 London Mission SE.

WARREN, John Francis, 16 Gainsborough Ave., St. Albans, Herts AL1 4NL. (0727-51834)—BD(Lond.). *b. 5 June 1934, Nottingham. m. 6 Aug 1960: 1d., 1s.*
Education: 1939–44 Scotland Rd. (Inf. and Jun.) Nottingham; 1944–45 The Ellis Sch. for Boys, Nottingham; 1945–51 The High Pavement Grammar Sch. for Boys, Nottingham; 1954–58 Wesley, Headingley.
Appointments: 1958–63 Retford; 1963–68 Lincoln (South); 1968–70 Runcorn; 1970–74 Colchester; 1974–81 Barnet; 1981– St. Albans; 1981– Secretary of the London NW District.
Connexional Committees: 1980– The London Committee (HM Division).
Hobbies and Recreations: Railway History, Steam Preservation, Model Railways, Singing, Music.

WARWICK, Frederick Stanley, 79 Park Avenue North, Northampton, NN3 2HX. (0604-717076) *b. 10 Feb 1916, Northampton. m. 28 Dec 1946: 1d., 2s.*
Education: 1921–27 Stimpson Ave. Elemen.; 1927–32 Northampton Town & County Grammar Sch.; 1946–47 Handsworth.
Appointments: 1945 Lincoln (Supply); 1945–46 Belper; 1947–50 Gateshead West; 1950–55 Skegness; 1955–58 Pontypool; 1958–62 March and Chatteris; 1962–68 Diss; 1968–73 Stewkley (1973–75 Joint with Leighton Buzzard); 1975–81 Biggleswade.
Special Interests: Counselling.
Hobbies and Recreations: Photography.

WASHBROOK, Alan James, 12 Victoria Cresc., Queen's Park, Chester CH4 7AX. (0244-675967)—BA. *b. 31 Jan 1939, Sutton Coldfield. m. 26 Aug 1966: 2s.*
Education: 1950–58 Bishop Vesey's Grammar Sch.; 1958–60 Westminster Coll., London and Oxford; 1962–65 Univ. of Leeds; 1962–65 Wesley, Headingley. *Appointments:* 1965–67 Durham; 1967–77 Nigeria Dt; 1977–82 Stevenage; 1982– Chester.
Special Interests: Pastoral Care and Worship. *Hobbies and Recreations:* Painting in Oils, Swimming, Passenger Transport, Walking.

WATERFIELD, Eric John, 11 Hall Close, Kettering, Northants NN15 7LQ. (0536-85690) *b. 13 Oct 1926, Thrapston, Northants. m. 6 Sept 1956: 2d.*
Education: 1931–36 Thrapston Council Sch.; 1936–41 Leicester Wyggeston Boys Grammar Sch.; 1951–54 Richmond. *Appointments:* 1954–57 Towcester; 1957–62 Sheffield South; 1962–66 Bristol, Bedminster; 1966–74 Swindon; 1974–80 Milton Keynes; 1980– Kettering and Corby.
Hobbies and Recreations: Walking, Motoring, Gardening.

WATERFIELD, Paul Trevor, Wesley Manse, 37 High St., Epworth, Doncaster, S. Yorks DN9 1EP. (0427-872319) *b. 20 Sept 1930, Bathley, Newark, Notts. m. 23 June 1956: 3s.*
Education: 1942–47 Magnus Grammar Sch.; 1950–51 Cliff Coll.; 1953–56 Handsworth.
Appointments: 1952–53 Cheddar Valley; 1956–62 Bahamas Dt; 1962–64 Spilsby; 1964–69 Matlock; 1969–72 Port Talbot; 1972–81 Retford; 1981– Epworth and Crowle.
Special Interests: Country Life.
Hobbies and Recreations: Gardening, Chess.

WATERHOUSE, Alfred, 32 Greenacres, Wick Lane, Downton, Salisbury, Wiltshire SP5 3NG. (994-20184) *b. 27 March 1905, Ancoats, Manchester. m. 22 Feb 1947: 1d., 1s.*
Education: 1910–16 St. Philips, Bradford Rd. CE; 1916–18 Manchester, Birley St., Higher Grade; 1927–28 Richmond; 1928–30 Didsbury. *Appointments:* 1930–32 Pateley Bridge, Cadishead; 1932–35 Spalding Broad St.; 1935–39 Manchester and Salford Mission; 1939–43 Linacre Mission, Liverpool; 1943–46 Chaplain HMF; 1946–48 Hungerford; 1948–51 Oldham Wesley; 1951–55 Liverpool, Anfield;

1955–57 Liverpool NE; 1957–60 Show and Royton; 1960–67 Haverfordwest and Milford Haven; 1967–70 Salisbury.
Hobbies and Recreations: Reading, Walking, Music, Gardening.

WATERHOUSE, John Malcolm, 3 Beechwood Ave., Coventry CV5 6DF. (0203-73036)–MA(Cantab.), BD(Lond.). *b. 19 March 1932, Halifax (Yorkshire). m. 16 Aug 1958: 1d.*
Education: 1943–48 Manchester Grammar Sch.; 1949–50 Plymouth Coll.; 1950–53 St. Catherine's Coll., Cambridge Univ.; 1953–56 London Univ.; 1953–56 Richmond.
Appointments: 1956–58 Attleborough; 1958–63 Leeds (Richmond Hill); 1963–68 Sheffield North-East; 1968–75 Carlisle; 1975–82 Elland and Greetland; 1982– Coventry.
Connexional Committees: 1972– Connexional Candidates Examining Committee; 1977–82 Division of Ministries Board. *Publications: Beware the Church* (Editor 1968). *Special Interests:* Tutor-Counselling (Open Univ.). *Hobbies and Recreations:* Reading, Singing, Travel.

WATERMAN, David Leonard Ralph, 1 Snape Drive, Great Horton Rd., Bradford 7, West Yorkshire BD7 4LZ. (0274-571670)–BA(Bristol). *b. 31 May 1936, Ilford, Essex. m. 3 Aug 1963: 3s.*
Education: 1941–45 Heatherlands Jun. Sch., Parkstone, Dorset; 1945–47 Cleveland Rd. Jun. Sch., Ilford, Essex; 1947–55 Ilford County High Sch. for Boys, Barkingside, Ilford, Essex; 1959–61 Edinburgh Univ.; 1961–64 Bristol Univ.; 1976–77 Stirling Univ.; 1961–64 Didsbury, Bristol.
Appointments: 1964–67 Glasgow, Parkhead and Burnbank; 1967–81 Falkirk, Wallacestone and Stirling; 1981– Bradford, Great Horton.
Local Council Committees: 1970–75 Chairman Stirling Burgh Children's Panel; 1975–77 Chairman Central Region Children's Panel.
Special Interests: Sociology, Psychology, Criminology, Univ. and Sch. Chaplain 14 years, Marriage Guidance Counsellor and Chairman Central Scotland MGC, 8 years Social Worker in Dept of Child and Family Psychiatry. *Hobbies and Recreations:* Cricket, Stirling County and Stirling Univ. Staff XI, Music, Reading, Art–Oil Painting and Cartoon.

WATKIN, Gilbert, Methodist Manse, Town Centre, Peterlee, Co. Durham SR8 1AD. (0783-862525) *b. 8 Jan 1918, Buxton, Derbyshire. m. 5 June 1950: 1d.*
Education: 1923–32 Kents Bank Boy's Sch., Buxton; 1945–47 Hartley Victoria. *Appointments:* 1944–45 HM Forces; 1947–50 Berwick on Tweed; 1950–51 Redcar, Saltburn and Guisborough; 1951–56 Armble; 1956–59 Redcar, Saltburn and Guisborough; 1959–62 Sunderland West; 1962–66 Coatbridge and Airdrie; 1966–73 South Bank and Eston; 1973–80 Durham and Dearness Valley; 1980– Durham Coast and Peterlee.
Council Member: 1967–68 Chaplain to Chairman of Eston Urban District Council.
Hobbies and Recreations: Music.

WATKINS, David Albert, 41 Lawn Heads Ave., Littleover, Derby DE3 6DR. (0332-42814) *b. 23 May 1930, Romford. m. 5 April 1975: 1d.*
Education: 1935–41 Albert Rd. Inf. and Jun. St. Edwards Jun. Sch.; 1941–46 Leyton County High Sch. (Boys); 1958–62 Richmond. *Appointments:* 1962–63 Aylesham; 1963–68 North Walsham; 1968–73 Buckingham and Brackley; 1973–82 Rotherham.
Special Interests: Evangelism, Holy Spirit Renewal, including Divine Healing, Personal Counselling.
Hobbies and Recreations: Gardening, Walking, Interest in Sport.

WATKINSON, Peter, 32 The Chine, Saltburn-by-the-Sea, Cleveland TS12 1QL. (0287-22335)–BA.
Education: 1952–55 Headingley.
Appointments: 1951–52 Glasgow, Claremont St.; 1955–57 Stamford; 1957–61 Melton Mowbray; 1962–65 Bolsover; 1965–69 Witney and Faringdon; 1969–74 Leicester (North); 1974–82 Ashfield; 1982– Redcar, Saltburn and Guisborough.
d. 27.12.85

WATSON, David Wilfred, 113 Elsdon Ave., Seaton Delaval, Whitley Bay, Tyne and Wear NE25 0JL. (0632-371527) *b. 7 Nov 1944, Middlesbrough. m. 26 Aug 1973: 1d., 2s.*
Education: –1958 Green Lane Prim. Sch., Middlesbrough; 1958–63 Stainsby Boys Sch., Middlesbrough; 1967–71 Hartley Victoria.
Appointments: 1971–73 Elland and Greetland; 1973–79 Blyth and Seaton Delaval; 1979– Blyth Valley.
Connexional Committees: 1981– Board of Property.
Special Interests: Finance, Building.
Hobbies and Recreations: Methodist History, Football, Sports.

WATSON, Edward, 30 Cleveland Ave., Bishop Auckland, Co. Durham DL14 6AR. (0388-603460) *b. 27 Sept 1937, Orton, Westmoreland. m. 28 March 1964: 2s.*
Education: 1942–49 Orton Prim. Sch.; 1949–54 Appleby Grammar Sch.; 1961–65 Headingley.
Appointments: 1965–67 Welshpool; 1967–74 Workington; 1974–80 Liverpool North; 1980– Bishop Auckland.
Hobbies and Recreations: Building, Engineering.

WATSON, John T., 16 Beverington Rd., Eastbourne, Sussex BN21 2SD. (0323-29838)–BA(Lond.), DD(Buchanan, USA), LTCL, FLCM. *b. 13 Jan 1904, Sutton Bridge. m. 3 May 1933: 2d., 3s.*
Education: Moulton Grammar Sch.; 1922–24 Westminster Training Coll.; 1926–29 Didsbury.
Appointments: 1929–34 French West Africa Dt; 1934–35 Kilburn and Hampstead; 1935–38 Plymouth; 1938–46 Kilburn and Hampstead; 1946–69 British and Foreign Bible Society.
Connexional Committees: Overseas General Committee. *Publications: Seen Heard in Dahomey* (1934); *How to Play a Hymn Tune* (1950); *Daily Prayers for the Methodist Church* (1951, 52, 53, 55, 57);

Intercessions for Methodists (1975); 2 Anthems.
Special Interests: Music. *Hobbies and Recreations:* Music Composition.

WATSON, Philip Saville, 60 Court Ave., Old Coulsdon, Surrey CR3 1HE. (07375-54675)–MA(Durham), MA, DD(Camb.), DD(Glasgow), Hon DD(Ohio Wesleyan). *b. 15 Oct 1909, Idle, Bradford, Yorks. m. 30 June 1942: 1d., 1s.*
Education: 1914–21 Thorp Sch., Idle; 1921–28 Bradford Grammar Sch.; 1928–31 St. John's Coll., Durham; 1931–34 Fitzwilliam House, Cambridge; 1934–35 Univ. of Tübingen; 1935–36 Univ. of Lund; 1931–34 Wesley House.
Appointments: 1936–39 Assistant Tutor, Headingley Coll.; 1939–44 Paisley Mission; 1944–46 Bristol, Clifton; 1946–55 Tutor in Systematic Theology and Philosophy of Religion, Handsworth Coll.; 1955–59 Tutor in Systematic and Pastoral Theology, Wesley House; 1959–73 Rall Professor of Systematic Theology, Garrett Theological Seminary, Evanston, Illinois.
Publications: The State as a Servant of God (SPCK 1946); *Let God be God* (the Fernley-Hartley Lecture for 1947, Epworth 1947, Muhlenberg 1948, Fortress paperback 1970); *Neoplatonism and Christianity* (Transactions of the Victoria Institute, vol. lxxxvii, 1955); *The Concept of Grace* (Epworth, Muhlenberg 1959); *The Message of the Wesleys* (Macmillan, Epworth 1964, Asbury Coll., 1983); (trans.) *A. Nygren, Agape and Eros* (1938–39, rev. edn 1953, Harper paperback 1970); *Essence of Christianity* (1960, Eerdmanns paperback 1973); *Meaning and Method* (Epworth, Fortress 1972) (trans. and ed.) *Luther's Commentary on Galatians* (Jas. Clarke, Revell, 1953); *The Bondage of the Will* (Concordia 1972); *Luther and Erasmus* (SCM Westminster 1969); (contrib.) *The Catholicity of Protestantism* (1950); *Lutherforschung Heute* (1958); *World Lutheranism of Today* (1960); *The Christian Replies* (1960); *The Doctrine of the Church* (1964); *A Dictionary of Christian Theology* (1969); and numerous journals.
Special Interests: The Charismatic Movement.

WATSON, Reginald Bliss, 6 Village Close, Kirby Cross, Frinton-on-Sea CO13 0PF.–BA(Canada). *b. 11 March 1922, Snider Mt., Kings Co., NB Canada. m. 30 March 1948: 1d., 2s.*
Education: Lower Millstream, Inf.; Lower Millstream Prim.; Sussex High Sch.; 1940–41, 1941–42, 1945–46 Acadia Univ., Canada; 1946–47 Edinburgh Univ.; 1947–48 Basel Univ.; Zurich Univ.; 1942–43 Mount Allison Univ., Canada. *Appointments:* 1946–72 American Baptist Church; 1972–73 Loftus and Staithes; 1973–77 Manchester Mission; 1977–82 Coningsby.
Publications: Lectures at Hartwick Univ., Onconta, NY, USA.
Special Interests: Travel, Gardening, Interior Decorating. *Hobbies and Recreations:* Reading, Music, Stamp Collecting, Coin Collecting.

WATSON, Roy Morgan, 6 Heathfield Drive, Barry, S. Glam CF6 7UG. (0446-735613)–BA. *b. 28 June 1939, Barry. m. 18 Aug 1962: 1d., 2s.*
Education: 1944–51 Gladstone Prim. and Jun. Sch.; 1951–58 Barry Boys Grammar; 1958–62 Univ. Coll., Cardiff; 1964–67 Didsbury, Bristol. *Appointments:* 1967– Barry.
Special Interests: The Church on Council Housing Estates, The Church and The Working Classes. *Hobbies and Recreations:* Football Referee, Welsh Football Association, Table Tennis, Cricket.

WATSON, Victor John, 54 Camberwell Rd., London SE5 0EN. (01-703-2477)–BD(Lond.). *b. 15 Oct 1928, Manchester. m. 5 Jan 1956: 1d., 2s.*
Education: 1938–44 Chorlton High Sch. for Boys; Wesley, Headingley.
Appointments: 1954–56 Bedale; 1957–65 Panama/Costa Rica; 1965–71 Manchester SE; 1971–77 London NW; 1977– London Mission (Clubland).
Connexional Committees: 1966–69 MMS; 1970– DSR (Community Relations Methodist Relief Fund); 1978– NGH (Fund for Human Need).
Council Member: Freedman of City of Colon, Panama; Master Keyholder of Panama Canal Zone; Commander of the Order of Vasconunez De Balboa, Republic of Panama.
Special Interests: Police/Community Relations, Unemployment. *Hobbies and Recreations:* Music, Reading, Organ, Piano.

WATTS, Francis Ernest, 16 Dover Rd., Wanstead, London E12 5EA. (01-989-5362) *b. 11 Aug 1923, Lambeth. m. 20 Aug 1955: 1s.*
Education: 1929–38 Garden City Boys Sch., Woodford Bridge, Essex; 1946–48 Cliff Coll.; 1949–52 Handsworth. *Appointments:* 1948–49 Camelford and Wadebridge; 1952–55 Newbury; 1955–58 Leicester South; 1958–64 Aldershot and Farnborough; 1964–69 Wolverton and Bletchley; 1969–76 High Wycombe; 1976– Leytonstone and Forest Gate.
Special Interests: History, National and Methodist, Church Architecture, Pre-Roman Britain. *Hobbies and Recreations:* Ornithology, Rambling, Gardening.

WEARING, George Michael, 20 Bowers Way, Harpenden, Herts AL5 4EW. (05827-2431)–BA(Leeds), MA(Leeds), BD(Manch.). *b. 25 April 1936, Scarborough, Yorkshire. m. 31 July 1963: 1d., 1s.*
Education: Gladstone Rd., Scarborough, Inf. and Jun. Sch.; Scarborough Coll.; Leeds Univ.; Manchester Univ.; 1961–63 Hartley Victoria. *Appointments:* 1963–69 Blackpool (North); 1969–74 Harrogate; 1974–81 Preston (Trinity); 1981– Harpenden; 1979–81 North Lancashire District Synod Secretary.
Connexional Committees: Local Preachers; Local Preachers Study Board (past); Division of Ministries; General Purposes (present); Faith and Order; National Childrens' Home (General Committee).
Hobbies and Recreations: Sport, Travel, Caravanning.

WEARY, Stanley Maurice, 20 De Merley Rd., Morpeth, Northumberland NE61 1HZ. (0670-513650) *b. 28 July 1928, Finchley. m. (2) 22 Oct 1977: 1d., 1s.*
Education: 1939–46 Harrow County Sch.; 1950–53 Handsworth.
Appointments: 1949 Buckingham and Brackley; 1953–55 Banbury; 1955–60 Watford; 1960–65 Cleethorpes; 1965–73 Preston (Lune St. and Orchard); 1973–82 Kingston upon Thames; 1982– Morpeth.

WEATHERILL, George William, 7 Sussex Way, Darlington, Co. Durham DL1 2LQ. (0325-61919) *b. 19 Dec 1902, Heworth-on-Tyne. m. 9 Aug 1933: 1d.*
Education: 1907–16 Coundon CE; 1926–29 Hartley Victoria.
Appointments: 1929–33 London, Balham; 1933–35 Hull (Fountain Rd.); 1935–40 Sunderland SE; 1940–47 Scarborough (St. Sepulchre St.); 1947–54 Darlington S; 1954–59 Walkden; 1959–64 Morecambe; 1964–69 Sale.
Connexional Committees: 1943–47 Christian Citizenship. *Publications: The Story of Darlington Methodism 1753-1953.*
Hobbies and Recreations: Woodwork.

WEATHERSPOON, Alan, 7 Priory Rd., Linlithgow, West Lothian EH49 6BP. (050-684-4855)–BA, BD.
Education: 1957–63 Manchester Univ.; 1957–63 Hartley Victoria.
Appointments: 1963–65 Holyhead; 1965–70 Leek; 1970–75 Nottingham West; 1975–78 Edinburgh Mission; 1978– Airdrie and Armadale (Scottish Marriage Guidance Council).

WEBB, Brian Hugh Fallon, 59 Mitchall Lane, Streatham, London SW16 6LW. (01-769-7652) *b. 27 Jan 1930, London. m. 13 Aug 1960: 2s.*
Education: 1935–43 Winchmore Hill Collegiate; 1943–46 Highgate Sch.; 1951–54 Handsworth.
Appointments: 1954–55 Ampthill; 1955–56 Walton-on-Thames; 1956–58 Doncaster Coalfields Mission (Caravan Ministry);1958–60 Home Mission Department; 1960–65 Chelmsford; 1965–70 Southend-on-Sea; 1970–76 East Dereham; 1976– Streatham and Dulwich.
Connexional Committees: 1962–69 MAYC, Education, Youth Committees. *Publications: Minds in Touch* (Methodist Publishing House 1978).
Special Interests: Rehabilitation of Mentally Disordered, Music and the Arts, Inter-Faith Relationships, Community Service, Youth Work.
Hobbies and Recreations: Music, Amateur Dramatics, Photography, Cricket, Playing Piano and Organ, Chess.

WEBB, John Thomas, Benison, 75 Hollies Drive, Bayston Hill, Shrewsbury SY3 0NP. *b. 30 March 1902, London. m. 1 Aug 1929.*
Education: 1913–18 Wisbech Grammar Sch.; 1923–26 Richmond.
Appointments: 1922–23 Merthyr Tydfil; 1926–29 Towcester; 1929–31 Knaresborough; 1931–34 Hebden Bridge; 1934–37 Rugby; 1937–40 Kettering; 1940–44 Tadcaster; 1944–48 Sheffield (Norfolk); 1948–52 Haworth; 1952–55 Newbury; 1955–58 Tenby; 1958–61 Monmouth; 1961–67 Leintwardine.
Special Interests: Pastoral Work.
Hobbies and Recreations: Bird Watching, Nature Studies, especially Coleoptera and Lepidoptera.

WEBBER, George Westacott, The Manse, Coads Green, Launceston, Cornwall PL15 7LY. (056-682-240) *b. 9 March 1924, South Norwood, London. m. 30 July 1952: 1s.*
Education: 1935–40 Reigate Grammar Sch., 1947–48 Cliff Coll.; 1950–52 Didsbury, Bristol.
Appointments: 1952–56 Ringsash; 1956–61 Andover; 1961–66 Reading; 1966–71 Newquay; 1971–79 Radstock; 1979– North Hill; 1969–71 Cornwall District Local Preachers' Secretary.
Connexional Committees: 1970–71 Local Preachers.
Hobbies and Recreations: Collecting Novels of Joseph and Silas Hocking.

WEBSTER, Gordon Eric, St Kilda, 137 Wootton Rd., King's Lynn, Norfolk PE30 4DR. (0553-671750)–BA(Dunelm), MA(Cantab.). *b. 13 Sept 1937, Ditchingham, Bungay, Suffolk. m. 2 July 1960: 1d., 1s.*
Education: 1942–46 Kirby Cane Prim.; 1947–48 Ditchingham Prim.; 1948–55 Bungay Grammar; 1955–58 Durham Univ. (St. Cuthberts); 1958–60 Cambridge Univ. (Fitzwilliam); 1958–60 Wesley House.
Appointments: 1960–63 Boroughbridge; 1963–67 Rotherham; 1967–71 Leicester West; 1971–75 Sheffield North East; 1975–82 Wymondham, Attleborough and Watton; 1982– King's Lynn Circuit.
Connexional Committees: 1973–75 Ministries; 1982– Social Responsibility. *Publications:* Chapter entitled *Psychology and Christian Mission* in *Investigations: Essays on Church and Society* (Epworth 1968).
Special Interests: Mental Health, Ecumenism, Social Responsibility, Church and Community. *Hobbies and Recreations:* Ornithology, Sport, Cartooning, Music.

WEBSTER, John Keith, 63 Londonderry Lane, Smethwick, Warley, West Midlands B67 7EZ. (021-558-7051)–BSc(Lond.), MA(Cantab.). *b. 3 Aug 1928, Raunds, Northants. m. 24 July 1962: 2d., 1fd., 1s.*
Education: 1932–35 Raunds Inf.; 1935–39 Raunds CE Jun. Mixed; 1939–46 Kimbolton Grammar Sch.; 1946–49 Univ. Coll., London; 1949–50 Westminster Training Coll.; 1958–60 Wesley House.
Appointments: 1960–72 Jamaica Dt; 1972–82 Birmingham, Sutton Park; 1982– Birmingham South West.
Connexional Committees: 1974–77, 1978–81 Central Committee, Overseas Division.
Special Interests: Community Relations. *Hobbies and Recreations:*Walking, Reading.

WEBSTER, John Meynell, 16 Redwood Ave., Dudley, West Midlands DY1 3TT. (093-73-3331) *b. 22 Oct 1934, Cookridge, Leeds. m. 27 Sept 1957: 1d., 2s.*
Education: 1939–43 Far Headingley Prep. Sch.; 1943–45 Leeds Grammar Sch.; 1945–51 Reeds Sch, Cobham,

Surrey; 1951–52 Hertfordshire Coll. of Agriculture; 1969–71 Hartley Victoria. *Appointments:* 1971–77 Bolton; 1977–82 Ryedale (N. Yorks); 1982– Gornal and Sedgley. *Connexional Committees:* 1973–76 Youth and Education. *Special Interests:* Holy Spirit Renewal, Expository Preaching, Audio/Visual Media. *Hobbies and Recreations:* Tape Recording, Travel, Creative Art.

WEDGEWOOD, Roy, Longholme Parsonage, 2 Bacup Rd., Rawtenstall, Rossendale, Lancs BB4 7ND. (0706-216110) *b. 1920. m.* *Education:* 1962–63 Richmond. *Appointments:* 1963–68 Todmorden; 1968–73 Harpenden; 1973–76 Darwen; 1976–81 Blaydon; 1981– Rossendale.

WEEKS, David Geoffrey, Belvoir Lodge, Northdown Rd., Bideford, Devon EX39 3LT. (02372-2440)–BA. *b. 23 May 1935, Bristol. m. 22 July 1961: 2d., 1s.* *Education:* 1940–46 Two Mile Hill Jun. Mixed Sch.; 1946–53 Bristol Grammar Sch.; 1953–56 Bristol Univ.; 1956–59 Richmond. *Appointments:* 1959–60 Home Missions, Caravan Missions; 1960–64 Stourbridge and Brierley Hill; 1964–70 Luton South; 1970–81 Kenya Conf.; 1981– Chaplain to Edgehill Coll. *Special Interests:* Third World, Economics, Politics, Preaching, Pastoral Care, Group Work (not necessarily in order of importance), Education. *Hobbies and Recreations:* Philately, Ornithology, Books, Music.

WELBOURNE, Thomas Charles Sydney, 5 Oakfield Rd., Street, Somerset BA16 0RD. (0458-43479)–BA(Open), TD. *b. 5 June 1926, Hull. m.: 1d., 2s.* *Education:* 1937–42 Riley High Sch., Hull; 1970–72 St. John's Teacher Training Coll.; 1951–54 Headingley. *Appointments:* 1954–57 Pickering; 1957–63 Tadcaster; 1963–68 York (Centenary); 1968–70 Hull (West); 1970–72 Easingwold; 1972–79 Hull (East); 1979– Somerset Mission. *Connexional Committees:* 1963–68 Education and Youth. *Special Interests:* TA Chaplain. *Hobbies and Recreations:* Lyke Wake Walker, Philatelist, Indoor Sports.

WELCH, James, 7 Gorse Grove, Helmhore, Rossendale, Lancs BB4 4JE. (0706-215633) *b. 13 Aug 1936, Chorley, Lancs. m. 1962: 1d., 2s.* *Education:* Rivington and Blackrod Grammar Sch.; 1952–53 Cliff Coll.; 1956–60 Hartley Victoria. *Appointments:* 1960–62 Knighton; 1962–67 Kendal; 1967–72 Ilkley; 1972–76 Scunthorpe; 1976–83 Accrington and Haslingden. *Connexional Committees:* 1966–67 Local Preachers. *Local Council Committees:* 1964–67 Westmorland CC Education Sub Committee; 1982– Lancs County Council District Education Liaison Committee. *Special Interests:* Youth Work. *Hobbies and Recreations:* Walking.

WELCH, Thomas Joseph, Braemar, 3 Stanmore Rise, Dawlish, Devon EX7 0DF. (0626-865578). *Education:* 1936–39 Hartley Victoria. *Appointments:* 1939–40 Scarborough, Queen St.; 1940–43 Ambleside and Windermere; 1943–47 Lowestoft; 1947–50 Cannock Chase; 1950–55 High Wycombe; 1955–60 Portsmouth and Southsea; 1960–66 Watford; 1966–71 London, Finchley and Hendon; 1971–76 Sevenoaks; 1976–79 Raunds.

WELLER, William Henry, 28 Manse Rd., Hadley, Telford, Salop TF1 4NH. (0952-44034)–MBE. *b. 6 May 1898, Hepworth, Suffolk. m. 21 March 1927: 3d., 1s.* *Education:* 1901–10 Elem.; 1919–21 Army; Non-Collegiate. *Appointments:* 1949–50 Tamworth; 1950–54 Ashton and Stalybridge; 1954–59 Patricroft and Eccles; 1959–64 Crewe; 1964–67 Wellington, Salop.

WELLS, Anthony Philip, 8 Rosehill Rd., Montrose, Angus DD10 8RY. (0674-2373)–BA, BSc. *b. 15 Feb 1950, Nottingham. m. 19 July 1980: 1s.* *Education:* 1961–68 Carlton le Willows Grammar Sch., Wood Lane, Gealing, Nottingham; 1968–72 Leeds Univ.; 1977–80 Bristol Univ.; 1977–81 Wesley, Bristol. *Appointments:* 1981– Arbroath and Montrose. *Special Interests:* General Paper Tutor for Connexional Candidates Exams. *Hobbies and Recreations:* Music, Table-Tennis, Badminton.

WENDT, S. Maurice, 4 Queensgate, Castle, Northwich, Cheshire CW8 1DX. (0606-75002) *b. 22 Aug 1921, Widnes, Lancashire. m. 29 July 1950: 1d., 1s.* *Education:* 1933–38 Wade Deacon Grammar Sch., Widnes; 1947–49 Hartley Victoria. *Appointments:* 1945–47 Kidderminster and Stourport; 1949–51 Holyhead; 1951–55 Crewe; 1955–60 Wellington (Shropshire); 1955–60 Chaplain HMF; 1960–66 Newbury; 1966–76 Reading; 1976–82 Chichester and Bognor; 1982– Northwich. *Hobbies and Recreations:* The Countryside.

WENT, Peter John, St. Andrews Manse, Brownley Rd., Wythenshawe, Manchester M22 6DW. (061-437-4887) *b. 19 Dec 1935, Wolverhampton, Staffordshire. m. 13 Aug 1966: 1d., 1s.* *Education:* 1940–46 St. Judes CE Prim. Sch., Wolverhampton; 1946–50 Whitmore Secondary Modern Sch.; 1960–62 Cliff Coll.; 1962–66 Handsworth. *Appointments:* 1966–68 Coningsby; 1968–72 Padiham; 1972–76 Burnley; 1976– Manchester and Salford Mission. *Council Member:* 1976– South Manchester Council of Churches; 1973–76 Founder Secretary of West Burnley Council of Churches. *Special Interests:* Folk Music. *Hobbies and Recreations:* Watching Soccer.

WESCOTT, William Joseph Richard, 75 Park St., Bridgend, Mid Glamorgan CF31 4AZ. (0656-4120) *b. 17 Feb 1920, Frogmore, St. Kea, Nr. Truro, Cornwall. m. 13 March 1948: 2d.*

Education: 1925–31 St. Feock CE Sch.; 1931–32 Daniell Rd., Council Sch., Truro; 1932–34 Truro Boys Sch., Union Place, Truro; 1946–47 Cliff Coll. *Appointments:* 1955–58 Church of Nazerene; 1958–63 Camelford and Wadebridge; 1963–68 Launceston; 1968–76 Barry; 1976–81 St. Ives and Hayle; 1981– Bridgend. *Connexional Committees:* 1974–76 Memorials Committee. *Special Interests:* Methodist Doctrine and Biographies.

WEST, Graham, 59 Barton Drive, Barton on Sea, New Milton, Hants BH25 7JH. (0425-612510)–BD(Lond.) *b. 7 Feb 1923, Walsall, Staffordshire. m. 19 Sept 1963.* *Education:* 1928–34 Walsall Bluecoat Sch.; 1934–38 Elmore Green Central Sch., Bloxwich; 1948–51 London Univ. External Undergraduate; 1947–50 Wesley, Headingley. *Appointments:* 1945–46 Barton on Humber; 1946–47 Market Weighton; 1950–52 Beverley; 1952–57 Hull Waltham St.; 1957–64 Birmingham Elmdon; 1964–66 Wantage and Abingdon; 1966–73 Leicester Central Mission; 1973–80 Liskeard and Looe; 1980– Christchurch and Lymington. *Connexional Committees:* 1954–57 Education; 1957–69 Local Preachers. *Publications: A Plain Methodist Looks at Church Membership* (1978). *Special Interests:* Local Preacher Training. *Hobbies and Recreations:* National Trust, The Countryside, Soccer and Tennis.

WEST, Ronald Gareth, 10 Devon Cresc., Skelton, Saltburn, Cleveland TS12 2BS. (0287-50409)–MA. *b. 22 May 1947, Morriston, Swansea. m. 16 Aug 1969: 2d.* *Education:* 1958–65 Whitchurch Grammar Sch., 1965–68 Univ. Coll. of North Wales, Bangor; 1969–71 Wesley, House. *Appointments:* 1971–74 Gateshead and Jarrow; 1974–77 Lerwick, North Roe and North Isles; 1977– Redcar, Saltburn and Guisborough. *Connexional Committees:* 1974–77 Division of Social Responsibility. *Hobbies and Recreations:* Photography, Tropical Fish.

WESTINGTON, Douglas Richard, Wesley Manse, Dinghurst Rd., Churchill, Bristol BS19 5NQ. (0934-852314) *b. 19 June 1920, Shirley, Addiscombe, Surrey. m. 4 Nov 1950: 1d., 2s.* *Education:* 1925–28 Three Small Private Schs.; 1928–32 Boscombe Council Sch.; 1932–36 Bournemouth Sch.; 1946–48 Didsbury, Bristol. *Appointments:* 1948–50 Frome (Wesley); 1950–52 Brynmawr; 1952–56 Willington; 1956–61 Grantham; 1961–66 London, Finsbury Park and Southgate; 1966–72 Barnstaple; 1972–76 Portsmouth and Southsea; 1976–81 Manchester (Cheetham Hill and Prestwich); 1981– Cheddar Valley. *Connexional Committees:* 1979– Ministers' Retirement Fund. *Special Interests:* Member of Society of Cirplanologists, 1962– Council Member of Homeless Childrens Aid and Adoption Society. *Hobbies and Recreations:* Steam Railways, Model Railways, Travel.

WESTWOOD, George Brian, Epworth, 87 Rhuddlan Rd., Rhyl, Clwyd LL18 2RE.–MA, PhD. *b. 4 Dec 1929. m. 1956.* *Education:* 1941–46 West Bromwich Grammar; 1953–56 Richmond. *Appointments:* 1956–59 Forest of Dean; 1959–63 Oldham West; 1963–66 Cheetham Hill and Prestwich; 1966–74 Congleton (Wagg St.), Biddulph and Mow Cop; 1974–79 Leek; 1979– Rhyl and Prestatyn. *Publications: Grant of Achievement of Arms* (1980). *Hobbies and Recreations:* Photography, Heraldry.

WHALE, Arthur Leslie, 2 Highfield Rd., Little Sutton, South Wirral L66 4PL. (051-339-2304) *b. 30 June 1921, Dudley, West Midlands. m.* *Education:* 1932–37 Dudley Grammar Sch.; 1952–55 Richmond. *Appointments:* 1955–57 Brighton (Dome Mission); 1957–62 Wellington (Salop); 1962–69 Burnley; 1969–74 Cannock; 1974–79 Southend-on-Sea; 1979– South Wirral.

WHALING, Frank, 29 Ormidale Terrace, Murrayfield, Edinburgh EH12 6EA. (031-337-5119)–BA(Cantab.), MA(Cantab.), ThD(Harvard). *b. 5 Feb 1934, Pontefract, Yorkshire. m. 6 Aug 1960: 1d., 1s.* *Education:* 1945–53 King's Sch., Pontefract; 1955–57 Christ's Coll., Cambridge; 1969–73 Harvard Univ.; 1957–59 Wesley House. *Appointments:* 1960–62 Birmingham Mission; 1962–66 Lucknow and Banaras Dt (N.India); 1966–69 Eastbourne; 1973 Lecturer in and Co-ordinator of Religious Studies at Edinburgh Univ. *Connexional Committees:* 1967–69 Overseas Missions; 1978– Inter-faith Dialogue. *Council Member:* 1978– Farmington Council. *Publications: An Approach to Dialogue: Hinduism and Christianity* (Lucknow Publishing House 1966); *The Rise of the Religious Significance of Rama* (Motilal Banarsidass 1980); *John and Charles Wesley* in the *Classics of Western Spirituality* (Paulist and SPCK 1981); *Contemporary Approaches to the Study of Religion* (Editor, Mouton, The Hague 1982–83); *Contemporary Issues of Religious Education* (Editor, Crossroads, New York 1982–83); *Christian Theology and World Religions* (Marshall Morgan and Scott 1983); 26 Articles and 24 Book Reviews in numerous journals, 1973–. *Special Interests:* Wesley Studies, Methodist Spirituality, Indian Religion, World Religions, Comparative Religion, History of Religions, Religious Studies, Theology of Religion, Non-Western Christian Theology, Global Studies. *Hobbies and Recreations:* Writing, Sport, Music.

WHEAL, Bryan Arthur, 50A New Hey Rd., Huddersfield, W. Yorks HD3 4AJ. (0483-31780)–BA. *b. 25 May 1944, Hadleigh, Essex. m. 8 May 1954: 2d., 2s.* *Education:* 1944–49 Westcliff High

Sch.; 1971–74 Manchester; 1971–74 Hartley Victoria. *Appointments:* 1974–81 Birstall and Birkenshaw; 1981– Huddersfield.
Special Interests: Care of Elderly (Age Concern), Early Retirement.
Hobbies and Recreations: Photography.

WHEELER, David John, 43 Himley Cresc., Goldthorn Park, Wolverhampton WV4 5DE. (0902-336913) *b. 2 May 1938, Birmingham. m. 12 Aug 1967: 1d., 1s.*
Education: 1949–55 Varndean Grammar Sch.; 1973–74 Matlock Coll. of Education; 1961–65 Handsworth. *Appointments:* 1965–67 Nottingham Mission; 1967–73 Nottingham North; 1974–78 The Anthony Gell Sch., Wirksworth, Derbyshire, Head of RE; 1978– Moreton Sch., Wolverhampton, Head of Year.

WHEELHOUSE, Derek, 23 Cold Overton Rd., Oakham, Leics LE15 6NT. (0572-2239) *b. 12 Oct 1926, Leeds. m. 25 June 1955: 3d., 1s.*
Education: 1931–40 Armley Park Sch.; 1940–42 Leeds Jun. Tech.; 1951–54 Hartley Victoria.
Appointments: 1955–58 N. Rhodesia District; 1958–61 Haslingden; 1961–65 Hindley; 1965–68 Aylsham; 1968–75 Alford; 1975–82 Melton Mowbray; 1982– Leek.
Connexional Committees: 1978–82 OM Central Committee.
Hobbies and Recreations: Gardening, Car Maintenance.

WHITE, Brian, 9 Stiles Ave., Marple, Stockport, Cheshire SK6 6LR. (061-427-2509).
Education: 1953–56 Bristol.
Appointments: 1956–57 Isles of Scilly; 1957–61 Manchester and Salford Mission; 1961–64 Edinburgh (Leith-Tranent); 1964–69 Blaydon; 1969–76 Keswick and Cockermouth; 1976– Romiley.

WHITE, Donald Victor Philip, 44 Westmount Rd., Eltham SE9 1JE. (01-850-2406) *b. 12 Nov 1917, Cardiff. m. 7 Aug 1948: 1d.*
Education: 1922–30 Gladstone Elem.; 1930–33 Kings Coll., (both in Cardiff); 1942–44 Cardiff Univ.; 1946–48 Didsbury, Bristol.
Appointments: 1945–46 Marlborough; 1948–52 Llanelly and Carmarthen; 1952–55 Huddersfield, Gledholt (West); 1955–59 Woodhouse Grove, Bradford; 1959–65 Medway Towns; 1965–70 Tunbridge Wells; 1970–77 Finchley and Hendon; 1977– Blackheath and Lewisham.
Hobbies and Recreations: Gardening, Photography.

WHITE, Frank Albert, 54 Horton View, Banbury OX16 9HP. (0295-3349) *b. 15 Aug 1908, Preston, Nr. Canterbury, Kent. m. 1 Oct 1937: 1d., 1s.*
Education: 1919–24 Chatham House Secondary Sch., Ramsgate, Kent; 1930–33 Richmond. *Appointments:* 1929–30 Wellington, Salop; 1933–45 South China Dt; 1946–49 Redruth; 1949–53 Perranporth and St. Agnes; 1953–58 Gloucester; 1958–65 Northampton; 1966–74 Hong Kong Dt.
Hobbies and Recreations: Reading, Gardening.

WHITE, Herbert Wilfred, 20 Beech Hill, Wellington, Somerset TA21 8ES. (082347-3847)–BA(Open Univ.). *b. 21 May 1931, Guernsey, Channel Islands. m. 31 July 1957: 1d., 1s.*
Education: 1936–40 Hautes Capelles, Guernsey; 1940–45 Birchgrove, Cardiff; 1951–54 Univ. of London; 1951–54 Richmond. *Appointments:* 1954–57 Bude; 1966– Kingsmead Sch., Wiveliscombe (Head of RE Dept.).
Publications: Proceedings Wesley Historical Association (Various Dates 1951–).
Special Interests: Methodist History, Antique Furniture Restoration, Visual Arts in Religious Education, Upholstery. *Hobbies and Recreations:* Photography, Gardening, Travel.

WHITE, Ian Thomas, 20 Victoria Rd., Hanham, Bristol BS15 32QH. (0272-673882) *b. 6 July 1939, Manchester. m. 1 April 1967: 2d.*
Education: 1945–49 Adlington County Prim. Sch.; 1949–50 Poynton County Prim. Sch.; 1950–54 Poynton County Secondary; 1961–65 Hartley Victoria. *Appointments:* 1965–69 Hull (Trinity); 1969–72 Retford; 1972–78 Bristol (South); 1978– Bristol (Kingswood); 1978– Bristol Synod Secretary.
Connexional Committees: 1975–76 Youth and Community.
Special Interests: The Handicapped.
Hobbies and Recreations: Rug Making, Jig Saws, Logic Problems.

WHITE, Leonard Edward, 109 Chiltern Ave., Bushey, Herts WD2 3QE. (01-950-4560)–BD. *b. 6 Oct 1908, London. (w.): 1d., 1s.*
Education: 1933–37 Richmond.
Appointments: 1938–41 Walton on Thames; 1941–45 Truro; 1945–50 Wanstead and Woodford; 1950–56 London, Barry Rd.; 1956–62 Ilford; 1962–68 Ealing and Acton; 1968–72 Staines and Feltham.
Hobbies and Recreations: Gardening, Woodwork, Walking.

WHITE, Malcolm Wesley, 93 Maidenhead Rd., Windsor, Berks SL4 5EY. (07535-64846)–MA(Cantab.), BSc(Lond.). *b. 14 Dec 1937, Bath. m. 9 Nov 1963: 1d., 1s.*
Education: 1949–56 Exeter Sch., Exeter; 1956–60 Plymouth Technical Coll.; 1960–62 Wesley House.
Appointments: 1982– Windsor and Maidenhead, Headmaster of Abbotsfield Sch., Hillingdon.
Publications: Courage of Your Doubts (1978).
Special Interests: Education. *Hobbies and Recreations:* Walking, Camping, Foreign Travel.

WHITE, Robert, 67 Baker St., Potters Bar, Herts EN6 2EX. (0707-52978).
Education: 1956–59 Richmond.
Appointments: 1959–61 Poole; 1963–67 Madras, Church of South India; 1968–77 Torquay and Paignton; 1977– Potters Bar, Barnet.
Hobbies and Recreations: Philately (particularly Postal History), Writing Articles, Reading, Walking.

WHITE, Thomas, 2 Orkney Close, Hollycroft, Hinckley, Leics LE10 0TA. (0455-637786)–DipAEd(Manch.), BA(Open Univ.). *b. 22 May 1934, Bothwell, Strathclyde. m. 13 Aug 1963: 1s., 1d.*
Education: 1946–49 Bellskill Academy; 1971–74 Manchester Univ. (Part Time); 1976–78 The Open Univ.; 1957–61 Hartley Victoria. *Appointments:* 1961–63 Barnsley (West); 1963–66 Tunstall; 1966–70 Crewe; 1970–74 South Cheshire Coll., Crewe, Lecturer in Adult Education; 1974 Assistant Principal, The John Cleveland Coll., Hinckley.
Special Interests: Adult and Continuing Education. *Hobbies and Recreations:* Philately, Photography, Model Railways.

WHITE, Wallace Hardy, 9 Queen's Ave., Byfleet, Weybridge, Surrey. (09323-42093) *b. 22 Dec 1919, London. m. 16 June 1945: 1d., 1s.*
Education: 1932–38 The Mercers Sch.; 1945–47 Handsworth.
Appointments: 1947–50 Birmingham (Great Barr and Kingstanding); 1950–54 Manchester Mission; 1954–59 Ealing and Acton; 1959–64 Richmond; 1964–71 Guildford; 1971–76 Winchester; 1976– Woking and Walton.
Connexional Committees: 1964–80 Local Preachers (Division of Ministries).
Special Interests: Psychotherapy.

WHITE, William John Anthony, The Manse, Canworthy Water, Launceston, Cornwall PL15 8UW. (056681-204)–BD(Lond.). *b. 2 May 1936, Redruth, Cornwall. m. 19 Aug 1961: 1d., 1s.*
Education: Penzance Grammar Sch., Cornwall; 1958–60 Hartley Victoria.
Appointments: 1961–64 South Derbyshire, 1964–81 Church of South India, Tiruchiradalli and Coimbatore Diocese; 1981– Week St. Mary.

WHITEHALL, David William, 299 Mercer Heights, Westvale, Kirkby, Liverpool L32 4TS. (051-546-1977)–BA(Manch.). *b. 27 Nov 1946, Birmingham. s.*
Education: 1958–65 St. George GS (Bristol); 1967–70 Manchester Univ.; 1967–71 Hartley Victoria; 1971 Kingsmead; 1971–79 Kenya Dt; 1979– Liverpool North.
Special Interests: Church History.
Hobbies and Recreations: Hiking, Cricket.

WHITEHEAD, James Kay, Elmside, Elmside Walk, Hitchin, Herts SG3 1HD. (0462-50297)–BA(Birmingham). *b. 28 March 1893, Bacup, Lancs. m. 9 Aug 1922 (w.): 1d., 1s.*
Education: 1905–10 Kingswood Sch.; 1919–21 Birmingham Univ.; 1919–21 Handsworth.
Appointments: 1915–19 HM Forces; 1921–24 Manchester and Salford Mission; 1924–27 Stockport, Trinity; 1927–33 Liverpool, Linacre Mission; 1933–43 Exeter; 1943–51 General Secretary, Methodist Youth Dept.; 1951–57 Chairman Exeter District; 1957–59 Chairman, Plymouth and Exeter District.
Connexional Committees: 1927–31 Temperance and Social Welfare; 1943–57 Methodist Youth Dept.; 1943–54 Home Mission Dept.; 1943–51 Overseas; 1943–51 NCHO; 1943–51 Chapel Committee; 1945–51 President's Council; 1934–39, 1943–54 General Purpose; 1965–75 Methodist Homes for Aged.
Special Interests: Wesley Guild Holidays, Methodist History, Art.
Hobbies and Recreations: Rugby Football, Cricket, Painting.

WHITTAKER, Harold, 34 Charmandean Rd., Worthing, Sussex BN14 9LQ. (0903-202195) *b. 15 July 1895, Madeley, Salop. m. 12 Aug 1924: 1d., 1s.*
Education: Madeley Wesleyan; Stafford Technical; 1915–16 Headingley; 1919–21 Didsbury and Handsworth. *Appointments:* 1916–19 HM Forces; 1919–21 Handsworth Coll.; 1921–24 Birmingham Mission; 1924–27 West Bromwich, Hill Top; 1927–30 West Bromwich, Wesley; 1930–35 Runcorn; 1935–39 Burnley Wesley; 1939–47 Warrington; 1947–53 Croydon; 1953–60 Luton.
Hobbies and Recreations: Gardening.

WHITTAKER, Peter, Wesley House, 2A Offa Rd., Bedford MK42 9HA. (0234-54329)–BA. *b. 20 March 1946, Huddersfield, Yorkshire. m. 30 Sept 1967: 2d., 1s., fc.*
Education: 1951–57 Outlane County Sch.; 1957–59 Salendinenook Secondary Modern; 1959–63 Royds Hall Grammar Sch.; 1971–74 Manchester Univ.; 1970–74 Hartley Victoria. *Appointments:* 1974–79 Glasgow, St. John's; 1979– Bedford South and Ampthill.
Connexional Committees: 1978– Connexional Ecumenical Committee; 1981– Connexional Faith and Order Committee; 1978– Methodist Rep. on Bristol Council of Church Assembly. *Publications:* Presenter of Religious Programme, Childrens Radio each Sunday Morning, 7.00–8.30pm.
Special Interests: Ecumenical Matters, Development Issues, Member World Development Movement, Communication, especially Local Radio, Foster Parents. *Hobbies and Recreations:* Photography, Walking, Music.

WHITTLE, Donald Carey Grenfell, Novelli, Lansdown Rd., Bath BA1 5SU. (0225-310500)–MA(Oxon), MA(Cantab.), MEd(Bristol). *b. 3 Nov 1925, Burnley, Lancs. m. 28 July 1951: 2s.*
Education: 1936–42 Bury Grammar Sch.; 1943, 1947–49 Magdalen Coll., Oxford; 1949–51 Wesley House.
Appointments: 1951–52 Gravesend, 1952–55 Leeds (Armley); 1955–64 Ashville Coll., Harrogate; 1964–67 Chaplain, Homerton Coll., Cambridge; 1967– Senior Lecturer in Religious Studies, Bath Coll. of Higher Education; Principal Lecturer in Religious Studies.
Local Council Committees. 1972–76 Agreed Syllabus Conference of Bath; 1976– Avon; 1978– Wiltshire; 1980– Somerset. *Publications: Prayers and Services* (Epworth 1962); *Christianity and the Arts* (Mowbrays 1966).
Special Interests: Religious

Education. *Hobbies and Recreations:* Piano (Classical and Jazz), Walking, Cinema.

WHITTLE, John, 7 Gledhow Park Rd., Leeds LS7 4JX. (622332)–BD, MPhil. *b. 10 Jan 1937, London. m. 18 July 1959: 1d., 3s.*
Education: 1942–48 Prim. Sc.; 1948–52 Leigh Grammar; 1975–76 St. John's Teachers Coll., York; 1959–63 Hartley Victoria.
Appointments: 1963–66 Pocklington; 1966–69 Oltey; 1969–81 Caribbean Conference; 1981– Leeds North East.
Special Interests: Education, Philosophy of Religion, Relation of Science to Religion. *Hobbies and Recreations:* Reading.

WHITTLE, William, 7 The Knoll, Tupsley, Hereford HR1 1RU. *b. 13 Jan 1894, Lincoln. m. 29 Sept 1979: 1d., 1s.*
Education; 1905–11 St. Botolph's Sch., Lincoln; 1911–15 Lincoln Sch.; 1914–15 Headingley; 1919–21 Didsbury. *Appointments:* 1921–27 Gold Coast (Ghana); 1927–31 Halifax, St. Johns; 1931–34 Warrington; 1934–38 Bury (Union St.); 1938–42 Bolton, Park; 1942–45 Eccles; 1945–47 Gold Coast (Ghana); 1947–50 Farnworth; 1950–55 Hull North; 1955–58 Oldbury.
Hobbies and Recreations: Wood Carving and Wood Turning, Gardening, Golf.

WHITTON, Cresswell John Henry, 147 Kirby Rd., Walton on the Naze, Essex Co14 8RL. (025-56-5336) *b. 30 Oct 1935, Highbridge, Nr. Eastleigh, Hants. m. 30 Aug 1956: 1d., 1s.*
Education: 1941–47 Ringwood Rd., Prim. Sch., Totton, Hants.; 1947–52 The Gregg Sch., Southampton; 1969–70 Farnborough Technical Coll., Business Studies; 1977–79 Wesley, Bristol. *Appointments:* 1979– Clacton on Sea.
Special Interests: Methodist History, Liturgy and Worship, Member of the Methodist Sacramental Fellowship. *Hobbies and Recreations:* Astronomy, Steam Railways, Walking.

WHORTON, Robert Osborne, Claremont, Dobwalls, Liskeard, Cornwall PL14 6JB. (0579-20627)–BSc. *b. 22 Aug 1956, Kirkby-in-Furness, Lancashire. m. 18 Sept 1976: 1d., 1s.*
Education: 1966–69 Queen Mary's Grammar, Basingstoke; 1969–72 Queen Mary's/Charles Chute Comp., Basingstoke; 1972–74 Queen Mary's 6th Form Coll.; 1975–78 Univ. Coll. Swansea; 1978–80 Univ. Birmingham; 1978–81 Queen's. *Appointments:* 1981– Liskeard and Looe.
Special Interests: Writing Songs.

WHYTE, John Jess, Ingleside, Chester Rd., Gresford, Nr. Wrexham, Clwyd LL12 8PA. (2883) *b. 30 July 1937, Stranraer, Scotland. m. 22 Sept 1962: 2d., 1s.*
Education: 1942–48 Kirkcolm Prim. Sch.; 1948–53 Stranraer High Sch.; 1958–59 GCHD Training Coll., Bletchley Park; 1969–72 Wesley, Bristol. *Appointments:* 1972–78 Bristol, Bedminster; 1978– Wrexham.
Special Interests: Youth Evangelism, Hospital Chaplain, Local Radio. *Hobbies and Recreations:* Music, Football, Athletics, Reading.

WIFFEN, Albert John, Flat 1, Clint House, Armathwaite, Carlisle CA4 9PB. (06-992-232)–BA(Manch.). *b. 4 Feb 1905, Chelmsford, Essex. m. 10 Oct 1936 (w.).*
Education: 1909–13 The Friars British Sch., Inf., Chelmsford; 1913–18 Trinity Rd. Council Sch., Boys; 1930–33 Victoria Univ. of Manchester; 1928–33 Hartley Victoria. *Appointments:* 1933–34 President's List; 1934–35 Hunts Mission; 1935–36 Market Drayton; 1936–39 Deal; 1939–45 Thetford; 1945–60 Downham Market; 1950–56 Weardale; 1956–61 Wigton; 1961–67 Kirkoswald; 1967–71 Alston, Carlisle.
Local Council Committees: 1958–67 Carlisle (now Cumbria) District Probationers' Secretary; Served on various District Committees in London SE, SE Anglia, Middlesbrough and Darlington, and in Carlisle (now Cumbria) over the years.
Special Interests: A Member of the Wesley Historical Society and Vice-President of Cumbria Branch, Overseas Missions. *Hobbies and Recreations:* Gardening and Swimming.

WIGGALL, John William, 30 Southbrae Drive, South Jordan Hill, Glasgow G13 1PY. (041-959-2432) *b. 16 Oct 1939, Birmingham. m. 30 July 1966: 3d.*
Education: 1953–56 Wednesbury County Commercial Secondary Sch.; 1963–67 Headingley. *Appointments:* 1967–69 Leeds (Richmond Hill); 1969–72 Harrogate; 1972–76 Corby; 1976– Glasgow (West).
Special Interests: Visual Aids, Ecumenics. *Hobbies and Recreations:* Photography, Painting, Keep Fit.

WIGLEY, Alfred Lanceley, 11 Apsin Ave., Knaresborough, North Yorkshire HG5 8EJ. (863151)–BA, BD(Manch.). *b. 7 Jan 1901, Liverpool. w: 1s.*
Education: 1911–13 Primitive Methodist Day Sch., Banks, Nr. Southport; 1913–18 Preston Grammar Sch.; 1923–28 Manchester Univ.; 1923–28 Hartley Victoria.
Appointments: 1928–34 Glasgow 2nd; 1934–38 Warrington; 1938–42 Sheffield North East; 1942–47 Southport North; 1947–52 Harrogate; 1952–58 Darlington North; 1958–66 Grimsby West.

WIGNALL, Arthur Ranulph, 39 Elvaston Rd., Hexham, Northumberland NE46 2HD. (0434-603139)–BA(Lond.), BD(Lond.). *b. 5 Sept 1924, Scarborough. m. 1951: 2d.*
Education: Scarborough High Sch.; NE Grammar Sch., Sheffield; London and Sheffield Univ.; 1947–49 Handsworth. *Appointments:* 1945–47 East Dereham; 1949–52 Hastings; 1952–57 Burslem; 1957–60 Biddulph; 1960–62 Sheffield Brunswick; 1962–71 Chesterfield; 1971–81 Maghull UR; 1981– Hexham.
Special Interests: History, Poetry, Cricket, Dogs. *Hobbies and Recreations:* Boating, Walking, Driving.

WIKTORSKA EVERATT, Julia (Mrs), 34 Greenways, Sunnybrow, Crook, County Durham DL15 0LX. (0388-746258)–BSc. *b. 28 Jan 1954, Edinburgh. m. 12 March 1976.*
Education: 1965–72 Holme Valley Grammar Sch., Honley; 1972–75 Univ. of East Anglia, Norwich; 1976–77 Urban Theology Unit, Sheffield; 1977–80 Wesley House.
Appointments: 1980–82 Hemel Hempstead and Berkhamsted; 1982– Willington.

WILDGUST, Michael John, 51 Ascot Rd., Moseley, Birmingham B13 9EN. (021-449-5857) *b. 8 Jan 1944, Oldham, Lancs. m. 2 Sept 1967: 1d., 1s.*
Education: 1949–52 St. Paul's Methodist Day Sch., Shaw, Lancs.; 1952–56 Carter Knowle Council Sch., Sheffield; 1956–60 Silverdale Secondary Sch., Sheffield; 1969–73 Hartley Victoria. *Appointments:* 1973–77 Manchester and Salford Mission; 1977– Birmingham Mission.
Special Interests: Inner City. *Hobbies and Recreations:* Model Railway, Football, Golf, Camping, Reading.

WILES, Carlos Edward, 15 Lowerside Rd., Glastonbury, Somerset BA6 9BE. (0458-32259)–BA, DipEd. *b. 15 Feb 1904, Wisbech. m. 31 July 1929: 1d., 1s.*
Education: 1915–16 Nottingham High Sch.; 1916–21 Elmfield Coll., York; 1922–26 Manchester Univ.; 1922–26 Hartley Victoria.
Appointments: 1926–32 Eastern Nigeria District, Methodist Coll., Vzuakoli; 1932–38 Oron Boys' High Sch.; 1941–44 Supervisor UF Sch.; 1938–40 Ramsgate; 1945–56 Oron Boys' High Sch.; 1956–62 Midsomer Norton; 1962–67 Gillingham.
Special Interests: Education, Social and Economic History. *Hobbies and Recreations:* Cricket, Football, Tennis, Swimming.

WILKES, David Edward, Army Service Chaplain, Serving Overseas, c/o Rev. R. Wolsey Gilbert, RN, Army and RAF Board, 1 Central Buildings, Westminster, London SW1H 9NH. *b. 7 June 1947, Nantwich, Cheshire. m. 8 March 1967: 2d., 1s.*
Education: 1952–58 Wistaston County Prim.; 1958–63 Sandbach Sch.; 1971–73 Manchester Univ.; 1970–73 Hartley Victoria.
Appointments: 1973–78 Worsley; 1978–80 Kettering and Corby; 1980– Chaplain HMF.
Special Interests: Christian Marriage, Counselling. *Hobbies and Recreations:* Squash, Rugby, Photography, Hill Walking.

WILKES, Donald Morley, 169 Forest Rd., Loughborough, Leics LE11 3HS. (0509-266189)–BA. *b. 12 July 1936, Colombo, Sri Lanka. m. 7 July 1962: 1d., 2s.*
Education: 1944–47 Colleygate Prim., Cradley; 1947–50 Truro Sch., Cornwall; 1950–54 Barnstaple Grammar Sch.; 1954–58 Univ. of Liverpool; 1958–62 Handsworth; 1962–63 St. Andrews; 1965 Bangalore. *Appointments:* 1963–65, 1965–68 Batticaloa, Eastern Province, Sri Lanka; 1968–73 Kimberley; 1973–78 Nottingham South; 1978– Loughborough.
Connexional Committees: 1975–78 Overseas Division Central and GP Committees; 1973–74 Overseas Division Home Committee; Connexional Allowances Committee.
Publications: International Bible Reading Association *Light for our Path* (1975–84).
Special Interests: Christian Unity, Third World, Liberal Party. *Hobbies and Recreations:* Rugby Football, Cricket, Table Tennis, Gardening, Walking, Photography.

WILKES, Robert Joseph Morley, 33 Danesfield Drive, Leominster, Herefordshire HR6 8HP. (0568-3128) *b. 3 June 1907, Jaffna, Northern Province, Sri Lanka. m. 15 Aug 1935: 1d., 4s.*
Education: 1917–23 Kingswood, Bath; 1923–25 Truro Sch.; 1927–30 Handsworth. *Appointments:* 1930–32 Jaffna, Sri Lanka; 1932–33 Kalmunai, Sri Lanka; 1933–38 Batticaloa, Sri Lanka; 1938 Furlough, England; 1939–40 Trincomalee, Sri Lanka; 1940–41 Batticaloa; 1941–44 Trincomalee; 1944–47 Stourbridge and Brierley Hill; 1947–50 Plymouth East; 1953–58 South Molton; 1958–63 Leominster; 1963–68 Selby; 1968–74 Pickering.
Connexional Committees: 1951–53, 1954–58 Overseas Missions.
Special Interests: Overseas Missions.
Hobbies and Recreations: Rugby and Association Football, Hockey, Cricket, Tennis, Fishing, Stamp Collecting, Gardening.

WILKINSON, Geoffrey, 17 Ryders Hayes Lane, Pelsall, Walsall WS3 4EG. (0922-682205) *b. 22 Feb 1925, Garstang, Lancs. m. 9 July 1949: 1d., 2s.*
Education: 1932–37 Hoghton, Lancs., CE Prim. Sch.; 1937–41 Queen Elizabeth's Grammar Sch., Blackburn; 1975–77 Wesley, Bristol.
Appointments: 1977–82 Downham Market; 1982– Brownhills and Pelsall.
Connexional Committees: 1956–67 Connexional Youth Committee.
Hobbies and Recreations: Gardening, Walking.

WILKINSON, Harry Reginald, Beechwood, 6 Hill Rise, Market Weighton, York YO4 3JX. (0696-73523) *b. 25 Nov 1908, Pontefract. m. 18 Aug 1936: 1d.*
Education: 1913–20 Council Sch., Pontefract; 1920–24 Kings Sch., Pontefract; 1930–33 Didsbury.
Appointments: 1929–30 South Hants Mission; 1933–34 Truro Sch.; 1934–36 Hunmanby Sch., Filey; 1936–39 Bridlington (Quay); 1939–41 Wisbech; 1941–45 Hornsea (Trinity); 1945–49 Ormskirk; 1949–53 Ipswich (Museum St.); 1953–58 Retford; 1958–63 Uttoxeter; 1963–68 Snaith; 1968–72 Selby.
Hobbies and Recreations: Gardening, Music, Chess.

WILKINSON, Henry, 2 The Green, Cranswick, Driffield YO25 9QU. (0377-70362) *b. 25 Jan 1933, Gateshead. m. 24 June 1961: 2d., 1s.*
Education: 1959–63 Headingley.
Appointments: 1963–57 Malton; 1967–70 Douglas; 1970–76

Motherwell and Wishaw; 1976– Driffield.
Connexional Committees: 1973–76 Divisional Board Education and Youth.
Hobbies and Recreations: Gardening, Philately, Sport.

WILKINSON, James, 7 Forest Rd., Heswall, Wirral, Merseyside L60 5SN. (051-342-2195) *b. 30 Oct 1905, Preston. m. 12 Aug 1933 (w.): 1s.*
Education: 1926–29 Hartley Victoria.
Appointments: 1929–33 Whitehaven; 1933–34 Swindon and Richmond; 1934–37 Leominster; 1937–48 Smethwick; 1948–53 Warrington; 1953–59 Fleetwood; 1959–63 Liverpool South; 1963–72 St. Helens; 1967–70 Haslingden.
Publications: In Search of God (Epworth 1934); *In Search of Man* (Epworth 1935); *Many Things by Parables* (1942); *More Things by Parables* (1947); *Wednesday at Three* (1968).
Special Interests: Christian Apologetics.

WILKINSON, Thomas, 199 Liverpool Rd., Crosby, Liverpool L23 0RX. (051-928-2141)– MA(Liverpool), BD(Lond.). *b. 15 March 1921, Bebington, Cheshire. m. 16 Nov 1948: 1d.*
Education: 1925–31 Barnton Prim. Sch.; 1931–37 Sir John Deane's Grammar Sch., Northwich; 1950–53 Liverpool Univ. (Part Time); 1945–48 Hartley Victoria. *Appointments:* 1941–45 HM Forces; 1948–53 Liverpool (North); 1953–60 Birkenhead; 1960–63 Woodhouse Grove Sch., (Chaplain); 1963–68 Wolverhampton (Trinity); 1968–78 Wallasay; 19078– Liverpool (Crosby).
Local Council Committees: 1964–68 Wolverhampton Education Committee.

WILKINSON, Thomas George, 8 Bradford Rd., Shipley, West Yorkshire BD18 3NP (0274-583356)– BA(Lond.), BD(Lond.). *b. 6 July 1945, Greenock, Scotland. m.: 2s.*
Education: 1950–57 Highlanders Academy; 1957–63 Greenock High Sch.; 1963–65 Glasgow Univ.; 1968–71 Cliff Coll.; 1968–71 Richmond Coll. *Appointments:* 1971– 73 Lerwick and North Isles; 1973–75 Whitehaven; 1975–76 Chaplain HM Forces; 1976–81 Motherwell and Wishaw; 1981– Shipley and Bingley.
Special Interests: Church Music, Hymnody. *Hobbies and Recreations:* Football Referee, Cricket, Music, Poetry.

WILKINSON, Thomas Gordon (A.), Acacia House, Millfield Sch., Street, Somerset BA16 0YD. (0458-46105)–BA(Bristol), MEd(Bristol). *b. 9 Dec 1931, Wettenhall, Nr. Nantwich, Cheshire. m. 24 Aug 1958: 1d., 2s.*
Education: 1936–44 Calveley Council Sch., Cheshire; 1944–50 Nantwich and Alton Grammar Sch., Nantwich, Cheshire; 1953–56 Univ. of Bristol; 1953–57 Didsbury, Bristol.
Appointments: 1957–59 Dursley and Stonehouse; 1959–63 Somerset Mission; 1963–66 Durham Coast and Peterlee; 1966– Chaplain, Millfield Sch., Street.
Special Interests: Education, Inter Church and Inter Faith Relationships.
Hobbies and Recreations: Golf, Cricket, Soccer.

WILLIAMS, Benjamin Ifor, 16 Heswall Ave., Higher Bebington, Wirral, Merseyside L63 5QD. (051-608-1632) *b. 19 April 1925, Llanrhaeadr-ym-Mochnant. m. 16 April 1949: 2d.*
Education: 1930–40 Llanrhaeadr-ym-Mochnant; 1959–61 Headingley.
Appointments: 1961–68 Rhuthun (Ruthin); 1968–75 Yr Wyddgrug (Mold); 1975–78 Liverpool and Manchester (Welsh); 1978– Y Giannau (including Liverpool and Manchester).
Connexional Committees: Property Division (Board Meeting).
Hobbies and Recreations: Reading, Walking, Motoring, Football.

WILLIAMS, Dennis, 291 Billing Rd. East, Northampton NN3 3LG. (0604-30128)–BSc(Lond.), MA(Cantab.). *b. 7 Feb 1929, Acton, London W3. m. 4 Dec 1954: 2d., 1s.*
Education: 1934–39 Behmont Sch., Chiswick; 1939–40 Llandow, South Wales, Village Sch.; 1940–46 Chiswick County Secondary Sch.; 1947–49 Acton Technical Coll., London Univ.; 1949–52 Fitzwilliam House; 1949–52 Wesley House.
Appointments: 1952–65 Methodist Church, Sierra Leone District; 1965–70 Basingstoke; 1970–76 Eastbourne; 1976– Chairman Oxford and Leicester District.
Connexional Committees: 1969–74 Central Committee of Overseas Division; 1970–73 Western Committee Candidates; 1976– GP, HM Board, OM Pastoral.
Special Interests: The Mende People and Vernacular of Sierra Leone, Ecumenica Movement. *Hobbies and Recreations:* Reading, Fishing, Painting.

WILLIAMS, Elfyn Griffith, Ty Gwyn, Chester Rd., Mold, Clwyd, N. Wales CH7 1UQ. (0352-59764) *b. 6 June 1926, New Broughton, Nr. Wrexham, N. Wales. m. 29 Dec 1951: 1d., 1s.*
Education: 1938–44 Grove Park Grammar Sch., Wrexham; 1946–48 Bangor Normal Coll., N. Wales; 1950–51 Birmingham Univ.
Appointments: 1981– Yr Wyddgrug.
Connexional Committees: 1981– Property Committee Cymru District.
Publications: Articles for *Symposium* (1971); Screen Education, Edge-Hill Coll. and Moral Education Teaching Kits.
Special Interests: Preparing Films for Public Viewing especially Sound Tracks. *Hobbies and Recreations:* Hi-Fi, Filming (Slides and Movies), Writing Plays, Audio-Visual, Aids in RE.

WILLIAMS, Emlyn, Argoed, Heol Cwm Bowydd, Blaenau, Ffestiniog, Gwynedd. (301-076681) *b. 4 Nov 1915, Llanbedr, Merioneth, Gwynedd. m. 28 June 1947: 1d., 1s.*
Education: 1920–29 Cwmnantcol Prim.; 1936–38 Rhyl, Clwyd Preparatory Sch.; 1946–47 Richmond. *Appointments:* 1940–43 Nat. Service; 1943 Leeds, Welsh; 1945–46 Dinas Mawddwy; 1946–47 Richmond Coll.; 1947–49 Pwllheli, Welsh; 1949–050 Abercynon, do;

1950–52 Yatum-tuen, do; 1952–55 Lampeter, do; 1955–60 Llanwrst, do; 1960–62 Holyhead, do; 1962–70 Bangor, do; 1970–80 Blaenau, Ffestiniog, do.
Publications: Two Welsh Novels 1970, 1974.
Special Interests: Chairman of Welsh Youth, Chairman of Free Church Council, Membere (Padre) Toc H, Chairman of CND Committee, Preaching. *Hobbies and Recreations:* Fishing, Gardening, Writing.

WILLIAMS, Gareth, c/o RN, Army and RAF Board, 1 Central Buildings, Westminster, London SW1H 9NH. *b. 5 Mar 1936, Merthyr Tydfil, South Wales. m. 18 Aug 1962.*
Education: 1947–52 Central Secondary Technical Sch., Gloucester; 1957–61 Didsbury, Bristol. *Appointments:* 1961–63 Trowbridge and Bradford-on-Avon; 1963–66 Tavistock; 1966–68 Melton Mowbray; 1968– Chaplain HMF.
Special Interests: Liturgy, Adult Christian Education. *Hobbies and Recreations:* Aviation Art, Film History, Road Marching, Gliding.

WILLIAMS, Gerald E., 27 Pendarves Rd., Camborne, Cornwall TR14 7QF. (713128).
Education: 1950–52 Didsbury.
Appointments: 1949–50 Market Weighton; 1952–54 Isles of Scilly; 1954–59 Falmouth; 1959–64 Porthleven; 1964–69 Birmingham, Elmdon; 1969–74 Salisbury; 1974– Camborne.

WILLIAMS, Hugh Lawley, 10 Sunridge Park, Midsomer Norton, Bath BA3 2NZ. (0761-418100) *b. 4 Jan 1915, Crewe, Cheshire. m. 31 Jan 1948: 2s.*
Education: Crewe Grammar Sch.; 1935–38 Headingley. *Appointments:* 1938–39 Coventry; 1939–42 Stour Valley; 1942–46 HMF Chaplain; 1946–49 Rochdale; 1949–54 Stretford and Urmston; 1954–58 Blackpool; 1958–65 Shrewsbury; 1965–72 Colwyn Bay and Llandudno; 1972–78 Bournemouth.
Connexional Committees: 1965–72 Standing Committee for Methodism in Wales.
Hobbies and Recreations: Camping.

WILLIAMS, John Marshall, 2 Burton St., Loughborough, Leics LE11 2DT. (0509-262668) *b. 13 July 1939, Leigh-on-Sea, Essex. m. 21 Aug 1968: 1d., 1s.*
Education: County Grammar Sch. for Boys, Maidenhead; 1963–66 Richmond Coll. *Appointments:* 1966–71 Louth; 1971–79 Grimsby West; 1979– Loughborough.

WILLIAMS, Joseph Edward, Wesley Manse, 13 Clwyd Ave., Prestatyn, Clwyd LL19 9NG. (07456-4204)–BD(Lond.). *b. 7 June 1921, Ffynnongroyw. m. 10 Jan 1970.*
Education: 1924–32 Ffynnongroyw Prim. Sch.; 1932–35 Holywell Grammar Sch.; 1950–53 Headingley.
Appointments: 1953–55 Llanfaircaereinion; 1955–57 Pwllheli; 1957–60 Machynlleth; 1960–64 Holywell; 1964–70 Corwen; 1970–80 De Gwynedd; 1980– Dyffryn Clwyd.
Hobbies and Recreations: Accompanist for Soloists and Choirs on Piano and Organ.

WILLIAMS, Joseph George Alan, 2 Sunnycroft Rd., Leicester LE3 6FT. (0533-857407)–BA. *b. 19 June 1925, Winsford, Cheshire. m. 17 July 1954: 2d., 1s.*
Education: 1947–48 Cliff Coll.; 1950–53 Richmond. *Appointments:* 1949–50 Presteigne and Kington; 1953–57 Bude; 1957–63 Yeovil; 1963–70 Bristol North; 1970–73 Shildon; 1973–78 Altrincham; 1978 Leicester West.
Connexional Committees: 1974–77 Candidates Committee; 1958–62 Local Preachers Committee.
Special Interests: Walking, Photography, Music, Theatre.

WILLIAMS, Maldwyn Owen,, 41 Arncliffe Rd., Harrogate HG2 8NB. (0423-887415)–DipTheol(Lond.). *b. 30 Mar 1913, Birmingham. m. 19 July 1941: 1d., 1s.*
Education: 1913–19 George Dixon Grammar Sch., Birmingham; 1934–38 London Univ.; 1934–38 Richmond.
Appointments: 1938–41 Edinburgh Mission; 1942–45 Barton-on-Humber; 1945–50 Luton; 1950–54 South Shields; 1954–58 Cardiff; 1958–65 London, Highgate; 1965–71 Luton; 1971–77 Lincoln.
Connexional Committees: 1972 Retirement Fund (Connexional Committee).
Special Interests: Poetry and Literature.

WILLIAMS, Peter S., 10 Wellington Rd., Bebington, Wirral, Merseyside L63 7NF. (051-645-1304) *b. 23 Oct 1923, Porthleven, Cornwall. m. 16 Nov 1945: 2d., 1s.*
Education: Porthleven Elem.; Helston Grammar; 1964–66 Didsbury, Bristol.
Appointments: 1966–71 North Scotland Mission, 1971–79 Manchester North and Middleton; 1979– South Wirral.

WILLIAMS, Philip Deryk, Wesley Manse, 2 Lafrowda Villas, South Place, St. Just, Penzance, Cornwall TR19 7HL. (0736-788506) *b. 10 Aug 1929, Penzance, Cornwall. m. 9 Jan 1952: 2d.*
Education: 1933–41 Mairon Board Sch., Heamoor, Penzance; 1941–43 Daniels End (CE) Sch., Mairon, Penzance, Cornwall; 1945–48 Army Apprentices Coll.; 1959–61 Richmond. *Appointments:* 1961–65 South East Asia; 1965–69 Camelford and Wadebridge; 1969–74 Perranporth and St. Agnes; 1974–81 St. Columb and Padstow; 1981– St. Just.
Connexional Committees: 1969–75 Methodist Missionary Society General Committee; 1972–75 Methodist Missionary Society Home Committee.
Council Member: 1967–69 Camelford Parish Council; 1970–74 St. Agnes Parish Council; 1975–81 St. Dennis Parish Council; 1981– St. Just Age Concern Council.
Special Interests: 1976–81 Chaplain, English China Clays; 1969– Chaplain, Cornwall Army Cadet Force; 1965– Chaplain, Agricultural Community
Hobbies and Recreations: Snooker, Male Voice Choirs, Brass Band Contests, Involvement in Local Community Activities, Carnival Committees.

WILLIAMS, Richard Thompson Falcus, 35 Long Hill Rise, Hacknall, Nottingham NG15 6GL. (0602-632356)–BD(Lond.). *b. 15 Jan 1922, Newcastle upon Tyne. m. July 30 1949: 2s.*
Education: 1933–38 Heaton Secondary Sch.; 1947–50 Richmond. *Appointments:* 1950–54 Blyth and Seaton Delaval; 1954–59 South Shields; 1959–63 Lancaster; 1963–69 Hull West; 1969–76 Sheffield, Ecclesall; 1976–81 Bramhall; 1981– Nottingham North.
Special Interests: Travel, Sport. *Hobbies and Recreations:* Sport, Golf, Cricket.

WILLIAMS, Robert Glyn, Llys Myfyr, Yr Ala, Pwllheli, Gwynedd LL53 5BW. (0758-2608)–BA(Lampeter), BD(Wales). *b. 27 July 1924, Penmachno, Gwynedd. m. 6 Oct 1953: 2d.*
Education: 1928–39 Penmachno Council Sch.; 1942–43, 1945–47 Treveca Coll.; 1960–64 St. David's Univ. Coll.; 1965–68 United Theol. Coll., Aberystwyth; 1949–51 Handsworth. *Appointments:* 1947–48 Machynlleth; 1948–49 Llanfaircaereinion; 1951–54 Lampeter; 1954–60 Caernarfon; 1960–65 Lampeter; 1965–70 Machynlleth; 1970–81 London Welsh; 1981– De Guynedd.
Council Member: Gwynedd County Council.
Special Interests: Education. *Hobbies and Recreations:* Walking, Visiting Places of Historical Interest.

WILLIAMS, Thelma L., 6 Fair View, Dalton in Furness, Cumbria LA15 8RZ. (0229-62500).
Education: Deaconess Coll., Ilkley. *Appointments:* 1977–82 Carlisle; 1982– South West Cumbria.

WILLIAMS, Tom Torkington, 37 Bron-yr-Eglwys, Mynydd Isa, Mold, Clwyd. (56132) *b. 17 June 1915, Stockport, Cheshire. m. 26 July 1946: 1d., 1s.*
Education: 1920–27 Prim. Sch.; 1927–31 Stockport Technical Coll.; 1939–41 Richmond; 1941–42 Headingley. *Appointments:* 1942–46 Preston, Clubland; 1947–48 W. Nigeria; 1947–52 Burslem Hill Top; 1952–56 Stourbridge; 1956–68 Bolton Wesley; 1968–77 Buckley and Deeside; 1977–80 Kidsgrove.
Connexional Committees: 1968–80 Property Division.
Local Council Committees: 1956–68 Education Committees and School Governor.
Hobbies and Recreations: Woodwork, Photography.

WILLIAMSON, Douglas C., 14 Compton Rd., Shepton Mallet, Somerset BA4 5QR. (0749-2462).
Education: 1951–54 Didsbury, Bristol. *Appointments:* 1950–51 Kent Mission; 1954–56 South Molton; 1956–60 Ringsash; 1960–63 Swindon; 1963–66 Bath; 1966–71 Somerset Mission; 1971–75 Bude; 1975–79 Aberdare; 1979– Frome.

WILLIAMSON, Eric Stanley, Lynchmere, 35 Western Ave., Barton-on-Sea, New Milton, Hants BH25 7PY. (0425-612712) *b. 6 Jan 1905, Leicester. m. 10 Aug 1938: 1d., 3s.*
Education: 1916–19 Burton-on-Trent Grammar Sch.; 1926–29 Hartley Victoria. *Appointments:* 1929–33 Brighton and Hove; 1933–34 Liphook; 1934–36 Chichester; 1936–42 Ryde (East Wight); 1942–47 Shaftesbury and Gillingham; 1947–48 Eastleigh; 1948–51 Ilkeston; 1951–54 Mansfield; 1954–60 Silchester; 1960–65 Buckfastleigh; 1965–69 Southwold.
Special Interests: Social Welfare, Peace and Disarmament. *Hobbies Recreations:* Stamp Collecting, Photography, Bowls.

WILLIAMSON, Ian Arthur, 41 Harewood Cresc., North Hykeham, Lincoln LN6 8JG. (0522-681282) *b. 30 Jan 1933, Derby. m. 5 Mar 1967.*
Education: Various Secondary Moderns in Birmingham Area; 1959–60 Cliff Coll.; 1961–63 Handsworth. *Appointments:* 1963–64 Bradford, Woodhouse Grove; 1964 Peterlee and Durham Coast; 1965–68 Middlesbrough; 1968–73 Coventry; 1973–81 Derby, Derwent Mission; 1981– Lincoln Central.
Connexional Committees: 1965–68 Div. of Education and Youth; 1965–68 District Youth Secretary; 1978–80 Overseas Division; 1982 Overseas Secretary, Nottingham and Derby District; 1982– Lincoln.
Special Interests: History, Travel, Walking, Music.

WILLIAMSON, Peter Booth, 4 The Elms, Stoke, Plymouth PL3 4BR. (0752-52982) *b. 25 March 1942, Marple, Cheshire. m. 16 Aug 1976.*
Education: 1947–53 Compstall County Prim.; 1953–57 Bredbury Secondary Modern; 1957–59 Hyde County Grammar; 1964–68 Hartley Victoria. *Appointments:* 1968–71 Leeds North East; 1971–76 Leeds (Horsforth and Bramley); 1976–82 South Molton; 1982– Devonport.
Connexional Committees: 1978– Divisional Board Education and Youth. *Local Council Committees:* 1977–82 Education and Youth Provisions.
Special Interests: Religious Broadcasting, Drama, Church in Inner City, Church and Community Projects, Education for Adults and Children, Youth Work. *Hobbies and Recreations:* Travel, Genealogy, Photography, Social and Political History of England from the 17th Century, Gardening, Philately.

WILLIE, David Frederick, 2 Thorn Rd., Bramhall, Stockport, Cheshire SK7 1HQ. (061-439-1204)–MA. *b. 25 July 1939, York. m. 3 July 1965: 1d., 2s.*
Education: 1944–47 St. Thomas Sch., York; 1947–50 Brighton Grove Sch., Gateshead; 1950–57 Jarrow Grammar Sch.; 1962-65 Fitzwilliam Coll., Cambridge; 1962–65 Wesley House. *Appointments:* 1965–68 Filey; 1968–73 York (Centenary); 1973–78 Harpenden; 1978– Bramhall.
Connexional Committees: 1970–75 Division of Education and Youth Board and Executive; 1981– Ministers Retirement Fund Committee. *Local Council Committees:* 1968–73 Youth Committee, York Education Authority.
Special Interests: Youth Work,

Healing Mission. *Hobbies and Recreations:* Walking, Badminton, Methodist Philately.

WILLINGHAM, Reginald John, 9 Goad Ave., Trevol, Torpoint, Cornwall PL11 2ND. (0752-813472)—BD(Lond.). *b. 28 Dec 1930, Ilford, Essex. m. 29 June 1968: 2d.*
Education: 1935–41 Downshall and William Torbitt Elem.; 1941–46 Ilford County High Sch. for Boys; 1951–54 London Univ.; 1951–54 Richmond. *Appointments:* 1954–57 Devonport; 1957–62 Ashton-under-Lyne; 1962–75 Leeward Island Dt; 1975– Devonport.
Connexional Committees: 1976–82 Central Committee (Overseas Division).

WILLIS, Derek, 2 Carlton Terrace, Cross Keys, Newport, Gwent NP1 7BU. (0495-270621).
Education: March Grammar; 1948–50 Hartley Victoria. *Appointments:* 1947–48 Llandrindod Wells; 1948–50 Hartley Victoria; 1950–51 Wymondham; 1951–54 Chaplain HMF; 1954–55 Nelson, Lancs.; 1955–58 Pocklington; 1958–59 Sheffield, Surrey St.; 1959–61 Sheffield South; 1961–66 Blaydon; 1964–67 Hebden Bridge; 1967–70 Leigh; 1970–73 Crook; 1973–76 Wath and Mexborough; 1976–78 North Shields and Whitley Bay; 1978–80 Risca and Cross Keys.
Special Interests: Politics, Education, Mental Health. *Hobbies and Recreations:* Rugby Union, Music, Brass Bands.

WILLIS, Ernest Charles, 17 Upgang Lane, Whitby, N. Yorks YO21 3DT. (0947-602248) *b. 23 Feb 1921, Derby. m. Carr, 8 April 1944: 1d.*
Education: 1925 35 Horninglow and Victoria, Burton-on-Trent.
Appointments: 1949–52 Lay Pastor, East End Mission; 1952–54 Lay Pastor, Devon and Dorset Mission; 1954–58 Southampton; 1958–63 Burton-on-Trent; 1962–63 Newall and Woodville; 1963–71 Tadcaster; 1971–79 Scarborough; 1979– Whitby.
Special Interests: Forces Chaplaincy, Journalism. *Hobbies and Recreations:* Photography, Letterpress Printing.

WILLS, Nicholas Mann, Ashfield, Low Worsall, Yarm, N. Yorks TS15 9PJ. (0642-780040) *b. 4 Oct 1901, Devonport. m. 28 Nov 1964: 3s.*
Education: Porth County Grammar; 1925–27 Hartley. *Appointments:* 1927–29 Swindon; 1929–33 Frome; 1933–38 Calne; 1938–44 Pontefract; 1944–50 Middlesbrough; 1950–55 Darlington; 1955–60 York; 1960–64 Thirsk.
Connexional Committees: 1933 Christian Citizenship.
Special Interests: Youth Work.
Hobbies and Recreations: Angling, Gardening, Lapidary.

WILLS, N. Trevelyan, 32 Chapel St., Ely, Cambs CB6 1AD. (0353-2426) *b. 18 Dec 1932. m. 13 June 1959: 2d., 1s.*
Education: 1957–60 Hartley Victoria.
Appointments: 1960–64 Darlaston; 1964–69 Barnsley (East); 1969–74 Wolverhampton (Trinity); 1974–81 Wymondham, Attleborough and Watton; 1981– Ely.

WILLSHAW, Thomas Mervyn, 11 Cherry Ave., Canterbury, Kent CT2 8EN. (0227-64179)—MA, BD. *b. 15 July 1934, Stoke-on-Trent. m. 9 Aug 1958: 1d., 2s.*
Education: 19445–50 Hanley High Sch.; 1975–76 Bristol Univ.; Univ. of Kent; 1954–58 Hartley Victoria.
Appointments: 1958–61 Dewsbury; 1961–66 Leeds (Headingley); 1966–71 York (Centenary); 1971–78 Bristol (Clifton and Redland); 1978– Chaplain Kent Coll., Canterbury.
Connexional Committees: 1961–66 Education Committee; 1980– Connexional Probationers' Oversight Committee; 1982– Connexional Candidates Committee. *Publications:* Essay in *The Testing of the Churches 1932–82* (Epworth 1982); Regular contributor to *Worship and Preaching* (1978–80, 1982–84); Occasional Sermons in *The Expository Times* (1972–82).
Special Interests: Preaching, 19th and 20th Century Church, Theological Education. *Hobbies and Recreations:* Cricket, Collecting Records, Badminton.

WILLSON, Philip Michael, 57 Priory Cresc., Bridlington, North Humberside YO16 5SE. (0262-74275) *b. 4 June 1938, York. m. 23 March 1963: 2d.*
Education: Fulford CE Prim., York; Archbishop Holgates Grammar Sch., York; 1963–67 Headingley.
Appointments: 1967–70 Cheadle; 1970–75 Barrow-in-Furness; 1975–80 Wakefield; 1980– Bridlington.
Local Council Committees: 1980– Youth Committee, Bridlington; 1971–75 Youth Committee, Barrow-in-Furness; 1978–79 Sch. Governor, Wakefield.
Special Interests: Music, Education.
Hobbies and Recreations: Playing the Piano.

WILMSHURST, Peter Eric, Wesley Manse, The Sands, Brampton, Cumbria CA8 1ET. (069-77-2452) *b. 25 July 1930, Sydenham, London. m. 21 June 1958: 2s.*
Education: 1954–58 Handsworth.
Appointments: 1958–60 Llandrindod Wells; 1960–66 Cradley Heath; 1966–69 Birmingham, Blackheath; 1969–76 Middlesbrough; 1976–82 Birmingham (Asbury); 1982– Brampton.

WILSON, David Dunn, 87 Willingdon Rd., Eastbourne BN21 1TZ. (0323-21551)—MA, BD, M.Phill, PhD. *b. 11 Aug 1933, Plumsted. m. 16 Aug 1958: 2d., 1s.*
Education: 1941–45 Worcester Royal Grammar Sch.; 1945–52 King Edward VI Grammar Sch., Stourbridge; 1952–56 Univ. of Birmingham; 1956–57 Univ. of Dubuque, USA; 1962–64 Univ. of Nottingham; 1965–68 Univ. of Leeds; 1975–77 Univ. of Kent; 1980–82 Univ. of Sussex; 1954–56 Handsworth. *Appointments:* 1957–58 Home Mission Evangelist; 1958–61 Doncaster District Coalfields Mission; 1962–67 Liverpool South East; 1968–75 Romford; 1975- Eastbourne.
Connexional Committees: 1972–76 Methodist Archives Committee;

1977–80 The President's Council; 1973– Fernley-Hartley Trust Committee. *Publications: Stories for Children* (1973); *How to Begin a Family Worship Programme* (1964); *Many Waters Cannot Quench* (1969).
Special Interests: Preaching, Church History. *Hobbies and Recreations:* Music, Railways.

WILSON, Derek, 14 Vista Rd., Runcorn, Cheshire WA7 4PB. (092-85-73651) *b. 9 March 1928, Manchester, m. 4 Aug 1956: 1d., 3s.*
Education: 1939–44 North Manchester High Sch.; 1952–55 Handsworth. *Appointments:* 1956–58 Stour Valley Mission; 1958–66 Ludlow; 1971–78 Sunderland North; 1966–71 Cannock Chase; 1978– Runcorn.
Connexional Committees: 1974–78 Property Division.

WILSON, Ewart Townend, 1 St. John's Ave., Filey, N. Yorks YO14 9AZ. (0723-512168) *b. 28 June 1922, Kingston-upon-Hull. m. 28 July 1951.*
Education: 1927–30 Endsleigh Convent, Hull; 1930–37 Marist Coll., Hull; 1937–38 Woods Commercial Coll.; 1947–49 Handsworth. *Appointments:* 1946–49 Wolverton and Bletchley; 1949–50 Marlborough; 1950–52 Pateley Bridge; 1952–56 Hull (St. George's Rd.); 1956–59 Middlesbrough; 1959–64 Cross Hills, Silsden and Cowling; 1964–71 Hillingdon; 1971–74 Hull Mission; 1974–78 Wimbledon; 1978– Filey.
Connexional Committees: 1965–79 SRD Politics and Economics Standing Committee; 1979– SRD Working Party on South African Investments; 1965–73 Inter-Departmental Youth Committee.
Special Interests: Politics, Sociology, Civic Affairs, History. *Hobbies and Recreations:* Reading, Music, Football, Swimming, Travel.

WILSON, Frank Waller, 21 The Ave., Richmond, N. Yorks DL10 7AZ. (0748-3149)–BA, BD(Lond.). *b. 4 Jan 1922, Hull, Yorks. m. 5 Aug 1969.*
Education: 1931–39 Hymers Coll., Hull; 1948–50 Headingley.
Appointments: 1946–48 Barton-on-Humber; 1950–52 Gibraltar; 1952–57 Blyth and Seaton Delaval; 1957–64 Ripon; 1964–69 Hull West; 1969–74 Filey; 1974–82 Huddersfield West and Pennine; 1982– Richmond (Yorks).
Special Interests: Work of the Ministry, History, Politics. *Hobbies and Recreations:* Fell Walking, Philately, Gardening.

WILSON, George Leslie, 39 Upper Boundary Rd., Derby DE3 3NU. (0332-44709) *b. 29 May 1904, Eastwood, Notts. m. 2 Aug 1937: 3s.*
Education: Elem.; 1930–33 Hartley Victoria. *Appointments:* 1933–35 President's List; 1935–39 Bottesford; 1939–42 Kirby, Stephen; 1942–47 Barrow; 1947–50 Blackburn, Clayton St.; 1950–54 Church Gresley; 1954–59 Workington; 1959–64 Gateshead South West; 1964–69 Old Hill; 1969–72 Derby, Derwent.
Local Council Committees: 1945–46 Barrow Youth Committee; 1965–69 Social Services, Rowley Regis.

WILSON, Gordon Leighton, 13 Endcliffe Rise Rd., Sheffield S11 8RU. (0742-666490)–BA(Open). *b. 19 Dec 1937, Derby. m.: 1d., 2s.*
Education: 1948–53 Bemrose Sch., Derby; 1981– Hull Univ. (Part Time); 1960–64 Handsworth.
Appointments: 1964–66 Wednesbury Mission; 1966–72 Wolverhampton (Darlington St.); 1972–74 Doncaster; 1974– Sheffield Mission (Industrial Chaplain).
Connexional Committees: 1967–72 Christian Citizenship; 1974–81 Church in Industry; 1981– Social Questions.
Special Interests: Mission, Theological Understanding of Industrial Society. *Hobbies and Recreations:* Caravanning, Photography, Walking, Model-Making.

WILSON, Joseph, 5 Parliament Sq., Castletown, Isle of Man. (0624-822244) *b. 19 Aug 1901, Liverpool. m. 26 Aug 1930: 3s.*
Education: 1911–15 Oakes Institute, Liverpool; 1915–17 Toxteth Technical, Liverpool; 1917–21 Skerries Coll. of Engineering; 1923–26 Didsbury. *Appointments:* 1930–33 Pateley Bridge; 1933–36 Birkenhead; 1936–39 Waterloo; 1939–43 Manchester Mission; 1943–49 Douglas (IoM); 1949–56 Lincoln; 1956–61 Spalding; 1961–66 Castle (IoM); 1956–59 Chairman of IoM District; 1943–49 Secretary IoM District; 1966– Appointed Government Chaplain House of Keys, IoM.
Connexional Committees: 1956–61 Cliff Coll.; 1943–49 Home Missions Committee; General Purposes etc.
Council Member: Holland (Lincs.) County Council Education Committee; 1956–61 Notts. Univ. Advanced Technical Committee.
Special Interests: Archaeology, Engineering, Motoring. *Hobbies and Recreations:* Reading.

WILSON, Joseph Arthur, 358 Edenfield Rd., Rochdale OL12 7NH. (0706-47648)–BA(Open), BD(Lond.). *b. 7 Nov 1935, Bingley, Yorkshire. m.: 2s.*
Education: 1941–47 Farnworth, St. Lukes CE, Widnes; 1947–52 Wade Deacon Grammar Sch., Widnes; 1960–61 Westhill; 1956–60 Hartley Victoria. *Appointments:* 1961–64 Regional Youth Organiser (MYD); 1964–69 Linacre Mission; 1969–76 Newark; 1976– Rochdale.
Connexional Committees: Day Schools. *Council Member:* 1972–75 Balderton Parish Council, Newark.
Local Council Committees: 1964–69 Bootle CB Education; 1978–81 Rochdale MB Education.

WILSON, Kenneth, 26 Debdale Rd., Wellingborough, Northamptonshire NN8 3AA. (0933-222560) *b. 14 July 1924, Wakefield, West Yorkshire. m. 23 Aug 1952: 2s.*
Education: 1929–31 Prim. Sch., Westgate, Wakefield; 1931–35 Tamworth, Bolehall Boys Sch.; 1935–41 Tamworth Grammar Sch.; 1948–50 Headingley. *Appointments:* 1946 Carlisle; 1947–49 Kendal; 1950–58 Salisbury; 1958–63 Chester Hunter

St.; 1959–63 Chester, Grosvenor Park; 1963 Chester; 1965–72 Leicester South; 1972–78 Leicester South East; 1978 Wellingborough.
Special Interests: Family. *Hobbies and Recreations:* Gardening, Music.

WILSON, Kenneth Brian, Westminster Coll., North Hinksey, Oxford OX2 9AT. (0865-47644)–MA(Cantab.), MLitt(Bristol), PhD(Bristol). *b. 10 April 1957, Bangor, Caernarvonshire, N. Wales. m. 31 July 1962: 2d., 1s.*
Education: 1950–56 Kingswood Sch., Bath; 1957–61 Trinity Hall, Cambridge; 1961–64 Univ. of Bristol; 1961–64 Wesley, Bristol.
Appointments: 1964–66 London, Hinde St.; 1966–69 Bath Circuit and Kingswood Sch. Assistant Chaplain; 1969–73 Kingswood Sch. Chaplain; 1973–80 Wesley Coll., Bristol, Tutor Philosophy and Ethics; 1980– Westminster Coll., (Principal).
Connexional Committees: 1974–82 Faith and Order. *Publications:* Fernley Hartley Lecturer (1973); *Making Sense of It* (Epworth 1973); *Living it Out* (1977); *The Experience of Ordination* (1979).
Special Interests: Philosophy, Systematic Theology, Science and Religion, Economics and Theology, EEC, Theology of Education. *Hobbies and Recreations:* Proust and Wittgenstein, Poetry, Gardening, Music.

WILSON, Robert, 211 Gloucester Rd., Cheltenham, Glos Gl51 8NJ. (0242-516078) *b. 22 Dec 1934, Bedlington, Northumberland. m. 27 May 1970: 2d., 3s.*
Education: 1939–44 Barrington Prim. Sch.; 1944–49 Bedlington Secondary Modern Sch.; 1960–61 Cliff Coll., 1962–65 Headingley.
Appointments: 1965–69 Halifax Wesley; 1969–72 St. Austell; 1972–79 Watford; 1979– Cheltenham.
Special Interests. People. *Hobbies and Recreations:* American Square Dancing, Counted Cross-Stitch.

WILSON, William, 12 Grassington Way, Chapleton, Sheffield S30 4ER. (463279)–MEd. *b. 19 Jan 1938, Durham. m. 11 June 1962: 1d., 1s.*
Education: 1956 Stockton Technical; 1957–60 Teeside Poly.; 1960–61 Bradford Univ.; 1973–76 Manchester Univ.; 1961–64 Hartley Victoria.
Appointments: 1964–65 Denby Dale; 1965–68 Birstal and Berkenshaw; 1968–72 Stockton and Billingham Technical Coll.; 1972– Stocksbridge Coll., Sheffield.
Publications: Decision Making (European International Journal 1976); Contributor to *Humanising the Workplace* (Croom & Helm 1977); *Towards Industrial Democracy in GB* (Manchester Univ. 1978).
Special Interests: Politics, Industrial Relations, Social Structures. *Hobbies and Recreations:* Reading, Walking, Music.

WINDSOR, Anthony, 7 Wentwood Gdns., Estover, Plymouth, Devon PL6 8TD, (0752-706490) *b. 5 May 1933, Poplar, London. m. 26 July 1958: 3d.*
Education: 1940–44 Benfleet (Essex) Prim. Sch.; 1944–46 Benfleet (Essex) Jun. Sch.; 1946–49 Southend-on-Sea (Essex) Municipal Coll.; 1955–58 Richmond. *Appointments:* 1958–61 Brigg; 1961–67 Downham Market; 1967–73 Manchester (Withington); 1973–82 Kings Lynn; 1975–81 East Anglia District, Synod Secretary; 1982– Plymouth (Devon).
Local Council Committees: 1975–77 Kings Lynn Community Health Council.
Special Interests: Ecumenical Work, Liturgy. *Hobbies and Recreations:* Walking, Music, Industrial Archaeology.

WINFIELD, Samuel, Pavia, Boon St., Eckington, Pershore, Worcs WR10 3BL. (0386-750639) *b. 17 Jan 1901, Awsworth, Notts. m. May: 1d., 1s.*
Education: 1906–15 Answorth County Sch.; 1924–27 Victoria Park.
Appointments: 1932–37 Blyth; 1937–46 Oakengates; 1946–52 Wolverhampton; 1952–58 Birmingham South; 1958–63 Derby South; 1963–68 Worsley.
Special Interests: Reading, Music. *Hobbies and Recreations:* Gardening, Painting.

WINN, Keith Kessell, 6 Hounslow Rd., Feltham, Middlesex TW14 9DG. (01-890-2783) *b. 4 June 1933, Troon, Camborne, Cornwall. m. 22 Aug 1959: 2d., 2s.*
Education: 1938–44 Troon Prim. and Jun.; 1944–49 Redruth Grammar; 1956–59 Didsbury, Bristol.
Appointments: 1959–62 Pontefract; 1962–67 St. Austell; 1967–72 Holsworthy; 1972–75 Devonport; 1975–82 Staines and Feltham; 1982– Nottingham North.
Connexional Committees: 1964–67 Social Responsibility.
Special Interests: Renewal and Church Growth Movement. *Hobbies and Recreations:* Caravanning, Walking, Photography.

WINTER, Harold Ernest, 41 Ashford Ave., London N8 8LN. (01-340-4185)–BD(Lond.). *b. 21 May 1921, Norwich. m. 15 Aug 1947: 1d., 1s.*
Education: 1925–32 Crooks Place, Norwich; 1932 City of Norwich Secondary Sch.; 1946–47 Headingley.
Appointments: 1943–46 Bedale; 1947–49 Bishop Auckland; 1949–53 East Suffolk; 1953–56 Hinckley (Stockwell Head); 1956–63 Luton; 1963–64 Leeds (Richmond Hill); 1964–72 Watford; 1972–81 St. Albans; 1981– London (Highgate); 1969–81 Synod Secretary, London NW District.
Special Interests: Music. *Hobbies and Recreations:* Gardening, Model Railways.

WINWOOD, David James, 9 Coniston Rd., Muswell Hill, London N10. (01-833-9312) *b. 21 July 1944, London. m. 11 April 1970.*
Education: 1955–57 Crouch End Secondary Boys Sch.; 1957–60 Enfield Secondary Technical Sch.; 1964–68 London Univ.; 1964–68 Richmond. *Appointments:* 1968–72 Glasgow Mission; 1972–79 Medway Towns; 1979– National Secretary MAYC Division of Education and Youth.
Connexional Committees: 1974–79 Education and Youth Board.

Publications: Sexuality under Discussion (1982); *Value and Vision* (1982); *I Want to Begin* (1983); *I Want to Belong* (1983); *Time for Talking* (Ed 1980); *Before it's too Late* (1980); *Ways to Work with the Young Unemployed* (1981); *Riots: Urgent need for Ministry among Young People* (1981). *Special Interests:* Counselling, Evangelism, Urban Mission, Community Work. *Hobbies and Recreations:* Guitar, Drums, Art, Photography, Camping.

WISBEY, Harry Lewis, Flat 4, Heathcliffe, Redhills Rd., Arnside, Carnforth, Lancs LA5 0AT. (761139) *b. 21 Jan 1905, Brightlingsea, Essex. m. 4 June 1932: 1d.*
Education: 1910–19 Wesleyan Day Sch., Brightlingsea. *Appointments:* 1950–51 Carlisle, Fisher St.; 1951–56 North Scotland Mission.
Special Interests: Preaching and Pastoral Work. *Hobbies and Recreations:* Gardening.

WITHERS, Stanley James, 6 The Drive, Dalby Rd., Melton Mowbray, Leics LE13 0BT. (0664-62501) *b. 3 Feb 1923, Whalley Range, Manchester. m. 30 July 1952: 1d., 2s.*
Education: 1928–34 Chorlton Park Prim., Manchester; 1934–40 Chorlton High, Manchester; 1947–49 Handsworth. *Appointments:* 1949–52 Raunds; 1952–56 Ossett and Horbury; 1956–61 Leigh; 1961–66 Marple; 1966–74 Hillingdon; 1974–79 West Somerset; 1979– Melton Mowbray.
Council Member: 1969–74 Gerrards Cross (Bucks) Parish Council.
Publications: Local Methodist Church Histories, Thornhill Combs (Youth 1955), Denham (Bucks 1970).
Special Interests: Mental Handicapped, Geriatrics. *Hobbies and Recreations:* Golf, Gardening, Travel.

WOLLEN, Douglas Albert, 51 Derwent House, Southern Grove, London E3 4PU. (01-980-2552)–MA(Lond.), BA(Lond.). *b. 22 June 1909, Woodford, Essex. m. 21 Aug 1937: 1d., 2s.*
Education: 1919–27 Chigwell Sch.; 1930–31 Westminster Training Coll.
Appointments: 1930–40 Temperance and Social Welfare Dept.; 1940–44: Ramsor and Uttoxeter; 1944–47 Macclesfield; 1947–50 Bromley; 1950–55 Exeter; 1955–60 Penarth; 1960–64 Chesterfield; 1964–72 Sydenham and Forest Hill; 1972–78 Poplar; 1978– Hon. Historian of Wesley Chapel.
Connexional Committees: TOSW and CC for many years; Faith and Order; Secretary of Connexional Church Membership Committee for many years. *Publications: John Wesley, Christian Citizen* (with E. C. Urwin 1937); *The Life of a Circuit Minister* (Reprinted from Pelican, Work 2, by Ministerial Training Dept.)
Special Interests: Arts Correspondent of Methodist Recorder after many years writing on the arts for the Times.

WOLLEN, Leslie Macauley, Rose Cottage, Kidnalls Rd., Pillowell, Lydney, Glos GL15 4RD. (0594-562046)–BSc(Lond.), MA(Cantab.). *b. 10 Jan 1911, Woodford, Essex. m. 23 July 1938: 3d.*
Education: Churchfields, Woodford (LEA Elem.); Bancrofts Sch., Woodford, Wells; 1927–31 London Univ.; 1935–36 Finch Scholar, Univ. of Heidelberg; 1932–35 Wesley House. *Appointments:* 1931–Wanstead and Woodford; 1936–41 Bristol, Bishopston; 1941–49 London, Deptford and Greenwich Mission; 1949–54 Finchley and Hendon; 1954–60 Buckingham and Brackley; 1960–63 Newcastle, Brunswick; 1963–75 Bristol District Chairman.
Connexional Committees: 1950–60 Church Membership, and many others, including Stationing, as Chairman of District. *Local Council Committees:* 1964–75 Bristol Education Committee; 1964–75 Bristol Community Relations.
Special Interests: Non-conformist History, Politics, United Nations Association. *Hobbies and Recreations:* Gardening, Walking.

WONG, John Yuk-Lun, 28 Gibbon Rd., East Acton, London W3 7AF. (01-743-5216)–BTh, BD. *b. 14 Jan 1926, Hong Kong. m. 27 Mar 1954.*
Education: 1931–42 Kong Kim Coll., Hong Kong; 1959–62 Trinity Theol. Coll. *Appointments:* 1963–67 Hong Kong District; 1967–68 London Mission/Overseas Division; 1968–80 Hammersmith (Chinese Chaplaincy); 1980–81 Overseas Division.
Local Council Committees: 1975–78 Executive Member of the Hammersmith Community, Relations Council of the Hammersmith Borough of London.
Special Interests: Psychology, Philosophy, Sociology. *Hobbies and Recreations:* Mechanical Engineering, Electronics and Carpentry, Jogging.

WOOD, Alfred Henry, 15 Mead Close, Paignton, Devon TQ3 2AS. (0803-527427) *b. 19 Jan 1917, London, Wandsworth, East Battersea. m.: 1d., 1s.*
Education: Fords Endowed, Dagenham, Essex; 1939–42 Headingley. *Appointments:* 1942–44 Southend on Sea; 1944–47 Chaplain HMS; 1947–51 Radcliffe; 1951–54 Bolton (Bridge St.); 1954–60 Okehampton; 1960–68 Plymouth (King St.); 1968–76 Holsworthy; 1976–82 Saltash and St. Germans.
Connexional Committees: Youth.
Publications: Faith for Life (Television Broadcasts, Westward TV, 1975).

WOOD, Arthur Skevington, Cliff Coll., Calver, Sheffield S30 1XG. (024-688-2321/2)–BA(Lond.), PhD(Edinburgh). *b. 21 April 1916, Ashbourne, Derbyshire. m. 1 Jan 1943.*
Education: 1921–26 Privately; 1926–33 Yarm Grammar Sch.; 1948–51 New Coll., Univ. of Edinburgh; 1936–40 Headingley. *Appointments:* 1940–43 Glasgow, Parkhead and Burnbank; 1943–46 Brierley Hill; 1946–51 Coatbridge and Airdrie; 1951–57 Paisley Mission; 1957–59 Sunderland West; 1959–62 York Wesley; 1962–70 Movement for World Evangelisation; 1970 Cliff Coll. (Tutor); 1977 Cliff Coll. (Principal).

Connexional Committees: 1945–51 Local Preachers; 1977– Home Mission; 1970–77 Methodist Study Centre; 1981– Epworth Press Editoral Sub-Committee. *Publications:* Eighteen Books on Biblical and Historical Subjects; Numerous Articles and Reviews; *The Drew Lecture on Immortality* (1979). *Special Interests:* The Protestant Reformation, The History of Revivals, Evangelism. *Hobbies and Recreations:* Cricket, Music.

WOOD, Cledwyn, 4 Roundle Ave., Felpham, Bognor Regis, West Sussex PO22 8LQ. (024-369-2982) *b. 3 May 1914, Stockton-on-Tees. m. 21 Dec 1945: 1s.*
Education: 1941–42 Hartley Victoria; 1942–43 Headingley; 1943–44 Wesley House. *Appointments:* 1939–41 Presteigne and Kington; 1944–46 New Forest Mission; 1946–49 Redditch; 1949–54 Birmingham (Wesley); 1954–59 East Wight; 1959–64 Portsmouth; 1964–71 New Forest Mission and Wimborne; 1971–78 Birmingham (Moseley Rd. and Sparkhill); 1978– Chichester and Bognor.
Hobbies and Recreations: Garden, Photography.

WOOD, David Ronald, 8 Brooksby Close, Oadby, Leicester LE2 5AB. (0533-712404)–MA(St. Andrews), MPhil(Cantab.). *b. 19 Dec 1951, Shipley, West Yorkshire. m. 10 Aug 1974: 1s.*
Education: 1956–60 Sandals Prim. Sch., Baildun; 1960–70 Bradford Grammar Sch.; 1970–73 St. Andrew's Univ.; 1976–79 Wesley House. *Appointments:* 1979 Leicester South East.
Special Interests: Hebrew and Old Testament Studies. *Hobbies and Recreations:* Walking, Model Railways.

WOOD, Raymond, The Manse, 45 Mulgrave Ave., Ashton-on-Ribble, Preston PR2 1HJ. (0772-726216) *b. 20 May 1930, Birmingham. m. 17 Dec 1960: 1d., 2s.*
Education: 1937–38 Dixon Rd. Prim. Sch., Small Heath, Birmingham; 1938–43 Billesley Prim., Jun., Sch; 1943–46 Bllesley Secondary Modern Sch.; 1953–55 Cliff Coll.; 1955–59 Hartley Victoria; 1959–60 St. Andrews. *Appointments:* 1961–74 Dahomey-Togo District, Lay Training and Christian Literature Secretary; 1971–76 Kirkoswald; 1976– Preston Trinity.
Connexional Committees: 1972–76, 1977– Overseas Division.
Hobbies and Recreations: Fly Fishing and Sea Fishing, Sport in General.

WOOD, Thomas, 19 St. John's Walk, Kirby Hill, Boroughbridge, Yorks YO5 9DJ. (090-12-2994) *b. 26 Mar 1908, Bedlington, Northumberland. m. 9 Nov 1943: 1s.*
Education: 1932–36 Headingley. *Appointments:* 1936–44 Barbados Dt; 1949–53 Kidderminster; 1953–58 Southampton; 1958–61 London, Finsbury Park; 1961–68 Buckley; 1968–73 Pateley Bridge.
Hobbies and Recreations: Gardening.

WOOD, Thomas Harold, 51 Cranmore Rd., Chislehurst West, BR7 6EP. (01-857-8690) *b. 28 June 1915, Barton-on-Humber, Lincs. m. 27 Dec 1954: 1d., 1s.*
Education: 1937–40 Richmond. *Appointments:* 1940–45 Brighton (Dome Mission); 1945–51 London, Paddington; 1951–57 South London Mission; 1957–63 Bromley; 1963–72 Canterbury; 1972–80 Chislehurst.
Connexional Committees: General Purposes Committee; Property Divisional Board; Permission to Serve External Organisations; Advisory Committee on Ministerial Appointments; Connexional Candidates Examination Committee.
Hobbies and Recreations: Camping and Caravanning, Foreign Travel, Photography.

WOODLEY, Alexander John, 71 Tynewydd Rd., Barry, S. Glamorgan CF6 6BA. (0446-734508) *b. 10 Feb 1923, Birmingham. m. 16 Aug 1952: 2d.*
Education: 1928–34 Hall Green Prim. and Jun. Sch., Birmingham; 1934–39 Moseley Grammar Sch., Birmingham; 1949–51 Hartley Victoria. *Appointments:* 1948–49 Worcester; 1951–53 Leominster; 1953–58 Wolstanton and Audley; 1958–63 Hull (West); 1963–70 York (Wesley); 1970–77 Ulverston; 1977–80 Cheddar Valley; 1980– Barry.
Connexional Committees: 1963–64 National President MAYC; 1958 Youth Committee.
Special Interests: Related to Church as a Family, Geriatric Chaplaincy.
Hobbies and Recreations: Painting, Photography.

WOODS, Bertram Ernest, 53 Daniel Place, Penzance, Cornwall TR18 4DU. (0736-4470) *b. 17 May 1900, Norwich. m. 1962: 1s.*
Education: Brighton; 1922–25 Didsbury. *Appointments:* 1921–22 Sittingbourne; 1925–28 Scarborough; 1928–31 North Isles; 1931–34 Swindon; 1934–37 Sunderland North; 1937–44 Glasgow, Cathcart Rd.; 1944–49 London Mission, Wandsworth Rd.; 1949–56 London, Brixton Hill; 1956–64 Redhill.
Connexional Committees: Home Missions Committee; Healing Committee. *Council Member:* Wandsworth Borough Council 3 Years. *Publications:* Book *Ministry of Healing;* Book of Anthems of his own composing.
Special Interests: Music, Spiritual Healing.

WOODS, Francis John, Woodlands, 68 Hill View Rd., Minehead, Somerset TS24 8EF. (0643-5297) *b. 28 Oct 1913, Seven Kings, Ilford. m. 7 Aug 1943.*
Education: 1918–25 Downshall Sch., Seven Kings, Ilford; 1925–30 County High Sch., Ilford; 1934–37 Headingley. *Appointments:* 1937–39 London, Walthamstow; 1939–42 London, Ilford; 1942–46 Harpenden; 1946–50 St. Albans; 1950–56 Nottingham West; 1956–60 Williton; 1960–69 Nottingham East; 1969–74 Liverpool, Crosby; 1974 Cardiff, Roath; 1975 Cardiff.
Connexional Committees: 1945–50 Methodist Study Centre; 1951–61,

1966–69 Church Membership; 1969–78 Prison.
Hobbies and Recreations: Music, Walking, Travel.

WOODS, John Wesley, 156 Greenhill Ave., Little Norton, Sheffield 8. *b. 10 Dec 1916, Eastbourne, Sussex. m. 7 July 1955: 1s.*
Education: St. Philips Inf., Eastbourne; St. Andrews Jun., Eastbourne; Berewell CE Central Sch.; 1946–48 Bristol, Didsbury.
Appointments: 1945–48 Bridgwater; 1948–49 Loughbrough; 1949–54 Derby South; 1954–59 Sheffield, Brunswick; 1959–64 Sheffield North; 1964–71 Walthamstow; 1971–77 Bishops Stortford; 1977–82 Sunderland North.

WOODWARD, David, Nantwyn, 3 Holyrood Ave., Old Colwyn, Colwyn Bay, Clwyd LL29 8BA. (0492-55612) *b. 14 Dec 1942, Norton Green, Stoke-on-Trent. m. 17 June 1967: 2d., 1s.*
Education: 1953–60 Leek High Sch.; 1963–67 Hartley Victoria.
Appointments: 1967–69 Milton Keynes; 1969–70 Biggleswade; 1970–74 Hitchin and Letchworth; 1974–80 Stoke (South); 1980- Colwyn Bay and Llandudno.
Connexional Committees: 1980–82 District Representative to Divisional Board, Education and Youth.
Special Interests: Amnesty International. *Hobbies and Recreations:* Gardening, Ornithology, Football, Music.

WOODWARD, Max Wakerley, 6A Field End Rd., Pinner, Middlesex HA5 2QL. (01-429-0608) *b. 29 Jan 1908, Sunderland, Co. Durham. m. 3 Nov 1934: 1d., 3s.*
Education: 1917–20 Aldershot County Sch.; 1920–22 Orme Boys Sch., Newcastle-under-Lyne; 1922-24 Kingswood Sch.; 1926–29 Handsworth. *Appointments:* 1929–42 Ceylon Dt; 1942–46 Chaplain HMF; 1946–50 Leamington Spa; 1950–54 London, Finsbury Park; 1954–58 London, Harrow; 1958–64 Wesley's Chapel, London; 1964–59 World Methodist Council (Secretary); 1969–73 Bromley, Kent.
Council Member: World Methodist Council. *Publications: One at London* (1966).
Hobbies and Recreations: Reading, Gardening, Stamp Collecting.

WOOLLEY, Arthur Richard Butler, 26 Cross St., Skipton, North Yorks BD23 2AH. (0756-5163) *b. 8 Sept 1911, Woodchurch, Ashford, Kent. m. 2 July 1938: 2d., 2s.*
Education: 1916–25 Woodchurch Prim. Sch.; 1950–51 Headingley.
Appointments: 1950–56 Skipton; 1956–59 British Guiana; 1959–65 Hawarth and Oakworth; 1965–69 Widnes; 1969–76 Liverpool H/E.

WOOSLEY, David Andrew, 435 Aigburth Rd., Liverpool L19 3PA. (051-427-1351)–BA(Dunelm), MA(Cantab.). *b. 23 Aug 1936, Croydon, Surrey. m. 29 July 1961: 2d., 1s.*
Education: 1947–55 Kingswood Sch.; 1955–59 Kings Coll., Newcastle-upon-Tyne (Durham Univ.); 1959–61 Wesley House. *Appointments:* 1961–63 Beechamville and Bensonton (Jamaica); 1963–1968 Colon (Panama); 1968–72 Panama (Panama); 1972–81 Liverpool North Central; 1981– Liverpool South.
Connexional Committees: 1979– President's Council.
Hobbies and Recreations: Drawing, Listening to Music.

WORTH, Creasey, 15 Denby Lane, Heaton Chapel, Stockport SK4 2QX. (061-442-9712) *b. 22 Feb 1916, West Bergholt, Colchester, Essex. m. 23 Dec 1929: 2d., 1s.*
Education: 1921–29 CE Prim. Sch., W. Bergholt; 1929–32 Colchester Technical Coll.; Handsworth.
Appointments: 1954–59 South Derbyshire; 1959–64 Stockport (South); 1964–69 Ashton-u-Lyne; 1969–72 Burnley; 1972–75 Hanley (Trinity); 1975–81 Colne.
Special Interests: Music. *Hobbies and Recreations:* Male Voice Choir, Gardening.

WRAGG, Eileen Muriel, 41 Station Rd., Brimington, Chesterfield, Derbyshire S43 1JU. (0246-73663) *b. 10 March 1923, Ambergate, Derbyshire.*
Appointments: 1973–74 York North; 1974–77 Hull West; 1977– Bolsover and Staveley.

WRAY, Martin Howard, 53 Fetherston Rd., Stanford-le-Hope, Essex SS17 0BU. (0375-672120)–BD(Lond.). *b. 21 July 1946, Halifax, Yorkshire. m. 12 Aug 1967: 1d., 1s.*
Appointments: 1973–77 Tonbridge; 1977– Grays.

WREN, John David Hugh, The Manse, St. Ann's Chapel, Gunnislake, Cornwall PL18 9HW. (0822-832462) *b. 1 Aug 1947, Broxbourne, Hertfordshire. m: 2d.*
Education: 1958–60 Hertford Grammar Sch.; 1960–66 Barnstaple Boys' Grammar Sch.; 1969–72 Wesley House. *Appointments:* 1972–77 Downham Market; 1977–82 Hinckley; 1982– Callington and Gunnislake.

WRIGHT, Alan Leonard, 137 Shardlow Rd., Alvaston, Derby DE2 0JR. (0332-71405) *b. 13 Aug 1952, Leicester. m. 5 July 1980.*
Education: 1957–63 Newbold Verdon (Leics.) Prim.; 1963–68 Ibstock High Sch.; 1974–78 Wesley, Bristol. *Appointments:* 1978–82 Bingham; 1982– Derby South.
Special Interests: Community Work.
Hobbies and Recreations: Photography, Hi-Fi (Classical), Citizens' Band Radio, Hill Walking.

WRIGHT, Donald, 2 The Paddocks, Crowle, Nr. Scunthorpe, South Humberside DN17 4HB. (0724-710311)–MA. *b. 13 Nov 1925, Stalybridge, Cheshire. m. 3 Sept 1949: 2d., 4s.*
Education: 1937–43 Manchester Grammar Sch.; 1943–44, 1947, 1950 Exeter Coll., Thetford.
Appointments: 1978– Epworth and Crowle.

WRIGHT, Eileen Joyce, 10 Knowler Hill, Liversedge, West Yorkshire WF15 6PH. (0924-402219) *b. 13*

June 1937, Alsager, Cheshire. *Education:* Nantwich and Action Grammar Sch.; 1959–61 Wesley Deaconess Coll.; 1974–75 Wesley, Bristol. *Appointments:* 1975–78 Crook; 1978– Spen Valley. *Hobbies and Recreations:* Jigsaws, Knitting, Walking.

WRIGHT, Ewart Burton, Lawithick, 23 Cogos Park, Mylor Bridge, Falmouth, Cornwall TR11 5SF. (0326-72084)–BD(Lond.). *b. 2 July 1919, Kirkby-in-Ashfield, Notts. m. 31 Oct 1945: 1d., 3s.* *Education:* 1924–29 Vernon Rd. Elem. Sch., Kirkby-in-Ashfield; 1929–30 Kirkby-in-Ashfield, Higher Grade Sch.; 1930–37 Queen Elizabeth Grammar Sch., Mansfield; 1937–41 Richmond. *Appointments:* 1941–48 South West China; 1948–52 Louth; 1952–58 Birkenhead; 1958–64 Buxton; 1964–69 Reading; 1969–77 West Somerset; 1977– Falmouth. *Special Interests:* Chinese Studies, World Church. *Hobbies and Recreations:* Sport, Stamp Collecting.

WRIGHT, James, 19 Mosley St., Barnoldswick, Colne, Lancs BB8 5BP. (0282-813225) *b. 9 Oct 1913, Barnoldswick. m. 12 Aug 1944.* *Education:* 1918–27 Rainhall Road Council Sch.; 1937–40 Didsbury. *Appointments:* 1940–44 Manchester, Hulme and Whalley Range; 1944–49 Otley; 1949–56 Clitheroe; 1956–64 Southport South; 1964–70 Altrincham; 1970–78 Southport. *Hobbies and Recreations:* Gardening (Heathers and Bonsai), Music, Walking, Embroidery.

WRIGHT, John, Tan-y-Graig, Deganwy Rd., Deganwy, Conway LL31 9DG. (0492 83608) *b. 19 July 1908, Hogsthorpe, Lincs. m. 3 Aug 1938. 1s.* *Education:* Alford, Queen Elizabeth's Grammar Sch.; 1932–36 Richmond. *Appointments:* 1931–32 Sussex Mission; 1936–37 President's List; 1937–40 London Mission, Downham; 1940–41 Liverpool South; 1941–45 St. Helens; 1945–50 Stockton, Brunswick; 1950–53 Middlesbrough; 1953–59 Mansfield, Bridge St.; 1959–65 Skegness and Wainfleet; 1965–73 Tarporley. *Publications: A Brief History of Wesley's Octagonal Chapel at Yarm, Yorks.* *Hobbies and Recreations:* Garden, Music, Reading, Motor Cars.

WRIGHT, John Brian, Headquarters, Northern Ireland BFPO 825. (08462-5222 Ext. 2343) *b. 2 Nov 1930, Southport. m. 11 Aug 1956: 1s.* *Education:* 1943–48 King George V Sch., Southport; 1951–54 Hartley Victoria. *Appointments:* 1954–57 Wath-on-Dearne and Mexborough; 1957–62 Ormskirk; 1962 Chaplain HMF. *Special Interests:* History. *Hobbies and Recreations:* Music.

WRIGHT, John Robert, 53 Westray Drive, Hinckley LE10 0TL. (0455-634705) *b. 8 June 1910, Ipswich, Suffolk. m. 5 Aug 1937: 2d., 1s.* *Education:* Ipswich Secondary; 1930–33 Didsbury. *Appointments:* 1933–52 Sri Lanka; 1952–56 Worksop; 1956–62 Coventry; 1962–68 Nottingham Central; 1968–72 Birmingham Wesley; 1972–75 Rochdale North. *Connexional Committees:* 1963–67 Overseas Mission. *Special Interests:* Languages. *Hobbies and Recreations:* Wood Carving.

WRIGHT, Kenyon Edward, Scottish Churches House, Dunblane FK15 0AJ (0786-824712)–MA(Glasgow), MA(Cantab.), MTh(Sevanpore, India). *b. 31 Aug 1932, Paisley, Scotland. m. 18 Aug 1955: 3d.* *Education:* 1938–40 Paisley Grammar Sch.; 1950–53 Glasgow Univ.; 1953–55 Cambridge Univ.; 1953–55 Wesley House. *Appointments:* 1955–70 Bengal District (Durgapub and Calcutta); 1963–70 Director of Ecumenical, Social and Industrial Institute; 1970–81 Director of International Ministry, Coventry Cathedral; 1974–81 Canon Residentiary of Coventry; 1981–Now Canon Emeritus; 1981– General Secretary Scottish Churches Council.

WRIGHT, Maurice Harold, Shelsey Castle St., Bishops Castle, Salop SY9 5BU. (0588-638300)–BA(Manch.). *b. 9 July 1936, Dawley, Shropshire. m. 23 April 1962: 1d., 1s.* *Education:* 1942–47 The Grove; 1947–55 Coalbrookdale High Sch.; 1957–60 Manchester Univ.; 1957–61 Hartley Victoria. *Appointments:* 1961–65 Leominster; 1965–70 Doncaster South; 1970–77 Stourbridge and Brierley Hill; 1977– Bishops Castle and Clun. *Connexional Committees:* 1966– Methodist Peace Fellowship Executive; 1972–82 Methodist Peace Fellowship Membersip Secretary. *Council Member:* 1979– Bishops Castle Town Council. *Publications: Balby Road Methodist Church 1968* (16pp Doncaster). *Special Interests:* 18th Century English Porcelain. *Hobbies and Recreations:* Collecting and Studying Porcelain 1774–1799.

WRIGHT, Neville Walter, 6 Kenwood Park Rd., Sheffield S7 1NF. (0742-52695)–BA(Leeds), BD(Lond.). *b. 31 July 1921, Bradford, Yorks. m. 29 July 1950: 1d., 2s.* *Education:* 1931–37 Grange Hill Sch., Bradford; Leeds Univ.; London Univ.; 1947–50 Headingley. *Appointments:* 1950–54 Isle of Man; 1954–59 Bury; 1959–67 Longton Mission; 1967–74 Leeds Mission; 1974–75 Edinburgh (Nicholson Sq.); 1975–82 Sheffield, Brunswick; 1982– Grimsby Mission. *Connexional Committees:* 1974–82 Connexional Finance Committee. *Publications: Another Paul* (Epworth Press 1954). *Hobbies and Recreations:* Sport.

WRIGHT, Peter Donald, Woodville, Redesmouth Rd., Bellingham, Hexham, Northumberland NE48 2EH. (0660 20283) *b. 9 Jan 1940, Sheffield. m. 5 Sept 1962: 1d., 1s.* *Education:* 1945–47 Western Rd Inf., Sheffield; 1947–51 Western Rd. Jun., Sheffield; 1951–54 Western Rd. Seniors, Sheffield; 1970–72 Wesley, Bristol; 1972–73 Kingsmead. *Appointments:* 1973–75 Jamaica District; 1975–80 Shipley; 1980– Hexham.

Connexional Committees: 1981– Radio and Television Sub Committee.
Special Interests: Local Commercial Radio (ILR Religious Broadcasting), Computers (Relevant to Church Administration). *Hobbies and Recreations:* Cooking, Walking, Folk Music, Photography, Squash.

WRIGHT, Raymond, 3101 Teton St., Boise, Idaho 83705, USA. (208-342-4949)–BA. *b. 11 May 1929, Stoke-on-Trent, Staffs. m. 14 July 1956: 2s.*
Education: 1939–45 Leek High Sch.; 1953–56 Leeds Univ.; 1952–56 Headingley. *Appointments:* 1956–63 Batley; 1963–71 Derby (South); 1971–79 Hull (West); 1979–82 Jerome, Idaho, USA; 1982– Boise (Whitney), Idaho.
Council Member: Free Church Federal Council (National). *Local Council Committees:* 1975–79 Hull Community Health Council; 1971–79 Methodist Home for the Aged, Willerby.
Special Interests: Industrial Chaplain, Rolls Royce Aero Engine Division Derby 1963–71, British Aerospace Division Brough (Nr. Hull) 1971–79, Hospital Chaplain, Shardlow Hospital, Derby 1964–71, Hull Royal Infirmary.
Hobbies and Recreations: Considerable Experience in Drama as Actor, Director, Singing, Mixed and Male Voice Choirs, Most Sports, Photography, Walking, Travel, Barn and Square Dancing.

WROE, John Henry, 2 Bramley Drive, Bramhall, Stockport, Cheshire SK7 2DR. (061-440-0572)–BD(Lond.). *b. 13 May 1911, Liverpool. m. 26 July 1941: 2d.*
Education: 1916–25 Matthew Arnold, Dingle, Liverpool; 1937–38 Manchester Univ.; 1938–41 London Univ. (External Student); 1932–33 Cliff Coll.; 1934–38 Hartley Victoria.
Appointments: 1938–41 Truro Sch. (Chaplain); 1941–42 Hazel Grove and Poynton; 1942–45 Sirhowy Valley; 1945–50 Ashton-u-Lyne; 1950–57 Morecambe; 1957–60 Woodhouse Grove (Chaplain); 1960–67 Blackpool North; 1967–74 Bramhall; 1974–78 Crosby.
Hobbies and Recreations: Water Colour Painting, Bowls, Gardening.

WYATT, Leslie Edward, 6 Werneth Rd., Woodley, Stockport, Cheshire SK6 1HW. ;061-430-2964)–BA. *b. 31 Oct 1925, Liverpool. m. July 1959: 3d., 1s.*
Education: 1948–52 Leeds Univ.; 1954–57 Manchester; 1954–57 Hartley Victoria. *Appointments:* 1957–59 Barnstaple; 1959–63 Durham; 1963–68 Leeds (Richmond Hill); 1968–72 Stockton-on-Tees; 1972–79 Stockport; 1979– Romiley.

WYLIE, Malcolm McLeod, 30 Humbie Rd., Kirkliston, West Lothian EH29 9AH. (031-333-3435) *b. 2 Oct 1901, Glasgow. m.: 2s.*
Education: Provanside Higher Grade, Glasgow; 1924–27 Hartley Coll.
Appointments: 1927–28 Supply; 1927–34 Fernado Po., West Africa; 1934–46 Glasgow (Parkhead); 1946–53 Glasgow, Claremont; 1953–62 Edinburgh, Leith; 1962–67 North Scotland Mission.

WYNNE, John Gordon, Lake House, Shebbear Coll., Shebbear, Devon EX21 5SJ. (040928-442)–BA(Dunelm), BA(Cantab.), MA(Cantab.). *b. 27 Mar 1937, Newcastle-upon-Tyne. m. 19 Aug 1961: 2s.*
Education: 1942–48 Chillingham Rd., Prim. and Jun.; 1948–56 Heaton Grammar Sch.; 1956–59 Kings Coll., Durham Univ.; 1959–61 Fitzwilliam House, Cambridge Univ.; 1959–61 Wesley House; 1961–62 St. Andrews Coll., Selly Oak. *Appointments:* 1962–66 Sierra Leone; 1966–67 Sunderland North; 1968–69 Letchworth Grammar Sch.; 1969–70 Univ. of Ibadan, Faculty of Education; 1971–77 Univ. of the S. Pacific, Fiji; 1977–82 Heaton and Wallsend; 1982– Shebbear Coll.
Connexional Committees: 1978– Asia Advisory Group, Methodist Church Overseas Divison. *Local Council Committees:* 1978–81 Chairman Central Sch. Board of Governors, Wallsend. *Publications:* Various Articles in Religious Education and Distance Education.
Special Interests: Continuing Education, Theatre, Music, The Mission of the Church. *Hobbies and Recreations:* Drama, Music, Stamps, Gardening, Walking, Reading.

YATES, George Hatton, 30 Fernside Rd., Winton, Bournemouth BH9 2LB. (0202-528802) *b. 22 Dec 1925, Gee Cross, Cheshire. m. 26 July 1952: 1d., 1s.*
Education: 1930–39 Gee Cross Sch.; 1948–50 Handsworth.
Appointments: 1947–48 Minehead and Dunster; 1950–52 Oldbury (Wesley); 1952–55 Newcastle (Staffs.); 1955–61 Birmingham (Moseley Rd. and Sparkhill); 1961–68 Southampton; 1968–73 Birmingham (Smethwick); 1973–80 Poole; 1980– Bournemouth.
Connexional Committees: 1979–82 Property Board; 1961– Minsters Retirement Fund.
Special Interests: Methodist History and Wesleyana. *Hobbies and Recreations:* Gardening.

YATES, Gilbert Ian, 2 Ridge Close, Portishead, Bristol BS20 8RQ. (0272-843440)–BA(Dunelm), BA(Cantab.), MA(Cantab.). *b. 4 Oct 1944, Worcestershire. m. 14 Aug 1970: 2d.*
Education: 1956–61 Cambridgeshire High Sch.; 1961–63 Cambridgeshire Coll. of Arts and Technology; 1963–66 St. John's Coll., Univ. of Durham; 1966–69 Wesley House.
Appointments: 1969–71 Bournemouth; 1971–75 Cleckheaton and Heckmondwike; 1975–82 Clevedon; 1982– Gloucester.
Connexional Committees: 1970– Local Preachers' Studies Board.
Publications: Introducing the Old Testament (1974 Part); *Hudson Hebrew Old Testament Prize* (1976).
Special Interests: Old Testament Studies. *Hobbies and Recreations:* Walking, Gardening.

YATES, Ian, OVSM, 121–131 East India Dock Rd., London E14 6DF. (01-515-7067).
Education: Handsworth.
Appointments: 1969–76 Rhodesia

Dt; 1976–78 London, Tottenham and Stoke Newington; 1978– London Mission, Poplar.

YATES, Ralph, Bethany, 2 Higher Croft, Tower Hill, Williton, Taunton, Somerset TA4 4NT. (32115) *b. 11 Oct 1909, Gunwed, Luxulyan, Bodmin, Cornwall. m. 1946.* *Education:* Lickingate, Bugle, Cornwall District; Lanivet, Bodmin, Cornwall District; 1931–32 Cliff Coll. *Appointments:* 1963–64 Barnstaple; 1964–69 Camborne; 1969–74 Truro. *Publications:* Did Hospital Leaflet *You Are Not Alone;* Also published two small books of talks and devotions for young people. *Special Interests:* Gardening, Reading. *Appointments:* Enjoying Countryside Walks.

YATES, Roy, 9 The Crescent, Hipperholme, Halifax, W. Yorks HX3 8NQ. (0484-202564)–MA, BD, MLitt. *Education:* 1964–69 Richmond. *Appointments:* 1969–74 St. Helens; 1974–79 Huddersfield NE; 1979– Halifax.

YELLAND, Stephen George, Thorncroft, 213 Kingsway, Ossett, West Yorkshire WF5 8ED. (0924-272290) *b. 10 May 1949, Epping, Essex. m. 10 July 1982.* *Education:* 1954–60 Alderton Hall Lane Prim. and Jun. Sch, Loughton, Essex; 1960–65 Brook County Secondary Modern Sch., Loughton, Essex; 1973–77 Wesley, Bristol. *Appointments:* 1977–80 Stoke on Trent (Tunstall); 1980– Ossett and Horbury. *Connexional Committees:* 1981–82 Divisional Board of Education and Youth. *Special Interests:* Drama. *Hobbies and Recreations:* Tennis, Squash, Reading, The Cinema, Photography.

YELLOWLEY, Brian, 207 Sunderland Rd., South Shields, Tyne and Wear NE34 6AQ. (0632-553244) *b. 13 Oct 1929, New York, Shiremoor, Northumberland. m. 18 July 1953.* *Education:* 1934–41 Murton Council Sch.; 1941–46 Tynemouth High Sch. (Grammar); 1946–47 Jarrow Grammar Sch.; 1947–50 Rutherford Coll. of Technology; 1946–51 Reyrolle Apprenticeship (Electrical Engineering); 1967–70 Richmond. *Appointments:* 1970–74 Lancaster; 1974–79 Hazel Grove; 1979– South Shields. *Special Interests:* Worship, Preaching, Christian Education, Listening and Healing, The Church's Ministries, Marriage Guidance Council, YMCA, Music, Social Reponsibility and Development, Hospitals. *Hobbies and Recreations:* Music, Photography, Reading, Gardening, Handicrafts, Walking.

YEOMANS, Martin Hugh, 31 Duchy Ave., Bradford, West Yorkshire BD9 5ND. (0274-497617)–MA(Cantab.), Post Graduate Diploma in Psychotherapy (Leeds). *b. 1922, Jersey, CI. m. 1951. 1d., 3s.* *Education:* 1933–38 Exmouth Grammar Sch.; 1938–41 Royal Grammar Sch.; 1941–42- 1946–48 Jesus Coll., Cambridge; 1946–48 Wesley House. *Appointments:* 1948–51 Hupeh Dt, China; 1951–54 Falmouth; 1954–58 Teddington; 1958–65 Bristol, Kingswood; 1963–68 Huddersfield West; 1968–77 Bradford, Manningham; 1977– Pastoral Consultant, Administrative Director and Acting Director, with the Clinical Theology Association. *Connexional Committees:* 1963–68 Book Committee; 1959–63 Didsbury Coll. (Bristol) Committee; 1973–77 Board of the Division of Ministries; 1981–82 Healing and Pastoral Ministry Committee. *Special Interests:* Pastoral Counselling, Psychotherapy, Adult Group Week.

YOUNG, Ernest George, 77 Withies Park, Midsomer Norton, Bath BA3 2PB. (0761-418176) *b. 7 April 1904, Porth, Rhondda, South Wales. m. 18 Aug 1932.* *Education:* 1909–15 Elem.; 1915–20 Evening Classes; 1929–30 Kingsmead, Selly Oak, Birmingham; 1927–29 Hartley. *Appointments:* 1925–27 Sheerness; 1930–48 Eastern Nigeria District; 1948–57 Midsomer Norton; 1957–64 Winchester; 1964–69 Portsmouth. *Connexional Committees:* 1951–57 Overseas Mission, Bristol District; 1959–64 Overseas Missions, Southampton District. *Publications:* 1967–72 Weekly Religious Articles for *Portsmouth News;* 1975–80 Religious Articles for *Somerset Guardian; History of High Street, Methodist Church, Midsomer Norton 1746–81.* *Hobbies and Recreations:* Male Voice Choir, Bowls.

YOUNG, Ian Dexter, The Manse, Prospect, Okehampton, Devon EX20 1JD. (0837-2302)–BA(Bristol). *b. 1929, Plymouth. m. 1954: 1d., 2s.* *Education:* 1940–45 Crypt (Gloucester); 1951–54 Didsbury, Bristol. *Appointments.* 1957–59 Marlborough; 1959–62 Downham Market; 1962–67 Sunderland (South); 1967–74 Hinckley; 1974–79 Nuneaton; 1979– Okehampton. *Connexional Committees:* 1972–73 Christian Citizenship Committee, District Rep.; 1973–74 Social Responsibility, District Rep.; 1982– Property.

YOUNG, John W., 63 Queen's Parade, Cleethorpes, South Humberside DN35 0DQ. (0472-691479)–BA(Leeds). *b. 7 Dec 1937, Fendrayton, Cambs. m. 30 May 1977: 1s.* *Education:* 1942–48 Cockton Hill Prim. and Jun., Bishop Auckland; 1948–57 Bishop Auckland Grammar Sch.; 1957–62 Leeds Univ.; 1959–62 Headingley. *Appointments:* 1962–65 Hull Trinity; 1965–71 Newton Abbot; 1971–78 Sheffield, Ecclesall; 1978– Cleethorpes. *Special Interests:* Theology, Hymnology. *Hobbies and Recreations:* Music, Reading, Football.

YOUNG, Terence John, 67 Wilbraham Rd., Manchester M14 7ON. (061-224-6048)–BA(Open). *b. 19 Dec 1944, Oxford. m. 16 Aug 1969: 2d., 1s.* *Education:* 1956–60 Forest Hill Comprehensive; 1970–71 West Hill

Coll.; 1967–70 Handsworth; 1970–71 Queens. *Appointments:* 1971–75 Bedford South and Ampthill; 1975–80 Purley; 1980– Manchester and Salford Mission.
Connexional Committees: Tutor with Methodist Study Centre. *Local Councl Committees:* 1971–73 Bedford Education and Youth Committee.
Special Interests: Local Radio, 1977–80 with BBC Radio London and 1980– with BBC Radio Manchester, currently Producer of BBC Radio Manchester's 'Focus' programme.

YOUNGS, David Ernest, 92 Debden Rd., Saffron Walden, Essex CB11 4AL. (0799-22037) *b. 8 Nov 1936, Upminster, Essex. m. 20 April 1963: 1d., 2s.*
Education: 1948–55 Coopers' Company's Sch., Bow E3; 1977–79 Wesley House. *Appointments:* 1979– Bishop's Stortford.
Connexional Committees: 1972–76 Education and Youth.
Special Interests: Music, Young People, Photography. *Hobbies and Recreations:* Model and Steam Railways, Canals and Narrow Boats.

ZIESLER, John Anthony, 7 Florence Park, Redland, Bristol BS6 7LS. (0272-24161 Ext 111)–BA(NZ), BD(Lond.), MA(Bristol), PhD(Lond.). *b. 7 Dec 1930, Timaru, New Zealand. m. 30 Jan 1960: 3d.*
Education: 1942–48 Timaru Boys' High Sch., NZ; 1949–52 Otago (NZ); 1953–56 London; 1956–58 Bristol; 1953–56 Richmond.
Appointments: 1956–58 Didsbury Coll. (Assistant Tutor); 1958–62 Hastings (NZ); 1962–67 Trinity Coll., Auckland, NZ; 1967–69 Wesley House, Cambridge; 1970–72 Trinity Coll., Auckland, NZ; 1972–77 St. Matthias Coll., Bristol; 1977– Univ. of Bristol.
Local Council Committees: 1981– Avon LEA Standing Advisory Committee on RE.
Publications: The Meaning of Righteousness in Paul (CUP 1972); *Christian Asceticism* (SPCK 1973, Eerdman's 1974); *The Jesus Question* (1980) and articles on New Testament Matters.
Special Interests: The Study of the New Testament. *Hobbies and Recreations:* Walking, Camping, Crosswords.

Methodist Church in Ireland

ABBOTT, Ivan Samuel, 4 Craigavon Rd., Fintona, Co. Tyrone, N. Ireland. (0662-841333)–Dip Theol(Queens Univ. Belfast). *b. 14 Feb 1956, Dublin. m. 17 Oct 1981.*
Education: 1968–74 Mount Temple Sch., Dublin; 1978–80 Queens Univ., Belfast; 1977–80 Edgehill.
Appointments: 1980–81 Lisburn Rd and Osborne Park, Belfast; 1981– Omagh and Fintona.
Hobbies and Recreations: Printing, Sports.

AGNEW, Wilfred Arthur, 64 Millisle Rd., Donaghadee, Co. Down, N. Ireland BT21 0HZ. (0247-883534)–BA. *b. 6 July 1921, Dublin. m. 5 Sept 1952: 2s.*
Education: 1928–38 Foyle Coll., Londonderry, N. Ireland; 1938–39 Ardmore Coll., Belfast; Univ. of London (External Student); 1948–50 Edgehill. *Appointments:* 1945–47 Cregagh; 1947–48 Belfast Central Mission; 1950–53 Knock (Dundwald); 1953–56 Dunkineely; 1956–61 Agnes St. (Woodsale); 1961–65 Tandragee; 1965–67 Superintendent of Evangelism; 1967–74 Londonderry Methodist City Mission; 1974–81 Ballyclere; 1981– Donaghadee.
Connexional Committees: 1968–73 Stationing Committee; 1976– Editorial Secretary of the Conference; 1970–74 Secretary of Londonderry District; 1974–78 Secretary of North East District; Other Committees too numerous to mention.
Special Interests: Ministry of Divine Healing. *Hobbies and Recreations:* Golf.

ALFORD, William Laird, 46 Seymour St., Lisburn, Co. Antrim BT27 4XG. (08462-2303). *b. 2 Dec 1927, Sligo, Co. Sligo. m. 20 April 1954: 3s.*
Education: 1938–41 Dundalk Grammar Sch.; 1941–47 Bishop Foy Sch., Waterford; 1960–63 Edgehill.
Connexional Committees: Member, Board of Governors, Edgehill Coll.; Stipends and Allowances Treasurer.

ALLEN, David John, 7 Hillside Drive, Belfast BT9 5EJ, N. Ireland. (0232-668724). *b. 3 July 1911, Loughgall, Co. Armagh, N. Ireland. m. 27 Aug 1941: 1d., 1s.*
Education: 1917–25 Ternagreevagh Prim. Sch.; 1927–30 Portadown Technical Coll.; 1934–37 Edgehill; 1940–43 Dublin Technical Coll.
Appointments: 1933–34 Newtownbutler; 1937–39 Waterford; 1939–40 Irvinestown; 1940–43 Dublin Central Mission; 1943–47 Moira; 1947–52 North Belfast Mission; 1952–55 Dungannon; 1955–60 Fivemiletown; 1960–64 Ballymena; 1964–69 Belfast, Crumlin Rd.; 1969–77 Coleraine, Portrush and Portsteward.
Connexional Committees: 1965–70 General Committee as Treasurer of the Chapel Fund; 1970–74 General Committee as Secretary of Property Board; 1973–76 Chairman of Londonderry District; 1973–76 Board of Examiners; 1966– A Trustee of the Methodist Church in Ireland.
Special Interests: Building and Design. *Hobbies and Recreations:* Wood Turning, Printing.

ANDERSON, Samuel Denis, 26 Great George's St., Warrenpoint, Co. Down BT34 3HR. (069-372-3642)–BA, BD. *b. 9 July 1952, Belfast. m. 15 Oct 1976: 2d.*
Education: 1963–70 Belfast Royal Academy; 1970–73 Queen's Univ., Belfast; 1973–76 Edgehill.
Appointments: 1976 Londonderry Mission; 1977 Dublin Central Mission; 1981– Newry.
Special Interests: Theology, Charismatic Renewal. *Hobbies and Recreations:* Sport, Gardening, Reading, Rock Music.

ARMITAGE, James Steward Smith, 8 Wellington Drive, Bangor, Co. Down BT20 4PN, N. Ireland. (0247-60548) *b. 10 Jan 1909, Co. Tipperary, Rep. of Ireland. m. 3 Oct 1940: 1d., 1s.*
Education: 1914–17 Newtown National, Co. Tipperary; 1918–21 Sopwell National, Co. Tipperary; 1921–28 Wesley Coll., Dublin; 1931–32 Cliff Coll.; 1933–36 Edgehill. *Appointments:* 1936–38 Portstewart; 1938–39 Falls Rd., Belfast; 1939–43 Kilkenny; 1943–47 Abbeyleix; 1947–52 Dublin; 1952–57 Rathkeale; 1957–62 Belfast; 1962–67 Larne; 1967–75 Dublin (Sandymount); 1975–78 Dumfries (Scotland); 1978–81 Roscreo.
Connexional Committees: 1971–73 Secretary Dublin District Synod; 1973–74 Deputy Chairman Dublin District.
Special Interests: Methodist History, Hebrew History. *Hobbies and Recreations:* Gardening, Athletics, Rugby, Football, Cricket.

ARMSTRONG, John Mostyn, Epworth, 4 Charlemont Gdns., The Mall, Armagh BT61 9BB. (0861-522014) *b. 31 May 1919, Newtownstewart, Co. Tyrone. m. 1955: 1d., 2s.*
Education: 1930–35 Bangor Grammar; 1935–39 Belfast.

ARMSTRONG, Robert H., 8 Old Park Rd., Ballymena, Co. Antrim BT42 1AY, N. Ireland. (0266-6693)

b. 21 July 1927, Lisbellaw, Co. Fermanagh, N.I.. m. 23 July 1964: 1d., 1s.
Education: Littlemount Primary Sch.; 1947–48 Cliff Coll.; 1952–54 Edgehill. *Appointments:* 1950–52 Castleclery; 1954–56 Sligo; 1956–59 Ballina; 1959–64 Swanlebar; 1964–67 Coleraine; 1967–80 Caribbean Conf.; 1980– Ballymena.
Connexional Committees: 1982– Overseas Missionary Committee.
Special Interests: Interested in Third World Needs.

BAIN, Charles Henry, 3 Old Rectory Park, Banbridge, Co. Down, N. Ireland BT32 4QA. (08206-22234)–BD(Lond.). *b. 17 Oct 1919, Drumaness. m. 7 Sept 1946: 1d., 1s.*
Education: 1925–33 Drumaness; 1933–35 Belfast Mercantile Coll.; 1935–37 Oranges' Civil Service Academy; 1937–38 Private Study; 1940–43 Edgehill. *Appointments:* 1943–47 North Belfast Mission; 1947–48 Moira; 1949–52 Ardara; 1952–57 Belfast, University Rd.; 1957–62 Larne; 1962–65 Londonderry (Carlisle Rd.); 1965–70 Portadown; 1970–82 North Belfast Mission; 1982– Banbridge.
Connexional Committees: District Chairman: 1963–65 Londonderry; 1967–70 Portadown; 1971–73 Belfast; 1973–76/1978–82 North East; General Committee; Trustees, Budget Committee; Board of Examiners; Church's Ministry of Healing.
Special Interests: Holy Spirit Renewal, The Healing Ministry. *Hobbies and Recreations:* Woodwork, Trout Fishing, Gardening.

BAIN, Desmond Charles, Atlantis, South Circular Rd., Limerick, Republic of Ireland. (061-28929)–Dip Theol(Belfast). *b. 19 March 1949, Belfast. m. 4 July 1974: 2s.*
Education: 1960–62 Methodist Coll., Belfast; 1962–65 Foyle Coll., Londonderry; 1965–68 Portadown Coll., Portadown; 1970–73 Queen's Univ., Belfast; 1969–72 Edgehill.
Appointments: 1972–75 Cork; 1975–80 Dunmanway and Bantry; 1980– Christ Church (United Methodist Presbyterian) Limerick.
Connexional Committees: 1975–76, 1978– Youth Council; 1979– Local Preachers; 1980– Social Welfare; 1982– Board of Examiners; 1981– Stipend and Allowances; 1982– General Committee; 1982– General Purposes. *Council Member:* 1980–82 Secretary; 1982– Chairman; 1972– Midland and Southern District Member. *Local Council Committees:* 1972– Youth Council; 1972–73, 1980– Home Mission; 1980– Overseas; 1980– Property.
Special Interests: Drama, Education.
Hobbies and Recreations: Fishing, Reading, but mostly Family Activities.

BAMBRICK, W. Denis, 22 My Lady's Mile, Holywood, Co. Down, N. Ireland BT18 9EW. (02317-2061)–BSc, BD. *b. 2 April 1931, Belfast. m. 29 June 1959: 3d., 1s.*
Education: 1943–49 Methodist Coll., Belfast; 1937–40 Belmont Inf.; 1940–43 Strandtown Prim.; 1943–49 Methodist Coll.; 1949–52, Queens Univ., Belfast; 1954–57 Edgehill.
Appointments: 1957–58 North Belfast Mission; 1959–61 Dungannon; 1961–63 Arklow; 1963–68 Sutton, Dublin and Superintendent of Colportedge and Open Air Work; 1968–74 Ghana, West Africa (Chaplain to Schools and Colleges, Kurmasi); 1974–78 Lynn Memorial, Belfast; 1978–80 Lisburn; 1980– Holywood.
Connexional Committees: 1976– General Secretary, Methodist Missionary Society (Ireland).
Hobbies and Recreations: Golf.

BEST, Kenneth, Methodist Manse, Ballinamallard, Co. Fermanagh, N. Ireland. (036581-200) *b. 2 May 1944, Portadown, N. Ireland. m. 3 July 1971: 2d.*
Education: 1949–55 Hart Memorial Prim. Sch., Portadown; 1955–60 Clounagh Sec. Sch., Portadown; 1967–70 Edgehill. *Appointments:* 1970–73 Dublin Central Mission; 1973–76 Clonakilty and Skibbereen; 1976– Ballinamalard.
Connexional Committees: 1979–81 Secretary of Synod; 1981– Chairman of District; 1981– District Stationer; Property Board; Council on Social Welfare; Mission Board; General Committee; Board of Examiners; General Purposes Board.
Hobbies and Recreations: Gardening, Reading.

BINGHAM, Walter, 27 Edgcumbe Gardens, Belfast BT4 2E6. (0232-657863) *b. 17 June 1914, Feddan, Ballyganley, Co. Tyrone. m. (1) 17 Aug 1944; (2) 27 Dec 1980.*
Education: 1932–33 Cliff Coll.; 1935–38 Edgehill. *Appointments:* 1934–35 Dungannon; 1938–39 Carlisle Rd., Derry; 1939–44 Derry City Mission; 1944–48 Ballintra; 1948–53 Irvinestown; 1953–58 Lurgan (Queen St.); 1958–63 Newtownards; 1963–68 Finaghy; 1968–76 Knock; 1976–80 Ligoniel and Oldpark, Joanmount.
Parliamentary Service: 1968–72 Methodist Chaplain to N.I. Parliament (Stormont). *Connexional Committees:* 1946–48 Secretary Sligo District; 1978–80 Chairman, Belfast District.
Hobbies and Recreations: Golf, Gardening.

BOLSTER, Herbert Lancelot Frank, 24 Limavady Rd., Londonderry, Co. Londonderry BT47 6GD. (0504-42644) *b. 28 Oct 1923, Belfast. m. 20 Aug 1954: 2d., 1s.*
Education: Belfast Technical Coll.; 1945–46 Cliff Coll.; 1949–51 Edgehill. *Appointments:* 1951–53 Enniskillen; 1953–54 Clonakilty; 1954–55 Montserrat; 1955–56 Antigua; 1956–60 Curacao; 1960–61 Dunmanway; 1961–65 Fivemiletown; 1965–73 Donaghadee; 1973–80 Armagh; 1980– Londonderry; 1975–80 Chairman of Synod; 1981 Londonderry.
Connexional Committees: Overseas Mission; 1971–76 Gen. Sec. Council on Social Welfare; Board of Education; Irish Methodist Youth Council; Board of Examiners; General Committee.
Special Interests: Social Welfare, Youth, Wesley Historical Soc.
Hobbies and Recreations: Collecting Wesleyana, Amateur Radio, Photograpy, Philately, Golf.

BOOTH, Alan Richard, Carters, Wickham Bishops, Witham, Essex CM8 3JB. (0621-891405)–MA, BD, LL/B. *b. 10 May 1911, Dublin. m. 1944.*
Education: 1920–25 Wesley Coll., Dublin; 1925–29 Leys Sch., Cambridge; 1929–33 Trinity Coll., Dublin; 1936–38 Edgehill.
Appointments: 1938–39 Belfast Central Mission; 1939–40 Junior Tutor, Edgehill Coll., Belfast; 1940–42 Per International Student Service; 1942–45 Per Christian Student Movement; 1951–55 Limerick; 1955–56 Cork; Per Church Committee and International Affairs; 1956–76 British Council of Churches; 1976– Lisburn.
Publications: Christian and Power Politics (1961); *Not only Peace* (1967); *Christian Responsibility in International Affairs* (Beckley Lecture 1970).
Special Interests: Ecumenism, International Affairs and Defence, University Life. *Hobbies and Recreations:* Music, Gardening.

BRADLEY, William Kenneth, 3 Ballygomartin Rd., Belfast BT13 3LA. (0232-743823) *b. 15 June 1944, Coalisland, Co. Tyrone, N. Ireland. m. 16 Aug 1969: 2s.*
Education: 1948–56 Killyman Prim. Sch.; 1956–63 Dungannon Royal Sch.; 1963–64 Queen's Univ., Belfast; 1966–69 Edgehill. *Appointments:* 1969–70 Belfast under direction of Chairman of District; 1970–71 Swanlinbar; 1971 Kingsmead Coll., Birmingham; 1972 L'Accueil Fraternel in Le Chambon sur Lignon, Haute-Loire, France for French language study; 1972–73 Stationed in Contonou and Bohicon in Dahomey, Benin/Togo District; 1973–78 Portadown; 1978–82 Sutton and Skerries; 1982– Belfast, Agnes St.
Connexional Committees: 1973–77 Portadown District Ministerial Youth Secretary; 1980–82 Dublin District Ministerial Representative on Budget Committee; 1973–78 Portadown Youth Council; 1978–82 Dublin District Youth Council and Overseas Committee; 1980–82 Secretary of Dublin District Synod; 1980–82 Dublin District Property Committee and Home Mission Committee. *Local Council Committees:* 1983– Member of Management Committee of Woodvale Youth Training Project Ltd.
Special Interests: Healing Ministry, Counselling in depth, Pastoralia. *Hobbies and Recreations:* Gardening.

BUCHANAN, William Thomas, 17 Glengarry Park, Jordanstown, Co. Antrim BT37 0QR, N. Ireland. (0231-63036) *b. 26 Nov 1934, Enniskillen, Co. Fermanagh, N. Ireland. m. 16 June 1960: 1d., 1s.*
Education: 1940–46 Tamlaght Prim. Sch., Co. Fermanagh; 1946–49 Model Sch., Enniskillen; 1949–53 Portora Royal Sch., Enniskellen; 1956–59 Queens Univ., Belfast; 1956–59 Edgehill. *Appointments:* 1954–56 Irvinestown; 1959–67 North Belfast Mission; 1967–70 Adare; 1970–76 Ballinamallard; 1976–82 Cregagh and Glenburn; 1982– North Belfast Mission.
Connexional Committees: 1971–76, 1977–82 Stationing Committee; 1977–81 Youth Council; 1978– Board of Examiners. *Local Council Committees:* 1978–80 Castlereagh Community Association.
Special Interests: 1978–82 Served as Prison Chaplain in Hydebank Wood Young Offenders Centre, Social Needs and Problems. *Hobbies and Recreations:* Camping and Caravanning, Golf, Squash, Bowls.

BURCH, Samuel, 9 Rosepark, Belfast BT5 7RG. (02318-3542)–Dip Theol(Lond.).*b. 11 Aug 1930, Belfast. m. 8 Aug 1963: 2d.*
Education: 1936–45 Grosvenor P.E.; 1955–58 Edgehill.
Appointments: 1959 Ballynafeigh and Knockbreda; 1959–65 Carrickfergus, 1965–72 Portadown; 1972–80 Shankill Team Ministry; 1980– Belfast, Knock.
Connexional Committees: 1960–82 Youth Dept.

CALLAGHAN, William Sydney, 41 Bawnmore Rd., Belfast BT9 6LB, N. Ireland. (0232-660716)–BA(Dublin), Dip Ed(Belfast), DD(Hon)(De Pauw Univ., Indiana, USA). *b. 20 March 1926, Dublin. m. 29 Dec 1968: 1d., 1s.*
Education: 1932–38 Rathgar Prim. Sch.; 1938–44 High Sch., Dublin; Trinity Coll., Dublin (Dublin Univ.); 1966–69 Queen's Univ., Belfast; 1948–50 Edgehill. *Appointments:* 1944–45 Lay Evangelist, Londonderry; 1945–47 Charlemont; 1947–48 Dunlaoghaire; 1950–55 Dublin Central Mission; 1955–62 Superintendent of Evangelism; 1961–62 Resident Chaplain, Edgehill; 1962–68 Agnes St., Belfast; 1968–76 Donegall Square, Belfast; 1976– Belfast South Circuit; 1980– President Methodist Church in Ireland.
Connexional Committees: 1955– General Committee; 1974– General Secretary of the Council on Social Welfare; 1974– Board of Education; 1956–81 Psychological and Spiritual Healing; 1970– Board of Examination.
Council Member: Board of Governors, Methodist Coll., Belfast; Board of Governors, Edgehill Theol. Coll., Belfast; Northern Ireland Hospice Ltd.; Northern Ireland Housing Ltd.; Northern Ireland Mental Health Review Tribunal.
Publications: Articles in various Journals in both the UK and America, eg *The Christian Century, The Agony of Ireland* (A.D.S.R. Publication); *The Beamer Lecture* (De Pauw Univ., Indiana, USA 1980); The R. R. Cunningham Theol. Foundation Lecturer and Preacher (Vancouver 1982).
Special Interests: Housing—Membership of Housing Association, The Care of the Terminally Ill, Founding Member and Treasurer of N.I. Hospice Ltd., Mental Health—Part time Lecturer in Dept. of Mental Health, QUB, Founding Member and Director of Samaritans, Belfast, Industrial Chaplain. *Hobbies and Recreations:* Sporting and Cultural Activities Generally.

CAMPBELL, James Patrick, 13 Greenhill Park, Newcastle, Co. Down, N. Ireland. (03967-23778) *b. 1 Oct 1908, Portadown, Co. Armagh. m. 14 July 1943 (w.): 3s.*
Education: 1912–23 Corcrain

Convent and Curran St. National (Prim.); 1935–39 Edgehill. *Appointments:* 1939–40 Waterford; 1940–43 Omagh; 1943–46 Skibbereen; 1946–49 Lisburn; 1949–52 Birr; 1952–56 Charlemont; 1956–57 Springfield; 1957–62 Brookborough; 19062–70 Lisburn; 1970–74 Ballyclare. *Connexional Committees:* 1962–66 Elected Secretary Enniskillen, Clones and Sligo District Synod; 1966–70 Chairman. *Special Interests:* Evanglism, Home and Oversea Missions. *Hobbies and Recreations:* Walking, Reading (particularly English Literature Biography and Auto), History, Travel.

COOKE, Alfred Wesley, 5 Carolhill Park, Bangor, BT20 5PP, N. Ireland. (0247-62419)–BA(Belfast). *b. 24 May 1935, Barbados. m. 24 June 1961: 4s.* *Education:* 1945–52 Methodist Coll., Belfast; 1958–62 Queens Univ.; 1958–61 Edgehill. *Appointments:* 1955–57 North Belfast Mission; 1957–58 Larne; 1961-63 Mission House; 1963–66 Church of South India; 1966–68 Cloughjorden; 1968– Per Religious Education.

COOKE, William Dennis Davison, 11 Upper Malone Rd., Belfast BT9 6TD, N. Ireland. (0232-665863)–BA, BD, MTh, PhD. *b. 3 Dec 1938, Grenada, West Indies. m. 3 July 1968: 1d., 2s.* *Education:* 1950–57 Methodist Coll., Belfast; 1957–60, 1962–65, 1975–80 Queens Univ. of Belfast; 1965–66 Lexington Theol. Seminary, Kentucky, USA; 1962–65 Edgehill. *Appointments:* 1960–61 Castlederg; 1961–62 Enniskillen; 1966–68 Belfast, Cregagh; 1968–71 Portstewart; 1971–75 Dublin, Centenary; 1977–80 Belfast, Agnes St.; 1980– Edgehill Theol. Coll. (Tutor). *Connexional Committees:* 1971– Faith and Order; 1979–82 Home Missions; 1970– Pastoral Efficiency; 1971– Tripartite Conversations. *Council Member:* 1972–77 Glencree Centre for Reconciliation (Dublin). *Publications: The Religious Dimension in the Northern Ireland Problem* (Lexington, Theol. Quarterly, USA July 1981); Public Lecture *Authority and Dissent* (Union Theol. Coll. Oct 1981). *Special Interests:* Church History, Ecumenism. *Hobbies and Recreations:* Swimming, Gardening.

COONEY, Dudley Alexander Leviston, The Manse, Newtownbutler, Co. Fermanagh, N. Ireland. (036573-221) *b. 2 Oct 1932, Dublin.* *Education:* 1938–44 Castlewood Sch., Dublin; 1944–48 The High Sch., Dublin; 1967–69 Edgehill. *Appointments:* 1969–71 Waterford; 1971–74 Carlow; 1974–82 Cloughjordan; 1982– Upper Erne. *Connexional Committees:* 1957–67 Local Preachers; 1959–63 Dublin Central Mission; 1961–67 Overseas Missions; 1970–75 Youth Department; 1971–79 World Development and Relief; 1972– Gurteen Agricultural Coll., Governor, 1975– Trustee, 1974–80 Secretary; 1980– Chairman; 1975– Budget Committee; 1979– Secretary; 1977–81 Stipends and Allowances Board; 1978–79 Council on Social Welfare; 1980– General Committee; 1982– Connexional Finance Committee Secretary. *Other Methodist Committees:* 1954–64 Dublin Methodist Council; 1956–60 Dublin District Laymen's Fellowship Secretary; 1960–63 Chairman; 1975–80 Midlands and Southern District Synod Secretary; 1980–82 Chairman. *Inter-Church Bodies:* 1974–75 Christian Endeavour, President, Central Ireland Union; 1971–79 Irish Union Treasurer; 1979–80 President; 1979–80 Irish Council of Churches—Forum on Human Rights; 1979– Commission on Unity Week. *Publications: The Ormond Methodists* (1975); *A History of the Christian Endeavour Movement in Ireland* (1977); *Methodism in Galway* (1978). *Special Interests:* Poeple, Places, History. *Hobbies and Recreations:* Books, Old Postcards.

COOPER, Robert, Suncroft, Brownshill Rd., Carlow, Eire. (0503-31129)–DipTh(Belfast). *b. 21 March 1945, Belfast. m. 3 July 1976.* *Education:* 1950–53 Riddle Memorial PE Sch.; 1953–56 Wheatfield PE Sch.; 1956–62 Oranges Academy; 1973–76 Edgehill. *Appointments:* 1976–78 Enniskillen; 1978– Carlow/Kilkenny. *Connexional Committees:* 1978– Council on Social Welfare. *Special Interests:* Ecumenics, Local Broadcasting. *Hobbies and Recreations:* Reading, Conversation.

COOPER, Thomas David, Epworth, 16 Brooklands Rd., Newtownards, Co. Down, N. Ireland BT23 4TL. (0247-815959) *b. 12 May 1943, Belfast. m. 5 Sept 1966: 3d., 1s.* *Education:* Regent House, Newtownards; 1963–66 Edgehill. *Appointments:* 1962–63 Fivemiletown; 1966–68 Belfast, Knock; 1968–72 Cloughjordan; 1972–80 Dun Laoghaire; 1980– Newtownards. *Connexional Committees:* 1972– Mission Board; 1977– Inter-Church Relations.

CURRAN, Stephen Desmond, Methodist Manse, Sackville St., Dunmanway, Co. Cork, Republic of Ireland. *b. 5 Oct 1950, Portadown, Co. Armagh.* *Education:* 1955–62 Moy (Co. Tyrone) Prim.; 1962–67 Portadown Technical Coll.; 1975–76 Cliff Coll.; 1980–82 Edgehill. *Appointments:* 1982– Dunmanway and Bantry. *Special Interests:* Farming, Evangelism.

DOWSE, John Walton, 16 Viewfort, Killymeal Rd., Dungannon, Co. Tyrone BT71 6LP. (08687-22674)–BA(Dublin) *b. 6 June 1935, Dublin. m. 8 Aug 1962: 1d., 1s.* *Education:* 1941–44 Mount Temple Sch.; 1944–53 High Sch., Dublin; 1953–57 Dublin Univ.; 1960–62 Edgehill. *Appointments:* 1957–59 Kilkenny; 1959–60 Castlederg; 1962–63 Lisburn; 1963–68 Gorey and Wexford; 1968–71 Sligo; 1971–78 Omagh and Fintona; 1978– Dungannon.

Connexional Committees: 1965–68, 1970–71 Overseas Missionary; 1965–68 Council on Social Welfare; 1965– Local Preachers Committee; 1976–78, 1980– Stipends and Allowances Board. *Publications: History of Drumquin Methodist Church* (Edited with Additional Chapter).
Special Interests: Pastoral Ministry.
Hobbies and Recreations: Gardening.

DUNCAN, Eric, Methodist Manse, Laghey, Co. Donegal, Eire. (08462-625) *b. 20 Sept 1938, Carlisle, Cumberland. m. 26 Aug 1963.*
Education: 1943–49 Skegoneil Prim.; 1949–55 Belfast Royal Academy; 1975–77 Edgehill.
Appointments: 1974–75 Wicklow; 1977–81 Sligo and Drumshanbo; 1981– Donegal and Ballintra.
Connexional Committees: 1979–81 Youth; 1981– Social Welfare; 1982– Property Board.
Hobbies and Recreations: Jogging, Squash, Gardening.

EDGAR, Sydney Carson, The Manse, Mountmellick, Co. Laois. (0502-24190) *b. 24 Jan 1916, Newtownards, Co. Down, N. Ireland. m. 14 Sept 1946.*
Education: 1920–28 Model Sch., Newtownards, Co. Down; 1928–34 Regent House, Newtownards; 1936–38 Queen's Univ., Belfast; 1936–40 Edgehill. *Appointments:* 1940–42 Portadown; 1942–43 Newry; 1943–46 Belfast, Agnes St.; 1946–47 Enniskillen; 1947–52 Ballina; 1952–56 Dublin Central Mission; 1956–61 Athlone; 1961–64 Youghal; 1964–68 Cookstown; 1968–74 South Derry Mission; 1974–78 Carlow; 1978– Portlaoise.
Connexional Committees: 1954–56 Secretary Dublin District Synod; Education Board.
Special Interests: Architecture, English Literature. *Hobbies and Recreations:* Photography, Gardening.

EDWARDS, Edward Arnold, 23 Knockview Park, Newtownabbey, Co. Antrim, N. Ireland BT36 6TY. (02313-48167) *b. 7 Oct 1913, North Beechburn, Co. Durham. m. 23 June 1949: 1d., 1s.*
Education: 1918–27 Local Prim. Sch., Blackhall, Co. Durham; 1935–36 William Booth Memorial Training Coll., London; 1940–43 Edgehill.
Appointments: 1943–45 Cregagh (Belfast); 1945–46 Newry; 1946–48 Castlederg; 1948–49 Joanmount (Belfast); 1949–53 Wexford/Corey (R of I); 1953–58 Manorhamilton/Blacklion; 1958–61 Lurgan; 1961–64 Glengormley; 1964–70 Ballymena; 1970–74 Ormeau Rd., Belfast; 1974–76 Dromore, Co. Down.
Connexional Committees: 1955–58 Secretary Sligo District Synod; 1970–74 Psychological and Spiritual Healing Committee; 1970–76 N.I. Chaplains' Executive (Rep. Meth. Church). *Local Council Committees:* 1970–74 Carolan Grammar Sch., Committee; Hospital Chaplain, Lurgan, Ballymena, Belfast.
Publications: Poems to Papers.
Special Interests: Poetry, Music, Choral and Solo Singing, Blind and Aged Welfare. *Hobbies and Recreations:* Carpentry, Printing (for Churches), Ceramics, Writing Poems (Humorous and Serious); Gardening.

EYRE, Charles George, 3 Upper Malone Rd., Belfast BT9 6TJ. (0232-668458)—BA(Belfast). *b. 2 June 1925, Belfast. m. 12 Dec 1951: 2d., 1s.*
Education: 1938–44 Coleraine Academical Institution; 1944–47 Queen's Univ., Belfast; 1945–47 Edgehill. *Appointments:* 1947–49 Londonderry City Mission; 1949–53 Belfast, Carlisle Circus; 1953–57 Waterford; 1957–65 Jamaica District; 1965–68 Youth Department; 1967–70 University Rd.; 1970–75 Belfast, Carlisle Circus; 1975–77 Portadown; 1977– Secretary of Conference.
Connexional Committees: 1965–68 Youth Council; 1973– Stipends and Allowances Board; 1977 All Connexional Committees (ex Officio); 1982 President Methodist Church in Ireland.
Special Interests: Church Music.
Hobbies and Recreations: Music.

FEE, John Alexander Thompson, 6 Thornleigh Drive, Antrim Rd., Lisburn BT28 2DA, N. Ireland. (08462-77164) *b. 28 Dec 1910, Trillick-A-Temple, Longford, Eire. m. 8 Aug 1939: 1d.*
Education: 1926–30 Armagh Royal Sch., Armagh; 1930–31 Cliff Coll.; 1933–36 Edgehill. *Appointments:* 1936–38 Language Sch., Peking; 1938–41 Engaged in Evangelistic work in and around Wutingfu, Shantung, N. China; 1941–45 Interned by Japanese first at Tsinanfu, later in Shanghai; 1947–49 Engaged in production of Visual Aids for Evangelistic work in N. China; 1950 Engaged in intensive missionary deputation work throughout Ireland; 1950–53 Appointed secretary Missionary Education Dept. at Mission House, London; 1953–57 On loan to Colonial Office as Resettlement Officer in Malaya; 1957–61 Portadown; 1961–65 Omagh; 1965–70 Ballynafeigh; 1971–75 Lisburn.
Connexional Committees: 1965–80 Overseas Missionary Committee.
Special Interests: Preparation and use of audio visual aids in missionary propaganda. *Hobbies and Recreations:* Photography, Gardening, Philately (especially China).

FENNELL, George Mathew, 19 Thistlemount Park, Ballymacash Rd., Lisburn, Co. Antrim, N. Ireland. (08462-2989) *b. 2 Sept 1895, Dublin, Southern Ireland. m. 29 Sept 1925: 1d., 1s.*
Education: 1900–14 Model Sch., Dublin; 1920–21 Edgehill.
Appointments: 1919–20 Wexford Cir.; 1920–21 Skibbereen; 1921–22 Moville; 1922–25 Clones; 1925–27 Ballybay; 1927–30 Bantry; 1930–33 Cookstown; 1932–38 Fivetmiletown; 1938–42 Aughnacloy; 1943–48 Warrenpoint; 1948–53 Rich Hill; 1953–58 Monaghan; 1958–63 Clones.

FERGUSON, Aian Wesley, Methodist Manse, Ardaghowen, Sligo, Republic of Ireland. (0015-2346) *b. 26 Oct 1953, Lisburn, Co.*

Antrim, N. Ireland. m. 1 July 1977: 1d.
Education: 1958–65 Lisburn Central Prim. Sch.; 1965–70 Wallace High Grammar Sch.; 1970–71 Lisburn Technical Coll.; 1974–77 Edgehill.
Appointments: 1977– Londonderry Methodist City Mission and Moville.
Connexional Committees: 1979– Connexional Youth Council.
Special Interests: New Testament Theology.

FORKER, William George Wilbert, PO Box N7776, Nassau, The Bahamas. (809-3274168) *b. 15 July 1935, Portadown, Co. Armagh, N. Ireland. m. 29 June 1959: 1d., 1s.*
Education: 1952–54 Shaftesbury House, Belfast; 1955–58 Edgehill.
Appointments: 1959–62 Georgetown, Guyana; 1964–66 Kingstown, St. Vincent; 1966–68 Bridgetown, Barbados; 1968–72 World Council of Churches, Geneva; 1972– Templeton.
Publications: The Templeton Foundation (1977).
Hobbies and Recreations: Stamp Collecting, Golf.

FORSYTHE, William Samuel, 20 Killycomaine Park, Portadown, Craigavon BT63 5JL, N. Ireland. (0762-339591) *b. 2 July 1915, Belfast. m. 12 Aug 1949: 1d., 1s.*
Education: 1945–47 Edgehill.
Appointments: 1943–45 Portlaoise; 1947–48 Moy; 1948–49 North Belfast Mission; 1949–50 Castlederg; 1950–54 Castlebar; 1954–59 Cranagill; 1959–62 Brookeborough; 1962–67 Springfield, Churchill; 1967–72 Rich Hill; 1972–77 Donacloney and Moira; 1977–80 Lisbellaw.

FRAME, Sydney, 55 Donaghadee Rd., Bangor, Co. Down BT20 4QY. (0247-60098) *b. 22 Dec 1929, Belfast, N. Ireland. m. 8 Sept 1955: 2d., 1s.*
Education: 1935–38 Corry's Jun.; 1938–41 Mountcollyer PE; 1941–42 Knockagh; 1942 Bangor PE; 1942–46 Belfast Technical High Sch.; 1951–52, 1953–55 Edgehill. *Appointments:* 1949–51 Charlemont; 1952–53 Sydenham; 1955–60 Longford; 1960–65 Lisbellaw and Maguiresbridge; 1965–68 Cavehill; 1968–74 Finaghy; 1974–82 Bangor, Queen's Parade.
Connexional Committees: 1958–60 Secretary of Sligo Synod; 1978–82 Chairman of Down District; 1968–80 An Assistant Secretary of Conference; 1970–82 General Committee; 1979–81 Stationing Committee.
Special Interests: Methodist Guild Holidays. *Hobbies and Recreations:* Golf, Swimming.

GALLAGHER, Ernest William, Edgehill College, Lennoxvale, Belfast BT9 5BY. (0232-665870)–BA, BD. *b. 24 Aug 1918, Kinsale, Co. Cork, Ireland. m. 11 Oct 1950: 2d., 2s.*
Education: 1929–36 Masonic Boys' Sch., Dublin; 1936–40 Trinity Coll., Dublin; 1940–43 Edgehill.
Appointments: 1944–66 India, Hyderabad District; 1967–75 Dublin, Charleston Rd.; 1975–82 Dublin, Centenary; 1982– Principal, Edgehill Coll.; 1981– President Methodist Church in Ireland.
Connexional Committees: Innumerable Connexional Committees in Ireland; 1969–77 MCOD Central Committee, as Irish Rep.
Special Interests: Modern Theology, Religion and Science, Comparative Religion, Philosophy, Irish History.
Hobbies and Recreations: Bird Watching, Photography.

GALLAGHER, Robert David Eric, 5 Vauxhall Park, Belfast BT9 5GZ, N. Ireland. (0232-660445)–OBE, MA, BD(Dublin), DD(Hon. Queen's Univ., Belfast). *b. 24 Aug 1913, Ballybay, Co. Monaghan. m. 30 June 1945: 2d., 1s.*
Education: 1921–24 Model Sch., Londonderry; 1924–25 Thomas St. Sch., Portadown; 1925–32 Methodist Coll., Belfast; 1932–36 Trinity Coll., Dublin Univ.; 1936–38 Edgehill.
Appointments: 1938–42 Woodvale Belfast; 1942–50 Methodist Coll., Belfast; 1950–54 Cregagh, Belfast; 1954–57 Belfast, University Rd.; 1957–79 Belfast Central Mission; 1958–67 Secretary Irish Conference; 1967 President Methodist Church in Ireland.
Connexional Committees: Several.
Council Member: 1967–69 Irish Council of Churches (Chairman); 1977–80 British Council of Churches (Vice President); Press Council of UK. *Publications: A Better Way for Irish Protestants and Roman Catholics* (Methodist Mission Board 1973); *Ecumenism in Ireland: Experiments and Achievements* (with Michael Ledwith, Irish Catholic Bishops' Conference and Irish Council of Churches 1981); *Christians in Ulster 1978–80* (with Stanley Worrall, Oxford University Press 1982).
Special Interests: Mission, Education, Ecumenism, Politics. *Hobbies and Recreations:* Golf, Reading.

GILLILAND, Arthur Desmond, The Manse, Dunkineely, Co. Donegal, Republic of Ireland. (52)–BA(Belfast), MA(Dublin). *b. 4 Oct 1921, Bantry, Co. Cork, Rep. of Ireland. m. 6 Aug 1948: 2d., 2s.*
Education: 1926–30 Dunkineely National Sch.; 1930–32 Drumblass Public Elem. Sch., Dungannon, Co. Tyrone; 1932–39 Wesley Coll., Dublin; 1940–43 Queen's Univ., Belfast; 1940–43 Edgehill.
Appointments: 1943–46 Glengormley, Belfast N.I.; 1946–50 Hupeh District, China; 1951–54 Tullamore; 1954–58, 1959–63 Hong Kong; Centenary Church Dublin, and Dean of Methodist Students in Dublin Universities; 1971–77 Bandon; 1977–82 United Methodist and Presbyterian Churches of Co. Wexford; 1982– Dunkineely.
Connexional Committees: 1963– Overseas Missionary Committee (now MMS Ireland); 1967– Board of Examiners; 1977– Council on Social Welfare (1979– Sec. of Southern Executive); 1975– World Development and Relief Committee (Sec.); 1976–77 Chairman of Midland and Southern District.
Special Interests: World Development and Relief. *Hobbies and Recreations:* Tennis, Reading, Verse, Writing, Watercolour Painting.

GILPIN, Henry Alexander, 20 Victoria Rd., Ballyhalbert, Newtownards, Co. Down, N. Ireland BT22 1DG. (210) *b. 6 Feb 1922, Hollybank House, Ardress, Annaghmore, Portadown. m. 4 Sept 1957: 1d., 1s.*
Education: 1928–33 Tullyroan PS; 1934–40 Royal Sch., Dungannon; 1940 Queen's Univ., Belfast; 1948–50 National Young Life Campaign Training Coll.; 1947 Army Education Course, Dalkeith; 1964–65 Edgehill.
Appointments: 1962–64 Dungannon; 1964–65 Belfast, Agnes St.; 1965–69 Lisbellaw; 1969–73 Belfast, Crumlin Rd.; 1973–78 Larne; 1978–82 Antrim; 1982– Glastry.
Connexional Committees: 1980–81 Mission Board. *Publications:* 60 Tracts and Articles for Victory Tract Club, London.
Special Interests: Evangelism.
Hobbies and Recreations: Golf, Reading, Rugby.

GOOD, George Edward, 30 Malone View Rd., Belfast BT9 5PH, N. Ireland. (0232-617441)–MA(Dublin). *b. 6 Oct 1915, Sligo, Ireland. m. 12 Sept 1944: 2d.*
Education: 1929–33 Sligo Grammar Sch.; 1933–34 Wesley Coll., Dublin; 1934–38 Trinity Coll., Dublin Univ.; 1938–40 Edgehill. *Appointments:* 1940–43 North Belfast Mission; 1943–45 Enniskillen; 1945–47 Portstewart; 1947–52 Omagh; 1952–54 Secretary, Methodist Youth Department; 1954–58 Donegall Sq., Belfast; 1958–61 University Rd., Belfast; 1961–65 Colombo, Sri Lanka; 1965–71 Cork; 1971–74 Sri Lanka; 1974–81 Enniskillen; 1981– Donegall Sq., Belfast; 1968–71 Chairman, Cork and Limerick District; 1974–80 Chairman, Enniskillen, Clones and Sligo District; 1969– President, Methodist Church in Ireland.
Connexional Committees: General Committee; Board of Examiners—Methodist Missionary Society (Ireland); Youth Council; Mission Board; General Purposes Board; Council on Social Welfare; Pastoral Efficiency. *Publications: The Code of Life* (1951); In Sri Lanka—*Lord, Teach us to Pray* (1964);*The Name is What You Are* (1973); *Living Stones* (1974).

GOOD, George Harold, 7 Tullybeg Fort, Ballynahinch, Co. Down, N. Ireland. (0238-562378)–STM, MBE. *b. 27 April 1937, Londonderry, N. Ireland. m. 11 Aug 1964: 3d., 2s.*
Education: 1945–49 Strandtown Prim., Belfast; 1949–55 Methodist Coll., Belfast; 1966–68 Christian Theol. Seminary, Indianapolis, Indiana, USA; 1959–62 Edgehill.
Appointments: 1956–58 Newry (Bessbrook); 1958–59 Dublin Central Mission; 1962–64 Waterford; 1964–66 First Methodist Church, Warren, Ohio; 1966–68 Imch and Methodist Hospital, Indianapolis; 1968–72 Agnes St., Belfast; 1972–73 Greenisland; 1973–78 Corrymella Community; 1978–79 Lynn Memorial and Crumlin Rd., HM Prison; 1979– Ballynahinch.
Connexional Committees: 1975–80 Supplementary Benefits Commission (N.I.); 1980–82 Social Security Advisory Committee (U.K.); 1975–80 Central Personal Social Services Advisory Committee (N.I.); 1974–78 British Council of Churches, Dept. of Ecumenical Affairs and Youth Division.
Hobbies and Recreations: Photography, Boating and Fishing, Travel.

GOOD, John Winston, 46 Diamond Gardens, Finaghy, Belfast BT10 0HE. (0232-619849) *b. 19 March 1934, Dungarvan, Co. Waterford. m. 1 Aug 1962: 1d., 2s.*
Education: 1939–45 Dungarvan Church of Ireland National Sch.; 1945–52 Sandford Park Sch., Dublin (Grammar Sch.); 1959–62 Edgehill.
Appointments: 1956–58 Castlederg; 1958–59 Fivemiletown; 1962–66 Manorhamilton and Blacklion; 1966–71 Finaghy; 1971–78 Lisburn and Dromore; 1978– General Secretary, Methodist Youth Dept.
Connexional Committees: 1978– General Committee, Council on Social Welfare, Board of Education, Mission Board, M.M.S. Ireland Special Evangelistic Agency, Church Extension; 1964– Connexional Youth Council. *Local Council Committees:* 1980– Northern Ireland Youth Committee; 1978– Standing Conference of Youth Organisations (N.I.); 1978– National Youth Council of Ireland.
Special Interests: Youth. *Hobbies and Recreations:* Gardening, Tropical Fish, Watching Sport.

GOOD, Peter Allen, 1 Corby Drive, Lurgan, Craigavon, Co. Armagh BT66 7AF. (076-22-3367) *b. 10 Dec 1933, Ballyclare, Co. Antrim. m. 4 July 1962: 2d., 1s.*
Education: 1938–39 Foyle Coll., Londonderry; 1939–45 Model Sch., Londonderry; 1945–50 Methodist Coll., Belfast; 1967–69 Edgehill.
Appointments: 1969–72 Dunkineely and Ardara; 1972–79 Whiteabbey; 1979– Lurgan (High St.).
Connexional Committees: 1975– Committee on Ministry of Healing; 1980– Social Responsibility; 1982– World Development; 1975–79 Mission Board.
Special Interests: Church Growth, World Mission, World Development.
Hobbies and Recreations: Marathons and Jogging, Model Railways.

GRIFFIN, Brian Desmond, Eglise Protestante Methodiste, 01 BP 1282, Abidjan 01, Ivory Coast, West Africa. (36-24-57)–BA, BD. *b. 20 Aug 1949, Dublin, Irish Republic. m. 22 June 1972: 1d., 2s.*
Education: 1954–61 St. Lukes Prim. Sch., Douglas, Cork; 1961–68 Cork Grammar and High Sch.; 1968–70 Univ. Coll., Cork; 1970–73 Queen's Univ., Belfast; 1970–73 Edgehill; 1978–79 Kingsmeade, Birmingham.
Appointments: 1973–78 Dublin South; 1979– Abidjan South.
Connexional Committees: Irish Conference; 1975–78 Education, Gurteen Agricultural Coll.; Ivory Coast District, 1980–81 Lay Training; 1982– Social Welfare; 1980– Board of Examiners; 1980– Urban Ministry; 1980– Reflection; 1981– Evangelism.
Special Interests: Newspapers.
Hobbies and Recreations: Hockey, Swimming.

HAMILTON, William Graham, Wesley Coll., Ballinteer, Dublin 16, R. of Ireland. (01-987012)–BA, BD(Lond.), HDipEd(Dublin). *b. 14 June 1936, Dublin. m. 4 July 1964: 1d., 3s.*
Education: Prim. Sch.; Private Education to Matriculation; Extern Student London Univ.; 1960–63 Edgehill. *Appointments:* 1957–58 Moy; 1958–60 Newry; 1963–64 Cork; 1964–66 Donegal; 1966–71 Upper Eire; 1971– Chaplain to Wesley Coll.; 1976– General Secretary Board of Education; 1979– Methodist Representative Radio Telefis Eireain.
Connexional Committees: 1965–71 District Secretary; Youth Department; Council on Social Welfare; General Committee; Board of Education; Governor, Edgehill Theol. Coll., Belfast.
Special Interests: Education, Television-Radio.

HAMILTON, William Irwin, 1 Green Rd., Knock, Belfast BT5 6JA. (0232-653413) *b. 5 June 1929, Belfast. m. 27 May 1968: 2d., 2s.*
Education: 1934–43 Woodvale and Glenwood P.E. Sch.; 1943–45 Technical High Sch., Belfast; 1949–50 Shaftesbury House, Belfast; 1951–54 Queens Univ.; 1951–54 Edgehill. *Appointments:* 1950–51 Newtownbutler; 1954–55 Knock; 1955–57 Cregagh and Glenburn; 1958–61 Knock; 1961–64 Carlow; 1964–68 Portadown; 1968–76 Sydenham; 1976– Knock.
Connexional Committees: 1969–72 Orphan Society; 1973–76 Property Board; 1977– Stipends and Allowances Board.
Special Interests: Care of the Elderly. *Hobbies and Recreations:* Gardening, Houses, Golf.

HANNA, Alan Gordon, 13b Woodland Park, Lisburn, Co. Antrim BT28 1LD. (08462-6678)–BA, B(Comm.). *b. 12 May 1913, Donegal. m. 4 Aug 1948: 1d., 2s.*
Education: 1924–31 Wesley Coll., Dublin; 1931–35 Trinity Coll., Dublin; 1939–41 Edgehill. *Appointments:* 1941–43 Ballyholme; 1943–45 Portstewart; 1945–47 Carlisle Memorial; 1947–48 Woodvale; 1948–52 Drumshanbo; 1952–57 Carlow; 1957–62 Holywood; 1962–66 Whiteabbey; 1966–74 Enniskillen; 1974–80 Glenavy; 1980– Retired.
Connexional Committees: 1968–69 Secretary Board of Examiners; 1970–74 Chairman Enniskillen District; 1973–79 Secretary Budget Committee.

HART, John, 7 Stirling Ave., Belfast BT6 9LN. (0232-794453) *b. 6 June 1902, Gilford, Co. Down, N. Ireland. m. (1) 8 Aug 1929, (2) 30 July 1963: 2d., 1s.*
Education: 1907–18 PE Sch., Gilford; 1918–20 Portadown Technical Sch.; 1921–22 Cliff Coll.; 1924–26 Edgehill. *Appointments:* 1923–24 Sligo; 1926–27 Londonderry City Mission; 1927–29 Falls Rd., Belfast; 1929–31 Donacloney; 1931–36 Youghal; 1936–40 Shankhill Rd., Belfast; 1940–45 Lisburn; 1945–50 Ormeau Rd., Belfast; 1950–55 Lynn Memorial, Belfast; 1955–60 Knock, Belfast; 1960–63 Downpatrick; 1963–66 Lurgan.
Connexional Committees: Past Psychological and Spiritual Healing, Property, Childrens Fd., Standing Committee, General Committee; Present, Trustees of Meth. Church in Ireland.
Special Interests: Hymnology. *Hobbies and Recreations:* Woodwork, Gardening.

HARTLEY, Thomas Alfred, 414 Upper Newtownlands Rd., Belfast BT4 3EZ, N. Ireland. (650743) *b. 14 Sept 1905, Belfast. m. 29 July 1936: 1d., 1s.*
Education: 1911–18 Mount Pottinger Boys National Sch.; 1918–21 Methodist Coll., Belfast; 1930–32 Edgehill. *Appointments:* 1927– Waterford; 1927–30 Dungannon; 1932–34 Maryborough; 1934–36 Killeshandra; 1936–39 Swanlinbar; 1939–42 Portarlington; 1942–47 Dolphin's Barn, Dublin; 1947–52 Newtownbutler; 1952–57 Whiteabbey; 1957–58 Omagh; 1958–63 Springfield Rd., Belfast; 1963–68 Sydenham, Belfast; 1968–71 Moy.
Connexional Committees: 1942–50 Bureau of Membership, Secretary; 1966–75 Trustees of the Methodist Church in Ireland; 1952–58 Methodist Orphan Society, Secretary; 1958–73 Treasurer.
Special Interests: Christian Endeavour, Evangelism, Social Welfare. *Hobbies and Recreations:* Woodwork, Do-it-yourself.

HASSARD, Austin Noel, 9 Belfast Rd., Glenavy, Co. Antrim, N. Ireland BT29 4LL. (0849-52494) *b. 25 Dec 1926, Church Hill, Co. Fermanagh, N. Ireland. m. 6 Dec 1958: 1d., 2s.*
Education: 1932–41 Church Hill PE; 1952–54 Edgehill. *Appointments:* 1948–50 Newcastle; 1951–52 Newry; 1954–57 Lisburn; 1957–58 North Belfast Mission; 1958–63 Cloughjordan; 1963–65 Ballintra; 1965–73 Castlederg; 1973–80 Cookstown; 1980– Glenavy.
Connexional Committees: 1976– Property Board.
Hobbies and Recreations: Golf, Bowls.

HENDERSON, Ian David, The Manse, Bayview Rd., Wicklow, Co. Wicklow. (0404-2216)–BA, BD. *b. 11 Sept 1946, Belfast. m. 20 June 1975: 1d.*
Education: 1950–53 Model Sch., Carrickfergus, Co. Antrim; 1953–64 Wesley Coll., Dublin; 1965–69 Trinity Coll., Dublin; 1970–73 Queens Univ., Belfast; 1970–73 Edgehill. *Appointments:* 1973–75 Dublin Central Mission; 1975–80 Cavan and Longford; 1980– Wicklow and Arklow.
Connexional Committees: 1982– Property Board.
Special Interests: History, Literature. *Hobbies and Recreations:*Stamp Collecting, Indoor Bowling, Badminton, Music, Gardening.

HILL, Alfred Wesley, 5 Windsor Drive, Wrexham, Clwyd LL11 2BD. (0978-262247)–BA(Queens Univ., Belfast); MB BCh BAO(Queens Univ., Belfast). *b. 16 Nov 1889, Belfast. m. 4 April 1981: 2d., 1s.*
Education: 1903–06, 1911–12 Methodist Coll., Belfast; 1909–12, 1922–27 Queen's Belfast; *Appointments:* 1912–13 Cork; 1913–16 Liuyang Hunan, China;

1916–49 Resigned; 1949– Without Pastoral Charge.
Council Member: British Medical Association, Local Medical Committee (NHS). *Publications: John Wesley Among the Physicians* (1958); *Introduction to Wesley's Primitive Physic* (1960).
Special Interests: Theology. *Hobbies and Recreations:* Gardening, Reading.

HOLLOWAY, Thomas Henry, 10 Kennedy Drive, Lisburn, Co. Antrim BT27 4HY. (084-62-70589) *b. 12 Jan 1907, Belfast. m. 14 July 1937: 1d., 3s.*
Education: 1910–20 Belfast Model; 1930–32 Edgehill. *Appointments:* 1929–30 Killeshandra; 1932–33 Carrickfergus; 1933–35 Newry; 1935–37 Osborne Park (Dunmurry); 1937–38 Clonakilty; 1938–40 Cootehill and Ballybay; 1940–41 Newtownstewart; 1941–46 Donegal; 1946–51 Portrush; 1951–56 Tandragee; 1956–60 Banbridge; 1960–65 Portadown; 1965–70 Belfast, Sandy Row; 1970–73 Donegall Road and Sandy Row; 1973–78 Belfast, Crumlin Rd.; 1948–50 Secretary of the Londonderry District Synod; 1953–65 Secretary of the Portadown District Synod; 1975–78 Chairman of the Belfast District; 1965–78 Hospital Chaplain (Belfast); 1973–78 Prison Chaplain (Crumlin Rd.); 1965–71 Secretary of the Council on Social Welfare, and still a Member of the Council.
Connexional Committees: 1965–71 Council on Social Welfare, Secretary, 1965– Member; 1954–56, 1958–63, 1975–78 Member of Stationing Committee. *Publications:* I write a column for weekly newspapers (26 years).
Special Interests: Journalism. *Hobbies and Recreations:* Caravanning, Photography, Writing.

HOUSTON, David, The Methodist Manse, Main St., Brookborough, County Fermanagh, N. Ireland. (036-553-219) *b. 23 Oct 1940, Eden, Carrickfergus, County Antrim, N. Ireland. m. 7 Aug 1973.*
Education: Prim. Education at Eden, Carrickfergus, and Harrogate, Yorkshire; 1950–56 Belfast High Sch.; 1957–59 Magee Univ. Coll., Londonderry; 1962–65 Edgehill.
Appointments: 1965–66 North Belfast Mission; 1966–67 Irvinestown; 1967–69 Waterford; 1969–70 Belfast Central Mission; 1970–71 Knock; 1971–73 Enniskillen District; 1973–75 Londonderry City Mission; 1975–80 Springfield and Churchill; 1980– Upper Erne.
Special Interests: A member of 'The Methodist Sacramental Fellowship'. *Hobbies and Recreations:* Philately, Sports.

IRVINE, Kenneth Irvine, 31 Colebrooke Rd., Fivemiletown, Co. Tyrone, N. Ireland BT75 0QG. (035-552-264) *b. 24 Feb 1945, Belfast. m. 30 May 1970: 1d., 2s.*
Education: 1950–55 Blenheim Jun., Prim. Sch.; 1955–60 Hemsworth Square Public Elem. Sch.; 1960–65 Belfast Coll. of Technology; 1965–67 Shaftsbury House Tutorial Coll.; 1967–70 Edgehill. *Appointments:* 1970–73 Londonderry and Inishowen; 1973–81 Belfast, Knock; 1981– Fivemiletown.
Connexional Committees: 1974–80 Property Board; 1971–73 Youth Council; 1982– Mission Board.
Special Interests: Preaching, Counselling, Church Renewal, Personal Renewal. *Hobbies and Recreations:* Squash, Badminton, Jogging, Swimming.

JOHNSTON, Thomas Alexander, 9A Fortwilliam Drive, Belfast, N. Ireland BT15 4EB. (0232-771496) *b. 4 May 1914, Newtowngore, Co. Leitrim, Ireland. w.*
Education: Methodist Coll., Belfast; 1936–39 Edgehill. *Appointments:* 1946–75 Nigeria Dt; 1976–78 Sierra Leone Dt; 1978–80 Nigeria Dt.
Connexional Committees: 1962–73 Chairman, Northern Nigeria District.

KELLS, John Alexander, 1 Mount Brandon, St. Luke's, Cork, Eire. (021-506182) *b. 29 Sept 1907, Derrylane, Co. Cavan. m. 4 Jan 1949.*
Education: National Sch.; Technical Sch.; 1928 Cliff Coll.; 1932–34 Edgehill. *Appointments:* 1932–33 Castlederg; 1934–35 Killishandra; 1935–37 Newry; 1937–40 Dublin, Abbey St.; 1940–45 Cork; 1945–50 Dublin, Rathmines; 1950–62 Bombay and Punjab Dt, Pakistan; 1962–67 Dublin, Sandymount; 1967–73 Clonakilty.

KELSO, Herbert, 67 Marlborough Park South, Belfast BT9 6HS, N. Ireland. (0232-666149) *b. 24 March 1923, Derryhubbert, Co. Armagh, N. Ireland. m. 17 June 1964: 1d., 2s.*
Education: 1930–38 Tamnamore Prim. (Co. Tyrone); 1939–40 Killyman Prim. (Co. Tyrone); 1947–48 Shaftesbury House, Belfast; 1945–46 Cliff Coll., Derbyshire; 1950–52 Presbyterian Coll., Belfast (Theol.), joint course with Edgehill Coll.; 1953 St. Andrew's Coll., Selly Oak, Birmingham; 1967–68 Magee Univ. Coll., Londonderry; 1950–53 Edgehill, joint course with Presbyterian, Belfast. *Appointments:* 1949–50 Mountpottinger (Belfast); 1953–64 Nigeria; 1964–67 Bailieborough; 1967–69 Dunkineely and Ardaragh; 1969–75 Athy/Mountmellick; 1975–78 Banbride; 1978–82 Sandy Row (Belfast); 1982– Belfast Cent. Mission.
Connexional Committees: 1967–69 Overseas Mission.
Special Interests: Methodist History, Church History, Ecumenics, World Mission, Philately, Numismatics, Genealogy. *Hobbies and Recreations:* Reading in Various Disciplines.

KER, Donald Paul, 32 South Hill, Dartry, Dublin 6. (974103)–BA(Dublin); BD(Belfast). *b. 19 June 1950, Belfast. m. 24 June 1972: 2d., 1s.*
Education: 1955–68 Methodist Coll., Belfast; 1968–72 Trinity Coll., Dublin; 1973–76 Edgehill.
Appointments: 1976–81 Dun Laoghaire; 1981– Dublin Centenary.
Connexional Committees: 1978– Connexional Youth Dept.; 1980– Faith and Order Committee; 1981– Council of Social Welfare.
Special Interests: New Testament Studies, Christian Education. *Hobbies and Recreations:* Music, Enjoying the Irish Countryside.

KERR, David James, 39 Rosetta Park, Belfast, N. Ireland BT6 0DL. (0232-643599) *b. 28 May 1937, Belfast. m. 8 Oct 1966: 1d., 3s.* *Education:* 1942–49 Strandtown Prim. Sch., Belfast; 1949–55 Sullivan Upper Grammar Sch., Holywood; 1961–64 Edgehill. *Appointments:* 1958–60 Irvinestown; 1960–61 Belfast (Sandy Row); 1964–69 North Belfast Mission; 1969–75 Limerick; 1975–81 Bangor; 1981– Belfast (Ballynafeig and Knockbreda). *Connexional Committees:* 1975–79 Mission Board; 1969–77 Council of Social Welfare; 1970–74 Sec. of Southern Executive; 1974 Stationing Committee; 1972–75 Sec. of Midlands and Southern Synod; 1976– Irish Council of Churches. *Special Interests:* Liturgy, Ecumenical Affairs. *Hobbies and Recreations:* Reading, Squash, Walking.

KEYS, John, 97 Orritor Rd., Cookstown, Co. Tyrone BT80 8BN. (06487-62157) *b. 3 Aug 1907, Drumbulcan, Irvinestown, Co. Fermanagh. m. 27 Aug 1940: 4s.* *Education:* 1913–22 Irvinestown National Sch.; 1932–35 Edgehill. *Appointments:* 1935–39 Moy and Charlemont; 1939–40 Ballineen; 1940–45 Dundalk; 1945–50 Fivemiletown; 1950–55 Edenderry; 1955–60 Ballinamallard; 1960–64 North Belfast Mission; 1964–72 Cullybackey; 1942–45 Aughnacloy. *Special Interests:* Pastoral Visiting. *Hobbies and Recreations:* Gardening.

KEYS, John Henry Francis, 1 Malone Rd., Belfast BT9 6BY. (0232-669559)–BA, MSc. *b. 14 May 1942, Newry. m. 1965: 2d., 1s.* *Education:* 1955–60 Portora Royal Sch.; 1962–66 Queen's Univ.; 1962–66 Edgehill. *Appointments:* 1967–73 Haiti, Carribean Conf.; 1973– Chaplain, Methodist Coll., Belfast. *Special Interests:* RE Curriculum Development.

KINGSTON, Paul, Aldersgate, Palmerston Park, Dublin 6, Eire. (971183) *b. 28 Dec 1932, Drimoleague, Co. Cork, Eire. m. 10 Dec 1960: 1d., 1s.* *Education:* 1943–50 Wesley Coll., Dublin; 1960–61 St. Andrews Coll., Selly Oak, Birmingham; 1958–60 Edgehill. *Appointments:* 1960–69 Idoma, N. Nigeria; 1969–76 Cregagh, Belfast; 1976– Dublin Central Mission. *Connexional Committees:* Mission Board, Board of Examiners, General Committee, Methodist Orphan Society (Secretary 1974–82), Governor of Edgehill Coll.; 1981– Chairman of Board of Governors Wesley Coll., Dublin. *Hobbies and Recreations:* Oil Painting.

KINGSTON, Paul, Kana, Drimoleague, Co. Cork, Eire. (028-31150) *b. 6 Feb 1899, Meenies, Drimoleague, Co. Cork. m. 24 May 1926: 1d., 2s.* *Education:* 1904–14 Meenies Prim.; 1923–26 Edgehill. *Appointments:* 1921–22 Castlederg; 1922–23 Sligo; 1926–40 Kana; 1940–41 Agbani; 1941–55 Port Harcourt (Chairman of District); 1955–60 Bible Translation, Ogoni Bori; 1961–63 Dunmanway; 1965–66 Skibbereen. *Publications: Ogoni Bible* (1966).

LAVERTY, Maurice, 50 Regent St., Newtownards, Co. Down BT23 4LP. (0247-812130) *b. 14 Feb 1950, Lurgan.* *Education:* 1961–68 Portadown Coll.; 1980–81 Edgehill. *Appointments:* 1982– Movilla Abbey and Comber. *Connexional Committees:* 1979–80 General Committee; 1978–80 Connexional Youth Council.

LINDSAY, Edward Rowlette, Mayo House, 61 Rathdown Park, Dublin 6, Republic of Ireland. (906998) *b. 25 June 1916, Roscrea, Co. Tipperary. m. 30 Aug 1945: 3d.* *Education:* 1924–30 Model Sch., Birr; 1930–32 Wesley Coll., Dublin; 1933–35 Cliff Coll.; 1936–39 Edgehill. *Appointments:* 1939–40 Belfast, Agnes St.; 1940–42 Clonakilty (Ballineen); 1942–45 Belfast, Agnes St.; 1945–46 Sandymount; 1946–51 Dun Laoghaire; 1951–56 Adare and Rathkeale; 1956–59 Cork; 1959–65 Ballynafeigh; 1965–68 Belfast, Knock; 1968– Home Missions General Secretary. *Parliamentary Service:* 1965–68 Northern Ireland Parliament Methodist Chaplain. *Connexional Committees:* 1968–82 Council on Social Welfare; 1947–51 Youth Dept.; 1959–58 Church Extension; 1968–82 General Committee; 1971–82 Mission Board; 1971–77 Property Board; 1971–77 General Purposes Board; 1977–82 Stipends and Allowances Board; 1968–82 Board of Education.

LINDSAY, Robert Kenneth, 136 Beechpark, Lucan, Co. Dublin, Eire. (280593)–BSc, BAgr, BD. *b. 4 Sept 1947, Bangor, Co. Down. m. 24 July 1980: 1d.* *Education:* 1952–59 Regent House Sch., Newtownards (Prep. Dept.); 1959–62 Regent House Sch., Newtownards (Grammar); 1962–67 Methodist Coll., Belfast; 1967–72, 1977–80 Queens Univ., Belfast; 1977–80 Edgehill. *Appointments:* 1979–80 Belfast, Cregagh and Glenburn; 1980– Dublin Central Mission. *Special Interests:* The Pastoral Ministry. *Hobbies and Recreations:* Gardening.

LIVINGSTONE, Robert George, Ceol na Mara, 18 The Point, Portavogie, Co. Down, N. Ireland. (02477-71333)–BA(Lond.), MA(Dublin). *b. 16 Oct 1913, Drum, Co. Monaghan, Ireland. m. (1) 31 Aug 1939, (2) 24 Sept 1966: 1d., 2s.* *Education:* 1923–29 Corrinshigo National Sch.; 1929–33 Drum National Sch.; 1936–40 Univ. of London; 1941–45 Univ. of Dublin; 1933–36 Edgehill. *Appointments:* 1945–50 Cork; 1950–55 Dublin Centenary; 1955–59 Dunlaoghaire; 1959–63 Principal of Gurteen Agriculture Coll.; 1963–72 Director of Agricultural Development in Church of South India; 1972–79 Leader of Shankill Team Ministry in Belfast; 1977 President of the Methodist Church in Ireland; 1961–63 Member of the National Council of the Irish Farmers Association; 1960–62 Chairman of the Irish

Farmers Association in North Tipperary.
Connexional Committees: 1975– Faith and Order Committee of Methodist Church; 1973–75 Convener of Commission on the Ministry; 1974–79 Member of the Council on Social Welfare; 1974–79 Member of Committee on World Development; 1976– Co-Secretary of Joint Standing Committee of Roman Catholics and Protestants on Mixed Marriages. *Publications: Church Come Alive* (Christian Journals 1977); *A Study Tour of Agriculture in Japan* (Church of South India 1969); Contributions to various Theological and Agricultural Journals.
Special Interests: Modern Poetry, United Church in Ireland, The Power of Non-Violence. *Hobbies and Recreations:* Gardening, Fishing.

LOANE, George William, 8 Richhill Crescent, Belfast BT5 6HF, N. Ireland. (0232-653476) *b. 22 April 1935, Dublin. m. 27 June 1962: 2d., 2s.*
Education: 1948–53 Wesley Coll., Dublin; 1959–62 Edgehill.
Appointments: 1962–64 North Belfast Mission; 1964–66 Drumshanbo and Boyle; 1966–70 Londonderry (Carlisle Rd.); 1970–76 Joanmount; 1976–80 Wesley Chapel, Cork; 1980– Mountpottinger.
Special Interests: TV and Broadcasting.

MacCORMACK, James T., 2 Balmoral Ave., Whitehead, Carrickfergus, Co. Antrim BT38 9QA. (06903-73327)–BA, BD. *b. 11 March 1926, Dublin.*
Education: 1938–44 Wesley Coll., Dublin; 1944–48 Dublin Univ.; 1949–52 Dublin Univ.; 1949–52 Edgehill. *Appointments:* 1947–49 Dublin Central Mission; 1952–63 Zambia; 1963–66 Springfield and Churchill; 1966–71 Zambia; 1971–77 Finaghy; 1977– Carrickfergus.
Connexional Committees: 1977– Budget Committee; 1976– Board of Examiners. *Publications:* I.B.R.A. Notes; *Should we Drink* (African Christian Press); Various translations in Zambian language.
Hobbies and Recreations: Mountain Walking, Photography.

MAGOWAN, Thomas Walker, Aldersgate, 47 Chanterhill Rd., Enniskillen, Co. Fermanagh, N. Ireland. (0365-22244)– DipTheol(Lond.). *b. 8 April 1929, Belfast, N. Ireland. m: 2d., 2s.*
Education: Skegoniel Prim. Sch.; Technical High Sch.; Belfast Coll. of Technology, Belfast; 1959–62 Edgehill. *Appointments:* 1958–61 Enniskillen; 1962–63 Londonderry; 1971–74, 1963–68 Caribbean Conference (Jamaica District); 1968–71 Belfast, Woodvale; 1974–81 Finaghy; 1981– Enniskillen.
Connexional Committees: Local Preachers Secretary Methodist Church in Ireland; Local Preachers Secretary Jamaica District; Overseas Missions Committee Methodist Church in Ireland.
Special Interests: Training of Local Preachers. *Hobbies and Recreations:* Golf, Boating, Fishing.

MAWHINNEY, Edmund Thomas Irwin, 33 Grange Rd., Coleraine, Co. Londonderry BT52 1NG. (0265-3158) *b. 26 Oct 1938, Moira, Co. Down. m. 29 July 1964: 1d., 2s.*
Education: 1944–50 Moira Prim. Sch.; 1950–56 Methodist Coll., Belfast; 1961–64 Edgehill.
Appointments: 1957–58 Ballyclare (Lay Evangelist); 1958–59 Lisbellaw; 1959–61 Enniskillen; 1964–66 Killeshandra; 1966–68 Killeshandra and Longford; 1968–75 Lurgan (High St.); 1975–81 Carlisle Circus, Duncairn Gardens and Cavehill, Belfast; 1981– Coleraine, Portrush and Portstewart; Secretary of District Synods: 1966–68 Enniskillen, Clones and Sligo; 1972–75 Portadown; 1979–81 Belfast; 1982– Londonderry; 1980 Journal Secretary of Conference.

McCAFFREY, Samuel Edwin, 67 Strand Rd., Portstewart, Co. Londonderry, N. Ireland BT55 7LX. (026583-2593) *b. 7 Jan 1897, Cregban, Omagh, Co. Tyrone. m. 14 July 1926.*
Education: Caranacew Sch., Omagh, Co. Tyrone; 1925–26 Edgehill.
Appointments: 1920–22 Coleraine; 1923–25 Castlederg; 1926–28 Cavan; 1928–32 Portadown; 1932–35 Coleraine; 1935–40 Armagh; 1940–45 Belfast, Ormeau Rd.; 1945–50 Coleraine; 1950–55 Cork; 1955–60 Dublin, Charleston Rd.; 1960–66 Enniskillen.
Connexional Committees: Chairman of four Districts, 1945–50 Londonderry District; 1950–55 Cork District; 1956–60 Dublin District; 1960–66 Enniskillen District; 1956–57 President of Methodist Church in Ireland. *Local Council Committees:* Many Local Committees.

McCONNELL, Henry Ormonde, 7 Palmerston Park, Belfast BT4 1PZ, N. Ireland. (0232-651004)–MBE, BA(Queen's Univ., Belfast). *b. 27 Feb 1904, Clonakilty, Co. Cork, Ireland. m. 6 July 1934: 2d., 2s.*
Education: 1917–20 Methodist Coll., Belfast; 1930–33 Queen's Univ., Belfast; 1930–33 Edgehill.
Appointments: 1928–30 Belfast, Agnes St.; 1936–70 Haiti, West Indies; Deputy Chairman of the Haitian Sub-District (of the Jamaica District) for many years; 1968–70 following the creation of the Methodist Church in the Caribbean and the Americas in 1967, Chairman of the Haiti District.
Publications: You can learn Creole (in collaboration wtih Eugene Swan 1945); *Haiti Diary 1933–70* (1976); The following were published in Haiti in French and in Creole *Manuel d'Instruction à l'usage des Croyants* (2nd Edition printed in 1951); *Esquisses de Doctrines Chrétiennes etc* (2nd Edition printed in 1957), *Le Dieu Qui Nous Parle* (Printed in French 1960 and in Creole in 1969).
Special Interests: Adult Literacy Campaign in Haitian Creole. *Hobbies and Recreations:* Golf, Photography.

McCONNELL, Patrick Morrison, 28 Margretta Park, Portadown, Co. Armagh BT63 5DF, N. Ireland. (0762-32616)–BA. *b. 10 June 1935, Cap Haitien, Haiti, Grandes Antilles (W.I.). m. 12 Aug 1961: 3d., 2s.*

Education: 1946–53 Methodist Coll., Belfast; 1974–77 New Univ. of Ulster, Coleraine; 1955–58 Edgehill. *Appointments:* 1958–72 Haiti, West Indies; 1973–75 Portstewart; 1975–77 Portstewart; 1973–75 Chaplain N.U.U. 2 years study leave; 1975–77 N.U.U.; 1977–81 Dunkineely and Ardara; 1981– Portadown. *Connexional Committees:* 1973–81 District O.M. Secretary (Londonderry). *Special Interests:* Cultural and Religious Links between Africa and Caribbean. *Hobbies and Recreations:* Walking, Rugby, Athletics, Painting, Music, Writing, Golf.

McELHINNEY, Robert Ivan, 3 Dromore Rd., Irvinestown, Co. Fermanagh, N. Ireland. (036-56-21203) *b. 6 July 1946, Donegal, Ireland. m. 29 May 1972: 3s.* *Education:* 1967–68 Cliff Coll.; 1969–72 Edgehill; 1973–74 Selly Oak. *Appointments:* 1972–73 North Belfast Mission; 1974–76 South Eleuthera (M.C.C.A.); 1976–80 North Eleuthera (M.C.C.A.); 1980– Pettigo and Irvinestown. *Publications: Now* magazine articles 1976, 1982.

MEARA, Alan, 2 Lyndhurst Ave., Bangor, Co. Down BT19 1AY. (0247-3400)–DipTheol(Belfast). *b. 26 May 1940, Dunmanway, Co. Cork. m. 12 July 1966: 1d., 1s.* *Education:* 1945–52 Model Sch., Dunmanway, Co. Cork; 1952–57 St. Ronan's Coll., Dunmanway; 1962–65 Edgehill. *Appointments:* 1961–62 Irvinestown; 1965–67 Belfast, Carlisle Circus; 1967–70 Swanlinbar; 1970–78 Dublin, Clontarf, Sutton and Skerries; 1978– Bangor. *Connexional Committees:* 1976– General Committee; 1973– Council on Social Welfare; 1968–74 Youth Council; 1976–79, 1981– General Purposes Board; 1982– Down District Synod Secretary. *Hobbies and Recreations:* Golf.

MOORE, John Raymond James, Methodist Manse, 35 Upper Green, Dunmurry, Co. Antrim BT17 0EL. (0232 622192) *b. 7 March 1948, Donegal. m. 31 Aug 1963.* *Education:* 1952–62 Ballintra Prim. Sch.; 1962–66 Donegal Secondary Sch.; 1972–73 Cliff Coll.; 1974–77 Edgehill. *Appointments:* 1977–81 North Belfast Mission; 1981– Finaghy. *Special Interests:* Preaching, Pastoring. *Hobbies and Recreations:* Model Railways, Photography.

MORRIS, Robert Desmond, 30 Killeaton Crescent, Dunmurry, Belfast BT17 9HD. (0232-617679) *b. 21 Feb 1916, Tullamore, Co. Offaly. m. 9 Aug 1945: 2d., 1s.* *Education:* 1921–29 Tullamore National; 1929–34 Wesley Coll., Dublin; 1938–40 Edgehill. *Appointments:* 1938–39 Fivemiletown; 1940–43 Dungannon; 1943–44 Bessrook; 1944–46 Dalkey; 1946–51 Portadown; 1951–54 Youghal; 1954–59 Secretary of Youth Dept.; 1959–63 Sydenham; 1963–71 Lisburn; 1971–76 Cork; 1976–81 Coleraine; 1971–76 Chairman of Midlands and Southern District; 1976–81 Chairman, Londonderry District. *Parliamentary Service:* 1974 President Methodist Church in Ireland. *Connexional Committees:* 1971–81 General Committee; 1971–81 Chairman's Committee; 1971–81 Board of Examiners; 1971–81 Stationing Committee. *Special Interests:* 1964–74 Music, Precentor of Irish Conference. *Hobbies and Recreations:* Past: Rugby, Hockey, Badminton, Tennis, Cricket, Present: Gardening, Music, Walking, Reading.

MORRIS, Steward Rowlett, Syngefield, Birr, Co. Offaly, Republic of Ireland. (200)–BA, BD(Hons)–*b. 15 June 1955, Dublin. M. 28 June 1980.* *Education:* 1959–66 St. Matthew's National, Irishtown, Dublin 4; 1966–72 Wesley Coll., Ballinteer, Dublin 16; 1972–76 Trinity Coll., Dublin; 1977–80 Queens Univ., Belfast. *Appointments:* 1980–82 Belvoir—on the Belfast (Ballynafeigh, Knockbreda, Belvoir) Circuit; 1982– Birr, Athlone and Tullamore Circuit. *Connexional Committees:* 1982– Youth Department. *Special Interests:* Travel, World Development. *Hobbies and Recreations:* Tennis, Jogging, Reading.

MORRISON, George Robert, 52 Maryville Park, Belfast BT9 6LP. (0232 667181) *b. 10 April 1925, Killeshandra, Co. Cavan, Ireland. m. 6 Aug 1955: 2d.* *Education:* 1930–39 Killegar N.S., Co. Leitrim; 1951–54 Edgehill. *Appointments:* 1949–51 Sligo; 1954–58 Belfast Central Mission; 1958–61 Carlow; 1961–65 Sligo; 1965–73 Londonderry; 1973–78 Carrickfergus; 1978– Belfast, University Road. *Connexional Committees:* (Various dates) General Committee; 1967–76 Property Board and Chapel Fund; 1961–83 Inter-Church Relations: various periods Board of Examiners; 1971–77 Stipends and Allowances Board. *Hobbies and Recreations:* Gardening, Walking.

MYLES, Gerald Garland, Claremont, Ballinclea Rd., Killiney, Co. Dublin, Republic of Ireland. (855442)–MA DipEd. *b. 22 June 1907, Adare, Co. Limerick. m. 16 Oct 1946: 1s.* *Education:* 1911–17 Adare, Co. Limerick National Sch.; 1917–24 Wesley Coll., Dublin; 1932–44 The Queen's Univ., Belfast; 1932–36 Edgehill Theological Coll. *Appointments:* 1931–32 Lisburn; 1936–42 Chaplain, Methodist Coll., Belfast; 1942–43 Shankill, Woodvale and Belfast Falls Rd.; 1943–46 Chaplain HMF; 1946–47 Univ. Rd., Belfast; 1947–72 Principal and Chaplain Wesley Coll., Dublin; 1972–74 Cloughjordan and Borrisokane. *Connexional Committees:* 1974–77 Secretary to the Trustees of the Methodist Church in Ireland; 1968–69 President of the Methodist Church in Ireland. *Council Member:* 1947– Trustee of Methodist Church in Ireland; 1947–80 Board of Examiners; 1974–80 Property Board. *Special Interests:* History, Literature. *Hobbies and Recreations:* Rugby, Hockey, Swimming, Rowing, Stamp Collection, Music (recorded).

NELSON, John Jones, 35 Tweskard Park, Belfast BT4 2JZ. (084 63792)–BA, DipSocSt. *b. 6 Jan 1939, Belfast. m. 8 Sept 1966: 2s.*
Education: 1947–57 Royal Belfast Academical Institution; 1964–66 Queen's Univ., Belfast; 1975–79 The Open Univ.; 1962–65 Edgehill.
Appointments: 1960–62 Irvinestown and Castlederg; 1965–71 Carnalea; 1971–74 Greencastle; 1974–77 Belfast, Central Mission; 1977– Campbell Coll., Belfast, Chaplain.
Connexional Committees: 1971–77 Youth Committee; 1975–82 Council of Social Welfare.
Special Interests: Presently reading for Research Degree in Ecumenics MA(Th) Hull Univ. in conjunction with Irish Sch. of Ecumenics.

NELSON, Robert Alexander, 49 Highfield Park, Dundrum, Dublin 14. (982152) *b. 6 Nov 1905, Broughmore, Lisburn, N. Ireland. m. 13 Aug 1930: 1d., 2s.*
Education: Seymour Street National Sch., Lisburn; Lisburn Intermediate Sch.; Edgehill. *Appointments:* 1924–25 Belfast Central Mission; 1925–26 Castledeig; 1926–28 List of Reserve; 1928–30 Mountmellick; 1930–45 Missionary Service in Ceylon (Sri Lanka); 1945–48 Carlow (Irish Conference); 1948–61 Colombo South (Sri Lanka); 1961–67 Univ. Rd., Belfast; 1967–72 Rathgar.
Connexional Committees: 1965– President Methodist Church in Ireland; 1962–81 Member Faith and Order Committee; 1962– Board of Examiners; 1964– Trustees of Methodist Church in Ireland; 1962–70 Edgehill Coll. Board Governors; 1961– M.M.S. (Ireland); 1962–78 Irish Council of Churches; 1965– Irish Tripartite Conversations. *Local Council Committees:* 1962–67 Secretary Dublin Council of Churches; 1952– Faith and Order, represented Ceylon M. Church at Lund; 1963 Faith and Order, represented Irish M. Church at Montreal; 1964 represented Irish M. Church at Nottingham Conference.
Publications: Contributor to *The Ecumenical Review, International Review of Missions, London Quarterly and Halloms Review, Ceylon Church Record.*
Special Interests: Ecumenical Theology. *Hobbies and Recreations;* Walking, Reading, Gardening, Classical Music.

NEWELL, Cecil Andred, 40 Larne Rd., Carrick Fergus, County Antrim, N. Ireland BT38 7DZ. (09603 62202)–BD(Lond.). *b. 28 Oct 1925, Belfast, N. Ireland. m. 7 Aug 1954: 1d., 1s.*
Education: 1931–39 Rosetta Public Elem. Sch.; 1939–40 Belfast Coll. of Technology. *Appointments:* 1945–47 Irvinestown; 1947–48 Newtown Butler and Lisnaskea; 1950–54 North Belfast Mission; 1955–71 Zimbabwe; 1971–78 Bangor; 1978– Carrick Fergus.
Connexional Committees: 1978– Stipend and Allowances Board; 1972– Board of Examiners; 1974–81 M.M.S. Ireland; 1976–78 Mission Board; 1974– General Committee; 1971–82 World Development and Relief; 1976–81 National Insurance Officer of Methodist Church in Ireland.
Special Interests: People and Music.
Hobbies and Recreations: Photography, Golf.

NICHOLL, William. 21 Old Cavehill Rd., Belfast, N. Ireland BT15 5GT. (0232 779929)–BD(Lond.), MTh(Queen's, Belfast). *b. 4 March 1926, Londonderry. m. 9 Sept 1954: 3d., 1s.*
Education: 1931–39 Clooney Public Elem. Sch., Londonderry; 1939–40 Londonderry Technical Coll.; 1948–50 Edgehill. *Appointments:* 1946–47 Maryborough; 1947–48 Dungannon; 1950–51 Waterford; 1951–53 Coleraine; 1953–54 Sligo; 1954–59 Tullamore; 1959–63 Portadown; 1963–66 Glenavy and Antrim; 1966–74 Oldpark Rd., Belfast; 1974–79 Ballynahinch; 1979–81 Glasgow South; 1981– Belfast, Carlisle Circus Rd., Cavehill.
Connexional Committees: 1960–79 Board of Examiners; 1965– Inter-Church Relations Committee.
Special Interests: Inter-Church Relations. *Hobbies and Recreations:* Golf and Chess.

OWENS, Cecil, 6 Beechcote Ave., Portadown, Co Armagh, Northern Ireland BT63 5DG. (0246 33709)–MA(Trinity Coll., Dublin). *b. 7 July 1916, Castlederg, Co. Tyrone, N. Ireland. m. 29 Sept 1949: 2d.*
Education: 1922–28 Model Sch., Londonderry; 1928–34 Foyle Coll., Londonderry; 1935–39 Magee Univ. Coll., Londonderry; 1935–39 Univ. of Dublin, Trinity Coll.; 1940–42 Edgehill Coll. *Appointments:* 1939–40 Dungannon; 1942–46 Portadown; 1946–48 North Belfast Mission; 1948–49 Carlisle Memorial, Cavehill; 1949–54 Cullybackey; 1954–59 Antrim; 1959–64 Cranagill; 1964–67 Armagh, Richhill; 1967–75 Banbridge.
Connexional Committees: 1950– Psychological and Spiritual Healing.
Hobbies and Recreations: Historical Studies, Natural History, Art, Gardening.

PARKER, Arthur, 4 Drumlin Rd., Donachlowey, Craigavon, N. Ireland BT66 7NJ. (0762-881255) *b. 6 Jan 1935, Belfast. m. 10 Sept 1955: 2d.*
Education: 1946 Fane St. Secondary; 1966–68 Edgehill Coll.
Appointments: 1968–69 Belfast Central Mission; 1969–73 Donegal and Ballintra; 1973–78 Dungannon; 1978–81 Belfast Central Mission; 1981– Moira.
Connexional Committees: 1972–82 Property Board; 1979– General Committee.
Hobbies and Recreations: Painting, Table Tennis, Reading.

PARKIN, Vincent, 37 Beechdene Gardens, Lisburn, Co. Antrim, N. Ireland BT28 3JH. (084-62-72908)–BSc, MA. *b. 7 June 1915, Washington, Co. Durham. m. 16 May 1942: 1s.*
Education: 1920–26 Washington Glebe Sch.; 1926–33 Washington Grammar Sch.; 1933–37 Durham Univ.; 1937–40 Cambridge Univ.; 1937–40 Wesley House.
Appointments: 1940–41 Edinburgh, Nicolson Square; 1941–47 Chaplain HMF; 1947–53 Kingswood Sch. Chaplain; 1953–67 Headingley Coll., Resident Tutor; 1967–73 Bristol Coll., Resident Tutor; 1973–82

Edgehill Coll., Principal; 1979 President Methodist Church in Ireland.

PLUNKETT, Hedley Washington, The Manse, Sandys Street, Newry, Co. Down, Northern Ireland BT34 1EN. (0693-2078)–Hon.DD(The American Univ., Washington DC, 1959). *b. 26 Jan 1917, Lisnaskea, Co. Fermanagh, N. Ireland. m. 21 Nov 1950: 2d., 2s.*
Education: 1940–42 Edgehill Coll. *Appointments:* 1939 Sligo, 1942–46 Portadown; 1946–50 Sydenham; 1950–52 Belfast Central Mission; 1952–55 Superintendent of Evangelism; 1956–59 Rathgar; 1959–64 Carlisle Memorial; 1964–69 Donegall Square; 1969–76 Cregagh; 1976– Newry; 1975 President Methodist Church in Ireland. *Connexional Committees:* 1953–73 Ministerial Treasurer of Edgehill Coll.; 1982 Chairman of the Board of Governors; 1967–69 Chairman of the Northern Evangelistic Agency; 1953–69 Member of the Connexional Youth Committee; 1961–74 Member of the Pastoral Efficiency; 1953–73, 1978–82 Member of the Board of Education; 1962–75 Member of the Broadcasting and Television Committee; 1964–68 Member of the Stewardship Committee; 1964–68 Member of the Psychological and Healing Committee; 1966–73 Member of the Memorials Committee; 1980–82 Chairman of the Portadown District; 1970 Secretary of Church Extension Committee; 1977–82 Chairman of Property Board; 1980–82 Stationing Committee; 1977–80 Inter-Church Relations; 1977–82 Faith and Order. *Council Member:* 1948–59 Secretary of the Irish Christian Endeavour Union; 1960 President of the Irish Christian Endeavour Union; 1961–64 Member of the N. Ireland Religious Advisory Committee of the B.B.C.; 1973–76 Chairman of the Bible Society of Ireland; 1968–69 Chairman of the Irish Council of Healing; 1973 Co-Founder of the East Belfast Good-Neighbour Movement; 1979–82 Chairman of the Management Committee of the Newry Model and Windsor Hill Primary Schs. and of the Daisy Hill Hospital Sch.; 1977–82 Member of the Executive and Vice-President of the N. Ireland Chaplains' Association; 1954 Delegate to the 2nd Assembly of the World Council of Churches, Evanston, Illinois; 1954 Delegate to the 11th World Christian Endeavour Convention, Washington DC; 1957 Missioner to the East Washington Conference of the American Methodist Church. *Publications: Adventure and Faith of the Irish Pioneers* (1964); *Methodists and The Lord's Supper* (1981); *Two and a Quarter Centuries of Methodism in Newry* (1981). *Hobbies and Recreations:* Gardening, Bee-keeping, Travel.

REDMAN, Malcolm Edward Geddis, 20 Towerview Ave., Bangor, Co. Down BT19 2BB. (0247/62745) *b. 9 Mary 1913, Harry's Harbour, Notre Dame Bay, Newfoundland. m. 5 Sept 1951: 1s.*
Education: 1923–29 Bangor, Co. Down; 1940–42 Edgehill Coll. *Appointments:* 1939–40 Carrickfergus; 1942–45 Dungarvan; 1946–47 Belfast, Falls Rd.; 1949–59 Belfast, Joanmount; 1959–63 Bangor; 1963–69 Belfast, Bloomfield; 1969–75 Belfast, Springfield Rd.; 1975–78 Newcastle, Co. Down.
Special Interests: Antiques, Adult Literacy Campaign. *Hobbies and Recreations:* Travel, Walking, Conversation.

RITCHIE, John Derek Hosford, 10 Edgcumbe View, Belfast BT4 2EL. (0232-654782)–BA. *b. Clonmel, Co. Tipperary. m. 1 July 1958: 1d., 1s.*
Education: 1942–45 Wesley Coll., Dublin; 1945–48 Dublin Univ.; 1951–53 Edgehill Coll.
Appointments: 1948–49 Newtownbutler; 1949–51 Irvinestown; 1953–58 Bloomfield; 1958–63 Clonakilty; 1963–66 Cloughjordan; 1966–73 Lurgan, Queen St.; 1973–81 Knockbreda; 1981– Sydenham.
Connexional Committees: 1971–77 Ministerial Treasurer, Youth Dept.; 1970– Convenor, Pastoral Efficiency Committee.
Special Interests: Music, the Hymn-book, Methodist History. *Hobbies and Recreations:* Watching sport (especially Rugby Football), Crosswords, Reading detective stories.

ROBINSON, Kenneth John, Epworth, 19 Londonderry Rd., Strabane, Co. Tyrone BT82 8DU. (0504-883594)–BD. b. 6 Feb 1953, Omagh, Co. Tyrone. m. 27 Dec 1974: 2s.
Education: 1957–59 Omagh Model Sch.; 1959–62 Omagh County Prim. Sch.; 1962–64 Omagh Academy Prep.; 1964–70 Omagh Academy; 1970–72 Foyle Coll., Londonderry; 1972–76 Edinburgh Univ.; 1976–77 Queen's Univ., Belfast; 1976–77 Edgehill Coll. *Appointments:* 1977–81 Larne; 1981– Londonderry.

RODDIE, Robin Parker, 40 Knutsford Drive, Belfast, N. Ireland BT14 6NA. (0232 747952) *b. 17 Oct 1938, Bandon, Co. Cork, Ireland. m. 10 July 1981.*
Education: 1951–57 Midleton Coll., Midleton, Co. Cork; 1961–63 Edgehill Coll. *Appointments:* 1958–59 Charlemont; 1959–61 Kilkenny; 1963–70 Dublin Central Mission; 1970–72 Dunlaoghiare; 1972–75 Sydney, Australia; 1975–78 Belfast Central Mission; 1978– Shankill Team Ministry; 1977– Producer of Religious Programmes with Ulster Television.
Connexional Committees: 1964–67 Youth Department; 1967–72 Broadcasting and Television; 1971–72 Mission Board; 1976– Board of Education; 1976– Negotiating Committee (Tripartite Consultation) Church of Ireland-Presbyterian-Methodist-Conversations; 1982– Secretary of Tripartite Consultation.
Publications: Editor of *Witness,* selection of scripts published by Ulster Television (1982).
Special Interests: Music and the Cinema, Psychology. *Hobbies and Recreations:* Cookery, Badminton, Photography.

RUSSELL, Derek, 10 Waterloo Gardens, Antrim Rd., Belfast, N. Ireland BT15 4EX. (0232-776778)

b. 7 May 1935, Belfast. m. 1 July 1961: 3s.
Education: 1940–44 Prim. Sch.; 1944–49 Porters P.E.S.; 1952–53 Cliff Coll.; 1965–67 Edgehill.
Appointments: 1967–68 Carrick Fergus Circuit; 1968–71 Bailie Borough; 1971–76 Upper Erne; 1976 Belfast Jennymount.
Connexional Committees: 1982– Orphan Society, Secretary.
Special Interests: Singing, Youth Work. *Hobbies and Recreations:* Badminton, Football, Table Tennis, P.T.

SLEATH, Arthur Douglas Lawrence, 15 Windmill Hill, Portaferry, Newtownards, Co. Down, N. Ireland BT22 1RH. (0247-28172) *b. 17 July 1914, Rathdowney, Co. Laois, Ireland. m. 14 July 1948: 2d., 2s.*
Education: 1917–18 Rathdowney National Sch.; 1921, 1923–30 Birr Model Sch.; 1942–43 Edgehill Coll; 1943–44 Renshaw's Tutorial Coll., Belfast. *Appointments:* 1944–50 North Belfast Mission; 1950–55 Tinahely; 1955–58 Clonakilty; 1958–63 Charlemont; 1963–69 Belfast Central Mission; 1969–72 Belfast, Sandy Row; 1972–79 Lurgan, High St.
Publications: The Methodist Doctrine of Scriptural Holiness (1976).
Special Interests: Preaching Church History and Doctrine, Evangelism, The deepening of spiritual life, Group Bible Fellowship. *Hobbies and Recreations:* Oil Painting, General Reading.

SLEATH, George Douglas Woods, 2 Kinghill Drive, Newcastle, Co. Down BT33 0DF. (03967-22226) *b. 16 Feb 1919, Birr, Co. Offaly, R. of Ireland. m. 15 Sept 1953: 2d., 2s.*
Education: 1940–44 Edgehill Coll., Belfast. *Appointments:* 1944–47 Pettigo; 1947–48 Killeshandra; 1948–49 Omagh; 1949–50 Kisnaskea; 1950–53 Sligo; 1953–58 Superintendent of Cavan; 1958–63 Ardara; 1963–71 Dunmanway; 1971–77 Lisbellaw; 1977–82 Charlemont.
Special Interests: Music in Worship.

SLOAN, Harold, 12 Ballymacormick Ave., Bangor, Co. Down BT19 2AY. (0247 57531) *b. 28 April 1908, Liverpool. m. 3 Aug 1939: 1d., 1s.*
Education: 1932–35 Edgehill Coll.
Appointments: 1935–36 Belleek; 1936–39 North Belfast Mission; 1939–40 Enniskillen; 1940–41 Fintona; 1941–46 Chaplain H.M.F.; 1946–50 Lisbellaw; 1950–55 Enniskillen; 1955–58 Ormeau Rd., Belfast; 1958–63 Donegall Square, Belfast; 1963–67 Rathgar, Dublin; 1967–77 Secretary of the Irish Conference; 1973– President of the Methodist Church in Ireland.

STAFFORD, Herbert Wilfred, 1 Station Walk, Bangor, N. Ireland BT19 1EX. (0247-62524)–BComSc, BA. *b. 22 Jan 1902, Belfast. m. 4 Nov 1931: 1d., 2s.*
Education: Campbell Coll., Belfast, 1917–21 and 1924–27 Queens Univ., Belfast; 1924–27 Edgehill.
Appointments: 1927–50 S.India; 1950–53 Cork; 1953–58 Newtownards; 1958–63 Lurgan; 1963–68 Bangor.
Connexional Committees: 1953–58 Irish O.M. Comm.
Hobbies and Recreations: Golf, Gardening.

STOREY, Robert James, 3 Ben Caom Park, Newcastle, Co. Down, N. Ireland. (03967-22905) *b. 6 Feb 1913, Scotstown, Co. Monaghan, S. Ireland. m. 30 Sept 1942 (w.).*
Education: Mullahara National Sch., Co. Monaghan; High Sch., Clones, Co. Monaghan; 1935–38 Edgehill
Appointments: 1938–40 Fivemiletown; 1940–42 Newtownbutler; 1942–43 Conakilty; 1943–46 Portartington; 1946–49 Tralee; 1949–54 Killeshandra; 1954–59 Donegal; 1959–60 Drogheda; 1960–64 Youghal; 1966–74 Drumshanbo; 1974–81 Adare.'
Connexional Committees: 1977–80 Chairman of the Midlands and Southern District, Ireland.

TAGGART, Norman Wilson, Grosvenor Hall, Glengall St., Belfast, N. Ireland BT9 5AD. (0232 241917)–BA, PhD, BD. *b. 31 Oct 1935, Belfast. m. 6 Sept 1960: 2d., 2s.*
Education: Woodvale Public Elem. Sch., Belfast; Springfield Public Elem. Sch., Belfast; 1948–54 Royal Belfast Academical Institution; 1954–60 Queen's Univ., Belfast; 1960–61 Kingsmead Coll., Selly Oak Colls.; 1956–60 Edgehill. *Appointments:* 1961–62 Sandy Row, Primitive St.; 1962–66 Medak Diocese, CSI; 1966–68 Sligo; 1968–72 Carrickfergus–Organising Secretary of Irish Council of Churches at same time; 1972–77 Home Secretary, MMS, London; 1977–79 Post-graduate Research; 1979– Belfast Central Mission.
Connexional Committees: 1972–77 MMS Committees; 1972–77 HMD General Committee; 1972–77 DSR World Development, Community Relations Committees. *Publications: The Irish Factor in World Methodism in the Eighteenth and Nineteenth Centuries* (April 1981, unpublished thesis); *The Irish in Canadian Methodism* (Toronto, Sept 1982, The Canadian Methodist Historical Society).
Special Interests: Methodist History, Especially Irish, Missionary Outreach, Ecumenism, World Development, Racial Justice.

TAYLOR, Richard Henry, 125 Orion Way, Northwood, Middlesex HA6 3EP. (Northwood 29263)–BA. *b. Belfast, N. Ireland. m. 24 Sept 1959: 1d., 1s.*
Education: 1932–34 Broadway Prim. Sch., Belfast; 1934–42 Springfield Public Elem. Sch., Belfast; 1944–48 Combined Engineering Course, College of Technology; 1954–57 Assemblies Coll., Belfast (Constituent Colls. of Queen's Univ. Belfast); 1954–57 Edgehill
Appointments: 1952–54 Kilkenny; 1957–59 Waterford; 1959–61 Dunkineely; 1961– Chaplain HMF; 1980– Assistant Principal Chaplain.
Special Interests: Political Science, Sociology, Military History. *Hobbies and Recreations:* Ex. Soccer International (Irish and British Universities and RAF), Soccer, Hockey, Tennis, Reading, Nature Study, DIY (car repairs).

TAYLOR, Thomas Wesley, 30 Castle Rd., Cookstown. (06487-62920) *b. 1 June 1903, Mullaghbane, Co. Fermanagh. m. 8 April 1953: 1d., 1s.* *Education:* 1908–17 Blacklion National Sch.; 1924–25 Cliff Coll.; 1928–30 Edgehill Coll. *Appointments:* 1926–28 Irvinestown; 1930–31 Pettigo; 1931–33 South Derry Mission; 1933–35 Moira; 1935–36 Newry; 1936–39 Sligo; 1940–42 Killeshandra; 1942–47 Chaplain HMF; 1947–63 Jamaica Dt; 1963–68 South Derry Mission; 1968–74 Cookstown. *Connexional Committees:* 1972–82 Overseas MMS (Ireland). *Special Interests:* Overseas Mission and Community Service, Christian Aid, Chaplain to Cookstown Royal British Legion Branch. *Hobbies and Recreations:* Golf, Gardening, Bowls, Photography.

THOMPSON, Kenneth Hamilton, The Manse, Church Rd., Sutton, Dublin 13, N. Ireland. (323143)–MA(Cantab.). *b. 14 Nov 1934, Dublin. m. 9 March 1960: 3d.* *Education:* 1938–41 Miss Ludlow's Prep. Sch.; 1941–45 Rathgar National Sch.; 1945–50 The High Sch., Dublin; 1954–55 Bolton Technical Coll., Lancs.; 1974–77 Fitzwilliam Coll., Cambridge; 1970–72 Edgehill Coll., Belfast; 1974–77 Wesley House, Cambridge. *Appointments:* 1972–74 Larne; 1977–82 Sligo and Drumsanbo; 1982 Clontarf, Sutton and Skerries. *Connexional Committees:* (Irish Conference); 1973–74 Property Board; 1978– Mission Board (Hon. Sec.); 1977– Faith and Order; 1978– Council on Social Welfare; 1967–70 and 1978– Governor of Wesley Coll., Dublin. *Special Interests:* Home Mission and Ecumenical Understanding, Modern Irish Church History, New Testament Studies. *Hobbies and Recreations:* Squash, Badminton, Golf, Car Maintenance, Reading.

TODD, Samuel Kenneth, 220 Barton Rd. East, Dundrum, Dublin 14, Republic of Ireland. (986559)–MA, BD. *b. 24 Oct 1943, Armagh. m. 6 April 1968: 2s., 1s.* *Education:* 1955–61 Royal Sch., Armagh; 1961–64 Queen's Univ., Belfast; 1963–66 Edgehill. *Appointments:* 1966–78 Sierra Leone Dt; 1978– Dublin South. *Connexional Committees:* 1978– M.C.O.D.; 1980– Faith and Order; 1980– General Committee. *Hobbies and Recreations:* Squash.

TURNER, James Bernard, Palmerston Guest Home, 17 Palmerston Rd., Belfast BT4 1QA. (0232-658291) *b. 23 April 1910, Cork City. m. 25 July 1945 (w.): 1d., 1s.* *Education:* 1916–23 National Sch.; 1923–26 Cork Grammar Sch.; 1934–37 Edgehill. *Appointments:* 1937–38 Beleek; 1938–40 Lisburn; 1940–42 Dungarvin; 1942–45 Sligo; 1945–46 Univ. Rd., Belfast; 1946–51 Dunmanway; 1951–52 Birr; 1952–56 Ballintra; 1956–61 Dundonald, Knock; 1961–66 Seymour Hill, Lisburn; 1966–74 Glenavy; 1974–75 Newry. *Connexional Committees:* 1970–78 Sec. and Treas. of Childrens Fund; 1970–78 Governor of Methodist Coll., Belfast; 1948–51 Sec. of Cork and Limerick District; 1952–56 Sec. of Sligo District; 1970–78 Sec. of Stipend and Allowances Board.

TURTLE, Thomas David, 24 Elmwood Ave., Belfast BT9 6AY. (0232 663443)–BD(Lond.). *b. 1 March 1922, Co. Tyrone. m. 7 May 1953: 1d., 2s.* *Education:* 1928–38 Stewartstown Public Elem.; 1946–49 Edgehill Coll. *Appointments:* 1944–45 Newry; 1945–46 Castlederg; 1949–53 Belfast, Sandy Row; 1953–64 Burma; 1965– Queen's Univ., Belfast. *Connexional Committees:* 1968–83 Board of Examiners; 1970–83 Board of Education. *Special Interests:* Counselling, Marriage Problems, Christians Abroad. *Hobbies and Recreations:* D.I.Y., Car Maintenance, Painting.

TWINEM, Frederick, Palmerston Guest House, Palmerston Rd., Belfast BT4 1QA. (0232-657447)–BA. *b. 13 Sept 1911, Lurgan, Co. Armagh. s.* *Education:* 1917–24 National Sch.; 1924–30 Lurgan Coll.; 1930–34 Queen's Univ., Belfast; 1935–37 Edgehill. *Appointments:* 1937–40 Mountmellick; 1940–42 Belleek; 1942–45 Belturbet; 1945–47 Sligo; 1947–48 Ringsend; 1948–49 Kinsale; 1949–51 Beragh; 1951–56 Donegal; 1956–59 Bantry; 1959–60 Tralee; 1960–64 Donegal; 1964–69 Dundalk; 1969–74 Strabane; 1974–79 Magherafelt.

WALPOLE, Christopher Gilling, 41 St. Kevin's Park, Dartry, Dublin 6, Republic of Ireland. (Dublin 976055) *b. 18 Aug 1929, Skerries, Co. Dublin. m. 1. 4 Oct 1962, 2. 21 June 1967: 1d., 1s.* *Education:* 1936–41 Newry Model Sch.; 1941–43 Newry Intermediate Sch.; 1944–46 Technical Colls.; 1958–61 Edgehill Coll. *Appointments:* 1956–58 Fivemiletown; 1961–62 Belfast Central Mission; 1962–65 Birr; 1965–68 Belfast, Sandy Row; 1968–75 Belfast, Cavehill; 1975–83 Dublin South. *Connexional Committees:* 1967–75 Synod Secretary; 1974–80 Journal Secretary of Conference; 1980– Assistant Secretary of Conference. *Special Interests:* Audio Visual Aids. *Hobbies and Recreations:* Squash, Model Railways.

WHITTINGTON, Thomas Stanley, 63 Rashee Rd., Ballyclare, Northern Ireland BT39 9HT. (09603 22272) *b. 23 Sept 1926, Londonderry. m. 23 Aug 1957: 1d., 1s.* *Education:* 1931–45 Model Sch., Londonderry; 1945–47 Technical Coll., Londonderry; 1951–52, 1953–55 Edgehill. *Appointments:* 1952 Newtownbutler; 1955–57 North Belfast Mission; 1957–1963 The Gambia, West Africa; 1963–65 Clonakilty; 1965–70 Portadown; 1970–71 Florence, Ontario, Canada (United Church of Canada); 1971–76 Mountpottinger; 1976–81 Belfast Central Mission; 1981– Ballyclare. *Connexional Committees:* 1952–56 Youth Council; 1963–70, 1971– Methodist Missionary Soc. (Ireland) Committee; 1971–74, 1980– General Committee.

Special Interests: Overseas Mission, Third World needs. *Hobbies and Recreations:* Photography, Golf, Swimming, Classical Records.

WILSON, Kenneth Alexander, 7 Upper Knockbreda Rd., Belfast, N. Ireland BT6 9QH. (0232-792446)– BA(Lond.), BD(Lond.). *b. 19 June 1939, Belfast, N.I. m. 14 July 1965: 1d., 1s.*
Education: 1951–53 Royal Sch., Dungannon, N.I.; 1953–58 Portadown Coll., Portadown, N.I.; 1970–73, 1975–78 London Univ. (extern.); 1981– Queen's Univ., Belfast; 1962–65 Edgehill. *Appointments:* 1961–62 Dublin Central Mission; 1965–69 Nevis, West Indies; 1970–73 Dominica, W.I.; 1973–76 Antigua, W.I.; 1976–77 Missionary Guest House, Birmingham; 1977–82 Cullybackey, N.I.; 1982– Glenburn, Belfast; 1969–70 Furlough.
Connexional Committees: 1978– Overseas Missions; 1979– Youth Department; 1978– Local Preachers; 1982– Board of Examiners; 1982– Faith and Order. *Local Council Committees:* School Management Committee of Lisnasharragh Prim. Sch. *Publications:* Lectures on *Evangelism* at Leeward Islands Synod (1976); *Methodist Doctrine of Conversion* at Glenstall Abbey, Ecumenical Conference (1981). *Special Interests:* Link between John Wesley's Spirituality, B.C.P. and the 18th Century Methodist Societies, have been asked to lead several Evangelical Missions. *Hobbies and Recreations:* All types of sport.

WISHEART, James, 14 Wynard Park, Belfast, N. Ireland BT5 6NS. (0232-798594) *b. 26 Dec 1900, Strabane, Co. Tyrone. m. 9 Sept 1931: 1d., 1s.*
Education: 1923–24 Cliff Coll.; 1914–16 Methodist Coll.; 1926–28 Edgehill. *Appointments:* 1931–34 Carlow; 1934–37 South Derry Mission; 1937–41 Enniskillen; 1941–45 Cregagh; 1945–52 Superintendent of Evangelism; 1952–57 Belfast, Agnes St.; 1957–61 Carrickfergus; 1961–67 Lurgan; 1962 President Methodist Church in Ireland. *Connexional Committees:* 1939–52, 1961–67 General Committee of the Methodist Church in Ireland; 1961–67 Stationing Committee. *Council Member:* 1961– Trustee of the Methodist Church. *Local Council Committees:* 1937–41 Co. Fermanagh Education Committee.

YOUNG, John Wright, 58 Kent Ave., Larne, Co. Antrim BT40 1ND. (0274 4458) *b. 10 Oct 1907, Belfast. m. 25 June 1940: 1d., 1s.*
Education: 1913–19 Whitehead National Sch.; 1919–27 Municipal Coll. of Technology; 1931–34 Edgehill Coll. *Appointments:* 1929–31 Fivemiletown; 1934–36 Irvinestown; 1936–40 Newry; 1940–45 Richill, Armagh; 1945–50 Dundum and Newcastle; 1950–55 Ballynafeigh; 1955–60 Belfast, Mountpottinger; 1960–67 Londonderry City Mission; 1967–73 Larne.
Connexional Committees: 1950–75 Council on Social Welfare (Secretary); 1960–82 Orphan Committee. *Local Council Committees:* 1973–82 North Eastern Education and Library Board. *Special Interests:* 1973– Regional Representative, Ireland, C.T.V.C. and Lord Rank Film Schemes. *Hobbies and Recreations:* Photography, Audio Visual Aids, Gardening.

Abbreviations

A

ALA—Associate of the Library Association
AKC—Associate of King's College (London)
ARCO—Associate of the Royal College of Organists
ARHS—Associate of the Royal Historical Society
Assoc.—Association

B

b.—born
BA—Bachelor of Arts
BD—Bachelor of Divinity
Bd—Board
BSc—Bachelor of Science

C

CERM—Conservative Evangelicals Revival Fellowship
Cert.Ed.—Certificate of Education
CE Prim.—Church of England Primary
Chmn.—Chairman
Coll.—College
Comm.—commercial/commerce
Cpln.—Chaplain
CP Sch—County Primary School
Cttee—Committee

D

d.—daughter/s
Dev.—Development
DD—Doctor of Divinity
Dip.Ed.—Diploma in Education
Div.—Division
DSR—Division of Social Responsibility
Dt./Dist.—District

E

Ecum.—ecumenical
edn.—edition
El./Elem.—Elementary
Eng.—English

F

FBA—Fellow of the British Academy
FPS—Fellow of the Philosophical Society
FRS—Fellow of the Royal Society
FRSE—Fellow of the Royal Society of Edinburgh

G

GP—General Purposes
Gramm.—Grammar (school)
Gt.—great

H

HM—Home Mission Division
HMF—Her Majesty's Forces

I

Inf.—Infants (school)
Inst.—Institute

J

JP—Justice of the Peace
Jun./Jnr.—Junior (school)

L

LCC—London County Council (now GLC)
LLB—Bachelor of Law
LLD—Doctor of Law
LP—Local Preachers
LRAM—Licentiate of the Royal Academy of Music
LSE—London School of Economics and Political Science

M

m.—married
M./Miss.—Mission
MA—Master of Arts
MAYC—Methodist Association of Youth Clubs
MC—Military Cross
MCCA—Methodist Church in the Caribbean and Americas
MCOD—Methodist Church Overseas Division
MM—Military Medal
MMS—Methodist Missionery Society
MRF—Methodist Revival Fellowship
MSc—Master of Science
MTh—Master of Theology

N

NABC—National Association of Boys' Clubs
NCH—National Children's Home
NT—New Testament

O

OCF—Officiating Chaplain to the Forces
OM—Overseas Mission Division
OT—Old Testament

P

Per—Permission
PGCE—Postgraduate Certificate of Education
PhD—Doctor of Philosophy
Poly.—Polytechnic
President's List—(supply minister) list of reserve
Prim.—Primary (school)
Prin.—Principal
p/t—part-time

R

Rd.—Road
Rep.—Representative

S

s.—son/s
Sch.—school
Sec.—secondary
Sec.—Secretary
Sec. Mod.—Secondary Modern
Soc.—Society
SR—Special Reserve
St.—Saint/Street
STM—Master of Sacred Theology
Supt.—Superintendant

T

TD—Territorial Decoration
Tech.—technical
Theol.D/ThD—Doctor of Theology
TocH—Talbot House (Soldiers' Club)

U

UCL—University College, London
Univ.—University

V

VDC—Volunteer Decoration
VMA—Voice of Methodism Association
VP—Vice President

W

(w.)—widower
WEA—Workers' Educational Association
WHS—Wesleyan Historical Society
WMS—World Methodist Council

Appendices

Appendix I

1744-1932

APPENDIX I

PRESIDENTS OF THE WESLEYAN METHODIST CONFERENCE: 1744-1932

The first Wesleyan Methodist Conference met at the Foundery, London, in 1744, and thereafter every year, 'but it does not appear that any Minutes taking the form of an Annual Record, were published, after the year 1749, till 1765.' In 1784 John Wesley drew up a Deed of Declaration, which has been called The Magna Charta of Wesleyan Methodism, and enrolled it in Chancery, which gave the Conference legal authority. The Legal Conference was composed of one hundred Preachers. The only condition the Deed required was that they must have, 'been admitted with the Conference, as a preacher and expounder of God's Holy Word, for twelve months.' The Deed provided regulations for elections to the Conference in place of those who died, had absented themselves without a dispensation, were superannuated, had resigned or had been expelled. The sixth clause required the Conference to elect a President and Secretary annually, and that the Journal of the Conference must be signed by these two officers. There is no record in the Journal of any elections taking place between 1784 and 1790, when it was signed by John Wesley, President, and Thomas Coke, Secretary, but from 1791 to 1932 elections were made as required by the Deed. In 1792 the Conference directed that there must be an interval of eight years before the re-election of a President. The offices of President and Secretary of the Conference (or as some preferred "the Assembly") were used by all the subsequent branches of Methodism, though the powers differed according to their individual constitutions.

Year	Place	President	Station or Appointment
1791	Manchester	William Thompson	Wakefield
1792	London	Alexander Mather	Hull
1793	Leeds	John Pawson	Liverpool
1794	Bristol	Thomas Hanby	Leeds
1795	Manchester	Joseph Bradford	Bristol
1796	London	Thomas Taylor	Oldham
1797	Leeds	Thomas Coke, LL.D.	London
1798	Bristol	Joseph Benson	Hull
1799	Manchester	Samuel Bradburn	Manchester
1800	James Wood	London	London
1801	Leeds	John Pawson, 2nd time	Birstall
1802	Bristol	Joseph Taylor	Burslem
1803	Manchester	Joseph Bradford, 2nd time	Plymouth Dock
1804	London	Henry Moore	Birmingham
1805	Sheffield	Thomas Coke, LL.D., 2nd time	London, General Superintendent of Missions
1806	Leeds	Adam Clarke, M.A.	London
1807	Liverpool	John Barber	Sheffield
1808	Bristol	James Wood, 2nd time	Bristol
1809	Manchester	Thomas Taylor, 2nd time	Wakefield
1810	London	Joseph Benson, 2nd time	London, Connexional Editor
1811	Sheffield	Charles Atmore	Hull
1812	Leeds	Joseph Entwisle	Bristol
1813	Liverpool	Walter Griffith	Rochester
1814	Bristol	Adam Clarke, M.A., LL.D., 2nd time	London, East
1815	Manchester	John Barber, 2nd time	Bristol
1816	London	Richard Reece	Manchester
1817	Sheffield	John Gaulter	Rochester
1818	Leeds	Jonathon Edmondson, M.A.	Birmingham
1819	Bristol	Jonathan Crowther	Burslem
1820	Liverpool	Jabez Bunting, M.A.	London, East
1821	Manchester	George Marsden	Leeds
1822	London	Adam Clarke, M.A., LL.D., 3rd time	Salford
1823	Sheffield	Henry Moore, 2nd time	London, City Road
1824	Leeds	Robert Newton	Salford
1825	Bristol	Joseph Entwisle, 2nd time	Birmingham
1826	Liverpool	Richard Watson	London, City Road
1827	Manchester	John Stephens	London, City Road
1828	London	Jabez Bunting, M.A., 2nd time	Manchester, Irwell Street
1829	Sheffield	James Townley, D.D.	London, Missionary Society
1830	Leeds	George Morley	London, Deptford
1831	Bristol	George Marsden, 2nd time	London, Great Queen Street
1832	Liverpool	Robert Newton, 2nd time	Manchester, Grosvenor Street
1833	Manchester	Richard Treffry	Bristol, Langton Street
1834	London	Joseph Taylor	London, City Road
1835	Sheffield	Richard Reece, 2nd time	London, Spitalfields
1836	Birmingham	Jabez Bunting, M.A., D.D., 3rd time	London, Missionary Society
1837	Leeds	Edmund Grindrod	London, City Road
1838	Bristol	Thomas Jackson	London, Connexional Editor
1839	Liverpool	Theophilus Lessey	London, Hinde Street
1840	Newcastle-upon-Tyne	Robert Newton, 3rd time	Leeds, Oxford Place
1841	Manchester	James Dixon, D.D.	Manchester, Grosvenor Street
1842	London	John Hannah, D.D.	Didsbury College
1843	Sheffield	John Scott	London, City Road
1844	Birmingham	Jabez Bunting, M.A., D.D., 4th time	London, Missionary Society
1845	Leeds	Jacob Stanley	London, Southwark
1846	Bristol	Willian Atherton	London, Hinde Street
1847	Liverpool	Samuel Jackson	London, Islington
1848	Hull	Robert Newton, D.D., 4th time	Stockport, Tiviot Dale
1849	Manchester	Thomas Jackson	Richmond College
1850	London	John Beecham, D.D.	London, Missionary Society
1851	Newcastle-upon-Tyne	John Hannah, D.D., 2nd time	Didsbury College
1852	Sheffield	John Scott, 2nd time	Westminster College
1853	Bradford	John Lomas	Manchester, Oxford Road
1854	Birmingham	John Farrar	Richmond College
1855	Leeds	Isaac Keeling	London, Islington

Year	Place	President	Station or Appointment
1856	Bristol	Robert Young	London, City Road
1857	Liverpool	Francis A. West	London, Hackney
1858	Hull	John Bowers	Didsbury College
1859	Manchester	Samuel D. Waddy	Sheffield, Wesley College
1860	London	William W. Stamp	London, Hinde Street
1861	Newcastle-upon-Tyne	John Rattenbury	London, Bayswater
1862	Camborne	Charles Prest	London, Home Missions Department
1863	Sheffield	George Osborn, D.D.	London, Missionary Society
1864	Bradford	*William L. Thornton, M.A.	London, Connexional Editor
1865	Birmingham	William Shaw (A)	London, Chelsea
1866	Leeds	William Arthur, M.A.	London, Missionary Society
1867	Bristol	John Bedford	Manchester, Chapel Committee
1868	Liverpool	S. Romilly Hall	Manchester, Irwell Street
1869	Hull	Frederick J. Jobson, D.D.	London, Book Steward
1870	Burslem	John Farrar, 2nd time	Headingley College
1871	Manchester	John H. James, D.D.	London, Islington
1872	London	Luke H. Wiseman, M.A.	London, Missionary Society
1873	Newcastle-upon-Tyne	George T. Perks, M.A.	London Missionary Society
1874	Camborne	W. Morley Punshon, LL.D.	London, Kensington
1875	Sheffield	Gervase Smith, D.D.	London, Metropolitan Building Fund
1876	Nottingham	Alexander McAuley	London, Home Missions Department
1877	Bristol	W. Burt Pope, D.D.	Didsbury College
1878	Bradford	James H. Rigg, D.D.	London, Westminster College
1879	Birmingham	Benjamin Gregory, D.D.	London, Connexional Editor
1880	London	Ebenezer E. Jenkins, M.A.	London, Missionary Society
1881	Liverpool	George Osborn, D.D., 2nd time	Richmond College
1882	Leeds	Charles Garrett	Liverpool Mission
1883	Hull	Thomas McCullagh	Liverpool, Wesley
1884	Burslem	Frederic Greeves, D.D.	Bromley, Kent
1885	Newcastle-upon-Tyne	Richard Roberts	London, Lambeth
1886	London	Robert N. Young, D.D.	Handsworth College
1887	Manchester	John Walton, M.A.	London, Mostyn Road
1888	Camborne	Joseph Bush	Newcastle-upon-Tyne, Brunswick
1889	Sheffield	Charles H. Kelly	London, Book Steward
1890	Bristol	William F. Moulton, M.A., D.D.	Cambridge, The Leys School
1891	Nottingham	T. Bowman Stephenson, B.A., D.D.	London, National Children's Home
1892	Bradford	James H. Rigg, D.D., 2nd time	London, Westminster College
1893	Cardiff	Henry J. Pope, D.D.	Manchester, Chapel Department
1894	Birmingham	Walford Green	London, Connexional Funds Office
1895	Plymouth	David J. Waller, D.D., LL.D.	London, Education Department
1896	Liverpool	Marshall Randles, D.D.	Didsbury College
1897	Leeds	William L. Watkinson, D.D.	London, Connexional Editor
1898	Hull	Hugh Price Hughes, M.A.	London Mission, west
1899	London	Frederic W. Macdonald	London, Missionary Society
1900	Burslem	Thomas Allen, D.D.	Handsworth College
1901	Newcastle-upon-Tyne	W. Theophilus Davison, M.A., D.D.	Handsworth College
1902	Manchester	John S. Banks, D.D.	Headingley College
1903	Camborne	Marshall Hartley	London, Missionary Society
1904	Sheffield	Silvester Whitehead	Bradford, Great Horton
1905	Bristol	Charles H. Kelly, 2nd time	London, Book Steward
1906	Nottingham	Albert Clayton	London, Twentieth Century Fund
1907	London	John S. Simon, D.D.	Didsbury College
1908	York	J. Scott Lidgett, M.A., D.D.	London, Bermondsey Settlement
1909	Lincoln	William Perkins	London, Missionary Society
1910	Bradford	John Hornabrook	Manchester, Chapel Department
1911	Cardiff	Henry Haigh, D.D.	Newcastle-upon-Tyne, Elswick
1912	Liverpool	F. Luke Wiseman, B.A.	Birmingham Mission
1913	Plymouth	Samuel F. Collier	Manchester and Salford Mission
1914	Leeds	Dinsdale T. Young	London, Westminster Central Hall
1915	Birmingham	R. Waddy Moss, D.D.	Didsbury College
1916	London	John G. Tasker, D.D.	Handsworth College
1917	London	Simpson Johnson	London, London Mission and Extension Fund
1918	Manchester	Samuel Chadwick	Cliff College
1919	Newcastle-upon-Tyne	William A. T. Barber, M.A., D.D.	Cambridge, The Leys School
1920	Hull	J. T. Wardle Stafford, D.D., D.C.L.	Newcastle-upon-Tyne, Brunswick
1921	Middlesborough	J. Alfred Sharp, S.T.D., D.D.	London, Book Steward
1922	Sheffield	John E. Wakerley	East Anglia, District Missionary
1923	Bristol	T. Ferrier Hulme, M.A., LL.D.	Bath and Bristol, District Missionary
1924	Nottingham	Amos Burnet	London, Missionary Society
1925	Lincoln	John H. Ritson, M.A., D.D.	London, British and Foreign Bible Society
1926	York	W. Russell Maltby, D.D.	Wesley Deaconess College
1927	Bradford	W. Hodson Smith	London, National children's Home
1928	Liverpool	John W. Lightley, M.A., B.D., D.Litt.	Leeds, Headingley
1929	Plymouth	William F. Lofthouse, M.A., D.D.	Handsworth College
1930	Leeds	Herbert B. Workman, M.A., D.D., D.Litt.	London, Education Department
1931	Birmingham	C. Ryder Smith, B.A., D.D.	Richmond College
1932	Manchester	H. Maldwyn Hughes, M.A., D.D.	Cambridge, Wesley House.

* Died in office, 1865.

WESLEYAN METHODIST CONNEXION

SECRETARIES OF THE CONFERENCE

1791-1795	Thomas Coke, LL.D.
1796-1798	Samuel Bradburn
1799	Thomas Coke, LL.D.
1800	Samuel Bradburn
1801-1804	Thomas Coke, LL.D.
1805	Joseph Benson
1806-1808	Thomas Coke, LL.D.
1809	Joseph Benson
1810-1813	Thomas Coke, LL.D.
1814-1819	Jabez Bunting, M.A.
1820	George Marsden
1821-1823	Robert Newton, D.D.
1824-1827	Jabez Bunting, M.A., D.D.
1828-1831	Robert Newton, D.D.
1832-1833	Edmund Grindrod
1834-1839	Robert Newton, D.D.
1840-1841	John Hannah, D.D.
1842-1847	Robert Newton, D.D.
1848	Joseph Fowler
1849-1850	John Hannah, D.D.
1851-1853	John Farrar
1854-1858	John Hannah, D.D.
1859-1869	John Farrar
1870	John H. James, D.D.
1871	Luke H. Wiseman, M.A.
1872	George T. Perks, M.A.
1873-1874	Gervase Smith, D.D.
1875-1877	Henry W. Williams, D.D.
1878-1880	Marmaduke C. Osborn
1881-1885	Robert N. Young, D.D.
1886-1894	David J. Waller, D.D., LL.D.
1895-1902	Marshall Hartley
1903-1909	John Hornabrook
1910-1916	Simpson Johnson
1917-1921	John E. Wakerley
1922-1927	Thomas Kirkup
1927-1932	Robert Bond, D.D.

CONNEXIONAL COMMITTEE SECRETARIES

In most cases the Connexional Committees were appointed much earlier than that indicated when a minister was set apart as Secretary. The first named is in most cases the General Secretary.

CHAPEL DEPARTMENT

1854-1855	William Kelk, George T. Perks
1855-1856	William Kelk, John Bedford, George T. Perks
1856-1858	William Kelk, John Bedford, William Davison
1858-1860	William Kelk, John Bedford, John Martin
1860-1861	John Bedford, Luke H. Wiseman, James H. Rigg
1861-1863	John Bedford, Luke H. Wiseman, James Rigg, William Edwards
1863-1864	John Bedford, James Rigg, John V. B. Shrewsbury, William Edwards
1864-1865	John Bedford, Julius Brigg, William Edwards, John V. B. Shrewsbury
1865-1873	John Bedford, William Edwards
1873-1876	William Edwards, Edwin H. Tindall
1876-1883	Edwin H. Tindall, Henry J. Pope
1883-1895	Henry J. Pope
1895-1897	Henry J. Pope, D.D., John Jackson
1897-1909	John Hornabrook, John Jackson
1909-1928	John Hornabrook, Albert H. Walker, M.A.
1928-1932	John Hornabrook, William Humphrey

HOME MISSION DEPARTMENT

1857-1876	Charles Prest
1876-1886	Alexander M'Auley, John W. Greeves
1886-1894	John W. Greeves, James E. Clapham
1894-1897	James E. Clapham
1897-1898	Henry J. Pope, D.D.
1898-1902	Henry J. Pope, D.D., James Bell (B)
1902-1910	Henry J. Pope, D.D., James Bell (B), Simpson Johnson
1910-1912	Henry J. Pope, D.D., James Bell (B), Thomas Kirkup
1912-1913	James Bell (B), Thomas Kirkup
1913-1915	F. Luke Wiseman, B.A., James Bell (B), Thomas Kirkup
1915-1928	F. Luke Wiseman, B.A., Thomas Kirkup
1928-1932	F. Luke Wiseman, B.A., J. Oliver Hornabrook, O.B.E.

ROYAL NAVY, ARMY AND ROYAL AIR FORCE BAND

1904-1909	Richard W. Allen
1909-1932	Joseph H. Bateson, C.B.E.

METROPOLITAN CHAPEL BUILDING FUND

1873-1881	Gervase Smith, M.A., D.D.
1881-1904	John Bond
1904-1908	Albert Clayton
1908-1910	Enoch Salt

Amalgamated with the London Committee 1910.

EXTENSION OF METHODISM IN GREAT BRITAIN

1874-1875	G. Stringer Rowe
1875-1879	Theophilus Woolmer
1879-1886	Joseph Hargreaves (Supernumerary)

Amalgamated with the Metropolitan Chapel Building Fund 1886.

LONDON WESLEYAN METHODIST MISSION

1889-1910	William D. Walters

Amalgamated with the London Committee 1910.

LONDON COMMITTEE

1910-1913	Simpson Johnson, William D. Walters
1913-1921	Simpson Johnson, C. Ensor Walters
1921-1924	C. Ensor Walters
1924-1928	C. Ensor Walters, Walter H. Armstrong
1928-1930	C. Ensor Walters,

TEMPERANCE COMMITTEE 1891-1918.
TEMPERANCE AND SOCIAL WELFARE DEPARTMENT 1919-1932.

1891-1905	G. Armstrong Bennetts, B.A.
1905-1906	J. Surman Cooke, (Supernumerary)
1906-1911	J. Alfred Sharp
1911-1920	Henry Carter
1920-1925	Henry Carter, E. Benson Perkins
1925-1926	Henry Carter
1926-1932	Henry Carter, Edwin Finch

SUNDAY SCHOOL COMMITTEE 1863-1907
SUNDAY SCHOOL DEPARTMENT 1907-1932

1864-1875	John Clulow
1875-1889	Charles H. Kelly
1889-1907	J. Williams Butcher
1907-1923	J. Williams Butcher
1923-1932	Alfred J. G. Seaton, B.D.

EDUCATION COMMITTEE

1851-1866	Michael C. Taylor
1866-1871	George W. Olver, B.A.
1871-1881	George O. Bate
1881-1912	David J. Waller, D.D.
1912-1919	Enoch Salt
1919-1920	William T. A. Barber, M.A., D.D.
1920-1932	Herbert B. Workman, M.A., D.D., D.Litt.

CONNEXIONAL FUNDS OFFICE

1885-1903	Walford Green, D.D.
1903-1908	Albert Clayton
1908-1919	Enoch Salt
1919-1926	Marshall Hartley
1926-1932	William H. Hart (Supernumerary)

WESLEY GUILD

1901-1920	W. Blackburn Fitzgerald
1920-1932	George Allen, B.A.

THE WESLEYAN METHODIST MISSIONARY SOCIETY

The Wesleyan Methodist Missionary Society was founded in 1786. The first non-colonial missionary station was Antigua. The man who did most to further the work of the Missionary Society was Dr. Thomas Coke, "the Father of Methodist Missions". In 1796 the Conference appointed him Superintendent of Foreign Mission, which he remained till his death on the way to Ceylon in 1814. It was not until 1818 that a minster was set aside as Secretary of the Society. The first named was known as the Senior Secretary, changed later to General Secretary.

MISSIONARY SECRETARIES

1818-1821	Joseph Taylor, Jun.
1821-1824	Jabez Bunting, Joseph Taylor, Jun., Richard Watson
1824-1826	George Morley, Richard Watson, John Mason, Jun.
1826-1827	George Morley, Robert Newstead, John Mason, Jun.
1827-1830	George Morley, James Townley, D.D., John James
1830-1831	James Townley, D.D., John James, Thomas Edwards
1831-1832	James Townley, D.D., John James, John Beecham, D.D.
1832-1833	John Beecham, D.D., John James
1833-1834	Jabez Bunting, M.A., John Beecham, D.D., Robert Adler, D.D.
1834-1836	Jabez Bunting, M.A., John Beecham, D.D., Robert Adler, D.D., Elijah Hoole
1836-1837	John Beecham, D.D., Robert Adler, D.D., Elijah Hoole

1837-1850	Jabez Bunting, M.A., D.D., John Beecham, D.D., Robert Adler, D.D., Elijah Hoole
1850-1851	Jabez Bunting, M.A., D.D., Robert Adler, D.D., Elijah Hoole, John Beecham, D.D.
1851-1856	John Beecham, D.D., Elijah Hoole, George Osborn, William Arthur, M.A.
1856-1861	Elijah Hoole, D.D., George Osborn, William Arthur, M.A. (1859-60. William B. Boyce)
1861-1866	Elijah Hoole, D.D., George Osborn, William B. Boyce, William Arthur, M.A.
1866-1867	William Arthur, M.A., Elijah Hoole, D.D., George Osborn, William B. Boyce
1867-1868	Elijah Hoole, George Osborn, William B. Boyce, William Arthur, M.A., George T. Perks, M.A.
1868-1872	Elijah Hoole, D.D., William B. Boyce, George T. Perks, M.A., Luke H. Wiseman, M.A.
1872-1873	William B. Boyce, Luke H. Wiseman, M.A., George T. Perks, M.A.
1873-1874	George T. Perks, M.A., William B. Boyce, Luke H. Wiseman, M.A.
1874-1875	William B. Boyce, George T. Perks, M.A., Luke H. Wiseman, M.A.
1875-1976	William B. Boyce, George T. Perks, M.A., W. Morley Punshon, LL.D.
1876-1877	George T. Perks, M.A., W. Morley Punshon, LL.D.
1877-1881	W. Morley Punshon, LL.D., John Kilner, Ebenezer E. Jenkins, M.A.
1881-1888	John Kilner, Ebenezer E. Jenkins, M.A., Marmaduke C. Osborn, George W. Olver, B.A.
1888-1891	John Walton, M.A., Marmaduke C. Osborn, George W. Olver, B.A., Marshall Hartley
1891-1896	George W. Olver, B.A., Frederic W. Macdonald, Marshall Hartley
1896-1898	George W. Olver, B.A., Frederic W. Macdonald, Marshall Hartley, William T. A. Barber, M.A., D.D.
1898-1900	George W. Olver, B.A., Frederic W. Macdonald, William Perkins, Marshall Hartley
1900-1905	Frederic W. Macdonald, William Perkins, Marshall Hartley, William H. Findlay, M.A.
1905-1910	William Perkins, John M. Brown, Marshall Hartley, William H. Findlay, M.A., William Goudie
1910-1912	William Perkins, John M. Brown, Marshall Hartley, William Goudie, Charles W. Andrews, B.A., B.D.
1912-1913	William Perkins, Marshall Hartley, Henry Haigh, D.D., William Goudie, Charles W. Andrews, B.A., B.D.
1913-1914	William Perkins, Marshall Hartley, Henry Haigh, D.D., Charles W. Andrews, B.A., B.D.
1914-1917	Marshall Hartley, Henry Haigh, D.D., Charles W. Andrews, B.A., B.D.
1917-1919	Marshall Hartley, William Goudie, Charles W. Andrews, B.A., B.D.
1919-1922	Amos Burnet, William Goudie, Charles W. Andrews, B.A., B.D., Edgar W. Thompson, M.A.
1922-1927	Amos Burnet, Charles W. Andrews, B.A., B.D., Edgar W. Thompson, M.A., Walter J. Noble
1927-1930	Charles W. Andrews, B.A., B.D., Edgar W. Thompson, M.A., Walter J. Noble, G. E. Hickman Johnson
1930-1932	Edgar W. Thompson, M.A., Walter J. Noble, G. E. Hickman Johnson

THE WESLEYAN METHODIST BOOK ROOM AND PUBLICATIONS

The first Methodist Book Room was situated in John Wesley's first London Chapel, the Foundery, and it remained there until the "new Chapel" in the City Road was built in 1778, in which a warehouse for stock, a packing room, and offices were provided. The Book Room was actually the rear house on the left hand side, near the morning chapel. In 1808 the Book Room was moved to 14 City Road, and in 1818 to help trade with the booksellers, premises were also opened at 66 Paternoster Row. In 1838 the last before Methodist Union took place, when three houses were bought in Windmill Street (now Worship Street) and a small cottage in Castle Street (now Epworth Street) were adapted, and at various times were enlarged.

BOOK STEWARDS

1739-1753	John Wesley, M.A.
1753-1759	Mr. Thomas Butts and Mr. William Briggs
1759-1773	Mr. Sam Francks
1773-1788	John Atlay
1788-1804	George Whitfield (Assistant, 1804-1805)
1804-1808	Robert Lomas
1808-1823	Thomas Blanchard
1823-1827	John Kershaw
1827-1864	John Mason
1864-1879	Frederick J. Jobson, D.D.
1879-1889	Theophilus Woolmer
1889-1907	Charles H. Kelly
1907-1910	Robert Culley
1910-1911	John Telford, B.A.
1911-1932	J. Alfred Sharp, D.D.

CONNEXIONAL EDITORS

1739-1791	John Wesley, M.A.
1776-1789	Thomas Olivers (Corrector of the Press)
1789-1793	James Creighton, B.A.
1793-1804	George Story (Corrector of the Press, 1793-1794)
1804-1821	Joseph Benson
1811-1816	James Macdonald (Assistant)
1821-1924	Jabez Bunting
1824-1842	Thomas Jackson
1842-1851	George Cubitt
1842-1849	John S. Stamp (Assistant)
1851-1865	William L. Thornton, M.A. (Associate from 1848)
1831-1857	William H. Rule (Joint Editor)
1857-1864	J. Gilchrist Wilson
1865-1875	Benjamin Frankland, B.A.
1876-1893	Benjamin Gregory (Joint from 1868)
1893-1904	William L. Watkinson
1904-1905	W. Theophilus Davison, M.A., D.D.
1905-1932	John Telford, B.A.

MONTHLY OR QUARTERLY PUBLICATIONS OF THE WESLEYAN METHODIST BOOK ROOM

In some cases the original title of the publication was changed. The list below indicates the title as it was with dates.

1778-1797	The Arminian Magazine
1798-1821	The Methodist Magazine
1822-1913	The Wesleyan Methodist Magazine
1914-1926	The Magazine of the Wesleyan Methodist Church
1927-1932	The Methodist Magazine
1817-1855	Youth's Instructor
1824-1845	The Child's Magazine
1846-1916	Early Days
1917-1932	The Kiddies' Magazine
1835-1836	The Illuminator
1837-1845	The Cottager's Friend
1846-1876	The Christian Miscellany and Family Visitor
1877-1900	The Christian Miscellany and Family Visitor
1841-1849	The Wesleyan Tract Reporter
1850-1852	The Wesleyan Vindicator and Constitutional Methodist
1853-1858	The London Quarterly Review
1858-1862	The London Review
1863-1932	The London Quarterly Review
1857-1880	The Wesleyan Sunday School Magazine
1881-1932	The Wesleyan Methodist Sunday School Magazine
1868-1906	The Methodist Temperance Magazine
1907-1911	The Temperance Pioneer
1912-1925	The Pioneer
1871-1876	The City Road Magazine
1871-1872	The Methodist Messenger
1872-1896	The King's Highway
1881-1927	Experience
1887-1905	Our Boys and Girls
1890-1927	The Preacher's Quarterly
1928-1932	The Preacher's and Class Leader's Magazine
1890-1892	The Monthly Greeting
1897-1901	The Guild
1909-1911	Hope
1924-1932	Home and Empire Magazine

THE FERNLEY LECTURE — 1870-1932

This Lecture was founded by Mr. John Fernley of Southport. It was his wish that it should take the form of an Annual Sermon, or Lectureship, in connection with the Conference, for the purpose of explaining and defending the theological doctrines, or ecclesiastical policy, of the Wesleyan Methodist Connexion. The Draft Deed of Foundation was presented to the Conference of 1869, and approved. The Conference appointed members to act as a Board of Management. The first Lecture was delivered at the Burslem Conference in 1870.

Year	Lecture	Lecturer
1870	The Mission and Work of the Holy Spirit	George Osborn, D.D.
1871	The Person of Christ	W. Burt Pope, D.D.
1872	Jesus Christ, the Propitiation for our Sins	John Lomas
1873	The Holy Catholic Church	Benjamin Gregory, D.D.
1874	The Doctrine of the Future Life as contained in the Old Testament Scriptures	J. Dury Geden, D.D.
1875	NO LECTURE	—
1876	The Priesthood of Christ	Henry W. Williams, D.D.
1877	Modern Atheism: Its Position and Promise	Ebenezer E. Jenkins, M.A.
1878	Life and Death, The Sanction of the Law of Love	George W. Olver, B.A.
1879	Life, Light and Love	Alfred J. French, B.A.
1880	Christianity and the Science of Religion	John S. Banks, D.D.
1881	The Dogmatic Principle in Relation to Christian Belief	Frederic W. Macdonald
1882	The Witness of the Spirit	Robert N. Young, D.D.
1883	The Difference between the Physical and Moral Law	William Arthur, M.A.
1884	The Universal Mission of the Church of Christ	Benjamin Hellier
1885	Methodism in the Light of the Early Church	William F. Slater, M.A.
1886	The Influence of Scepticism on Character	William L. Watkinson
1887	The Creator and what we may know of the Method of Creation	William H. Dallenger, D.D., LL.D., D.Sc., F.R.S.
1888	The Christian Conscience	W. Theophilus Davison, M.A., D.D.
1889	The Credentials of the Gospel	J. Agar Beet, D.D.
1890	The Mission of Methodism	Richard Green
1891	The Inspiration of the Holy Scriptures	Francis Starr
1892	The Design and Use of Holy Scripture	Marshall Randles, D.D.
1893	Christianity and Socialism	William Nicholas, M.A., D.D.
1894	Christian Doctrine and Morals	George G. Findlay, B.A.
1895	Jesus Christ and the Present Age	James Chapman
1896	The Theology of Modern Fiction	Thomas G. Selby
1897	The Spiritual Principle of the Atonement	J. Scott Lidgett, M.A.
1898	The Range of Christian Experience	R. Wadd Moss, D.D.
1899	The Evangelical Succession	Thomas F. Lockyer, B.A.
1900	Christianity and the Nineteenth Century	Charles J. Little, D.D.
1901	Spiritual Religion	John G. Tasker, D.D.
1902	Some Leading Ideas of Hinduism	Henry Haigh, D.D.
1903	Methodism in Canada	Alexander Sutherland
1904	The Hymn Book of the Modern Church	Arthur E. Gregory, D.D.
1905	The Unrealized Logic of Religion	William H. Fitchett, B.A., LL.D.
1906	Persecution in the Early Church	Herbert B. Workman, M.A., D.Litt.
1907	The Revival of Religion in England	John S. Simon, D.D.
1908	Man's Partnership with a Divine Providence	John Telford, B.A.
1909	The Witness of Israel	Wilfrid J. Moulton, M.A., B.D.
1910	The Spiritual Sense in the Sacred Ledgend	Edward J. Brailsford
1911	The Christ of the Gospels	W. West Holdsworth, M.A.
1912	The Preacher and the Modern Mind	George Jackson, B.A.
1913	Religions and Religion	J. Hope Moulton, M.A., D.D., D.Litt., D.Th.
1914	Personality and Fellowship	William Bradfield, B.A.
1915	Immanence and Christian Thought	Frederic Platt, M.A., D.D.
1916	Christian Reality in Modern Light	Frank Ballard, M.A., B.Sc., D.D.
1917	The Unfolding Life	William T. A. Barber, M.A., D.D.
1918	NO LECTURE	—
1919	Jewish Sect and Parties in the Time of Christ	John W. Lightley, M.A., B.D.
1920	Christian Responsibility for the Social Order	Samuel E. Keeble
1921	Altar, Cross and Community	William F. Lofthouse, M.A.
1922	The Kingdom of Heaven	H. Maldwyn Hughes, M.A., D.D.
1923	The Church which is His Body	Henry Howard
1924	Early Christianity and the Modern Church	R. Martin Pope, M.A.
1925	Evangelical Humanism	Lynn H. Hough
1926	The Evangel of the Hebrew Prophets	Alfred S. Geden, M.A., D.D.
1927	The Sacramental Society	C. Ryder Smith, B.A., B.D.
1928	Israel's Debt to Egypt	Edward H. Sugden, M.A., D.Litt.
1929	Popular Preaching	Dinsdale T. Young
1930	Divine Providence in the Light of Personality	T. Bowman Stephenson, B.A., B.D.
1931	The Fourth Gospel in Recent Criticism and Interpretation	Wilbert F. Howard, B.D.
1932	The Word of the Cross and Hinduism	Edgar W. Thompson, M.A.

KINGSWOOD SCHOOL, BRISTOL: 1748-1851
KINGSWOOD SCHOOL, BATH: 1851

Kingswood School, Bristol, was opened by John Wesley as a Boarding School for children of Methodist parentage. It is not to be confused with the school he opened for the miner's children of Kingswood. During his lifetime John Wesley was the Governor. After his death in 1791 till 1795 the school was put under the care of a small committee appointed by the Conference. We are not sure of the exact date, but most authorities agree that it was in 1794 that Kingswood was used for the education of the sons of Methodist Preachers only, and the Connexion was responsible fo. the financial commitments. In 1851 larger and more convenient premises were erected at Bath, and since then a number of extensions have been made.

In 1922 an important change was made because of the financial burden. The Conference directed that £15 p.a. should be paid by ministers in respect of children at the school, and that the children of laymen should be admitted. Kingswood is now a Methodist Public School, but assistance is still given from the Ministers' Children's Fund for both sons and daughters of ministers.

KINGSWOOD SCHOOL, BRISTOL

GOVERNORS

1748-1791	Revd. John Wesley, M.A.
1795-1802	Revd. Joseph Bradford
1802-1807	Revd. John Pritchard
1807-1809	Mr. William Wragge
1809-1811	Revd. Thomas Pinder
1811-1812	Revd. Joseph Wormersley
1812-1813	Revd. Thomas Stanley
1813-1820	Revd. Thomas Johnson
1820-1851	Revd. Joseph Cusworth

HEADMASTERS

1748-1750	Revd. Walter Sellon
1750-1752	Revd. John Jones
1752-1754	Revd. James Rouquet
1754-1758	Mr. John Parkinson
1760-1768	Revd. Thomas Greaves
1768-1770	Revd. Joseph Benson
1779-1783	Mr. Thomas Simpson, M.A.
1783-1794	Revd. Thomas McGeary, M.A.
1794-1795	Mr. John Clarke, M.A.
1795-1802	Mr. Andrew Mayer
1802-1804	Revd. Thomas Fletcher
1804-1809	Mr. William G. Horner
1809-1817	Mr. William Wragge
1817-1819	Mr. William Grear
1819-1823	Revd. John Lomas
1823-1826	Revd. Jonathan Crowther
1826-1829	Mr. Edmund Shaw
1829-1832	Mr. Samuel Griffith
1832-1833	Revd. William P. Burgess, M.A.
1833-1845	Mr. Samuel Griffith
1845-1850	Revd. Samuel Jones, M.A.
1850-1851	Mr. Henry McEffer Shera, M.A., LL.D.

KINGSWOOD SCHOOL, BATH

GOVERNORS

1851-1857	Revd. Joseph Cusworth
1857-1858	Revd. Theophilus Woolmer

GOVERNOR AND CHAPLAIN

1858-1860	Revd. Theophilus Woolmer
1860-1867	Revd. Francis A. West
1867-1873	Revd. William H. Sargent
1873-1885	Revd. John H. Lord
1885-1892	Revd. George Bowden, D.D.
1892-1901	Revd. Wesley Brunyate
1901-1904	Revd. T. Ferrier Hulme, M.A.

HEADMASTERS

1851-1854	Mr. Henry McEffer Shera, M.A., LL.D.
1854-1855	Mr William J. Shera, M.A.
1855-1865	Mr. William Jefferson, M.A.
1865-1866	Mr. William Elton, M.A.
1866-1885	Mr. Thomas G. Osborn, M.A.
1885-1889	Mr. Henry Jefferson, M.A.
1889-1918	Mr. Walter P. Workman, M.A., B.Sc.
1919-1928	Mr. Hubert A. Wootton, M.A.
1928-1932	Mr. Alfred B. Sackett, M.C., M.A.

VISITORS

1911-1926	Revd. Marshall Hartley
1926-1932	Revd. Owen S. Watkins, C.M.G., C.B.E., K.C.H.

WOODHOUSE GROVE SCHOOL

Woodhouse Grove School, Apperley Bridge, Yorkshire, was opened in January 1812. It was provided for the sons of Wesleyan ministers who were stationed in the north of England. The conditions of entry were the same as those that obtained at Kingswood School, and the financial commitments provided by the Schools' Fund. In the early 1870's the financial condition of the Schools' Fund was such that some began to think that Woodhouse Grove should be closed and sold, and the proceeds should provide additional accommodation at Kingswood. As might be expected the northern Methodists protested. The outcome of long negotiations was that Kingswood and Woodhouse Grove were amalgamated in 1875. Woodhouse Grove was responsible for boys age nine (the Lower Division) and pass on to Kingswood, (the Upper Division) at thirteen. The amalgamation was not to last very long. In 1883 the "Woodhouse Grove School Limited Liability Company" was formed, and it ceased to be a Connexional School solely for ministers' sons.

GOVERNORS

1812-1813	Mr. John Fennell
1813-1814	James Wood
1814-1816	Thomas Stanley
1815-1824	Miles Martindale
1824-1831	John Stamp
1831-1843	George Morley
1843-1848	William Lord

GOVERNORS AND CHAPLAIN

1858-1868	John Farrar
1868-1876	Henry H. Chettle
1876-1883	George Fletcher

HEADMASTERS

1813-1814	Revd. Thomas Fletcher
1814-1816	Revd. J. M. Bletsoe, M.A.
1816-1817	Revd. Jonathan Crowther
1817-1832	Mr. Samuel E. Parker
1832-1835	Mr. John Gardiner
1835-1838	Revd. Joshua Wood
1838-1854	Mr. William Greer
1854-1857	Mr. Samuel Sharpe, M.A., ..LD.
1857-1875	Mr. John M. Rabey, B.A., B.Sc., LL.D.
1875-1883	Mr. Thomas G. Osborn, M.A.

From 1813 all the Governors and Chaplains were Wesleyan ministers appointed by the Conference. The two clerical Headmasters, the Revd. J. M. Bletsoe, was an Anglican, and the Revd. Joshua Wood, was Church of Ireland, the son an Irish Methodist minister.

WESTMINSTER COLLEGE: 1851-1932 (MEN)

By the time of the Centenary of Wesleyan Methodism in 1839 there were a 101 day-schools, most of them connected with local Methodist Chapels. In many cases the hall or rooms used on weekdays were used for Sunday schools. In the early 1840's the Conference saw the need of providing teachers for the schools and a Committee was appointed to investigate and if possible produce a plan. The first Methodist students were trained at David Stow's Institution at Glasgow. One of the leading ministers in the field of education at the time was the Revd. John Scott. 'He knew better than any other man living, every aspect of education as it affected Methodism'. Westminster Normal Institution was opened in Horseferry Road, Westminster, London, in 1851. At this time there were 369 Methodist day-schools with 37,972 pupils.

PRINCIPALS

1851-1868	Revd. John Scott
1868-1903	Revd. James H. Rigg, D.D.
1903-1930	Revd. Herbert B. Workman, M.A., D.Litt., D.D.
1930-1932	Revd. Archibald W. Harrison, M.C., B.A., B.Sc., D.D.

VICE-PRINCIPALS

1851-1881 Mr. William Sugden
1881-1888 Mr. Charles Mansford
1888-1903 Mr. Henry A. Reatchlous, M.A., B.Sc.
1904-1918 Mr. Alfred G. D. Barriball, B.A.
1918-1921 Dr. Egbert H. Magson, M.A.
1921-1930 Revd. Archibald W. Harrison, M.C., B.A., B.Sc., D.D.
1930-1932 Mr. James H. Ross, M.A., B.Sc.

CHAPLAINS

1930-1931 Revd. J. Neilson Morrison, B.A., B.Sc.
1931-1932 Revd. J. Alan Kay, B.A.

TUTORS

1919-1921 J. Eric Dixon, M.C., B.A., B.D.

TEACHER TRAINING COLLEGE (WOMEN) — BATTERSEA, LONDON: 1871-1927 DOVER: 1927-1929. SOUTHLANDS COLLEGE, WIMBLEDON: 1929-1932

PRINCIPALS

1872-1881 Revd. George Olver, B.A.
1881-1886 Revd. George O. Bate
1886-1895 Revd. Frederic Greeves, D.D.
1895-1913 Revd. James Chapman, D.D.
1914-1918 Miss M. Atkinson Williams, M.A.
1918-1931 Miss Christine E. Brunyate, M.A.
1931-1932 Miss Florence M. Wood, M.A.

CHAPLAINS

1913-1928 Revd. James Critichison
1928-1932 Revd. Alfred H. Lowe, B.D.

JOYFUL NEWS HOME: 1889-1904 CLIFF COLLEGE: 1904

PRINCIPALS

1899-1903 Thomas Champness
1903-1904 Thomas Cook
1904-1912 Thomas Cook
1913-1932 Samuel Chadwick

TUTORS

1907-1912 Samuel Chadwick
1912-1916 W. Fiddian Moulton, M.A.
1916-1919 College closed
1919-1929 W. Fiddian Moulton, M.A.
1927-1929 Joseph I. Brice
1930-1932 Norman G. Dunning, M.A., LL.B.
1930-1932 Joseph I. Brice, B.A.

NATIONAL CHILDREN'S HOME: 1873-1883 — CHILDREN'S HOME AND ORPHANAGE: 1883-1909 — NATIONAL CHILDREN'S HOME AND ORPHANAGE: 1909-1932

PRINCIPALS

1873-1900 T. Bowman Stephenson, B.A., D.D.
1900-1912 Arthur E. Gregory, D.D.
1912-1932 W. Hodson Smith

STAFF

1886-1887 Danile Heaton
1887-1888 Nehemiah Curnock (B)
1891-1892 R. Bevan, Shepherd, B.A.
1898-1900 Arthur E. Gregory
1900-1901 Henry Martin, M.A.
1901-1907 R. Bevan Shepherd, B.A.
1906-1908 W. Herbert Spencer
1908-1909 Benjamin A. Gregory
1909-1917 S. Carroll Myers
1917-1927 Herbert J. Sugden
1917-1932 John H. Litten
1927-1932 George A. Parkinson

WITHOUT PASTORAL CHARGE PERMITTED TO SERVE

1920-1922 John Leal
1921-1931 G. Beesley Austin
1927-1931 Herbert J. Sugden
1931-1932 Cecil F. Walpole

THE WESLEY ORDER — WARDENS

1903-1907 T. Bowman Stephenson, B.A., D.D.
1907-1920 William Bradfield, B.A.
1920-1932 W. Russell Maltby, D.D.

Both the National Children's Home and the Wesley Deaconess Order were founded by the Revd. T. Bowman Stephenson.

THE WESLEYAN THEOLOGICAL INSTITUTION — 1834-1929
THE MINISTERIAL TRAINING FUND — 1929-1932

Theological training in Wesleyan Methodism began in 1834. The first Institution House (College) was opened at Hoxton, London, and it had accommodation for about thirty students. In 1839 Abney House, Stoke Newington was opened and had room for about thirty students. It soon became desirable for better and larger accommodation, and it was decided that there should be facilities in the South and North of the country. Suitable premises which lended themselves to adaptation were found at Didsbury, Manchester. Didsbury was opened in 1842, and Hoxton was closed. In 1843 Richmond, Surrey, was opened, and Abney House was closed. In 1865 it was decided that it would be better to train missionary students exclusively, and Richmond was chosen for this purpose. It was a bad decision that was not rectified until 1885. Meanwhile accommodation was needed for candidates for the home work, and in 1868 Headingley, Leeds was opened. Still further accommodation was required by the late 1870's, and in 1881 Handsworth, Birmingham was opened. In 1921 largely as the result of two benefactors, Wesley House, Cambridge was opened, for the benefit of those students who could avail themselves of a post-graduate course of studies.

At the beginning the minister appointed in charge of the building and having pastoral care of the students was called the Governor. From 1888 the Governor was also responsible for Pastoral Theology and Church History. In 1910 Principals replaced the Governors, and the care of college property and pastoral care of the students was the responsibility of the Resident Tutor. The Theological tutor was responsible for subjects as his title suggests, and the Classical tutor for Biblical Languages and Literature, Classics, and in some cases Mathematics in the early days till the subject was dropped. The Classical tutor generally had the help of an Assistant tutor, who was usually, though not always a probationer.

HOXTON

GOVERNORS

1834-1838 Joseph Entwisle
1838-1840 Richard Treffy
1840-1842 Philip C. Turner

THEOLOGY

1834-1842 John Hannah, D.D.

BIBLICAL LITERATURE AND CLASSICS

1835-1841 Samuel Jones, M.A.
1841-1842 William L. Thornton, M.A.

ABNEY HOUSE

GOVERNOR

1839-1843 John Farrar

THEOLOGY

1839-1842 John Hannah, D.D. (Part-time)
1842-1843 Thomas Jackson

DIDSBURY

GOVERNORS

1842-1843 Philip C. Turner

1843-1864 John Bowers
1864-1888 William Jackson
1888-1900 Richard Green
1900-1901 James Crabtree
1901-1913 John S. Simon, D.D.

RESIDENT TUTORS
1913-1915 George Jackson, B.A.
1919-1932 Thomas H. Barratt, B.A.

PRINCIPALS
1913-1915 R. Waddy Moss, D.D.
1919-1924 Wilfred J. Moulton, M.A., B.D.
1925-1932 Thomas H. Barratt, B.A.

THEOLOGY
1842-1867 John Hannah, D.D.
1867-1886 W. Burt Pope, D.D.
1886-1902 Marshall Randles, D.D.
1902-1915 R. Waddy Moss, D.D.
1919-1924 Wilfred J. Moulton, M.A., B.D.
1925-1930 J. Arundel Chapman, M.A., B.D.
1930-1932 Charles J. Wright, B.A., Ph.D.

BIBLICAL LITERATURE AND CLASSICS
1842-1849 William L. Thornton, M.A.
1849-1856 Jonathan Crowther
1856-1883 John D. Geden, D.D. (From 1874-1883, Old Testament and Classics)
1871-1888 Alfred J. French, B.A. (Mathematics, Classics, and Philosophy)
1887-1903 William F. Slater, M.A.
1888-1902 R. Waddy Moss, D.D.
1902-1915 J. Hope Moulton, M.A., D.D., D.Litt., D.Th., D.C.L. (New Testament Language and Literature)
1903-1905 Arthur Moorhouse, M.A., B.D. (Old Testament Language and Literature)
1905-1910 Frederic Platt, M.A., D.D. (Old Testament Language and Literature)
1910-1915 Charles Bedale, M.A. (Old Testament Language and Literature)
1919-1932 J. Alexander Findlay, M.A., D.D. (New Testament Language and Literature)
1929-1932 W. Bardsley Brash, M.A., B.D., M.Litt.

ASSISTANT TUTORS
1842-1843 Theophilus Woolmer
1845-1846 John Hebb
1847-1851 Benjamin Hellier
1851-1853 George W. Olver, B.A.
1858-1859 Charles H. Kelly (P.A.)
1858-1861 Frederick E. Toyne
1861-1863 George Fletcher
1863-1867 Theophilus Chubb
1867-1871 George Oyston, B.A.
1869-1870 Bernard G. Wilkinson
1871-1873 R. Waddy Moss
1873-1874 John Thackray, B.A.
1874-1876 John A. Vanes, B.A.
1876-1878 Robert M. Rees, M.A.
1877-1878 George A. Bennetts, B.A., (P.A.)
1878-1882 George A. Bennetts, B.A.
1882-1887 F. Luke Wiseman, B.A.
1883-1884 Alfred S. Geden, M.A.
1883-1888 Herbert B. Workman, M.A.
1888-1891 Albert H. Walker, B.A.
1891-1894 John H. Ritson, M.A.
1894-1897 Edwin D. Jackson, B.A.
1896-1897 Trevor H. Davies
1897-1900 Henry C. J. Sidnel, B.A.
1900-1903 Sherwin Smith, M.A.
1903-1906 Charles Bedale, M.A.
1906-1909 Archibald W. Harrison, B.Sc., B.D.
1907-1908 Wilbert F. Howard, B.D. (P.A.)
1907-1912 C. Kingsley, B.A.
1912-1913 Arthur H. Bray, M.A., B.D.
1914-1916 John Leale, M.A.
1915-1916 John R. S. Hutchinson
1919-1920 Joseph W. Jones, B.A.
1920-1922 Frank Whittaker, M.A.
1922-1924 Magnus Nicholson, M.A.
1924-1928 Frederic Greeves, M.A.
1928-1931 Hedley Hodkin, M.A.
1931-1932 John W. Waterhouse, M.A., B.D.

RICHMOND

GOVERNORS
1843-1846 Philip C. Turner
1846-1848 William W. Stamp, D.D.
1848-1855 Samuel Jackson
1855-1858 William M. Harvard
1858-1868 Alfred Barrett
1868-1891 Daniel Sanderson
1891-1909 George Fletcher

RESIDENT TUTORS
1910-1915 Thomas H. Barratt, B.A.
1920-1929 William T. A. Barber, M.A., D.D.
1929-1932 Leslie F. Church, B.A., Ph.D.

PRINCIPALS
1910-1920 W. Theophilus Davison, M.A., D.D.
1920-1929 William T. A. Barber, M.A., D.D.
1929-1932 C. Ryder Smith, B.A., D.D.

THEOLOGY
1843-1861 Thomas Jackson
1861-1868 John Lomas
1868-1885 George Osborn, D.D.
1885-1905 J. Agar Beet, D.D.
1905-1915 W. Theophilus Davison, M.A., D.D.
1920-1932 C. Ryder Smith, B.A., D.D.

BIBLICAL LITERATURE AND CLASSICS
1843-1857 John Farrar
1857-1868 Benjamin Hellier
1868-1874 William F. Moulton, M.A.
1875-1881 George G. Findlay, B.A.
1875-1883 Frederick P. Napier, B.A.
1881-1891 W. Theophilus Davison, M.A., D.D.
1887-1891 John G. Tasker
1891-1915 Alfred S. Geden, M.A., D.D. (Old Testament Language and Literature)
1910-1915 Harry Bisseker, M.A.
1920-1932 F. Bertram Clogg, M.A., B.D. (New Testament Language and Literature)

CHURCH HISTORY, HISTORY OF DOCTRINE, AND PASTORAL THEOLOGY
1925-1932 Leslie F. Church, B.A., Ph.D.

PHILOSOPHY OF RELIGION
1920-1942 Eric S. Waterhouse, M.A., D.D.

ASSISTANT TUTORS
1847-1851 J. Dury Geden
1851-1853 Robert N. Young
1854-1855 William Gibson, B.A.
1858-1868 William F. Moulton, M.A.
1868-1872 Marshall Hartley
1871-1876 James Cooling
1872-1875 Frederick P. Napier, B.A.
1874-1875 George G. Findlay, B.A.
1876-1880 John G. Tasker
1880-1882 William H. Findlay, M.A.
1882-1884 William T. A. Barber, M.A.
1884-1887 John G. Tasker
1886-1889 Frederick W. Kellett, M.A.
1889-1891 Ernest O. Barrett, M.A.
1891-1893 W. Percy Hutton, B.A.
1891-1894 Thomas Stephenson, B.A.
1893-1896 Harold C. Morton, B.A.
1894-1896 James H. Darrell, B.A.
1896-1898 Charles F. Hunter, B.A.
1896-1898 William F. Lofthouse, M.A.
1898-1904 Thomas Stephenson, B.A., B.D.
1902-1904 Percy M. Wright, B.Sc.
1904-1906 Ernest G. Loosley, B.D.
1906-1909 R. Idwal Hopwood, M.A.
1909-1912 F. Bertram Clogg, M.A.
1912-1915 Conrad Skinner, B.A.
1915-1916 * William H. Dyson
1920-1925 H. Douglas Anthony, M.A., B.Sc.
1925-1928 Stanley R. Hayward, B.A.

1928-1930 John T. Jones, B.A.
1930-1932 A. Marcus Ward, M.A.
1931-1932 Kenneth G. Bloxham, B.D.

* Killed in action, 1916; appointed, but never served.

HEADINGLEY

GOVERNORS
1868-1876 John Farrar
1876-1887 Benjamin Hellier
1887-1904 G. Stringer Rowe
1904-1916 T. Hardwick Mawson

PRINCIPALS
1930-1932 John W. Lightley, M.A., B.D., D.Litt.

RESIDENT TUTORS
1930-1932 John W. Lightley, M.A., B.D., D.Litt.

THEOLOGY
1868-1973 John Lomas
1873-1879 Samuel Coley
1880-1910 J. S. Banks, D.D.
1910-1916 Wilfred J. Moulton, M.A., B.D.
1930-1932 J. Arundel Chapman, M.A., B.D.

BIBLICAL LITERATURE AND CLASSICS
1868-1876 Benjamin Hellier
1896-1881 Robert N. Young, D.D.
1881-1916 George G. Findlay, B.A., D.D.
1930-1932 Vincent Taylor, D.D. Ph.D.

CHURCH HISTORY AND HISTORY OF DOCTRINE
1930-1923 H. Watkin-Jones, M.A., D.D.

Headingley was closed during the First World War, and did not reopen again until 1930.

ASSISTANT TUTORS
1868-1870 William Stevenson, B.A.
1870-1874 George G. Findlay, B.A.
1874-1880 Edward H. Sugden, B.A., B.Sc.
1880-1881 William Foster, B.A.
1881-1885 Francis J. Nance, B.A.
1885-1887 Thomas H. Banks, B.A.
1887-1890 J. Anthony Barnes, B.A.
1890-1903 Arthur Moorhouse, M.A., B.D.
1893-1896 Wilfred J. Moulton, M.A.
1896-1899 C. Ryder Smith, B.A.
1899-1902 Arthur A. Fuller, B.A.
1902-1903 George H. Bamford
1902-1904 Stuart Wilson, M.A., B.Sc.
1903-1907 J. Hugh Michael, B.A.
1907-1910 Charles H. Pitt, B.A.
1909-1912 J. Arundel Chapman, M.A., B.D.
1910-1911 Joseph W. Hunkin, B.A.
1911-1913 Cecil T. Groves, B.A.
1912-1915 Ernest J. Nuttall, M.A.
1913-1916 William H. Findlay, M.A.
1930-1932 C. Leslie Mitton, B.A.

HANDSWORTH

GOVERNORS
1881-1892 John Hartley
1892-1897 Robert N. Young, D.D.
1897-1905 Thomas Allen, D.D.
1905-1910 Silvester Whitehead

RESIDENT TUTORS
1910-1923 John G. Tasker, D.D.
1923-1932 Henry Bett, M.A., D.Litt.

PRINCIPALS
1910-1923 John G. Tasker, D.D.
1923-1925 Frederic Platt, M.A., D.D.
1924-1932 William F. Lofthouse, M.A., D.D.

THEOLOGY
1881-1891 Frederic W. Macdonald
1891-1904 W. Theophilus Davison, M.A., D.D.
1904-1910 John G. Tasker, D.D.
1910-1916 Frederic Platt, M.A., D.D.
1919-1925 Frederic Platt, M.A., D.D.
1925-1932 William F. Lofthouse, M.A., D.D. (And Philosophy of Religion)

BIBLICAL LITERATURE AND CLASSICS
1881-1892 Robert N. Young, D.D.
1892-1904 John G. Tasker
1904-1915 W. West Holdsworth, M.A., B.D. (New Testament Language and Literature)
1904-1915 William F. Lofthouse, M.A., D.D. (Old Testament Language and Literature)
1919-1932 William F. Howard, M.A., D.D. (New Testament Language and Literature)
1919-1925 William F. Lofthouse, M.A., D.D. (Old Testament Language and Literature, and Philosophy of Religion)
1925-1932 Christopher R. North, M.A. (Old Testament Language and Literature)

CHURCH HISTORY
1910-1916 John G. Tasker, D.D. (And Apologetics)
1919-1923 John G. Tasker, D.D. (And Apologetics)
1923-1932 Henry Bett, M.A., D.Litt. (And Pastoral Theology)

ASSISTANT TUTORS
1881-1883 William Foster, B.A.
1883-1886 Arthur E. Sharpley, B.A., B.D.
1886-1888 Charles W. Andrews, B.A., B.D.
1886-1887 Arthur W. Ward, B.A.
1888-1891 R. Martin Pope, M.A.
1891-1893 Arthur W. Cooke, M.A.
1893-1896 W. Hubert Thorpe, B.A.
1896-1899 George Allen, B.A.
1899-1901 William F. Lofthouse, M.A.
1900-1901 R. Winboult Harding, B.A.
1901-1904 George Allen, B.A.
1901-1903 Frederick H. Benson, B.A.
1902-1904 Alfred R. Fuller, B.A.
1904-1907 J. Alexander Findlay, M.A.
1907-1909 R. Thackray Morrison, M.A.
1909-1910 J. Arundel Chapman, M.A., B.D.
1910-1913 R. Newton Flew, B.A.
1913-1915 Ronald D. Rees, M.A.
1915-1916 Hugh M. Brook, B.Sc.
1919-1921 Cecil H. Rose, M.A.
1921-1922 Theophilus S. Gregory, M.A.
1922-1924 Arthur D. Philipson, B.A., B.D.
1924-1926 Arthur S. Gregory, M.A.
1926-1930 William F. Flemington, M.A.
1929-1930 Maldwyn L. Edwards, M.A.
1930-1931 Gordon C. Johnson, B.A., B.D.
1931-1932 Noel J. Chew, B.A.

WESLEY HOUSE, CAMBRIDGE

PRINCIPAL
1921-1932 H. Maldwyn Hughes, M.A., D.D.

THEOLOGY
1921-1932 H. Maldwyn Hughes, M.A., D.D.

ASSISTANT TUTORS
1924-1926 Harold Roberts, M.A.
1926-1927 W. Pearson Baker, B.A.

BIBLICAL LANGUAGES AND LITERATURE
1927-1932 R. Newton Flew, M.A., B.D.

THE WELSH WESLEYAN METHODIST ASSEMBLY OF WALES: 1898-1932

The Conference of 1898 confirmed the creation of a Welsh Wesleyan Methodist Assembly of Wales. The reason for the formation of the Assembly was the hope that it would create among the Welsh Churches a sense of unity which could not exist while Welsh Methodism was split into unequal and unrelated fragments. The Assembly met each year in June, and was presided over by the President of the British Conference. The Assembly elected each year a Minister in the Welsh Work to be its President. The chief function of the President of the Assembly was to preside over all the Connexional Committees, all of which had ministerial and lay representatives. The Assembly consisted of two Sessions, the Representative and the Pastoral, the functions of which were as in the British Conference. The Assembly could only act within the constitution, and all acts and resolutions were subject to the Legal Conference.

Year	President	Year	President	Year	President
1899	Edward Humphreys	1910	J. Cadvan Davies	1922	A. Colin Pearce
1900	Rice Owen	1911	Thomas J. Pritchard	1923	D. Mon Hughes
1901	Hugh Jones	1912	Richard Morgan (B)	1924	D. Gwynfryn Jones
1902	Hugh Hughes	1913	Thomas Jones (C)	1925	Hugh Evans
1903	Ishmael Evans	1914	W. Owen Evans	1926	Thomas Rowlands
1904	Thomas Manual	1915	Owen Evans	1927	Robert W. Jones
1905	R. Lloyd Jones	1916	John Felix	1928	T. Charles Roberts
1906	T. Jones-Humphreys	1917	Evan Isaac	1929	D. Tecwyn Evans, M.A.
1907	Thomas Hughes (B)	1918	T. Isfryn Hughes	1930	E. Berwyn Roberts
1908	Evan Jones	1919	Thomas O. Jones	1931	E. Mostyn Jones
1909	P. Jones Roberts	1920	O. Madoc Roberts	1932	Evan D. Thomas
		1921	Philip Price		

SECRETARIES OF THE WELSH WESLEYAN METHODIST ASSEMBLY OF WALES: 1898-1932

1899-1904	P. Jones Roberts	1911-1914	Hugh Evans	1921	Hugh Evans	1922-1932	H. Meirion Davies
1905-1910	John Humphreys	1915-1920	E. Tegryd Davies		H. Meirion Davies		

METHODIST NEW CONNEXION: 1797-1907
PRESIDENTS OF THE CONFERENCE

Year	Place	President	Station or Appointment
1797	Leeds	William Thom	Leeds and Huddersfield
1798	Sheffield	William Thom, 2nd time	Leeds and Huddersfield
1799	Nottingham	John Grundell	Manchester
1800	Manchester	Stephen Eversfield	Manchester
1801	Leeds	William Thom, 3rd time	Book Steward
1802	Sheffield	William Thom, 4th time	Book Steward
1803	Hull	William Thom, 5th time	Book Steward
1804	Nottingham	William Driver	Nottingham and Leicester
1805	Manchester	James Mort	Nottingham
1806	Hanley	William Styan	Sheffield
1807	Leeds	William Brown	London
1808	Huddersfield	Edward Oakes	Huddersfield
1809	Sheffield	George Wall	Ashton
1810	Hull	Thomas Shore	Sheffield
1811	Chester	William Thom, 6th time	Book Steward
1812	Nottingham	Joseph Manners	Nottingham
1813	Manchester	William Haslam	Dewsbury
1814	Hanley	George Hendley	Halifax
1815	Leeds	George Wall, 2nd time	Huddersfield
1816	Huddersfield	William Drive, 2nd time	Hanley
1817	Halifax	Abraham Scott	Newcastle-upon-Tyne
1818	Sheffield	Thomas Waterhouse	Ashton
1819	Hull	Abraham Jackson	Manchester
1820	Chester	John Harrison	Hull
1821	Nottingham	James Mort, 2nd time	Chester
1822	Manchester	Thomas Allin	Bolton
1823	Hanley	William Driver, 3rd time	Liverpool
1824	Liverpool	William Haslem, 2nd time	Ashton
1825	Leeds	William Styan, 2nd time	Halifax
1826	Ashton	Simeon Woodhouse	Chester
1827	Huddersfield	William Shuttleworth	Connexional Editor and Book Steward
1828	Longton	William Chapman	Sunderland
1829	Halifax	Christopher Atkinson	Barnsley
1830	Sheffield	William R. Wood	Todmorden
1831	Hull	William Salt	Stockport
1832	Chester	George Wall, 3rd time	Halifax
1833	Nottingham	James Wilson (A)	Macclesfield
1834	Manchester	Thomas Waterhouse, 2nd time	Leeds
1835	Hanley	William Ford	Halifax
1836	Liverpool	Thomas Scattergood	Ashton
1837	Leeds	Abraham Scott, 2nd time	Stockport
1838	Ashton	Joseph Livingston	Sheffield
1839	Huddersfield	Simeon Woodhouse, 2nd time	Nottingham
1840	Longton	George Goodhall	Dudley
1841	Halifax	John Wilson, 2nd time	Newcastle-upon-Tyne
1842	Sheffield	Samuel Hulme	Dudley
1843	Hull	William Cooke	Newcastle-upon-Tyne

Year	Place	President	Station or Appointment
844	Chester	John Bakewell	London
845	Nottingham	William Ford, 2nd time	London
846	Manchester	Thomas Allin, 2nd time	Manchester (Supernumerary)
847	Hanley	William Burrows	Stockport
848	Liverpool	James Henshaw	Stockport
849	Dudley	Parkinson T. Gilton	Hanley
1850	Leeds	William Baggaly	Liverpool
851	Hanley	Thomas Waterhouse, 3rd time	Leeds
852	Huddersfield	Philip J. Wright	Leeds
853	Longton	John Hudston	Huddersfield
854	Halifax	William Mills	Hanley
855	Sheffield	Samuel Hulme 2nd time	Hanley
856	Chester	Haenry Watts	Burslem
857	Nottingham	Law Stoney	Stalybridge
858	Hull	John Addyman	Stalybridge
859	Manchester	William Cooke, 2nd time	London
860	Hanley	James Stacey	Sheffield, South
861	Liverpool	Henry O. Crofts, D.D.	Leeds
862	Dudley	Thomas W. Ridley	Stalybridge
863	Leeds	William Cocker	Sheffield, South
864	Ashton	Robert Henshaw	Manchester, North
865	Newcastle-upon-Tyne	William Baggaly, 2nd time	Stockport
866	Birmingham	Samuel Hulme, 3rd time	Manchester, South
867	Huddersfield	John Taylor	Stockport
868	Longton	Charles Hibbert	Sheffield, North
869	Hanley	William Cooke, D.D., 3rd time	London
870	Sheffield	Thomas Smith	Sheffield, North
871	Nottingham	Alexander McCurdy	Nottingham
872	Manchester	Joseph H. Robinson	London, III
873	Hull	George Grundy	Dewsbury
874	Hanley	William B. Wilshaw	Stockport
875	Dudley	Henry Piggin	York
876	Dewsbury	C. Dewick Ward, D.D.	Leeds, I
877	Leeds	John Medicraft	Nottingham
878	Ashton	John Ogden	Manchester, North
879	Huddersfield	James C. Watts, D.D.	Sheffield, South
880	Longton	William Cocker, D.D., 2nd time	Principal, Ranmoor College
881	Halifax	James Stacey, D.D., 2nd time	Sheffield, West
882	Batley	William Longbottom	Hanley
883	Sheffield	Thomas Rider	Ashton
1884	Nottingham	Thomas D. Crothers, D.D.	Stalybridge
1885	Manchester	Alexander McCurdy, 2nd time	Leicester
886	Newcastle-upon-Tyne	William J. Townsend, D.D.	Newcastle-upon-Tyne
887	Stockport	John K. Jackson	Southport
888	Hanley	Thomas T. Rushworth	Manchester, South
889	Dudley	Alfred R. Pearson	Longton (Supernumerary)
890	Dewsbury	James Le Huray	Southport
891	Leeds	Henry T. Marshall, D.D.	Ashton
892	Ashton	Joseph C. Milburn	Oldbury and Tipton
893	Huddersfield	Thomas Scowby	Bradford
894	Longton	Michael Bartram	Ashton
895	Halifax	George Packer, D.D.	Huddersfield
896	Batley	Elisha Holyoake	Ripon
897	Sheffield	John Innocent	Stockport (On furlough from China)
1898	Nottingham	David Heath	Sheffield, West
1899	Manchester	John E. Radcliffe	Leeds
1900	Newcastle-upon-Tyne	George S. Hornby	Halifax, North
1901	Hanley	George T. Candlin, D.D.	Leeds
1902	Stockport	Martin J. Birks	Rochdale
1903	Dudley	William Hookins	Leeds, Hunslet
1904	Dewsbury	Thomas M. Rees	Halifax, South
1905	Leeds	Francis H. Robinson	Liverpool, Park Place
1906	Ashton	Joseph Foster	Mossley
1907	Huddersfield	John S. Clements, B.A., B.D.	Principal, Ranmoor College

METHODIST NEW CONNEXION — SECRETARIES OF THE CONFERENCE

The office of Secretary of the Conference could be held either by a minister or laymen. For some years the Conference appointed two Secretaries, and is sometimes referred to as the Financial Secretary. This practice ceased in 1844.

Years	Secretary
1797-1798	Revd. Alexander Kilham
1799-1800	Mr. Robert Hall
1801	Mr. Samuel Heginbottom
1802	Revd. George Beaumont
1803	Revd. Edward Oakes
1804	Mr. Charles Sutton
1805	Mr. Thomas Steele
1806	Mr. William Huddlestone
1807-1808	Revd. Richard Watson
1809	Mr. John Garlick
1810	Mr. James Burne
1811	Revd. Richard Watson
	Mr. W. Wawne
1812	Mr. William Huddlestone
1813	Mr. James Burne
1814	Mr. John Raines
1815	Mr. John Horner
1816	Revd. Joseph Manners
1817	Mr. William Makinson
1818	Mr. Richard Reynolds
1819	Mr. John Raines
1820	Mr. James Burne
1821	Revd. Simeon Woodhouse
	Mr. William Makinson

Years	Secretary
1822	Mr. John Blackweel
	Mr. William Ridgway
1823	Mr. James Burne
	Mr. T. Hanmer
1824	Mr. Richard Sutton
	Mr. John Milner
1825	Mr. Benjamin Jackson
1826	Revd. David Barker
	Mr. Richard Reynolds
1827	Mr. John Blackwell
1828-1830	Mr. John Robinson
1831	Mr. Benjamin Jackson
1832	Mr. Bryan J. Proctor
1833	Revd. William Hughes
1834	Mr. William Makinson
1835	Mr. Richard Sutton
1836	Mr. William Halliwell
1837	Mr. John Robinson
1838	Mr. James Dean
1839	Mr. John Milner
1840	Mr. John Robinson
1841-1843	Revd. John Bakewell
	Revd. William Baggaly
1844	Mr. W. H. Waterhouse
1845	Mr. Josiah Bates
1846	Mr. John Robinson
1847	Mr. Edward W. Makinson, M.A.
1848	Mr. Josiah Bates
1849	Mr. George L. Robinson
1850	Mr. Edward W. Makinson, M.A.
1851	Mr. George L. Robinson
1852	Mr. Edwin Lumby
1853	Mr. William G. Tate
1854	Mr. John Robinson
1855	Mr. George L. Robinson
1856-1857	Mr. John Robinson
1858	Mr. John F. Sutton
1859	Mr. John Robinson
1860	Mr. Edwin Lumby
1861-1862	Mr. John Robinson
1863	Mr. Edwin Lumby
1864	Mr. John Cunliffe
1865	Mr. Joshua Pollard
1866	Mr. Thomas Fenton
1867	Mr. John W. Longbottom
1868	Revd. Thomas D. Crothers, D.D.
1869	Mr. Alfred Ramsden
1870-1871	Mr. Richard Hankinson
1872-1873	Revd. James C. Watts, D.D.
1874	Mr. Richard Hankinson
1875	Revd. James C. Watts, D.D.
1876	Mr. Joshua Pollard
1877	Revd. William J. Townsend, D.D.
1878	Mr. George Goodall
1879	Mr. John Runton
1880	Mr. Richard Hankinson
1881	Mr. George Goodhall
1882	Revd. Thomas Addyman
1883	Mr. Alfred Ramsden
1884	Revd. John F. Goodhall
1885	Revd. Thomas Addyman
1886	Mr. Thomas Cunliffe
1887	Mr. Alfred Ramsden
1888	Revd. George Packer
1889	Mr. Alfred Ramsden
1890	Revd. Samule Walker
1891	Mr. Charles D. Heaps
1892	Revd. David Heath
1893	Mr. John W. Cunliffe, M.A., D.Litt.
1894	Revd. Elisha Holyoake
1895	Mr. William P. Burnley
1896	Mr. Charles F. Robinson
1897	Sir Charles T. Skelton
1898	Mr. Edward R. Noall
1899	Mr. John Derbyshire
1900	Revd. Martin J. Birks
1901	Revd. Joseph Foster
1902	Mr. John G. Watson
1903	Revd. J. Capes Story
1904	Mr. James S. Newsome
1905	Revd. George Parker
1906	Mr. Darley Terry
1907	Revd. John W. Walls

METHODIST NEW CONNEXION — CONNEXIONAL SECRETARIES

GENERAL MISSION COMMITTEE

1837-1838	James Dixon (Mr)
1838-1842	Thomas Berry
1842-1849	William Cooke
1849-1859	Thomas Allin
1859-1863	James Stacey
1863-1879	Samuel Hulme
1879-1886	James Stacey, D.D.
1886-1891	William J. Townsend
1891-1892	John Medicraft
1892-1897	John K. Jackson
1897-1907	George Parker, D.D.

CHAPEL COMMITTEE

1840-1841	William Ford
1841-1842	William Baggaly
1842-1844	William Ford
1844-1845	Thomas Scattergood
1845-1846	John Bakewell
1846-1859	William Ford
1859-1867	George L. Robinson (Mr)
1867-1877	William Baggaly
1877-1889	Alexander M'Curdy
1889-1891	Alfred R. Pearson
1891-1892	Charles D. Ward, D.D.
1892-1902	William Longbottom
1892-1907	Martin J. Birks

HOME MISSION AND EXTENSION COMMITTEE

1866-1879	Samuel Hulme
1879-1886	James Stacey, D.D.
1886-1891	William J. Townsend
1891-1901	James Ogden
1901-1907	George Packer, D.D.

TEMPERANCE AND BAND OF HOPE COMMITTEE

1874-1879	David Heath
1879-1883	James C. Storey
1883-1888	Francis H. Robinson
1888-1892	Alfred Colbeck
1892-1893	John W. Sims
1893-1898	William F. Newsam
1898-1903	Samuel T. Nicholson
1903-1907	William Matthews

SUNDAY SCHOOL AND YOUNG PEOPLE'S COMMITTEE

1877-1884	Samuel Walker
1884-1892	James Gibson
1892-1897	Enoch Hall
1897-1902	Thomas Stoneley
1902-1907	John Young

BOOK STEWARDS

1797-1801	Mr. Thomas Hannam
1801-1803	George Beaumont
1803-1811	William Thom
1811-1816	Mr. John Ridgway
1816-1827	Mr. Thomas Allbut
1827-1844	William Shuttleworth
1844-1849	John Bakewell
1849-1870	William Cooke
1871-1874	Joseph H. Robinson
1874-1880	John Hudston
1880-1887	Charles D. Ward
1887-1893	James C. Watts

(From 1983 no minister was appointed as Book Steward; the Connexion appointed a lay officer.)

CONNEXIONAL EDITORS

1797-1801	Mr. Thomas Hannam
1801-1803	George Beaumont
1803-1811	William Thom
1812-1816	Mr. John Ridgway
1816-1827	Mr. Thomas Allbut
1827 1841	William Shuttleworth
1841-1848	John Bakewell
1848-1870	William Cooke
1871-1874	Joseph H. Robinson
1874-1880	John Hudston
1880-1887	Charles D. Ward
1887-1892	James C. Watts
1893-1897	William J. Townsend
1987-1901	Alfred Colbeck
1902-1903	William J. Townsend
1903-1905	Alfred Colbeck
1905-1907	Henry Smith

METHODIST NEW CONNEXION MAGAZINES

1796-1797	The Methodist Monitor
1798-1811	The Methodist Magazine or Evangelical Repository: The New Methodist Magazine (1812-1832) The Methodist New Connexion Magazine (1833-1907)
1824-1850	Sunday Scholars' Magazine: The Juvenile Instructor (1850-1898): Young People (1899-1907)
1842	The Beacon

METHODIST NEW CONNEXION — CONNEXIONAL INSTITUTIONS

Ministerial training in the Methodist New Connexion began in a very small way in 1835, when one of the leading ministers, the Revd. Thomas Allin, took into his home some accepted candidates and supervised their studies. Some years later the same arrangement was made under Dr. William Cooke and Dr. James Stacey. In the early 1860's the Conference determined to commence an Institution, Ranmoor College, Sheffield, was opened in 1864. It was retained at the formation of the United Methodist Church in 1907, but closed during the First World War, and did not re-open again. It was sold in 1919.

RANMOOR COLLEGE

PRINCIPALS AND RESIDENT TUTORS

1864-1867	James Stacey, D.D.
1867-1886	William Cocker, D.D.
1886-1898	Thomas D. Crothers, D.D.
1898-1907	John S. Clements, B.A., D.D.

TUTORS

1864-1866	Samuel Hulme
1866-1879	James Stacey, D.D.
1879-1880	Benjamin B. Turnock, M.A.
1880-1882	James C. Watts, D.D.
1903-1907	E. Wales Hurst, M.A., B.Sc.

During the periods 1866-1876 and 1882-1903 there were a number of part-time lecturers. After 1883 some of the students were able to attend Firth College, the forerunner of Sheffield University.

PRIMITIVE METHODIST CONNEXION: 1810-1932
PRESIDENTS OF THE PRIMITIVE METHODIST CONFERENCE

The Primitive Methodist Connexion began in 1810, but the first Conference was not held until 1820. The constitution permitted both Ministers and Laymen to be elected President, and in a few cases the President was a supernumeray minister. Unfortunately for some years between 1820-1841, there is no record of the name of the President.

Year	Place	President	Station or Appointment
1820	Hull	George Handford	Loughborough
1821	Tunstall	No Record	
1822	Loughborough	No Record	
1823	Leeds	No Record	
1824	Halifax	No Record	
1825	Sunderland	Thomas King	Nottingham
1826	Nottingham	James Bourne	Bemersley, Book Steward
1827	Manchester	No Record	
1828	Tunstall	No Record	
1829	Scotter	James Bourne, 2nd time	Bemersley, Book Steward
1830	Hull	No Record	
1831	Leicester	No Record	
1832	Bradford	No Record	
1833	Sunderland	No Record	
1834	Birmingham	No Record	
1835	Tunstall	No Record	
1836	Lyme Regis	No Record	
1837	Sheffield	No Record	
1838	Darlaston	No Record	
1839	Bradford	No Record	
1840	Manchester	No Record	
1841	Reading	No Record	
1842	Newcastle-upon-Tyne	James Bourne, 3rd time	Bemersley, Book Steward
1843	Nottingham	John Garner	London, Missionary Secretary
1844	Lyme Regis	William Clowes	Hull, Supernumerary
1845	Hull	William Clowes, 2nd time	Hull, Supernumerary
1846	Tunstall	William Clowes, 3rd time	Hull, Supernumerary
1847	Halifax	John Garner, 2nd time	London, Missionary Secretary
1848	Leeds	Thomas King, 2nd time	Manchester
1849	Sunderland	Mr. Stephen Longdin	
1850	Nottingham	John Garner, 3rd time	Epworth, Supernumerary
1851	Yarmouth	John Garner, 4th time	Epworth, Supernumerary
1852	Sheffield	John Garner, 5th time	Epworth, Supernumerary
1853	York	Mr. Joseph Bailey	Epworth Supernumerary
1854	Manchester	John Garner, 6th time	Epworth, Supernumerary
1855	Hull	George Tetley	Bedford
1856	Darlaston	Sampson Turner	Kendal
1857	Cambridge	Mr. Thoma Bateman	Kendal
1858	Doncaster	Sampson Turner, 2nd time	Kendal, Supernumerary
1859	Newcastle-upon-Tyne	William Garner	Driffield
1860	Tunstall	John Petty	Hull I
1861	Derby	William Garner, 2nd time	Hull II
1862	Sheffield	William Harland	Gainsborough
1863	Leeds	William Antliff, D.D.	London, Connexional Editor
1864	York	James Garner	London, Missionary Secretary
1865	Hull	William Antliff, D.D., 2nd time	London, Connexional Editor
1866	Chester	George Lamb	Hull II
1867	Luton	Mr. Thomas Bateman, 2nd time	Hull II
1868	Sunderland	William Lister	London Book Steward
1869	Grimsby	Philip Pugh	London, Connexional Editor
1870	Nottingham	Moses Lupton	Sunderland, Supernumerary
1871	Oldham	James Garner, 2nd time	Liverpool, Supernumerary
1872	Yarmouth	James Macphearson	London, Connexional Editor
1873	London	Samuel Antliff, D.D.	London, Missionary Secretary
1874	Hull	William Rowe	London, Missionary Secretary
1875	Leicester	Robert Smith	Kingston
1876	Newcastle-upon-Tyne	John Dickinson	London, Book Steward

Year	Place	President	Station or Appointment
1877	Scarborough	Thomas Smith	York Governor, Elmfield School
1878	Manchester	Henry Phillips	Whitby
1879	Leeds	Thomas Newell	Keighley I
1880	Grimsby	Colin C. McKechnie	London, Connexional Editor
1881	Hull	Charles Kendall	Driffield
1882	Sheffield	Joseph Wood, M.A., B.D.	Grimsby I
1883	South Shields	William Cutts	Sheffield II
1884	Tunstall	George Lamb, 2nd time	London, Book Steward
1885	Reading	Ralph Fenwick	London, Balham and Clapham
1886	Derby	John Atkinson	London, Missionary Secretary
1887	Scarborough	Thomas Whitehead	London, General Committee Secretary
1888	Liverpool	Thomas Whittaker, D.D.	Manchester IV
1889	Bradford	Joseph Toulson	London, Book Steward
1890	Sunderland	John Hallam	Newcastle-upon-Tyne I
1891	Northampton	Joseph Ferguson, D.D.	Darlaston
1892	Norwich	James Travis	London, General Committee Secretary
1893	Nottingham	John Stephenson	Nottingham III
1894	Chester	John Wenn	Leicester I
1895	Edinburgh	John Watson, D.D.	Manchester, Hartley College
1896	Burnley	William Jones	Tunstall
1897	Manchester	James Jackson	Barnard Castle
1898	Leeds	John Smith	London, Missionary Secretary
1899	Grimsby	William Goodman	Kingston
1900	Bristol	Joseph Odell	Birmingham IV
1901	Sheffield	H. Bickerstaffe Kendall, B.A.	Folkestone
1902	Hull	Thomas Mitchell, D.D.	London, Church Extension Fund Secretary
1903	Newcastle-upon-Tyne	T. Hankey Hunt	Liverpool, IV
1904	Birmingham	Robert Harrison	Hull III
1905	Scarborough	George E. Butt	London, Special Deputations
1906	Manchester	George Parkin, M.A., B.D.	Oldham
1907	Leicester	Henry Yooll	Manchester IV
1908	London	James Pickett	London, Harringay
1909	Southport	Sir William P. Hartley	
1910	Tunstall	Samuel S. Henshaw	Nottingham II
1911	Bradford	Edwin Dalton, D.D.	Hull I
1912	Norwich	Thomas Jackson	London, Whitechapel Mission
1913	Derby	Joseph Ritson	Luton I
1914	Middlesbrough	George Bennett	London, Forest Hill
1915	Reading	John D. Thompson	Cambridge
1916	Nottingham	Arthur T. Guttery, D.D.	Liverpool I
1917	London	J. Tolfree Parr	Aldershot
1918	Northampton	William A. Hammond	Brighton
1919	Grimsby	James Watkin	Chesterfield
1920	Hull	Matthew P. Davison	Hexham, Supernumerary
1921	Sheffield	Samuel Horton	London, Kensington Park
1922	Leeds	Henry J. Taylor	Liverpool I
1923	Liverpool	George Armstrong	Haltwhistle
1924	Newcastle-upon-Tyne	Joseph T. Barkby	London, Special Missions
1925	Scarborough	James Lockhart	Birmingham V
1926	Manchester	A. Lewis Humphries, M.A.	Manchester, Hartley College
1927	Leicester	George Armitage	Dartford
1928	Southport	John G. Bowran	Newcastle-upon-Tyne II
1929	Tunstall	John H. Saxton	Northampton
1930	Bradford	W. Musson Kelley	Bournemouth I
1931	Derby	Edward McLellan	Southport
1932	Middlesbrough	William Younger	Hull VIII

PRIMITIVE METHODIST — VICE PRESIDENTS OF THE CONFERENCE

The office of Vice-President of the Conference was begun in 1872, and the constitution permitted either a minister or layman to be elected.

1872	Revd. Samuel Antliff
1873	Revd. Thomas Newall
1874	Revd. George Lamb
1875	Revd. Thomas Smith
1876	Mr. George Charlton
1877	Revd. Henry Phillips
1878	Revd. Thomas Newall
1879	Revd. Colin C. McKechnie
1880	Revd. Michael Clarke
1881	Revd. Thomas Wood
1882	Revd. William Cutts
1883	Revd. Thomas Southron
1884	Mr. Thomas Bateman
1885	Mr. Thomas Lawrence
1886	Mr. Henry Hodge
1887	Mr. John Coward
1888	Mr. Henry Adams
1889	Mr. John Caton
1890	Mr. Elijah Jennings
1891	Mr. Robert Clapham
1892	Mr. William P. Hartley
1893	Mr. John Jones
1894	Mr. Thomas Robinson
1895	Mr. William E. Parker
1896	Mr. Levi E. Morse
1897	Mr. William McNeil
1898	Mr. William Glass
1999	Mr. William Windsor
1900	Mr. Adam Adams
1901	Mr. Robert Foster
1902	Mr. Frederick C. Lindfield
1903	Mr. James Bell
1904	Mr. George Green
1905	Mr. Edmund C. Rawlings
1906	Mr. Stephen Hilton
1907	Mr. Richard Fletcher

1908	Mr. Mark Harrison	1917	Mr. James Gray	1926	Mr. Moses Bourne
1909	Revd. John Welford	1918	Mr. Charles Lewis	1927	Mr. James W. Arnold
1910	Mr. James Sivil	1919	Mr. Harvey Robinson	1928	Mr. William E. Clegg
1911	Mr. Tom Fletcher	1920	Mr. Joseph Longstaff	1929	Mr. William H. Hawthorne
1912	Mr. Ernest H. Brown	1921	Mr. Charles K. Watkinson	1930	Mr. Charles Wass
1913	Mr. William M. Patterson	1922	Mr. Thomas L. Gerrard	1931	Mr. James Black
1914	Mr. Henry Speed	1923	Sir Thomas Robinson, K.B.E.	1932	Mr. A. Victor Murray, M.A., B.Litt.
1915	Mr. Charles S. Parkin	1924	Mr. James Skinner		
1916	Mr. Albert Shaw	1925	Mr. W. Ewart Morse		

PRIMITIVE METHODIST CONNEXION — CONNEXIONAL COMMITTEE SECRETARIES

The constitution of the Primitive Methodist Connexion did not provide for a number of separate Connexional Departments. In most cases a number of Departments were grouped together with one Secretary over the whole. The General Connexional Committee had oversight over all the Committees. In order to save confusion I have indicated the changes as they have occured and added notes.

MISSIONARY COMMITTEE

1834-1848 John Garner
1848-1854 William Garner
1854-1859 John Bywater
1859-1865 Moses Lupton
1865-1869 Thomas Jobling
1869-1874 Samuel Antliff, D.D.
1874-1878 William Rowe
1878-1883 William Cutts
1883-1889 John Atkinson
1889-1894 James Travis
1894-1899 John Smith
1899-1902 Richard W. Burnett
1902-1903 John Slater
1903-1908 James Pickett
1908-1913 Arthur T. Guttery, D.D.
1913-1918 Samuel Horton
1918-1923 Joseph T. Barkby
1923-1928 John H. Hirst
1938-1932 George Ayre

GENERAL CONNEXIONAL COMMITTEE

(Up to 1864 the Missionary Secretary was also the Secretary of the General Connexional Committee)

1865-1869 James Garner
1869-1874 Robert Smith
1874-1879 Charles Smith
1879-1884 Robert Cheeseman
1884-1889 Thomas Whitehead
1889-1894 John Wenn
1894-1899 William Goodman
1899-1904 John Hallam
1904-1909 John Welford
1909-1914 John D. Thompson
1914-1919 Matthew P. Davison
1919-1924 George Armitage
1924-1929 W. Musson Kelley
1929-1932 Jacob Walton

HOME MISSIONS COMMITTEE

(From 1864 till 1924 the Missionary Secretary was also General Superintendent of Home Missions)

1924-1929 William J. Ward
1929-1932 George E. Wiles

CHURCH EXTENSION COMMITTEE

1906-1909 Thomas Mitchell, D.D.

CHURCH EXTENSION AND CHAPEL COMMITTEE

1906-1909 Thomas Mitchell, D.D.
1909-1914 Henry J. Taylor
1914-1919 John Mayles
1919-1924 Arthur Baldwin

From 1924 to 1932 the Home Mission Secretary became responsible for this Committee.

SUNDAY SCHOOL COMMITTEE

1875-1882 Joseph Wood, D.D.
1882-1887 Thomas Whittaker, D.D.
1887-1892 Joseph Ferguson, D.D.
1892-1897 Thomas H. Hunt
1897-1902 Dnazy Sheen
1902-1907 Samuel H. Henshaw
1907-1912 George Bennett
1912-1917 William Spedding
1917-1922 German Hunt
1922-1927 Samuel Palmer
1927-1932 John W. Clifford, M.A.

THE PRIMITIVE METHODIST CONNEXION — BOOK STEWARDS AND CONNEXIONAL EDITORS

BOOK STEWARDS

1820-1838 James Bourne
1838-1846 John Hallam
1843-1848 Thomas Holliday (Assistant)
1846-1848 Thomas Holliday and William Garner
1848-1854 Thomas Holliday
1854-1858 Thomas King
1859-1860 John Day
1859-1865 Richard Davies
1865-1870 William Lister
1870-1875 George Lamb
1875-1880 John Dickenson
1880-1885 Ralph Fenwick
1885-1890 Joseph Toulson
1890-1895 James B. Knapp
1895-1900 Thomas Mitchell
1900-1905 Robert Bryant
1905-1910 Edwin Dalton
1910-1915 William Hammond
1915-1920 Joseph Johnson
1920-1921 Matthew T. Pickering
1921-1926 Wilfred R. Wilkinson
1926-1931 John Swinden
1931-1932 Ernest Barrett, M.A.

CONNEXIONAL EDITORS

1819-1842 Hugh Bourne
1842-1852 John Flesher
1851-1852 John Petty (Assistant)
1852-1857 John Petty
1857-1862 William Harland
1862-1867 William Antliff
1867-1871 Philip Pugh
1871-1876 James Macpherson
1876-1887 Colin C. McKechnie
1887-1892 Thomas Newall
1897-1901 H. Bickerstaffe Kendall, B.A.
1901-1906 Henry Youll
1906-1911 Joseph Ritson
1911-1916 J. Dodd Jackson
1916-1921 John G. Bowran
1921-1926 Edward McLellan
1926-1931 Joseph C. Mantripp
1931-1932 B. Aquila Barber

PUBLICATIONS OF THE PRIMITIVE METHODIST BOOK ROOM

1818-1819 A Methodist Magazine
1820-1899 The Primitive Methodist Magazine
1900-1932 The Aldersgate and Primitive Methodist Magazine

1824-1851	The Primitive Methodist Children's Magazine
1852-1900	The Primitive Methodist Juvenile Magaaine
1901-1932	Morning
1832-1913	The Primitive Methodist Preacher's Magazine
1914-1932	The Primitive Methodist Preacher's and Class Leader's Magazine
1865-1932	The Christian Messenger
1865-1914	The Child's Friend
1873-1895	The Teacher's Assistant
1896-1907	The Sunday School Journal and Teacher's Magazine
1908-1913	The Teacher and Preacher
1914-1932	The Primitive Methodist Sunday School Magazine
1886-1929	Springtime
1892-1896	Joyful Tidings
1897-1903	Joyful Tidings and PSA Messenger
1923-1932	Advance

THE HARTLEY LECTURE

The Hartley Lecture founded in 1896. Mr. William P. Hartley, of Liverpool provided for a Connexional Lectureship by donating ten guineas per annum for twenty years or by investing such sum with the Chapel Aid Association as will with interest provide the required amount. The Conference was responsible for making arrangements for the delivery of the Lecture as some time during the sitting of the Conference. Ten guineas was given to the Lecturer as an honorarium, but if the lecture was subsequently published, the manuscript was considered to be the property of the Primitive Methodist Connexion. The first Lecture was delivered at the Manchester Conference in 1897.

Year	Lecture	Lecturer
1897	The Holy Spirit	James Feruson, D.D.
1898	The Fatherhood of God	John Watson, D.D.
1899	Inspiration and Revelation	Robert Bryant
1900	Christ and Mission	John Smith
1901	Christ's Kingdom and the Church	H. Bickerstaffe Kendell, B.A.
1902	The Sabbath	Robert G. Graham
1903	Evangelism	Joseph Odell, M.A.
1904	The Problem of Suffering in the Old Testament	Professor Arthur S. Peake, M.A.
1905	Christian Beneficence	Thomas Mitchell, D.D.
1906	The Ethics of Evangelism	Henry Yooll
1907	The Doctrine of Immortality	John D. Thompson
1908	The New Testament Portrait of Jesus	George Parkin, M.A., B.D.
1909	The Romance of Primitive Methodism	John Ritson
1910	Sin and the Preacher	Robert Hind
1911	The Holy Spirit in Faith and Experience	A. Lewis Humphries, M.A.
1912	The Message and the Man	A. Dodd Jackson
1913	The Missionary Crisis	James Pickett
1914	The Permanent Values of Religion	Francis H. Simmin
1915	The Supreme Quest	James P. Langham
1916-1918	NO LECTURES	—
1919	The Revelation of St. John	Professor Arthur S. Peake, M.A., D.D.
1920	Conversion	Arthur T. Guttery, D.D.
1921	The Challenge of Freedom	Henry J. Taylor
1922	The Hebrew Prophets and the Modern Teacher	Henry J. Pickett
1923	Christianity and Culture	John G. Bowran
1924	The International View of Christian Ethics	William Younger
1925	Israel and Babylon	W. Lansdell Wardle, M.A., D.D.
1926	The Golden Stool	Edwin Smith
1927	Society, The Art of Living Together	Professor Atkinson Lee, M.A.
1928	Religious Experience	Wilfred R. Wilkinson
1929	Jesus the Reformer	Edward McLellan
1930	The Evangelism of Today	Robert Ferguson
1931	The Faith of a Christian	Joseph C. Mantripp
1932	The Oldest Versions of the Bible	Henry G. Meecham, M.A., B.D., Ph.D.

PRIMITIVE METHODIST CONNEXIONAL INSTITUTIONS

For some years the Conference discussed the possibility of a school for the sons of the ministers and the better-off parents of the Connexion. In 1863 the Conference authorised a Committee to seek for suitable premises, and they acquired a house in York which the previous owners had called "Elmfield", hence Elmfield College. After extensive rebuilding and renovation it was opened in 1864.

SCHOOLS

ELMFIELD COLLEGE (BOYS)

GOVERNORS

1864-1868	John Petty
1869-1880	Thomas Smith
1880-1889	Robert Smith
1889-1891	Robert Harrison
1891-1896	George Seaman
1896-1901	John Gair
1901-1904	William E. Crombie
1904-1907	George F. Fawcett

HEADMASTERS

1864-1871	J. K. Dall, LL.D.
1871-1878	W. J. Russell
1878-1879	Revd. J. M. Raby, B.A., B.Sc., LL.D.
1879-1886	Revd. T. Gough, B.A., B.Sc.
1886-1892	W. Johnson, B.A.B.Sc.
1892-1907	R. G. Heys, B.A.
1907-1929	S. R. Slack, B.A.
1929-1932	Revd. H. D. Anthony, M.A., B.Sc., Ph.D.

There was a dual control system of a Resident Governor and a Headmaster from 1864 until 1907. In 1932 Elmfield amalgamated with the former United Methodist school, Ashville College, Harrogate.

The first real attempt of theological training for candidates for the Primitive Methodist ministry was to send a small number into their Secondary School for Boys, Elmfield College, York, under the supervision of the Governor of the college, the Revd. John Petty, in 1865. While better than nothing, it was not a very satisfactory arrangement. In 1868 a building was purchased in Sunderland, which became known as the Sunderland Institution. In 1881 a second Institution was built in Manchester, and in 1883 the Sunderland Institute was closed. In 1897 and in 1906 extensive enlargements were made to the Manchester premises, largely through the genoristy of Mr. William P. Hartley, and in recognition of this it became known as Hartley College.

ELMFIELD COLLEGE

1865-1868	John Petty

SUNDERLAND INSTITUTE

Principals

1868-1881	William Antliff, D.D.
1881-1883	Thomas Greenfield

TUTOR

1877-1881	Thomas Greenfield

MANCHESTER INSTITUTE, 1881-1906
HARTLEY COLLEGE, 1906-1932

PRINCIPALS

1881-1889	James Macpherson
1889-1893	James Wood, D.D.
1893-1898	John Wilson, D.D.
1898-1903	George Parkin, M.A., B.D.
1903-1908	William Johnson
1908-1913	W. Jones Davies
1913-1916	Henry J. Pickett
1918-1923	James Lockhart
1923-1928	Henry J. Pickett
1928-1932	W. Lansdell Wardell, M.A., D.D.

TUTORS

1899-1902	James Macphearson
1892-1929	Professor Arthur S. Peake, M.A., D.D.
1902-1932	A. Lewis Humphries, M.A.
1903-1928	W. Lansdell Wardle, M.A., D.D.
1908-1932	Professor Atkinson Lee, M.A.
1930-1932	Henry G. Meecham, M.A., B.D., Ph. D.

NOTES

Professors Arthur S. Peake and Atkinson Lee were lay tutors. Dr. Peake covered a very wide range of subjects. Dr. Wardle was an Old Testament scholar, and Mr. Lewis and Dr. Meecham New Testament. Professor Lee was responsible for Philosophy or Religion.

THE BIBLE CHRISTIAN METHODISTS: 1815-1907
PRESIDENTS OF THE CONFERENCE

Year	Place	President	Station or Appointment
1819	Launceston	William O'Bryan	General Superintendent
1820	Launceston	William O'Bryan, 2nd time	General Superintendent
1821	Shebbear	William O'Bryan, 3rd time	General Superintendent
1822	Stoke Damerel	William O'Bryan, 4th time	General Superintendent
1823	Stoke Damerel	William O'Bryan, 5th time	General Superintendent
1824	Stoke Damerel	William O'Bryan, 6th time	General Superintendent
1825	Stoke Damerel	William O'Bryan, 7th time	General Superintendent
1826	Cawsand	William O'Bryan, 8th time	General Superintendent
1827	Stoke Damerel	William O'Bryan, 9th time	Devonport
1828	Shebbear	William Mason	Luxillian
1829	Shebbear	Andrew Cory	Luxillian
1830	Shebbear	Harry Major	Shebbear
1831	Hicks Mill	James Thorne	Kilkhampton and Canworthywater
1832		William Reed	Shebbear
1833	Burrington	Richard Sedwell	Shebbear
1834	Langtree	William Coutice	St. Ervan
1835	Shebbear	James Thorne, 2nd time	Shebbear, Book Steward
1836	St. Austell	Paul Robins	Kingsbrompton and Taunton Mission
1837	Langtree	William Reed, 2nd time	Holsworthy
1838	St. Austell	James Brooks	Shebbear
1839	Langtree	Richard Sedwell, 2nd time	Isle of Wight
1840	Langtree	Richard Kinsman	Shebbear
1841	Langtree	William Richards	Milverton and Taunton Mission
1842	Truro	James Thorne, 3rd time	Shebbear, Book Steward
1843	Shebbear	Paul Robins, 2nd time	St. Austell
1844	St. Austell	Henry Reed	Ringsash
1845	Holsworthy	William Reed, 3rd time	Liskeard
1846	Devonport	Matthew Robins	Holsworthy
1847	Langtree	James Way	Torrington
1848	Brentor	Richard P. Tabb	Launceston
1849	Plymouth	Jacob H. Prior	Shebbear
1850	Shebbear	Francis Martin	Portsea
1851	Hicks Mill	Richard Kinsman, 2nd time	Devonport
1852	Southsea	Matthew Robins, 2nd time	St. Austell
1853	Exeter	James Ching	Ringsash
1854	Morchard Bishop	Robert Kent	Isle of Wight, West
1855	Plymouth	William Reed, 4th time	Tawstone and North Devon
1856	Newport, Isle of Wight	William Cautice, 2nd time	Rackenford
1857	Bideford	James Thorne, 4th time	Shebbear, Book Steward
1858	Devonport	James Hinks	Bristol
1859	London	John Gammon	Faversham
1860	Exeter	Matthew Robins, 3rd time	Penzance
1861	Hicks Mill	Thomas W. Garland	Devonport
1862	Southsea	William Hopper	Shebbear
1863	Bideford	John Brown	Devonport
1864	Plymouth	William Luke	Southampton
1865	Exeter	James Thorn, 5th time	Shebbear, Book Steward
1866	Portsmouth	Matthew Robins, 4th time	Portland
1867	St. Austell	Frederick W. Bourne	Devonport
1868	Shebbear	Thomas P. Oliver (A)	Launceston
1869	Bristol	Robert Blackmore	Holsworthy
1870	Plymouth	William Gilbert	Portsmouth
1871	Hicks Mill	William J. Hocking	Abervan
1872	Bideford	William Rowe	Hicks Mill
1873	Portsmouth	Isaac B. Vanstone	London, Woolwich and Forest Hill
1874	London	John Tremelling	London

Year	Place	President	Station or Appointment
1875	Exeter	Frederick W. Bourne, 2nd time	London
1876	St. Austell	John Gammon, 2nd time	Shebbear, School Govenor
1877	Torquay	Thomas C. Penwarden	Chagford
1878	Southsea	John C. Honey	Portsmouth
1879	Truro	John Dymond	Devonport
1880	Bristol	James Horwill	Bideford
1881	Newport, Isle of Wight	William B. Reed	Exeter
1882	Plymouth	William B. Lark	Portsmouth
1883	Exeter	Peter Labdon	Shanklin
1884	London	John Martin	London, Kilburn
1885	Bideford	William Bray	Newport, Monmouth
1886	Southsea	Alexander Trengrove	Plymouth
1887	Swansea	John H. Batt	Torrington
1888	London	John O. Keen, D.D.	London, Forest Hill
1889	Holsworthy	Mark Brokenshire	Bristol
1890	Penzance	William Higman	Taunton
1891	Plymouth	Frederick W. Bourne, 3rd time	London, Clapham
1892	Newport, Isle of Wight	William Lee	Kilkhampton
1893	St. Austell	James Woolcock	Newport and Ryde
1894	Bristol	Samuel Allin	Exeter
1895	Barnstaple	John Thorne	London (Without Pastoral Charge)
1896	Southsea	Daniel Murley	Bideford
1897	Exeter	Alexander Trengrove, 2nd time	London, Jubilee
1898	Cardiff	William B. Lark, 2nd time	Abaravan
1899	Holsworthy	Thomas Braund	Shebbear (Supernumerary)
1900	Penzance	John Luke	Barnstaple
1901	Plymouth	John Luke, 2nd time	Barnstaple
1902	London	John Dale	Neath
1903	Newport, Isle of Wight	Arthur Hancock	Plymouth
1904	St. Austell	William R. K. Baulkwill	Newport and Ryde
1905	Exeter	Samuel R. Lane	Brighton
1906	Plymouth	John B. Stedeford	Bideford
1907	Portsmouth	William B. Lark, 3rd time	Shebbear, School Governor

BIBLE CHRISTIAN METHODISTS — SECRETARIES OF THE CONFERENCE

1819-1830	James Thorne
1831	William Reed
1832-1834	James Thorne
1835	Paul Robins
1836	Edward Hocken
1837	Richard Kinsman
1838	Paul Robins
1839-1840	William Reed
1841-1842	Paul Robins
1843	Richard Kinsman
1844-1845	Matthew Robins
1846	William Reed
1847	Henry Reed
1848	Jacob H. Prior
1849-1850	William Reed
1851	Jacob H. Prior
1852	William Reed
1853	James Thorne
1854	Richard Kinsman
1855-1856	Matthew Robins
1857	James Hinks
1858	Matthew Robins
1859	James Hinks
1860	William Luke
1861-1865	William Gilbert
1866-1867	Thomas P. Oliver (A)
1868	Robert Blackmore
1869-1870	Isaac B. Vanstone
1871	William Rowe
1872	Isaac B. Vanstone
1873	Samuel Jory
1874	James Horwill
1875-1876	John Dymond
1877	John C. Honey
1878-1879	William B. Reed
1880-1881	William B. Lark
1882	Peter Labdon
1883	John Martin
1884	William Lee
1885	Alexander Trengrove
1886	John H. Batt
1887	John O. Keen, D.D.
1888	Mark Brokenshire
1889	William Higman
1890	Frederick W. Bourne
1891-1892	James Woolcock
1893	Samuel Allin
1894-1895	Danile Murley
1896-1899	John Luke
1900	Thomas E. Munday
1901-1904	Samuel B. Luke
1905-1907	James H. Blackwell

CONNEXIONAL COMMITTEEE SECRETARIES

In 1821 the Conference appointed a General Missionary Committee, and in 1847 its work was more clearly defined with the appointment of a Secretary for the Home work, and one for Foreign.

GENERAL COMMITTEE: 1821-1847

1821-1822	William O'Bryan
1822-1823	James Thorne
1823-1825	Harry Major
1825-1826	William O'Bryan
1826-1827	William Mason
1827-1828	James Thorne
1828-1829	William O'Bryan
1829-1830	William Grigg
1830-1831	John H. Eynon
1831-1833	William Reed
1833-1834	Andrew Cory
1834-1836	Harry Major
1836-1837	Edward Hocken
1837-1839	James Thorne
1839-1841	Jacob H. Prior
1841-1842	Richard Kinsman
1842-1843	Henry Reed
1843-1844	Richard P. Tabb
1844-1846	Paul Robins
1846-1847	James Thorne

HOME MISSIONS. 1847-1907

1847-1851	Paul Robins
1851-1854	Jacob H. Prior
1854-1856	Cephas Barker
1856-1859	Robert Blackmore
1859-1866	Frederick W. Bourne
1866-1871	William Luke
1871-1886	John Tremelling
1886-1896	William J. Hocking
1896-1899	John Dymond
1899-1902	Samuel Allin
1902-1907	Arthur Hancock

FOREIGN MISSIONS: 1847-1907

1847-1848	James Thorne
1848-1849	James Wray
1849-1850	James Thorne
1850-1851	Jacob H. Prior
1851-1855	William Reed
1855-1856	Richard Kinsman
1856-1863	Jacob H. Prior
1863-1885	William Gilbert
1885-1904	Isaac B. Vanstone
1904-1907	Charles Stedeford

CHAPEL COMMITTEE: 1825-1907

1825-1826	Harry Major
1826-1827	James Thorne
1827-1828	Edward Hocken
1828-1829	John Adams

1829-1830	James Ford	1835-1836	John Thorne, Jun.	1842-1846	Paul Robins
1830-1831	William Daniel	1836-1837	James Straddon	1846-1849	Cephas Barker
1831-1832	Henry Reed	1837-1839	Richard Kinsman	1849-1879	James Hinks
1832-1834	James Thorne	1839-1841	Matthew Robins	1879-1899	Alexander Trengrove
1834-1835	James Straddon	1841-1842	Jacob H. Prior	1899-1907	John Luke

BOOK STEWARDS AND CONNEXIONAL EDITORS

BOOK STEWARDS

1819-1823	William O'Bryan
1823-1825	Samuel Thorne
1825-1826	Harry Major
1826-1827	Edmund Warne
1827-1837	Samuel Thorne
1837-1869	James Thorne
1869-1888	Frederick W. Bourne
1881-1882	Isaac B. Vanstone (Associate)
1888-1898	Alexander Trengrove
1898-1905	George Daniel
1905-1907	William H. Gregory
1901-1903	Cooper G. Hawken (Associate)

CONNEXIONAL EDITORS

1822-1828	William O'Bryan
1823-1828	James Thorne (Assistant)
1828-1869	James Thorne
1861-1866	Frederick W. Bourne (Assistant)
1866-1869	Frederick W. Bourne (Associate)
1869-1900	Frederick W. Bourne
1896-1900	Herbert W. Horwill, M.A. (Assistant)
1900-1907	John H. Batt

PUBLICATIONS OF THE BIBLE CHRISTIAN METHODIST BOOK ROOM

1822-1828	The Arminian Magazine
1829-1907	The Bible Christian Magazine
1825-1848	A Young People's Magazine
1849-1883	The Youth's Penny Miscellany
1884-1893	The Youth's Miscellany
1894-1907	The Young People's Magazine

CONNEXIONAL INSTITUTIONS

SHEBBEAR COLLEGE FOR BOYS

GOVERNORS

1841-1870	James Thorne
1870-1873	Robert Blackmore
1873-1885	John Gammon
1885-1899	John Martin
1899-1907	Robert Spencer

HEADMASTERS

1841-1842	Revd. H. C. O'Donohue, M.A.
1842-1864	No Record
1864-1907	Mr. Thomas Ruddle, B.A.

EDGEHILL COLLEGE FOR GIRLS

GOVERNORS

1883-1907	William B. Reed

HEADMISTRESSES

1884-1890	Miss R. A. Wooldridge (Miss Wooldridge married the Revd. William B. Reed, 1890)
1890-1907	Mrs. William B. Reed

The Bible Christians had no College for the specific training of its ministers. Some received instruction under the supervision of the Governor of Shebbear College, for one or two years.

PRESIDENTS OF THE WESLEYAN PROTESTANT METHODIST YEARLY MEETING: 1829-1836

Year	Place	President
1829	Leeds	Mr. James Sigston
1830	Leeds	Mr. Joseph Blythman
1831	Sheffield	Mr. George Turton
1832	Leeds	Mr. Matthew Johnson
1833	Leeds	Mr. James Sigston
1834	Preston	Mr. George Slater
1835	Leeds	Mr. George Cookman

SECRETARIES OF THE WESLEYAN PROTESTANT METHODIST YEARLY MEETING: 1829-1836

1829	Mr. Joah Mallinson and Mr. Matthew Johnson
1830-1831	Mr. Matthew Johnson
1832	Mr. Joseph Blythman
1833	Mr. Matthew Johnson
1834	*Mr. Joseph Blythman
1835	Mr. Matthew Johnson

* Joseph Blythman entered the Wesleyan Protestant ministry in 1835.

There was no Book Room, but there was a Wesleyan Protestant Methodist Magazine 1829-1835.

PRESIDENTS OF THE WESLEYAN METHODIST ASSOCIATION ASSEMBLY: 1836-1856

Year	Place	President	Station or Appointment
1836	Manchester	SAmuel Warren, LL.D.	Manchester
1837	Liverpool	Mr. James Livesey	
1838	Rochdale	James Molineux	Rochdale
1839	Leeds	Mr. James Sigston	
1840	Manchester	Mr. David Rowland	
1841	Liverpool	Robert Eckett	London, Connexional Editor
1842	Rochdale	Thomas Townend	Darlington
1843	Leeds	John Peters	Sunderland
1844	Manchester	Enoch Darke	Birmingham
1845	Liverpool	James Molineux, 2nd time	Bury and Bolton
1846	Rochdale	Robert Eckett, 2nd time	London, Connexional Editor
1847	Leeds	Robert Eckett, 3rd time	London, Connexional Editor
1848	Manchester	Henry Breedon	Salford
1849	Liverpool	George Smith	Liverpool
1850	Rochdale	William Patterson	Northwich
1851	Leeds	John Peters, 2nd time	Manchester, Grosvenor Street
1852	Manchester	Thomas A. Bayley	Liverpool
1853	Liverpool	Enoch Darke, 2nd time	Leeds
1854	Rochdale	Anthony Gilbert	Manchester, Lever Stret
1855	Manchester	William Dawson	Leeds
1856	Leeds	Matthew Baxter	London, Connexional Editor

SECRETARIES OF THE WESLEYAN METHODIST ASSOCIATION ASSEMBLY: 1836-1856

1836-1837	Mr. Matthew Johnson	1841	Mr. John Kipling	1847	John Peters
1838	Mr. Richard Farrar	1842-1843	Mr. Matthew Johnson	1848-1853	Robert Eckett
1839	James Molinuex	1844-1845	Robert Eckett	1854	Thomas A. Bayley
1840	Robert Eckett	1846	Mr. John Kipling	1855-1856	Robert Eckett

BOOK STEWARDS AND CONNEXIONAL EDITORS

BOOK STEWARDS

1838-1840	*James Jones
1840-1841	George Chesson
1841-1846	Emmanuel Pearson
1846-1850	Richard Abercrombie
1850-1854	Robert Eckett
1854-1855	Thomas A. Bayley
1855-1857	Matthew Baxter

CONNEXIONAL EDITORS

1838-1840	*James Jones
1840-1852	Robert Eckett
1852-1858	Thomas A. Bayley
1855-1857	Matthew Baxter

* James Jones was a layman and held both offices and conducted the affairs from Horseshoe Court, Ludgate Hill, London. At the time it is very probable that a minister could not be spared.

WESLEYAN METHODIST ASSOCIATION PUBLICATIONS

1834-1835	The Watchman's Lanters
1838-1857	The Wesleyan Methodist Association Magazine

PRESIDENTS OF THE UNITED METHODIST FREE CHURCHES: 1857-1907

The United Methodist Free Churches was the name chosen when the Wesleyan Methodist Association (1836), amalgamated with the Wesleyan Reformers (1849).

Year	Place	President	Station or Appointment
1857	Rochdale	James Everett	Newcastle-upon-Tyne
1858	London	Robert Eckett	London, Missionary Secretary
1859	Sheffield	John Mann	Norwich
1860	Manchester	Thomas Hacking	Bristol
1861	Leeds	Samuel S. Barton	Rochdale
1862	Bristol	William Reed	London I
1863	Rochdale	John Gutteridge	Sheffield, Mout Tabor
1864	Manchester	Joseph Coleman	Scarborough
1865	Nottingham	William R. Brown	Bury
1866	Sheffield	Thomas Newton	Exeter
1867	Manchester	Richard Chew	Newcastle-upon-Tyne
1868	Louth	Marmaduke Miller	Huddersfield, Brunswick Street
1869	Sunderland	John Mather	Newcastle-upon-Tyne
1870	Leeds	John Myers	Leeds, West
1871	London	Edward Boaden	Haslingdon
1872	Bristol	John S. Withington	Leeds, Lady Lane
1873	Rochdale	John Adcock	Bradford
1874	Newcastle-upon-Tyne	Joseph Garside	Louth
1875	Nottingham	Joseph Kirsop	Norwich
1876	Sheffield	Thomas M. Booth	Rochdale, Baillie Street
1877	Louth	Anthony Holliday	Huddersfield, Brunswick Street
1878	Manchester	William Boyden	Burnley
1879	Sunderland	Thomas W. Townend	Oldham
1880	Leeds	William Hunter	Bristol, North
1881	London	Richard Chew, 2nd time	Lincoln, Silver Street
1882	Bristol	Arthur Hands	Harrogate
1883	Rochdale	Mr. Henry T. Mawson	
1884	Newcastle-upon-Tyne	Edwin Askew	Derby, Beckett Street
1885	Nottingham	Alfred Jones (A)	Huddersfield, Brunswick Street
1886	Sheffield	Thomas Sherwood	Heywood
1887	Louth	James S. Balmer	Blackpool
1888	Manchester	Thomas Wakefield	Leeds, West
1889	Redruth	Ralph Abercrombie, M.A.	Shrewsbury
1890	Leeds	Matthias T. Myers	Rochdale, Baillie Street
1891	Sunderland	Matthias T. Myers	Rochdale, Baillie Street
1892	London	John Truscott (A)	Burslem
1893	Bristol	Samuel Wright	Lincoln, Silver Street
1894	Rochdale	Mr. James Duckworth	
1895	Norwich	William R. Sunman	Burton-on-Trent
1896	Newcastle-upon-Tyne	George Turner	Sheffield, Hanover
1897	Nottingham	Robert Swallow, M.D.	On Furlough from China
1898	Lincoln	Ebenezer D. Cornish	Manchester IV
1899	Sheffield	James C. Brewitt	Cleckheaton
1900	Manchester	Frederick Galpin	Clitheroe
1901	Redruth	David Brook, M.A., D.C.L.	Southport, Duke Street
1902	Leeds	William Redfern	Wakefield
1903	Sunderland	W. H. Cory Harris	Manchester IV
1904	London	Jabez King	Norwich
1905	Rochdale	Thomas J. Dickinson	Rochdale, Castlemere
1906	Bristol	David Irving, M.A., D.C.L.	West Hartlepool
1907	Newcastle-upon-Tyne	William Barnes	Farsley and Pudsey

It was constituionally allowable for a Layman to be elected President of the Assembly, but only two were elected, 1883 and 1894.

UNITED METHODIST FREE CHURCHES
SECRETARIES OF THE CONFERENCE

1857	Robert Eckett
1858	William Reed
1859	Robert Eckett
1860	Matthew Baxter
1861-1863	Joseph Coleman
1864-1865	Marmaduke Miller
1866	Richard Chew
1867-1868	John Myers
1869-1870	Robert Bushell
1871	John S. Withington
1872	John Adcock
1873-1874	Anthony Holliday
1875	Thomas M. Booth
1876-1877	William Boyden
1878	Thomas W. Towend
1879	John Adcock
1880-1883	Edwin Askew
1884-1885	Thomas Sherwood
1886	John S. Balmer
1887-1888	George Turner
1889	Matthias T. Myers
1890-1891	John Truscott (A)
1892-1894	William R. Sunman
1895-1897	Ebenezer D. Cornish
1898	James C. Brewitt
1899	Jabez King
1900-1902	W. H. Cory Harris
1903-1904	Thomas J. Dickinson
1905	David Irving, M.A., D.C.L.
1906	William Barnes
1907	John Baxter

SECRETARIES OF CONNEXIONAL COMMITTEES

GENERAL MISSIONARY COMMITTEE

1860-1862	Robert Eckett
1862-1871	Samuel S. Barton
1871-1881	Robert Bushell
1881-1889	John Adcock
1889-1895	George Turner
1895-1904	Henry T. Chapman

Until 1904 this Committee was responsible for Home and Foreign Missions.

FOREIGN MISSIONS

1904-1907 Henry T. Chapman

HOME MISSIONS

1904-1907 John Moore

CHAPEL COMMITTEE

1857-1859	Samuel S. Barton
1859-1863	Marmaduke Miller
1863-1901	Edward Boaden
1901-1907	Ebenezer D. Cornish

LONDON MISSION AND EXTENSION

1877-1879	George Lowndes
1879-1882	Charles Worboys
1882-1885	Richard E. Abercrombie
1885-1891	John Roberts (A)
1891-1893	Jabez King
1893-1896	George Lowndes
1896-1897	Edward C. Dinsley
1897-1906	Henry Mann
1906-1907	John Moore

FREE METHODIST TEMPERANCE LEAGUE

1880-1882	James S. Balmer
1882-1904	John Thornley
1904-1907	John B. Stonman

BOOK STEWARDS AND CONNEXIONAL EDITORS

BOOK STEWARDS

1857-1860	Matthew Baxter
1860-1871	William Reed
1871-1875	Thomas Barlow
1875-1883	Thomas Newton
1883-1907	Andrew Crombie

CONNEXIONAL EDITORS

1857-1860	Matthew Baxter
1860-1871	William Reed
1871-1875	Marmaduke Miller
1875-1877	Thomas Newton
1877-1883	J. Swann Withington
1883-1892	Ralph Abercrombie
1892-1907	Andrew Crombie

UNITED METHODIST FREE CHURCHES PUBLICATIONS

1858-1891	The United Methodist Free Churches Magazine
1892-1907	The Methodists Monthly
1867-1891	Welcome Words
1885-1894	The Brooklet

CONNEXIONAL INSTITUTIONS

Ministerial training in the United Methodist Free Churches began in 1871. The first Institution House was in Stockport Road, Manchester. In 1875 three adjoining houses were purchased and adapted in the area of Victoria Park, Manchester, hence the name of the College.

VICTORIA PARK COLLEGE

PRINCIPALS AND RESIDENT TUTORS

1871-1881	Thomas Hacking
1882-1895	Anthony Holliday
1897-1907	Thomas Sherwood

During the whole period the Principal was assisted by part-time lecturers. Some of the students later were able to attend Owens College, the forerunner of Manchester University. Among those who served the College at various times were: the Revds. Ralph Abercrombie, Arthur T. Jones, M.A., D.Litt., Joseph Kirsop, William Redfern, John Taylor (A), J. Twigg Taylor, and two notable laymen, Professor Arthur S. Peake, M.A., D.D., and Dr. R. J. Lloyd, M.A.

ASHVILLE COLLEGE (Boarding School, Boys)

HEADMASTERS

1877-1890	Mr. William Richardson, B.A., LL.D.
1890-1905	Mr. John Bowick, M.A., LL.D.
1905-1907	Revd. Alfred Soothill, B.A.

THE DEACONESS INSTITUTE

WARDENS

1891-1907 Thomas J. Cope

THE UNITED METHODIST CHURCH: 1907-1932
PRESIDENTS OF THE CONFERENCE

The United Methodist Church was formed by the union of the Methodist New Connexion (1797), the Bible Christians (1815), and the United Methodist Free Churches (1857).

Year	Place	President	Station or Appointment
1907	London	Edward Boaden	Leamington (Supernumerary)
1908	Sheffield	William J. Townsend, D.D.	Hawarden (Supernumerary)
1909	Plymouth	William B. Lark	Stratton and Bude
1910	Nottingham	Henry T. Chapman	Leeds, Lady Jane
1911	Manchester	George Packer, D.D.	Leeds, Connexional Secretary
1912	Hanley	John Luke	Todmorden
1913	Halifax	William Redfern	Bristol

1914	Redruth	George Parker	Sheffield, Assessments Funds Office
1915	Exeter	John B. Stedeford	Hull, Bethel
1916	Rochdale	Thomas J. Cox	Bristol, South
1917	Sheffield	James Wright	Bristol West
1918	Leeds	John W. Walls	Huddersfield, High Street
1919	Bristol	John Moore	Nottingham, Home Missions Department
1920	London	Henry Smith	London, Army and Navy Chaplains Committee
1921	Newcastle-upon-Tyne	William Treffry	Plymouth
1922	Birmingham	Ernest H. F. Capey	Whitley Bay
1923	Huddersfield	Charles Pye	Cardiff, Newport Road
1924	Plymouth	Joseph Lineham, B.A., Ph.D.	Newcastle-upon-Tyne
1925	Manchester	W. Alexander Grist	Bristol
1926	Nottingham	Henry James	Ashton-under-Lyne
1927	Rochdale	Richard Pyke	Plymouth
1928	Hanley	Charles Stedeford	Birmingham, Missionary Society
1929	Halifax	R. H. Bowden Shapland	Burton-on-Trent
1930	Sheffield	Arthur E. J. Cosson	London, Lee
1931	Redruth	J. Ford Reed	Shebbear College
1932	Kingswood	William C. Jackson, M.A.	Manchester, Chapel Committee

SECRETARIES OF THE CONFERENCE

1907	Revd. George Packer, D.D.
1908-1910	Revd. John Baxter
1911	Mr. William S. Skelton
1912	Mr. John E. Le Huray
1913	Mr. George F. Dymond, M.A.
1914	Mr. Isaac W. Schofield
1915	Mr. James A. Loram
1916	Mr. John R. Bennett
1917	Mr. Richard W. Carr
1918-1919	Mr. Thomas Gill
1920	Mr. William S. Welch
1921	Mr. Richard Norman
1922	Mr. J. Percival Bridgwater
1923	Mr. Lawrence Crowther, O.B.E.
1924	Mr. Ernest E. Nicholls
1925	Mr. William A. Lewins
1926	Mr. Harry Harris
1927	Mr. James Duckworth
1928	Mr. W. Bert Jones
1929	Mr. William Patterson
1930	Mr. John. Hardy
1931	Mr. George P. Bunt
1932	Sir Charles Bird, C.B.E.

SECRETARIES OF CONNEXIONAL DEPARTMENTS

CONNEXIONAL COMMITTEE

1907-1920 George Packer, D.D.
1920-1925 David Brook, M.A., D.C.L.
1925-1932 Henry Smith

HOME MISSIONS

1907-1910 George Packer, D.D., John Moore, Arthur Hancock
1910-1920 John Moore
1920-1928 Thomas Sherwood
1928-1932 Joseph Lineham, B.A., Ph.D.

FOREIGN MISSIONS

1907-1910 George Packer, D.D., Henry T. Chapman, Charles Stedeford
1910-1929 Charles Stedeford
1929-1930 W. Alexander Grist, Charles Stedeford
1930-1932 Charles Stedeford

CHAPEL COMMITTEE

1907-1910 Martin J. Birks, Ebenezer D. Cornish, John Luke
1910-1919 Ebenezer D. Cornish
1919-1932 William C. Jackson, M.A.

LONDON MISSION AND EXTENSION

1907-1910 Henry Mann
1910-1912 Mr. Isaac W. Bullen
1912-1915 Andrew Crombie
1915-1916 Charles H. Buxton
1916-1932 Charles H. Poppleton

LOCAL PREACHERS

1907-1911 Thomas M. Rees
1911-1912 Joseph Foster
1912-1927 John B. Stedeford
1927-1932 Mr. Herbert Ibberson

YOUNG PEOPLE'S AND TEMPERANCE LEAGUE

1907-1910 Thomas Stoneley, Thomas P. Dale, John Thornley
1910-1918 Samuel C. Challenger
1918-1928 Thomas A. Jeffries, M.Sc.
1928-1932 H. Vincent Capsey

BOOK STEWARDS AND CONNEXIONAL EDITORS

BOOK STEWARDS

1907-1912 Andrew Crombie
1912-1932 Henry Hooks

CONNEXIONAL EDITORS

1907-1923 Henry Smith
1923-1932 Henry Hooks

PUBLICATIONS OF THE UNITED METHODIST BOOK ROOM

1908-1932 The United Methodist Magazine
1907-1912 The Pleasant Hour

CONNEXIONAL INSTITUTIONS

VICTORIA PARK COLLEGE (U.M.F.C.)

PRINCIPALS AND RESIDENT TUTORS

1907-1913 Thomas Sherwood
1913-1919 David Brook, M.A., D.C.L.
1919-1932 John T. Brewis, M.A., B.D.

TUTORS

1912-1919 John T. Brewis, M.A., B.D.
1919-1932 E. Wales Hirst, M.A., B.Sc., D.Litt.
1920-1932 George G. Hornby, M.A., B.D.

RANMOOR COLLEGE (M.N.C.)

PRINCIPAL AND RESIDENT TUTOR

1907-1916 John S. Clemens, B.A., B.D.
1907-1912 E. Wales Hurst, M.A., B.Sc.

Ranmoor closed during the First World War, and did not re-open again. It was sold in 1919, the proceeds of sale were used to endow and extend Victoria Park College.

THE DEACONESS INSTITUTE

WARDENS

1907-1912 Thomas J. Cope
1912-1918 Henry Smith
1918-1920 John Moore
1920-1922 Thomas Sunderland
1922-1932 Robert W. Gair

CONNEXIONAL SCHOOLS

SHEBBEAR COLLEGE (B.C.) BOYS

GOVERNORS

1907-1909 William B. Lark
1909-1915 William R. K. Baulkwill
1915-1922 Richard Pyke
1922-1932 J. Ford Reed

HEADMASTERS

1907-1932 Mr. John Rounsefell, M.A., B.Sc.

EDGEHILL COLLEGE (B.C.) GIRLS

GOVERNORS

1907-1909 William B. Reed
1909-1916 William Treffry
1916-1919 Richard S. Hall
1919-1920 David Brook, M.A., D.C.L.
1920-1923 John Moore
1923-1932 William Treffry

HEADMISTRESSES

1907-1909 Mrs. R. A. Reed
1909-1932 Miss Edith O. Johnson, B.A.

ASHVILLE COLLEGE (U.M.F.C.) BOYS

HEADMASTERS

1907-1927 Revd. Alfred Soothill, B.A.
1927-1932 Mr. J. T. Lancaster, B.A., M.Litt.

NEW COLLEGE (U.M.) BOYS

HEADMASTERS

1930-1932 Mr. J. L. Hawkins

In 1932 Elmfield College (P.M.), New College (U.M.), amalgamated with Ashville College.

THE DEACONESS INSTITUTE (U.M.F.C.)

WARDENS

1907-1912 Thomas J. Cope
1912-1918 Henry Smith
1918-1920 John Moore
1920-1922 Thomas Sunderland
1922-1932 Robert W. Gair

Appendix II

1932-1982

APPENDIX II

PRESIDENTS OF THE METHODIST CONFERENCE

Year	Place	President	Station or Appointment
1932	London	J. Scott Lidgett, C.H., M.A., D.D., LL.D.	London, Methodist Settlement
1933	London	F. Luke Wiseman, B.A., D.D., Litt.D.	London, Home Missions Department
1934	Leicester	William Younger	Hull, Analbly Road
1935	Bristol	William C. Jackson, M.A.	Manchester, Chapel Department
1936	Newcastle-upon-Tyne	C. Ensoe Walters	London, London Mission Committee
1937	Bradford	Robert Bond, D.D.	London, Connexional Funds Office
1938	Hull	W. Lansdell Wardle, M.A., D.D.	Manchester, Hartley Victoria College
1939	Liverpool	Richard Pyke	Southport South
1940	Sheffield	Henry Bett, M.A., Litt.D.	Birmingham, Handsworth College
1941	Leeds	Walter H. Armstrong	East Anglia, District Missionary
1942	Manchester	Walter J. Noble, D.D.	London, Missionary Society
1943	Birmingham	Leslie F. Church, B.A., Ph.D.	London, Connexional Editor
1944	Leeds	Wilbert F. Howard, F.B.A., M.A., D.D.	Birmingham, Handsworth College
1945	Nottingham	*Archibald W. Harrison, M.C., B.A., B.Sc., D.D.	London, Education Department
1946	London	R. Newton Flew, M.A., D.D.	Cambridge, Wesley House
1947	Newcastle-upon-Tyne	William E. Farndale, D.D.	Lincoln, District Missionary
1948	Bristol	E. Benson Perkins, M.A., LL.D.	Manchester, Chapel Department
1949	Liverpool	Harold B. Rattenbury, B.A.	London, Missionary Society
1950	Bradford	W. Edwin Sangster, M.A., Ph.D., LL.D.	London, Westminster Central Hall
1951	Sheffield	H. Watkin-Jones, M.A., D.D.	Leeds, Headingley College
1952	Preston	Colin A. Roberts, D.D.	London, Home Mission Department
1953	Birmingham	The Lord Soper, M.A., Ph.D.	London, Kingsway Hall
1954	London	W. Russell Shearer, M.A.	Birmingham, District Missionary
1955	Manchester	Leslie D. Weatherhead, C.B.E., M.A., D.D., Ph.D., D.Litt.	London, City Temple
1956	Leeds	H. Crawford Walters	North Lancashire, District Missionary
1957	Nottingham	Harold Roberts, M.A., D.D., Ph.D.	London, Richmond College
1958	Newcastle-upon-Tyne	Norman H. Snaith, M.A., D.D., Litt.D.	Leeds, Headingley College
1959	Bristol	Eric W. Baker, M.A., D.D., Ph.D., LL.D.	London, Secretary of the Conference
1960	Liverpool	Edward Rogers, M.A., B.D.	London, Christian Citizenship Department
1961	Bradford	Maldwyn L. Edwards, M.A., D.D., Ph.D.	Cardiff and Swansea District Chairman
1962	Stoke-on-Trent	Leslie Davison, D.D., L.H.D.	London, Home Mission Department
1963	Preston	Frederic Greeves, M.A., LL.D.	Bristol, Didsbury College
1964	Sheffield	A. Kingsley Lloyd	London, Connexional Funds Office
1965	Plymouth	W. Walker Lee, M.A.	Bolton and Rochdale District Chairman
1966	Wolverhampton	Douglas W. Thompson	London, Missionary Society
1967	Middlesborough	Irvonwy Morgan, M.A., B.D., Ph.D.	London, London Mission Committee
1968	London	E. Gordon Rupp, F.B.A., M.A., D.D., D.Theol.	Cambridge, Wesley House
1969	Birmingham	Brian S. O'Gorman	Wolverhampton and Shrewsbury District Chairman
1970	Manchester	Rupert E. Davies, M.A., B.D.	Bristol, Wesley College
1971	Harrogate	Kenneth L. Waights	Newcastle-upon-Tyne District Chairman
1972	Nottingham	Harry O. Morton, M.A.	London, Missionary Society
1973	Newcastle-upon-Tyne	Donald R. Lee, M.B.E., B.D.	Southampton District Chairman
1974	Bristol	J. Russell Pope	Plymouth and Exeter District Chairman
1975	Liverpool	A. Raymond George, M.A., B.D.	Bristol, WesleyCollege
1976	Preston	Colin M. Morris, G.C.O.F., B.A., Litt.D., LL.D.	London, Missionary Society
1977	Hull	B. Arthur Shaw, D.Univ.	Chester and Stoke-on-Trent District Chairman
1978	Bradford	Donald English, M.A.D.D.	Bristol, Wesley College
1979	London	William Gowland	Luton Industrial Mission
1980	Sheffield	Kenneth G. Greet, D.D.	London, Secretary of the Conference
1981	Norwich	John A. Newton, M.A., Ph.D.	London Mission, West
1982	Plymouth	Norwyn E. Denny, B.D.	Liverpool District Chairman

* Died in office, January 1946.

VICE-PRESIDENTS OF THE METHODIST CONFERENCE

The only Branch of the Methodist Church previous to Methodist union with the office of Vice-President, was the Primitive Methodists. The office was not created till 1872, and it could be held by a minister or layman, but in fact only one minister was so elected (1907). The constitution of the Methodist Church, 1932, S.O. 6. 'There shall be a Vice-President of the Conference, who shall be a Layman of the Methodist Church, and he shall be elected by ballot vote and by a clear majority of the votes cast.' The first Laywoman was not elected till 1948.

Year	Vice-President
1932	Sir Robert W. Perks, Bart
1933	Moses Bourne
1934	George P. Dymond, M.A.
1935	Edmund S. Lamplough
1936	James Gray
1937	Rt. Hon. Isaac Foot, D.Litt.
1938	Robert P. Tomlinson
1939	Sir Isaac Holden, Bart, M.A.
1940	William E. Clegg
1941	The Lord Rochester
1942	Herbert Ibberson
1943	Charles C. Nightingale, S.S.C.
1944	Wilfred Turner, O.B.E.
1945	Sir George Knight
1946	Richard J. Soper
1947	A. Victor Murray, M.A., B.D., B.Litt., S.T.D.
1948	Mrs. Mildred C. Lewis
1949	John A. Stead
1950	Clifford W. Towlson, M.A., B.D., Ph.D.
1951	Cecil H. Pawson, M.B.E., M.Sc., F.R.S.E.
1952	Sister Dorothy H. Farrar, B.A., Ph.D., Litt.D.
1953	L. Ward Kay, M.B., Ch.B.
1954	H. Guylee Chester, O.B.E.
1955	Thomas E. Jessop, O.B.E., M.C., M.A., Litt.D., D.Litt.
1956	Douglas P. Blatherwick, O.B.E.
1957	Philip H. Race
1958	John M. Gibbs, O.B.E., M.A., L.H.D.
1959	Charles A. Coulson, M.A., D.Sc., Ph.D., F.R.S., F.R.S.E.
1960	Rt. Hon. George T. Thomas

1961	Mrs. Marjorie W. Lonsdale, O.B.E., M.A., B.D., Ph.D.
1962	A. Lowry Creed, M.A.
1963	David Foot Nash
1964	Douglas V. Brown
1965	Miss Pauline M. Webb, B.A., S.T.M.
1966	Albert Bailey
1967	Percy L. Backus, M.D., C.M., M.C.P.S.
1968	John C. Blake, C.B., M.A.
1969	Kenneth J. T. Leese, M.B., Ch.B.
1970	W. Russell Hindmarsh, M.A., D.Phil.
1971	John W. Kellaway
1972	Howard Souster, M.R.C.S.
1973	John I. Miller
1974	Ernest Armstrong, M.P.
1975	William A. Cockell
1976	Cyril J. Bennett
1977	Mrs. Esther M. Waterhouse, M.B., B.S.
1978	Mrs. Mary I. Lenton, M.A.
1979	Patrick W. Welch, B.A.
1980	Mrs. Elsie Moult
1981	David Ensor
1982	Mrs. Pamela Luke

SECRETARIES OF THE METHODIST CONFERENCE

1932-1936 Robert Bond, D.D.
1937-1950 Edwin Finch
1951-1970 Eric W. Baker, M.A., D.D., Ph.D., LL.D.
1971 Kenneth G. Greet, D.D.

ASSISTANTS TO THE SECRETARY OF THE CONFERENCE

1946-1948 Harold Spencer, B.A.
1947-1953 Walter A. Goss, M.A.
1953-1967 J. Bernard Sheldon
1968 W. N. Charles Wooldridge, B.D.

THE METHODIST CHURCH
SECRETARIES OF DEPARTMENTS AND CONNEXIONAL COMMITTEES

At Methodist Union the various Departments and Connexional Committees of the three uniting churches were merged together, and the Conference appointed the Secretariat. The first named is the General Secretary.

HOME MISSIONS DEPARTMENT

1932-1937 F. Luke Wiseman, B.A., George E. Wiles, Joseph Lineham, B.A., Ph.D.
1937-1939 F. Luke Wiseman, B.A., J. Oliver Hornabrook, O.B.E., Joseph Lineham, B.A., Ph.D.
1939-1947 J. Oliver Hornabrook, O.B.E., William Upright, Colin A. Roberts
1947-1955 Colin A. Roberts, Ernest W. Odell, B.A., B.D., C. Leonard Tudor
1955-1957 W. Edwin Sangster, M.A., Ph.D., LL.D., Ernest W. Odell, B.A., B.D., C. Leonard Tudor
1957-1959 W. Edwin Sangster, M.A., Ph.D., LL.D., C. Leonard Tudor, Leslie Davison, B.D.
1959-1965 C. Leonard Tudor, Leslie Davison, B.D., Donald Shaw, M.A.
1965-1966 Leslie Davison, D.D., L.D.H., H. Sinclair Walker, Donald Shaw, M.A.
1966-1969 Leslie Davison, D.D., L.D.H., H. Sinclair Walker, George Sails, B.D.
1969-1971 Leslie Davison, D.D., L.D.H., H. Sinclair Walker, George Sails, B.D., Alan J. Davies, M.A.
1971-1973 Leslie Davison, D.D., L.DH., George Sails, B.D., Jeffrey Harris, M.A., B.D., Alan J. Davies, M.A.

ROYAL NAVY, ARMY AND ROYAL AIR FORCE BOARD

1932-1936 Joseph H. Bateson, C.B.E.
1936-1938 H. Peverley Dodd, O.B.E.
1938-1945 George Standing, C.B.E., D.S.O., M.C.
1945-1956 Joseph Firth, M.C.
1956-1962 F. Wilfred Hilborne
1962-1970 Roland S. Hamblin
1970-1973 Douglas A. Spear, C.B.E., M.A.

LONDON MISSION DEPARTMENT

1932-1936 C. Ensor Walters
1936-1939 C. Ensor Walters, Robinson Whittaker
1939-1940 Robinson Whittaker
1940-1947 Robinson Whittaker, Charles H. Hulbert
1947-1951 Robinson Whittaker
1951-1973 Irvonwy Morgan, M.A., B.D., Ph.D.

CHAPEL COMMITTEE

1932-1933 William Humphrey
1933-1939 William Humphrey, William C. Jackson, M.A.
1939-1942 William C. Jackson, M.A., E. Benson Perkins
1942-1952 E. Benson Perkins, Albert Hearn
1952-1958 Albert Hearn, W. Oliver Phillipson, M.A.
1958-1966 W. Oliver Phillipson, M.A., Herbert Simpson
1966-1973 Herbert Simpson, George W. Dolbey, M.A., B.D.

TEMPERANCE AND SOCIAL WELFARE DEPARTMENT: 1932-1950
CHRISTIAN CITIZENSHIP DEPARTMENT: 1950-1973

1932-1933 Henry Carter, Edwin Finch
1933-1942 Henry Carter, E. Clifford Urwin, M.A., B.D.
1942-1948 E. Clifford Urwin, M.A., B.D., Maldwyn L. Edwards, M.A., Ph.D.
1948-1950 E. Clifford Urwin, M.A., B.D., Noel Hutchcroft
1950-1953 E. Clifford Urwin, M.A., B.D., Edward Rogers, M.A., B.D.
1953-1954 Edward Robers, M.A., B.D.
1954-1972 Edward Rogers, Kenneth G. Greet
1972-1973 Edward Rogers, M.A., B.D., John H. Atkinson, M.A.

EDUCATION DEPARTMENT

1932-1940 Herbert B. Workman, M.A., D.D., D.Litt.
1940-1945 Archibald W. Harrison, M.C., B.A., B.Sc., D.D.
1946-1951 Eric W. Baker, M.A., Ph.D.
1951-1970 George Osborn, M.A.
1970-1973 Douglas S. Hubery, Douglas A. Brown, M.A.

SUNDAY SCHOOL DEPARTMENT: 1932-1943
YOUTH DEPARTMENT: 1943-1973

1932-1933 Alfred J. G. Seaton, B.D., F. Clifford Taylor, M.A., B.D., H. Vincent Capsey
1933-1943 H. Vincent Capsey, F. Clifford Taylor, M.A., B.D., J. Eric Dixon, M.C., B.A., B.D.
1943-1949 James K. Whitehead, B.A., Douglas A. Griffiths, Wilfrid J. Doidge, B.A., B.D.
1949-1951 James K. Whitehead, B.A., Wilfrid J. Doidge, B.A.,B.D., Leonard P. Barnett, B.D.
1951-1953 Gerald Lansley, Kenneth J. Meir, B.A., Leonard P. Barnett, B.D.
1953-1958 Bryan H. Reed, B.D., J. Kenneth Meir, B.A.
1958-1960 Bryan H. Reed, B.D., J. Kenneth Meir, B.A., Reginald C. Bedford, B.A.
1960-1961 Bryan H. Reed, B.D., Douglas S. Hubery, Reginald C. Bedford, B.A.
1961-1967 Douglas S. Hubery, Christopher C. Bacon, B.A., B.D., Reginald C. Bedford, B.A.
1967-1969 Douglas S. Hubery, Christopher D. Bacon, B.A., B.D., George W. Cloke, B.D.
1969-1970 Douglas S. Hubery, Gordon Turner, George W. Cloke, B.D.
1970-1973 Gordon Turner, George W. Cloke, B.D.

LOCAL PREACHERS' DEPARTMENT

1937-1946 Fred A. Farley, M.A., B.D.
1946-1958 Greville P. Lewis, B.A., B.D.
1958-1967 David N. Francis, M.A.
1967-1973 John Stacey, B.D.

CONNEXIONAL FUNDS DEPARTMENT

1932-1937 William H. Hart (Supernumerary)
1937-1942 Robert Bond, D.D.
1942-1949 W. Lorne Cornish
1949-1952 A. Simpson Leck
1952-1969 A. Kingsley Lloyd
1969-1973 Derek R. Farrow, B.A.

GENERAL SUSTENTATION FUND

1932-1933 Robert Bond, D.D.

1933-1937 Robert Bond, D.D., George E. Wiles, Joseph Lineham, B.A., Ph.D.
1937-1942 Robert Bond, D.D.
1942-1949 W. Lorne Cornish
1949-1952 A. Simpson Leck
1952-1966 A. Kingsley Lloyd

This Fund was discontinued in 1966.

METHODIST MISSIONARY SOCIETY

1932-1934 Edgar W. Thompson, M.A., Walter J. Noble, G. E. Hickman Johnson, W. Alexander Grist, George Ayre
1934-1939 Walter J. Noble, G. E. Hickman Johnson, W. Alexander Grist, George Ayre, Harold B. Rattenbury, B.A.
1939-1945 Walter J. Noble, G. E. Hickman Johnson, Harold B. Rattenbury, B.A., Frederick W. Dodds
1945-1947 Walter J. Noble, G. E. Hickman Johnson, Harold B. Rattenbury, B.A., Frederick W. Dodds, Fred W. J. Cottrell
1947-1948 G. E. Hickman Johnson, Harold B. Rattenbury, B.A., Frederick W. Dodds, Fred W. J. Cottrell, Basil Clutterbuck, M.A.
1948-1949 Harold B. Rattenbury, B.A., Frederick W. Dodds, Fred W. J. Cottrell, Basil Clutterbuck, M.A., Wilfred Easton, B.D.
1949-1950 Harold B. Rattenbury, B.A., Frederick W. Dodds, Fred W. J. Cottrell, Basil Clutterbuck, M.A., Wilfred Easton, B.D., Donald B. Childe
1950-1951 Basil Clutterbuck, M.A., T. Allan Beetham, M.A., Donald B. Childe, Wilfred Easton, B.D.
1951-1958 Basil Clutterbuck, M.A., T. Allan Beetham, M.A., Donald B. Childe, Wilfred Easton, B.D., N. Allen Birtwhistle, M.A., B.Sc.
1958-1959 Basil Clutterbuck, M.A., T. Allan Beetham, M.A., Donald B. Childe, Wilfred Easton, B.D., Wilfred R. Pile, B.D.
1959-1960 Douglas W. Thompson, T. Allan Beetham, M.A., Donald B. Childe, Wilfred Easton, B.D., R. Wilfrid R. Pile, B.D.
1960-1961 Douglas W. Thompson, Donald B. Childe, Wilfred Easton, B.D., Kenneth Johnson, B.D., Wilfrid R. Pile, B.D.
1961-1963 Douglas W. Thompson, Donald B. Childe, Kenneth Johnson, B.D., Wilfrid R. Pile, B.D., Philip A. Potter, M.Th.
1963-1965 Douglas W. Thompson, Donald B. Childe, Wilfrid R. Pile, B.D., Philip A. Potter, M.Th., Harry O. Morton, M.A.
1965-1966 Douglas W. Thompson, Cyril J. Davey, Wilfrid R. Pile, B.D., Philip A. Potter, M.Th., Harry O. Morton, M.A.
1966-1967 Douglas W. Thompson, Cyril J. Davey, Wilfrid R. Pile, B.D., Hugh E. Thomas, B.A., B.D., Harry O. Morton, M.A.
1967-1968 Douglas W. Thompson, Cyril J. Davey, Wilfrid R. Pile, B.D., Hugh E. Thomas, B.A., B.D., Harry O. Morton, M.A.
1968-1972 G. Thackray Eddy, M.A., B.D., Cyril J. Davey, Wilfred R. Pile, B.D., Hugh E. Thomas, B.A., B.D., Harry O. Morton, M.A.
1972-1973 Harry O. Morton, M.A., Cyril J. Davey, Wilfrid R. Pile, B.D., Hugh E. Thomas, B.A., B.D., Norman W. Taggart, B.A., B.D.

THE DIVISIONS

In 1973 there was a restructuring of the Conference, Connexional Departments and Committees, and Seven Divisions were formed. The first named where appropriate is the General Secretary of the Division.

HOME MISSION

1973-1979 George W. Sails, B.D., Irvonwy Morgan, M.A., B.D., Ph.D. (London Committee), Jeffrey W. Harris, M.A., B.D., Alan J. Davies, M.A.
1979-1982 George W. Sails, B.D., Jeffrey W. Harris, M.A., B.D. (London CommittEe), Alan J. Davies, M.A., J. David Bridge, B.A., B.D.
1982 Donald English, M.A., D.D., Jeffrey W. Harris, M.A., B.D. (London Committee), Alan J. Davies, M.A., J. Davis Bridge, B.A., B.D.

ROYAL NAVY, ARMY AND ROYAL AIR FORCE BOARD

1973-1975 Douglas A. Spear, M.A.
1975-1977 Gordon T. Brigg, M.A.
1977 C. R. Wolsey Gilbert

PROPERTY

1973-1975 Herbert Simpson, George W. Dolbey, M.A., B.D.
1975-1979 George W. Dolbey, M.A., B.D., Peter A. Kerridge
1979 Peter A. Kerridge, Ralph E. Fennell, M.A.

FINANCE

1973 Derek R. Farrow, B.A.

SOCIAL RESPONSIBILITY

1973-1975 Edward Rogers, M.A., B.D., John H. Atkinson, M.A.
1975-1978 John H. Atkinson, M.A., John P. Hastings, B.A., B.D.
1978-1979 John H. Atkinson, M.A., John P. Hastings, B.A., B.D., Norman J. Richardson
1979-1981 Gerald M. Burt, M.A., John P. Hastings, B.A., B.D., Norman J. Richardson
1981 Gerald M. Burt, M.A., Norman J. Richardson, Brian Ducker, M.A.

EDUCATION AND YOUTH

1973-1978 Douglas S. Hubery, Douglas A. Brown, M.A., Gordon Turner, Martin V. Caldwell
1978-1979 Douglas A. Brown, M.A., Wilfred Tooley, M.A., B.D., N. Keith Hurt, M.A., B.D., S.T.M.
1979 Douglas A. Brown, M.A., Wilfred Tooley, M.A., B.D., N. Keith Hurt, M.A., B.D., S.T.M., David J. Winwood

MINISTRIES

1973-1974 Christopher D. Bacon, B.A., B.D., John Stacey, B.D. (Local Preachers), Gerald M. Burt, M.A.
1974-1979 Christopher D. Bacon, B.A., B.D., John Stacey, B.D. (Local Preachers), Gerald M. Burt, M.A., Ralph E. Fennell, M.A. (Sector Ministers)
1979 Trevor T. Rowe, M.A., B.Sc., B.D., John Stacey, B.D. (Local Preachers)

OVERSEAS

1973-1975 Colin M. Morris, G.C.O.F., B.A., L.H.D., LL.D., Cyril J. Davey, Hugh E. Thomas, B.A., B.D., Graeme C. Jackson, M.A., Norman W. Taggart, B.A., B.D.
1975-1976 Colin M. Morris, G.C.O.F., B.A., L.H.D., LL.D., Cyril J. Davey, Hugh E. Thomas, B.A., B.D., Graeme C. Jackson, M.A., Gordon Shaw, M.A., LL.B., Norman W. Taggart, B.A., B.D.
1976-1977 Colin M. Morris, G.C.O.F., B.A., L.H.D., LL.D., Hugh E. Thomas, B.A., B.D., Graeme C. Jackson, M.A., Gordon Shaw, M.A., LL.D., Norman W. Taggart, B.A., B.D.
1977-1978 Colin M. Morris, G.C.O.F., B.A., L.H.D., LL.D., Albert W. Mosley, M.A., Ph.D., Graeme C. Jackson, M.A., Gordon Shaw, M.A., LL.D.
1978-1982 Albert W. Mosley, M.A., Ph.D., Graeme C. Jackson, M.A., Sidney N. Groaves, B.D., B.Comm., Gordon Shaw, M.A., LL.D., Michael Sheard, B.A.
1982 Albert W. Mosley, M.A., Ph.D., Graeme C. Jackson, M.A., Sidney N. Groves, B.D., B.Comm., David R. Cruise, B.A., M.Th., Michael Sheard, B.A.

THE METHODIST BOOK ROOM

BOOK STEWARDS

1932-1933 Henry Hooks
1932-1934 Ernest Barrett, M.A.
1932-1948 Edgar C. Barton
1948-1969 Frank H. Cumbers, B.A., D.D.

CONNEXIONAL EDITORS

1932-1934 John Telford, B.A.
1932-1935 B. Aquila Barber
1935-1953 Leslie F. Church, B.A., Ph.D.
1953-1962 J. Alan Kay, M.A., Ph.D.
1963-1972 Gordon S. Wakefield, M.A., B.Litt.

CONNEXIONAL ARCHIVISTS

1961-1962 Wesley F. Swift
1962-1976 John C. Bowmer, M.A., B.D., Ph.D.
1976-1978 Mrs. Shiela Himsworth (Acting)
1978 Revd. William Leary, B.A.

METHODIST PUBLICATIONS

1932-1970	The Methodist Magazine
1932-1968	The London Quarterly Review
1932-1958	The Kiddies' Magazine
1932-1954	The Preacher's and Class Leader's Magazine
1932-1954	The Choir and Musical Journal
1955-1964	The Choir
1933-1949	The Methodist Church Record and Home Magazine
1950-1958	The Church Record
1933-1947	The Methodist Teacher's Magazine
1954-1969	The Preachers' Quarterly
1964-1968	New Directions
1965-1967	Mosaic
1971	Worship and Preaching
1974	The Epworth Review

THE FERNLEY HARTLEY LECTURE

After Methodist Union the Conference took the necessary legal measures to amalgamate the Fernley Trust and the Hartley Trust. The first Fernley Hartley Lecture was delivered in 1933.

Year	Lecture	Lecturer
1933	The Philosophical Approach to Religion	Eric S. Waterhouse, M.A., D.D.
1934	Jesus and the Primitive Need	Charles P. Groves, B.A., D.D.
1935	Jesus and the Moralists	Edward W. Hirst, M.A., B.Sc., D.Litt.
1936	Motive and Method in a Christian Order	Sir Josiah C. Stamp
1937	The Spirit of Methodism	Henry Bett, M.A., D.Litt.
1938	Jesus and His Church	R. Newton Flew, M.A., D.D.
1939	Personal Experience and the Historic Faith	Professor A. Victor Murray, M.A., B.D., B.Litt., S.T.D.
1940	The Atonement in New Testament Teaching	Vincent Taylor, D.D., Ph.D.
1941	The Evangelical Doctrines of Charles Wesley's Hymns	J. Ernest Rattenbury, D.D.
1942	The Evangelical Revival and Christian Reunion	Archibald W. Harrison, M.A., B.A., B.Sc., D.D.
1943	The Christ Character in the Early Church	F. Bertram Clogg, M.A., B.D.
1944	The Distinctive Ideas in the Old Testament	Norman H. Snaith, M.A., D.D.
1945	John Wesley and William Law	J. Brazier Green, M.A., B.D.
1946	The Old Testament Interpretation of History	Christopher R. North, M.A., D.D.
1947	Let God be God	Philip S. Watson, M.A.
1948	The Early Methodist People	Leslie F. Church, B.A., Ph.D.
1949	The Theology of the Reformation	H. Watkin-Jones, M.A., D.D.
1950	Jesus and His Parables	J. Alexander Findlay, M.A., D.D.
1951	A Commentary of Communism	Edward Rogers, M.A., B.D.
1952	The Old Testament Apocalyptic	Stanley B. Frost, M.A.
1953	Communion with God in the New Testament	A. Raymond George, M.A., B.D.
1954	Jesus and the Kingdom of God	Harold Roberts, M.A., D.D., Ph.D
1955	The Makers of Protestantism	E. Gordon Rupp, M.A., D.D.
1956	The Meaning of Sin	Frederic Greeves, M.A., LL.D.
1957	Puritan Devotion	Gordon S. Wakefield, M.A., B.Litt.
1958	The Faith of a Methodist	Eric W. Baker, M.A., D.D., Ph.D., LL.D.
1959	Jesus and the Future Life	William Strawson, M.Th., Ph.D.
1960	Origin and the Doctrine of Grace	Benjamin Drewery, M.A.
1961	They Who will Hear	N. Allen Birtwhistle, M.A., B.Sc.
1962	1662, and after three Centuries of English Nonconformity	John T. Wilkinson, M.A., D.D.
1963	The Biblical Concept of Power	Cyril H. Powell, B.A., Ph.D., M.Litt.
1964	I Launch at Paradise	Frederick A. Rowe, M.A.
1965	Called to Preach	W. Russell Shearer, M.A.
1966	Man in Society	John H. Chamberlayne, M.A., M.Th., Ph.D.
1967	The Use of Praying	J. Neville Ward, M.A., B.D.
1968	Religious Authority in an Age of Doubt	Rupert E. Davies, M.A., B.D.
1969	Israel, People of God	George Anderson, M.A., D.D.
1970	Baptism in Early Methodism	G. Bernard Holland, M.A., M.Th., Ph.D.
1971	The Deists and the Bible	Henry Rack, M.A.
1972	Ulrich Zwingli, The Swiss Reformer	Peter W. Stephens, M.A., B.D.
1973	Making Sense Of It All, Philosophy of Religion	Kenneth B. Wilson, M.A.
1974	The Theology of St. Augustine of Hippo	Trevor T. Rowe, M.A., B.Sc., B.D.
1975	Pastor and People	John C. Bowmer, M.A., B.D., Ph.D.
1976	The Concept of Christian Experience	Graham Slater, M.A.
1977	Mark, The Storyteller	David Blatherwick, B.A., LL.B.
1978	Christian Character in the Gospel of Luke	Brian E. Beck, M.A.
1979	The Praise of God in Worship	Geoffrey Wainwright, M.A., B.D., D.Theol.
1980	The Lukan School	David Deeks, M.A.
1981	Moral Conviction and Belief in God	John A. Harrod, M.A., B.Sc.
1982	Conflict and Reconciliation	J. Muncey Turner, M.A.

THE WESLEY HISTORICAL SOCIETY

The Wesley Historical Society was founded by the Revd. Richard Green in 1893, though he tells us that the idea was first suggested to him by a friend, Mr. George Stampe, of Grimsby. The first Annual Meeting of the Society took place during the sitting of the Birmingham Conference in 1894. The first resolution of that meeting was that the Society should be called the Wesley Historical Society. Richard Green was responsible for starting the Manuscript Journal which lasted until 1934. The Proceedings of the Society began in 1896, the first volume contained five parts. Later the number was increased to eight quarterly parts, and recently it has been reduced to six. The current volume is No. XLIII. In addition to the Proceedings there are occasional publications (see below). In 1933 an Annual Lecture was inaugurated, and the first was delivered at the Leicester Conference in 1934.

In 1956 the then President of the Society, the Revd. Francis F. Bretherton, B.A., died. His family generously made a gift of his Methodist Library (of over 2,000 volumes) to the Society to serve as a nucleus for the Society Library. The Library was opened in April 1959, in the Crypt of Wesley's Chapel, London. Since that time many more accessions have been added, and the Library is now housed at Southlands College, Wimbledon.

OCCASIONAL PUBLICATIONS

1896 John Bennet's Copy of the Minutes of the Conferences of 1744, 1745, 1747, and 1748, with John Wesley's Copy for 1746. The Minutes of the Conference for 1749, 1755, and 1758 from Wesley's Copy.
1897 Articles of Religion prepared by order of the Conference of 1806.
1898 Mrs. Wesley's Conference with her Daughter (Emilia). An Essay by Mrs. Susanna Wesley, hitherto unpublished.
1899 The Index to the Library Edition of Thomas Jackson's, Life of Charles Wesley, by Francis M. Jackson.
1906 The Index to The Life and Times of Selina, Countess of Huntingdon, Aaron C. H. Seymour, by Francis M. Jackson.
1908 An Itinerary of John Wesley's Journeys, 1736-1790.
1909 An Index to the Memoirs, and Obituary Notices, and recent Deaths, together with the references to the Local Histories of Methodism as contained in The Arminian Magazine, 1778-1797; The Methodist Magazine, 1798-1821; and The Wesleyan Methodist Magazine, 1822-1839, by Francis M. Jackson.
1958 John Cennick. A Handlist of his Writings. Frank Baker, B.A., B.D., Ph.D.
1960 A General Index to the Proceedings of the Wesley Historical Society.
1964 How to Write a Local History of Methodism. Wesley F. Swift.
1971 John Wesley and Methodism. Thomas Shaw.
1972 John Jones — First after the Wesleys? Alfred B. Sackett, M.C., M.A.
1972 James Rouquet and his part in Early Methodism. Alfred B. Sackett, M.C., M.A.
1974 Some Early Methodist Tune Books. Francis B. Westbrook, B.A., Mus.D.
1977 Samuel E. Keeble: The Rejected Prophet. Michael S. Edwards, M.A., M.Litt.
1978 The 1851 Religious Census. A Select Bibliography of materials relating to England and Wales. Clive D. Field, M.A., D.Phil., Cert.Ed.

ANNUAL LECTURES OF THE WESLEY HISTORICAL SOCIETY

Year	Lecture	Lecturer
1933	The Early Methodist Preachers	Revd. Henry Bett, M.A., Litt.D.
1936	The Rank and File of the Early Methodists*	Revd. Leslie F. Church, B.A., Ph.D.
1937	Haworth Parsonage	Mrs. G. Elsie Harrison
1938	John Wesley's Journal	Revd. R. Lee Cole, M.A., B.D.
1939	Wesley's Anglican Contemporaries	Dr. John H. Whiteley
1940	The Countess of Huntingdon	Revd. Francis F. Bretherton, B.A.
1941	The Early Bible Christians	Revd. Richard Pyke
1942	Adam Clarke	Revd. Maldwyn L. Edwards, M.A., D.D., Ph.D.
1943	John Wesley and his Letters*	Revd. Wilbert F. Howard, M.A., D.D., F.B.A.
1944	John Wesley, His Conferences and his Preachers	Revd. W. Lamplough Doughty, B.A., B.D.
1945	The Separation of Methodism from the Church of England	Revd. Archibald W. Harrison, M.C., B.A., B.Sc., D.D.
1946	John Wesley's London Chapels	Revd. J. Henry Martin
1947	Methodism in Scotland	Revd. Wesley F. Swift
1948	Charles Wesley as Revealed in his Letters	Revd. Frank Baker, B.A., B.D., Ph.D.
1949	The Significance of 1849	Revd. E. Clifford Urwin, M.A., B.D.
1950	The Secret of Mow Cop	Revd. William E. Farndale, D.D.
1951	Howell Harris	Revd. Griffith T. Roberts, M.A., B.D.
1952	Methodist Preaching Houses and the Law	Revd. E. Benson Perkins, M.A., LL.D.
1953	The Hymns of Charles Wesley	Revd. R. Newton Flew, M.A., D.D.
1954	Thomas Jackson, Methodist Patriarch	Revd. E. Gordon Rupp, M.A., D.D., D.Theol., F.B.A.
1955	Jabez Bunting, The Last Wesleyan	Revd. John H. S. Kent, M.A., Ph.D.
1956	The Book Room	Revd. Frank H. Cumbers, B.A., D.D.
1957	The United Methodist Free Churches	Revd. Oliver A. Beckerlegge, M.A., Ph.D.
1958	John Wesley among the Physicians	Revd. A. Wesley Hill, B.A., M.B., B.Ch.
1959	Methodism and the Trade Unions	Revd. Robert F. Wearmouth, M.A., B.Sc., Ph.D.
1960	Shropshire Saint	Revd. George Lawton
1961	The Lord's Supper in Methodism 1791-1960	Revd. John C. Bowmer, M.A., B.D., Ph.D.
1962	A Portrait in Pottery	Revd. Arthur D. Cummings
1963	The Architectural Expression of Methodism	Revd. George W. Dolby, M.A., B.D.
1964	Thomas Coke, Apostle of Methodism	Mr. John A. Vickers, B.A., B.D.
1965	The Bible Christians	Revd. Thomas Shaw
1966	Methodist Devotion	Revd. Gordon S. Wakefield, M.A., B.Litt.
1967	John Wesley and the Coming Great Church	Revd. Frederick Hunter, M.A., B.D.
1968	The Labourers Hire, 1744-1813*	Revd. A. Kingsley Lloyd
1969	Methodist Theology*	Revd. William Strawson, M.Th., Ph.D.
1970	The Wednesbury Riots	Revd. J. Leonard Waddy
1971	My Dear Sister	Revd. Maldwyn L. Edwards, M.A., D.D., Ph.D.
1972	S. E. Keeble and Methodist Social Thinking, 1880-1939	Revd. Michael S. Edwards, M.A., M.Litt.
1973	Methodism and the Irish Problem	Mr. Frederick Jeffrey, O.B.E., B.A.
1974	Some early Methodist Tune-Books	Revd. Francis B. Westbrook, B.A., Mus.D.
1975	Adam Clarke Controversialist	Dr. Ian Sellars, M.A., B.Litt.
1976	Samuel Warren and the Methodist Reformers of Lancashire*	Dr. David A. Gowland, B.A.
1977	Wesleyanism and the World of the Nineteenth Century	Revd. Henry D. Rack, M.A.
1978	The People at the Grass-roots within the great Haworth Round: 1738-1791	Miss Joanna M. G. Dawson
1979	The Origin of Religious Revival. The International Setting of Early Methodism*	Dr. W. Reginald Ward, M.A.
1980	Methodism in its Industrial Setting*	Mr. Barrie Trinder, B.A.
1981	John Wesley and the Poor*	Dr. John Walsh, M.A.
1982	Methodist Union of 1932 and its Fruits*	Revd. Rupert E. Davies, M.A., B.D.

* Lectures not published.

MINISTERIAL TRAINING — MINISTERIAL TRAINING COMMITTEE

SECRETARIES

1932-1934 John H. Ritson, M.A., D.D.
1934-1943 Thomas Naylor, B.A.
1943-1948 Sydney G. Dimond, M.A., D.D.
1948-1958 Arthur N. Rose, M.A.
1958-1973 N. Allen Birtwhistle, M.A., B.Sc.

All the Colleges of the three uniting Churches were retained at the beginning, Didsbury, Richmond, Headingley, Handsworth and Wesley House, Wesleyan Methodist. Hartley, Primitive Methodist, and Victoria Park, United Methodist. For some years before Hartley College and Victoria Park had close links and the tutors shared classes. Hartley College being very much larger than Victoria Park provided extra accommodation for United Methodist students. In 1934 Victoria Park was closed and amalgamated with Hartley College, hence, Hartley Victoria. All the Colleges with the exception of Wesley House, Cambridge were closed during the war. They all re-opened in 1945, with the exception of Didsbury College, Manchester. The building was sold and the proceeds of sale provided for a new College at Bristol, designated Didsbury College, Bristol. By the middle 1860's it was apparent that there were insufficient condidates for the available places in the six Colleges. In 1967 Wesley College, Headingley, was closed, and amalgamated with Didsbury, Bristol, which was renamed, Wesley College, Bristol. In 1970 Handsworth College, Birmingham, was closed. The building was sold and Handsworth amalgamated with the Anglican Queen's College, Birmingham. Part of the proceeds of sale of the Methodist property has provided a new building called the Handsworth Building. The necessary steps were taken to make Queen's an Ecumenical College. In 1972 Richmond, Surrey, was closed. In 1868 the Missionary Society purchased Richmond from the Technological Institution for the training of missionary students. When this mistaken practice ceased in 1885, the property remained in the hands of the Missionary Society, and to the proceeds of sale of Richmond went to the Society. In 1973 Hartley Victoria, Manchester, building was vacated and sold, and we share facilities provided by the Manchester Baptist College.

DIDSBURY COLLEGE, MANCHESTER. 1932-1940

PRINCIPLES

1932-1939 Thomas H. Barratt, B.A.
1939-1940 W. Bardsley Brash, M.A., B.D., M.Litt.

RESIDENT TUTORS

1932-1939 Thomas H. Barratt, B.A.
1939-1940 Harold S. Darby, M.A.

THEOLOGY

1932-1940 Charles J. Wright, B.A., Ph.D

BIBLICAL LANGUAGES AND LITERATURE

1932-1940 J. Alexander Findlay, M.A., D.D.
1932-1939 W. Bardsley Brash, M.A., B.D., M.Litt.

ASSISTANT TUTURS

1932-1935 John W. Waterhouse, M.A.B.D.
1935-1937 John F. Butler, M.A., Ph.D.
1937-1940 John H. Blamey, M.A., B.D.

DIDSBURY COLLEGE, BRISTOL: 1945-1967

PRINCIPALS AND RESIDENT TUTORS

1945-1949 W. Bardsley Brash, M.A., B.D., M.Litt.
1949-1967 Frederic Greeves, M.A., LL.D.

THEOLOGY

1946-1967 Frederic Greeves, M.A.

BIBLICAL LANGUAGES AND LITERATURE

1946-1949 W. Bardsley Brash, M.A., B.D., M.Litt (English and the English Bible, and Hebrew)
1946-1949 J. Alexander Findlay, M.A., D.D. (New Testament Language and Literature)
1949-1956 Stanley B. Frost, M.Th., Ph.D. (Old Testament Language and Literature)
1949-1965 Kenneth Grayson, M.A. (New Testament Language and Literature)
1956-1962 Islywn Blythin, M.A. (Old Testament Language and Literature)
1962-1967 W. David Stacey, M.A. (Old Testament Language and Literature)
1965-1967 John A. Newton, M.A., Ph.D. (New Testament Language and Literature)

CHURCH HISTORY

1952-1967 Rupert E. Davies, M.A., B.D.

ASSISTANT TUTORS

1948-1949 Arthur Candeland, M.A.
1949-1950 Ivor S. W. Reith
1950-1952 Howard W. Marratt, B.A., B.D.
1952-1954 Ronald Williamson, B.A.
1954-1956 Donald E. Henry, M.A.
1956-1958 John A. Ziesler, B.A., B.D.
1958-1960 J. Cedric Arnold, B.A.
1960-1962 Howard Marshall, M.A., B.D.
1962-1964 Albert Jewell, B.A.
1964-1965 John S. Curnow, M.A.
1965-1967 Brian G. Powley, B.A.

WESLEY COLLEGE, BRISTOL

PRINCIPALS

1967-1973 Rupert E. Davies, M.A., B.D.
1973-1978 John A. Newton, M.A., Ph.D
1978 W. David Stacey, M.A., Ph.D.

RESIDENT TUTORS

1967-1973 Vincent Parkin, M.A., B.Sc.
1973-1978 John A. Newton, M.A., Ph.D.
1978 W. David Stacey, M.A., Ph.D

THEOLOGY

1967-1973 Rupert E. Davies, M.A., B.D.
1973-1980 W. Peter Stephens, M.A., B.D., D. es SR.
1981 Christopher D. Wiltsher, B.A., B.Sc., M.Litt.

BIBLICAL LANGUAGES AND LITERATURE

1967-1973 Vincent Parkin, M.A., B.Sc. (New Testament Language and Literature)
1967-1971 W. David Stacey, M.A., Ph.D (Old Testament Language and Literature)
1973-1981 A. Raymond George, M.A., B.D. (Biblical Subjects and Liturgy)
1973 Ivor H. Jones, M.A., Ph.D. (Biblical Subjects)
1978 W. David Stacey, M.A., Ph.D. (Biblical Studies)

CHURCH HISTORY

1967-1972 John A. Newton, M.A., Ph.D
1972-1973 A. Raymond George, M.A., B.D.

PRACTICAL THEOLOGY AND METHODISM

1973-1982 Donald English, M.A., D.D.
1982 Donald M. Cadie

PHILOSOPHY AND PSYCHOLOGY OF RELIGION

1967-1973 Bernard E. Jones, M.A., B.D., Ph. D.
1973-1980 Kenneth B. Wilson, M.A., M.Litt., Ph.D

ASSISTANT TUTORS

1967-1969 John E. Richardson, B.A.
1969-1971 John C. A. Barratt, B.A.
1970-1971 Neil Dixon, B.A. (P.A.)
1971-1973 Neil Richardson, B.A.
1975-1976 Stuart Jordan, B.A. (P.A.)

P.A. President's Assistant.

RICHMOND COLLEGE, SURREY: 1932-1972

PRINCIPLES

1932-1940 C. Ryder Smith, B.A., D.D.
1945-1951 Eric S. Waterhouse, M.A., D.D.
1951-1955 F. Bertram Clogg,a M.A., B.D.
1955-1968 Harold Roberts, M.A., D.D., Ph.D.
1968-1972 A. Raymond George, M.A., B.D.

RESIDENT TUTORS

1932-1935 Leslie F. Church, B.A., Ph.D.
1935-1940 Sydney G. Dimond, M.A.
1945-1951 Eric S. Waterhouse, M.A., D.D.
1951-1955 F. Bertram Clogg, M.A., B.D.
1955-1972 S. Clive Thexton, M.Th.

THEOLOGY

1932-1940 C. Ryder Smith, B.A., D.D.
1946-1968 Harold Roberts, M.A., D.D., Ph.D.
1968-1972 A. Raymond George, M.A., B.D.

BIBLICAL LANGUAGES AND LITERATURE

1932-1940 F. Bertram Clogg, M.A., B.D. (New Testament Language and Literature')
1954-1955 F. Bertram Clogg, M.A., B.D. (New Testament Language and Literature)
1951-1972 S. Clive Thexton, M.Th. (Old Testament Language and Literature)
1955-1972 A. Marcus Ward, M.A., D.D. (New Testament and Literature)

CHURCH HISTORY AND PASTORAL THEOLOGY

1932-1935 Leslie F. Church
1935-1940 Sydney G. Dimond, M.A.
1947-1952 E. Gordon Rupp, M.A., B.D.
1952-1971 Norman P. Goldhawk, M.A.

PHILOSOPHY AND PSYCHOLOGY OF RELIGION

1920-1951 Eric S. Waterhouse, M.A., D.D.
After 1951 Philosophy of Religion was taught by the Theological Tutor.

ASSISTANT TUTORS

1932-1937 George A. E. Cornforth, M.A.
1937-1939 Charles F. Davey, M.A., B.D.
1939-1940 George Anderson, M.A.
1945-1946 Charles F. Davey, M.A.B.D.
1946-1951 S. Clive Thexton, B.D.
1951-1953 David H. G. Head, M.A.
1953-1956 Amos S. Cresswell, M.A.
1956-1958 E. Michael Newman, M.A.
1957-1958 Robert W. Fulcher, M.A., B.D.
1958-1961 John A. Newton, B.A., Ph.D.
1961-1963 Rodney C. Cocks, B.A.
1963-1966 Philip McR, Beuzeval, B.A., LL.B.
1966-1970 David G. Deeks, B.A.
The College was closed from 1940-1945 owing to the war.

WESLEY COLLEGE, HEADINGLEY, LEEDS: 1932-1967

PRINCIPALS

1932-1936 John W. Lightley, M.A., B.D., D.Litt.
1936-1943 Vincent Taylor, D.D., Ph.D.
1946-1953 Vincent Taylor, D.D., Ph.D., F.B.A.
1953-1954 H. Watkin-Jones, M.A., D.D.
1954-1961 Norman H. Snaith, M.A., D.D., Litt.D.
1961-1967 A. Raymond George, M.A., B.D.

RESIDENT TUTORS

1932-1936 John W. Lightley, M.A., B.D., D.Litt.
1936-1943 Vincent Taylor, D.D., Ph.D.
1946-1953 Vincent Taylor, D.D., Ph.D., F.B.A.
1953-1967 Vincent Parkin, M.A., B.Sc.

THEOLOGY, PASTORAL THEOLOGY AND PHILOSOPHY

1932-1934 J. Arundel Chapman, M.A., B.D.
1934-1940 Harold Roberts, M.A., Ph.D.
1940-1943 R. Idwal Hopwood, M.A.
1946-1967 A. Raymond George, M.A., B.D.

BIBLICAL LANGUAGES AND LITERATURE

1932-1936 John W. Lightley, M.A., B.A., D.Litt.
1932-1943 Vincent Taylor, D.D., Ph.D. (New Testament Language and Literature)
1946-1953 Vincent Taylor, D.D., Ph.D., F.B.A. (New Testament Language and Literature)
1946-1961 Norman H. Snaith, M.A., D.D., Litt.D. (Old Testament Language and Literature)
1953-1967 Vincent Parkin, M.A., B.Sc. (New Testament Language and Literature)
1961-1967 Herbert J. Cook, M.A. (Old Testament Language and Literature)

CHURCH HISTORY AND HISTORY OF DOCTRINE

1932-1943 H. Watkin-Jones, M.A., D.D.
1946-1954 H. Watkin-Jones, M.A., D.D.
1954-1967 H. Morlet Rattenbury, M.A.

ASSISTANT TUTORS

1932-1933 C. Leslie Mitton, B.A.
1933-1936 Leslie A. Hewson, B.A.
1936-1939 Philip S. Watson, M.A.
1939-1940 Thomas C. Baird, B.A., B.D.
1940-1942 Christopher D. Bacon, B.A., B.D.
1942-1943 C. Kingsley Barrett, M.A.
1946-1948 Lawrence Proctor, B.D.
1948-1952 Owen E. Evans, M.A., B.D.
1951-1953 John H. S. Kent, M.A., Ph.D. (P.A. 1952-1953)
1953-1955 Kenneth R. Tucker, B.A.
1955-1957 Brian J. N. Galliers, B.D.
1957-1959 Francis N. Jasper, B.A. (P.A. 1958-1959)
1958-1960 John Dover, M.A.
1960-1962 Donald English, B.A.
1962-1964 David Blatherwick, M.A., LL.B.
1964-1967 David G. A. Calvert, B.A., B.D.
P.A. President's Assistant.
The College was closed 1943-1946 owing to the war.

HANDSWORTH COLLEGE, BIRMINGHAM: 1932-1970
QUEEN'S COLLEGE, BIRMINGHAM: 1970

HANDSWORTH

PRINCIPALS

1932-1940 William F. Lofthouse, M.A., D.D.
1945-1951 Wilbert F. Howard, M.A., D.D., F.B.A.
1951-1955 Philip S. Watson, M.A., B.D.
1955-1970 C. Leslie Mitton, B.A., M.Th., D.D., Ph.D.

RESIDENT TUTORS

1932-1940 Henry Bett, M.A., D.Litt.
1945-1952 Harold S. Darby, M.A.
1953-1956 G. Ernest Long, M.A.
1956-1970 C. Leslie Mitton, B.A., M.Th., D.D., Ph.D.

THEOLOGY AND PHILOSOPHY

1932-1940 William F. Lofthouse, M.A., D.D.
1945-1955 Philip S. Watson, M.A., B.D.
1955-1970 William Strawson, M.Th., Ph.D.

BIBLICAL LANGUAGES AND LITERATURE

1932-1940 Christopher R. North, M.A. (Old Testament Language and Literature)
1932-1940 Wilbert F. Howard, M.A., D.D., F.B.A. (New Testament Language and Literature)
1945-1951 Wilbert F. Howard, M.A., D.D., F.B.A. (New Testament Language and Literature)
1946-1956 George Anderson, M.A. (Old Testament Language and Literature)
1951-1970 C. Leslie Mitton, B.A., M.Th., D.D., Ph.D. (New Testament Language and Literature)
1956-1967 Cyril S. Rodd, M.A. (Old Testament Language and Literature)

CHURCH HISTORY AND PASTORAL THEOLOGY

1932-1940 Henry Bett, M.A., D.Litt.
1945-1952 Harold S. Darby, M.A.
1953-1970 G. Ernest Long, M.A.

ASSISTANT TUTORS

1932-1934 Harold S. W. Page, B.A.
1934-1936 Thomas W. Taylor, M.A.
1936-1938 William G. B. Ream, M.A.
1938-1940 A. Raymond George, M.A.
1946-1951 Michael J. Skinner, M.A.
1951-1953 W. David Stacey, B.A.

1953-1957 Arthur W. Wainwright, M.A.
1957-1959 Brian E. Beck, B.A.
1959-1961 Graham Slater, B.A.
1961-1964 Ivor H. Jones, M.A.
1964-1965 Peter W. Ludlow, B.A.
1965-1967 Raymond Goodburn, B.A.
1967-1970 Graham A. Patrick, B.A., B.D.

The College was closed from 1940-1945 owing to the war.

QUEEN'S COLLEGE, BIRMINGHAM: 1970

PRINCIPALS
1970-1973 John S. Hapgood, M.A., D.D. (Anglican)
1974-1979 Arthur P. Bird, M.A., M.B., B.Ch. (Anglican)
1979 Gordon S. Wakefield, M.A., B.Litt. (Methodist)

SENIOR METHODIST TUTORS
1970-1975 William Strawson, M.Th., Ph.D.
1975-1979 Trevor T. Rowe, M.A., B.Sc., B.D.

THEOLOGY
1970-1975 William Strawson, M.Th., Ph.D.
1975-1979 Geoffrey Wainwright, M.A., B.D., D.Theol.
1979 John Taylor, B.A., B.D.

BIBLICAL STUDIES
1973-1975 Geoffrey Wainwright, M.A., B.D., D.Theol.

PASTORAL STUDIES
1970-1979 Trevor T. Rowe, M.A., B.Sc., B.D.

CHURCH HISTORY
1970-1981 J. Muncey Turner, M.A.
1981 W. Peter Stephens, M.A., B.D., D es R.

LITURGY AND SPIRITUALITY
1979 Gordon S. Wakefield, M.A., B.Litt.

VICTORIA PARK COLLEGE, MANCHESTER: 1932-1934
HARTLEY COLLEGE, MANCHESTER: 1932-1934
HARTLEY VICTORIA COLLEGE, MANCHESTER: 1934-1973
HARTLEY VICTORIA COLLEGE — MANCHESTER BAPTIST COLLEGE: 1973

VICTORIA PARK

PRINCIPAL
1932-1934 John T. Brewis, B.A., B.D.

TUTORS
1932-1934 E. Wales Hirst, M.A., B.Sc.

HARTLEY

PRINCIPAL
1932-1934 W. Lansdell Wardle, M.A., D.D.

TUTORS
1932-1934 A. Lewis Humphries, M.A.
1932-1934 Henry G. Meecham, M.A., B.D., Ph.D.
1932-1934 Professor Atkinson Lee, M.A.

HARTLEY VICTORIA

PRINCIPALS
1934-1942 W. Lansdell Wardle, M.A., D.D.
1945-1948 John T. Brewis, B.A., B.D.
1948-1953 Henry G. Meecham, M.A., B.D., Ph.D.
1953-1959 John T. Wilkinson, M.A., D.D.
1959-1973 Percy Scott, B.D., D.Theol.

RESIDENT TUTORS
1946-1953 Henry G. Meecham, M.A., B.D., Ph.D.
1953-1964 J. Yoeman Muckle, B.A.
1964-1973 Percy Scott, B.D., D.Theol.

THEOLOGY
1934-1940 John T. Brewis, B.A., B.D.
1940-1942 Charles J. Wright, B.A., Ph.D.
1946-1947 John T. Wilkinson, M.A., D.D.
1947-1973 Percy Scott, B.D., Ph.D.

APPLIED THEOLOGY
1969-1973 Richard G. Jones, M.A., B.D.

HISTORICAL THEOLOGY
1972-1973 Donald English, M.A.

BIBLICAL LANGUAGES AND LITERATURE
1934-1942 W. Lansdell Wardle, M.A., D.D. (Old Testament Language and Literature)
1934-1942 Henry G. Meecham, M.A., B.D., Ph.D. (New Testament Language and Literature)
1945-1948 John T. Brewis, B.A., B.D. (Old Testament Language and Literature)
1945-1953 Henry G. Meecham, M.A., B.D., Ph.D. (New Testament Language and Literature)
1948-1970 J. Yoeman Muckle, B.A., (Old Testament Language and Literature)
1953-1969 Owen E. Evans, M.A., B.D. (New Testament Language and Literature)
1970-1973 Ivor H. Jones, M.A., M.Litt. (Biblical Languages and Literature)

CHURCH HISTORY
1934-1940 George G. Hornby, M.A., B.D.
1940-1942 W. Bardsley Brash, M.A., B.D., B.Litt.
1945-1946 John T. Wilkinson, M.A., D.D.
1947-1959 John T. Wilkinson, M.A., D.D.
1959-1965 John H. S. Kent, M.A., Ph.D.
1965-1970 Henry D. Rack, M.A.
1970-1973 W. Peter Stephens, M.A., B.D., D es R.

PHILOSOPHY
1934-1942 Professor Atkinson Lee, M.A.
1945-1947 Professor Atkinson Lee, M.A.
1957-1967 Bernard E. Jones, M.A., B.D., Ph.D.

Between 1947-1957, and 1967-1973 Philosophy was taught by the Theological tutor.

ASSISTANT TUTORS
1940-1942 A. Raymond George, M.A.
1948-1950 Stanley J. Metcalf, B.A.
1950-1952 John R. Farley, B.A.
1952-1955 J. Clifford Hindley, B.A.
1955-1958 Alan S. Warren, B.A.
1958-1961 W. Peter Stephens, B.A.
1961-1963 G. Michael Wearing, B.A., B.D.
1963-1967 Kenneth S. J. Hext, B.A.
1967-1969 John A. Rudge, B.A.
1969-1971 Michael R. Fielding, B.A.
1971-1973 John A. Harrod, B.A., B.Sc.

The College was closed 1942-1945 owing to the war.

HARTLEY VICTORIA — MANCHESTER BAPTIST COLLEGE: 1973

PRINCIPALS
1973-1981 Richard G. Jones, M.A., B.D.
1981 Graham Slater, M.A.

TUTORS
1973-1975 John A. Harrod, B.A., B.Sc.
1975-1981 Graham Slater, M.A.
1981 Thomas J. Stuckey, M.Th., B.Sc.

WESLEY HOUSE, CAMBRIDGE: 1932

PRINCIPALS
1932-1937 H. Maldwyn Hughes, M.A., D.D.
1937-1955 R. Newton Flew, M.A., D.D.
1955-1967 William F. Flemington, M.A.
1967-1974 E. Gordon Rupp, M.A., D.D., D.Theol., F.B.A.
1974-1980 Michael J. Skinner, M.A.
1980 Brian E. Beck, M.A.

THEOLOGY
1932-1937 H. Maldwyn Hughes, M.A., D.D.
1937-1955 R. Newton Flew, M.A., D.D.
1955-1959 Philip S. Watson, M.A., D.D.
1959-1960 Michael J. Skinner, M.A.
1980 David G. Deeks, M.A.

NEW TESTAMENT LANGUAGE AND LITERATURE

1932-1937	R. Newton Flew, M.A., D.D.
1937-1967	William F. Flemington, M.A.
1968	Brian E. Beck, M.A.

CLIFF COLLEGE

PRINCIPALS

1932	Samuel Chadwick
1933-1948	John A. Broadbelt
1948-1957	J. Edward Eagles, M.C.
1957-1965	Thomas D. Meadley, B.A., B.D.
1965-1977	Howard A. G. Belben, M.A., B.D.
1977	A. Skevington Wood, B.A., Ph.D.

TUTORS

1932-1934	Norman G. Dunning, M.A., LL.B.
1934-1942	George Allen, B.A.
1937-1940	Joseph I. Brice, M.A.
1943-1946	George Allen, B.A.
1946-1948	J. Edward Eagles, M.C.
1946-1947	Maurice Barnett, M.A., B.D.
1947-1953	Howard A. G. Belben, M.A., B.D.
1953-1956	Cyril H. Powell, M.A., M.Litt., Ph.D.
1956-1961	Leonard E. Sutch
1959-1960	David R. Hall, M.A.
1960-1965	Howard A. G. Belben, M.A., B.D.
1961-1966	Amos S. Cresswell, M.A.
1965-1970	Malcolm W. White, M.A., B.Sc.
1966-1969	H. J. Royston Emms, B.Sc., B.D.
1969-1975	David G. Sharp, M.A., B.D.
1970-1977	A. Skevington Wood, B.A., Ph.D.
1975	John B. Job, M.A., B.D.
1977	Brian R. Hoare, B.D.

NATIONAL CHILDREN'S HOME AND ORPHANAGE; 1932-1965
NATIONAL CHILDREN'S HOME: 1965

1932-1933	W. Hodson Smith, John H. Litten, George A. Parkinson
1933-1944	John H. Litten, Alfred J. G. Seaton, B.D., Ernest Raithby
1944-1945	John H. Litten, Alfred J. G. Seaton, B.D., George A. Parkinson, Cecil F. Walpole, John W. Waterhouse, M.A., B.D.
1945-1950	John H. Litten, Cecil F. Walpole, John W. Waterhouse, M.A., B.D.
1950-1957	John W. Waterhouse, M.A., B.D., Cecil F. Walpole
1957-1968	John W. Waterhouse, O.B.E., M.A., B.D., Gordon E. Barritt, M.A.
1968-1969	John W. Waterhouse, O.B.E., M.A., B.D., Gordon E. Barritt, M.A., Raymond J. Jones, M.A., B.D.
1969-1976	Gordon E. Barritt, M.A., Raymond J. Jones, M.A., B.D.
1976-1977	Gordon E. Barritt, M.A.
1977	Gordon E. Barritt, M.A., E. Michael Newman, M.A.

The first named is the Principal.

WESLEY DEACONESS ORDER

WARDENS

1932-1940	W. Russell Maltby, D.D.
1940-1952	W. Harold Beales, M.A.
1952-1964	Thomas M. Morow, M.A.
1964-1972	Geoffrey Litherland, M.A., B.D.
1972-1980	Brian J. N. Galliers, M.A., M.Th.

The Order has now ceased.

The National Children's Home and Orphanage (1873) and the Wesley Deaconess Order (1903), were both founded by the Revd. Dr. T. Bowman Stephenson, B.A.

KINGSWOOD SCHOOL: 1932

HEADMASTERS

1932-1959	Mr. A. Barrett Sackett, M.C., M.A.
1959-1970	Mr. A. Lowry Creed, M.A.
1970	Mr. Laurence J. Campbell, M.A.

CHAPLAINS

1935-1947	Revd. Rupert E. Davies, M.A., B.D.
1947-1953	Revd. Vincent Parkin, M.A., B.Sc.
1953-1961	Revd. J. Clifford Culshaw, M.A.
1961-1969	Revd. Gerald D. Needham, M.A.
1969-1973	Revd. Kenneth B. Wilson, M.A.
1972-1973	Revd. Graham G. Fergusson, B.A. (Assistant)
1973	Revd. John C. A. Barrett, M.A.

VISITORS

1932-1936	Revd. Owen S. Watkins, G.M.G., C.B.E.
1936-1938	Revd. C. Ryder Smith, B.A., D.D.
1938-1944	Revd. Owen S. Watkins, G.M.G., C.B.E.
1944-1955	Revd. Leonard J. W. Babb, M.C.
1955-1974	Revd. A. Kingsley Lloyd
1974	The President of the Conference

WESTMINSTER COLLEGE, LONDON: 1932-1959
WESTMINSTER COLLEGE, NORTH HINKSEY, OXFORD: 1959

PRINCIPALS

1932-1940	Revd. Archibald W. Harrison, M.C., B.A., B.Sc., D.D.
1940-1953	Mr. James S. Ross, M.A., B.Sc.
1953-1968	Revd. H. Trevor Hughes, M.A.
1968-1982	Mr. Donald Crompton, M.A.
1982	Revd. Kenneth B. Wilson, M.A., M.Litt., Ph.D.

VICE-PRINCIPALS

1932-1940	Mr. James S. Ross, M.A., B.Sc.
1946-1953	Revd. H. Trevor Hughes, M.A.
1953-1961	Dr. Thomas B. Shepherd, M.A.
1962-1969	Dr. D. Geoffrey Harrison, M.A.
1969-1971	Mr. Christopher T. Eddy, M.A.
1971-1981	Mr. Donald Tranter, M.A.
1981-1982	Revd. Kenneth B. Wilson, M.A., M.Litt., Ph.D.
1982	Mr. Stephen G. Phillipson, M.A.

CHAPLAINS

1932-1934	Revd. J. Alan Kay, B.A.
1934-1935	Revd. Stanley T. Vincent, B.A.
1935-1938	Revd. Reginald Kissack, B.A., B.D.
1945-1955	Revd. H. Trevor Hughes, M.A.
1955-1962	Revd. Anthony H. Barraclough, M.A.
1962-1963	Revd. John Job, M.A., B.D.
1963-1968	Revd. Kenneth Underwood, B.D.
1968-1969	Revd. John C. A. Barrett, M.A.
1981	Revd. Ralph Waller, M.Th.

SOUTHLANDS COLLEGE, WIMBLEDON: 1932

PRINCIPALS

1932-1949	Miss Florence M. Wood, M.A.
1949-1965	Miss Myra S. Johnson, B.A.
1965-1977	Miss Pauline M. Callard, B.Comm.
1977	Mr. J. Douglas Milbank, B.A.

VICE-PRINCIPALS

1944-1949	Miss Gwendoline E. Hughes, M.A.
1949-1968	Miss Margaret E. Gibbs, O.B.E., M.Sc.
1968-1977	Mr. J. Douglas Milbank, B.A.
1977-1981	Mrs. Irene Elloway, M.A., Ph.D., A.K.C.
1981	Mr. William Hart, B.A., M.Phil.

CHAPLAINS

1932-1940	Revd. Alfred H. Lowe, B.D.
1940-1943	Revd. Derrick A. Greeves, M.A.
1943-1946	Revd. Howard G. A. Belben, M.A., B.D.
1951-1957	Revd. B. Arthur Shaw
1957-1962	Revd. Arnold H. Cooper, B.A.
1962	Revd. James B. Bates, B.A.

Between 1940 and 1946 the College was evacuated to Weston-super-Mare. The Revds. Derrick Greeves and Howard A. G. Belben acted in a part-time capacity. On the return to Wimbledon in 1946 there was no Chaplain until 1951. From 1951 to 1962, the Revds. B. Arthur Shaw and Arnold H. Cooper, who were ministers at Hinde Street, London, acted in a part-time capacity.

CHAIRMEN OF THE DISTRICTS

The office of Chairman of the District was inaugurated by the Conference of 1792 in Wesleyan Methodism. The regulation for election at first was: 'All the Preachers of every District respectively, who shall be present at the Conference from time to time, shall meet together, as soon as possible, after the Stations of the Preachers are finally settled, and choose a Chairman for their District, out of the present or absent members of the District Committee.' In 1797 the regulation was changed: 'The Chairman of every District shall be chosen by the ballot of the Conference.' In 1812 the Conference directed that: 'The President of the Conference shall always be, ex officio, Chairman of the District in which he is stationed, during the year of his presidency.' These regulations with little alteration remained in force till 1932. At Methodist Union the office of Chairman of the District was retained, and the former Wesleyan mode of election was used. In 1957 the Districts were reduced from 46 to 34, and the Chairman of the District was separated (i.e. no Circuit or other appointment), except for the Channel Islands, the Isle of Man, the three Welsh Districts, and Shetland. In 1974 the three Welsh Districts were amalgamated and the District became Cymru with a Chairman. The other three Districts remain as they were, and now there are 32 Districts. The method of choosing a Chairman is now done by a Committee composed of representatives from the Connexion and the District. The nomination is made to the Conference which usually confirms the choice.

1. LONDON NORTH EAST

1957-1966 Percy D. Beckwith
1966-1972 Frank C. Eden
1972-1982 Deryck C. Collingwood, B.A.
1982 Brian J. N. Galliers, M.A., M.Th.

2. LONDON NORTH WEST

1957-1962 Lawrence O. Brooker
1962-1974 A. Kingsley Turner, M.A.
1972-1980 Richard L. J. Kaye
1980 Stanley K. Chesworth

3. LONDON SOUTH WEST

1957-1965 George H. Simpson
1965-1976 Cyril Wainwright, B.A., B.D.
1976-1981 Wilfrid H. Jones
1981 Colin G. Rowe

§. LONDON SOUTH EAST

1957-1969 F. Ronald Ducker, B.Comm.
1969-1980 Norman V. Dowson, M.A., B.Sc.
1980 Peter W. Sutcliffe, B.A.

5. BIRMINGHAM

1957-1963 W. Russell Shearer, M.A.
1963-1974 Wilfred H. Bridge
1974 C. Hughes Smith, M.A.

6. BOLTON AND ROCHDALE

1957-1966 W. Walker Lee, M.A.
1966-1970 Norman C. Parsons
1970-1980 Ronald Jobling
1980 Geoffrey Stone, B.D.

7. BRISTOL

1957-1963 Fred W. J. Cottrell
1963-1975 Leslie M. Wollen, M.A.
1975 Ian C. Lunn, M.A., B.Sc.

8. CARDIFF AND SWANSEA

1957-1971 Maldwyn L. Edwards, M.A., D.D., Ph.D.
1971 Wyndham E. Bold

9. CUMBRIA

1957-1965 Ernest Hardy
1965-1974 M. Wesley Earl, M.A., B.D.
1974-1980 Alan O. Barber
1980 J. Norman Pickering, B.D.

10. CHANNEL ISLANDS

1957-1959 E. Eccleston Potts, M.B.E., T.D.
1959-1962 William Moralee
1962-1966 J. Reginald Bailey
1962-1972 Hedley C. Browning
1972-1976 Herbert Lindley
1976-1979 S. Theodore Thomas, B.A.
1979 Kenneth E. Street, M.A.

11. CHESTER AND STOKE-ON-TRENT

1957-1962 Arthur G. Utton, M.A., B.D.
1962-1980 B. Arthur Shaw, D.Univ.
1980 J. Stuart Rhodes, M.A.

12. CORNWALL

1957-1963 Wilfred Wade
1963-1973 R. Hubert Luke
1973-1980 A. Bernard Franklin
1980 Ian Haile, B.Met.

13. DARLINGTON

1957-1961 Arthur Simmons, B.A.
1961-1968 Thomas Sutcliffe
1968-1975 E. Lincoln Minshull, B.A.
1979 Geoffrey Kemp

14. EAST ANGLIA

1957-1972 Hubert J. Martin, M.A., B.D.
1972 G. Thackray Eddy, M.A., B.D.

15. ISLE OF MAN

1957-1958 Leonard Emerson
1958-1963 Christopher Ross
1963-1965 Joseph Wilson
1965-1969 John Dodds
1969-1972 Edward J. Le Poidevin
1969-1975 Kenneth A. Bear, B.A.
1975-1976 Harold Hughes
1976-1981 Ronald W. J. Pearce
1981 Arthur Harris

16. LEEDS

1957-1966 Edward J. Prentice
1966-1978 W. Walker Lee, M.A.
1978 W. Stanley Rose, B.D.

17. LINCOLN

1957-1973 Frederic O. Le Sueur, B.A.
1963-1967 G. Thackray Eddy, M.A., B.D.
1967-1973 C. Vincent Corner
1973 W. Eric Jones

18. LIVERPOOL

1957-1962 Gilberthorpe Harrison
1962-1965 H. Sinclair Walker
1965-1975 Reginald Kissack, M.A., B.D.
1975 Norwyn E. Denny, B.D.

19. MANCHESTER AND STOCKPORT

1957-1959 J. Herbert Price, M.A.
1959-1971 Kenneth H. Crosby, B.A., B.D., Ph.D.
1971-1979 Gordon S. Wakefield, M.A., M.Litt.
1979 Ronald C. W. Hoar, B.D.

20. NEWCASTLE-UPON-TYNE

1957-1958 John G. Lane
1958-1966 William V. Harper
1966-1974 Kenneth L. Waights
1974-1980 M. Wesley Earl, M.A., B.D.
1980 John G. Mitchell

21. NORTH LANCASHIRE

1957-1969 Gordon A. Maland
1969-1980 G. Herbert Raynor
1980 George W. S. Knowles, M.A.

22. NOTTINGHAM AND DERBY

1957-1963 John W. Swarbrick, M.A., B.D.
1963-1969 Wilfred Wade
1969-1973 Christopher D. Bacon, B.A., B.D.
1973 Brian A. Greet, B.A., B.D., S.T.M.

23.OXFORD AND LEICESTER

1957-1969 Wilfred Shepherd
1969-1971 William F. Hewitson, B.A., B.D.
1971-1976 Gordon W. Argyle, B.D.
1976 Dennis Williams, M.A., B.Sc.

24. PLYMOUTH AND EXETER

1957-1959 James K. Whitehead, B.A.
1959-1976 J. Russell Pope
1976 Amos S. Cresswell, M.A.

25. SHEFFIELD
1957-1969 George Percival
1969-1978 Frank Amery, M.A.
1978 Sidney Booth

26. SOUTHAMPTON
1957-1968 Reginald C. Stonham
1968-1977 Donald R. Lee, M.B.E., B.D.
1977 Laurence A. Ashman, B.D.

27. WEST YORKSHIRE
1957-1962 Harold Key, O.B.E.
1962-1965 Cyril Wainwright, B.A., B.D.
1965-1974 Thomas M. Morrow, M.A.
1974-1979 Ralph E. Fennell, M.A.
1979 John H. Atkinson, M.A.

28. WOLVERHAMPTON AND SHREWSBURY
1957-1975 Brian S. O'Gorman
1975 Nigel L. Gilson, D.F.C., M.A.

29. YORK AND HULL
1975-1964 F. Pratt Green
1964-1970 J. Cyril T. Downes, M.B.E., M.A., B.D.
1970-1975 Peter A. Kerridge
1975 Ronald Atkinson

30. FIRST NORTH WALES
1957-1971 I. Elfyn Ellis, M.A.
1971-1974 Gwilym R. Tilsley, M.A.

31. SECOND NORTH WALES
1957-1962 J. Gwyn Jones, M.A.
1962-1974 Griffith T. Roberts, M.A., B.D.

32. SOUTH WALES
1957-1963 D. Llewelyn Jones, B.A.
1963-1964 J. Henry Griffiths, B.A.

First North Wales, Second North Wales, and South Wales amalgamated in 1974, and renamed Cymru, and became District No. 30, now making 32 Districts in all.

30. CYMRU
1974-1980 Hugh Rowlands
1980 William O. Thomas

31. SCOTLAND
1957-1969 Frederick A. Rowe, M.A.
1969-1982 H. Haddow Tennant
1982 Alan P. Horner, B.A., B.D.

32. SHETLAND (ZETLAND 1957-1969)
1957-1960 Alan H. Grant
1960-1967 Frank C. Searle
1967-1972 Henry E. Foss
1972-1977 Eric Wright, B.D.
1977 David Monkton

CANDIDATES FOR THE MINISTRY: 1974-1982
THEOLOGICAL COLLEGE TO WHICH CANDIDATES HAVE BEEN DESIGNATED

The date indicates the year of acceptance.

WESLEY HOUSE, CAMBRIDGE

ENTERED 1974
1974 Anderson, Brian J., B.Sc.
1974 Davies, Keith, M.Theol
1974 Ensor, Peter W., M.A.
1974 Hall, Margaret M., B.A.
1974 Hannah, Nigel J.
1974 Hoar, Philip C., B.A.
1974 Jackson, Richard J., B.A., B.Sc., Ph.D.
1974 Kingsnorth, Stephen L., B.A.
1974 Lavender, David F., M.A.
1974 McCall, Malcolm J., M.A., D.Phil.
1974 Moyle, D. Joan
1974 Roseblade, Graham C., B.A.

ENTERED 1975
1975 Amery, Martin J., B.A.
1975 Bolt, Alistair V.C., B.A., B.Sc.
1975 Cornell, Christine E., B.A. (nee Potter)
1975 Frudd, David J.
1975 Gifford, A. Margaret
1975 Land, Derek, B.A., B.Sc.
1975 Pine, Norman, B.Eng.

ENTERED 1976
1976 Barber, Peter, E.
1976 Bowden, Jill B.
1976 Cornell, Geoffrey R.
1976 Demore Timothy P.
1976 Mares, Stephen R.
1975 Wood, David R.

ENTERED 1977
1977 Clarke, Philip A., B.A.
1977 Everatt, Julia W., B.Sc.
1977 Mullins, David H., B.Sc.
1976 Pye, Jonathan H. B.A.
1976 Richardson, Kathleen M.
1977 Shreeve, Christopher J.
1977 Sneddon, Robert, B.Sc.
1976 Taylor, Kathleen, B.A.
1977 Wilson, Michael P., B.A., B.Sc.
1977 Youngs, David E.

ENTERED 1978
1978 Cross, J. Donald, B.Sc.
1978 Davies, Judith M. (nee Phillips)
1978 Drysdale, Peter, B.Sc.
1978 Easton, David P., B.Ed.
1978 Jackson, Roy McP., M.A.
1977 Jones, James W., B.A., B.Sc.
1978 Jones, Robert L., B.Sc.
1978 Smithson, Martin T.
1978 Such, Royston J., LL.B.
1977 Suttie, Ian, B.A.
1978 Tunnicliffe, Michael, M.A.

ENTERED 1979
1979 Berry, Philip J., F.A.
1979 Jones, Nicola G.
1979 Jones, Susan A., B.A.
1978 Levitt, J. Peter F.
1979 Souter, Ian, B.A.
1979 Wilkinson, Marlene H., B.Sc.

ENTERED 1980
1980 Bosworth, David
1980 Firth, Christopher J.
1980 Golighthly, Paul A., B.A.
1979 Hoggard, Trevor, B.A.
1980 Howcroft, Kenneth G., M.A.
1980 Kreschnak, H. Frieder
1980 Lee, Geoffrey, M.Sc.
1980 Parker, Ian W. L., LL.B.
1980 Summerscales, Ian, B.A.

ENTERED 1981
1981 Burrow, J. Keith, B.A.
1981 Champley, Andrew P., B.A.
1981 Cobb, Jessie E.D., B.Sc.
1981 Edwards. Peter, B.A.
1981 Gibson, David C., B.A.
1981 Godfrey, Mark R., B.A.
1981 Howard, John D., B.Sc.
1981 Kilby, Kenneth E.
1979 Palmer, David G., B.Sc.
1981 Robinson, Jennifer M., B.Ed.
1981 Simmonds, Stafford J.
1980 Titley, Robert J., B.A.

ENTERED 1982
1982 Bean, A. Robert, Ph.D.

1982 Blake, Christopher, B.Sc., Ph. D.
1982 Cockburn, Paul, B.Sc.
1982 Forecast, Hazel M., B.A.
1982 Fox, Nigel D., B.Tech.
1982 Haynes, Gregory S., M.A.
1982 Hurst, Edmee W.
1981 Jones, Gareth P., B.A.
1982 Parr, Keith J.

QUEEN'S, BIRMINGHAM

ENTERED 1974
1974 Cluterbuck, Richard N., B.A.
1974 Jones, David L.
1974 Moore, Roger G., B.A.
1974 Nixon, Melvyn, B.A., B.Ed.
1974 Pugh, Neville
1974 Reynolds, Dennis G.
1974 Sharrock, Malcolm J., B.A.
1973 Walton, Roger L., B.A., B.Sc.

ENTERED 1975
1975 Anderson, William E.
1975 Gilchrist, Eileen
1974 Hamfleet, David G.
1975 Hughes, Michael
1975 Lowe, Roger E.
1972 Poxon, Stephen J., B.Sc.
1975 Rolls, Olive
1975 Sharman, John R.

ENTERED 1976
1976 Bales, Stephen D.
1976 Baxendale, Janet A.
1976 Cox, Anthony C.
1976 Donoghue, Stephen
1976 Fisher, Geoffrey R.
1976 Hall, David B.
1976 Johnson, Maurice F.
1976 Pillinger, Peter F.
1976 Smith, David J.D.
1976 Sowler, Peter
1976 Spencer, Terence
1976 Toze, Stephen J.

ENTERED 1977
1977 Armson, Barry R.
1977 Brown, Stephen J., B.Sc.
1977 Burgess, Stephen J., B.Sc.
1977 Etheridge, W. Gordon, B.Sc.
1977 Hamilton, Ian H.
1977 Ludlow, Shirley
1977 Thomas, Bertram J., B.A.
1976 Trethowan, Christine M., B.A.

ENTERED 1978
1978 Ball, Ian C., B.A.
1978 Chapple, Richard R.
1978 Edwards, Kerrin R.
1977 Hancock, Alan P.
1978 Hinton, Alan, B.Sc.
1978 Howes, Paul R.
1978 Jones, David B.
1978 Lewis, Michael J.
1978 Maizel, Judith L., B.A.
1978 Stoyle, Eleanor M.A., B.A.
1978 Taylor, David G.
1977 Unsworth, Gordon
1978 Whorton, Robert, B.Sc.

ENTERED 1979
1979 Annand, Alexander R.
1979 Betts, Jacqueline C.
1979 Davis, Paul H.
1979 Hallworth, Arthur J.
1979 Ireland, Frederick C.
1979 Powell, Robert J.
1979 Pratt, Andrew E., M.Sc.
1979 Pugh, John H.
1979 Ramsey, Virginia
1979 Stabler, John
1979 Safford, Maurice E. M.A.

ENTERED 1980
1980 Blandford, Gwen
1979 Bryant, C. Jill
1980 Cheeseman, Christopher J.
1980 Fowle, Clive R.
1980 Hobson, David
1980 Howard, John A.
1980 Howes, Sandra M. (nee Crabb)
1980 Jackson, Ian, B.A.
1980 Leslie, Roger M.
1979 Warner, Pauline, B.A.
1980 Waterfield, Nigel, B.A.

ENTERED 1981
1981 Ashmore, Richard L., B.D.
1981 Clarke, Peter S., B.Ed.
1981 Coke-Woods, Nigel
1981 Dawes, Martin C.
1981 Goodhand, Mark G., B.A.
1981 Hall, Graham
1981 Hallett, Graham
1981 Hedworth, Paul S.J.
1981 Hoggar, Stephen A.
1981 Holmes, Susan
1981 Howard, Roy E.
1981 Young, Frances M., M.A., Ph.D.

ENTERED 1982
1981 Allison, John L.H., B.Sc.
1982 Bolas, Ann M.
1982 Brown, Stanley, B.A.
1982 Fairhurst, D. Wesley
1982 Hill, Andrew J., B.A.
1982 Howarth, Ian, M.A.
1982 Leckey, Alexander
1982 Longbottom, Peter
1982 Mawditt, Robert S., B.A.
1982 Morton, Derek
1982 Newton, Alistair
1982 Pakes, Andrew
1982 Smith, Margaret C.
1982 Snellgrove, Brian J.
1982 Stacey, J. Neil, LL.B
1982 Stinger, David C., M.A.

HARTLEY VICTORIA, MANCHESTER

ENTERED 1974
1974 Cooke, K. Hilary
1974 Hill, Michael J., B.A.
1974 Seaton, Philip
1974 Tewkesbury, Keith, B.A., B.D.

ENTERED 1975
1975 Bedford, Peter, B.A.
1975 Bhogal, Indejit S.
1975 Burton, A. Dennis
1975 Fenner, John E., B.A.
1974 Jones, Christine, B.A., M.Phil. (nere Vose)
1975 McIntosh, Graham
1975 Morley, Barrie, B.A.
1975 Morton, Robert G.
1975 Robinson, Stephen J.
1975 Torpey, Angela E., B.A.

ENTERED 1976
1976 Clarke, John R., M.A., B.D.
1976 Izzard, John R.
1976 Saville, John R.
1976 Sharp, Christopher J.

ENTERED 1977
1977 Allen Derek M.
1977 Atkins, Martyn D.
1977 Burchell, Keith, B.Sc.
1977 Knight, Keith, B.A.
1977 Richter, Rosemary J., B.A. (nee Cook)
1977 Short, Colin E.
1977 Summers, Peter L.

ENTERED 1978
1978 Henderson, Robert
1978 Little, Robert

1978 Lockhart, Graham
1978 Maguire, Andrew P., B.A.
1978 Rush, Pamela E., B.Ed.
1977 Stears, Alan A.B., M.A., B.Sc.
1978 Town, Keith E.

ENTERED 1979
1979 Bradley, Peter M.
1979 Creamer, Robert B.
1979 Foster, Andrew, M.A.
1979 Gunstone, Andrew L., B.A.
1979 Hall, Stanley
1979 Hare, Doreen C.
1979 Taylor, M. Peter, B,Met

ENTERED 1980
1980 Blundell, Nicholas C., B.A.
1980 Dobson, James
1979 Ferry, Marian
1979 Lunt, Raymond, F.C.A.
1980 Wren, Philip J.
1980 Young, Nigel J., B.Sc.

ENTERED 1981
1981 Albans, Keith R., B.A.
1981 Archer, David J., M.A.
1981 Atkinson, John P., B.Sc.
1981 Fletcher, I. Peter, M.A., D. Phil.
1981 Johnston, Ieuan A., B.Sc.
1981 Lambrick, Jeanette M.
1981 Newman, Paul R.
1981 Sheasby, Peter D., B.A.
1980 Standing, Roger C.
1981 Tomlin, Alison F., B.A.

ENTERED 1982
1982 Bamford, M. Glennys, B.A.
1982 Bishop, Neil A., B.A.
1982 Dixon, J. Trevor
1982 Floyd, Geoffrey D., B.A.
1982 Gayle, Albert C.
1982 Gibson, Ian B.Ed
1982 Hunter, William J., B.A.
1982 Pearce, Daniel
1982 Sparrow, G. Michael, LL.B
1982 Thompson, T. Neil

WESLEY COLLEGE, BRISTOL

ENTERED 1974
1974 Bradshaw, Richard J.
1974 Crow, Patrick L.
1974 Curnow, Howard, B.Sc.
1974 Evans, Graham A.
1974 Hand, Peter G.
1974 Hucknall, John N.
1974 Hughes, Michael C.
1974 Jones, Marian J.
1974 Lander, Derrick R.
1974 Locking, Graham R.
1974 Maymand, Malcolm T.
1974 Paterson, Daniel J.R.

ENTERED 1975
1975 Ashton, Alan
1975 Barnett, John P.
1975 Bennett, Christopher J.
1975 Broad, R. Anthony
1975 Deans, Lynne
1975 Forsaith, Peter S.
1975 Hunter, Ronald
1974 Jobling, Helen M.
1974 Kent, Graham R.
1975 King, David
1974 McBride, Patricia M., B.A., M.Th.
1975 Savage, Kevin G.
1975 Smarth, Judith A. (nee Winsor)
1975 Stillwell, Martin J.
1975 Tanner, Richard J.
1975 Wales, Ian H.
1975 Wilkinson, Geoffrey
1975 Williams, John

ENTERED 1976
1976 Aldridge, Derek A.
1976 Bradshaw, Raymond J.
1975 Braithwaith, Gilbert D., B.A.
1976 Bridges, John A.
1976 Buglass, Anthony E.
1976 Burton, David
1976 Clay, Graham C.
1976 Dybdahl, Christine A.
1976 Evans, Andrew J.
1976 Jones, David B., B.Sc.
1976 Lambrick, Laurence R.
1976 McQueeney, Joyce
1976 Pawlett, Kathryn E. (nee Humble)
1976 Payne, John F. W.
1976 Phipps, Keith M.
1976 Trainer, Neil
1976 Vale, David G.

ENTERED 1977
1977 Bowe, Kathleen M.
1977 Bunkum, Jacqueline C.
1977 Cordy, Andrew
1977 Davis, Peter W.
1977 Edwards, Cecil
1977 Garner, Keith V.
1977 Gillman, David J.
1977 Grasby, Derek
1976 Hildred, Linda
1977 Horsley, Graham
1977 Jackson, Margaret C.
1977 Jackson, Stanley
1977 Jones, Maureen E.
1977 Kirkwood, A. Cameron
1977 Marshall, David
1977 Martin, David F.
1977 Palmer, W. Andrew
1977 Styles, Richard M.
1977 Wells, Anthony
1977 Whitton, Creswell H. J.

ENTERED 1978
1978 Barker, Stanley J.
1978 Bayliss, Roger O.
1978 Bradshaw, Timothy J.
1978 Brazier, Anthony
1978 Broadbridge, James A.
1978 Calver, Martin V.
1978 Cocking, Graham G.
1978 Cole, Peter J.
1978 Dare, Jeremy C.
1978 Featherstoner, Peter F.
1978 Fanning, Phyn N., B.A.
1978 Gardner, Helen D.
1978 Gregory, Henry M.
1978 Harris, Robert G.
1978 Hodgson, Peter W.
1978 Jaggard, Derek W. W.
1978 Richards, Robert A.
1978 Roskilly, Margaret L.
1978 Sankey, Andrew P.
1978 Skelding, Nicholas J.
1978 Sowden, Andrew D.
1978 Speed, David R.
1978 Staton, John E.
1978 Stopford, Michael

ENTERED 1979
1978 Barker, Alan M.., B.Tech.
1979 Bucktrout, David B.
1979 Davies, T. John
1979 Farthing, Geoffrey P. M.A.
1979 Fish, Nigel P.
1979 Hardman, Roger B.
1979 Harrison, Philip N.
1979 Huxtable, Anthony G., B.Theol.
1979 Jackson, R. Paul
1979 Knowles-Berry, Janet M.
1978 Meachem, David T.
1979 Morgan, Gareth G., B.A.
1979 Palmer, John E.

1979 Shaw, Sally, B.A. (nee Dallimore)
1979 Short, Jeffrey M.
1979 Snook, Barrie D.
1979 Teal, Richard J.
1979 Turner, Joan M., B.A.

ENTERED 1980
1980 Baines, Geoffrey
1980 Booth, Mark S.
1980 Carne, F. John
1980 Fielding, Andrew
1980 Gates, Bryan P.
1980 Groves, Martin L., M.Theol.
1980 Haley, John M., B.A.
1980 Harrison, Timothy J.
1980 Hill, Charles J.
1980 Himsworth, Keith
1980 Hughes, Ann
1980 Ingrouille, Rodney F.
1980 Jennings, Stuart R.
1980 Johnson, David M.
1980 Nuttall, George
1980 Perkins, David J.
1980 Riddell, Robert G., B.Sc.
1980 Ridley, Brian
1980 Salter, Keith
1980 Spencer, Ian McRae
1980 Walker, David M.
1980 Wild, Steven J.
1980 Williams, Stephen E., B.A.

ENTERED 1981
1981 Atkinson, Paul, B.Sc.
1981 Ashby, Paul H., B.Sc.
1981 Barton, Nigel F.
1981 Bates, Peter K.
1981 Blyth, Mona, M.B., Ch.B.
1981 Bolton, David, M.A., Ph.D.
1981 Feast, Michael P.
1981 Giles, Elaine E.
1981 Gregory, David R.
1981 Hart, David J., B.Ed.
1981 Hellyer, John, B.Sc.
1981 Hill, Stehen
1981 Leese, Robert T.
1981 Letchford, Colin W.
1981 McInerney, Thomas
1981 Martin, Paul, B.A.
1981 Needham, Cynthia R.
1981 Peacock, Malcolm, B.Sc.
1981 Read, Tom D.
1981 Shawcross, David G.
1981 Shipley, Barry
1981 Singleton, Stephen B.
1981 Spencer, Susan E.
1981 Tabraham, Barrie W., B.A.
1981 Taylor, Ronald J.
1981 Wheeler, David J.C.
1981 Wilde, Richard W.
1981 Wright, Stephen

ENTERED 1982
1982 Davies, K. Rhian
1982 Davis, Stuart
1982 Dunbar, Geoffrey L.
1982 Easton, David J.
1982 Fellows, Cedric J.
1982 Fenn, John P.
1982 Graff, Anthony J.
1982 Guidi, Cesar A.
1981 Hart, Kevin M.
1981 Heath, Stephen N.
1982 Humphreys, Teifon
1982 Hunt, Brian J.
1982 Jay, Stephen A.
1982 Nadin, Geoffrey F.
1982 Oliver, Malcolm J.
1982 Prime, David A.
1982 Ritson, John D.
1982 Rowbottom, Keith
1982 Walter, David C.

NON-RESIDENTIAL TRAINING
1974 Curran, David J.
1975 Faulks, Veronica M.S.
1976 Burgess, Alan S.
1978 Brant, Peter M.
Timms, Peter
1979 Taylor, Jane E.
1980 Bartlett, Roger N.
Featherstone, Susan V.H.
1981 Booth, James A.
Chapman, Valerie
Dawson, Peter
Foreman, Sheila
Hall, Grahame
Humphries, Hazel
Prichard, Eric C.
Trotter, James
Walton, Terence E.
1982 Pocock, Christine M.

PRESIDENTS OF THE WELSH ASSEMBLY

1932	Evan D. Thomas
1933	Arthur W. Davies, M.C.
1934	H. Meirion Davies
1935	R. Jones Williams
1936	Robert J. Parry
1937	E. Tegla Davies, M.A., D.Litt
1938	D Egwyn Jones
1939	R. Garrett Roberts
1940	Edward Davies
1941	Charles Jones
1942	Richard Jones, B.A.
1943	J. Lloyd Hughes
1944	J. Hopkin Morgan
1945	Lewis Edwards
1946	W. Morris Jones
1947	T. Gabriel Hughes, B.A.
1948	J. Roger Jones, M.A., B.D.
1949	Robert W. Davies
1950	David R. Rogers, M.A.
1951	Joseph Jenkins
1952	D. Llewelyn Jones, B.A.
1953	J. Ellis Williams
1954	John Price
1955	David H. Thomas, B.A.
1956	John Hughes
1957	Robert G. Hughes
1958	G. Lloyd Brookes
1959	J. Gwyn Jones, M.A.
1960	D. Arthur Morgan
1961	I. Elfyn Ellis, M.A.
1962	H. Baldwyn Pugh
1963	D. Henriw Mason
1964	David R. Evans
1965	O. Prys Davies
1966	Rufus Roberts, M.A.
1967	Rheinallt L. Jones
1968	Griffith T. Roberts, M.A., B.D.
1969	Gwilym R. Tilsley, M.A.
1970	Enoc T. Davies
1971	W. Lslwyn Morgan
1972	Eric Edwards
1973	D. James Evans
1974	D. James Evans

SECRETARIES OF THE WELSH ASSEMBLY

1932-1934	H. Meirion Davies
1935-1955	John Hughes
1956-1962	D. Henriw Mason
1963	W. Islwyn Morgan
1964-1974	Hugh Rowlands

The Conference of 1974 approved the amgamation of the three Welsh Districts, and it was named the Cymru District with a Chairman. The functions of the Welsh Assembly to be performed by the Synod.

THE METHODIST CHURCH IN IRELAND

The first Wesleyan Methodist Conference in Ireland was held at Dublin in 1756, and was presided over by John Wesley. Between 1756 and 1790 sixteen Conferences were held in Ireland. From 1792 they have been held annually.

IRISH CONFERENCES: 1756-1790

Year	Place	President
1756	Dublin	John Wesley, M.A.
1758	Limerick	John Wesley, M.A.
1760	Limerick	John Wesley, M.A.
1767	Dublin	John Wesley, M.A.
1769	Dublin	John Wesley, M.A.
1771	Dublin	John Wesley, M.A.
1778	Dublin	John Wesley, M.A.
1782	Dublin	Thomas Coke, LL.D.
1783	Dublin	John Wesley, M.A.
1784	Dublin	Thomas Coke, LL.D.
1785	Dublin	John Wesley, M.A.
1786	Dublin	Thomas Coke, LL.D.
1787	Dublin	John Wesley, M.A.
1788	Dublin	Thomas Coke, LL.D.
1789	Dublin	John Wesley, M.A.
1790	Dublin	Thomas Coke, M.A.

From 1792 to 1813 the Irish Conference met each year in Dublin presided over by Dr. Thomas Coke.

1814	Dublin	Adam Averill
1815	Dublin	Walter Griffith
1816	Dublin	Adam Clarke, M.A., LL.D.
1817	Dublin	Richard Reece
1818	Dublin	John Gaulter

From 1818 to 1932 the President of the British Conference presided over the sessions of the Irish Conference.

In 1814 some of the Irish Preachers and members petitioned the Conference to allow the Irish Preachers to administer the Sacraments. (The Plan of Pacification which had settled the matter in England had not applied to Ireland). For the next three years it was debated, and in 1818 those who wanted no change seceded and formed themselves into the Primitive Wesleyan Connexion, and they remained separate until they reunited in 1878.

Until 1868 'the British President came to the Irish Conference armed with what was termed the "Power of the Delegate". In other words, he was commissioned to be the Legal Conference in his own person.' This was very unsatisfactory and the British Conference of 1867 resolved: 'That one of the members appointed by the Conference from year to year shall be one of the Irish members of the Legal Conference, (there were always ten members), to be nominated and presented to the British Conference by the Irish representatives.' The Irish Conference concurred and the minister so nominated became known as the Vice-President of the Conference. The British President had no authority outside the sessions of the Conference. The Vice-President presided over all Connexional Committees and acted between Conferences in his official capacity. In 1921 the Vice-President of the Conference became known also as the President of the Methodist Church in Ireland. After 1932 though the British President is still the President of the Conference, the Vice-President and President of the Methodist Church in Ireland is elected at the Irish Conference.

VICE-PRESIDENTS OF THE CONFERENCE

1868 Henry Price
1869 James Tobias
1870 Joseph W. McKay
1871 Robinson Scott, D.D.
1872 William P. Applebe, LL.D.
1873 George Vance
1874 Wallace McMullen
1975 Gibson McMillan
1876 Joseph W. McKay, 2nd time
1877 James Tobias, 2nd time
1878 Wallace McMullen, 2nd time
1879 William G. Price
1880 William P. Applebe, LL.D., 2nd time
1881 James Tobias, 3rd time
1882 Oliver McCutcheon
1883 William Crook, D.D.
1884 James Donnelly
1885 Thomas A. McKee, D.D.
1886 Joseph W. McKay, 3rd time
1887 John D. Powell
1888 Wallace McMullen, 3rd time
1889 William G. Price, 3rd time
1890 Oliver McCutcheon, 2nd time
1891 John W. Ballard
1892 William Gorman
1893 Wesley Guard
1894 William Nicholas, D.D.
1895 Wallace McMullen, D.D., 4th time
1896 William Crook, D.D., 2nd time
1897 James Robertson
1898 R. Crawford Johnson, D.D.
1899 Charles H. Crookshank, M.A.
1900 William Crawford, M.A.
1901 John O. Park
1902 Wesley Guard, 2nd time
1903 William Nicholas, M.A., D.D., 2nd time
1904 Thomas Knox
1905 George R. Wedgwood
1906 James Robertson, D.D., 2nd time
1907 William Crawford, M.A., 2nd time
1908 James D. Lamont
1909 Joseph W. R. Campbell, M.A.
1910 John O. Park, M.A.
1911 Wesley Guard, 3rd time
1912 George R. Wedgwood, 2nd time
1913 Samuel T. Boyd, B.A.
1914 William R. Budd
1915 John O. Price
1916 Pierce Martin
1917 William Maguire
1918 Hugh McKeag
1919 James Kirkwood
1920 Henry Shire

VICE-PRESIDENTS OF THE CONFERENCE. PRESIDENTS OF THE METHODIST CHURCH IN IRELAND

1921 William H. Smyth, M.A.
1922 James M. Alley
1923 James W. Parkhill
1924 William Corrigan
1925 Edward B. Cullen
1926 Robert M. Ker
1927 William H. Smyth, M.A., 2nd time
1928 Randall C. Phillips
1929 John C. Robinson, M.A., B.D.
1930 William Moore
1931 Frederick E. Harte, M.A.
1932 John A. Duke, B.A.
1933 R. Lee Cole, M.A., B.D.
1934 John A. Walton, M.A.
1935 Thomas J. Irwin, D.Litt.
1936 William H. Massey
1937 C. Henry Crookshank
1938 Thomas J. Allen
1939 Alexandre McCrea, M.A.
1938 Hugh M. Watson, M.A.
1939 John N. Spence
1940 Beresford S. Lyons
1941 George A. Joynt, M.A.
1942 William L. Northridge, M.A., D.D.
1943 Edward Whittaker
1946 Robert H. Gallagher, B.A.
1947 John England
1948 W. E. Morley Thompson
1949 John W. Stutt
1950 J. R. Wesley Roddie
1951 Henry N. Medd
1952 John Montgomery
1953 Richard M. L. Waugh, M.A., B.D.
1954 Ernest Shaw
1955 Albert Holland

1956	Samuel E. McCaffrey
1957	J. Wesley McKinney
1958	Robert J. Good
1959	R. Ernest Ker, M.A.
1960	Robert W. McVeigh
1961	Charles W. Ranson, B.Litt., D.Theol.
1962	James Wiseheart
1963	Frederick E. Hill, B.A.
1964	Samuel H. Baxter, M.A., D.D.
1965	Robert A. Nelson
1966	Samuel J. Johnston
1967	R. D. Eric Gallagher, M.A., B.D.
1968	Gerald G. Myles, M.A., H.Dip.Ed.
1969	George E. Good, M.A.
1970	James Davison, O.B.E.
1971	Charles H. Bain, B.D.
1972	Edward R. Lindsay
1973	Harold Sloan
1974	R. Desmond Morris
1975	Hedley W. Plunkett, D.D.
1976	Richard Greenwood, M.A., B.D.
1977	Robert G. Livingstone, M.A.
1978	John Turner, D.D.
1979	Vincent Parkin, M.A., B.Sc.
1980	W. Sydney Callaghan, B.A.
1981	Ernest W. Gallagher, B.A., B.D.
1982	Charles G. Eyre, B.A.

SECRETARIES OF THE IRISH CONFERENCE

1792	John Crook
1793	Walter Griffith
1794-1795	John Crook
1796	William Smith
1797	John Crook
1798	Andrew Hamilton, Jun.
1799	John Kerr
1800	John Dinnen
1801	Adam Averell
1802	John Kerr
1803	Andrew Hamilton, Jun.
1804	William Smith
1805	Samuel Steele
1806	John Grace
1807	Matthew Tobias
1808	William Ferguson
1809	Charles Mayne
1810	Samuel Wood
1811	Matthew Langtree
1812	James MacKeown
1813	Robert Banks
1814	William Stewart
1815	Robert Crozier
1816-1817	Samuel Wood
1818-1819	William Smith
1820	Samuel Woods
1821-1822	Andrew Hamilton, Jun.
1823	Samuel Wood
1824	Andrew Hamilton
1825	Samuel Wood
1826	Andrew Hamilton
1827-1828	Samuel Wood
1829-1830	William Stewart
1831-1839	Thomas W. Doolittle
1840-1847	William Stewart
1848-1860	John F. Matthews
1861-1869	James Tobias
1870-1880	Joseph W. McKay, D.D.
1881-1892	James Donnelly
1893-1897	R. Crawford Johnson, D.D.
1898-1900	John O. Park, B.A.
1900-1904	Caleb S. Laird, M.A.
1905-1907	James D. Lamont
1908-1912	Samuel T. Boyd, B.A.
1913-1921	James M. Alley
1922-1925	Robert M. Ker
1926-1932	R. Lee Cole, M.A., B.D.
1933-1936	C. Henry Crookshank
1937-1940	John N. Spence, M.B.E.
1941-1947	W. E. Morley Thompson
1948-1955	Joseph B. Jameson
1956-1957	Richard S. Morris, M.A.
1958-1966	R. D. Eric Gallagher, M.A., B.D.
1967-1977	Harold Sloan
1978	Charles G. Eyre, B.A.

THE PRIMITIVE WESLEYAN CONNEXION IN IRELAND: 1816-1877

PRESIDENTS OF THE CONFERENCE

Year	Place	President
1816-1818	Clones	Samuel Moorhead
1819	—	—
1820-1846	Dublin	Adam Averell
1847-1852	Dublin	Alexander Stewart
1853	Dublin	Joseph McCormac
1854	Dublin	Thomas McFarr
1855	Dublin	William Herbert
1856	Dublin	Dawson D. Heather
1857	Dublin	William Craig
1858	Dublin	John White
1859	Dublin	John Wherry
1860	Dublin	George Hamilton
1861	Dublin	William H. Mervyn
1862	Dublin	Joseph McCormac
1863	Dublin	William Craig
1864	Dublin	William Robinson
1865	Dublin	James Griffin
1866	Dublin	John Henning
1867	Dublin	Joseph McCormac
1868	Dublin	James Wilson
1869	Dublin	Thomas A. Jones
1870	Dublin	George Hamilton
1871	Dublin	Robert Kerr
1872	Dublin	John Henning
1873	Dublin	James Irwin
1874	Dublin	James Wilson
1875	Dublin	Thomas Abraham
1876	Dublin	Thomas C. Maguire
1877	Dublin	James Griffin

For the years 1838-1846 there was a Vice-President of the Conference, Alexander Stewart.

SECRETARIES OF THE CONFERENCE

1816-1817	Andrew Swenzy
1818	Samuel Moorhead
1819	—
1820-1821	Robert Smith
1822	Alexander Stewart
1823-1824	Robert Smith
1825-1826	Alexander Stewart
1827-1828	George Revington
1829	Alexander Stewart
1830	Thomas McFarr
1831	John Stephenson
1832	John Mallin
1833	John Buttle
1834	Alexander Stewart
1835	Thomas McFarr
1836	Robert Connolly
1837-1838	Alexander Stewart
1839	Thomas McFarr
1840-1842	George Robinson
1843	Thomas McFarr
1844	John Wherry
1845	Joseph McCormac
1846	Richard Robinson
1847-1848	George H. Irwin
1849	Harry Taylor
1850-1851	Thomas McFarr
1852-1853	William H. Mervyn
1854	James Griffin
1855	Robert Kerr
1856	John White
1857	Robert Kerr
1858	Thomas Wilson
1859	Thomas C. Maguire
1860	John White
1861-1862	William Flarherty
1863	Robert Kingsborough

1864	William Flarherty	1867-1868	Thomas C. Maguire	1875	James Wilson
1865	Thomas C. Maguire	1869-1870	James Wilson	1876	Robert Kingsborough
1866	James Wilson	1870-1874	Thomas C. Maguire	1877	Thomas C. Maguire

Appendix III

The Independent Methodist Church

The Wesleyan Reform Union

Glossary

APPENDIX III

THE INDEPENDENT METHODIST CHURCH: 1806
PRESIDENTS OF THE ANNUAL MEETING

The Independent Methodist Church has no ordained or salaried ministry.

Year	Place	President	Representative From
1806	Manchester	No Record	No Record
1807	Macclesfield	No Record	No Record
1808	Macclesfield	Richard Harrison	Warrington
1809	Manchester	No Record	No Record
1810	Warrington	John Berisford	Macclesfield
1811	Macclesfield	J. Crawshaw	Manchester
1812	Manchester	No Record	No Record
1813	Warrington	Peter Ashley	Stockport
1814	Oldham	Peter Ashley	Stockport
1815	Sheffield	Peter Ashley	Stockport
1816	Blackburn	Peter Phillips	Warrington
1817	Stockport	Benjamin Daffin	Sheffield
1818	Warrington	Richard Mills	Warrington
1819	Manchester	Peter Ashley	Stockport
1820	Sheffield	Peter Phillips	Warrington
1821	Oldham	Benjamin Daffin	Sheffield
1822	Warrington	Peter Phillips	Warrington
1823	Manchester	Peter Ashley	Ashton-under-Lyne
1824	Bolton	Peter Phillips	Warrington
1825	Sheffield	Peter Phillips	Warrington
1826	Oldham	Peter Phillips	Warrington
1827	Warrington	William Morton	Sheffield
1828	Manchester	Peter Thornley	Bolton
1829	Bolton	Benjamin Daffin	Sheffield
1830	Oldham	Gamaliel Swindells	Stockport
1831	Oldham	John Lees	Oldham
1832	Warrington	Peter Phillips	Warrington
1833	Manchester	Alexander Donavan	Glasgow
1834	Bolton	Thomas Jones	Liverpool
1835	Wigan	Thomas Jones	Liverpool
1836	Oldham	Humphrey Harper	Salford
1837	Warrington	Humphrey Harper	Salford
1838	Bradford	Thomas Oxley	Manchester
1839	Manchester	Alexander Donavan	Glasgow
1840	Bolton	Samuel Johnson	Manchester
1841	Wigan	Peter Phillips	Warrington
1842	Oldham	Peter Phillips	Warrington
1843	Warrington	Alexander Donavan	Glasgow
1844	Stockport	Joseph Armitt	Manchester
1845	Liverpool	Alexander Donavan	Glasgow
1846	Manchester	Alexander Donavan	Glasgow
1847	Bolton	Alexander Donavan	Glasgow
1848	Oldham	Alexander Donavan	Glasgow
1849	Lancaster	William Sanderson	Liverpool
1850	Liverpool	Alexander Donavan	Glasgow
1851	Glasgow	Alexander Donavan	Glasgow
1852	Warrington	Alexander Donavan	Glasgow
1853	Manchester	Alexander Donavan	Glasgow
1854	Bolton	Alexander Donavan	Glasgow
1855	Liverpool	Alexander Donavan	Glasgow
1856	Nelson	Alexander Donavan	Glasgow
1857	Lancaster	Thomas Oxley	Manchester
1858	Wigan	William Sanderson	Liverpool
1859	Oldham	John Nield	Oldham
1860	Manchester	Alexander Donavan	Glasgow
1861	Liverpool	Alexander Donavan	Glasgow
1862	Nelson	Alexander Donavan	Glasgow
1863	Bolton	Alexander Donavan	Glasgow
1864	Warrington	Alexander Donavan	Glasgow
1865	Liverpool	Alexander Donavan	Glasgow
1866	Roe Green and Sindsley	Edward Twiss	Warrington
1867	Oldham	Alexander Donavan	Glasgow
1868	Nelson	Alexander Donavan	Glasgow
1968	Glasgow	Alexander Donavan	Glasgow
1870	Lancaster	Alexander Donavan	Glasgow
1871	Bolton	William Sanderson	Liverpool
1872	Liverpool	John Knowles	Lymm
1873	Warrington	Alexander Donavan	Glasgow
1874	Colne, Bristol	Alexander Donavan	Glasgow
1875	Cleckheaton	Alexander Donavan	Glasgow
1876	Oldham, Smith St.	Alexander Donavan	Glasgow

Year	Place	President	Representative From
1877	Bolton, Noble St.	Alexander Donavan	Glasgow
1878	Glasgow	Alexander Donavan	Glasgow
1879	Ashton-under-Lyne	William Oxley	Manchester
1880	Sindsley	William Sanderson	Liverpool
1881	Warrington	William Oxley	Manchester
1882	Nelson, Salem	Matthew Kennedy	Wigan
1883	Sunderland	Matthew Kennedy	Wigan
1884	Liverpool	William Brimelow	Bolton
1885	Pendleton	Alfred Roscoe	Bolton
1886	Oldham	James Proe	Wigan
1887	Colne	William Crumblehulme	Bolton
1888	Bolton, Noble St.	William Crumblehulme	Bolton
1889	Stretford	Thomas Worthington	Wigan
1890	Nelson, Barkerhouse Rd.	Thomas Worthington	Wigan
1891	Pendleton	Thomas Worthington	Wigan
1892	Wigan	William Boote	Liverpool
1893	Bolton, Folds Rd.	Benjamin Dyson	Oldham
1894	Barnoldswick	William Brimelow	Bolton
1895	Oldham	William Brimelow	Bolton
1896	Bingley	William Brimelow	Bolton
1897	Warrington	Richard Lee	Wigan
1898	Moorside	Richard Leed	Wigan
1899	Nelson, Salem	William Branfoot	Sunderland
1900	Stretford	John Crumblehulme	Bolton
1901	Leigh	John Crumblehulme	Bolton
1902	Colne, Bethel	Arthur Watson	Nelson
1903	Sunderland	George Hunter	Leigh
1904	Liverpool	George Hunter	Leigh
1905	Oldham	Robert W. Collin	Sunderland
1906	Roe Green	Robert W. Collin	Sunderland
1907	Bristol	Ward H. Riding	Colne
1908	Lancaster	Ward H. Riding	Colne
1909	Burnley	Ellis Barker	Morecambe
1910	Manchester	Ellis Barker	Morecambe
1911	Barnoldswick	Will Price	Wigan
1912	Norwich	Will Price	Wigan
1913	Wigan, Kendle St.	John W. Johnson	Sunderland
1914	Colne, Waterside	John W. Johnson	Sunderland
1915	Oldham, Smith St.	Edward Ralphs	Westhoughton
1916	Leigh	Edward Embleton	Sunderland
1917	Manchester	Edward Embleton	Sunderland
1918	Bolton, Noble St.	Robert Henshall	Warrington
1919	Moorside	Robert Henshall	Warrington
1920	Nelson, Salem	W. H. Hindley	Farnworth
1921	Bolton, Beverley Rd.	W. H. Hindley	Farnworth
1922	Sunderland, Cairo St.	T. Lomax	Bolton
1923	Colne, Bethel	T. Lomax	Bolton
1924	Pendleton	J. Evans	Warrington
1925	Oldham, King St.	T. R. Openshaw	Gargrave
1926	Barnoldswick	Richard Brimelow	Southport
1927	Roe Green	Henry Barrett	Nelson
1928	Liverpool	Abraham Dean	Bingley
1929	Bingley	A. J. Winnard	Wigan
1930	Wigan	Hartley Barrett	Colne
1931	Nelson, Salem	Thomas Bruce	Pendleton
1932	Bolton, Noble St.	George Hunter	Leigh
1933	Colne, Bethel	William Grundy	Leigh
1934	Leigh, Avenue	Mrs. Edward Embleton	Sunderland
1935	Sunderland, Bethany	William Foreman	Sunderland
1936	Moorside	T. Perry	Wigan
1937	Oldham, Smith St.	R. J. Hubbard	Nelson
1938	Barnoldswick	G. Proudfoot	Bishop Auckland
1939	Friars Green	C. Thornton	Ashton-under-Lyne
1940	Bolton, Chalfont St.	T. Darlington	Wistaston
1941	Newtown, Bethel	T. Darlington	Wistaston
1942	Moorside	T. R. Openshaw	Gargrave
1943	Stretford	W. Burrows	St. Helens
1944	Wigan, New Springs	W. Burrows	St. Helens
1945	Oldham, Smith St.	A. Walker	Oldham
1946	Roe Green	A. J. Winnard	Wigan
1947	Nelson, Salem	A. Shires	Thornhill Edge
1948	Bolton, Beverley Rd.	W. Eccleston	Golborne
1949	Wigan, Pemberton	T. Grey	Hetton-le-Hole
1950	Prescot	E. J. Higham	Warrington
1951	Colne, Waterside	W. Imeson	Bristol
1952	Southport, Sussex Rd.	J. S. Hassall	Wistaston
1953	Horwich	A. Lambley	Loughborough
1954	New Silksworth	N. Eccleson	Manchester

Year	Place	President	Representative From
1955	Friars Green		Sunderland
1956	Liverpool, Mill Lane	John Lawson	Southport
1957	New Seaham	J. Groom	Crewe
1958	Wigan, New Springs	A. J. Winnard	Wigan
1959	Tyldesley	Walter Hill	Wigan
1960	Liverpool, Tetlow St.	T. W. Stout	Hetton-le-Hole
1961	Colne, Bethel	Miss. D. Barber	Cleckheaton
1962	Horwich	Dr. W. W. Kay	Epsom
1963	New Silksworth	H. Sharples	Bolton
1964	Tyldesley	Mrs. F. Tetlow	Thornton Cleveleys
1965	Lamberhead Green	Dr. W. W. Kay	Bedford
1966	Colne, Providence	W. J. V. Hills	Houghton-le-Spring
1967	Brandon	Granville Mason	Tyldesley
1968	Bingley	Edith A. Bevan	Swinton
1969	Friars Green	H. Sharples	Bolton
1970	New Seaham	W. Drummond Brown	Swinton
1971	Barnoldswick	Charles F. Grey, C.B.E.	Hetton-le-Hole
1972	Lamberhead Green	W. Stokes	Horwich
1973	Oldham, Chamber Rd.	J. Edwards	Sunderland
1974	Horden	H. G. Gleave	Warrington
1975	Liverpool	A. Kell	Sedgefield
1976	Friars Green	J. Kay	Bury
1977	Durham	Dr. T. Backhouse	Liverpool
1978	Manchester	J. R. Johnson	Wigan
1979	Oldham, Chamber Rd.	T. W. Savage	Seaham
1980	Newtown, Bethel	G. S. Turner	Bristol
1981	Frairs Green	Miss. E. Tyson	Oldham
1982	Bolton	Miss. E. Tyson	Oldham

SECRETARIES OF THE CONFERENCE

1806-1807	No Record
1808	T. Gregory
1809	No Record
1810-1811	Peter Ashley
1812	No Record
1813	J. Goodier
1814	William McGuinness
1815	W. Massey
1816-1817	J. Higson
1818	J. Shaw
1819	William McGuinness
1820	George Turton
1821	W. H. Stephenson
1822	Alexander Donavan
1823	Samuel Balmer
1824	John Mallinson
1825	William McMillan
1826	George Turton
1827	Alexander Donavan
1828	William Morton
1829	J. Davies
1830	Henry Perkins
1831	John Mayall
1832	S. Peacock
1833	William Davis
1834	Alexander Donavan
1835	T. H. Massey
1836	John Mayall
1837	John Kelly
1838-1839	Samuel Roberts
1840	John Kelly
1841	Joseph Holmes
1842-1844	James Bentley
1845	William Sanderson
1846	Thomas Dunning
1847-1848	James Bentley
1849	J. Furniss
1850-1851	William Sanderson
1852	James Gandy
1853-1856	William Sanderson
1857-1858	Samuel Fitzgerald
1859-1862	William Sanderson
1863-1866	Edward Twiss
1867-1868	James Vickers
1869-1870	William Oxley
1871	William Bamber
1872	Jasper Isterling
1873	William Wright
1874-1878	William Oxley
1879-1880	Alfred Roscoe
1881	Silas Cooke
1882-1883	Alfred Roscoe
1884	Matthew Kennedy
1885	William Oxley
1886-1887	John Wild
1888-1892	Robinson Foulds
1893-1898	Frederick Wilkinson
1899-1901	Ward H. Riding
1902-1908	Ellis Barker
1909-1920	James Vickers
1921-1925	Henry Barrett
1926-1940	James Murray
1941-1942	James Murray and W. P. Lockley
1943-1947	W. P. Lockley
1948-1952	Norman Eccleson
1952-1964	W. Drummond Brown
1965-1972	W. Drummond Brown and Dennis S. Downing
1973-1977	Dennis S. Downing
1978	John M. Day, B.Sc.

THE WESLEYAN REFORM UNION: 1859-

According to rule at the time until 1864, the same persons did not, with one or two exceptions, preside over the sitting of the Conference, and so until then in some cases two Presidents are named. The office was open to both ministers and laymen.

Year	Place	President
1859	Sheffield	Mr. T. Chamberlain
1860	Bradford	Mr. J. Andrew and Revd. W. Griffith
1861	Doncaster	Mr. J. Andrew, 2nd time
1866	Birmingham	Mr. E. Hibbert
1867	Sheffield	Mr. S. Hereman
1868	High Wycombe	Mr. J. Neal
1869	Bradford	Mr. T. Chamberlain, 5th time
1870	Grantham	Revd. J. Lord
1871	Wibsey	Mr. T. H. Richard
1872	Middlesbrough	Mr. J. Neal, 2nd time
1873	Bakewell	Mr. S. Hereman, 2nd time
1874	Masborough	Mr. W. Wilkinson
1875	Sheffield	Revd. E. Barley
1876	Bradford	Mr. S. H. Burrows
1877	Birmingham	Mr. E. Dickinson
1878	Northampton	Revd. R. Nichols
1879	Grantham	Mr. M. Nash
1880	Bradford	Mr. S. H. Burrows, 2nd time
1881	Middlesbrough	Mr. W. Marsden
1882	High Wycombe	Revd. E. Barley, 2nd time
1883	Sheffield	Mr. J. Neal, 3rd time
1884	Mexborough	Mr. J. Parker
1885	High Wycombe	Mr. E. Benson, 3rd time
1886	Wibsey	Revd. T. Bromage
1887	Northampton	Revd. A. Holland
1888	Bakewell	Mr. W. Marsden, 2nd time
1889	Skelmanthorpe	Mr. S. Carr
1890	Wombwell	Revd. G. Green
1891	Shipley	Revd. T. Bromage
1892	High Wycombe	Mr. H. Turner
1893	Sheffield	Mr. J. T. Law
1894	Barnsley	Mr. T. Johnson
1895	Wellingborough	Mr. J. T. Beale
1896	Bradford	Mr. H. Heaton
1897	Mexborough	Mr. W. Shirley
1898	Clayton West	Mr. W. Brookes
1899	Sheffield, Jubilee	Mr. G. Carr
1900	Bakewell	Mr. J. H. Freeborough
1901	Wibsey	Revd. W. Clough
1902	High Wycombe	Revd. E. Bromage
1903	Rushden	Mr. W. Marsden
1904	Foleshill	Mr. T. R. Green
1905	Barnsley	Revd. T. G. Harper
1906	Skelmanthorpe	Mr. T. Pears
1907	Shipley	Mr. W. Brookes
1908	Hucknall Torkard	Revd. G. E. Stone
1909	Mexborough	Revd. W. Clough
1910	Sheffield	Mr. J. H. Freeborough
1911	Rushden	Mr. J. H. Freeborough
1912	Bradford, Muff Field	Mr. T. Barron
1913	High Wycombe	Revd. W. C. Smith
1914	Youlgrave	Mr. J. Jaques
1915	Barnsley	Revd. E. Dennis
1916	Hucknall	Revd. J. Clark
1917	Sheffield	Revd. J. Clark
1918	Bradford, Muff Field	Revd. S. Bastow
1919	Bradford, Muff Field	Revd. S. Bastow
1920	Wombwell	Revd. W. Robinson
1921	Mansfield	Revd. W. Ronbinson
1922	Sheffield, Sharrow	Revd. J. Abbott
1923	Rushden, High St.	Revd. G. E. Stone
1862	London	Mr. T. Chamberlain, 2nd time and Mr. E. Courtnell
1863	Retford	Mr. E. Benson and Mr. T. Chamberlain, 3rd time
1864	Grantham	Mr. T. Chamberlain, 4th time
1865	Manchester	Mr. E. Benson, 2nd time
1924	Youlgrave	Mr. W. Brookes, J.P.
1925	Foleshill	Revd. E. Bromage
1926	Barnsley	Mr. W. H. Vaughan
1927	Skelmanthorpe	Revd. A. Wortley
1928	Kiskeard	Mr. G. Clamp
1929	Norwich	Revd. S. J. Smith
1930	Wibsey	Mr. T. R. Green
1931	Hucknall	Mr. J. T. Waterhouse
1932	Wombwell	Revd. G. A. Metcalf, D.D.
1933	Grimesthorpe	Mr. L. F. Milner, O.B.E., J.P.
1934	Rushden, High St.	Revd. G. E. Stone
1935	Youlgrave	Mr. G. F. Nuttall
1936	Liskeard	Revd. N. S. Lobb
1937	Barnsley	Mr. C. Fowler
1938	Coventry	Revd. E. E. Bromage
1939	Mexborough	Revd. W. S. Goodwin
1940	Hucknall	Revd. W. T. Burkitt
1941	Sheffield	Mr. A. Brown
1942	Wibsey, Slackside	Revd. W. H. Jones, D.D.
1943	Skelmanthorpe	Revd. E. Dennis
1944	Sheffield	Revd. E. Dennis
1945	Wombwell	Mr. T. Tomlinson, J.P.
1946	Mansfield	Mr. P. Johnson
1947	Rushden, High St.	Revd. W. T. Burkitt, D.D.
1948	Liskeard	Mr. Grant
1949	Grimesthorpe	Revd. N. S. Lobb
1950	Bradford, Muff Field	Revd. A. Wortley
1951	Barnsley, Salem	Mr. T. O. Roberts
1952	High Wycombe	Revd. A. Halladay
1953	Bakewell	Mr. R. Furness
1954	Wombwell	Revd. C. E. Finnemore
1955	Rushden	Revd. W. T. Burkitt, D.D.
1956	Hucknall	Mr. P. Johnson
1957	Grimesthorpe	Mr. E. G. Nagle
1958	Philadelphia, Sheffield	Revd. C. Mackinder
1959	Wibsey	Mr. C. W. Hodson, J.P.
1960	High Wycombe	Revd. G. Bellamy
1961	Barnsley, Salem	Mr. T. O. Roberts
1962	Youlgrave	Revd. F. C. Wilson
1963	Mexborough	Mr. A. Fisher
1964	Rushden, High St.	Mr. C. Race
1965	Foleshill	Revd. A. Halladay
1966	Grimesthorpe	Mr. H. Sykes
1967	Bradford, Muff Field	Revd. G. D. Lee, B.D.
1968	Barnsley, Salem	Mr. T. Ashby
1969	Bakewell	Revd. D. A. Morris
1970	Wombwell	Mr. P. Johnson
1971	Rushen, High St.	Mr. R. Sowerby
1972	Coventry	Revd. R. Taylor
1973	Sheffield	Mr. F. W. Bruntlett
1974	Wibsey	Revd. A. Halladay
1975	Barnsley, Staincross	Revd. R. Graves
1976	Bakewell	Mr. L. Cook
1977	Mexborough	Revd. E. W. Downing
1978	Rushden, High St.	Revd. J. Barton
1979	Grimesthorpe	Mr. I. Fairhurst
1980	Wibsey	Revd. A. J. Williams
1981	Nuneaton	Revd. J. W. Goulder
1982	Barnsley	Revd. D. A. Morris

CONNEXIONAL COMMITTEE SECRETARIES

Home and Colonial Missions were begun in 1860. In 1929 Home and Overseas Mission Committees were formed. The General Secretary is also the Home Missions Secretary.

OVERSEAS MISSIONS

1929-1946	Revd. J. S. Smith
1946-1962	Mr. P. Johnson, Sen.
1962	Mr. P. Johnson, Jun.

YOUNG PEOPLE'S DEPARTMENT

1907-1922	Revd. G. A. Metcalfe
1922-1943	Revd. E. E. Bromage
1943-1948	Revd. F. G. Gunn
1948-1951	Revd. A. Halladay
1951-1952	Mr. C. Race
1952-1962	Miss J. Banks
1962-1969	Mr. D. Cartledge
1969-1972	Mr. G. Sharp
1972-1978	Mr. D. Russell
1978	Miss J. Senior

TEMPERANCE AND SOCIAL SERVICE LEAGUE

1908-1920	Revd. W. S. Goodwin
1920-1939	Mr. P. J. Squire
1939-1948	Revd. W. T. Burkitt, D.D.
1948-1954	Revd. W. Kendrick
1954-1958	Revd. C. Mackinder
1958-1963	Revd. W. T. Burkitt, D.D.
1963	Revd. R. Graves

PUBLICATIONS

1861-1865	The Wesleyan Union Magazine
1866	Christian Words

WESLEYAN REFORM UNION

The Wesleyan Reform Union did not appoint a Secretary of the Conference, but a General Secretary of the Union. Until 1910 the office was honorary. From that time a minister has been appointed.

GENERAL SECRETARIES

1910-1923	E. Bromage
1923-1943	G. A. Metcalfe, D.D.
1943-1953	W. H. Jones, D.D.
1953-1955	G. A. Metcalfe, D.D.
1955-1973	A. Halladay
1973	D. A. Morris

GLOSSARY

1. **Conference or Assembly** — the supreme legislative body of the Methodist Connexions.
2. **The Legal Hundred** — the Legal Conference of the Wesleyan Methodist Connexion consisting of one hundred ministers 1784-1932.
3. **District Synod** — known in the early days as the District Meeting, formed in Wesleyan Methodism in 1792, a pattern followed by the other connexions.
4. **Circuit** — a group of local Methodist churches, differing in size according to locality.
5. **Society** — this was a term used by John Wesley to indicate groups of people who had joined him. It was not uncommon in the eighteenth century for this word to be used with this meaning. It should always be understood that Wesley never intended to found a new church or sect.
6. **Trustees** — persons legally appointed according to the law of the land and the church to administer all Methodist properties.
7. **Leaders** — originally these men and women were Class Leaders (a Class consisted of about 12 persons). In later development the term applied to any in charge of groups within the local Society (Church).
8. **Preacher** — this was a term used by John Wesley of all those who had been called into the work. They were the forerunners of the Methodist Ministry. Ordination in Wesleyan Methodism by the imposition of hands did not begin until 1836.
9. **Superintendant** — the word originally used by John Wesley of the Preacher (minister) in charge of a Circuit was Assistant. Superintendent superceded Assistant in later development.
10. **Station** — another word used for the appointment of a minister to a Circuit or institution. The appointments are made by the Stationing Committee and confirmed by the Conference.
11. **Connexion** — the opposite of independence. All Methodist churches are in a Circuit, which are in a District, and are subject to the constitution of the Conference.